What's What

What's What

A Visual Glossary of the Physical World

REVISED EDITION

Reginald Bragonier Jr. and David Fisher

HAMMOND®
INCORPORATED
MAPLEWOOD, NEW JERSEY

Printed in the United States of America

Library of Congress Cataloging-in-Publication Data

Bragonier, Reginald.
   What's what, a visual glossary of the physical world/
Reginald Bragonier Jr., and David Fisher.—Rev. ed.
      p. cm.
   Includes index
   Summary: Pictures of common objects and their parts, each identified individually by name, are classed under such general categories as living things, transportation, and personal items.
   ISBN 0-8437-3322-5
   1. Picture dictionaries, English. [1. Picture dictionaries.
2. Vocabulary. 3. English language—Terms and phrases.
4. Technology—Dictionaries.] I. Fisher, David, 1946-
II. Title. III. Title: What's what.
AG250.B7 1990   89-51862
031.02—dc20   CIP
                                                                AC

BOMC offers recordings and compact discs, cassettes and records. For information and catalog write to BOMR, Camp Hill, PA 17012.

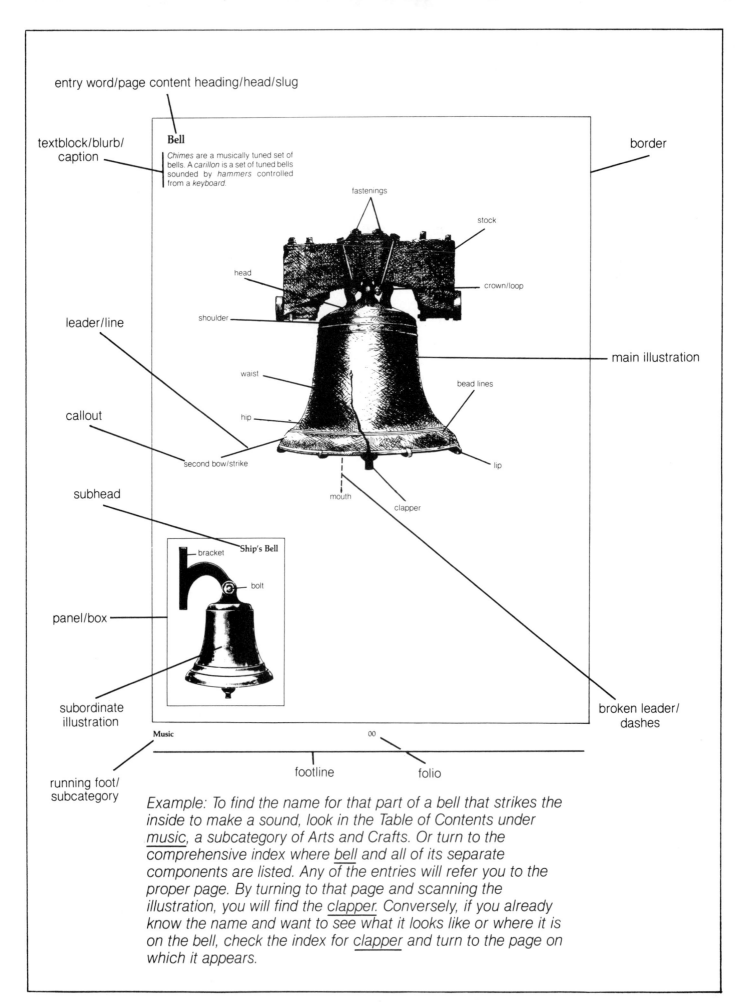

entry word/page content heading/head/slug

textblock/blurb/caption

border

Bell

Chimes are a musically tuned set of bells. A *carillon* is a set of tuned bells sounded by *hammers* controlled from a *keyboard.*

fastenings

stock

head

crown/loop

shoulder

leader/line

main illustration

waist

bead lines

callout

hip

second bow/strike

lip

mouth

clapper

subhead

Ship's Bell

bracket

bolt

panel/box

subordinate illustration

broken leader/ dashes

footline

folio

running foot/ subcategory

Example: To find the name for that part of a bell that strikes the inside to make a sound, look in the Table of Contents under music, a subcategory of Arts and Crafts. Or turn to the comprehensive index where bell and all of its separate components are listed. Any of the entries will refer you to the proper page. By turning to that page and scanning the illustration, you will find the clapper. Conversely, if you already know the name and want to see what it looks like or where it is on the bell, check the index for clapper and turn to the page on which it appears.

What It Is

Until now, it has been all but impossible to find words you've forgotten or never knew to begin with. The reason for this is obvious: to use a dictionary you need to know the word in order to find it. WHAT'S WHAT provides access to words in an entirely new way—*visually*. Readers can now find words they are seeking by turning to detailed illustrations in which all the visible parts are identified and labeled. This system of visual classification puts within verbal reach of everyone, for the first time, the words used to describe the myriad objects in our everyday world.

The objects chosen for inclusion in WHAT'S WHAT have been selected on the basis of their usefulness to contemporary readers; and although no single volume of this kind can be encyclopedic in its coverage, WHAT'S WHAT is both comprehensive in its scope and practical in its treatment of individual items. Thus, illustrations generally include only the visible parts of objects. However, when it is necessary or desirable to identify part of an item not actually shown, its location is indicated by a broken line. Variations and styles of objects have been presented only when the object's parts make it so distinctive that the item itself has a unique name—lorgnette, for example, which appears on the eyeglasses page. In addition, considerable use has been made of composite illustrations—nonliteral representations combining diverse elements found among similar objects.

How It Works

The book's system of classification is simple and straightforward. Since every object in the physical world is part of a larger whole, the reader can find any detail by locating the larger item. All objects fall naturally into one of the following twelve categories: *The Earth; Living Things; Shelters and Structures; Transportation; Communications; Personal Items; The Home; Sports and Recreation; Arts and Crafts; Machinery, Tools and Weapons; Uniforms, Costumes and Ceremonial Attire;* and *Signs and Symbols.*

To locate an item, turn first to the Table of Contents, where each entry is arranged by category and subcategory according to the object's nature and use. There you will readily determine in what part of the book the item is located. An automobile, for example, is listed under Transportation. An object, or the name of a part, can also be found by consulting the all-inclusive index at the back of the book. A collar stay, for example, can be located by looking under "shirt," "collar," or any other part of a shirt known to the reader, since all these entries will refer to the page on which a shirt is illustrated and all its parts are identified. Rigorous cross-referencing makes the task of finding any item or detail in the book even simpler.

And Why

WHAT'S WHAT is far more than an ordinary reference book. Aided by well-known artists and experts in the visual-arts fields, the editors have made every effort to produce a book that is as engaging as it is informative. Its use, it is hoped, will entertain as well as enlighten.

TABLE OF CONTENTS

THE EARTH – 1

The Planetary System (2–3): the universe
The Earth (4–6): inner world, cartographer's world, wind and ocean currents
Terrains (7–12): land features, mountains, volcano, cave, glacier
Water Systems (13–15): river, wave, shoreline and continental margin
Weather (16–19): clouds, storm systems, weather monitoring equipment, weather map
Maps (20–22): geographic, political, thematic, nautical chart, topographic map

LIVING THINGS – 23

Human Anatomy (24–31): the human body, literary anatomy, skeletal and muscular systems, internal
    organs, circulatory system and heart, nervous system and brain, sense organs, the
    extremities
Edible Animals (32–35): cow, lamb, pig, poultry
Domestic Animals (36–38): dog, cat, horse
Wild Animals (39–49): bird, spider, insects, reptiles, dinosaurs, amphibians, fish, marine life, shellfish,
    ultimate beast
Plants (50–58): tree, root system, leaf, flower, vegetables, fruit, succulents, special plants, grass

SHELTERS AND STRUCTURES – 59

House (60–69): foundation, frame, exterior, house styles, door, window, staircase, fence, building
    materials, brick wall
Architectural Designs from Other Lands (70–73): international architecture, arch, column
Special Purpose Buildings (74–96): Capitol, White House, prison, skyscraper, elevator, escalator,
    castle, fortifications, tepee, domed structures, church, temple, courtroom, circus,
    amusement park, airport, railroad yard
Other Structures (97–104): bridge, tunnel, canal lock, dam, offshore oil rig, supermarket, barn and silo

TRANSPORTATION – 105

Automobile (106–114): exterior, cutaway, car types and body styles, interior, engine, gasoline pump,
    traffic control devices, highway
Public Transportation (115–119): railroad crossing, railroad, bus, subway
Carriers (120–121): truck, trailer
Emergency Vehicles (122–125): police car, ambulance, fire engine
Public Service Vehicles (126–127): tow truck, street cleaner, garbage truck
Cycles (128–129): bicycle, motorcycle
Recreational Vehicles (130): camper, snowmobile
Carriages (131): stagecoach, hansom cab
Boats and Ships (132–145): nautical terminology, rowboat, sailboat, sail, outboard engine, powerboat,
    tanker, passenger ship, tugboat and fireboat, hovercraft and hydrofoil
Aircraft (146–151): helicopter, private aircraft, glider, civil aircraft, cockpit, blimp
Spacecraft (152–156): space shuttle, launch pad, flight deck, lunar lander, lunar buggy, flight suit

COMMUNICATIONS – 157

Print Communications (158–171): pen and pencil, correspondence, résumé, typewriter, personal
    computer, printers, fax machine and copier, typography, printing, book, newspaper,
    magazine cover, contents page and feature
Visual Communications (172–176): still camera and film, instant cameras, movie camera, projectors,
    accessories
Aural Communications (177–183): tape recorder, audio equipment, telephone, cellular telephone,
    answering machine, portable radios and cassette players, transceiver
Audiovisual Communications (184–186): video recorder, television, satellite

TABLE OF CONTENTS *(Continued)*

PERSONAL ITEMS – 187

Men's Apparel (188–194): jacket and vest, shirt, belt and suspenders, pants, neckwear, underwear

Women's Apparel (195–198): foundation garments, jacket and pants, blouse and skirt, dress

Unisex Clothing (199–201): sweater, outerwear

Headwear (202–203): men's hats, women's hats

Footwear (204–207): man's shoe, woman's shoe, boot and sandal, shoe accessories

Fasteners (208–209): pin, zipper, buttons

Hairstyles and Facial Hair (210–214): shavers, men's hair, hair grooming implements, women's hairstyles, hairstyling implements

Cosmetics (215–217): toothbrush, makeup, beauty products

Jewelry (218–219): gemstone, ring, pendant

Timepieces (220): wristwatch, pocket watch

Eyeglasses (221): lens shapes, lorgnette, monocle, contact lens

Bags (222): handbag

Wallet and Currency (223–227): paper money, coin, personal banking, credit card account, traveler's check

Smoking Materials (228–229): cigar, cigarette, pipe

Umbrella (230)

THE HOME – 231

Living Room (232–241): fireplace, clock, chair, lounger, sofa, candelabrum, lamps and lighting, window coverings

Dining Room (242–246): table, side pieces, place setting, dessert setting, carpet

Kitchen (247–269): sink and compactor, stove and microwave oven, refrigerator, dishwasher, openers, coffee makers, toaster, blenders, juicers, knives, pots and pans, mixing and measuring tools, preparation utensils, strainers and drainers, grinders and graters, food ingredients, prepared foods, desserts, snack foods, containers, labeling and packaging

Bedroom (270–272): bed and bedding, dressers

Bathroom (273–275): faucet and sink, bath and shower, toilet

Playroom/Utility Room (276–285): desk, desktop equipment, sewing machine, iron, washer and dryer, broom and mop, vacuum cleaners, fire extinguisher, luggage

Yard (286–288): children's gear and playground equipment, barbecue, chaise longue, hammock

SPORTS AND RECREATION – 289

Team Sports (290–299): baseball, football, ice hockey, basketball, soccer, lacrosse, polo

Competitive Sports (300–319): track and field, running shoe, field events equipment, hurdle, pole vault, gymnastics, trampoline, boxing, golf, tennis, handball and squash, jai alai, fencing, swimming and diving, bowling, shuffleboard and croquet, volleyball and badminton

Table Games (320–321): pool and billiards, ping-pong

Individual Sports (322–334): darts, kites, roller skating and skateboarding, ice skates, skiing, sledding and tobogganing, water skiing, windsurfing and surfing, skin diving, hot air ballooning, parachuting and hang gliding, mountain climbing

Equestrian Sports (335–337): riding equipment, flat and harness racing

Automobile Racing (338–339): Grand Prix, drag racing

Outdoor Sports (340–343): fishing, camping and backpacking

Body Building (344)

Board Games (345): chess and checkers, backgammon and mahjong

Casino Games (346–348): slot machine, roulette wheel, craps table, dice, cards

ARTS AND CRAFTS – 349

Performing Arts (350–351): stage, theater

Music (352–367): bell (see page iv), sheet music, orchestra, violin, woodwinds, brasses, organ, piano, guitar, electric guitar and synthesizer, drums, bagpipe, accordion and folk instruments, musical accessories

Fine Arts (368–379): elements of composition, painting equipment, sculpting tools, potting, woodcut printing, silk screen and scrimshaw, lithography, intaglio and etching, stained glass, framing

Cartooning (380–381)

Fireworks (382–383)

Crafts (384–388): sewing, decorative stitching, knitting, weaving, sewing pattern

TABLE OF CONTENTS *(Continued)*

MACHINERY, TOOLS AND WEAPONS – 389

Power Systems (390–399): wind systems, solar power, nuclear power, particle accelerator, lasers, power line, vacuum tube and transistor, battery, receptacle and plug, meter and fuse box

Climate Control Units (400–404): furnace, hot water heater, air conditioner, heat exchanger, woodburning stove

Engines (405–407): steam engine, internal combustion engine, jet engines

Household Tools (408–426): workbench, vise, nails and screws, nuts and bolts, hammer, screwdriver, pliers, wrench, handsaw, power saw, drills, planing and shaping tools, sander, plumbing tools, electrician's tools, measuring tools, painting tools, Swiss Army knife

Gardening Tools (427–431): hoe and rake, shovel and shears, sprinkler and nozzles, lawn mower, wheelbarrow and seeder, chain saw

Rancher's Equipment (432): lariat, branding iron, barbed wire

Trapping Devices (433): mousetrap, bear trap, lobster trap

Agricultural Tools (434): tractor, hitch and harrow

Construction Equipment (435–436): bulldozer, transit and jackhammer

Computing Tools (437–441): voting booth, computer workstation, computer system, cash register, calculators

Scientific Tools (442–443): microscope, telescope and binoculars

Sensing Devices (444–447): radar and sonar, detectors, laboratory equipment

Medical Tools (448–456): examination equipment, medical tables, treatment aids, supportive devices, dental corrective devices, dental unit, dental equipment, tooth chart

Security Devices (457–460): safe, door locks, key and padlock, hinge and hasp

Chain and Pulley (461)

Execution Devices (462): electric chair, gallows, guillotine

Weapons (463–482): cutting and thrusting weapons, medieval arms, armor, bow and arrow, cannon and catapult, shotgun and rifle, handguns, automatic rifle and machine gun, mortar and bazooka, grenade and land mine, tank, fighting ships, aircraft carrier, submarines and torpedo, combat jet fighter, pilot's instrument panel, missiles

UNIFORMS, COSTUMES AND CEREMONIAL ATTIRE – 483

Royal Vestments (484–485): attire, crown, orb and scepter

Religious Attire (486–487): vestments and ritual items

Wedding Attire (488): bride and groom

Servants' Attire (489): domestic staff

Native Attire (490–491): cowboy and Indian, Arab and Chinese dress

Historical Costumes (492): general, pirate, miser and wizard

Performers' Costumes (493–495): clown, ballet dancer, drum major

Military Attire (496–497): dress and combat

Municipal Uniforms (498–500): policemen, firemen

SIGNS AND SYMBOLS – 501

Flags (502)

Heraldry (503)

Road Signs (504–505)

Public Signs (506)

Gestures (507)

Religious Symbols (508)

Signs of the Zodiac (509)

Symbols of Science, Business and Commerce (510–511)

Sign Alphabet and Braille (512)

Grammatical Symbols (513)

Proofreader's Marks (514)

Graffiti (515)

TOMBSTONE AND COFFIN – 516

The Earth

This section offers various ways of looking at the earth, ranging from showing the earth as a small planet in the larger space it shares with other heavenly bodies to physical features and symbolic depictions illustrating aspects and details of the earth's surface.

Nonliteral renditions, such as the illustration of the universe, condense information visually by pulling together disparate elements for labeling. Cutaway illustrations like the one of the earth's inner layers are used only when elements considered essential to show and identify are not readily visible. The cave illustration, on the other hand, is rendered in cross section in order to show parts and details which might not be apparent in a traditional illustration.

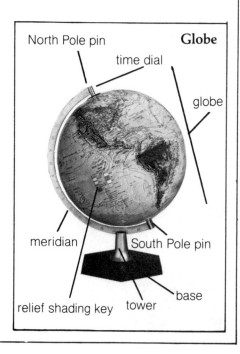

Globe

North Pole pin

time dial

globe

meridian

South Pole pin

relief shading key   tower

base

The Universe

This whimsical creation of the universe includes such bits and pieces of the entire *cosmic mass* as the *solar system, local galaxies* and *external galaxies*. Observable *planets* are illuminated by the light of our sun. *Meteors,* or *shooting stars,* are seen as streaks of light in the *sky* as they are vaporized on entering earth's atmosphere.

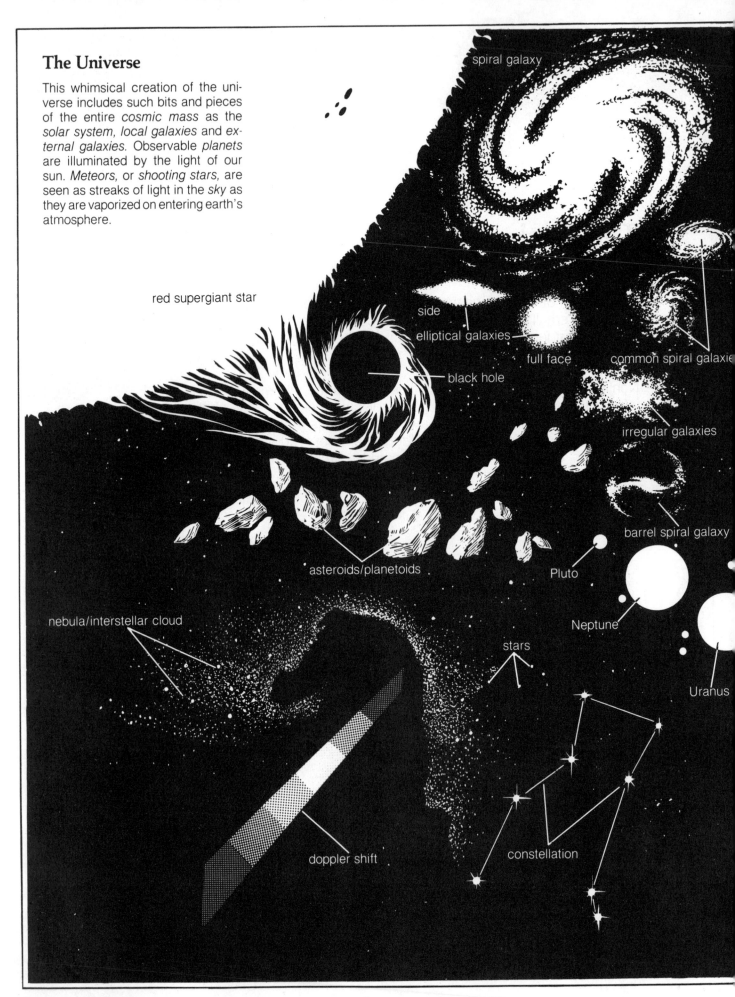

spiral galaxy

red supergiant star

side

elliptical galaxies

full face

common spiral galaxie

black hole

irregular galaxies

asteroids/planetoids

barrel spiral galaxy

Pluto

nebula/interstellar cloud

Neptune

stars

Uranus

doppler shift

constellation

mystery gas cloud

pulsar

quark

quasar

radiation belt

tail

comet

head/coma

binary stars/double stars

white dwarf star

ion particle cloud

radio waves

supernova

satellite

Cassini division

rings

Saturn

Jupiter

solar flare/solar prominence

Titan

Mars

Earth

Venus

moon/satellite

Mercury

Milky Way Galaxy

Sun

Sun spots

cosmic rays

The Planetary System

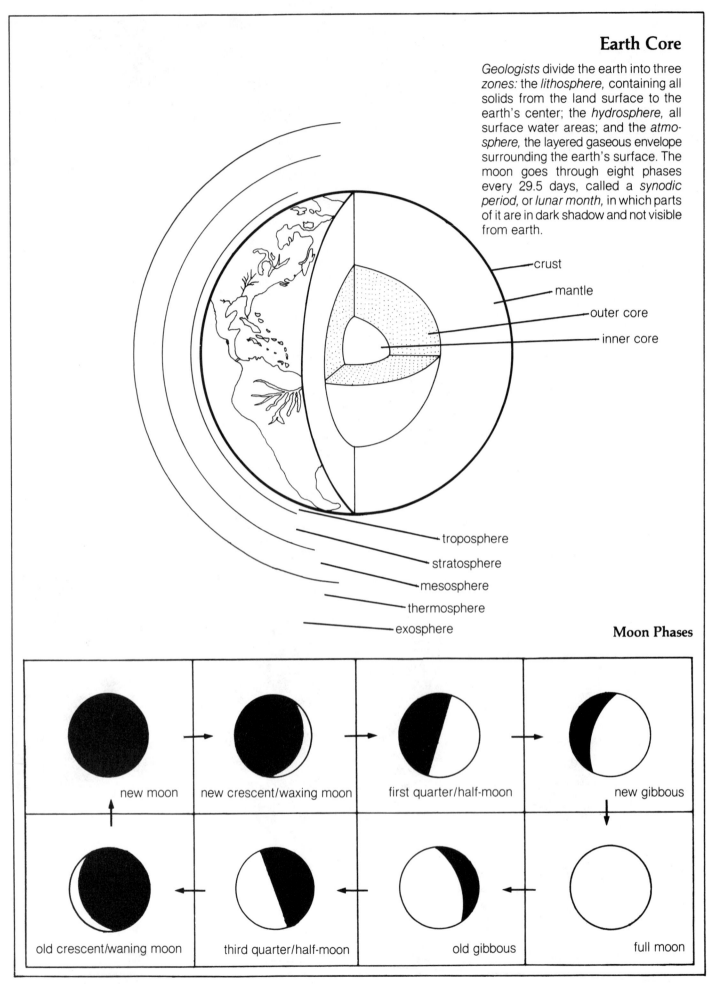

Earth Core

Geologists divide the earth into three *zones:* the *lithosphere,* containing all solids from the land surface to the earth's center; the *hydrosphere,* all surface water areas; and the *atmosphere,* the layered gaseous envelope surrounding the earth's surface. The moon goes through eight phases every 29.5 days, called a *synodic period,* or *lunar month,* in which parts of it are in dark shadow and not visible from earth.

crust

mantle

outer core

inner core

troposphere

stratosphere

mesosphere

thermosphere

exosphere

Moon Phases

new moon

new crescent/waxing moon

first quarter/half-moon

new gibbous

old crescent/waning moon

third quarter/half-moon

old gibbous

full moon

Cartographer's World

Position on the earth's *grid* can be determined by finding exact *latitude, north* or *south* of the equator, and *longitude, east* or *west* of the prime meridian. As the earth makes its daily rotation, the sun crosses every meridian once each day. When this occurs, all points on the meridian experience *noon* at the same instant. At the same time on the opposite side of the earth it is *midnight* and a new *calendar day* is beginning. There is a difference of one hour in *solar time* every 15 *degrees*. The world time zone map shows how the theoretical division of the world into 24 equal *time belts* has been modified to follow *political* or *geographical boundaries*.

pole

rhumb line

parallels of latitude/
latitude lines

meridians/
longitude lines

prime meridian/
first meridian

equator

Central
Time

Greenwich
Mean Time

Mountain
Time

Eastern
Time

Pacific
Time

Time Zones

International
Date Line

equator

Greenwich
prime meridian

The Earth

Wind and Ocean Currents

The *zonal patterns* of wind are displaced northward and southward seasonally. Those shown here prevail in winter. *Seasonal currents* change speed and direction due to seasonal winds, whereas *permanent currents* experience relatively little change.

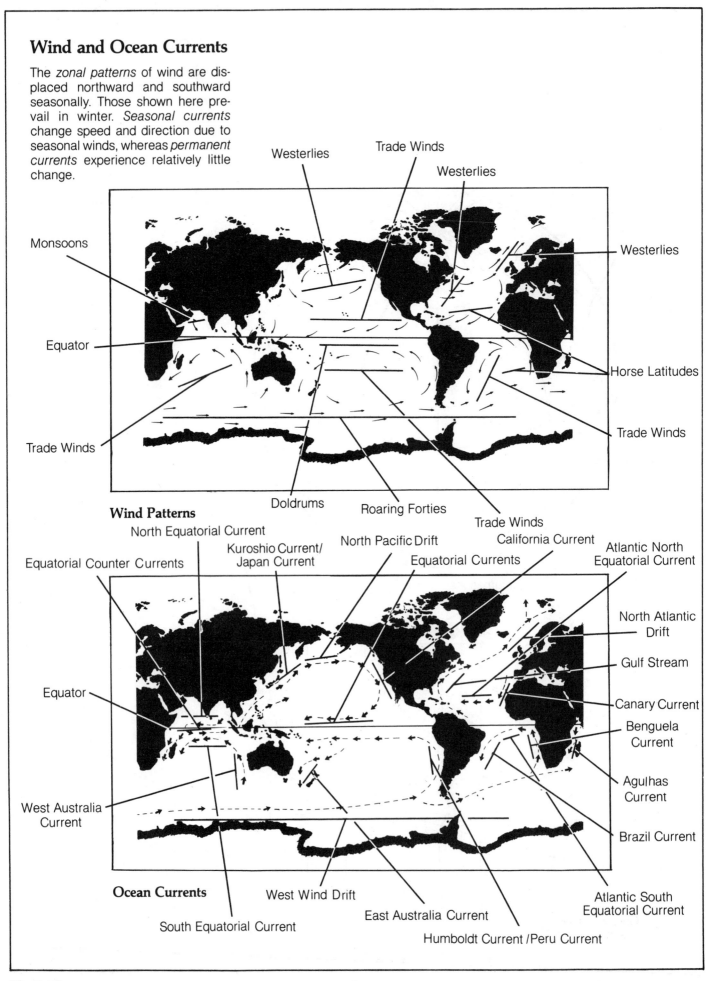

Westerlies

Trade Winds

Westerlies

Monsoons

Westerlies

Equator

Horse Latitudes

Trade Winds

Trade Winds

Doldrums

Roaring Forties

Trade Winds

Wind Patterns

North Equatorial Current

North Pacific Drift

California Current

Equatorial Counter Currents

Kuroshio Current/Japan Current

Equatorial Currents

Atlantic North Equatorial Current

North Atlantic Drift

Gulf Stream

Equator

Canary Current

Benguela Current

Agulhas Current

West Australia Current

Brazil Current

Ocean Currents

West Wind Drift

Atlantic South Equatorial Current

South Equatorial Current

East Australia Current

Humboldt Current /Peru Current

Land Features

A part of an *ocean* or *sea* extending into the land is a *gulf*. A narrow finger of land extending into the water is a *spit*. A sand or gravel bar connecting an island with the *mainland* or another island is a *tombolo*.

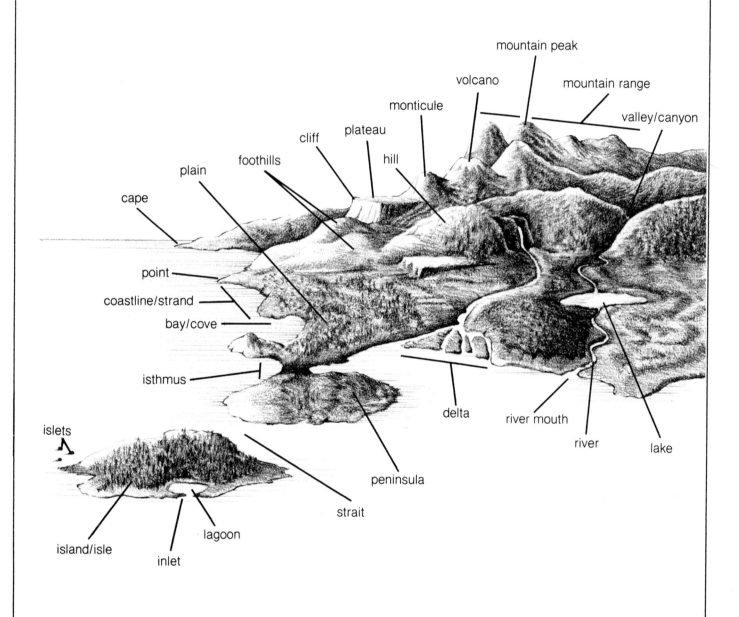

mountain peak

volcano

mountain range

monticule

valley/canyon

cliff

plateau

foothills

hill

plain

cape

point

coastline/strand

bay/cove

isthmus

delta

river mouth

river

lake

islets

peninsula

strait

island/isle

inlet

lagoon

Terrains

Mountains

A series of mountains, such as the Alpine mountains shown here, is a *range*. A circular space in mountains is a *cirque*, or *cwm*. A *kame* is a ridge or material left by a retreating *ice sheet*. An isolated hill or mountain rising abruptly from the surrounding land is a *butte*.

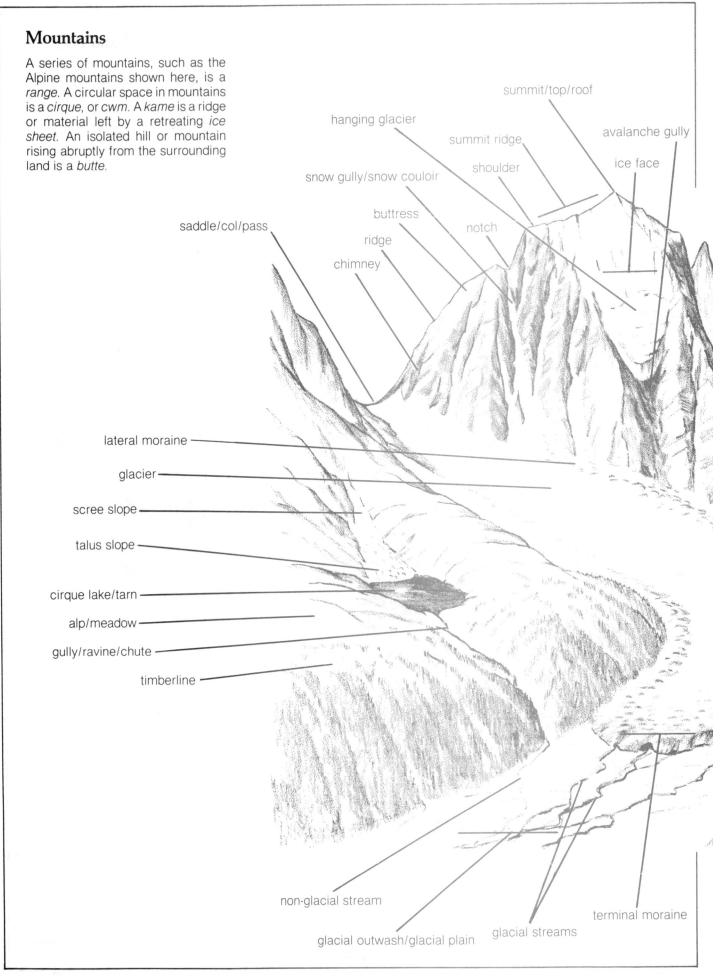

summit/top/roof

hanging glacier

summit ridge

avalanche gully

shoulder

ice face

snow gully/snow couloir

saddle/col/pass

buttress

notch

ridge

chimney

lateral moraine

glacier

scree slope

talus slope

cirque lake/tarn

alp/meadow

gully/ravine/chute

timberline

non-glacial stream

glacial outwash/glacial plain

glacial streams

terminal moraine

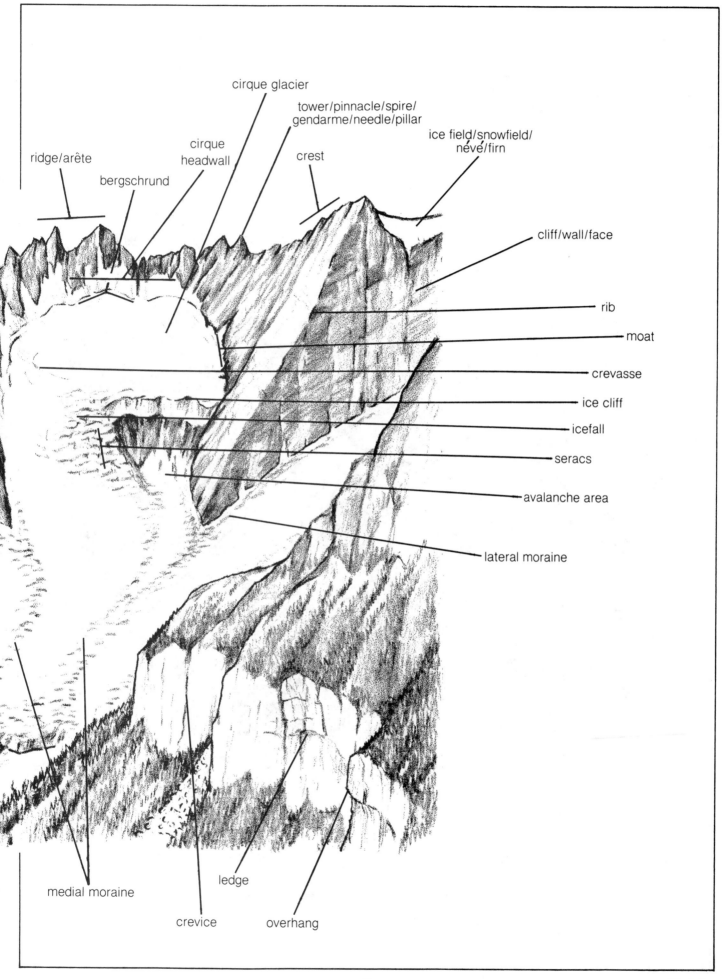

ridge/arête
bergschrund
cirque headwall
cirque glacier
tower/pinnacle/spire/gendarme/needle/pillar
crest
ice field/snowfield/névé/firn
cliff/wall/face
rib
moat
crevasse
ice cliff
icefall
seracs
avalanche area
lateral moraine
medial moraine
crevice
ledge
overhang

Terrains

Volcano

In *central-vent volcanoes,* such as the one shown here, material erupts from a single pipe. *Fissure volcanoes* extrude material along extensive *fractures.*

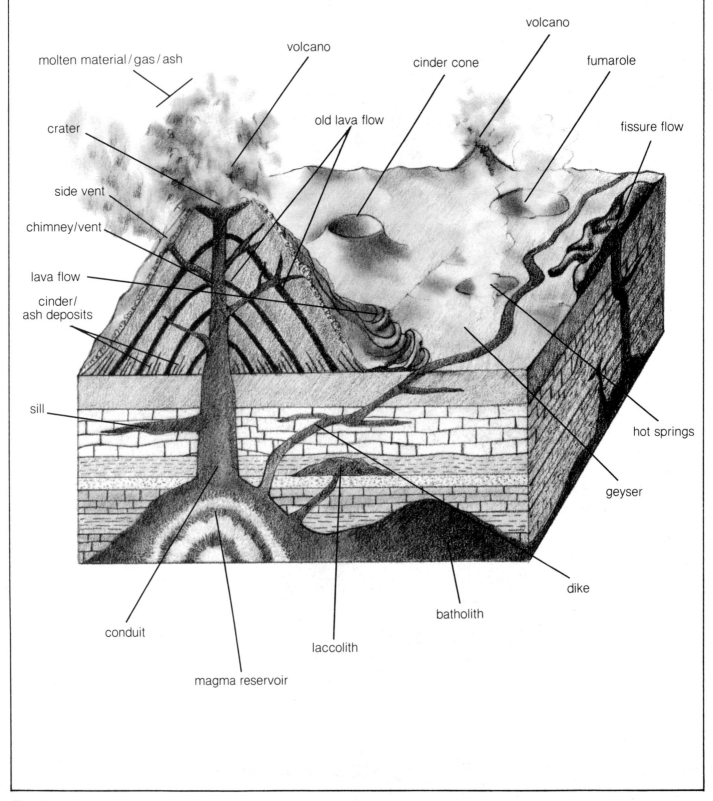

molten material / gas / ash

volcano

volcano

cinder cone

fumarole

fissure flow

crater

old lava flow

side vent

chimney/vent

lava flow

cinder/
ash deposits

sill

hot springs

geyser

dike

conduit

batholith

laccolith

magma reservoir

Cave Cross Section

The exploration of caves, or *caverns* is called *spelunking* or *caving*. The area lighted by daylight just inside a cave entrance is the *twilight zone*. An underground structure containing many *galleries, chambers* or *rooms* is a *cave system*. Anything formed inside a cave, *cavern* or *grotto*, by dripping water is *dripstone*. Knobby calcite growths often found on *walls* and *floors* of once-submerged caves are called *cave coral* or *cave popcorn*.

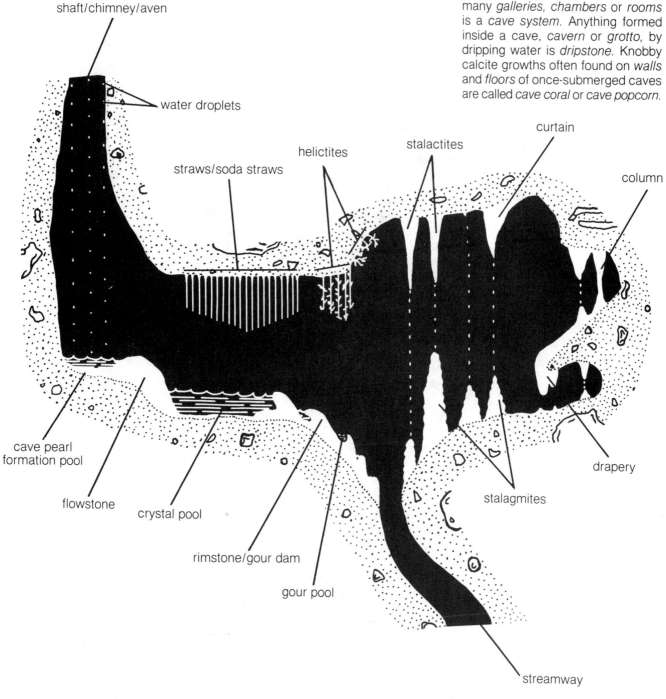

shaft/chimney/aven

water droplets

helictites

straws/soda straws

stalactites

curtain

column

cave pearl
formation pool

flowstone

crystal pool

rimstone/gour dam

gour pool

stalagmites

drapery

streamway

Glacier

When a glacier terminates at the water's edge, sections break off, or *calve*, to form icebergs. Icebergs often break apart to form smaller, separate *bergs, bergy bits* or *bitty bergs*. Even smaller sections are called *growlers*. *Ice packs*, formed when the water surface between floating ice freezes, are called *floes*. Sections that break off are called *floebergs*.

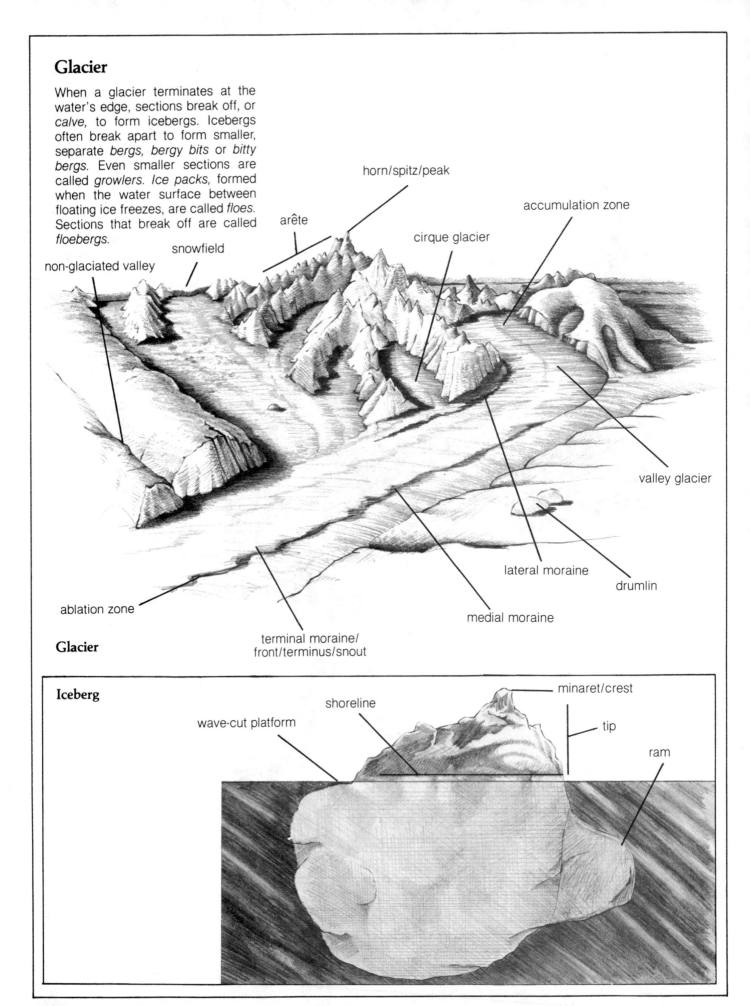

non-glaciated valley

snowfield

arête

horn/spitz/peak

cirque glacier

accumulation zone

valley glacier

lateral moraine

drumlin

medial moraine

ablation zone

terminal moraine/
front/terminus/snout

Glacier

Iceberg

wave-cut platform

shoreline

minaret/crest

tip

ram

River

A *river system* consists of the main river and its tributaries or branches. It drains from a *river basin,* and flows along a *course,* or *watercourse,* cutting a *channel* through the land. A *flood* occurs when it overflows its banks.

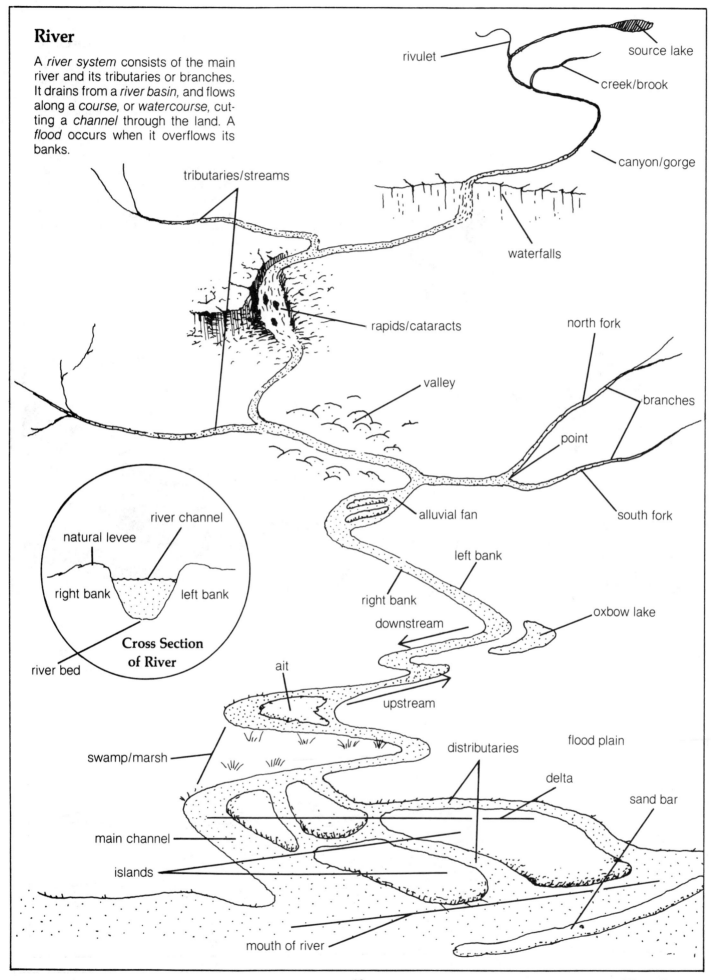

rivulet

source lake

creek/brook

canyon/gorge

tributaries/streams

waterfalls

rapids/cataracts

north fork

branches

valley

point

south fork

alluvial fan

left bank

right bank

oxbow lake

downstream

natural levee

river channel

right bank

left bank

river bed

Cross Section of River

ait

upstream

flood plain

swamp/marsh

distributaries

delta

sand bar

main channel

islands

mouth of river

Water Systems

Wave and Shoreline

Wavelength is the linear distance between two wave crests, *period* is the time it takes two crests to pass a given point, and *wave height* is the vertical distance measured from the trough to the crest of a wave. There are *surface waves, tidal waves, internal waves, tsunamis, storm surges* and *seiches.* Long, crestless waves are *swells.* The rapid flow of water up onto the *beach face* following the breaking of *surf* is the *uprush* or *swash.*

crest

whitecap/spindrift

scend

curl/tunnel/
tube/pipeline

back

shoulder/wall

trough

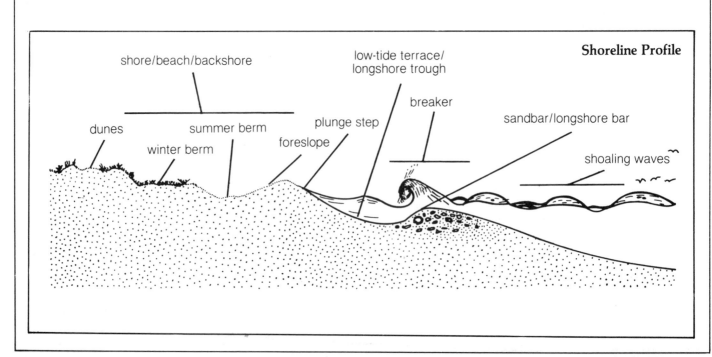

Shoreline Profile

shore/beach/backshore

low-tide terrace/
longshore trough

breaker

dunes

summer berm

plunge step

sandbar/longshore bar

winter berm

foreslope

shoaling waves

Coastline and Continental Margin

The *littoral zone* is that part of the shoreline that lies between *high* and *low tides*. The continental shelf is the submerged border of *landmasses* extending into the *ocean basin*. The *100-fathom curve* has long been used as the outer limit of the continental shelf.

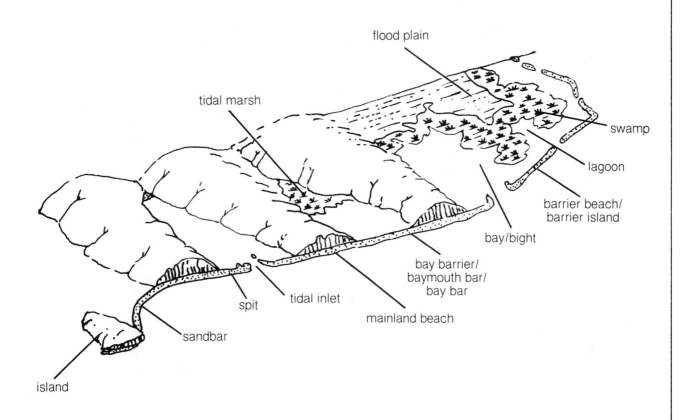

flood plain

tidal marsh

swamp

lagoon

barrier beach/
barrier island

bay/bight

bay barrier/
baymouth bar/
bay bar

mainland beach

spit

tidal inlet

sandbar

island

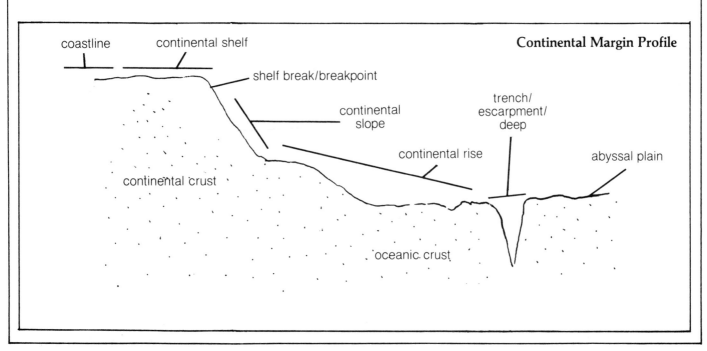

Continental Margin Profile

coastline

continental shelf

shelf break/breakpoint

continental
slope

trench/
escarpment/
deep

continental rise

abyssal plain

continental crust

oceanic crust

Water Systems

Clouds

The name of a cloud describes both its appearance and its height above the ground. Clouds are formed from tiny droplets of water or *ice crystals* and continually change shape due to evaporation, wind and *air movements*.

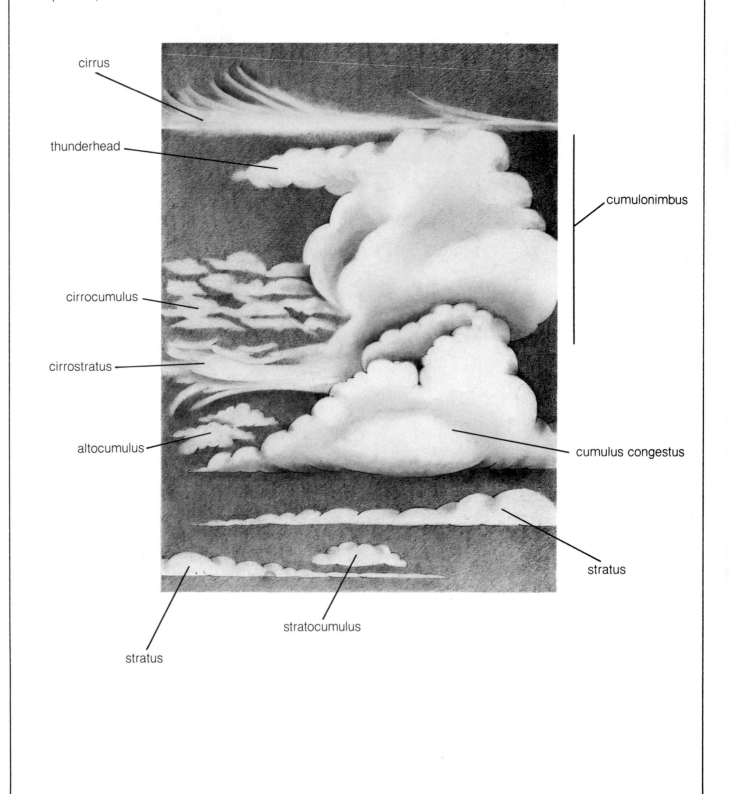

cirrus

thunderhead

cumulonimbus

cirrocumulus

cirrostratus

altocumulus

cumulus congestus

stratus

stratus

stratocumulus

Storm Systems

Thunderstorms carry the same general features: lightning, *thunder*, strong gusts of *wind*, heavy *showers*, and occasionally *hailstones*. When hurricanes occur in the Pacific, they are called *typhoons*. Tornados are also known as *twisters*.

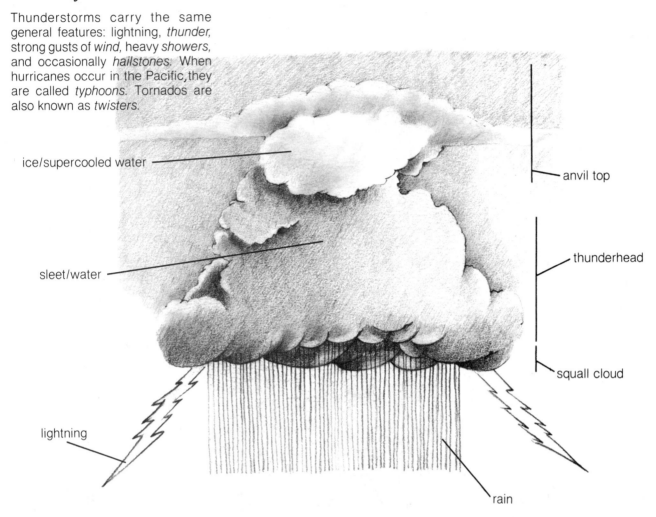

ice/supercooled water

sleet/water

lightning

anvil top

thunderhead

squall cloud

rain

Thunderstorm

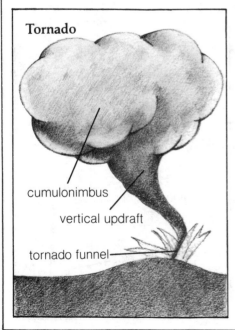

Tornado

cumulonimbus

vertical updraft

tornado funnel

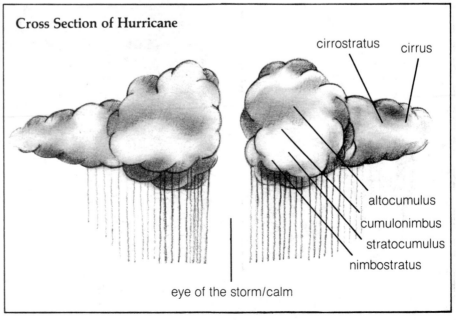

Cross Section of Hurricane

cirrostratus

cirrus

altocumulus

cumulonimbus

stratocumulus

nimbostratus

eye of the storm/calm

Weather Monitoring Equipment

Equipment, such as that shown here, helps a *meteorologist* predict weather and make *weather forecasts*.

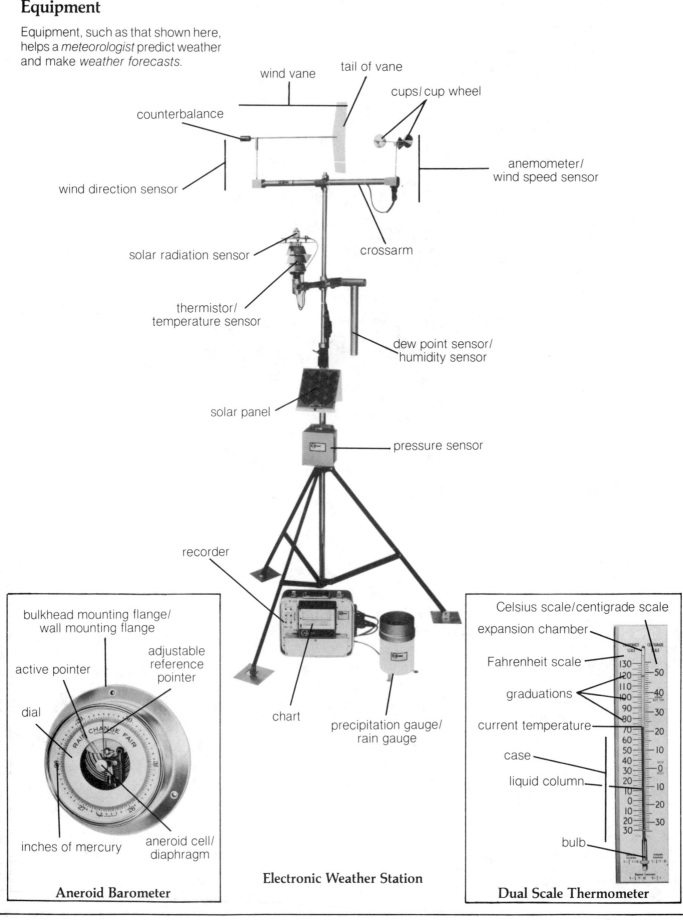

wind vane

tail of vane

cups/cup wheel

counterbalance

anemometer/ wind speed sensor

wind direction sensor

crossarm

solar radiation sensor

thermistor/ temperature sensor

dew point sensor/ humidity sensor

solar panel

pressure sensor

recorder

Aneroid Barometer

bulkhead mounting flange/ wall mounting flange

adjustable reference pointer

active pointer

dial

RAIN   CHANGE   FAIR

chart

inches of mercury

aneroid cell/ diaphragm

precipitation gauge/ rain gauge

Electronic Weather Station

Dual Scale Thermometer

Celsius scale/centigrade scale

expansion chamber

Fahrenheit scale

graduations

current temperature

case

liquid column

bulb

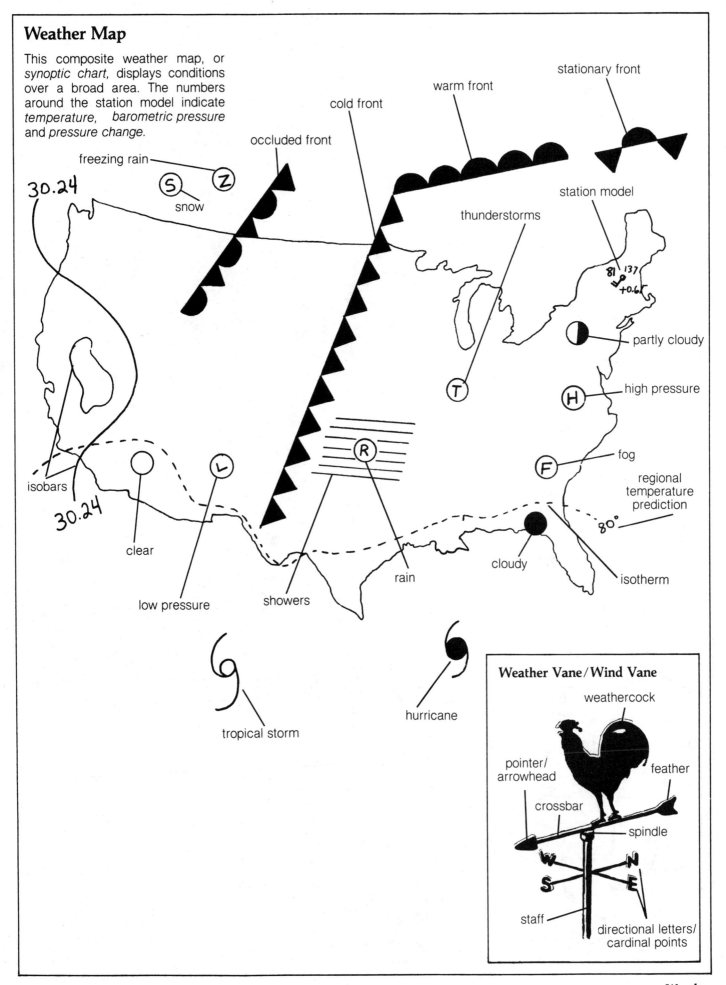

Weather Map

This composite weather map, or *synoptic chart,* displays conditions over a broad area. The numbers around the station model indicate *temperature, barometric pressure* and *pressure change.*

freezing rain

30.24

occluded front

snow

cold front

warm front

stationary front

thunderstorms

station model

81 137
+0.6

partly cloudy

high pressure

fog

regional temperature prediction

80°

isobars

30.24

clear

low pressure

showers

rain

cloudy

isotherm

tropical storm

hurricane

Weather Vane/Wind Vane

weathercock

pointer/arrowhead

feather

crossbar

spindle

staff

directional letters/cardinal points

Map

The science of *mapmaking* is also known as *cartography*. The *projection* of a map is the framework on which its main components, *linework,* point or area symbols and type are placed.

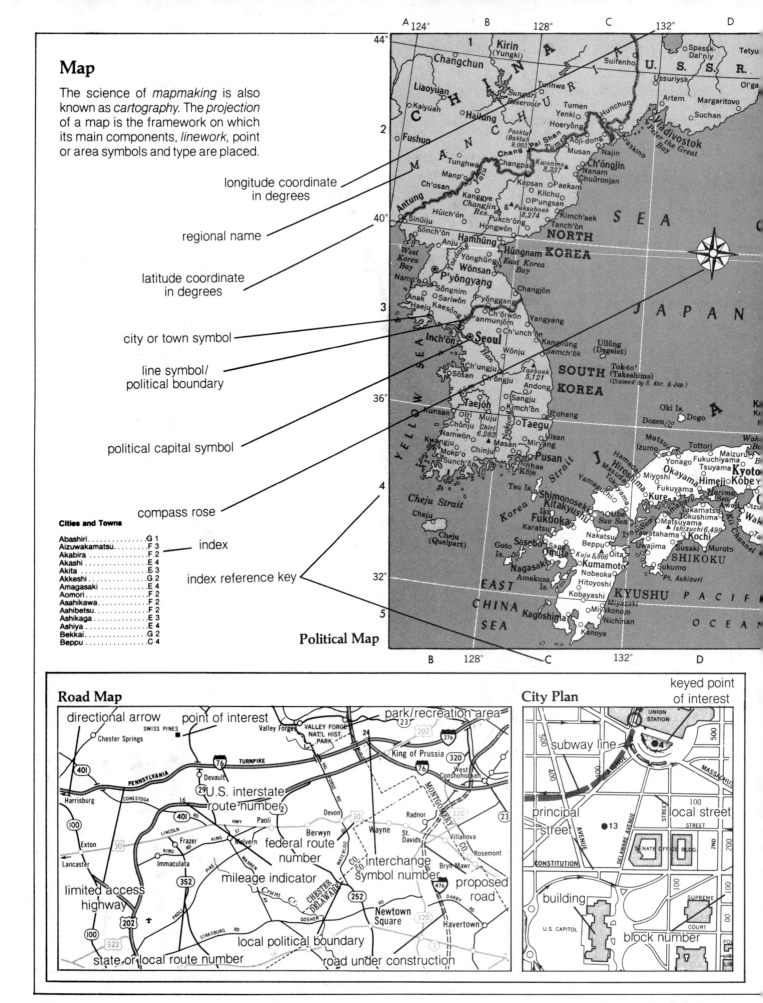

longitude coordinate in degrees

regional name

latitude coordinate in degrees

city or town symbol

line symbol/ political boundary

political capital symbol

compass rose

Cities and Towns

Abashiri..............G 1 — index
Aizuwakamatsu.........F 3
Akabira ....F 2
Akashi ....E 4
Akita ....E 3
Akkeshi ....G 2
Amagasaki ....E 4
Aomori ....F 2
Asahikawa ....F 2
Ashibetsu ....F 2
Ashikaga ....E 3
Ashiya ....E 4
Bekkai ....G 2
Beppu ....C 4

index reference key

Political Map

Road Map

directional arrow   point of interest   park/recreation area

U.S. interstate route number

federal route number

mileage indicator

limited access highway

interchange symbol number

proposed road

state or local route number   local political boundary   road under construction

City Plan

keyed point of interest

subway line

principal street

local street

building

block number

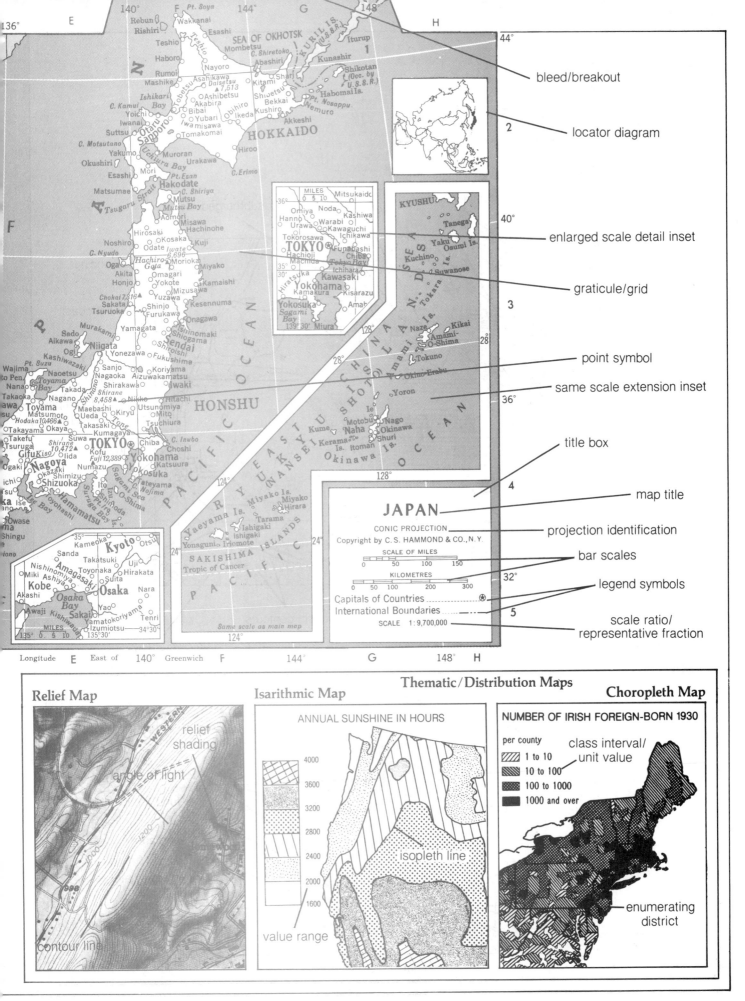

bleed/breakout

locator diagram

enlarged scale detail inset

graticule/grid

point symbol

same scale extension inset

title box

map title

projection identification

bar scales

legend symbols

scale ratio/
representative fraction

JAPAN

CONIC PROJECTION
Copyright by C.S. HAMMOND & CO., N.Y.

SCALE OF MILES
0   50   100   150

KILOMETRES
0   50   100   200   300

Capitals of Countries .... ⊛
International Boundaries ....

SCALE 1:9,700,000

Longitude   E   East of   140°   Greenwich   F   144°   G   148°   H

Thematic/Distribution Maps

Relief Map

relief shading

angle of light

contour line

Isarithmic Map

ANNUAL SUNSHINE IN HOURS

4000
3600
3200
2800
2400
2000
1600

isopleth line

value range

Choropleth Map

NUMBER OF IRISH FOREIGN-BORN 1930

per county
1 to 10
10 to 100
100 to 1000
1000 and over

class interval/
unit value

enumerating district

Nautical Chart and Topographic Map

On nautical charts, *sounding datum reference* is stated in the *chart title*. *Depth conversion scales* are provided to enable the mariner to work in *meters, fathoms,* or *feet.* The space outside a chart or map, used to identify and explain the map, is the *map margin.*

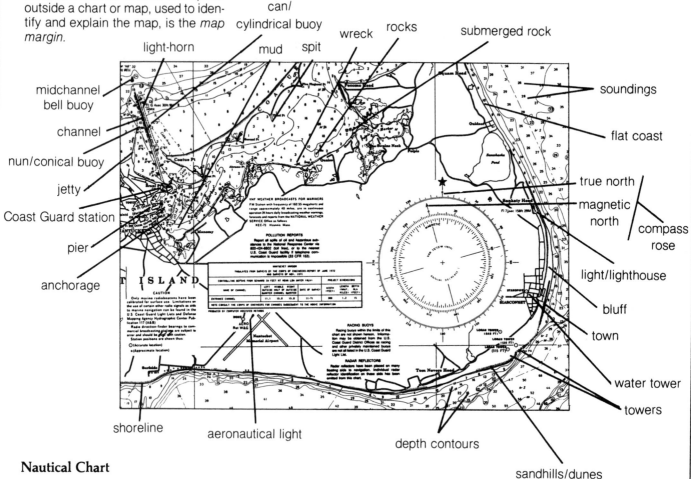

Nautical Chart

Labels: light-horn, can/cylindrical buoy, mud, spit, wreck, rocks, submerged rock, midchannel bell buoy, channel, nun/conical buoy, jetty, Coast Guard station, pier, anchorage, soundings, flat coast, true north, magnetic north, compass rose, light/lighthouse, bluff, town, water tower, towers, shoreline, aeronautical light, depth contours, sandhills/dunes

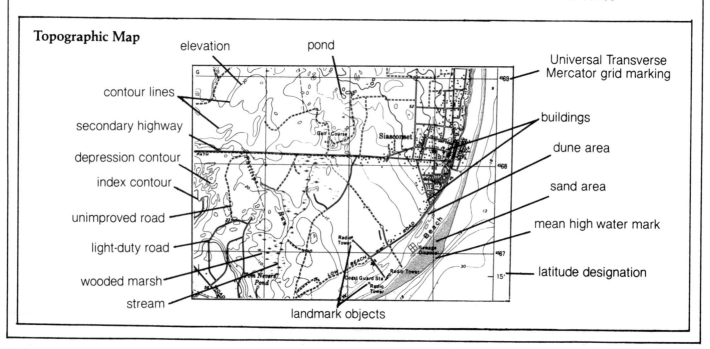

Topographic Map

Labels: elevation, pond, contour lines, secondary highway, depression contour, index contour, unimproved road, light-duty road, wooded marsh, stream, landmark objects, Universal Transverse Mercator grid marking, buildings, dune area, sand area, mean high water mark, latitude designation

Living Things

For ease of reference, this section has been divided into five subcategories: man, edible animals, domestic animals, wild animals, and plants. The animals and plants selected for inclusion within each subsection contain most of the parts common to all members of the major families they represent.

With the exception of man, examined more closely than any other subject in this section because of his obvious importance to us, only the external parts of living things have been identified. However, edible animals have been illustrated in such a way as to show those parts which supply our daily food. Domestic and wild animals, some of them grouped by habitat, are represented by single members of a species. But because there are parts which are unique to certain animals, a composite "beast" has been created to illustrate some of them.

The plant kingdom is represented from the roots up, literally, including coverage of parts of a flower, special plants, and edible portions called fruits and vegetables.

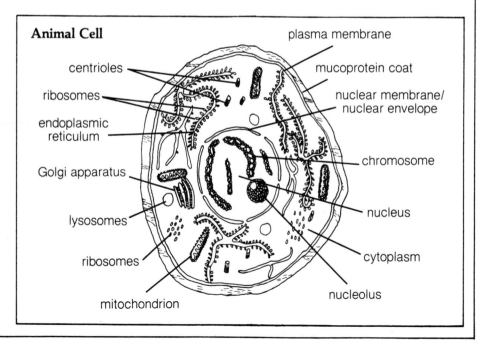

Animal Cell

plasma membrane

centrioles

mucoprotein coat

ribosomes

nuclear membrane/ nuclear envelope

endoplasmic reticulum

chromosome

Golgi apparatus

nucleus

lysosomes

ribosomes

cytoplasm

nucleolus

mitochondrion

The Human Body

The body, less the *head* and *limbs,* is referred to as the *trunk* or *torso.*

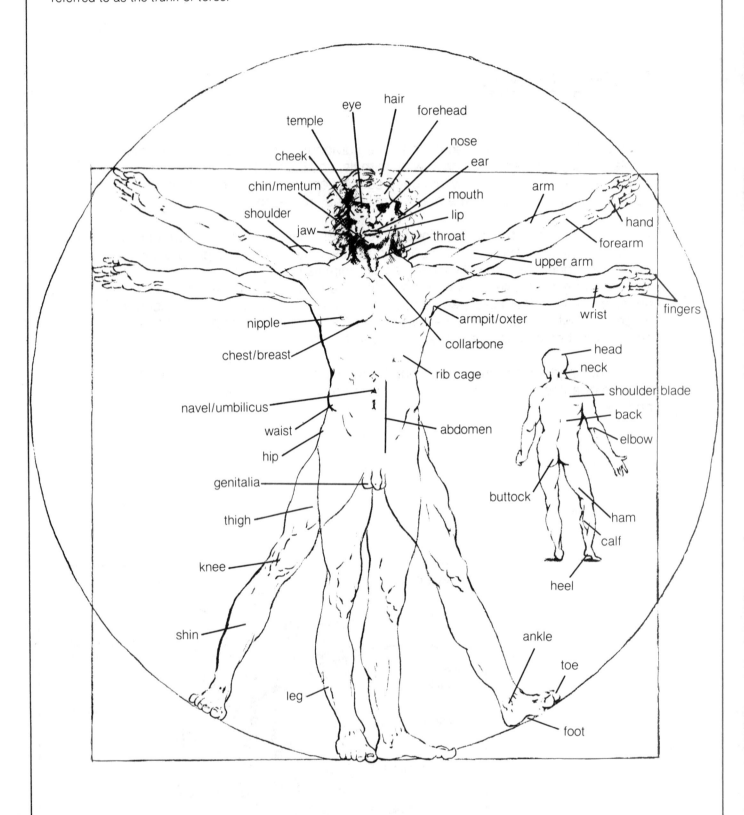

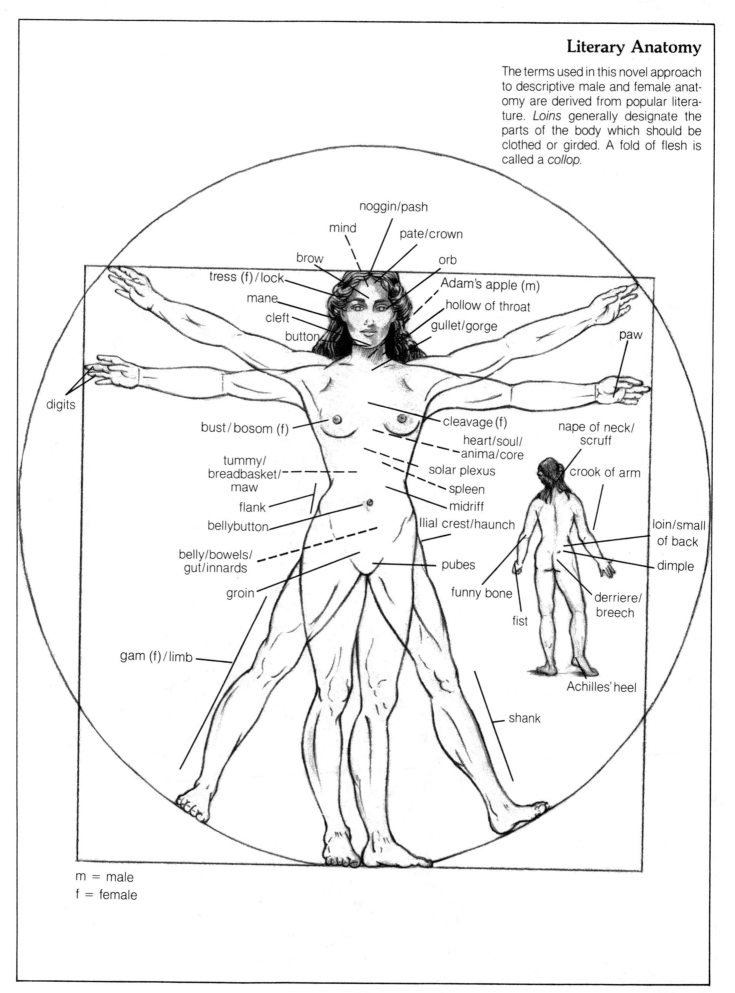

Literary Anatomy

The terms used in this novel approach to descriptive male and female anatomy are derived from popular literature. *Loins* generally designate the parts of the body which should be clothed or girded. A fold of flesh is called a *collop*.

noggin/pash

mind

brow

pate/crown

orb

tress (f)/lock

Adam's apple (m)

mane

hollow of throat

cleft

gullet/gorge

button

paw

digits

bust/bosom (f)

cleavage (f)

nape of neck/scruff

heart/soul/anima/core

crook of arm

tummy/breadbasket/maw

solar plexus

flank

spleen

loin/small of back

bellybutton

midriff

dimple

Ilial crest/haunch

belly/bowels/gut/innards

pubes

derriere/breech

groin

funny bone

fist

Achilles' heel

gam (f)/limb

shank

m = male
f = female

Skeletal and Muscular System

Voluntary muscles are subject to or controlled by will, pulling on *bones* of the *skeleton* to produce movement. *Involuntary muscles*, like the heart, act independently of volition. Where one bone meets another is a *joint*. *Cartilage*, or *gristle*, is a flexible type of connective tissue. The bony structure in which the brain is housed is the *cranium*.

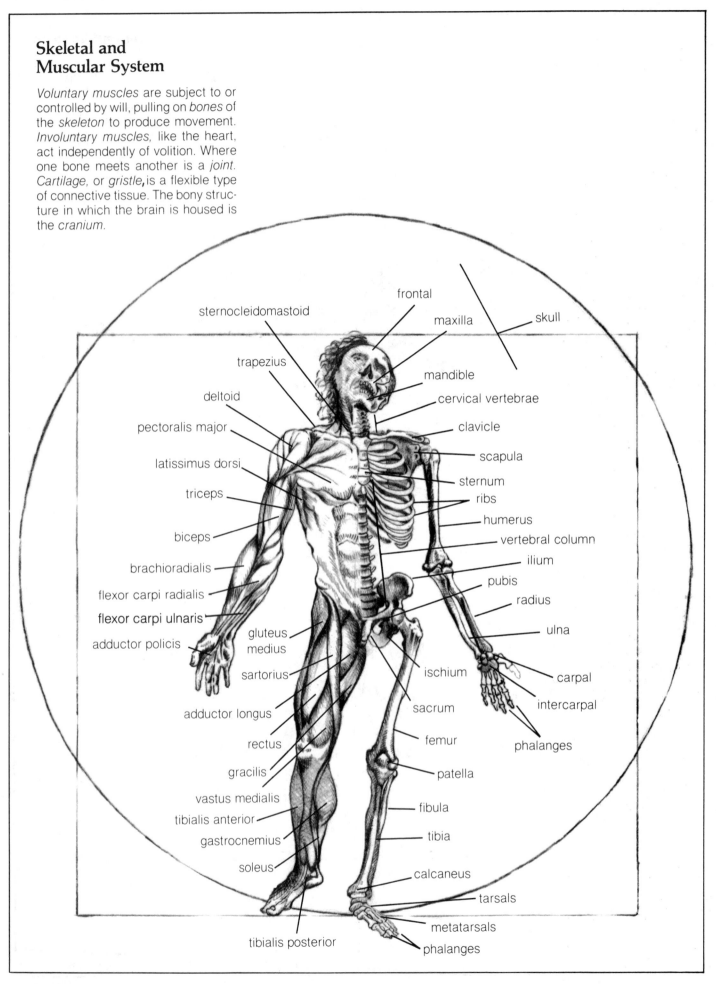

frontal

sternocleidomastoid

maxilla

skull

trapezius

mandible

deltoid

cervical vertebrae

pectoralis major

clavicle

latissimus dorsi

scapula

triceps

sternum

biceps

ribs

brachioradialis

humerus

flexor carpi radialis

vertebral column

flexor carpi ulnaris

ilium

adductor policis

pubis

gluteus medius

radius

sartorius

ulna

adductor longus

ischium

rectus

carpal

gracilis

sacrum

intercarpal

vastus medialis

femur

phalanges

tibialis anterior

patella

gastrocnemius

fibula

soleus

tibia

tibialis posterior

calcaneus

tarsals

metatarsals

phalanges

Internal Organs

The stomach and intestines are the principal organs of the *digestive system*, or *alimentary canal*, and the *pancreas*, liver and *gall bladder* all aid in the nutrition process and the elimination of wastes. The heart is the pump of the *circulatory system*, sending blood through *arteries, veins* and *capillaries*. The lungs are the center of the *respiratory system*.

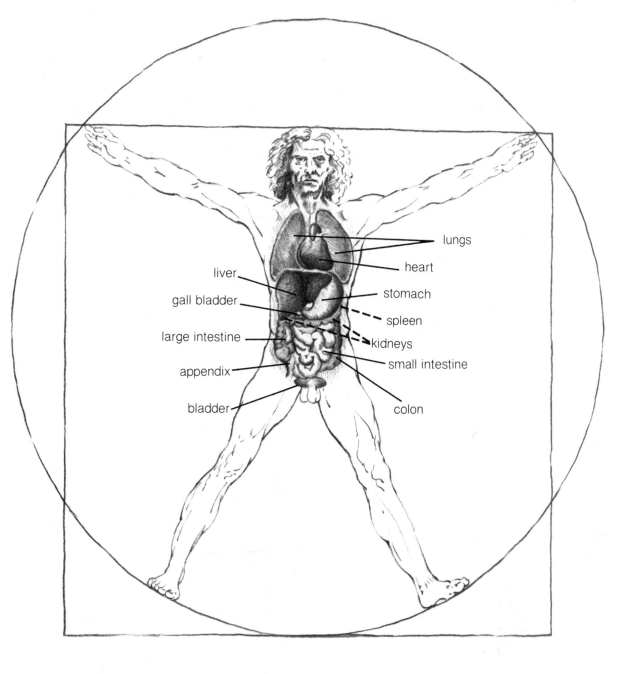

lungs

heart

liver

stomach

gall bladder

spleen

large intestine

kidneys

small intestine

appendix

bladder

colon

Circulation System and Heart

The heart pumps oxygenated and nutrient-rich blood throughout the body via arteries and their smaller branches, *arterioles*. Blood flows across body tissue through a network of small vessels, collectively called a *capillary bed*. Deoxygenated blood collects in small vessels called *venules*, which join to form veins.

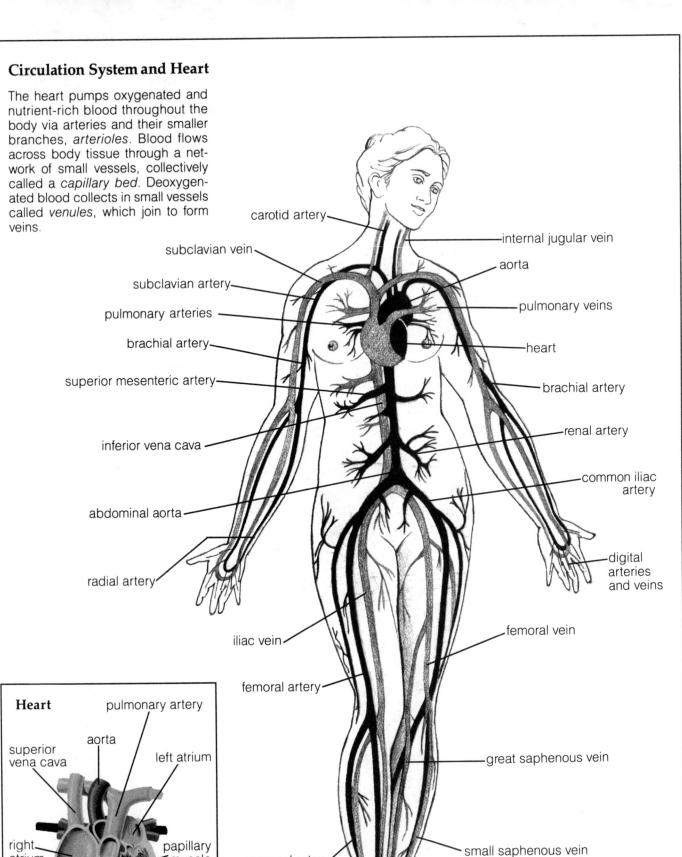

carotid artery

subclavian vein

subclavian artery

pulmonary arteries

brachial artery

superior mesenteric artery

inferior vena cava

abdominal aorta

radial artery

iliac vein

femoral artery

peroneal artery

internal jugular vein

aorta

pulmonary veins

heart

brachial artery

renal artery

common iliac artery

digital arteries and veins

femoral vein

great saphenous vein

small saphenous vein

Heart

pulmonary artery

aorta

superior vena cava

left atrium

right atrium

papillary muscle

inferior vena cava

left ventricle

right ventricle

septum

cerebrum

brain

brain stem

spinal cord

brachial plexus

thoracic nerves

lumbrosacral plexus

spinal nerves

median nerve

ulnar nerve

radial nerve

femoral nerve

sciatic nerve

posterior tibial nerve

common peroneal nerve

sural nerve

tibial nerve

Nervous System and Brain

Nerve tissue is composed of specialized cells called *neurons. Nerves* are composed of *fibers* and accessory *sheaths. Sensory,* or *afferent nerves* carry impulses from *receptors* in the *sense organs* to the *central nervous system. Motor,* or *efferent nerves* lead in the other direction, out to muscles and other *effectors.*

frontal lobe

cerebral cortex

Brain

meninges

parietal lobe

corpus callosum

thalamus

hypothalamus

occipital lobe

pituitary gland

pons

cerebellum

temporal lobe

medulla

Human Anatomy

Sense Organs

The eye, which is located in an *eye socket*, or *orbit*, is covered with a transparent layer called the *cornea*. The angle formed where upper and lower eyelids come together is called the *canthus*. The junction nearest the nose is the *inner canthus*, the other is the *outer canthus*. The tongue rubs against the *palate* at the top of the mouth. The *pharynx* is the beginning of the *throat*, or *gullet*.

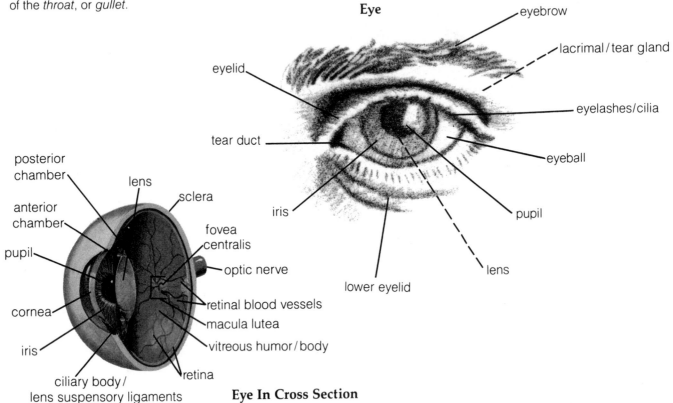

Eye

eyebrow

lacrimal / tear gland

eyelashes/cilia

eyeball

pupil

lens

lower eyelid

eyelid

tear duct

iris

posterior chamber

anterior chamber

pupil

cornea

iris

lens

sclera

fovea centralis

optic nerve

retinal blood vessels

macula lutea

vitreous humor / body

ciliary body / lens suspensory ligaments

retina

Eye In Cross Section

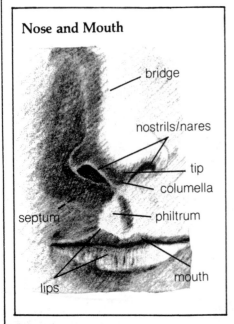

Nose and Mouth

bridge

nostrils/nares

tip

columella

septum

philtrum

lips

mouth

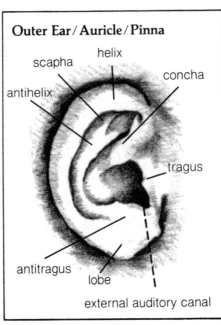

Outer Ear / Auricle / Pinna

helix

scapha

concha

antihelix

tragus

antitragus

lobe

external auditory canal

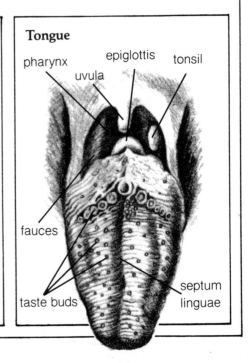

Tongue

pharynx

uvula

epiglottis

tonsil

fauces

taste buds

septum linguae

The Extremities

The space between the thumb and extended forefinger is the *purlicue*. A *fingerprint* is an ink impression of the *arches, loops* and *whorls* created by ridges of skin in the finger pad. The *back of the hand* is called the *opisthenar.*

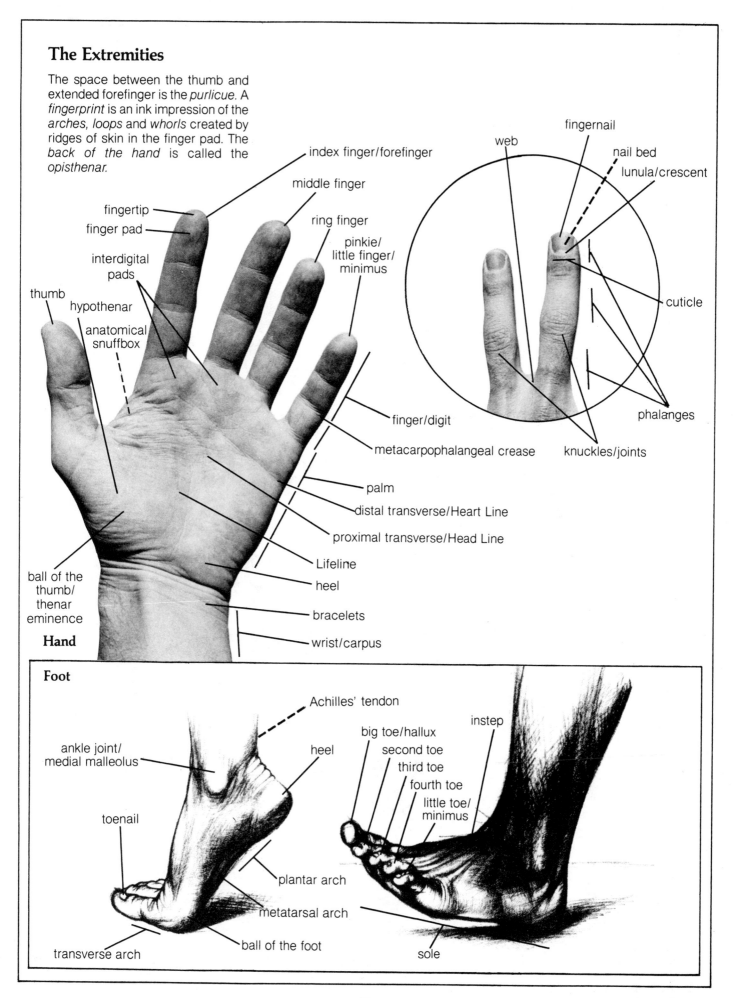

index finger/forefinger

middle finger

ring finger

pinkie/
little finger/
minimus

web

fingernail

nail bed

lunula/crescent

cuticle

fingertip

finger pad

interdigital
pads

thumb

hypothenar

anatomical
snuffbox

finger/digit

metacarpophalangeal crease

knuckles/joints

phalanges

palm

distal transverse/Heart Line

proximal transverse/Head Line

Lifeline

heel

bracelets

wrist/carpus

ball of the
thumb/
thenar
eminence

Hand

Foot

Achilles' tendon

big toe/hallux

second toe

third toe

fourth toe

little toe/
minimus

instep

ankle joint/
medial malleolus

heel

toenail

plantar arch

metatarsal arch

transverse arch

ball of the foot

sole

Human Anatomy

Cow

Young *cattle* are *calves;* females are *heifers* until they give birth and are then cows; males are *bulls.* Castrated males, raised for *beef,* are *steers.* Castrated males, raised as draft animals, are *oxen.* The body, or *torso,* of a cow is known as the *barrel.*

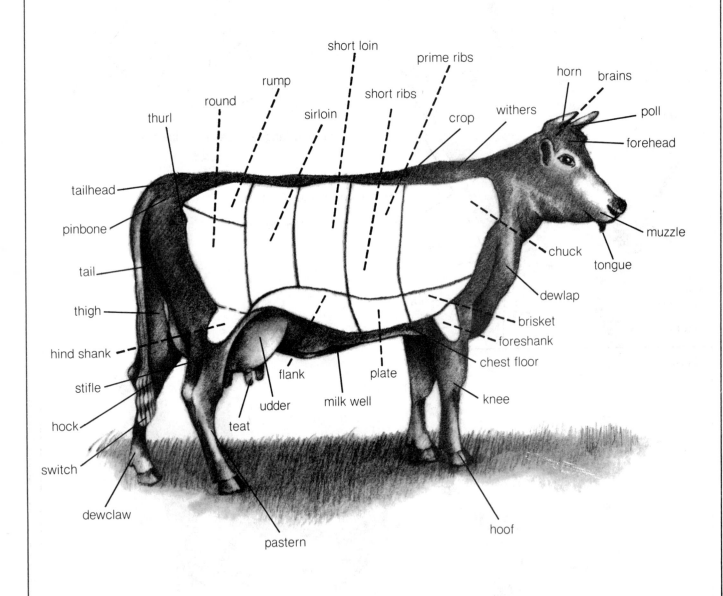

short loin

prime ribs

rump

round

horn   brains

thurl

sirloin

short ribs

crop

withers

poll

forehead

tailhead

pinbone

muzzle

chuck

tongue

tail

dewlap

thigh

brisket

hind shank

foreshank

stifle

flank   plate

chest floor

hock

udder   milk well

knee

switch

teat

dewclaw

pastern

hoof

Sheep

A young sheep is called a *lamb*. An adult male is a *ram;* an adult female is a *ewe*. The meat of a young sheep is called *lamb*, while that of an animal over eighteen months old is called *mutton*.

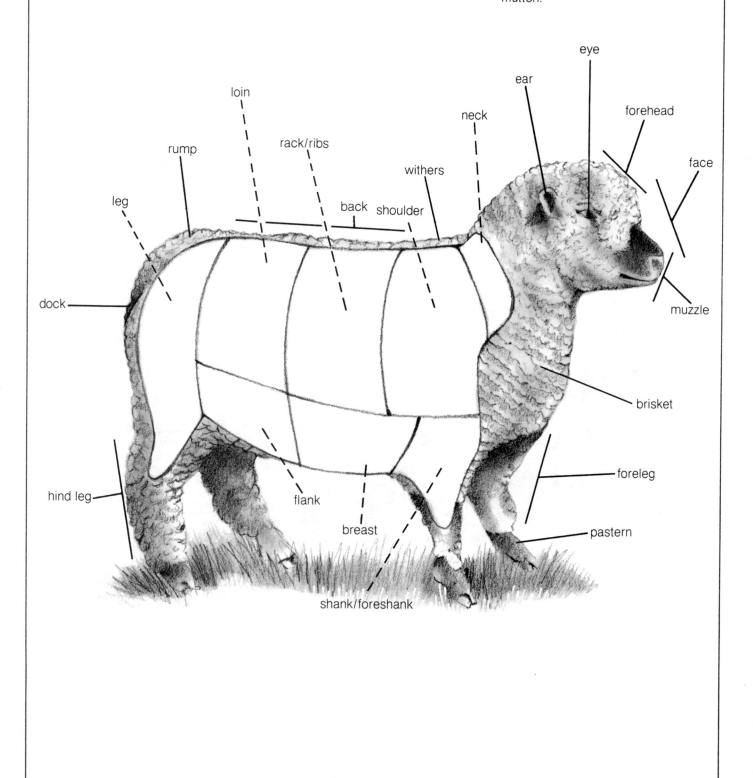

eye

ear

forehead

loin

neck

face

rack/ribs

rump

withers

leg

back   shoulder

dock

muzzle

brisket

foreleg

hind leg

flank

pastern

breast

shank/foreshank

Edible Animals

Pig

Young pigs are called *shoats*. Small or sub-adult domestic animals are *pigs* or *gruntlings*. If they weigh over 120 pounds, they are called *hogs*. Adult males are *boars*. Adult females are *sows*. Pigs, hogs, boars and sows are referred to as *swine*. Pig meat is called *pork*.

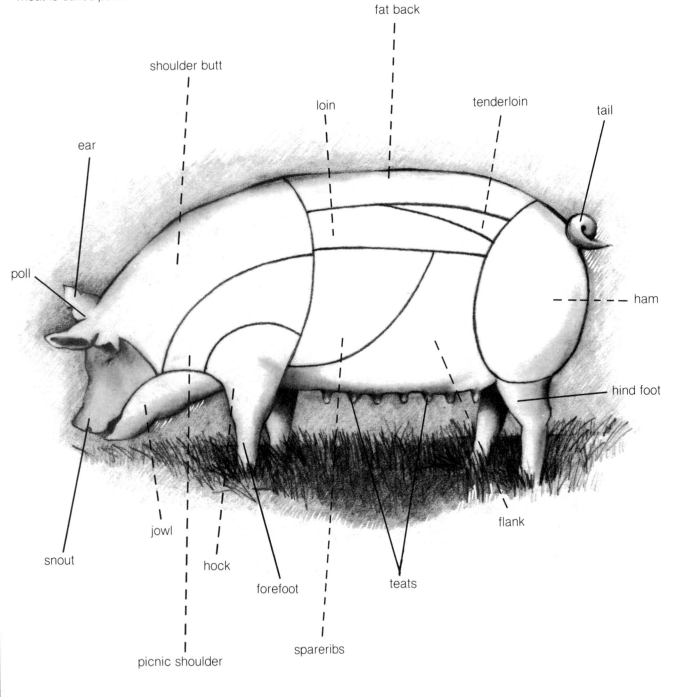

fat back

shoulder butt

loin

tenderloin

tail

ear

poll

ham

snout

jowl

hock

forefoot

teats

flank

hind foot

picnic shoulder

spareribs

Poultry

Chickens, turkeys, *ducks*, *geese* and *pheasants* are known collectively as *fowl* in the wild, as *poultry* if domesticated. A male chicken is a *rooster*; a female is a *hen*. A male turkey is a *tom*. Young chickens are *chicks*; young turkeys are *poults*. A *capon* is a male chicken that has been castrated before sexual maturity. Ducks have *webbed feet* and broad, flat *bills* with small teeth-like ridges. Among the *entrails* of a fowl, the most edible are the *giblets*: the *heart*, the *liver* and the *gizzard*.

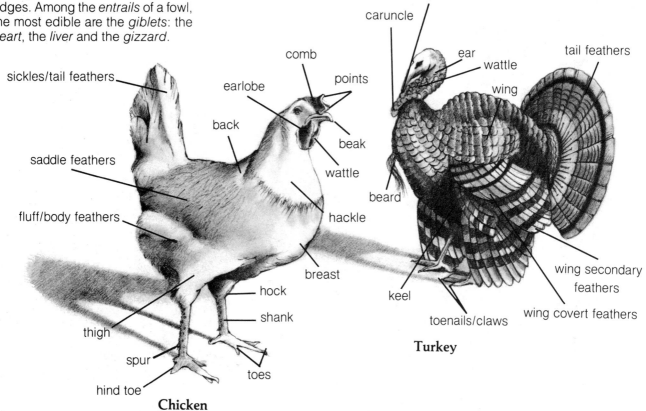

Chicken

Turkey

Poultry Parts

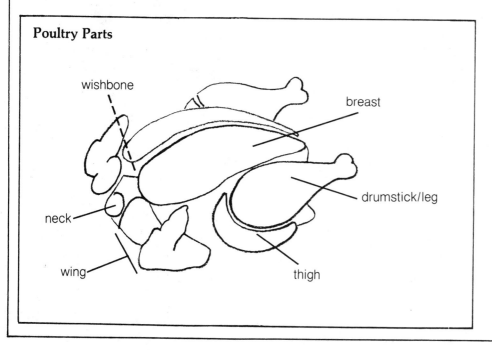

Edible Animals

Dog

Dogs are digitigrade animals; they walk on what are anatomically their four *fingertips*, or pads. The fifth finger, or *thumb*, a functionless inner claw, is known as a *dewclaw*, and does not reach the ground. The bushy tail of a rough-coated dog is called a *brush*. A smooth-coated dog's tail is a *stern*.

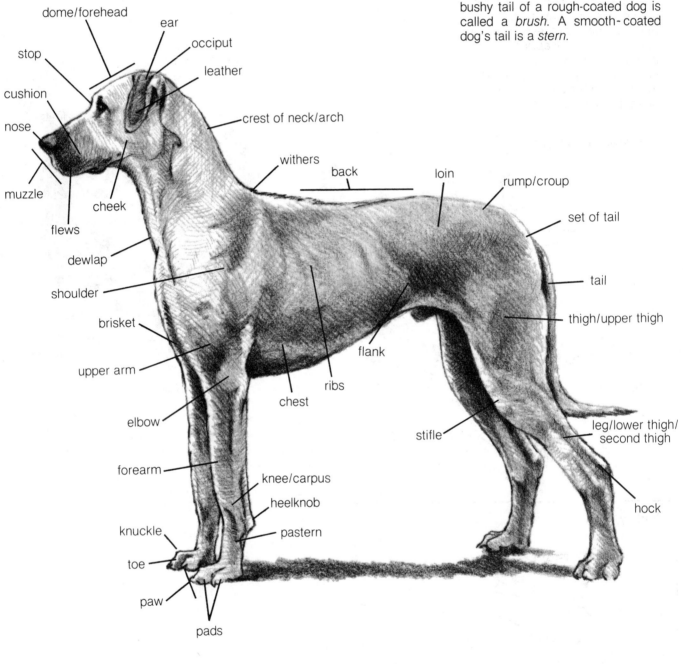

dome/forehead
ear
occiput
stop
leather
cushion
nose
crest of neck/arch
muzzle
withers
back
loin
rump/croup
cheek
flews
set of tail
dewlap
tail
shoulder
thigh/upper thigh
brisket
flank
upper arm
ribs
chest
elbow
stifle
leg/lower thigh/ second thigh
forearm
knee/carpus
heelknob
hock
knuckle
pastern
toe
paw
pads

Cat

Newborn cats are called *kittens*, adult males are *tomcats*, and adult females are *cattas*. Cats are capable of drawing their *toenails*, or *claws*, into *sheaths* located above the *pads* of their feet. A cat's *muzzle* consists of the *nose* and *jaw* sections of its face.

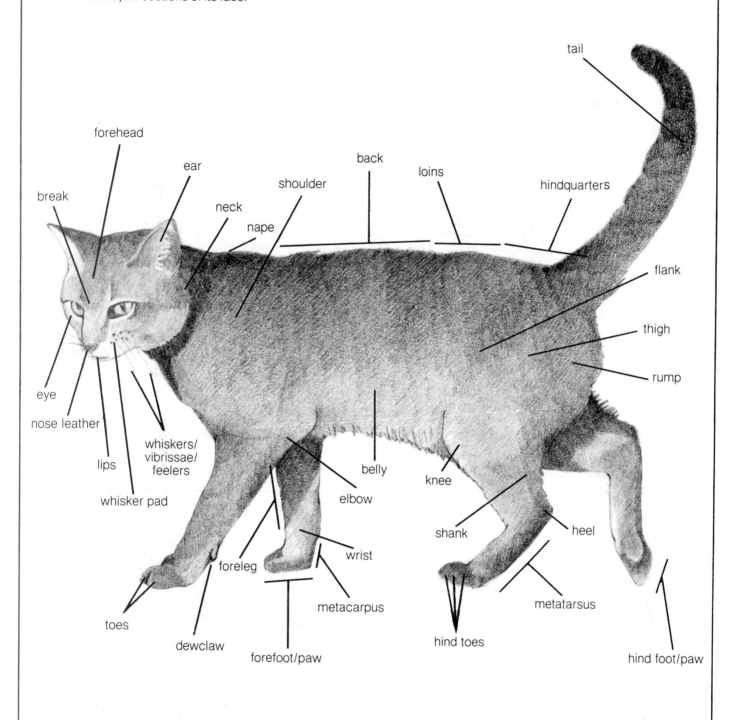

forehead

ear

break

neck

shoulder

nape

back

loins

hindquarters

tail

flank

thigh

rump

eye

nose leather

lips

whiskers/
vibrissae/
feelers

whisker pad

belly

elbow

knee

shank

heel

toes

foreleg

wrist

dewclaw

metacarpus

forefoot/paw

hind toes

metatarsus

hind foot/paw

Domestic Animals

A horse less than a year old is a *foal*. Male foals are *colts*, females are *fillies*. A mature male is a *stallion*, a female is a *mare*. In breeding, the male parent is a *sire*, the female is a *dam*. A castrated male is called a *gelding*.

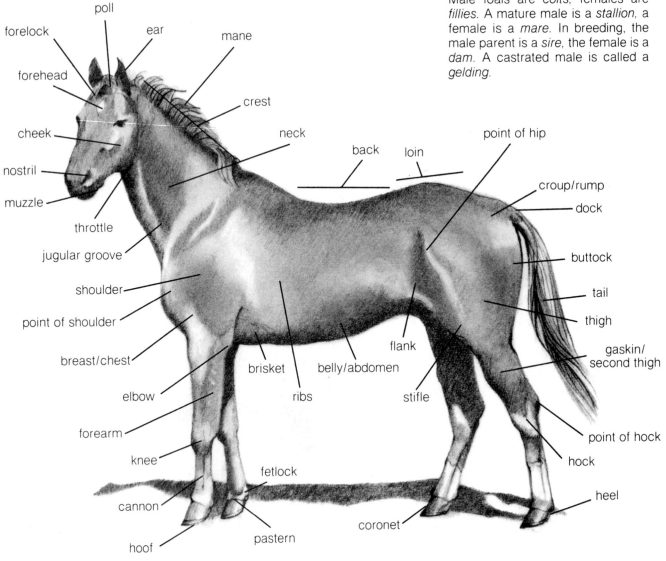

poll
forelock
ear
mane
forehead
crest
cheek
neck
nostril
back
loin
point of hip
muzzle
croup/rump
throttle
dock
jugular groove
buttock
shoulder
tail
point of shoulder
thigh
flank
breast/chest
gaskin/second thigh
brisket
belly/abdomen
elbow
ribs
stifle
forearm
point of hock
knee
hock
fetlock
cannon
heel
coronet
hoof
pastern

Foot

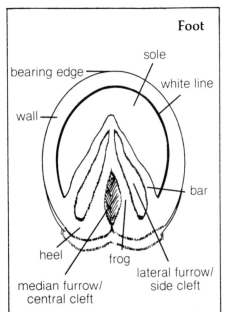

bearing edge
sole
white line
wall
bar
heel
frog
median furrow/central cleft
lateral furrow/side cleft

Hoof

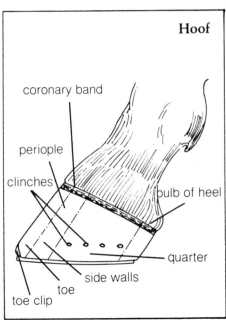

coronary band
periople
clinches
bulb of heel
quarter
toe clip
toe
side walls

Shoe

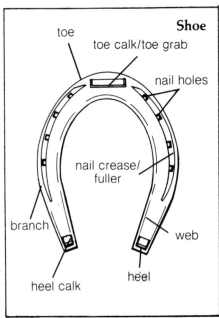

toe
toe calk/toe grab
nail holes
nail crease/fuller
branch
web
heel calk
heel

Bird

A *flight feather* consists of tightly meshed *barbs* along the vane. *Contour feathers* and an *undercoat* of fine *down* cover the bird's body. A featherless portion of a bird's skin is called an *apterium*.

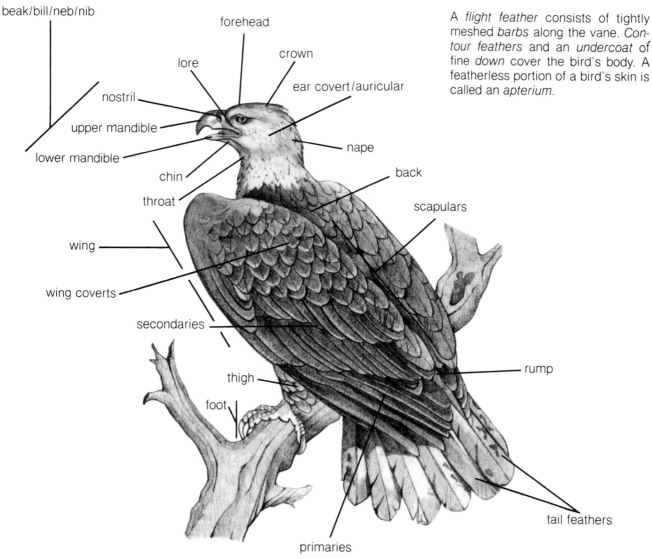

beak/bill/neb/nib

forehead

lore

crown

ear covert/auricular

nostril

upper mandible

nape

lower mandible

chin

back

throat

scapulars

wing

wing coverts

secondaries

rump

thigh

foot

tail feathers

primaries

Grasping Foot

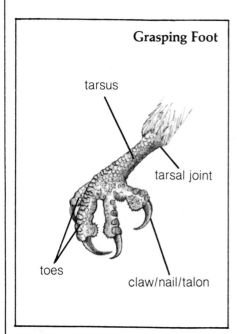

tarsus

tarsal joint

toes

claw/nail/talon

Swimming Foot/Webbed Foot

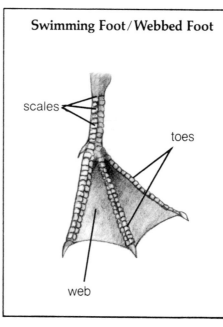

scales

toes

web

Feather

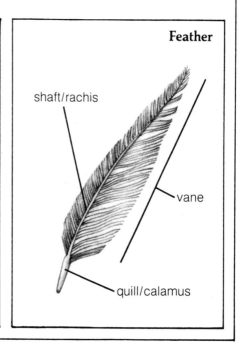

shaft/rachis

vane

quill/calamus

Wild Animals

Spider

Spiders produce *silk threads* which they use to make webs, *nests* or *parachutes* that allow the wind to carry them from one location to another. When a spider spins a web, it first constructs a *bridge* between two supports and fashions an *orb* beneath. A *scaffolding web* of dry thread is then used to lay down a *viscid spiral* of sticky thread.

pedipalpi

eyes

pedicel

coxa

trochanter

femur

patella

tibia

metatarsus

tarsus

leg

claws

scopula

cephalothorax

abdomen

spinnerets

Face

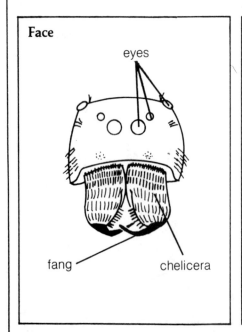

eyes

fang

chelicera

Web

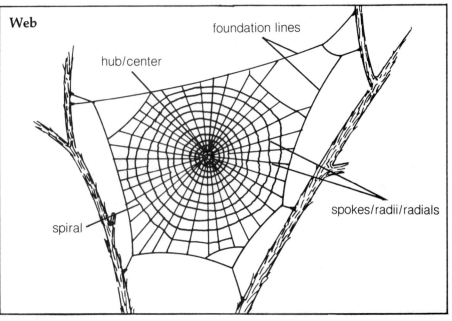

foundation lines

hub/center

spiral

spokes/radii/radials

Insects

Insects have shell-like outer coverings called *exoskeletons.* Most undergo four stages during *metamorphosis:* the *egg,* the *larva,* the *pupa,* and the *adult.*

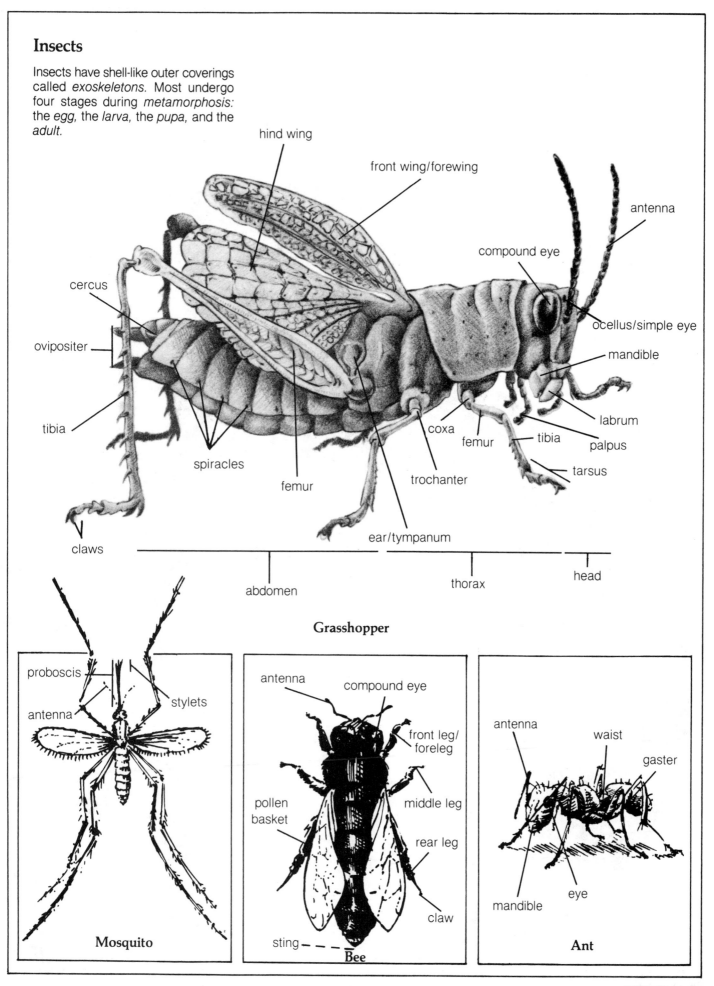

hind wing

front wing/forewing

antenna

compound eye

cercus

ocellus/simple eye

ovipositer

mandible

labrum

tibia

palpus

spiracles

coxa

tarsus

femur

femur

tibia

trochanter

claws

ear/tympanum

abdomen

thorax

head

Grasshopper

proboscis

stylets

antenna

compound eye

antenna

front leg/foreleg

pollen basket

middle leg

rear leg

claw

sting

Mosquito

Bee

antenna

waist

gaster

mandible

eye

Ant

Wild Animals

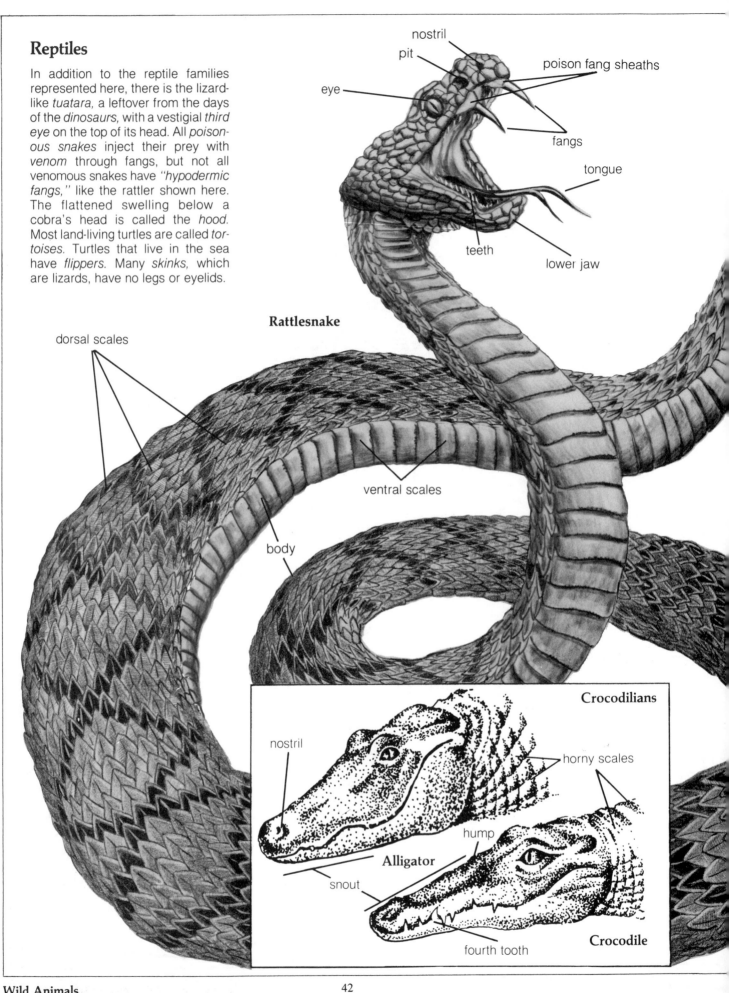

Reptiles

In addition to the reptile families represented here, there is the lizard-like *tuatara*, a leftover from the days of the *dinosaurs*, with a vestigial *third eye* on the top of its head. All *poisonous snakes* inject their prey with *venom* through fangs, but not all venomous snakes have *"hypodermic fangs,"* like the rattler shown here. The flattened swelling below a cobra's head is called the *hood*. Most land-living turtles are called *tortoises*. Turtles that live in the sea have *flippers*. Many *skinks*, which are lizards, have no legs or eyelids.

nostril
pit
poison fang sheaths
eye
fangs
tongue
teeth
lower jaw

Rattlesnake

dorsal scales

ventral scales

body

Crocodilians

nostril

horny scales

hump

Alligator

snout

fourth tooth

Crocodile

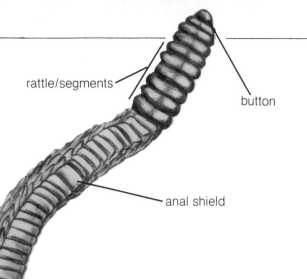

rattle/segments

button

anal shield

Dinosaurs/Extinct Reptiles

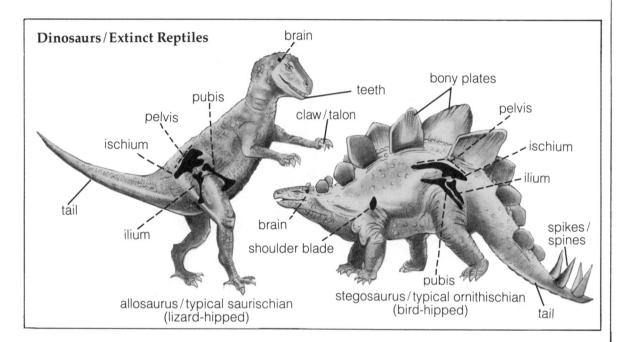

brain

teeth

bony plates

pelvis

pubis

claw/talon

ischium

pelvis

ischium

ilium

tail

brain

spikes/ spines

ilium

shoulder blade

pubis

allosaurus/typical saurischian
(lizard-hipped)

stegosaurus/typical ornithischian
(bird-hipped)

tail

Turtle/Tortoise

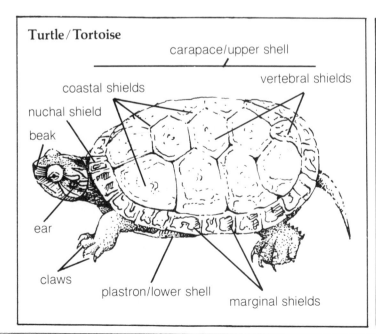

carapace/upper shell

coastal shields

vertebral shields

nuchal shield

beak

ear

claws

plastron/lower shell

marginal shields

Lizard/Iguana

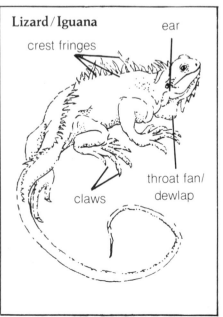

ear

crest fringes

throat fan/
dewlap

claws

Amphibians

Frogs and toads resemble one another closely, but toads are characteristically more terrestrial and have rougher, drier skin.

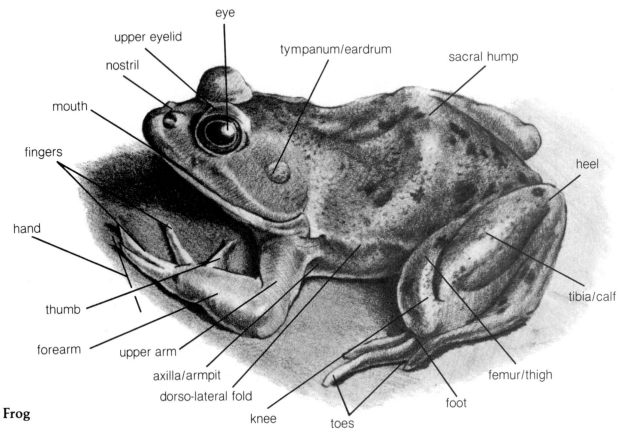

eye

upper eyelid

nostril

tympanum/eardrum

sacral hump

mouth

fingers

heel

hand

thumb

forearm

upper arm

tibia/calf

axilla/armpit

dorso-lateral fold

femur/thigh

knee

toes

foot

Frog

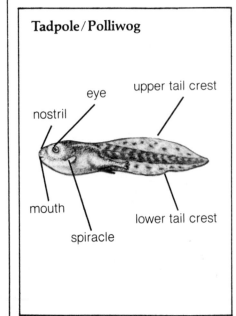

Tadpole/Polliwog

eye

upper tail crest

nostril

mouth

spiracle

lower tail crest

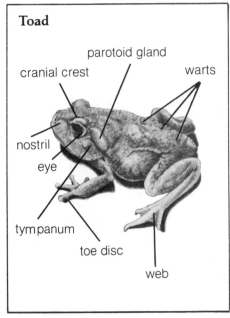

Toad

parotoid gland

cranial crest

warts

nostril

eye

tympanum

toe disc

web

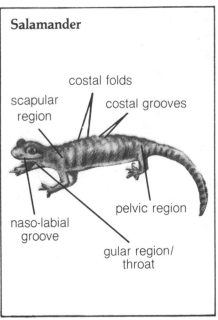

Salamander

costal folds

scapular region

costal grooves

naso-labial groove

pelvic region

gular region/throat

Marine Life

Fish often swim in groups, called *schools,* and reproduce by depositing eggs, or *spawning.* Recently hatched or small adult fish are called *fry.*

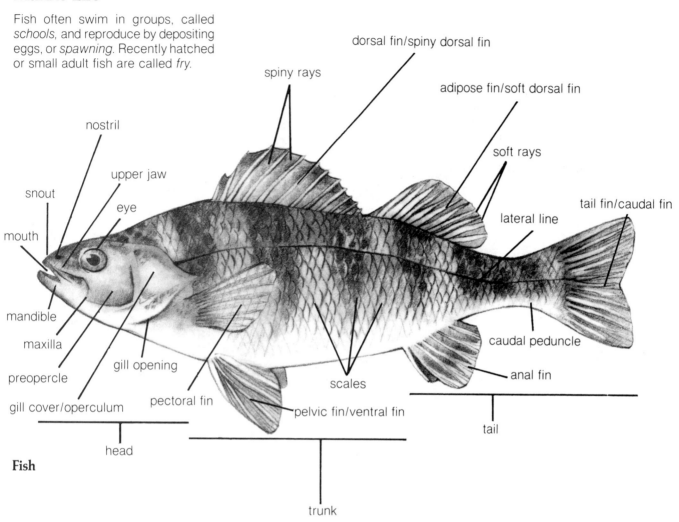

spiny rays

dorsal fin/spiny dorsal fin

adipose fin/soft dorsal fin

soft rays

nostril

upper jaw

snout

eye

mouth

lateral line

tail fin/caudal fin

mandible

maxilla

preopercle

gill opening

gill cover/operculum

pectoral fin

scales

caudal peduncle

anal fin

pelvic fin/ventral fin

tail

head

Fish

trunk

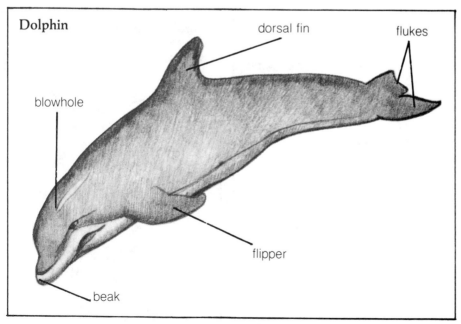

Dolphin

dorsal fin

flukes

blowhole

flipper

beak

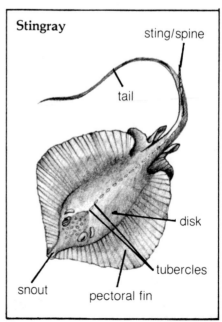

Stingray

sting/spine

tail

disk

snout

pectoral fin

tubercles

Wild Animals

Marine Life

The *mantle* of an octopus is the tough protective wrapper that covers the body and gives it shape. Octopuses and squid have *chromatophores*, or *pigment cells*, which enable them to change color, as well as *ink glands*, or *sacs*, that secrete protective *"ink."* Starfish have *mouths* on their *oral surfaces*. Coral polyps live within limestone *skeletons*, which form the basis for *coral reefs*.

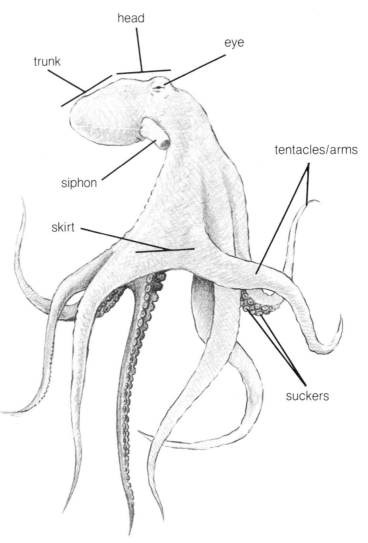

head

eye

trunk

tentacles/arms

siphon

skirt

suckers

Octopus/Devilfish

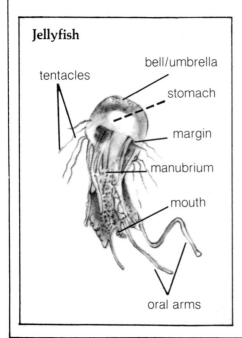

Jellyfish

tentacles

bell/umbrella

stomach

margin

manubrium

mouth

oral arms

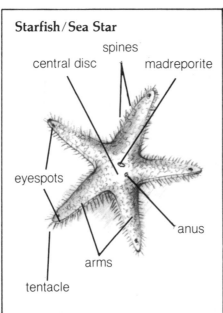

Starfish/Sea Star

spines

central disc

madreporite

eyespots

anus

arms

tentacle

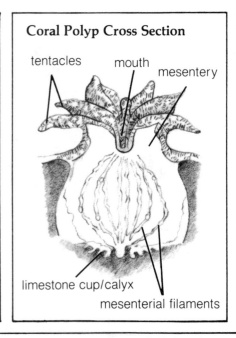

Coral Polyp Cross Section

tentacles

mouth

mesentery

limestone cup/calyx

mesenterial filaments

Shellfish

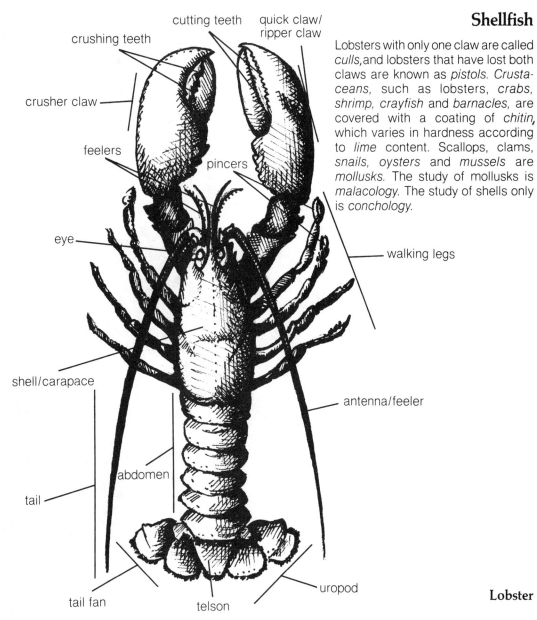

crushing teeth

cutting teeth

quick claw/ripper claw

crusher claw

feelers

pincers

eye

walking legs

shell/carapace

antenna/feeler

abdomen

tail

tail fan

telson

uropod

Lobster

Lobsters with only one claw are called *culls,* and lobsters that have lost both claws are known as *pistols. Crustaceans*, such as lobsters, *crabs, shrimp, crayfish* and *barnacles*, are covered with a coating of *chitin,* which varies in hardness according to *lime* content. Scallops, clams, *snails, oysters* and *mussels* are *mollusks*. The study of mollusks is *malacology*. The study of shells only is *conchology*.

Univalve Shell/Snail

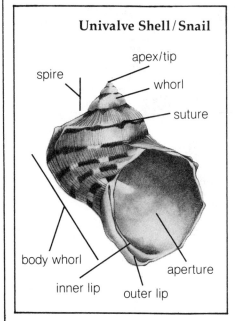

spire

apex/tip

whorl

suture

body whorl

inner lip

outer lip

aperture

Bivalve Shell/Scallop

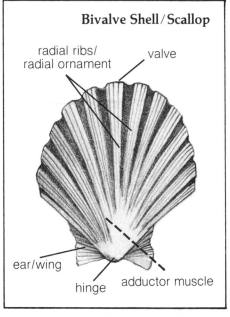

radial ribs/radial ornament

valve

ear/wing

hinge

adductor muscle

Bivalve Shell/Clam

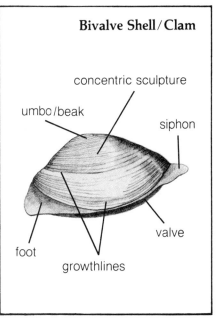

concentric sculpture

umbo/beak

siphon

foot

growthlines

valve

Wild Animals

Ultimate Beast

This remarkable *creature* calls attention to those parts of animals which are distinctive to particular species. Missing are posterior extensions, or *tails,* which vary from long, thin tails that end in a *brush* and have a horny appendage called a *thorn* in the middle, such as a lion's, to brushy fox tails and stubby boar tails. Another composite animal is the legendary *manticore,* which combined the head of a man, the body of a lion, and the tail of a *dragon* or *scorpion.*

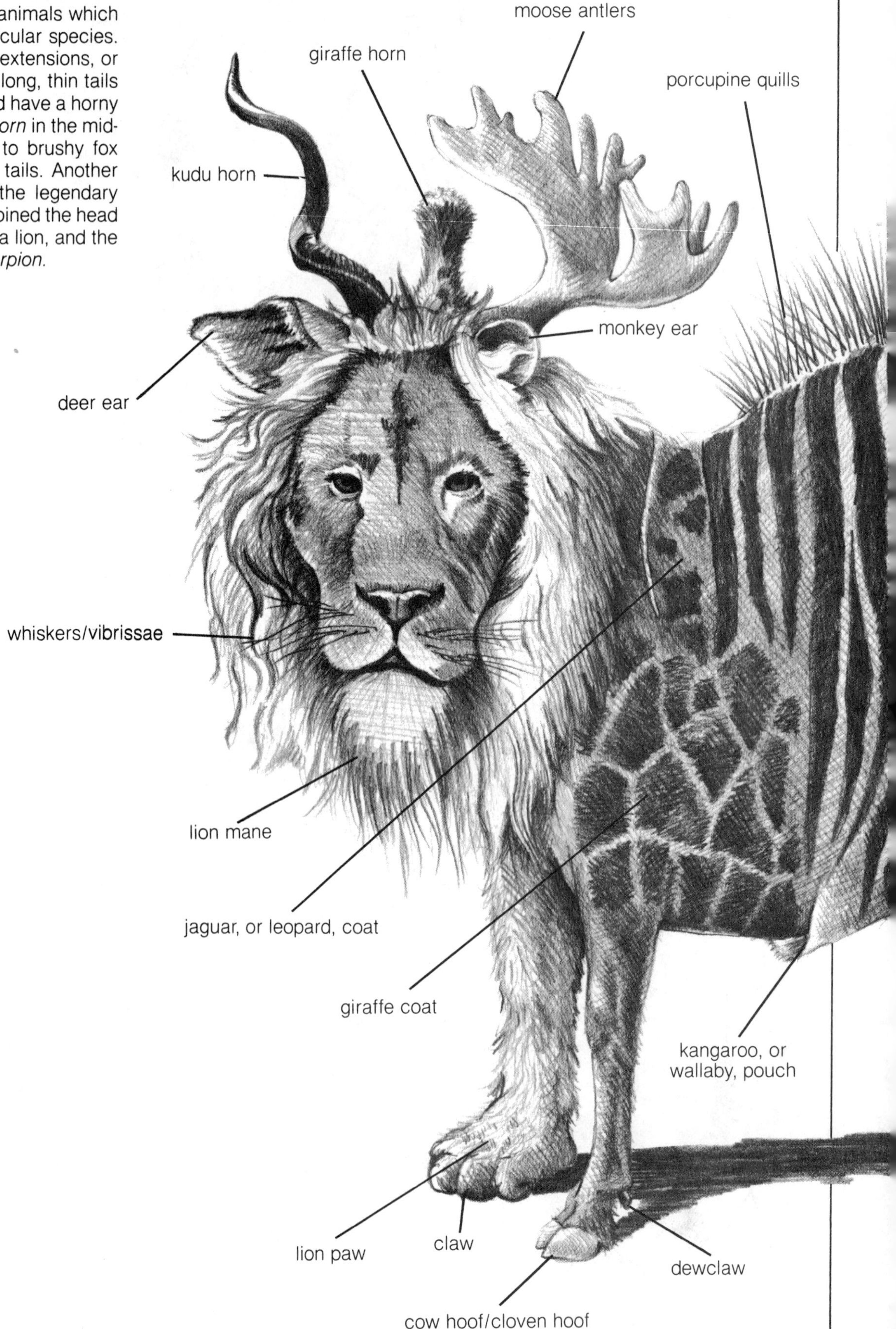

moose antlers

giraffe horn

porcupine quills

kudu horn

monkey ear

deer ear

whiskers/vibrissae

lion mane

jaguar, or leopard, coat

giraffe coat

kangaroo, or wallaby, pouch

lion paw

claw

dewclaw

cow hoof/cloven hoof

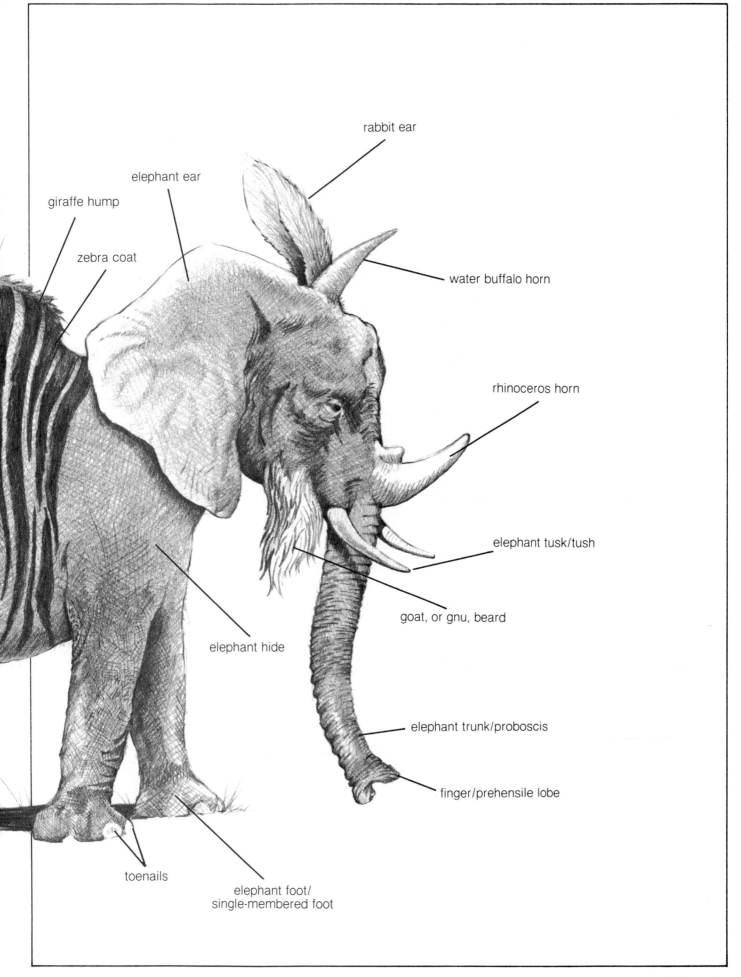

rabbit ear

elephant ear

giraffe hump

zebra coat

water buffalo horn

rhinoceros horn

elephant tusk/tush

goat, or gnu, beard

elephant hide

elephant trunk/proboscis

finger/prehensile lobe

toenails

elephant foot/
single-membered foot

Tree

When a tree is cut down, what remains attached to the *root* is called a *stump*.

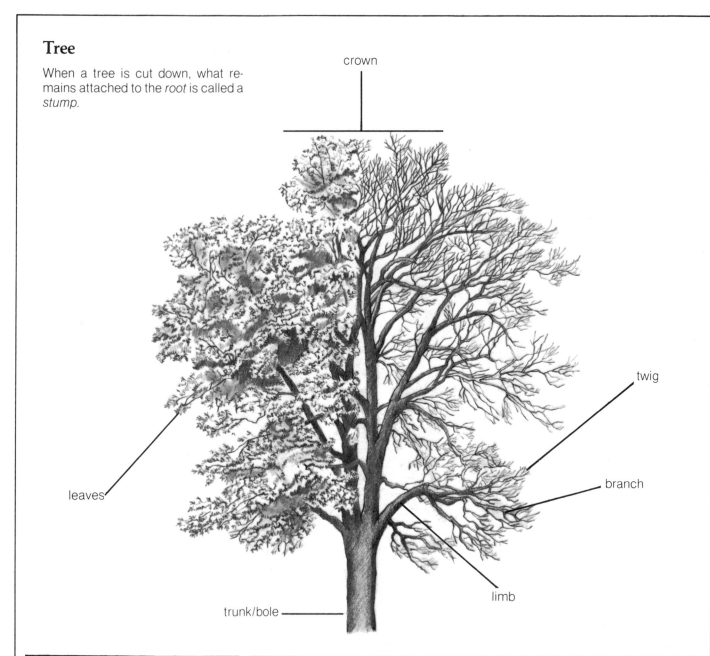

crown

twig

branch

leaves

limb

trunk/bole

Tree Trunk Cross Section

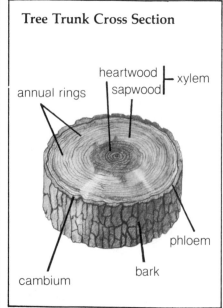

annual rings

heartwood
sapwood
$\}$ xylem

cambium

bark

phloem

Twig

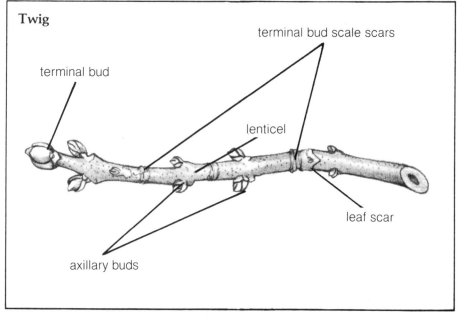

terminal bud scale scars

terminal bud

lenticel

leaf scar

axillary buds

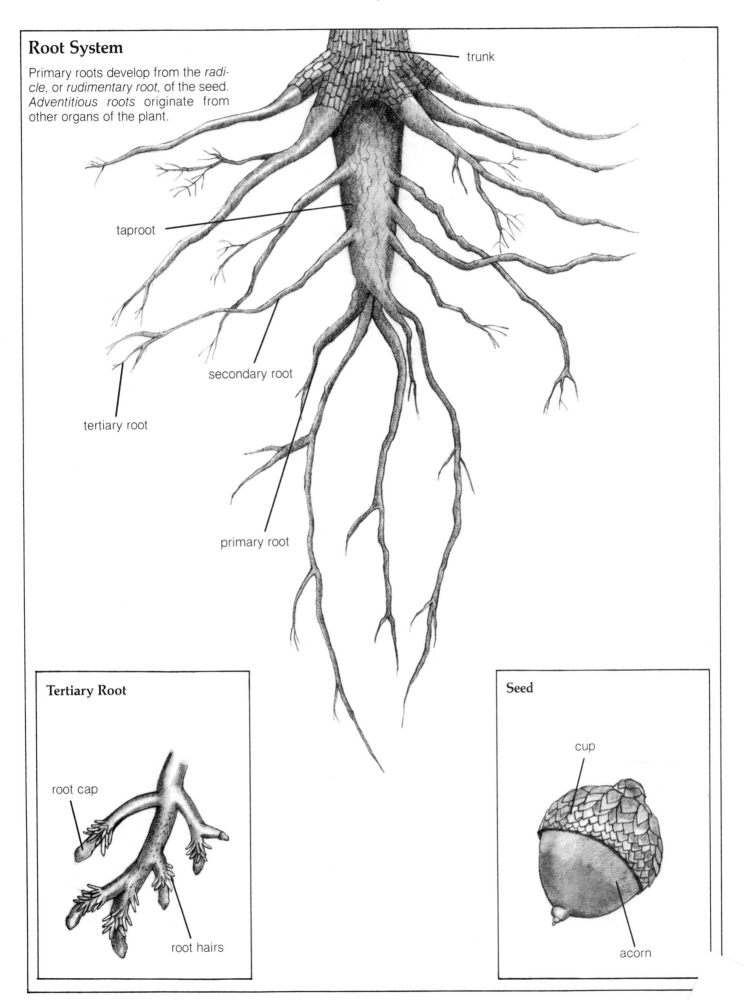

Root System

Primary roots develop from the *radicle*, or *rudimentary root*, of the seed. *Adventitious roots* originate from other organs of the plant.

trunk

taproot

secondary root

tertiary root

primary root

Tertiary Root

root cap

root hairs

Seed

cup

acorn

51

Leaf

The waxy layer covering the outer leaf is the *cuticle*. Tiny leaves, spines or growths at the base of a leaf stem are called *stipules. Compound leaves* are made up of two or more blades, or *leaflets*. The aggregate of leaves produced by one or more plants is called *foliage*.

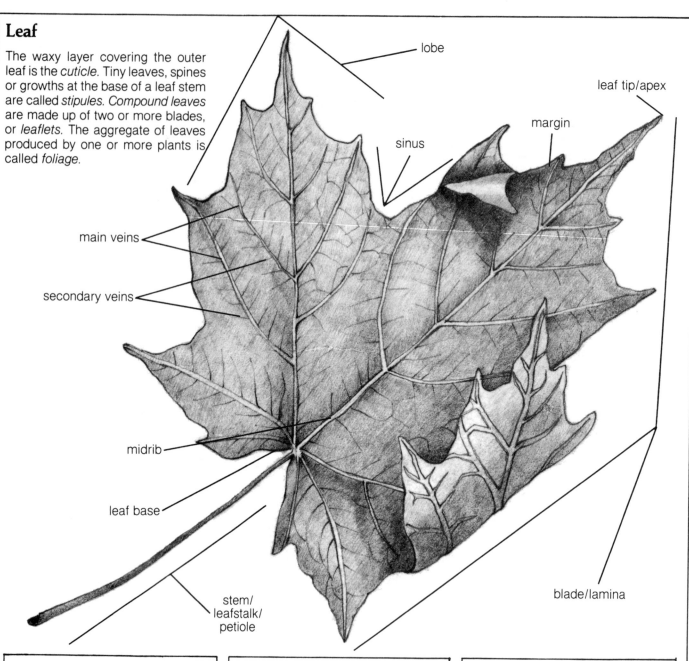

lobe

leaf tip/apex

margin

sinus

main veins

secondary veins

midrib

leaf base

stem/ leafstalk/ petiole

blade/lamina

Pine Cone

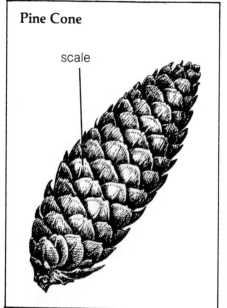

scale

Samara/Key

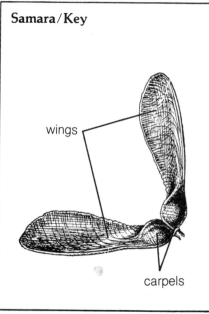

wings

carpels

Palm

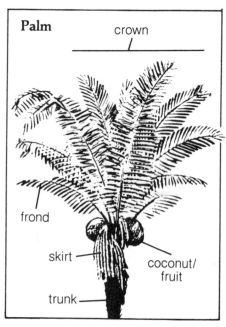

crown

frond

skirt

coconut/ fruit

trunk

Flower

Most flowers have an outer covering of leaflike *sepals* protecting an inner whorl of bright-colored, scented *petals*. When sepals and petals are almost identical, as they are in the lily shown here, they are called *tepals*. Flower *seeds* are created when *pollen* from the anther fertilizes *ovules,* or *egg cells,* in the stigma.

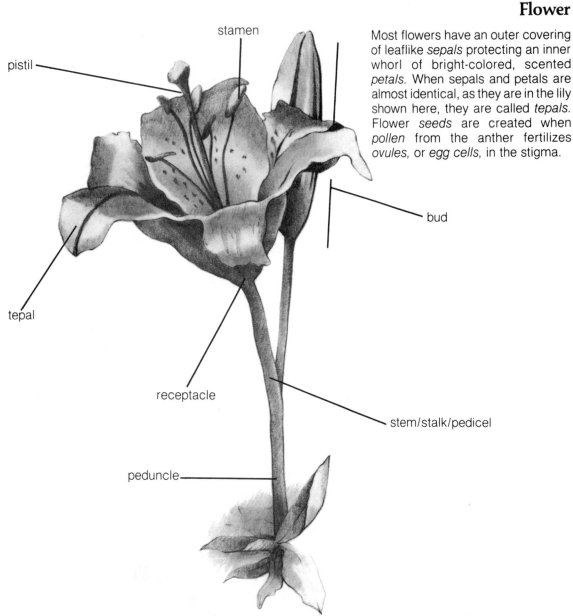

pistil

stamen

tepal

bud

receptacle

stem/stalk/pedicel

peduncle

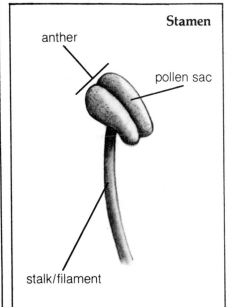

Stamen

anther

pollen sac

stalk/filament

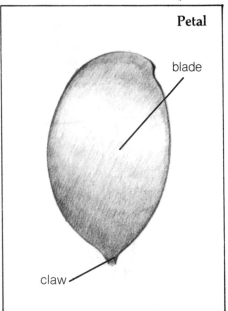

Petal

blade

claw

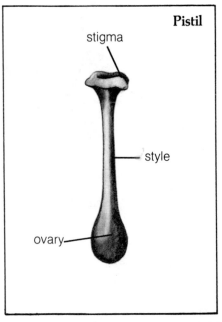

Pistil

stigma

style

ovary

Vegetables

A vegetable is that part of a plant that can be eaten. The roots of carrots, beets and turnips are edible, as are asparagus stems, potato tubers, leek and onion leaf bases, cabbage, lettuce and spinach leaves, the *immature fruit,* or *ovary,* of cucumbers, peas and summer squash, and the *mature fruit* of tomatoes and winter squash.

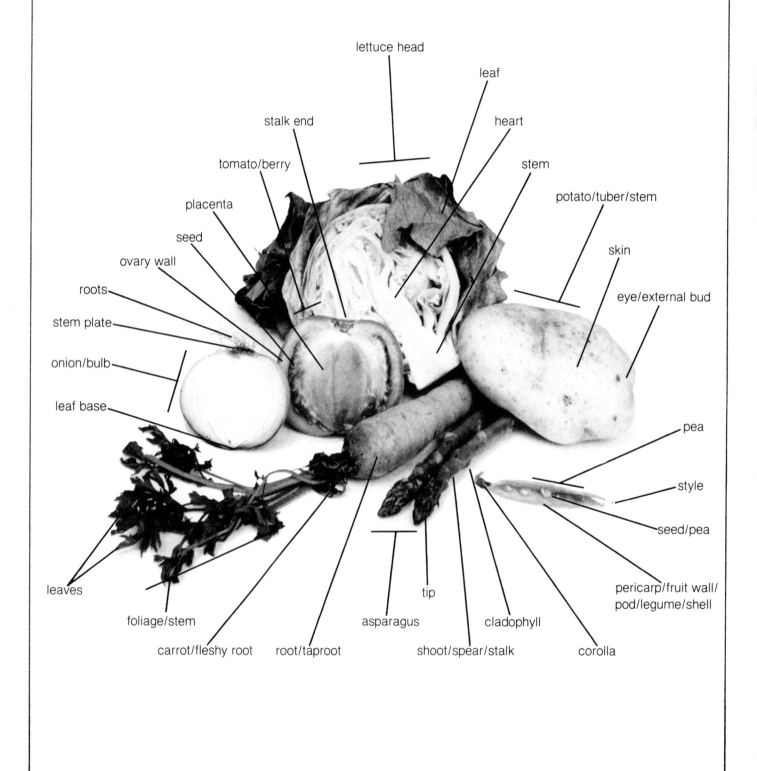

lettuce head

leaf

stalk end

heart

tomato/berry

stem

placenta

potato/tuber/stem

seed

skin

ovary wall

roots

eye/external bud

stem plate

onion/bulb

leaf base

pea

style

seed/pea

leaves

pericarp/fruit wall/
pod/legume/shell

foliage/stem

tip

carrot/fleshy root

root/taproot

asparagus

cladophyll

corolla

shoot/spear/stalk

Nuts and crops commonly referred to as vegetables, such as tomatoes and melons, are actually *vegetable fruits*. Fruits are classed according to the number of ovaries they have: They range from simple fruits, such as peaches, to aggregate fruits, such as strawberries. Each segment of *multiple fruits,* such as pineapples and figs, is edible.

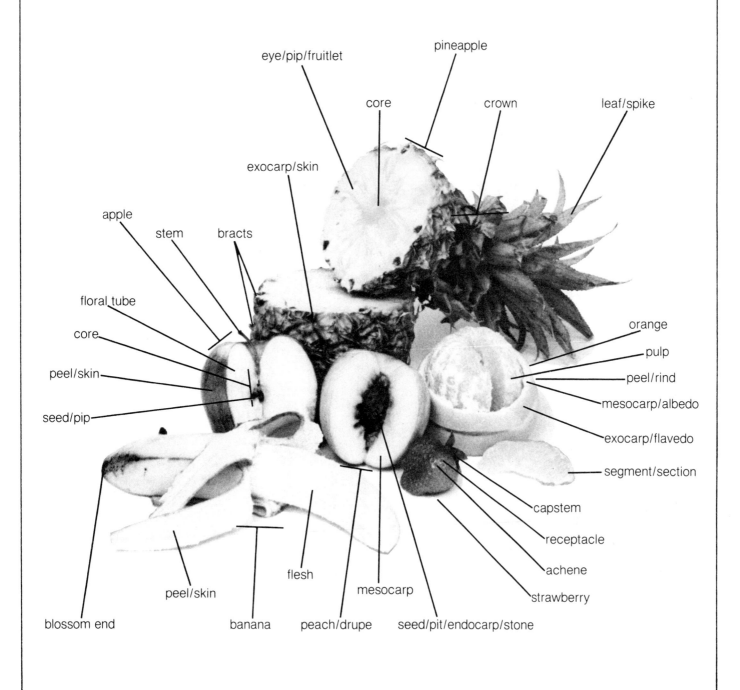

eye/pip/fruitlet

pineapple

core

crown

leaf/spike

exocarp/skin

apple

stem

bracts

floral tube

core

peel/skin

seed/pip

orange

pulp

peel/rind

mesocarp/albedo

exocarp/flavedo

segment/section

capstem

receptacle

achene

strawberry

blossom end

peel/skin

banana

flesh

peach/drupe

mesocarp

seed/pit/endocarp/stone

Succulents

Succulents are plants with *fleshy tissue* that have the ability to store moisture for long periods of time in their stem. Some cacti have protective *glochidia,* razor-sharp hairlike bristles, in addition to spines and flowers.

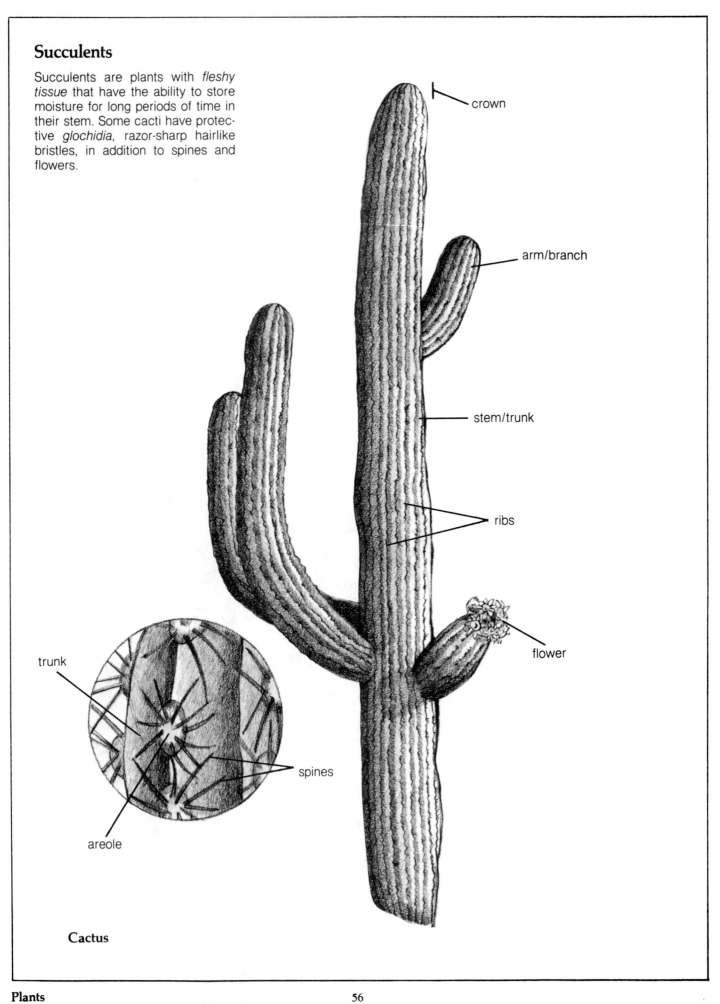

crown

arm/branch

stem/trunk

ribs

flower

trunk

spines

areole

Cactus

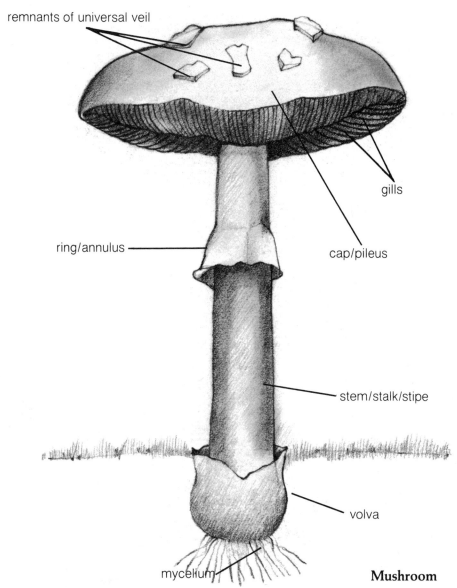

remnants of universal veil

gills

ring/annulus

cap/pileus

stem/stalk/stipe

volva

mycelium

Mushroom

Toadstools are inedible mushrooms, or *fungi*. Flowerless, seedless ferns reproduce by means of *spores* carried in spore cases on the underside of the leaves. Seaweed, such as the *marine algae* shown here, attaches itself to the ocean floor by means of a *holdfast*.

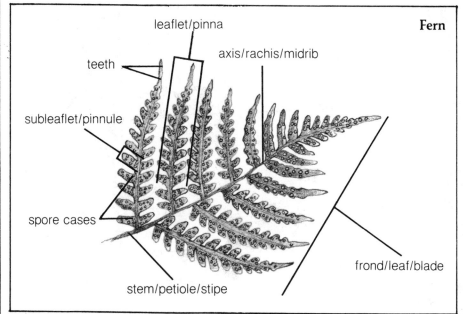

Fern

leaflet/pinna

axis/rachis/midrib

teeth

subleaflet/pinnule

spore cases

frond/leaf/blade

stem/petiole/stipe

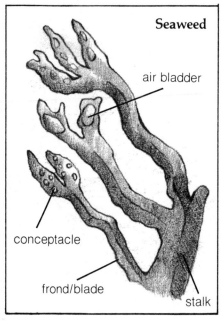

Seaweed

air bladder

conceptacle

frond/blade

stalk

57

Plants

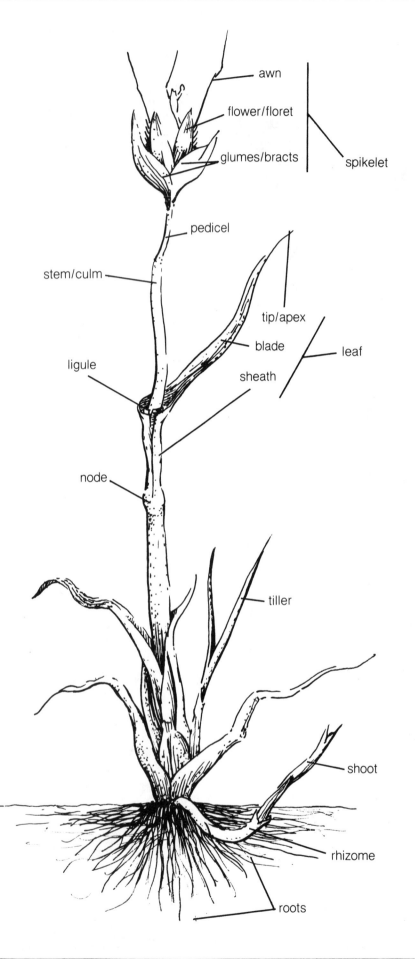

awn

flower/floret

glumes/bracts

spikelet

pedicel

stem/culm

tip/apex

blade

leaf

ligule

sheath

node

tiller

shoot

rhizome

roots

Grass

There are two parts to grass plants, the *vegetable organs* and the *floral organs*. *Cereal grasses*, such as *wheat, oat, barley* and corn, produce edible *fruit, seed* or *kernels*. Rhizomes and *stolons*, or *runners*—above-ground stems—spread out from grass plants to produce new plants. The *inflorescence*, or *flower cluster*, of grasses consists of many spikelets. Grass leaves are *parallel-veined*.

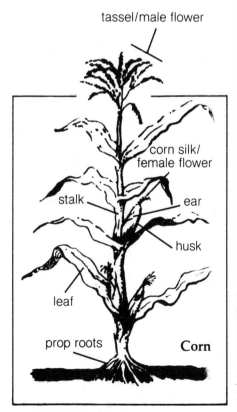

tassel/male flower

corn silk/
female flower

stalk

ear

husk

leaf

prop roots

Corn

Shelters and Structures

Since man's most basic shelter is a house, it is illustrated in a variety of ways, from foundation and frame to windows and walls.

The shelters and structures in the rest of the section are grouped in three subcategories: designs from other lands, which range from pagodas to pyramids; special-purpose buildings such as the Capitol and the White House, skyscrapers and prisons, amusement parks and airports; and other structures which bear on our everyday lives—bridges, tunnels, canals and dams.

The terms for the parts of objects found in most shelter interiors are the same as those found in a house, all of which have been illustrated. But those of a courtroom are sufficiently different to merit coverage, as are the parts of a skyscraper's elevator and escalator. In some cases floor plans and cross-section illustrations have been used to facilitate the reader's access to terms which are unique to a particular structure.

Building Connections

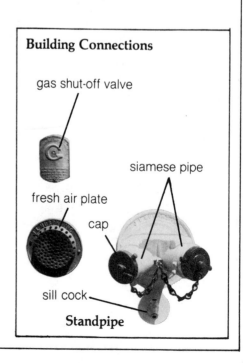

gas shut-off valve

fresh air plate

siamese pipe

cap

sill cock

Standpipe

Foundation

Some houses are built on sunken *posts,* or *piers.* Others are built on concrete floors, or *slabs.* The area of a house built below ground level is the *basement.* Houses without basements usually have an area between the floor joists and the ground called a *crawl space,* through which access is gained to inspect pipes.

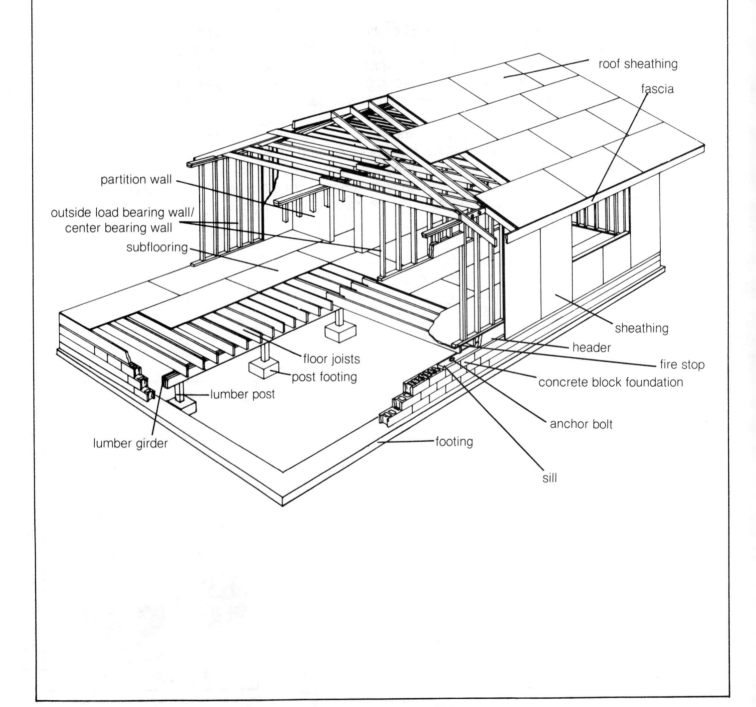

partition wall

outside load bearing wall/
center bearing wall

subflooring

floor joists

post footing

lumber post

lumber girder

roof sheathing

fascia

sheathing

header

fire stop

concrete block foundation

anchor bolt

footing

sill

Frame

Any diagonally placed piece of timber in a frame is a *brace*. A *cat* is a small piece of lumber nailed between studs for reinforcement. *Beams* are squared off pieces of timber, such as *joists*, used to support *floor* or *ceiling*, or *lintels*, horizontal *members* designed to carry loads above openings such as doors and windows.

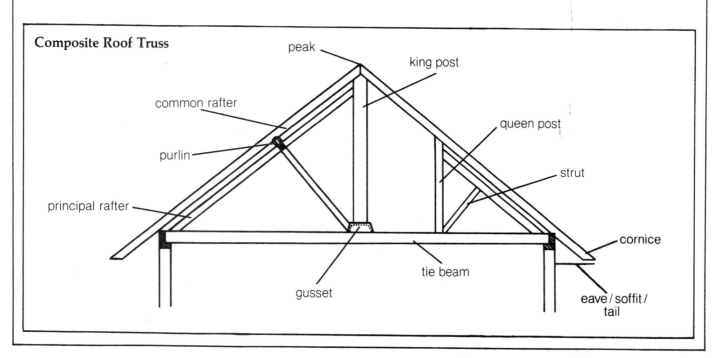

ridgepole/ridgeboard

wood splice

fascia rafter

collar beam

top plate

roof rafter

cripples

ceiling joist

jack stud

fascia

header

outrigger

door bucks

bottom plate/sole plate

header joist

stud

doubling

anchor bolt

corner post

sill plate

rough sill

Composite Roof Truss

peak

king post

common rafter

queen post

purlin

strut

principal rafter

cornice

tie beam

gusset

eave / soffit / tail

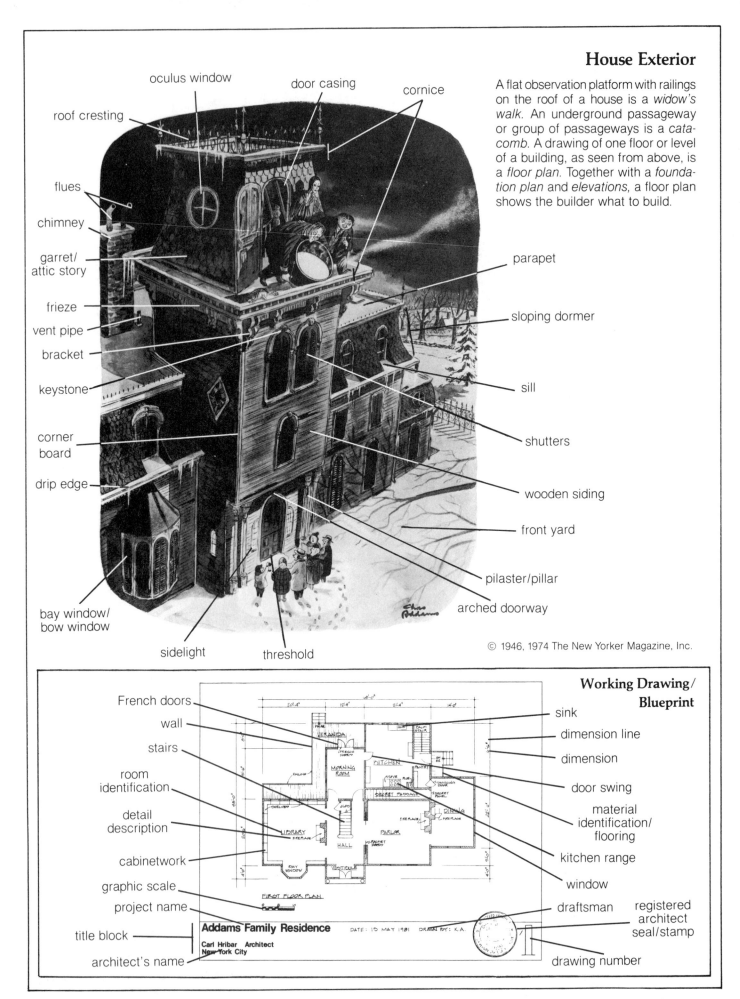

House Exterior

A flat observation platform with railings on the roof of a house is a *widow's walk*. An underground passageway or group of passageways is a *catacomb*. A drawing of one floor or level of a building, as seen from above, is a *floor plan*. Together with a *foundation plan* and *elevations*, a floor plan shows the builder what to build.

oculus window

door casing

cornice

roof cresting

flues

chimney

garret/ attic story

frieze

vent pipe

bracket

keystone

corner board

drip edge

bay window/ bow window

sidelight

threshold

parapet

sloping dormer

sill

shutters

wooden siding

front yard

pilaster/pillar

arched doorway

© 1946, 1974 The New Yorker Magazine, Inc.

Working Drawing/ Blueprint

French doors

wall

stairs

room identification

detail description

cabinetwork

graphic scale

project name

title block

architect's name

sink

dimension line

dimension

door swing

material identification/ flooring

kitchen range

window

draftsman

registered architect seal/stamp

drawing number

Addams Family Residence
Carl Hribar Architect
New York City

FIRST FLOOR PLAN

House Exterior

The room or space under the roof is the *attic*. The lowest story of a house is called the *basement* if it is at least partly below ground or street level. A part of a house projecting on one side or subordinate to the main structure is called a *wing*. *Patios, terraces, decks* and *porches* adjoin a house and are used for play or relaxation. An open *gallery* alongside a house with its own roof is a *veranda*.

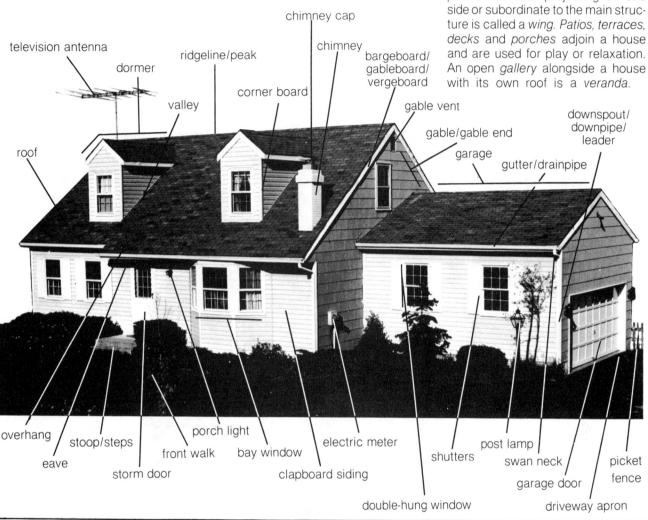

television antenna
dormer
ridgeline/peak
valley
corner board
roof
chimney cap
chimney
bargeboard/ gableboard/ vergeboard
gable vent
gable/gable end
garage
downspout/ downpipe/ leader
gutter/drainpipe

overhang
eave
stoop/steps
storm door
front walk
porch light
bay window
clapboard siding
electric meter
double-hung window
shutters
post lamp
swan neck
garage door
driveway apron
picket fence

House Styles

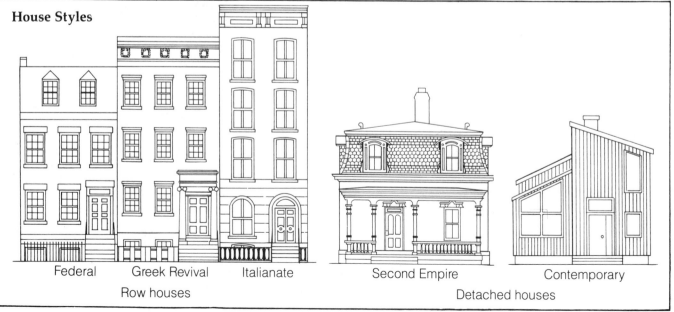

Federal   Greek Revival   Italianate

Row houses

Second Empire   Contemporary

Detached houses

House

Door

The *sill, threshold,* or *saddle* is that part directly beneath the door. Entrance doors are often covered by *screendoors*. A door cut in half horizontally whose two parts can be used independently is called a *Dutch door*. A door having glass panes throughout or nearly throughout its length is a *French door*. The rubber-tipped projection attached to the wall behind an opening door to protect it from the impact is a *doorstop*.

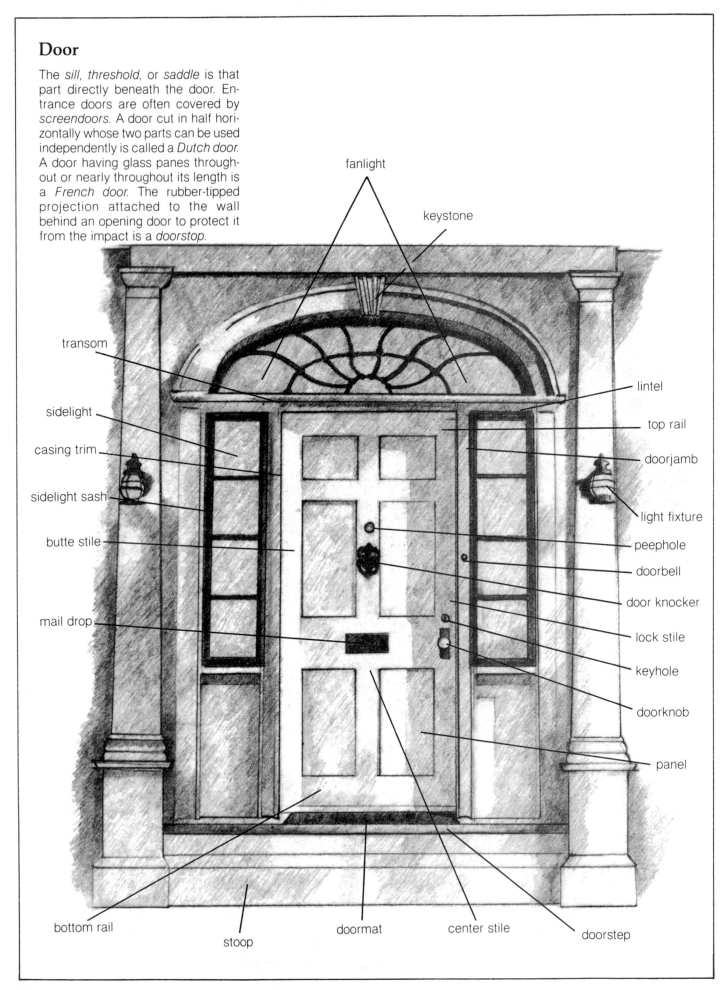

fanlight

keystone

transom

sidelight

casing trim

sidelight sash

butte stile

mail drop

lintel

top rail

doorjamb

light fixture

peephole

doorbell

door knocker

lock stile

keyhole

doorknob

panel

bottom rail

stoop

doormat

center stile

doorstep

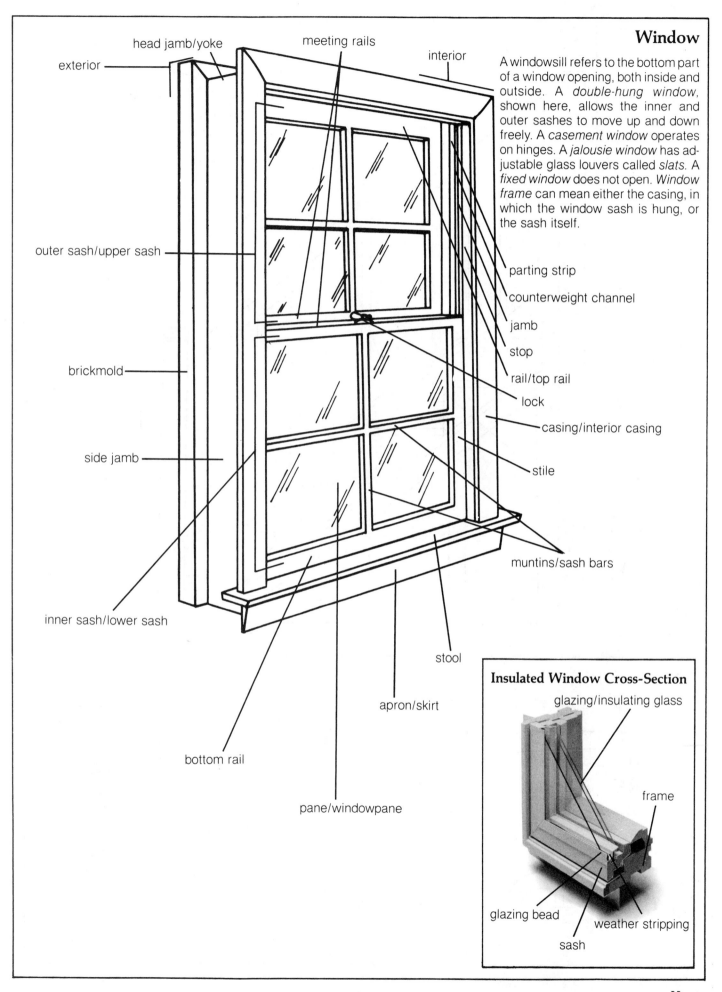

Window

A windowsill refers to the bottom part of a window opening, both inside and outside. A *double-hung window*, shown here, allows the inner and outer sashes to move up and down freely. A *casement window* operates on hinges. A *jalousie window* has adjustable glass louvers called *slats*. A *fixed window* does not open. *Window frame* can mean either the casing, in which the window sash is hung, or the sash itself.

head jamb/yoke

exterior

meeting rails

interior

parting strip

counterweight channel

jamb

stop

rail/top rail

lock

casing/interior casing

stile

outer sash/upper sash

brickmold

side jamb

muntins/sash bars

inner sash/lower sash

stool

apron/skirt

bottom rail

pane/windowpane

Insulated Window Cross-Section

glazing/insulating glass

frame

glazing bead

weather stripping

sash

House

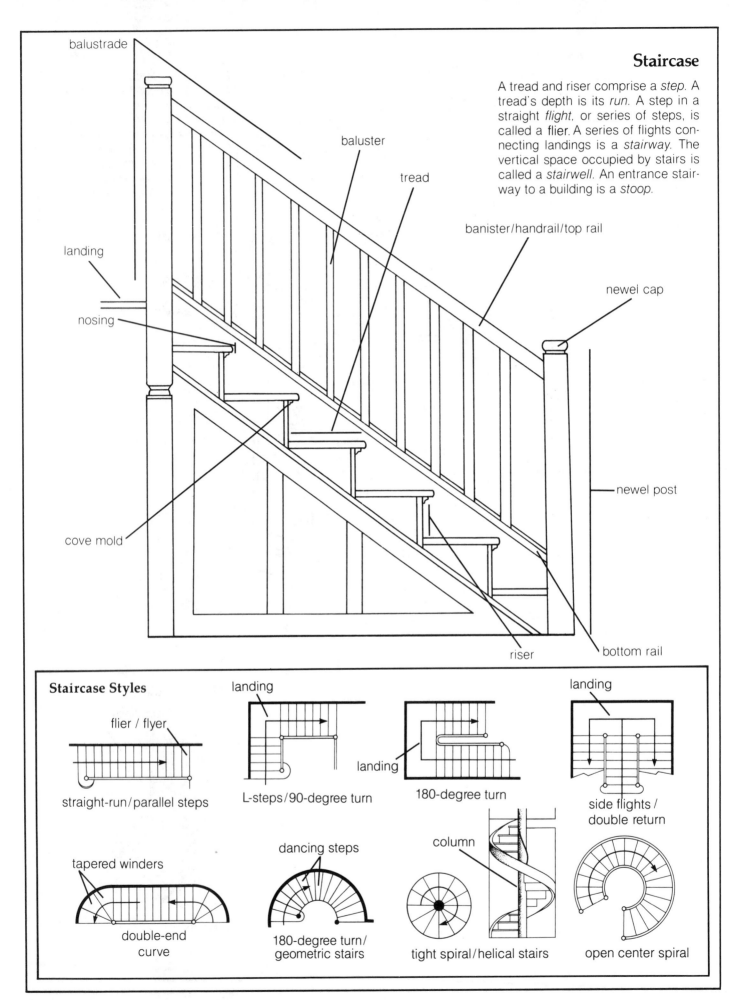

balustrade

baluster

tread

Staircase

A tread and riser comprise a *step*. A tread's depth is its *run*. A step in a straight *flight*, or series of steps, is called a **flier**. A series of flights connecting landings is a *stairway*. The vertical space occupied by stairs is called a *stairwell*. An entrance stairway to a building is a *stoop*.

banister/handrail/top rail

landing

newel cap

nosing

cove mold

newel post

riser

bottom rail

Staircase Styles

flier / flyer

straight-run/parallel steps

landing

L-steps/90-degree turn

landing

180-degree turn

landing

side flights / double return

tapered winders

double-end curve

dancing steps

180-degree turn/ geometric stairs

column

tight spiral/helical stairs

open center spiral

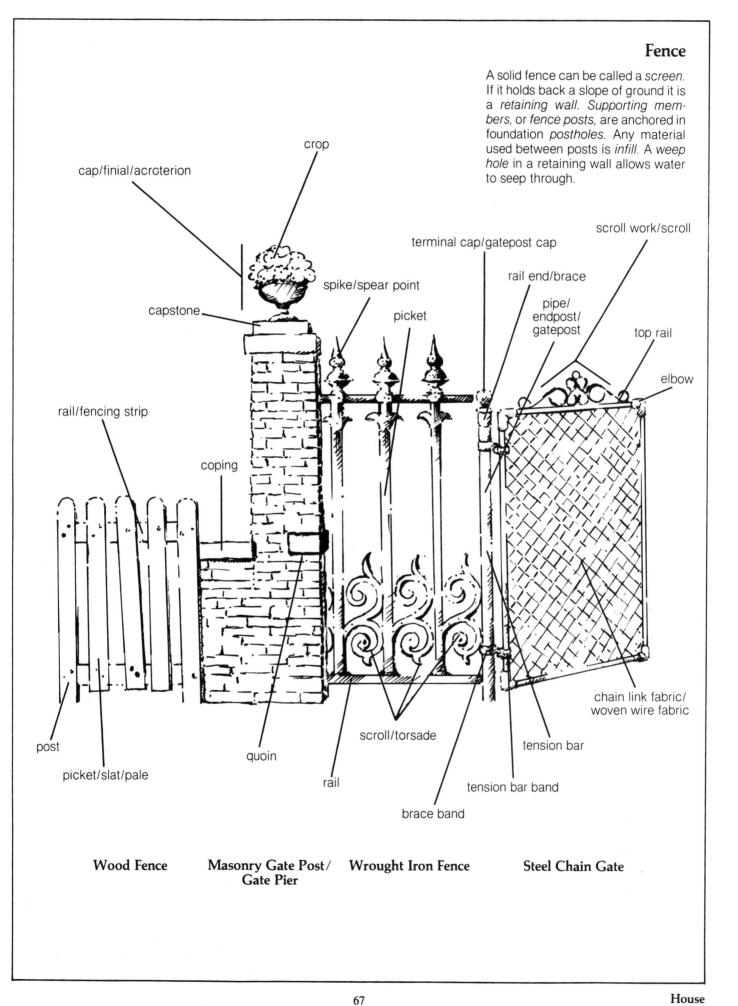

Fence

A solid fence can be called a *screen*. If it holds back a slope of ground it is a *retaining wall. Supporting members*, or *fence posts*, are anchored in foundation *postholes*. Any material used between posts is *infill*. A *weep hole* in a retaining wall allows water to seep through.

crop

cap/finial/acroterion

capstone

spike/spear point

picket

terminal cap/gatepost cap

scroll work/scroll

rail end/brace

pipe/
endpost/
gatepost

top rail

elbow

rail/fencing strip

coping

chain link fabric/
woven wire fabric

post

picket/slat/pale

quoin

rail

scroll/torsade

tension bar

tension bar band

brace band

Wood Fence   **Masonry Gate Post/
Gate Pier**   **Wrought Iron Fence**   **Steel Chain Gate**

Building Materials

Boards are *timber,* or lumber, cut in long, flat *slabs.* When used in construction, boards are referred to as *beams,* or *balks.* When they are used to support a pitched roof, they are called *rafters.* A *plank* is thicker than a board. *Shakes* are *wooden shingles,* but cracks in wood caused by wind or frost are also called shakes. A *spall* is a chip or flaking of brick.

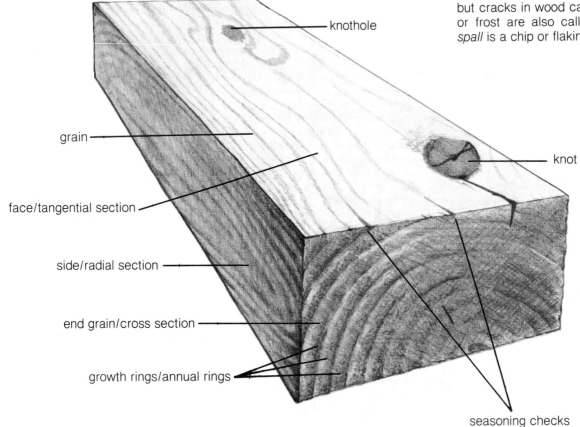

knothole

grain

face/tangential section

side/radial section

end grain/cross section

growth rings/annual rings

knot

seasoning checks

Lumber

Brick/Masonry Unit

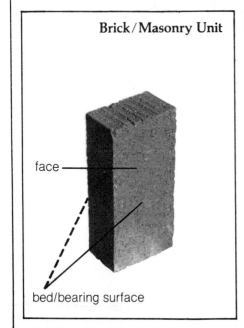

face

bed/bearing surface

Roofing Shingle

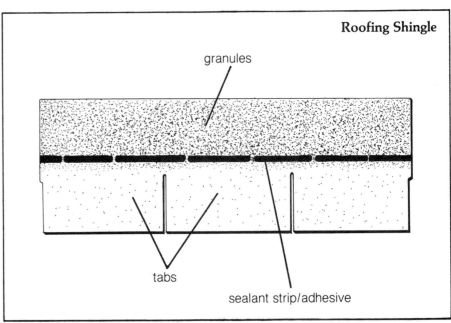

granules

tabs

sealant strip/adhesive

Brick Wall

Bricks and brick faces take on different names, depending on where and how they are used or exposed. Structures built of *stone* or brick are called *masonry.* The pattern in which a wall is laid is its *bond.* The exposed surface is the *face.* A piece of iron or steel used to brace a wall is a *cramp,* while a recess left within for pipes or ducts is a *chase.* A *tie* is any material that holds masonry together.

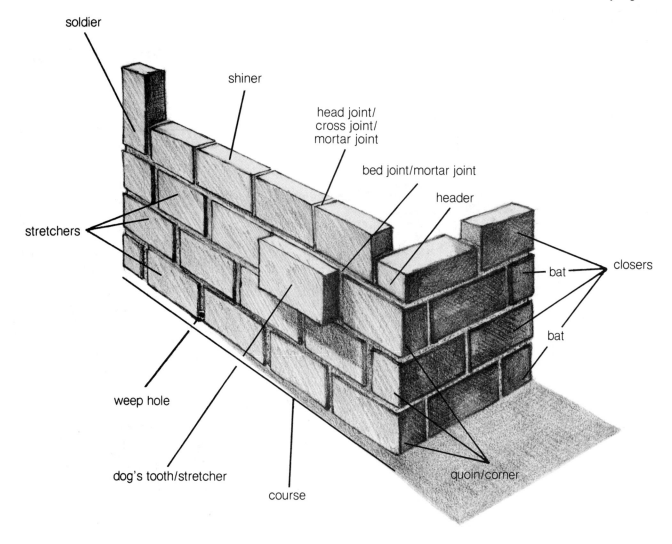

soldier

shiner

head joint/
cross joint/
mortar joint

bed joint/mortar joint

header

stretchers

closers

bat

bat

weep hole

dog's tooth/stretcher

course

quoin/corner

International Architecture

The Japanese developed the *whole-timbered building,* with *interlocking timbered joints.* Minarets, from which *criers,* or *muezzins,* call people to prayer, are normally attached or annexed to a mosque. Obelisks were often surrounded by *pillars,* or stelae, erected in honor of gods. Pyramids, *quadrilateral structures,* were used as tombs or temples. Flat-topped pyramids called *mastabas* were strictly *funerary structures,* while *ziggurats,* stepped pyramids supporting a *shrine,* were used for worship.

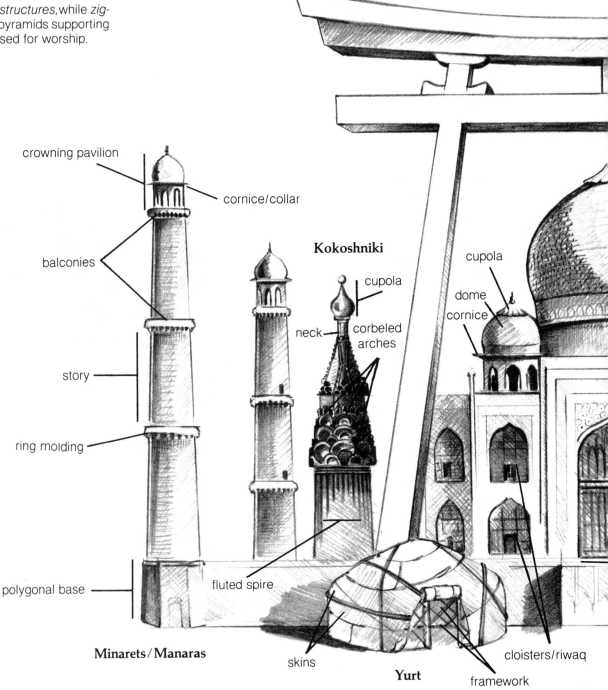

Torii/Shinto Temple Gateway

crowning pavilion

cornice/collar

balconies

Kokoshniki

cupola

neck

corbeled arches

cupola

dome

cornice

story

ring molding

polygonal base

fluted spire

Minarets/Manaras

skins

Yurt

cloisters/riwaq

framework

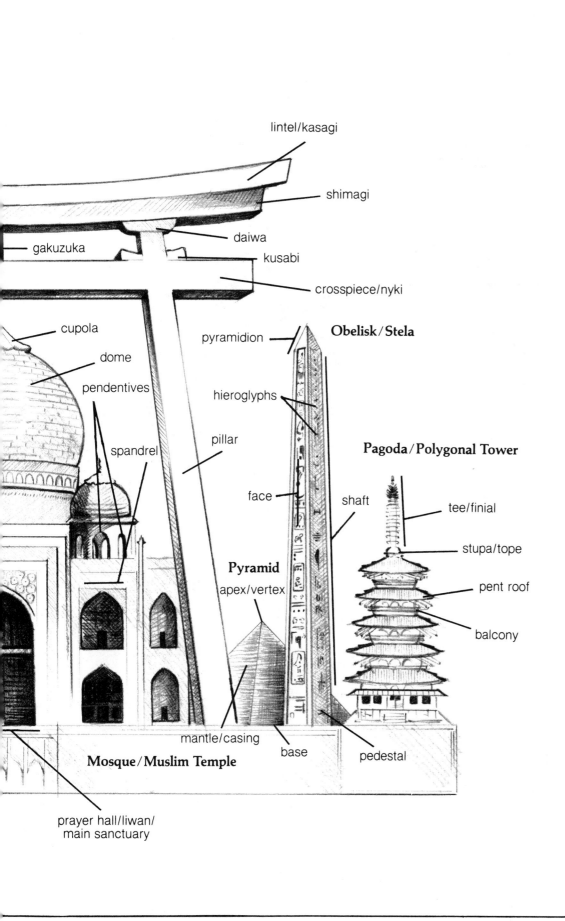

lintel/kasagi

shimagi

gakuzuka

daiwa

kusabi

crosspiece/nyki

cupola

Obelisk/Stela

pyramidion

dome

pendentives

hieroglyphs

Pagoda/Polygonal Tower

spandrel

pillar

shaft

tee/finial

face

stupa/tope

pent roof

Pyramid

apex/vertex

balcony

mantle/casing

base

pedestal

Mosque/Muslim Temple

prayer hall/liwan/
main sanctuary

Arch

The distance between the imposts is called the *span*. The *rise* is the distance between the top of the imposts and the highest point of the intrados. The *crown* is the highest point of the extrados. The area of an arch extending from the crown to the impost is the *haunch*, or *hance*.

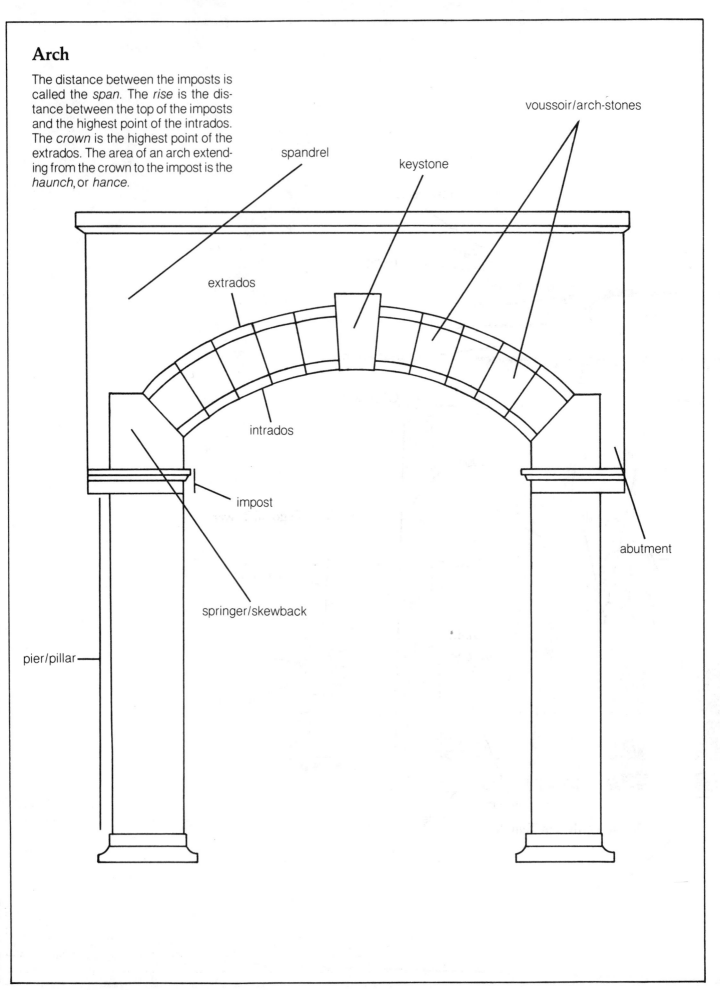

spandrel

keystone

voussoir/arch-stones

extrados

intrados

impost

abutment

springer/skewback

pier/pillar

Column

The clear space between two columns is *intercolumniation*.

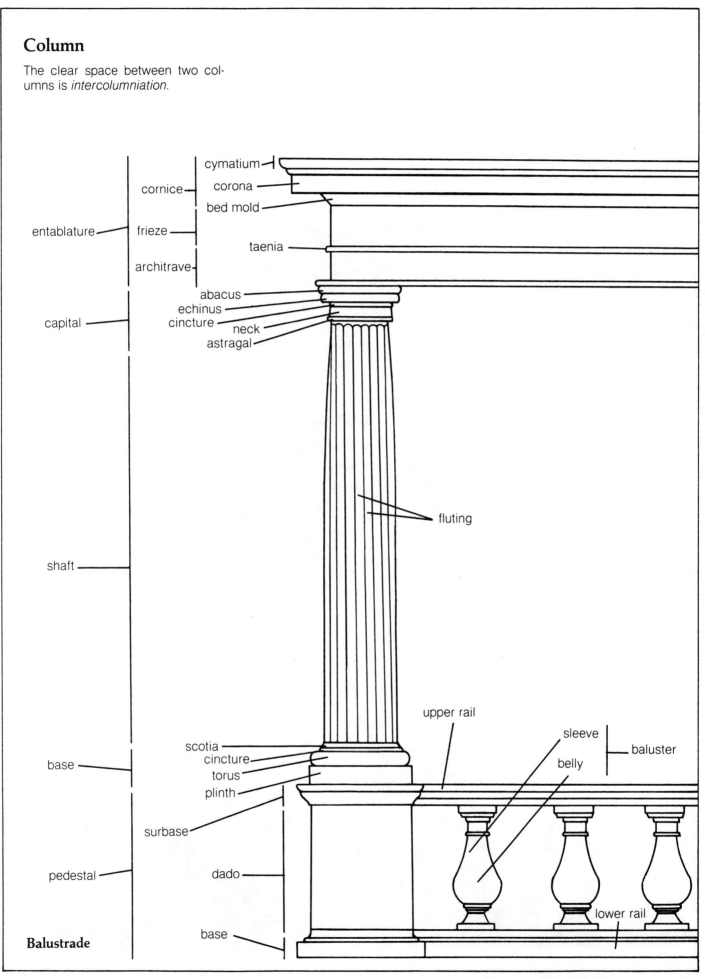

entablature
- cornice
  - cymatium
  - corona
  - bed mold
- frieze
  - taenia
- architrave

capital
- abacus
- echinus
- cincture
- neck
- astragal

shaft
- fluting

base
- scotia
- cincture
- torus
- plinth
- surbase

pedestal
- dado
- base

upper rail

sleeve
belly
baluster

Balustrade

lower rail

Capitol

The first floor of the Capitol contains the *Hall of Columns, House* and *Senate corridors, committee rooms, restaurants, transportation offices* and a *post office.* When the House is called to order, the *Mace of the House of Representatives* is placed on a cylindrical *pedestal* to the right of the Speaker's desk. On the Senate side is a *chandelier* with two bulbs below it. The red one indicates an executive session; the white, a regular session. Visitors to the chambers of Congress sit in *galleries.*

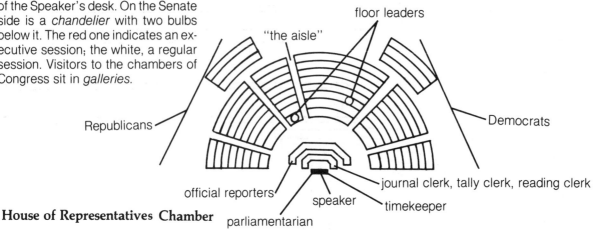

floor leaders

"the aisle"

Republicans

Democrats

journal clerk, tally clerk, reading clerk

official reporters

speaker

timekeeper

House of Representatives Chamber

parliamentarian

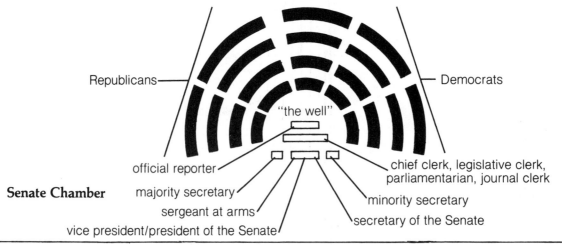

Republicans

Democrats

"the well"

official reporter

chief clerk, legislative clerk, parliamentarian, journal clerk

Senate Chamber

majority secretary

minority secretary

sergeant at arms

secretary of the Senate

vice president/president of the Senate

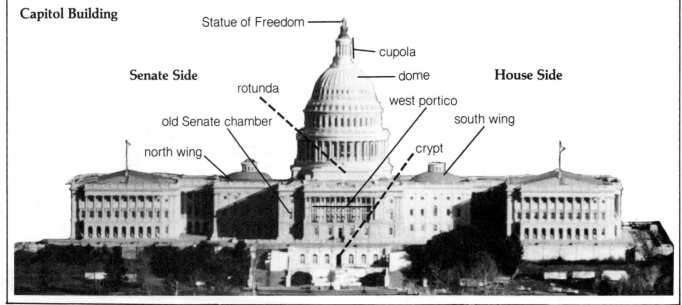

Capitol Building

Statue of Freedom

cupola

Senate Side

rotunda

dome

House Side

west portico

old Senate chamber

south wing

north wing

crypt

Special Purpose Buildings

White House

The White House, a historic *mansion* that serves as the President's *home* and *office*, contains *portraits, antiques* and *memorabilia.* In addition to the rooms and offices shown here, there is a bombproof *command post* in the cellar and a *helipad* on the south lawn.

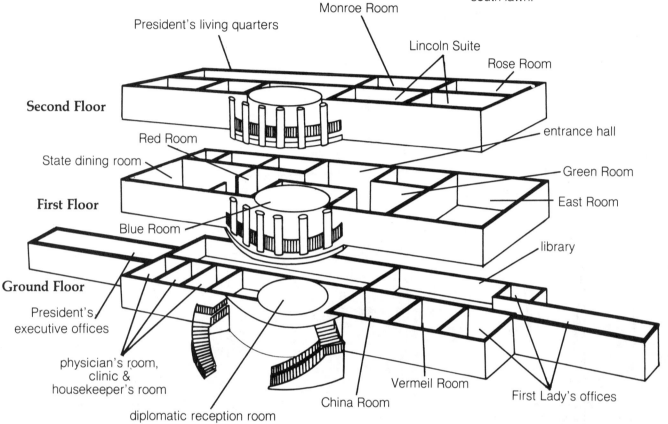

Monroe Room

President's living quarters

Lincoln Suite

Rose Room

Second Floor

entrance hall

Red Room

State dining room

First Floor

Green Room

East Room

Blue Room

library

Ground Floor

President's executive offices

physician's room, clinic & housekeeper's room

diplomatic reception room

China Room

Vermeil Room

First Lady's offices

House Plan

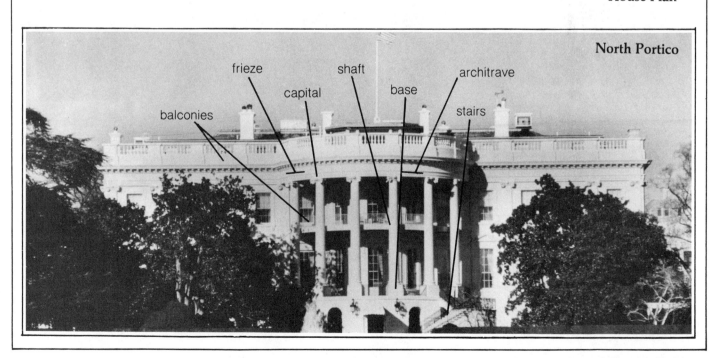

North Portico

frieze

shaft

architrave

capital

base

balconies

stairs

Special Purpose Buildings

Prison

Maximum security prisons, such as the one seen here, are characterized by high *walls, armed guards* and *security checkpoints. Minimum security prisons* may be surrounded by *chainlink fences* and have *security systems* that are largely electronic, with *doors, alarms, TV monitors* and *intercoms* monitored by *central computers. Prisoners,* or *inmates,* in all *correctional facilities,* including *jails,* live in *cells* with *barred doors.*

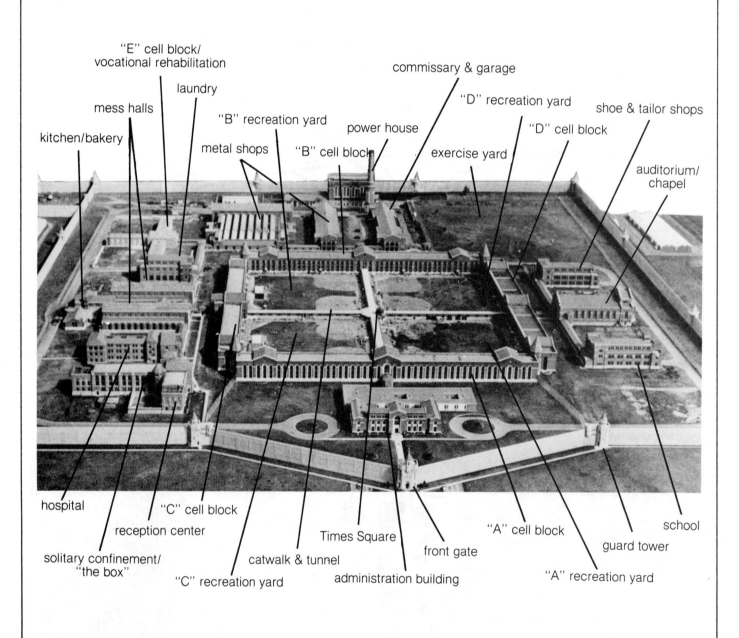

"E" cell block/ vocational rehabilitation

laundry

commissary & garage

mess halls

"B" recreation yard

"D" recreation yard

shoe & tailor shops

kitchen/bakery

metal shops

"B" cell block

power house

exercise yard

"D" cell block

auditorium/ chapel

hospital

"C" cell block

reception center

Times Square

front gate

"A" cell block

school

solitary confinement/ "the box"

catwalk & tunnel

guard tower

"C" recreation yard

administration building

"A" recreation yard

Skyscraper

A skyscraper, or *building* more than twenty stories high, is built on a *foundation* of reinforced concrete *piers* supported by *piles* driven into soil or bedrock. The center of the building, or *core,* usually contains the *elevator bank.* The machinery needed to operate the building's systems is located on the *mechanical floors.* A *cornerstone* is a stone laid at a formal inauguration ceremony.

kangaroo crane

columns

roof

beams/girders

skeleton/frame

tarpaulin cover

stories/tenant floors

skylobby/transfer to local elevators

television & radio mast

fastigiated top

Completed

dirigible mooring mast

observation deck

curtainwall/ skin/facing

setbacks

plaza

lobby/foyer

Under Construction

Special Purpose Buildings

Elevator

There is padding which makes up the *safety edges* on the *shafts,* or innermost sides, of elevator doors. Most elevator cars have *emergency top exits* in the *canopy* or real ceiling as well as *service cabinets* which contain *fan switches, light* and *start switches.* An individual who directs people to the next available car in a *bank* of elevators is called a *starter.*

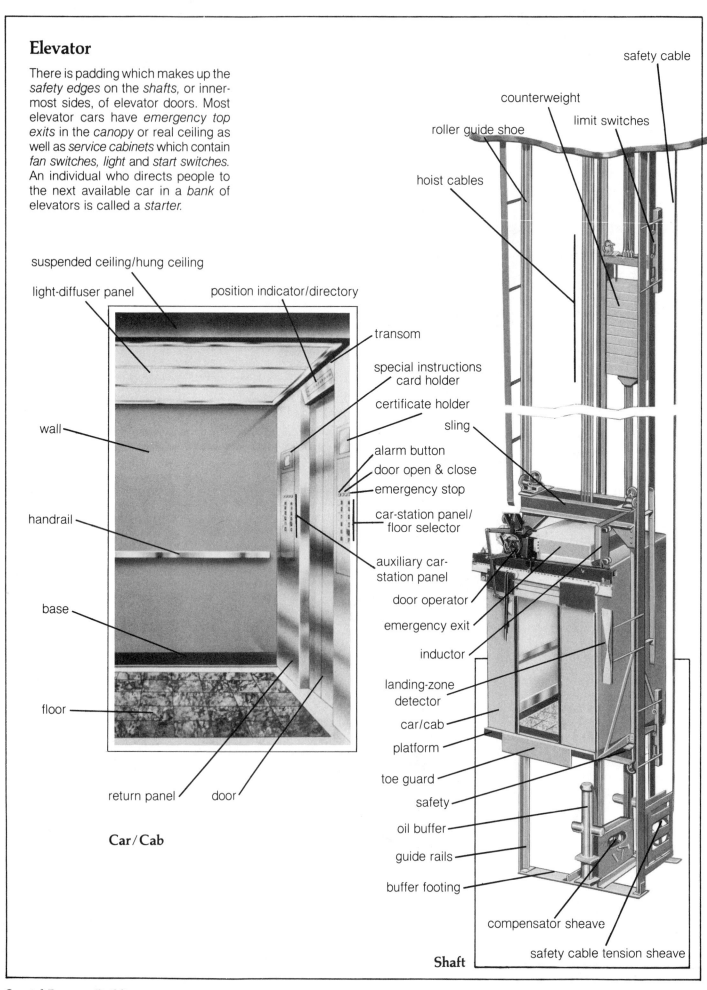

suspended ceiling/hung ceiling

light-diffuser panel

position indicator/directory

transom

special instructions card holder

certificate holder

wall

alarm button

door open & close

emergency stop

car-station panel/ floor selector

auxiliary car-station panel

handrail

base

door operator

emergency exit

inductor

landing-zone detector

car/cab

platform

toe guard

floor

safety

oil buffer

guide rails

buffer footing

return panel   door

Car/Cab

safety cable

counterweight

roller guide shoe

limit switches

hoist cables

sling

compensator sheave

safety cable tension sheave

Shaft

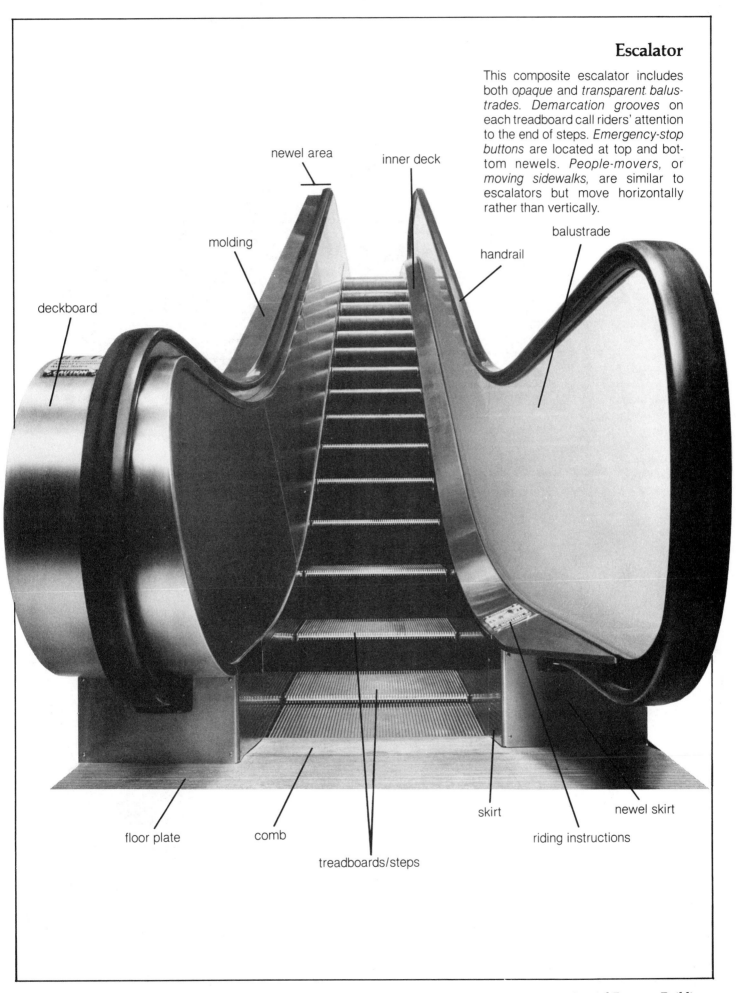

Escalator

This composite escalator includes both *opaque* and *transparent balustrades*. *Demarcation grooves* on each treadboard call riders' attention to the end of steps. *Emergency-stop buttons* are located at top and bottom newels. *People-movers*, or *moving sidewalks*, are similar to escalators but move horizontally rather than vertically.

newel area

inner deck

molding

handrail

balustrade

deckboard

floor plate

comb

treadboards/steps

skirt

riding instructions

newel skirt

Castle

A castle was protected by a moat which could be crossed by a lowered *drawbridge*. Narrow openings in turret or tower floors, used to drop boiling liquids or stones on attackers, were called *machicolations*.

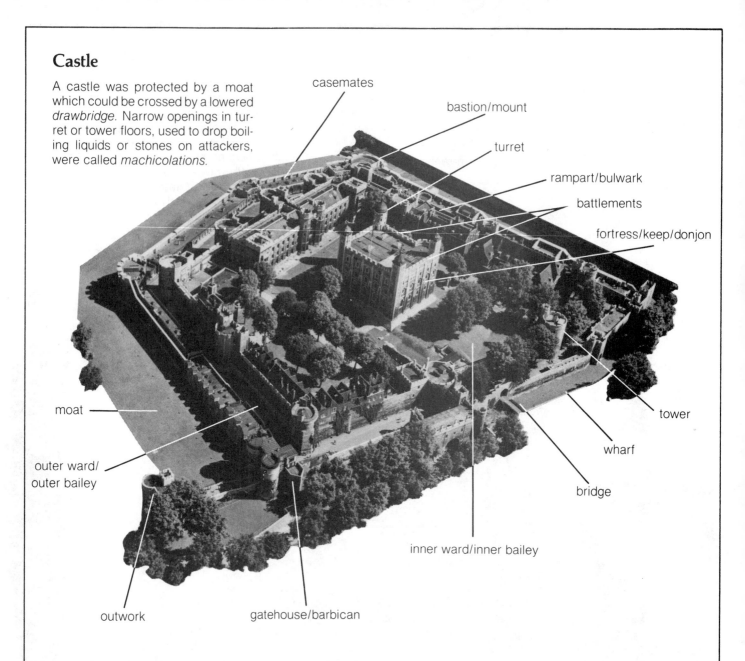

casemates

bastion/mount

turret

rampart/bulwark

battlements

fortress/keep/donjon

tower

wharf

bridge

inner ward/inner bailey

moat

outer ward/ outer bailey

outwork

gatehouse/barbican

Embattled Parapet

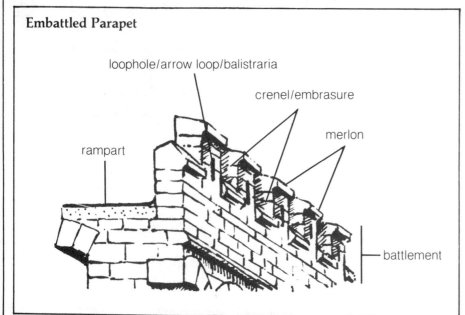

loophole/arrow loop/balistraria

crenel/embrasure

merlon

rampart

battlement

Bartizan/Turret

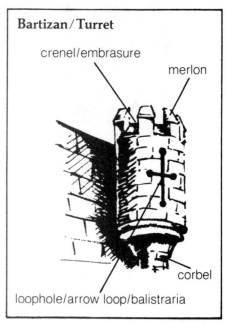

crenel/embrasure

merlon

corbel

loophole/arrow loop/balistraria

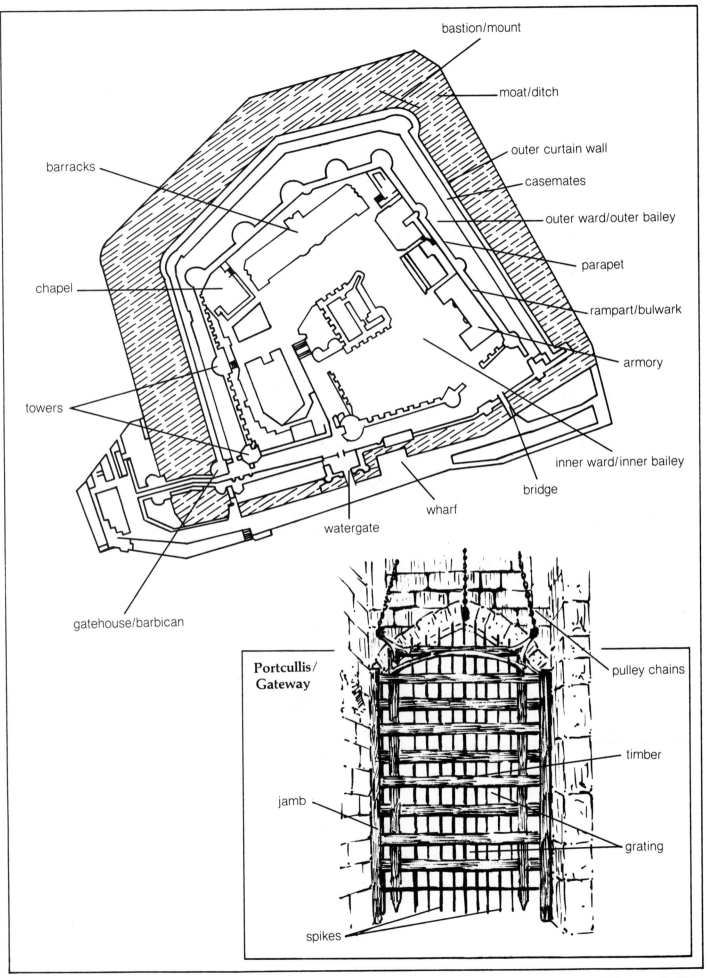

bastion/mount

moat/ditch

outer curtain wall

casemates

outer ward/outer bailey

parapet

rampart/bulwark

armory

inner ward/inner bailey

bridge

wharf

watergate

gatehouse/barbican

towers

chapel

barracks

Portcullis/ Gateway

pulley chains

timber

grating

jamb

spikes

81

Special Purpose Buildings

Fortifications

This *field fortification* or *trading post* was protected by wooden walls from behind which soldiers could fire on attackers from raised *parapets*. *Powder* and *ammunition* were stored in a building called a *magazine*.

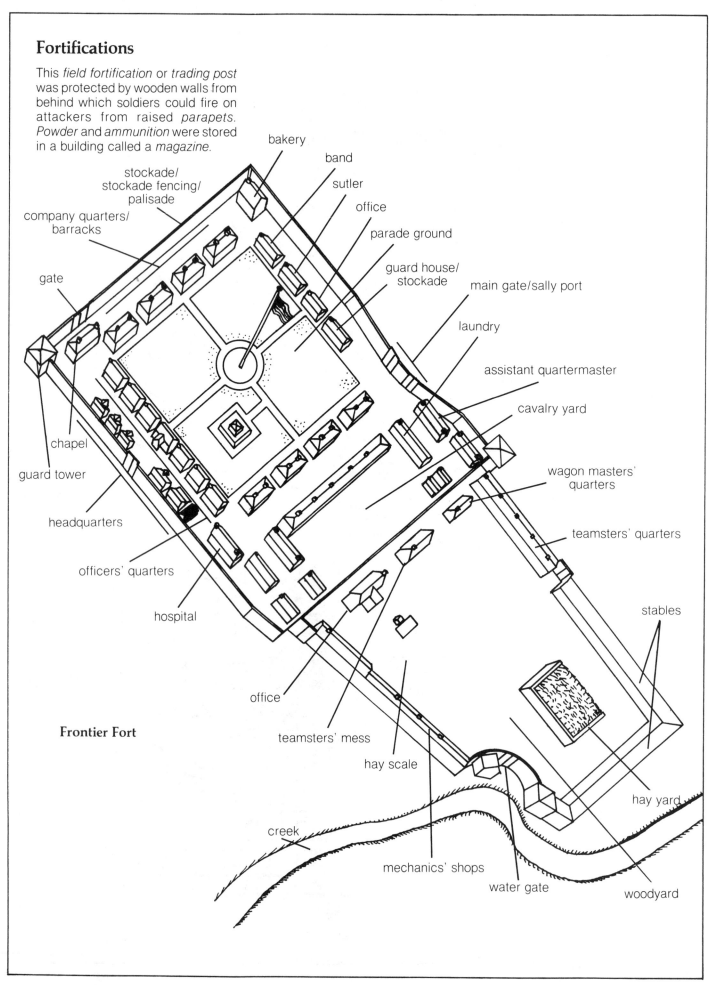

bakery

band

sutler

office

parade ground

guard house/ stockade

main gate/sally port

laundry

assistant quartermaster

cavalry yard

wagon masters' quarters

teamsters' quarters

stables

hay yard

woodyard

water gate

mechanics' shops

hay scale

teamsters' mess

office

hospital

officers' quarters

headquarters

guard tower

chapel

gate

company quarters/ barracks

stockade/ stockade fencing/ palisade

creek

Frontier Fort

Fortifications

Permanent fortifications, such as the *point* of the star fort illustrated here, had *walls* and *slopes* made of *masonry* and earth. They often had *casemates; bombproofs,* walls impervious to explosives; *drawbridges* and *earthen breastworks,* breast-high protection for soldiers.

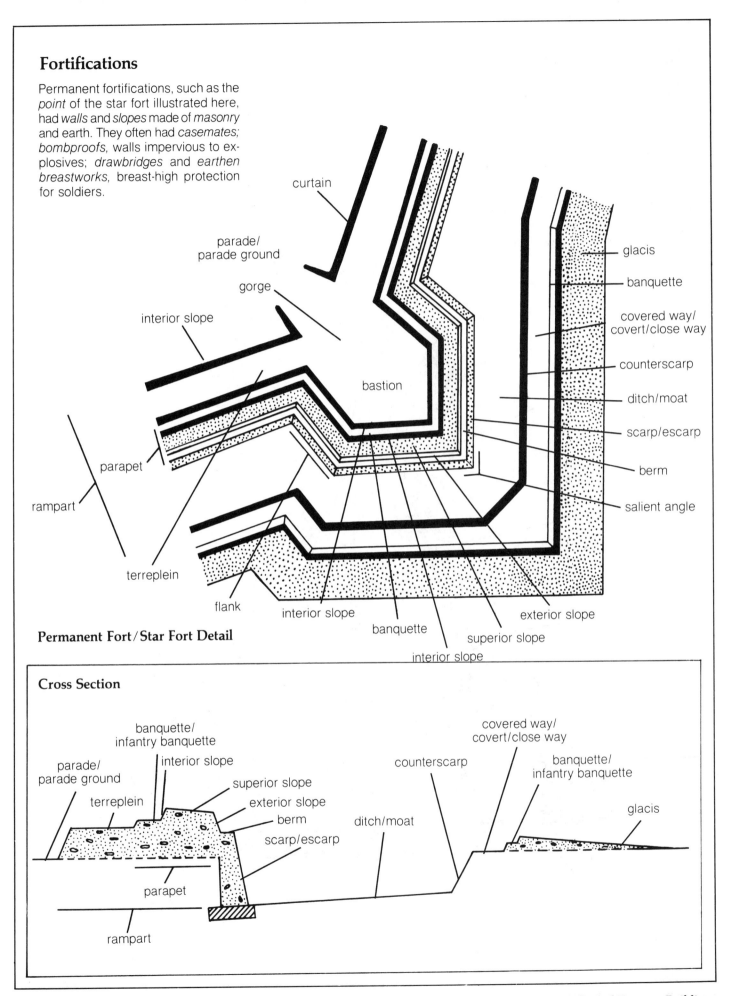

curtain

parade/ parade ground

gorge

interior slope

bastion

parapet

rampart

terreplein

flank

interior slope

banquette

superior slope

interior slope

exterior slope

glacis

banquette

covered way/ covert/close way

counterscarp

ditch/moat

scarp/escarp

berm

salient angle

Permanent Fort/Star Fort Detail

Cross Section

banquette/ infantry banquette

interior slope

parade/ parade ground

terreplein

superior slope

exterior slope

berm

scarp/escarp

parapet

rampart

covered way/ covert/close way

counterscarp

banquette/ infantry banquette

glacis

ditch/moat

Special Purpose Buildings

Tepee/Teepee/Tipi

The *pole frame* of an Indian tepee was held together at the top by a *hide rope*. It was covered with dressed buffalo *skins* and had a *fire pit* on the floor within. Other Indian dwellings included *wigwams*, rounded or oval-shaped lodges formed by poles overlaid with *bark*, *mats* or skins; *wickiups*, huts made of *brushwood* or covered with mats; and *hogans*, dwellings constructed of *earth* and *branches* and covered with *mud* or *sod*.

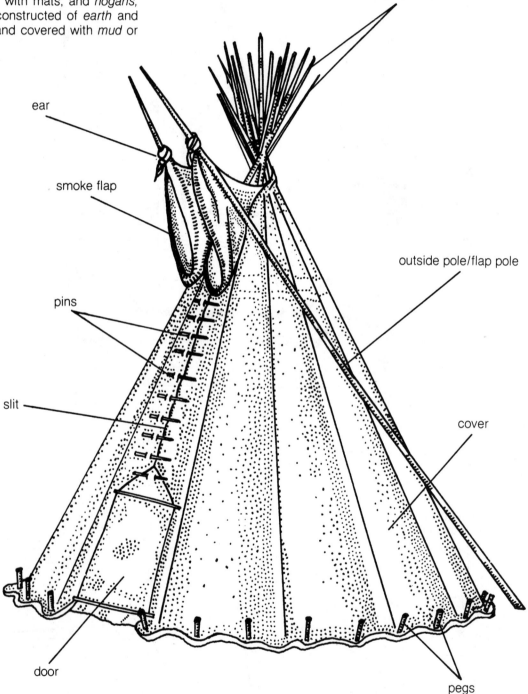

lodge poles

ear

smoke flap

pins

slit

outside pole/flap pole

cover

door

pegs

Domed Structures

Traditionally, a dome is a circular *vault* whose walls exert equal thrust in all directions, resisted by a *tension ring*. The geodesic dome consists of a *grid* of *compression* or *tension members* lying upon *great circles* running in three directions in any given area.

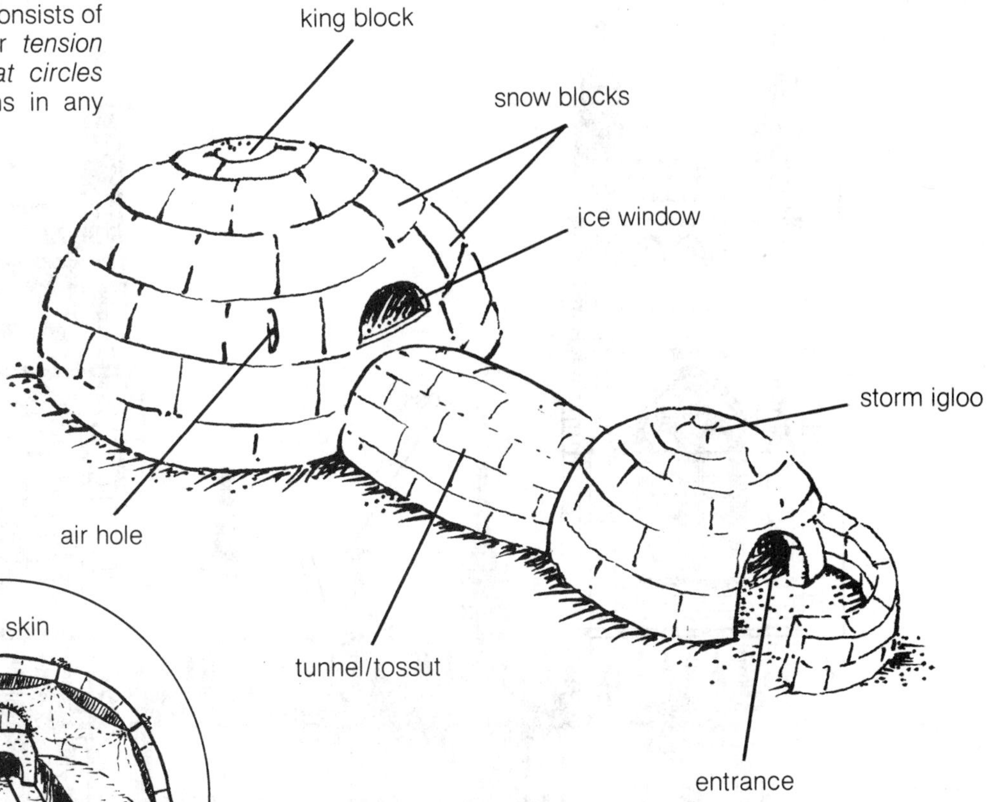

Igloo / Iglu

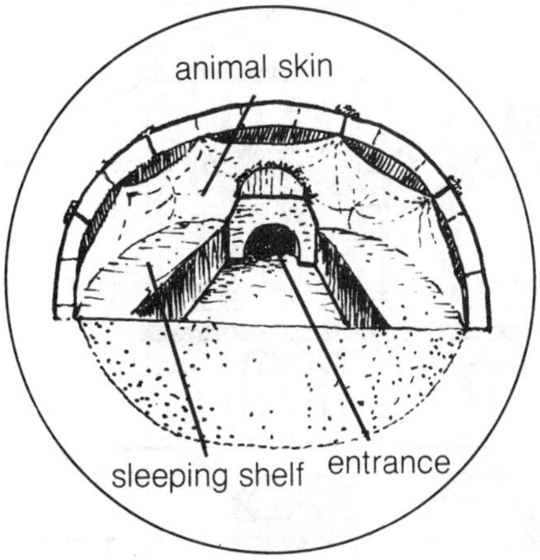

king block

snow blocks

ice window

storm igloo

air hole

tunnel/tossut

entrance

animal skin

sleeping shelf   entrance

Interior

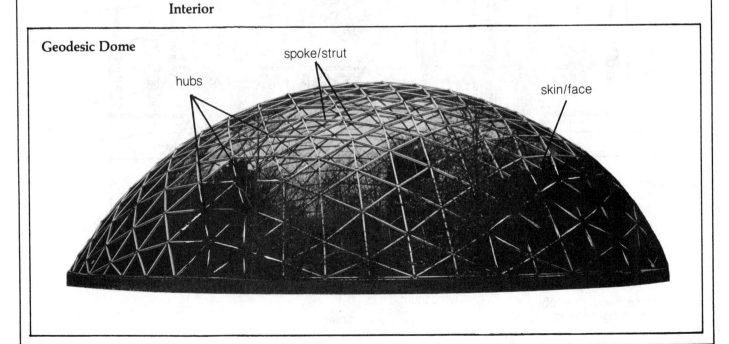

Geodesic Dome

hubs

spoke/strut

skin/face

Special Purpose Buildings

Church/Cathedral

A small building used for worship is called a *chapel*. Living quarters used by church clergy are the *rectory*. The office in which church business is conducted is the *chancellery*.

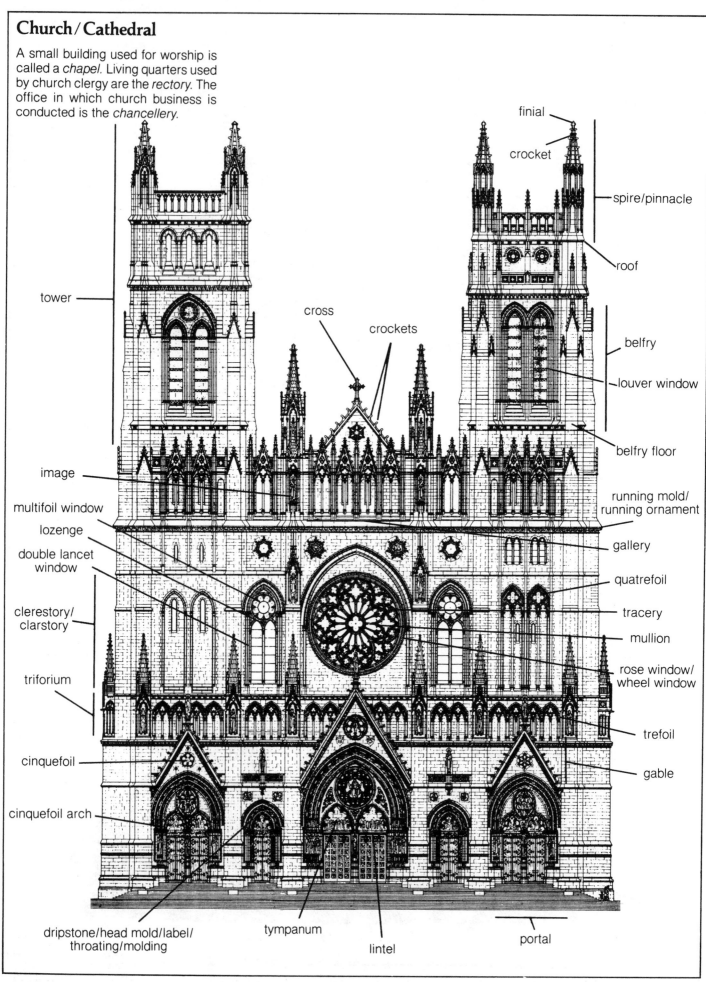

finial

crocket

spire/pinnacle

roof

tower

cross

crockets

belfry

louver window

belfry floor

image

running mold/ running ornament

multifoil window

lozenge

gallery

double lancet window

quatrefoil

tracery

clerestory/ clarstory

mullion

rose window/ wheel window

triforium

trefoil

cinquefoil

gable

cinquefoil arch

dripstone/head mold/label/ throating/molding

tympanum

lintel

portal

Church Interior

That part of a church containing the altar and seats for the clergy and choir is called the *chancel*. A *pulpit* is an elevated platform used in preaching or conducting a worship service. The *tabernacle* is a receptacle for consecrated elements of the Eucharist: the *pix*, the container in which Communion *wafers* are kept; the *paten*, a plate used to hold *Communion bread*; and the *chalice*, or *Communion cup*, used to dispense consecrated *wine*.

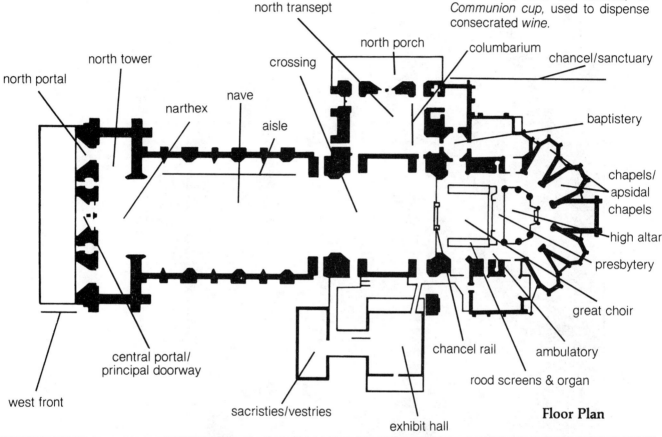

north transept

north porch

columbarium

chancel/sanctuary

north tower

crossing

north portal

nave

narthex

aisle

baptistery

chapels/
apsidal
chapels

high altar

presbytery

great choir

ambulatory

central portal/
principal doorway

chancel rail

rood screens & organ

west front

sacristies/vestries

exhibit hall

Floor Plan

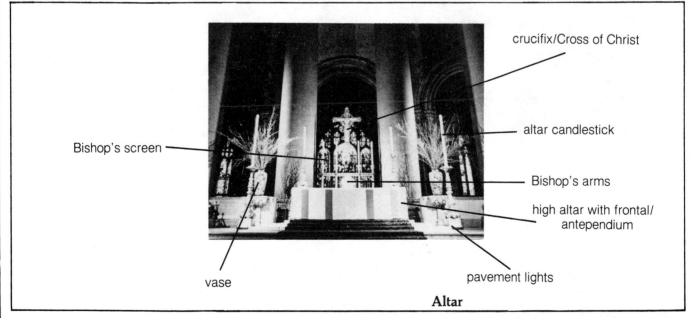

crucifix/Cross of Christ

altar candlestick

Bishop's screen

Bishop's arms

high altar with frontal/
antependium

vase

pavement lights

Altar

Synagogue/Temple

The Torah is a parchment or leather *scroll* containing the first five books of the *Scriptures*, or *Pentateuch*, written in Hebrew. It is tied closed with a beltlike *wrapper*.

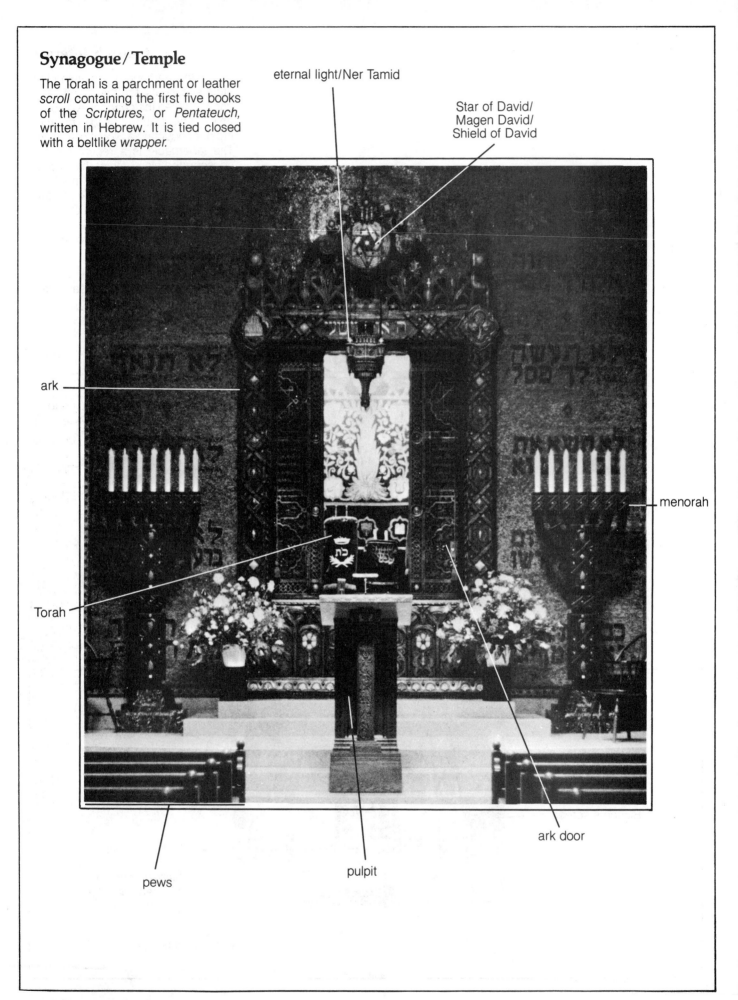

eternal light/Ner Tamid

Star of David/ Magen David/ Shield of David

ark

menorah

Torah

ark door

pews

pulpit

Courtroom

The small anteroom off the courtroom in which the *judge* changes into his *robes* and holds conferences is called the *judge's chambers*. After a *jury* has heard a case, it deliberates in a *jury room*. A judge may sometimes use a malletlike *gavel* during proceedings.

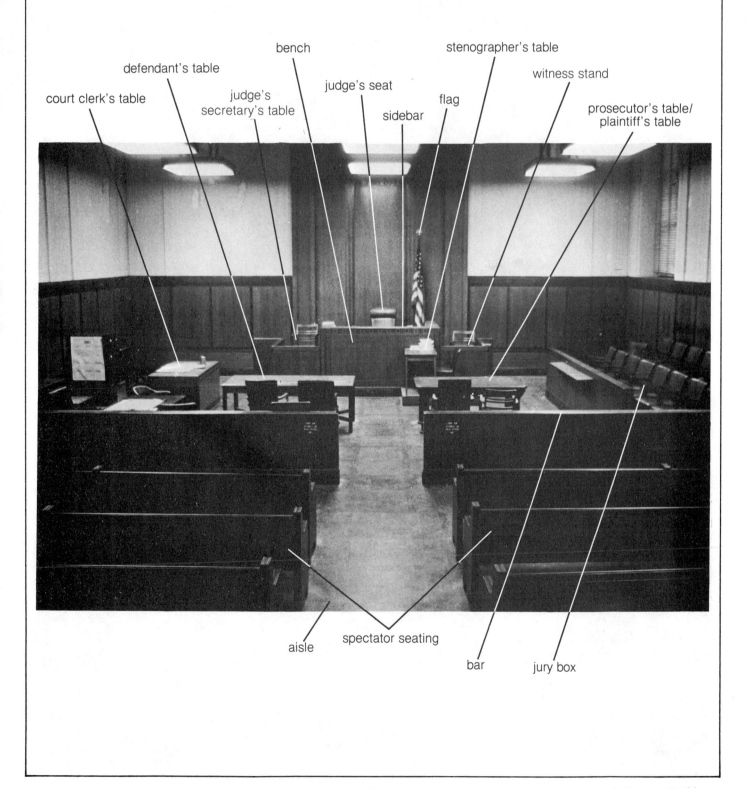

court clerk's table

defendant's table

judge's secretary's table

bench

judge's seat

sidebar

flag

stenographer's table

witness stand

prosecutor's table/ plaintiff's table

aisle

spectator seating

bar

jury box

Special Purpose Buildings

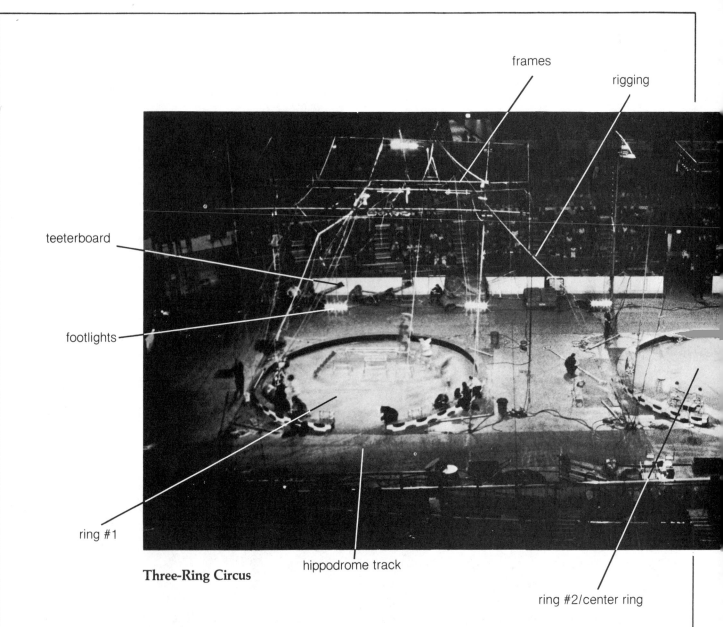

frames

rigging

teeterboard

footlights

ring #1

hippodrome track

Three-Ring Circus

ring #2/center ring

Aerialists/Flyers/Trapeze Artists

Animal Tamer

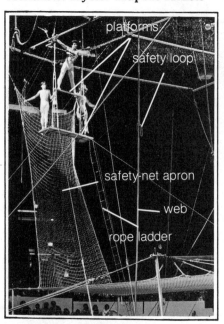

platforms

safety loop

safety-net apron

web

rope ladder

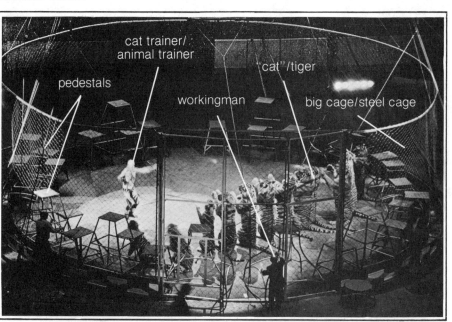

cat trainer/
animal trainer

"cat"/tiger

pedestals

workingman

big cage/steel cage

Circus

Circuses traditionally take place in tents erected by *roustabouts* and begin with a *parade* in which all the performers enter the *arena*. A *ringmaster*, usually clad in *top hat* and *tails*, announces acts, including *animal* and *clown acts; tightrope,* or *high-wire acts;* and *jugglers.* In the past, *sideshows,* which took place in an adjoining tent, featured *tattooed ladies, giants, midgets, sword-swallowers* and *fire-eaters.*

audience

ring curbs

animal cage

spotlight

ring #3

Circus Tent / Big Top / Top

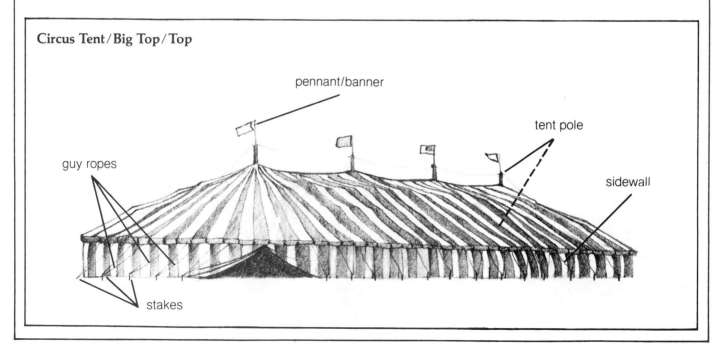

pennant/banner

tent pole

guy ropes

sidewall

stakes

Special Purpose Buildings

Amusement Park

A roller coaster consists of *hills, straightaways* and *loops. Upstop wheels* lock roller-coaster cars to the track, *guide wheels* are used for turns and tractor wheels are used for gliding.

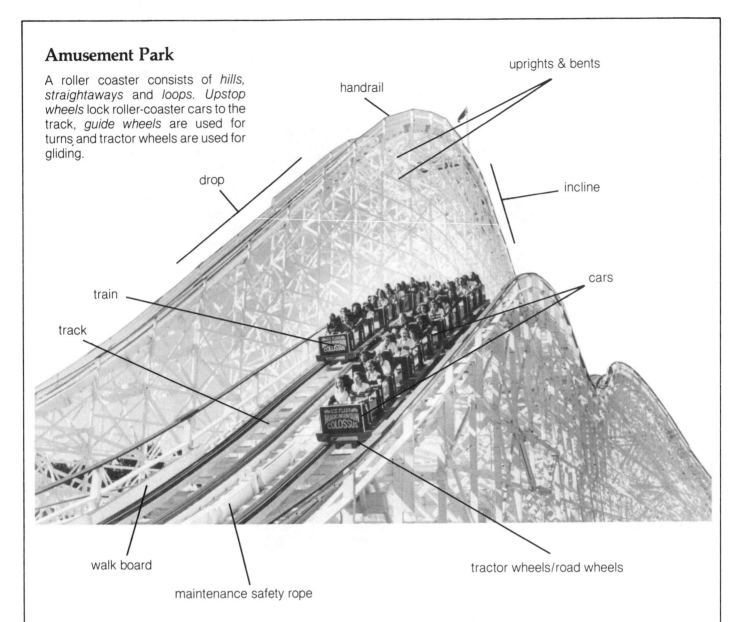

uprights & bents

handrail

incline

drop

cars

train

track

walk board

maintenance safety rope

tractor wheels/road wheels

Roller Coaster

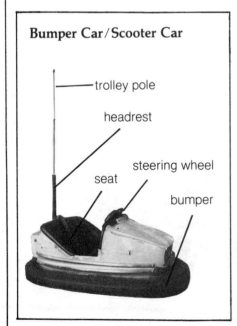

Bumper Car / Scooter Car

trolley pole

headrest

steering wheel

seat

bumper

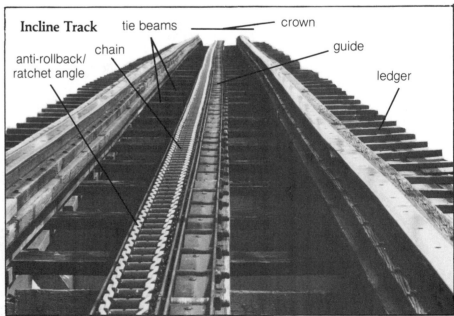

Incline Track

tie beams

crown

chain

guide

anti-rollback/ ratchet angle

ledger

Amusement Park

Immobile carousel horses are called *gallopers*. *Jumpers* move up and down on horse rods. *Flying horses* tilt outward as the carousel picks up speed. Merry-go-round music is traditionally provided by a mechanical *band organ*, often referred to as a *calliope*.

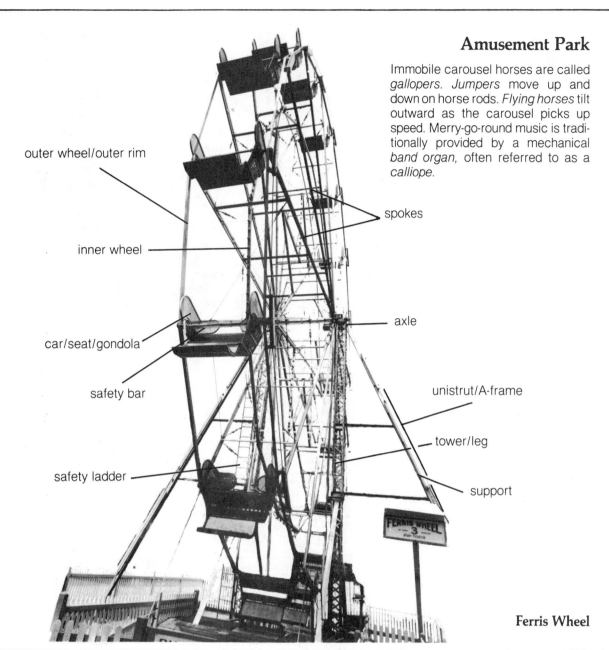

outer wheel/outer rim

inner wheel

spokes

axle

car/seat/gondola

safety bar

unistrut/A-frame

tower/leg

safety ladder

support

FERRIS WHEEL 3

Ferris Wheel

Merry-Go-Round/Carousel

panel painting

rim/rounding board/cornice/shield

rotating frame

inner cornice

horse rod

horse

gondola/chariot

platform

inside drive

Special Purpose Buildings

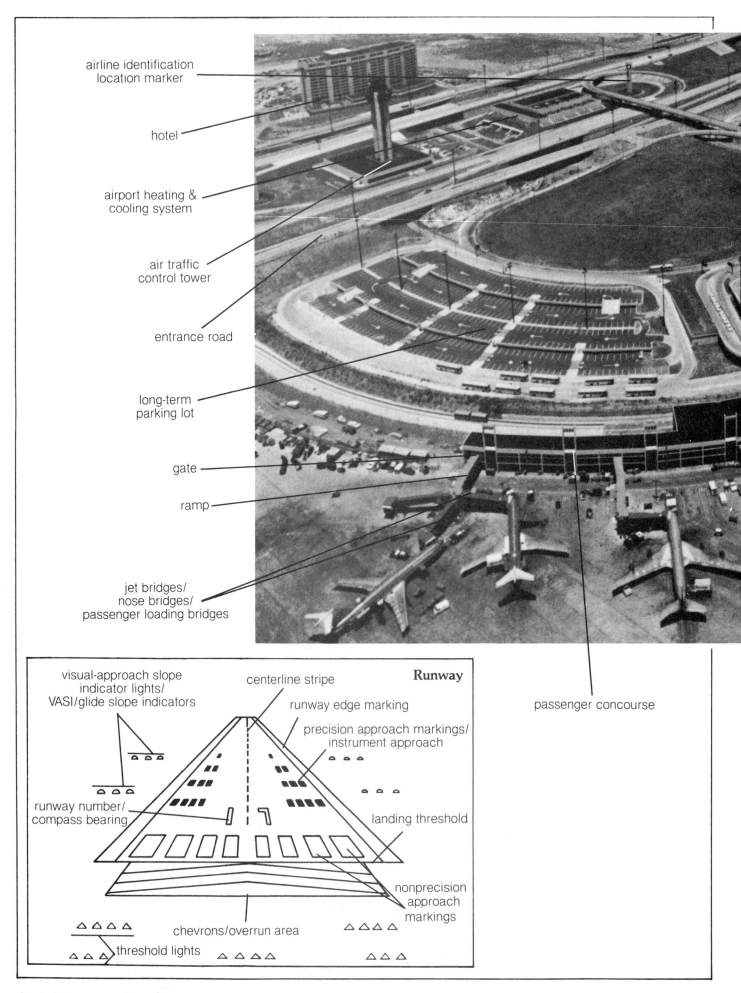

airline identification
location marker

hotel

airport heating &
cooling system

air traffic
control tower

entrance road

long-term
parking lot

gate

ramp

jet bridges/
nose bridges/
passenger loading bridges

passenger concourse

Runway

visual-approach slope
indicator lights/
VASI/glide slope indicators

centerline stripe

runway edge marking

precision approach markings/
instrument approach

runway number/
compass bearing

landing threshold

nonprecision
approach
markings

chevrons/overrun area

threshold lights

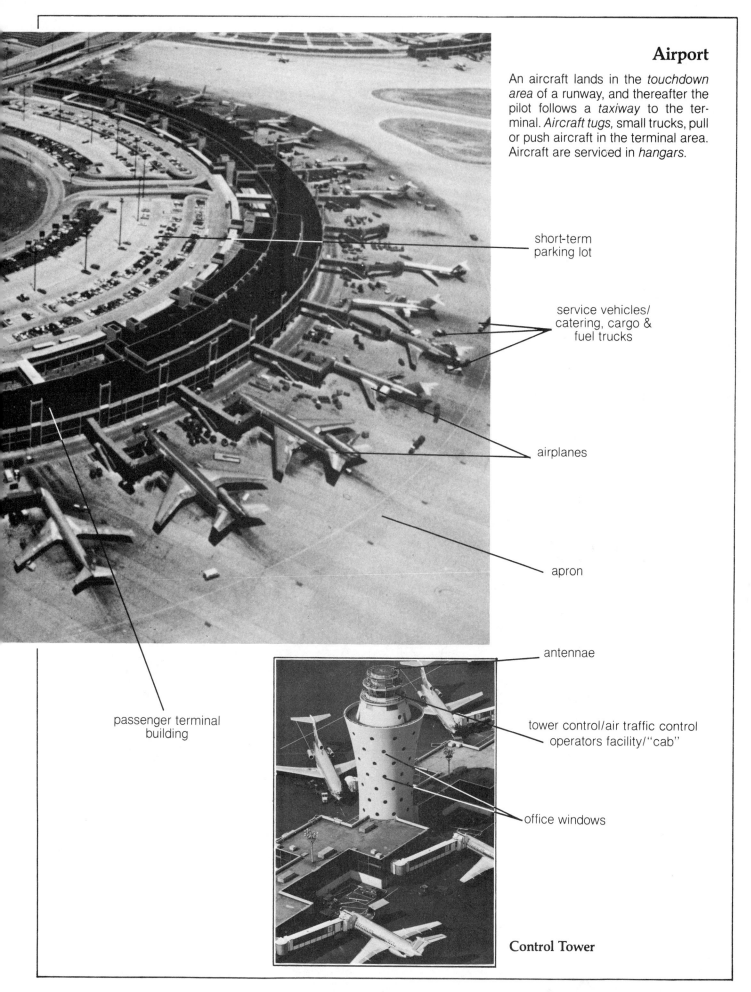

Airport

An aircraft lands in the *touchdown area* of a runway, and thereafter the pilot follows a *taxiway* to the terminal. *Aircraft tugs,* small trucks, pull or push aircraft in the terminal area. Aircraft are serviced in *hangars.*

short-term parking lot

service vehicles/ catering, cargo & fuel trucks

airplanes

apron

passenger terminal building

antennae

tower control/air traffic control operators facility/"cab"

office windows

Control Tower

Special Purpose Buildings

Railroad Yard

A railroad yard, or *marshalling yard,*
consists of a system of *parallel tracks,*
crossovers and *switches* where *cars*
are formed into *trains* and where
cars, *locomotives* and other *rolling*
stock are kept when not in use or
awaiting repair. In *hump yards,*
freight cars are pushed down a
hump onto a *siding,* determined by a
yardmaster, to be coupled to a form-
ing train. *Electropneumatic retarders*
control the speed of the cars as they
move along the tracks.

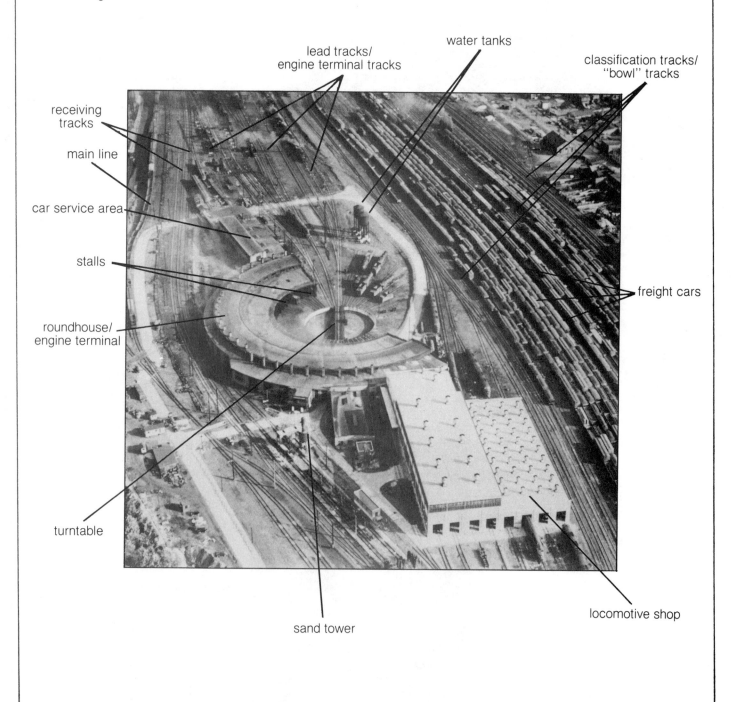

lead tracks/
engine terminal tracks

water tanks

classification tracks/
"bowl" tracks

receiving
tracks

main line

car service area

stalls

roundhouse/
engine terminal

freight cars

turntable

sand tower

locomotive shop

Bridge

A pedestrian walkway on a bridge is a *footpath*. *Fixed bridges* have no moving parts, while *movable bridges*, such as lift bridges, *drawbridges* and *bascule bridges* either lift of swing open. A *pontoon bridge* is built on *floating piers*.

safety rail

window

tower

main cable

stay rope

suspender cables

girder

stiffening trusses

side span

center span

tower leg

pier

Suspension Bridge

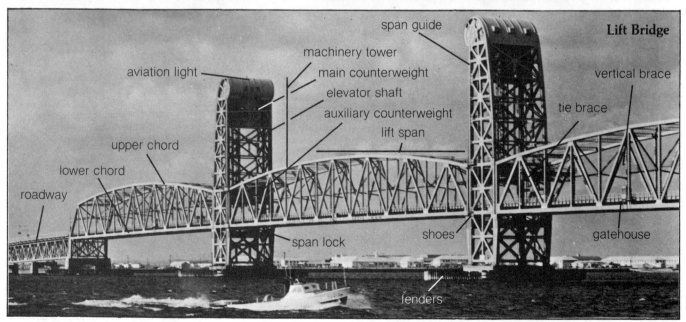

span guide

Lift Bridge

machinery tower

aviation light

main counterweight

elevator shaft

vertical brace

auxiliary counterweight

tie brace

lift span

upper chord

lower chord

roadway

span lock

shoes

gatehouse

fenders

97

Other Structures

Tunnel

Tunnels that take water to hydroelectric plants or to municipal waterworks and those that remove storm water and sewage are called *conduits*. Tunnels cut through rock frequently require no *lining*. Underwater tunnels can be ventilated by *shafts* leading to the surface or by *exhaust* or *booster fans* at the ends.

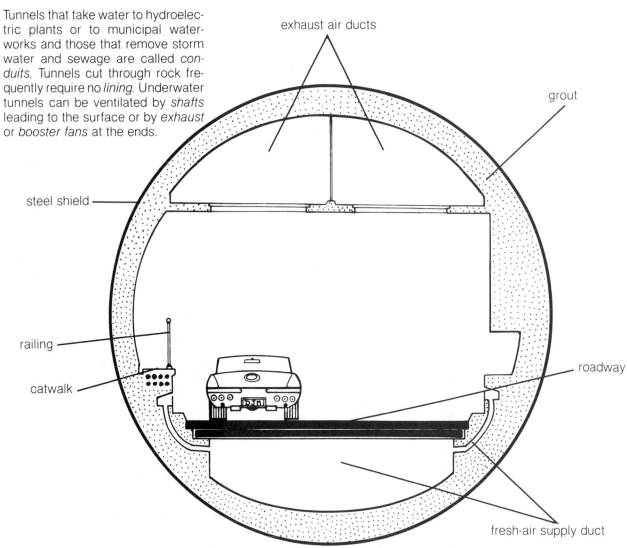

exhaust air ducts

grout

steel shield

railing

catwalk

roadway

fresh-air supply duct

Cross Section

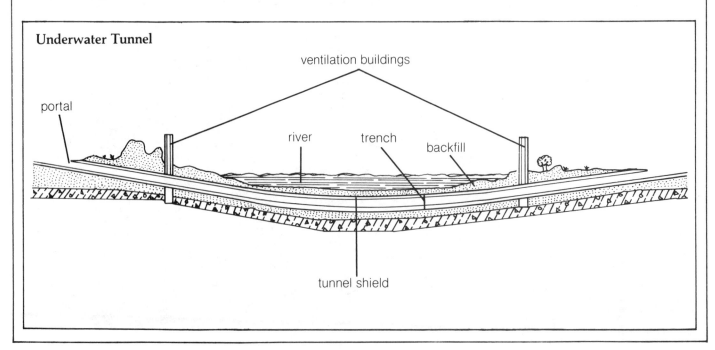

Underwater Tunnel

ventilation buildings

portal

river

trench

backfill

tunnel shield

Canal Lock

The water level in a canal lock is raised or lowered through *sluice gates* in the lock wall or *floor. Shipboard lines* or *hawsers* secured to *bollards* along the lockside hold the vessel steady while the lock is in operation. Before *electric locomotives* were used, animals would haul boats through locks following a *towpath*.

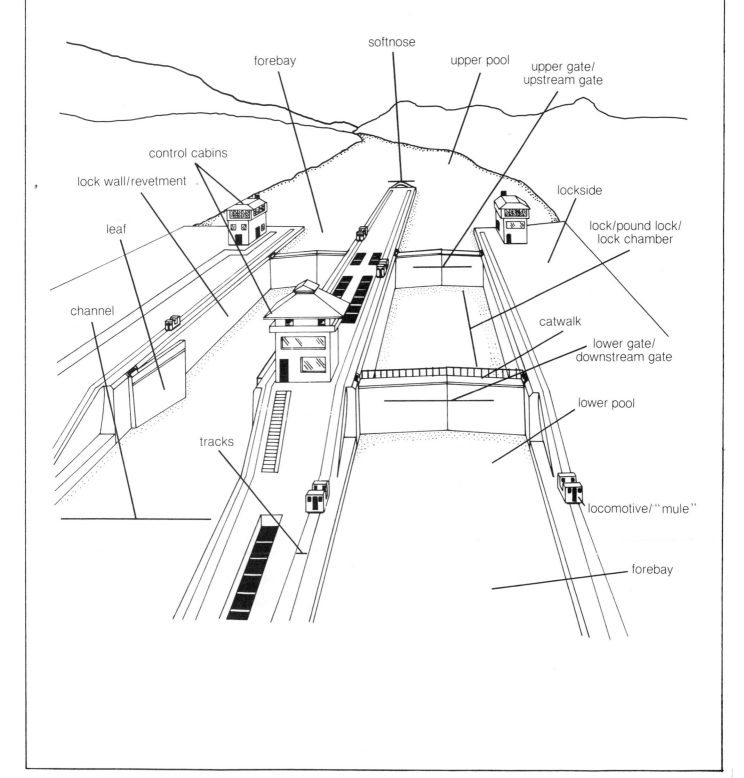

forebay

softnose

upper pool

upper gate/
upstream gate

control cabins

lock wall/revetment

leaf

channel

lockside

lock/pound lock/
lock chamber

catwalk

lower gate/
downstream gate

lower pool

tracks

locomotive/"mule"

forebay

Other Structures

Dam

Many dams have steep channels divided by partitions into pools, called *fishways* or *fish ladders*, that enable fish to swim upriver. Other dams have *log chutes* designed to allow logs to pass through. A *dike*, or *levee*, is an earthwork construction built to block water rather than to regulate its flow.

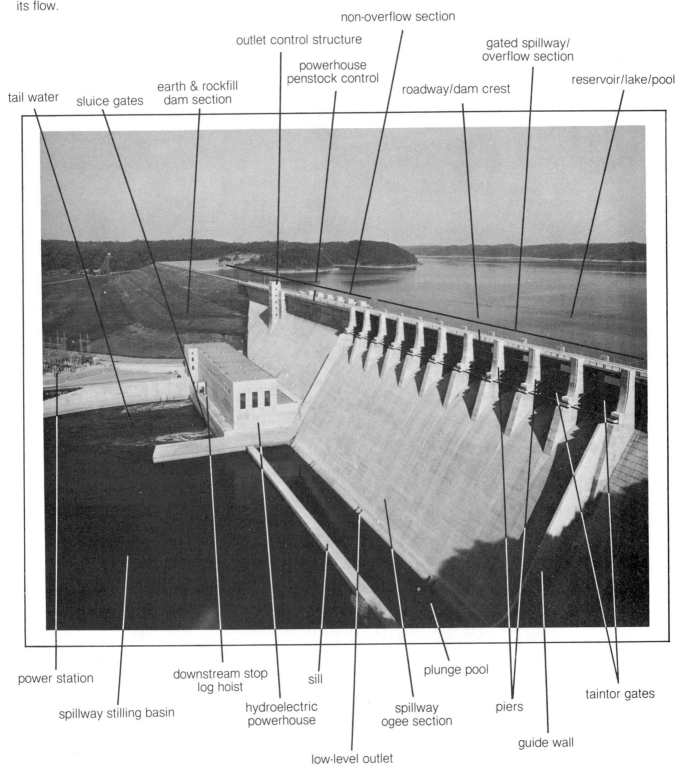

non-overflow section

outlet control structure

powerhouse penstock control

gated spillway/ overflow section

roadway/dam crest

reservoir/lake/pool

tail water

sluice gates

earth & rockfill dam section

power station

spillway stilling basin

downstream stop log hoist

hydroelectric powerhouse

sill

low-level outlet

plunge pool

spillway ogee section

piers

guide wall

taintor gates

Oil Drilling Platform/ Offshore Rig

In shallow water this *semisubmersible* rig drills in the floating position. When drilling at greater depths the motion compensator, a *hydraulic-pneumatic device,* moves up and down as the rig does in the sea to keep the *pipe* stationary in the *hole.* The "driller" controls the *drill, bit* changes and large hydraulic valves, or *blowout preventors.*

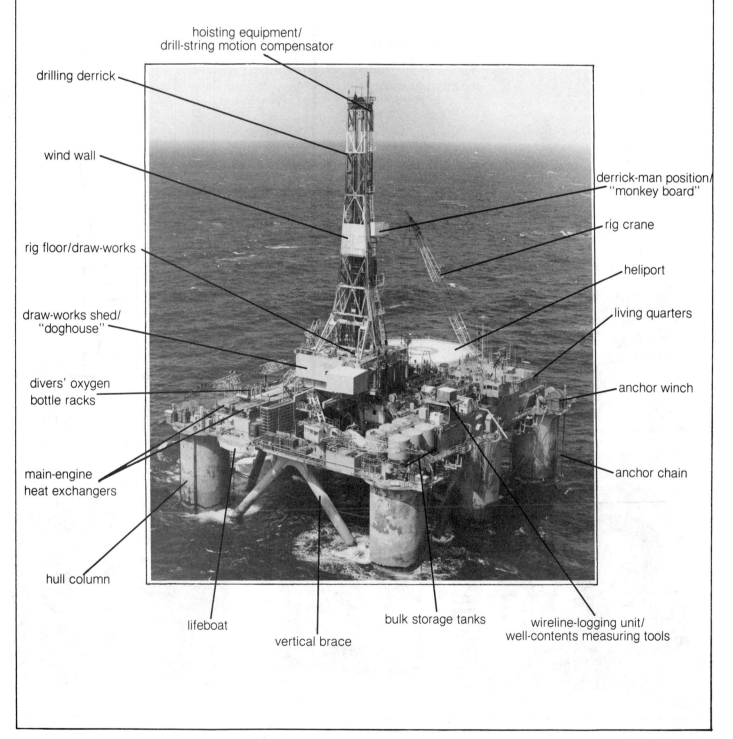

hoisting equipment/
drill-string motion compensator

drilling derrick

wind wall

derrick-man position/
"monkey board"

rig crane

rig floor/draw-works

heliport

draw-works shed/
"doghouse"

living quarters

divers' oxygen
bottle racks

anchor winch

main-engine
heat exchangers

anchor chain

hull column

lifeboat

vertical brace

bulk storage tanks

wireline-logging unit/
well-contents measuring tools

Other Structures

Supermarket

The representative floor plan shown here is of a typical *superstore*, or *supercombo*, a combination drug store and food store, with emphasis on *perishables* and *preprepared* foods. The supermarkets of the future will be *warehouse stores*, or *hypermarkets*.

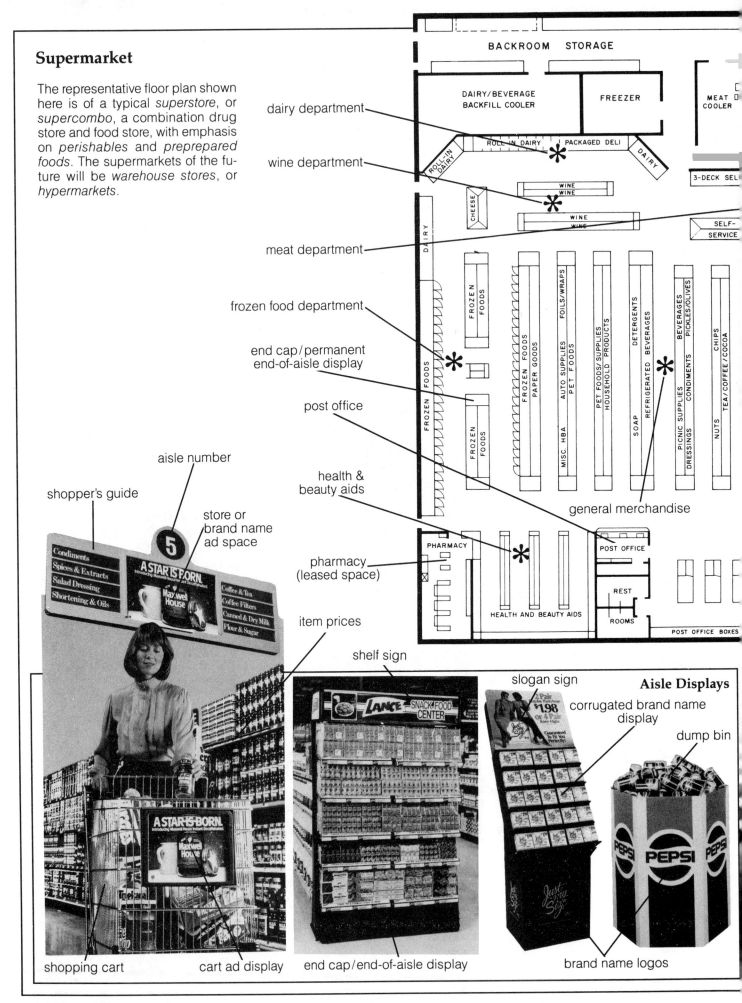

BACKROOM STORAGE

DAIRY/BEVERAGE BACKFILL COOLER

FREEZER

MEAT COOLER

dairy department

ROLL-IN DAIRY   PACKAGED DELI

ROLL-IN DAIRY

DAIRY

3-DECK SEL

wine department

WINE
WINE

CHEESE

WINE

WINE
WINE

SELF-SERVICE

meat department

DAIRY

frozen food department

FROZEN FOODS

FROZEN FOODS

FROZEN FOODS

FROZEN FOODS

FROZEN FOODS

PAPER GOODS

FOILS/WRAPS

AUTO SUPPLIES

PET FOODS

PET FOODS/SUPPLIES

HOUSEHOLD PRODUCTS

DETERGENTS

BEVERAGES

REFRIGERATED BEVERAGES

SOAP

PICKLES/OLIVES

BEVERAGES

CONDIMENTS

PICNIC SUPPLIES

DRESSINGS

NUTS

CHIPS

TEA/COFFEE/COCOA

MISC. HBA

end cap/permanent end-of-aisle display

post office

general merchandise

health & beauty aids

aisle number

shopper's guide

store or brand name ad space

5

A STAR IS BORN.
Introducing Maxwell House and Decaffeinated.

Condiments
Spices & Extracts
Salad Dressing
Shortening & Oils

Maxwell House

Coffee & Tea
Coffee Filters
Canned & Dry Milk
Flour & Sugar

pharmacy (leased space)

PHARMACY

POST OFFICE

REST ROOMS

HEALTH AND BEAUTY AIDS

POST OFFICE BOXES

item prices

shelf sign

slogan sign

Aisle Displays

corrugated brand name display

dump bin

A STAR IS BORN.
Introducing Maxwell House Instant Decaffeinated.

Maxwell House

LANCE   SNACK FOOD CENTER

$1.98

PEPSI   PEPSI   PEPSI

shopping cart

cart ad display

end cap/end-of-aisle display

brand name logos

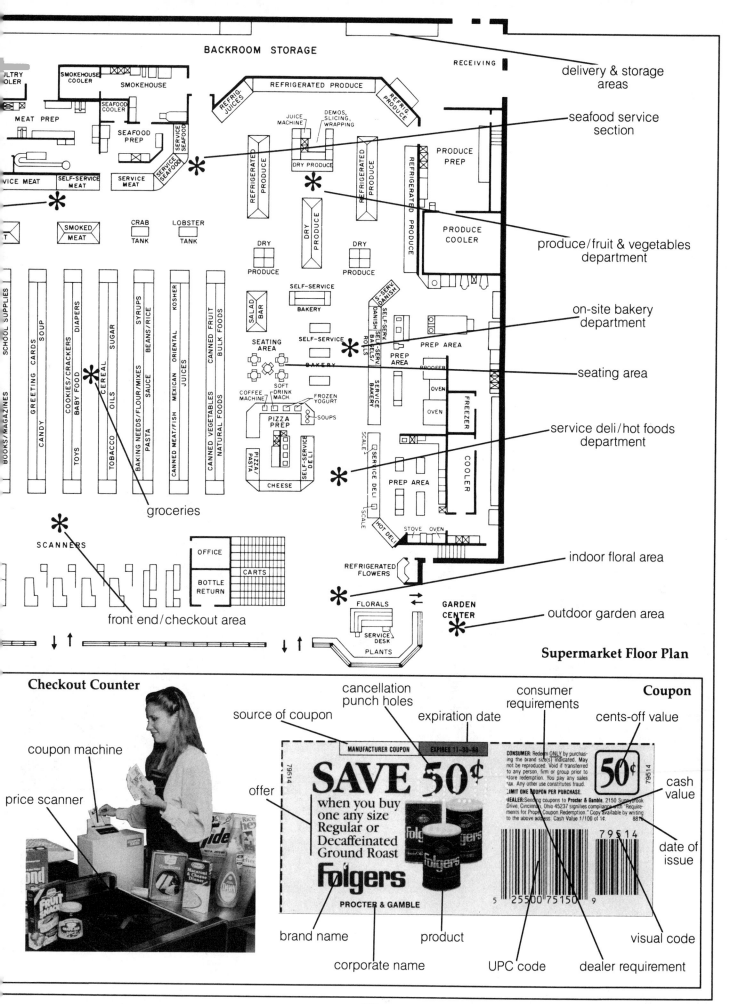

BACKROOM STORAGE

RECEIVING

delivery & storage areas

POULTRY COOLER

SMOKEHOUSE COOLER

SMOKEHOUSE

SEAFOOD COOLER

MEAT PREP

SEAFOOD PREP

SERVICE SEAFOOD

SERVICE MEAT

SELF-SERVICE MEAT

SERVICE MEAT

REFRIG. JUICES

REFRIGERATED PRODUCE

REFRIG PRODUCE

JUICE MACHINE

DEMOS, SLICING, WRAPPING

DRY PRODUCE

REFRIGERATED PRODUCE

REFRIGERATED PRODUCE

REFRIGERATED PRODUCE

PRODUCE PREP

PRODUCE COOLER

seafood service section

produce/fruit & vegetables department

SMOKED MEAT

CRAB TANK

LOBSTER TANK

DRY PRODUCE

DRY PRODUCE

DRY PRODUCE

SCHOOL SUPPLIES

BOOKS/MAGAZINES

GREETING CARDS

CANDY

SOUP

COOKIES/CRACKERS

BABY FOOD

DIAPERS

TOYS

TOBACCO

SUGAR

OILS

CEREAL

BAKING NEEDS/FLOUR/MIXES

PASTA

SAUCE

BEANS/RICE

SYRUPS

CANNED MEAT/FISH

MEXICAN

ORIENTAL

JUICES

KOSHER

CANNED VEGETABLES

NATURAL FOODS

CANNED FRUIT

BULK FOODS

SALAD BAR

SELF-SERVICE BAKERY

SELF-SERVICE BAKERY

SEATING AREA

SELF-SERV DANISH

SELF-SERV DANISH BAGELS

SELF-SERV ROLLS

SERVICE BAKERY

PREP AREA

PREP AREA

PROOFER

OVEN

OVEN

FREEZER

COOLER

on-site bakery department

seating area

COFFEE MACHINE

SOFT DRINK MACH.

FROZEN YOGURT

SOUPS

PIZZA PREP

PIZZA/PASTA

SELF-SERVICE DELI

CHEESE

SERVICE DELI

PREP AREA

SCALE

SCALE

HOT DELI

STOVE

OVEN

service deli/hot foods department

groceries

SCANNERS

OFFICE

CARTS

BOTTLE RETURN

front end/checkout area

REFRIGERATED FLOWERS

FLORALS

SERVICE DESK

PLANTS

GARDEN CENTER

indoor floral area

outdoor garden area

Supermarket Floor Plan

Checkout Counter

coupon machine

price scanner

cancellation punch holes

source of coupon

expiration date

consumer requirements

Coupon

cents-off value

offer

MANUFACTURER COUPON   EXPIRES 11-30-88

79514

SAVE 50¢

when you buy one any size Regular or Decaffeinated Ground Roast

Folgers

PROCTER & GAMBLE

CONSUMER: Redeem ONLY by purchasing the brand size(s) indicated. May not be reproduced. Void if transferred to any person, firm or group prior to store redemption. You pay any sales tax. Any other use constitutes fraud. LIMIT ONE COUPON PER PURCHASE.

DEALER: Sending coupons to Procter & Gamble, 2150 Sunnybrook Drive, Cincinnati, Ohio 45237 signifies compliance with "Requirements for Proper Coupon Redemption." Copy available by writing to the above address. Cash Value 1/100 of 1¢.

50¢

79514

cash value

date of issue

5 25500 75150 9

79514

brand name

corporate name

product

UPC code

dealer requirement

visual code

103

Barn and Silo

A barn *floor* is divided in the center by a *feed passage* that may be lined with *stanchions* to hold cows. On either side are *manure gutters,* and on each side of these are *mangers, boxes* or *troughs,* from which horses or cattle eat. Hay is stored in a *loft,* a storage room next to the roof. Surrounding a barn is a *yard* with a *manure pit* large enough to back a wagon into. Other barnyard structures, adjoining the main barn or built nearby, include *grain pits,* or *bins; springhouses; smokehouses,* and *pigpens.*

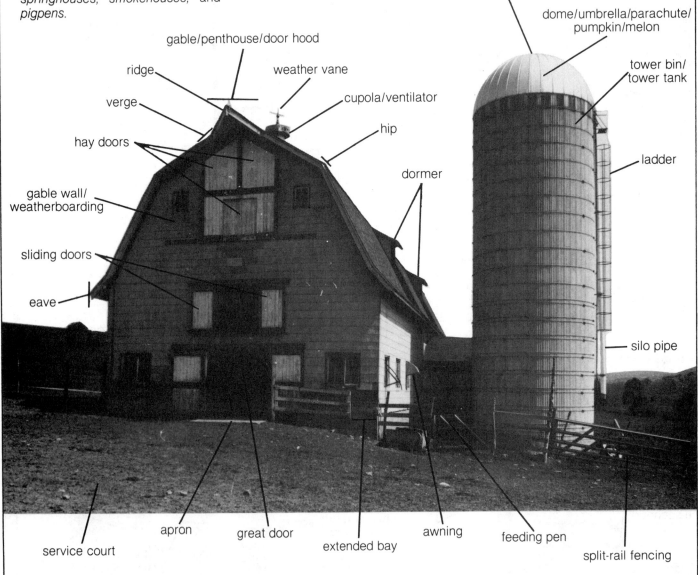

intake

dome/umbrella/parachute/pumpkin/melon

tower bin/tower tank

gable/penthouse/door hood

ridge

weather vane

verge

cupola/ventilator

hip

ladder

hay doors

gable wall/weatherboarding

dormer

sliding doors

eave

silo pipe

apron

great door

awning

feeding pen

service court

extended bay

split-rail fencing

Barn

Silo

Transportation

All the major forms of transportation are incorporated in this section, beginning with the most ubiquitous mode of everyday travel—the automobile. Coverage of the car begins with an illustration of a specially built model displaying all the exterior parts that appear or have appeared on recent designs. Also included is a cutaway drawing that shows the major but often unseen interior components of a car as well as illustrations of a car engine, interior dash and traffic control devices.

The other major subcategories cover public conveyances; emergency, public service and recreational vehicles; boats and ships; aircraft and spacecraft. Vehicles used for military purposes, such as fighting ships and aircraft, are included in this section as well.

Cutaway illustrations have been used to show the reader the interior parts of an ocean liner and the cockpits of a jumbo jet, military fighter and space shuttle.

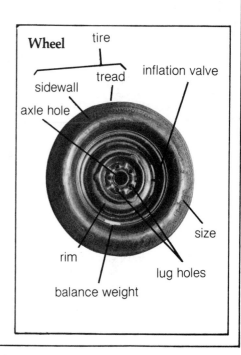

Wheel
tire
tread
inflation valve
sidewall
axle hole
size
rim
lug holes
balance weight

Automobile/Car Exterior

The *body* of this specially designed car, or *customized automobile,* rests on a *chassis* consisting of a *frame* and wheels. Older cars often had *rumble seats* instead of trunks. On *convertibles,* the entire top folds into a compartment called the *boot.* Many contemporary cars have sliding *sun roofs* or *moon roofs.* A *sedan* usually has four doors and full-width front and rear seats. A *coupe* is a smaller version of a sedan, having only two doors. A *station wagon* is a boxlike car with storage space behind the rear seat, which may have *fold-down seats* for additional passenger seating. A high-performance car with a low-slung body is a *sports car.*

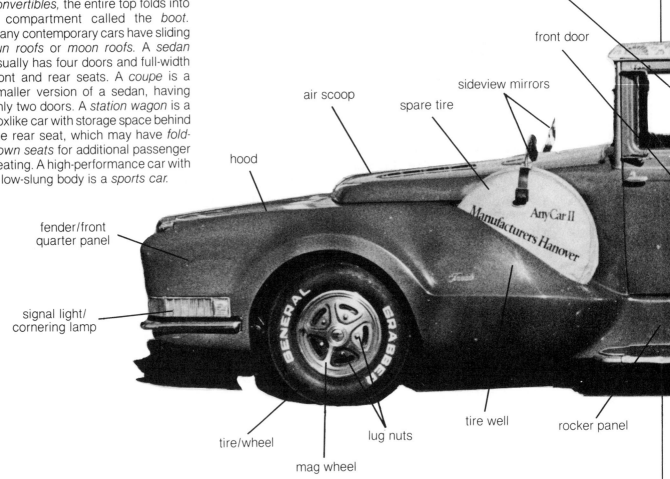

front window/front door window

front door

sideview mirrors

air scoop

spare tire

hood

AnyCar II

Manufacturers Hanover

fender/front quarter panel

signal light/cornering lamp

tire well

rocker panel

tire/wheel

lug nuts

mag wheel

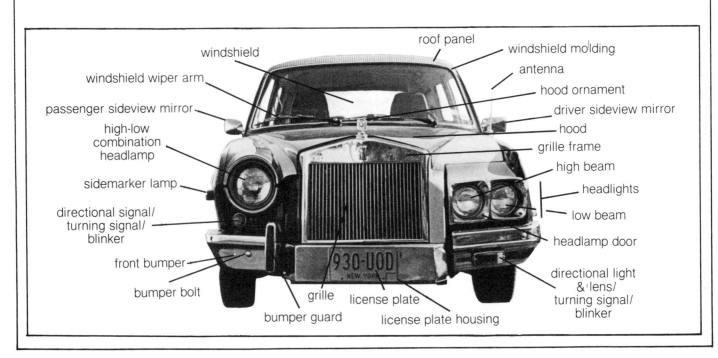

windshield

roof panel

windshield molding

windshield wiper arm

antenna

passenger sideview mirror

hood ornament

driver sideview mirror

high-low combination headlamp

hood

grille frame

sidemarker lamp

high beam

headlights

directional signal/ turning signal/ blinker

low beam

headlamp door

front bumper

directional light & lens/ turning signal/ blinker

bumper bolt

grille

license plate

bumper guard

license plate housing

930-UOD
NEW YORK

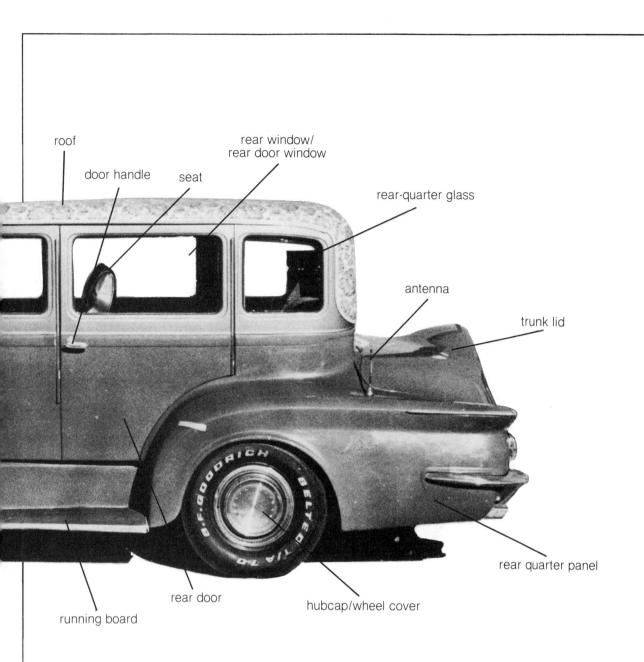

roof

rear window/
rear door window

door handle

seat

rear-quarter glass

antenna

trunk lid

running board

rear door

hubcap/wheel cover

rear quarter panel

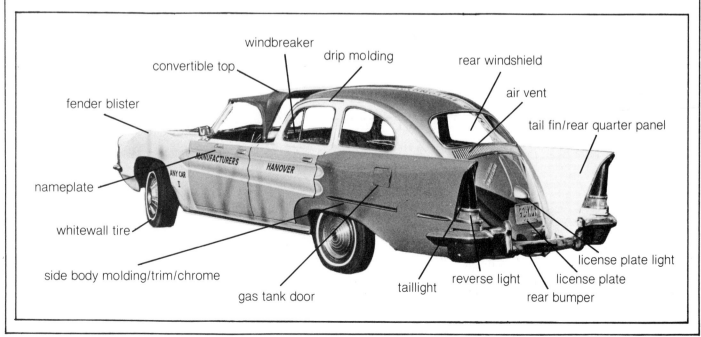

windbreaker

convertible top

drip molding

rear windshield

air vent

fender blister

tail fin/rear quarter panel

nameplate

whitewall tire

side body molding/trim/chrome

gas tank door

taillight

reverse light

license plate light

license plate

rear bumper

Automobile Cutaway

Various systems are incorporated in a car: a *power train,* which consists of *clutch,* transmission, driveshaft and rear axle; a *cooling system* designed to control engine temperature; an *electrical system* to power the engine *starter motor,* accessories and lights; a *suspension system* to provide a smooth ride; and a *braking system.*

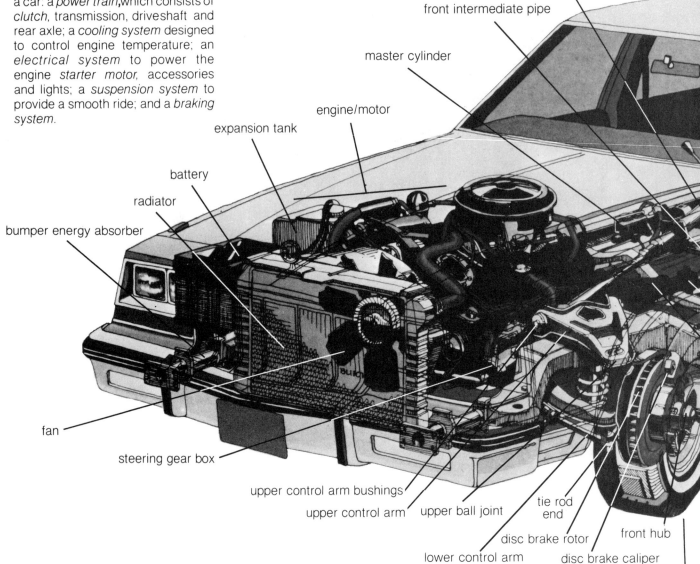

steering column
front intermediate pipe
master cylinder
engine/motor
expansion tank
battery
radiator
bumper energy absorber
fan
steering gear box
upper control arm bushings
upper control arm
upper ball joint
tie rod end
disc brake rotor
front hub
lower control arm
disc brake caliper

Passenger Car Types and Body Styles

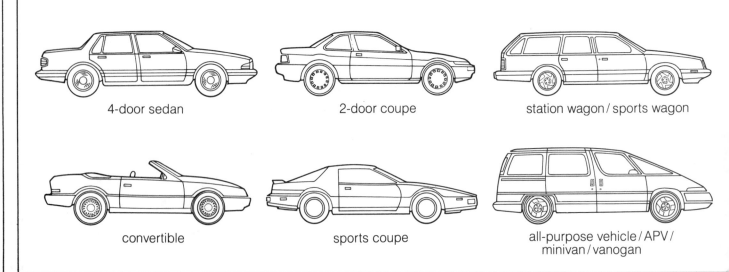

4-door sedan

2-door coupe

station wagon / sports wagon

convertible

sports coupe

all-purpose vehicle / APV / minivan / vanogan

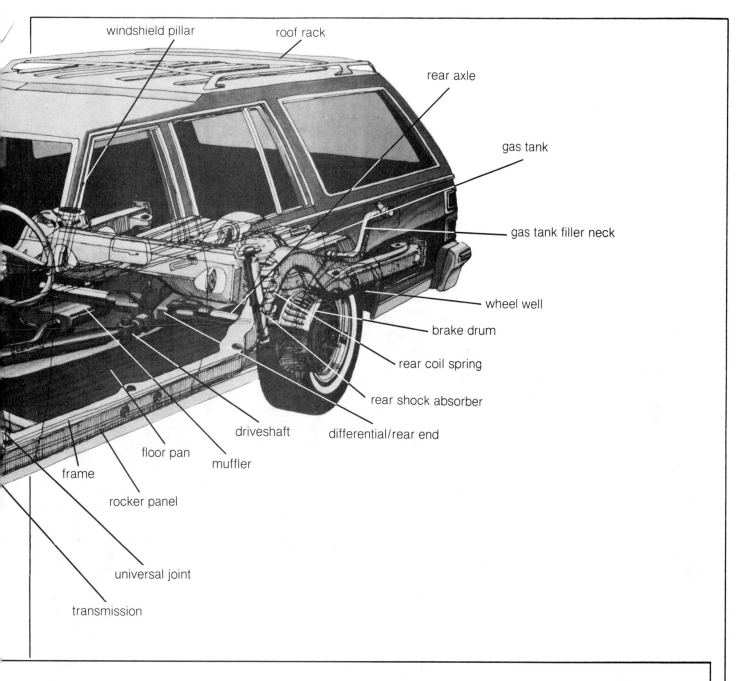

windshield pillar

roof rack

rear axle

gas tank

gas tank filler neck

wheel well

brake drum

rear coil spring

rear shock absorber

differential/rear end

driveshaft

muffler

floor pan

frame

rocker panel

universal joint

transmission

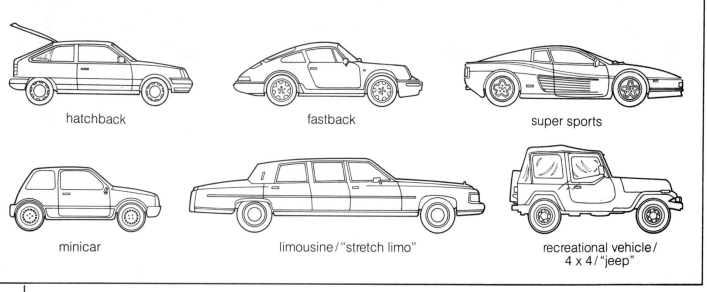

hatchback

fastback

super sports

minicar

limousine/"stretch limo"

recreational vehicle/
4 x 4/"jeep"

Automobile Interior

In addition to parts shown on this *dash*, or *dashboard*, are *headlight* and *warning light controls*, *hood release*, *engine choke* and *hand throttle*, *windshield wiper speed control* and *directional signal switch*. Above the dash, there is usually a *rearview mirror*. Flip-down *sun visors* are located above the windshield. Car seats are equipped with *seat belts* or *safety belts*.

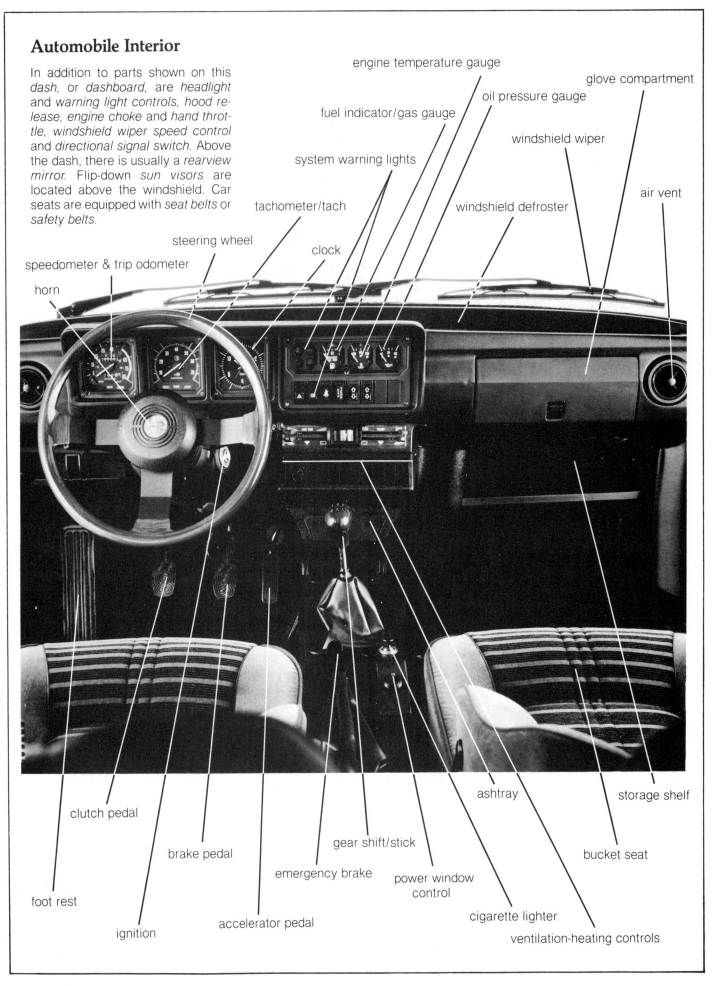

engine temperature gauge

glove compartment

oil pressure gauge

fuel indicator/gas gauge

windshield wiper

system warning lights

air vent

windshield defroster

tachometer/tach

steering wheel

clock

speedometer & trip odometer

horn

clutch pedal

brake pedal

gear shift/stick

ashtray

storage shelf

emergency brake

power window control

bucket seat

foot rest

cigarette lighter

ignition

accelerator pedal

ventilation-heating controls

Automobile Engine

The parts of an engine are fitted into or on the *engine block* or within the *head.* Common engine configurations include the *horizontally opposed,* or *flat four-cylinder;* the *in-line six;* and the *V-8.*

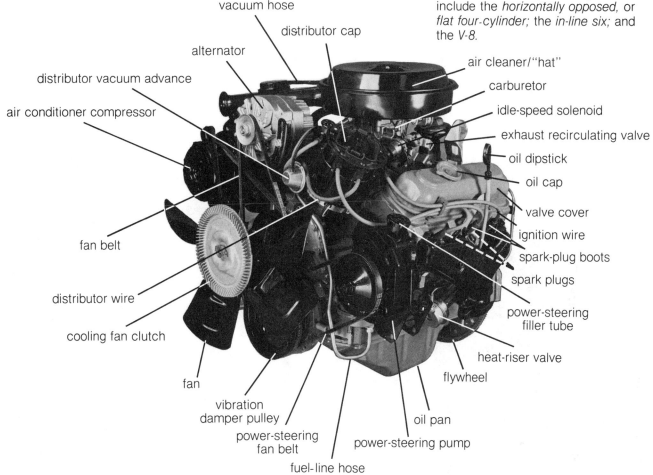

vacuum hose
distributor cap
alternator
distributor vacuum advance
air conditioner compressor
fan belt
distributor wire
cooling fan clutch
fan
vibration damper pulley
power-steering fan belt
fuel-line hose
power-steering pump
oil pan
flywheel
heat-riser valve
power-steering filler tube
spark plugs
spark-plug boots
ignition wire
valve cover
oil cap
oil dipstick
exhaust recirculating valve
idle-speed solenoid
carburetor
air cleaner/"hat"

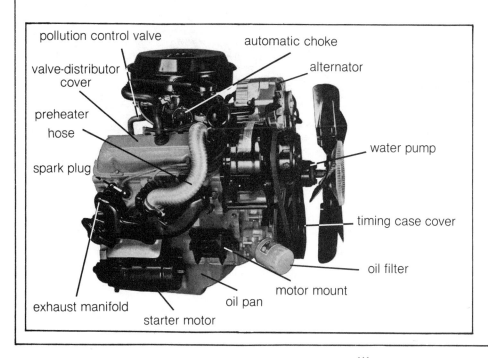

pollution control valve
automatic choke
valve-distributor cover
alternator
preheater hose
spark plug
water pump
timing case cover
oil filter
motor mount
exhaust manifold
oil pan
starter motor

Automobile

Gasoline Pump

Service station islands can be *self-service* or *full-service*. Gas pumps draw supplies from underground *storage tanks*. Gasoline is purchased in different *grades* determined by *octane number*.

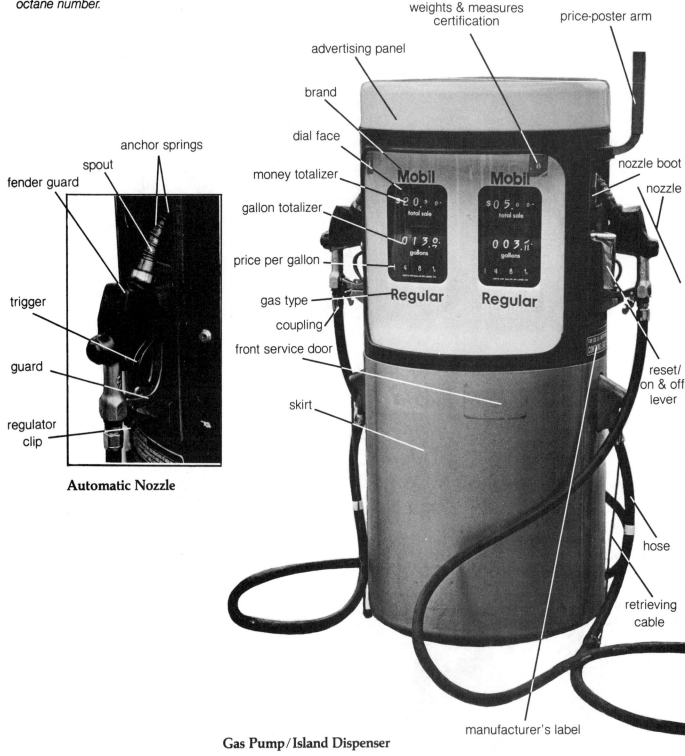

fender guard

spout

anchor springs

trigger

guard

regulator clip

Automatic Nozzle

advertising panel

brand

dial face

money totalizer

gallon totalizer

price per gallon

gas type

coupling

front service door

skirt

weights & measures certification

price-poster arm

nozzle boot

nozzle

Mobil

Mobil

reset/ on & off lever

hose

retrieving cable

manufacturer's label

Gas Pump/Island Dispenser

Traffic Control Devices

Four-face traffic signals, or lights, are operated manually by a traffic-control official or run automatically by an electric *timer.* Parking meters, set atop *pipe standards,* contain *self-starting timers.* Jammed meters activate a *slot closer* so that additional coins cannot be inserted in the *slot block.* Some meters have a *washer detector* that allows *washers* and *slugs* to pass through without registering time on the *dial.*

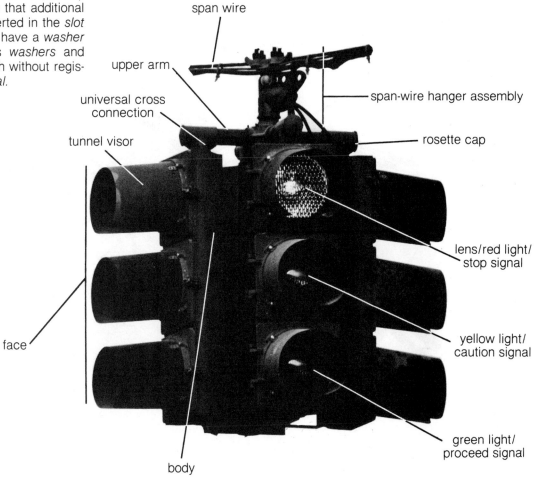

span wire

upper arm

universal cross connection

tunnel visor

face

span-wire hanger assembly

rosette cap

lens/red light/ stop signal

yellow light/ caution signal

green light/ proceed signal

body

Traffic Light

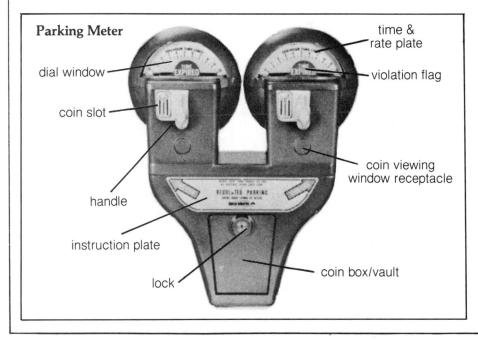

Parking Meter

dial window

coin slot

handle

instruction plate

lock

time & rate plate

violation flag

coin viewing window receptacle

coin box/vault

Highway

Energy absorbing barriers, or *impact attenuation devices,* are positioned in gore areas to reduce accidents. Some roads are lined with *guard-rails,* or *railings. Milestones,* or *mile markers,* provide distance information between specific points. Many *expressways, freeways* and *thruways* have *rest areas, scenic overlooks* and *service areas.*

entrance ramp

gore area

service road

exit ramp

road divider

shoulder

lane/roadway

roadbed/
divided highway

access road

median/island

entrance lane

loop ramp

underpass

overpass/bridge

major road

intersection/junction

minor road/
subsidiary road

Cloverleaf/Interchange

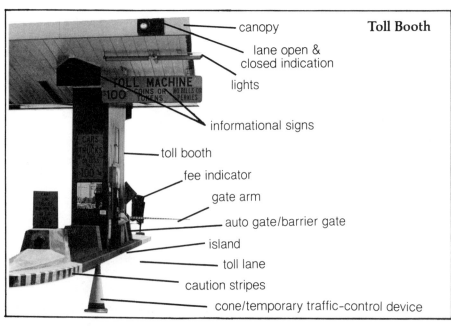

Toll Booth

canopy

lane open &
closed indication

lights

informational signs

toll booth

fee indicator

gate arm

auto gate/barrier gate

island

toll lane

caution stripes

cone/temporary traffic-control device

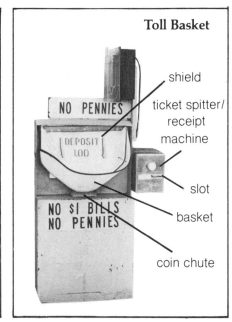

Toll Basket

shield

ticket spitter/
receipt
machine

slot

basket

coin chute

Railroad Crossing

A railroad *roadway* consists of two rails, or tracks, and all their supporting elements, including *railroad bridges, tunnels* and *embankments.* The roadway follows the *right of way.* The distance between rails is the *gauge,* while the degree of rise or fall in a *roadbed* is the *grade.* The top of a rail is the *railhead.* The bottom is the *rail foot.*

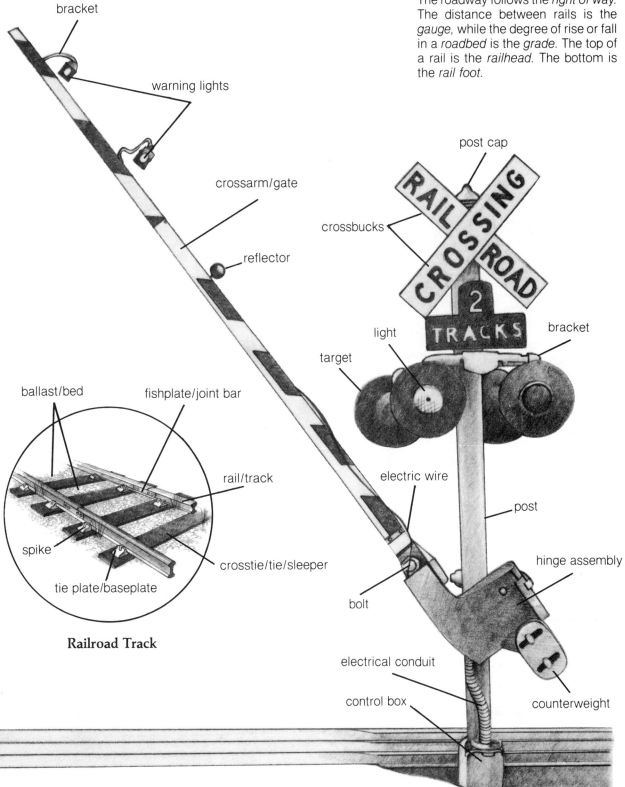

bracket

warning lights

crossarm/gate

reflector

post cap

crossbucks

RAIL CROSSING ROAD

2 TRACKS

light

target

bracket

electric wire

post

hinge assembly

bolt

electrical conduit

counterweight

control box

Crossing Signal

ballast/bed

fishplate/joint bar

rail/track

spike

crosstie/tie/sleeper

tie plate/baseplate

Railroad Track

Public Transportation

Railroad

In addition to the locomotives shown here, there are *diesel* and *electric locomotives*. *Open-top*, *box* and *flat cars* are the principal types of *freight cars*, while *passenger trains* consist of *coaches*, *buffet* and *dining cars*, *sleeping cars*, *lounge* or *observation cars* and *baggage cars*.

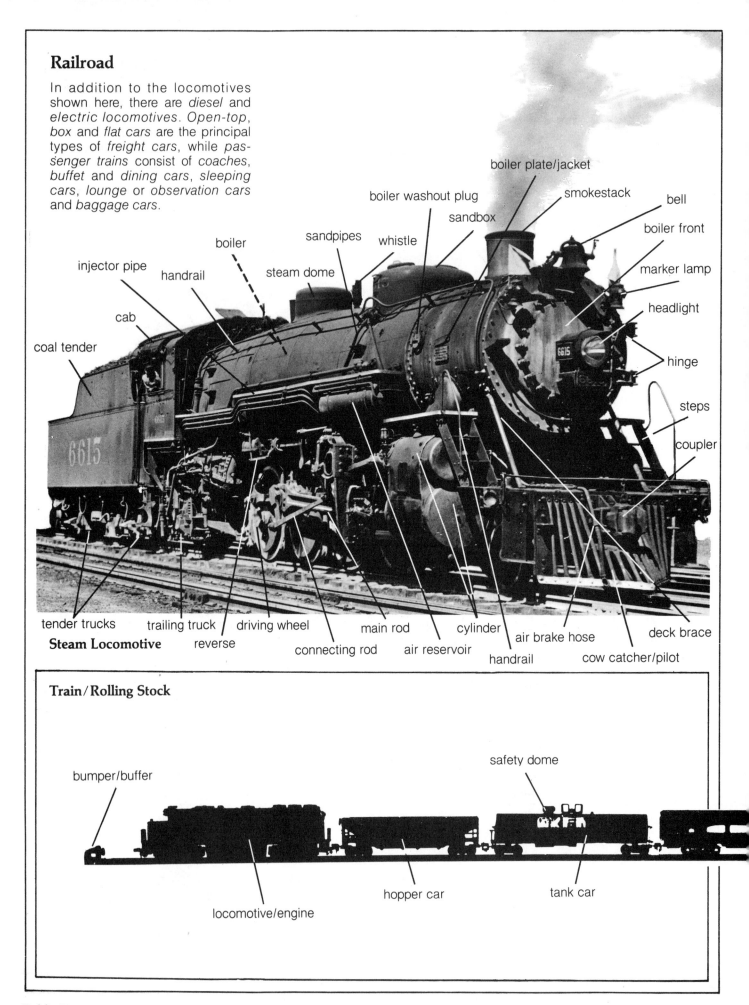

boiler plate/jacket

boiler washout plug

smokestack

bell

sandbox

boiler front

sandpipes

whistle

marker lamp

boiler

steam dome

headlight

injector pipe

handrail

hinge

cab

steps

coal tender

coupler

tender trucks

trailing truck

driving wheel

main rod

cylinder

deck brace

Steam Locomotive

reverse

connecting rod

air reservoir

handrail

air brake hose

cow catcher/pilot

Train/Rolling Stock

safety dome

bumper/buffer

hopper car

tank car

locomotive/engine

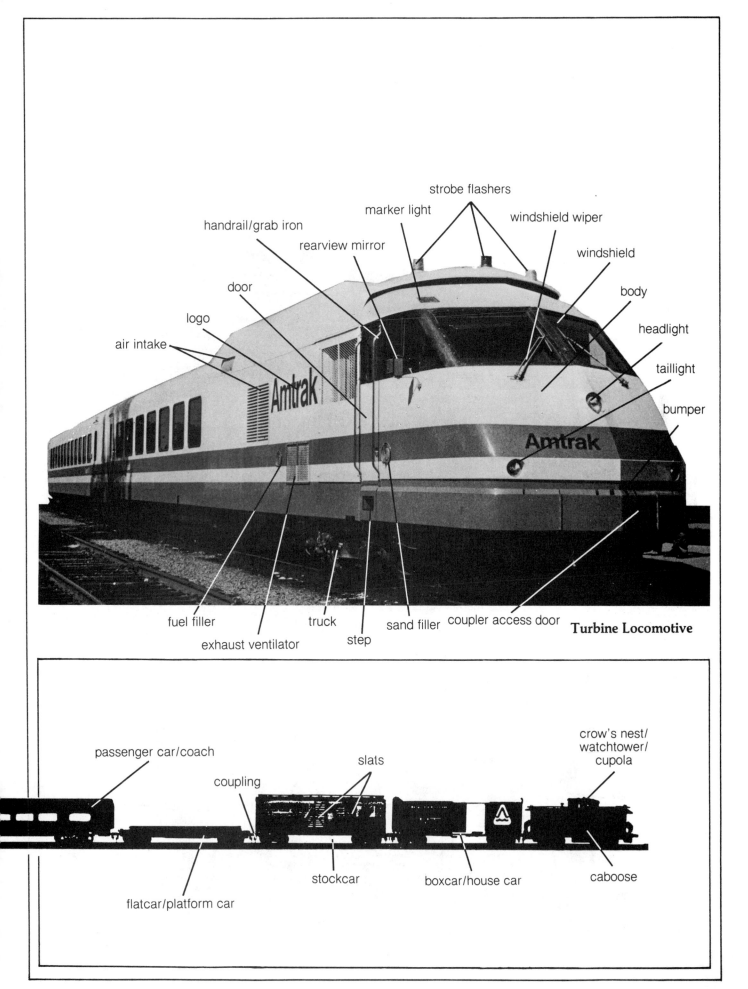

strobe flashers

marker light

windshield wiper

handrail/grab iron

rearview mirror

windshield

door

body

logo

headlight

air intake

taillight

bumper

Amtrak

Amtrak

fuel filler

truck

sand filler

coupler access door

Turbine Locomotive

exhaust ventilator

step

crow's nest/
watchtower/
cupola

passenger car/coach

slats

coupling

stockcar

boxcar/house car

caboose

flatcar/platform car

117

Public Transportation

Bus

Long-distance coaches have airplanelike *reclining seats* with *overhead baggage racks* and *reading lights.* They may also have *lavatories* and *roof ventilation hatches. Sightseeing buses* have *transparent roofs,* at least in part, to increase the viewing area.

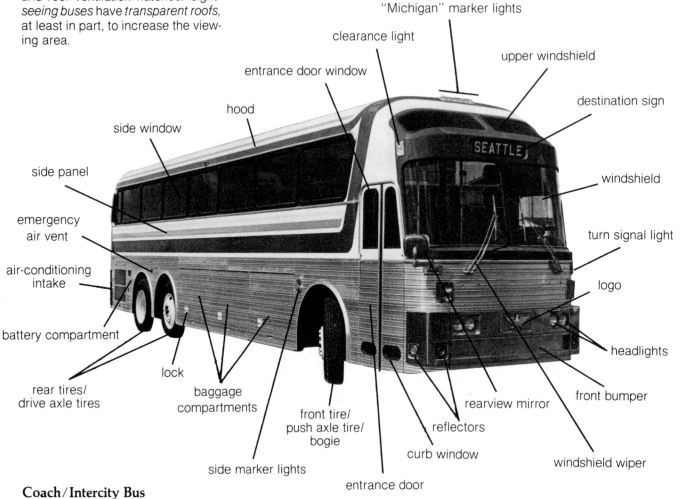

"Michigan" marker lights
clearance light
entrance door window
upper windshield
hood
destination sign
side window
windshield
side panel
turn signal light
emergency air vent
logo
air-conditioning intake
headlights
battery compartment
front bumper
rear tires/ drive axle tires
rearview mirror
lock
reflectors
baggage compartments
curb window
front tire/ push axle tire/ bogie
windshield wiper
side marker lights
entrance door

Coach/Intercity Bus

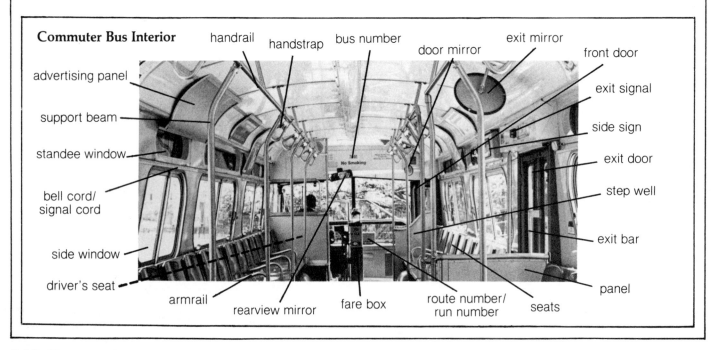

Commuter Bus Interior

advertising panel
handrail
handstrap
bus number
door mirror
exit mirror
front door
support beam
exit signal
standee window
side sign
bell cord/ signal cord
exit door
step well
side window
exit bar
driver's seat
panel
armrail
rearview mirror
fare box
route number/ run number
seats

A subway, or *rapid transit system*, usually consists of a *train* which derives its power from a *third rail*; subterranean *tunnels*, or *tubes*; *elevated tracks*; and *subway stations*, or *stops*, along each *route*.

window

ventilator

fan

light

emergency brake

advertising panels

handstraps

subway map

door panels

side handrail

seat

handrail/support beam

storm door

destination sign/ side sign

Taxi Roof Light

off-duty sign

medallion number

signal light

Motorman's Cab

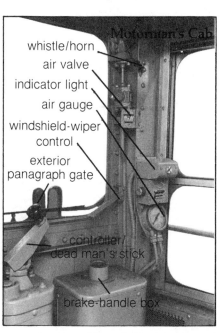

whistle/horn

air valve

indicator light

air gauge

windshield-wiper control

exterior panagraph gate

controller/ dead man's stick

brake-handle box

Truck

A *rig* consists of a tractor *coupled* with or *hooked up* to a trailer. A cab may have a partitioned section within, called a *sleeping box,* for the driver, and a *varashield,* a capelike device designed to deflect air and reduce resistance on the trailer, mounted on the roof. The *refrigeration van,* or *reefer,* shown on the opposite page, is a semi, meaning that the tractor bears some of its weight. A true trailer rests and rides on its own wheels.

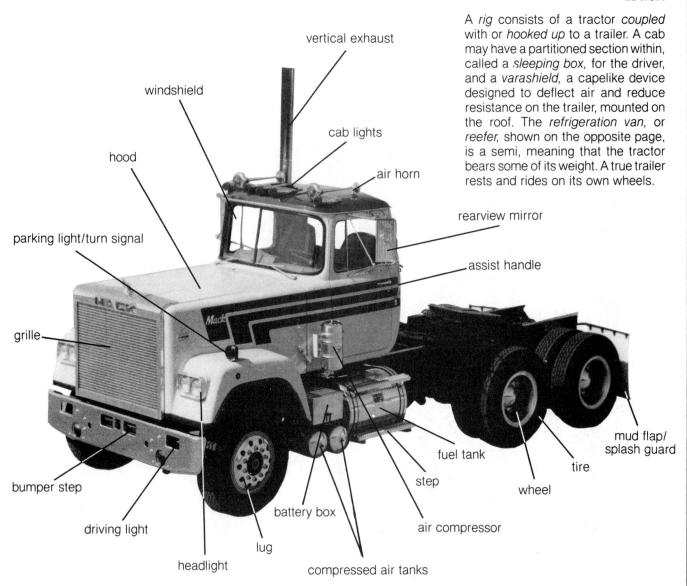

vertical exhaust

windshield

cab lights

hood

air horn

parking light/turn signal

rearview mirror

assist handle

grille

bumper step

mud flap/ splash guard

tire

driving light

wheel

battery box

fuel tank

step

air compressor

lug

headlight

compressed air tanks

Tractor/Cab

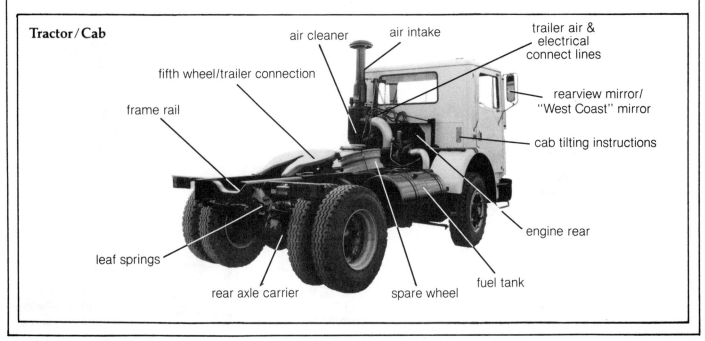

air cleaner

air intake

trailer air & electrical connect lines

fifth wheel/trailer connection

rearview mirror/ "West Coast" mirror

frame rail

cab tilting instructions

engine rear

leaf springs

fuel tank

rear axle carrier

spare wheel

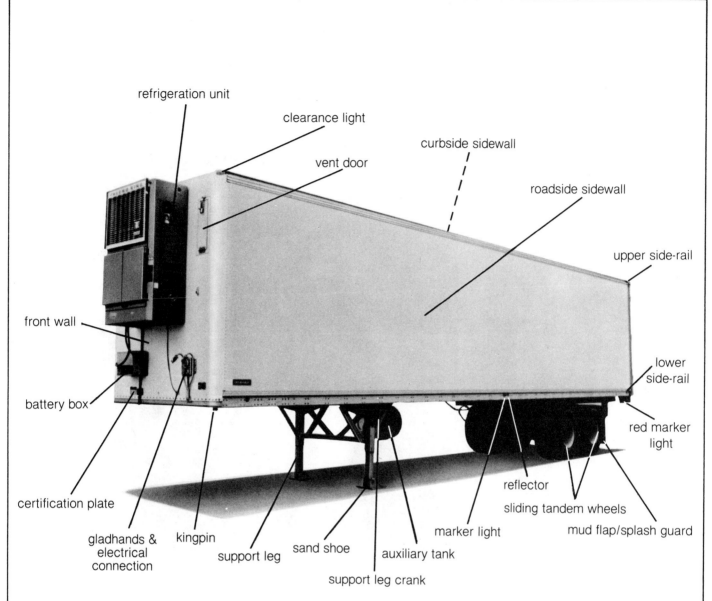

refrigeration unit

clearance light

vent door

curbside sidewall

roadside sidewall

upper side-rail

front wall

lower side-rail

battery box

red marker light

certification plate

reflector

sliding tandem wheels

mud flap/splash guard

gladhands & electrical connection

kingpin

support leg

sand shoe

auxiliary tank

marker light

support leg crank

Semitrailer/Van

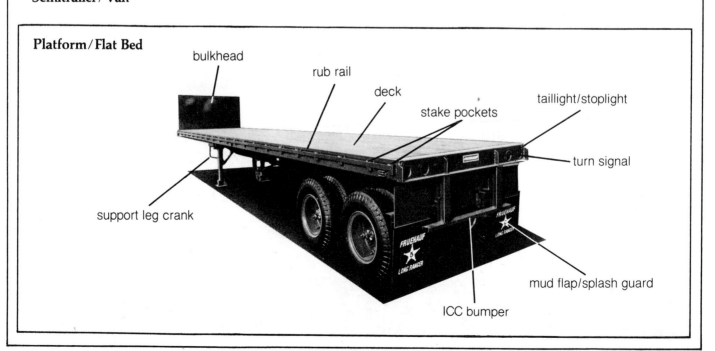

Platform/Flat Bed

bulkhead

rub rail

deck

stake pockets

taillight/stoplight

turn signal

support leg crank

mud flap/splash guard

ICC bumper

Carriers

Police Car

Many police cars have *alley lights,* strong floodlights at either end of the light bar on the roof. A wire screen between the driver's seat and the back seat of the car is called the *cage.* Contained in the trunk of many police cars are a *hurst tool,* or *jaws of life,* a *haligan tool,* an *oxygen unit, flares,* a *fire extinguisher,* a *riot gun,* a *first-aid kit, blankets* and a *pillow.*

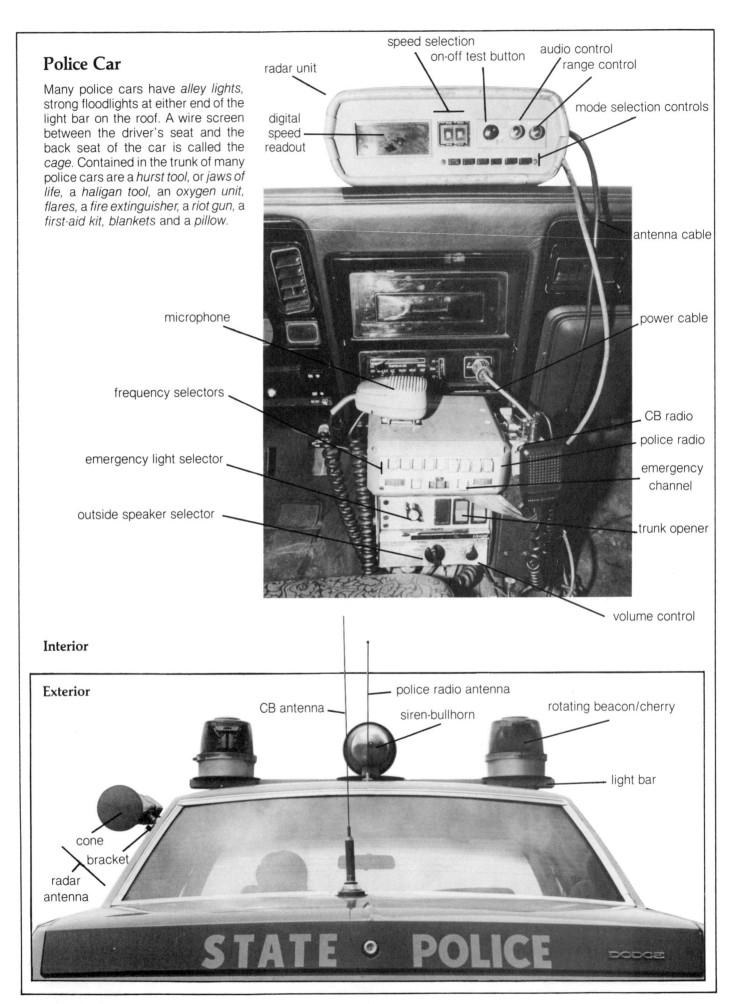

radar unit

speed selection
on-off test button

audio control
range control

mode selection controls

digital speed readout

antenna cable

microphone

power cable

frequency selectors

CB radio
police radio
emergency channel

emergency light selector

outside speaker selector

trunk opener

volume control

Interior

Exterior

police radio antenna

CB antenna

siren-bullhorn

rotating beacon/cherry

light bar

cone

bracket

radar antenna

STATE • POLICE

Ambulance

Additional equipment carried inside *advanced life-support units,* such as the one shown here, are *burn sheets, gauze, emesis basins, cervical collars, neck rolls, bitee sticks, tongue blades, peroxide* and *alcohol, extension tubes,* additional *oxygen tanks, splints, sandbags* (for traction), *linens,* a *scoop stretcher* and a *carrying chair.*

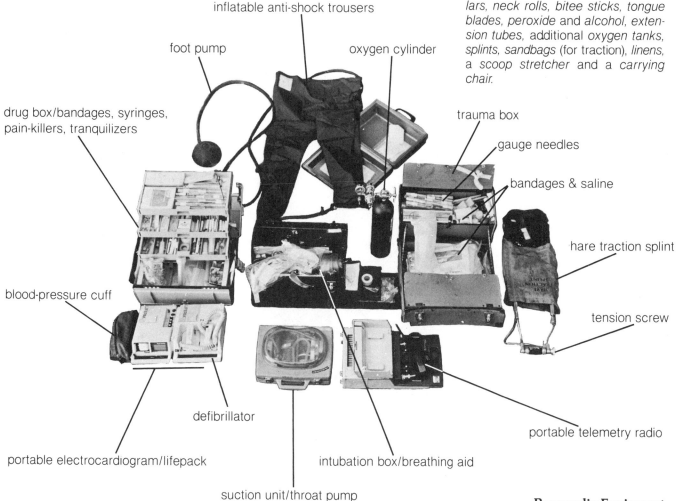

inflatable anti-shock trousers

foot pump

oxygen cylinder

drug box/bandages, syringes, pain-killers, tranquilizers

trauma box

gauge needles

bandages & saline

hare traction splint

blood-pressure cuff

tension screw

defibrillator

portable telemetry radio

portable electrocardiogram/lifepack

intubation box/breathing aid

suction unit/throat pump

Paramedic Equipment

Ambulance

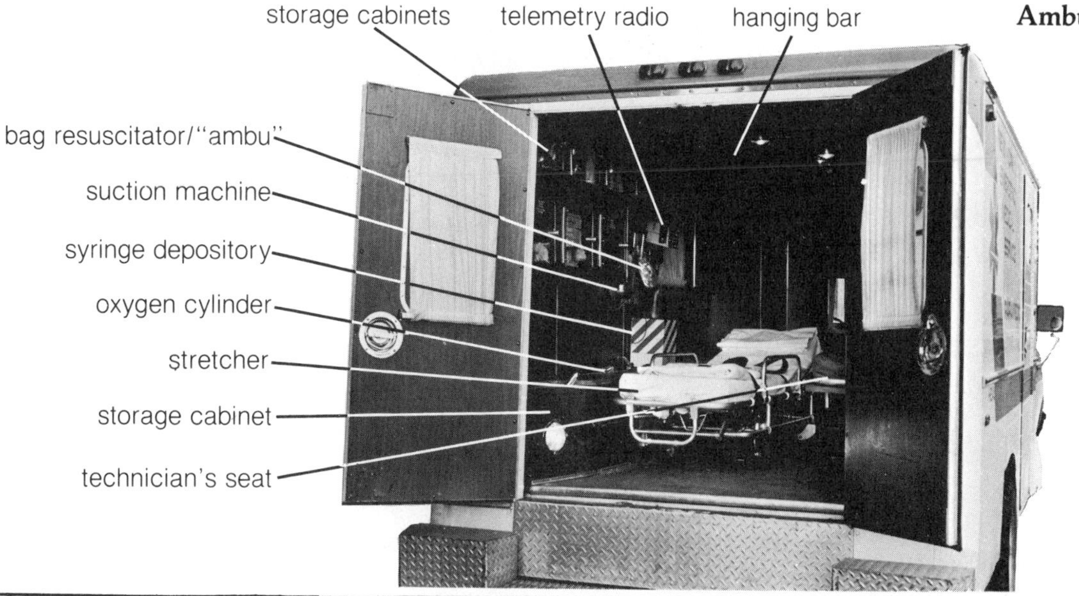

storage cabinets

telemetry radio

hanging bar

bag resuscitator/"ambu"

suction machine

syringe depository

oxygen cylinder

stretcher

storage cabinet

technician's seat

Emergency Vehicles

Fire Engine

On a fire truck, the entire tower ladder and control platform revolve on a *turntable.* Contained within a pumper is a water *booster tank* for fighting small fires, a *booster hose-reel,* for letting out hose line, and an *extension ladder.* Most fire fighting *apparatus* also carry *air tanks, lift-nets, EMT,* or *first aid boxes,* and *smoke ejectors.*

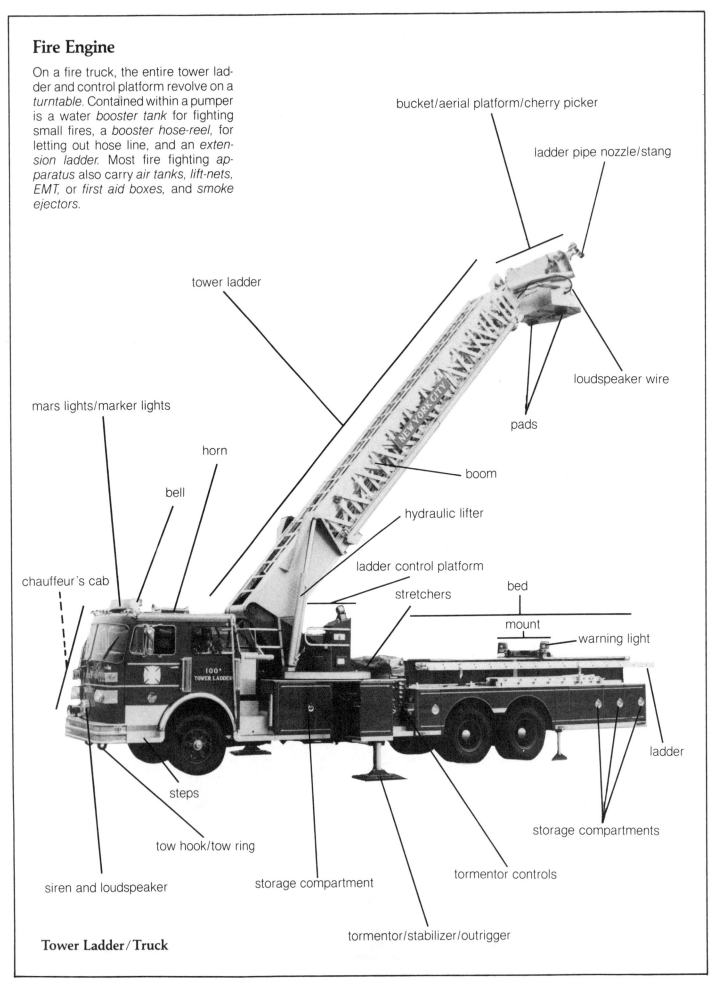

bucket/aerial platform/cherry picker

ladder pipe nozzle/stang

tower ladder

loudspeaker wire

mars lights/marker lights

pads

horn

boom

bell

hydraulic lifter

ladder control platform

bed

chauffeur's cab

stretchers

mount

warning light

steps

ladder

tow hook/tow ring

storage compartments

siren and loudspeaker

storage compartment

tormentor controls

tormentor/stabilizer/outrigger

Tower Ladder / Truck

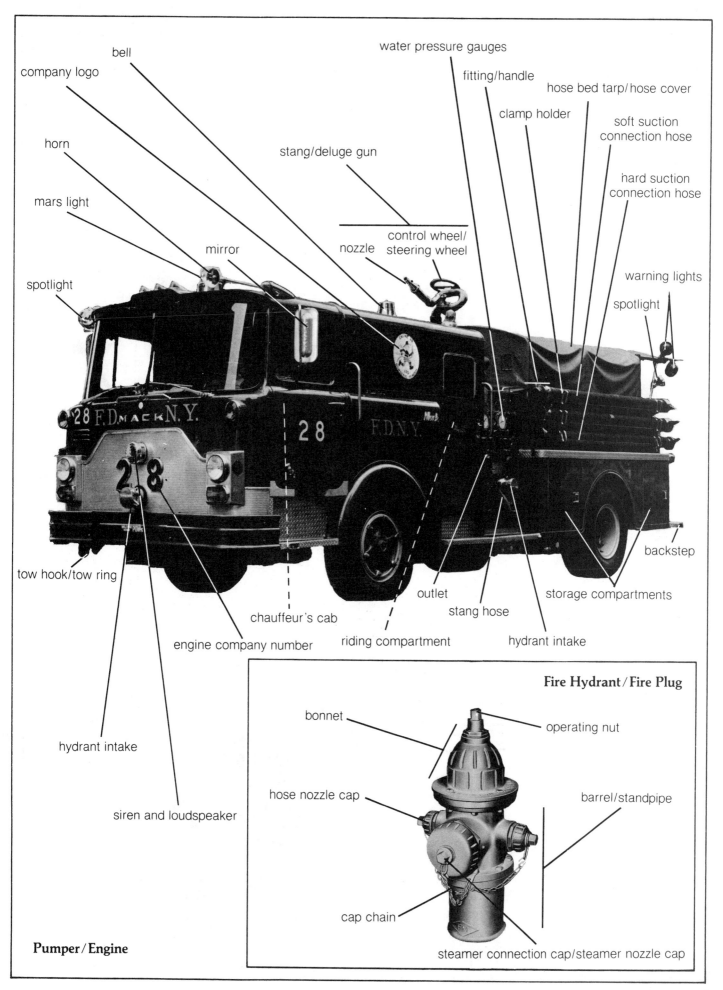

bell

company logo

water pressure gauges

fitting/handle

hose bed tarp/hose cover

horn

clamp holder

soft suction
connection hose

mars light

stang/deluge gun

hard suction
connection hose

mirror

control wheel/
steering wheel

spotlight

nozzle

warning lights

spotlight

28 F.D. MACK N.Y.

28

F.D.N.Y.

tow hook/tow ring

backstep

outlet

storage compartments

chauffeur's cab

stang hose

engine company number

riding compartment

hydrant intake

hydrant intake

siren and loudspeaker

Fire Hydrant/Fire Plug

bonnet

operating nut

hose nozzle cap

barrel/standpipe

cap chain

steamer connection cap/steamer nozzle cap

Pumper/Engine

Emergency Vehicles

Tow Truck/Wrecker

Tow trucks, or *rigs*, that respond to accident reports are called "chasers." A fully-equipped tow truck carries *fire extinguishers*, *battery charger*, *battery jumper cables*, and a two-pronged *lockout tool* which enables the operator to open locked car doors.

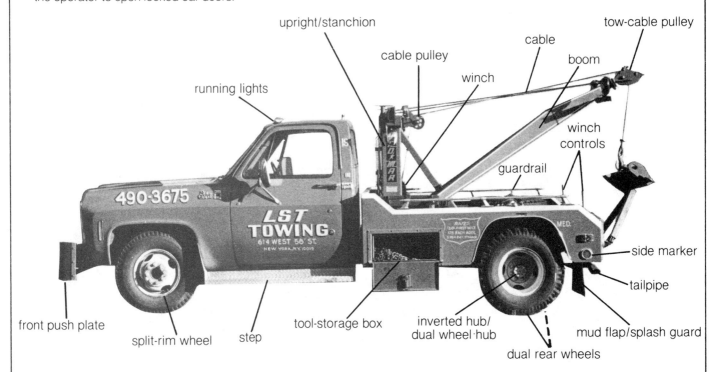

upright/stanchion

cable pulley

cable

boom

tow-cable pulley

winch

running lights

winch controls

guardrail

side marker

tailpipe

front push plate

split-rim wheel

step

tool-storage box

inverted hub/ dual wheel·hub

mud flap/splash guard

dual rear wheels

Truck Bed

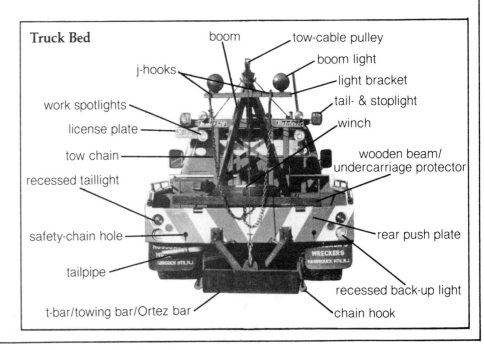

boom

tow-cable pulley

j-hooks

boom light

light bracket

work spotlights

tail- & stoplight

license plate

winch

tow chain

wooden beam/ undercarriage protector

recessed taillight

safety-chain hole

rear push plate

tailpipe

recessed back-up light

t-bar/towing bar/Ortez bar

chain hook

Sanitation Vehicles

Garbage collectors, sanitation men, or "sanmen," also use a large, water-carrying truck called a *flusher* to wet down and clean streets.

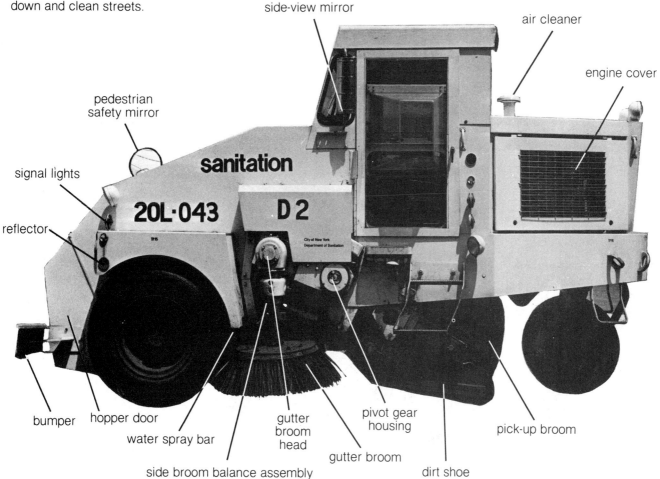

side-view mirror

air cleaner

engine cover

pedestrian safety mirror

signal lights

reflector

sanitation

20L·043

D 2

bumper

hopper door

water spray bar

gutter broom head

side broom balance assembly

gutter broom

pivot gear housing

dirt shoe

pick-up broom

Mechanical Sweeper / Street Cleaner

Side-Loading Collection Truck / Garbage Truck

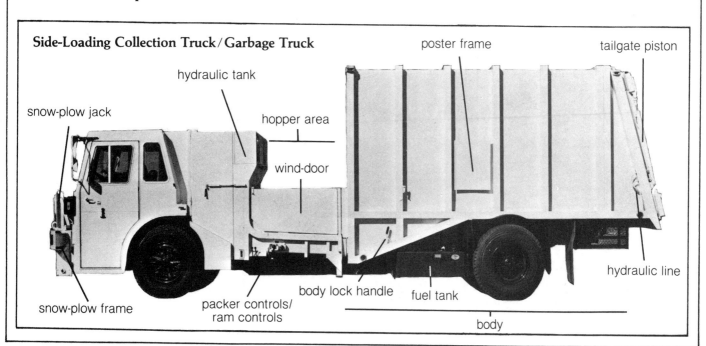

poster frame

tailgate piston

hydraulic tank

snow-plow jack

hopper area

wind-door

snow-plow frame

packer controls/ ram controls

body lock handle

fuel tank

hydraulic line

body

Bicycle

This illustration combines elements from the most popular bicycle styles. The *frame* is the skeleton to which the *wheels* and all other components are attached. A one-wheel cycle is called a *unicycle*. A three-wheeler is a *tricycle*.

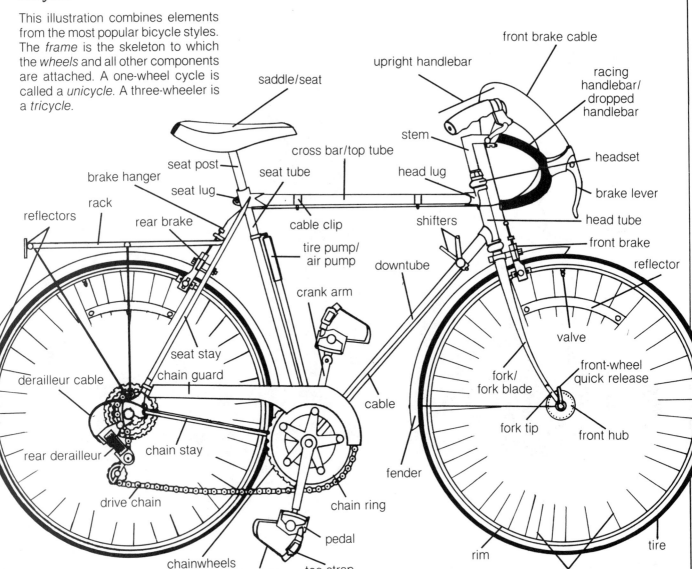

front brake cable

upright handlebar

racing handlebar/ dropped handlebar

saddle/seat

stem

cross bar/top tube

head lug

headset

seat post

seat tube

brake lever

brake hanger

seat lug

head tube

rack

cable clip

shifters

front brake

reflectors

rear brake

reflector

tire pump/ air pump

downtube

valve

crank arm

seat stay

fork/ fork blade

front-wheel quick release

derailleur cable

chain guard

cable

fork tip

front hub

rear derailleur

chain stay

drive chain

fender

chain ring

chainwheels

pedal

rim

tire

toe clip

toe strap

spokes

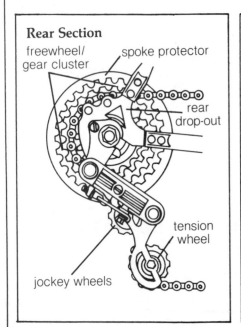

Rear Section

freewheel/ gear cluster

spoke protector

rear drop-out

tension wheel

jockey wheels

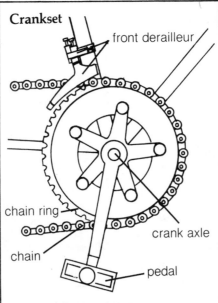

Crankset

front derailleur

chain ring

crank axle

chain

pedal

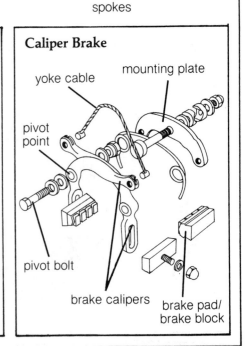

Caliper Brake

yoke cable

mounting plate

pivot point

pivot bolt

brake calipers

brake pad/ brake block

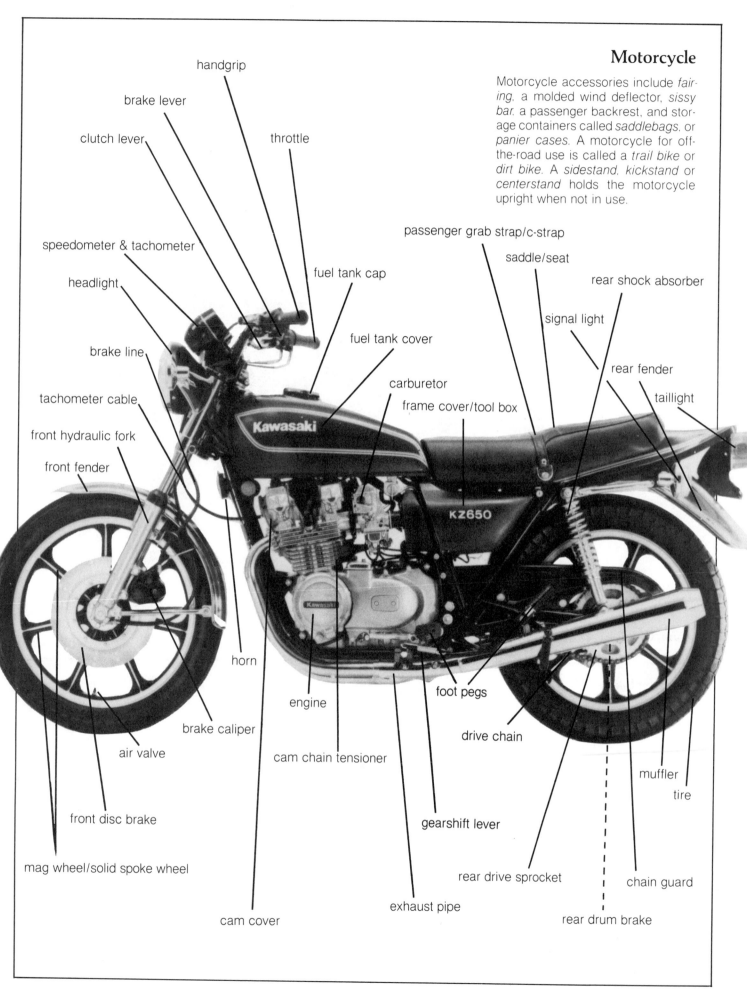

Motorcycle

Motorcycle accessories include *fairing*, a molded wind deflector, *sissy bar*, a passenger backrest, and storage containers called *saddlebags*, or *panier cases*. A motorcycle for off-the-road use is called a *trail bike* or *dirt bike*. A *sidestand*, *kickstand* or *centerstand* holds the motorcycle upright when not in use.

handgrip

brake lever

clutch lever

throttle

speedometer & tachometer

headlight

fuel tank cap

passenger grab strap/c-strap

saddle/seat

rear shock absorber

signal light

rear fender

taillight

fuel tank cover

brake line

carburetor

tachometer cable

frame cover/tool box

front hydraulic fork

front fender

Kawasaki

KZ650

horn

brake caliper

air valve

engine

cam chain tensioner

foot pegs

drive chain

muffler

tire

front disc brake

mag wheel/solid spoke wheel

cam cover

gearshift lever

exhaust pipe

rear drive sprocket

rear drum brake

chain guard

Cycles

Recreational Vehicles

The *heating* and *cooking units* in the rear *coach* of a camper run on *propane gas*. Unlike campers, which run under their own power, *trailers* are hitched behind a vehicle and towed. Other *off-the-road vehicles* include *four-wheel drive jeeps* and *dune buggies*.

running lights

side window

roof air conditioner

luggage rack

front window

side window

water fill

road light

sewer valve

power-cord compartment

fuel tank

hot water heater

storage compartment

Camper/Motor Home

Snowmobile

instrument panel

handlebars

windshield

tail section

headlight

nose cone/wedge

seat

bumper

snow spoiler

suspension wheel

cleats

slide rail

track

steering link

skis

shock absorber

shock absorber

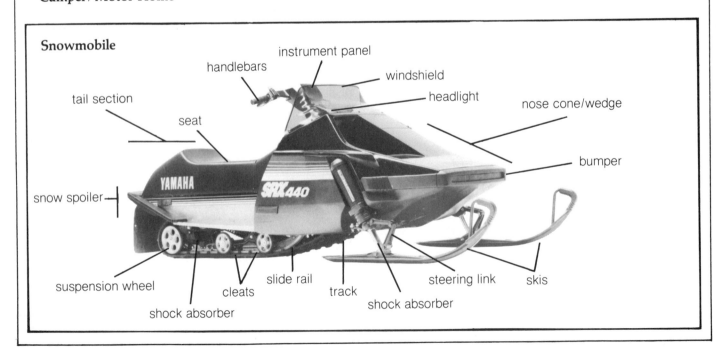

Horse-drawn Carriages

Stagecoaches were drawn by teams of horses and commanded by a *driver* called the *whip, Charlie* or *Jehu*. Protection was provided by a *guard*, or *shotgun*. A *buggy* was four-wheeled. A *gig* had two wheels. A *buckboard* had a spring-supported seat attached to a board directly connected to the axles. A *cabriolet* was a *hackney carriage*, or *cab*, with only two wheels and a folding top.

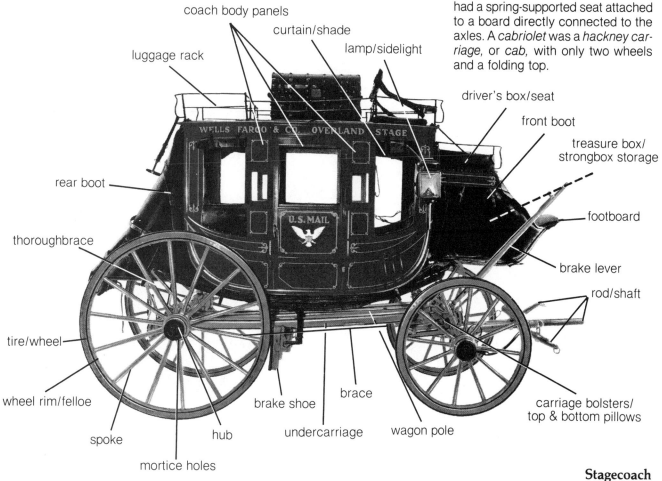

coach body panels

curtain/shade

lamp/sidelight

luggage rack

driver's box/seat

front boot

treasure box/ strongbox storage

rear boot

footboard

thoroughbrace

brake lever

rod/shaft

tire/wheel

wheel rim/felloe

carriage bolsters/ top & bottom pillows

brake shoe

brace

spoke

hub

undercarriage

wagon pole

mortice holes

Stagecoach

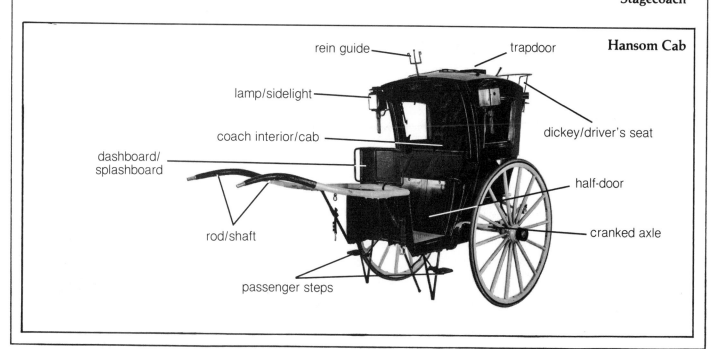

Hansom Cab

rein guide

trapdoor

lamp/sidelight

coach interior/cab

dickey/driver's seat

dashboard/ splashboard

half-door

rod/shaft

cranked axle

passenger steps

Nautical Terminology

The outer shell of a boat is the *hull*. A hull's greatest width is the *beam*. Any line running from one side of a boat to the other is said to run *athwartships*. That part of a boat facing the direction from which the wind is blowing is called the *windward* side. The opposite side is called the *leeward* side.

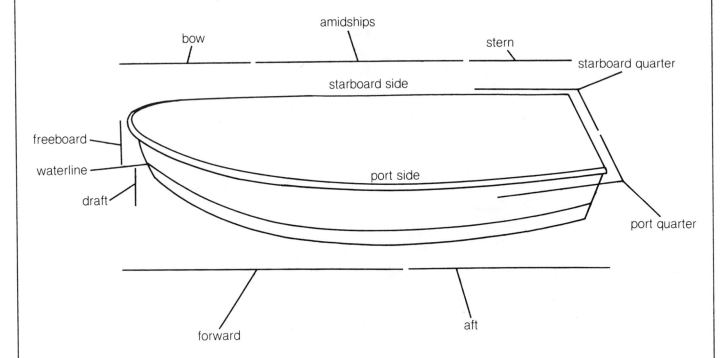

bow
amidships
stern
starboard quarter
starboard side
freeboard
waterline
port side
draft
port quarter
forward
aft

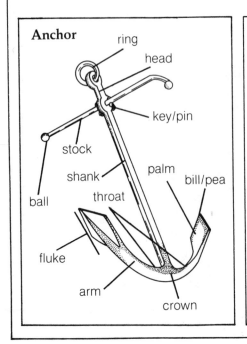

Anchor

ring
head
key/pin
stock
shank
palm
bill/pea
ball
throat
fluke
arm
crown

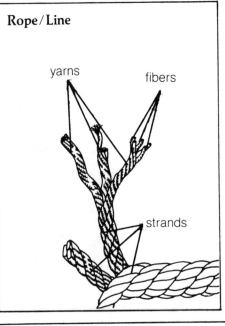

Rope/Line

yarns
fibers
strands

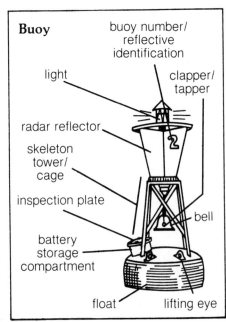

Buoy

buoy number/ reflective identification
light
clapper/ tapper
radar reflector
skeleton tower/ cage
inspection plate
battery storage compartment
bell
float
lifting eye

Rowboat

Any small *craft*, either *decked* or *open* and propelled by oars, is a rowboat, or *skiff*. If it is used to service a *yacht* or *motor cruiser*, it is called a *dinghy*, *dink* or *tender*.

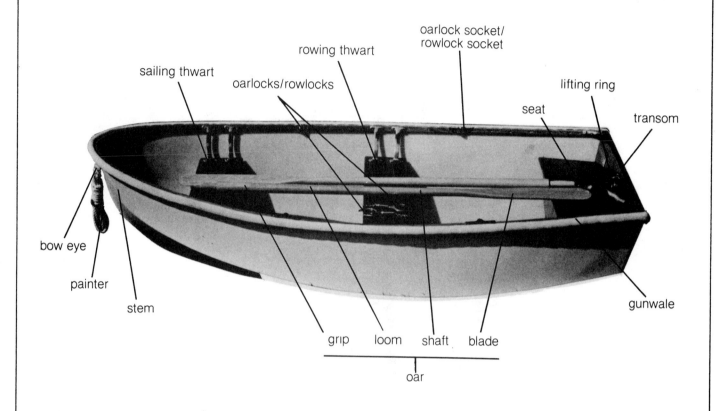

sailing thwart

oarlocks/rowlocks

rowing thwart

oarlock socket/ rowlock socket

lifting ring

seat

transom

bow eye

painter

stem

grip   loom   shaft   blade

oar

gunwale

Inflatable

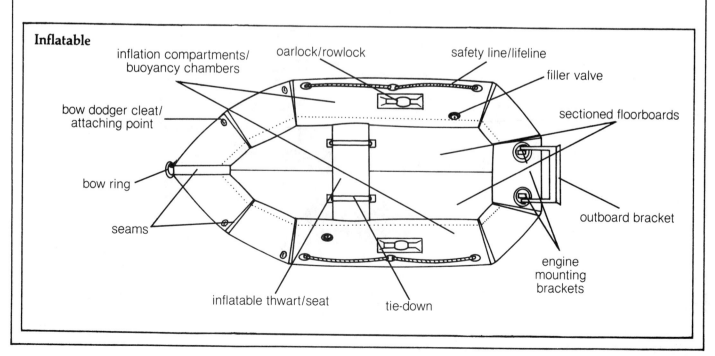

inflation compartments/ buoyancy chambers

oarlock/rowlock

safety line/lifeline

filler valve

bow dodger cleat/ attaching point

sectioned floorboards

bow ring

outboard bracket

seams

engine mounting brackets

inflatable thwart/seat

tie-down

Sailboat

Standing rigging, shrouds and stays, keep a sailing vessel's mast, or *spar,* upright. *Halyards* are used to hoist sails and *running rigging,* lines and *sheets,* control them. On some boats a *tiller* is used instead of a wheel to steer.

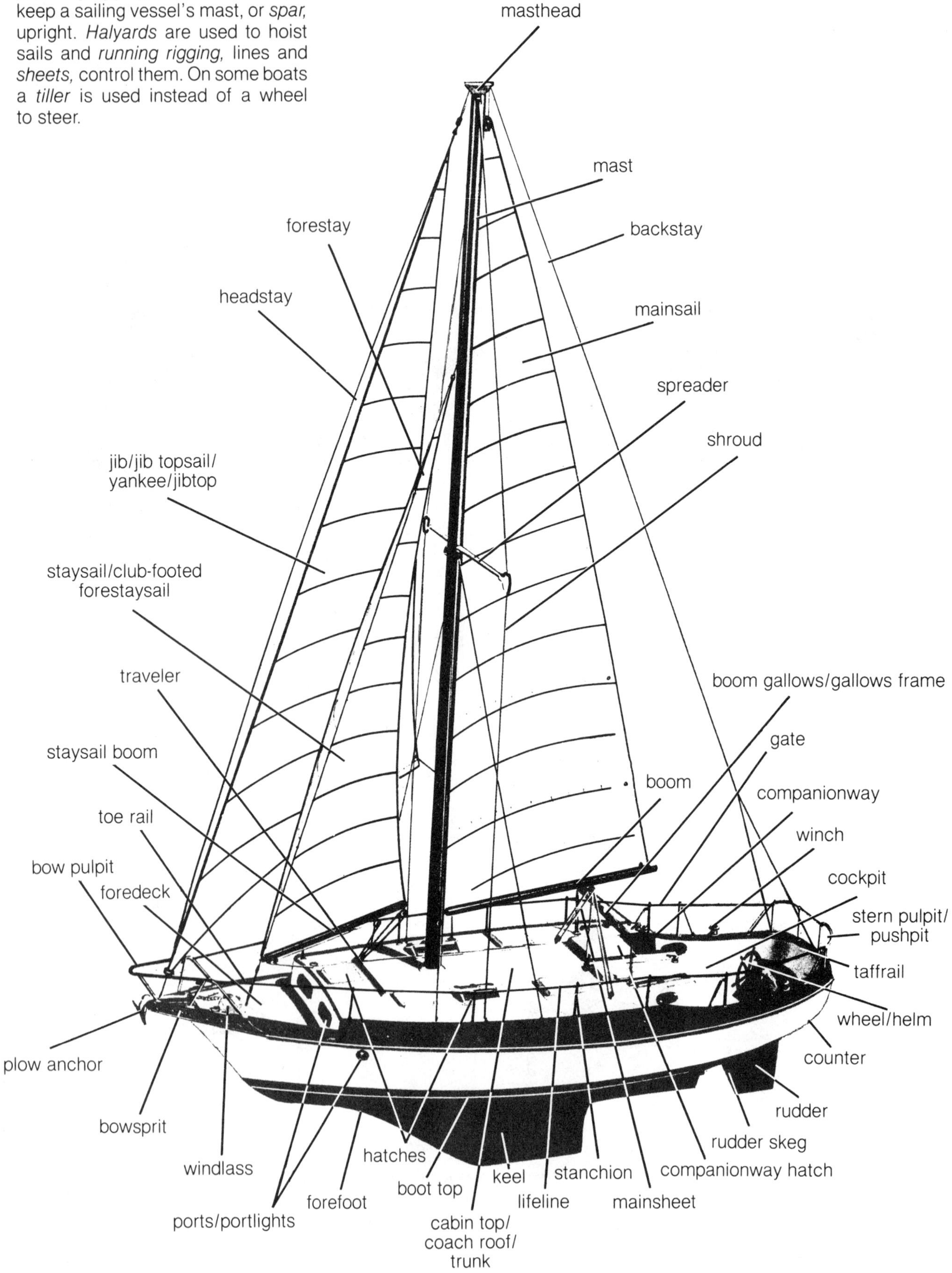

masthead

mast

forestay

backstay

headstay

mainsail

spreader

shroud

jib/jib topsail/ yankee/jibtop

staysail/club-footed forestaysail

traveler

boom gallows/gallows frame

gate

staysail boom

boom

companionway

toe rail

winch

bow pulpit

cockpit

foredeck

stern pulpit/ pushpit

taffrail

wheel/helm

plow anchor

counter

rudder

bowsprit

rudder skeg

windlass

hatches

stanchion

companionway hatch

ports/portlights

forefoot

boot top

keel

lifeline

mainsheet

cabin top/ coach roof/ trunk

Sailboat Accommodations

The area between a vessel's cabin sole and its hull is called the *bilge*. Boats with overnight accommodations usually have a *navigator's station*, featuring a *chart table*.

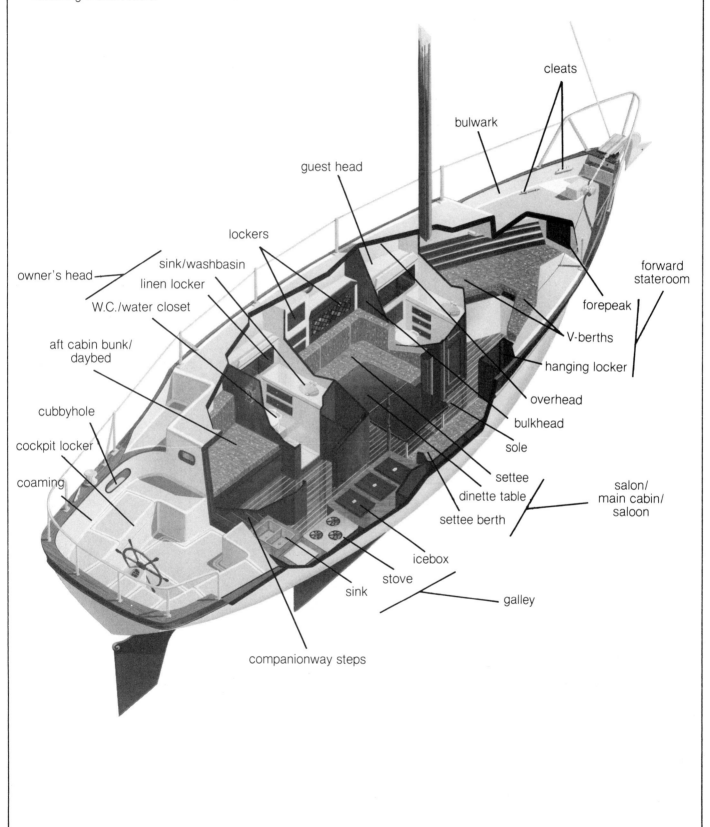

cleats

bulwark

guest head

lockers

sink/washbasin

owner's head

linen locker

W.C./water closet

aft cabin bunk/ daybed

cubbyhole

cockpit locker

coaming

forward stateroom

forepeak

V-berths

hanging locker

overhead

bulkhead

sole

settee

dinette table

settee berth

salon/ main cabin/ saloon

icebox

stove

sink

galley

companionway steps

Sail

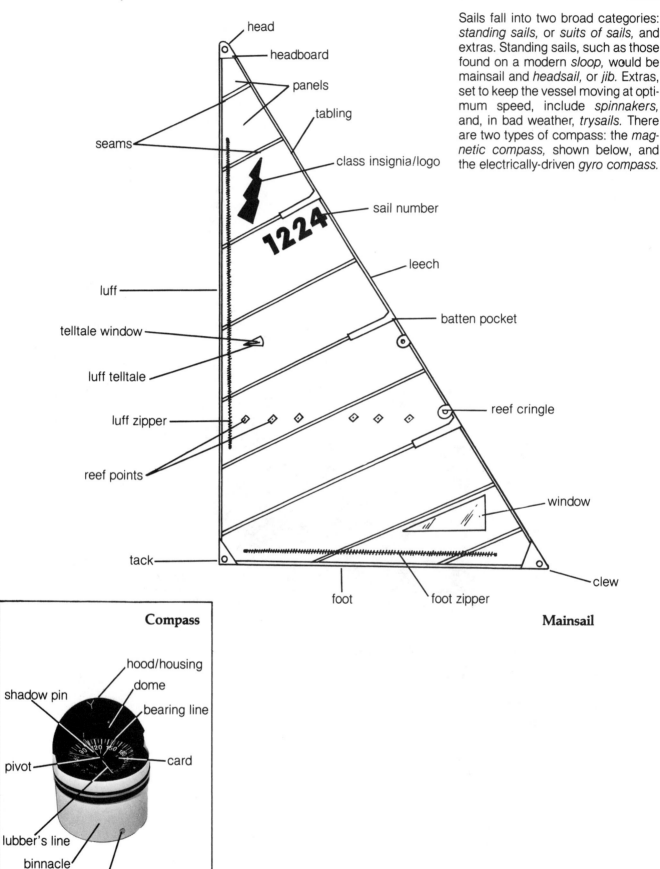

Sails fall into two broad categories: *standing sails,* or *suits of sails,* and extras. Standing sails, such as those found on a modern *sloop,* would be mainsail and *headsail,* or *jib.* Extras, set to keep the vessel moving at optimum speed, include *spinnakers,* and, in bad weather, *trysails.* There are two types of compass: the *magnetic compass,* shown below, and the electrically-driven *gyro compass.*

head

headboard

panels

tabling

seams

class insignia/logo

sail number

1224

leech

luff

batten pocket

telltale window

luff telltale

reef cringle

luff zipper

reef points

window

tack

clew

foot

foot zipper

Mainsail

Compass

hood/housing

dome

shadow pin

bearing line

pivot

card

lubber's line

binnacle

corrector magnet controls

Outboard Engine

Three basic types of engines are used to power vessels: outboards, *inboard-outboards,* or *sterndrives,* and *inboards.* A marine sextant, a successor to the *octant* and *quadrant,* is used to measure the angle between a celestial body and the earth's horizon to help mariners determine their position at sea.

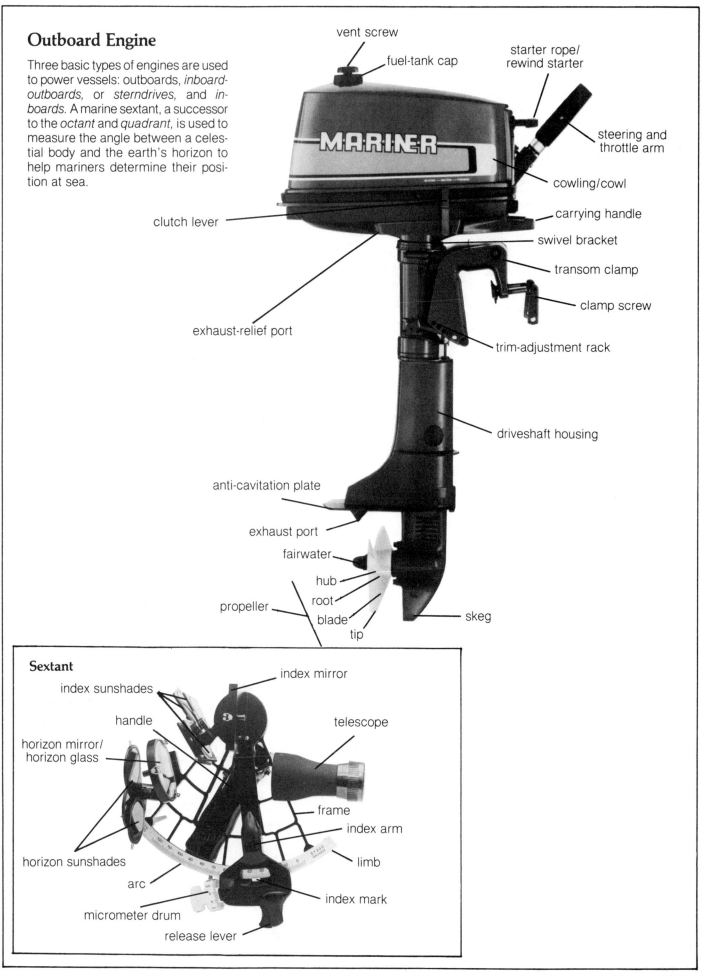

vent screw

fuel-tank cap

starter rope/ rewind starter

steering and throttle arm

cowling/cowl

carrying handle

swivel bracket

transom clamp

clamp screw

trim-adjustment rack

clutch lever

exhaust-relief port

driveshaft housing

anti-cavitation plate

exhaust port

fairwater

hub

root

propeller

blade

tip

skeg

Sextant

index sunshades

index mirror

handle

telescope

horizon mirror/ horizon glass

frame

index arm

limb

horizon sunshades

arc

micrometer drum

index mark

release lever

Powerboat

There are basically two kinds of powerboat *hull forms: displacement* and *planing.* Within these categories there are *V-bottom, cathedral, gullwing, flat-bottom* and *round-bottom hulls. Houseboats* are boxlike vessels designed to provide maximum living space aboard. Projecting steel fittings used to hoist and carry a dinghy on a yacht are called *davits.*

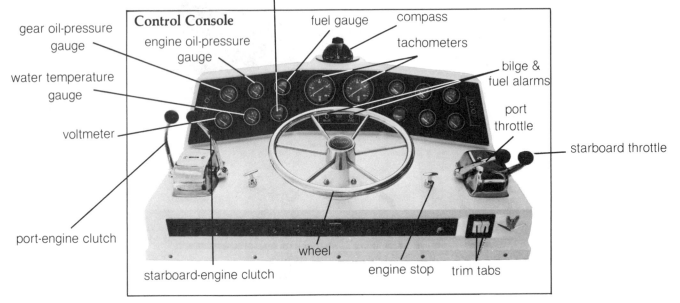

Control Console

engine hour meter

fuel gauge

compass

tachometers

gear oil-pressure gauge

engine oil-pressure gauge

water temperature gauge

bilge & fuel alarms

port throttle

voltmeter

starboard throttle

port-engine clutch

starboard-engine clutch

wheel

engine stop

trim tabs

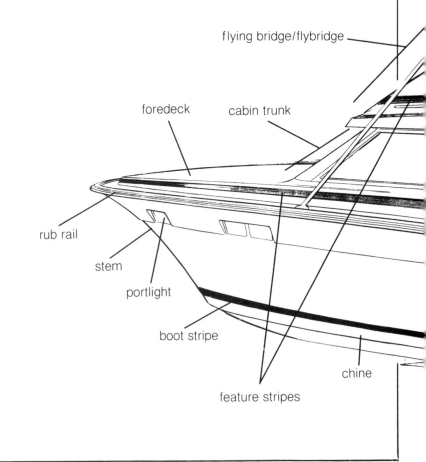

flying bridge/flybridge

foredeck

cabin trunk

rub rail

stem

portlight

boot stripe

chine

feature stripes

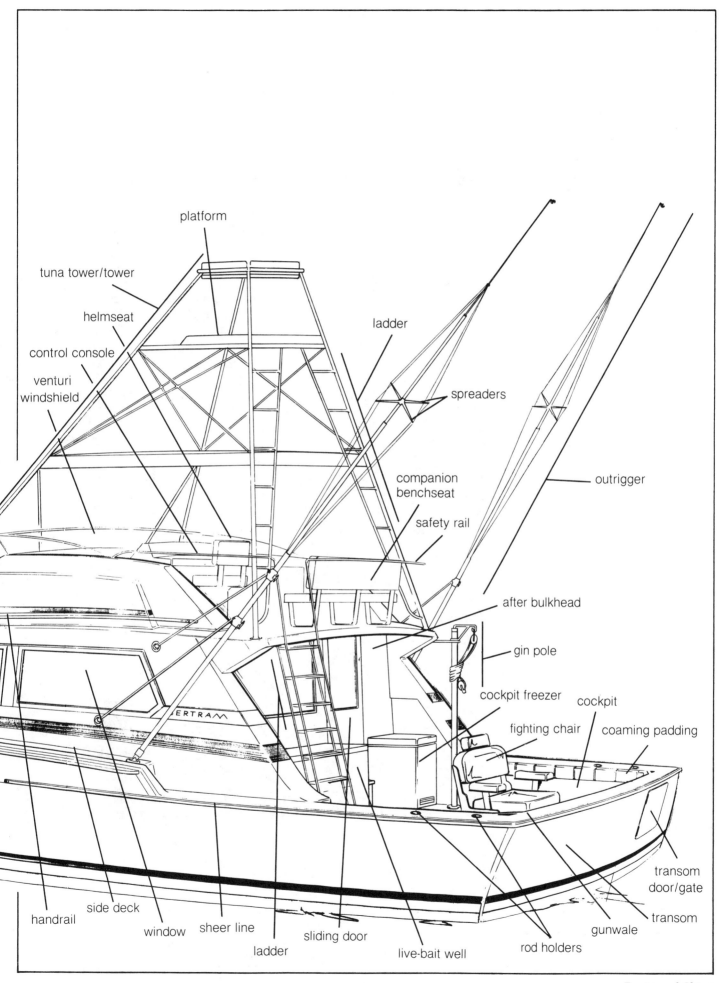

platform

tuna tower/tower

helmseat

control console

venturi
windshield

ladder

spreaders

companion
benchseat

safety rail

outrigger

after bulkhead

gin pole

cockpit freezer

cockpit

fighting chair

coaming padding

transom
door/gate

transom

handrail

side deck

window

sheer line

ladder

sliding door

live-bait well

rod holders

gunwale

Boats and Ships

Tanker

Cargo ships include *roll on-roll off ships; container ships; barge carriers; pallet ships; refrigerator ships,* or *reefers; dry-bulk carriers;* and *liquid-bulk carriers* such as the *super tanker* seen here. A *merchant ship* carrying *cargo* or *freight* is called a *liner* if it travels on scheduled routes at regular intervals, or a *tramp* if it does not have a fixed or scheduled route.

"catwalk"/ fore & aft gangway

foremast

"crow's nest"/ lookout area

pressure & vacuum relief valves

belowdeck storage entrance

anchor windlass & mooring winch

anchor windlass & mooring winch

radar mast & radar antennas

bridge/wheelhouse

bridge wing

wireless, telegraph & navigation aerials

king post

lifeboat

hose-handling derrick

"stowed" derrick brackets

aft superstructure/ deckhouse

pressure & vacuum relief valves

deck manifold

tank hatches

rail

foam monitors & fire-fighting stations

gas-vent lines

Boats and Ships

Passenger Ship/ Ocean Liner

Main bulkheads, steel walls running athwartships on a ship, are normally watertight. A *collision bulkhead* is a *watertight bulkhead* near the bow to prevent flooding in the event of collision. Circular windows aboard ship are called *ports* or *portholes.* A ship is boarded at the pier by a portable stairway, or *gangplank,* which fits in an opening in a ship's *rail* or *bulwark.* A metal shield on *berthing hawsers* to prevent rats from coming aboard is a *ratcatcher.*

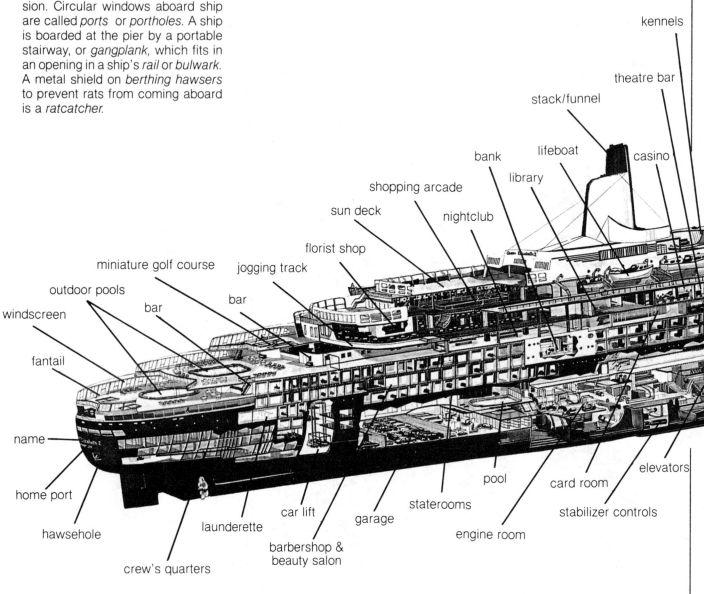

kennels

theatre bar

stack/funnel

bank   lifeboat   casino

shopping arcade   library

sun deck   nightclub

florist shop

miniature golf course   jogging track

outdoor pools

bar   bar

windscreen

fantail

name

home port

hawsehole

crew's quarters   launderette   car lift   garage   staterooms   pool   card room   elevators

barbershop & beauty salon   engine room   stabilizer controls

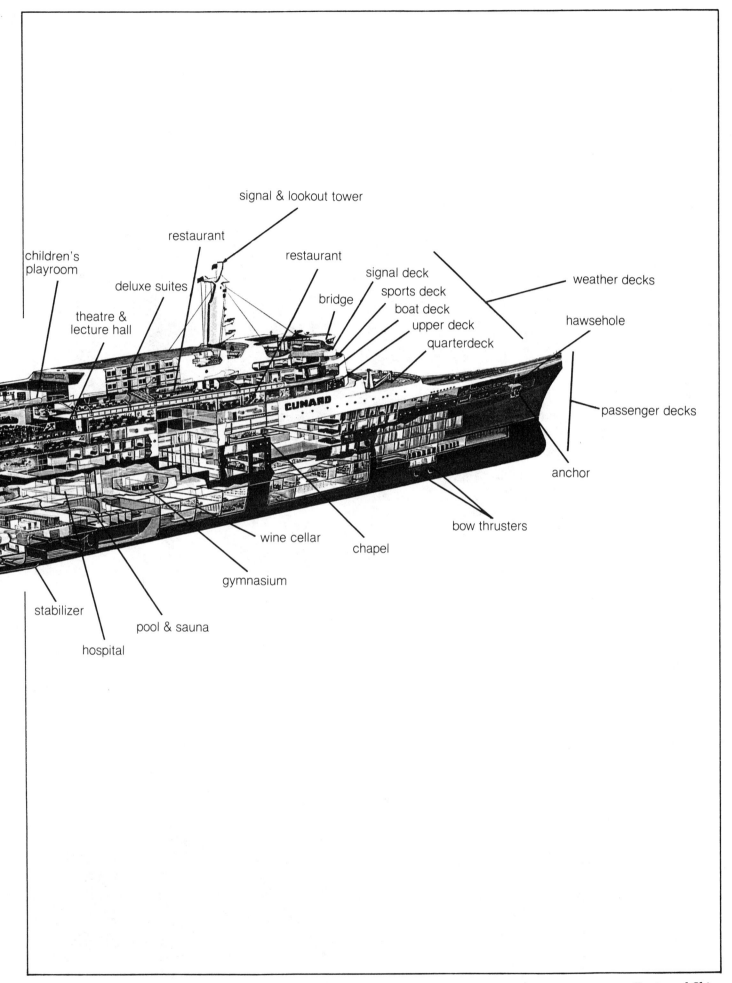

signal & lookout tower

restaurant

restaurant

children's playroom

signal deck

bridge

sports deck

boat deck

weather decks

deluxe suites

upper deck

hawsehole

theatre & lecture hall

quarterdeck

passenger decks

CUNARD

anchor

bow thrusters

wine cellar

chapel

gymnasium

stabilizer

pool & sauna

hospital

Boats and Ships

Tugboat and Fireboat

A *pudding fender* is a large fender made of old rope, formerly fitted to the bow of many *tugs,* or *towboats.* A *pusher tug,* also called a *pushboat,* is specially designed with a high flat bow for *barge cluster* push-towing. A fireboat is usually a tug fitted with such items as *high-pressure pumps, hoses* and *nozzles.*

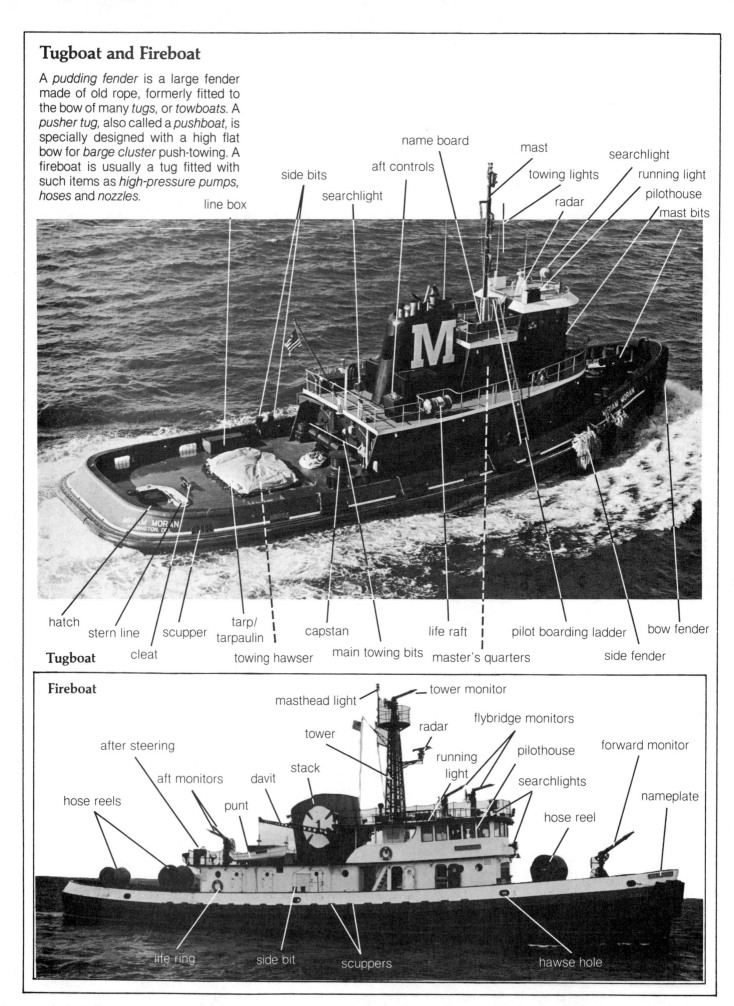

name board
mast
searchlight
aft controls
towing lights
running light
side bits
radar
pilothouse
searchlight
mast bits
line box

hatch
stern line
scupper
tarp/tarpaulin
capstan
life raft
pilot boarding ladder
bow fender
cleat
towing hawser
main towing bits
master's quarters
side fender

Tugboat

Fireboat

masthead light
tower monitor
flybridge monitors
tower
radar
after steering
running light
pilothouse
forward monitor
aft monitors
davit
stack
searchlights
hose reels
punt
hose reel
nameplate

life ring
side bit
scuppers
hawse hole

Hovercraft and Hydrofoil

Air Cushion Vehicles (ACV), or *ground-effect machines*, are *amphibious vehicles* that ride on a cushion of air blown by *lift fans* through *slots* or *jets* around the underside of the hull. There are four classes of hydrofoils: *ladder, depth-effect, surface-piercing* and *submerged foils*.

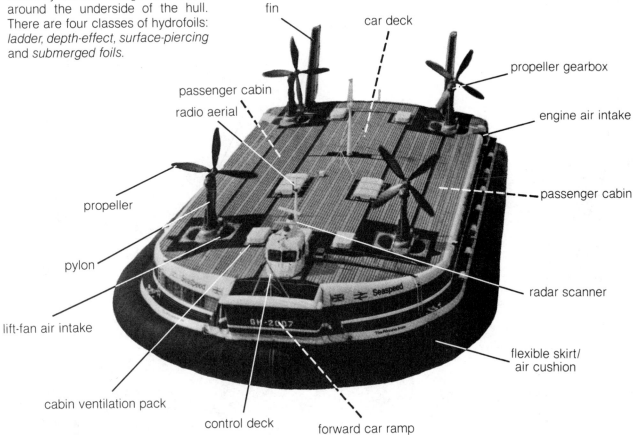

fin

car deck

propeller gearbox

passenger cabin

radio aerial

engine air intake

propeller

passenger cabin

pylon

radar scanner

lift-fan air intake

flexible skirt/ air cushion

cabin ventilation pack

control deck

forward car ramp

Hovercraft / Air Cushion Vehicle

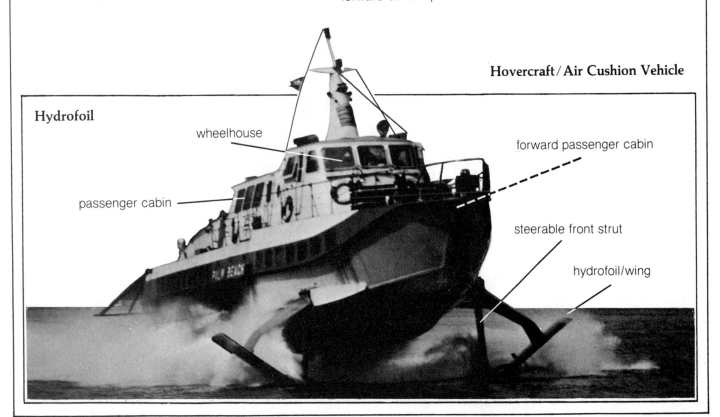

Hydrofoil

wheelhouse

forward passenger cabin

passenger cabin

steerable front strut

hydrofoil/wing

Boats and Ships

Helicopter

The main body of a helicopter, *chopper, whirlybird,* or *eggbeater,* is called the *fuselage.* The rescue helicopter shown here has an *amphibious hull.* Armed military helicopters are called *gunships.*

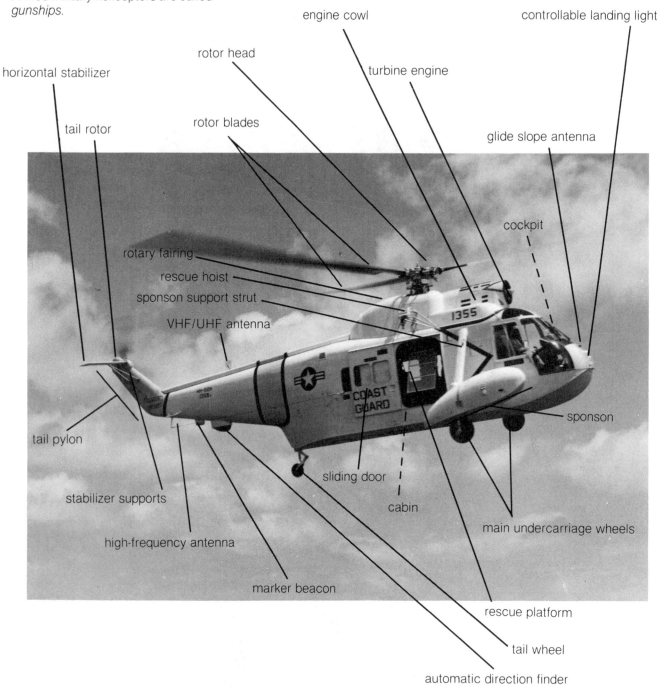

engine cowl

controllable landing light

rotor head

turbine engine

horizontal stabilizer

glide slope antenna

tail rotor

rotor blades

cockpit

rotary fairing

rescue hoist

sponson support strut

1355

VHF/UHF antenna

COAST GUARD

tail pylon

sponson

stabilizer supports

sliding door

high-frequency antenna

cabin

main undercarriage wheels

marker beacon

rescue platform

tail wheel

automatic direction finder

Private Aircraft

An aircraft's central body portion is called the *fuselage*. To land on water, an airplane uses *pontoons*. To become airborne and begin *soaring*, a glider is pulled behind a motor-driven airplane or car by a cable attached to a *tow hook*. A glider lands on either a *landing wheel* or a *skid*.

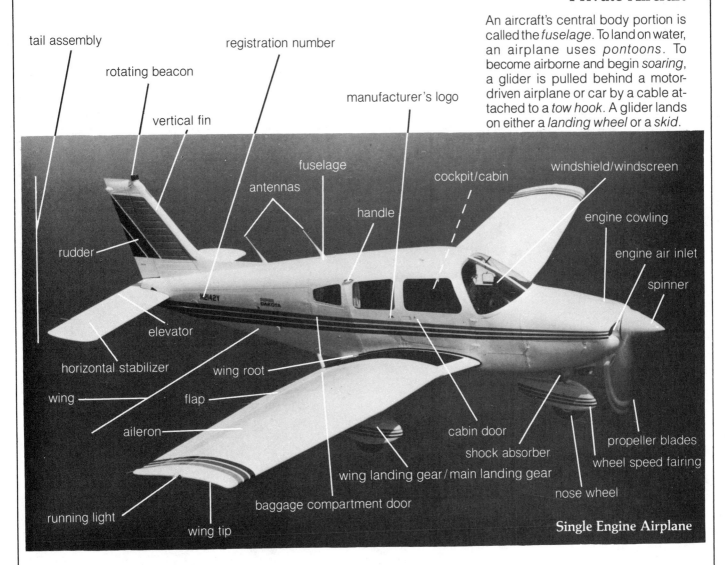

tail assembly

rotating beacon

vertical fin

registration number

manufacturer's logo

fuselage

antennas

handle

cockpit/cabin

windshield/windscreen

engine cowling

engine air inlet

spinner

rudder

elevator

horizontal stabilizer

wing root

wing

flap

aileron

cabin door

shock absorber

propeller blades

wheel speed fairing

wing landing gear/main landing gear

nose wheel

running light

baggage compartment door

wing tip

Single Engine Airplane

Glider/Sailplane

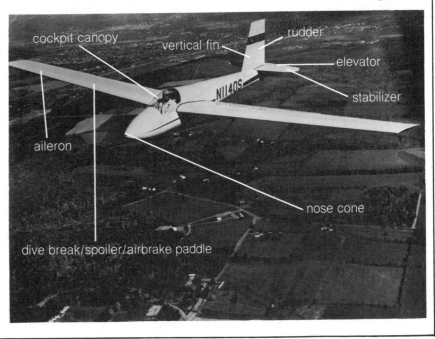

cockpit canopy

vertical fin

rudder

elevator

stabilizer

aileron

nose cone

dive break/spoiler/airbrake paddle

Aircraft

Civil Aircraft

The *trailing edge* of the wings on a *jumbo jet,* such as the one shown here, has small *static discharge wicks* to reduce electrical-charge buildup. Passengers store carry-on belongings in *overhead bins,* or *stowage compartments,* or in front *closets.* Aboard many aircraft, seat cushions double as *flotation devices. Life rafts* are stored in overhead ceiling compartments above the doors, and *emergency escape chutes* are folded inside the doors.

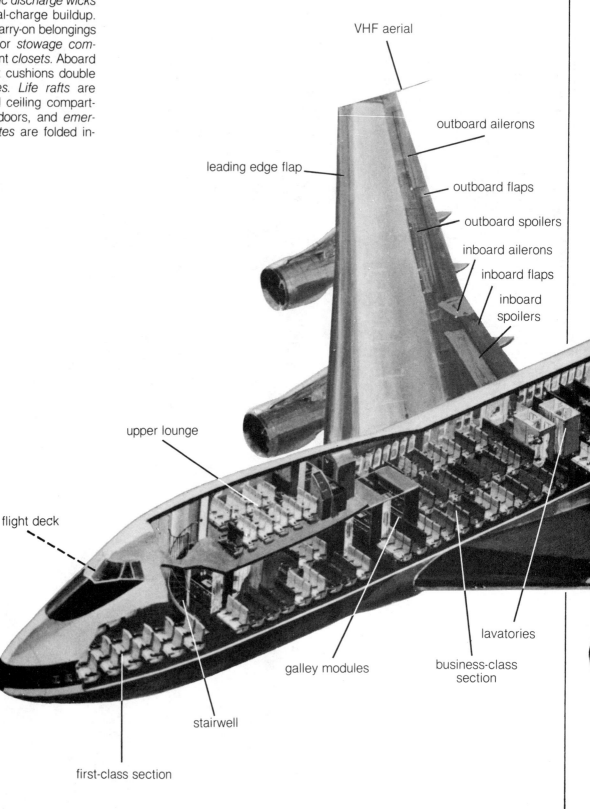

VHF aerial

outboard ailerons

leading edge flap

outboard flaps

outboard spoilers

inboard ailerons

inboard flaps

inboard spoilers

upper lounge

flight deck

radar cone

lavatories

galley modules

business-class section

stairwell

first-class section

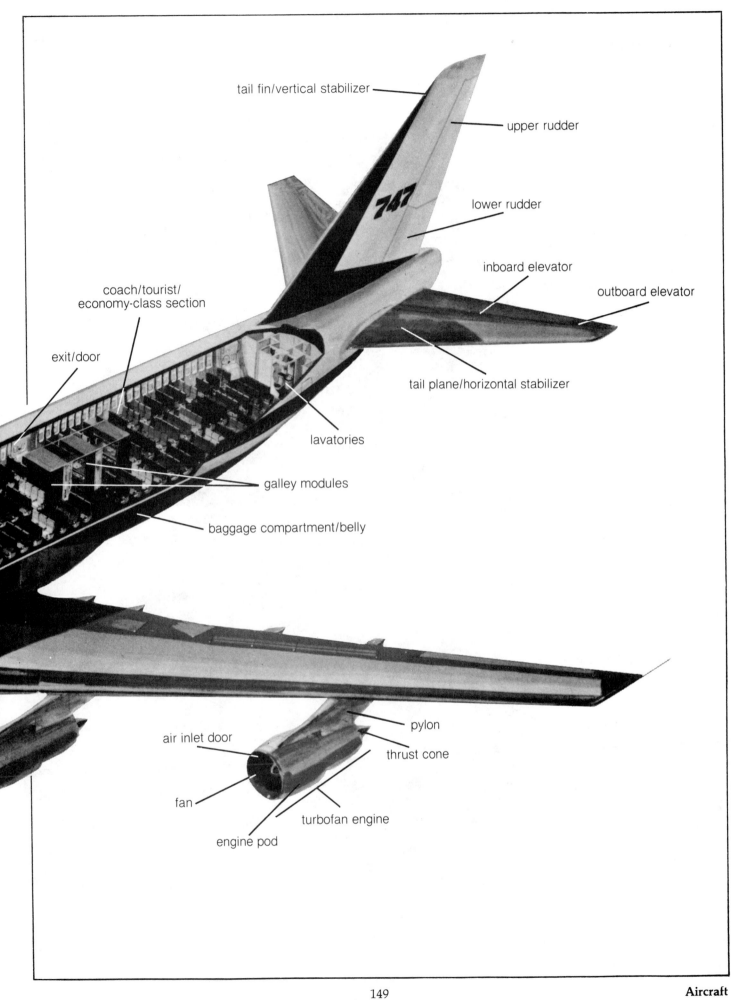

tail fin/vertical stabilizer

upper rudder

lower rudder

inboard elevator

outboard elevator

coach/tourist/
economy-class section

exit/door

tail plane/horizontal stabilizer

lavatories

galley modules

baggage compartment/belly

pylon

air inlet door

thrust cone

fan

turbofan engine

engine pod

Aircraft

747 Cockpit

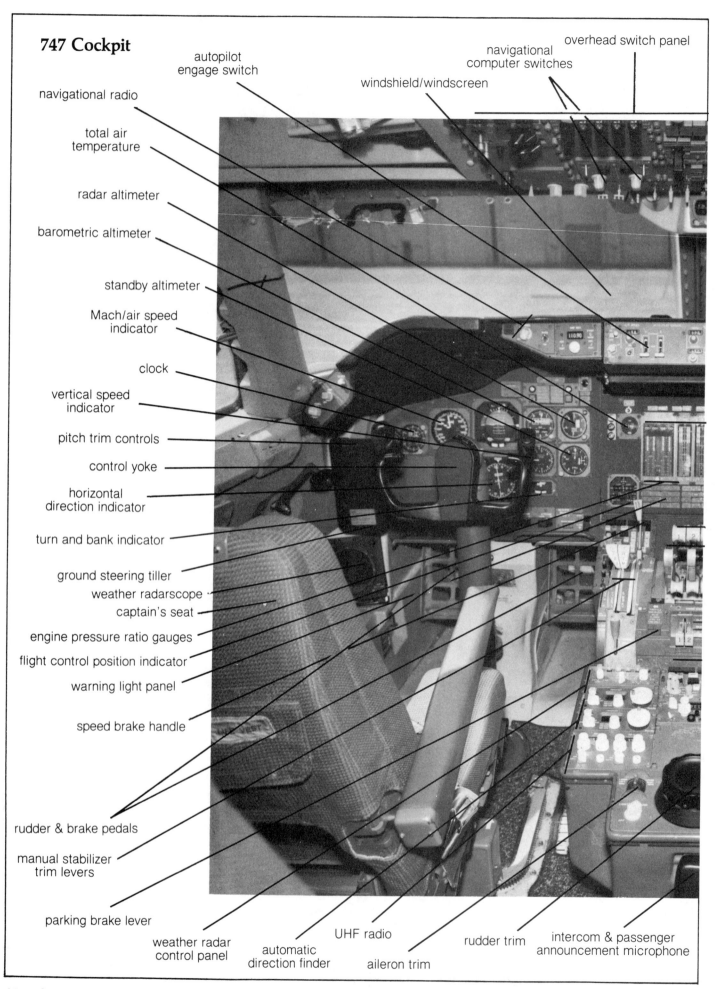

navigational
computer switches

overhead switch panel

autopilot
engage switch

windshield/windscreen

navigational radio

total air
temperature

radar altimeter

barometric altimeter

standby altimeter

Mach/air speed
indicator

clock

vertical speed
indicator

pitch trim controls

control yoke

horizontal
direction indicator

turn and bank indicator

ground steering tiller

weather radarscope

captain's seat

engine pressure ratio gauges

flight control position indicator

warning light panel

speed brake handle

rudder & brake pedals

manual stabilizer
trim levers

parking brake lever

weather radar
control panel

automatic
direction finder

UHF radio

aileron trim

rudder trim

intercom & passenger
announcement microphone

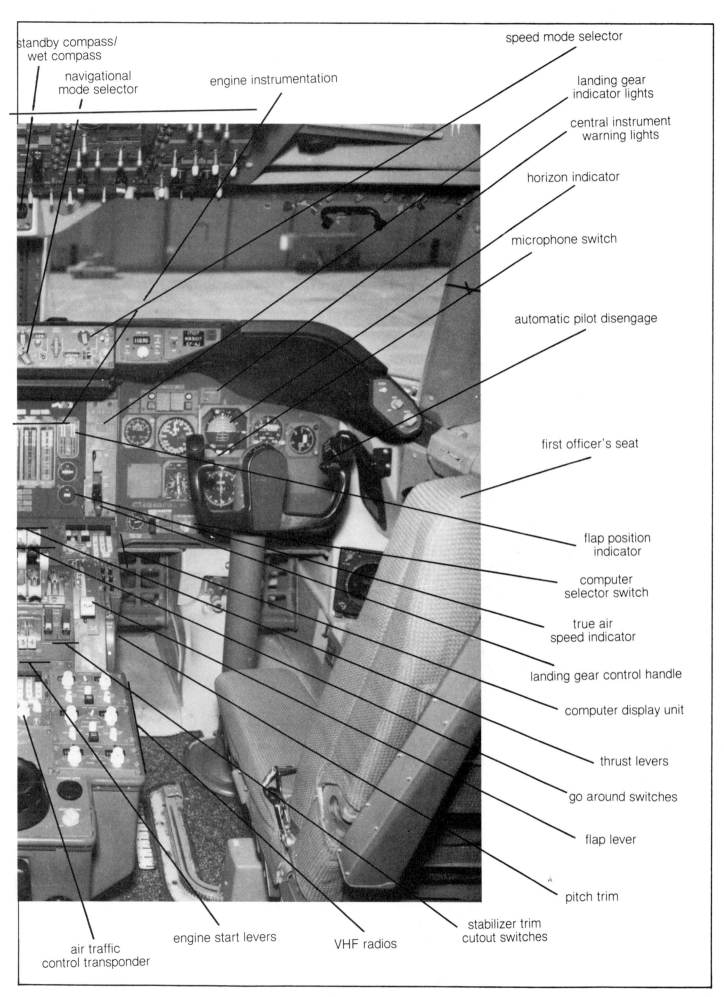

standby compass/ wet compass

navigational mode selector

engine instrumentation

speed mode selector

landing gear indicator lights

central instrument warning lights

horizon indicator

microphone switch

automatic pilot disengage

first officer's seat

flap position indicator

computer selector switch

true air speed indicator

landing gear control handle

computer display unit

thrust levers

go around switches

flap lever

pitch trim

stabilizer trim cutout switches

air traffic control transponder

engine start levers

VHF radios

Space Shuttle and Launch Pad

A shuttle has three main components: an orbiter, external tank and two solid-rocket boosters. Many launch pads have *flame buckets* designed to direct *fireballs* and steam away from the pad itself. A gantry is a movable structure used for erecting and servicing a rocket prior to launch.

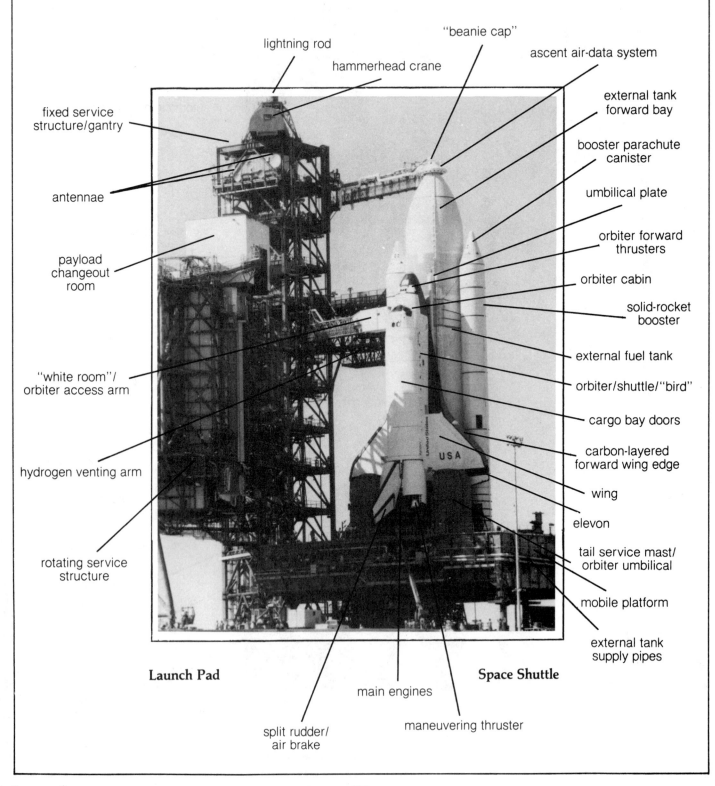

lightning rod

"beanie cap"

hammerhead crane

ascent air-data system

fixed service structure/gantry

external tank forward bay

booster parachute canister

antennae

umbilical plate

orbiter forward thrusters

payload changeout room

orbiter cabin

solid-rocket booster

external fuel tank

orbiter/shuttle/"bird"

"white room"/ orbiter access arm

cargo bay doors

carbon-layered forward wing edge

hydrogen venting arm

wing

elevon

tail service mast/ orbiter umbilical

rotating service structure

mobile platform

external tank supply pipes

Launch Pad

Space Shuttle

main engines

split rudder/ air brake

maneuvering thruster

Space Shuttle Flight Deck

Overhead controls include *circuit breakers, environmental monitors* and *fuel cell monitors.* The *orbiter* has work and living quarters for as many as seven people, including two pilots, *mission specialists* and *payload specialists.* It also features a *quad-redundant computer system,* including a fifth computer to arbitrate disputes among the first four.

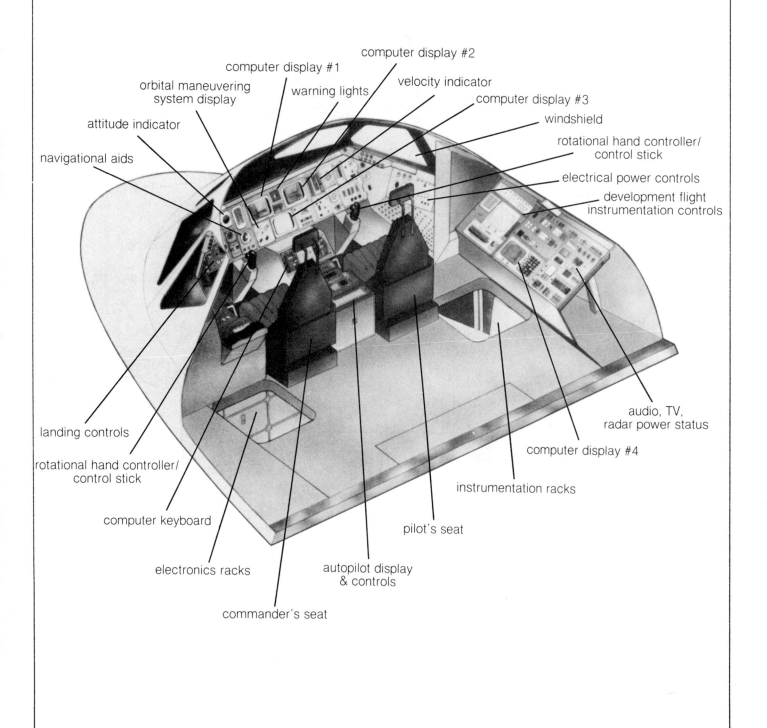

computer display #2

computer display #1

orbital maneuvering system display

warning lights

velocity indicator

computer display #3

attitude indicator

windshield

rotational hand controller/ control stick

navigational aids

electrical power controls

development flight instrumentation controls

landing controls

rotational hand controller/ control stick

computer keyboard

electronics racks

autopilot display & controls

commander's seat

pilot's seat

instrumentation racks

computer display #4

audio, TV, radar power status

Lunar Lander

The *lunar module* consists of a lower *descent stage* which houses the *landing engine, exploration equipment, secondary tanks* and landing gear. The *ascent stage* contains *crew compartment* and *controls, equipment compartment, tanks* and *take-off engine,* used to rejoin the *command module.*

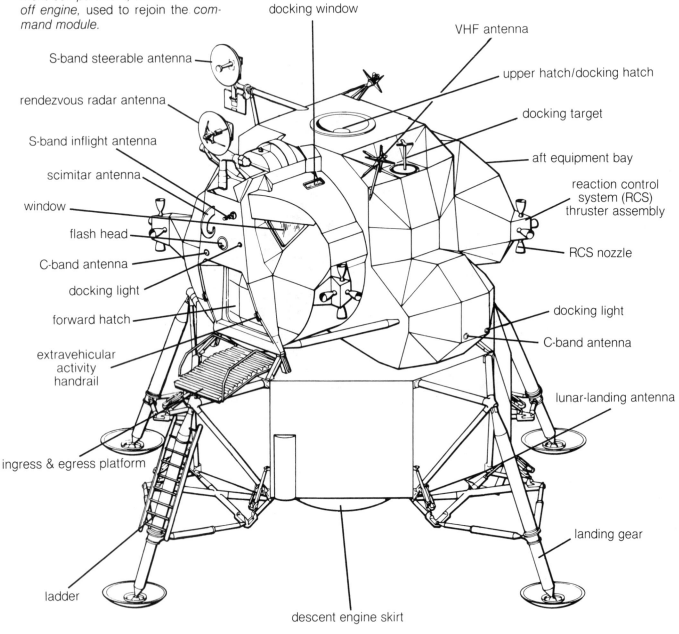

docking window

VHF antenna

S-band steerable antenna

upper hatch/docking hatch

rendezvous radar antenna

docking target

S-band inflight antenna

aft equipment bay

scimitar antenna

reaction control system (RCS) thruster assembly

window

flash head

RCS nozzle

C-band antenna

docking light

docking light

C-band antenna

forward hatch

extravehicular activity handrail

lunar-landing antenna

ingress & egress platform

landing gear

ladder

descent engine skirt

Lunar Rover

Officially called the *Lunar Roving Vehicle*, the *moon buggy* is folded in the Lunar Lander and deployed to transport astronauts and equipment on the lunar surface. The spacesuit, or *integrated thermal meteoroid garment*, is a many-layered structure laced to a *torso limb suit* which consists of an inner cloth *comfort lining*, a *bladder*, and a *restraint layer*.

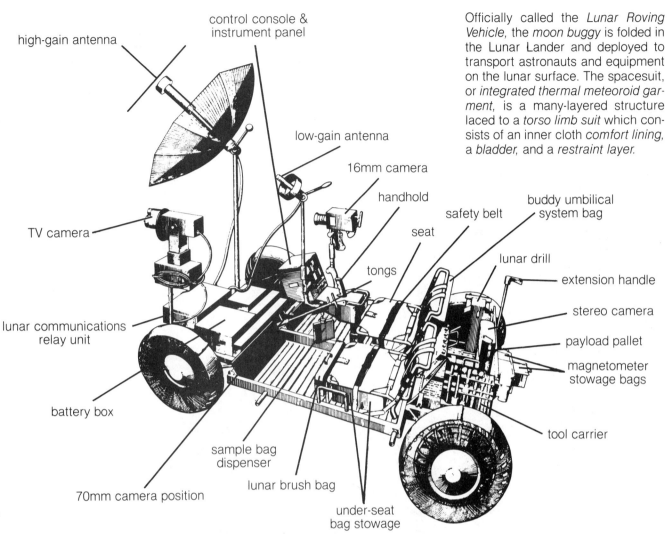

high-gain antenna

control console & instrument panel

low-gain antenna

16mm camera

handhold

safety belt

seat

buddy umbilical system bag

lunar drill

extension handle

stereo camera

payload pallet

magnetometer stowage bags

tongs

TV camera

lunar communications relay unit

battery box

sample bag dispenser

70mm camera position

lunar brush bag

under-seat bag stowage

tool carrier

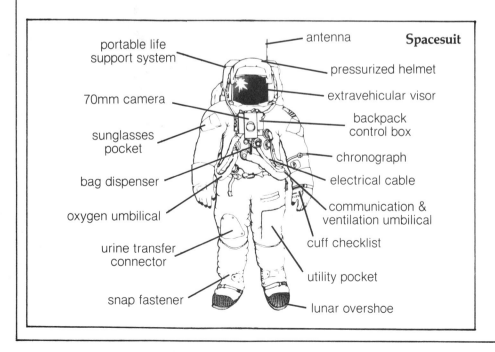

Spacesuit

antenna

pressurized helmet

extravehicular visor

backpack control box

chronograph

electrical cable

communication & ventilation umbilical

cuff checklist

utility pocket

lunar overshoe

portable life support system

70mm camera

sunglasses pocket

bag dispenser

oxygen umbilical

urine transfer connector

snap fastener

Spacecraft

Engine-driven, steerable lighter-than-air craft are called blimps, or dirigibles. They can be *nonrigid* or *semi-rigid*, dependent on interior *ballonets,* or *air bags,* to maintain their shapes. *Rigid airships,* with metal *frameworks* within their *envelopes,* are referred to as *Zeppelins.* Airships are tethered to *mooring masts* when not aloft.

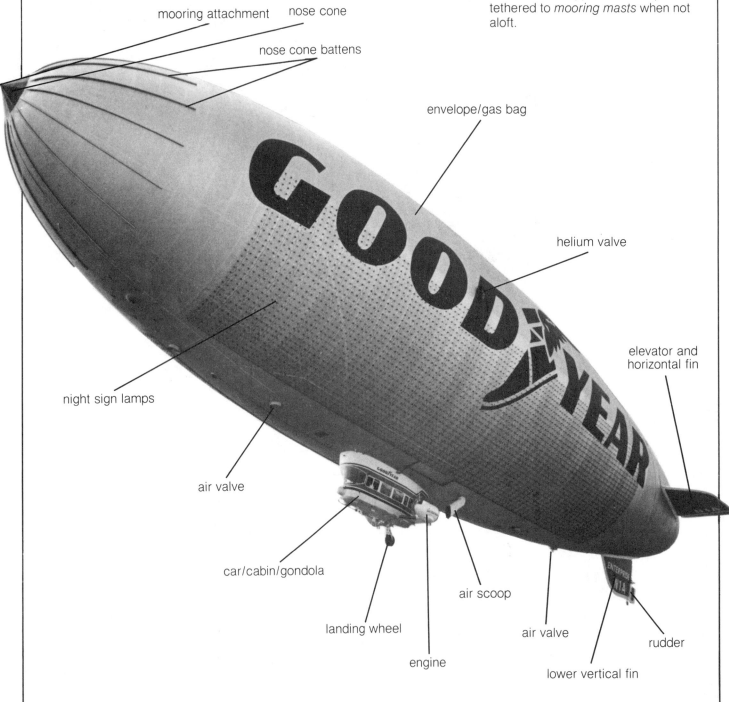

mooring attachment   nose cone

nose cone battens

envelope/gas bag

helium valve

elevator and horizontal fin

night sign lamps

air valve

car/cabin/gondola

air scoop

landing wheel

air valve

engine

rudder

lower vertical fin

Blimp/Dirigible

Communications

Communications ranks among the fastest-growing areas of modern life. Nevertheless, as this book is meant to demonstrate by providing visual access to language, print communications remains a vital part of the future. Print is therefore examined in some detail, up to and including a close look at the mailing label affixed to periodicals received every day by millions of subscribers.

Space limitations prevent presentation of industrial items such as transmitting stations and microwave towers, sound-recording and television studios and film-processing equipment.

But the devices used in all forms of communications—visual, aural and audiovisual—are represented by objects commonly used in most households. The single exception to this is the satellite which appears at the end of the section. It is included because of the vital role it plays in modern communications of all kinds.

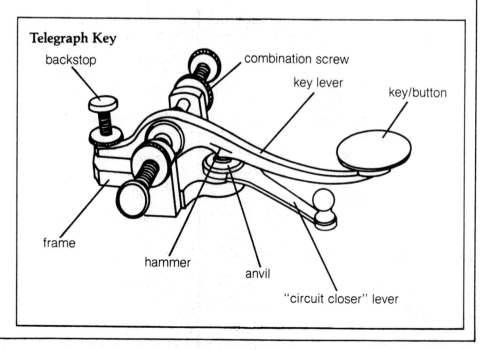

Telegraph Key

backstop

combination screw

key lever

key/button

frame

hammer

anvil

"circuit closer" lever

Pen and Pencil

In refillable *lead pencils* a *barrel cap* is turned in order to push new lead out the tip. Some fountain pens are *cartridge-loaded* but older models have a barrel, *ink reservoir* and *self-filling mechanism*. *Quills*, or *feather pens*, made from the horny, hollow barrel of bird feathers, were dipped in *ink wells*.

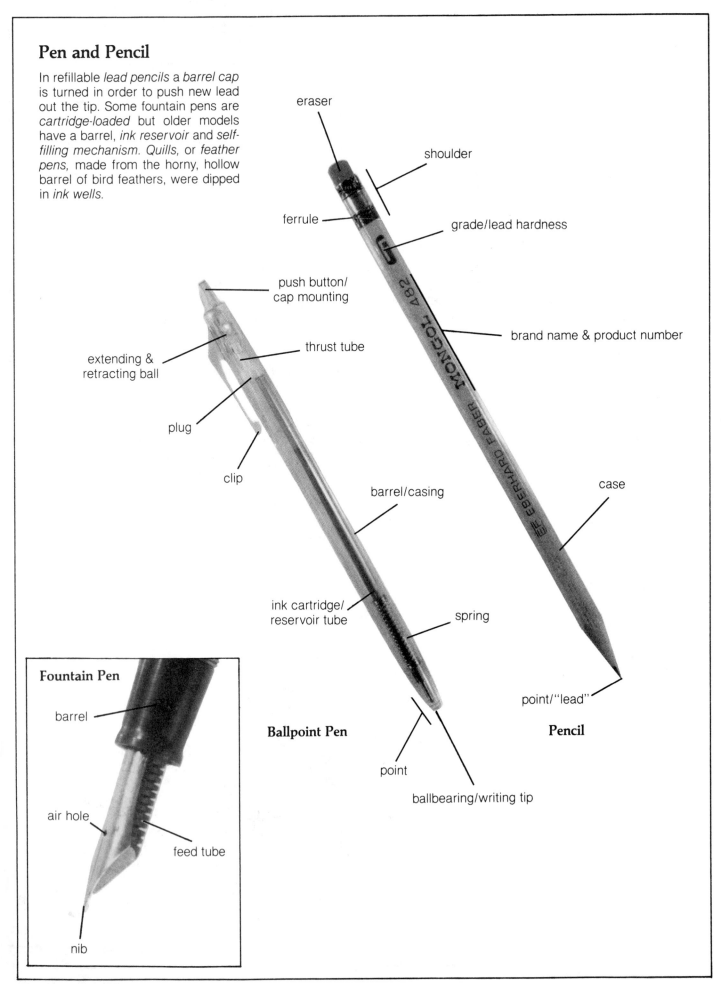

eraser

shoulder

ferrule

grade/lead hardness

push button/ cap mounting

brand name & product number

extending & retracting ball

thrust tube

plug

clip

barrel/casing

case

ink cartridge/ reservoir tube

spring

Fountain Pen

barrel

air hole

feed tube

nib

Ballpoint Pen

point

ballbearing/writing tip

point/"lead"

Pencil

Correspondence

A note appended to a completed letter is called a *postscript*, abbreviated as *P.S.* When items are enclosed with a letter they are indicated by the word *enclosure(s)* or *encl.* The back portion of an envelope which is glued down after a letter has been inserted is the *flap.* Postage stamps can be purchased in *books*, *strips*, *blocks*, *coils* and *sheets*, or *panes.*

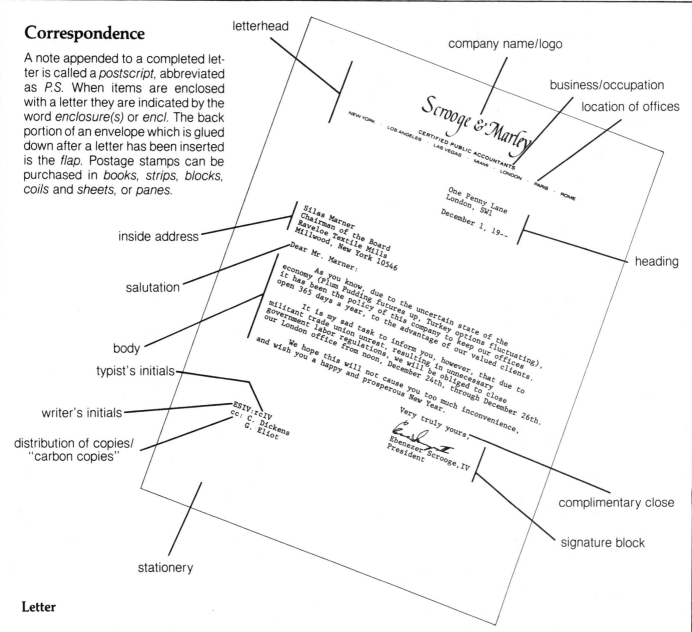

letterhead

company name/logo

business/occupation

location of offices

NEW YORK · LOS ANGELES · LAS VEGAS · MIAMI · LONDON · PARIS · ROME

Scrooge & Marley

CERTIFIED PUBLIC ACCOUNTANTS

One Penny Lane
London, SW1
December 1, 19--

heading

inside address

Silas Marner
Chairman of the Board
Raveloe Textile Mills
Millwood, New York 10546

salutation

Dear Mr. Marner:

body

As you know, due to the uncertain state of the economy (Plum Pudding futures up, Turkey options fluctuating), it has been the policy of this company to keep our offices open 365 days a year, to the advantage of our valued clients.

It is my sad task to inform you, however, that due to militant trade union unrest, resulting in unnecessary government labor regulations, we will be obliged to close our London office from noon, December 24th, through December 26th.

We hope this will not cause you too much inconvenience, and wish you a happy and prosperous New Year.

Very truly yours,

Ebenezer Scrooge, IV
President

typist's initials

writer's initials

ESIV:rcIV

distribution of copies/ "carbon copies"

cc: C. Dickens
    G. Eliot

complimentary close

signature block

stationery

Letter

Envelope

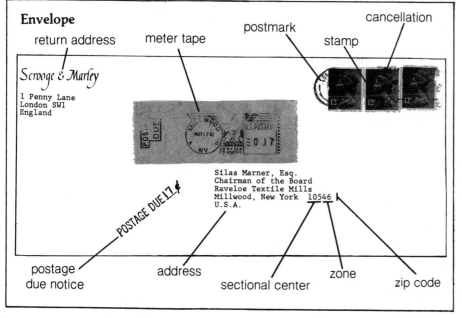

return address

Scrooge & Marley

1 Penny Lane
London SW1
England

meter tape

postmark

stamp

cancellation

POS. DUE

MILLWOOD
MAY 13 '81
NY

U.S. POSTAL

0.17

POSTAGE DUE 17¢

Silas Marner, Esq.
Chairman of the Board
Raveloe Textile Mills
Millwood, New York 10546
U.S.A.

postage
due notice

address

sectional center

zone

zip code

Stamp

commemorative subject

issuing government

BICENTENNIAL
EXECUTIVE BRANCH

USA
25

face value/ denomination

design

cancellation/ postmark

perforation

159

Print Communications

Résumé and Business Card

A summary of a job applicant's background and qualifications is called a résumé or *curriculum vitae*. In addition to brief descriptions of one's education and work experience, it may include *awards* and *honors*, *outside interests* and objectives or goals. Personal references may be listed or made available on request.

name/address

date of birth (optional)

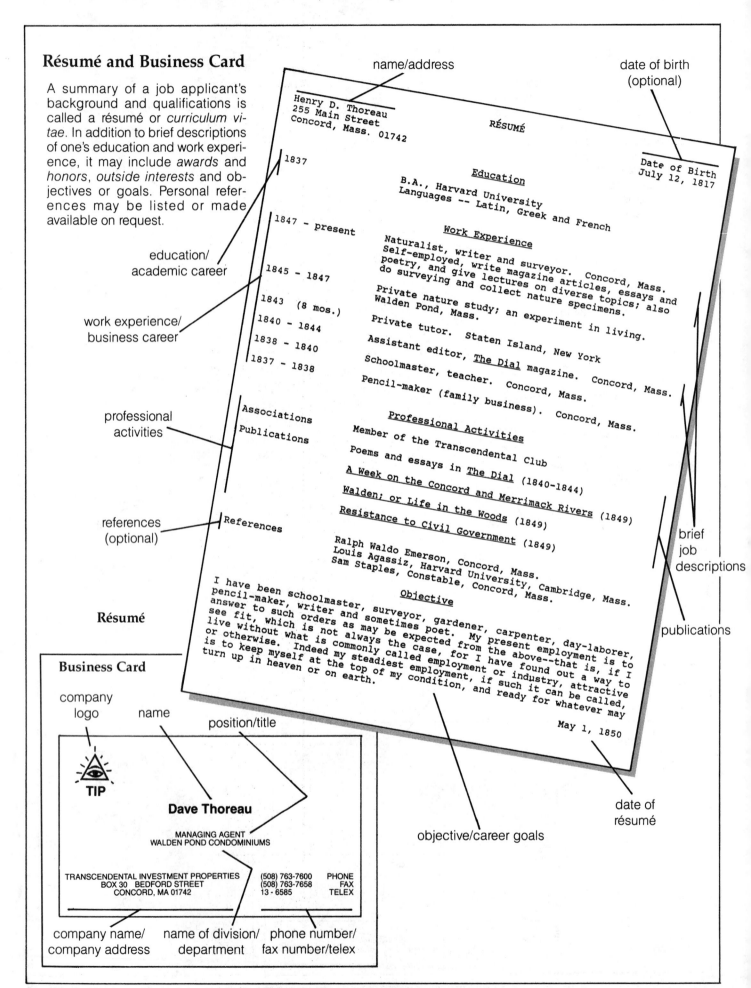

Henry D. Thoreau
255 Main Street
Concord, Mass. 01742

RÉSUMÉ

Date of Birth
July 12, 1817

1837

education/
academic career

Education
B.A., Harvard University
Languages -- Latin, Greek and French

1847 - present

work experience/
business career

1845 - 1847

1843 (8 mos.)
1840 - 1844
1838 - 1840
1837 - 1838

Work Experience
Naturalist, writer and surveyor. Concord, Mass.
Self-employed, write magazine articles, essays and poetry, and give lectures on diverse topics; also do surveying and collect nature specimens.
Private nature study; an experiment in living. Walden Pond, Mass.
Private tutor. Staten Island, New York
Assistant editor, The Dial magazine. Concord, Mass.
Schoolmaster, teacher. Concord, Mass.
Pencil-maker (family business). Concord, Mass.

professional
activities

Associations

Publications

Professional Activities
Member of the Transcendental Club
Poems and essays in The Dial (1840-1844)
A Week on the Concord and Merrimack Rivers (1849)
Walden; or Life in the Woods (1849)
Resistance to Civil Government (1849)

references
(optional)

References

Ralph Waldo Emerson, Concord, Mass.
Louis Agassiz, Harvard University, Cambridge, Mass.
Sam Staples, Constable, Concord, Mass.

Objective
I have been schoolmaster, surveyor, gardener, carpenter, day-laborer, pencil-maker, writer and sometimes poet. My present employment is to answer to such orders as may be expected from the above--that is, if I see fit, which is not always the case, for I have found out a way to live without what is commonly called employment or industry, attractive or otherwise. Indeed my steadiest employment, if such it can be called, is to keep myself at the top of my condition, and ready for whatever may turn up in heaven or on earth.

May 1, 1850

brief
job
descriptions

publications

date of
résumé

objective/career goals

Résumé

Business Card

company
logo

name

position/title

TIP

Dave Thoreau

MANAGING AGENT
WALDEN POND CONDOMINIUMS

TRANSCENDENTAL INVESTMENT PROPERTIES   (508) 763-7600   PHONE
BOX 30   BEDFORD STREET   (508) 763-7658   FAX
CONCORD, MA 01742   13 - 6585   TELEX

company name/
company address

name of division/
department

phone number/
fax number/telex

Typewriter

On standard manual or *office type-writers,* lightweight *portables* and older *electrics,* when a key labeled with a *character* is struck, it sends the appropriate type bar toward an inked *ribbon.* On modern electric typewriters type bars in the *type basket* have been replaced with a ball.

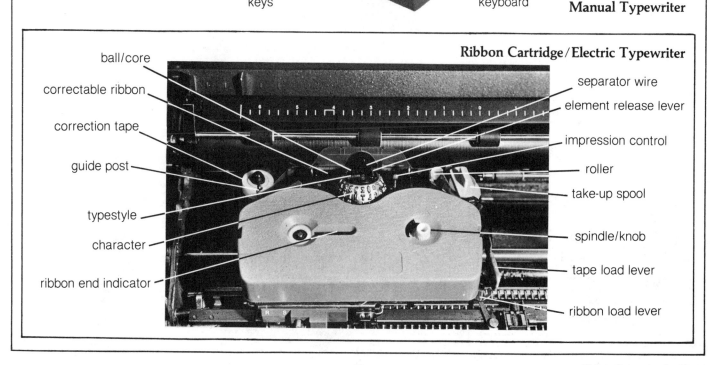

automatic line finder

carriage release

paper guide

erasure table

line space regulator

retractable paper support

variable spacer

platen

margin stop

bail roller

paper bail/ positioning scale

paper release

carriage return & line space lever

platen knob

type guide

carriage

margin release

ribbon color control

card holder

shift & lock key

card loop

shift key

top plate

type bars

tabulator control

space bar

backspace key

keys

keyboard

Manual Typewriter

Ribbon Cartridge/Electric Typewriter

ball/core

separator wire

correctable ribbon

element release lever

correction tape

impression control

guide post

roller

typestyle

take-up spool

character

spindle/knob

ribbon end indicator

tape load lever

ribbon load lever

Print Communications

Personal Computer

A personal computer is designed to use *programs*, or instructions, written in a *language* the computer understands, that enable the *computer operator* to use the speed and sophistication of the machine's computational abilities. Programs range from *finance* and *graphics* to *word processing* and *electronic games*. A *word processor* is a computer that is designed primarily to handle writing and editing tasks.

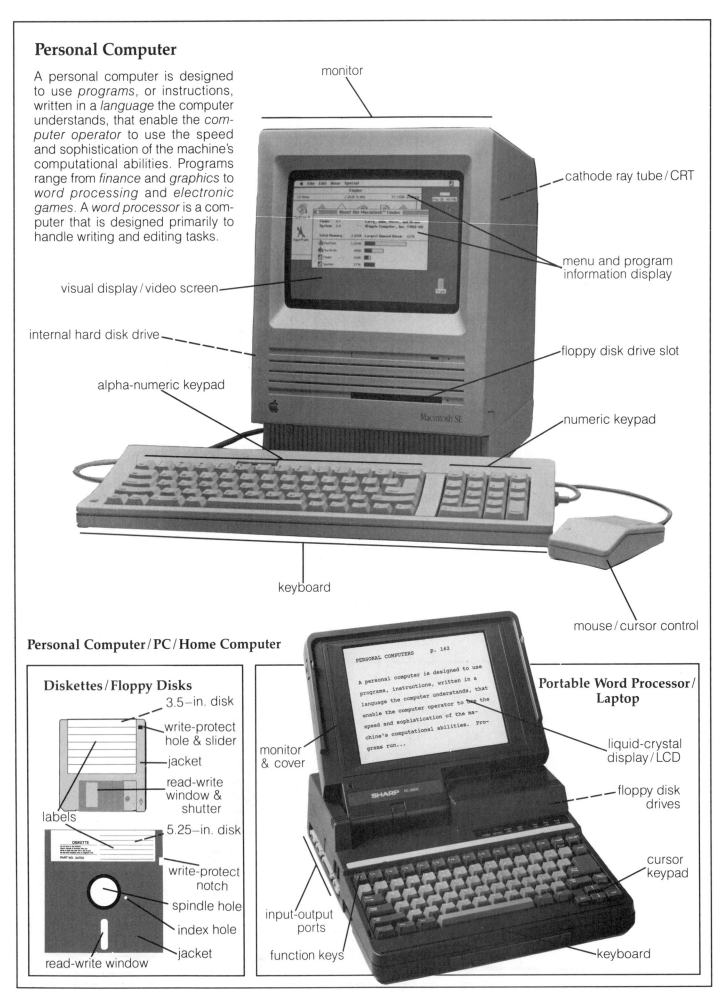

monitor

cathode ray tube / CRT

menu and program information display

visual display / video screen

internal hard disk drive

floppy disk drive slot

alpha-numeric keypad

numeric keypad

Macintosh SE

keyboard

mouse / cursor control

Personal Computer / PC / Home Computer

Diskettes / Floppy Disks

3.5–in. disk

write-protect hole & slider

jacket

read-write window & shutter

labels

5.25–in. disk

DISKETTE

PART NO. 34700

write-protect notch

spindle hole

index hole

jacket

read-write window

Portable Word Processor / Laptop

PERSONAL COMPUTERS   p. 162

A personal computer is designed to use programs, instructions, written in a language the computer understands, that enable the computer operator to use the speed and sophistication of the machine's computational abilities. Programs run...

monitor & cover

liquid-crystal display / LCD

floppy disk drives

cursor keypad

input-output ports

function keys

keyboard

SHARP PC-6600

Printers

Computer *output* printed on paper is called *hard copy*. The precise form this takes depends on the type of printer used. On dot matrix and laser printers, characters are built out of a series of dots, the laser's being smaller and more closely grouped to produce crisp detail. A *daisy-wheel printer* uses a wheel of type bars, similar to a typewriter's, to produce *"letter quality"* results.

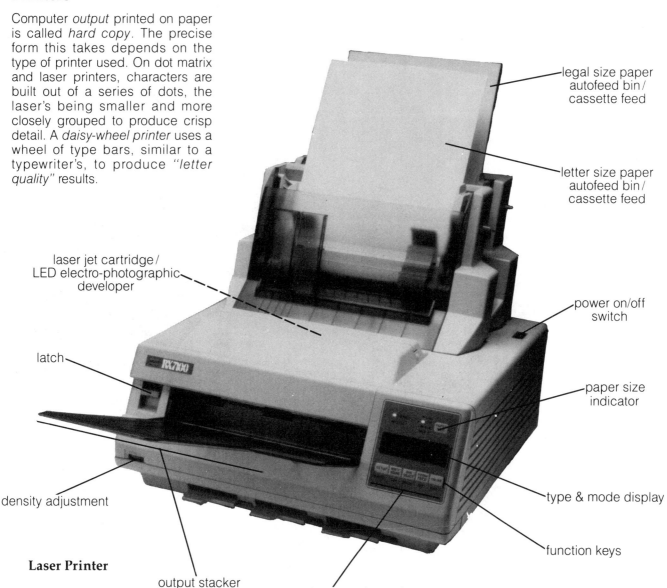

legal size paper
autofeed bin /
cassette feed

letter size paper
autofeed bin /
cassette feed

laser jet cartridge /
LED electro-photographic
developer

power on/off
switch

paper size
indicator

type & mode display

function keys

latch

density adjustment

Laser Printer

output stacker

operator control panel

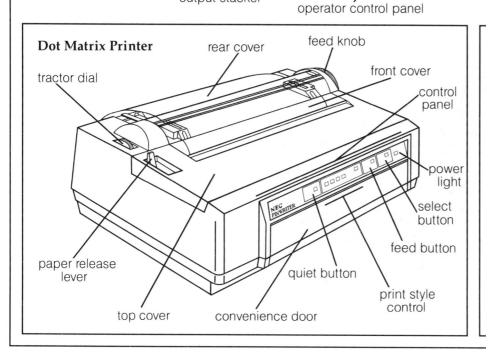

Dot Matrix Printer

rear cover

feed knob

tractor dial

front cover

control
panel

power
light

select
button

feed button

print style
control

paper release
lever

top cover

convenience door

quiet button

Print Samples

8-pin Matrix

24-pin Matrix

Laser Printer

enlarged type

8-pin Matrix

24-pin Matrix

Laser Printer

Fax Machine and Copier

Fax machines transmit clear, detailed paper *facsimilies* of documents quickly from one *terminal* to another over *telephone lines*. The fax operator may, in addition, couple the transmission with spoken conversation over the telephone handset. Copier, *answering machine, delayed transmission, unattended reception*, memory and automatic dialing capabilities may also be provided.

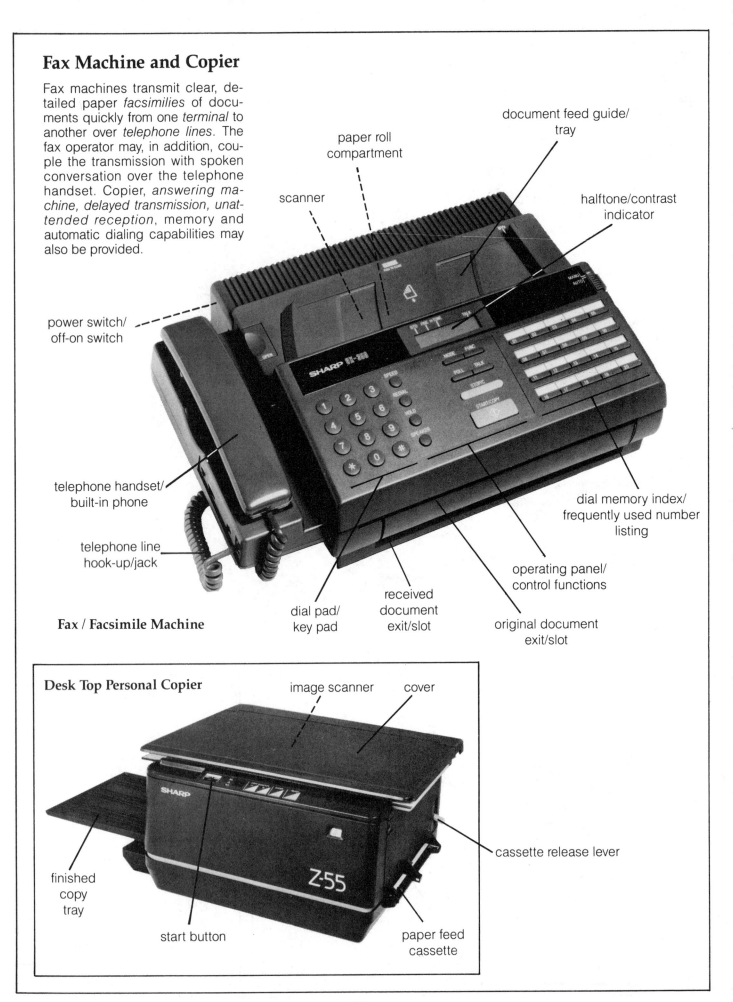

paper roll compartment

document feed guide/ tray

scanner

halftone/contrast indicator

power switch/ off-on switch

telephone handset/ built-in phone

telephone line hook-up/jack

dial memory index/ frequently used number listing

dial pad/ key pad

received document exit/slot

operating panel/ control functions

original document exit/slot

Fax / Facsimile Machine

Desk Top Personal Copier

image scanner

cover

cassette release lever

finished copy tray

start button

paper feed cassette

Type with serifs is called *book type*.
Type without serifs is *sans serif*.

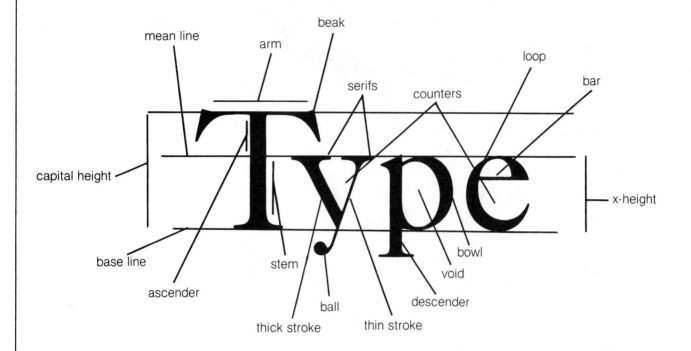

Typeface Composition

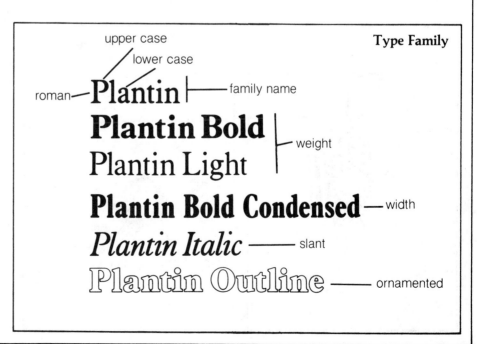

Type Family

Print Communications

Printing Processes

All *metal type* is known collectively as *hot metal,* in contrast to *cold type,* which is produced photographically. The letterpress method of printing uses a raised surface, or *relief,* while gravure uses a depressed surface, or *intaglio,* and lithography uses a *plane,* or *flat surface.* Printing is done on sheets of paper on *sheet-fed presses* or on rolls of paper on *web-fed presses.*

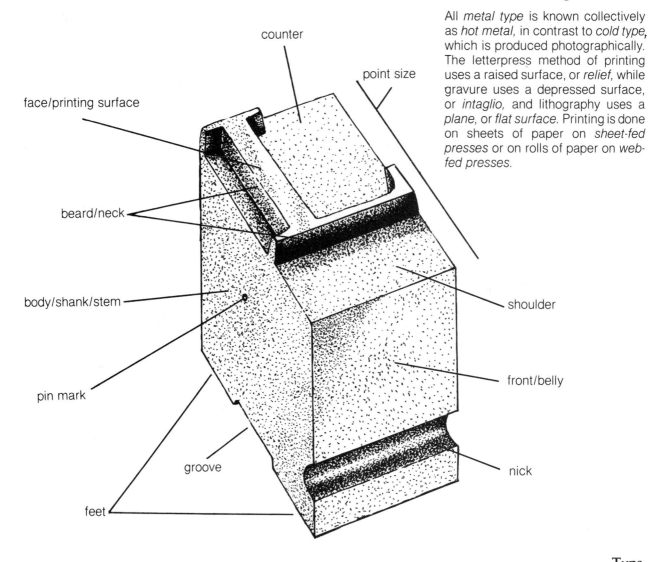

counter

point size

face/printing surface

beard/neck

body/shank/stem

pin mark

groove

feet

shoulder

front/belly

nick

Type

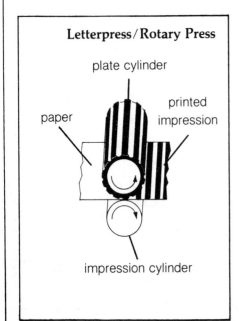

Letterpress/Rotary Press

plate cylinder

paper

printed impression

impression cylinder

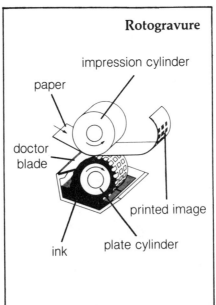

Rotogravure

impression cylinder

paper

doctor blade

printed image

ink

plate cylinder

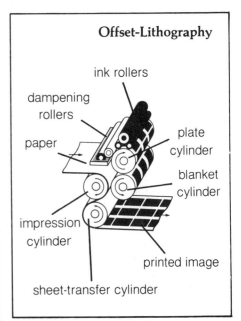

Offset-Lithography

ink rollers

dampening rollers

paper

plate cylinder

blanket cylinder

impression cylinder

printed image

sheet-transfer cylinder

Book

The *body* of a book is made up of *leaves,* each side of which is a *page.* Two facing pages form a *spread.* Pages leading up to the actual *text* are called *preliminaries* or *front matter.* Those pages following the text are *back matter, end matter* or *reference matter.* A box for a book, open at one end, is called a *slipcase* or *forel.*

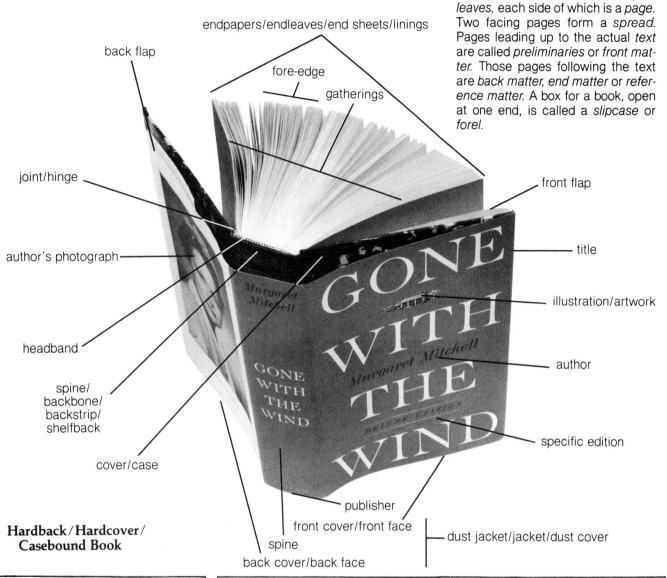

endpapers/endleaves/end sheets/linings

fore-edge

gatherings

back flap

joint/hinge

author's photograph

headband

spine/
backbone/
backstrip/
shelfback

cover/case

front flap

title

illustration/artwork

author

specific edition

publisher

front cover/front face

spine

back cover/back face

dust jacket/jacket/dust cover

Hardback/Hardcover/Casebound Book

Paperback/Softback/Softcover/Softbound Book

covers/wrappers

publisher

colophon/
trademark

price

spine

blurb

International
Standard
Book Number/
ISBN

order number/
inventory control
number

Spread

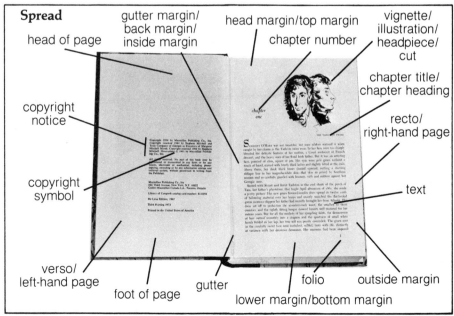

gutter margin/
back margin/
inside margin

head margin/top margin

chapter number

vignette/
illustration/
headpiece/
cut

head of page

copyright
notice

copyright
symbol

verso/
left-hand page

foot of page

gutter

folio

lower margin/bottom margin

outside margin

text

recto/
right-hand page

chapter title/
chapter heading

Print Communications

Newspaper

Terms vary from newspaper to newspaper. Those shown here are used at *The New York Times*. Small-size newspapers are called *tabloids*.

nameplate/flag/logo

skyline

out-of-town prices

weather ear

copyright

issue date

price

left ear

volume number

folio line

banner headline

head

deck/bank

bar line

byline

dateline

lead/lede

dingbat

readout dash

agate line

twinned stories

body of story

subhead

jump line

credit line

caption/cut line

italic refer

art

hairline rule

index

Magazine Cover and Contents Page

Periodicals may be consumer magazines, intended for the general public; *trade* or *technical magazines,* intended for particular industries and businesses; or *journals,* published for people engaged in professions. *House organs* are distributed within a specific company. Covers may have *cover blurbs* with *selling copy,* describing inside stories, and *cover captions.*

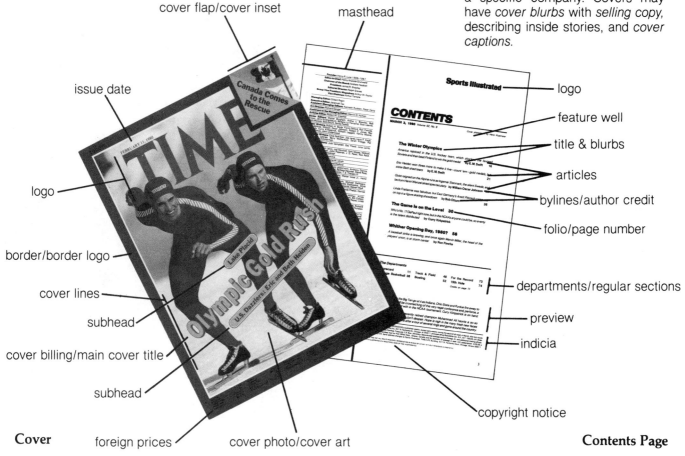

cover flap/cover inset

masthead

issue date

logo

border/border logo

cover lines

subhead

cover billing/main cover title

subhead

foreign prices

cover photo/cover art

copyright notice

logo

feature well

title & blurbs

articles

bylines/author credit

folio/page number

departments/regular sections

preview

indicia

Cover

Contents Page

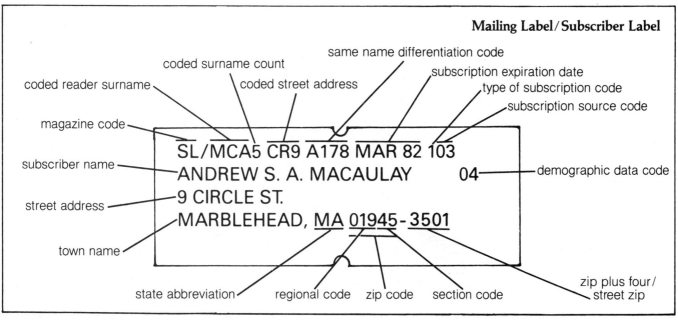

Mailing Label / Subscriber Label

same name differentiation code

coded surname count

subscription expiration date

coded reader surname

coded street address

type of subscription code

subscription source code

magazine code

subscriber name

street address

town name

demographic data code

```
SL/MCA5 CR9 A178 MAR 82 103
ANDREW S. A. MACAULAY          04
9 CIRCLE ST.
MARBLEHEAD, MA 01945-3501
```

state abbreviation

regional code

zip code

section code

zip plus four/ street zip

Magazine Feature

The design of a magazine page is called the *layout*. In the feature shown here *dummy type* has been substituted for *text* or *copy*. Two facing pages are called a spread, *double spread,* or *double-truck*. A *sidebar* is a self-contained, boxed *article* bearing on the main feature.

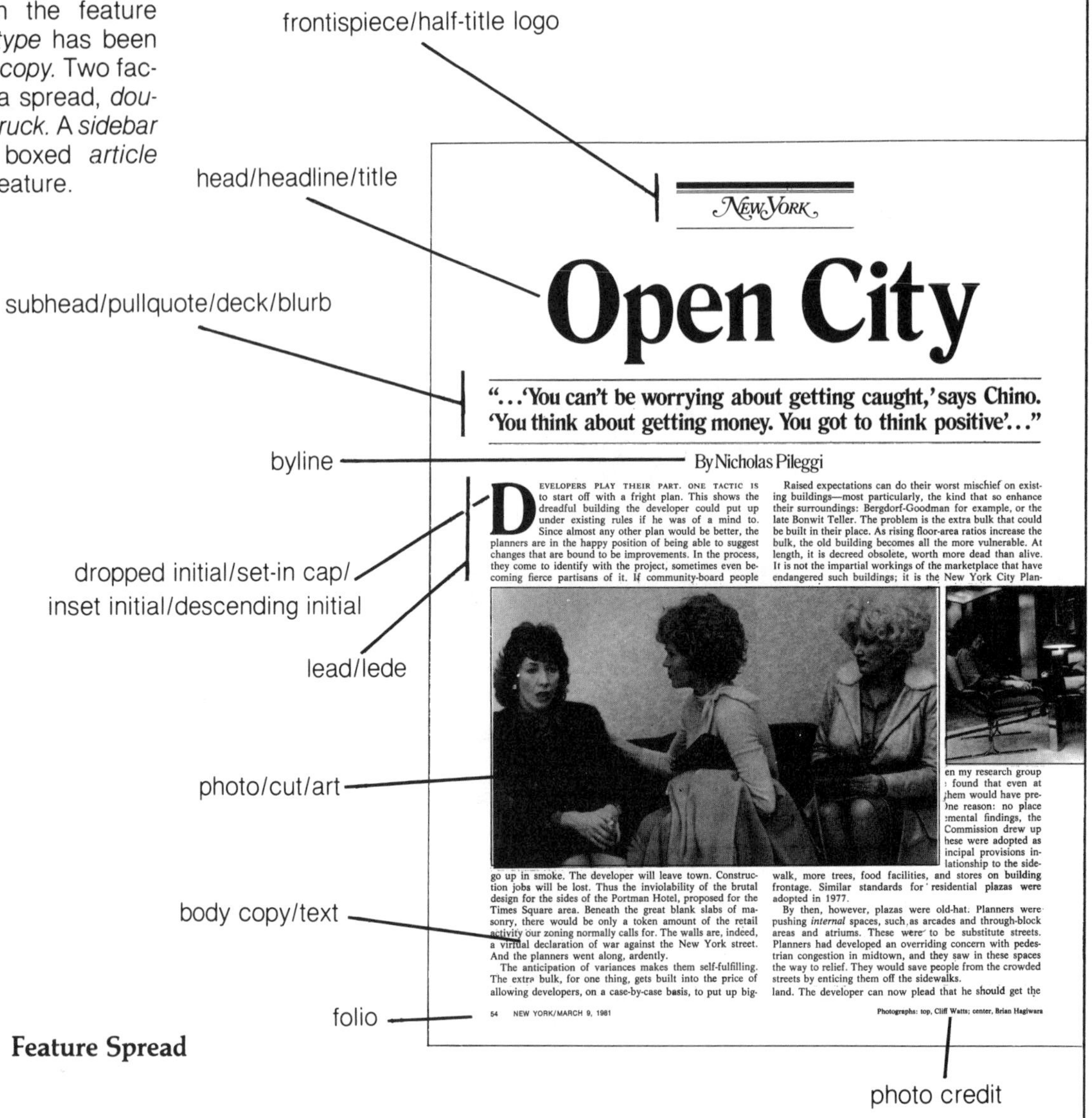

frontispiece/half-title logo

head/headline/title

subhead/pullquote/deck/blurb

byline

dropped initial/set-in cap/
inset initial/descending initial

lead/lede

photo/cut/art

body copy/text

folio

Feature Spread

photo credit

Service Articles

Reviews

scotch rule

art/illustration

oxford rule

head

column rule

special-feature photo treatment

sign-off

"nuts and bolts"

flush-left type

ragged-right type

running title

subhead

decorated initial

introduction

breaker

boldface/highlight

column

A page that folds out to twice the size of a regular page is called a *gatefold*. A *jump line,* or *continued line,* at the end of a page refers the reader to the remaining text of a story appearing elsewhere in the magazine. A brief descriptive headline above the main head, designed to attract the reader's attention, is a *kicker, teaser, eyebrow,* or *highline.* Subscription cards bound into a magazine are called *inserts.* Those not physically connected are called *blow-ins.*

gutter/gutter margin

italics

margin

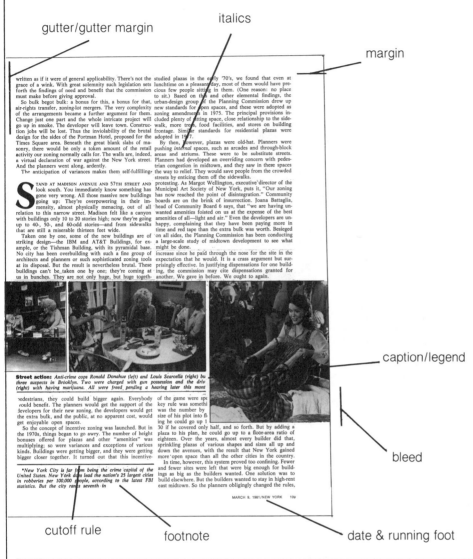

caption/legend

bleed

cutoff rule

footnote

date & running foot

Column

Back of the Book

slug

two-deck head

bold face lead-in

art

end slug/closed quad

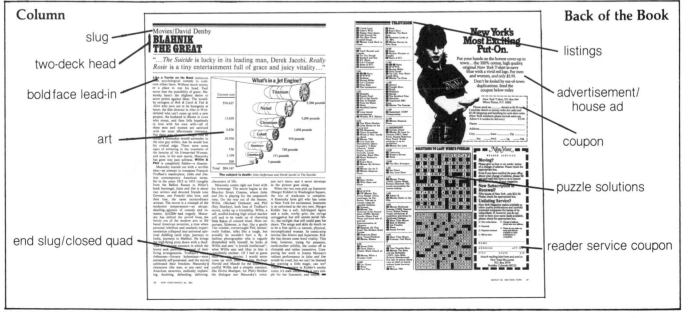

listings

advertisement/ house ad

coupon

puzzle solutions

reader service coupon

Still Camera and Film

To focus on an *image*, a photographer looks through the *viewfinder* on the back of the camera. Some cameras have *automatic focus* and *power winder* as in this model shown. Camera accessories include *interchangeable lenses—telephoto, wide-angle, zoom* and *special-purpose—lens caps* and *hoods, filters, focusing screens* and *eyecups*.

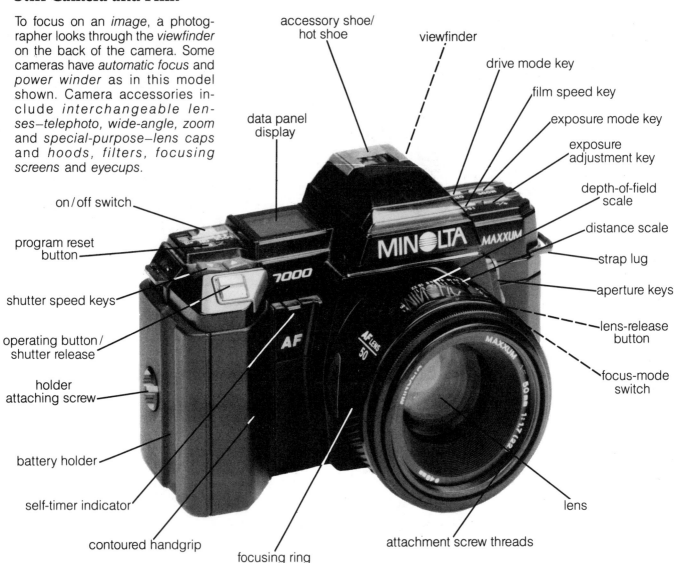

accessory shoe/ hot shoe

viewfinder

drive mode key

film speed key

exposure mode key

exposure adjustment key

depth-of-field scale

distance scale

strap lug

aperture keys

lens-release button

focus-mode switch

data panel display

on/off switch

program reset button

shutter speed keys

operating button/ shutter release

holder attaching screw

battery holder

self-timer indicator

contoured handgrip

focusing ring

attachment screw threads

lens

Single Lens Reflex/SLR/Autofocus 35 mm Camera

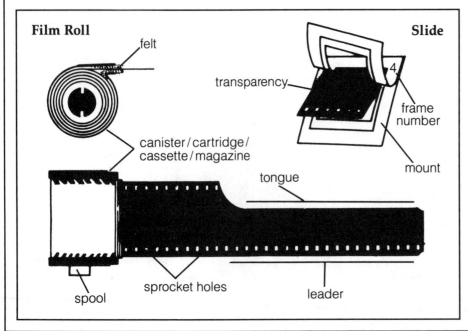

Film Roll

felt

transparency

canister/cartridge/ cassette/magazine

tongue

spool

sprocket holes

leader

Slide

frame number

mount

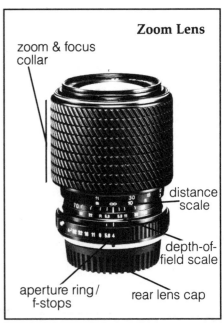

Zoom Lens

zoom & focus collar

distance scale

depth-of-field scale

aperture ring/ f-stops

rear lens cap

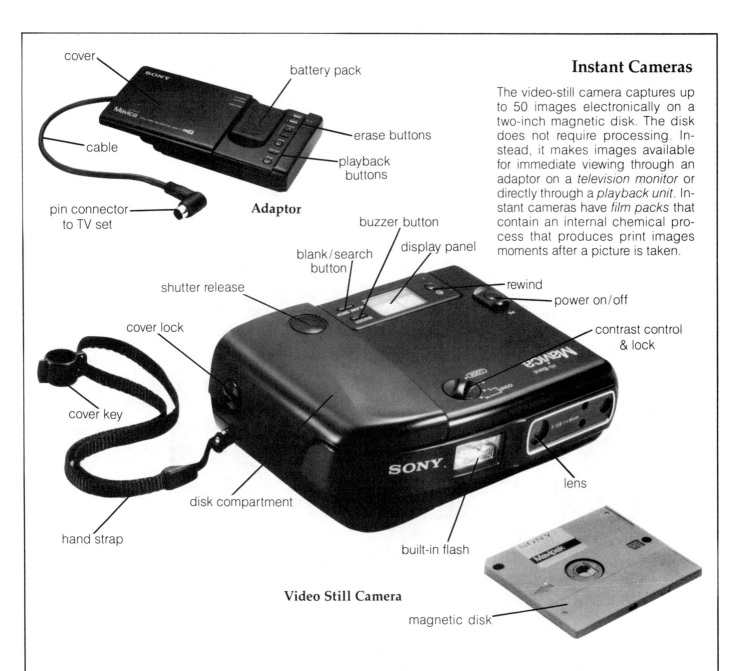

cover

battery pack

SONY Mavica

erase buttons

cable

playback buttons

pin connector to TV set

Adaptor

Instant Cameras

The video-still camera captures up to 50 images electronically on a two-inch magnetic disk. The disk does not require processing. Instead, it makes images available for immediate viewing through an adaptor on a *television monitor* or directly through a *playback unit*. Instant cameras have *film packs* that contain an internal chemical process that produces print images moments after a picture is taken.

buzzer button

blank/search button

display panel

shutter release

rewind

power on/off

cover lock

contrast control & lock

cover key

hand strap

disk compartment

SONY

lens

built-in flash

Video Still Camera

magnetic disk

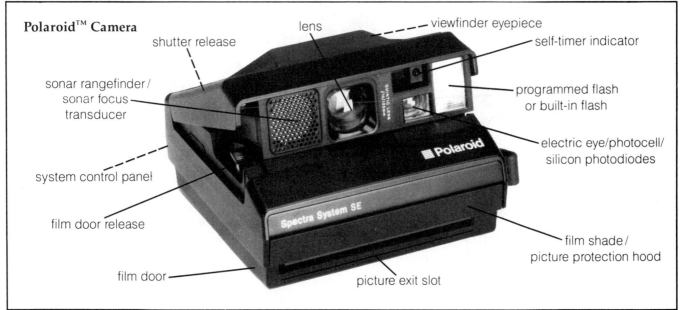

Polaroid™ Camera

lens

viewfinder eyepiece

shutter release

self-timer indicator

sonar rangefinder/ sonar focus transducer

programmed flash or built-in flash

electric eye/photocell/ silicon photodiodes

system control panel

Polaroid

film door release

Spectra System SE

film door

picture exit slot

film shade/ picture protection hood

Movie Camera

Home-movie cameras, such as the one shown here, use film contained in *drop-in cartridges.* In large commercial models, *unexposed film* moves through the body from the *supply reel* to the *take-up reel.* The reels in these cameras are often housed in a *blimp,* a soundproof device that fits on top of the body. *Single-system sound cameras* record both *image* and *sound* on the same film. Sound tracks on film may be either *optical* or *magnetic.*

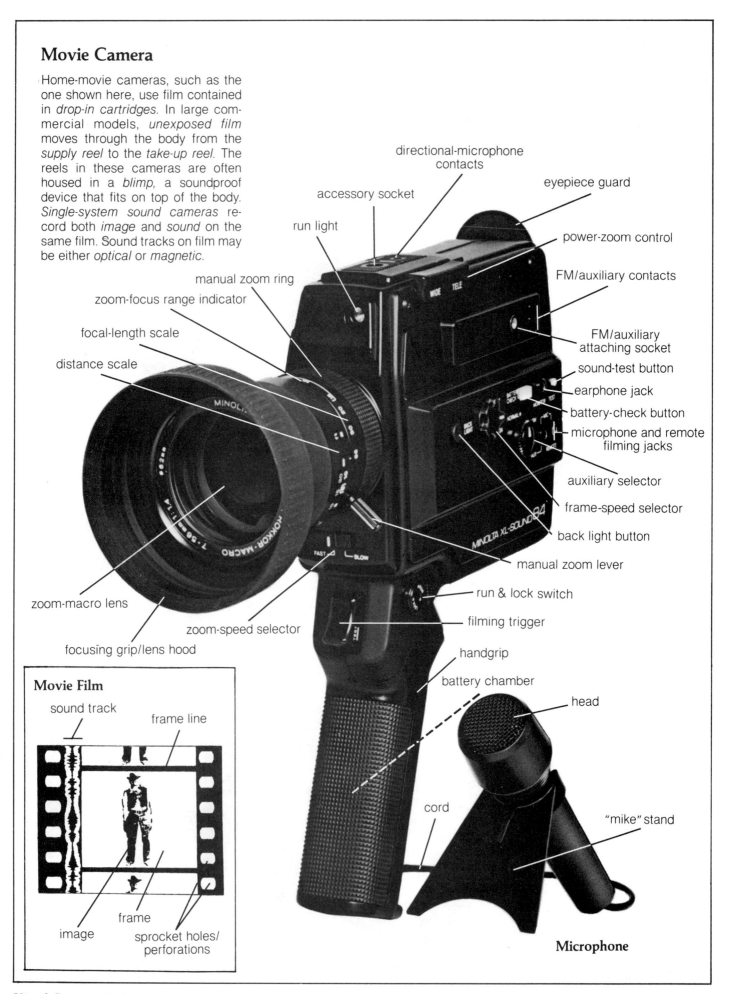

directional-microphone contacts

accessory socket

eyepiece guard

run light

power-zoom control

FM/auxiliary contacts

manual zoom ring

zoom-focus range indicator

focal-length scale

distance scale

FM/auxiliary attaching socket

sound-test button

earphone jack

battery-check button

microphone and remote filming jacks

auxiliary selector

frame-speed selector

back light button

manual zoom lever

zoom-macro lens

run & lock switch

filming trigger

zoom-speed selector

focusing grip/lens hood

handgrip

battery chamber

head

cord

"mike" stand

Movie Film

sound track

frame line

image

frame

sprocket holes/ perforations

Microphone

Projectors

The film projector shown here is a *self-threading, reel-to-reel model* with a built-in *speaker.* Slide projectors may have circular, or *carousel,* trays, *slide cubes* or *straight trays.*

carrying handle

framing knob

supply spindle

supply reel

take-up spindle

supply-reel arm

take-up reel

loop-former bar

film-loading port

operating control

zooming ring

volume control

lens

projection-speed selector

audio-input

microphone input plug

focusing knob

monitor

tilting knob

DIN socket

dubbing control

recording lever

recording-lever lock

Movie Projector

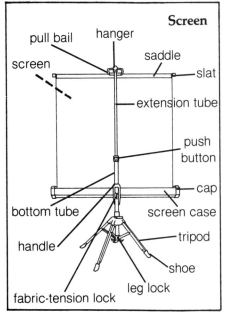

Screen

pull bail   hanger

saddle

screen

slat

extension tube

push button

bottom tube

cap

handle

screen case

tripod

shoe

fabric-tension lock   leg lock

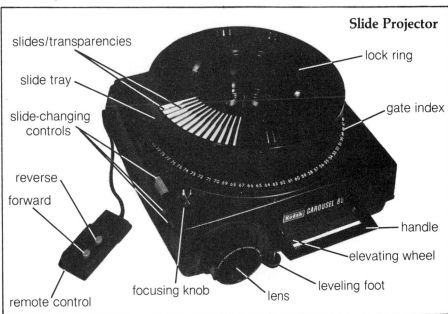

Slide Projector

slides/transparencies

lock ring

slide tray

slide-changing controls

gate index

reverse

forward

handle

elevating wheel

leveling foot

remote control

focusing knob

lens

Visual Communications

Photographic Accessories

In addition to the accessories shown here, *carrying straps, gadget bags,* and *cleaning supplies* such as *brushes, lens tissue* and *cleaning fluid* are used.

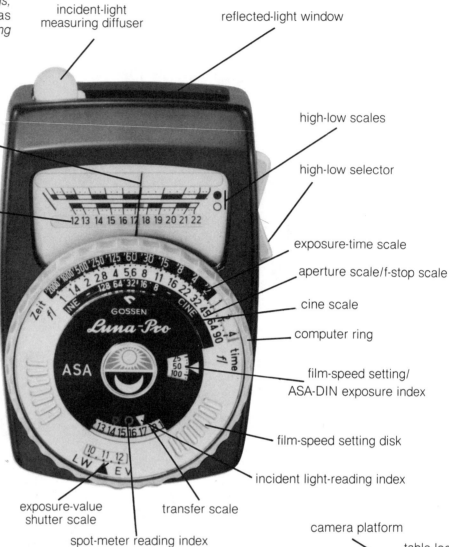

incident-light measuring diffuser

reflected-light window

high-low scales

high-low selector

indicator needle

light-reading scale/ indicator scale

exposure-time scale

aperture scale/f-stop scale

cine scale

computer ring

film-speed setting/ ASA-DIN exposure index

film-speed setting disk

incident light-reading index

exposure-value shutter scale

transfer scale

spot-meter reading index

Exposure Meter/Light Meter

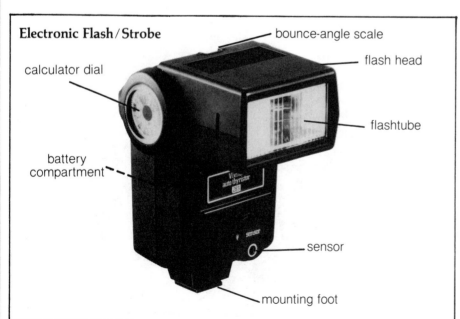

Electronic Flash/Strobe

bounce-angle scale

flash head

calculator dial

flashtube

battery compartment

sensor

mounting foot

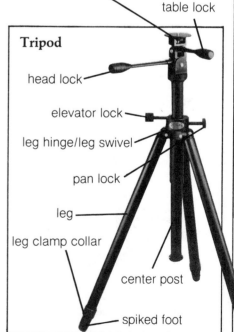

Tripod

camera platform

table lock

head lock

elevator lock

leg hinge/leg swivel

pan lock

leg

leg clamp collar

center post

spiked foot

Tape Recorders

Sound is recorded on *magnetic tape* by passing the tape over a *recording head.* Most cassette recorders have *built-in microphones* but are designed to work with *external mikes* as well. They are *battery-powered,* have *rechargeable battery packs* or *AC power cords.*

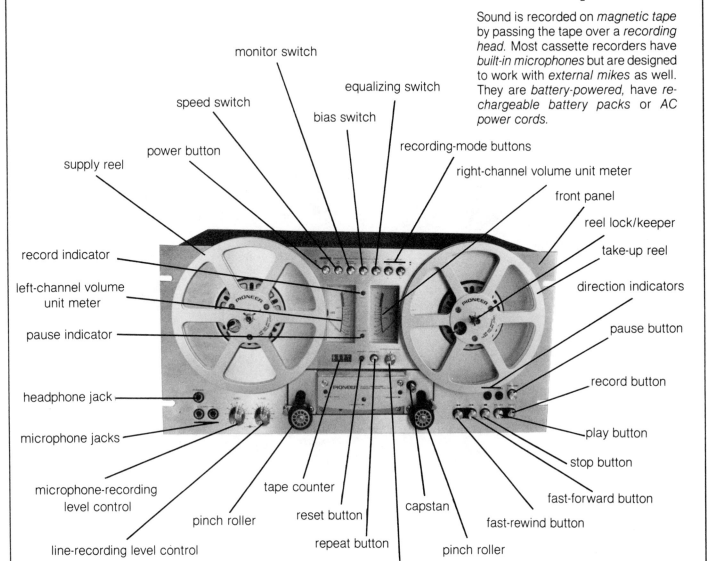

monitor switch

equalizing switch

speed switch

bias switch

power button

recording-mode buttons

right-channel volume unit meter

supply reel

front panel

reel lock/keeper

record indicator

take-up reel

left-channel volume unit meter

direction indicators

pause indicator

pause button

record button

headphone jack

microphone jacks

play button

stop button

microphone-recording level control

fast-forward button

tape counter

fast-rewind button

pinch roller

reset button

capstan

pinch roller

line-recording level control

repeat button

pitch-control dial

Reel-to-Reel Recorder and Playback Unit

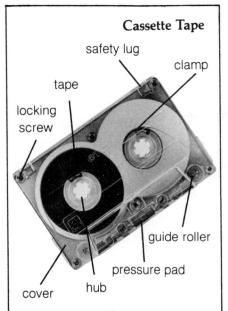

Cassette Tape

safety lug

clamp

tape

locking screw

guide roller

pressure pad

cover

hub

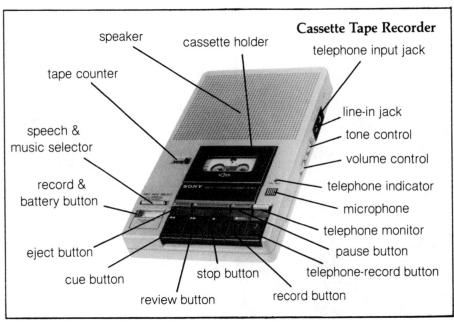

Cassette Tape Recorder

speaker

cassette holder

telephone input jack

tape counter

line-in jack

tone control

speech & music selector

volume control

telephone indicator

record & battery button

microphone

telephone monitor

eject button

pause button

cue button

telephone-record button

review button

stop button

record button

Aural Communications

Disc and Record Players

Compact disc players use a *laser tracking system* to play or repeat selections. Multiple albums can be programmed to play in any order on a *CD changer*, while a CD player holds only one album at a time. An optional *monster cable* improves sound by eliminating disc vibration. The amount of information a player can read off a disc is measured in *bits*.

Compact Disc Player/CD Player

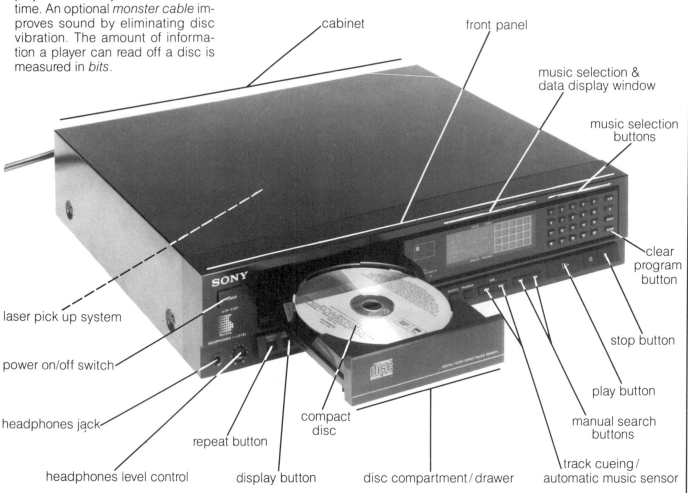

cabinet

front panel

music selection & data display window

music selection buttons

clear program button

laser pick up system

power on/off switch

headphones jack

headphones level control

repeat button

display button

compact disc

disc compartment/drawer

stop button

play button

manual search buttons

track cueing/ automatic music sensor

Record/Platter/Disc

lead-in groove

manufacturer

record title & artist

locked groove

grooves/ spiral

label

lead-out groove

center hole

master number

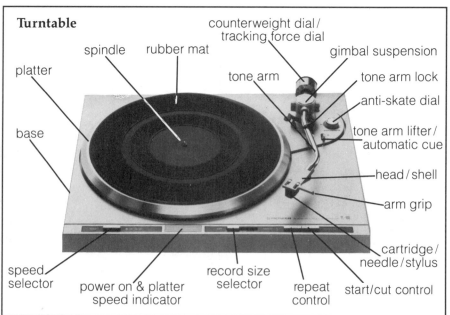

Turntable

counterweight dial/ tracking force dial

spindle

rubber mat

gimbal suspension

platter

tone arm

tone arm lock

anti-skate dial

base

tone arm lifter/ automatic cue

head/shell

arm grip

cartridge/ needle/stylus

start/cut control

speed selector

power on & platter speed indicator

record size selector

repeat control

Audio Equipment

A home audio system produces minimally distorted sound, or *high fidelity*. It is usually comprised of a *tuner*, a disc or record player, a *pre-amp*, and amplifier and speakers. Its power output is measured in *watts*.

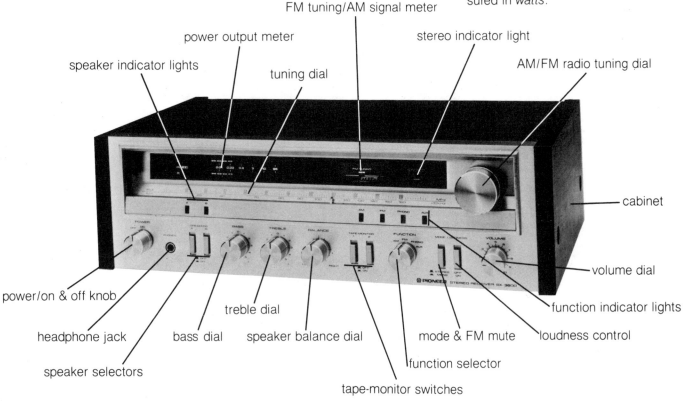

power output meter

speaker indicator lights

FM tuning/AM signal meter

tuning dial

stereo indicator light

AM/FM radio tuning dial

cabinet

volume dial

power/on & off knob

function indicator lights

loudness control

headphone jack

treble dial

bass dial

speaker balance dial

mode & FM mute

speaker selectors

function selector

tape-monitor switches

Receiver / Amplifier

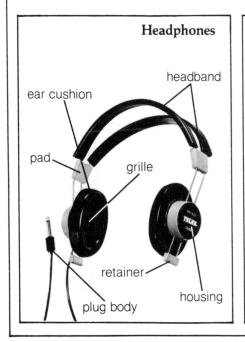

Headphones

headband

ear cushion

pad

grille

retainer

housing

plug body

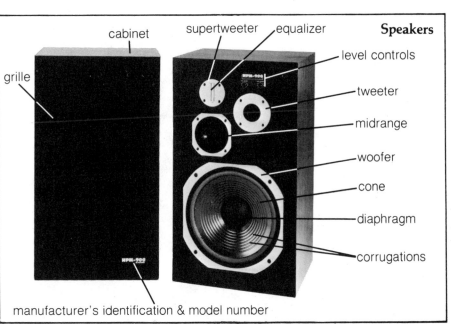

Speakers

cabinet

supertweeter

equalizer

level controls

grille

tweeter

midrange

woofer

cone

diaphragm

corrugations

manufacturer's identification & model number

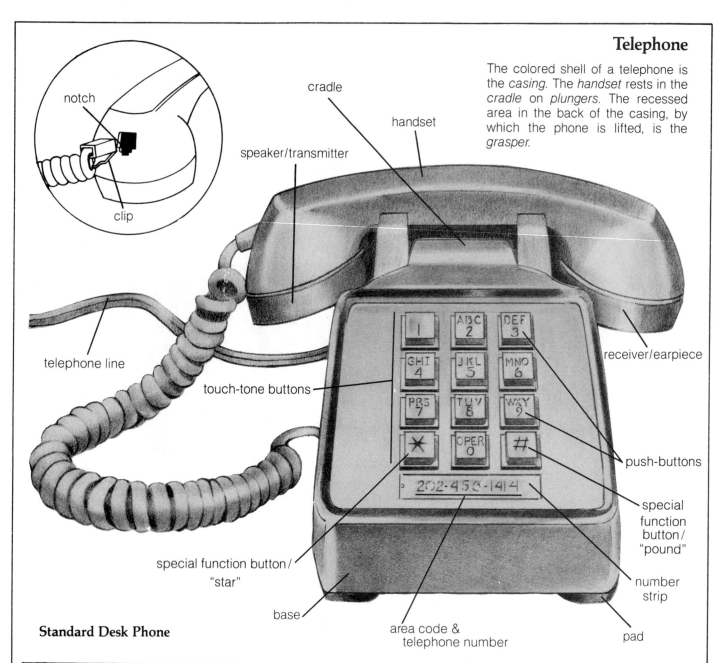

notch

clip

Telephone

The colored shell of a telephone is the *casing*. The *handset* rests in the *cradle* on *plungers*. The recessed area in the back of the casing, by which the phone is lifted, is the *grasper*.

cradle

handset

speaker/transmitter

receiver/earpiece

telephone line

touch-tone buttons

push-buttons

special function button/ "pound"

number strip

special function button/ "star"

base

area code & telephone number

pad

Standard Desk Phone

202-450-1414

Pay Phone

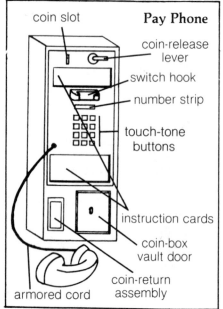

coin slot

coin-release lever

switch hook

number strip

touch-tone buttons

instruction cards

coin-box vault door

coin-return assembly

armored cord

Trimline Phone

number strip

rotary dial

plunger

finger hole

base

finger stop

bell adjuster

Cordless Phone

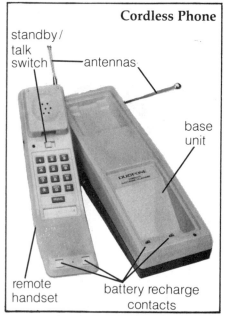

standby/ talk switch

antennas

base unit

remote handset

battery recharge contacts

Cellular Telephone

A *cell* is a circular service area of 16 mile radius, and calls are transmitted over radio waves and relayed from cell to cell over telephone wires. Available features include *memory redial* to recall numbers, *hands-off* operation, and an electronic lock to prevent unauthorized use. *Remote operation*, either with a *beeper* or *Touch-tone*™ phone, includes options like message retrieval, or leaving messages or *memos*. Many answering machines allow *call screening*, permitting calls to be heard without being answered.

antenna

liquid crystal display screen/LCD

auto redial

handset

illuminated menu keys

illuminated alpha-numeric keypad

battery pack

signal strength indicator

SIG
01 ABCDEF
1234567890

memory data

Display Screen

carrying handle

number being called

loudspeaker

stand/base/case

Cellular Telephone/Mobile Phone

electronic lock

cord

Answering Machine

message indicator lights

transfer call

telephone handset

play messages button

answer button

speakerphone

alpha-numeric keypad / telephone push buttons

control buttons

Aural Communications

Portable Radios and Cassette Players

A cassette player, or "Walkman"™, may be heard through headphones, a *built-in speaker* or *external speakers*. Portable radios often have detachable speakers. *Autoreverse*, or *continuous play*, automatically plays both sides of a tape. *Dolby*™ sound reduces tape hiss. Some players with recording capabilities have *high-speed dubbing*, which copies tapes at faster than normal playing speed, and *synchronized dubbing*, which starts the original tape and blank tape simultaneously.

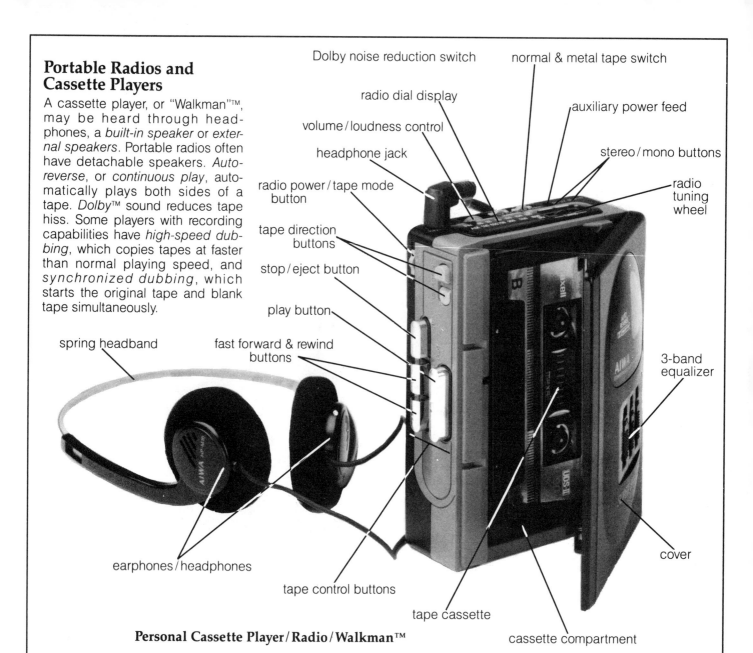

Dolby noise reduction switch

normal & metal tape switch

radio dial display

auxiliary power feed

volume/loudness control

stereo/mono buttons

headphone jack

radio tuning wheel

radio power/tape mode button

tape direction buttons

stop/eject button

play button

3-band equalizer

spring headband

fast forward & rewind buttons

earphones/headphones

cover

tape control buttons

tape cassette

cassette compartment

Personal Cassette Player/Radio/Walkman™

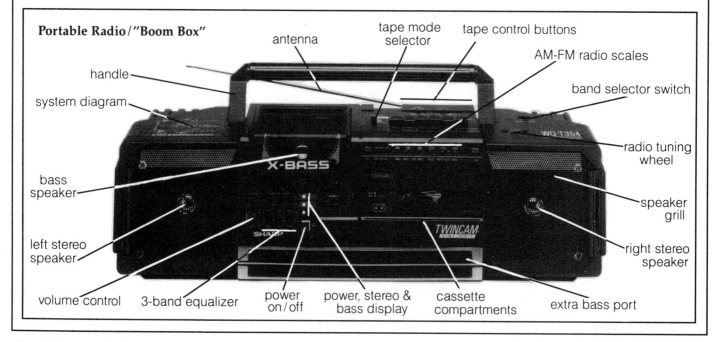

Portable Radio/"Boom Box"

antenna

tape mode selector

tape control buttons

handle

AM-FM radio scales

system diagram

band selector switch

radio tuning wheel

bass speaker

speaker grill

left stereo speaker

right stereo speaker

volume control

3-band equalizer

power on/off

power, stereo & bass display

cassette compartments

extra bass port

Transceiver

A *walkie-talkie* is a hand-held transceiver used to transmit and receive over short distances. *CBs,* or Citizens Band radios, like the one shown here, have greater but still limited range. *Amateur radio operators,* or "hams," use transceivers capable of communicating over vast distances.

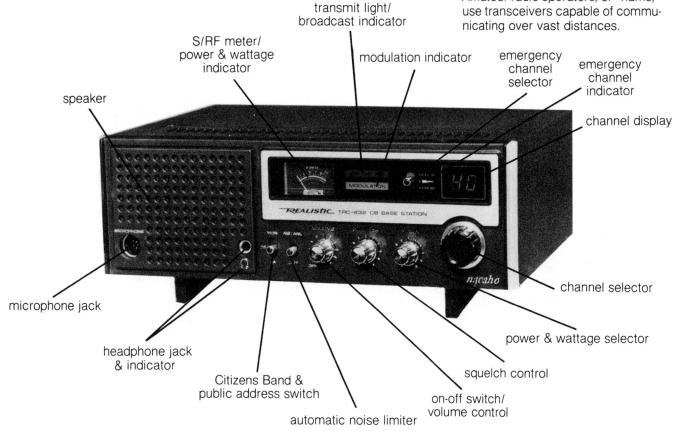

transmit light/
broadcast indicator

modulation indicator

emergency channel selector

emergency channel indicator

channel display

S/RF meter/
power & wattage indicator

speaker

microphone jack

channel selector

power & wattage selector

squelch control

on-off switch/
volume control

automatic noise limiter

Citizens Band &
public address switch

headphone jack
& indicator

Base Station

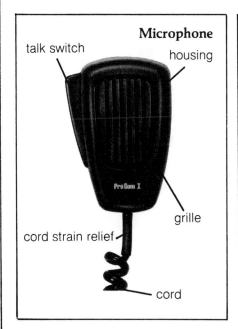

Microphone

talk switch

housing

grille

cord strain relief

cord

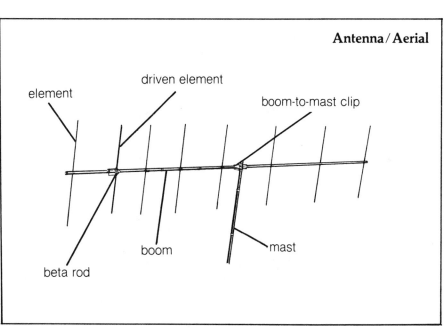

Antenna/Aerial

element

driven element

boom-to-mast clip

beta rod

boom

mast

Aural Communications

Video Recorder

Video recorders are used in conjunction with *television sets*, or *monitors*. They can be operated by hand-size *remote control units*. Some recorders use a grooveless *disc*, others use a *video cassette tape*.

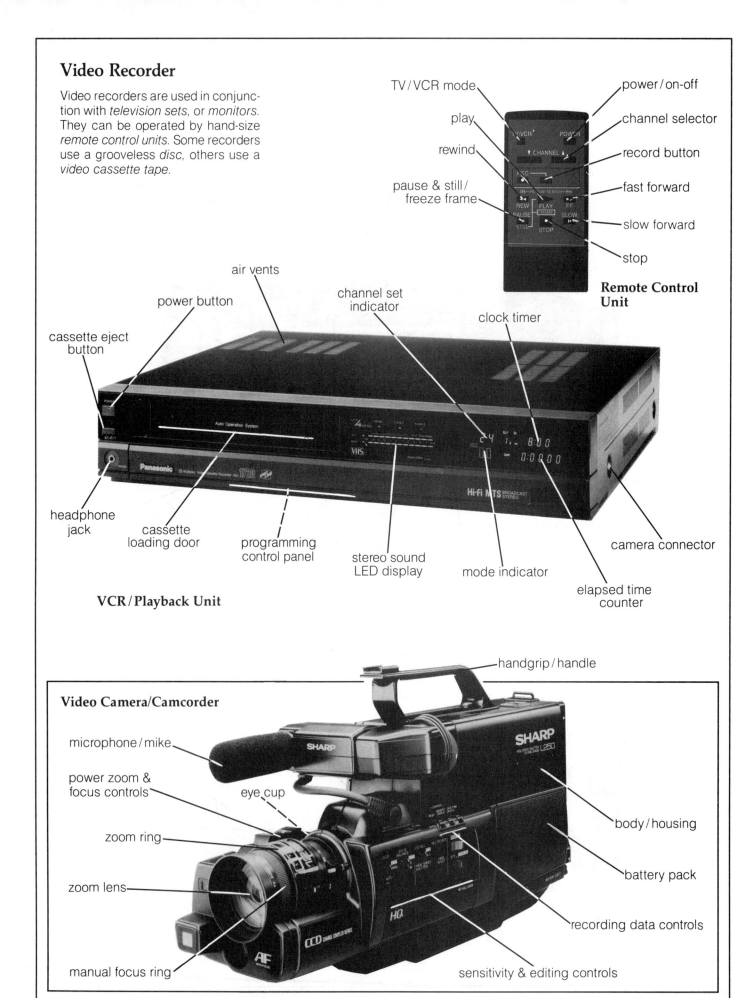

TV/VCR mode

play

rewind

pause & still/
freeze frame

power/on-off

channel selector

record button

fast forward

slow forward

stop

Remote Control Unit

air vents

power button

channel set indicator

clock timer

cassette eject button

headphone jack

cassette loading door

programming control panel

stereo sound LED display

mode indicator

camera connector

elapsed time counter

VCR/Playback Unit

handgrip/handle

Video Camera/Camcorder

microphone/mike

power zoom & focus controls

eye cup

zoom ring

zoom lens

body/housing

battery pack

recording data controls

manual focus ring

sensitivity & editing controls

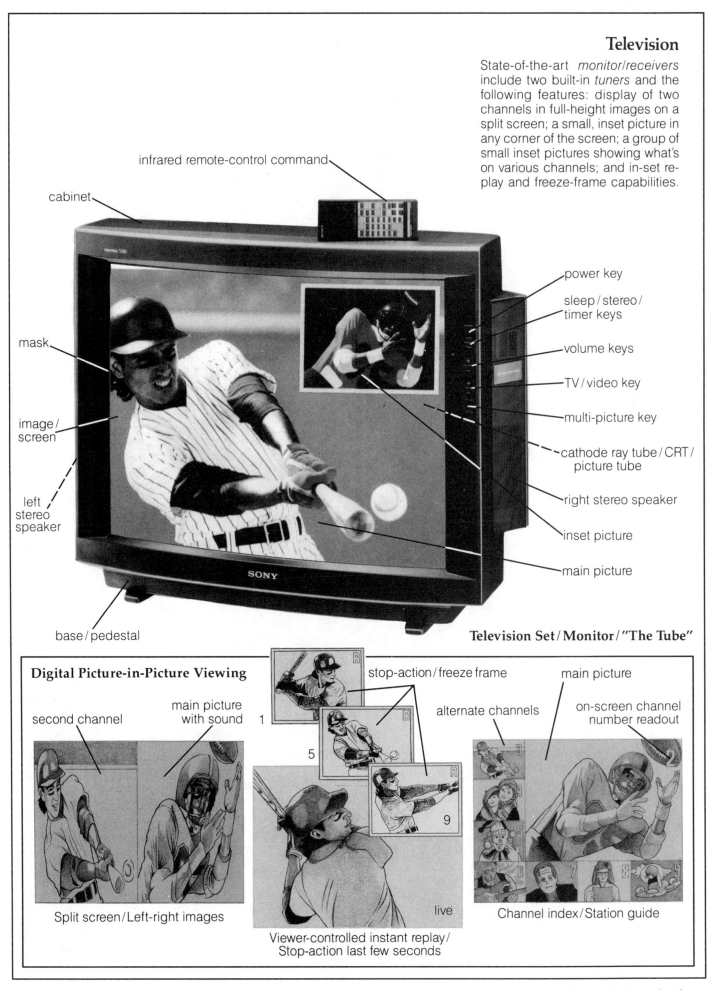

Television

State-of-the-art *monitor/receivers* include two built-in *tuners* and the following features: display of two channels in full-height images on a split screen; a small, inset picture in any corner of the screen; a group of small inset pictures showing what's on various channels; and in-set replay and freeze-frame capabilities.

infrared remote-control command

cabinet

mask

image / screen

left stereo speaker

base / pedestal

power key

sleep / stereo / timer keys

volume keys

TV / video key

multi-picture key

cathode ray tube / CRT / picture tube

right stereo speaker

inset picture

main picture

Television Set / Monitor / "The Tube"

Digital Picture-in-Picture Viewing

second channel

main picture with sound

stop-action / freeze frame

alternate channels

main picture

on-screen channel number readout

Split screen / Left-right images

Viewer-controlled instant replay / Stop-action last few seconds

Channel index / Station guide

Visual Communications

Satellite

Active repeater satellites are communications satellites that amplify signals beamed to them for retransmission. *Passive* or *reflector satellites* mirror signals without amplifying them. Satellites used for space exploration, such as the one shown here, make scientific measurements and transmit the information back to earth.

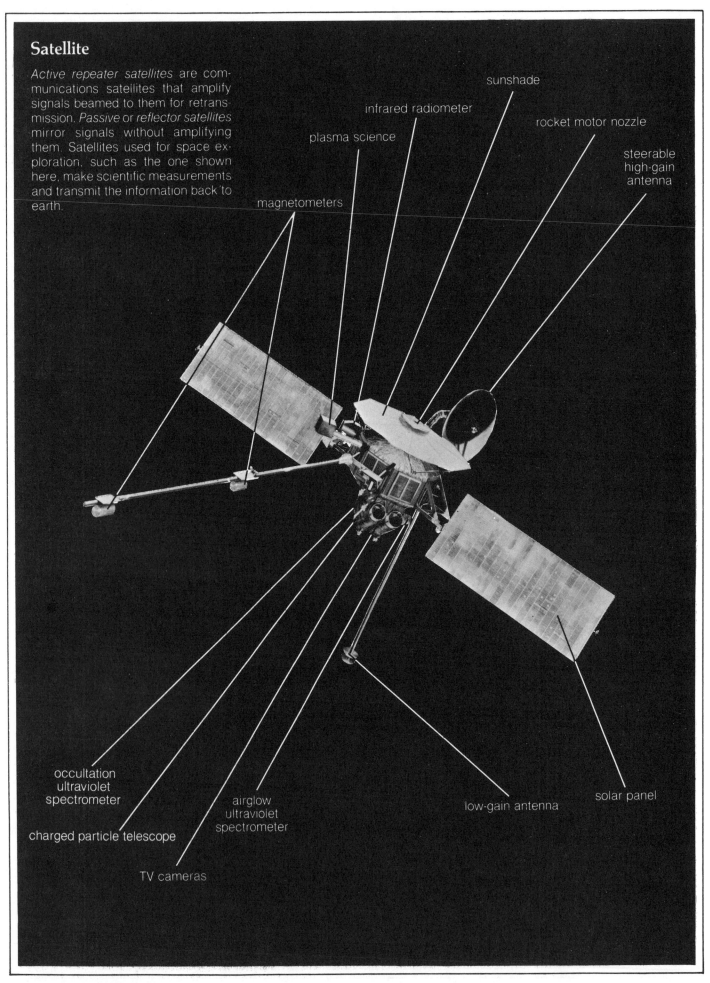

magnetometers

plasma science

infrared radiometer

sunshade

rocket motor nozzle

steerable high-gain antenna

occultation ultraviolet spectrometer

charged particle telescope

airglow ultraviolet spectrometer

TV cameras

low-gain antenna

solar panel

Personal Items

This section includes items people are likely to wear, carry or use in the course of their everyday lives. Thus, coverage includes clothing, hats, shoes, jewelry and money.

Wherever men's and women's apparel differ appreciably, items have been separated. But in the case of items such as sweaters and overcoats, articles worn by both sexes, only one version has been presented. Liberal use has been made to show the variations possible on single objects. However trendy clothing fashions or hairstyles may be, they share the same basic parts and details shown in the illustrations on the pages that follow.

Because cosmetics, grooming, hairstyles and jewelry are an important part of everyday life, they have been included in this section, as have such items as eyeglasses, handbags and wallets, timepieces and smoking materials. And because on rainy days an umbrella is essential to carry, it, too, appears here.

Identification Bracelet

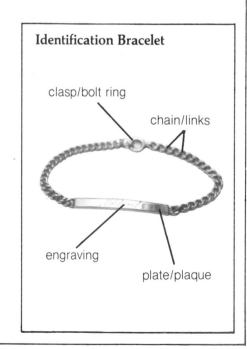

clasp/bolt ring

chain/links

engraving

plate/plaque

Jacket and Vest

A jacket, or *coat*, can be *single* or *double-breasted*. A *handkerchief pocket* or *breast pocket* is usually found on the upper left front panel. The pouch-like attachment inside a side pocket is called a *change pocket*. Most jackets have a *vent* or *double vent* cut into the hem in the back panel. Vests have an adjustable *backstrap* in the back.

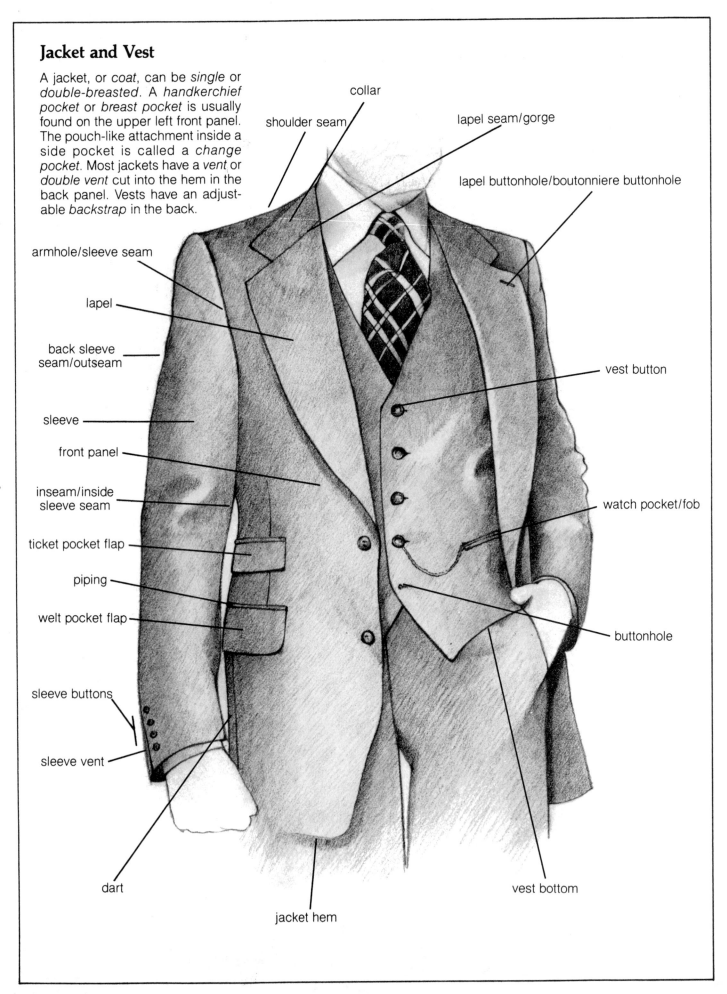

collar

shoulder seam

lapel seam/gorge

lapel buttonhole/boutonniere buttonhole

armhole/sleeve seam

lapel

back sleeve seam/outseam

sleeve

front panel

inseam/inside sleeve seam

ticket pocket flap

piping

welt pocket flap

sleeve buttons

sleeve vent

dart

jacket hem

vest button

watch pocket/fob

buttonhole

vest bottom

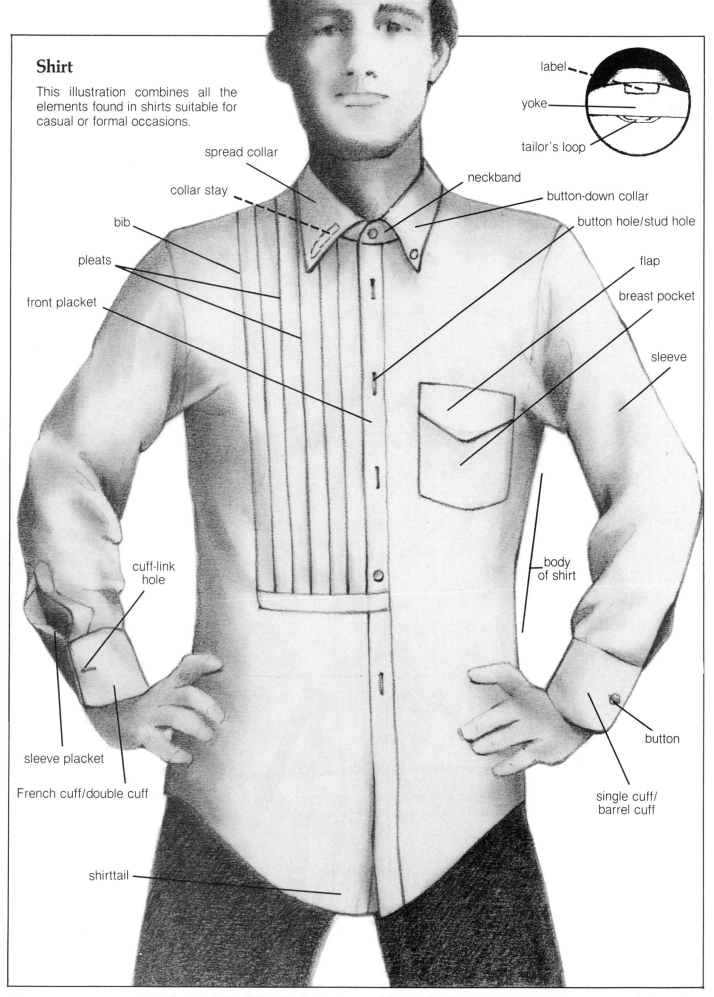

Shirt

This illustration combines all the elements found in shirts suitable for casual or formal occasions.

label

yoke

tailor's loop

spread collar

collar stay

bib

pleats

front placket

neckband

button-down collar

button hole/stud hole

flap

breast pocket

sleeve

cuff-link hole

body of shirt

sleeve placket

French cuff/double cuff

button

single cuff/barrel cuff

shirttail

Men's Apparel

Belt and Suspenders

Large, often elaborately engraved buckles are called *plaque buckles*. *Military buckles*, or *ratchet buckles*, are adjusted by pushing a *tension rod* inside the *frame*. Some belts come with reinforcing *eyelets* in the punch holes. The composite pair of suspenders shown here are *fireman's, policeman's*, or *working man's suspenders*. They all have a single elastic band at the back, whereas *dress suspenders* have crossed bands.

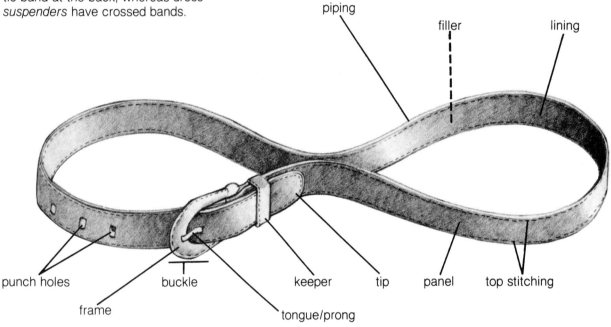

piping · filler · lining

punch holes · buckle · frame · keeper · tip · panel · top stitching · tongue/prong

Belt

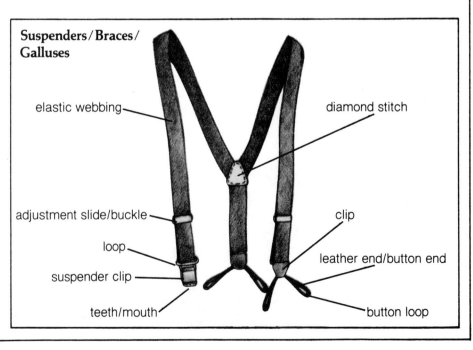

Suspenders / Braces / Galluses

elastic webbing · diamond stitch · adjustment slide/buckle · clip · loop · leather end/button end · suspender clip · teeth/mouth · button loop

Pants

The back of a *pair of pants* is called the *seat*. Mid-thigh or knee length pants are *shorts*. *Jeans* often have pockets and seams reinforced with *rivets*. *Waistband closures* on pants are secured with *button tab closings* or metal *hook and eye closings*.

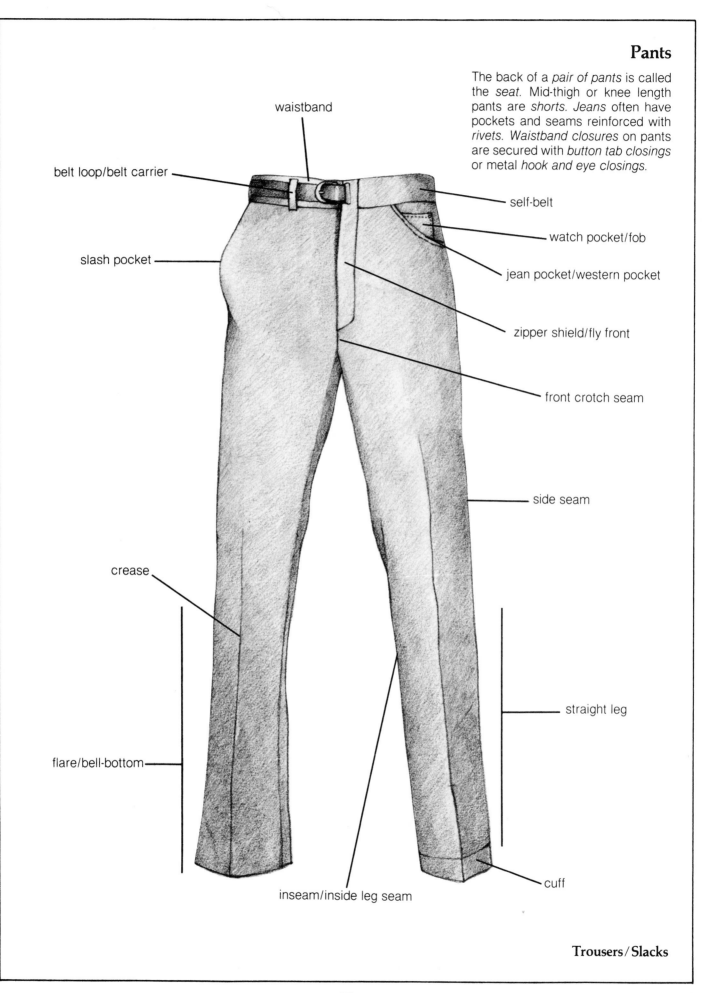

waistband

belt loop/belt carrier

self-belt

watch pocket/fob

slash pocket

jean pocket/western pocket

zipper shield/fly front

front crotch seam

side seam

crease

straight leg

flare/bell-bottom

cuff

inseam/inside leg seam

Trousers/Slacks

Men's Apparel

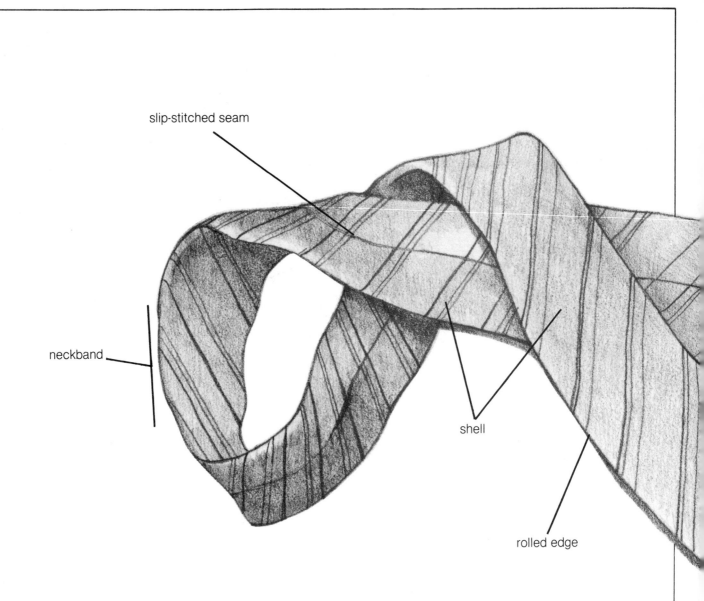

slip-stitched seam

neckband

shell

rolled edge

Necktie/Four-in-Hand

Bow Tie/Butterfly Tie

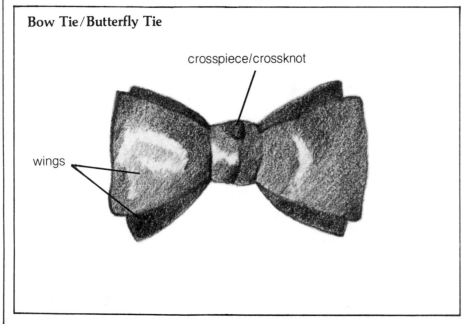

crosspiece/crossknot

wings

String Tie/Bolo Tie

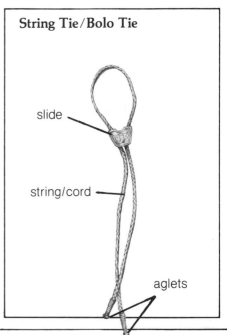

slide

string/cord

aglets

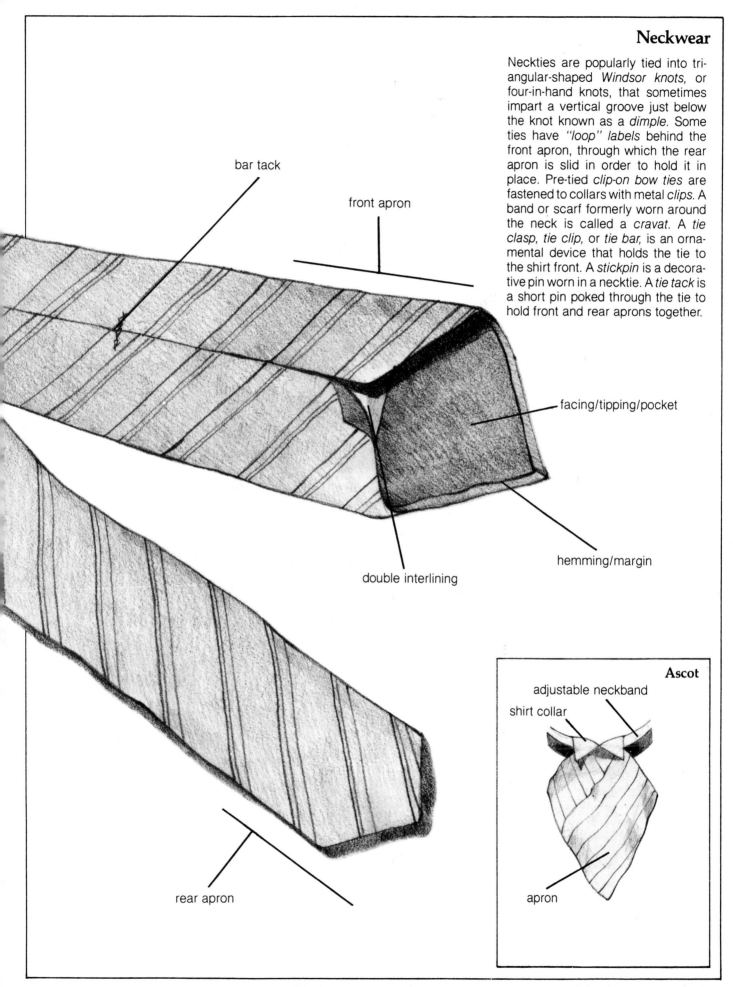

Neckwear

Neckties are popularly tied into triangular-shaped *Windsor knots*, or four-in-hand knots, that sometimes impart a vertical groove just below the knot known as a *dimple*. Some ties have "*loop*" labels behind the front apron, through which the rear apron is slid in order to hold it in place. Pre-tied *clip-on bow ties* are fastened to collars with metal *clips*. A band or scarf formerly worn around the neck is called a *cravat*. A *tie clasp*, *tie clip*, or *tie bar*, is an ornamental device that holds the tie to the shirt front. A *stickpin* is a decorative pin worn in a necktie. A *tie tack* is a short pin poked through the tie to hold front and rear aprons together.

bar tack

front apron

facing/tipping/pocket

hemming/margin

double interlining

rear apron

Ascot

adjustable neckband

shirt collar

apron

Men's Apparel

Underwear

A *T-shirt* has short sleeves rather than shoulder straps. Loose-fitting *boxer shorts* have short, trouserlike legs rather than leg openings. Some athletic supporters, or *jockstraps*, have pockets in the pouch to accommodate rubber-lined *protective cups*.

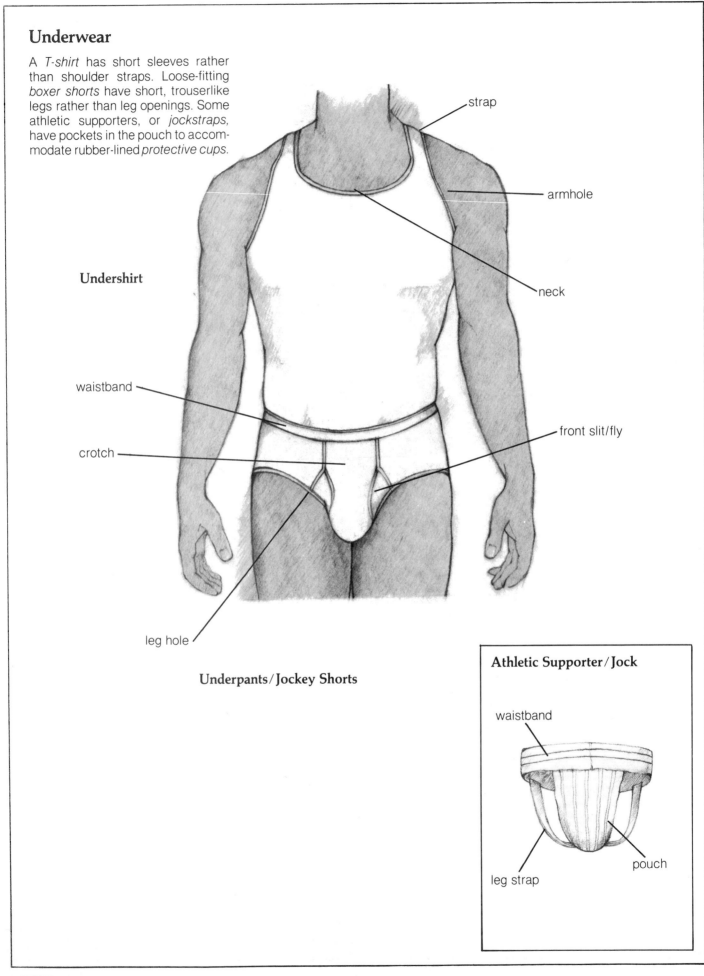

strap

armhole

neck

Undershirt

waistband

crotch

front slit/fly

leg hole

Underpants/Jockey Shorts

Athletic Supporter/Jock

waistband

pouch

leg strap

Foundation Garments

Most *bras* are secured with *hook-and-eye closures* either on a *back-strap* or in the front of the garment. Many have *underwiring* and/or *side-bones* for added support. *Cup padding* is another optional element. Girdles are sometimes stiffened with *spiral bones* or *stays*. Corsets are similar to girdles.

Brassiere

Girdle

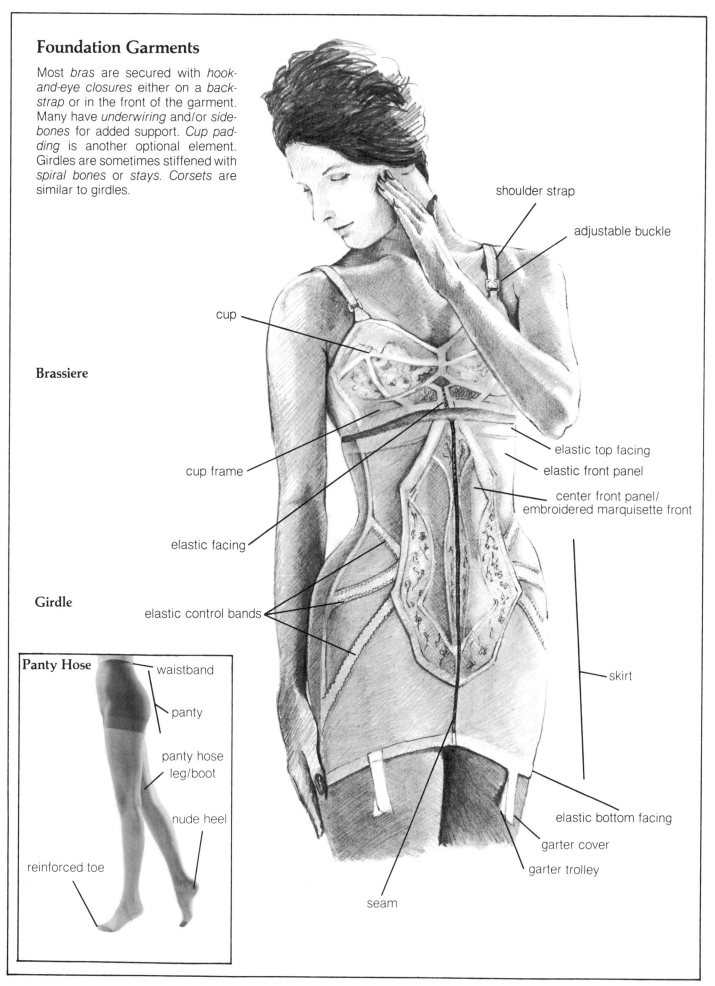

shoulder strap

adjustable buckle

cup

cup frame

elastic facing

elastic top facing

elastic front panel

center front panel/
embroidered marquisette front

elastic control bands

skirt

elastic bottom facing

garter cover

garter trolley

seam

Panty Hose

waistband

panty

panty hose
leg/boot

nude heel

reinforced toe

Jacket and Pants

Facing material is used on the underside of a lapel. *Lining* is used on the inside of a garment to cover up seamwork and provide body. A pair of lined pants has inside material from cuff to waist. In half-lined pants, the material stretches from waist to knee. In unlined garments, *seams* are clean finished with *bias tape,* or bias binding, sewn on a diagonal to provide stretch and support and to protect fabric from raveling.

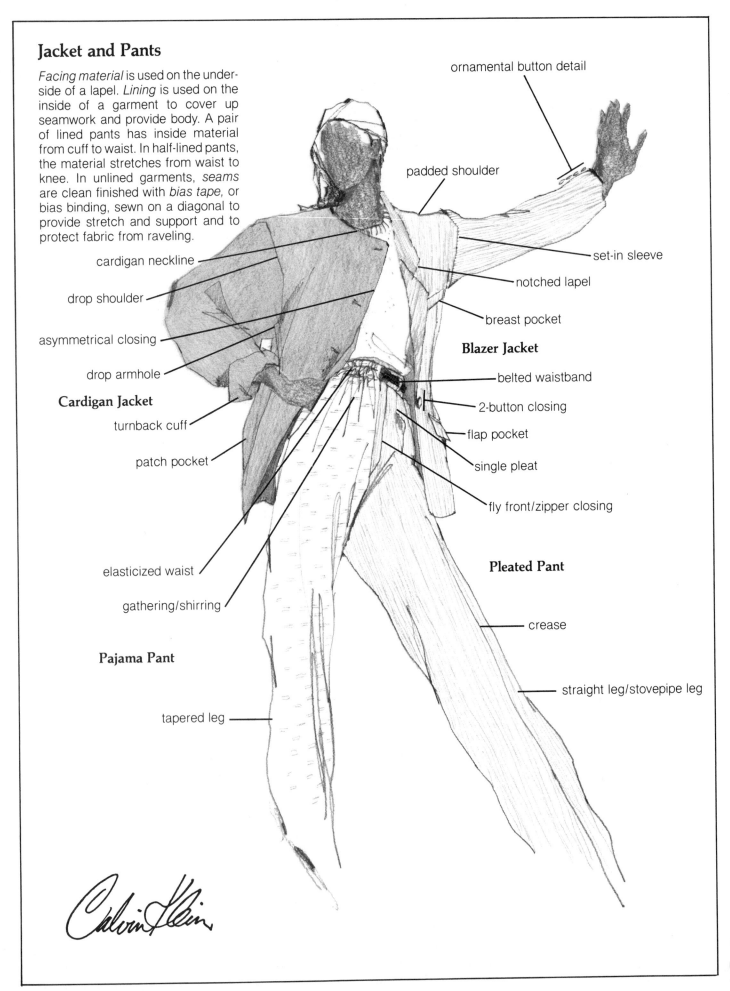

ornamental button detail

padded shoulder

set-in sleeve

notched lapel

breast pocket

cardigan neckline

drop shoulder

asymmetrical closing

drop armhole

Blazer Jacket

belted waistband

2-button closing

flap pocket

single pleat

fly front/zipper closing

Cardigan Jacket

turnback cuff

patch pocket

Pleated Pant

elasticized waist

gathering/shirring

crease

Pajama Pant

straight leg/stovepipe leg

tapered leg

Blouse and Skirt

The blouse and the skirt shown here are composites. Skirts can be secured at the waist with a *belt, tie, zipper, hook* and *eye,* or *buttons.*

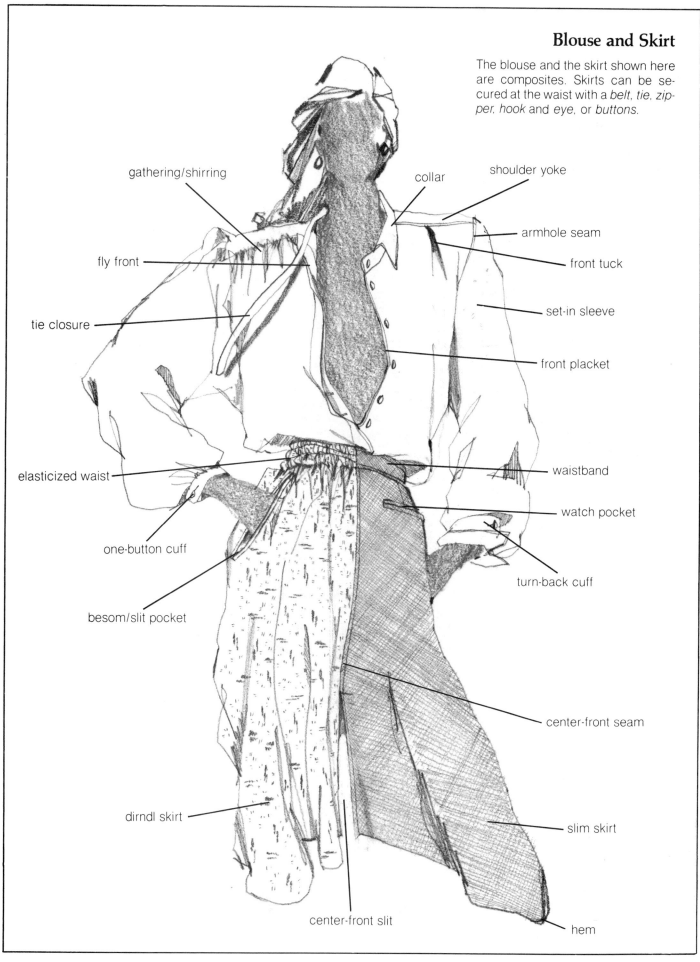

gathering/shirring

collar

shoulder yoke

armhole seam

front tuck

fly front

set-in sleeve

tie closure

front placket

elasticized waist

waistband

watch pocket

one-button cuff

turn-back cuff

besom/slit pocket

center-front seam

dirndl skirt

slim skirt

center-front slit

hem

Women's Apparel

Dress

This composite dress, or *gown,* has a *camisole top.* A dress hanging straight from the shoulders is a *chemise.* Some dresses have a fitted or shaped piece at the shoulder called a *yoke. Bratelles* are ornamental suspenderlike straps. Dresses are stored on hangers by means of *keepers, carriers, riders, loops* or *hangers.*

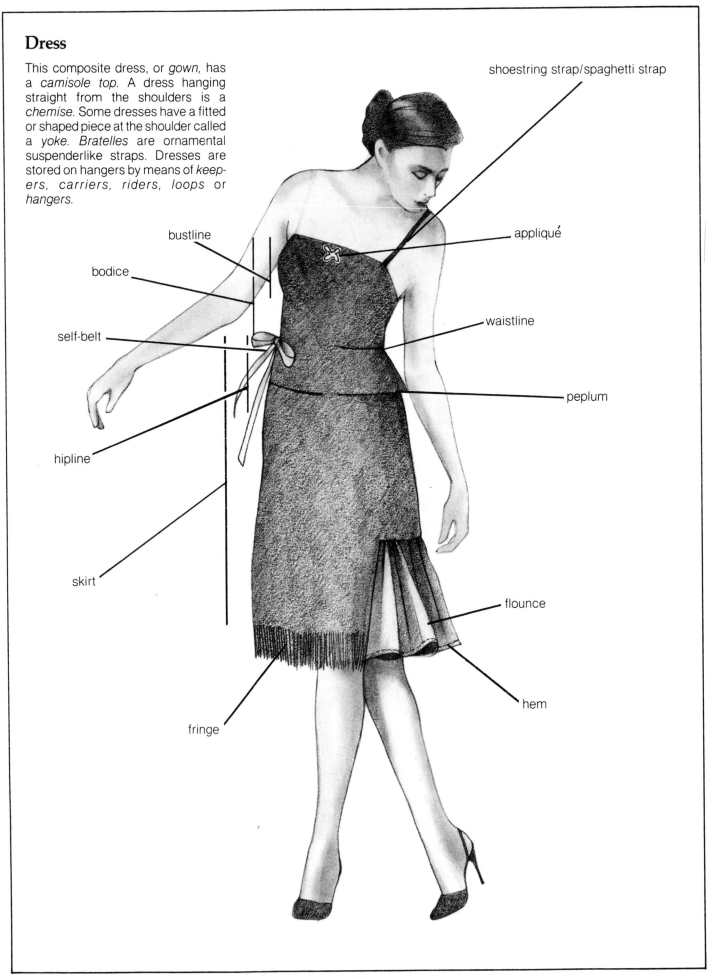

shoestring strap/spaghetti strap

bustline

bodice

self-belt

hipline

skirt

fringe

appliqué

waistline

peplum

flounce

hem

Sweater

A *crew neck sweater* is a pullover with a high, round neck. A *turtleneck* has a high neck that turns back over itself. A sweater with a neck opening that stretches from shoulder to shoulder is a *boat neck,* or *bateau neck.* A sweater without arms is a *vest,* or *knit vest.*

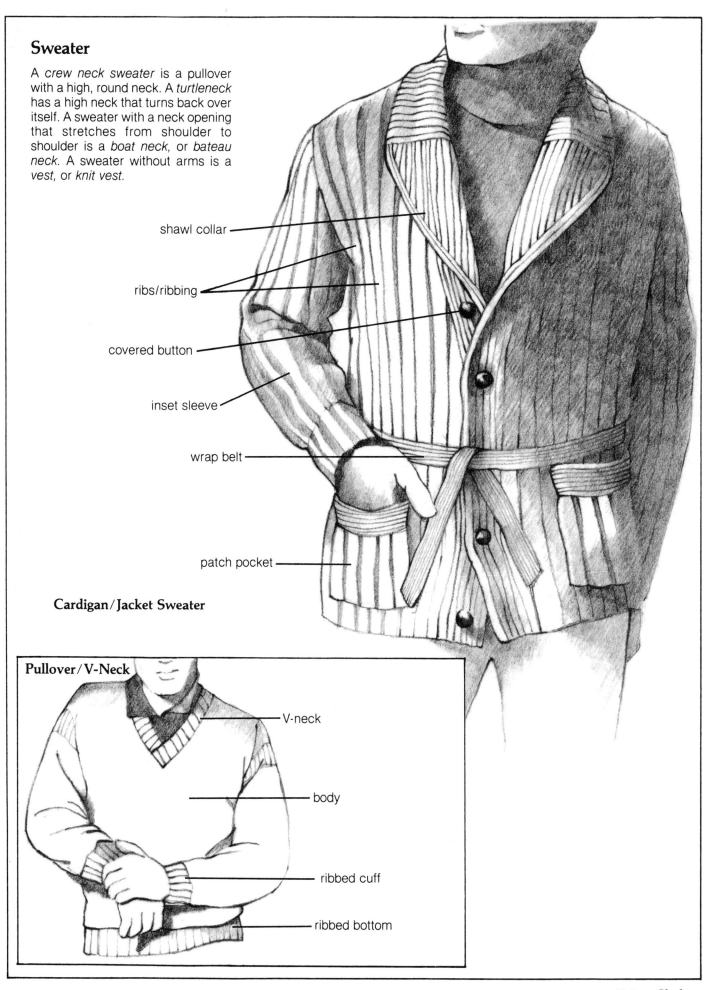

shawl collar

ribs/ribbing

covered button

inset sleeve

wrap belt

patch pocket

Cardigan/Jacket Sweater

Pullover/V-Neck

V-neck

body

ribbed cuff

ribbed bottom

Unisex Clothing

Outerwear

The type of combination *overcoat* and *raincoat* shown here usually has a *button-out* or *zip-out robe lining* which provides warmth in cold weather. It also has a *storm shield* on the back, ornamental *'D' rings* hanging from the back of the belt and sometimes a *throat latch* strap around the collar.

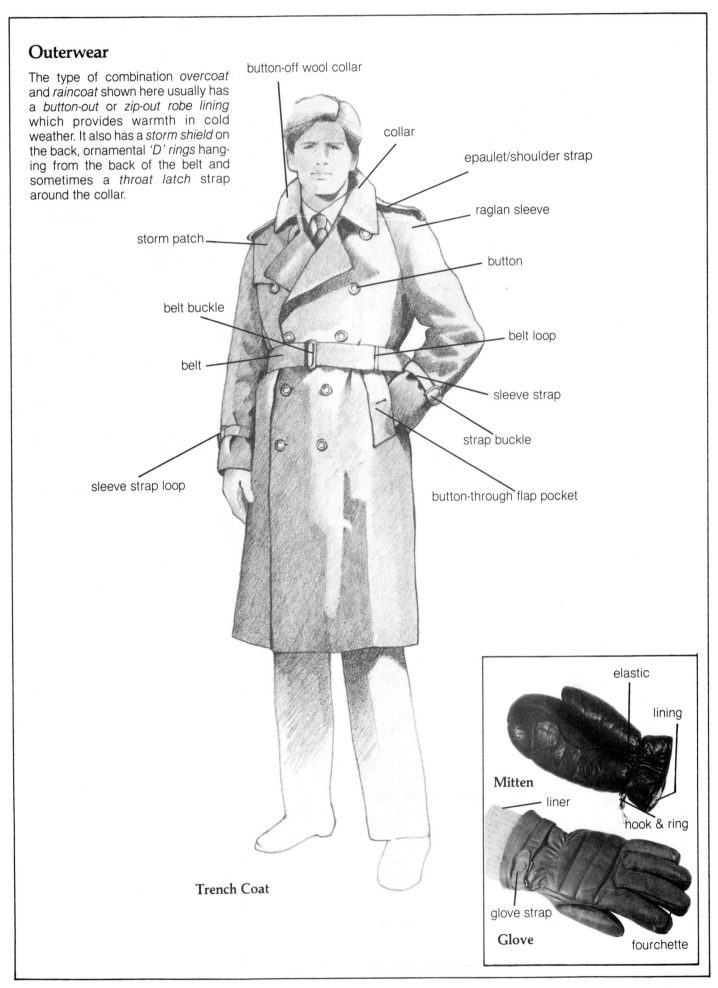

button-off wool collar

collar

epaulet/shoulder strap

raglan sleeve

button

belt loop

sleeve strap

strap buckle

button-through flap pocket

storm patch

belt buckle

belt

sleeve strap loop

Trench Coat

elastic

lining

Mitten

liner

hook & ring

glove strap

Glove

fourchette

Outerwear

Fur pelts used in apparel by *furriers* are first *dressed*, or cleaned, then fleshed, stretched and tanned. The furry parts of a pelt's facial hair are called *gills*.

hood

outer shell

raglan sleeve

drawstring closure/leather tab

map pocket

double slide zipper

bellows breast pocket

zipper pull

snap closure

hand warming slot

placket

bellows cargo pocket

Velcro cuff closure

hem

cloth lining

Parka / Anorak

Pelt

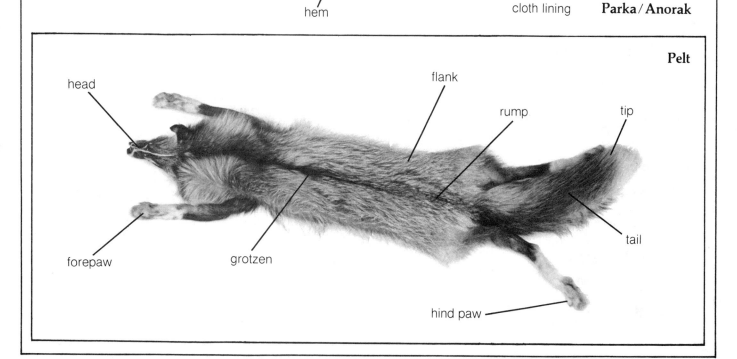

flank

head

rump

tip

forepaw

grotzen

tail

hind paw

Unisex Clothing

Men's Hats

Hats are *styled,* or *blocked,* by a *hat-maker* or *hatter.* Hats that have not been creased have an *open crown.* Some hats have *plastic linings.*

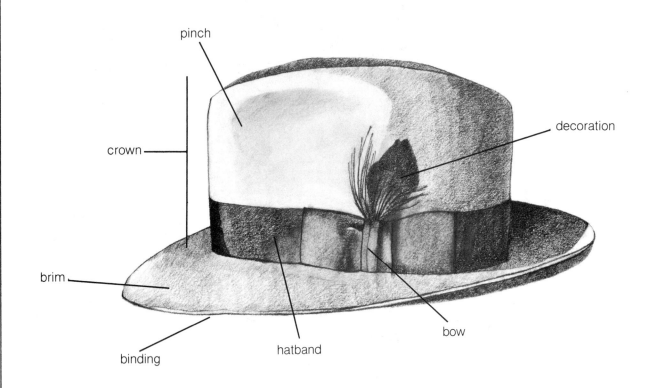

pinch

crown

decoration

brim

hatband

bow

binding

Cowboy Hat/Ten-Gallon Hat

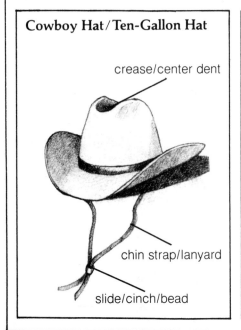

crease/center dent

chin strap/lanyard

slide/cinch/bead

Beret

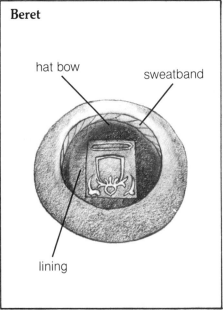

hat bow

sweatband

lining

Cap

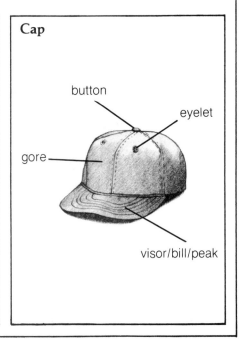

button

eyelet

gore

visor/bill/peak

Women's Hats

Women's hats are designed, made and sold by *milliners*. *Malines*, or stiff, fine *netting*, is often used as a veil. *Buckles, sequins, plastic fruit, fabric flowers, buttons, tassels* and *braids* are among the many items used as decorative *trimming*. Brimless, close-fitting hats include a *toque*, a *cloche*, and a *turban*. A *picture hat* has a broad flexible brim and is often decorated with trimming. A shallow, round hat with vertical sides is a *pillbox*. A netlike hat or part of a hat or the fabric that holds or covers the back of a woman's hair is a *snood*.

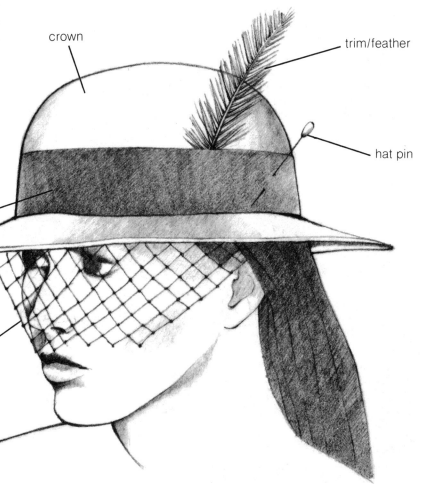

crown

trim/feather

hat pin

hatband

brim

veil

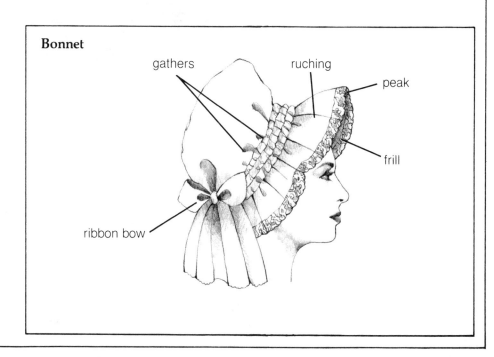

Bonnet

gathers

ruching

peak

frill

ribbon bow

Headwear

Man's Shoe

A shoe consists of a *bottom*, or heel and sole, an *inner sole*, or *insole*, and an *upper*. Shoes like the one shown here, in which the flaps fold over the tongue or vamp, are *bluchers*. Shoes without this construction are *barrels*. A step-in shoe without laces is a *loafer*, whereas a *moccasin* has neither laces nor a heel. The fringed leather decoration on some shoes that covers the laces is the *kiltie*.

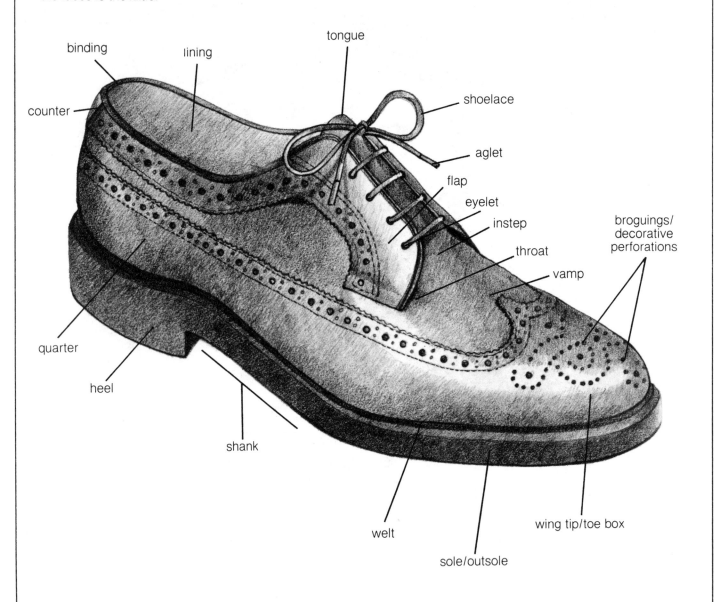

binding

lining

tongue

counter

shoelace

aglet

flap

eyelet

instep

throat

vamp

broguings/
decorative
perforations

quarter

heel

shank

welt

sole/outsole

wing tip/toe box

Woman's Shoe

A shoe with an open front is an *open-toed shoe,* whereas a shoe with an open back, held on by a strap, is a *slingback,* or *sling shoe.* The *high-heel shoe* seen here is similar to a *pump* in that it grips both the toe and the heel. A high, thin heel is a *spiked,* or *stiletto, heel.* A shoe with a thick layer between the *inner sole* and the outsole is a *platform.*

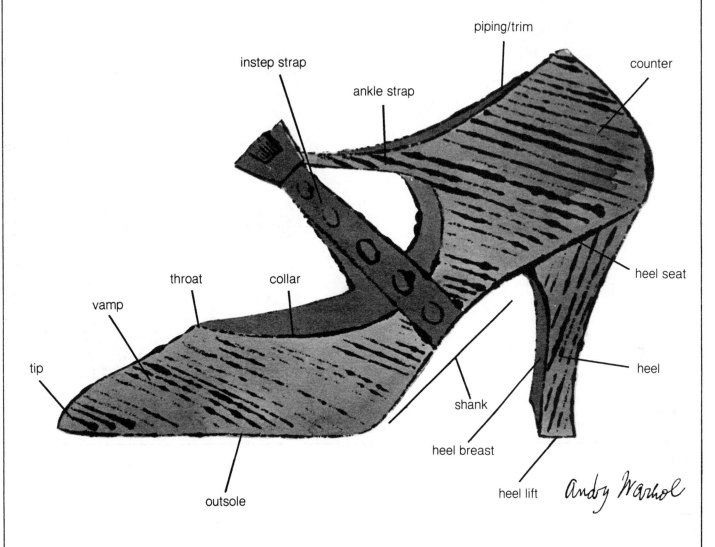

piping/trim

counter

instep strap

ankle strap

heel seat

throat

collar

vamp

heel

tip

shank

heel breast

heel lift

Andy Warhol

outsole

Footwear

Boot and Sandal

The upper section of a boot, called the *shaft*, may extend from ankle to knee. The lower section is called the *foot*. Many boots have a contoured steel *shank*, located between outsole and *insole*, to provide support for the arch area. A *thong* is a type of sandal in which the strap comes up between the big toe and the toe next to it.

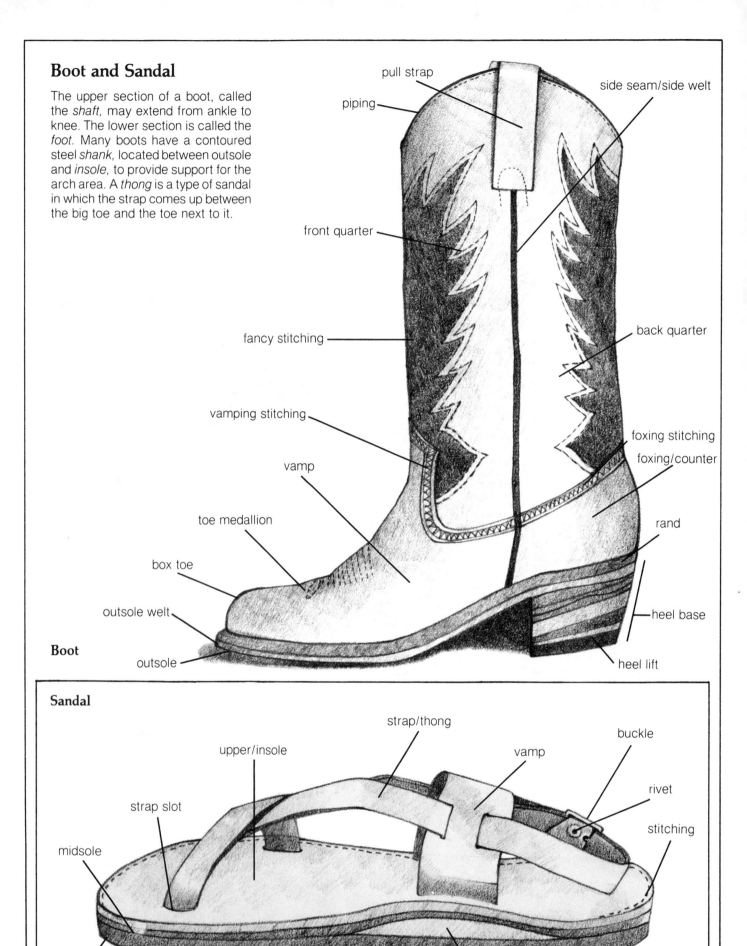

pull strap

piping

side seam/side welt

front quarter

fancy stitching

back quarter

vamping stitching

foxing stitching

foxing/counter

vamp

rand

toe medallion

box toe

outsole welt

heel base

Boot

outsole

heel lift

Sandal

strap/thong

buckle

upper/insole

vamp

strap slot

rivet

midsole

stitching

crepe sole

arch cookie/scaphoid pad

Shoe Accessories

Shoes can be protected in wet weather by *rubbers, rain boots* or *galoshes.* Socks, or *hose,* which extend to the ankle are *ankle socks,* whereas *knee socks* reach to the knee. *Support* hose have a higher *denier,* or mesh count, than regular hose, which provides additional support for the foot and leg. *Peds* are liners that cover the toes, sole and heel. *Boot hooks,* which fit into *boot loops,* help pull boots on, while V-shaped *bootjacks* hold the boot heel for easier removal. *Athletic socks,* or *sweat socks,* absorb perspiration. Shapeless *tube socks* mold to any foot shape.

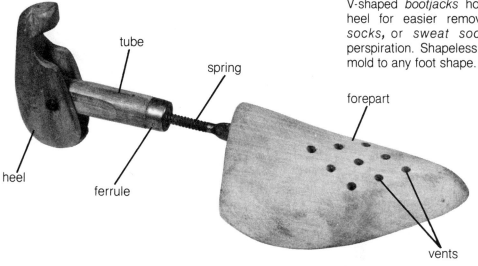

tube

spring

forepart

heel

ferrule

vents

Shoe Tree

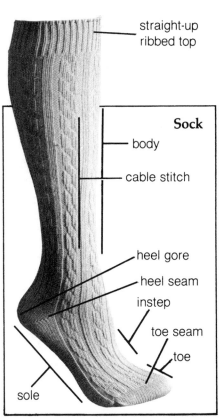

straight-up ribbed top

Sock

body

cable stitch

heel gore

heel seam

instep

toe seam

toe

sole

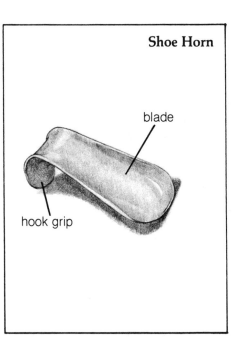

Shoe Horn

blade

hook grip

Fasteners

Heavy-duty hook-and-eye closures are called *hook and bars*. In a *cinch fastener*, a *strap* is pulled through two *rings* then back through the second ring to fasten. A *frog* consists of an intricately knotted *cord loop* through which a button is hooked.

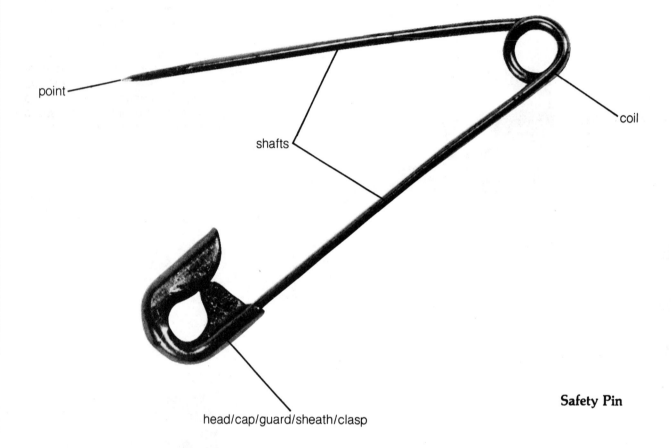

point

shafts

coil

head/cap/guard/sheath/clasp

Safety Pin

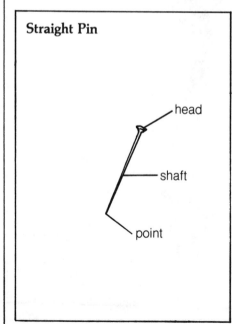

Straight Pin

head

shaft

point

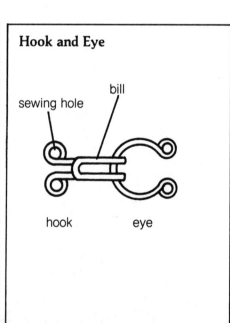

Hook and Eye

sewing hole

bill

hook

eye

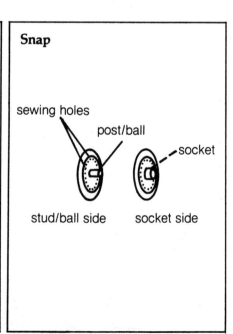

Snap

sewing holes

post/ball

socket

stud/ball side

socket side

Closures

A *divider* within the zipper slide separates teeth when it is moved downward. Some zippers have a *synthetic coil* rather than teeth. A *pull ring* is occasionally attached to the slide for decorative purposes. A *two-way zipper* can be opened from either end, while an *invisible zipper* is concealed when closed and appears to be a *seam*.

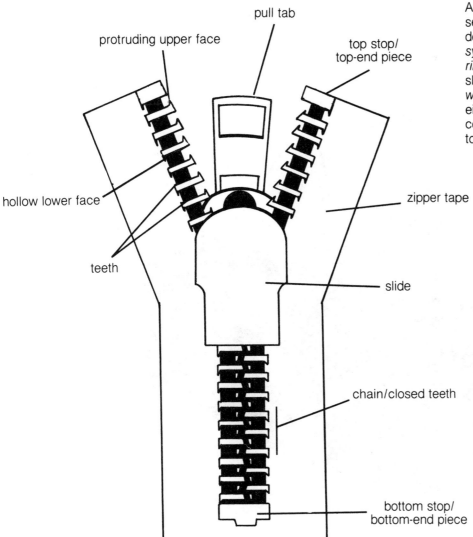

- pull tab
- protruding upper face
- top stop/ top-end piece
- zipper tape
- hollow lower face
- teeth
- slide
- chain/closed teeth
- bottom stop/ bottom-end piece

Zipper/Slide Fastener

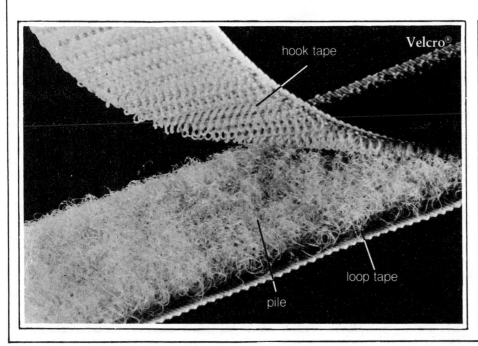

Velcro®

- hook tape
- loop tape
- pile

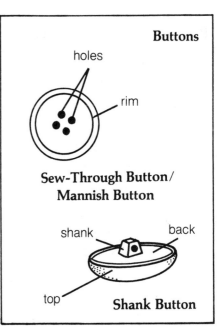

Buttons

- holes
- rim

Sew-Through Button/ Mannish Button

- shank
- back
- top

Shank Button

Fasteners

Shavers

A *straight razor* has a single, long blade which folds into a *handle*. It is sharpened on a long strip of leather called a *strop*. Other, older barbering equipment includes *shaving brushes* and *shaving mugs*. A *safety razor* has two *wings* on the *head* which are opened by a screw at the base of the handle. Bleeding from shaving cuts or nicks can be stopped with a *styptic pencil*.

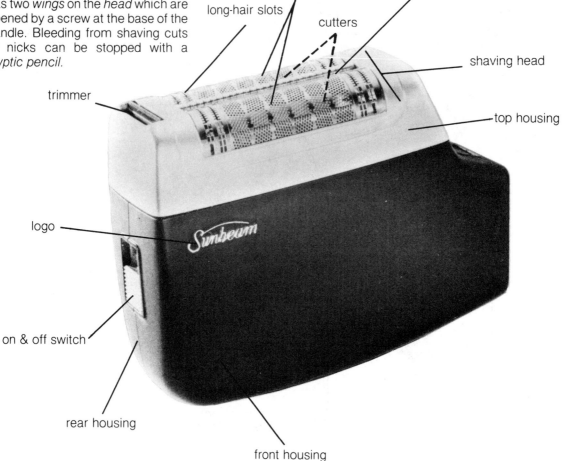

long-hair slots

combs

cutters

tension bar

trimmer

shaving head

top housing

logo

on & off switch

rear housing

front housing

Electric Razor

Razor Blade/Double-Edged Blade

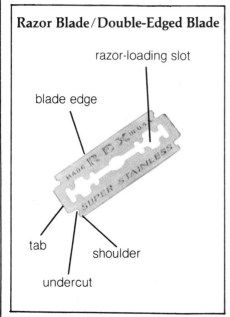

razor-loading slot

blade edge

tab

shoulder

undercut

Blade Injector

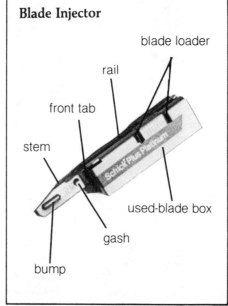

blade loader

rail

front tab

stem

used-blade box

gash

bump

Disposable Razor

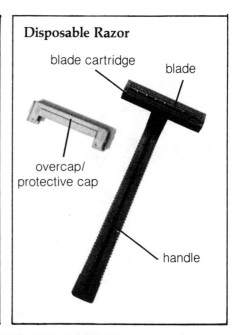

blade cartridge

blade

overcap/ protective cap

handle

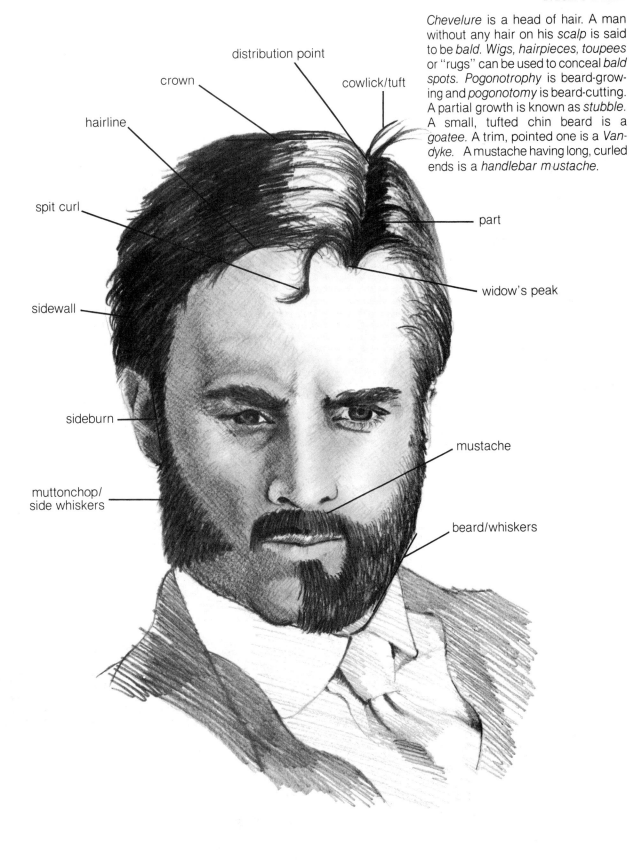

Men's Hair

Chevelure is a head of hair. A man without any hair on his *scalp* is said to be *bald*. *Wigs, hairpieces, toupees* or "rugs" can be used to conceal *bald spots*. *Pogonotrophy* is beard-growing and *pogonotomy* is beard-cutting. A partial growth is known as *stubble*. A small, tufted chin beard is a *goatee*. A trim, pointed one is a *Van-dyke*. A mustache having long, curled ends is a *handlebar mustache*.

distribution point

crown

cowlick/tuft

hairline

spit curl

part

sidewall

widow's peak

sideburn

mustache

muttonchop/
side whiskers

beard/whiskers

Hairstyles and Facial Hair

Hair Grooming Implements

Among other attachments available for use with a *pro-style dryer* are combs, brush and an *air-flow nozzle,* to limit the amount of hot air.

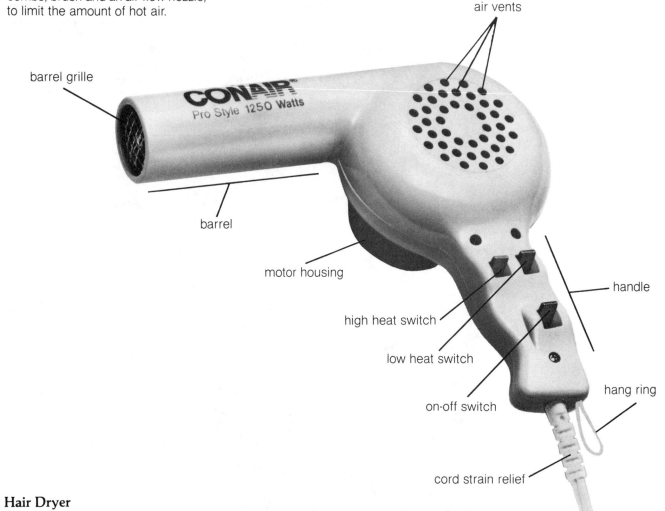

air vents

barrel grille

barrel

motor housing

high heat switch

low heat switch

on-off switch

handle

hang ring

cord strain relief

Hair Dryer

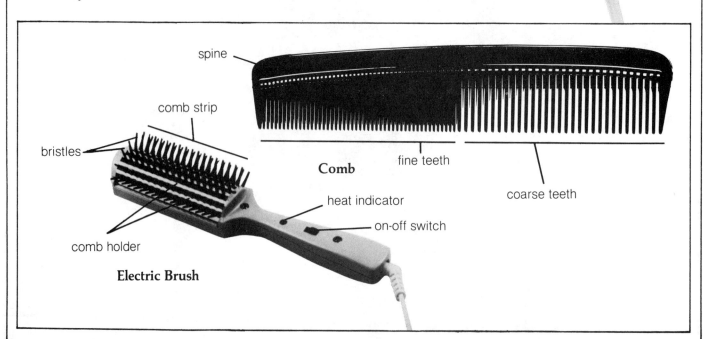

spine

comb strip

bristles

fine teeth

Comb

coarse teeth

heat indicator

on-off switch

comb holder

Electric Brush

Women's Hair

A small portion of hair in a woman's *hairdo,* or *coiffure,* is a *lock. Bouffant* is a puffed-out hairdo. *Teased,* or *back-combed, hair* is achieved by taking hold of a strand and pushing the short hairs toward the scalp with a comb. A braid on the back of the head is a *pigtail.* Hair that turns inward at the end, rather than outward, is a *pageboy.* A long piece of store-bought hair clipped to real hair is a *fall.*

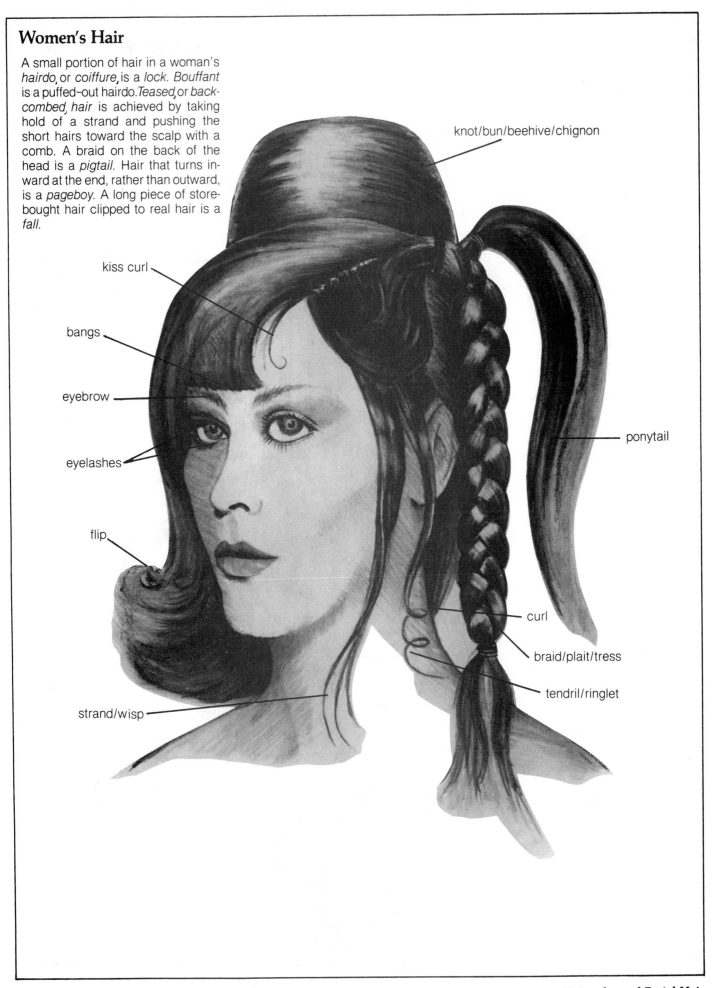

knot/bun/beehive/chignon

kiss curl

bangs

eyebrow

eyelashes

flip

ponytail

curl

braid/plait/tress

tendril/ringlet

strand/wisp

Hairstyles and Facial Hair

Hairstyling Implements

A curling iron is used to curl a *strand* of hair or to straighten it. Hair clips and bobby pins, which may be long or short, can be used to secure a roller while hair is being set. The roller shown here, however, is *self-clasping*. Barrettes, *combs, hair ribbons, headbands* and *hair bands* hold hair in place or serve as decorative *hair ornaments*. Professional *hairdressers* use *permanent rods* and *papers, applicator bottles* filled with *permanent lotion, setting lotion, rinse* or *dye*, plastic *caps, dryers* and *infrared lamps* to treat and style *hairdos*.

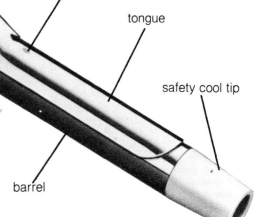

on-off switch

thumb press

power cord

strain relief

thermal dot

tongue

main housing

safety cool tip

stand

barrel

Curling Iron

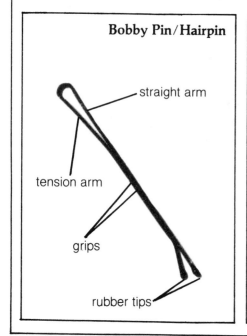

Bobby Pin/Hairpin

straight arm

tension arm

grips

rubber tips

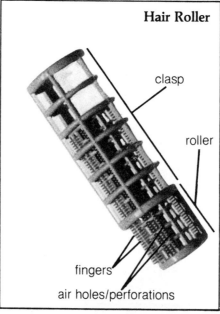

Hair Roller

clasp

roller

fingers

air holes/perforations

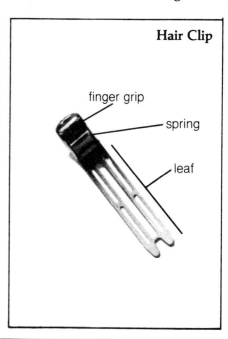

Hair Clip

finger grip

spring

leaf

Toothbrush

The stimulator tip on a toothbrush fits in what is called a *hang-up hole.* Teeth can also be cleaned with *dental floss,* a waxed string, and *high-pressure water-spray units.* Nails can be smoothed with an *emery board,* a cardboard strip covered with *powdered emery,* or a *nail file.*

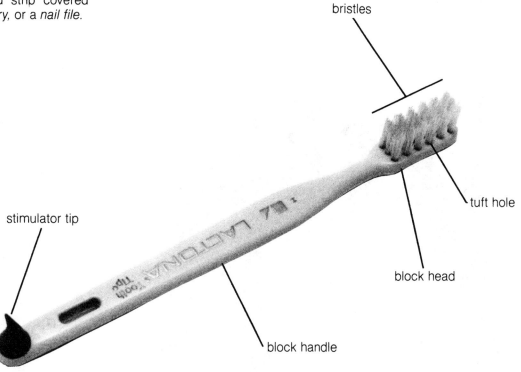

bristles

tuft hole

stimulator tip

block head

block handle

Toothbrush

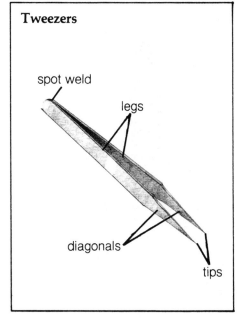

Tweezers

spot weld

legs

diagonals

tips

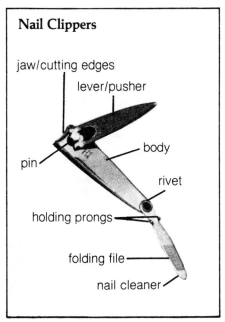

Nail Clippers

jaw/cutting edges

lever/pusher

body

pin

rivet

holding prongs

folding file

nail cleaner

Makeup

A skin-colored *concealer,* or *coverup,* can be used to cover blemishes or undesirable shadows under the eyes. *Pancake makeup* is a thick face powder used by actors and actresses as a foundation. Makeup can be removed with a *cleansing cream* or *cold cream.*

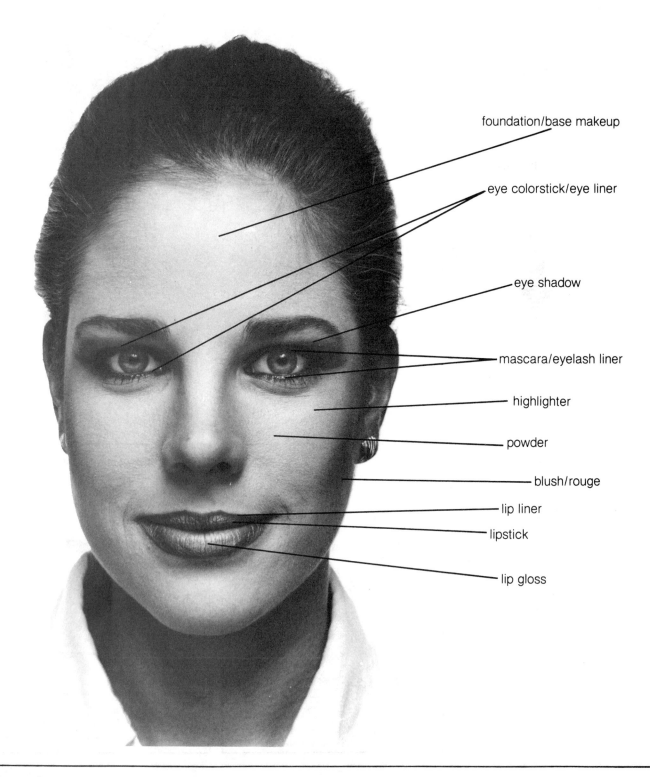

foundation/base makeup

eye colorstick/eye liner

eye shadow

mascara/eyelash liner

highlighter

powder

blush/rouge

lip liner

lipstick

lip gloss

Colored *nail polish* is often used to "paint" fingernails and toenails. In addition to those beauty products shown here, there are *scents*, such as *perfume*, applied by women to *pulse points; bath oils; body oils; moisturizers* and *lotions*. Men use *colognes* or *after-shave lotions*.

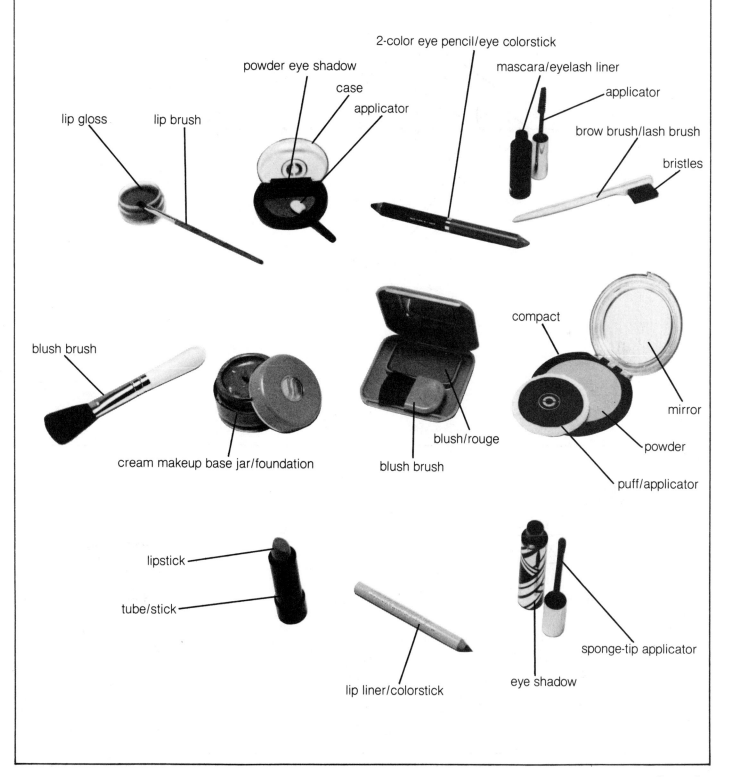

2-color eye pencil/eye colorstick

powder eye shadow

case

applicator

mascara/eyelash liner

applicator

lip gloss   lip brush

brow brush/lash brush

bristles

compact

blush brush

mirror

cream makeup base jar/foundation

blush/rouge

blush brush

powder

puff/applicator

lipstick

tube/stick

sponge-tip applicator

eye shadow

lip liner/colorstick

Gemstone

The shades of color a gemstone gives off are called *fire.* A matched set of jewelry, or *parure,* often includes a necklace, earrings and a *brooch.* A *cameo* is a gem on which a relief carving has been made. Nonprecious *costume jewelry* is made to simulate its precious counterparts. The end of a *cuff link* that is passed through the buttonhole and fastened is called a *wing-back,* or *airplane-back.*

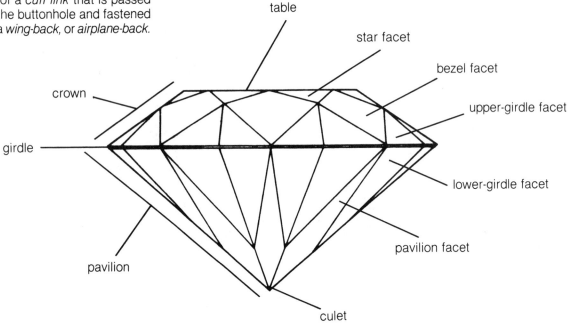

table

star facet

bezel facet

upper-girdle facet

crown

girdle

lower-girdle facet

pavilion facet

pavilion

culet

Cut Gemstone

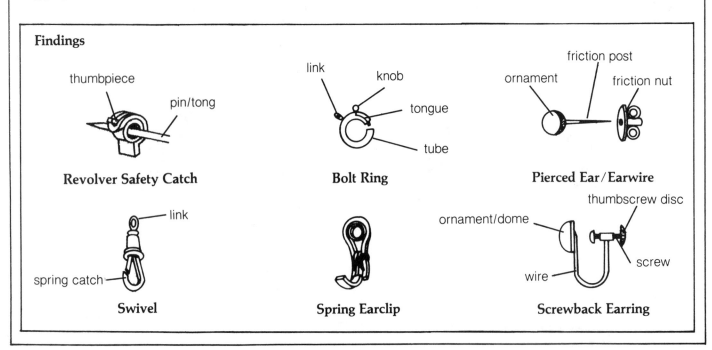

Findings

thumbpiece

pin/tong

Revolver Safety Catch

link

knob

tongue

tube

Bolt Ring

ornament

friction post

friction nut

Pierced Ear / Earwire

link

spring catch

Swivel

Spring Earclip

ornament/dome

thumbscrew disc

screw

wire

Screwback Earring

Ring

A *lavaliere* is a pendant worn on a chain as a necklace. A *charm* is a trinket worn on a bracelet or necklace, often having personal or symbolic meaning. An *ouch* is a brooch or a setting for a precious stone. *Spangles* are glittering pieces of metal used on clothing for decoration. A *riviere* is a multi-stringed necklace containing many precious stones.

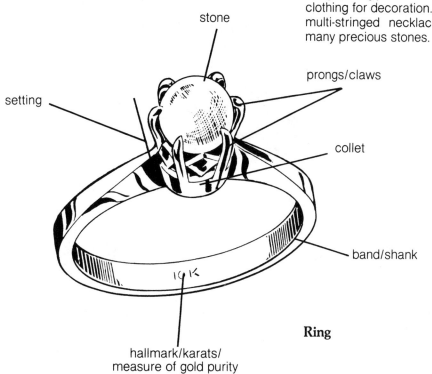

stone

prongs/claws

setting

collet

band/shank

hallmark/karats/
measure of gold purity

Ring

Pendant

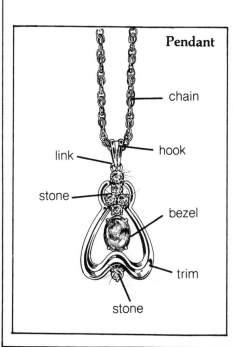

chain

link

hook

stone

bezel

trim

stone

Pieces

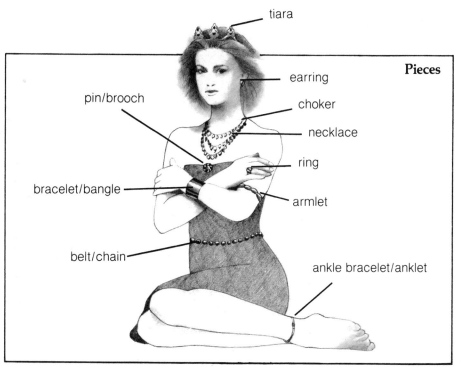

tiara

earring

pin/brooch

choker

necklace

ring

bracelet/bangle

armlet

belt/chain

ankle bracelet/anklet

Jewelry

Watches

The digital display on this watch can indicate date, seconds, time in a different time zone, and it can perform *stopwatch* functions. An extremely accurate timepiece is called a *chronometer*. A watchband, or *strap*, is attached to the case by *push-pins*, or *spring-bars*.

link

watchband/bracelet

zero mark

case

dial/face

minute hand

hour hand

protective shoulder

crown

Liquid Crystal Display (LCD)

LCD second time zone display control

LCD second and date display control

elapsed time bezel

luminous indices/markers

Wristwatch

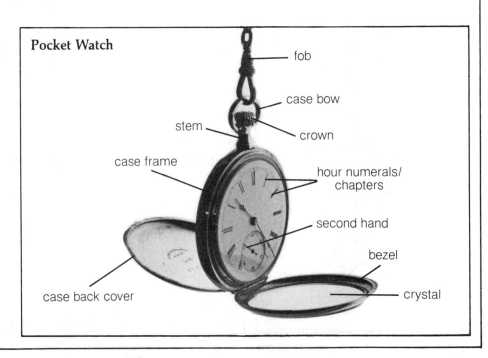

Pocket Watch

fob

case bow

stem

crown

case frame

hour numerals/chapters

second hand

bezel

case back cover

crystal

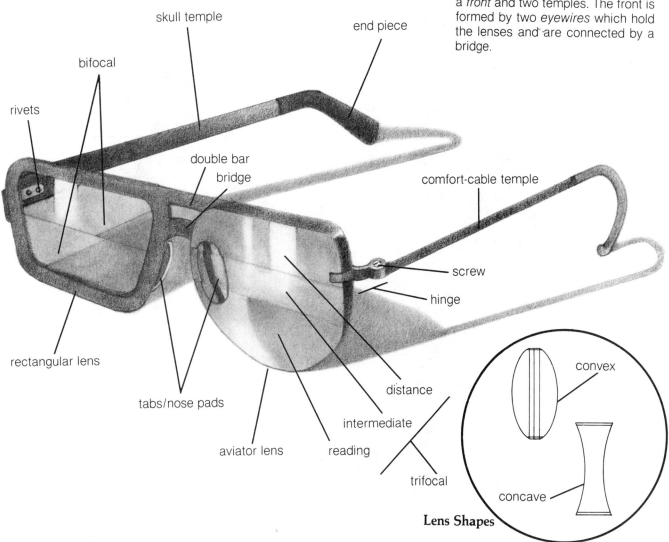

Eyeglasses

This is a composite pair of eyeglasses, or *spectacles*. The *frame* consists of a *front* and two temples. The front is formed by two *eyewires* which hold the lenses and are connected by a bridge.

skull temple

end piece

bifocal

rivets

double bar

bridge

comfort-cable temple

screw

hinge

rectangular lens

tabs/nose pads

aviator lens

reading

distance

intermediate

trifocal

Lens Shapes

convex

concave

Monocle

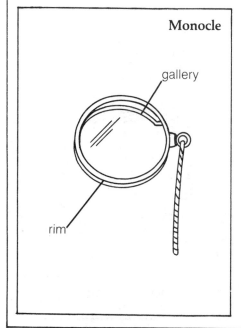

gallery

rim

Lorgnette

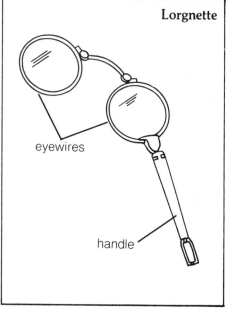

eyewires

handle

Contact Lens

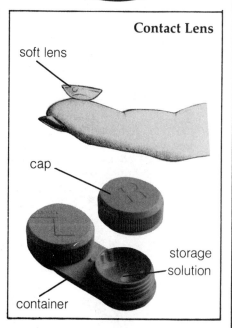

soft lens

cap

storage solution

container

Handbag

A handbag can also be referred to as a *pocketbook* or *purse*. A bag with no handles is a *clutch*. *East-west* describes a handbag which is wider than it is long. A *north-south* bag has a long, narrow shape. The metal ornaments and closures on bags are collectively called *hardware* or *fittings*.

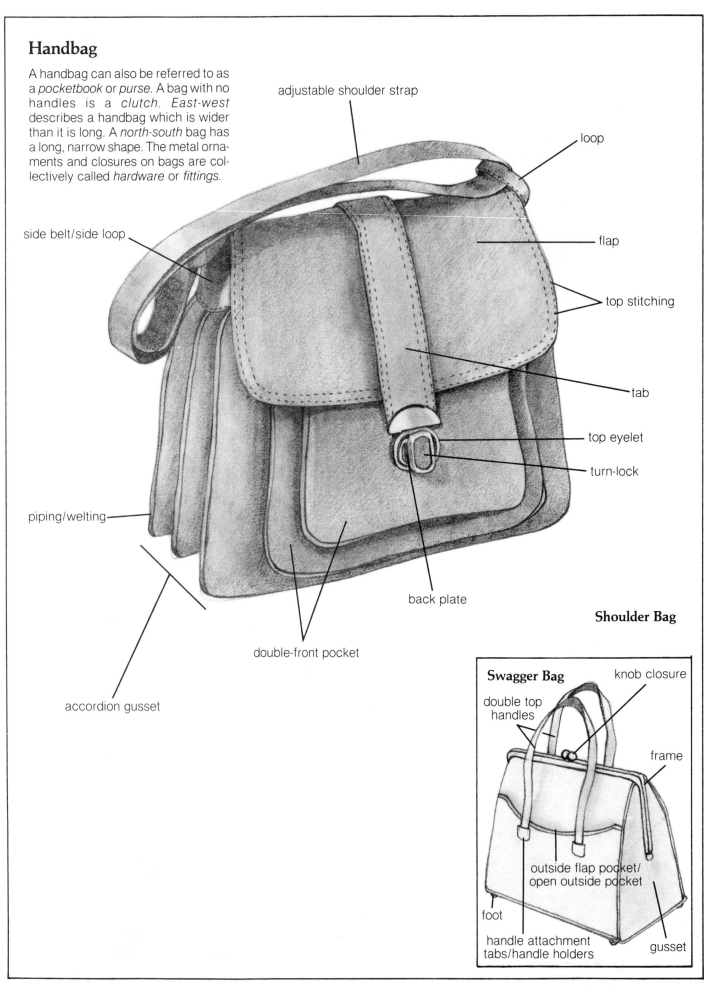

adjustable shoulder strap

loop

side belt/side loop

flap

top stitching

tab

top eyelet

turn-lock

piping/welting

back plate

double-front pocket

accordion gusset

Shoulder Bag

Swagger Bag

knob closure

double top handles

frame

outside flap pocket/ open outside pocket

foot

handle attachment tabs/handle holders

gusset

Wallet / Billfold

A wallet's exterior covering is called the *cover*. Women's wallets often have a *coin purse* within and a *tab closing* on the outside. *Photo holders* that unfold and become a long strip are called *accordion windows*.

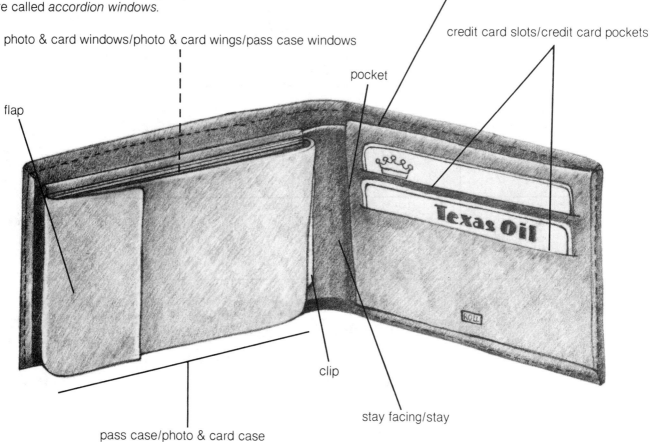

photo & card windows/photo & card wings/pass case windows

flap

bill compartment/currency pocket

credit card slots/credit card pockets

pocket

Texas Oil

clip

pass case/photo & card case

stay facing/stay

Checkbook Clutch

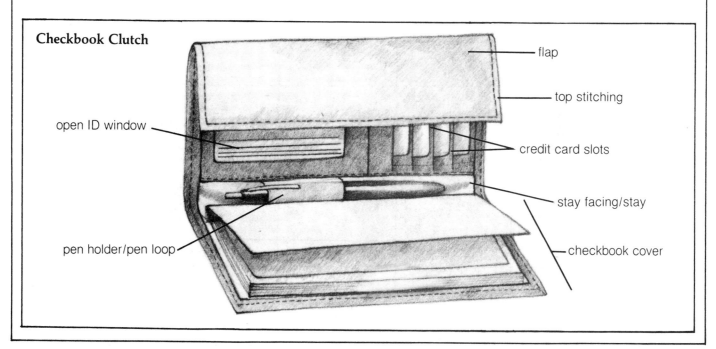

open ID window

pen holder/pen loop

flap

top stitching

credit card slots

stay facing/stay

checkbook cover

Money

United States paper currency in circulation today consists primarily of *Federal Reserve Notes* or "greenbacks" bearing a green seal, and a few *United States Notes* (mainly $100 bills) bearing a red seal. Other types of paper money, such as *Silver Certificates*, have been withdrawn from circulation. *Bills* are printed from *engraved plates* on paper containing colored *fibers*. Notes damaged during printing are replaced by *star notes*. Money printed illegally and passed off as *legal tender* is called *counterfeit money*.

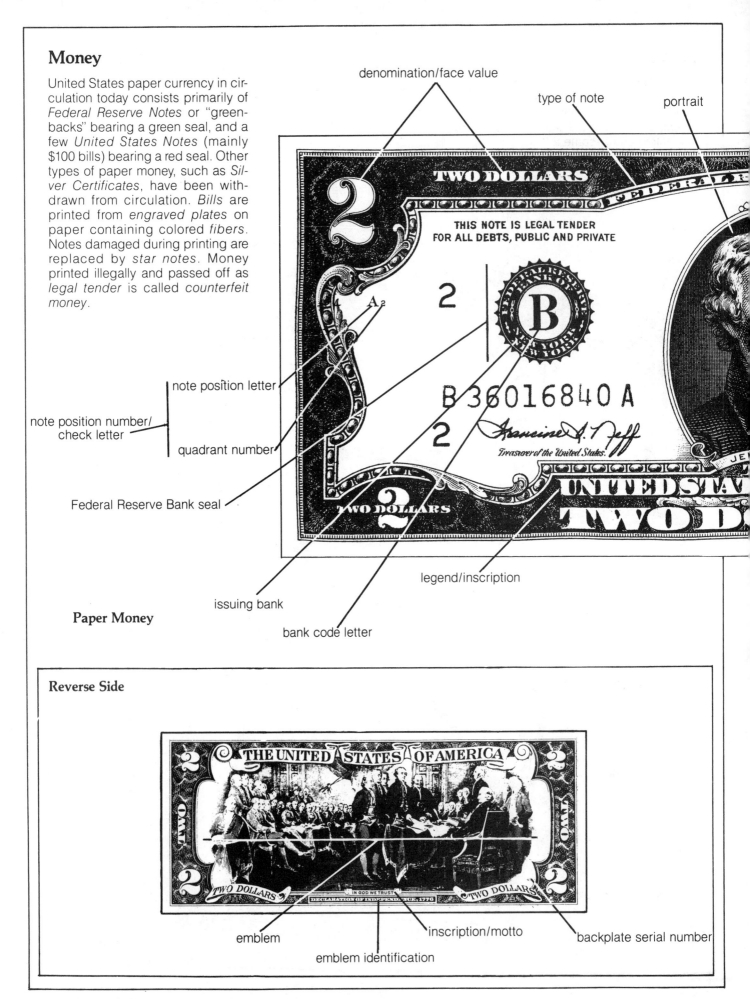

denomination/face value

type of note

portrait

TWO DOLLARS

THIS NOTE IS LEGAL TENDER
FOR ALL DEBTS, PUBLIC AND PRIVATE

note position letter

note position number/
check letter

quadrant number

Federal Reserve Bank seal

B 36016840 A

Francine I. Neff
Treasurer of the United States.

TWO DOLLARS

UNITED STA
TWO D

Paper Money

issuing bank

bank code letter

legend/inscription

Reverse Side

THE UNITED STATES OF AMERICA

IN GOD WE TRUST

DECLARATION OF INDEPENDENCE 1776

TWO DOLLARS

TWO DOLLARS

emblem

emblem identification

inscription/motto

backplate serial number

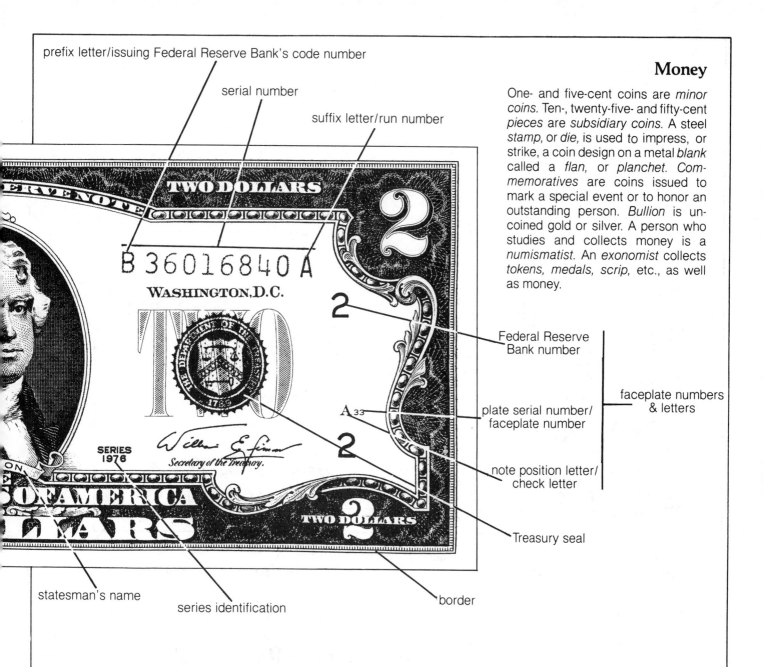

prefix letter/issuing Federal Reserve Bank's code number

serial number

suffix letter/run number

One- and five-cent coins are *minor coins.* Ten-, twenty-five- and fifty-cent *pieces* are *subsidiary coins.* A steel *stamp,* or *die,* is used to impress, or strike, a coin design on a metal *blank* called a *flan,* or *planchet. Commemoratives* are coins issued to mark a special event or to honor an outstanding person. *Bullion* is uncoined gold or silver. A person who studies and collects money is a *numismatist.* An *exonomist* collects *tokens, medals, scrip,* etc., as well as money.

Federal Reserve Bank number

faceplate numbers & letters

plate serial number/ faceplate number

note position letter/ check letter

Treasury seal

statesman's name

series identification

border

Coin

portrait

inscription

field

mint mark

motto

reeding/milled edge/serrations

symbolic date

Obverse Side/"Heads"/"Face"

main device

motto

designer's initials

denomination/ face value

Reverse Side/"Tails"/Back

Personal Banking

A check must be signed by the maker, and *endorsed* on the back by the payee to be valid. Banking at an automatic teller machine requires a bank card and a *Personal Identification Number*, or *PIN* number. *Cash machines* allow withdrawals and deposits to be made, while *banking centers* permit most banking functions to be performed.

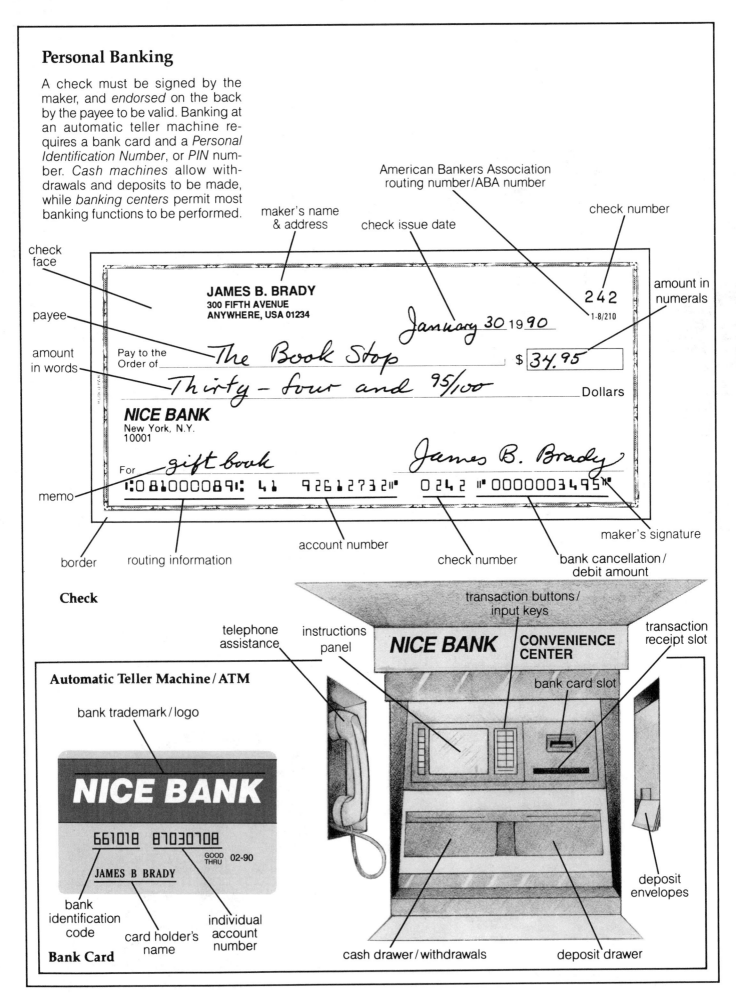

American Bankers Association routing number/ABA number

check issue date

check number

maker's name & address

check face

payee

amount in words

memo

border

routing information

account number

check number

amount in numerals

maker's signature

bank cancellation/ debit amount

JAMES B. BRADY
300 FIFTH AVENUE
ANYWHERE, USA 01234

January 30 19 90

242
1-8/210

Pay to the Order of *The Book Stop* $ 34.95

Thirty - four and 95/100 Dollars

NICE BANK
New York, N.Y.
10001

For *gift book*

James B. Brady

⑈081000089⑈ 41 926127321⑈ 0242 ⑈000000349 5⑈

Check

Automatic Teller Machine/ATM

bank trademark/logo

NICE BANK

661018   87030708

GOOD THRU 02-90

JAMES B BRADY

bank identification code

card holder's name

individual account number

Bank Card

transaction buttons/ input keys

telephone assistance

instructions panel

NICE BANK CONVENIENCE CENTER

transaction receipt slot

bank card slot

deposit envelopes

cash drawer/withdrawals

deposit drawer

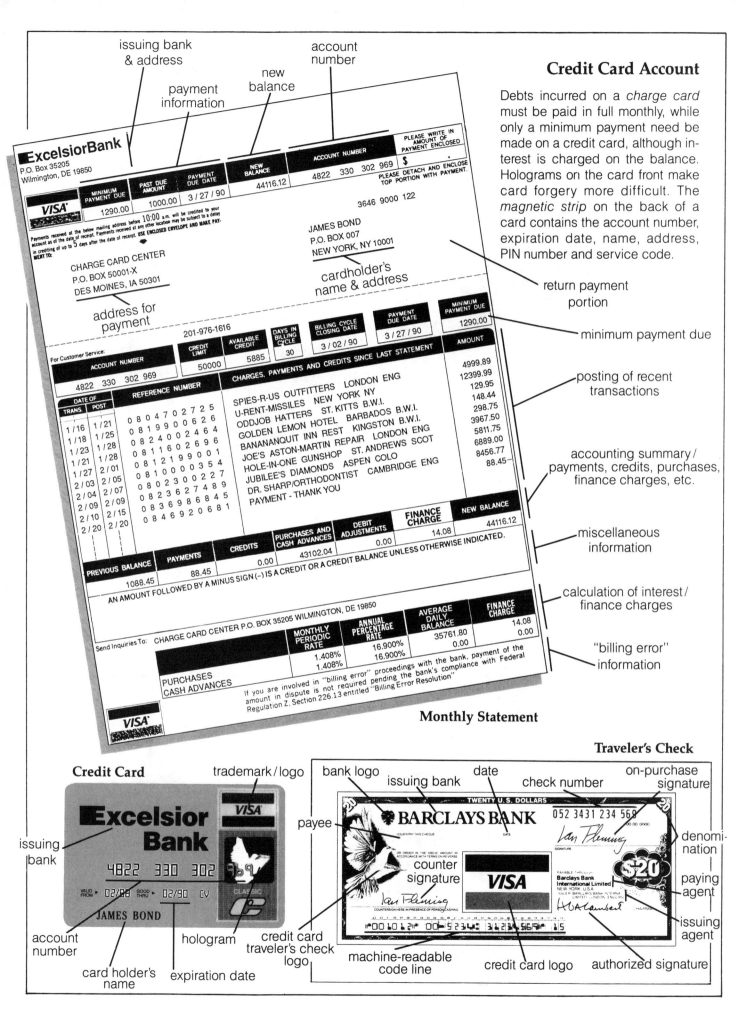

Credit Card Account

Debts incurred on a *charge card* must be paid in full monthly, while only a minimum payment need be made on a credit card, although interest is charged on the balance. Holograms on the card front make card forgery more difficult. The *magnetic strip* on the back of a card contains the account number, expiration date, name, address, PIN number and service code.

issuing bank & address

payment information

new balance

account number

return payment portion

minimum payment due

posting of recent transactions

accounting summary / payments, credits, purchases, finance charges, etc.

miscellaneous information

calculation of interest / finance charges

"billing error" information

address for payment

cardholder's name & address

Monthly Statement

Traveler's Check

Credit Card

trademark/logo

issuing bank

account number

card holder's name

hologram

expiration date

credit card traveler's check logo

bank logo

issuing bank

payee

counter signature

date

check number

on-purchase signature

machine-readable code line

credit card logo

authorized signature

denomination

paying agent

issuing agent

Cigar and Cigarette

The cigar wrapper, as well as the interior *binder,* is a spirally-rolled *leaf.* Cigars, or *"stogies,"* are stored in *humidors* to insure freshness. The residue of smoked tobacco is *ash.* The remains of a smoked cigar or cigarette is the *butt.* The abrasive striking surface or *friction strip* on which matches are struck is on the *back cover* of a matchbook.

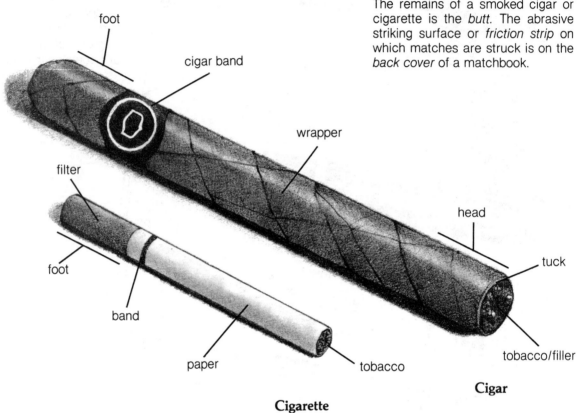

foot

cigar band

wrapper

filter

head

foot

tuck

band

paper

tobacco

tobacco/filler

Cigar

Cigarette

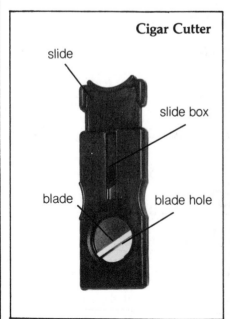

Cigar Cutter

slide

slide box

blade

blade hole

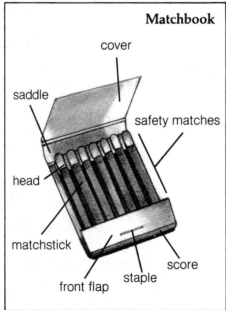

Matchbook

cover

saddle

safety matches

head

matchstick

front flap

staple

score

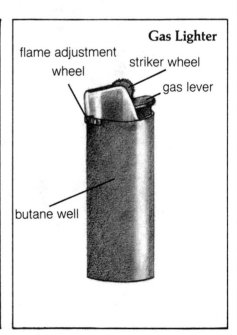

Gas Lighter

flame adjustment wheel

striker wheel

gas lever

butane well

Pipe

Pipe smoke is also called *lunt,* and un-smoked tobacco in the bottom of the bowl after smoking is called *dottle.* The pliable, tufted rod used to clean the inside of a pipe's stem is a *pipe cleaner.* Pipe tobacco is kept in a *pouch.* Some bowls are covered with a *pipe umbrella* or *bowl lid.* An Eastern pipe with a long, flexible tube by which the smoke is drawn through a jar of water and thus cooled is a *water pipe, hookah,* or *hubble-bubble.*

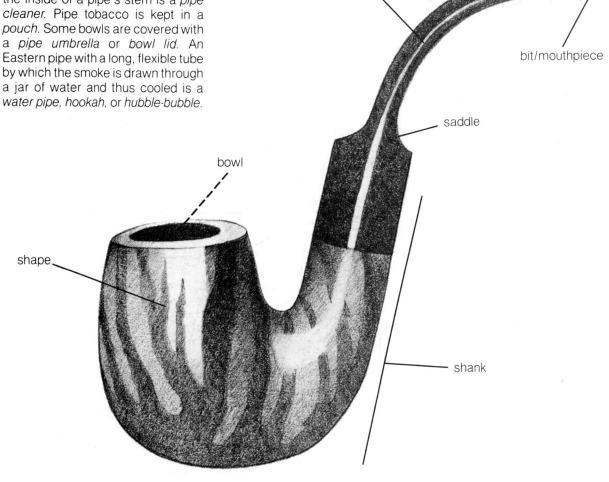

stem

bit/mouthpiece

saddle

bowl

shape

shank

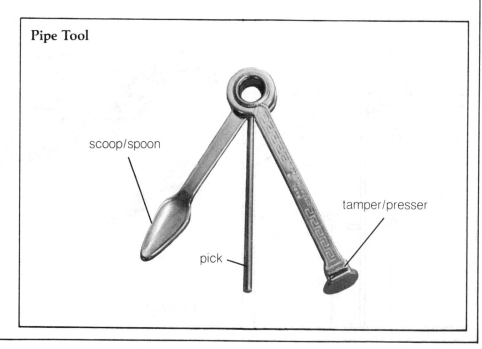

Pipe Tool

scoop/spoon

pick

tamper/presser

Smoking Materials

Umbrella

An umbrella's water-repellent *fabric* is attached to a *frame*, or *skeleton*. The specific points where the fabric is sewn to the skeleton are called *tacks*.

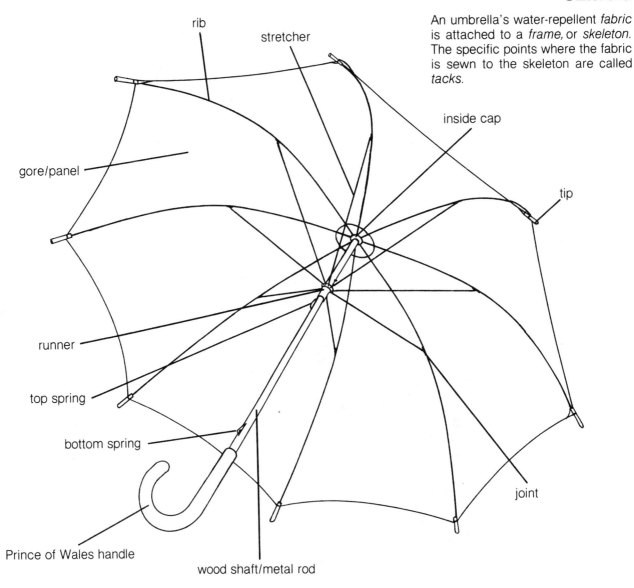

rib

stretcher

inside cap

tip

gore/panel

runner

top spring

bottom spring

joint

Prince of Wales handle

wood shaft/metal rod

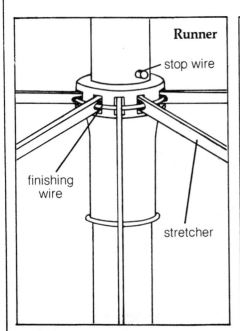

Runner

stop wire

finishing wire

stretcher

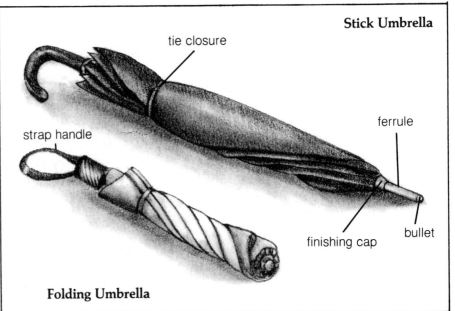

Stick Umbrella

tie closure

ferrule

strap handle

finishing cap

bullet

Folding Umbrella

The Home

To facilitate locating items found in the home, the objects in this section have been grouped according to where they are most likely to be encountered: living room, dining room, kitchen, bedroom, bathroom, playroom, utility room or yard.

The kitchen subsection, for example, includes implements for preparing food as well as appliances that make food preparation easier. In addition to identifying the parts of containers used to bring groceries into the kitchen, coverage includes all the terms used in the designing and packaging of food and kitchenware. Knowing the names for these components will surely change how the reader views his or her cereal box at the breakfast table in the future.

The terms for details of desk equipment, found in the playroom/utility room subsection, apply as well to office furnishings. The seven parts of a paper clip, for example, are valid wherever this unique little device is used.

Although a nursery is not included as a subsection, objects used for or by children—stroller, car seat, playpen, and swings—have been incorporated in the subcategory of yard equipment.

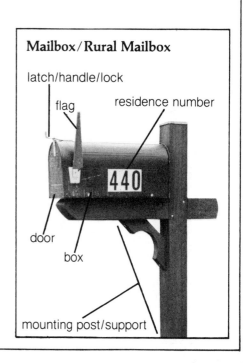

Mailbox/Rural Mailbox

latch/handle/lock

flag

residence number

440

door

box

mounting post/support

Fireplace

Many fireplaces have glass and metal *fire screens* to prevent heat loss and to keep sparks from flying into the room. Others have a low metal *fender* between the inner and outer hearth. A metal cover, used to shield a banked or dying fire, is called a *curfew*. Fireplace accessories include air-blowing *bellows, coal hods* and *wood carriers,* and *grates* or *heat exchangers* which can be used instead of andirons. A *firebrand* is a piece of burning wood.

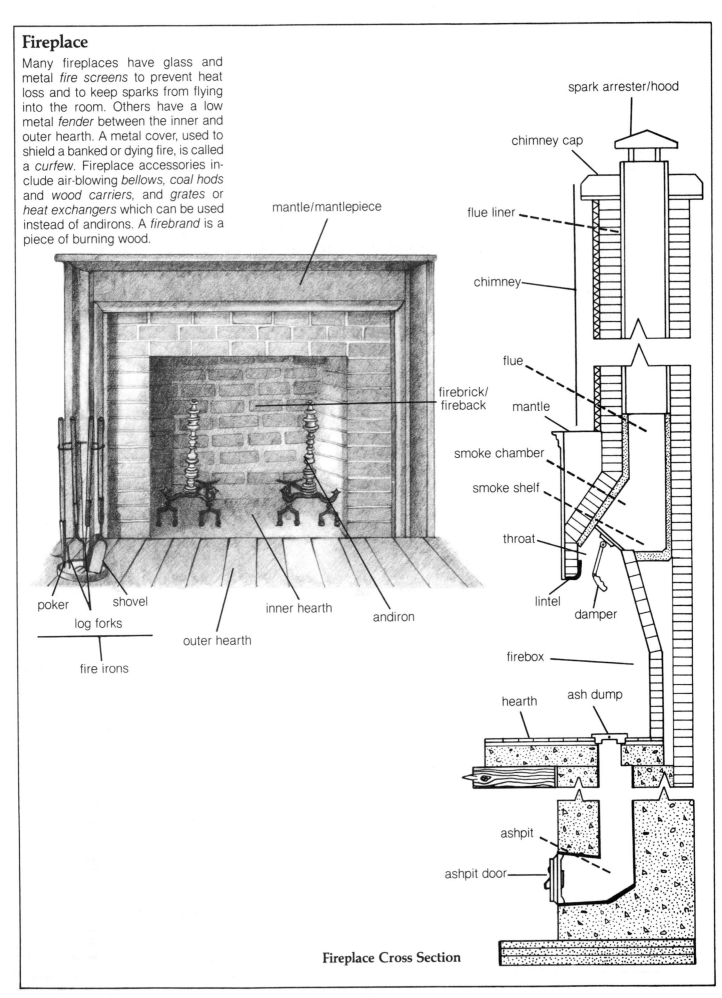

mantle/mantlepiece

firebrick/fireback

poker

shovel

log forks

fire irons

outer hearth

inner hearth

andiron

spark arrester/hood

chimney cap

flue liner

chimney

flue

mantle

smoke chamber

smoke shelf

throat

lintel

damper

firebox

hearth

ash dump

ashpit

ashpit door

Fireplace Cross Section

Clock

A *pendulum clock* tall enough to stand on the floor, either a grandfather or the shorter *grandmother clock,* is called a *tall-case clock.* The machinery or *movement* within is called the *clockworks.* A *rating,* the length of a pendulum swing, can be adjusted by a *rating nut,* usually found beneath the bob.

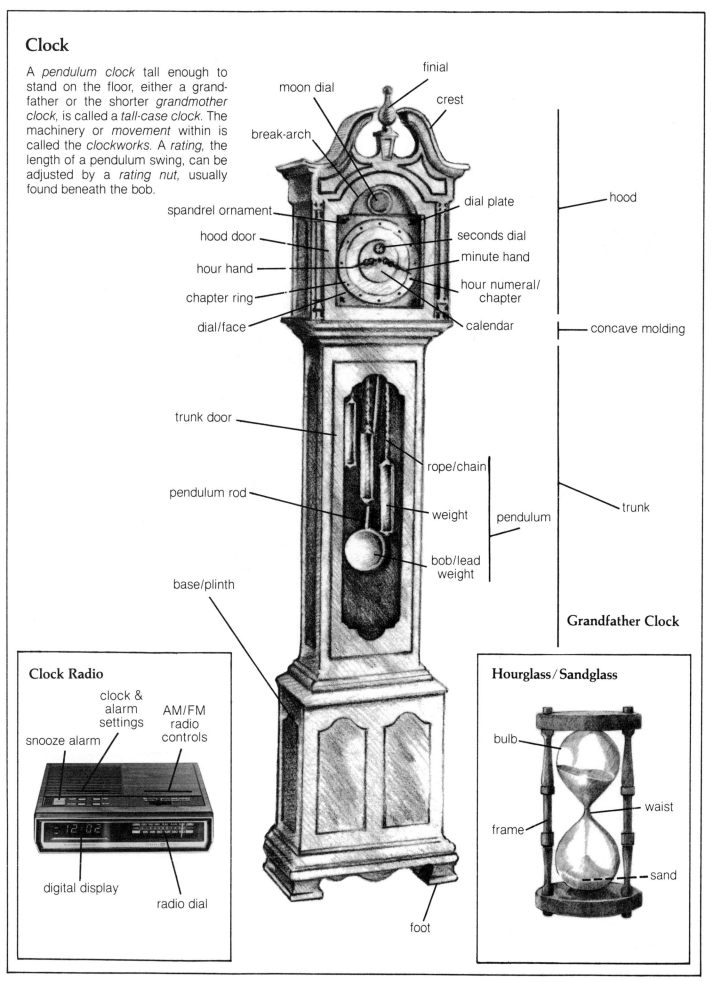

finial

moon dial

crest

break-arch

dial plate

spandrel ornament

seconds dial

hood door

hood

minute hand

hour hand

hour numeral/ chapter

chapter ring

dial/face

calendar

concave molding

trunk door

rope/chain

pendulum rod

weight

trunk

pendulum

bob/lead weight

base/plinth

Grandfather Clock

Clock Radio

clock & alarm settings

AM/FM radio controls

snooze alarm

digital display

radio dial

foot

Hourglass / Sandglass

bulb

waist

frame

sand

Chair

A single broad center upright used in place of spindles in a seat back is called a *splat*. Horizontal members across the seat back are called *slats*, or *crosspieces*. *Braces* are two spindles that form a "V" at the back of a chair seat. The crest of a chair may have a shape called a *handgrip, roll top* or *pillow*. A *slip seat* is a seat that is fitted into a molding and can be removed and covered with fabric, then replaced. An extended arm with a flat surface is called a *writing arm*.

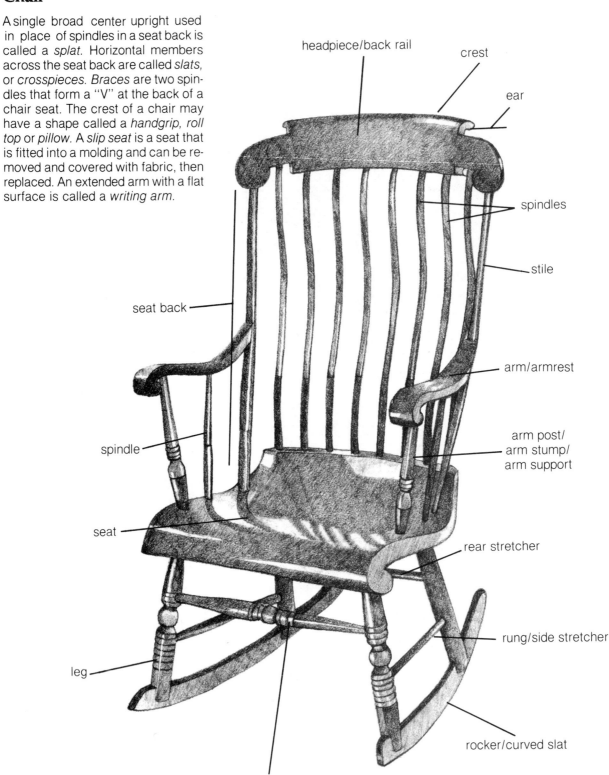

headpiece/back rail

crest

ear

spindles

stile

seat back

arm/armrest

arm post/
arm stump/
arm support

spindle

seat

rear stretcher

rung/side stretcher

leg

rocker/curved slat

front stretcher

Rocking Chair/Rocker

Lounger

When the backrest of this *recliner,* or *Barcalounger,* is pushed back, the *footrest* rises to seat level. The term *ottoman,* or *pouf,* is often used to refer to an overstuffed *footstool.* An *arm pad* on an *easy chair* is also called a *manchette.*

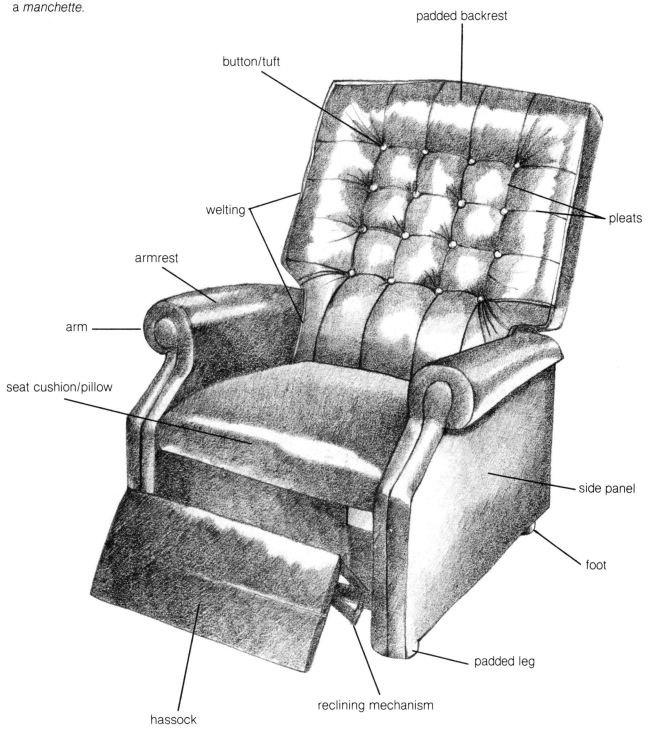

padded backrest

button/tuft

pleats

welting

armrest

arm

seat cushion/pillow

side panel

foot

hassock

reclining mechanism

padded leg

Living Room

Sofa

A sofa is an upholstered *couch* with a back and two arms or raised ends. If it is composed of several independent sections that can be arranged individually or in various combinations, it is a *sectional.* A *davenport* or *convertible* can be converted into a bed for nighttime use, whereas a *divan* is a large couch without back or arms that is often used as a bed. A sofa for two is a *loveseat,* or *courting seat.* Cylindrical pillows, or *bolsters,* and *fitted* or *tailored pillows* or *cushions* are often used on sofas.

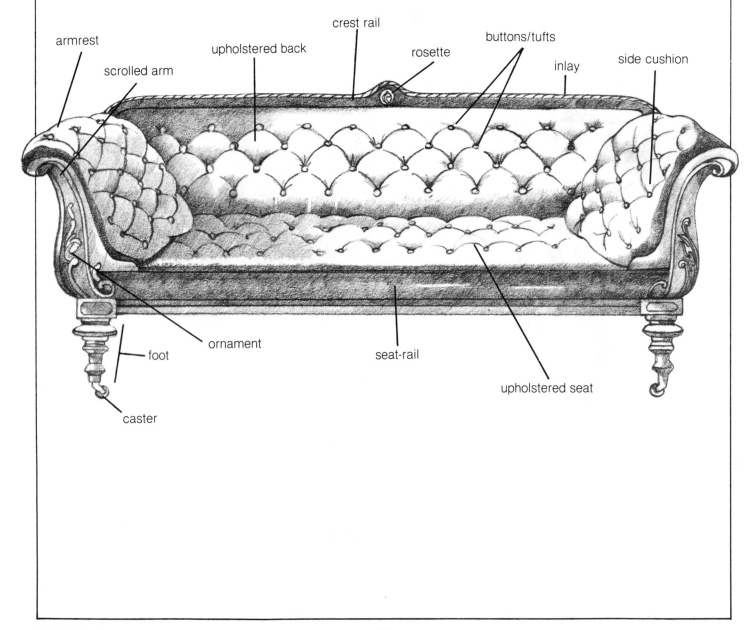

crest rail

armrest

buttons/tufts

upholstered back

rosette

inlay

side cushion

scrolled arm

ornament

foot

seat-rail

upholstered seat

caster

Candle and Candelabrum

Candles, or *tapers,* are made of *tallow, wax* or *paraffin.* Most are *dripless.* A collar placed at the top of a candle is a *burner.* The charred or partly consumed portion of a candle-wick, or *snaste,* is the *snuff,* formerly referred to as the *snot.* The remains of a used candle is the *stub.* Many candlesticks have a pointed *pricket* on which a candle is impaled, rather than a socket. Small candles used for religious purposes are called *devotionals* or *votive candles.*

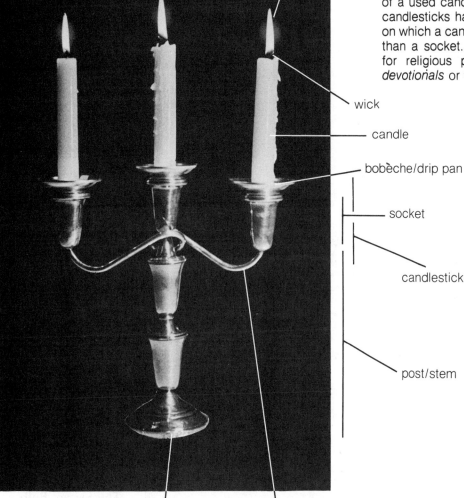

flame

wick

candle

bobèche/drip pan

socket

candlestick

post/stem

branch/arm

base

Candle Snuffer/Extinguisher

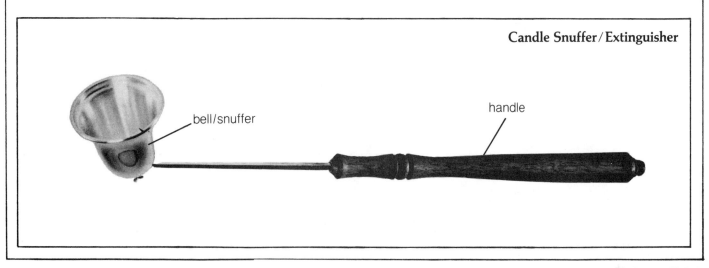

bell/snuffer

handle

Living Room

Lamps and Lighting

Light output, measured in *lumens*, depends on the amount of electricity used by a bulb. *Long-life bulbs* have heavier filaments. *Three-way bulbs* have two filaments, used separately for two of the light levels and together for the third. Two general types of bulb glass are soft, or *lime glass,* and hard, or *heat-resistant glass.* Lamp shades come in *drum, empire* and *bell* shapes. Lighting fixtures suspended from the ceiling are called *chandeliers.* The ceiling cap that covers the *junction box* for hanging lighting fixtures is the *canopy.*

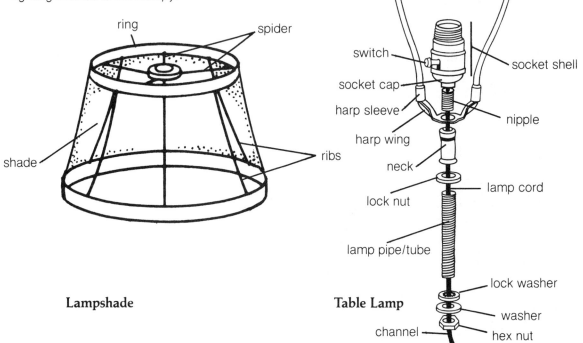

Lampshade

ring · spider · shade · ribs

Table Lamp

finial · harp · switch · socket shell · socket cap · harp sleeve · nipple · harp wing · neck · lamp cord · lock nut · lamp pipe/tube · lock washer · washer · channel · hex nut · power cord

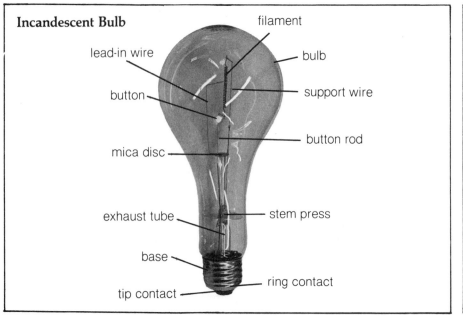

Incandescent Bulb

filament · lead-in wire · bulb · button · support wire · button rod · mica disc · exhaust tube · stem press · base · ring contact · tip contact

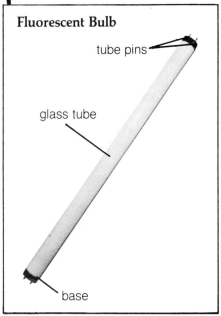

Fluorescent Bulb

tube pins · glass tube · base

Lamps and Lighting

Adjustable lamps, such as the one seen here, have an *inner reflector* around the bulb to help ventilate the shade. *Gooseneck lamps* have flexible shafts which permit the shade to be turned in any direction. *High-intensity* lamps produce a strong beam of light that illuminates only a small area.

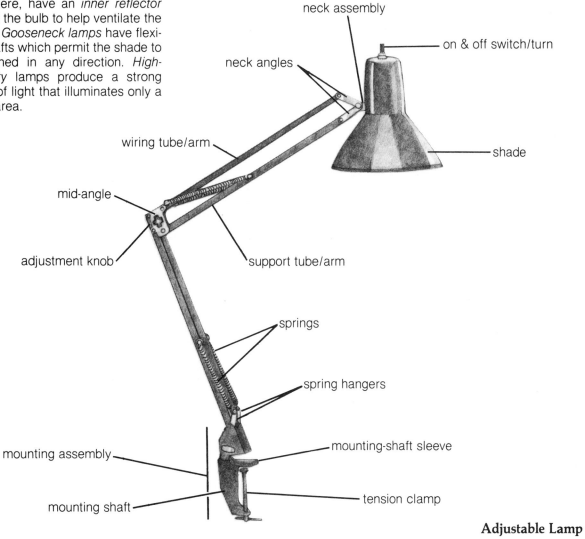

neck assembly

on & off switch/turn

neck angles

wiring tube/arm

shade

mid-angle

adjustment knob

support tube/arm

springs

spring hangers

mounting assembly

mounting-shaft sleeve

mounting shaft

tension clamp

Adjustable Lamp

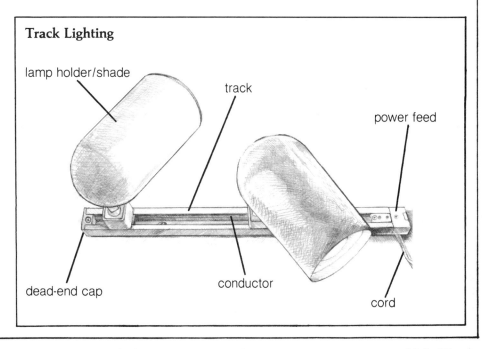

Track Lighting

lamp holder/shade

track

power feed

dead-end cap

conductor

cord

Window Coverings

The gathering of material at the top of draperies, hidden by the valance in this illustration, is called the *heading*. A *curtain rod* is a simple metal or wooden rod on which curtains are hung and moved by hand, without aid of pulley mechanisms. A curtain *panel* is a vertical section of fabric. *Cafe curtains* are suspended from rings and cover only part of a window.

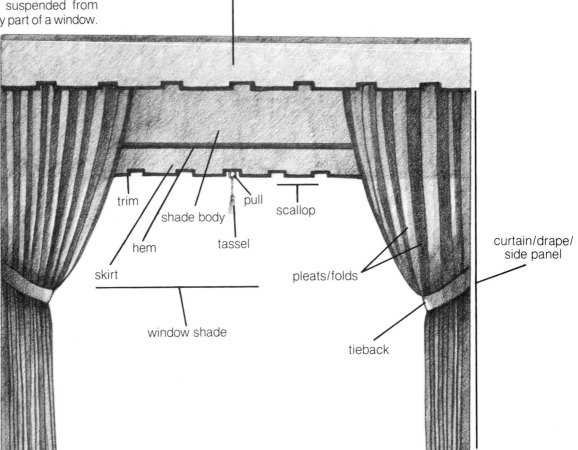

Curtains/Draperies and Shade

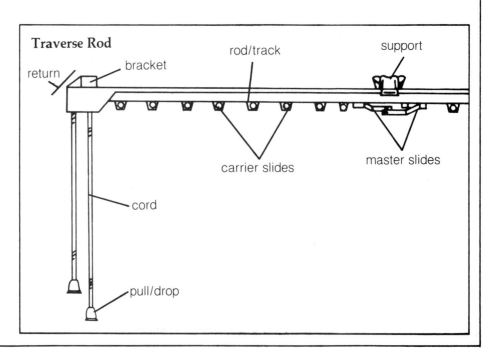

Window Coverings

Braided ladders are used in place of ladder tapes on some venetian blinds, and tubular *wands* are sometimes used instead of tilt cords. In *roll-up blinds*, slat tilt cannot be adjusted. A shutter consists of *panels*, each one of which contains louvers within a frame.

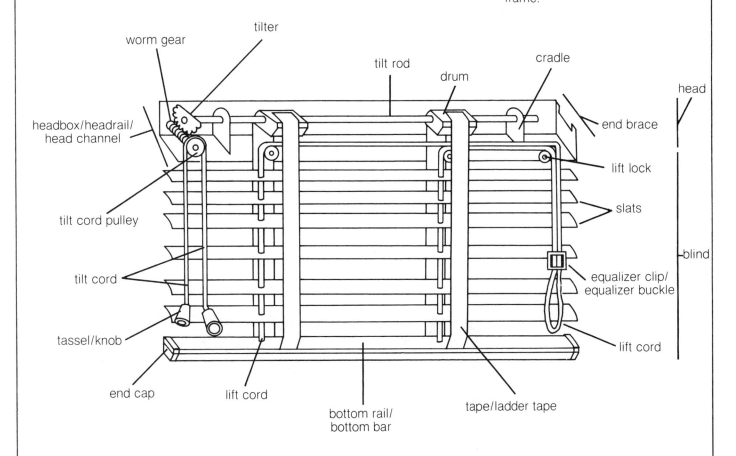

worm gear
tilter
tilt rod
drum
cradle
head
headbox/headrail/head channel
end brace
lift lock
tilt cord pulley
slats
blind
tilt cord
equalizer clip/equalizer buckle
tassel/knob
lift cord
end cap
lift cord
bottom rail/bottom bar
tape/ladder tape

Venetian Blinds

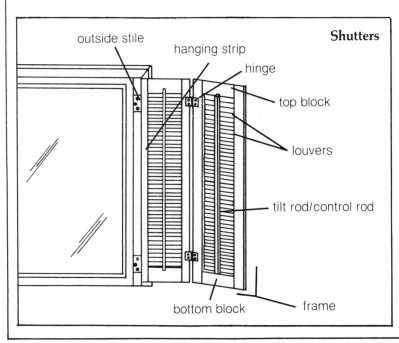

Shutters

outside stile
hanging strip
hinge
top block
louvers
tilt rod/control rod
bottom block
frame

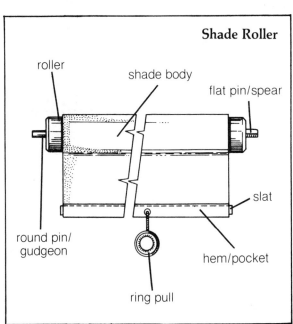

Shade Roller

roller
shade body
flat pin/spear
round pin/gudgeon
slat
hem/pocket
ring pull

Living Room

Table

A drop-leaf table is any table with a leaf that drops down to the side, such as a *gateleg* or a *butterfly table*. In a butterfly table, which has *splayed legs,* wooden wing-shaped *brackets* support the leaves. *Pedestal tables* rest on a single *base* rather than on legs. Some tables have an *apron,* wooden slats that run along the sides just beneath the top, to provide additional support. *Card tables,* or *bridge tables,* are lightweight, portable tables with folding *frames.*

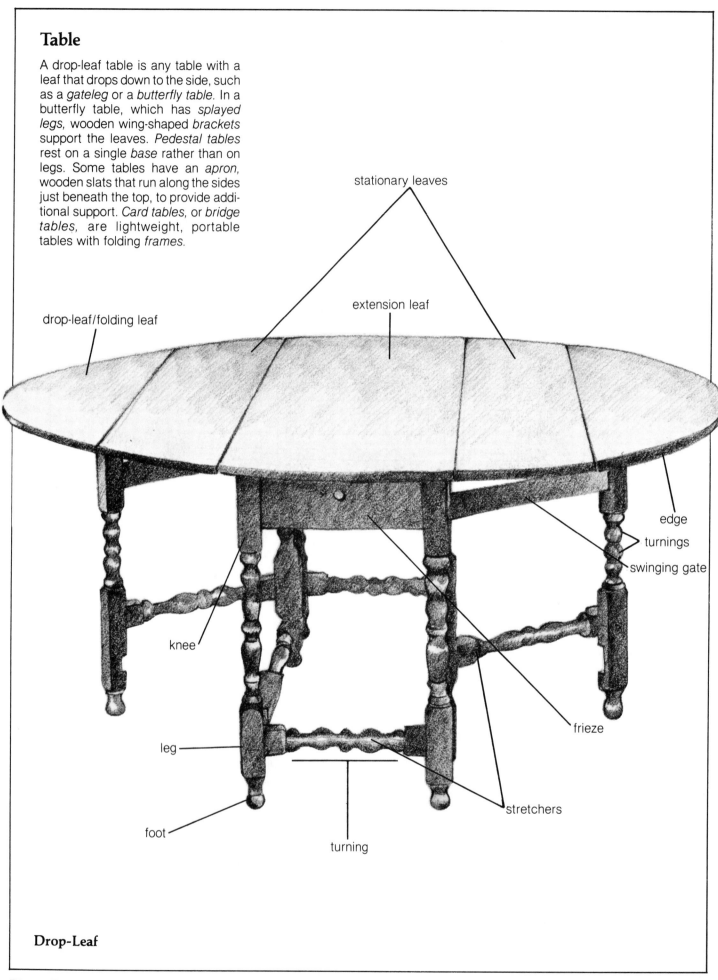

stationary leaves

extension leaf

drop-leaf/folding leaf

edge

turnings

swinging gate

knee

frieze

leg

stretchers

foot

turning

Drop-Leaf

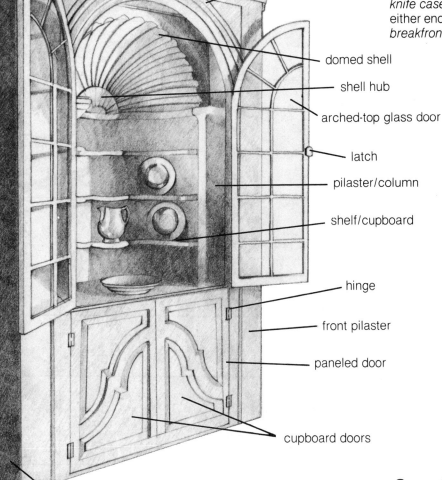

cornice

keystone

rosette

molding

domed shell

shell hub

arched-top glass door

latch

pilaster/column

shelf/cupboard

hinge

front pilaster

paneled door

cupboard doors

return end

Side Pieces

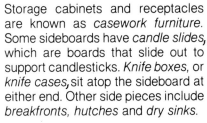

Side Pieces

Storage cabinets and receptacles are known as *casework furniture*. Some sideboards have *candle slides*, which are boards that slide out to support candlesticks. *Knife boxes*, or *knife cases*, sit atop the sideboard at either end. Other side pieces include *breakfronts, hutches* and *dry sinks*.

Corner Cupboard / China Cabinet

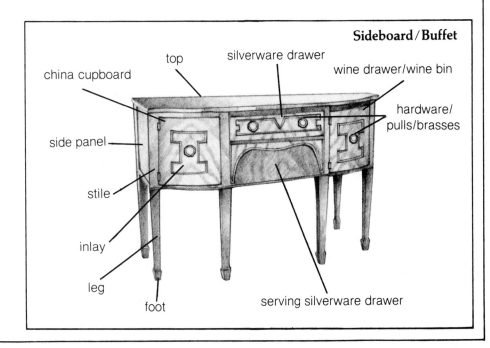

Sideboard / Buffet

china cupboard

top

silverware drawer

wine drawer/wine bin

hardware/
pulls/brasses

side panel

stile

inlay

leg

foot

serving silverware drawer

Place Setting

There is no universally accepted way of setting a table. The elements and their proper position vary. The arrangement shown here is based on that used by the White House on formal occasions.

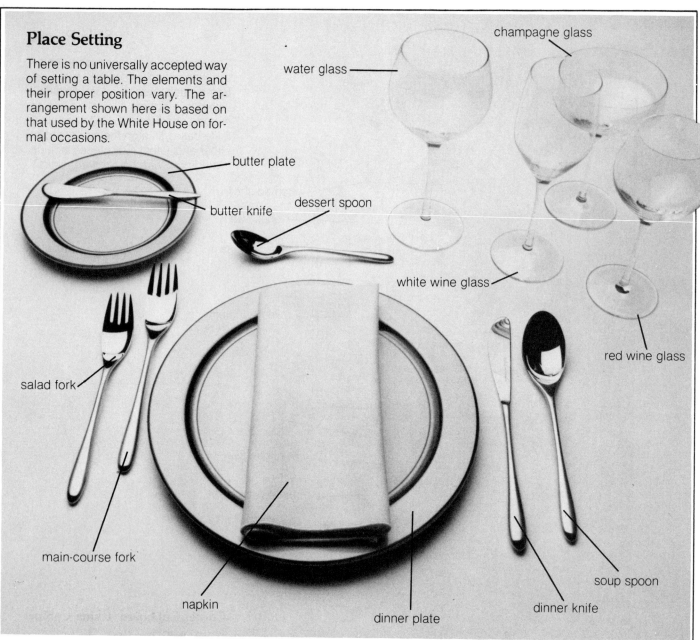

water glass

champagne glass

butter plate

butter knife

dessert spoon

white wine glass

red wine glass

salad fork

main-course fork

napkin

dinner plate

dinner knife

soup spoon

Flatware/Silverware

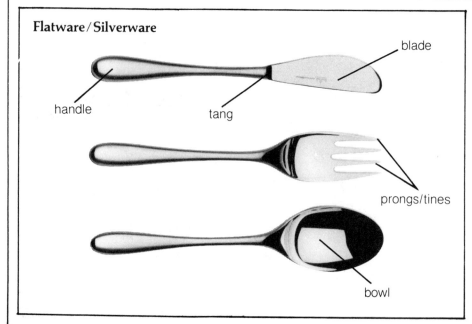

blade

handle

tang

prongs/tines

bowl

Stemware

rim/lip

head

bowl

stem

foot

Dessert Setting

Among other plates used for serving dessert and sweets are multi-tiered *terrace servers*, *serving trays*, *cake plates*, *fruit bowls* called *centerpieces*, and *compotes*. After-dinner drinks are often poured from ornamental glass bottles called *decanters*.

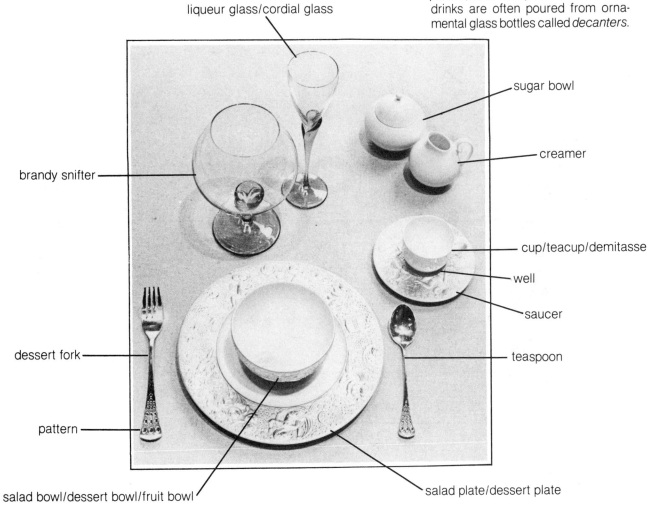

liqueur glass/cordial glass

brandy snifter

sugar bowl

creamer

cup/teacup/demitasse

well

saucer

dessert fork

teaspoon

pattern

salad bowl/dessert bowl/fruit bowl

salad plate/dessert plate

Chafing Dish

insulated handle

chafing dish/pan

stand

burner

Tea Set / Tea Service and Kettle

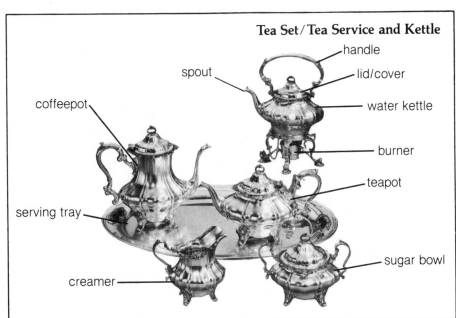

handle

spout

lid/cover

coffeepot

water kettle

burner

teapot

serving tray

sugar bowl

creamer

Carpet

Carpets, or *wall-to-wall carpets,* cover the entire floor of a room, while *rugs, area rugs, throw rugs* and narrow *runners* cover only a part, are not tacked down, and often rest on *rug pads. Tacks* are short nails with flat, broad heads. Much modern *carpeting* is tufted, made by stitching *yarn loops* into a *woven backing.*

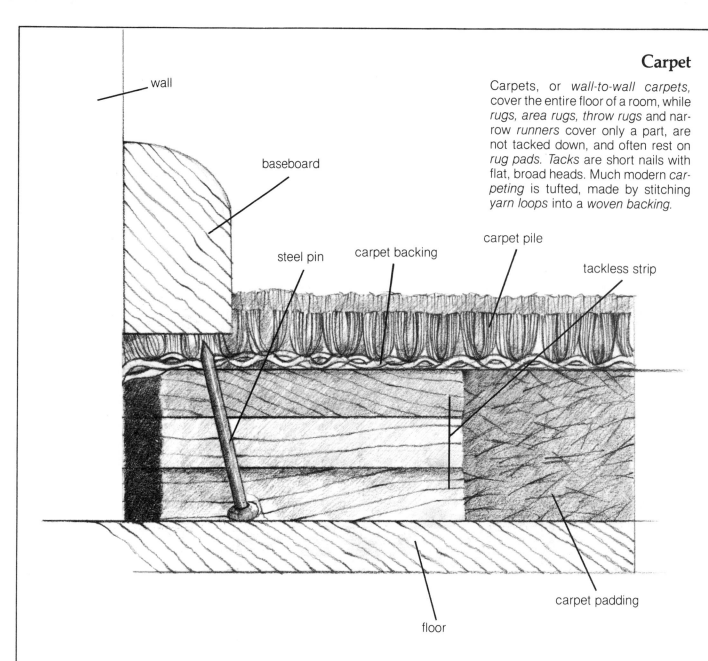

wall

baseboard

steel pin

carpet backing

carpet pile

tackless strip

floor

carpet padding

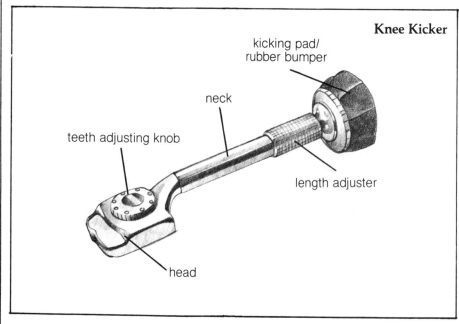

Knee Kicker

kicking pad/
rubber bumper

neck

teeth adjusting knob

length adjuster

head

Sink and Compactor

The hardware in a sink, the faucet handles and spout, are known as *fixtures*. Sink drains usually have perforated *drain baskets* which trap debris but allow water to pass through. Many baskets are two-piece units that form a watertight seal when the *inner basket* is twisted. *Instant hot-water devices* mounted on the spout of some sinks have a constantly heated coil that produces small amounts of hot water on demand.

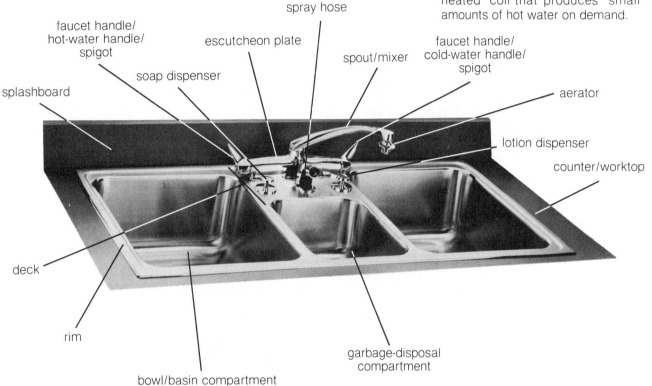

faucet handle/ hot-water handle/ spigot

soap dispenser

splashboard

spray hose

escutcheon plate

spout/mixer

faucet handle/ cold-water handle/ spigot

aerator

lotion dispenser

counter/worktop

deck

rim

bowl/basin compartment

garbage-disposal compartment

Kitchen Sink

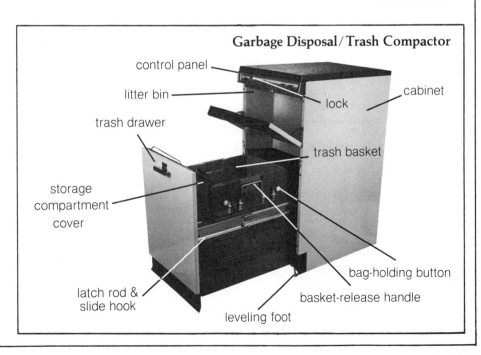

Garbage Disposal / Trash Compactor

control panel

litter bin

trash drawer

storage compartment cover

lock

cabinet

trash basket

latch rod & slide hook

bag-holding button

basket-release handle

leveling foot

Kitchen

Stove/Range

On an *electric range*, *heating elements* connected to *terminal blocks* are used in place of burner grates on a gas model. The permanent flame, used to ignite individual burners on a gas stove, is called a *pilot light.* Some models have an *electric pilot.* The walls of a self-cleaning oven are covered with a heat-resistant porcelain enamel finish.

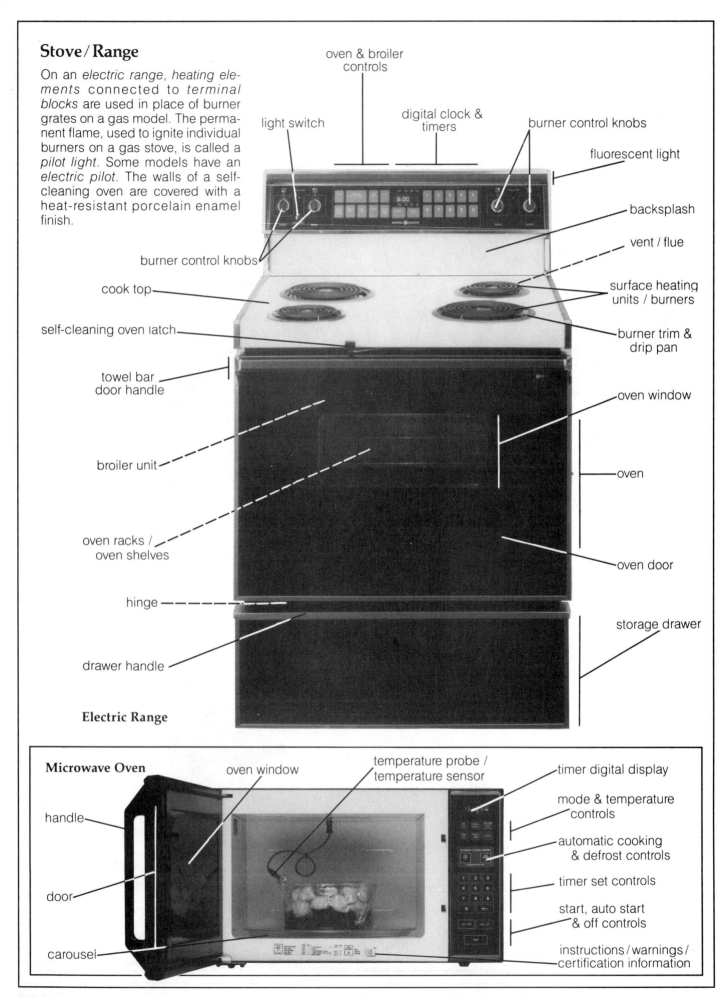

oven & broiler controls

light switch

digital clock & timers

burner control knobs

fluorescent light

backsplash

vent / flue

surface heating units / burners

burner trim & drip pan

burner control knobs

cook top

self-cleaning oven latch

towel bar door handle

broiler unit

oven window

oven

oven door

oven racks / oven shelves

hinge

drawer handle

storage drawer

Electric Range

Microwave Oven

oven window

temperature probe / temperature sensor

timer digital display

mode & temperature controls

automatic cooking & defrost controls

handle

timer set controls

start, auto start & off controls

door

carousel

instructions/warnings/ certification information

Refrigerator

Some refrigerators, or *iceboxes*, have an *ice dispenser* in the freezer section. Others have *ice trays*. A *frostfree*, or *no-frost*, model does not require defrosting.

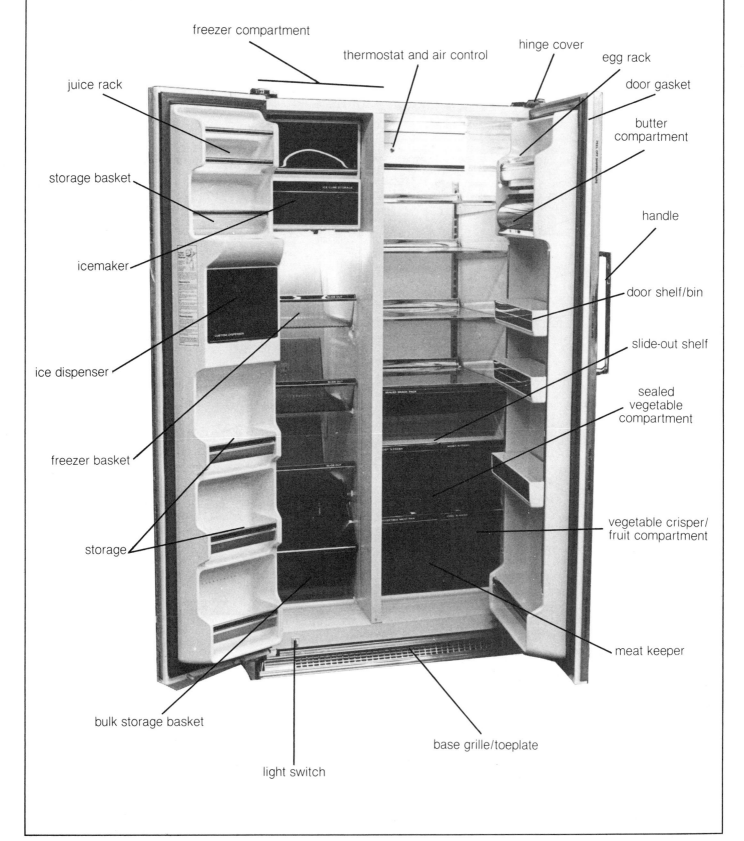

freezer compartment

thermostat and air control

hinge cover

egg rack

door gasket

juice rack

butter compartment

storage basket

handle

icemaker

door shelf/bin

slide-out shelf

ice dispenser

sealed vegetable compartment

freezer basket

storage

vegetable crisper/ fruit compartment

meat keeper

bulk storage basket

base grille/toeplate

light switch

Kitchen

Dishwasher

The *cycle-selector control panel* and *timer* are located on the outside of the door of this built-in dishwasher. The machine will operate only when the *external door switch,* or latch, is engaged.

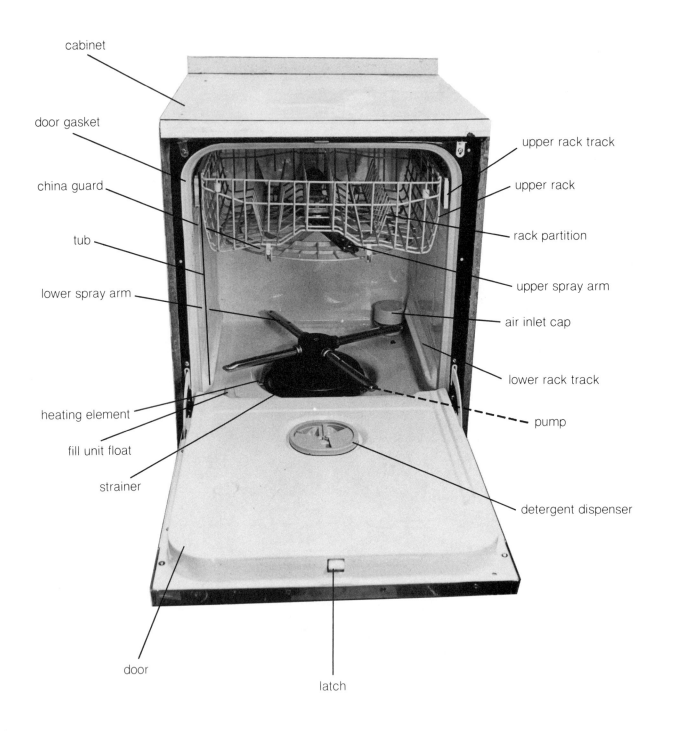

cabinet

door gasket

china guard

tub

lower spray arm

heating element

fill unit float

strainer

door

upper rack track

upper rack

rack partition

upper spray arm

air inlet cap

lower rack track

pump

detergent dispenser

latch

Openers

With manual openers, the can rim is held between a *cutting blade* and a *turning gear,* with pressure applied by squeezing two *handles* and the can rotated with a winged *key.* The blade and handle device used by military personnel to open food ration cans is called a *"John Wayne."* The corkscrew shown below is used by *sommeliers,* or *wine stewards.*

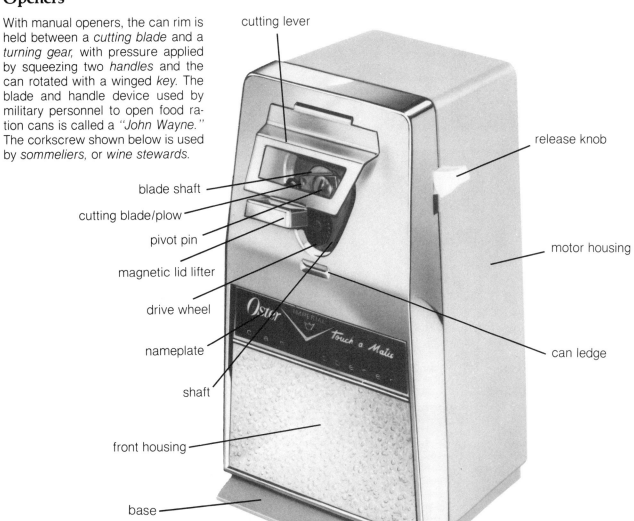

cutting lever

release knob

blade shaft

cutting blade/plow

pivot pin

magnetic lid lifter

drive wheel

nameplate

motor housing

shaft

can ledge

front housing

base

Electric Can Opener

Corkscrew

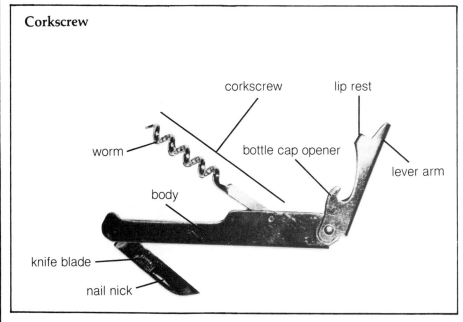

corkscrew

lip rest

worm

bottle cap opener

lever arm

body

knife blade

nail nick

"Church Key"/Can Piercer

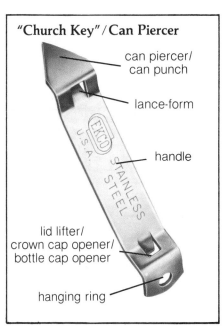

can piercer/ can punch

lance-form

handle

lid lifter/ crown cap opener/ bottle cap opener

hanging ring

Kitchen

Coffee Makers

Coffee is *brewed* by passing boiling water through *ground coffee* beans. *Espresso* is brewed by forcing steam through roasted beans. *Cappuccino* consists of espresso and steamed milk.

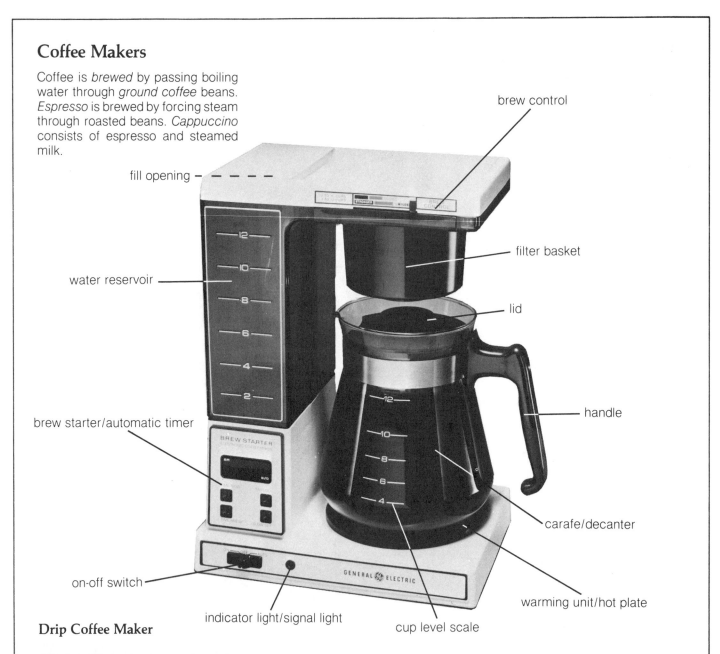

brew control

fill opening

filter basket

water reservoir

lid

handle

brew starter/automatic timer

carafe/decanter

on-off switch

warming unit/hot plate

indicator light/signal light

cup level scale

Drip Coffee Maker

Percolator

dome

spout

lid

pot/body

plug outlet

brewing & warming element

brew selector

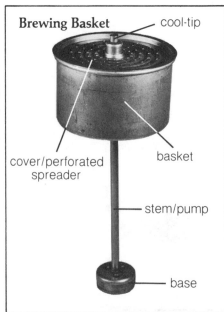

Brewing Basket

cool-tip

cover/perforated spreader

basket

stem/pump

base

Infusion Maker

knob/plunger

lip/spout

rod

frame

beaker/carafe/jug

filter assembly

Toaster

Many toasters have removable *crumb trays*. The heating elements in toasters are flat *nichrome wires*. Toasters have either a spring-and-cylinder *dash-pot* or a simple spring device to pop toast up once it is browned. Toaster ovens have removable *baking trays*.

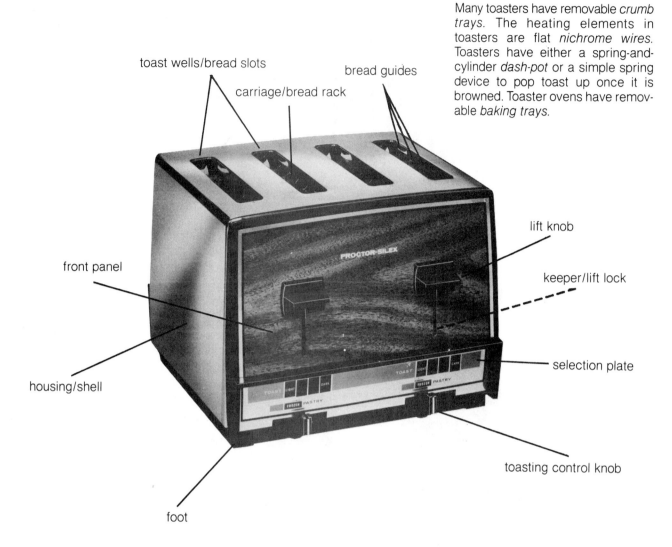

toast wells/bread slots

carriage/bread rack

bread guides

lift knob

keeper/lift lock

front panel

selection plate

housing/shell

toasting control knob

foot

Toaster Oven

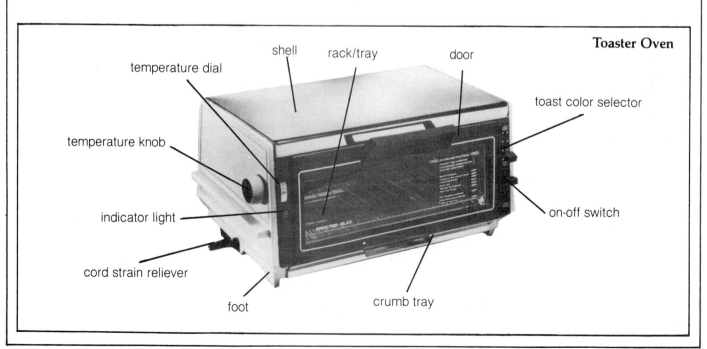

shell

rack/tray

door

temperature dial

toast color selector

temperature knob

indicator light

on-off switch

cord strain reliever

foot

crumb tray

Kitchen

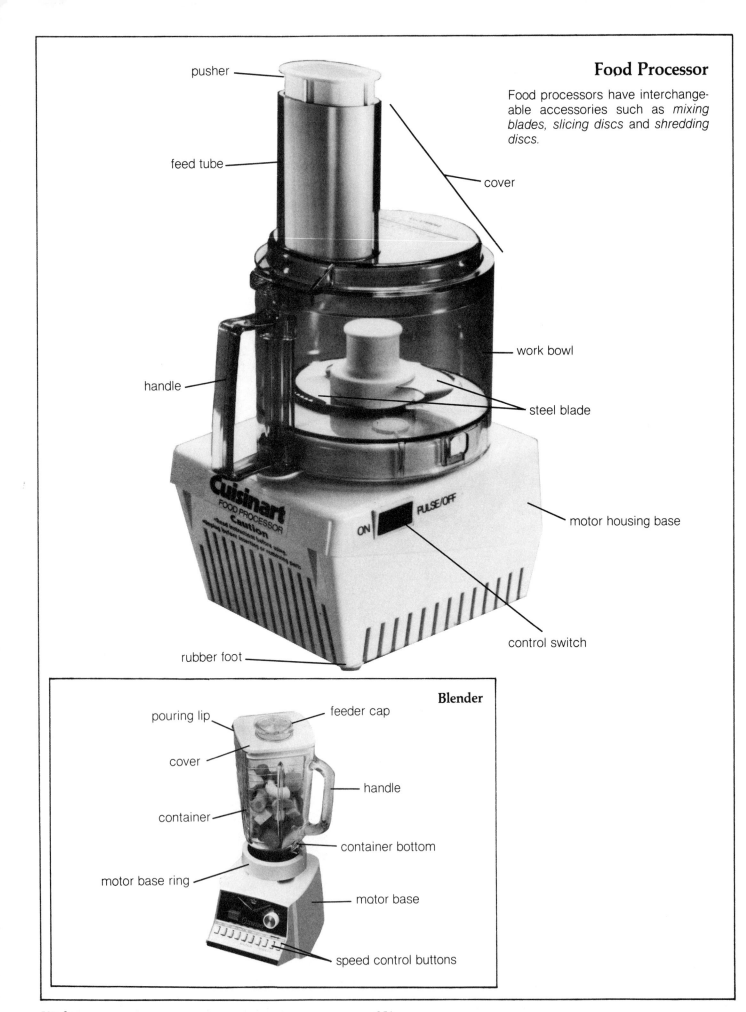

Food Processor

Food processors have interchangeable accessories such as *mixing blades, slicing discs* and *shredding discs.*

pusher

feed tube

cover

work bowl

handle

steel blade

motor housing base

control switch

rubber foot

Blender

pouring lip

feeder cap

cover

handle

container

container bottom

motor base ring

motor base

speed control buttons

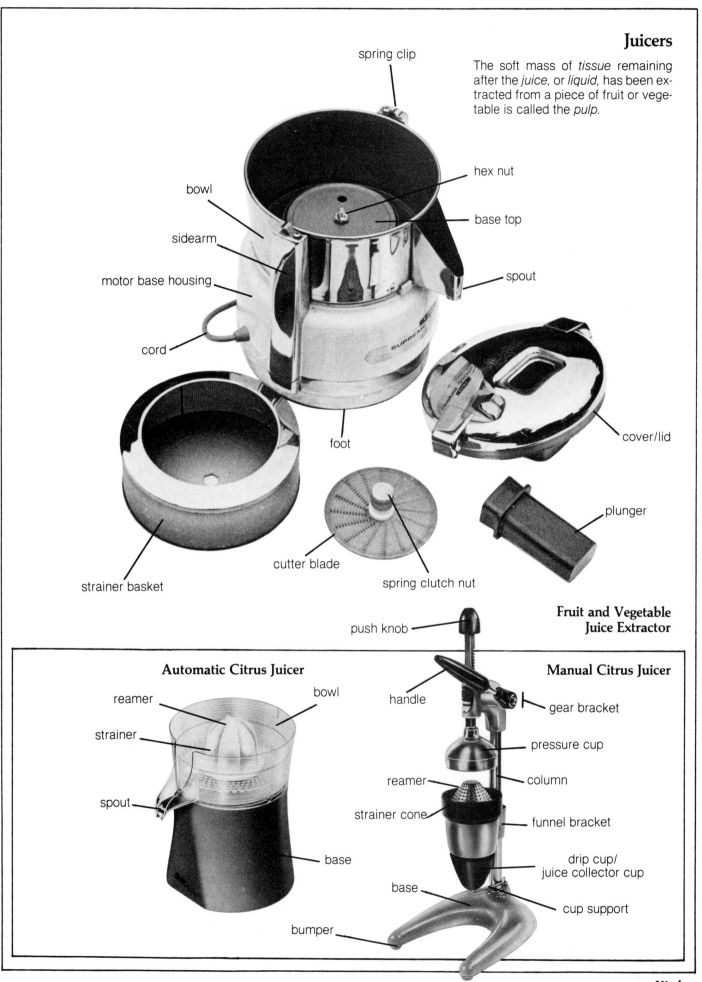

Juicers

The soft mass of *tissue* remaining after the *juice,* or *liquid,* has been extracted from a piece of fruit or vegetable is called the *pulp.*

spring clip

hex nut

base top

bowl

spout

sidearm

motor base housing

cord

cover/lid

foot

plunger

strainer basket

cutter blade

spring clutch nut

push knob

Fruit and Vegetable Juice Extractor

Automatic Citrus Juicer

Manual Citrus Juicer

reamer

bowl

handle

gear bracket

strainer

pressure cup

reamer

column

spout

strainer cone

funnel bracket

base

drip cup/ juice collector cup

base

cup support

bumper

Kitchen

Knife

The part of a knife blade that extends into the handle is called the *tang,* and the blade's formation is known as the *grind.* In a *flat grind,* the sides of the blade are smooth. In a *hollow grind* there is a marked curve or bevel along the length of the blade.

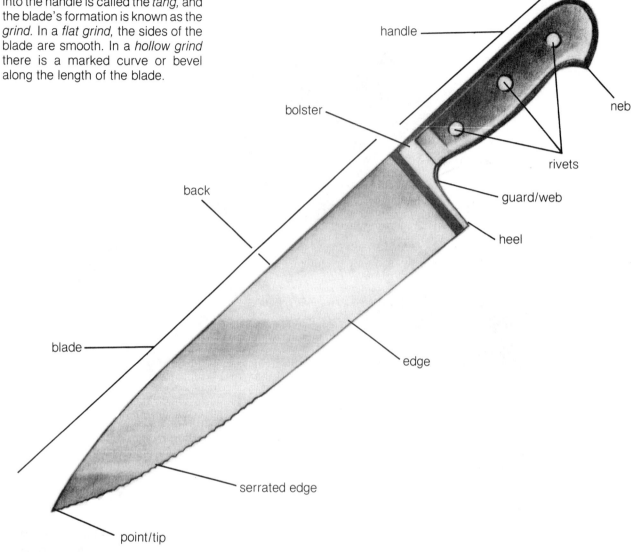

handle

neb

bolster

rivets

back

guard/web

heel

blade

edge

serrated edge

point/tip

Peeler

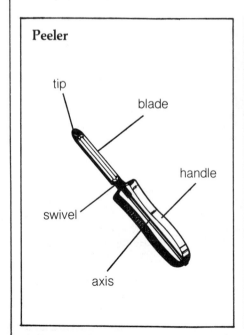

tip

blade

swivel

handle

axis

Sharpening Steel

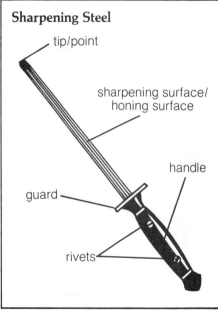

tip/point

sharpening surface/ honing surface

guard

handle

rivets

Cheese Plane / Cheese Slicer

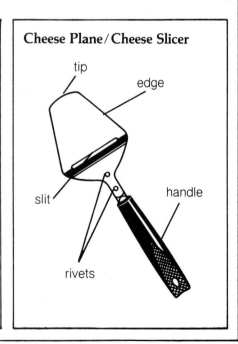

tip

edge

slit

handle

rivets

Pots and Pans

Pots and pans are often described by their function—for example, a *boiler* or *steamer. Crockpots* are pots made of earthenware. *Casseroles* are earthenware, glass or cast-iron pots in which food can be both baked and served. A *pipkin* is a small saucepan with a long handle used to melt butter.

knob

cover/lid

handle

Stock Pot/Stew Pot

lift-out stem

perforated panel

rim

Steamer Basket

leg/foot

Saucepan

side

tang

bottom

hanging ring

handle

Skillet/Frying Pan

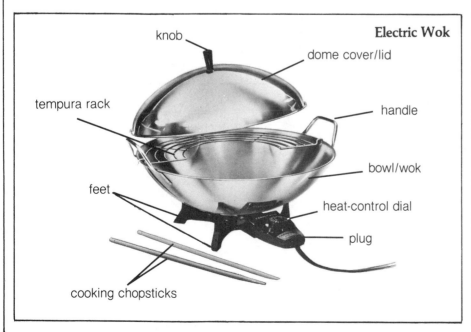

Electric Wok

knob

dome cover/lid

tempura rack

handle

bowl/wok

feet

heat-control dial

plug

cooking chopsticks

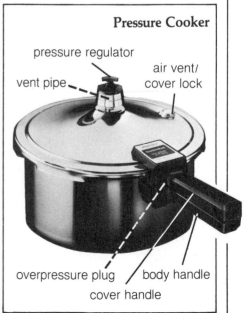

Pressure Cooker

pressure regulator

vent pipe

air vent/ cover lock

overpressure plug

body handle

cover handle

Kitchen

Mixing and Measuring Tools

In addition to the *meat,* or *rapid-response thermometer,* seen here, well-equipped kitchens have *oven* and *freezer thermometers, deep-frying thermometers, scales* and *funnels.*

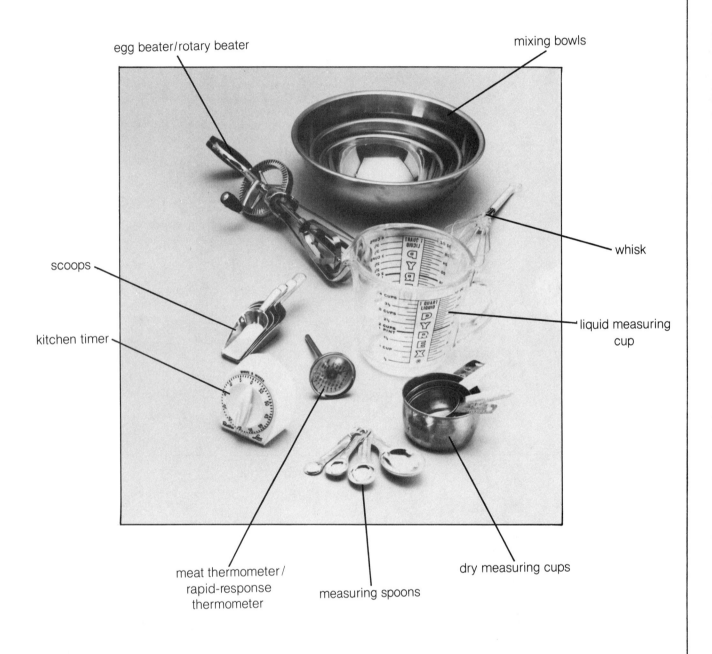

egg beater/rotary beater

mixing bowls

scoops

whisk

kitchen timer

liquid measuring cup

meat thermometer/ rapid-response thermometer

measuring spoons

dry measuring cups

Preparation Utensils

Additional preparation implements include *molding scoops,* for soft foods, wooden *spaghetti spoons* with long *prongs* to wrap pasta and lift it from boiling water, *basting ladles* with an egg-shaped *bowl* for easy pouring, and cylindrical one-piece *pastry pins.*

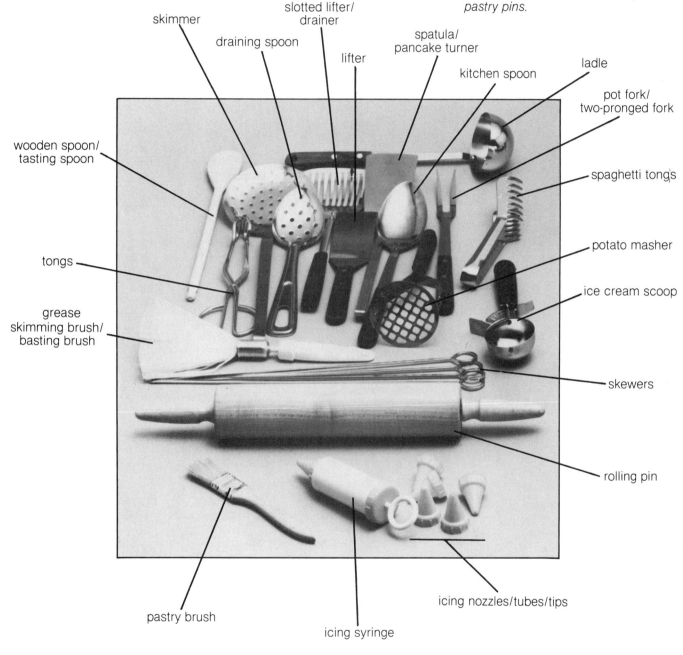

skimmer

slotted lifter/ drainer

draining spoon

lifter

spatula/ pancake turner

kitchen spoon

ladle

pot fork/ two-pronged fork

wooden spoon/ tasting spoon

spaghetti tongs

tongs

potato masher

grease skimming brush/ basting brush

ice cream scoop

skewers

rolling pin

pastry brush

icing syringe

icing nozzles/tubes/tips

Kitchen

Strainers and Drainers

Clean dishes, vegetables and fruits may be left on a *draining rack,* or *dish rack,* to dry. *Cooling racks* are used in conjunction with baked foods. A *sieve* has a mesh bottom for straining. A *food mill,* or *food foley,* is a heavy colander through which food is pressed by means of a flat *plate* attached to a *rotating handle.*

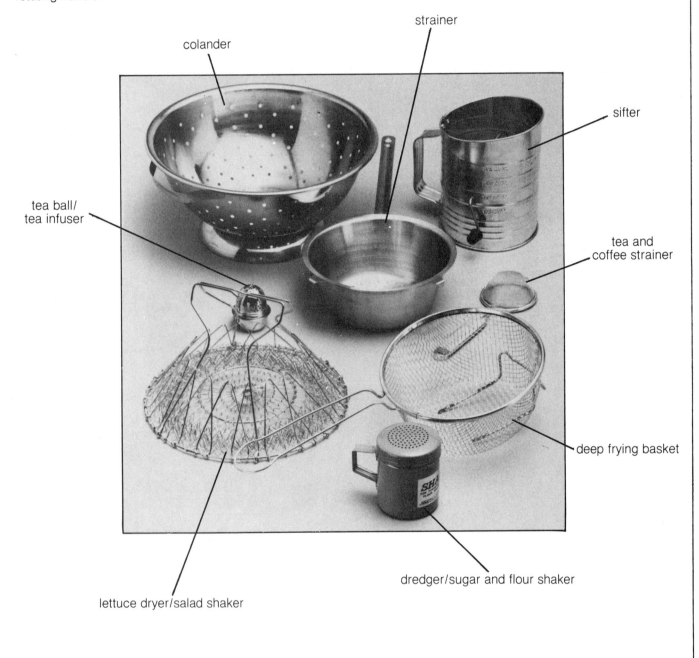

colander

strainer

sifter

tea ball/
tea infuser

tea and
coffee strainer

deep frying basket

dredger/sugar and flour shaker

lettuce dryer/salad shaker

Cutters, Grinders and Graters

A *potato peeler* has a swivel blade for following contours and a sharp tip for gouging. Hand-cranked *meat grinders* chop meats and other foods. A *zester* is a tool that shaves the thin surface off fruits.

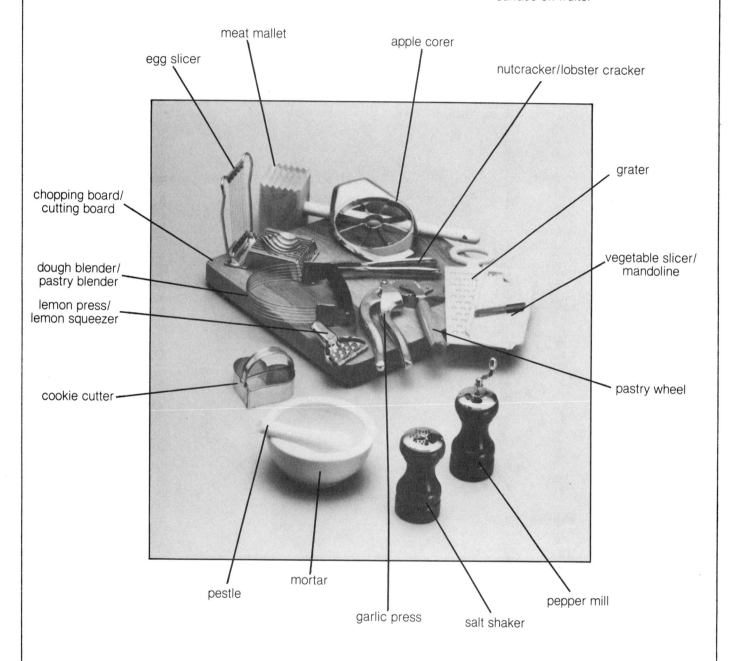

egg slicer

meat mallet

apple corer

nutcracker/lobster cracker

grater

chopping board/ cutting board

vegetable slicer/ mandoline

dough blender/ pastry blender

lemon press/ lemon squeezer

cookie cutter

pastry wheel

pestle

mortar

garlic press

salt shaker

pepper mill

Kitchen

Raw Ingredients

On *lettuce,* the entire mass of leaves is called the *head,* while the center leaves are the *heart.* A small slice of meat is a *collop.* A *peppercorn* is a dried berry of black pepper.

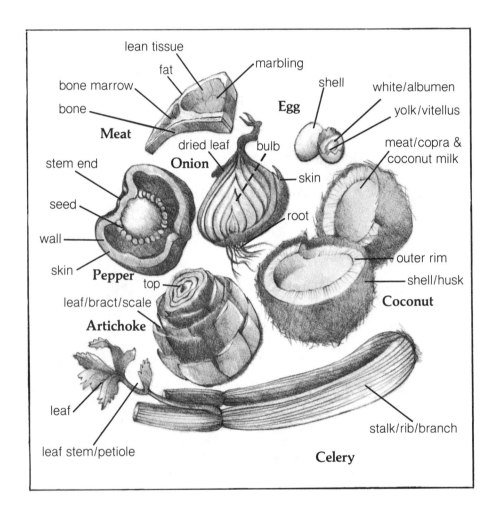

Prepared Foods

Appetizers, or *hors d'oeuvres,* are served before the main *course,* or *entree.* An ingredient, such as a *condiment, spice* or *herb,* added to food for the savor it imparts, is *seasoning.* Cheese is made by separating the *curd,* milk solids, from the *whey,* milk liquids. *Crumb* refers to both the soft inner portion of bread and any tiny piece that flakes off the loaf or a slice.

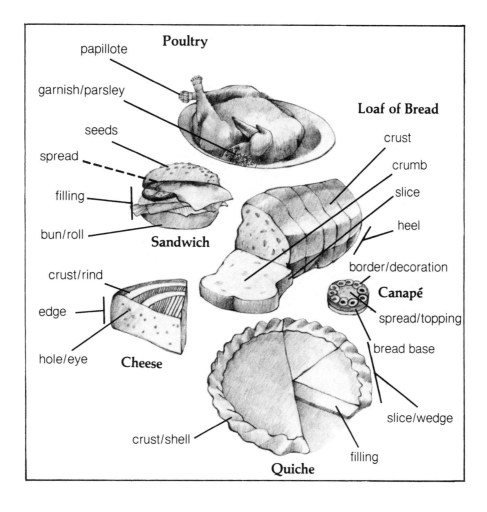

Poultry

papillote

garnish/parsley

seeds

spread

filling

bun/roll

Sandwich

Loaf of Bread

crust

crumb

slice

heel

border/decoration

Canapé

spread/topping

bread base

crust/rind

edge

hole/eye

Cheese

slice/wedge

crust/shell

filling

Quiche

Kitchen

Desserts

Baked desserts, or *sweet goods,* made of dough or having a crust made of enriched dough, such as *pies,* tarts and *turnovers,* are *pastries.* A *parfait* is similar to a sundae but may have layers of fruit and be frozen.

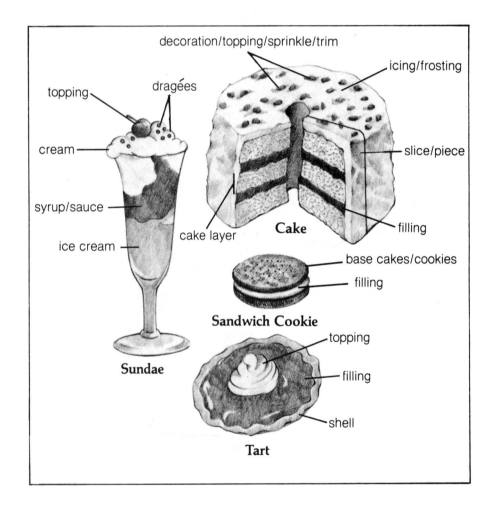

decoration/topping/sprinkle/trim

icing/frosting

topping

dragées

cream

slice/piece

syrup/sauce

ice cream

cake layer

filling

Cake

base cakes/cookies

filling

Sandwich Cookie

topping

filling

shell

Tart

Sundae

Snack Foods

Ice cream scoops are also put in flat-bottomed *wafer cones* and topped with other *fixings,* including *nuts* and *cherries.* When ice cream melts and drips down the cone, it forms *lickings.* The part of a hot dog roll that remains attached after the roll is sliced is the *hinge. Smoked sausages* are larger than franks and often include additional *seasonings.* Among other pizza toppings are *anchovies, extra cheese, pepperoni* and *onions.*

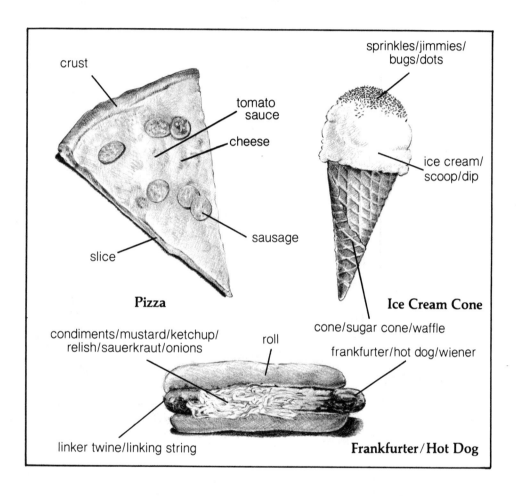

crust

tomato sauce

cheese

sausage

slice

Pizza

sprinkles/jimmies/ bugs/dots

ice cream/ scoop/dip

Ice Cream Cone

cone/sugar cone/waffle

condiments/mustard/ketchup/ relish/sauerkraut/onions

roll

frankfurter/hot dog/wiener

linker twine/linking string

Frankfurter/Hot Dog

Kitchen

Containers

Most baskets are made by weaving individual *strands* or *rods* in front of one *stake* of the *frame* and behind the next. Some baskets have a border, or *foot,* on the bottom, just above the *base,* as well as a *cover,* or *lid,* which often rests on an inside *ledge.* A small, oblong veneer basket with rounded ends, the kind used for mushrooms, is a *climax basket,* and a little wooden paillike container with one stave extending up for a handle is a *piggin.*

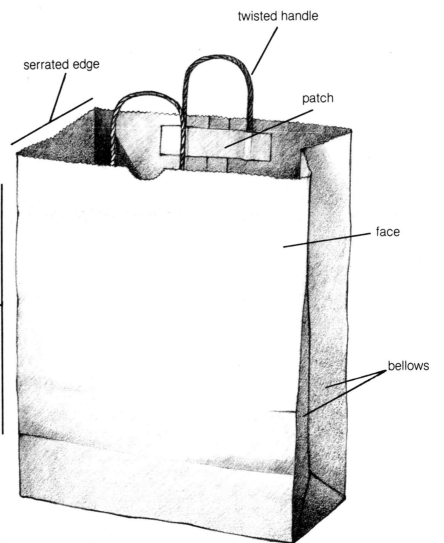

serrated edge

twisted handle

patch

face

body

bellows

Paper Bag

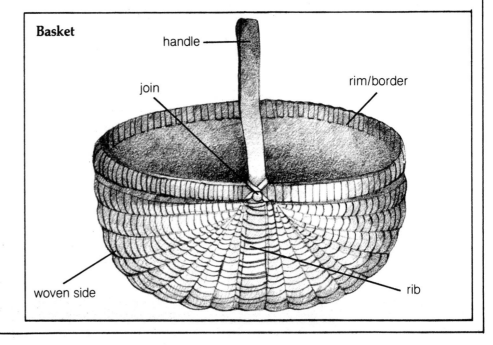

Basket

handle

join

rim/border

woven side

rib

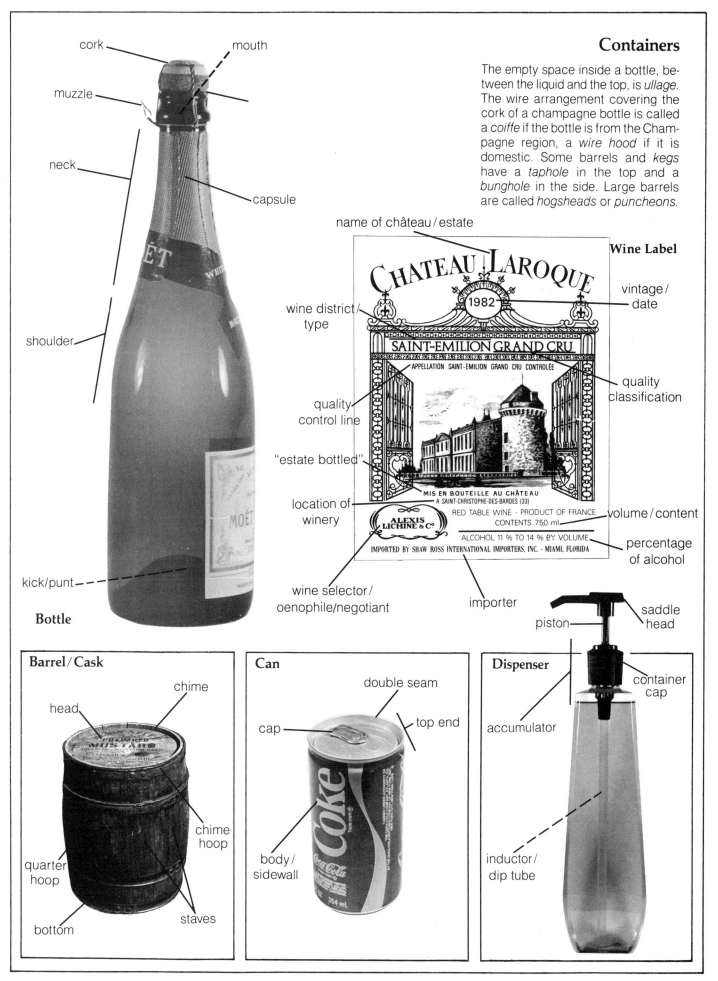

Containers

cork

mouth

muzzle

neck

capsule

shoulder

The empty space inside a bottle, between the liquid and the top, is *ullage*. The wire arrangement covering the cork of a champagne bottle is called a *coiffe* if the bottle is from the Champagne region, a *wire hood* if it is domestic. Some barrels and *kegs* have a *taphole* in the top and a *bunghole* in the side. Large barrels are called *hogsheads* or *puncheons*.

Wine Label

name of château/estate

wine district/type

vintage/date

CHATEAU LAROQUE

1982

SAINT-EMILION GRAND CRU

APPELLATION SAINT-EMILION GRAND CRU CONTROLÉE

quality control line

quality classification

"estate bottled"

location of winery

MIS EN BOUTEILLE AU CHÂTEAU
A SAINT-CHRISTOPHE-DES-BARDES (33)

RED TABLE WINE · PRODUCT OF FRANCE
CONTENTS 750 ml

ALCOHOL 11 % TO 14 % BY VOLUME

ALEXIS LICHINE & Cº

IMPORTED BY SHAW ROSS INTERNATIONAL IMPORTERS, INC. - MIAMI, FLORIDA

volume/content

percentage of alcohol

kick/punt

Bottle

wine selector/oenophile/negotiant

importer

Dispenser

piston

saddle head

container cap

accumulator

inductor/dip tube

Barrel/Cask

chime

head

chime hoop

quarter hoop

staves

bottom

Can

double seam

cap

top end

body/sidewall

Kitchen

Labeling and Packaging

Sketches or pictures on labels are called *vignettes*. When letters or vignettes on labels are raised, they are *embossed*. When they are recessed they are *debossed*. A seal of clear plastic that conforms to a product's shape is a *shrinkwrap*. A *promotional,* or *spot label,* often applied over the regular label, is a *tip-on*.

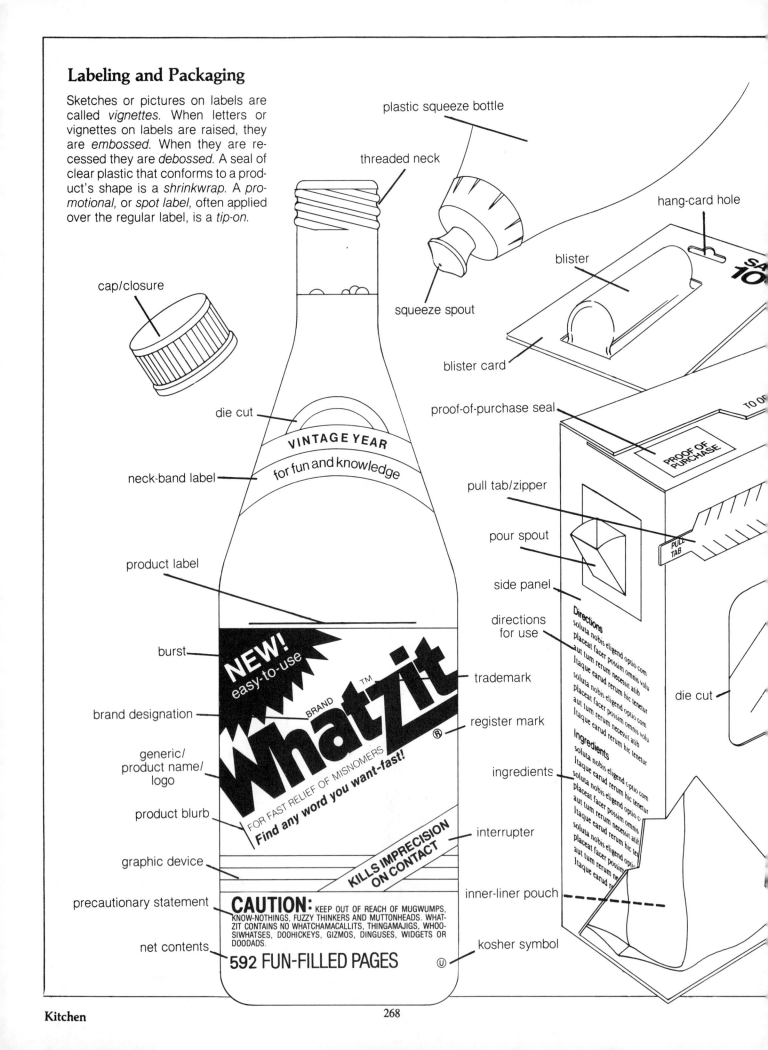

plastic squeeze bottle

threaded neck

hang-card hole

blister

squeeze spout

blister card

cap/closure

proof-of-purchase seal

PROOF OF PURCHASE

die cut

pull tab/zipper

VINTAGE YEAR
for fun and knowledge

neck-band label

pour spout

PULL TAB

side panel

product label

directions for use

die cut

burst

NEW! easy-to-use

BRAND

Whatzit ™

trademark

brand designation

®

register mark

FOR FAST RELIEF OF MISNOMERS

generic/ product name/ logo

Find any word you want–fast!

Directions

Ingredients

ingredients

product blurb

interrupter

KILLS IMPRECISION ON CONTACT

graphic device

inner-liner pouch

precautionary statement

CAUTION: KEEP OUT OF REACH OF MUGWUMPS, KNOW-NOTHINGS, FUZZY THINKERS AND MUTTONHEADS. WHATZIT CONTAINS NO WHATCHAMACALLITS, THINGAMAJIGS, WHOOSIWHATSES, DOOHICKEYS, GIZMOS, DINGUSES, WIDGETS OR DOODADS.

net contents

kosher symbol

592 FUN-FILLED PAGES

Ⓤ

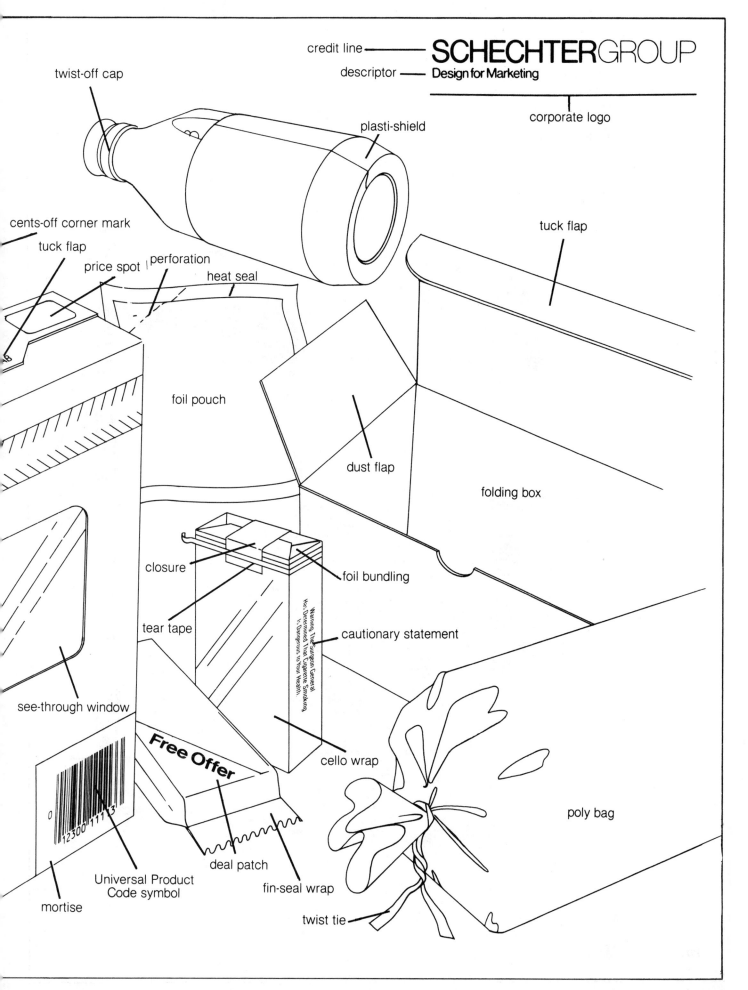

twist-off cap

SCHECHTERGROUP
Design for Marketing

corporate logo

plasti-shield

cents-off corner mark

tuck flap

tuck flap

price spot | perforation

heat seal

foil pouch

dust flap

folding box

closure

foil bundling

tear tape

cautionary statement

see-through window

Warning: The Surgeon General Has Determined That Cigarette Smoking Is Dangerous to Your Health.

cello wrap

Free Offer

poly bag

0 12300 11113

deal patch

Universal Product
Code symbol

fin-seal wrap

mortise

twist tie

Bed and Bedding

A bedstead or *bed frame* consists of *side rails,* or *bedrails,* which connect the headboard to the *footboard.* A *twin bed* is a single bed, or one of a matching pair or beds, while a *double bed* is large enough to sleep two adults. A *comforter* is a small, thick quilt, while a *throw* is a bedspread with a short *side drop* rather than long *skirts.*

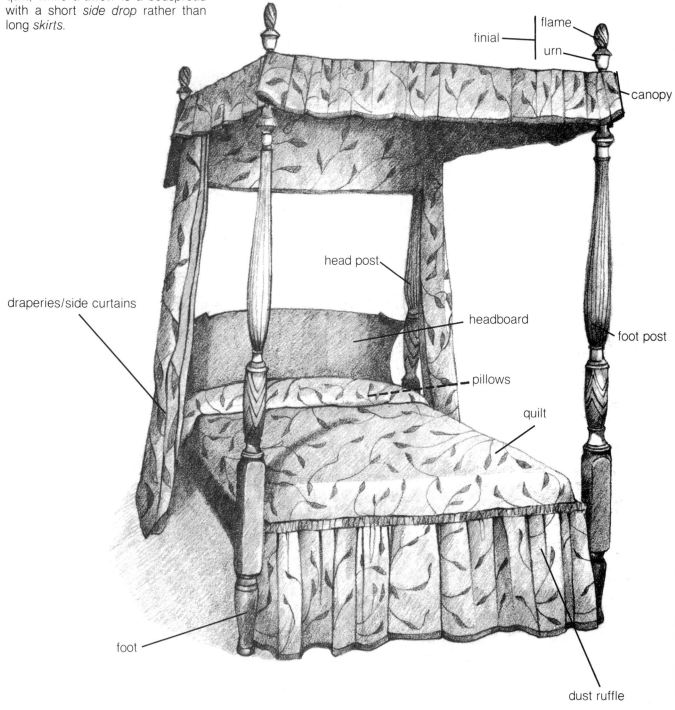

finial

flame

urn

canopy

head post

headboard

foot post

draperies/side curtains

pillows

quilt

foot

dust ruffle

Four-Poster / Canopy Bed

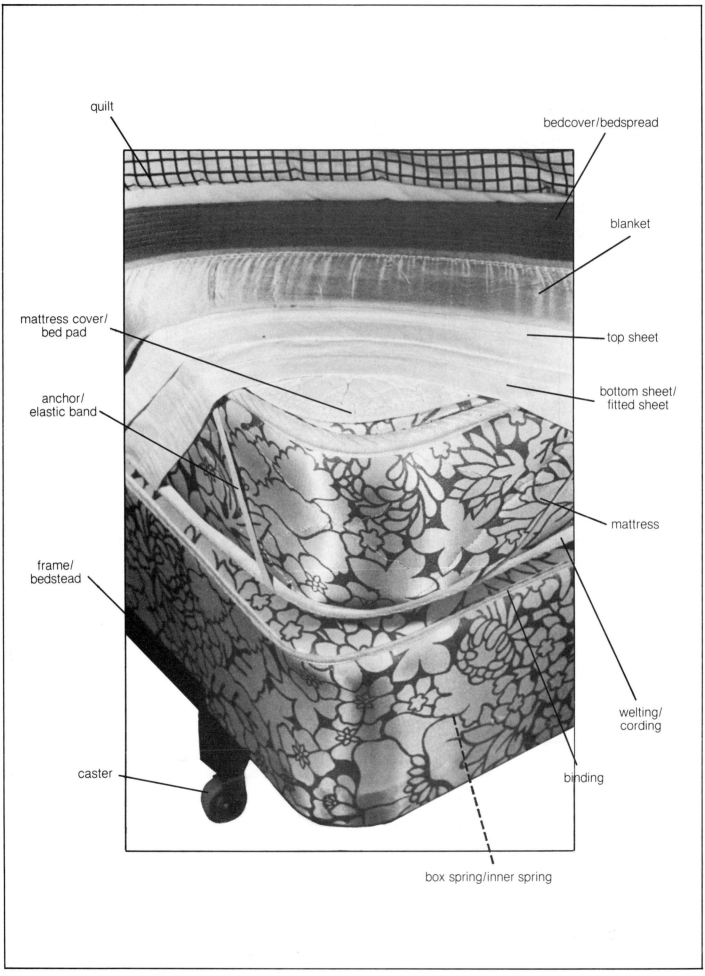

quilt

bedcover/bedspread

blanket

mattress cover/
bed pad

top sheet

anchor/
elastic band

bottom sheet/
fitted sheet

mattress

frame/
bedstead

welting/
cording

caster

binding

box spring/inner spring

271　　　　　　　　　　　　　　　　　　　　**Bedroom**

Dressers

A dresser without the drawers in it is called the *main body,* or *carcass.* The thin plywood sheets between drawers, to keep *drawer cases* rigid, are *dust panels.* An *armoire,* or *wardrobe,* is a tall, movable closet in which to hang clothes. A *chiffonier* is a high, narrow chest of drawers.

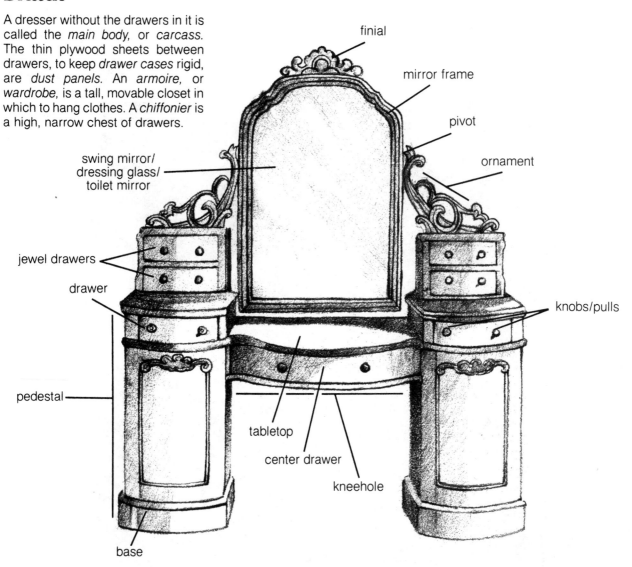

finial

mirror frame

pivot

ornament

swing mirror/
dressing glass/
toilet mirror

jewel drawers

drawer

knobs/pulls

pedestal

tabletop

center drawer

kneehole

base

Dressing Table/Vanity

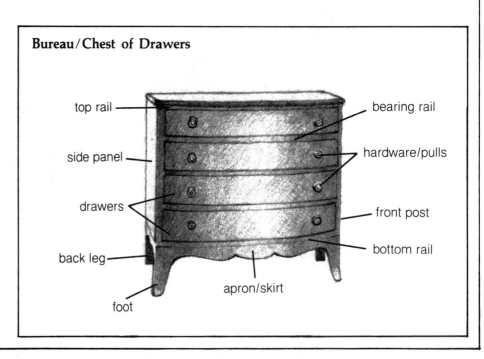

Bureau/Chest of Drawers

top rail

bearing rail

side panel

hardware/pulls

drawers

front post

back leg

bottom rail

foot

apron/skirt

Faucet and Sink

Some basins have *rubber plug* and *chain stoppers* to hold water, and *splash rims* or *lips* to prevent water from overflowing.

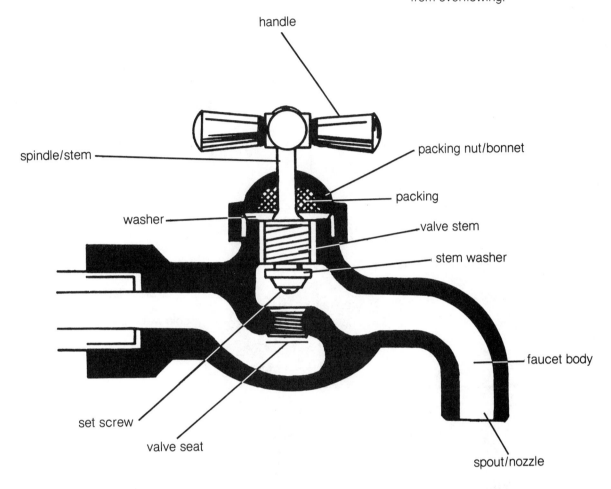

handle

spindle/stem

packing nut/bonnet

packing

washer

valve stem

stem washer

faucet body

set screw

valve seat

spout/nozzle

Faucet/Spigot/Tap/Bibcock

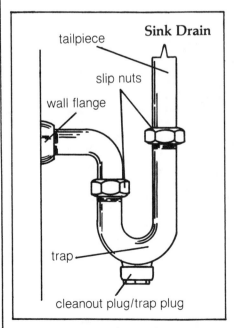

Sink Drain

tailpiece

slip nuts

wall flange

trap

cleanout plug/trap plug

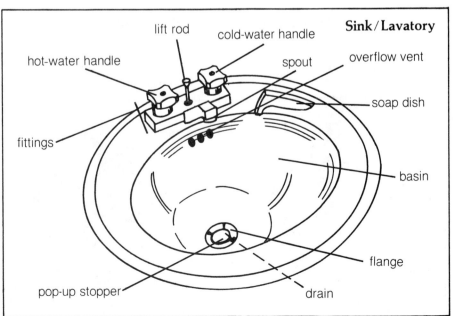

Sink/Lavatory

lift rod

cold-water handle

hot-water handle

spout

overflow vent

soap dish

fittings

basin

flange

pop-up stopper

drain

Bathroom

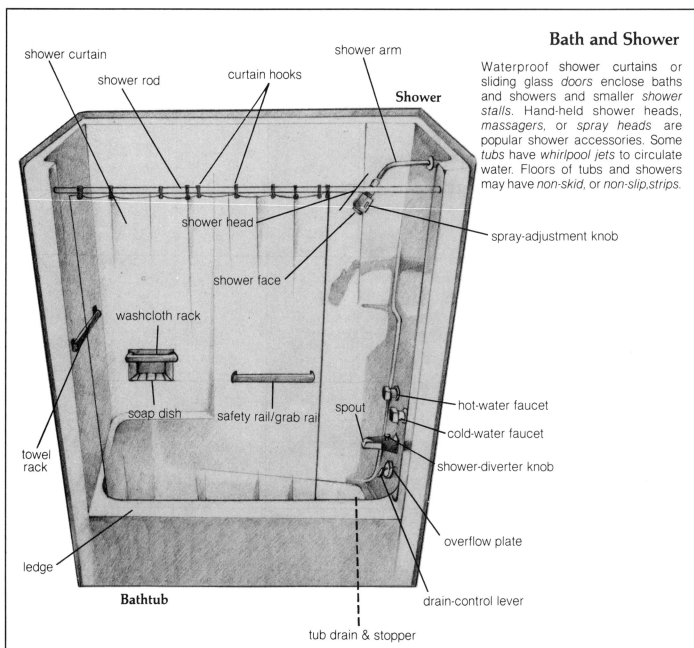

shower curtain

shower rod

curtain hooks

shower arm

Shower

Bath and Shower

Waterproof shower curtains or sliding glass *doors* enclose baths and showers and smaller *shower stalls*. Hand-held shower heads, *massagers*, or *spray heads* are popular shower accessories. Some *tubs* have *whirlpool jets* to circulate water. Floors of tubs and showers may have *non-skid*, or *non-slip, strips.*

shower head

spray-adjustment knob

shower face

washcloth rack

soap dish

safety rail/grab rail

spout

hot-water faucet

cold-water faucet

shower-diverter knob

towel rack

overflow plate

ledge

drain-control lever

Bathtub

tub drain & stopper

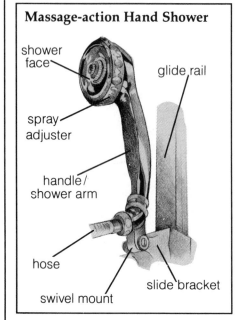

Massage-action Hand Shower

shower face

glide rail

spray adjuster

handle/ shower arm

hose

slide bracket

swivel mount

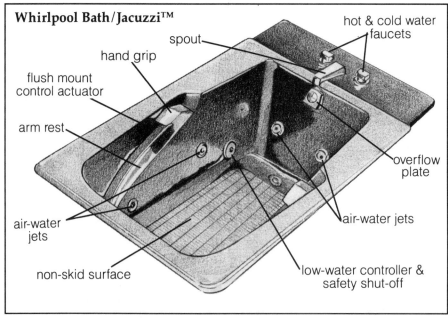

Whirlpool Bath/Jacuzzi™

spout

hand grip

flush mount control actuator

arm rest

hot & cold water faucets

overflow plate

air-water jets

air-water jets

non-skid surface

low-water controller & safety shut-off

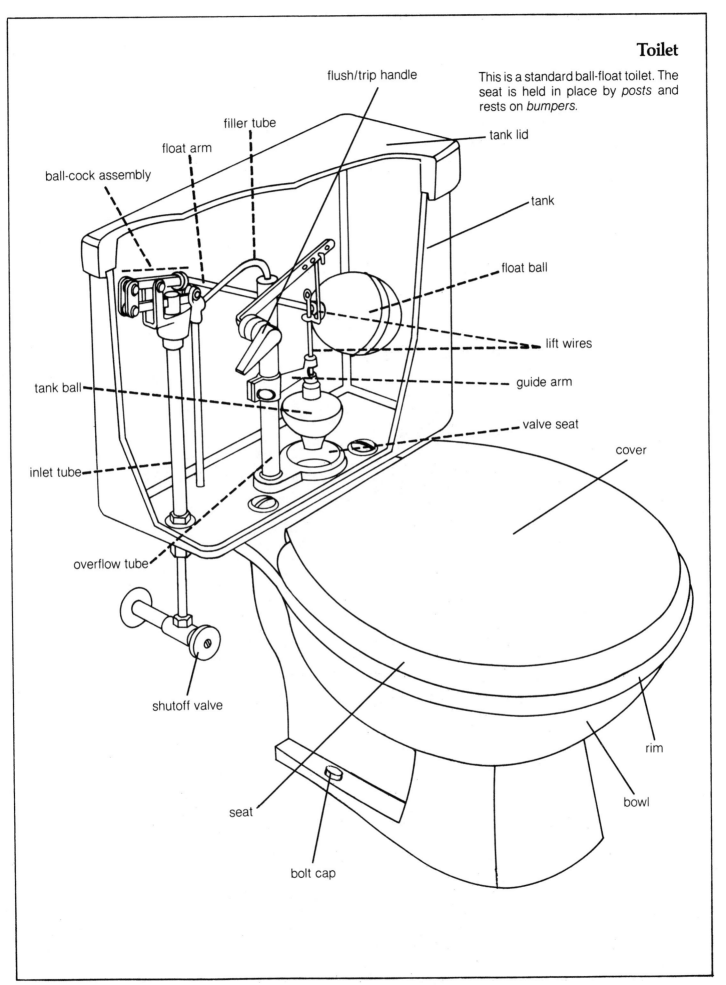

Toilet

This is a standard ball-float toilet. The seat is held in place by *posts* and rests on *bumpers*.

flush/trip handle

filler tube

float arm

ball-cock assembly

tank lid

tank

float ball

lift wires

guide arm

tank ball

valve seat

cover

inlet tube

overflow tube

shutoff valve

seat

rim

bowl

bolt cap

Desk

A *rolltop* or *cylinder desk* has a *sliding cover* that covers the desk's *writing area* when not in use. In *slant-front, falling-front* or *drop-lid desks*, the *front* flips down to offer a writing area which is supported by two *slide-out supports*. Some modern office desks have *elevator platforms* that can be raised and locked in place to hold a business machine, or lowered and closed behind a *cabinet door*.

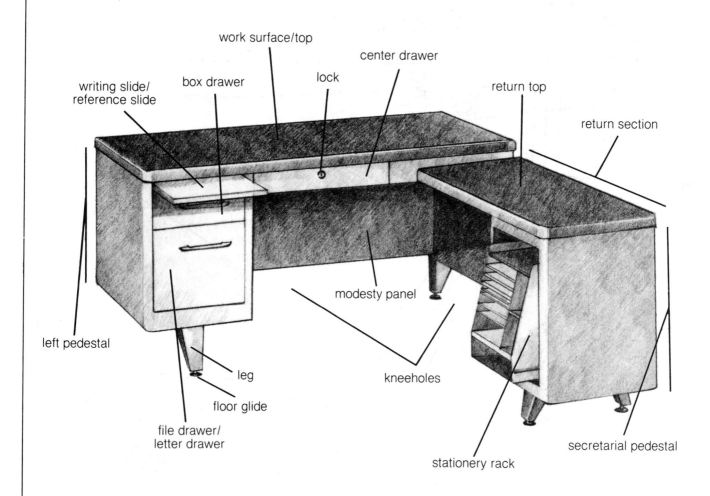

work surface/top

center drawer

writing slide/
reference slide

box drawer

lock

return top

return section

left pedestal

modesty panel

leg

floor glide

kneeholes

file drawer/
letter drawer

stationery rack

secretarial pedestal

Desktop Equipment

Strips of staples are loaded into a stapler's *channel*. Pencils are sharpened in a *carrier* which holds two grooved cylinders called *cutters*. A paper clip is a piece of bessemer stock wire given three *twists*.

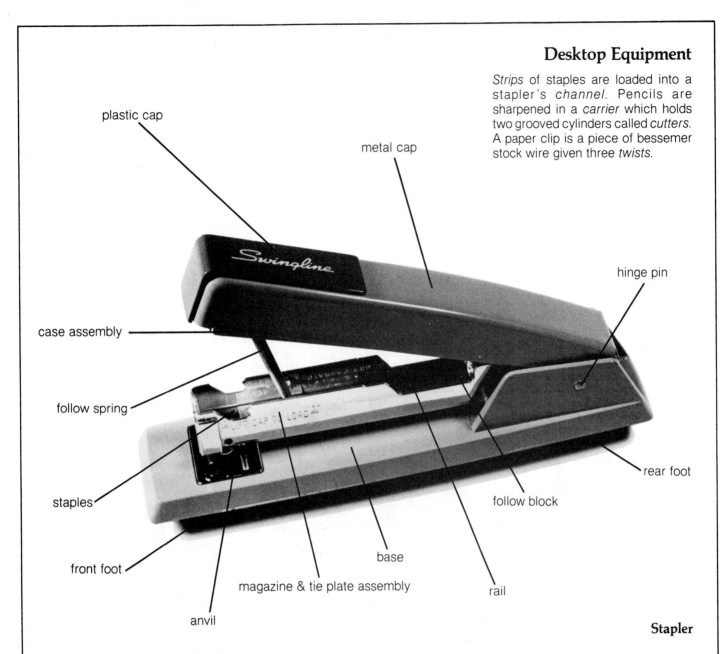

plastic cap

metal cap

hinge pin

case assembly

follow spring

rear foot

staples

follow block

front foot

base

magazine & tie plate assembly

rail

anvil

Stapler

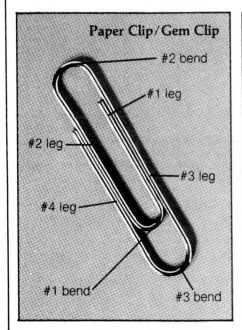

Paper Clip/Gem Clip

#2 bend

#1 leg

#2 leg

#3 leg

#4 leg

#1 bend

#3 bend

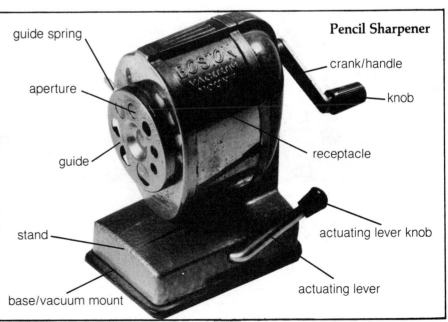

Pencil Sharpener

guide spring

crank/handle

aperture

knob

guide

receptacle

stand

actuating lever knob

base/vacuum mount

actuating lever

Sewing Machine

The standard presser foot can be replaced by a variety of special attachments, including a *zipper foot, hemmer foot* and *roller foot*. Some machines have a *slide plate* as well as a needle plate that opens to provide access to the bobbin case.

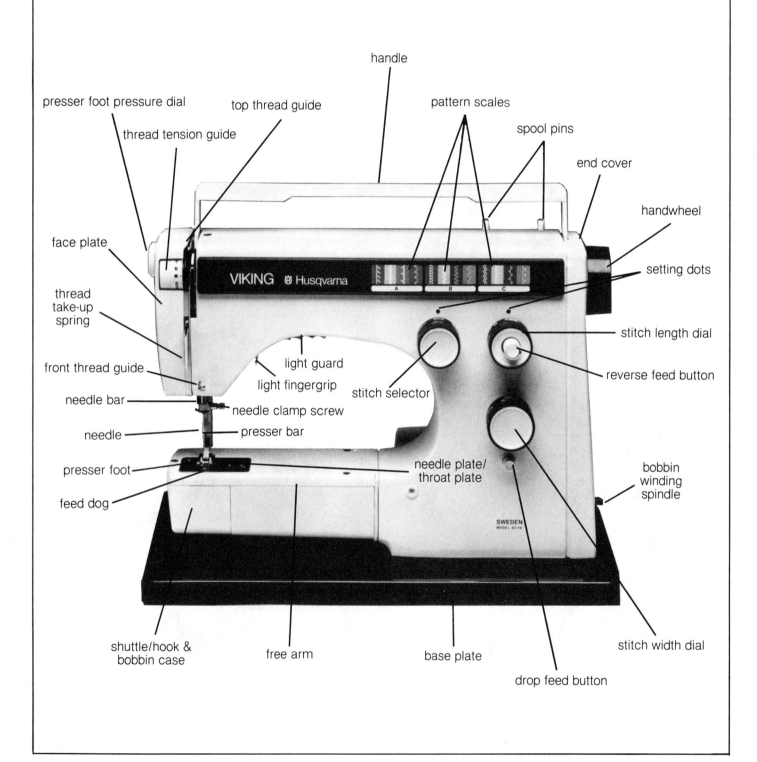

handle

presser foot pressure dial

top thread guide

pattern scales

thread tension guide

spool pins

end cover

handwheel

face plate

VIKING Husqvarna

setting dots

thread take-up spring

stitch length dial

front thread guide

light guard

light fingergrip

stitch selector

reverse feed button

needle bar

needle clamp screw

needle

presser bar

presser foot

needle plate/ throat plate

bobbin winding spindle

feed dog

SWEDEN MODEL 6370

shuttle/hook & bobbin case

free arm

base plate

stitch width dial

drop feed button

Iron

The *steam-and-dry iron,* or *flatiron,* shown here has *steam vents,* or *steam ports,* in the soleplate. Some irons have *front spray nozzles* as well.

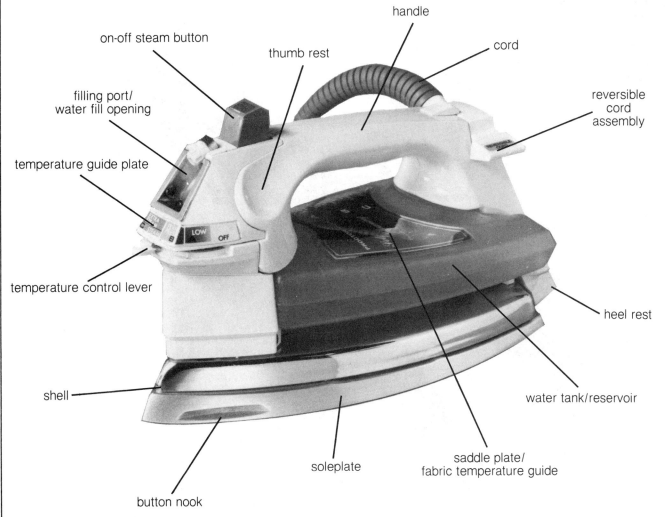

on-off steam button

thumb rest

handle

cord

reversible cord assembly

filling port/ water fill opening

temperature guide plate

temperature control lever

LOW   OFF

shell

heel rest

water tank/reservoir

button nook

soleplate

saddle plate/ fabric temperature guide

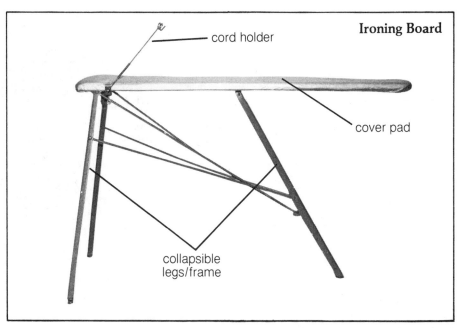

Ironing Board

cord holder

cover pad

collapsible legs/frame

Washing and Drying

Formerly, clothes were washed in a *washtub* with a *scrubboard* and *wringer* before being hung out to dry on *clotheslines,* or *washlines,* with clothespins. Wash-and-wear shirts are still air-dried on hangers. In automatic *top-loading washing machines* and *front-loading washers,* the basket, which has *drain holes* inside it, is contained within a metal *tub.* Some washers and dryers have a *window* in the *door* and a *tub light.*

gripping hole

spring slot

claw end

pinwood

handle

spring

Clothespin

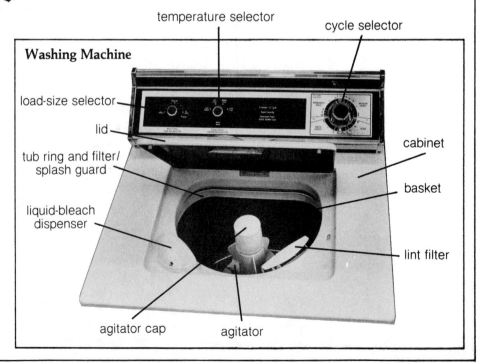

Washing Machine

temperature selector

cycle selector

load-size selector

lid

tub ring and filter/ splash guard

liquid-bleach dispenser

cabinet

basket

lint filter

agitator cap

agitator

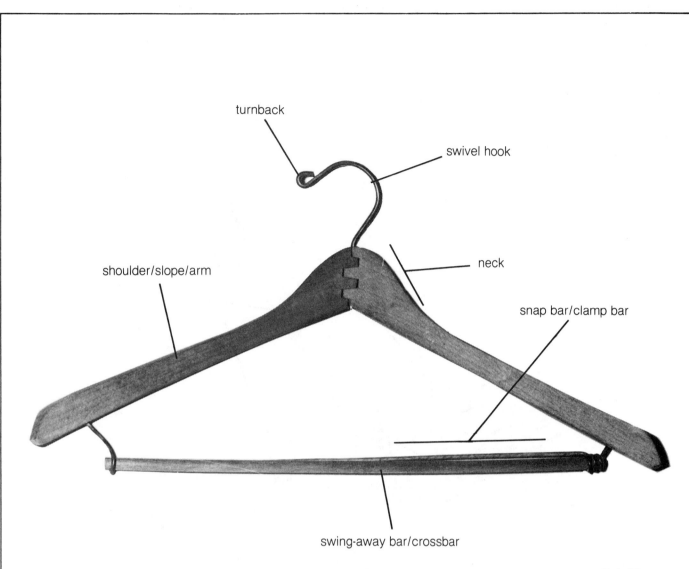

turnback

swivel hook

shoulder/slope/arm

neck

snap bar/clamp bar

swing-away bar/crossbar

Suit Hanger

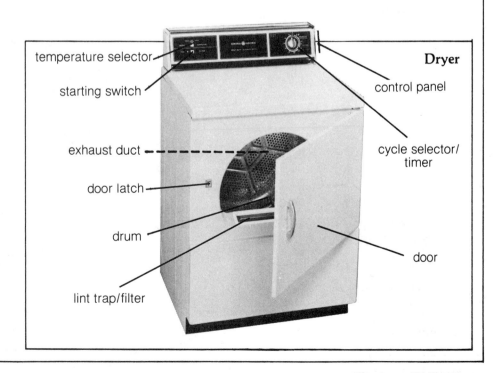

temperature selector

Dryer

starting switch

control panel

exhaust duct

cycle selector/
timer

door latch

drum

door

lint trap/filter

Household Cleaning Equipment

A conventional mop has absorbent *strands* rather than a sponge. An *electric broom* is a lightweight vacuum cleaner on a handle. A *carpet sweeper* contains two revolving brushes in a box at the end of a pushing handle.

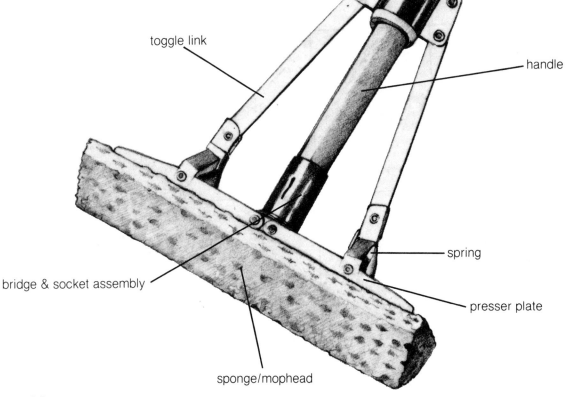

sleeve

rail

brace

toggle link

handle

spring

bridge & socket assembly

presser plate

sponge/mophead

Sponge Mop

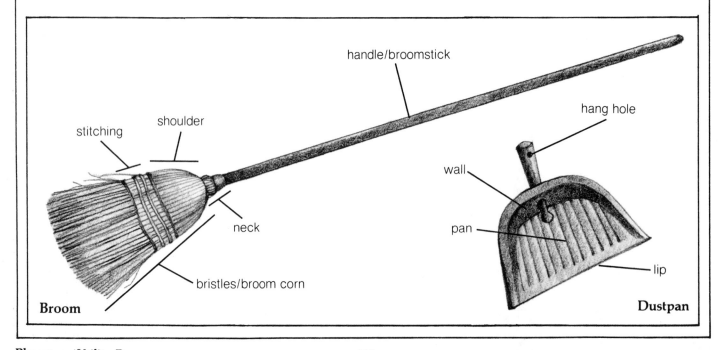

handle/broomstick

hang hole

shoulder

stitching

wall

neck

pan

bristles/broom corn

lip

Broom

Dustpan

Vacuum Cleaners

In an *upright vacuum cleaner,* shown here, *spiral brushes* under the hood and *beater bars* stir up dust and dirt. A *fan* blows these into a *disposable bag.* In a *cylinder model,* all the cleaning components are mounted horizontally. Dirt is sucked directly from the *intake tube* into a *vacuum bag,* or *dust bag.*

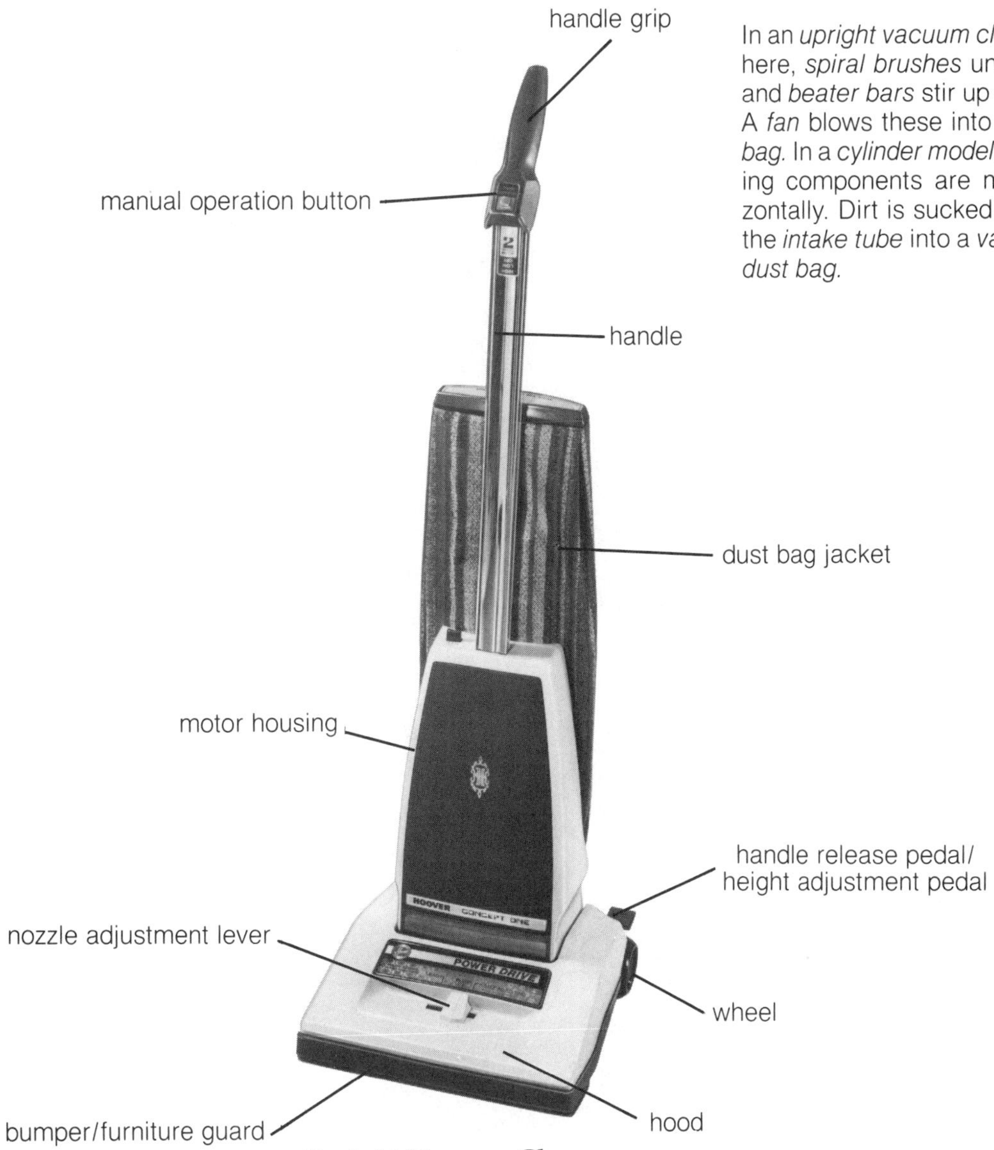

handle grip

manual operation button

handle

dust bag jacket

motor housing

handle release pedal/ height adjustment pedal

nozzle adjustment lever

wheel

bumper/furniture guard

hood

Upright Vacuum Cleaner

Attachments

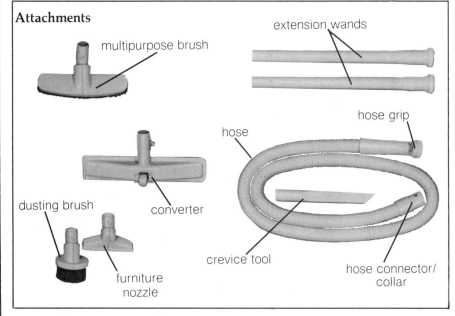

multipurpose brush

extension wands

hose grip

hose

converter

dusting brush

crevice tool

furniture nozzle

hose connector/ collar

Minivacuum

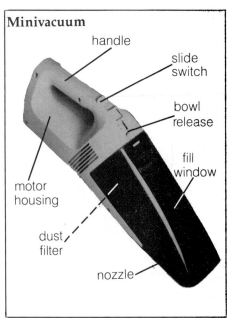

handle

slide switch

bowl release

fill window

motor housing

dust filter

nozzle

283

Firefighting Devices

Dry chemical extinguishers, containing chemicals and gas under pressure, are activated by squeezing or twisting the handle. *Soda-acid extinguishers,* inverted to mix the contents, produce a smothering *foam.*

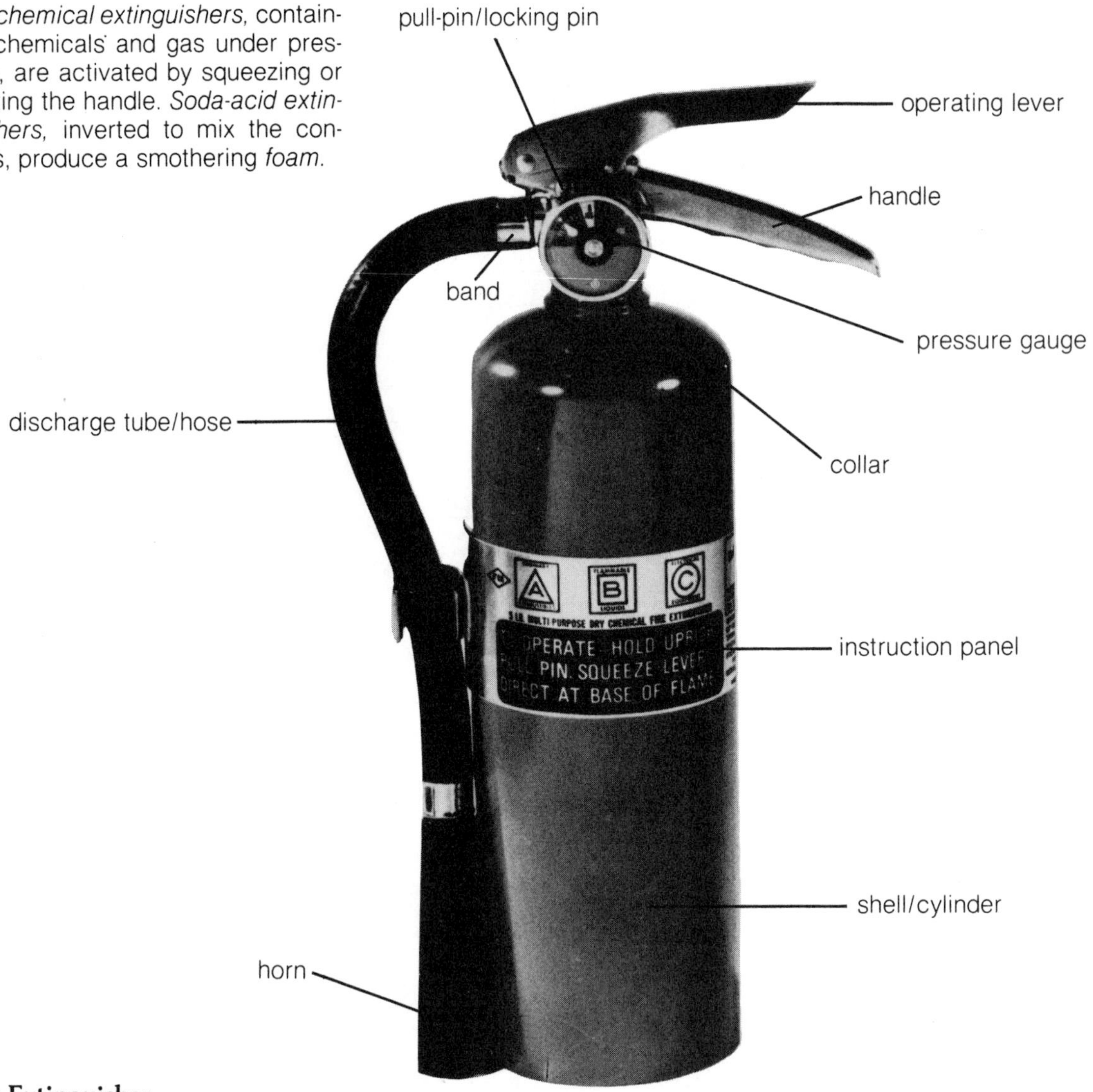

pull-pin/locking pin
operating lever
handle
band
pressure gauge
discharge tube/hose
collar
instruction panel
TO OPERATE HOLD UPRIGHT
PULL PIN. SQUEEZE LEVER
DIRECT AT BASE OF FLAME
shell/cylinder
horn

Fire Extinguisher

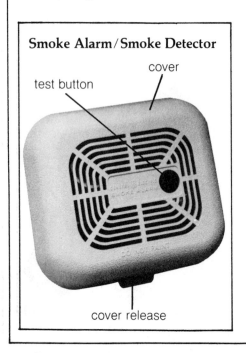

Smoke Alarm/Smoke Detector

cover
test button
cover release

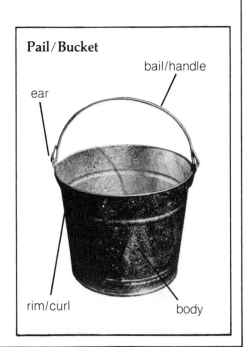

Pail/Bucket

bail/handle
ear
rim/curl
body

Luggage

The exterior parts of a *suitcase* or *bag* are identical to those of an *attaché case*. A suitcase that unfolds to be hung up is called a *garment bag*. Briefcases sometimes have zippered *file folders* or *portfolios* as well as paper storage *pockets*.

handle

identification tag

lock

shell

frame

foot

rivet

beading

Attaché Case/Briefcase

Overnight Bag

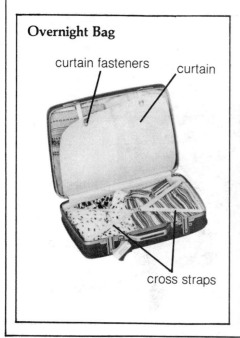

curtain fasteners

curtain

cross straps

Cosmetic Case

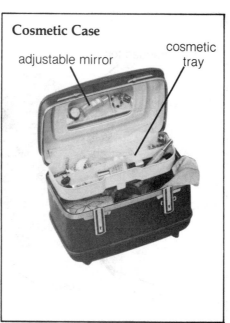

adjustable mirror

cosmetic tray

Two-Suiter

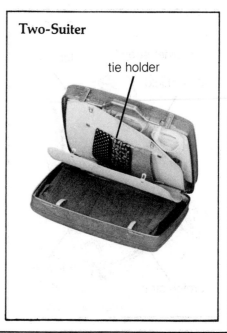

tie holder

Playroom/Utility Room

Children's Gear

Modern strollers have largely re-placed more elaborate *baby carriages,* or *perambulators.* A portable, basketlike infant bed, often with a *hood* at one end, is called a *bassinet.* An indoor *baby chair,* or *high chair,* has long legs, a *footrest* and a *serving tray.*

handle grip

canopy

handle

canopy support

backrest

backrest adjustment lever

wing

seat

frame

rear axle

footrest

swivel fork

wheel pin

swivel wheel holder

brake

wheel

Stroller

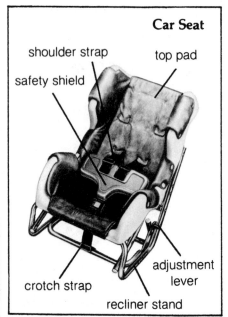

Car Seat

shoulder strap

top pad

safety shield

crotch strap

adjustment lever

recliner stand

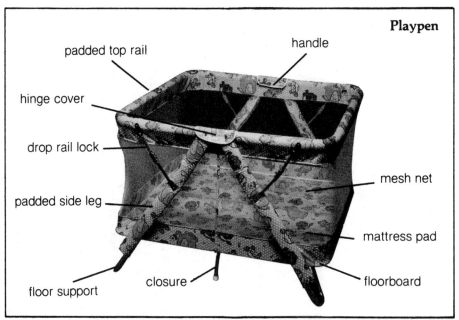

Playpen

padded top rail

handle

hinge cover

drop rail lock

mesh net

padded side leg

mattress pad

floor support

closure

floorboard

Backyard Equipment

Other popular backyard and *playground* equipment includes *seesaws*, or *teeter-totters*; *jungle gyms*, or *monkey bars*; *climbing nets*; *overhead ladders* and *sandboxes*.

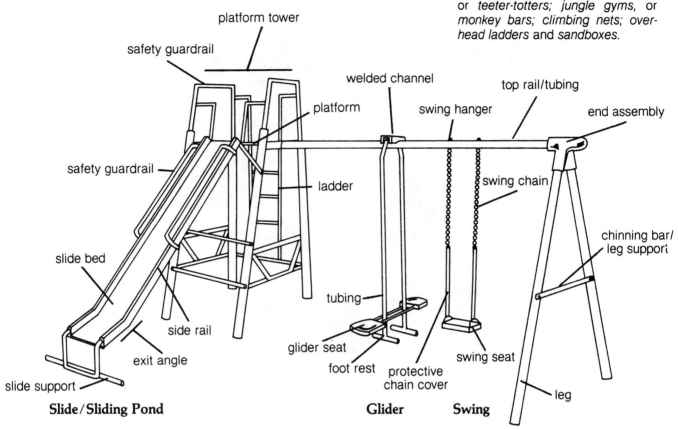

platform tower

safety guardrail

platform

safety guardrail

ladder

welded channel

swing hanger

top rail/tubing

end assembly

swing chain

slide bed

side rail

chinning bar/ leg support

exit angle

tubing

slide support

glider seat

foot rest

protective chain cover

swing seat

leg

Slide/Sliding Pond

Glider

Swing

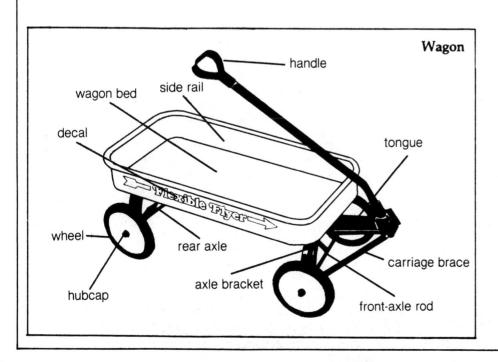

Wagon

handle

wagon bed

side rail

decal

tongue

wheel

rear axle

carriage brace

hubcap

axle bracket

front-axle rod

Flexible Flyer

287

Yard

Patio Accessories

On regular grills and *braziers*, food is cooked over *charcoal briquettes* resting in a *fire bowl*, whereas on gas and electric models food is grilled over *volcanic rock*. Other grills include *hibachis* and *kettle grills* featuring *damper controls*, *adjustable grills*, and *ash catchers*. On some outdoor lounges and *settees*, small springs, or *helicals*, connect the frame to metal supporting straps.

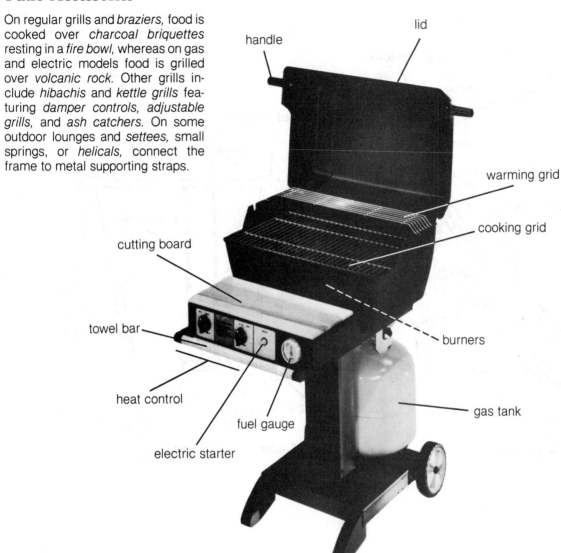

handle

lid

warming grid

cooking grid

cutting board

towel bar

heat control

fuel gauge

electric starter

burners

gas tank

Barbecue Grill/Gas Barbecue

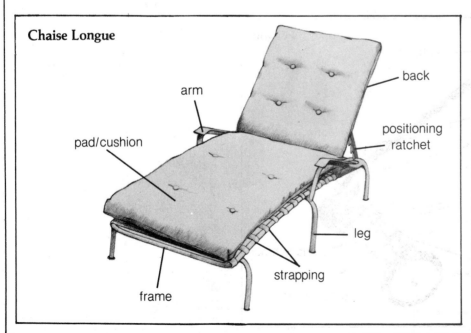

Chaise Longue

back

arm

positioning ratchet

pad/cushion

leg

strapping

frame

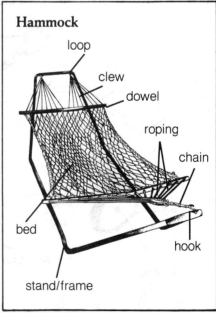

Hammock

loop

clew

dowel

roping

chain

bed

hook

stand/frame

Sports and Recreation

Emphasis in this section is given to major sports and forms of recreational activity which involve gear and equipment. Word and picture games, for example, have been omitted, since the nomenclature involved is so limited.

In order to enable the reader to find particular items quickly, recreational activities have been grouped in the following way: team sports, competitive sports, individual sports, equestrian sports, automobile racing, outdoor sports, bodybuilding, board games and casino games.

Because playing areas involved in team and competitive sports are an integral part of the activity, fields, courts and rinks have been diagramed with all the vital areas, lines and demarcations identified.

And to show the parts of clothing and equipment used by players, real athletes rather than models have been photographed: batter Rod Carew, football running back Bruce Harper, basketball guard Mike Glenn, hockey defenseman Ken Morrow and goalie Billy Smith.

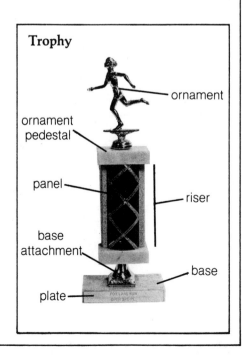

Trophy

ornament

ornament pedestal

panel

riser

base attachment

base

plate

Baseball

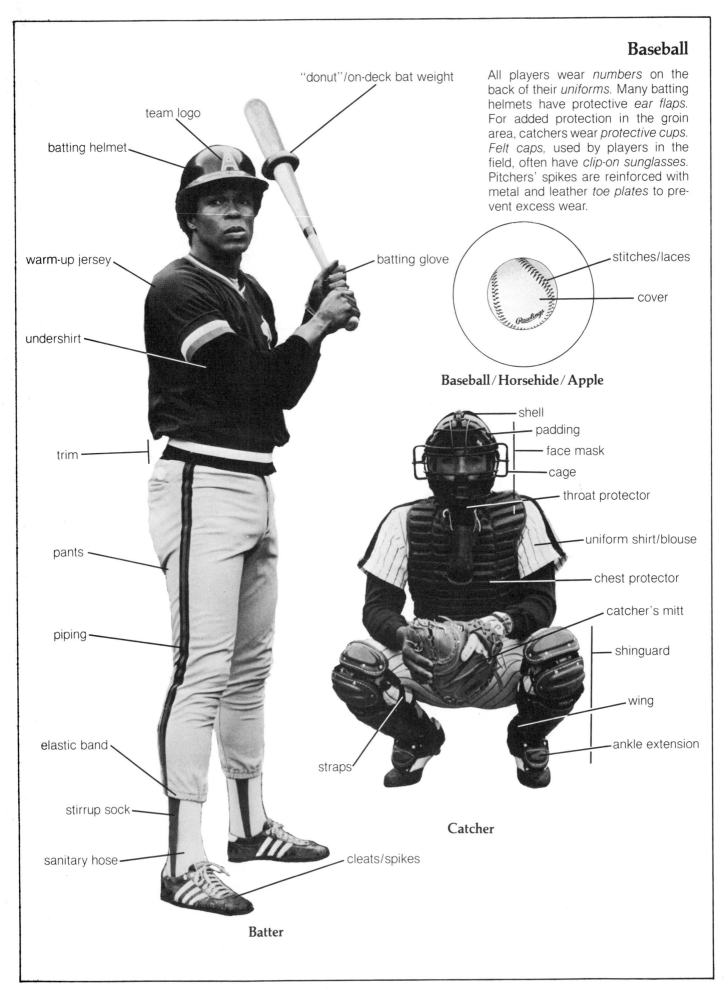

"donut"/on-deck bat weight

team logo

batting helmet

warm-up jersey

undershirt

trim

pants

piping

elastic band

stirrup sock

sanitary hose

cleats/spikes

batting glove

All players wear *numbers* on the back of their *uniforms*. Many batting helmets have protective *ear flaps*. For added protection in the groin area, catchers wear *protective cups*. *Felt caps,* used by players in the field, often have *clip-on sunglasses*. Pitchers' spikes are reinforced with metal and leather *toe plates* to prevent excess wear.

stitches/laces

cover

Baseball / Horsehide / Apple

shell

padding

face mask

cage

throat protector

uniform shirt/blouse

chest protector

catcher's mitt

shinguard

wing

ankle extension

straps

Catcher

Batter

Baseball

Artificial turf has replaced natural *grass* in the outfield and certain portions of the infield in many *stadiums,* or *ballparks.*

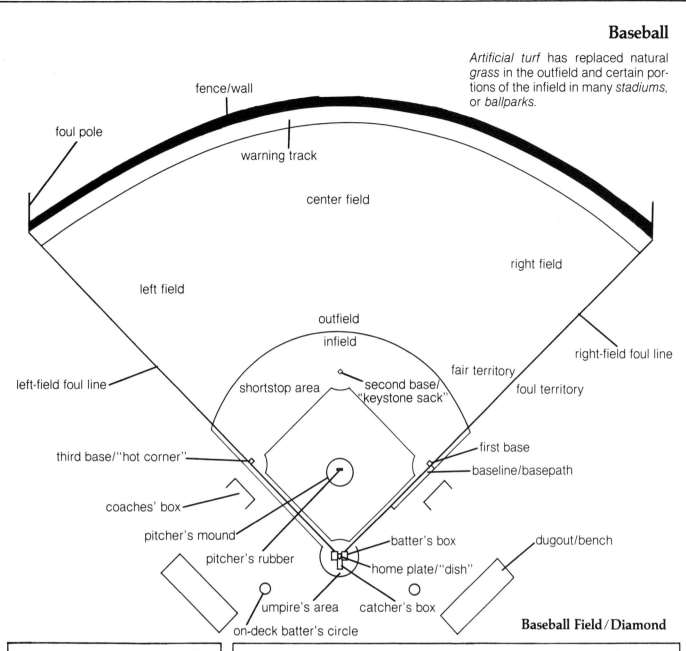

fence/wall

foul pole

warning track

center field

right field

left field

outfield

infield

right-field foul line

shortstop area

second base/
"keystone sack"

fair territory

left-field foul line

foul territory

third base/"hot corner"

first base

baseline/basepath

coaches' box

pitcher's mound

pitcher's rubber

batter's box

dugout/bench

home plate/"dish"

umpire's area

catcher's box

on-deck batter's circle

Baseball Field/Diamond

Bat

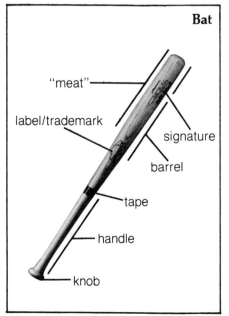

"meat"

label/trademark

signature

barrel

tape

handle

knob

Glove/Mitt

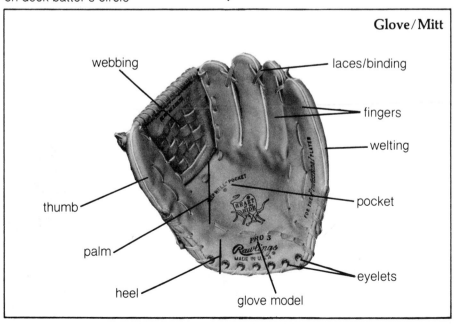

webbing

laces/binding

fingers

welting

thumb

pocket

palm

heel

glove model

eyelets

Football

Protective equipment worn on the upper body is covered with a *numbered jersey*. A *tear-away jersey* is loosely sewn and meant to rip apart when grabbed by an opponent. Helmets are manufactured with different *suspension systems*, some of which are air-inflated. Football covers have a rough *pebble finish* and an air-retaining *bladder* which is filled by inserting an *inflation needle* in the valve.

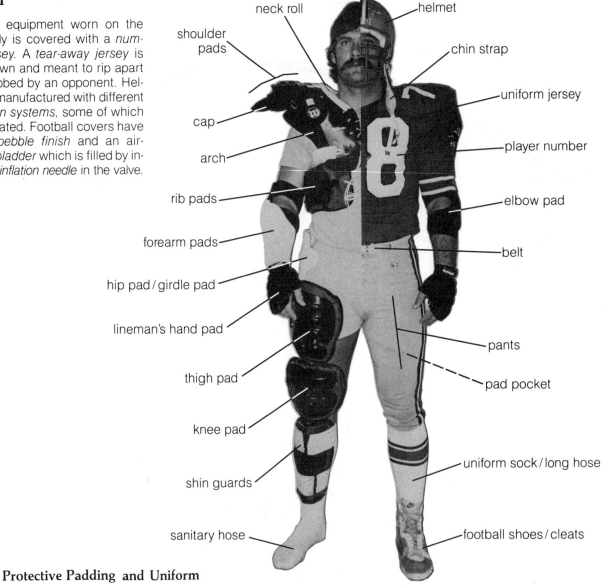

neck roll
helmet
shoulder pads
chin strap
cap
uniform jersey
arch
player number
rib pads
elbow pad
forearm pads
belt
hip pad / girdle pad
lineman's hand pad
thigh pad
pants
pad pocket
knee pad
shin guards
uniform sock / long hose
sanitary hose
football shoes / cleats

Protective Padding and Uniform

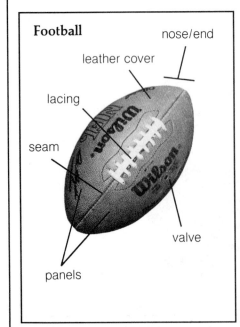

Football

nose/end
leather cover
lacing
seam
valve
panels

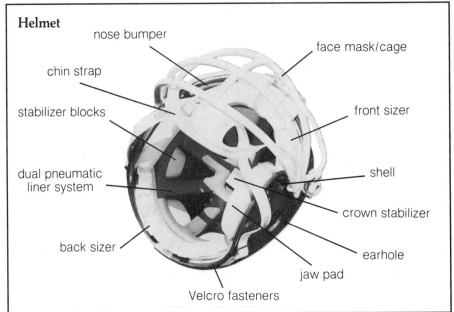

Helmet

nose bumper
face mask/cage
chin strap
front sizer
stabilizer blocks
shell
dual pneumatic liner system
crown stabilizer
back sizer
earhole
jaw pad
Velcro fasteners

Football

A *down marker* is used to mark the exact location of the ball on the field between downs. The *flip chart* at the top of the down marker has *flip panels* to indicate what down is about to be played. Yard lines cross the field every five yards. *Flags* are located at the junction of the goal line and sideline to mark in bounds. Small, rubber inverted V-shaped *yard markers* are placed at five-yard intervals along the sidelines.

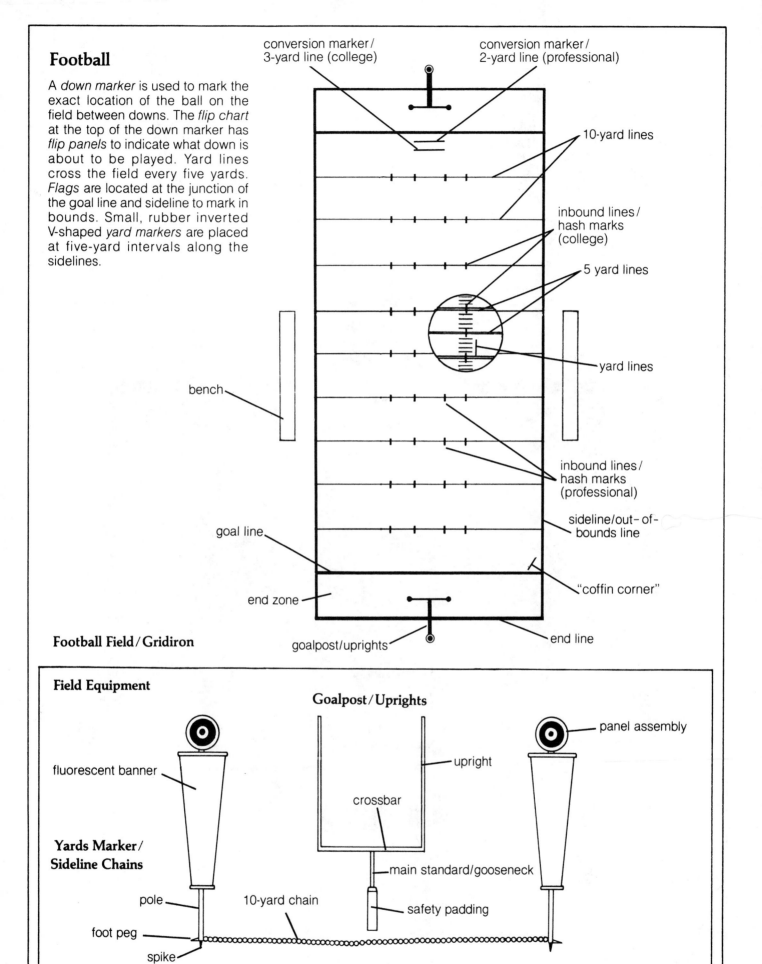

conversion marker/ 3-yard line (college)

conversion marker/ 2-yard line (professional)

10-yard lines

inbound lines/ hash marks (college)

5 yard lines

yard lines

bench

inbound lines/ hash marks (professional)

sideline/out-of-bounds line

goal line

"coffin corner"

end zone

end line

goalpost/uprights

Football Field/Gridiron

Field Equipment

Goalpost/Uprights

fluorescent banner

panel assembly

upright

crossbar

Yards Marker/ Sideline Chains

pole

10-yard chain

main standard/gooseneck

foot peg

safety padding

spike

Ice Hockey

Hockey players' pants are held up by *suspenders*. Socks are attached to a *garter belt*. The angle between the shaft of a hockey stick and the blade is called the *lie*. The game is played with a black vulcanized rubber *puck*. A blinking *red light* atop the goal judge's box indicates a goal.

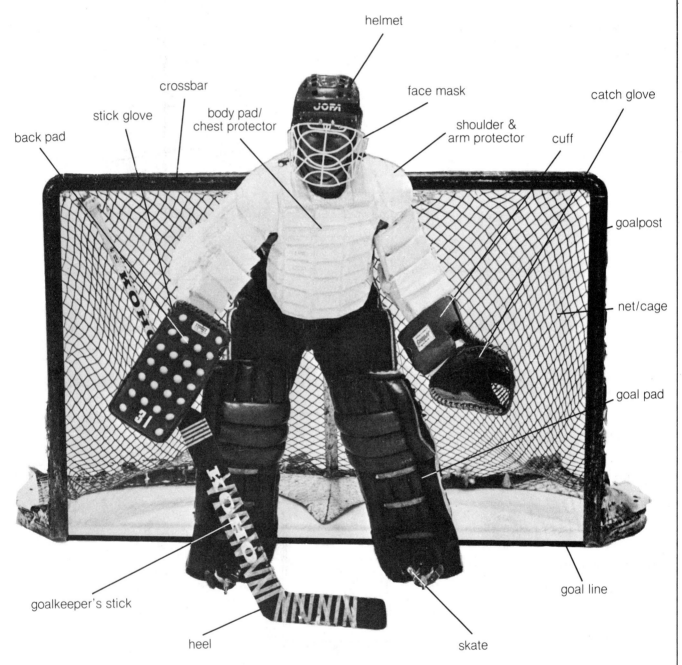

helmet

crossbar

stick glove

body pad/ chest protector

back pad

face mask

catch glove

shoulder & arm protector

cuff

goalpost

net/cage

goal pad

goalkeeper's stick

goal line

heel

skate

Goal and Goalie / Goalkeeper / Goaler

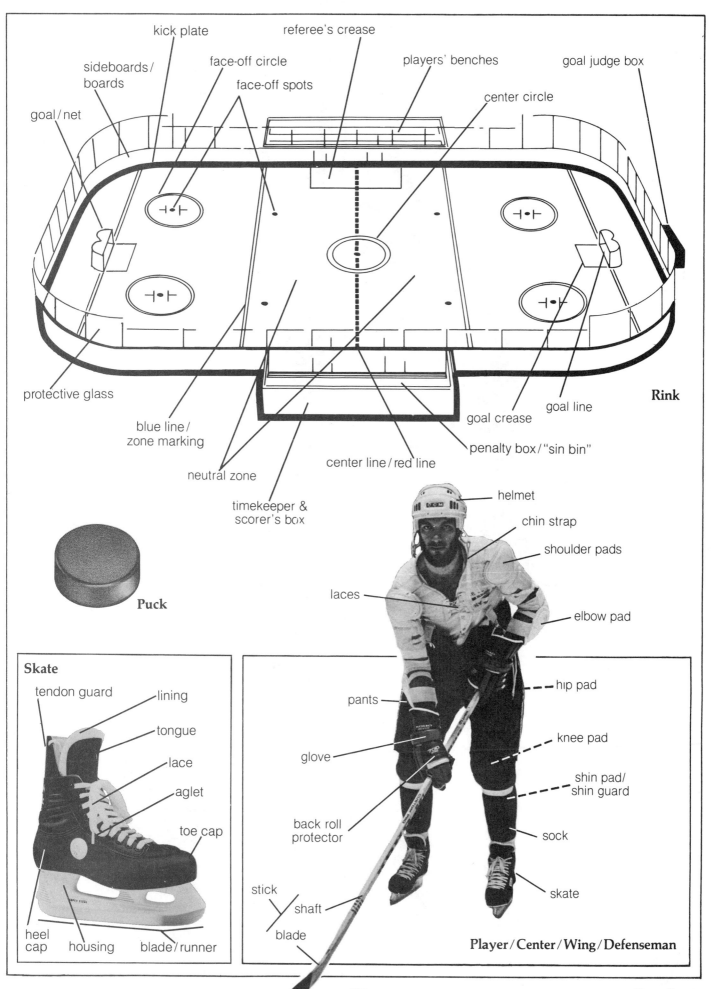

kick plate

referee's crease

sideboards/
boards

face-off circle

players' benches

goal judge box

face-off spots

center circle

goal/net

protective glass

blue line/
zone marking

goal crease

goal line

penalty box/"sin bin"

neutral zone

center line/red line

timekeeper &
scorer's box

Rink

Puck

Skate

tendon guard

lining

tongue

lace

aglet

toe cap

heel
cap

housing

blade/runner

helmet

chin strap

shoulder pads

laces

elbow pad

hip pad

pants

knee pad

glove

shin pad/
shin guard

back roll
protector

sock

stick

skate

shaft

blade

Player/Center/Wing/Defenseman

295

Team Sports

Basketball

The offensive team advances from its own *backcourt* into the *forecourt*. The area at the top of the free-throw lane, usually patrolled by the *center* (as opposed to one of two *guards* or two *forwards*), is called the *pivot*. Many players wear *kneepads* and *elbow pads* for protection, and *warm-up suits* prior to games.

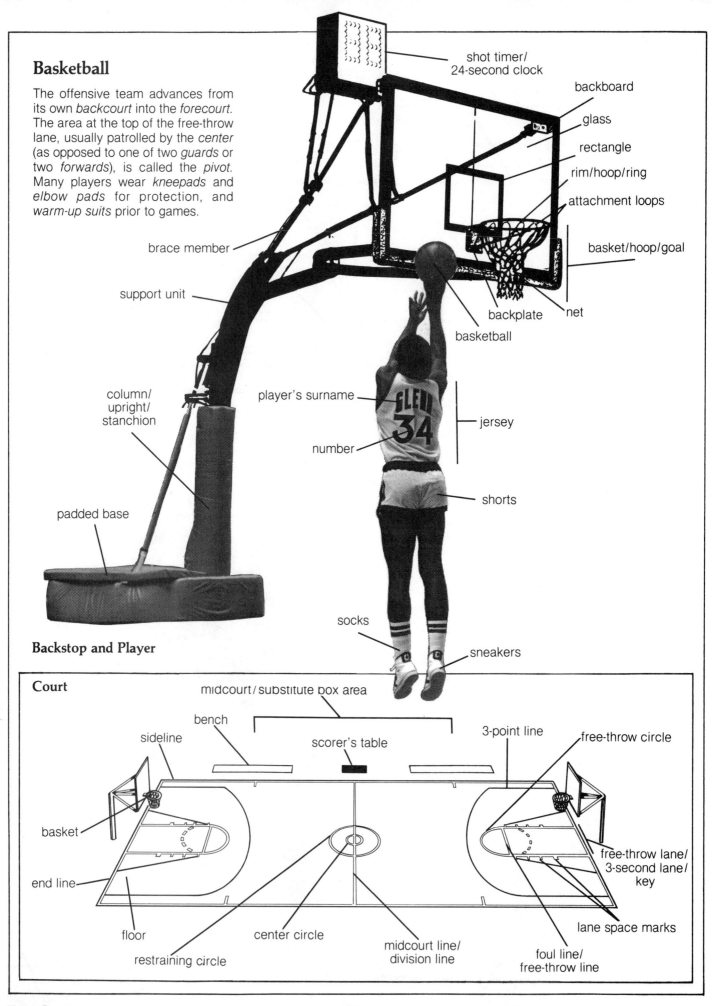

shot timer/ 24-second clock

backboard

glass

rectangle

rim/hoop/ring

attachment loops

basket/hoop/goal

brace member

support unit

net

backplate

basketball

column/ upright/ stanchion

player's surname

jersey

number

shorts

padded base

GLEN 34

socks

sneakers

Backstop and Player

Court

midcourt/substitute box area

bench

scorer's table

3-point line

free-throw circle

sideline

basket

free-throw lane/ 3-second lane/ key

end line

lane space marks

floor

restraining circle

center circle

midcourt line/ division line

foul line/ free-throw line

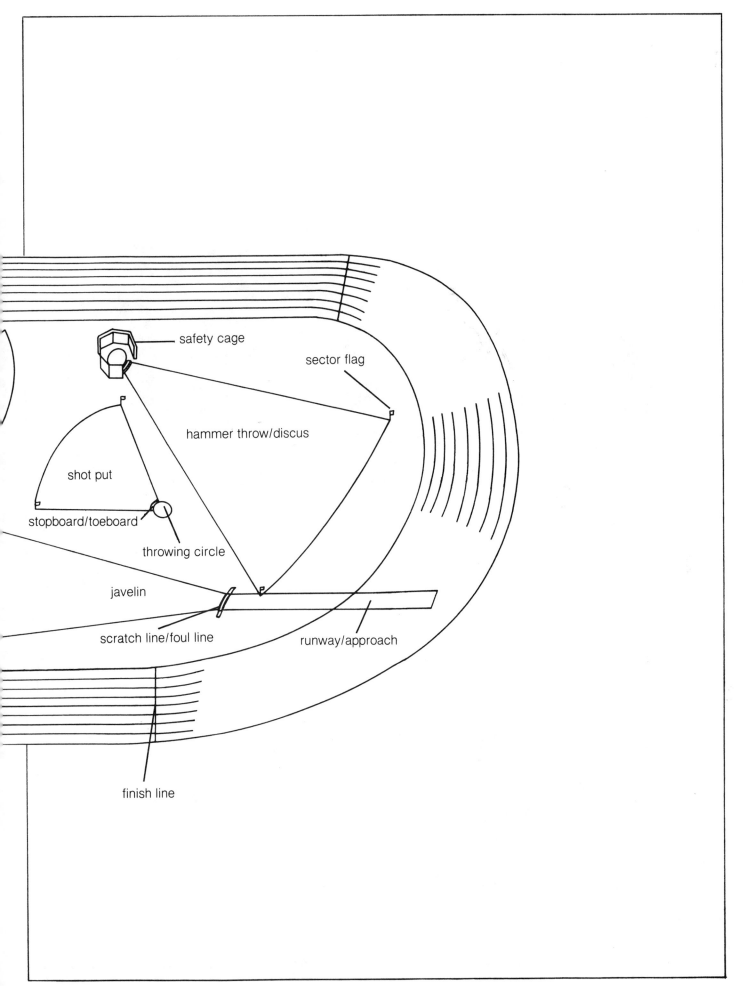

safety cage

sector flag

hammer throw/discus

shot put

stopboard/toeboard

throwing circle

javelin

scratch line/foul line

runway/approach

finish line

Running Shoe

These *training shoes*, or *trainers*, are more durable than lighter-weight *racing flats*. Lightweight running shoes are worn by *joggers* or *distance runners* in long races such as *marathons*. *Track shoes*, shoes with *spikes*, are used for most track-and-field events.

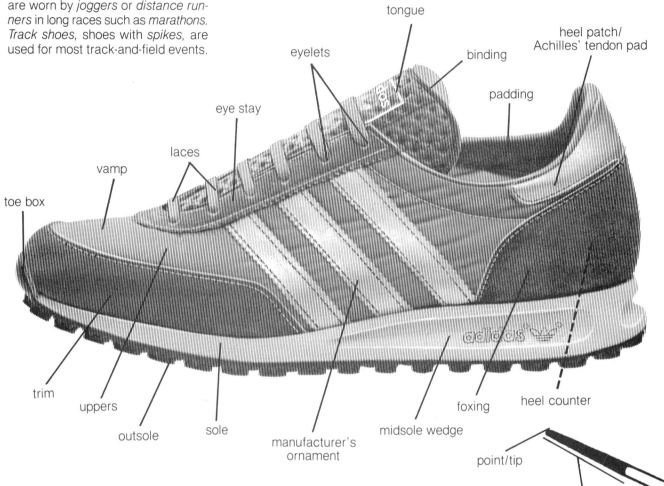

tongue

heel patch/
Achilles' tendon pad

eyelets

binding

padding

eye stay

laces

vamp

toe box

trim

uppers

outsole

sole

manufacturer's
ornament

midsole wedge

foxing

heel counter

point/tip

head

Tread

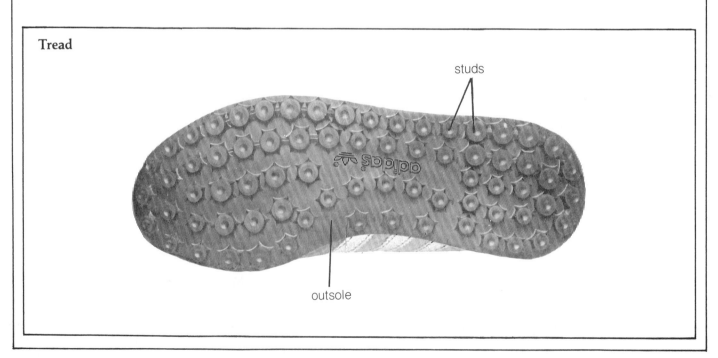

studs

outsole

Field Events Equipment

In addition to the equipment shown here, a round metal ball called a *shot put,* or *shot,* is also used in field events. Hammer throwers often wear *gloves* with padded palms.

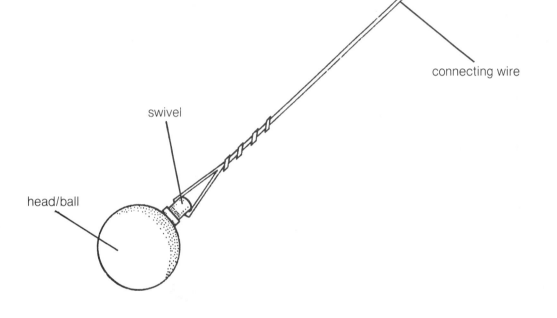

grip

handle

connecting wire

swivel

head/ball

Hammer

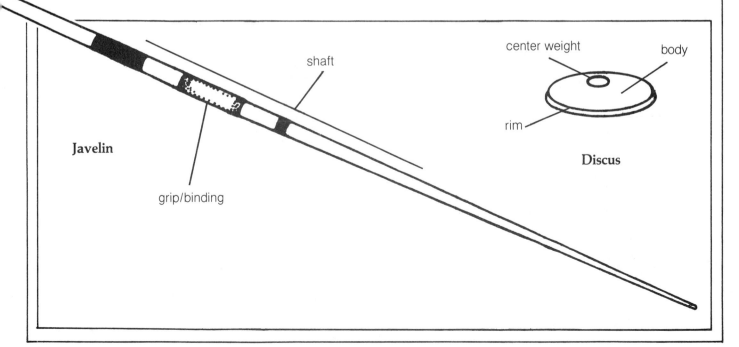

center weight

body

shaft

rim

Javelin

grip/binding

Discus

Competitive Sports

Hurdle

The height of hurdles can be adjusted for use in *high, intermediate* and *low hurdle* events. Base weights can also be adjusted to provide the proper *pull-over,* or *flipover,* the force required to knock them over. *Fixed hurdles* are used in a *steeplechase race,* an event that includes *water hazards.* Roller, or notched *lever locks* permit runners to adjust the slant on starting blocks, and a *plunger snap lock* allows them to position the blocks individually on the rail.

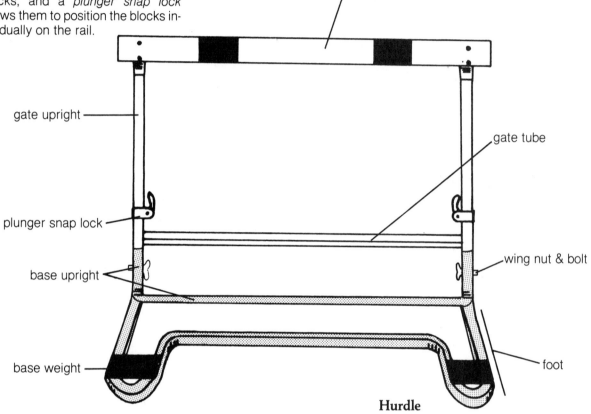

gatebar/top bar

gate upright

gate tube

plunger snap lock

base upright

wing nut & bolt

base weight

foot

Hurdle

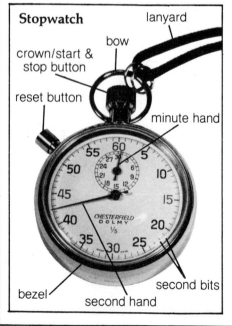

Stopwatch

lanyard

bow

crown/start & stop button

reset button

minute hand

CHESTERFIELD DOLMY 1/5

bezel

second hand

second bits

Starting Block/Blocks

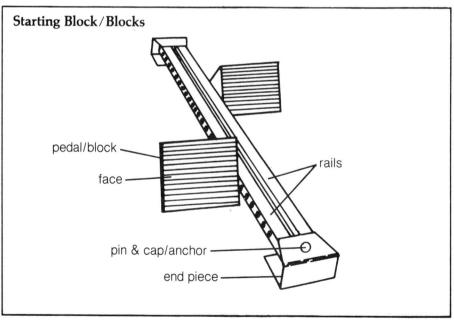

pedal/block

face

rails

pin & cap/anchor

end piece

Pole Vault

The *fiberglass pole,* which replaced traditional *bamboo* and *metal poles,* enables a *vaulter* to catapult over the *bar.* A *high-jump pit* is similar to the pole vault, but the crossbar is considerably lower and there is no *box* in the *take-off area.*

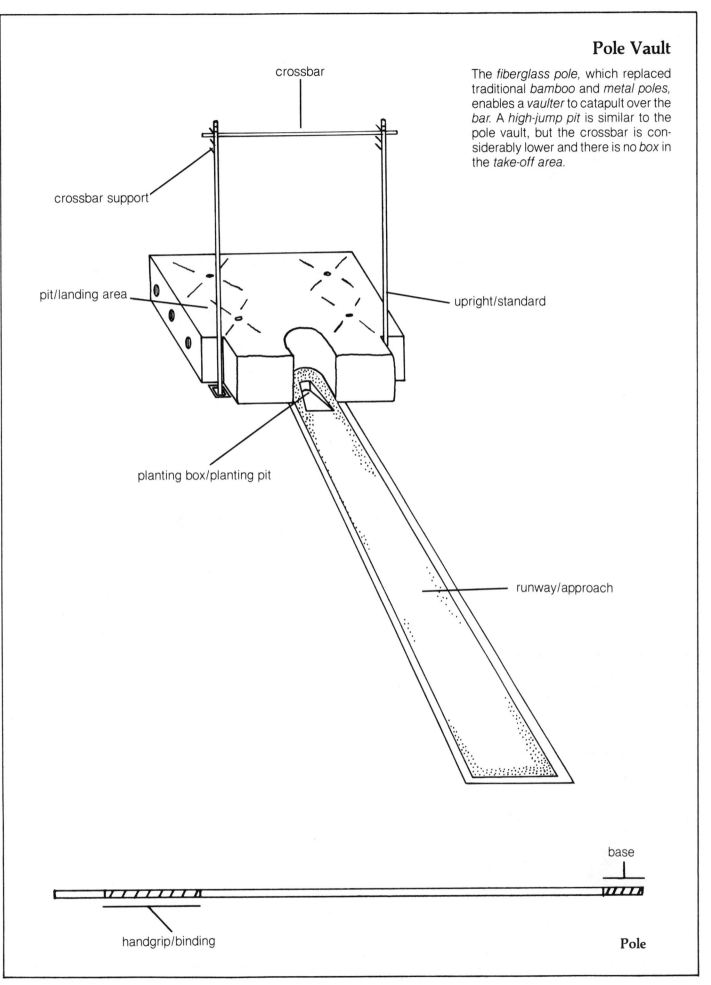

crossbar

crossbar support

pit/landing area

upright/standard

planting box/planting pit

runway/approach

base

handgrip/binding

Pole

Competitive Sports

Gymnastics

Protective *landing mats* are placed around each piece of gymnastic equipment when it is in use. In addition, during practice sessions, assistants called *spotters* stand by to aid the *gymnast*. Gymnastic competition called *floor exercises* takes place on lined *floor exercise mats*.

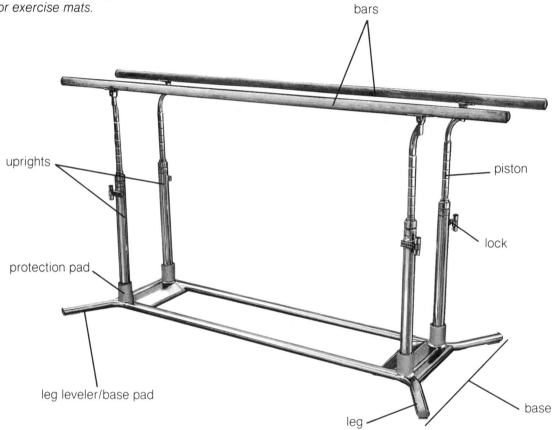

bars

uprights

piston

lock

protection pad

leg leveler/base pad

leg

base

Parallel Bars

Horizontal Bar/High Bar

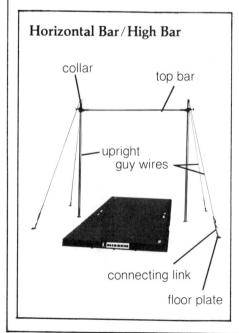

collar

top bar

upright
guy wires

connecting link

floor plate

Uneven Parallel Bars

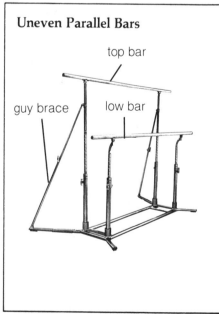

top bar

guy brace

low bar

Balance Beam

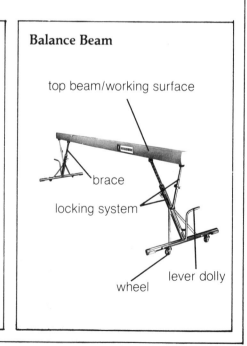

top beam/working surface

brace

locking system

wheel

lever dolly

Gymnastics

Some pommel horses, or *side horses,* can be converted into *vaulting,* or *long, horses* by removing the pommels and plugging the holes they fit in. *Vaulting boards,* or *springboards,* are used by *vaulters* to gain height when mounting the apparatus.

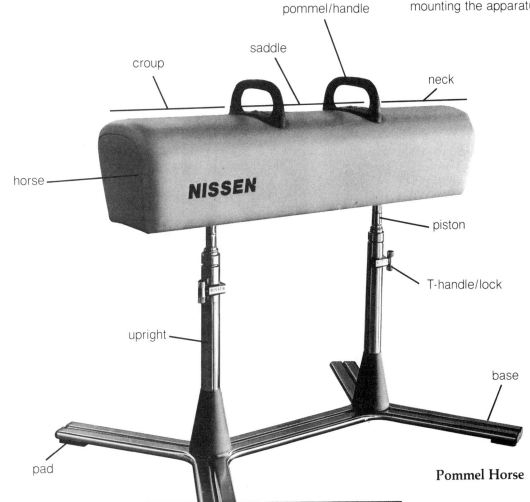

croup

saddle

pommel/handle

neck

horse

NISSEN

piston

T-handle/lock

upright

base

pad

Pommel Horse

Stationary Rings

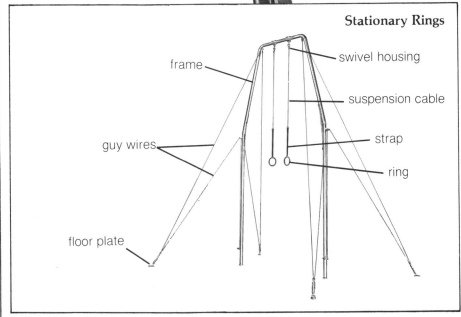

frame

swivel housing

suspension cable

guy wires

strap

ring

floor plate

Competitive Sports

Trampoline

Trampolining, trampoline tumbling, or *rebound tumbling* is performed on the canvas or elastic-webbing bed. Smaller *trampolets* are often used as *springboards* for mounting gymnastic apparatus.

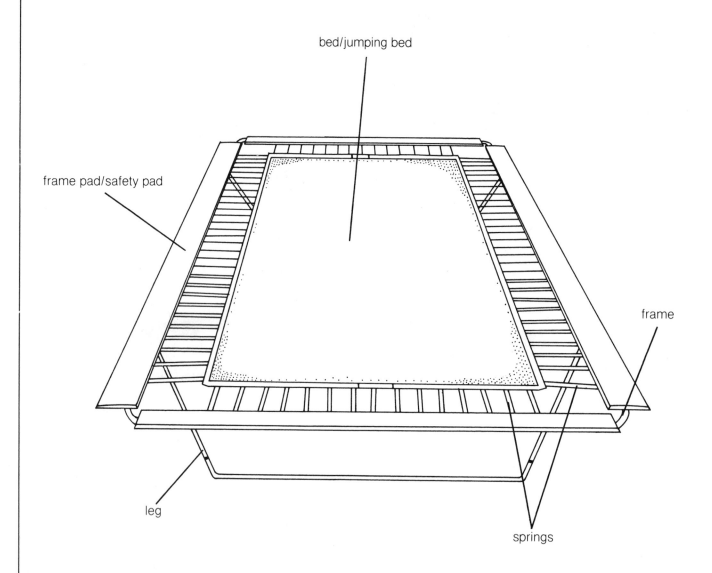

bed/jumping bed

frame pad/safety pad

frame

leg

springs

Boxing

In addition to the *sparring,* or practice, equipment shown here, *boxers* use a *mouthpiece* or *mouthguard* for protection of teeth. A *bell* at *ringside* is used to indicate the beginning and end of each *round.* Boxers rest on *stools* placed in their corners by assistants, or *handlers,* between rounds. Corners not used by fighters during these periods are called *neutral corners.*

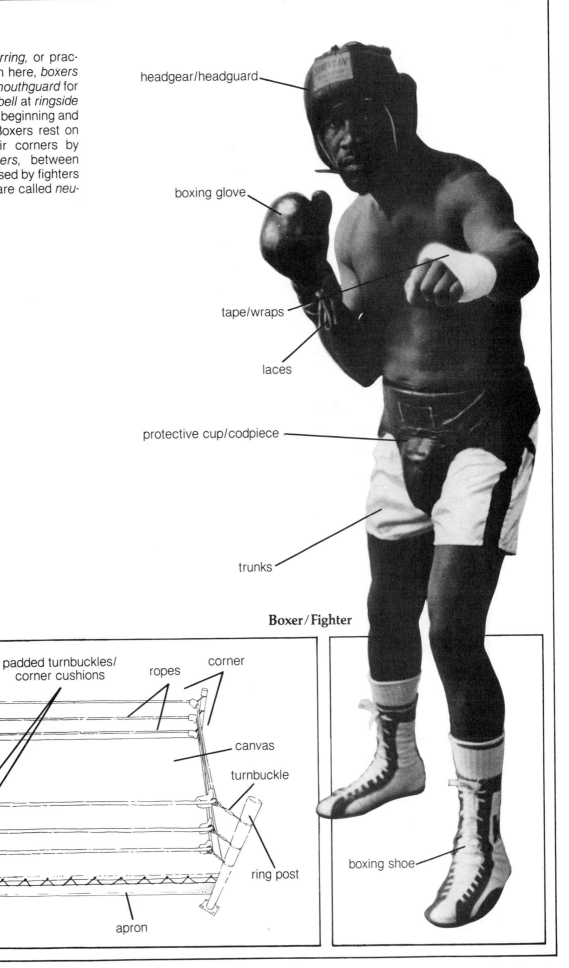

headgear/headguard

boxing glove

tape/wraps

laces

protective cup/codpiece

trunks

Boxer/Fighter

Boxing Ring

padded turnbuckles/
corner cushions

ropes

corner

canvas

turnbuckle

ring post

apron

boxing shoe

Competitive Sports

Golf

Clubs are numbered in order of increasing *loft,* the angle of the clubface from the vertical, with woods numbered from one to five and the irons numbered two through nine. A *golfer* may also carry a *pitching wedge,* a *sand wedge* and a putter. The spot where the ball lands after being hit is called the *lie.*

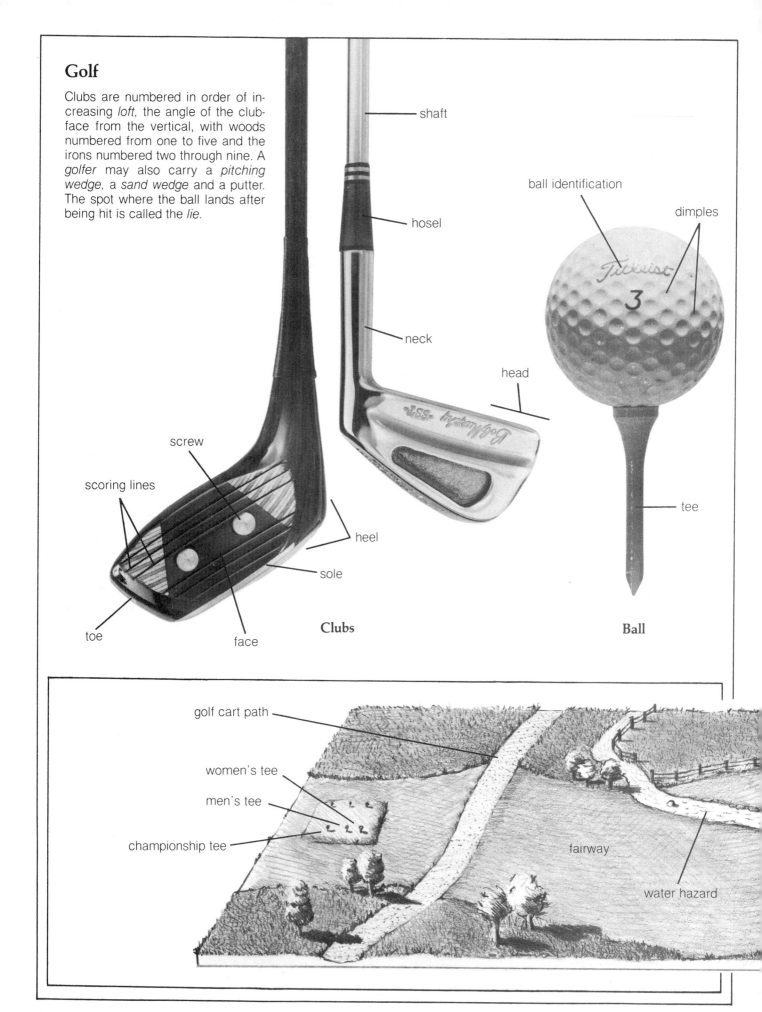

shaft

hosel

neck

head

ball identification

dimples

tee

screw

scoring lines

heel

sole

toe

face

Clubs

Ball

golf cart path

women's tee

men's tee

championship tee

fairway

water hazard

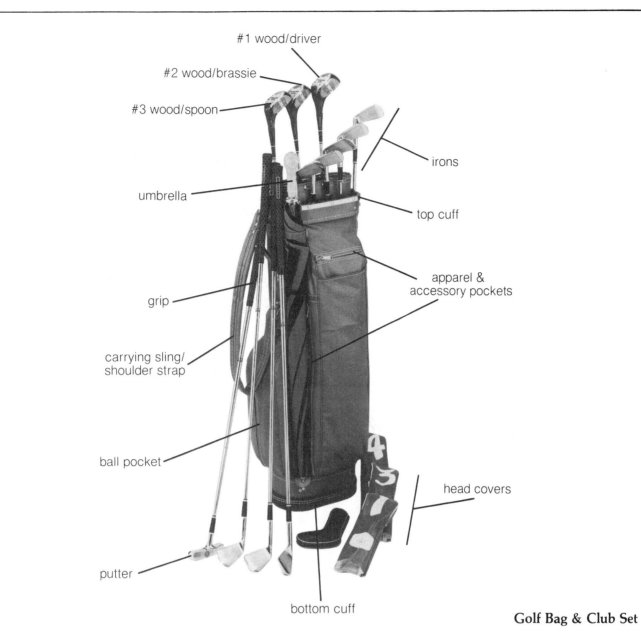

#1 wood/driver

#2 wood/brassie

#3 wood/spoon

irons

umbrella

top cuff

grip

apparel &
accessory pockets

carrying sling/
shoulder strap

ball pocket

head covers

putter

bottom cuff

Golf Bag & Club Set

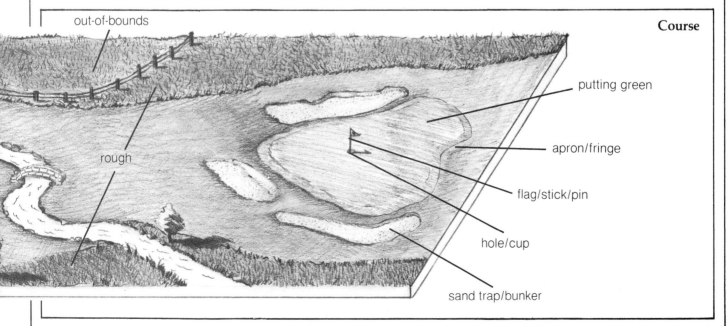

Course

out-of-bounds

putting green

apron/fringe

rough

flag/stick/pin

hole/cup

sand trap/bunker

Competitive Sports

Tennis

Some rackets have an interchangeable handle, or *pallet*, and a replaceable *throatpiece*, or *yoke*. The "sweet spot" is the prime hitting area of a racket *face*.

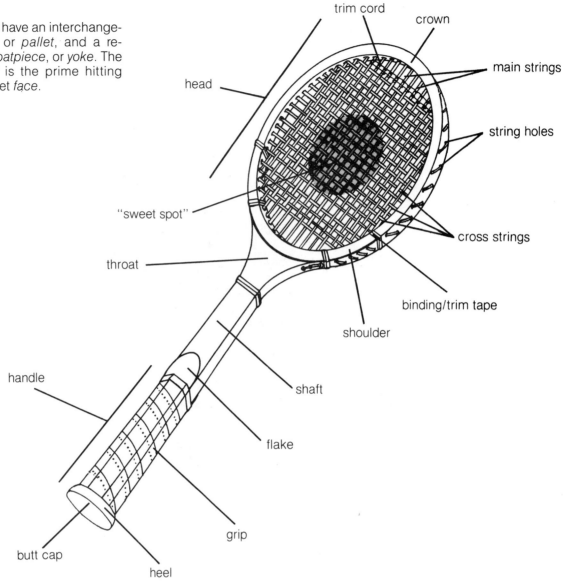

trim cord

crown

main strings

head

string holes

"sweet spot"

cross strings

throat

binding/trim tape

shoulder

handle

shaft

flake

grip

butt cap

heel

Racket

Court

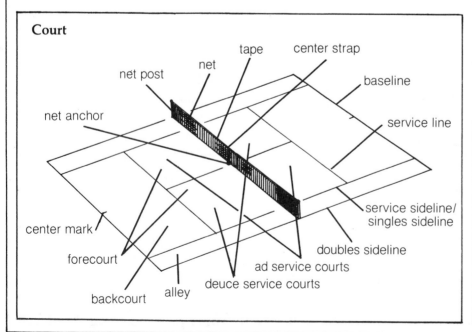

center strap

tape

net

baseline

net post

service line

net anchor

center mark

forecourt

service sideline/
singles sideline

doubles sideline

backcourt

alley

deuce service courts

ad service courts

Ball

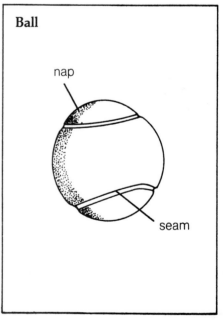

nap

seam

Handball and Squash Courts

The composite court shown here includes both handball and squash rackets terms. In each case, the court is entered through a small *door* in the *back wall*. In handball, players alternately hit a hard black *ball* with their hands, whereas in squash a soft rubber ball is hit with a *racket*.

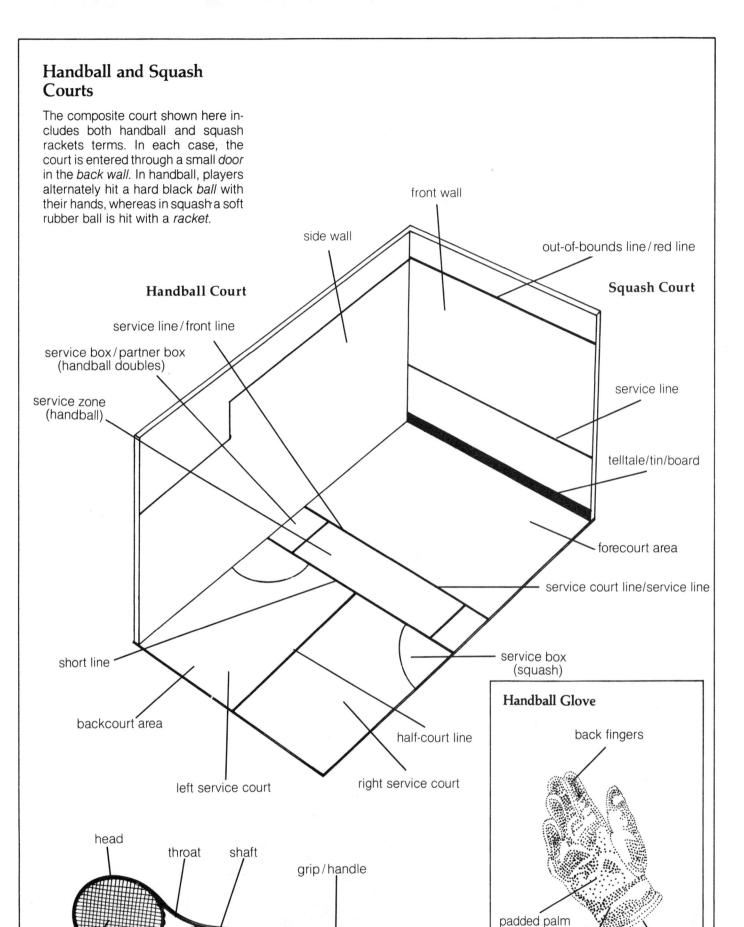

front wall

side wall

out-of-bounds line / red line

Handball Court

Squash Court

service line / front line

service box / partner box (handball doubles)

service line

service zone (handball)

telltale / tin / board

forecourt area

service court line / service line

short line

service box (squash)

backcourt area

half-court line

left service court

right service court

Handball Glove

back fingers

head

throat

shaft

grip / handle

padded palm

piping

strings

Squash Racket

strap

Competitive Sports

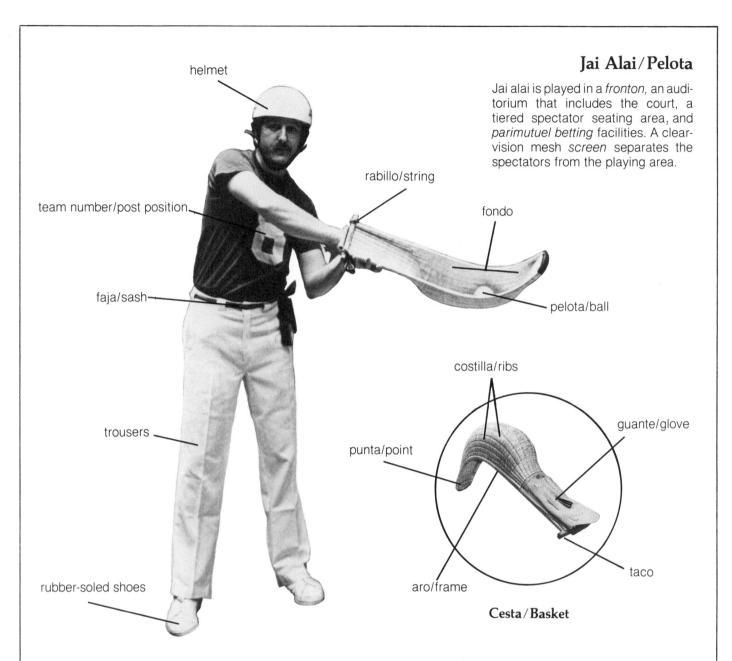

Jai Alai/Pelota

Jai alai is played in a *fronton,* an auditorium that includes the court, a tiered spectator seating area, and *parimutuel betting* facilities. A clear-vision mesh *screen* separates the spectators from the playing area.

helmet

rabillo/string

fondo

team number/post position

faja/sash

pelota/ball

trousers

costilla/ribs

punta/point

guante/glove

rubber-soled shoes

aro/frame

taco

Cesta/Basket

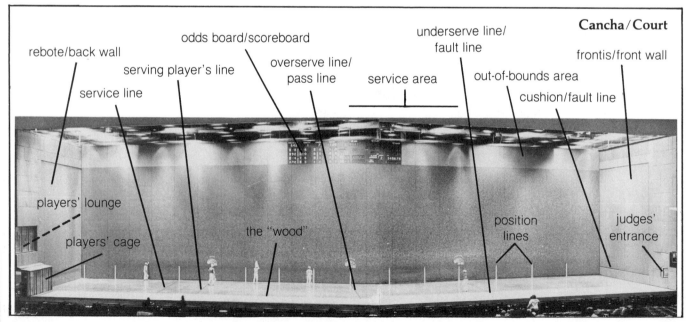

Cancha/Court

rebote/back wall

odds board/scoreboard

underserve line/
fault line

frontis/front wall

serving player's line

overserve line/
pass line

service line

service area

out-of-bounds area

cushion/fault line

players' lounge

players' cage

the "wood"

position
lines

judges'
entrance

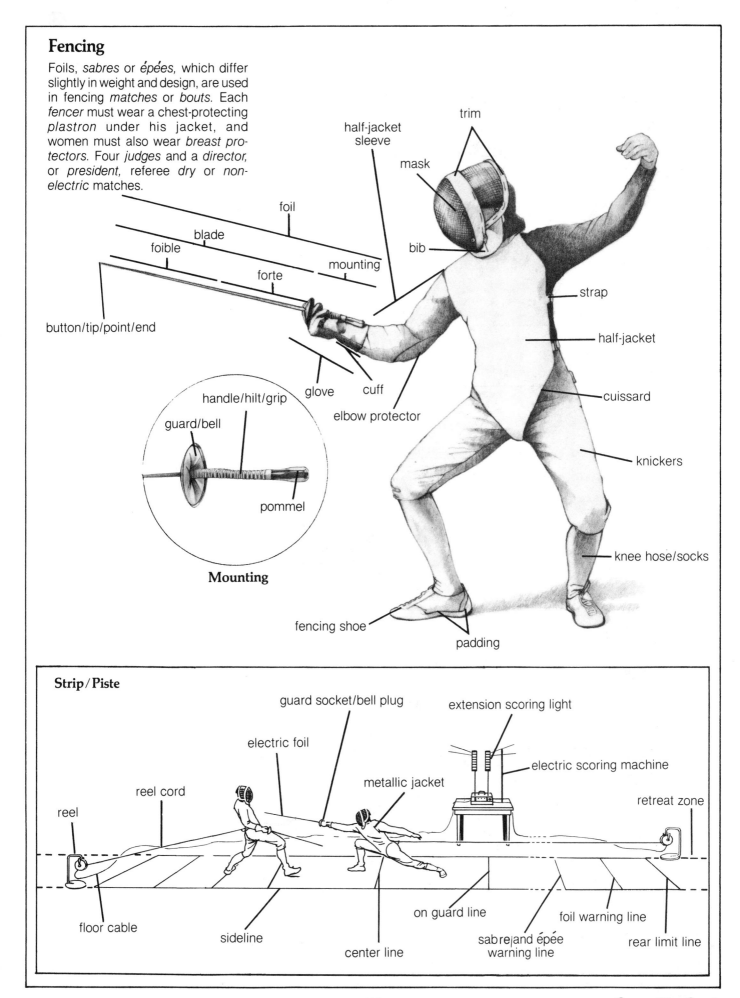

Fencing

Foils, *sabres* or *épées,* which differ slightly in weight and design, are used in fencing *matches* or *bouts.* Each *fencer* must wear a chest-protecting *plastron* under his jacket, and women must also wear *breast protectors.* Four *judges* and a *director,* or *president,* referee *dry* or *nonelectric* matches.

trim

half-jacket sleeve

mask

foil

bib

blade

foible

mounting

forte

strap

button/tip/point/end

half-jacket

glove

cuff

cuissard

elbow protector

handle/hilt/grip

guard/bell

knickers

pommel

knee hose/socks

Mounting

fencing shoe

padding

Strip/Piste

guard socket/bell plug

extension scoring light

electric foil

metallic jacket

electric scoring machine

reel cord

retreat zone

reel

floor cable

sideline

center line

on guard line

sabre and épée warning line

foil warning line

rear limit line

Competitive Sports

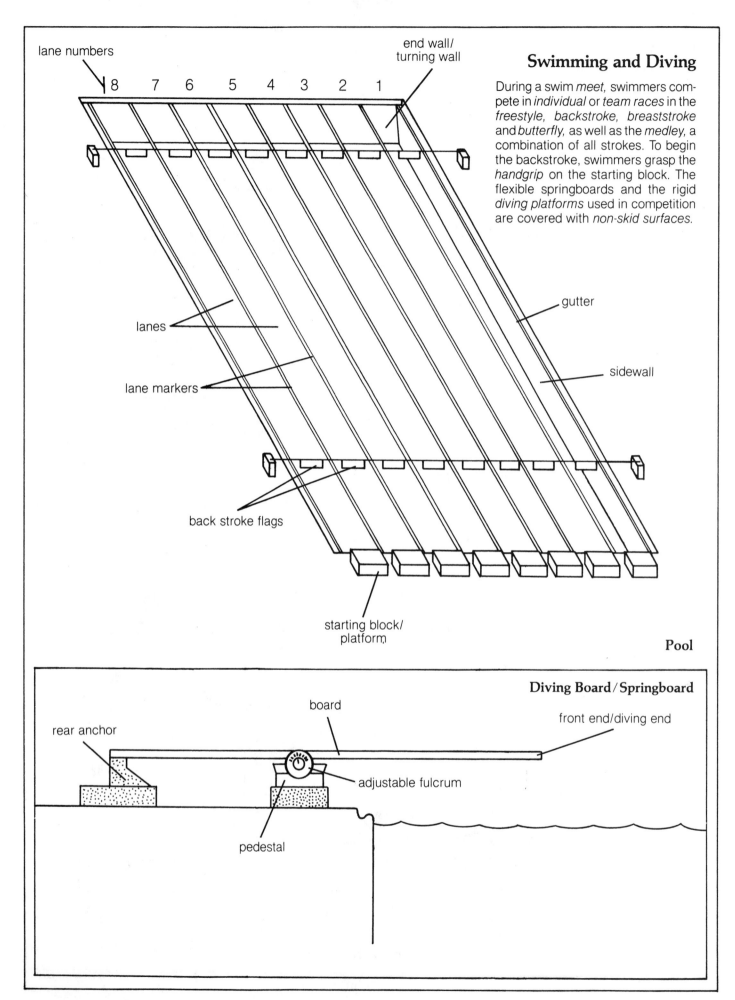

lane numbers

end wall/
turning wall

8 7 6 5 4 3 2 1

Swimming and Diving

During a swim *meet,* swimmers compete in *individual* or *team races* in the *freestyle, backstroke, breaststroke* and *butterfly,* as well as the *medley,* a combination of all strokes. To begin the backstroke, swimmers grasp the *handgrip* on the starting block. The flexible springboards and the rigid *diving platforms* used in competition are covered with *non-skid surfaces.*

gutter

sidewall

lanes

lane markers

back stroke flags

starting block/
platform

Pool

Diving Board / Springboard

board

front end/diving end

rear anchor

adjustable fulcrum

pedestal

Bowling

The strike pocket opposite to the hand delivering the ball is called the *Brooklyn pocket* or *Jersey pocket*. Pins are reset by a mechanical *pinsetter* or *pinspotter*. *Duckpins* and *candlepins* are forms of bowling in which differently shaped pins and lighter, smaller balls are used.

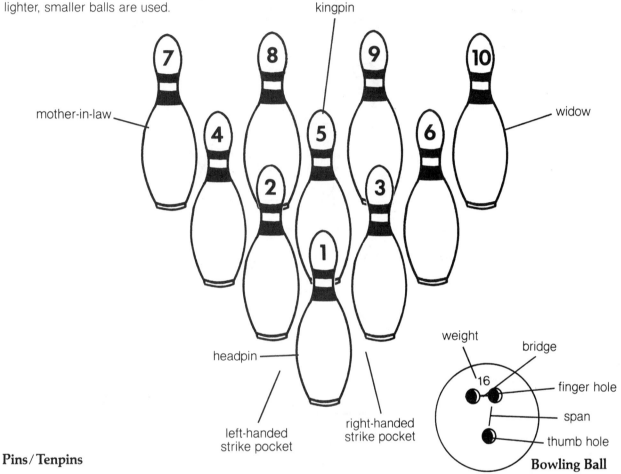

kingpin

mother-in-law

widow

headpin

left-handed strike pocket

right-handed strike pocket

Pins/Tenpins

weight

16

bridge

finger hole

span

thumb hole

Bowling Ball

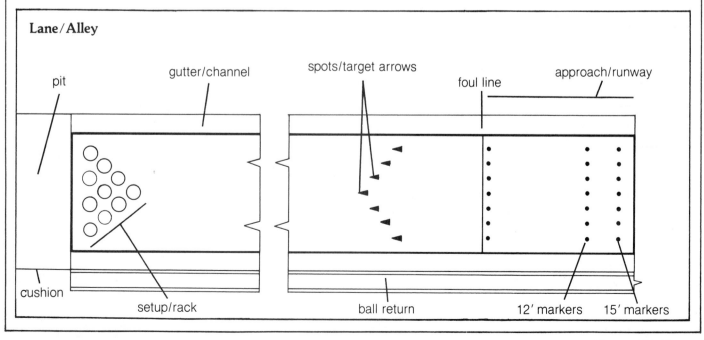

Lane/Alley

pit

gutter/channel

spots/target arrows

foul line

approach/runway

cushion

setup/rack

ball return

12' markers

15' markers

Shuffleboard and Croquet

A shuffleboard game may begin at either end of a *court.* That end is designated the *head.* The opposite end is the *foot.* In croquet, *strikers* start at the *home stake* and return to it after going through wickets and hitting the *turning stake.*

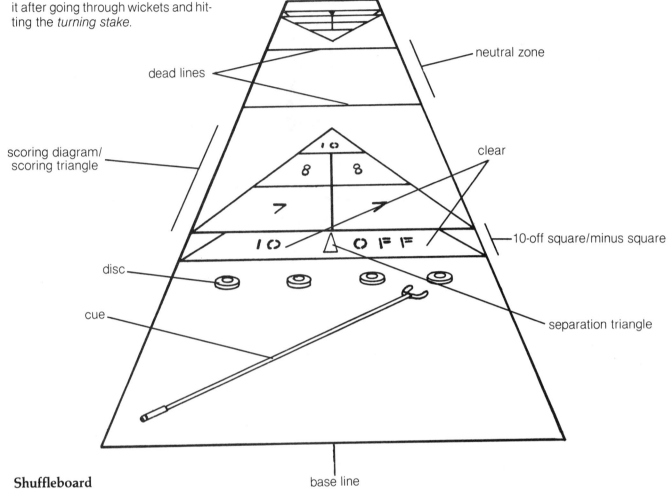

neutral zone

dead lines

scoring diagram/ scoring triangle

clear

10-off square/minus square

disc

cue

separation triangle

Shuffleboard

base line

Croquet

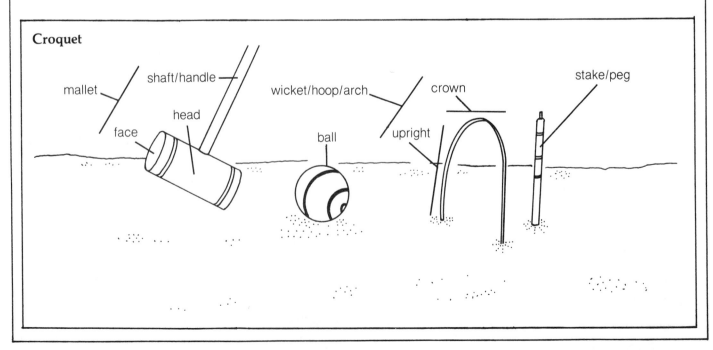

mallet

shaft/handle

wicket/hoop/arch

crown

stake/peg

head

face

ball

upright

Volleyball and Badminton

In volleyball, an inflated ball hit sharply is called a *spike* or *kill*. Badminton is played with a *racket* or *bat* whose parts are similar to those of a tennis racket. Some badminton shuttles have nylon *skirts* rather than feathers.

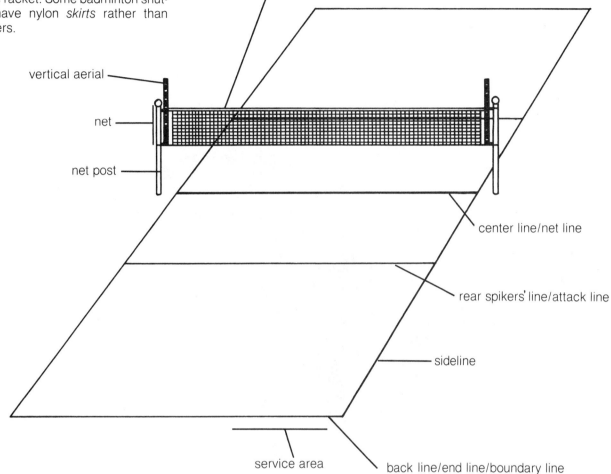

tape

vertical aerial

net

net post

center line/net line

rear spikers' line/attack line

sideline

service area

back line/end line/boundary line

Volleyball Court

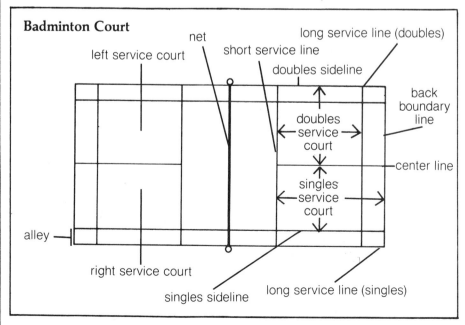

Badminton Court

net

left service court

short service line

long service line (doubles)

doubles sideline

back boundary line

doubles service court

center line

singles service court

alley

right service court

singles sideline

long service line (singles)

Shuttlecock / Bird / Shuttle

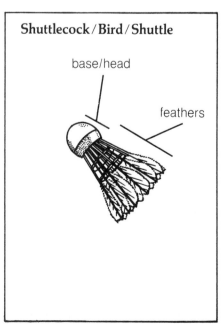

base/head

feathers

Competitive Sports

Billiards and Pool

Billiard and pool tables are usually covered with a dark green cloth called *felt,* or *bed cloth.* A triangular *rack* is used to position object balls at the beginning of a pool or *snooker* game. *Chalk* is used on cue tips. A point scored in billiards is called a *carom.*

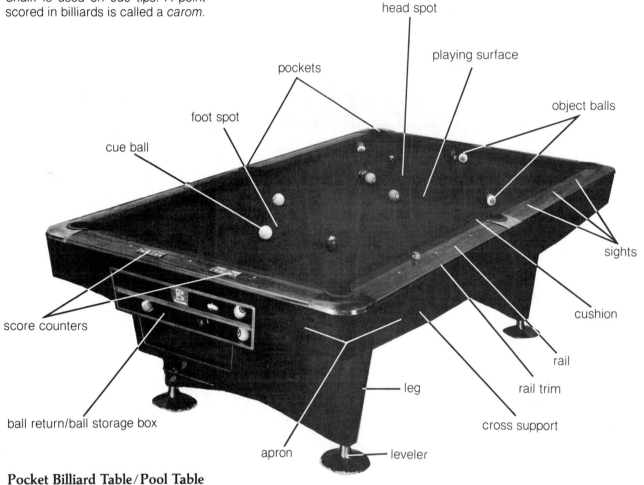

Pocket Billiard Table/Pool Table

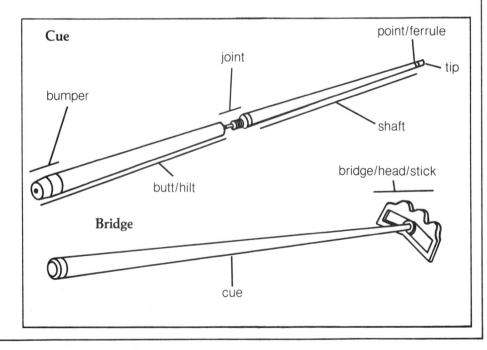

Ping-Pong/Table Tennis

Paddles have two types of grips, *shake-hands grips* and *penhold grips,* and two types of faces, *rubber* and *sponge.* The game is played with a ping-pong *ball.*

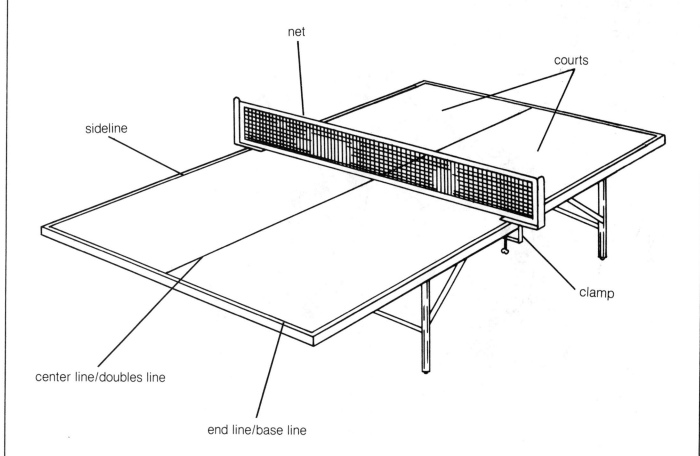

net

courts

sideline

clamp

center line/doubles line

end line/base line

Ping-Pong Table

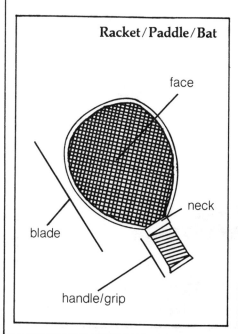

Racket/Paddle/Bat

face

blade

neck

handle/grip

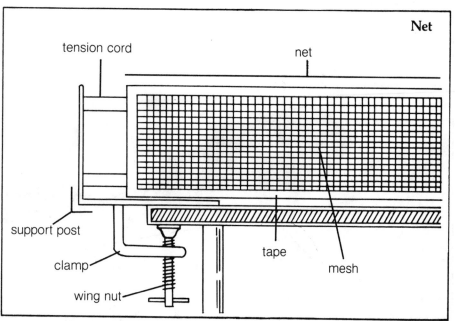

Net

tension cord

net

support post

clamp

wing nut

tape

mesh

Darts

Darts, or *darting*, is played by two *dartists* or teams of from two to eight. Darts are scored on *point of entry* on the board *face*. Of the *clock-face games*, *tournament darts* is the most popular. Other games include *round-the-clock, all-fives, baseball, high score, cricket, 51-in-5's, 14-stop, killer, Mulligan, 301, sudden death,* and *Shanghai.*

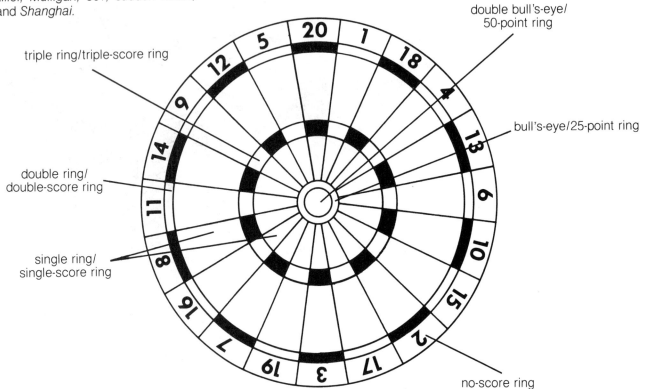

triple ring/triple-score ring

double bull's-eye/
50-point ring

double ring/
double-score ring

bull's-eye/25-point ring

single ring/
single-score ring

no-score ring

Dart Board/English Clock

Dart

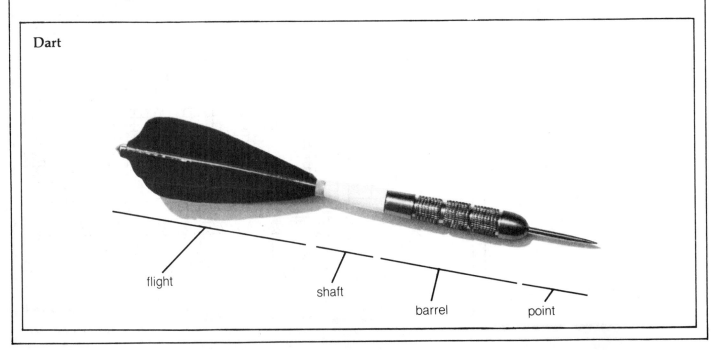

flight

shaft

barrel

point

Kites

Bridle lines are attached to the spine through holes in the front cover. They are shown here on the rear of the kite only for illustrative purposes. Among the limitless varieties of kites, there are six major categories: flat, *plane*, or *two-stick kites; bowed kites,* sometimes known by their classic example, the *Eddy;* box, or *cellular,* kites; *compound kites,* represented by the *Conyne kite; semiflexible kites,* such as *delta-keels;* and *Rogallos,* or *flexible,* kites. *Fighting kites* have two flying lines.

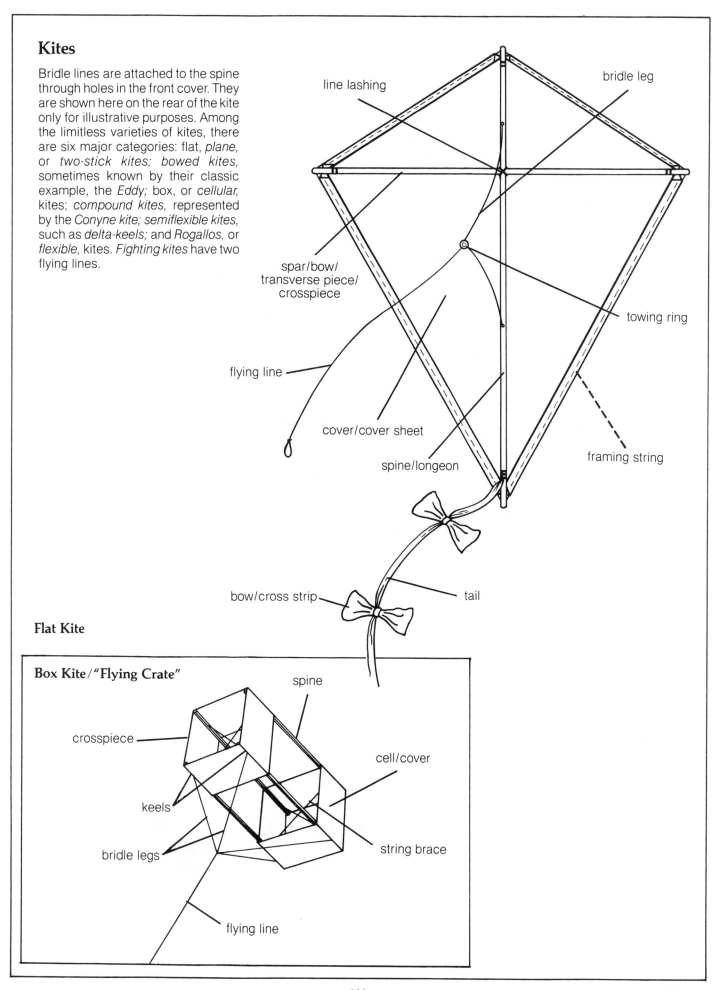

line lashing

bridle leg

spar/bow/
transverse piece/
crosspiece

towing ring

flying line

cover/cover sheet

framing string

spine/longeon

bow/cross strip

tail

Flat Kite

Box Kite/"Flying Crate"

spine

crosspiece

cell/cover

keels

string brace

bridle legs

flying line

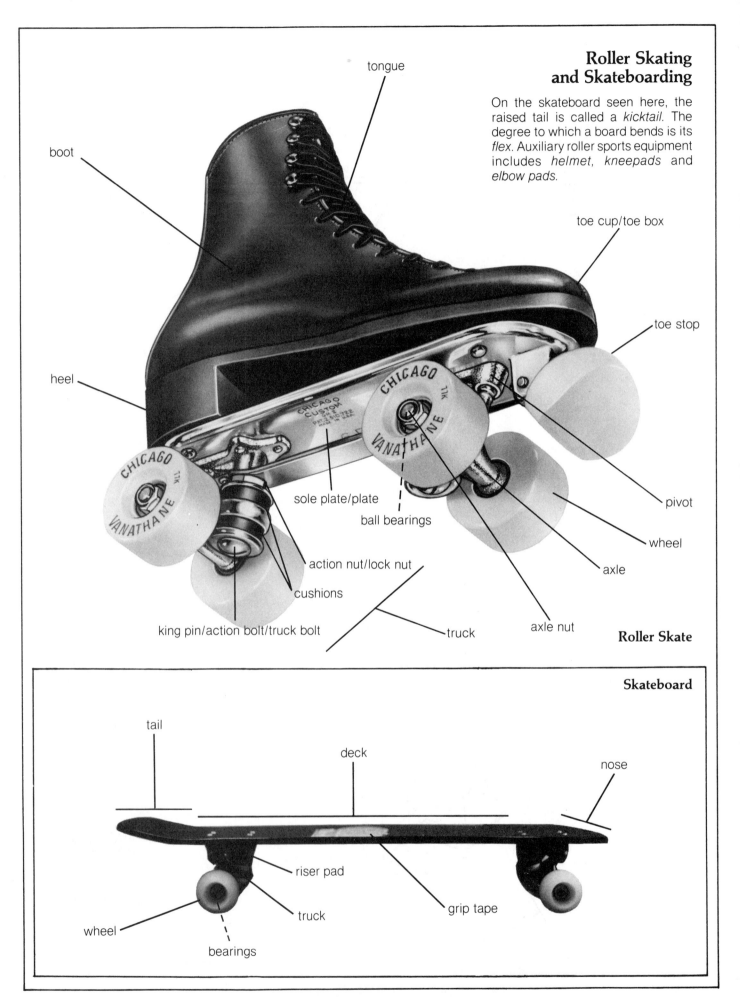

tongue

Roller Skating and Skateboarding

On the skateboard seen here, the raised tail is called a *kicktail*. The degree to which a board bends is its *flex*. Auxiliary roller sports equipment includes *helmet, kneepads* and *elbow pads*.

boot

toe cup/toe box

toe stop

heel

CHICAGO CUSTOM

CHICAGO VANATHANE 11K

CHICAGO VANATHANE 11K

sole plate/plate

ball bearings

pivot

wheel

axle

action nut/lock nut

cushions

axle nut

king pin/action bolt/truck bolt

truck

Roller Skate

Skateboard

tail

deck

nose

riser pad

truck

grip tape

wheel

bearings

Ice Skates

Uppers refer to the area of a skate above the sole. *Inserts* can be used to reinforce the uppers and tighten the heel, and *lunge pads* provide extra protection in the toe area. Hockey skates often have L-shaped *ankle guards* built into the boot. *Skate guards* or *blade booties* protect skate blades when not in use.

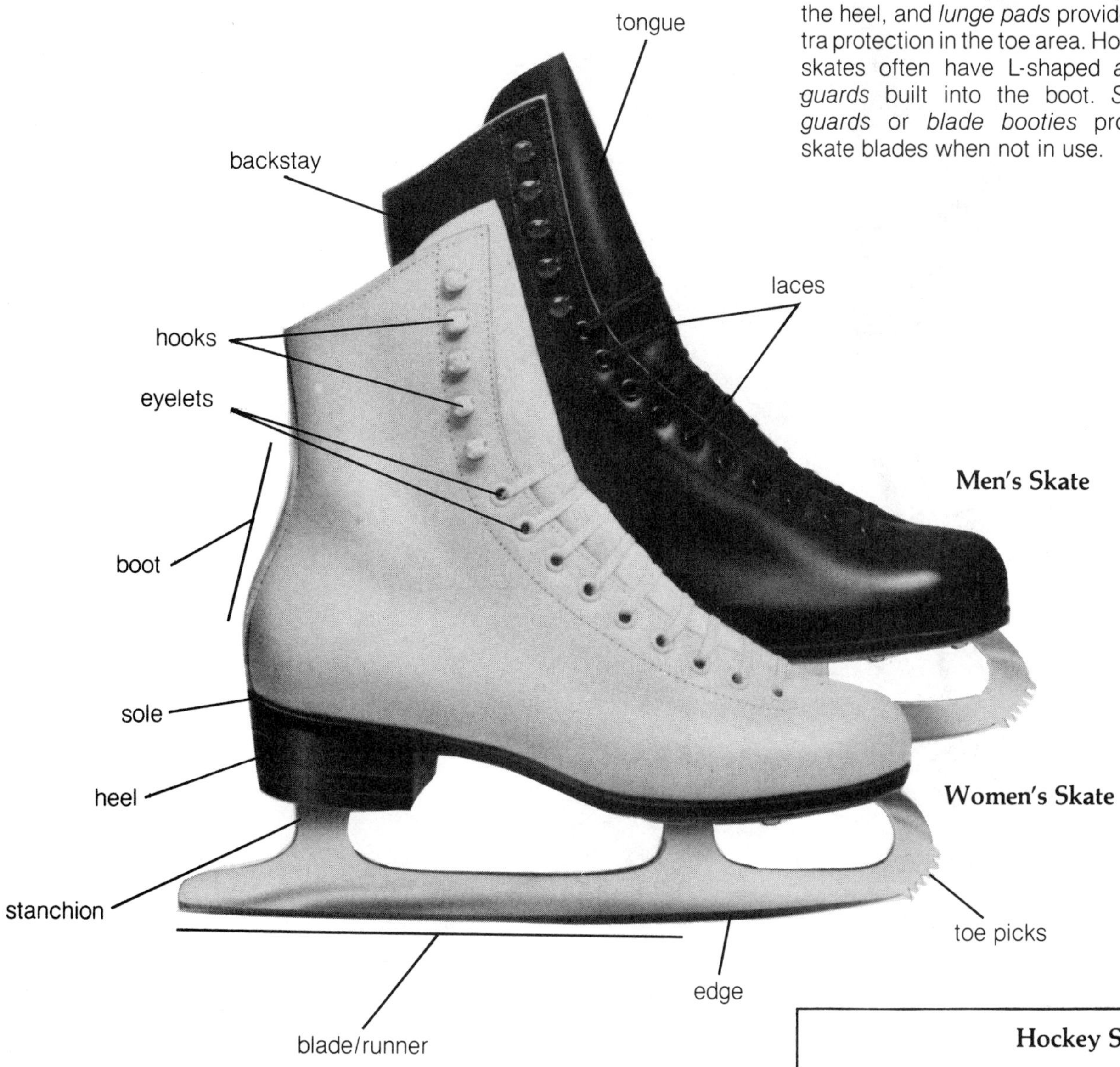

tongue

backstay

laces

hooks

eyelets

Men's Skate

boot

sole

heel

Women's Skate

stanchion

toe picks

edge

blade/runner

Figure Skates

Hockey Skate

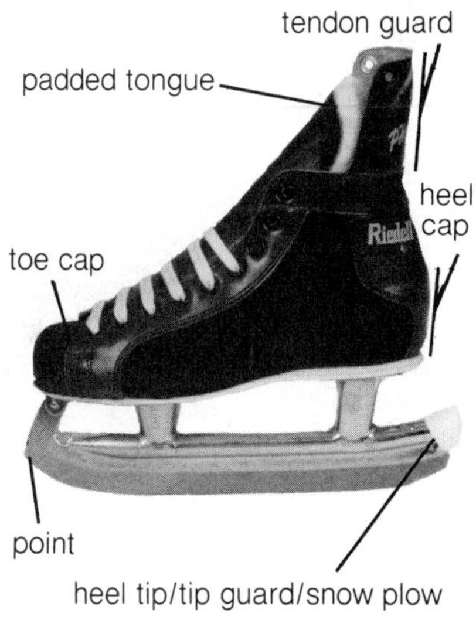

tendon guard

padded tongue

heel cap

toe cap

point

heel tip/tip guard/snow plow

Individual Sports

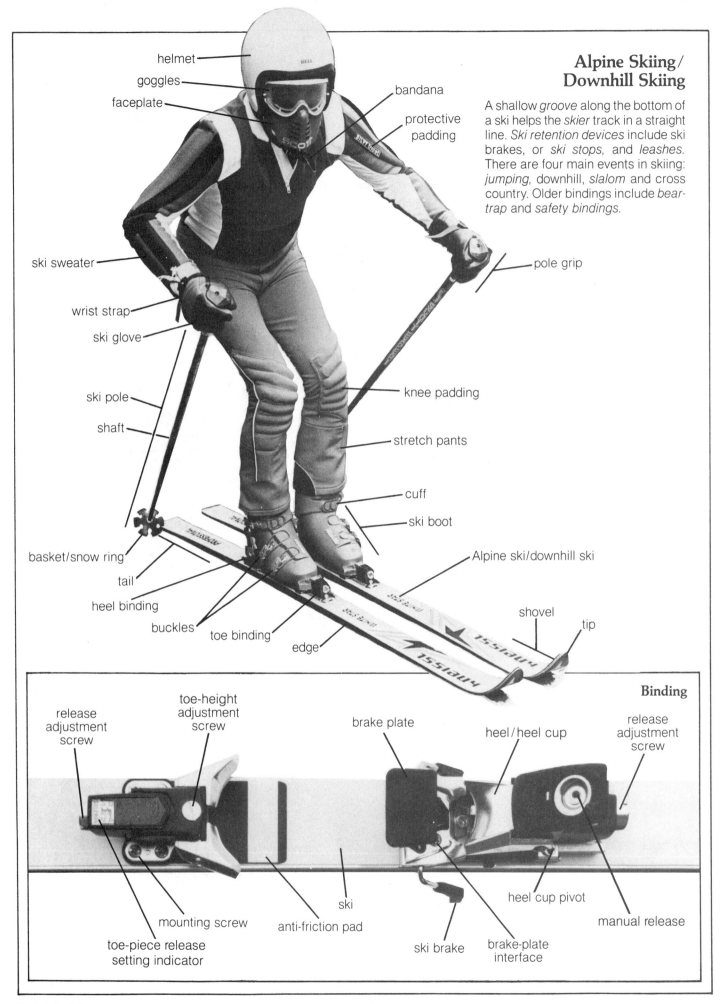

helmet

goggles

faceplate

bandana

protective padding

Alpine Skiing/ Downhill Skiing

A shallow *groove* along the bottom of a ski helps the *skier* track in a straight line. *Ski retention devices* include ski brakes, or *ski stops,* and *leashes.* There are four main events in skiing: *jumping,* downhill, *slalom* and cross country. Older bindings include *bear-trap* and *safety bindings.*

ski sweater

wrist strap

ski glove

ski pole

shaft

basket/snow ring

tail

heel binding

buckles

toe binding

edge

pole grip

knee padding

stretch pants

cuff

ski boot

Alpine ski/downhill ski

shovel

tip

Binding

release adjustment screw

toe-height adjustment screw

brake plate

heel/heel cup

release adjustment screw

mounting screw

toe-piece release setting indicator

anti-friction pad

ski

ski brake

brake-plate interface

heel cup pivot

manual release

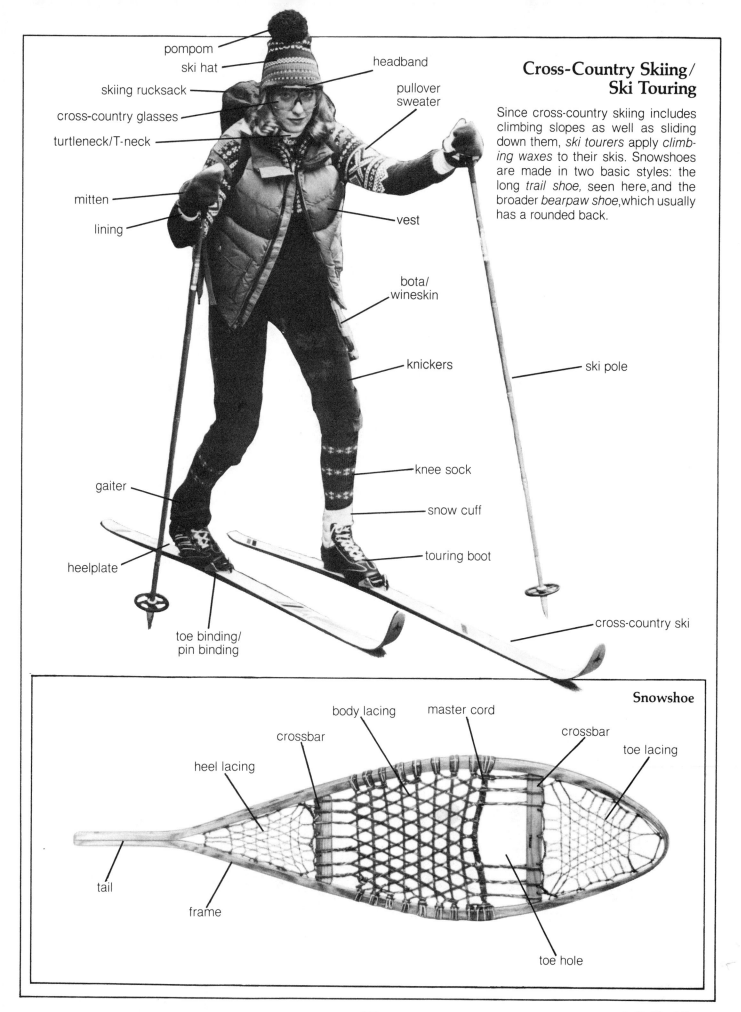

pompom

ski hat

headband

skiing rucksack

cross-country glasses

turtleneck/T-neck

pullover sweater

mitten

lining

vest

bota/ wineskin

knickers

ski pole

gaiter

knee sock

snow cuff

touring boot

heelplate

cross-country ski

toe binding/ pin binding

Cross-Country Skiing/ Ski Touring

Since cross-country skiing includes climbing slopes as well as sliding down them, *ski tourers* apply *climbing waxes* to their skis. Snowshoes are made in two basic styles: the long *trail shoe*, seen here, and the broader *bearpaw shoe*, which usually has a rounded back.

Snowshoe

body lacing

master cord

crossbar

crossbar

toe lacing

heel lacing

tail

frame

toe hole

Individual Sports

Sledding and Tobogganing

Bobsleds, driven by two- or four-man crews, have a racing *cowl* and toothed metal *brake.* Small racing sleds called *luges* are controlled by reclining drivers using their feet and *hand ropes.*

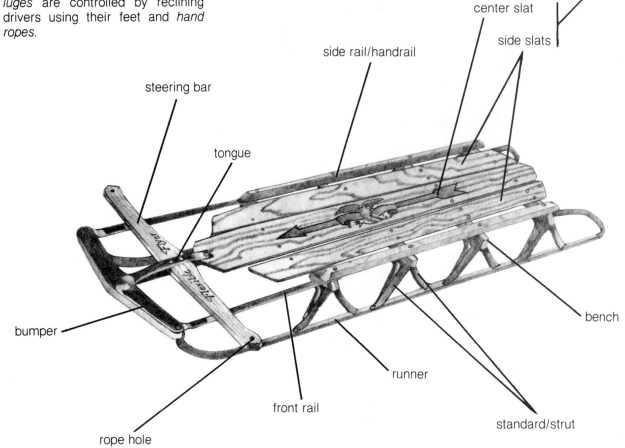

steering bar

tongue

side rail/handrail

center slat

side slats

deck

bumper

rope hole

front rail

runner

bench

standard/strut

Sled

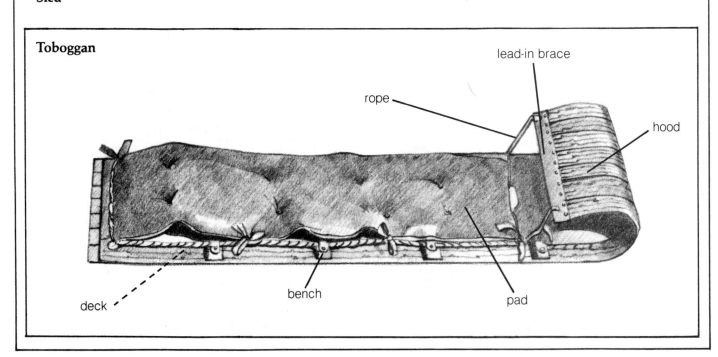

Toboggan

lead-in brace

rope

hood

deck

bench

pad

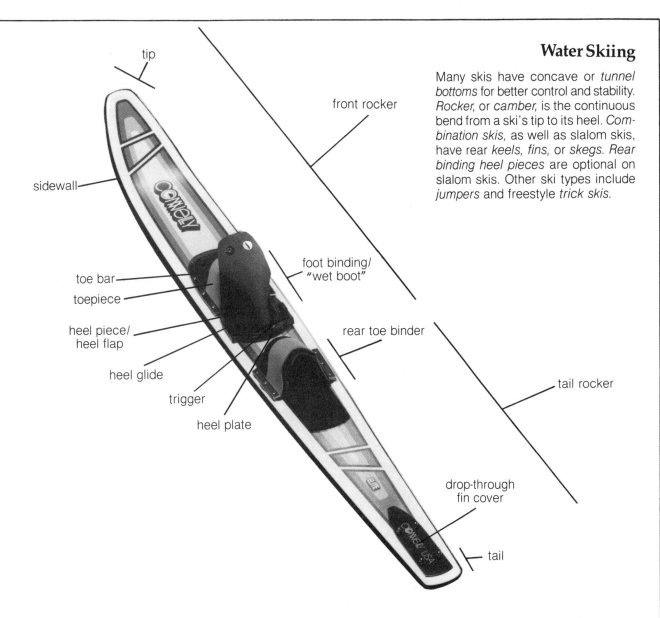

tip

front rocker

Water Skiing

Many skis have concave or *tunnel bottoms* for better control and stability. *Rocker,* or *camber,* is the continuous bend from a ski's tip to its heel. *Combination skis,* as well as slalom skis, have rear *keels, fins,* or *skegs. Rear binding heel pieces* are optional on slalom skis. Other ski types include *jumpers* and freestyle *trick skis.*

sidewall

foot binding/ "wet boot"

toe bar

toepiece

heel piece/ heel flap

rear toe binder

heel glide

trigger

heel plate

tail rocker

drop-through fin cover

tail

Slalom Ski

Ski Vest/Safety Jacket

reinforced shoulder

strap/belt

buckle

snap

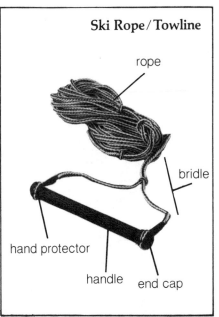

Ski Rope/Towline

rope

bridle

hand protector

handle

end cap

Individual Sports

Surfing

A windsurfer, or *sailboard,* is equipped with a *free-rotating mast* and *loose-footed sail,* or *free-sail system.* Surfboards range in size from heavy *big guns* to smaller *hotdogging boards.* A *pig board* or *tear drop* is a board shaped like a pie wedge.

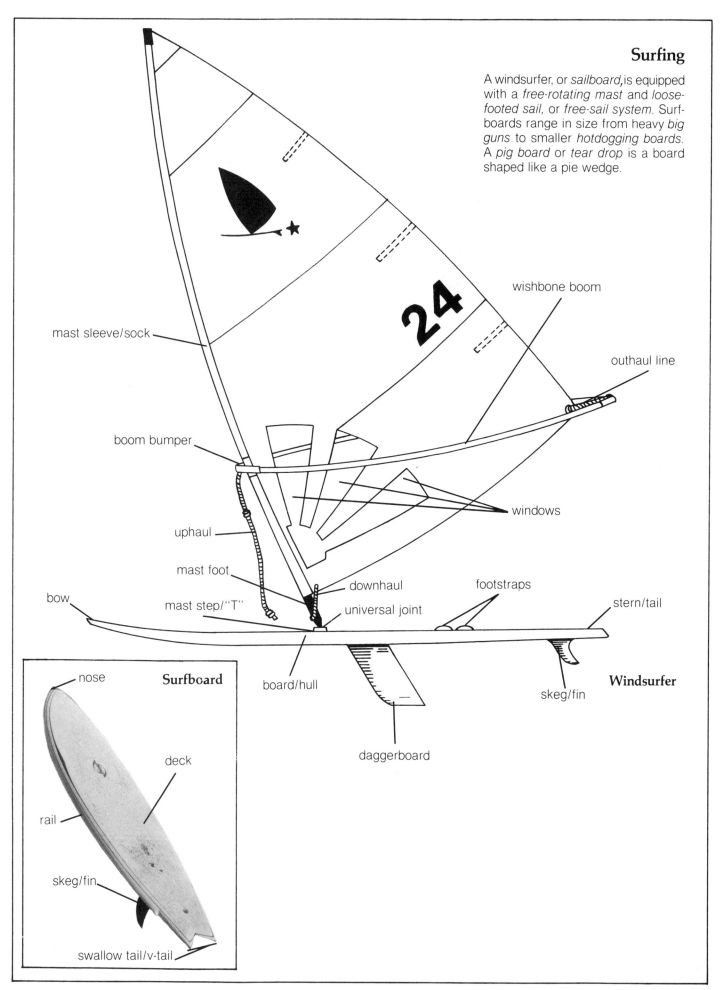

24

wishbone boom

outhaul line

mast sleeve/sock

boom bumper

windows

uphaul

mast foot

downhaul

footstraps

bow

mast step/"T"

universal joint

stern/tail

board/hull

Windsurfer

skeg/fin

daggerboard

Surfboard

nose

deck

rail

skeg/fin

swallow tail/v-tail

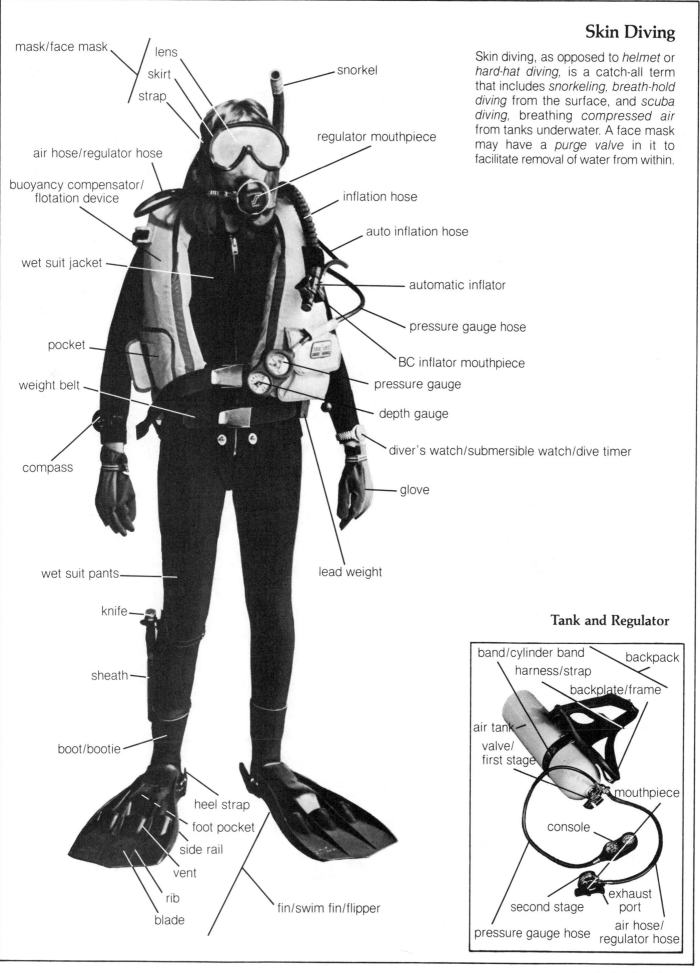

Skin Diving

Skin diving, as opposed to *helmet* or *hard-hat diving,* is a catch-all term that includes *snorkeling, breath-hold diving* from the surface, and *scuba diving,* breathing *compressed air* from tanks underwater. A face mask may have a *purge valve* in it to facilitate removal of water from within.

mask/face mask

lens

skirt

strap

snorkel

regulator mouthpiece

air hose/regulator hose

buoyancy compensator/
flotation device

inflation hose

auto inflation hose

automatic inflator

pressure gauge hose

wet suit jacket

BC inflator mouthpiece

pocket

pressure gauge

weight belt

depth gauge

diver's watch/submersible watch/dive timer

compass

glove

wet suit pants

lead weight

knife

Tank and Regulator

band/cylinder band

backpack

harness/strap

backplate/frame

sheath

air tank

valve/
first stage

mouthpiece

boot/bootie

console

heel strap

foot pocket

second stage

exhaust
port

side rail

vent

pressure gauge hose

air hose/
regulator hose

rib

blade

fin/swim fin/flipper

Individual Sports

Hot Air Balloon

A balloon, or *montgolfier*, rises when *ballast*, usually water or *sandbags*, is jettisoned. A *drag*, or *trail rope*, hangs from the balloon to give it stability in flight and slow it down upon landing. To deflate the balloon a *ripping panel*, or *rip panel*, near the top is opened.

parachute valve/
parachute vent

envelope/bag

registration number/
"N" number

envelope
graphic

panel seams

gore seams

load cords

panels

bottom girdle

skirt

skirt band

burner

suspension rope

load ring

padding

basket handle

mouth

valve line

burner support

basket/carriage

scuff leather

tether line

Parachuting and Hang Gliding

Unless attached to a *static line*, which automatically opens a *chute* once a *jumper* has cleared the *jump plane*, a *sky diver* can *free-fall* before pulling his *rip cord*.

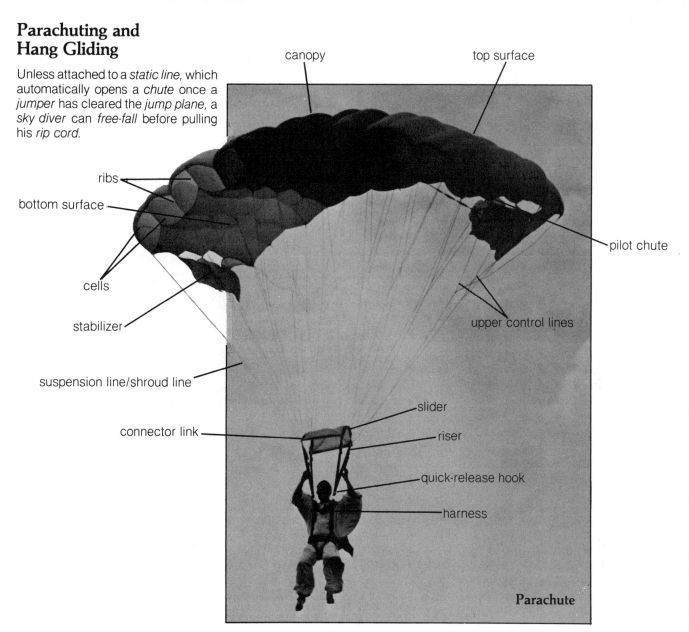

canopy

top surface

ribs

bottom surface

cells

stabilizer

pilot chute

upper control lines

suspension line/shroud line

connector link

slider

riser

quick-release hook

harness

Parachute

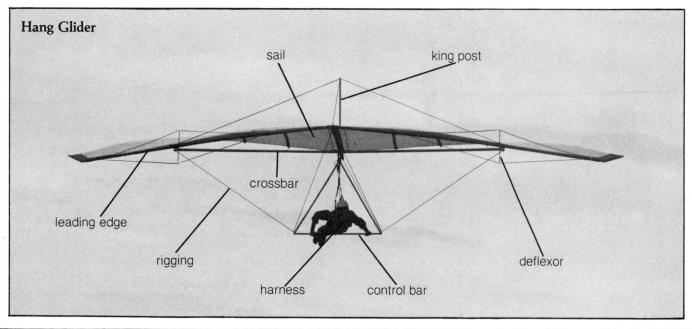

Hang Glider

sail

king post

crossbar

leading edge

rigging

deflexor

harness

control bar

Individual Sports

Mountain Climbing

Mountaineers use nylon webbing for *shoulder slings* and *swami belts.* Carabiners, either oval- or D-shaped, have spring-loaded *gates* for connecting various pieces of climbing equipment. Unlike *pitons,* which are hammered into cracks, nuts are wedged into cracks and easily removed. *Icescrews,* ring-topped threaded tubes, are actually screwed into the ice for protection.

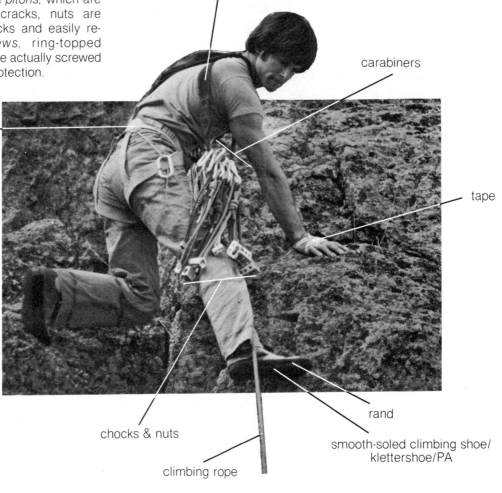

hardware sling

carabiners

tape

climbing harness

rand

smooth-soled climbing shoe/ klettershoe/PA

chocks & nuts

climbing rope

Ice Climbing Boot

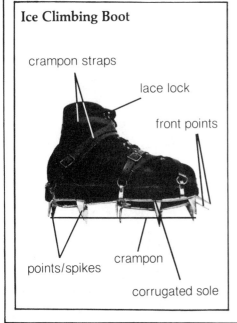

crampon straps

lace lock

front points

points/spikes

crampon

corrugated sole

Ice Tools

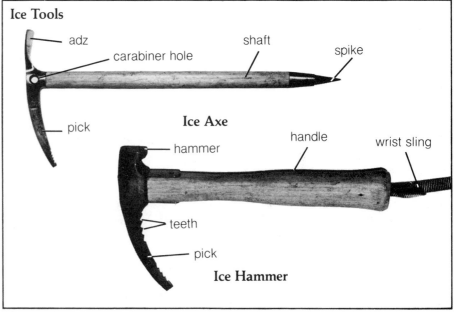

adz

carabiner hole

shaft

spike

pick

Ice Axe

hammer

handle

wrist sling

teeth

pick

Ice Hammer

A saddle is built on a frame called a *saddle tree*. A *saddle blanket* or *saddle pad* is placed between horse and saddle. Metal stirrups, or *stirrup irons*, are attached to the saddle by *stirrup leathers*. *Saddlebags* fit over the back of the saddle.

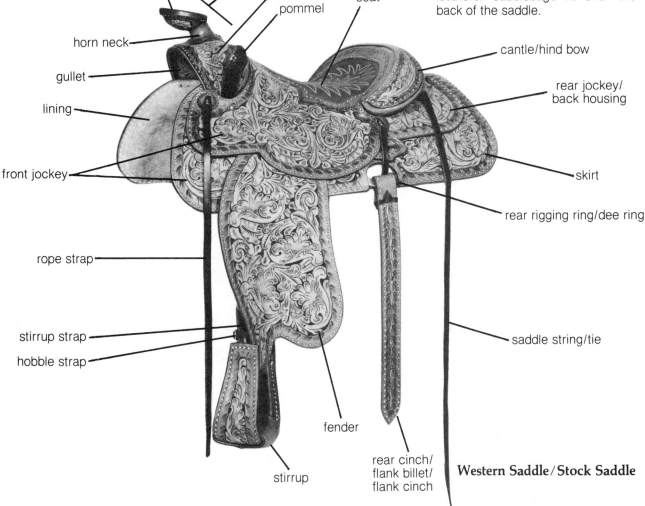

horn cap

horn

fork/swell

pommel

seat

horn neck

cantle/hind bow

gullet

rear jockey/ back housing

lining

front jockey

skirt

rear rigging ring/dee ring

rope strap

stirrup strap

hobble strap

saddle string/tie

fender

stirrup

rear cinch/ flank billet/ flank cinch

Western Saddle/Stock Saddle

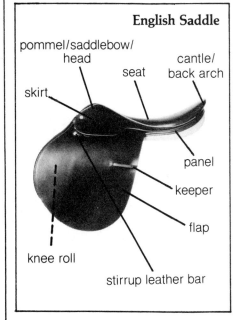

English Saddle

pommel/saddlebow/ head

cantle/ back arch

seat

skirt

panel

keeper

flap

stirrup leather bar

knee roll

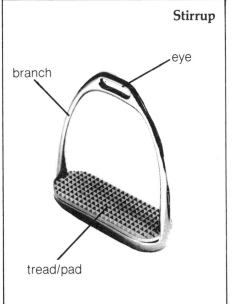

Stirrup

eye

branch

tread/pad

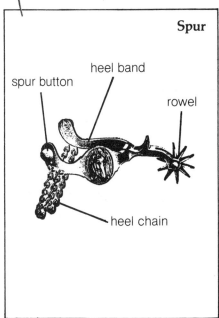

Spur

heel band

spur button

rowel

heel chain

Flat Racing

The equipment used on a racehorse is called the *tack*. *Thoroughbreds* start from a fixed *starting gate,* while harness racers start from a car-pulled *moving gate.* The most desirable *post position* in a race is gate number one, the *pole position* closest to the *rail.* Bettors pick horses to finish first, second and third, or *win, place* and *show.* Picking all three finishers in the right order is called a *trifecta.*

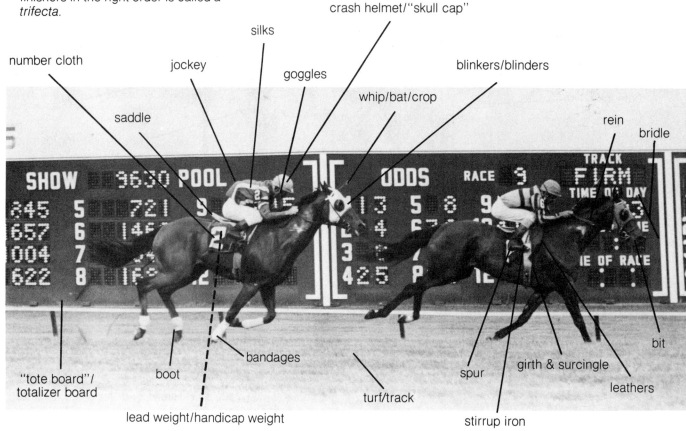

number cloth · jockey · silks · goggles · crash helmet/"skull cap" · whip/bat/crop · blinkers/blinders · rein · bridle · saddle · "tote board"/totalizer board · boot · bandages · turf/track · spur · girth & surcingle · bit · leathers · lead weight/handicap weight · stirrup iron

Racing Program Entry

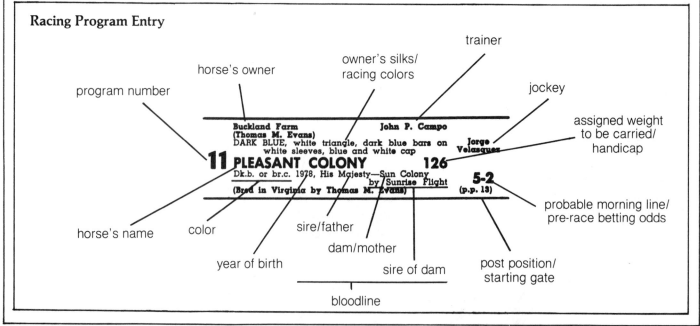

program number · horse's owner · owner's silks/racing colors · trainer · jockey · assigned weight to be carried/handicap · horse's name · color · year of birth · sire/father · dam/mother · sire of dam · post position/starting gate · probable morning line/pre-race betting odds · bloodline

Buckland Farm
(Thomas M. Evans)   John P. Campo
DARK BLUE, white triangle, dark blue bars on
white sleeves, blue and white cap   Jorge
Velasquez
11 PLEASANT COLONY 126
Dk.b. or br.c. 1978, His Majesty—Sun Colony
by Sunrise Flight   **5-2**
(Bred in Virginia by Thomas M. Evans)   (p.p. 13)

Harness Racing

Trotters and pacers race in *harness.* Trotters move front and opposing rear legs in unison, *laterally gaited,* while pacers move front and rear legs on the same side in unison, *diagonally gaited.* Horses are assembled, saddled and paraded in the *paddock area.*

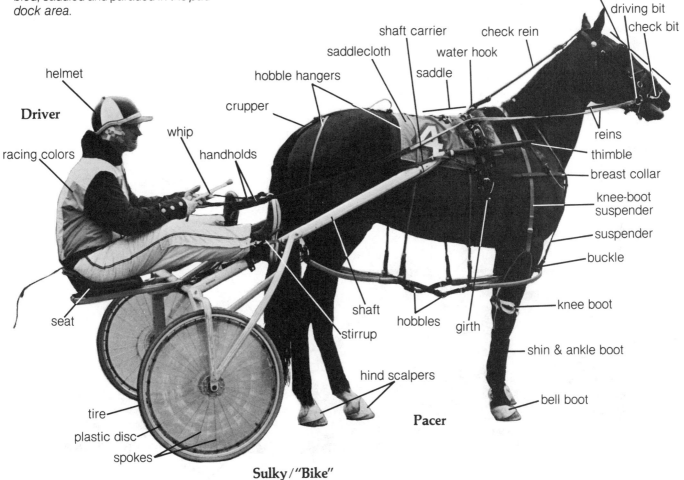

Driver

helmet

racing colors

whip

handholds

seat

tire

plastic disc

spokes

Sulky / "Bike"

crupper

hobble hangers

saddlecloth

shaft carrier

saddle

water hook

check rein

bridle

driving bit

check bit

reins

thimble

breast collar

knee-boot suspender

suspender

buckle

knee boot

shin & ankle boot

bell boot

shaft

stirrup

hobbles

girth

hind scalpers

Pacer

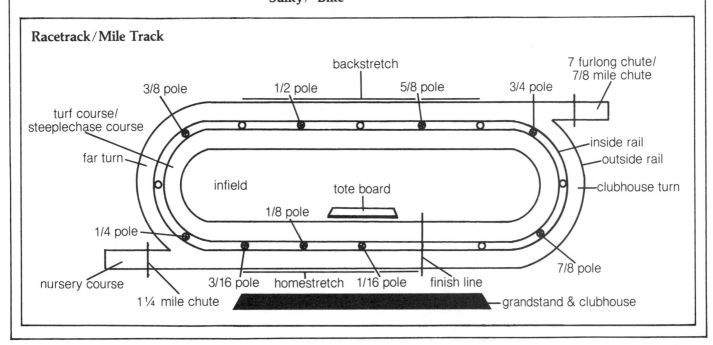

Racetrack / Mile Track

3/8 pole

turf course/
steeplechase course

far turn

1/4 pole

nursery course

1¼ mile chute

1/2 pole

backstretch

5/8 pole

3/4 pole

7 furlong chute/
7/8 mile chute

inside rail

outside rail

clubhouse turn

infield

tote board

1/8 pole

3/16 pole

homestretch

1/16 pole

finish line

7/8 pole

grandstand & clubhouse

Equestrian Sports

Grand Prix Racing

International *road racing* takes place on *closed-circuit tracks* laid out through the countryside, as opposed to *speedway racing,* which takes place on banked, oval-shaped *race tracks. Formulas* primarily limit engine size and car weight, and range from *Super-Vee* to *Formula One,* used in Grand Prix racing.

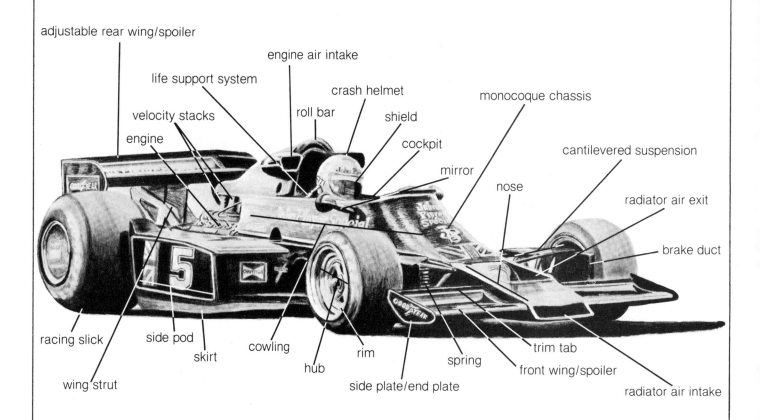

Formula One Racing Car

Drag Racing

Each drag racing *event,* or *acceleration contest,* involves two-car *heats,* the winner of which is deemed the *eliminator.* Vehicles include *slingshot dragsters* and *funny cars* whose mismatched bodies, or *"hulls,"* and *chassis* give them an unusual appearance. The Christmas Tree is situated in the middle of a divided, two-lane *straight-line course, drag strip* or *dragway. Elapsed time,* or *"ET,"* is computed from the moment a car breaks a *light beam* at the *starting line* until it breaks a similar beam at the *finish.* A car leaving the starting line prematurely, in either *handicap* or *heads-up racing,* is said to be *"red-lighting."*

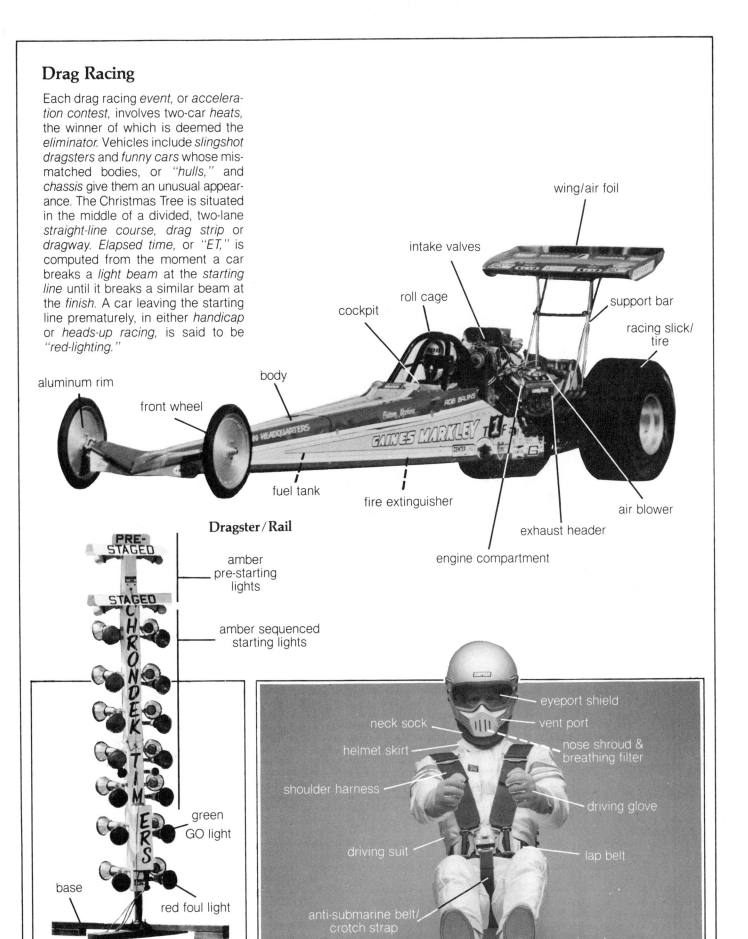

wing/air foil

intake valves

roll cage

cockpit

support bar

racing slick/ tire

aluminum rim

body

front wheel

fuel tank

fire extinguisher

air blower

exhaust header

engine compartment

Dragster / Rail

amber pre-starting lights

amber sequenced starting lights

green GO light

base

red foul light

Starting Lights / Christmas Tree

eyeport shield

neck sock

vent port

helmet skirt

nose shroud & breathing filter

shoulder harness

driving glove

driving suit

lap belt

anti-submarine belt/ crotch strap

racing shoe

Driver's Fire Suit

handle

foot/pole mount

leg/reel stem

crank handle

trip/dog

bail/pick-up arm

spool skirt

spool

anti-reverse lever

rear bearing

gear housing

bearing cover

silent
anti-reverse
housing

drag-adjustment knob/
drag knob

line roller/line guide

Reel/Spinning Reel

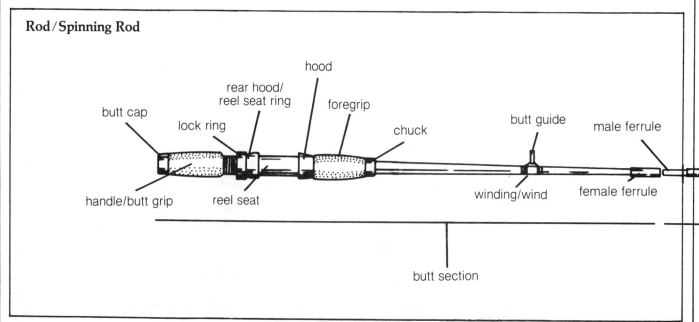

Rod/Spinning Rod

hood

rear hood/
reel seat ring

foregrip

butt cap

lock ring

chuck

butt guide

male ferrule

handle/butt grip

reel seat

winding/wind

female ferrule

butt section

Fishing

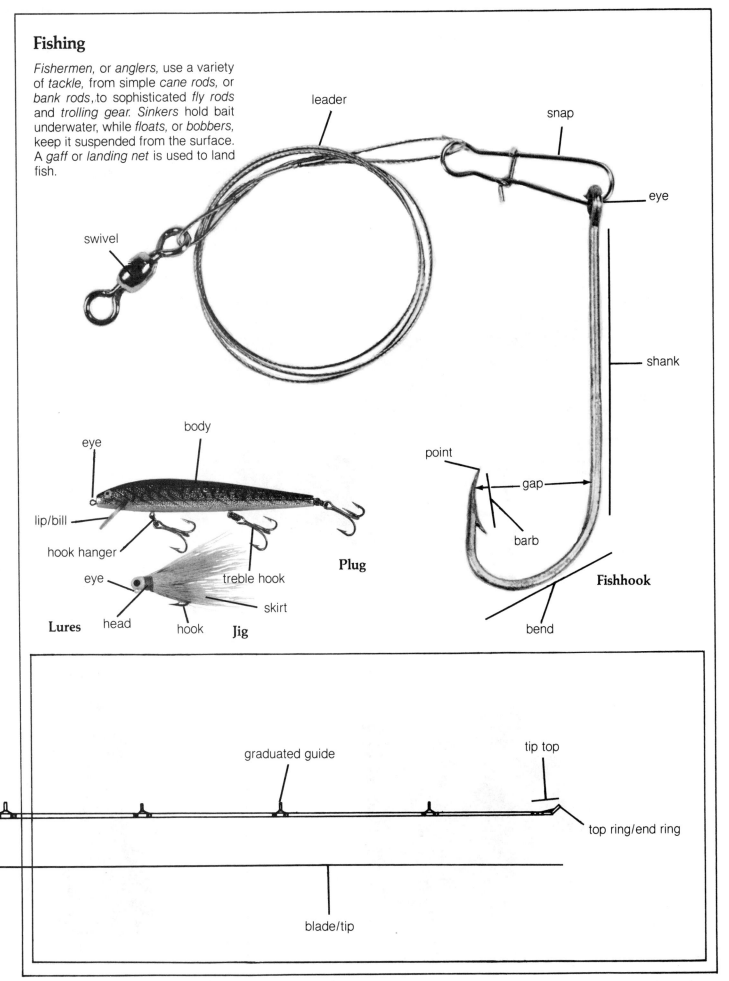

Fishermen, or anglers, use a variety of tackle, from simple cane rods, or bank rods, to sophisticated fly rods and trolling gear. Sinkers hold bait underwater, while floats, or bobbers, keep it suspended from the surface. A gaff or landing net is used to land fish.

leader

snap

swivel

eye

shank

body

eye

point

gap

lip/bill

barb

hook hanger

eye

treble hook

head

skirt

Lures

hook

Jig

Plug

Fishhook

bend

graduated guide

tip top

top ring/end ring

blade/tip

Camping

Wall tents and pup tents are held up by tent poles. Many modern tents have *exterior frame* construction. Features in all the above-mentioned tents include *lap-felled* or *French seams*, which provide four layers for keeping out water, webbed–tape *backing* and pressed-on *grommets* or sewn-in *rings* for *ropes* secured to the ground with *pegs* or *stakes*, and sewn-in *flooring*. A lantern is primed by pumping the *pump valve* and lit by a match placed in the *lighting hole*.

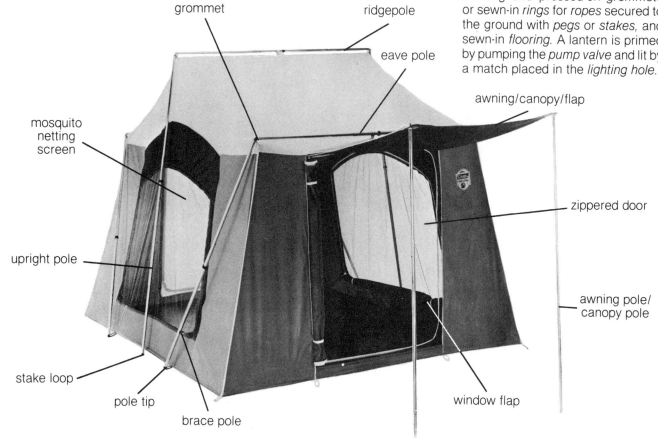

grommet

ridgepole

eave pole

mosquito netting screen

awning/canopy/flap

zippered door

upright pole

awning pole/ canopy pole

stake loop

pole tip

brace pole

window flap

Tent

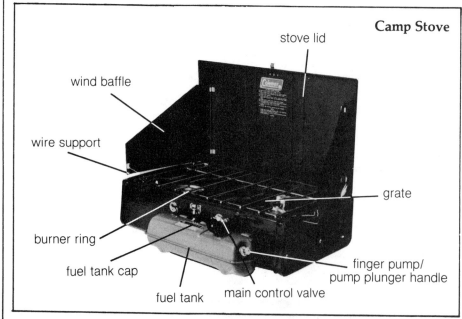

Camp Stove

stove lid

wind baffle

wire support

grate

burner ring

fuel tank cap

fuel tank

main control valve

finger pump/ pump plunger handle

Lantern

ventilator

bail

mantle

globe

heat shield

fuel valve

base rest

tank/fount

fuel cap

Backpacking

Loft is the trade term for fluffiness in sleeping bags. *Bonded insulation filling* eliminates the need for *quilting* and reduces "cold spots." The various pockets of backpacks, *knapsacks* or *rucksacks,* are called *local organizers.* Small camping items are packed in *stuffsacks,* which are then put inside a hiker's *pack.*

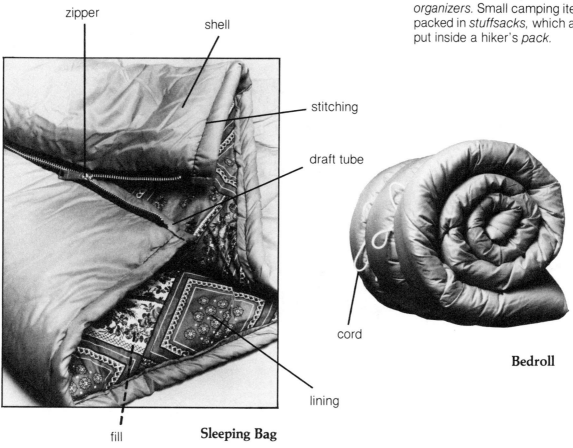

zipper

shell

stitching

draft tube

lining

fill

Sleeping Bag

cord

Bedroll

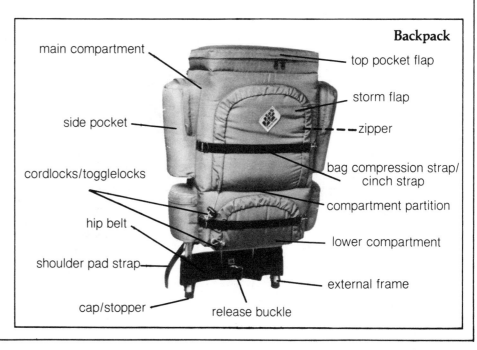

Backpack

main compartment

top pocket flap

storm flap

side pocket

zipper

cordlocks/togglelocks

bag compression strap/ cinch strap

compartment partition

hip belt

lower compartment

shoulder pad strap

external frame

cap/stopper

release buckle

Body Building

Among other *stations* in the universal gym, designed to improve muscle development through *isotonic exercises*, are *dead lift* and *low pulley*. Muscle-building and toning equipment includes *dumbbells, hand grips,* or *hand flexors, scissor grips, tone-up wheels, power twisters, exercise bikes, neck developers, ankle* and *wrist weights, triceps exercisers* and *waist trimmers*.

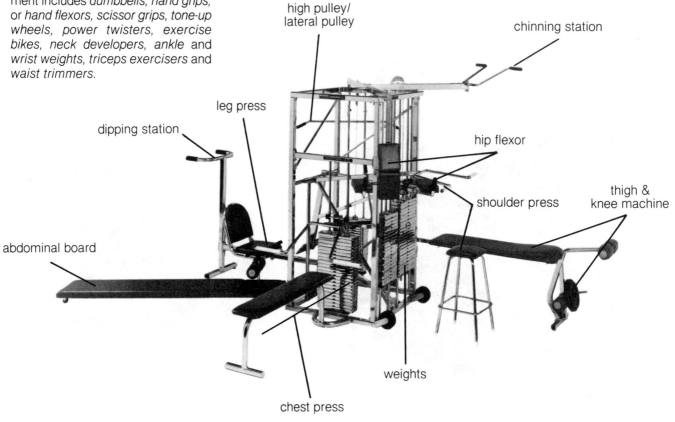

high pulley/
lateral pulley

chinning station

leg press

dipping station

hip flexor

shoulder press

thigh &
knee machine

abdominal board

weights

chest press

Universal Gym

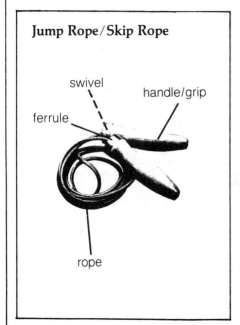

Jump Rope/Skip Rope

swivel

handle/grip

ferrule

rope

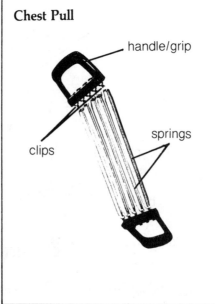

Chest Pull

handle/grip

springs

clips

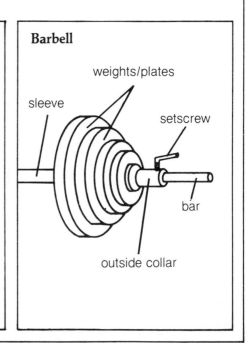

Barbell

weights/plates

sleeve

setscrew

bar

outside collar

Chess, Checkers, Backgammon and Tile Games

When chessmen and checkers are arranged at the start of a game, they are positioned in a *setup*. A chessboard's horizontal rows are called *ranks*. Vertical rows are *files*. In backgammon, a player increases the stakes by turning a dicelike *doubling cube*. A single backgammon piece on a point is called a *blot*. Two or more on a point make a *block*. In dominos, pieces with identical numbers on both ends are called *doubles* or *spinners*. Dominos that have been played form a *layout*. In mah-jongg, tiles are arranged in a *wall* to begin a game.

white square

double corner

checkers/checker men

king

single corner

king row

black square

chessmen/ chess pieces

queen rook/ queen castle

queen rook pawn/ queen castle pawn

queen knight

queen bishop

queen knight pawn

queen bishop pawn

queen pawn

queen

king pawn

king

king bishop pawn

king bishop

king bishop

king knight pawn

king knight

king rook/ king castle

king rook pawn/ king castle pawn

Chessboard/Checkerboard

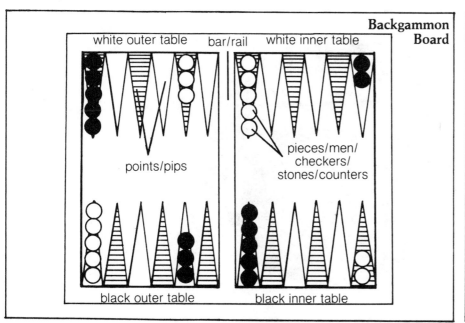

Backgammon Board

white outer table   bar/rail   white inner table

points/pips

pieces/men/ checkers/ stones/counters

black outer table   black inner table

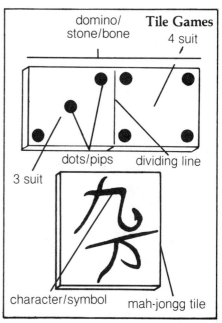

Tile Games

domino/ stone/bone

4 suit

dots/pips   dividing line

3 suit

character/symbol

mah-jongg tile

Gambling Equipment

A roulette wheel is operated by a *croupier.* Bets are placed on a *layout.* Slots are divided into *red* and *black* for betting purposes. Dice players bet either with the person rolling the dice, the *shooter,* or with the casino, or *house.* The blackjack dealer pushes money won by the house into a double-locked *drop box* below the betting table. Other casino games include *baccarat, chemin de fer, wheel of fortune,* and *chuck-a-luck,* a game played with three dice.

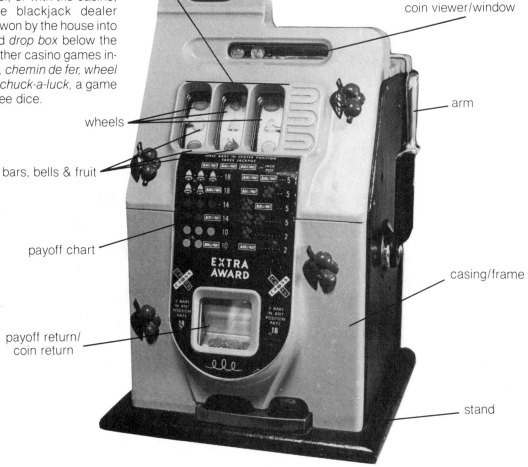

coin slot

face

coin viewer/window

arm

wheels

bars, bells & fruit

payoff chart

EXTRA AWARD

casing/frame

payoff return/ coin return

stand

Slot Machine / One-Arm Bandit

Roulette Wheel

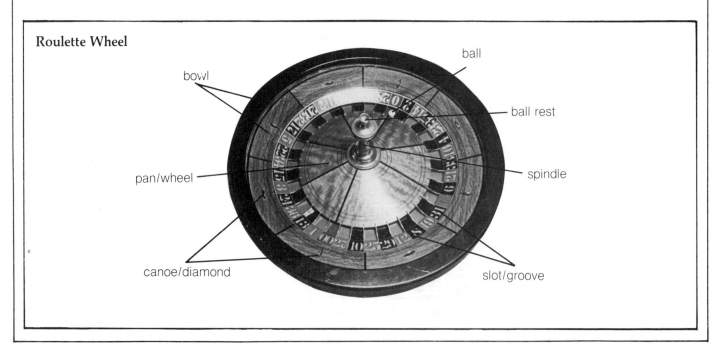

bowl

ball

ball rest

pan/wheel

spindle

canoe/diamond

slot/groove

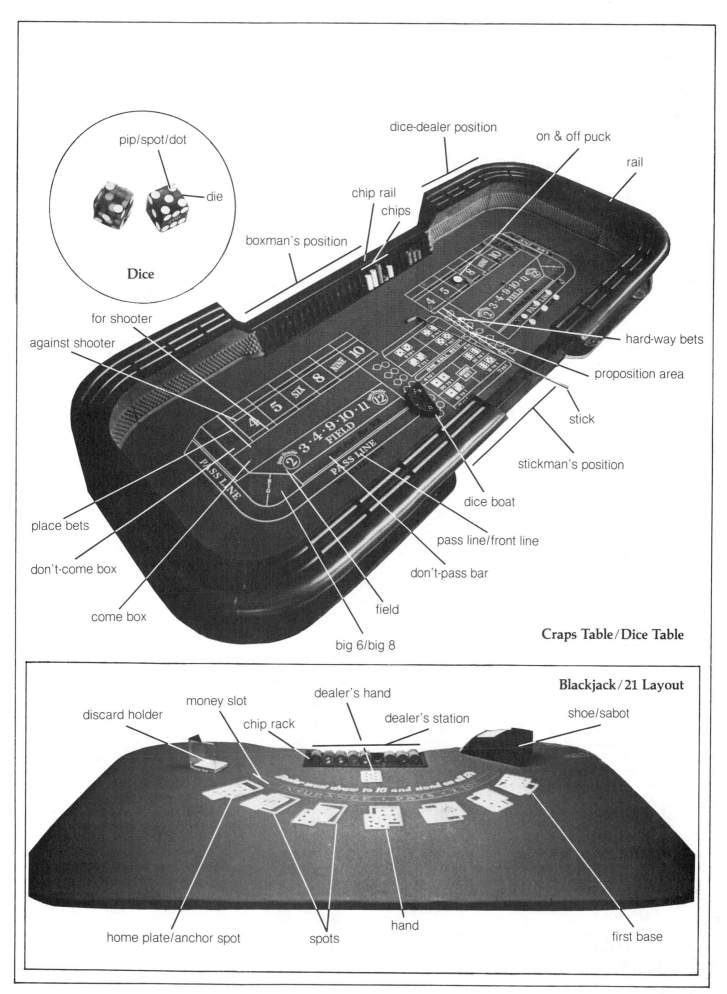

pip/spot/dot

die

Dice

dice-dealer position

on & off puck

rail

chip rail

chips

boxman's position

for shooter

against shooter

hard-way bets

proposition area

stick

stickman's position

4 5 SIX 8 NINE 10

2 3·4·9·10·11 FIELD 12

PASS LINE

dice boat

pass line/front line

place bets

don't-come box

don't-pass bar

come box

field

big 6/big 8

Craps Table/Dice Table

Blackjack/21 Layout

discard holder

money slot

dealer's hand

chip rack

dealer's station

shoe/sabot

home plate/anchor spot

spots

hand

first base

347

Casino Games

Playing Cards

There are 52 cards in a *deck* or, *pack*. The *aces*, shown below, and cards numbered two through ten, are called *spot cards* or *pip cards*. An additional card, the *joker*, or *mistigris*, is used in *card games* requiring a *wild card*. A *marked deck* is one in which the card *backs* have been altered slightly to allow a player to read their *values* illegally.

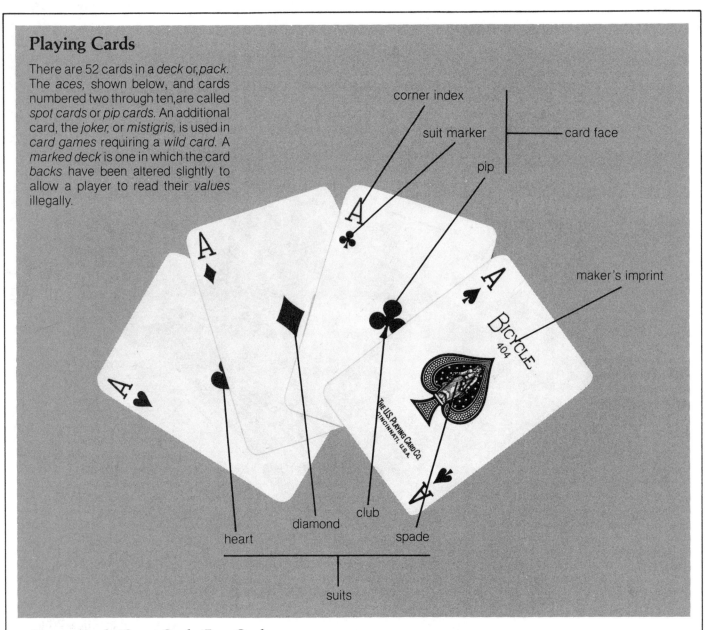

corner index

suit marker

card face

pip

maker's imprint

heart

diamond

club

spade

suits

Picture Cards / Court Cards / Face Cards

Jack / Knave

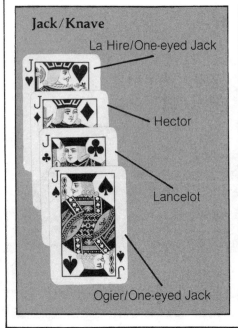

La Hire/One-eyed Jack

Hector

Lancelot

Ogier/One-eyed Jack

Queen

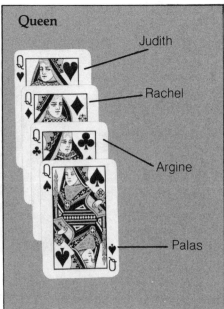

Judith

Rachel

Argine

Palas

King

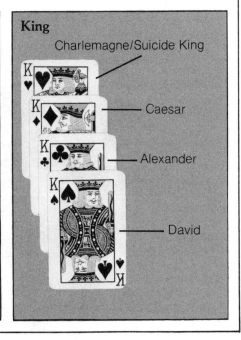

Charlemagne/Suicide King

Caesar

Alexander

David

Arts and Crafts

The main subsections here include the platforms on which the performing arts take place; coverage of the music field, ranging from the symbols that appear on sheet music to the parts of various musical instruments; the fine arts and crafts.

In the fine arts subsection an effort has been made to identify the terms for elements of style, rather than to cover styles themselves. The equipment used in everything from painting and sculpting to relief arts and stained glass are also illustrated and their parts labeled. The crafts subsection covers decorative stitching, knitting and weaving, and also includes the terms used to identify a sewing pattern.

Cartooning has a subsection all to itself. Here, for the first time, the reader will be able to identify everything from the beads of fear on a comic character (plewds) to the meaning of double XX's on a cartoon bottle (boozex). In addition the reader will henceforth be able to recognize the difference between a thought balloon, a speech balloon and an idea balloon in a cartoon panel.

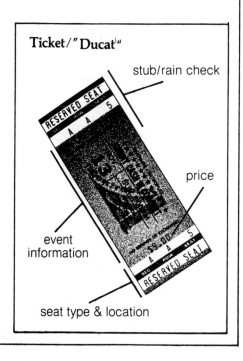

Ticket/"Ducat"

stub/rain check

price

event information

seat type & location

Stage

Also found on many stages are *tormentors,* or *legs* which frame the stage to narrow the acting area, a *trapdoor,* or *scruto,* an *elevator,* and a fabric backdrop, or *scrim.* Everything used on stages, or *boards,* are *props,* or *properties.* The arrangement of scenery, furniture and properties is called a set.

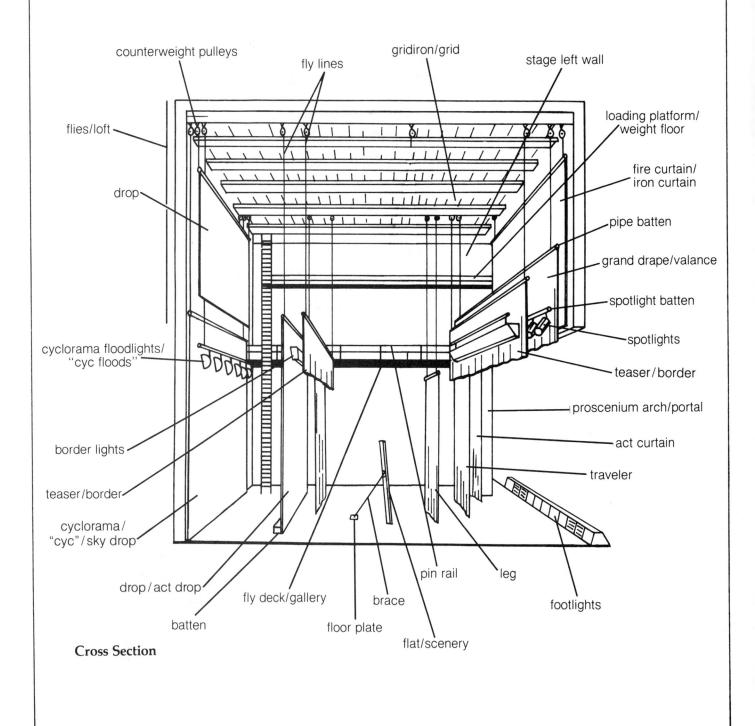

counterweight pulleys

fly lines

gridiron/grid

stage left wall

flies/loft

loading platform/ weight floor

drop

fire curtain/ iron curtain

pipe batten

grand drape/valance

spotlight batten

spotlights

cyclorama floodlights/ "cyc floods"

teaser/border

border lights

proscenium arch/portal

act curtain

teaser/border

traveler

cyclorama/ "cyc"/sky drop

pin rail

leg

footlights

drop/act drop

fly deck/gallery

brace

flat/scenery

batten

floor plate

Cross Section

Theater

In a *performance hall,* the orchestra sits in a sunken *orchestra pit* between the audience and the stage. For some shows a *runway,* or *ramp,* extends from the stage into the *center aisle.* The seating area above the orchestra is the *balcony.* In theaters with more than one balcony, the lowest one is the *mezzanine,* the front section of which is the loge.

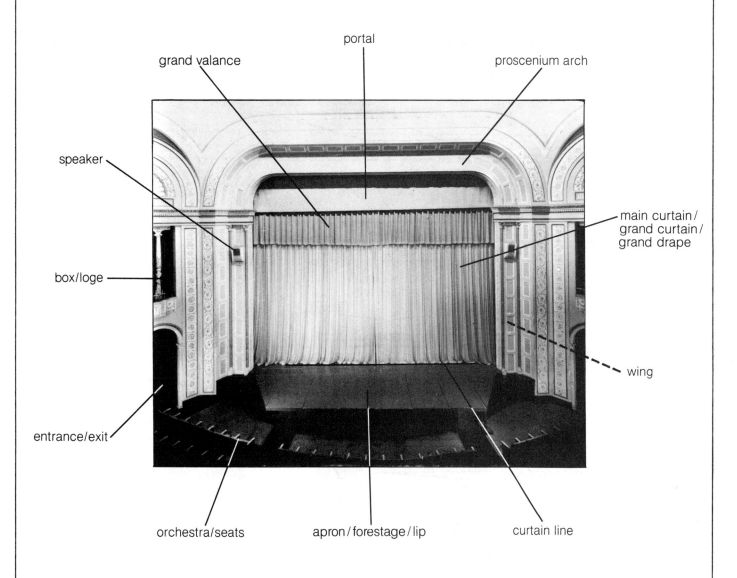

portal

grand valance

proscenium arch

speaker

main curtain/
grand curtain/
grand drape

box/loge

wing

entrance/exit

orchestra/seats

apron/forestage/lip

curtain line

Performing Arts

Sheet Music Notations

Words to be sung, or *lyrics,* appear below the staff on sheet music. The notation ' is a *breath mark* indicating that the singer or musician should briefly pause. A combination of tones that blend harmoniously is a *chord.* Sharps, flats and naturals appearing directly in front of specific notes are called *accidentals.* A *quasihemi-demisemiquaver* is a 128th note.

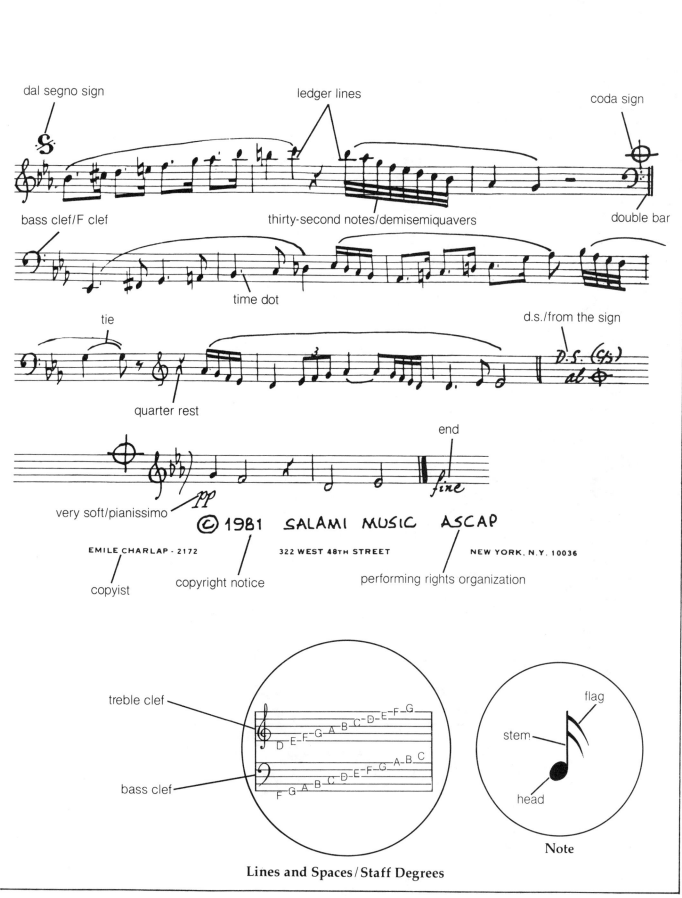

Lines and Spaces/Staff Degrees

Note

Orchestra

In symphony orchestras, string, woodwind and brass parts are performed by many *musicians.* In *chamber music ensembles,* each part is usually played by a single *player. Bands* do not normally include stringed instruments. *Marching bands* generally use no oboes or bassoons, and flutes are replaced with piccolos or *fifes. Dance bands* and *jazz bands* are loosely structured.

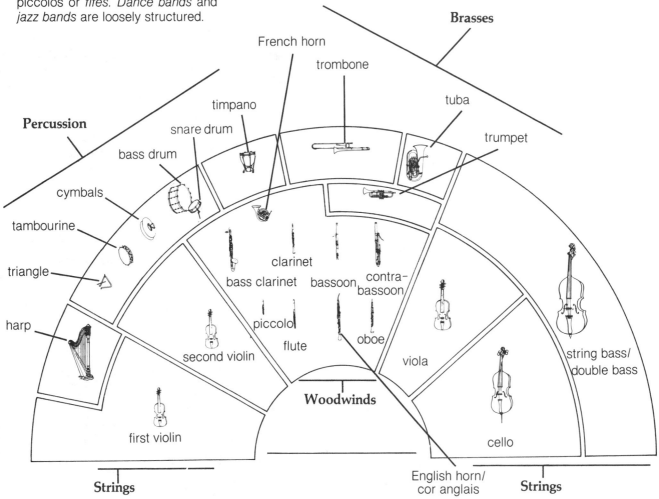

Brasses

French horn

trombone

tuba

trumpet

Percussion

timpano

snare drum

bass drum

cymbals

tambourine

triangle

harp

clarinet

bass clarinet

piccolo

flute

second violin

first violin

Strings

bassoon

contra-bassoon

oboe

viola

cello

English horn/ cor anglais

Woodwinds

string bass/ double bass

Strings

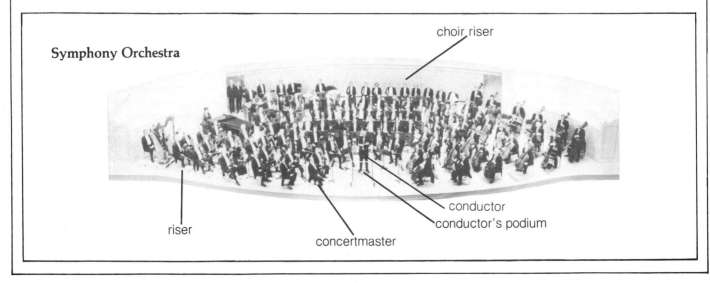

Symphony Orchestra

choir riser

conductor

conductor's podium

riser

concertmaster

Violin

Stringed instruments produce tones when a bow is drawn across the strings (*arco*) or they are finger-plucked (*pizzicato*). The sympathetic vibration produced between the instrument's belly and *back* adds *resonance* and *volume* to the sound.

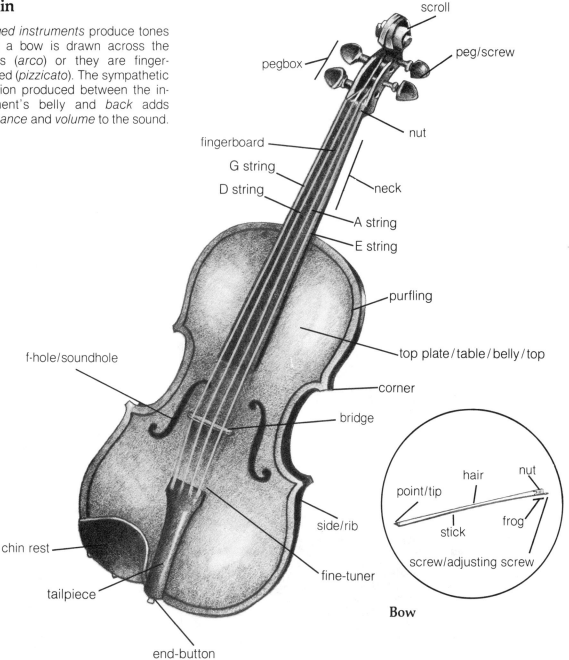

scroll

pegbox

peg/screw

nut

fingerboard

G string

D string

neck

A string

E string

purfling

top plate/table/belly/top

corner

f-hole/soundhole

bridge

side/rib

chin rest

fine-tuner

tailpiece

end-button

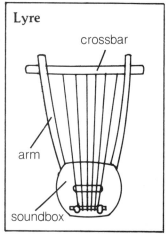

point/tip

hair

nut

stick

frog

screw/adjusting screw

Bow

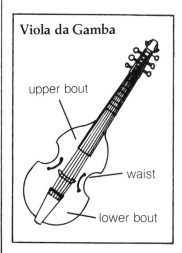

Viola da Gamba

upper bout

waist

lower bout

Cello / Violoncello

endpin

Lyre

crossbar

arm

soundbox

Double Bass / Bass / Bass Fiddle

E string

A string

D string

G string

Music

Woodwinds

Woodwinds produce *tones* by the vibration of one or two reeds of pliant cane in the mouthpiece or by the passing of air across a blow hole.

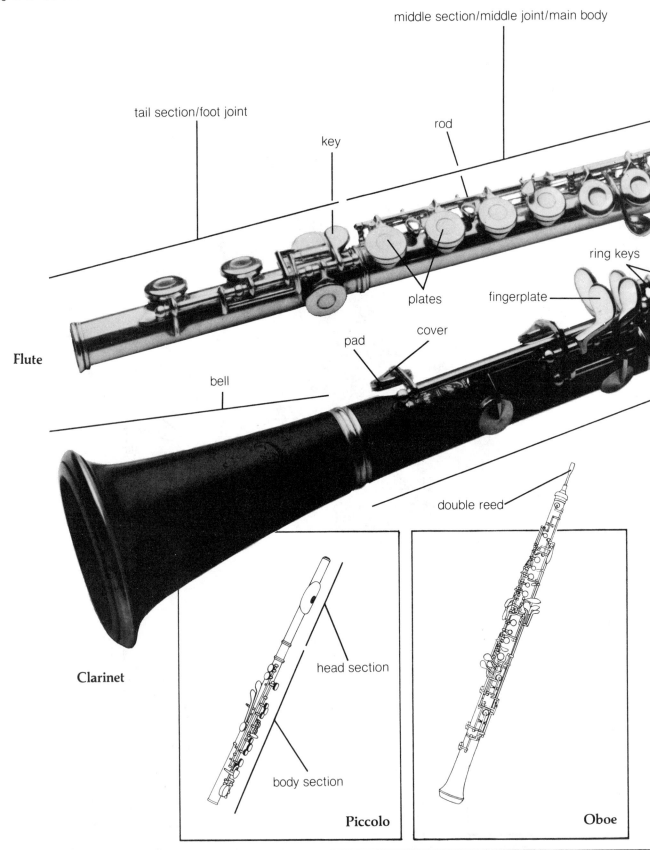

middle section/middle joint/main body

tail section/foot joint

key

rod

ring keys

plates

fingerplate

pad

cover

Flute

bell

double reed

Clarinet

head section

body section

Piccolo

Oboe

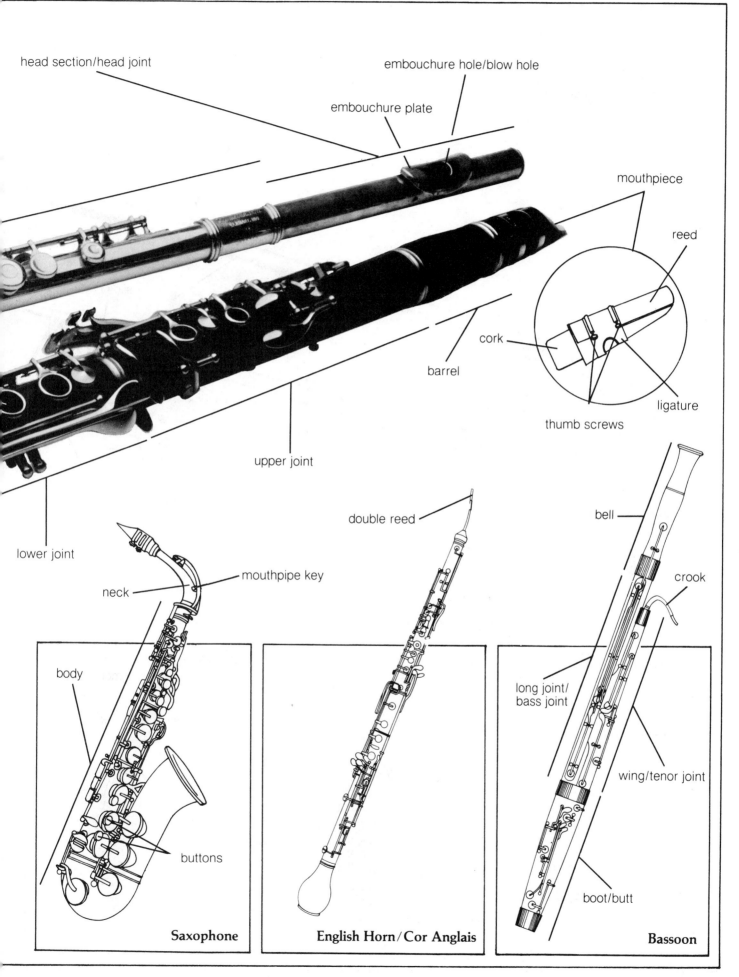

head section/head joint

embouchure hole/blow hole

embouchure plate

mouthpiece

reed

cork

barrel

ligature

thumb screws

upper joint

double reed

bell

crook

lower joint

mouthpipe key

neck

body

long joint/
bass joint

wing/tenor joint

buttons

boot/butt

Saxophone

English Horn/Cor Anglais

Bassoon

Music

Brasses

Brasses are *wind instruments* that produce *tones* when lips are buzzed against the mouthpiece. The range of brass instruments is increased by added lengths of tubing called *crooks* or *shanks*.

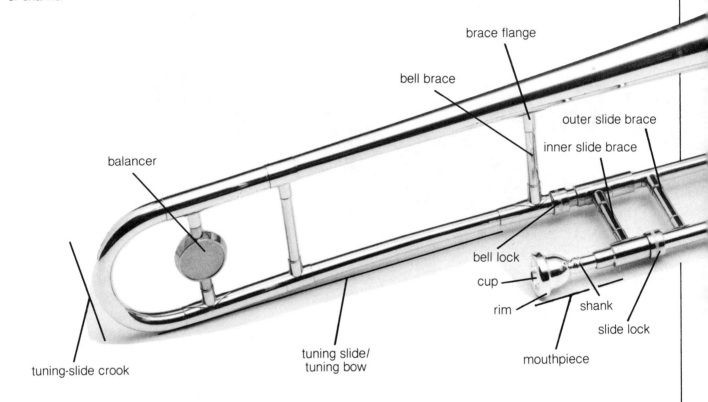

brace flange

bell brace

outer slide brace

inner slide brace

balancer

bell lock

cup

rim

shank

slide lock

mouthpiece

tuning-slide crook

tuning slide/
tuning bow

Trombone

Sousaphone

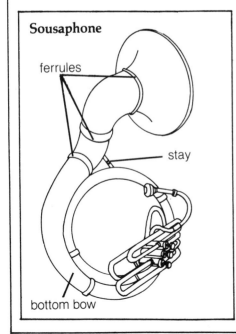

ferrules

stay

bottom bow

Tuba

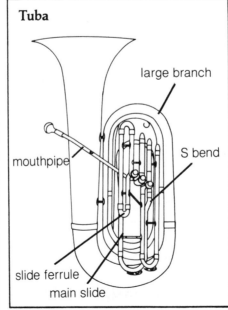

large branch

mouthpipe

S bend

slide ferrule

main slide

French Horn

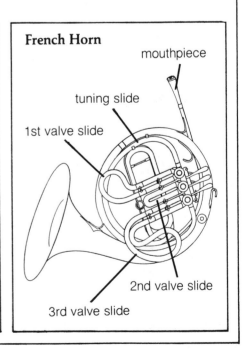

mouthpiece

tuning slide

1st valve slide

2nd valve slide

3rd valve slide

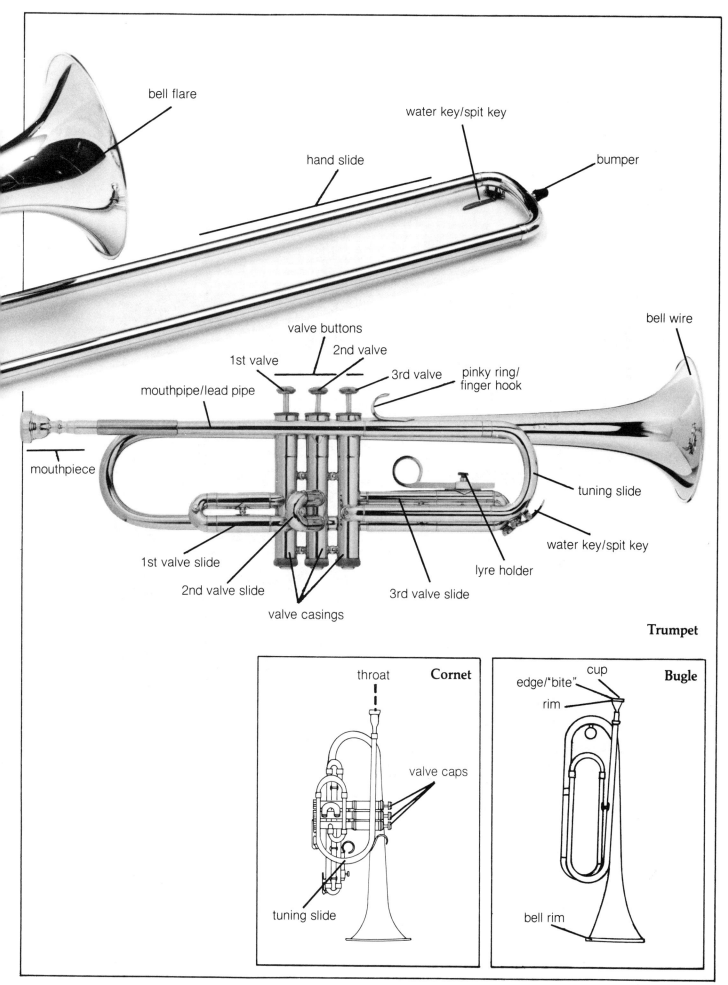

bell flare

water key/spit key

hand slide

bumper

valve buttons

bell wire

1st valve

2nd valve

3rd valve

pinky ring/
finger hook

mouthpipe/lead pipe

mouthpiece

tuning slide

1st valve slide

water key/spit key

2nd valve slide

lyre holder

3rd valve slide

valve casings

Trumpet

throat

Cornet

cup

edge/"bite"

Bugle

rim

valve caps

tuning slide

bell rim

359

Organ

The keyboards, or *manuals*, and pedal board, contained in a *console* or *keydesk*, as shown here, together with a number of *organ pipes*, separate from the console, comprise a pipe organ. Music is produced when air, sent into a *wind chest* by *bellows*, is directed into a selection of the organ's many pipes. An *electric organ* produces tones mechanically; an *electronic organ* uses integrated circuits and speakers to make *sounds*.

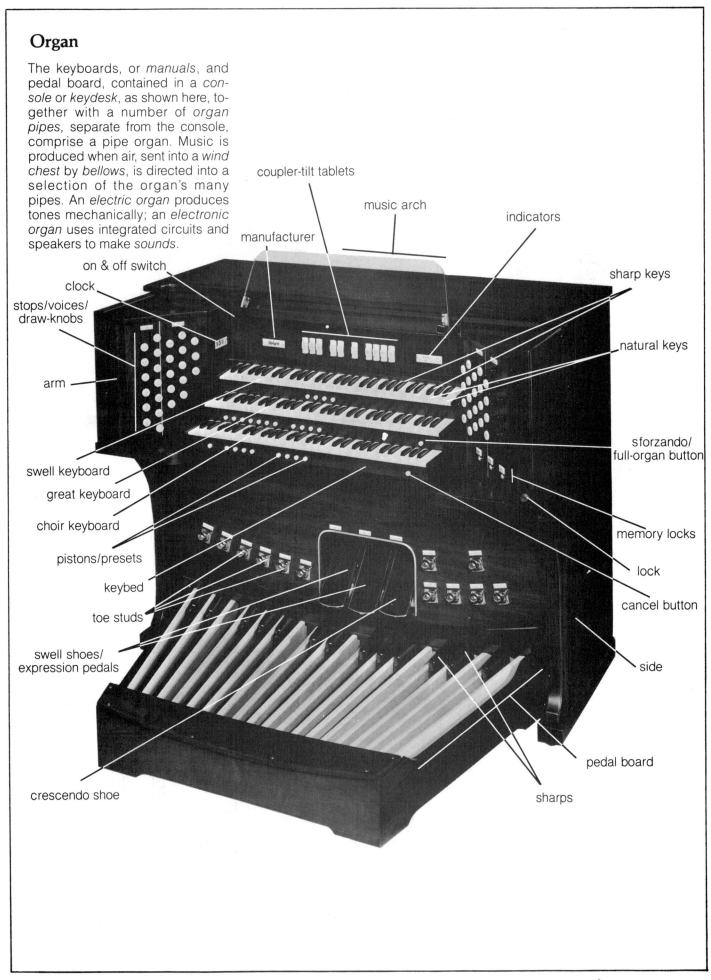

coupler-tilt tablets

music arch

indicators

manufacturer

sharp keys

on & off switch

clock

stops/voices/ draw-knobs

natural keys

arm

sforzando/ full-organ button

swell keyboard

great keyboard

choir keyboard

memory locks

pistons/presets

lock

keybed

cancel button

toe studs

swell shoes/ expression pedals

side

crescendo shoe

pedal board

sharps

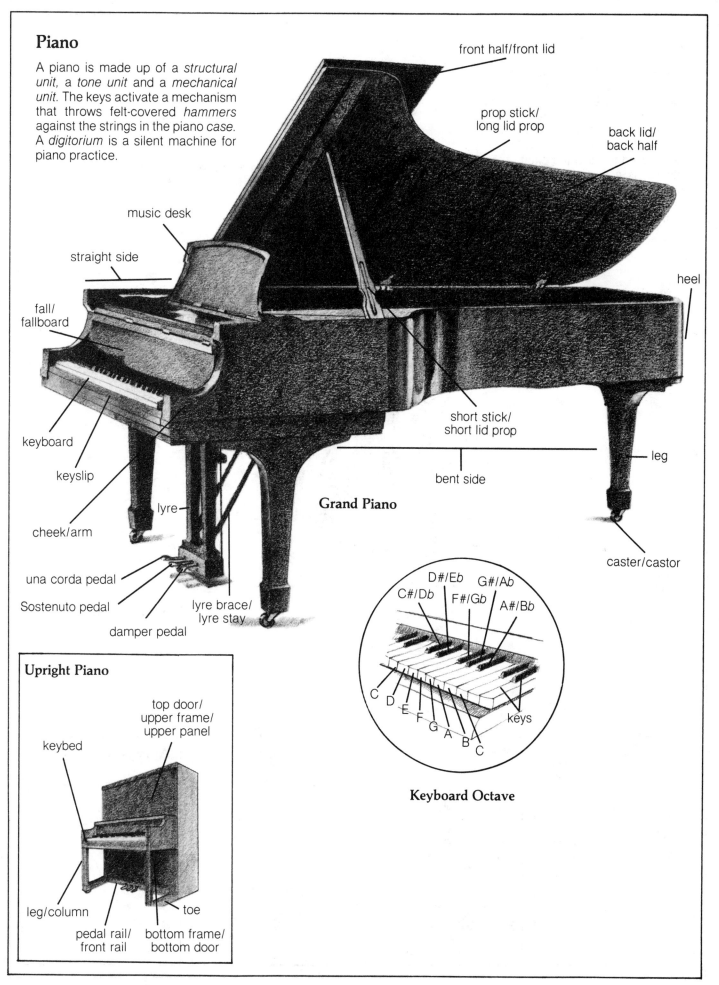

Piano

A piano is made up of a *structural unit*, a *tone unit* and a *mechanical unit*. The keys activate a mechanism that throws felt-covered *hammers* against the strings in the piano *case*. A *digitorium* is a silent machine for piano practice.

front half/front lid

prop stick/ long lid prop

back lid/ back half

music desk

straight side

heel

fall/ fallboard

keyboard

keyslip

lyre

cheek/arm

short stick/ short lid prop

leg

bent side

Grand Piano

una corda pedal

Sostenuto pedal

damper pedal

lyre brace/ lyre stay

caster/castor

Upright Piano

top door/ upper frame/ upper panel

keybed

leg/column

toe

pedal rail/ front rail

bottom frame/ bottom door

C#/Db

D#/Eb

F#/Gb

G#/Ab

A#/Bb

C
D
E
F
G
A
B
C

keys

Keyboard Octave

Music

Guitar

These *chordophones,* or *stringed instruments,* are members of the lute family. They are played by plucking or strumming the strings with the fingers or with a stiff *plectrum* or *pick.* A movable device attached to a guitar neck, used to raise the pitch of the strings, is a *capo.* There are *sympathetic strings* inside the hollow neck of a sitar that vibrate in response to the drone or melody strings.

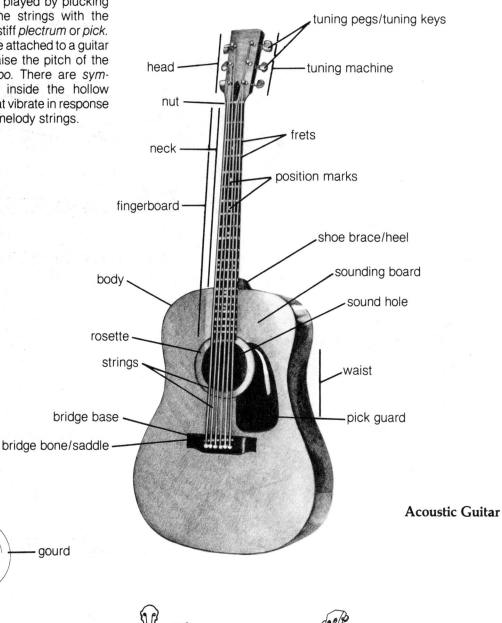

tuning pegs/tuning keys

head

tuning machine

nut

neck

frets

position marks

fingerboard

shoe brace/heel

sounding board

body

sound hole

rosette

strings

waist

bridge base

pick guard

bridge bone/saddle

Acoustic Guitar

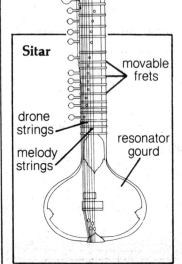

tuning pegs

gourd

Sitar

movable frets

drone strings

melody strings

resonator gourd

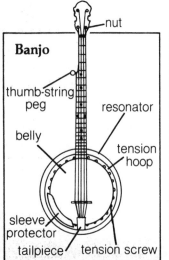

Banjo

nut

thumb-string peg

resonator

belly

tension hoop

sleeve protector

tailpiece

tension screw

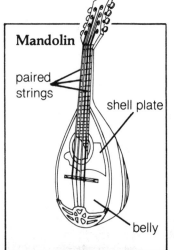

Mandolin

paired strings

shell plate

belly

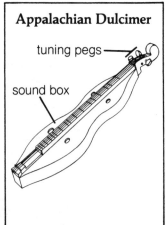

Appalachian Dulcimer

tuning pegs

sound box

Electric Guitar and Synthesizer

The electric guitar has a *solid body* rather than the *hollow* or *semi-hollow body* of an acoustic guitar. *Special-effects pedals*, among them *fuzz*, *fuzz-phaser*, *wah-wah* and *distortion*, can be linked to the amplifier. *Pre-amplifiers*, which serve to magnify weak signals, can also be hooked up to the amplifier.

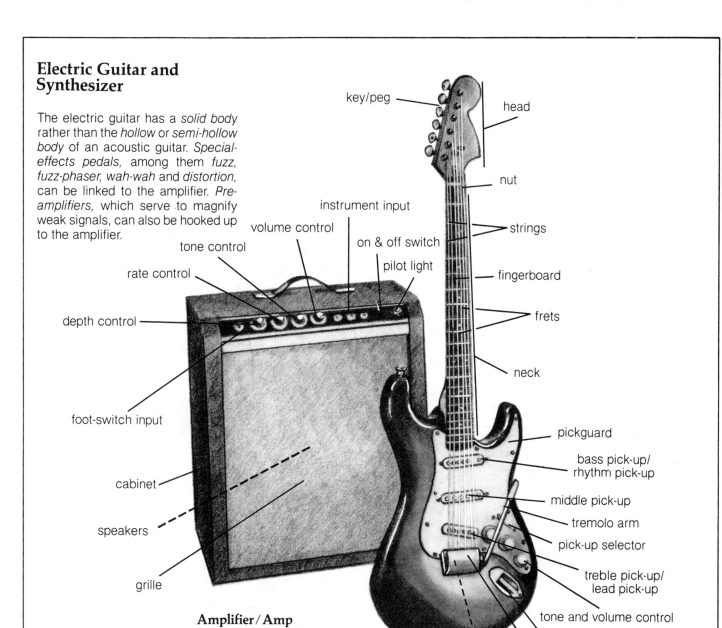

key/peg
head
nut
strings
fingerboard
frets
neck
pickguard
bass pick-up/ rhythm pick-up
middle pick-up
tremolo arm
pick-up selector
treble pick-up/ lead pick-up
tone and volume control
jack-plug socket
bridge cover
bridge

instrument input
volume control
on & off switch
tone control
pilot light
rate control
depth control
foot-switch input
cabinet
speakers
grille

Amplifier / Amp

Electric Guitar

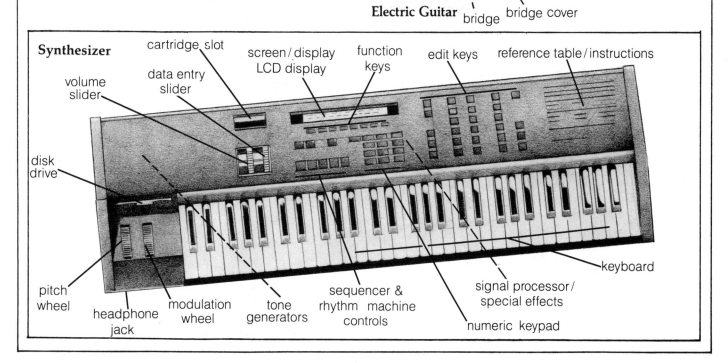

Synthesizer

cartridge slot
volume slider
data entry slider
screen/display LCD display
function keys
edit keys
reference table/instructions
disk drive
pitch wheel
headphone jack
modulation wheel
tone generators
sequencer & rhythm machine controls
numeric keypad
signal processor/ special effects
keyboard

Drums

Drums, or *membranophones*, in a *drum set* such as the one shown here, are played with *drumsticks*, *mallets* or *brushes*. A *gong* is struck with a *beater*. Adjustable metal, nylon or gut strings, called *snares*, are stretched across the bottom head, or *snare head*, of a snare drum. Timpani can be adjusted by screws or pedals to produce sounds of different pitches.

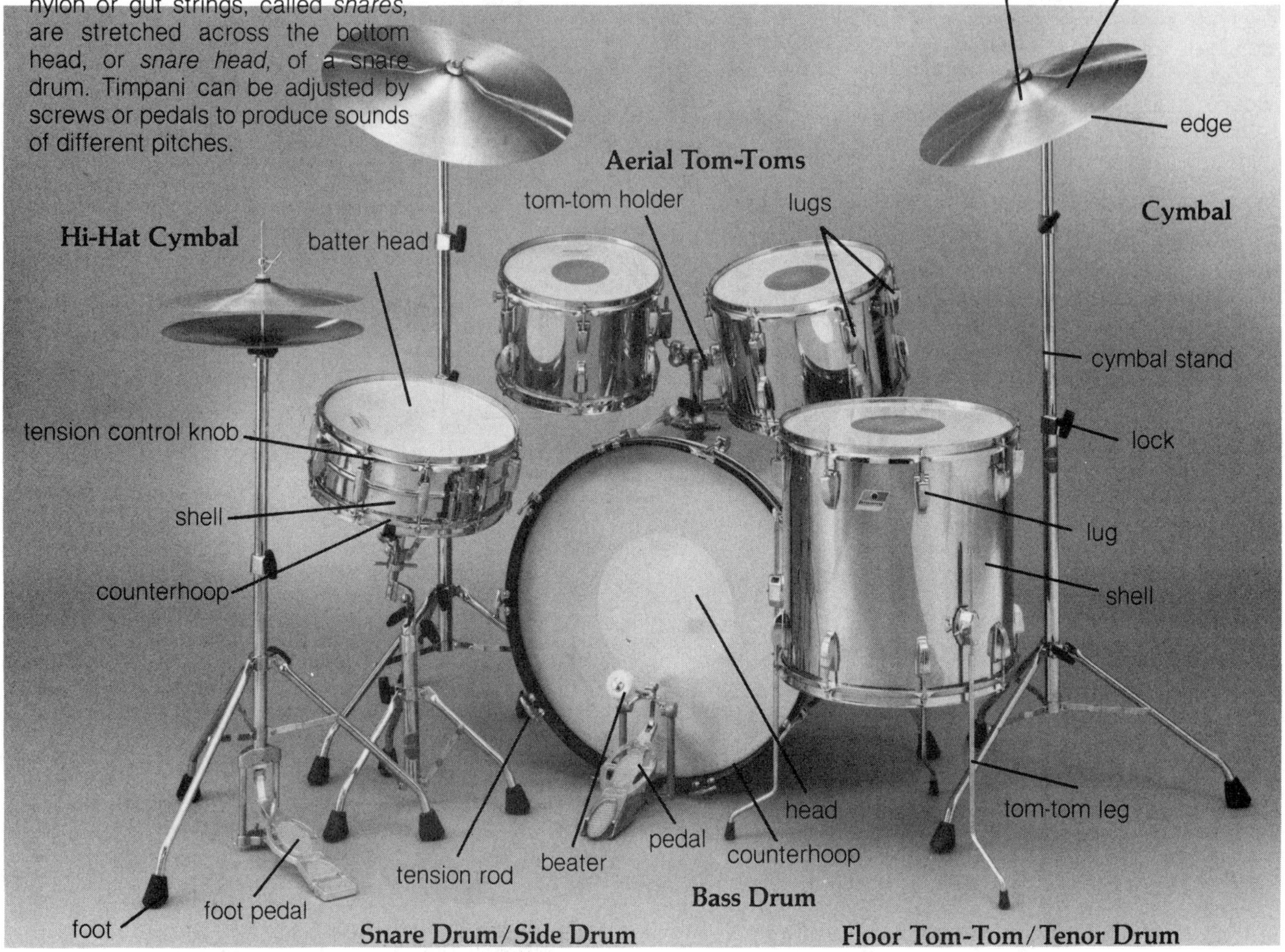

bell

bow

edge

Cymbal

Aerial Tom-Toms

tom-tom holder

lugs

cymbal stand

Hi-Hat Cymbal

batter head

lock

tension control knob

lug

shell

shell

counterhoop

head

tom-tom leg

pedal

tension rod

beater

counterhoop

foot

foot pedal

Bass Drum

Snare Drum / Side Drum

Floor Tom-Tom / Tenor Drum

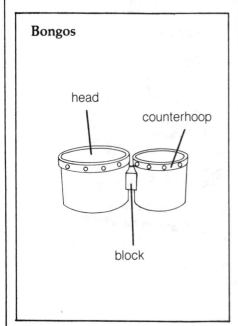

Bongos

head

counterhoop

block

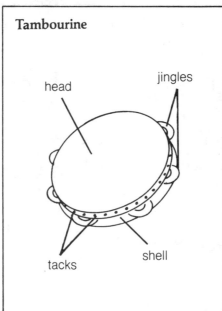

Tambourine

jingles

head

shell

tacks

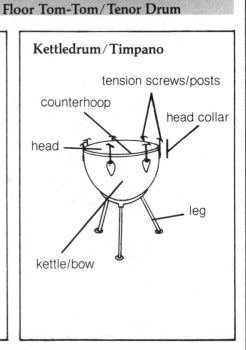

Kettledrum / Timpano

tension screws/posts

counterhoop

head collar

head

leg

kettle/bow

Bagpipe

A *drone reed,* or *double-reed,* held inside the chanter by a *tenon,* creates music when air is blown into the *pipes* by a *bagpiper* or by pumping *bellows* strapped to the *piper's* body. The melody is played on the eight *open holes* in the chanter. The *leather bag* is usually covered with a decorative *bag cover.*

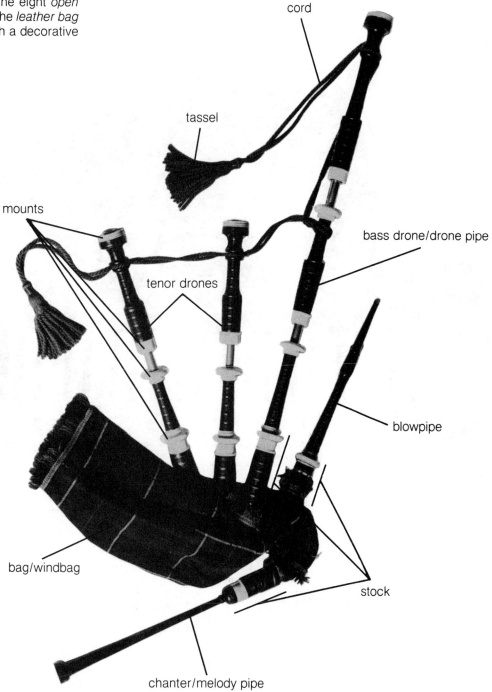

cord

tassel

mounts

tenor drones

bass drone/drone pipe

blowpipe

bag/windbag

stock

chanter/melody pipe

Folk Instruments

Like the harmonica, the accordion, or *piano-accordion,* is a *free-reed instrument.* Many accordions have *treble* and *bass register buttons* which allow the *accordionist* to change the tone of the instrument.

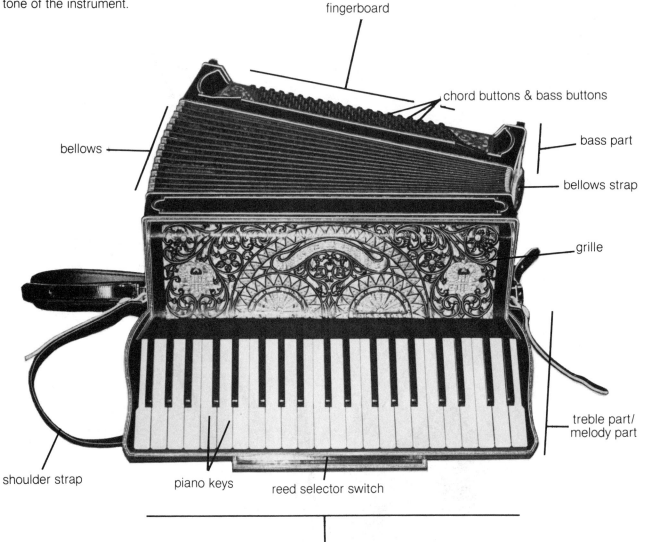

fingerboard

chord buttons & bass buttons

bass part

bellows strap

bellows

grille

shoulder strap

piano keys

reed selector switch

treble part/ melody part

keyboard

Accordion

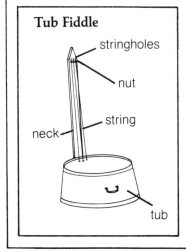

Tub Fiddle

stringholes

nut

string

neck

tub

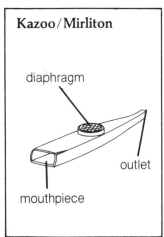

Kazoo/Mirliton

diaphragm

outlet

mouthpiece

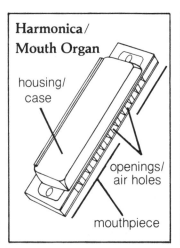

Harmonica/ Mouth Organ

housing/ case

openings/ air holes

mouthpiece

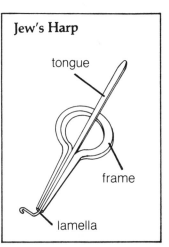

Jew's Harp

tongue

frame

lamella

Musical Accessories

A metronome, used to find the correct speed for music in beats per minute, can be spring wound or electric. A tuning fork is constructed and tempered so as to give a pure *tone* when caused to vibrate. It can be used in conjunction with a *resonance box* to amplify its sound.

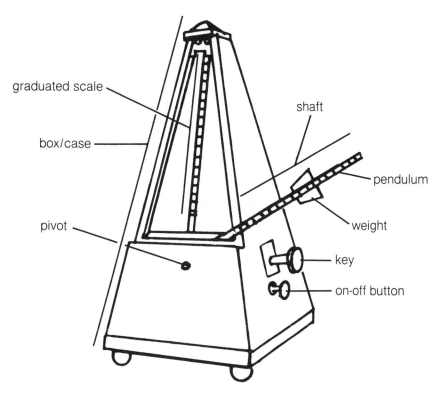

graduated scale

shaft

box/case

pendulum

weight

pivot

key

on-off button

Metronome

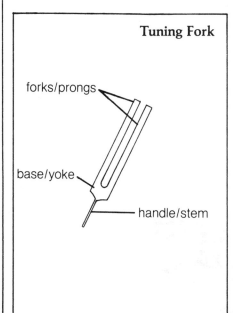

Tuning Fork

forks/prongs

base/yoke

handle/stem

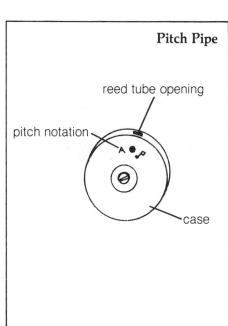

Pitch Pipe

reed tube opening

pitch notation

case

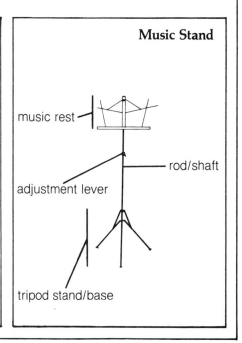

Music Stand

music rest

rod/shaft

adjustment lever

tripod stand/base

Elements of Composition

The forms of *linear perspective* illustrated here allow an artist or illustrator to show *dimension – height, width* and *depth* – on a *flat surface.* The central focus of a work of art is the *subject.* The way an artist renders a subject, which ranges from *literal rendition* to forms of *abstraction,* is called *style.*

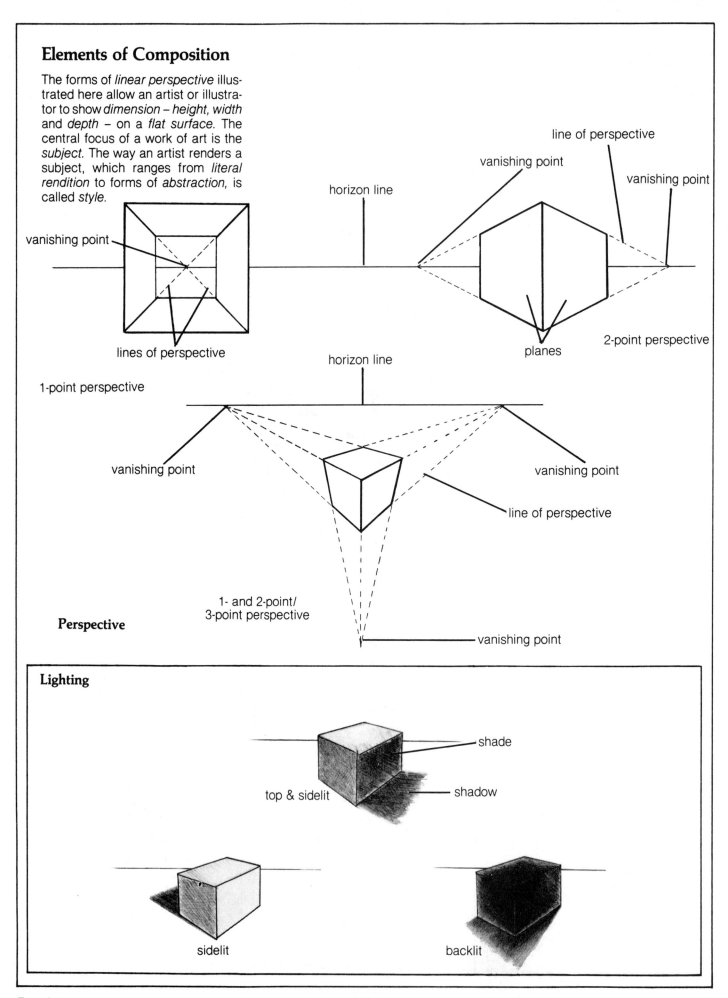

vanishing point

horizon line

line of perspective

vanishing point

vanishing point

lines of perspective

planes

2-point perspective

1-point perspective

horizon line

vanishing point

vanishing point

line of perspective

1- and 2-point/
3-point perspective

Perspective

vanishing point

Lighting

shade

shadow

top & sidelit

sidelit

backlit

Composition

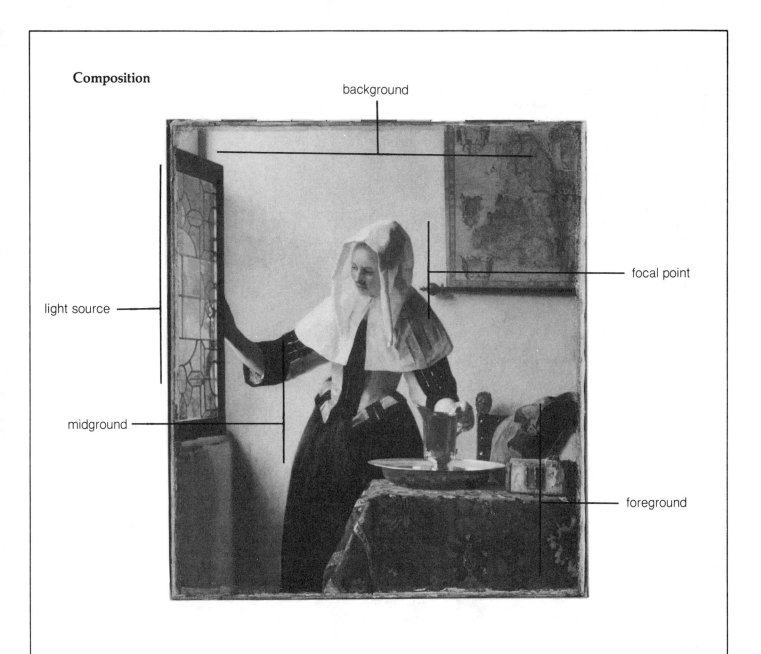

background

light source

midground

focal point

foreground

Texture

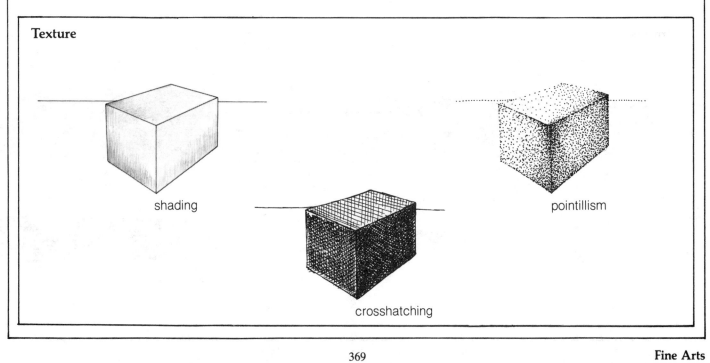

shading

crosshatching

pointillism

Painting

Before paint is applied to a *canvas* it must be drawn taut on a *stretcher* and the surface coated with *primer,* usually a substance called *gesso.* The *artist,* or *painter,* chooses a type of paint, or *medium,* in which to work, the most common of which are *tempera, acrylic* and *oil.* A thin blade set in a handle, used for mixing colors or applying them to a canvas, is a palette knife.

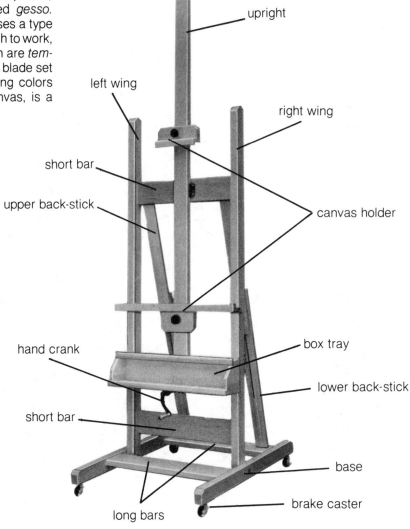

upright

left wing

right wing

short bar

upper back-stick

canvas holder

hand crank

box tray

lower back-stick

short bar

base

long bars

brake caster

Easel

Brushes

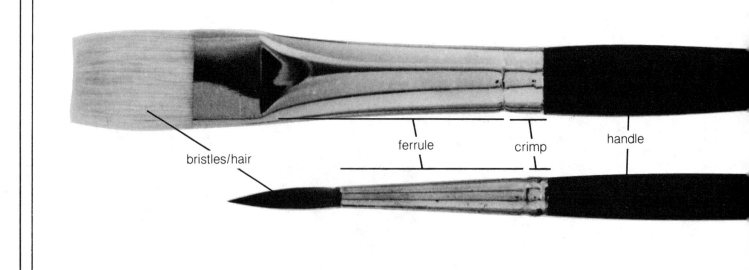

bristles/hair

ferrule

crimp

handle

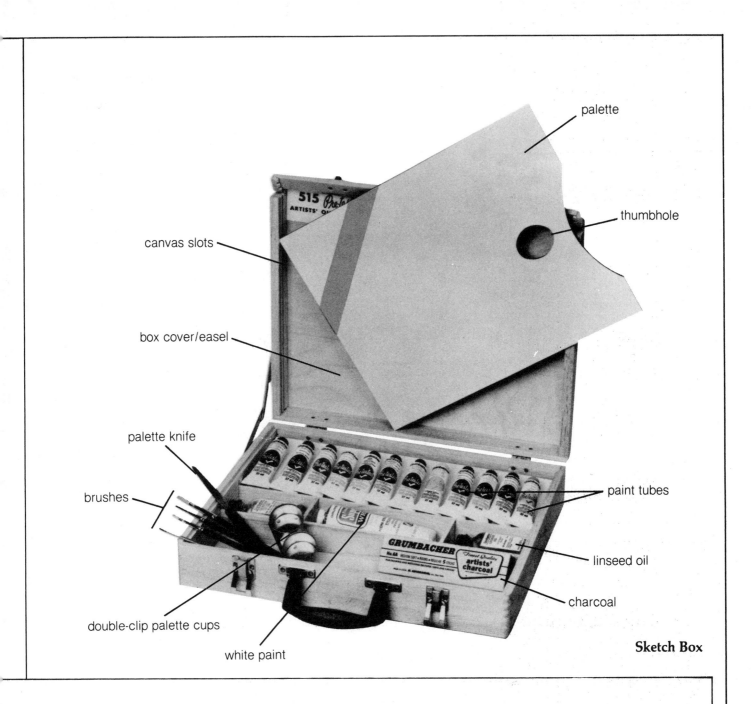

palette

thumbhole

canvas slots

box cover/easel

palette knife

brushes

paint tubes

linseed oil

charcoal

double-clip palette cups

white paint

Sketch Box

515 Pre-[...]
ARTISTS' Q[...]

GRUMBACHER
No.6A MEDIUM SOFT • ROUND • REGULAR 5 STICKS
Finest Quality
artists'
charcoal

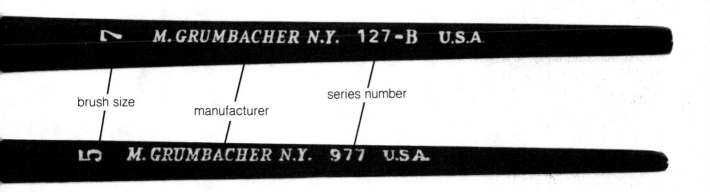

M. GRUMBACHER N.Y. 127-B U.S.A

M. GRUMBACHER N.Y. 977 U.S.A.

brush size

manufacturer

series number

Sculpting Tools

In stone sculpture, a *subtractive process,* forms or objects are created in *three dimensions* or in *relief.* Works may be carved or built up from some flexible material. Whenever a pliant material is used, it may be laid upon an inner skeleton, or *armature.* To make the finished product more durable, it may be fired or cast.

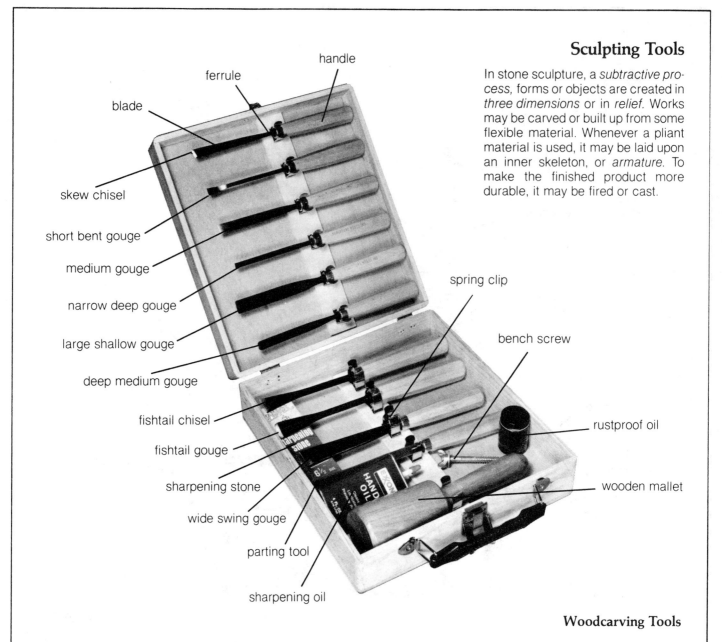

handle

ferrule

blade

skew chisel

short bent gouge

medium gouge

narrow deep gouge

large shallow gouge

deep medium gouge

fishtail chisel

fishtail gouge

sharpening stone

wide swing gouge

parting tool

sharpening oil

spring clip

bench screw

rustproof oil

wooden mallet

Woodcarving Tools

Clay Modeling Tools

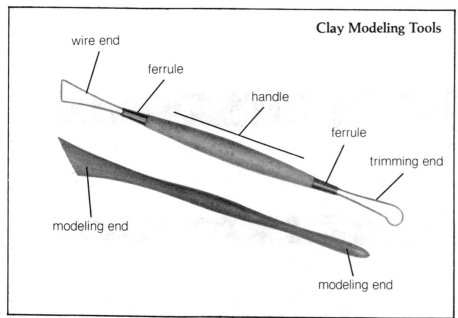

wire end

ferrule

handle

ferrule

trimming end

modeling end

modeling end

Stonecutting Tools

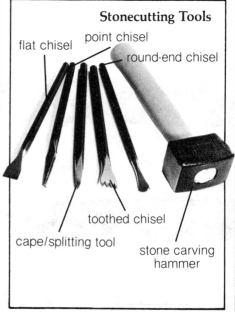

flat chisel

point chisel

round-end chisel

toothed chisel

cape/splitting tool

stone carving hammer

Potting

An object made on a potter's wheel is *thrown*. The object is then put in a kiln where it is *fired*, or hardened. Its surface is usually covered with a glasslike coating, or *glaze*. A knifelike *fettling tool* is used to cut and shape soft clay, as is a wooden strip called a *paddle*. A manually operated potter's wheel is called a *kick-wheel*.

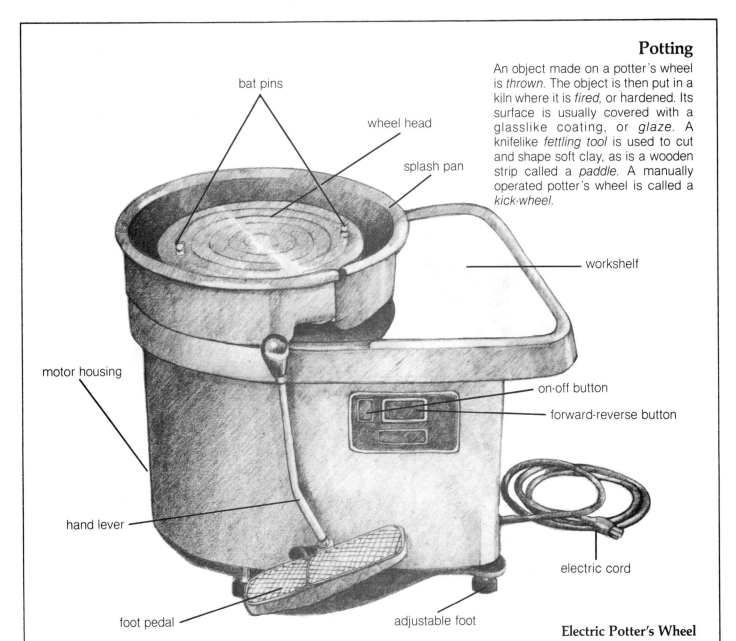

bat pins

wheel head

splash pan

worshelf

on-off button

forward-reverse button

motor housing

hand lever

electric cord

foot pedal

adjustable foot

Electric Potter's Wheel

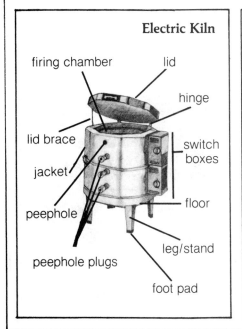

Electric Kiln

firing chamber

lid

lid brace

hinge

jacket

switch boxes

peephole

floor

peephole plugs

leg/stand

foot pad

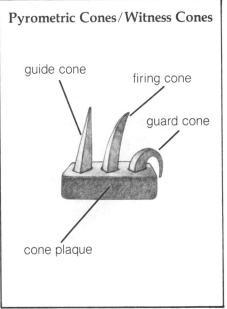

Pyrometric Cones / Witness Cones

guide cone

firing cone

guard cone

cone plaque

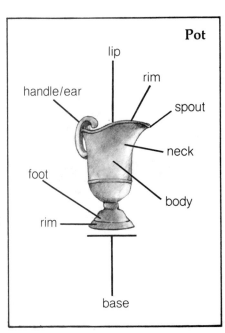

Pot

lip

rim

handle/ear

spout

foot

neck

rim

body

base

Fine Arts

Woodcut Printing

The art of making *engravings* with wooden blocks is *xylography,* and the tools used to create the designs are called *gravers.*

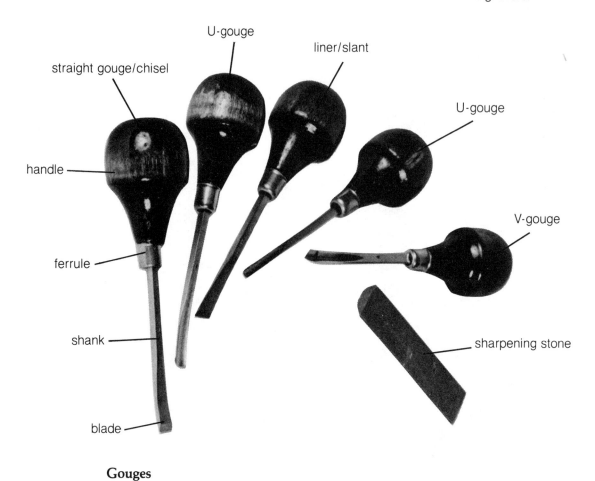

straight gouge/chisel

U-gouge

liner/slant

U-gouge

V-gouge

handle

ferrule

shank

blade

sharpening stone

Gouges

Wood Block

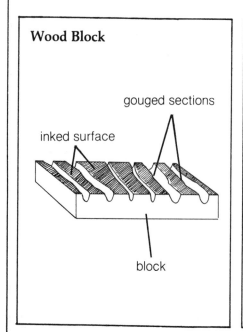

gouged sections

inked surface

block

Brayer/Roller

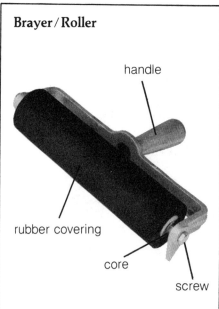

handle

rubber covering

core

screw

Baren

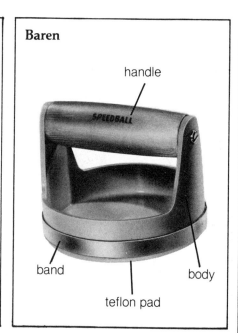

handle

SPEEDBALL

band

teflon pad

body

Silk Screen and Scrimshaw

The *silk-screen printmaking process* is called *serigraphy*. A *stopping medium*, called a *resist*, blocks out or *masks* an area of the screen. Ink or paint passes through the unprotected areas of the screen to become the print. A person who does *decorative engravings* or *carvings* in *ivory* or *whalebone* is called a *scrimshander*.

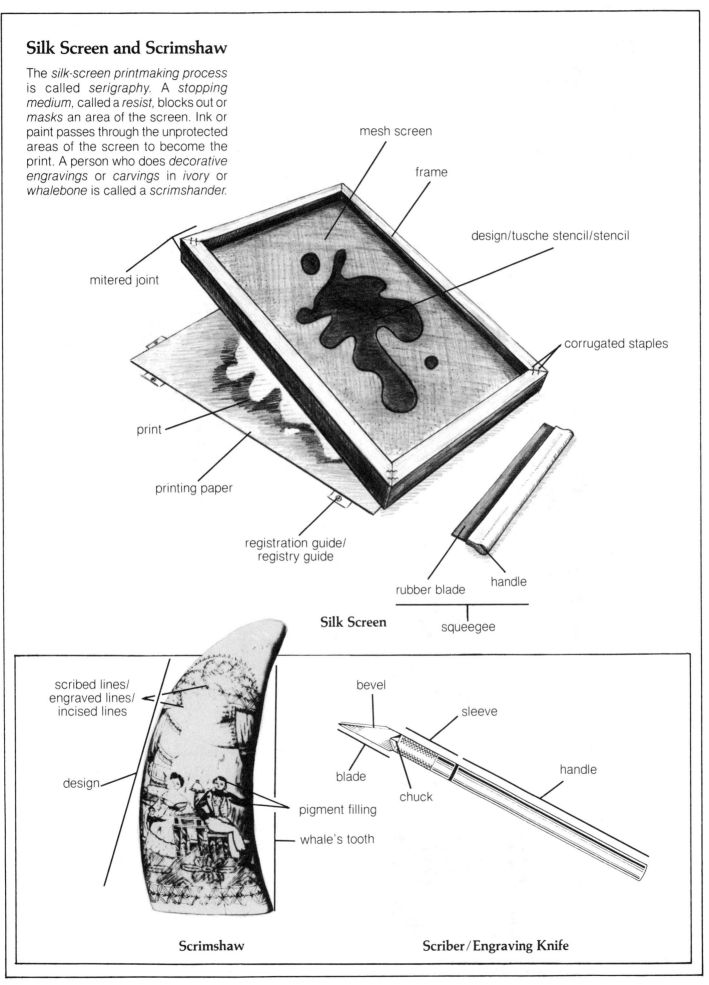

mesh screen

frame

design/tusche stencil/stencil

mitered joint

corrugated staples

print

printing paper

registration guide/ registry guide

rubber blade

handle

squeegee

Silk Screen

scribed lines/ engraved lines/ incised lines

bevel

sleeve

design

blade

handle

chuck

pigment filling

whale's tooth

Scrimshaw

Scriber/Engraving Knife

Lithography

Lithography is a form of *planographic printing*. The design is made on a stone, prepared, or "grained," by spinning the levigator over its surface, or on a metal *plate* with a *lithographic crayon, lithographic pencil, rubbing ink* or *asphaltum*.

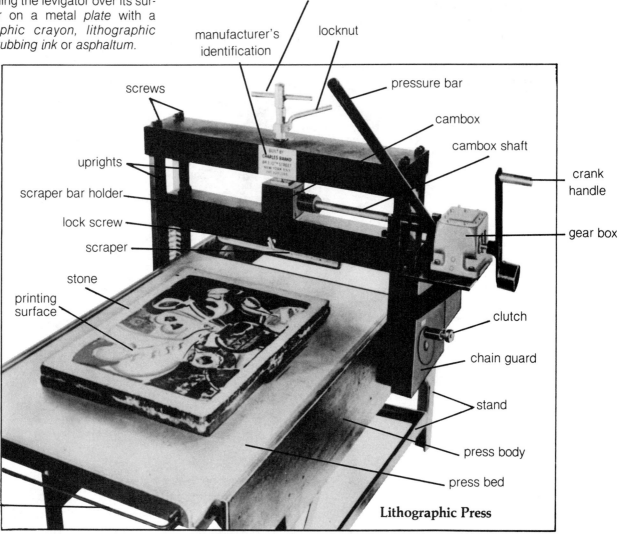

adjustment screw

locknut

manufacturer's identification

pressure bar

cambox

cambox shaft

crank handle

gear box

screws

uprights

scraper bar holder

lock screw

scraper

stone

printing surface

clutch

chain guard

stand

press body

press bed

bed handle

Lithographic Press

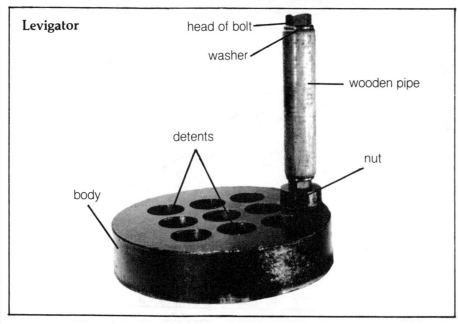

Levigator

head of bolt

washer

wooden pipe

detents

nut

body

Intaglio and Etching

Intaglio, or *incised printing,* is a type of *printmaking* in which a design is cut into a *plate* by techniques such as etching, *engraving, soft ground* or *aquatint.* A person who engraves metal is called a *chaser.*

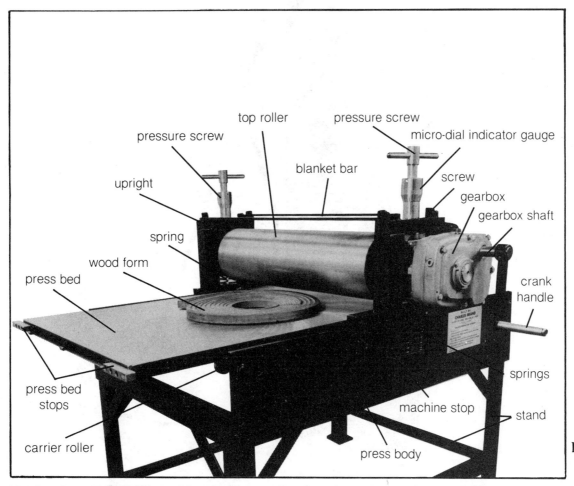

top roller
pressure screw
pressure screw
micro-dial indicator gauge
blanket bar
screw
upright
gearbox
gearbox shaft
spring
wood form
crank handle
press bed
springs
press bed stops
machine stop
stand
carrier roller
press body

Etching Press

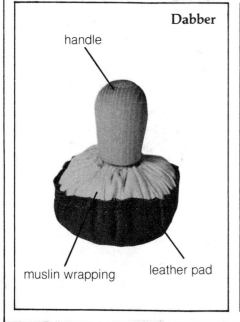

Dabber

handle
muslin wrapping
leather pad

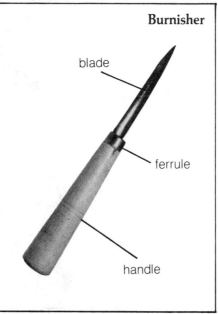

Burnisher

blade
ferrule
handle

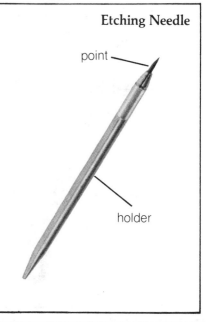

Etching Needle

point
holder

Stained Glass

Cut sections of *colored glass* are separated by *breakers. Grozing pliers* are used to grind or bite away irregular glass edges.

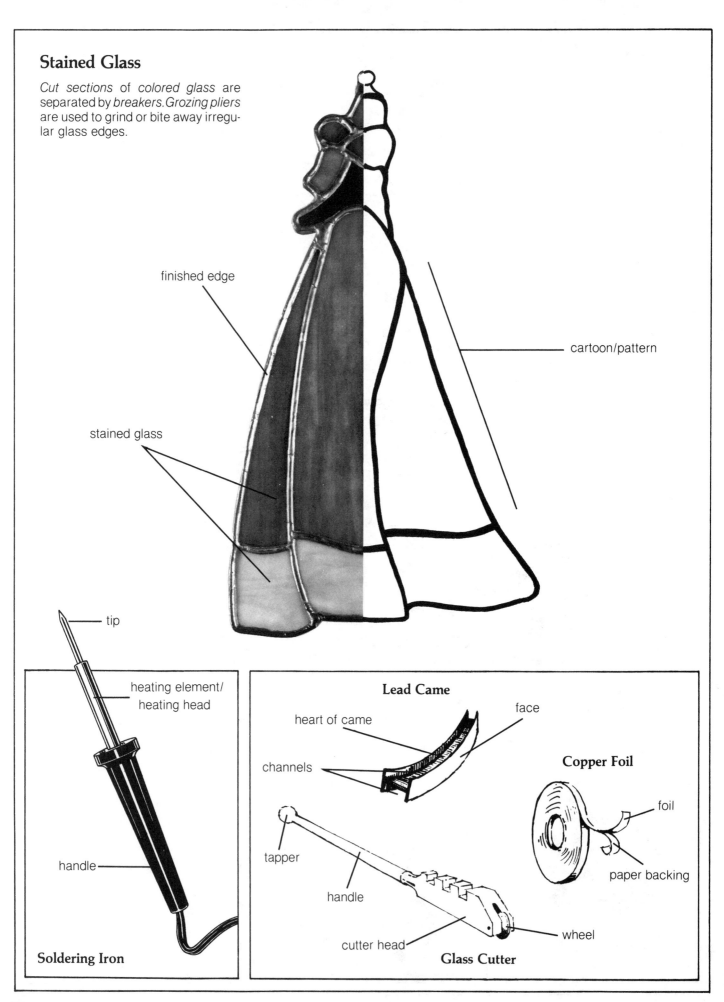

finished edge

cartoon/pattern

stained glass

tip

heating element/ heating head

handle

Soldering Iron

Lead Came

heart of came

face

channels

tapper

handle

cutter head

wheel

Glass Cutter

Copper Foil

foil

paper backing

Frame

The frame shown here is a long-lasting *archival frame*. The area cut out of the mat to reveal the artwork is the *mat window*. A wire hanger can be attached to L-shaped *shoulder hooks, picture hooks* or *nails* as well as to screw eyes. The process of permanently affixing artwork to a backing is called *mounting*. A *free-standing easel-back* or *piano frame* consists of an easel, backing and an angled support *stand*. In *passe-partout*, the framing elements are held together by strips of cloth or paper pasted over the edges.

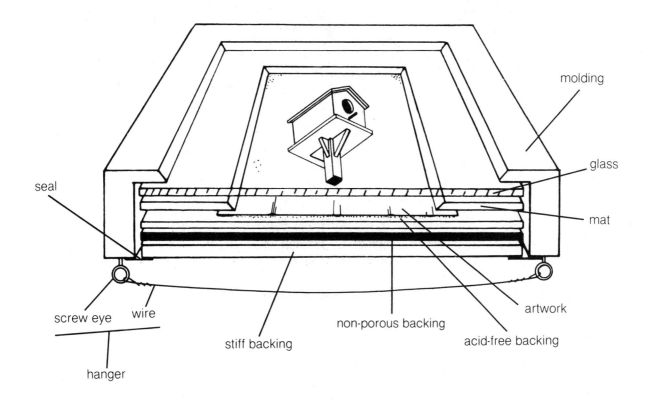

molding

glass

mat

seal

screw eye   wire

artwork

non-porous backing

acid-free backing

stiff backing

hanger

Cartooning

Many one-panel cartoons use *captions* or *labels* below the *illustration* for dialogue or explanation. Those appearing on the editorial pages of newspapers are called *editorial* or *political cartoons* and usually feature an exaggerated likeness, or *caricature*, of some well-known figure, as the main *character*. *Comics*, or *comic books*, use cartooning throughout. A complete *sphericasia*, or *swalloop*, is used by a *cartoonist* to depict a complete swing at an object, be it a golf ball or another person.

brick symbolia

thought balloon

agitrons

onomatopoeia

dites

lucaflect

staggeration

hites

briffit

vites

cross-hatching

artist's signature

Comic Strip

strip title

cartoonist

cartoon panel/frame

border

speech balloon

Cartooning

Fireworks

Fireworks makers, *pyrotechnists*, work in concrete block buildings called *magazines*. *Display rockets*, *aerial bombs*, *pin wheels* or *Catherine wheels*, and *fountains* derive their explosive force from a combination of *saltpeter*, *sulfur* and *charcoal*. Explosive *M-80s* and *cherry bombs* are now banned.

chrysanthemums

aerial flash

titanium salute

firing smoke

Grand Finale

twice-changing chrysanthemum

star shell

tails

palm trees

electric sparks

octopus

magnesium
star shells

peonies

Crystal Palace
set piece

lasers

flitter candles

flare

jetting fire crescendo

fountains

Aerial Shells

bare match end

fuse /
black match

twine ties

outside wrap /
shell wrap

label

lift section
wrap

Exterior case

fuse

shell fuse

fuse for lifting
charge

washer

quick match /
communications
fuse

lifting charge /
gunpowder

Interior assembly

stars /
metallic salts

shell case

bursting charge /
gunpowder

Rocket

cap

shell /
papier-mâché
case

bursting
charge

stars

propellant

clay choke /
plug

stick

fuse

Fireworks

Sewing

Each in-and-out movement of a threaded needle produces a *stitch*. A scissor's *bite* is the distance it cuts into a fabric on a single stroke. A small cushion into which pins or most-used needles are stuck until needed is called a *pincushion*.

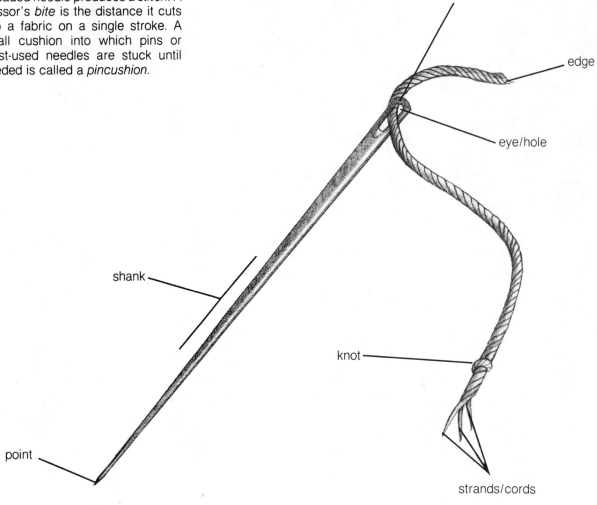

crown

edge

eye/hole

shank

knot

point

strands/cords

Needle and Thread

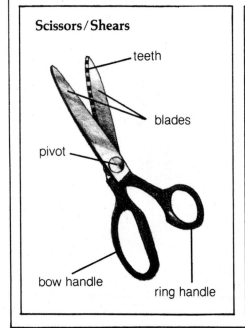

Scissors/Shears

teeth

blades

pivot

bow handle

ring handle

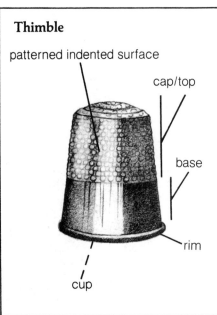

Thimble

patterned indented surface

cap/top

base

rim

cup

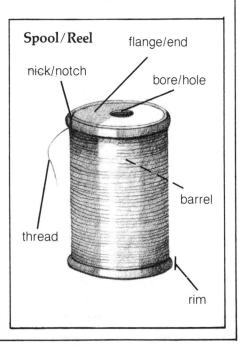

Spool/Reel

flange/end

nick/notch

bore/hole

barrel

thread

rim

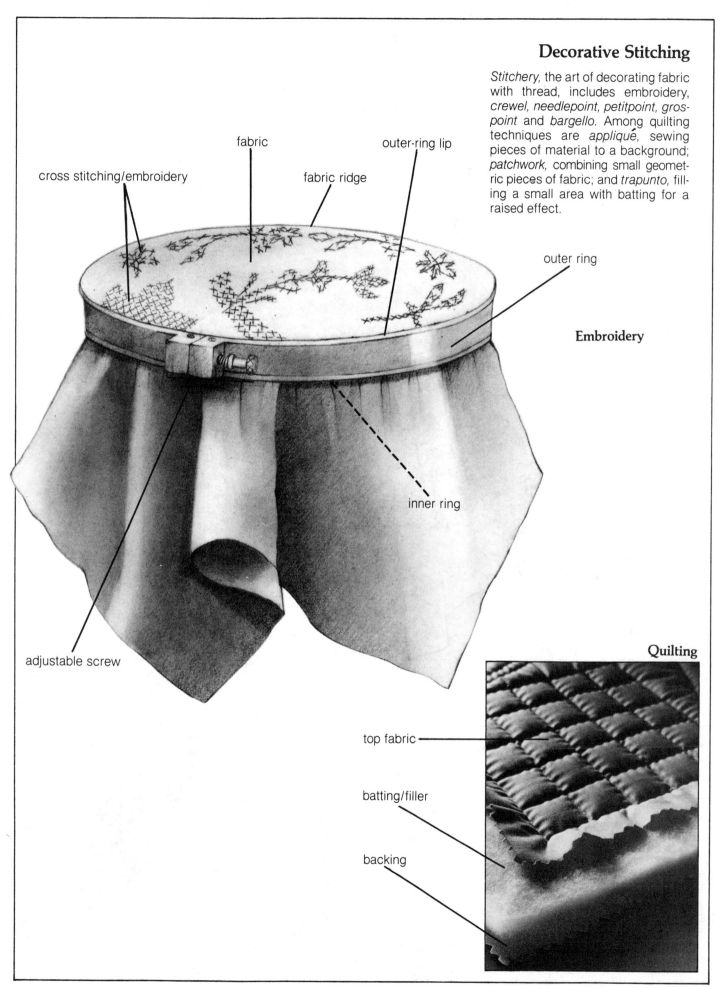

Decorative Stitching

Stitchery, the art of decorating fabric with thread, includes embroidery, *crewel, needlepoint, petitpoint, grospoint* and *bargello.* Among quilting techniques are *appliqué,* sewing pieces of material to a background; *patchwork,* combining small geometric pieces of fabric; and *trapunto,* filling a small area with batting for a raised effect.

cross stitching/embroidery

fabric

fabric ridge

outer-ring lip

outer ring

Embroidery

inner ring

adjustable screw

Quilting

top fabric

batting/filler

backing

Crafts

Knitting

Knitting is the interlacing of *loops.* The main stitches are the *knit stitch,* or *stitch,* and the *purl stitch,* or *purl. Crocheting* is a form of *needlework* done by looping thread with a *crochet needle. Macrame* is knotting, and *tatting* is done by looping and knotting with a single cotton thread and a small shuttle.

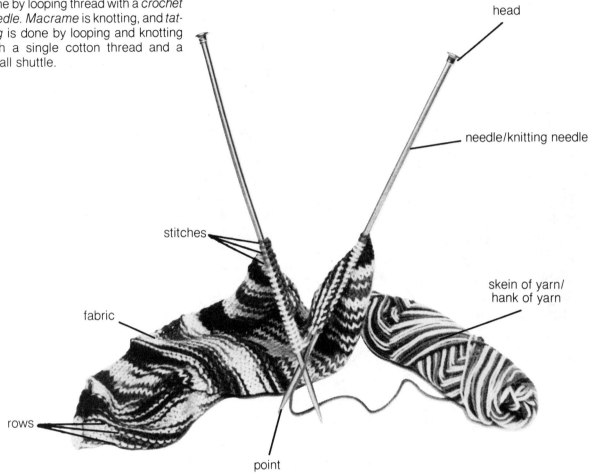

head

needle/knitting needle

stitches

fabric

skein of yarn/ hank of yarn

rows

point

Hand Knitting

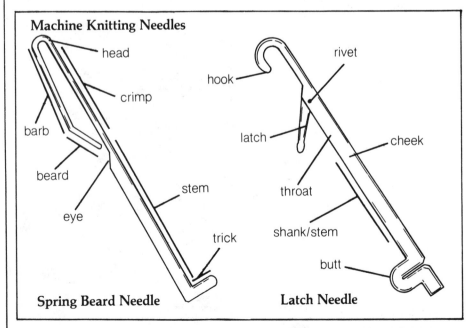

Machine Knitting Needles

head

crimp

hook

rivet

barb

latch

cheek

beard

eye

stem

throat

shank/stem

trick

butt

Spring Beard Needle

Latch Needle

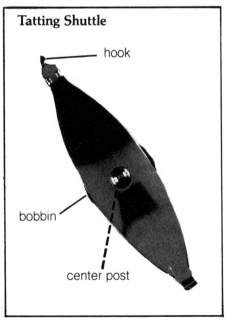

Tatting Shuttle

hook

bobbin

center post

Weaving

The lengthwise (front to back) *yarn* or *threads* on a loom are called the warp. Threads taken together which run from side to side, or from *selvage* to selvage, are called the *weft*. The weft is also often called the *woof*, although more correctly, the woof is the same as the *web*, or finished *fabric*.

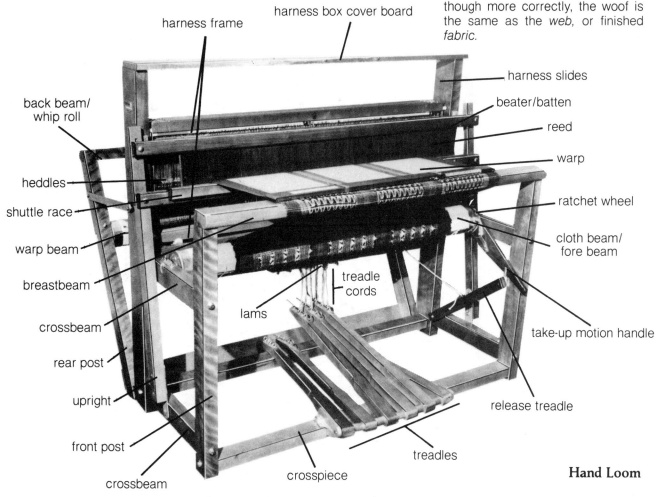

harness frame

harness box cover board

harness slides

beater/batten

reed

warp

ratchet wheel

cloth beam/ fore beam

take-up motion handle

release treadle

treadles

back beam/ whip roll

heddles

shuttle race

warp beam

breastbeam

crossbeam

rear post

upright

front post

crossbeam

crosspiece

treadle cords

lams

Hand Loom

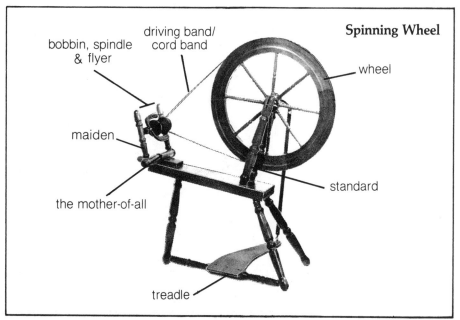

bobbin, spindle & flyer

driving band/ cord band

wheel

maiden

standard

the mother-of-all

treadle

Spinning Wheel

Sewing Pattern

A roll of fabric of a specified length is called a *bolt*. A sample of a fabric is a *swatch*. Fabrics sold at lengths specified by the customer are called *piece goods* or *yard goods*.

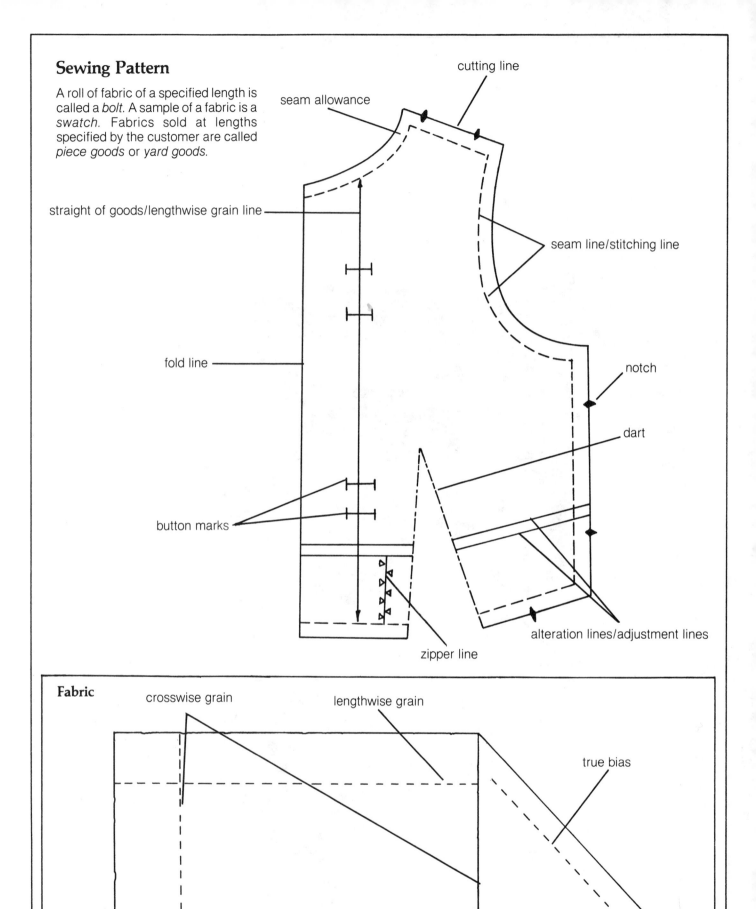

cutting line

seam allowance

seam line/stitching line

straight of goods/lengthwise grain line

fold line

notch

dart

button marks

alteration lines/adjustment lines

zipper line

Fabric

crosswise grain

lengthwise grain

true bias

selvage

Machinery, Tools and Weapons

Except for office and industrial equipment, which is outside the scope of this book, this section covers all the man-made equipment one is likely to encounter in everyday life, daily reading or classroom learning. It includes basic power systems and offshoots, everything from a nuclear power plant to an electrical plug, equipment used to control temperature in a house, and components of various engines.

Considerable space has been devoted to illustrating the parts of tools used around the home and in the yard while not ignoring the basic gear used by ranchers, trappers, farmers, scientists and doctors. Even penal equipment used for capital punishment has been included.

The weaponry subsection traces the names and parts of articles used in warfare from medieval times to objects used today. Thus, a student reading about King Arthur for the first time will be able to identify the parts of a sword as easily as a newspaper reader is able to identify the parts of a modern missile.

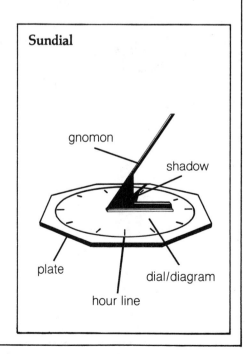

Sundial

gnomon

shadow

plate

dial/diagram

hour line

Wind Systems

The cloth sail on this *smock mill* is in a *first reef*, or *curled*, position, as opposed to *sword point*, *dagger point* or *full sail*. Sails or *shutters* on a fantail are called *vanes*. Some mills have *petticoats*, or vertical boards, below the cap, to provide protection where cap and tower meet, and *beards*, or decorated boards behind the cannister.

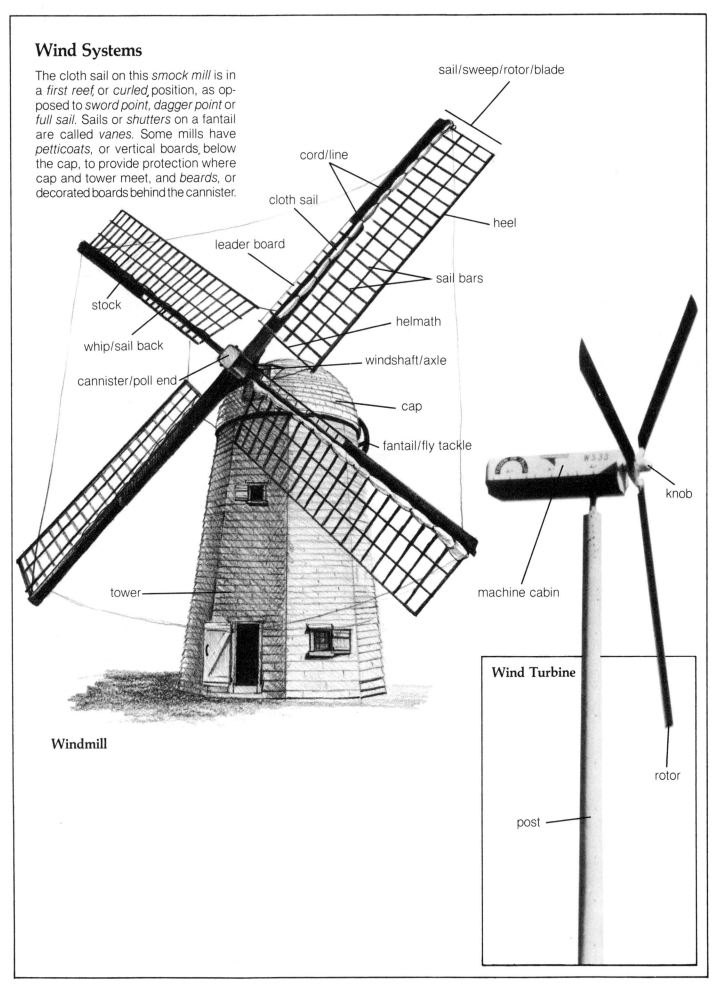

sail/sweep/rotor/blade

cord/line

cloth sail

heel

leader board

sail bars

stock

helmath

whip/sail back

windshaft/axle

cannister/poll end

cap

fantail/fly tackle

tower

Windmill

machine cabin

knob

Wind Turbine

rotor

post

Solar Power System

Solar energy can be collected by systems such as the one shown here, which operate like *radiators* working in reverse to produce hot water. The sun's energy can also be converted directly into *electricity* by *solar cells*. *Concentrating solar collectors* use *lenses* or *reflecting sufaces* to direct sunlight on a trough-type collector to produce large amounts of heat which can be converted into electricity.

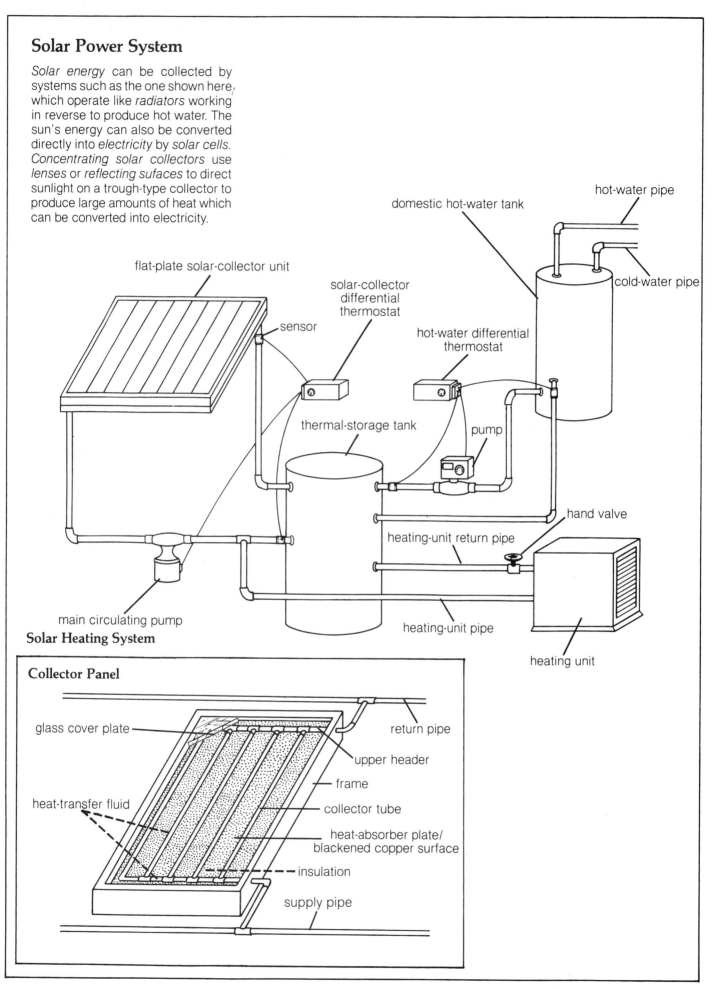

flat-plate solar-collector unit

solar-collector differential thermostat

sensor

domestic hot-water tank

hot-water pipe

cold-water pipe

hot-water differential thermostat

thermal-storage tank

pump

hand valve

heating-unit return pipe

main circulating pump

heating-unit pipe

heating unit

Solar Heating System

Collector Panel

glass cover plate

return pipe

upper header

frame

collector tube

heat-absorber plate/ blackened copper surface

heat-transfer fluid

insulation

supply pipe

Power Systems

Nuclear Power Reactor

In order to generate *electricity* by using the heat produced by *fission*, the *chain reaction* must be slowed down and controlled. To control the reaction rate in a reactor, or *pile*, *rods* of neutron-absorbing material are moved in and out as required. The smallest amount of *fissionable material* in which fission is self-sustaining is called the *critical mass*. If more fissionable material is produced than consumed, the reactor is called a *breeder reactor*.

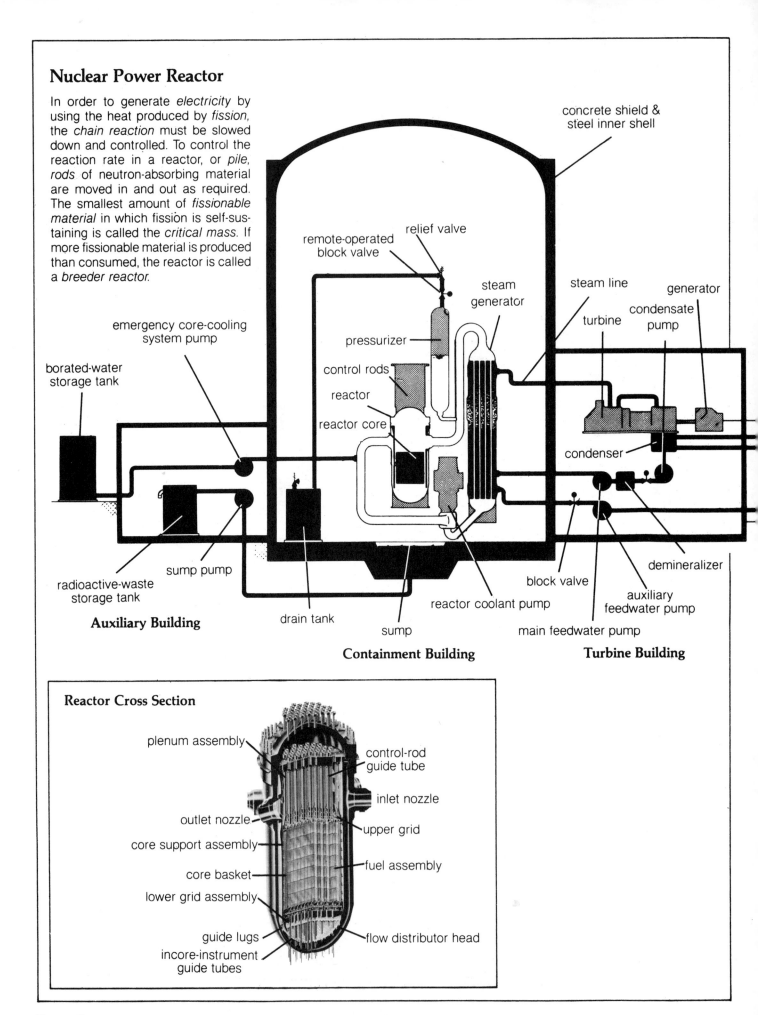

concrete shield & steel inner shell

relief valve

remote-operated block valve

steam generator

steam line

generator

condensate pump

turbine

pressurizer

emergency core-cooling system pump

control rods

reactor

reactor core

borated-water storage tank

condenser

radioactive-waste storage tank

sump pump

block valve

demineralizer

drain tank

reactor coolant pump

auxiliary feedwater pump

main feedwater pump

sump

Auxiliary Building

Containment Building

Turbine Building

Reactor Cross Section

plenum assembly

control-rod guide tube

inlet nozzle

outlet nozzle

upper grid

core support assembly

core basket

fuel assembly

lower grid assembly

guide lugs

incore-instrument guide tubes

flow distributor head

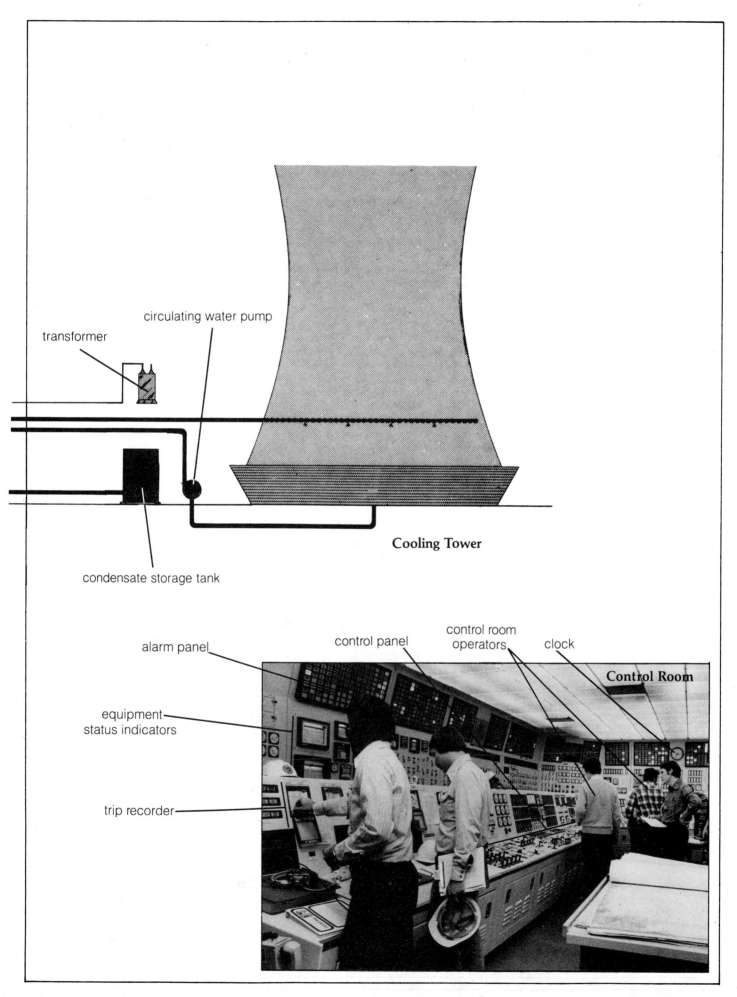

transformer

circulating water pump

condensate storage tank

Cooling Tower

alarm panel

control panel

control room operators

clock

Control Room

equipment status indicators

trip recorder

Power Systems

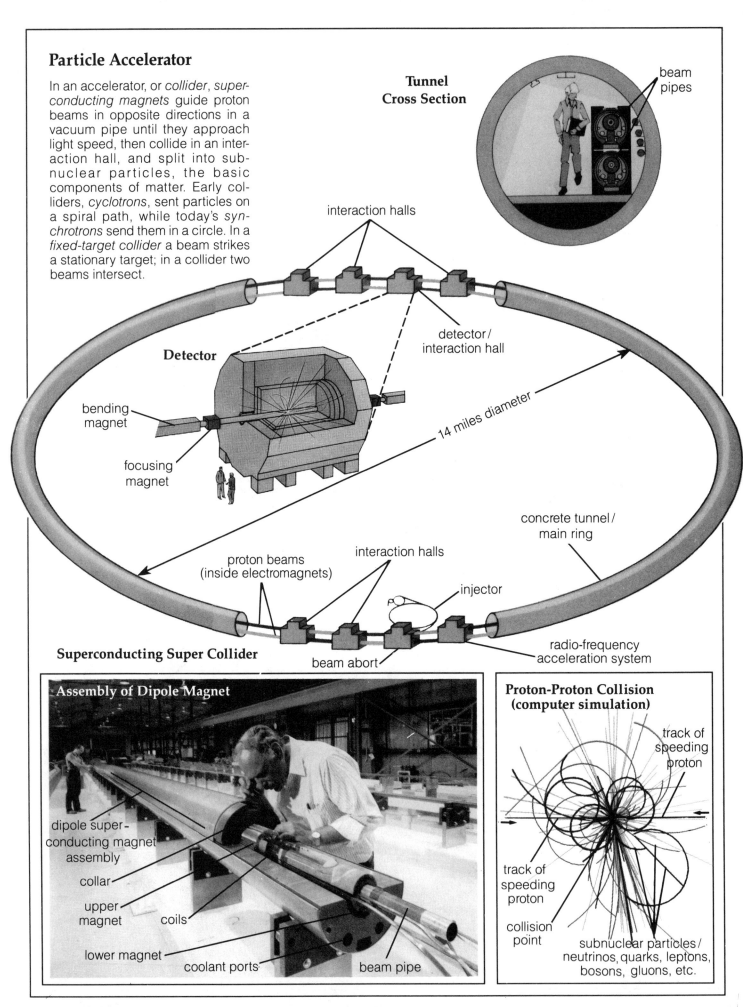

Particle Accelerator

In an accelerator, or *collider*, *superconducting magnets* guide proton beams in opposite directions in a vacuum pipe until they approach light speed, then collide in an interaction hall, and split into subnuclear particles, the basic components of matter. Early colliders, *cyclotrons*, sent particles on a spiral path, while today's *synchrotrons* send them in a circle. In a *fixed-target collider* a beam strikes a stationary target; in a collider two beams intersect.

Tunnel Cross Section

beam pipes

interaction halls

detector/ interaction hall

Detector

bending magnet

focusing magnet

14 miles diameter

concrete tunnel/ main ring

proton beams (inside electromagnets)

interaction halls

injector

radio-frequency acceleration system

Superconducting Super Collider

beam abort

Assembly of Dipole Magnet

dipole super- conducting magnet assembly

collar

upper magnet

coils

lower magnet

coolant ports

beam pipe

Proton-Proton Collision (computer simulation)

track of speeding proton

track of speeding proton

collision point

subnuclear particles/ neutrinos, quarks, leptons, bosons, gluons, etc.

Lasers and Holography

Laser, an acronym for Light Amplification by Stimulated Emission of Radiation, is a device that produces intense light from a laser tube, or *resonator*. Photons in a laser light race along a narrow, "coherent" *beam* in which all the rays are vibrating together, on exactly the same *wavelength* and at exactly the same phase. In holography, a laser's beam is split in two, the object beam, which lights the subject, and the reference beam, which goes to a film plate. In the resulting hologram, the image appears to be *three-dimensional*.

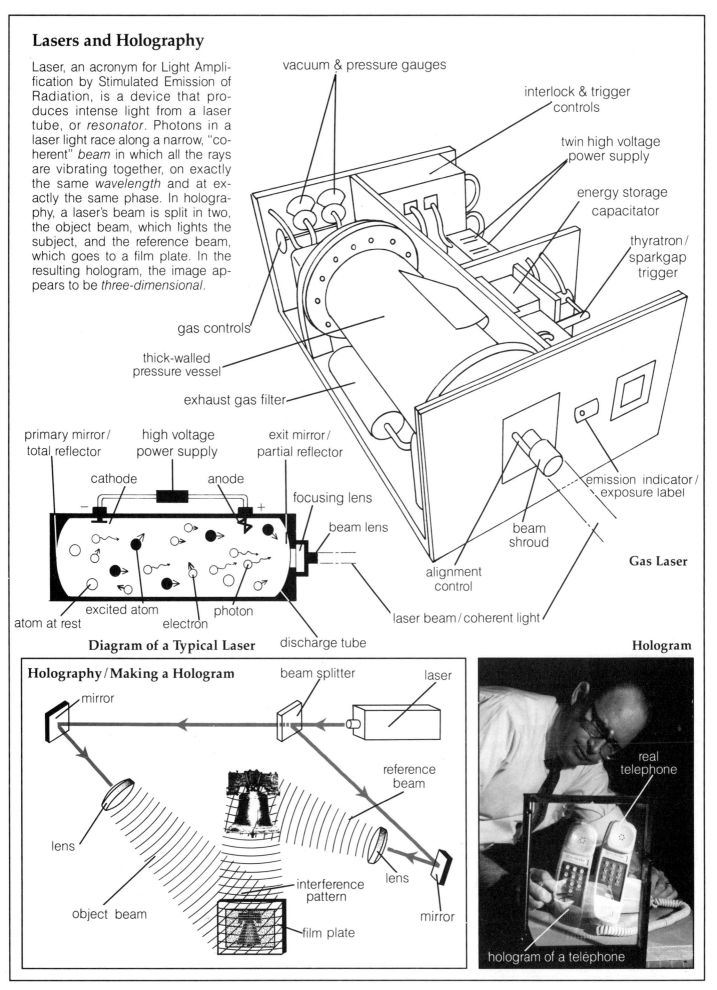

vacuum & pressure gauges

interlock & trigger controls

twin high voltage power supply

energy storage capacitator

thyratron / sparkgap trigger

gas controls

thick-walled pressure vessel

exhaust gas filter

emission indicator / exposure label

beam shroud

alignment control

laser beam / coherent light

Gas Laser

primary mirror / total reflector

high voltage power supply

exit mirror / partial reflector

focusing lens

beam lens

cathode

anode

excited atom

electron

photon

atom at rest

discharge tube

Diagram of a Typical Laser

Hologram

Holography / Making a Hologram

mirror

beam splitter

laser

reference beam

lens

object beam

interference pattern

film plate

lens

mirror

real telephone

hologram of a telephone

Power Line, Vacuum Tube and Transistor

An *overhead line support, lattice-work tower* or *double-circuit tower* transmits high-voltage electrical power from *generating plants* to various parts of a *power network*. A transistor consists of a small block of a *semiconductor* with at least three *electrodes*.

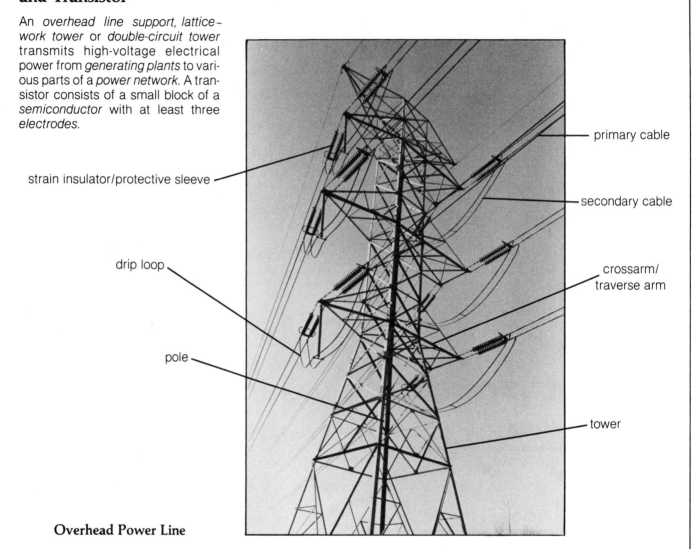

strain insulator/protective sleeve

primary cable

secondary cable

drip loop

crossarm/ traverse arm

pole

tower

Overhead Power Line

Transistor Chip

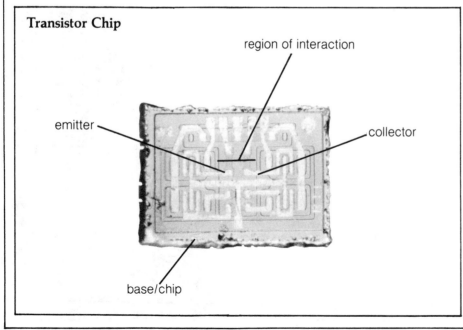

region of interaction

emitter

collector

base/chip

Vacuum Tube/Electron Tube

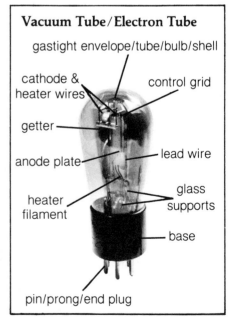

gastight envelope/tube/bulb/shell

cathode & heater wires

control grid

getter

anode plate

lead wire

heater filament

glass supports

base

pin/prong/end plug

Battery

Batteries are marked with *polarity symbols,* + identifying the positive terminal, − the negative. *Secondary cells* can be recharged, while *primary cells* cannot.

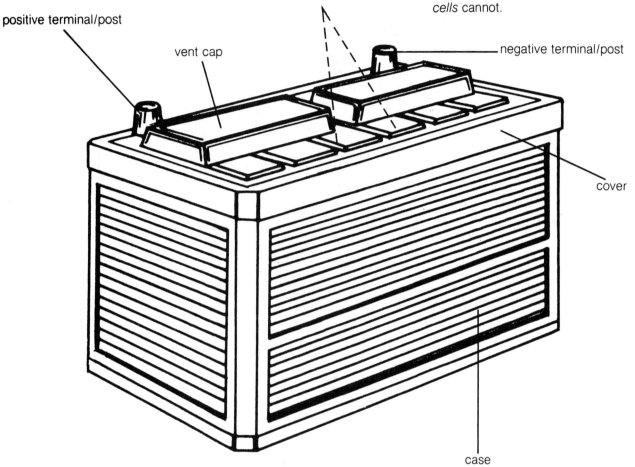

cell compartments

positive terminal/post

vent cap

negative terminal/post

cover

case

Lead Acid Battery

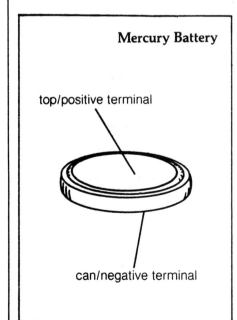

Mercury Battery

top/positive terminal

can/negative terminal

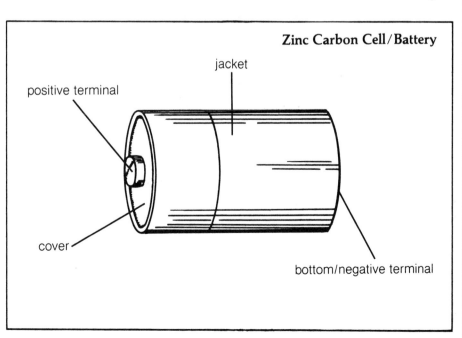

Zinc Carbon Cell/Battery

jacket

positive terminal

cover

bottom/negative terminal

Switch, Receptacle and Plug

A wall switch conducts *electrical current* only when it is in the up, or *on position*, as opposed to the down, or *off position*. *Ground wires* are located inside the junction box. *Attachment plugs*, or *"dead front" plugs*, such as the one shown here, have no exposed current-carrying parts except prongs, blades or *pins*. A *male plug* is fitted into a *female receptacle*.

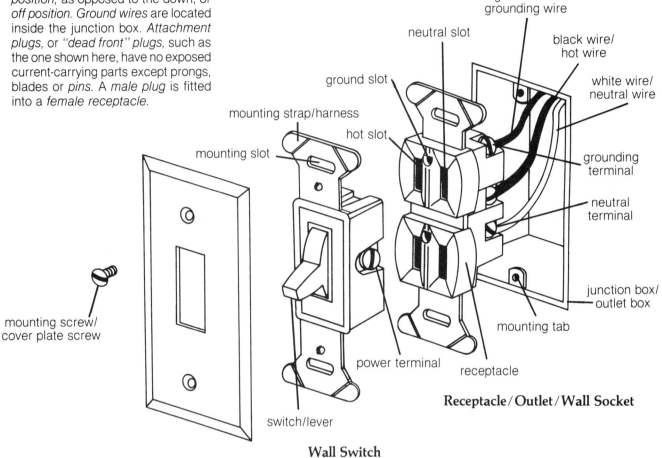

mounting screw/
cover plate screw

mounting strap/harness

mounting slot

neutral slot

ground slot

hot slot

green wire/
grounding wire

black wire/
hot wire

white wire/
neutral wire

grounding
terminal

neutral
terminal

junction box/
outlet box

mounting tab

receptacle

power terminal

switch/lever

Receptacle/Outlet/Wall Socket

Wall Switch

Cover Plate/Switch Plate

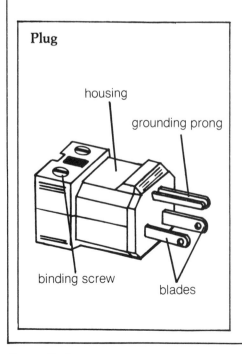

Plug

housing

grounding prong

binding screw

blades

Meter and Fuse Box

Fuses "blow" and circuit breakers "trip" when there is too much current in the wires of a particular *circuit.* The fuse or circuit breaker acts as a safety device to keep fire from starting by heat caused by an *overload* or by a *short circuit.*

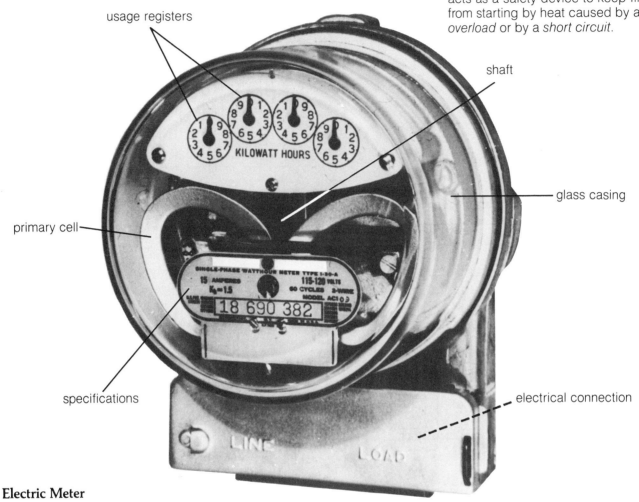

usage registers

shaft

glass casing

primary cell

KILOWATT HOURS

SINGLE-PHASE WATTHOUR METER TYPE I-30-A
15 AMPERES 115-120 VOLTS
$K_h=1.5$ 60 CYCLES 2-WIRE
MODEL AC10

18 690 382

specifications

electrical connection

LINE LOAD

Electric Meter

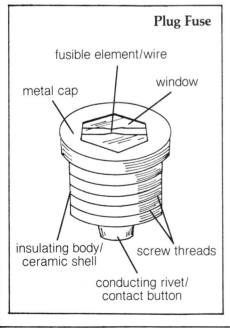

Plug Fuse

fusible element/wire

metal cap

window

insulating body/ceramic shell

screw threads

conducting rivet/contact button

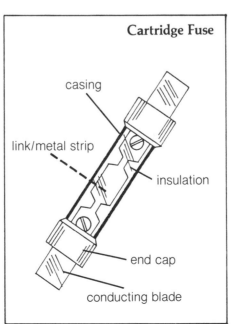

Cartridge Fuse

casing

link/metal strip

insulation

end cap

conducting blade

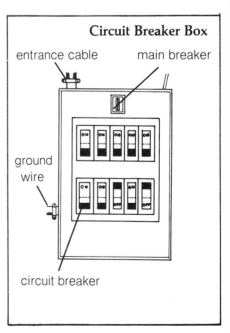

Circuit Breaker Box

entrance cable

main breaker

ground wire

circuit breaker

Power Systems

Furnace

The furnace shown in this schematic illustration provides *steam heat* to radiators located in various parts of a building.

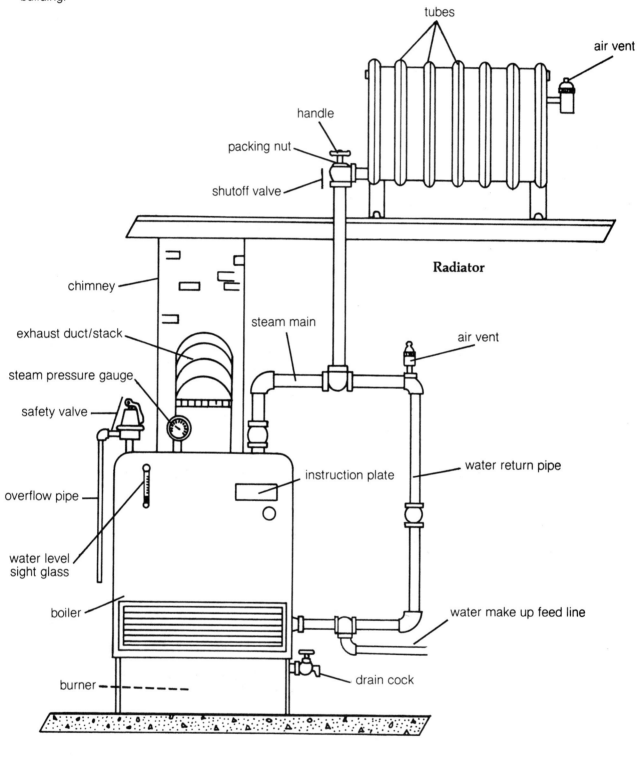

tubes

air vent

handle

packing nut

shutoff valve

Radiator

chimney

steam main

exhaust duct/stack

air vent

steam pressure gauge

safety valve

water return pipe

instruction plate

overflow pipe

water level sight glass

boiler

water make up feed line

burner

drain cock

Furnace

Hot Water Heater

The unit shown here is *gas-fired*.
Other models include *electric water heaters* and *oil water heaters*.

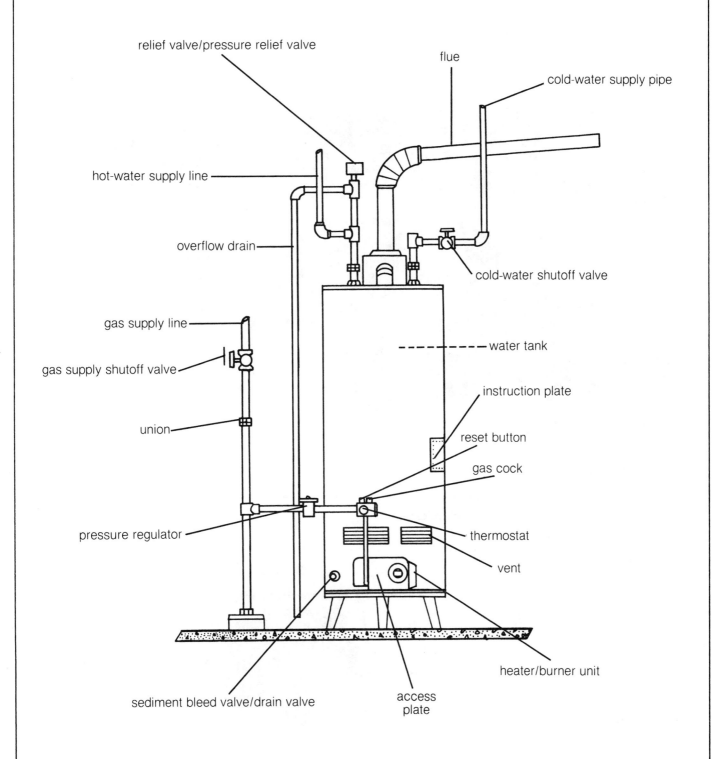

relief valve/pressure relief valve

flue

cold-water supply pipe

hot-water supply line

overflow drain

cold-water shutoff valve

gas supply line

water tank

gas supply shutoff valve

instruction plate

reset button

gas cock

union

pressure regulator

thermostat

vent

heater/burner unit

sediment bleed valve/drain valve

access plate

Climate Control Units

Air Conditioning

An air conditioner's *front grille* has *louvers* which allow cooled air to be directed to any part of a room. *Condenser coils* in the rear of the unit discharge heat outdoors. Hand-held *folding fans, overhead fans* and *rotary fans* circulate air without actually cooling it. A *dehumidifier* removes moisture from the air, whereas a *humidifier* adds moisture to it.

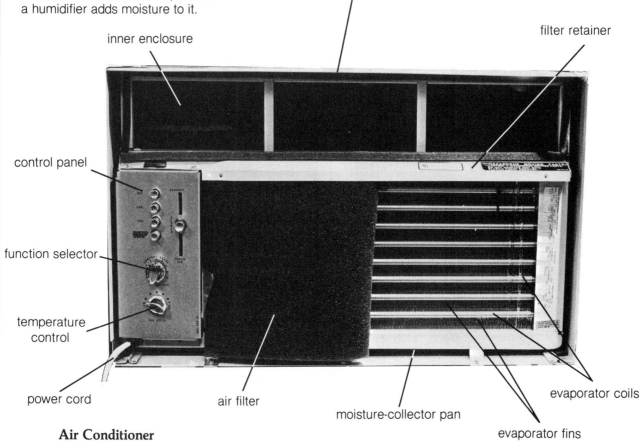

cabinet

filter retainer

inner enclosure

control panel

function selector

temperature control

power cord

air filter

moisture-collector pan

evaporator coils

evaporator fins

Air Conditioner

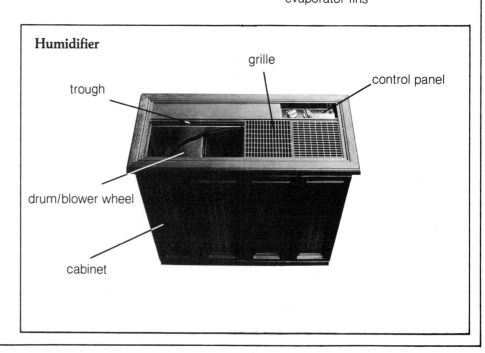

Humidifier

grille

control panel

trough

drum/blower wheel

cabinet

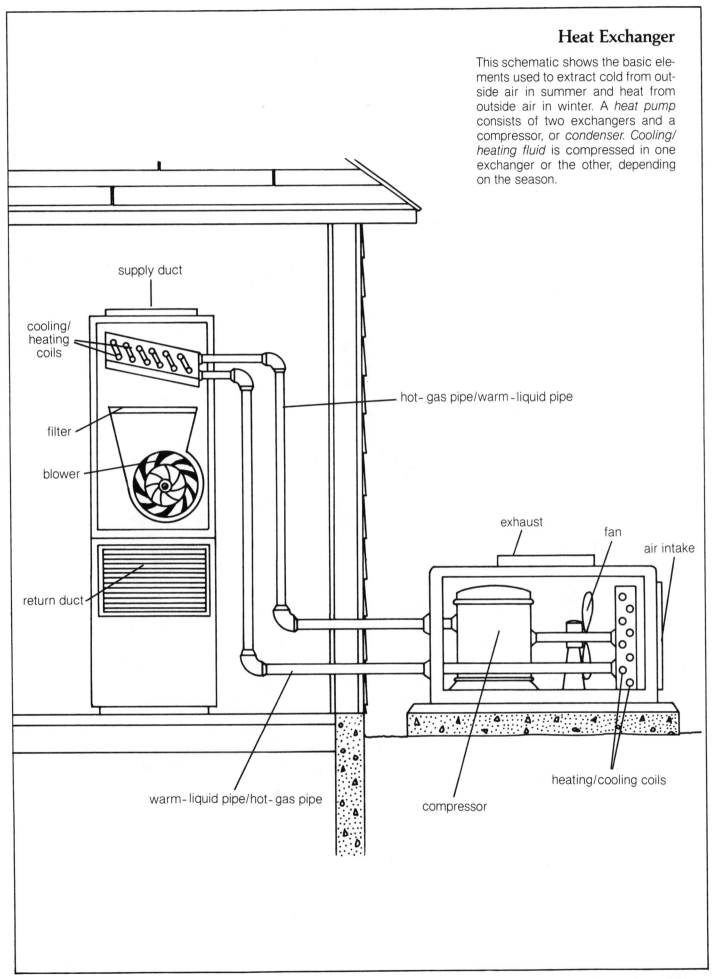

Heat Exchanger

This schematic shows the basic elements used to extract cold from outside air in summer and heat from outside air in winter. A *heat pump* consists of two exchangers and a compressor, or *condenser*. *Cooling/ heating fluid* is compressed in one exchanger or the other, depending on the season.

supply duct

cooling/ heating coils

filter

blower

return duct

hot-gas pipe/warm-liquid pipe

exhaust

fan

air intake

heating/cooling coils

warm-liquid pipe/hot-gas pipe

compressor

Climate Control Units

Woodburning Stove

When the *stove damper* is closed, interior *baffles* direct air into the *secondary combustion chamber,* then through the *smoke path* until it exits through the flue collar. A stovepipe led through a wall is attached to a *thimble.* The original *Franklin stove* was built into the wall, but three sides extended into the room to radiate heat.

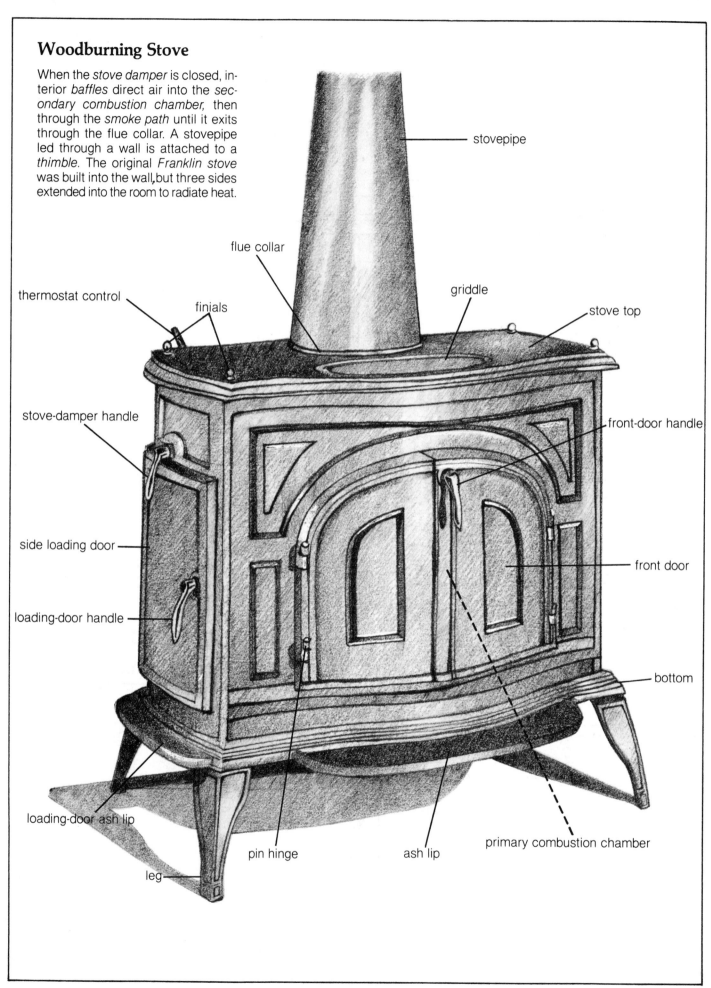

stovepipe

flue collar

griddle

thermostat control

finials

stove top

stove-damper handle

front-door handle

side loading door

front door

loading-door handle

bottom

loading-door ash lip

pin hinge

ash lip

primary combustion chamber

leg

Steam Engine

The steam engine was used to generate *mechanical power* from *thermal energy*. A *piston* inside the steam cylinder, or *engine cylinder*, was driven by *high-pressure steam*. It moved the crankshaft to provide *rotational motion*.

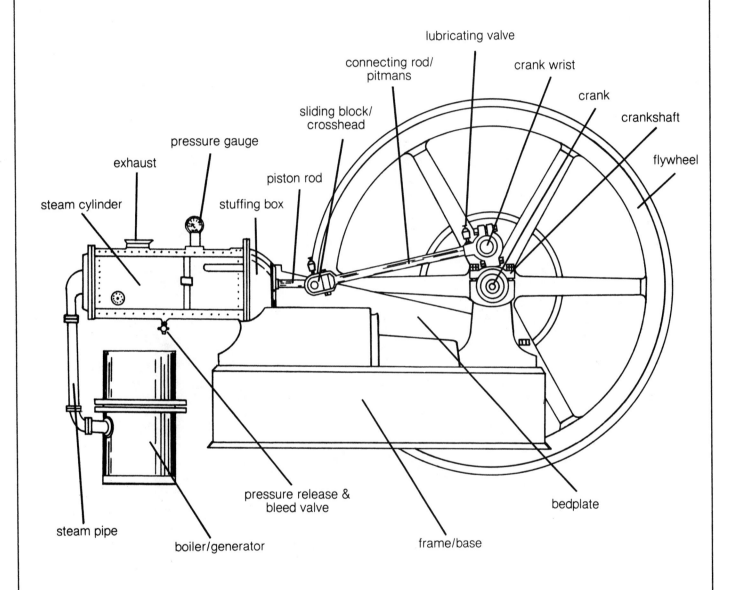

lubricating valve

connecting rod/ pitmans

crank wrist

crank

crankshaft

sliding block/ crosshead

flywheel

pressure gauge

exhaust

piston rod

steam cylinder

stuffing box

pressure release & bleed valve

bedplate

steam pipe

boiler/generator

frame/base

Internal Combustion Engine

The internal combustion engine is one in which combustion of fuel takes place within the *cylinder*, the product of which is measured in *horsepower*. Engines are *two-cycle*, *four-cycle*, or *Otto cycle*; *gas-* or *diesel-fueled*; *air-cooled* or *liquid-cooled*.

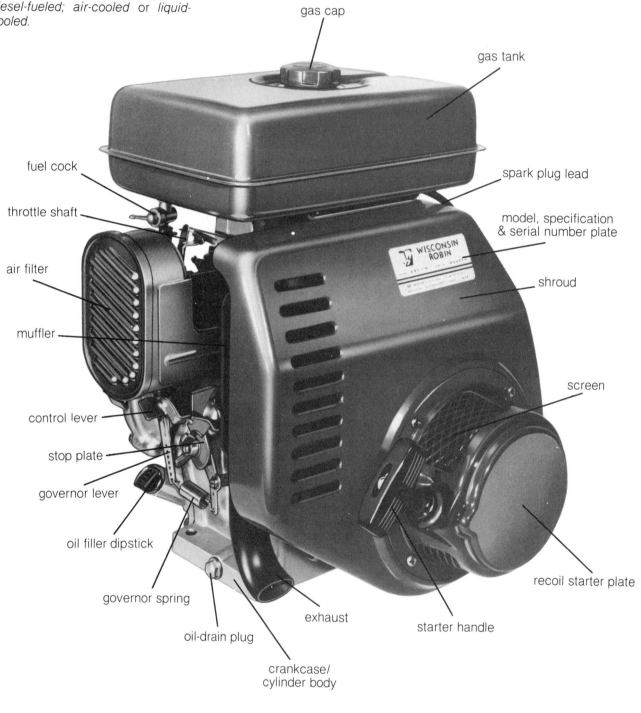

gas cap

gas tank

fuel cock

throttle shaft

spark plug lead

model, specification & serial number plate

air filter

shroud

muffler

control lever

screen

stop plate

governor lever

oil filler dipstick

governor spring

recoil starter plate

oil-drain plug

exhaust

starter handle

crankcase/ cylinder body

WISCONSIN ROBIN

Jet Engines

A *turboprop engine* is like a combustion jet engine or *turbofan jet,* except that its turbine wheel is attached to a *crankshaft* that turns a *propeller.* Unlike a rocket, a *ramjet,* or *flying stovepipe,* combines compressed incoming air with fuel injection and ignition for propulsion.

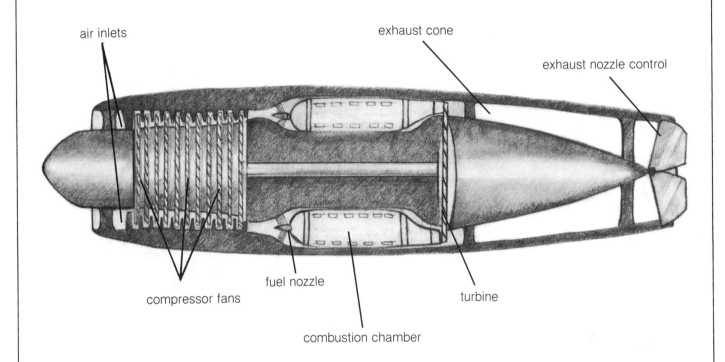

air inlets

exhaust cone

exhaust nozzle control

compressor fans

fuel nozzle

turbine

combustion chamber

Combustion Jet Engine

Rocket

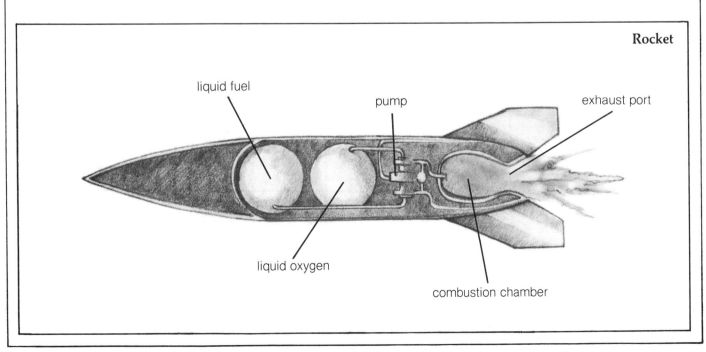

liquid fuel

pump

exhaust port

liquid oxygen

combustion chamber

Engines

Workbench

A *machinist's vise* has two parallel iron *jaws* with a wide *throat opening* to allow as much working room as possible. A *vise dog* is a steel pin in a vise which can be raised to hold materials between the vise and the bench dogs. A *backstop* is a raised portion at the rear of a workbench.

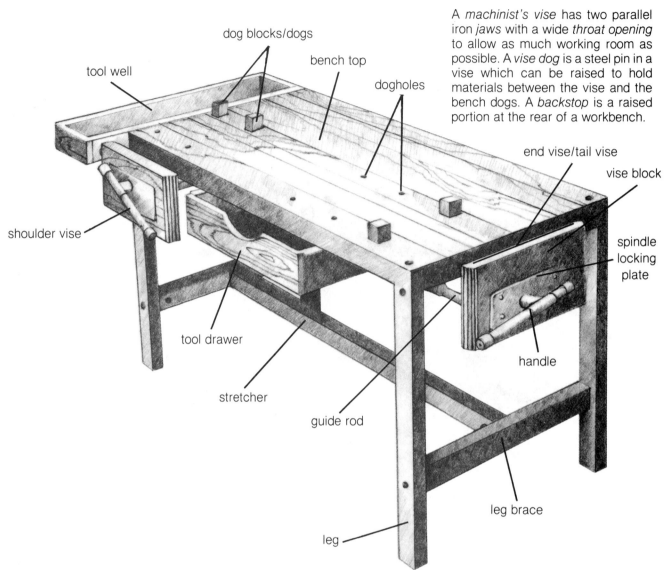

dog blocks/dogs

bench top

tool well

dogholes

end vise/tail vise

vise block

shoulder vise

spindle locking plate

tool drawer

handle

stretcher

guide rod

leg brace

leg

Sawhorse/Sawbuck

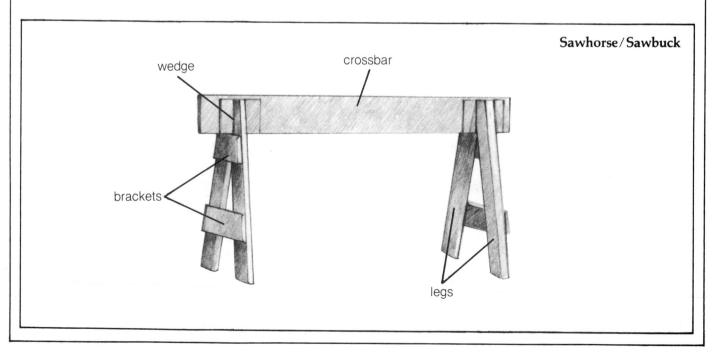

wedge

crossbar

brackets

legs

Clamps

In addition to the *holding tools* shown here, there are *hand screws, bar clamps, miter clamps, band clamps* and *spring clamps.* A *woodworking vise* is similar to a *metalworking vise* except that its jaws are padded in order to hold lumber without marring it. In wood clamps, the steel screws operate through *pivots* so that the jaws can be set at any required angle. *Adjustable C-clamps,* also known as *short bar clamps,* have an adjustable jaw that slides along a flat metal bar to the desired position.

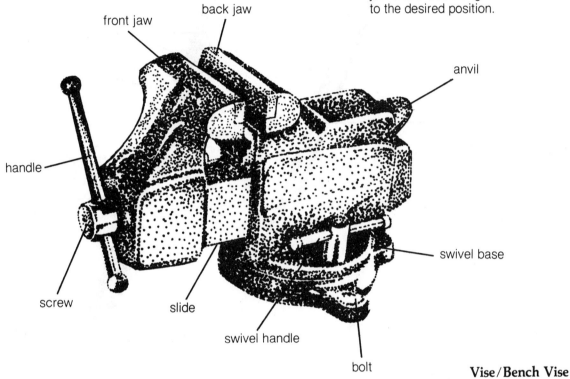

front jaw

back jaw

anvil

handle

screw

slide

swivel base

swivel handle

bolt

Vise/Bench Vise

Hand-Screw Clamp/
Wood Clamp

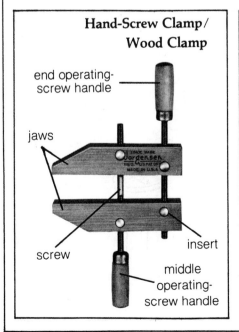

end operating-screw handle

jaws

screw

insert

middle operating-screw handle

C-Clamp

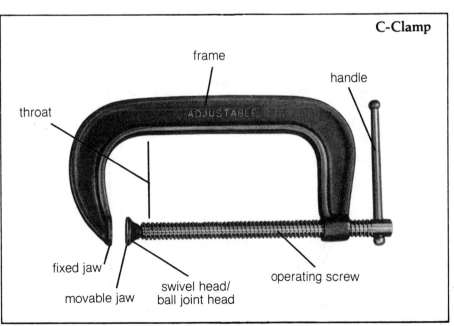

frame

handle

throat

ADJUSTABLE

fixed jaw

movable jaw

swivel head/
ball joint head

operating screw

Household Tools

Nails and Screws

A nail is measured in *penny sizes*. A *brad* is a thin *finishing nail* with a tiny *nailhead* used mainly in cabinetwork. *Spikes* are large, heavy nails. The small hole drilled prior to driving a screw is called a *pilot hole*.

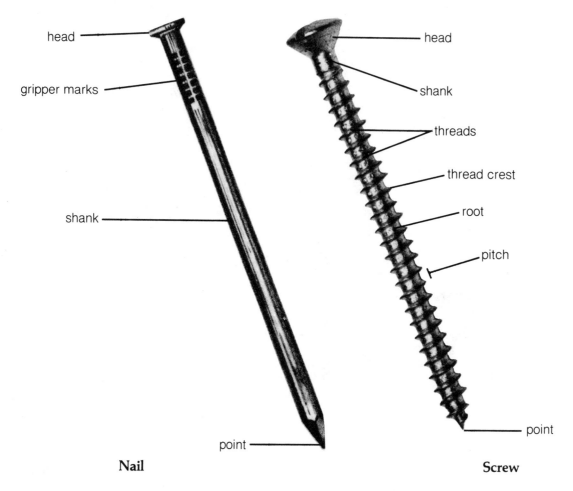

head
gripper marks
shank
point

Nail

head
shank
threads
thread crest
root
pitch
point

Screw

Fasteners

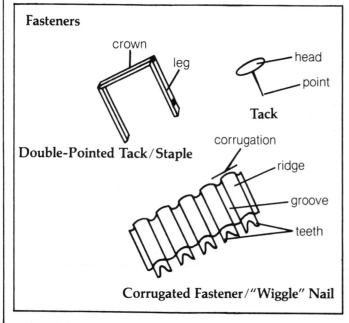

crown
leg

head
point

Tack

Double-Pointed Tack / Staple

corrugation
ridge
groove
teeth

Corrugated Fastener / "Wiggle" Nail

Screw Heads

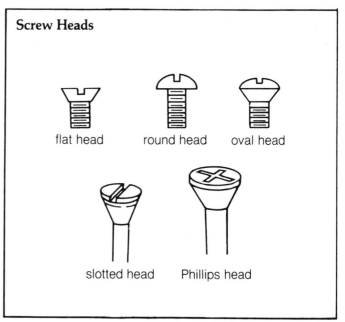

flat head   round head   oval head

slotted head   Phillips head

Nuts and Bolts

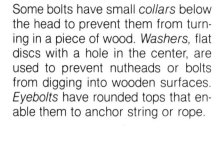

Some bolts have small *collars* below the head to prevent them from turning in a piece of wood. *Washers,* flat discs with a hole in the center, are used to prevent nutheads or bolts from digging into wooden surfaces. *Eyebolts* have rounded tops that enable them to anchor string or rope.

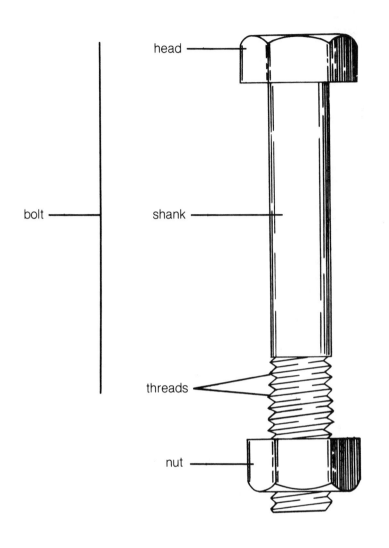

head

bolt — shank

threads

nut

Nuts

acorn nut/cap nut

hex nut/full nut

square nut

wing nut/butterfly nut

Bolts

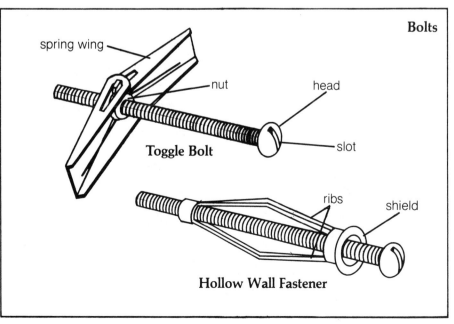

spring wing

nut

head

slot

Toggle Bolt

ribs

shield

Hollow Wall Fastener

Household Tools

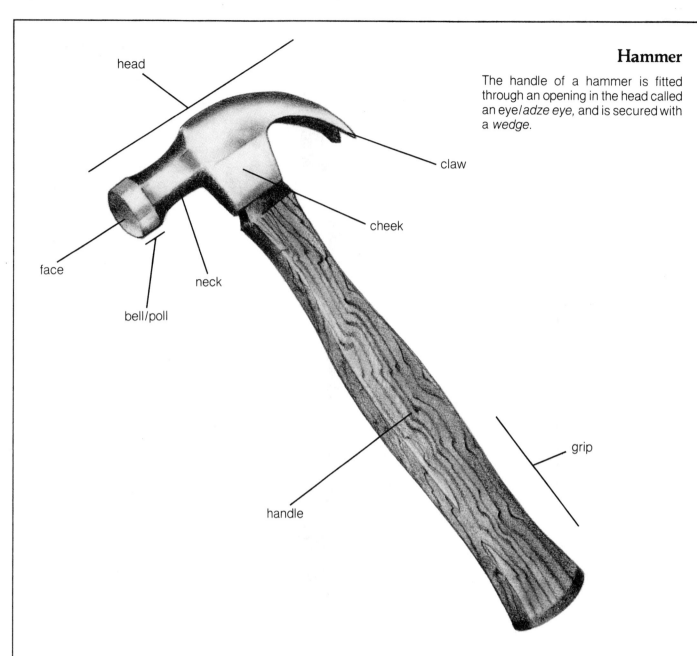

Hammer

The handle of a hammer is fitted through an opening in the head called an eye/*adze eye*, and is secured with a *wedge*.

head

claw

face

cheek

neck

bell/poll

grip

handle

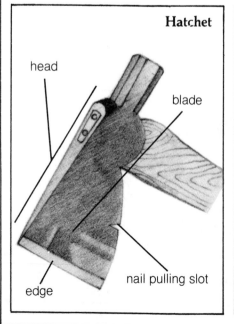

Hatchet

head

blade

edge

nail pulling slot

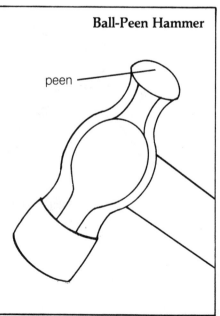

Ball-Peen Hammer

peen

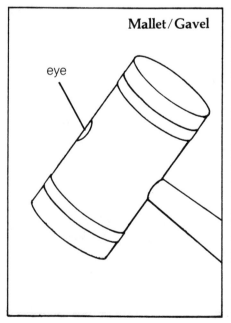

Mallet/Gavel

eye

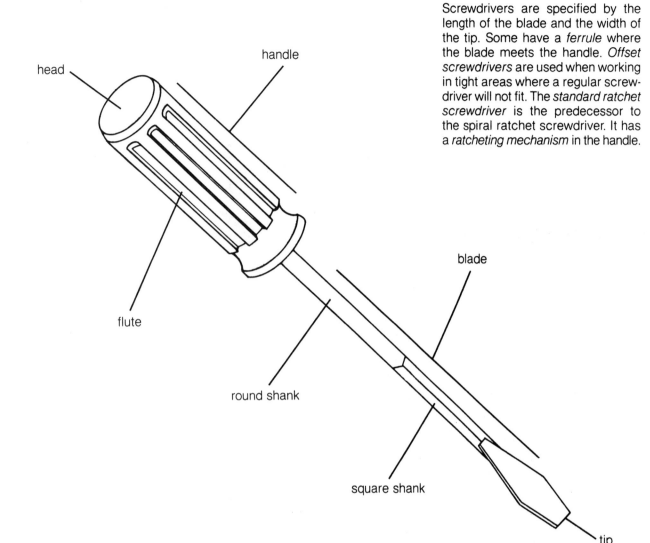

Screwdriver

Screwdrivers are specified by the length of the blade and the width of the tip. Some have a *ferrule* where the blade meets the handle. *Offset screwdrivers* are used when working in tight areas where a regular screwdriver will not fit. The *standard ratchet screwdriver* is the predecessor to the spiral ratchet screwdriver. It has a *ratcheting mechanism* in the handle.

head

handle

flute

blade

round shank

square shank

tip

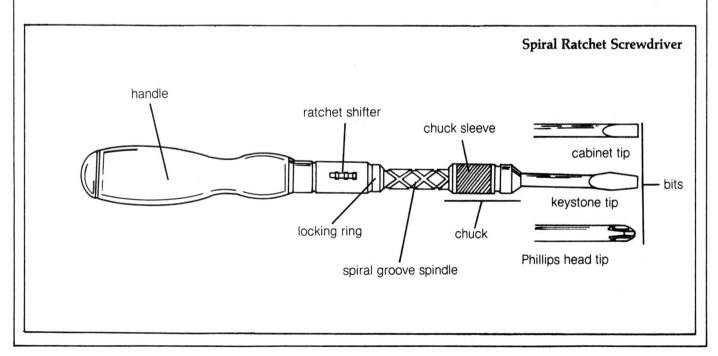

Spiral Ratchet Screwdriver

handle

ratchet shifter

chuck sleeve

cabinet tip

bits

locking ring

keystone tip

chuck

spiral groove spindle

Phillips head tip

Household Tools

Pliers

In addition to the pliers seen here, there are heavy-duty *bolt cutters;* *midget pliers* and *needle-nose pliers,* often used for jewelry work or electrical jobs; *music wire pliers,* used for cutting piano wire; and *duckbill pliers,* used primarily by telephone workers and weavers.

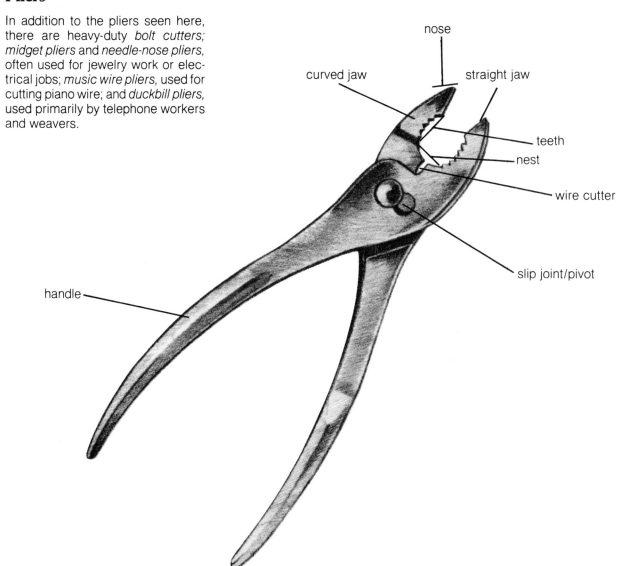

nose

curved jaw

straight jaw

teeth

nest

wire cutter

slip joint/pivot

handle

Combination Pliers/Slip-Joint Pliers

Tongue-and-Groove Pliers

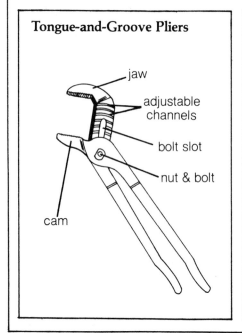

jaw

adjustable channels

bolt slot

nut & bolt

cam

Lineman's Pliers/ Electrician's Pliers

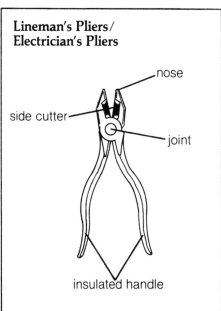

nose

side cutter

joint

insulated handle

Locking Pliers/ Lever-Wrench Pliers

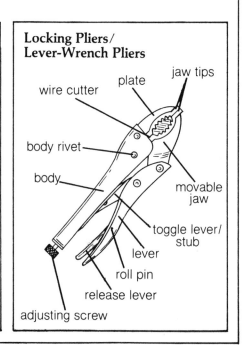

jaw tips

plate

wire cutter

body rivet

body

movable jaw

toggle lever/ stub

lever

roll pin

release lever

adjusting screw

Wrench

Adjustable wrenches come in two styles, *locking* and *non-locking*. A *"cheater"* is a handle extension used to increase leverage. Some wrenches have *offset handles* to provide clearance over obstructions. *Socket wrenches* combine an offset handle with a male *drive piece* which has a spring-loaded *bearing* to lock on various sized *sockets*. Many socket wrenches also have a *ratchet handle* so that reversing is possible.

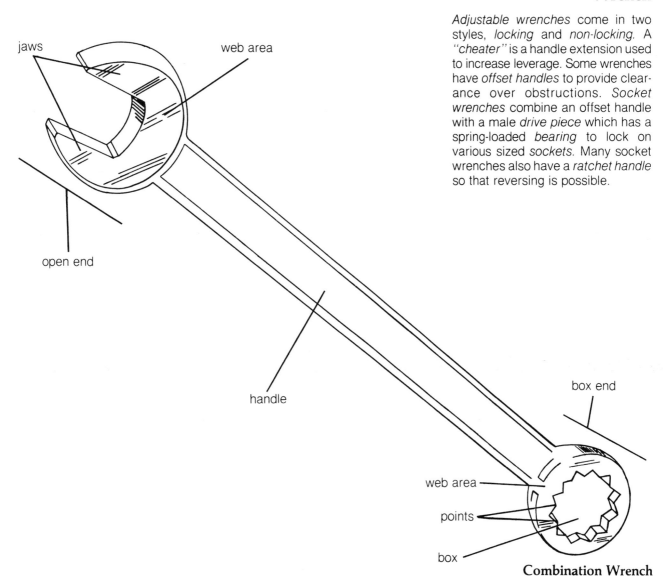

jaws

web area

open end

handle

box end

web area

points

box

Combination Wrench

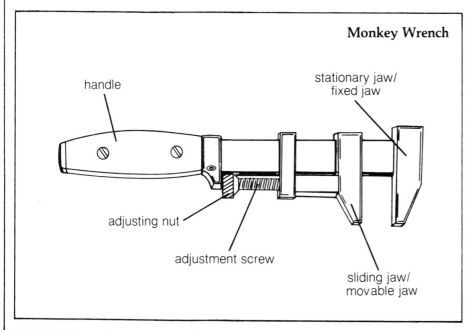

Monkey Wrench

handle

stationary jaw/
fixed jaw

adjusting nut

adjustment screw

sliding jaw/
movable jaw

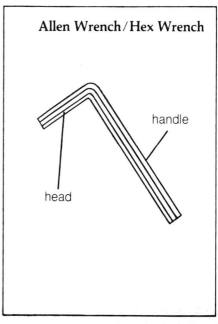

Allen Wrench / Hex Wrench

handle

head

Household Tools

Handsaws

The cut or incision made by a saw blade is the *kerf*. The carpenter's saw, shown here, occurs in two major varieties, the *ripsaw* (used for cutting with the grain) and the *crosscut saw* (for cutting across the grain). A *skewback handsaw* has an inwardly curved back. On a coping saw, the distance from the blade to the frame is the *throat* or *throat clearance*. A coping saw with a particularly long throat is called a *deep throat*.

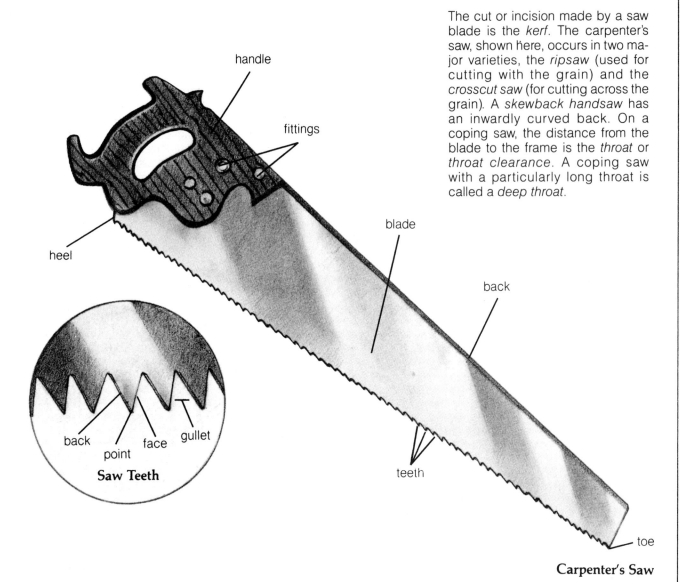

handle

fittings

heel

blade

back

teeth

toe

Carpenter's Saw

back point face gullet

Saw Teeth

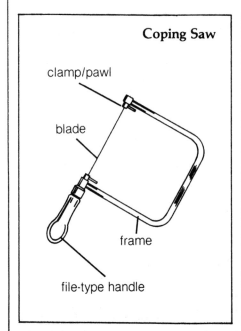

Coping Saw

clamp/pawl

blade

frame

file-type handle

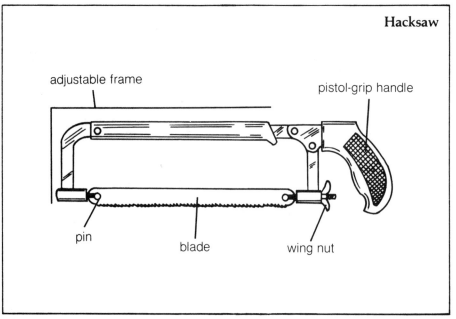

Hacksaw

adjustable frame

pistol-grip handle

pin

blade

wing nut

Power Saw

The round blades used in table and circular saws have either *crosscut teeth* or *rip teeth*. Circular saws can be equipped with a *rip guide* and an *ejector chute*, which routes sawdust to the rear or side. Saber units include *variable-speed controls* and a *roller support* behind the blade. The *band saw* derives its name from the fact that its blade is a continuous band revolving on two wheels.

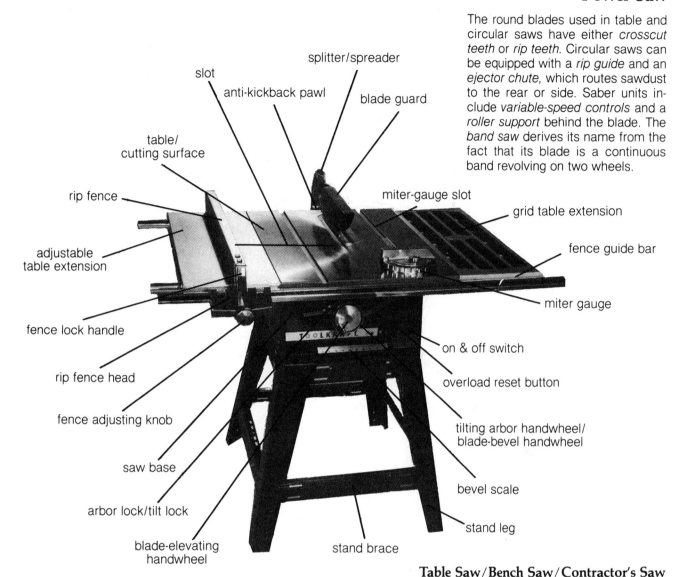

slot

splitter/spreader

anti-kickback pawl

blade guard

table/ cutting surface

miter-gauge slot

rip fence

grid table extension

adjustable table extension

fence guide bar

fence lock handle

miter gauge

rip fence head

on & off switch

fence adjusting knob

overload reset button

saw base

tilting arbor handwheel/ blade-bevel handwheel

arbor lock/tilt lock

bevel scale

blade-elevating handwheel

stand brace

stand leg

Table Saw/Bench Saw/Contractor's Saw

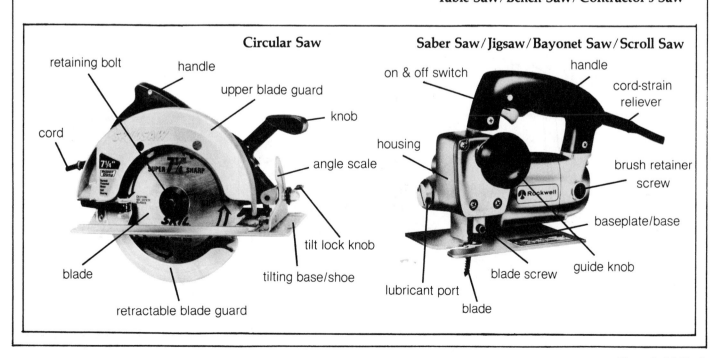

Circular Saw

Saber Saw/Jigsaw/Bayonet Saw/Scroll Saw

retaining bolt

handle

handle

on & off switch

cord-strain reliever

upper blade guard

cord

knob

housing

angle scale

brush retainer screw

tilt lock knob

baseplate/base

blade

tilting base/shoe

guide knob

retractable blade guard

blade screw

lubricant port

blade

417

Household Tools

Manual Drill

Drilling accessories include a *bit gage, reamer, auger bits, dowel bits, expanding bits, screwdriver bits, countersink bits, twist drill bits, spade bits* and *power bore bits.* The circle described by turning the handle of a brace is called the *sweep.*

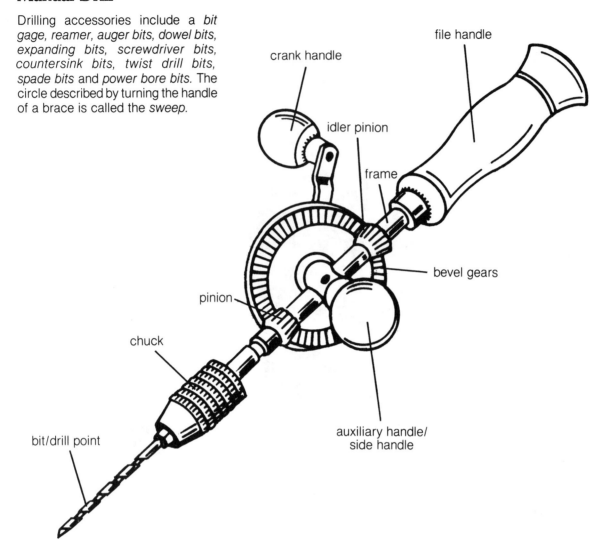

crank handle

file handle

idler pinion

frame

bevel gears

pinion

chuck

auxiliary handle/
side handle

bit/drill point

Hand Drill

Brace/Hand Brace

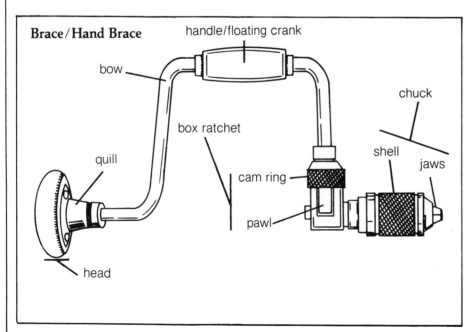

handle/floating crank

bow

box ratchet

chuck

quill

cam ring

pawl

shell

jaws

head

Gimlet

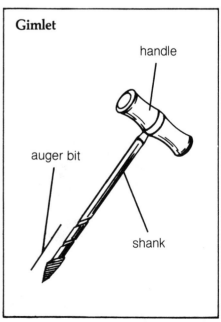

handle

auger bit

shank

Power Drills

A regular bit, or *drill,* consists of a *point, body* and shank. Some bits have specially configured *tangs* at the end of the shank. If a drill has a *geared key chuck,* the bit is locked in place with a key. Holes can be drilled to predetermined depths by clamping an *adjustable bit gauge* to the bit shank. A drill is classified by the largest bit its chuck will accept. Some drills have *reversible motors.*

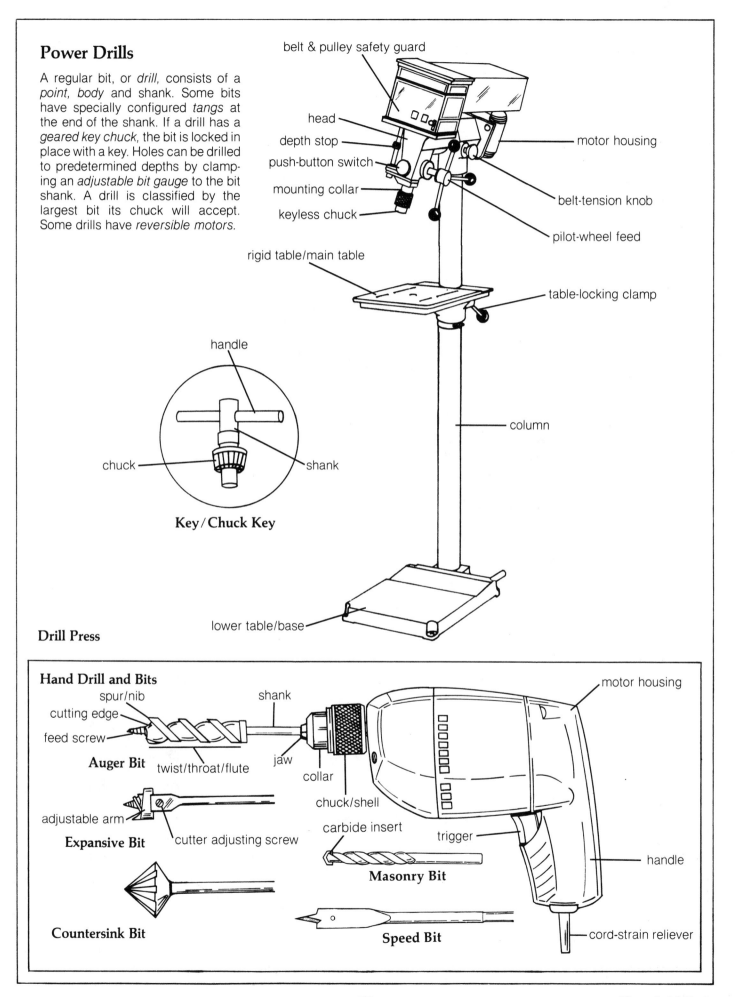

belt & pulley safety guard

head

depth stop

push-button switch

mounting collar

keyless chuck

motor housing

belt-tension knob

pilot-wheel feed

rigid table/main table

table-locking clamp

column

handle

chuck

shank

Key / Chuck Key

lower table/base

Drill Press

Hand Drill and Bits

spur/nib

cutting edge

feed screw

shank

Auger Bit

twist/throat/flute

jaw

collar

chuck/shell

adjustable arm

Expansive Bit

cutter adjusting screw

carbide insert

Masonry Bit

trigger

motor housing

handle

Countersink Bit

Speed Bit

cord-strain reliever

Household Tools

Planing and Shaping Tools

The body of a plane is the *frame*. The angle of the blade is the *pitch*. The flat side of a chisel is its *back*. *Cold chisels* are designed to cut metal and have no handles. *Gouges* are either *in-cannel*, with the bevel ground on the inside of the curved blade, or *out-cannel*, with the bevel ground on the outside. The rough side of a rasp or file is the *face*. The smooth side is called the *"safe" side*.

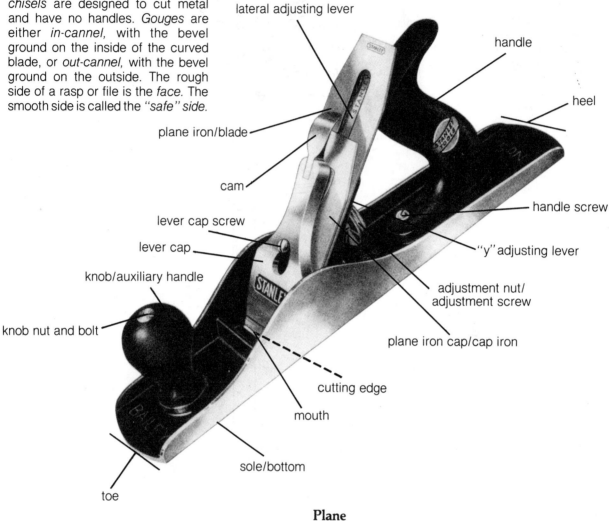

lateral adjusting lever

handle

heel

plane iron/blade

cam

handle screw

"y" adjusting lever

lever cap screw

lever cap

knob/auxiliary handle

adjustment nut/
adjustment screw

plane iron cap/cap iron

knob nut and bolt

cutting edge

mouth

sole/bottom

toe

Plane

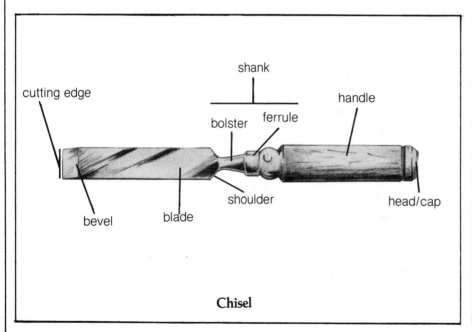

shank

cutting edge

handle

bolster

ferrule

shoulder

head/cap

bevel

blade

Chisel

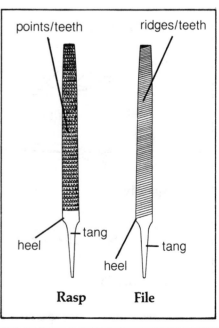

points/teeth

ridges/teeth

heel

tang

heel

tang

Rasp   **File**

Sander

In a finishing, or *straight-line*, sander, the pad moves back and forth, whereas in the similar-looking *orbital sander*, the pad moves in a small orbital pattern. *Belt sanders* use a continuous *belt* of either *natural* or *artificial abrasive material,* and are available with or without *dust bags.* Sandpaper has either an *open* or *closed coat,* depending on spacing between *grains.*

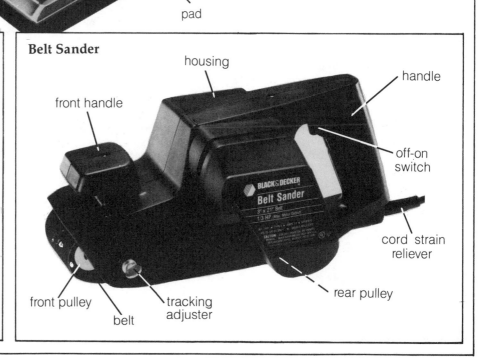

handle

cord strain reliever

trigger switch

front handle

paper clamp

upper housing

lower housing

shoe

paper clamp

pad

Finishing Sander

Sandpaper

grit/abrasive coating

36

grit number

backing

Belt Sander

housing

handle

front handle

off-on switch

BLACK & DECKER
Belt Sander
3" x 21" Belt
1/3 HP (Max. Motor Output)

cord strain reliever

front pulley

belt

tracking adjuster

rear pulley

Plumbing Tools

In addition to the basic plumbing tools shown here, there are *tubing*, or *pipe cutters*, some of which have built-in *polishers; reamers* for removing *burrs* inside cut *pipe;* and *flaring tools*, used to spread the ends of copper *tubing* for *flare fittings*. In *sweat soldering, flux* and *solder* are used. When working with *threaded pipe*, a *pipe threader* (which consists of a *die, diestock* and *handles*) and *joint-sealing tape* or *compound* are used. Other basic plumbing tools are *hacksaws* and *pipe wrenches*.

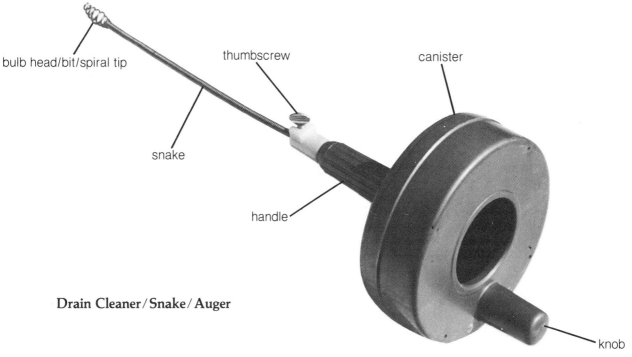

bulb head/bit/spiral tip

thumbscrew

canister

snake

handle

knob

Drain Cleaner/Snake/Auger

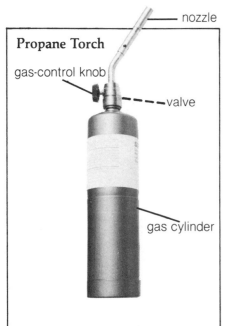

nozzle

Propane Torch

gas-control knob

valve

gas cylinder

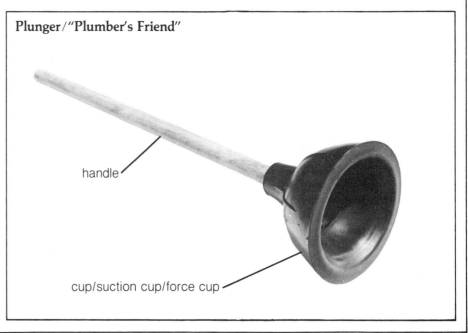

Plunger/"Plumber's Friend"

handle

cup/suction cup/force cup

Electrician's Tools

A volt-ohm meter, also known as a *multimeter* or *volt-ohm-milliammeter*, is used with test *leads* and *jacks* attached to needle-type *probes* or *alligator clips*. The markings on the sheath of a wire describe *wire size*, number of *conductors*, the existence of a ground wire and cable type.

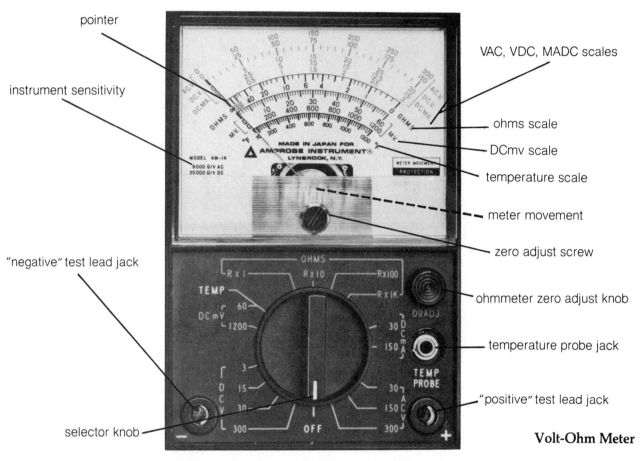

pointer

instrument sensitivity

VAC, VDC, MADC scales

ohms scale

DCmv scale

temperature scale

meter movement

zero adjust screw

"negative" test lead jack

ohmmeter zero adjust knob

temperature probe jack

"positive" test lead jack

selector knob

Volt-Ohm Meter

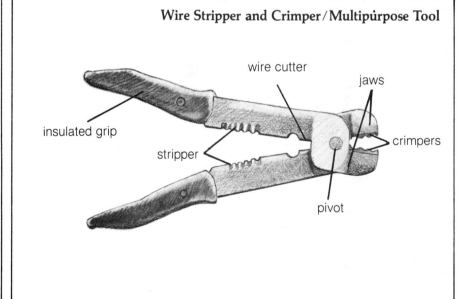

Wire Stripper and Crimper/Multipurpose Tool

insulated grip

wire cutter

jaws

crimpers

stripper

pivot

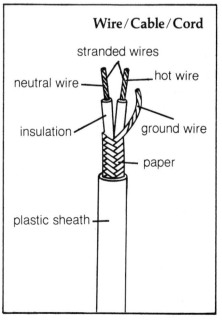

Wire/Cable/Cord

stranded wires

neutral wire

hot wire

insulation

ground wire

paper

plastic sheath

Household Tools

Measuring Tools

The basic measuring tool is the one-piece *bench rule*, or *ruler*. Tape measures also come in *reels* which can be manually rewound. An *L-shaped square* has two *arms* set at right angles. The longer arm is the *blade*, the shorter one is the *tongue*. They meet at the *heel*. A *combination square* substitutes for *try squares*, *depth gauges* and *marking gauges*. When the *air bubble* in a monovial stops between *marks*, the level is on the desired *plane*.

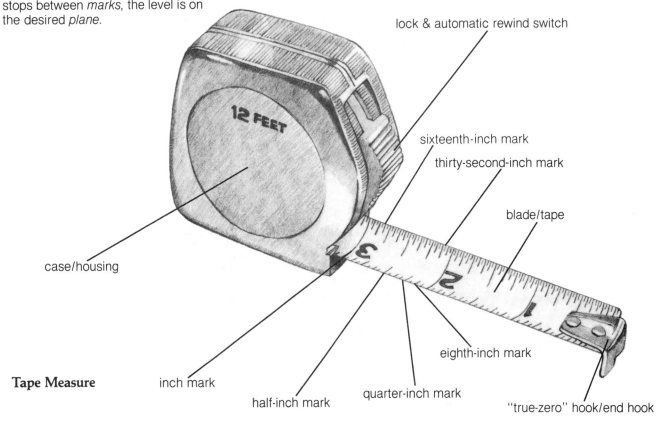

lock & automatic rewind switch

sixteenth-inch mark

thirty-second-inch mark

blade/tape

case/housing

eighth-inch mark

Tape Measure

inch mark

half-inch mark

quarter-inch mark

"true-zero" hook/end hook

Combination Square

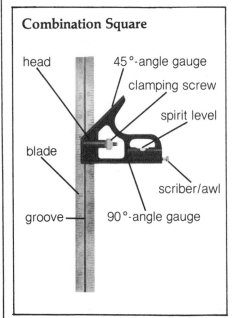

head

45°-angle gauge

clamping screw

spirit level

blade

scriber/awl

groove

90°-angle gauge

Folding Rule/Zigzag Rule

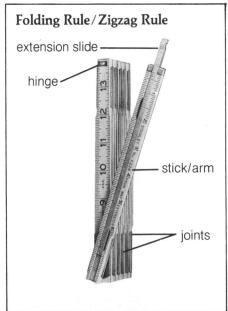

extension slide

hinge

stick/arm

joints

Carpenter's Level

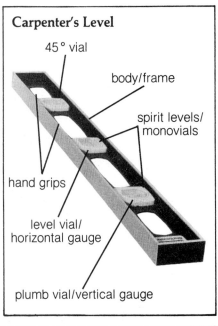

45° vial

body/frame

spirit levels/monovials

hand grips

level vial/horizontal gauge

plumb vial/vertical gauge

Painting Tools

A regular *paint brush* has *bristles* with *split,* or *flagged,* ends. The *heel* section of a brush is where the *butt ends* of bristles fit into a *ferrule* attached to the handle. Other paint-application tools include *pressure brushes, foam brushes* and *pad applicators.* Accessories include *pot* and *brush holders* and *brush spinners.* Paint rollers may have *threaded handles* to accommodate *extenders. Tack cloth* is used to clean surfaces to be painted, and a *drop cloth* protects objects and areas against paint spills.

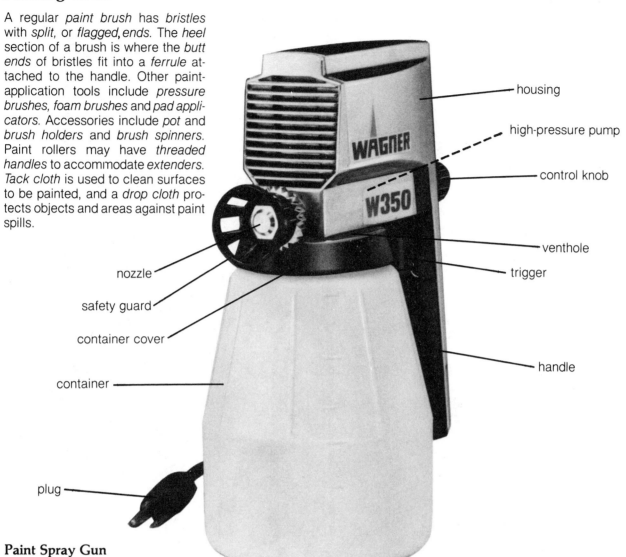

housing

high-pressure pump

control knob

venthole

trigger

handle

nozzle

safety guard

container cover

container

plug

Paint Spray Gun

Tray and Roller

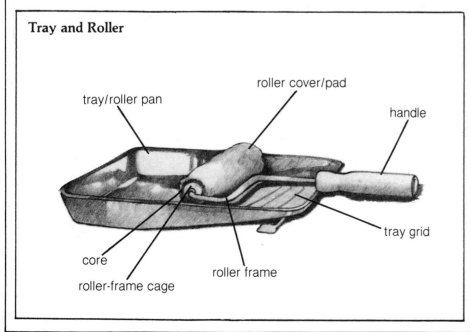

roller cover/pad

tray/roller pan

handle

core

roller-frame cage

roller frame

tray grid

Ladder / Stepladder

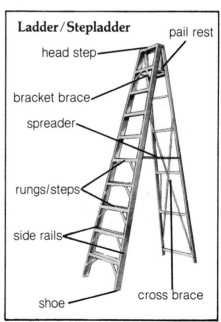

pail rest

head step

bracket brace

spreader

rungs/steps

side rails

shoe

cross brace

Household Tools

Swiss Army Knife

The *dividers* in the *handle* of a *jack-knife*, pocketknife or *camping knife* keep each blade or *tool* separate.

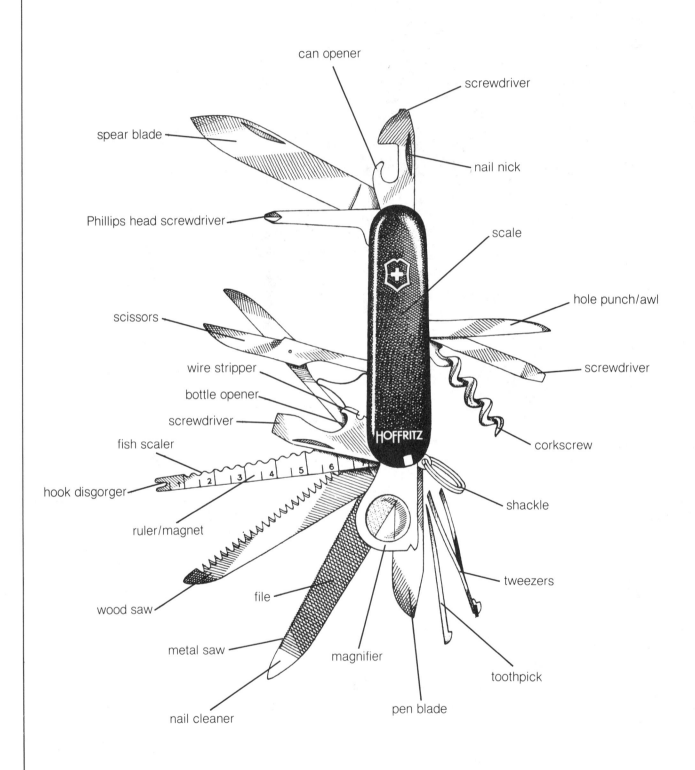

can opener

screwdriver

spear blade

nail nick

Phillips head screwdriver

scale

hole punch/awl

scissors

screwdriver

wire stripper

bottle opener

screwdriver

corkscrew

fish scaler

hook disgorger

shackle

ruler/magnet

tweezers

wood saw

file

metal saw

magnifier

toothpick

nail cleaner

pen blade

HOFFRITZ

Gardening Implements

A hand tool with a small scooped blade used for potting and planting is a *trowel*. A *spading fork* is used for turning soil. Shears are generally of two types: *anvil,* in which a blade cuts through a branch and stops against an anvil, and *by-pass,* which uses a shearing action to cut.

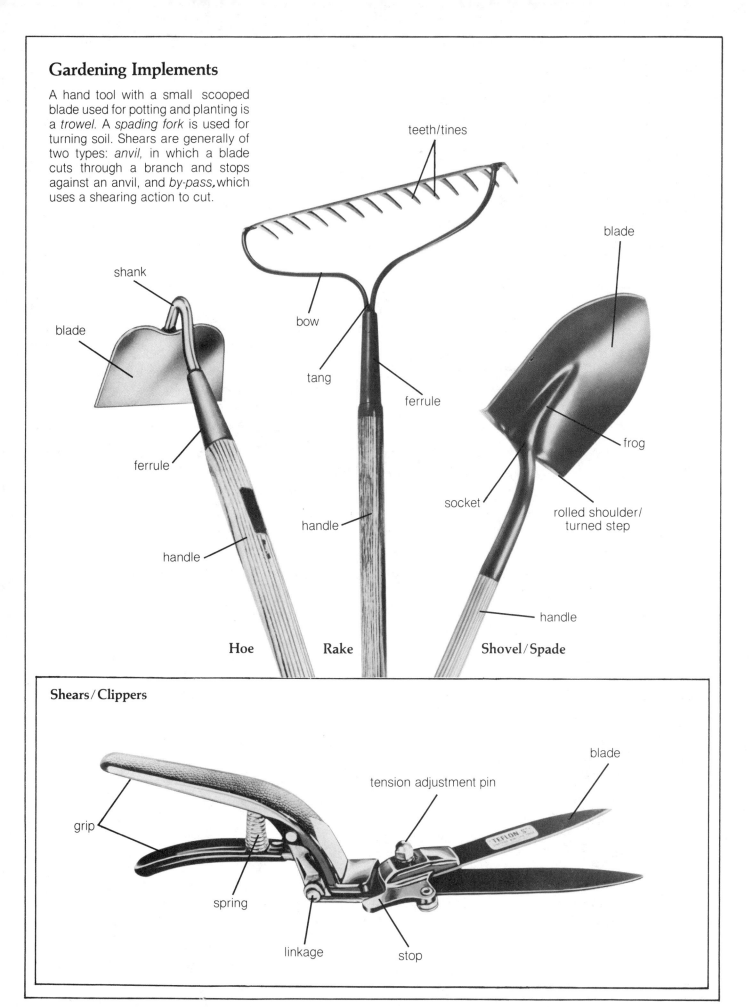

teeth/tines

blade

shank

bow

blade

tang

ferrule

frog

ferrule

socket

rolled shoulder/
turned step

handle

handle

handle

Hoe   **Rake**   **Shovel/Spade**

Shears/Clippers

blade

tension adjustment pin

grip

spring

linkage   stop

Gardening Tools

Sprinkler and Nozzles

Revolving sprinklers have rotating *arms* that spray water through nozzles at each end. An inverted Y-shaped *coupling,* or *siamese,* makes it possible to connect two *hoses* to a single *faucet.* In making a *hose connection,* the larger *female coupling* is fitted over the *male coupling* and turned until the connection is made fast. *Washers* inside couplings make seals watertight.

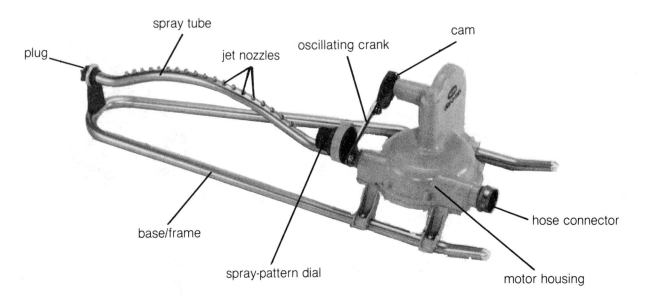

plug
spray tube
jet nozzles
oscillating crank
cam
hose connector
base/frame
spray-pattern dial
motor housing

Oscillating Lawn Sprinkler

Hose Nozzle

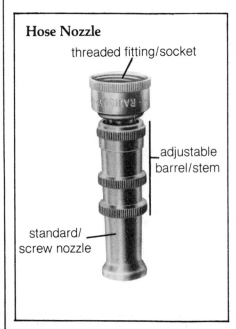

threaded fitting/socket
adjustable barrel/stem
standard/ screw nozzle

Pistol Nozzle

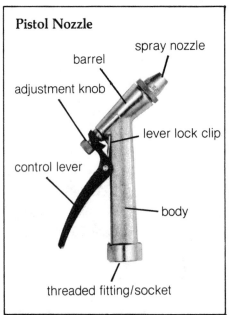

barrel
spray nozzle
adjustment knob
lever lock clip
control lever
body
threaded fitting/socket

Lawn Mower

Rotary mowers, such as the one shown here, use a single *blade* to slice off grass, as does a *scythe*. *Reel mowers,* such as the *sickle-bar mower,* use multiple blades, called a *reel,* to push grass against a stationary *bed knife* at the base of the mower. Cut grass is contained in a bag called a *grass-catcher.* With a *mulching mower,* bagging is unnecessary. A *lawn sweeper* uses a rotating sweeping action to pick up cuttings and leaves. *Lawn edgers* and *trimmers* are used to cut grass in areas where mowers cannot.

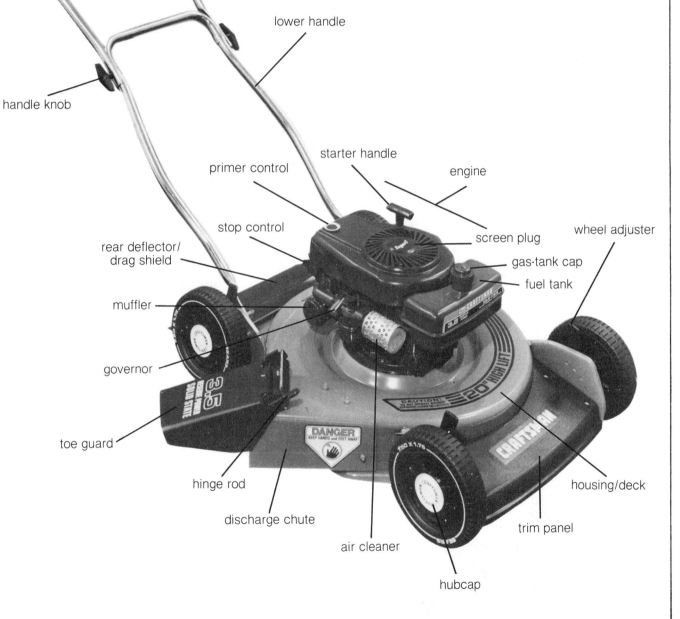

upper handle

lower handle

handle knob

starter handle

primer control

engine

stop control

screen plug

wheel adjuster

rear deflector/ drag shield

gas-tank cap

fuel tank

muffler

governor

toe guard

hinge rod

DANGER
KEEP HANDS and FEET AWAY

discharge chute

air cleaner

housing/deck

trim panel

hubcap

Power Mower

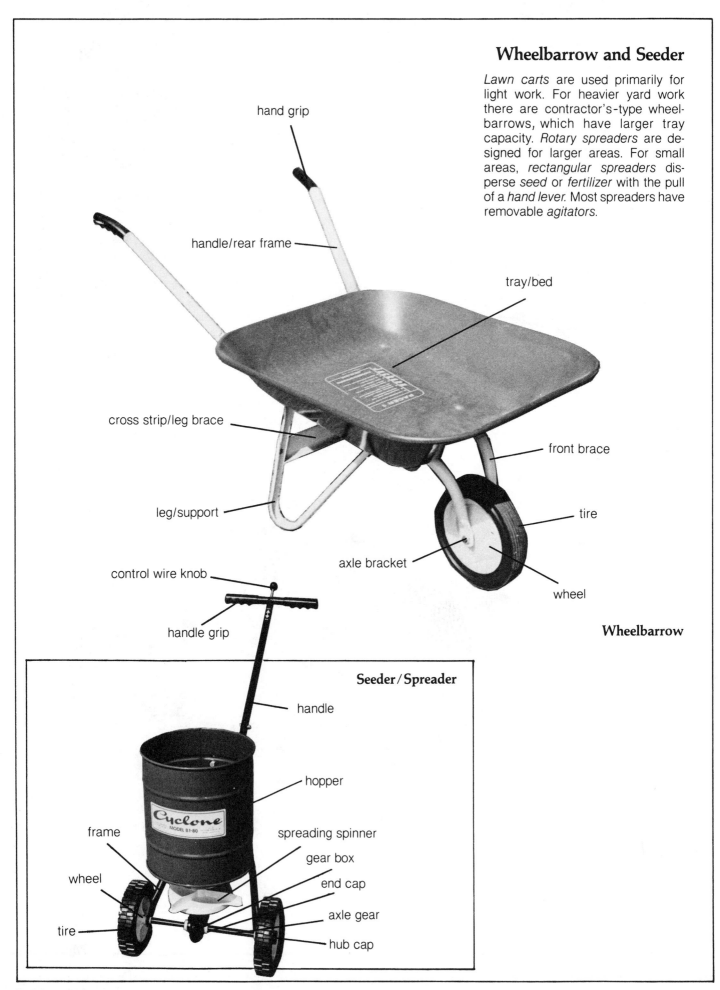

Wheelbarrow and Seeder

Lawn carts are used primarily for light work. For heavier yard work there are contractor's-type wheelbarrows, which have larger tray capacity. *Rotary spreaders* are designed for larger areas. For small areas, *rectangular spreaders* disperse *seed* or *fertilizer* with the pull of a *hand lever*. Most spreaders have removable *agitators*.

hand grip

handle/rear frame

tray/bed

cross strip/leg brace

front brace

leg/support

tire

axle bracket

wheel

Wheelbarrow

control wire knob

handle grip

Seeder / Spreader

handle

hopper

frame

Cyclone
MODEL 81-80

spreading spinner

gear box

wheel

end cap

tire

axle gear

hub cap

Chain Saw

Chain saws are either gasoline- or electric-powered. Power output is measured in cubic inches of *piston displacement* in the *power head* rather than in horsepower. The *cutting head* may be *direct drive* or *gear drive*. A *sprocket-tip cutting bar* increases cutting speed because it eliminates most of the friction around the *bar tip*. Safety devices include a *chain brake* intended to stop the moving chain when the saw begins to kick back, *throttle latches* for safer starting, *safety triggers* to prevent accidental acceleration, *muffler shields,* and *chain catchers* designed to protect the operator from a broken or slipped chain.

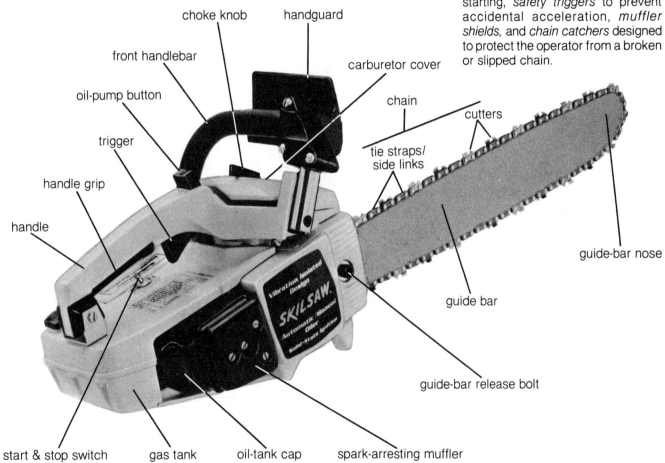

choke knob

handguard

front handlebar

carburetor cover

oil-pump button

chain

cutters

trigger

tie straps/ side links

handle grip

handle

guide-bar nose

guide bar

guide-bar release bolt

start & stop switch

gas tank

oil-tank cap

spark-arresting muffler

Gardening Tools

Ranching Gear

In the days of cattle ranching, *ketch hands* would rope *calves,* or "critters," an *iron man* would brand them, and, in some instances, a *knife man* would cut an additional identifying notch, or *earmark,* in their ears. A *tally man* would record the operation.

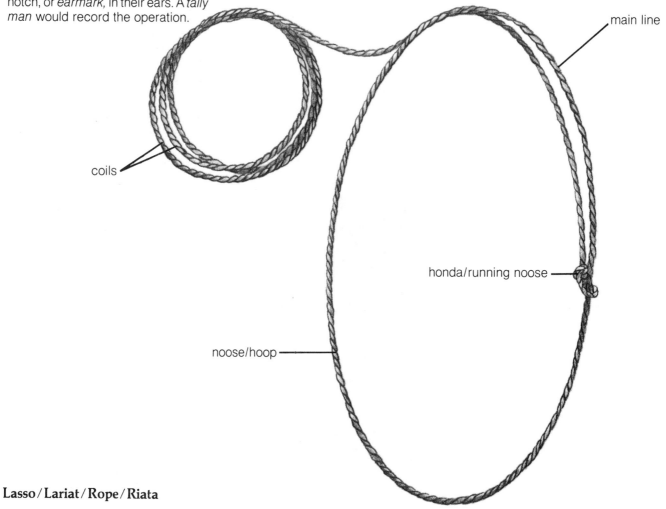

coils

main line

honda/running noose

noose/hoop

Lasso / Lariat / Rope / Riata

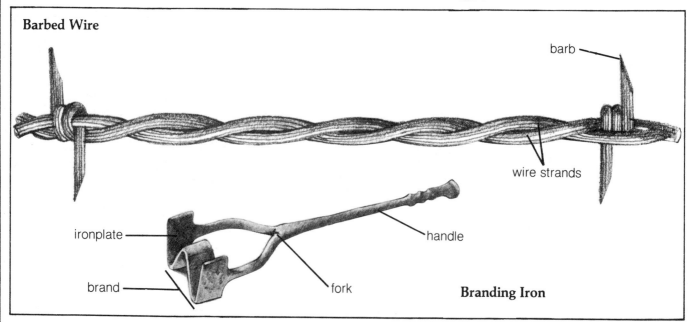

Barbed Wire

barb

wire strands

ironplate

handle

brand

fork

Branding Iron

Traps

Enclosing traps catch animals without hurting them. *Arresting traps,* such as the bear trap shown here, catch and hold animals in their teeth. *Killing traps* destroy animals and rodents.

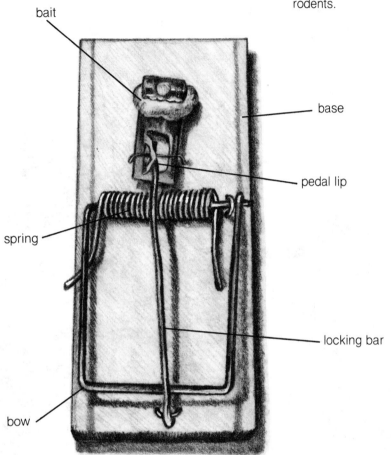

bait

base

pedal lip

spring

locking bar

bow

Mousetrap

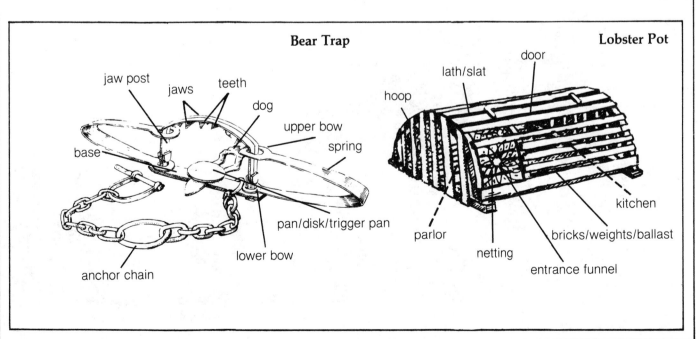

Bear Trap

jaw post

jaws

teeth

dog

upper bow

spring

base

pan/disk/trigger pan

lower bow

anchor chain

Lobster Pot

door

lath/slat

hoop

kitchen

parlor

netting

bricks/weights/ballast

entrance funnel

Trapping Devices

Tractor

Plows, reapers, cultivators, like the harrow seen here, and various *planting machines* are coupled to a tractor to work the land. The operating speed of attachments is controlled by a *power takeoff.* Optional *outboard planetaries* with *adjustable wheel treads* and *add-on segment weights* help boost traction.

front windows

cab

muffler

warning light

headlamp/ headlight

hood

air filter

grille

fender

front-end weights

rear axle

adapter plate

frame

wide tire

side panel

steps

Hitch and Harrow

SMV (slow-moving vehicle) symbol

parking stand

top link

lift link

universal drive joint

lower links

flywheel

drive yoke and rocker

tine bars

tines

crumble roller

depth adjusting screw

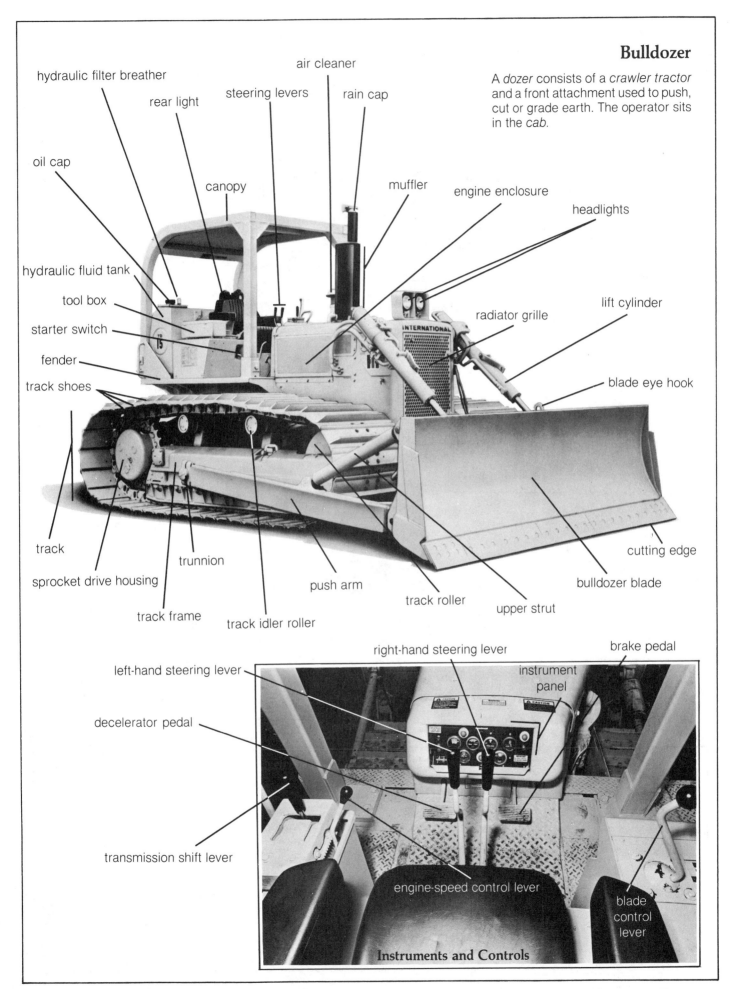

Bulldozer

A *dozer* consists of a *crawler tractor* and a front attachment used to push, cut or grade earth. The operator sits in the *cab*.

hydraulic filter breather

air cleaner

rear light

steering levers

rain cap

oil cap

canopy

muffler

engine enclosure

headlights

hydraulic fluid tank

radiator grille

lift cylinder

tool box

starter switch

blade eye hook

fender

track shoes

track

sprocket drive housing

trunnion

track frame

track idler roller

push arm

track roller

upper strut

cutting edge

bulldozer blade

right-hand steering lever

brake pedal

left-hand steering lever

instrument panel

decelerator pedal

engine-speed control lever

transmission shift lever

blade control lever

Instruments and Controls

Construction Equipment

Transit and Jackhammer

A transit is used by *engineers* and *surveyors* to determine *angles, bearings* and *levels.* It is mounted on a three-legged stand called a *tripod.* A weight, known as a *plumb* or *plumb bob,* is suspended directly below the telescope to determine *true vertical.*

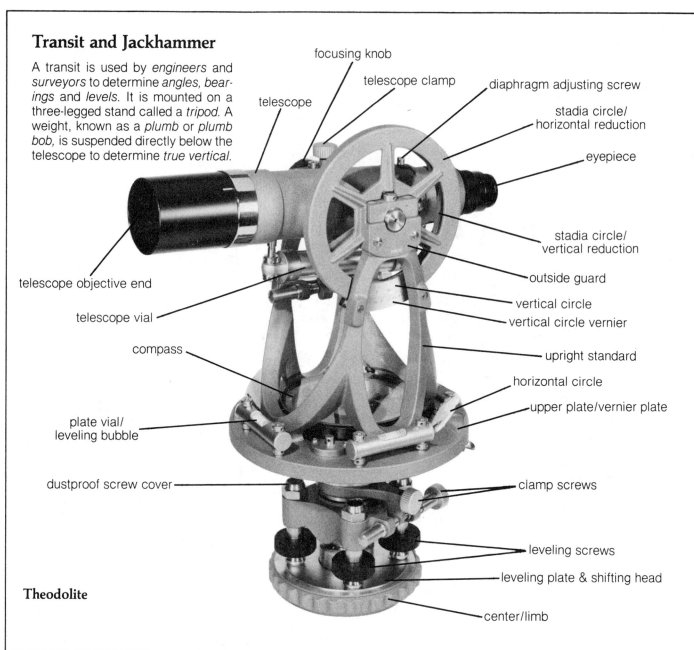

focusing knob

telescope clamp

diaphragm adjusting screw

telescope

stadia circle/ horizontal reduction

eyepiece

stadia circle/ vertical reduction

telescope objective end

outside guard

telescope vial

vertical circle

vertical circle vernier

compass

upright standard

horizontal circle

plate vial/ leveling bubble

upper plate/vernier plate

dustproof screw cover

clamp screws

leveling screws

leveling plate & shifting head

Theodolite

center/limb

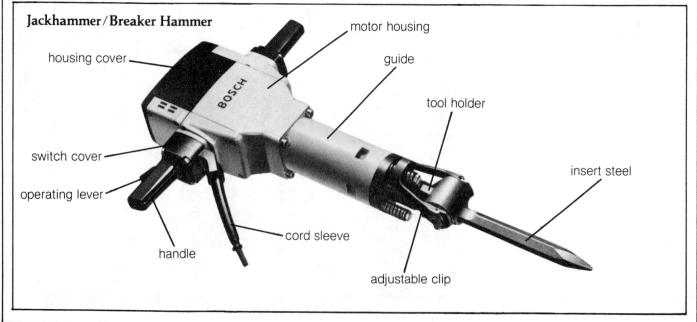

Jackhammer/Breaker Hammer

motor housing

housing cover

guide

tool holder

BOSCH

insert steel

switch cover

operating lever

cord sleeve

handle

adjustable clip

Voting Booth

Voting booths, or *mechanized voting machines*, are located at *polling places*, or *polls*. An *x-indication* appears next to a candidate's name when a lever is pressed. When a *voter* presses levers for every candidate of a single political party, it is called voting a *straight ticket*. Any variation is a *split ballot*.

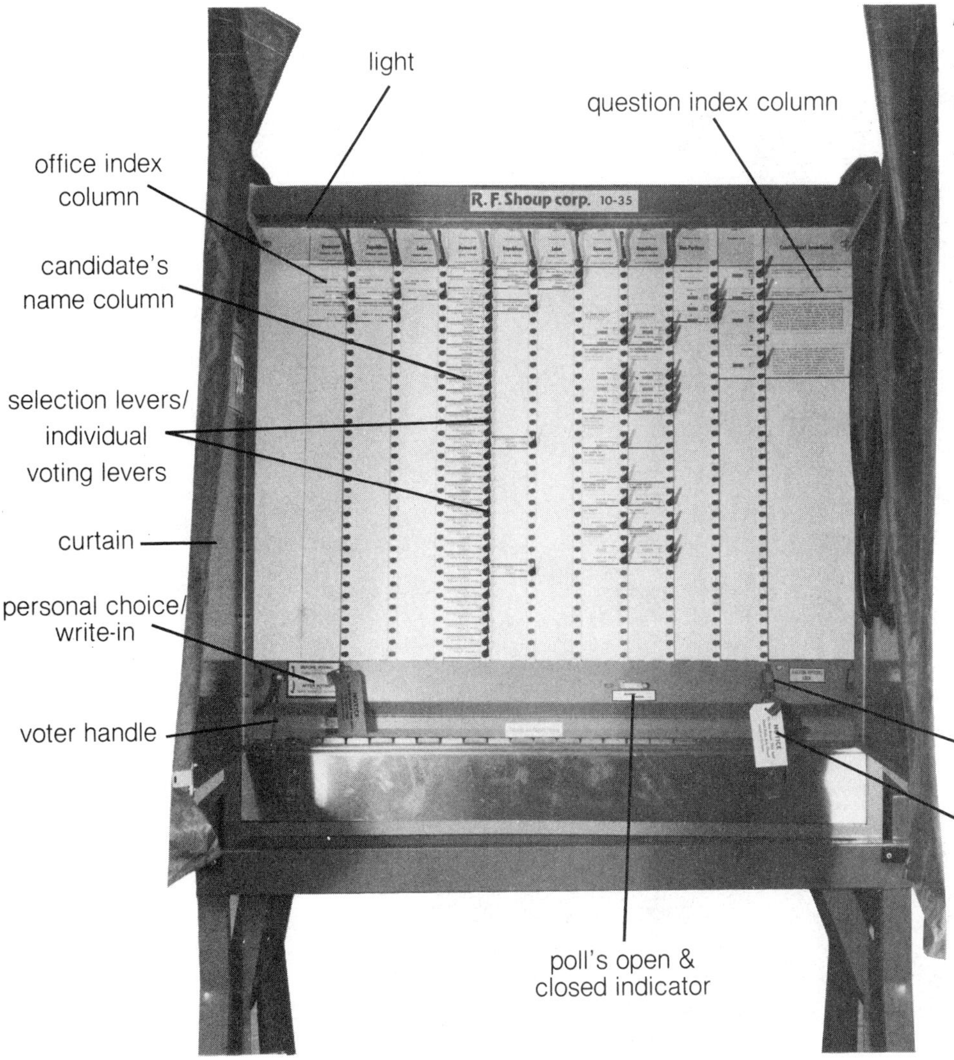

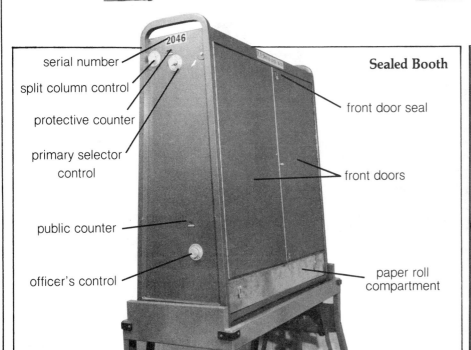

light

question index column

office index column

candidate's name column

selection levers/ individual voting levers

curtain

personal choice/ write-in

voter handle

ballot/face

custodian's seal

officer's lock & seal

poll's open & closed indicator

R. F. Shoup corp. 10-35

Mechanical Voting Booth

Electronic Voting System

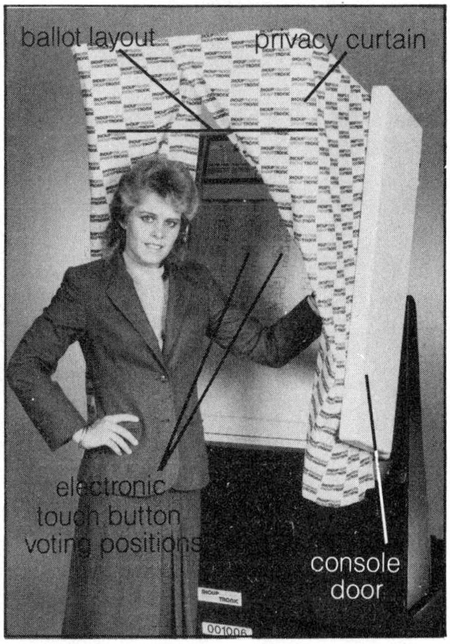

serial number

split column control

protective counter

primary selector control

public counter

officer's control

Sealed Booth

2046

front door seal

front doors

paper roll compartment

ballot layout

privacy curtain

electronic touch button voting positions

console door

Computing Tools

Computer Workstation

A workstation uses the computer's problem solving ability to generate drawings or perform complex design analyses. It is made up of a *central processing unit*, or *CPU*, and a *display monitor* and keypad, all of which is referred to as *hardware*. *Application packages*, or *software*, come on *digital tapes* and both *hard and floppy disks*. Within the CPU, data and files are stored in *random access memory*, or *RAM*, and *read only memory*, or *ROM*.

cathode ray tube/CRT

monitor/high-resolution display

Mexico, Central America & The West Indies

floppy disk drive

function keys

alpha-numeric keypad

keyboard

numeric keypad

cursor control/puck

reset switch

circuit boards/central processing unit/CPU

hard disk drive

tablet/menu/graphics functions selector

adjustable platform/ergostand

data file server/deskside electronics cabinet

pedestal

movable base

Computer Aided Design System/CAD

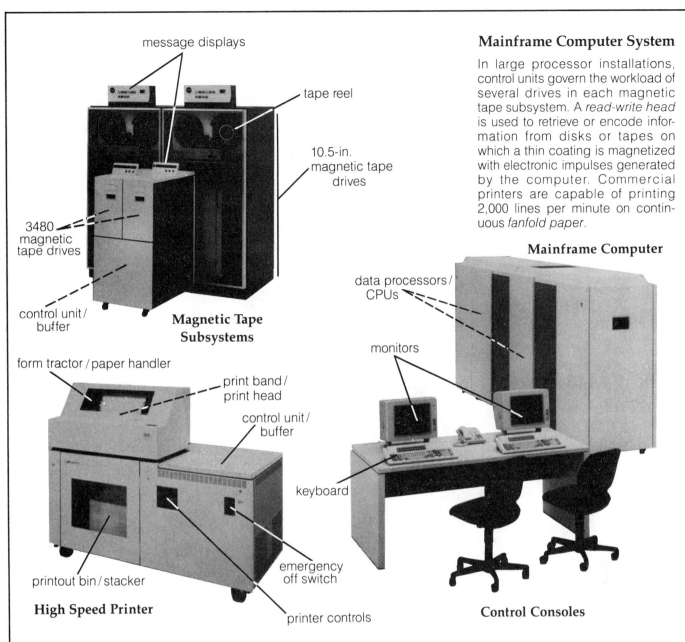

message displays

tape reel

10.5-in. magnetic tape drives

3480 magnetic tape drives

control unit / buffer

Magnetic Tape Subsystems

Mainframe Computer System

In large processor installations, control units govern the workload of several drives in each magnetic tape subsystem. A *read-write head* is used to retrieve or encode information from disks or tapes on which a thin coating is magnetized with electronic impulses generated by the computer. Commercial printers are capable of printing 2,000 lines per minute on continuous *fanfold paper*.

Mainframe Computer

data processors / CPUs

monitors

keyboard

form tractor / paper handler

print band / print head

control unit / buffer

printout bin / stacker

emergency off switch

High Speed Printer

printer controls

Control Consoles

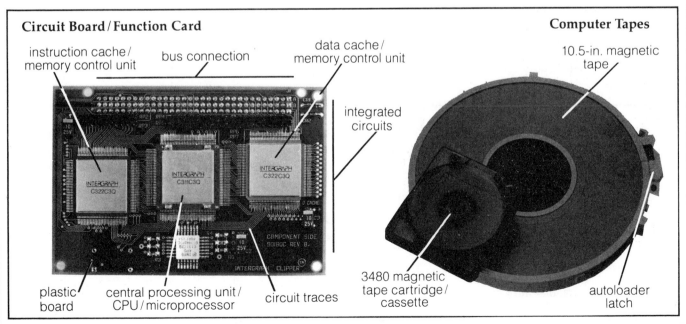

Circuit Board / Function Card

instruction cache / memory control unit

bus connection

data cache / memory control unit

integrated circuits

Computer Tapes

10.5-in. magnetic tape

plastic board

central processing unit / CPU / microprocessor

circuit traces

3480 magnetic tape cartridge / cassette

autoloader latch

Computing Tools

Cash Register

The money drawer of a cash register is the *cash box,* or *till.* A roll of coins put up in paper is a *rouleau.* A *checkout center,* such as the one shown here, is sometimes equipped with a penlike optical *scanner* that translates information on the Universal Product Code, or *UPC label,* into a *cash register receipt* or *item-by-item tape.* It can also feed data to a *central inventory control unit.*

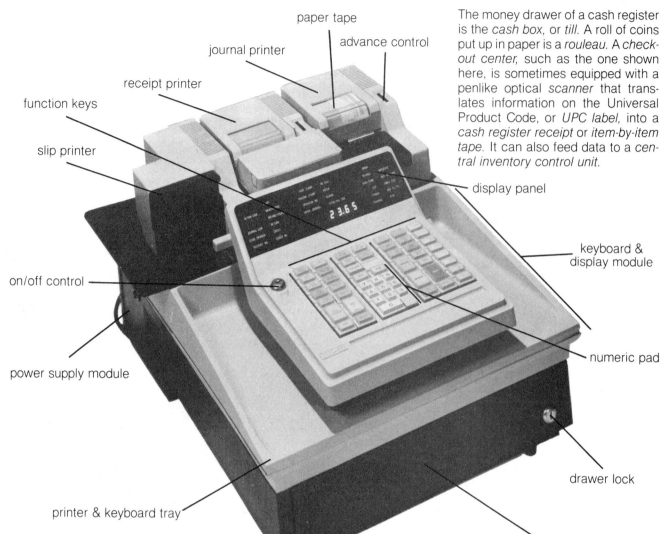

paper tape

advance control

journal printer

receipt printer

function keys

slip printer

display panel

keyboard & display module

on/off control

numeric pad

power supply module

drawer lock

printer & keyboard tray

cash drawer

Universal Product Code

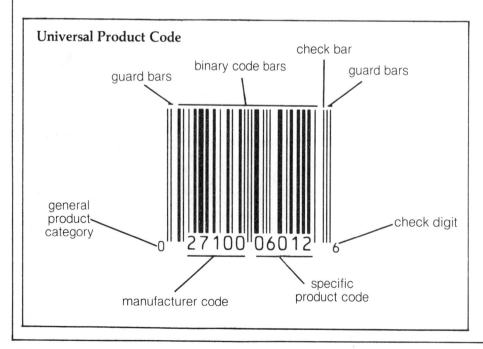

check bar

binary code bars

guard bars

guard bars

general product category

check digit

0 27100 06012 6

manufacturer code

specific product code

Calculators

The electronic calculator has generally replaced the *adding machine* today. The linear slide rule, seen here, often has scales on both sides. A *circular slide rule* can only be used for *multiplication* and *division*. A *cylindrical slide rule* is a series of long scales wound around a cylinder like a screw thread. The abacus is an ancient calculator used for solving problems of *addition*, *subtraction*, *multiplication* and *division*, all by the movement of beads. Other early devices include *counting rods*, or "*bones*."

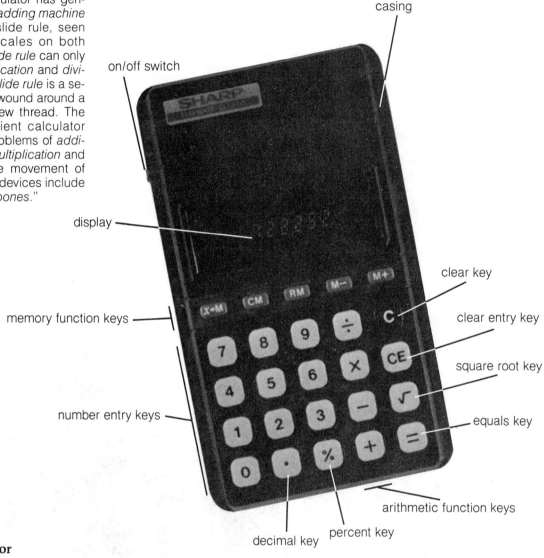

casing

on/off switch

display

clear key

memory function keys

clear entry key

square root key

number entry keys

equals key

arithmetic function keys

decimal key

percent key

Electronic Calculator

Linear Slide Rule

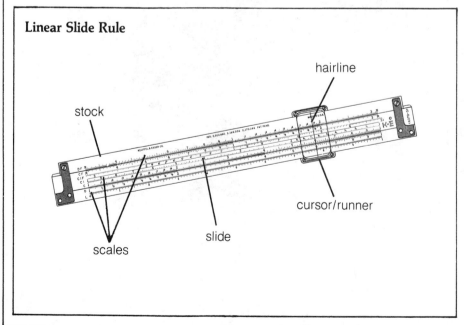

hairline

stock

cursor/runner

scales

slide

Abacus

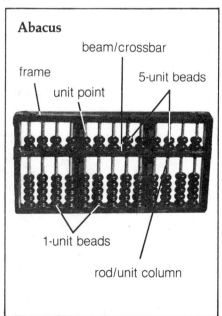

beam/crossbar

frame

5-unit beads

unit point

1-unit beads

rod/unit column

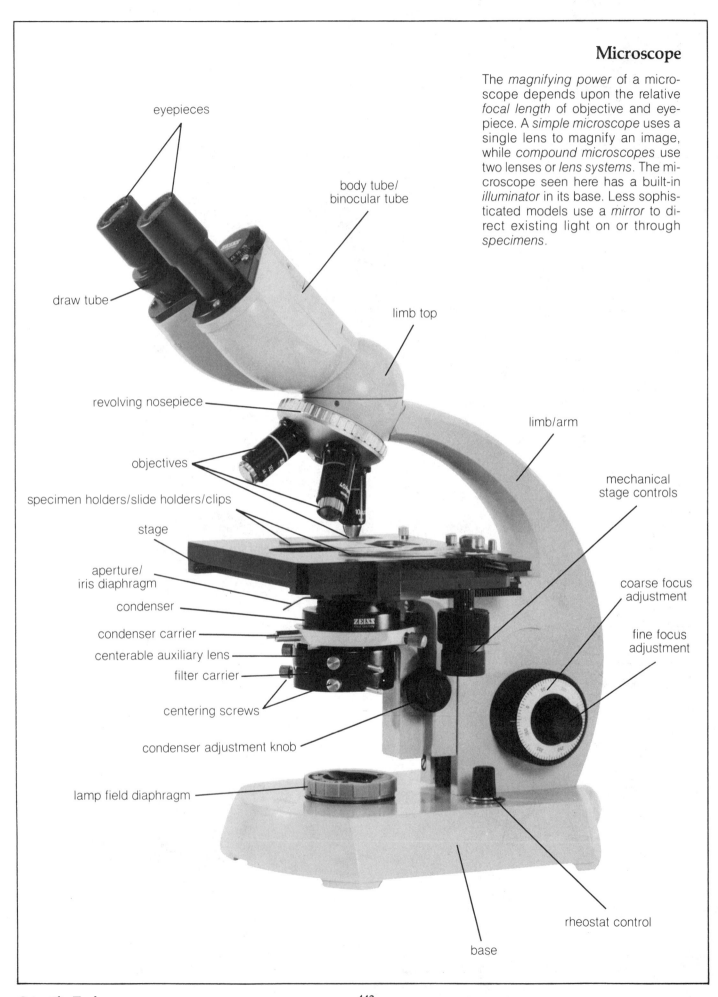

Microscope

The *magnifying power* of a microscope depends upon the relative *focal length* of objective and eyepiece. A *simple microscope* uses a single lens to magnify an image, while *compound microscopes* use two lenses or *lens systems*. The microscope seen here has a built-in *illuminator* in its base. Less sophisticated models use a *mirror* to direct existing light on or through *specimens*.

eyepieces

body tube/ binocular tube

draw tube

limb top

revolving nosepiece

limb/arm

objectives

specimen holders/slide holders/clips

mechanical stage controls

stage

aperture/ iris diaphragm

condenser

coarse focus adjustment

condenser carrier

fine focus adjustment

centerable auxiliary lens

filter carrier

centering screws

condenser adjustment knob

lamp field diaphragm

rheostat control

base

Telescope & Binoculars

A *refracting telescope,* such as the one seen here, relies on the objective lens to concentrate incoming light. A *reflecting telescope* employs a *concave mirror* to do the same task. Binoculars are composed of two similar telescopes, one for each eye. *Field glasses* are lightweight binoculars that employ *erecting telescopes* of the *spyglass* type, while *opera glasses,* designed for use inside, use *Galilean telescopes.*

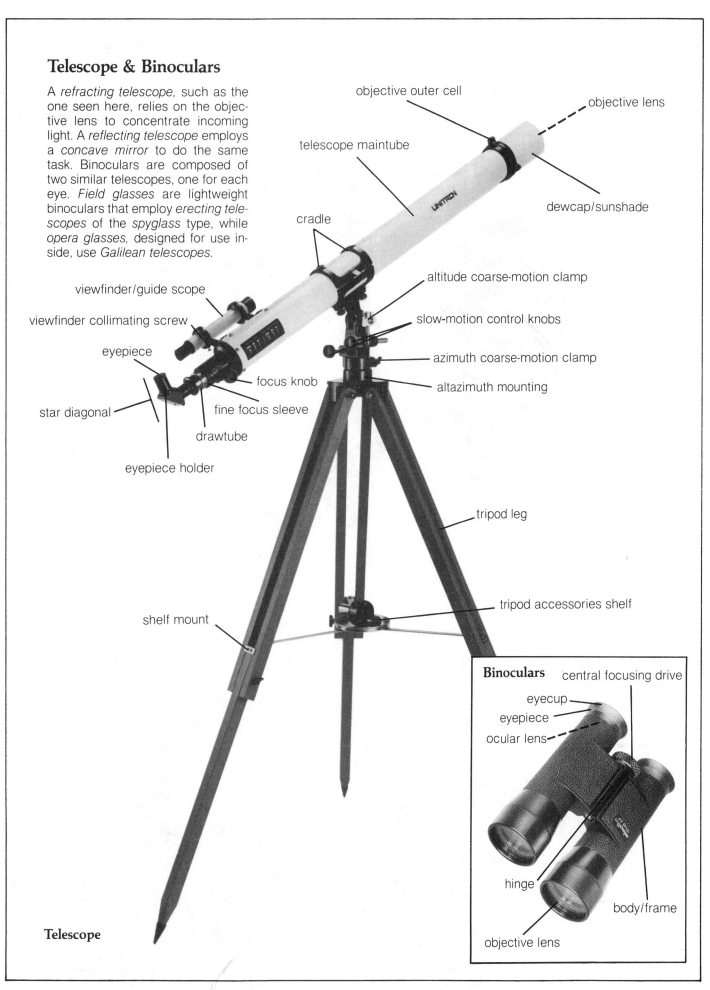

objective outer cell

objective lens

telescope maintube

dewcap/sunshade

cradle

altitude coarse-motion clamp

viewfinder/guide scope

slow-motion control knobs

viewfinder collimating screw

azimuth coarse-motion clamp

eyepiece

focus knob

altazimuth mounting

star diagonal

fine focus sleeve

drawtube

eyepiece holder

tripod leg

tripod accessories shelf

shelf mount

Binoculars

central focusing drive

eyecup

eyepiece

ocular lens

hinge

body/frame

objective lens

Telescope

Scientific Tools

Radar and Sonar

The cursor on a radar display unit is used to determine the *relative bearings* of *targets.* Most units come with a *viewing hood* and *magnifying lens.* Sonar, formerly known as *asdic,* uses a trainable *transducer* housed in a *soundome* beneath a vessel's hull.

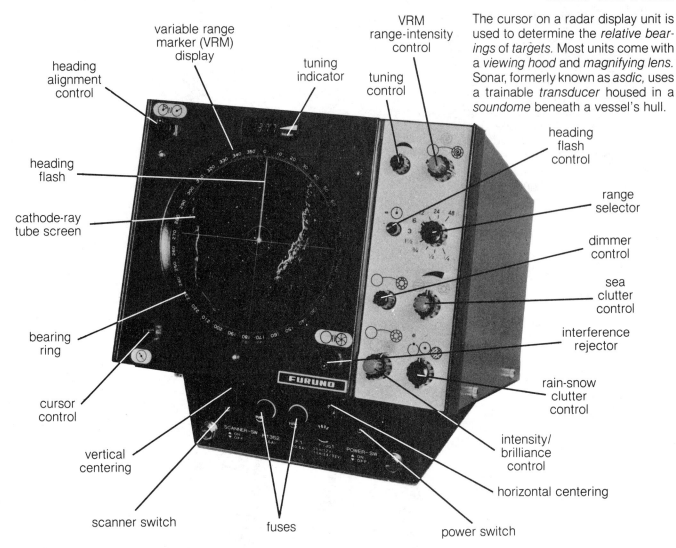

- variable range marker (VRM) display
- VRM range-intensity control
- tuning indicator
- tuning control
- heading alignment control
- heading flash control
- heading flash
- range selector
- cathode-ray tube screen
- dimmer control
- sea clutter control
- bearing ring
- interference rejector
- cursor control
- rain-snow clutter control
- vertical centering
- intensity/ brilliance control
- horizontal centering
- scanner switch
- fuses
- power switch

Radar Display Unit

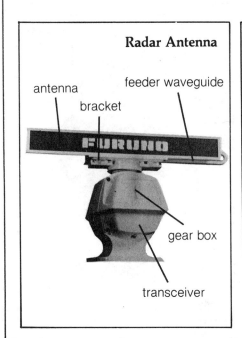

Radar Antenna

- antenna
- feeder waveguide
- bracket
- gear box
- transceiver

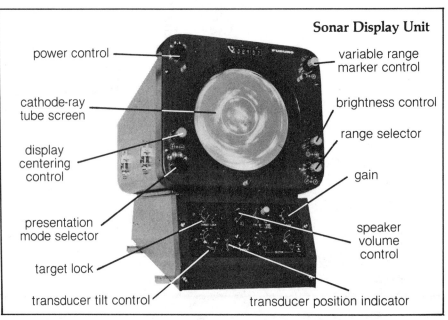

Sonar Display Unit

- power control
- variable range marker control
- cathode-ray tube screen
- brightness control
- display centering control
- range selector
- gain
- presentation mode selector
- speaker volume control
- target lock
- transducer tilt control
- transducer position indicator

Detectors

A *metal locator* works by subtracting a frequency produced by an *oscillator* from a frequency produced by internal circuitry. When the *search coil* is near a metal object, this produces an audio frequency in the speaker or headphones.

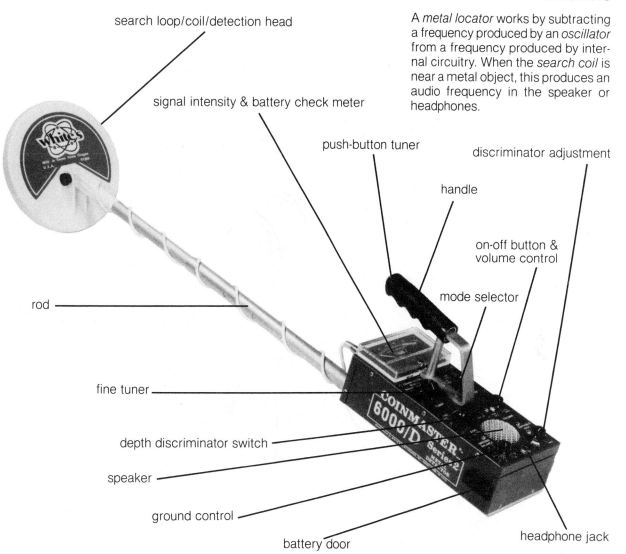

search loop/coil/detection head

signal intensity & battery check meter

push-button tuner

discriminator adjustment

handle

on-off button & volume control

mode selector

rod

fine tuner

depth discriminator switch

speaker

ground control

battery door

headphone jack

Metal and Mineral Detector

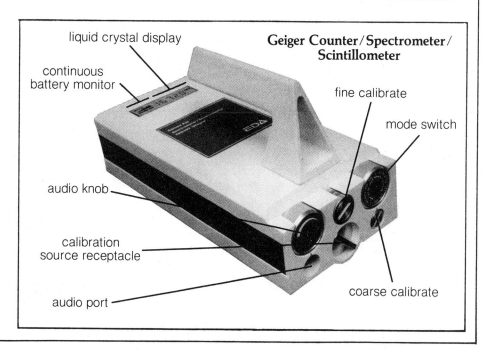

Geiger Counter/Spectrometer/ Scintillometer

liquid crystal display

continuous battery monitor

fine calibrate

mode switch

audio knob

calibration source receptacle

coarse calibrate

audio port

Sensing Devices

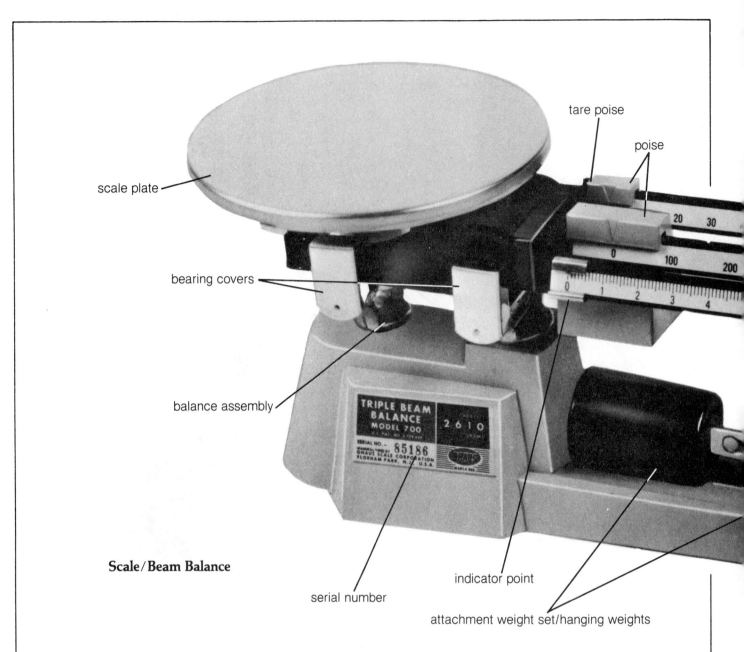

scale plate

tare poise

poise

20   30

0   100   200

bearing covers

0   1   2   3   4

balance assembly

TRIPLE BEAM
BALANCE
MODEL 700   2610

SERIAL NO. —   85186
MANUFACTURED BY
OHAUS SCALE CORPORATION
FLORHAM PARK, N.J. U.S.A.

Scale/Beam Balance

serial number

indicator point

attachment weight set/hanging weights

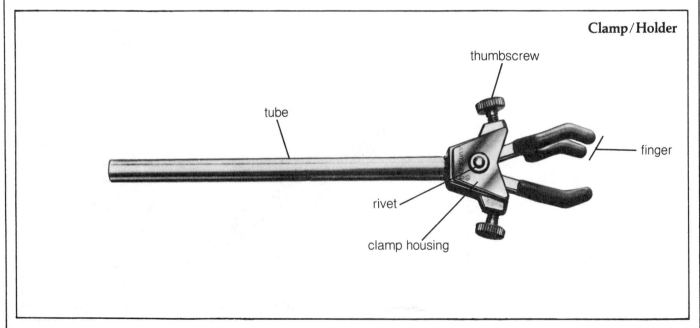

Clamp/Holder

thumbscrew

tube

finger

rivet

clamp housing

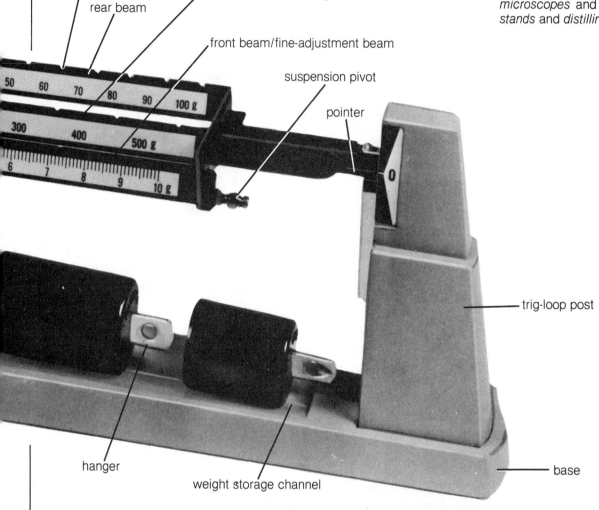

poise notch

rear beam

center beam/coarse-adjustment beam

front beam/fine-adjustment beam

suspension pivot

pointer

50 60 70 80 90 100 g

300 400 500 g

6 7 8 9 10 g

0

Other laboratory equipment includes *ring stands,* to hold various cylinders, *flasks, laboratory thermometers, burettes,* for measuring the volume of liquids, *hydrometers, vacuum jars, microscopes* and *slides, adjustable stands* and *distilling equipment.*

trig-loop post

hanger

weight storage channel

base

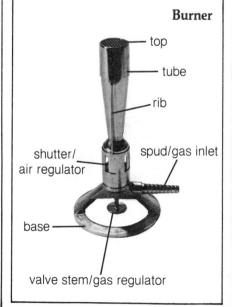

Burner

top

tube

rib

shutter/air regulator

spud/gas inlet

base

valve stem/gas regulator

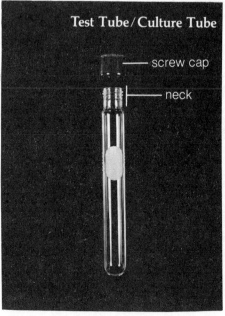

Test Tube/Culture Tube

screw cap

neck

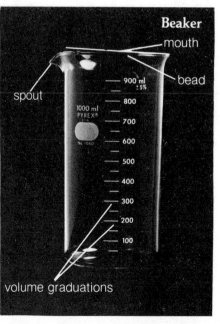

Beaker

mouth

bead

spout

900 ml ±5%

1000 ml
PYREX

800

700

600

500

400

300

200

100

volume graduations

Sensing Devices

Examination Equipment

The scopes seen below are used by *Eye, Ear, Nose and Throat Doctors,* or *EENT specialists.* The speculum is used by *gynecologists* and *obstetricians.* *Headlights* mounted on headbands provide a light source for doctors.

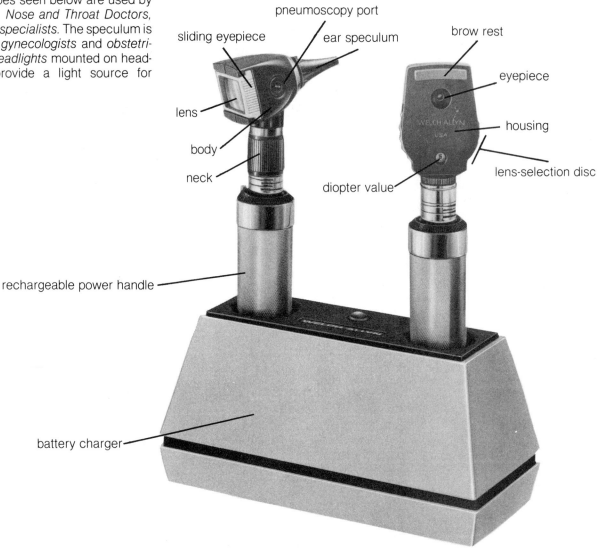

pneumoscopy port

sliding eyepiece

ear speculum

brow rest

eyepiece

lens

housing

body

lens-selection disc

neck

diopter value

rechargeable power handle

battery charger

Ear Scope/Otoscope

Eye Scope/Ophthalmoscope

Speculum

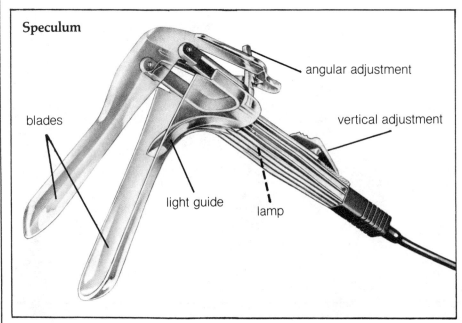

angular adjustment

vertical adjustment

blades

light guide

lamp

Physician's Mirror

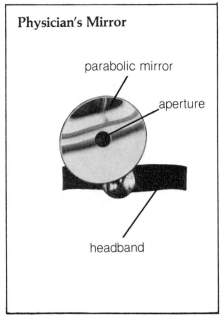

parabolic mirror

aperture

headband

In addition to the examination equipment shown here, doctors use *tongue depressors*, or *tongue blades*; and a *hammer* to test reflexes. Thermometers have *opaque backgrounds* and *celsius* (*centigrade*) and *fahrenheit scales*.

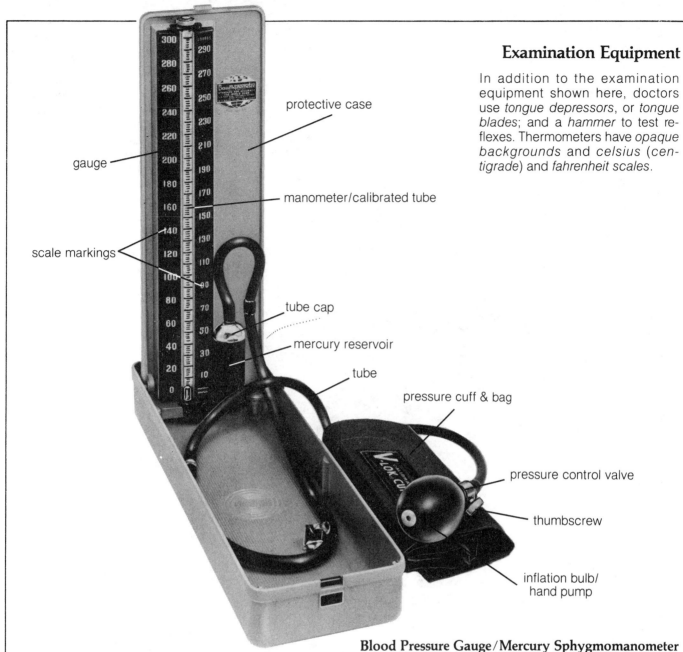

gauge

protective case

manometer/calibrated tube

scale markings

tube cap

mercury reservoir

tube

pressure cuff & bag

pressure control valve

thumbscrew

inflation bulb/
hand pump

Blood Pressure Gauge/Mercury Sphygmomanometer

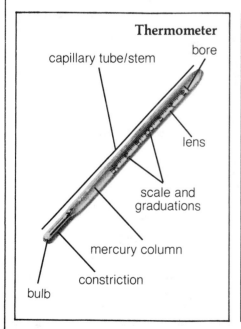

Thermometer

capillary tube/stem

bore

lens

scale and
graduations

mercury column

constriction

bulb

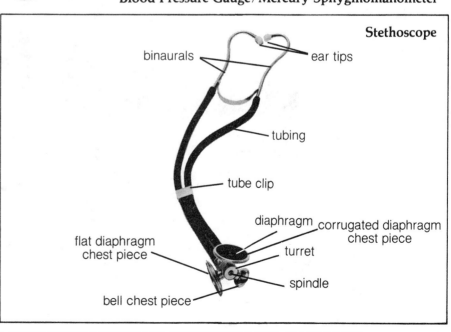

Stethoscope

binaurals

ear tips

tubing

tube clip

diaphragm

corrugated diaphragm
chest piece

flat diaphragm
chest piece

turret

spindle

bell chest piece

Medical Tools

Medical Tables

Surgical, or *operating room, tables,* have built-in *channels* for holding *x-ray cassettes.* Among the accessories that can be attached to them are *intravenous,* or *IV, equipment, arm-* and *footboard extensions, crutch sockets* for holding legs in position, and buckle-type *body-restraint straps.*

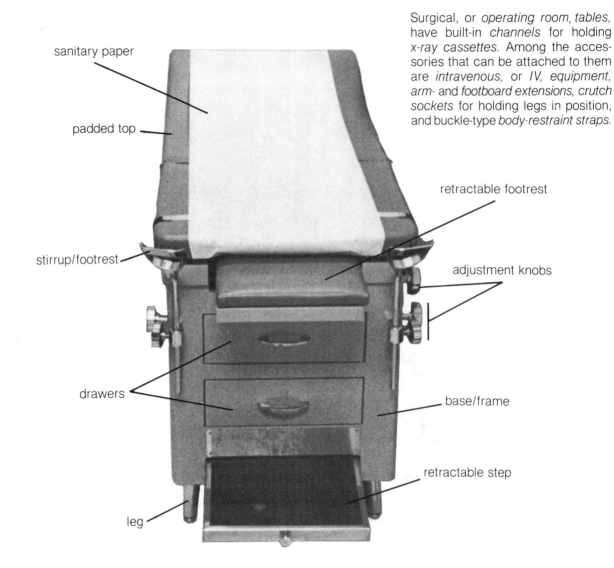

sanitary paper

padded top

retractable footrest

stirrup/footrest

adjustment knobs

drawers

base/frame

retractable step

leg

Examination Table

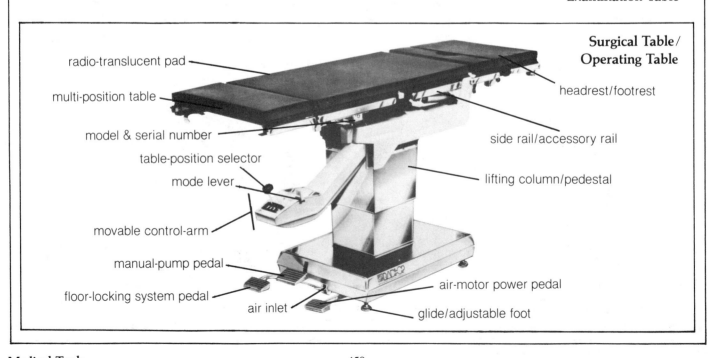

Surgical Table / Operating Table

radio-translucent pad

multi-position table

model & serial number

table-position selector

mode lever

movable control-arm

manual-pump pedal

floor-locking system pedal

air inlet

headrest/footrest

side rail/accessory rail

lifting column/pedestal

air-motor power pedal

glide/adjustable foot

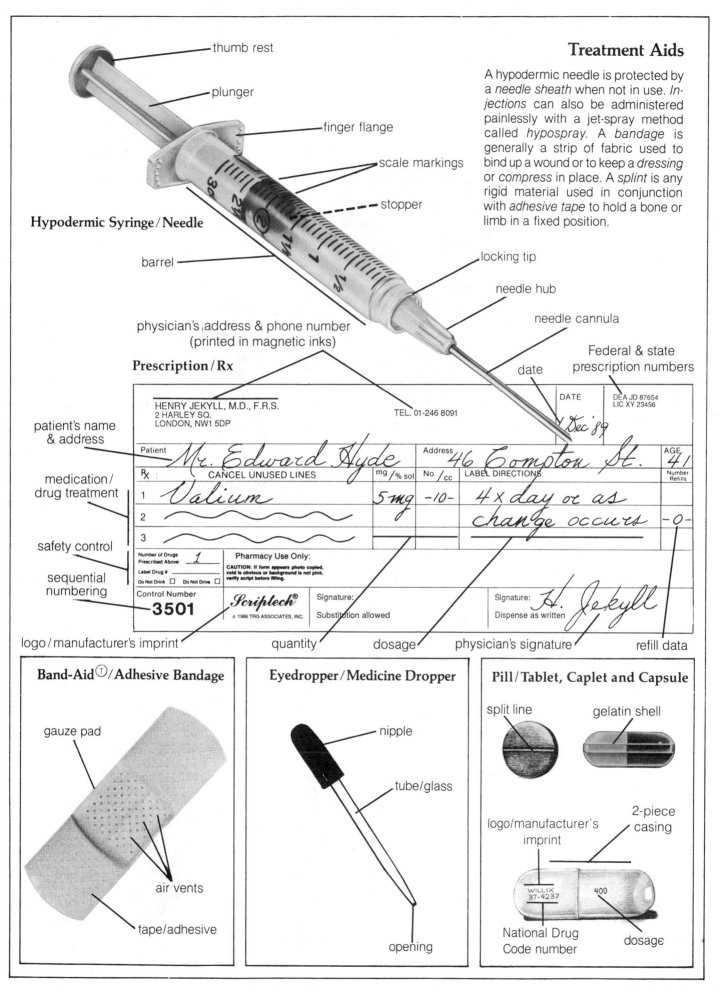

Treatment Aids

A hypodermic needle is protected by a *needle sheath* when not in use. *Injections* can also be administered painlessly with a jet-spray method called *hypospray*. A *bandage* is generally a strip of fabric used to bind up a wound or to keep a *dressing* or *compress* in place. A *splint* is any rigid material used in conjunction with *adhesive tape* to hold a bone or limb in a fixed position.

Hypodermic Syringe / Needle

thumb rest
plunger
finger flange
scale markings
stopper
barrel
locking tip
needle hub
needle cannula

physician's address & phone number
(printed in magnetic inks)

Prescription / Rx

date
Federal & state prescription numbers

patient's name & address

medication / drug treatment

safety control

sequential numbering

HENRY JEKYLL, M.D., F.R.S.
2 HARLEY SQ.
LONDON, NW1 5DP

TEL. 01-246 8091

DATE
Dec '89

DEA JD 87654
LIC XY 23456

Patient	*Mr. Edward Hyde*	Address *46 Compton St.*	AGE *41*

Rx	CANCEL UNUSED LINES	mg /% sol	No. /cc	LABEL DIRECTIONS:	Number Refills
1	*Valium*	*5 mg*	*-10-*	*4 × day or as*	
2				*change occurs*	*-0-*
3					

Number of Drugs Prescribed Above: *1*

Label Drug #

Do Not Drink ☐ Do Not Drive ☐

Pharmacy Use Only:
CAUTION: If form appears photo copied, void is obvious or background is not pink, verify script before filling.

Control Number
3501

Scriptech®
c 1986 TRG ASSOCIATES, INC.

Signature:
Substitution allowed

Signature: *H. Jekyll*
Dispense as written

logo / manufacturer's imprint
quantity
dosage
physician's signature
refill data

Band-Aid ⓣ / Adhesive Bandage

gauze pad
air vents
tape/adhesive

Eyedropper / Medicine Dropper

nipple
tube/glass
opening

Pill / Tablet, Caplet and Capsule

split line
gelatin shell

logo/manufacturer's imprint
2-piece casing

WILLIX 37-4237
400

National Drug Code number
dosage

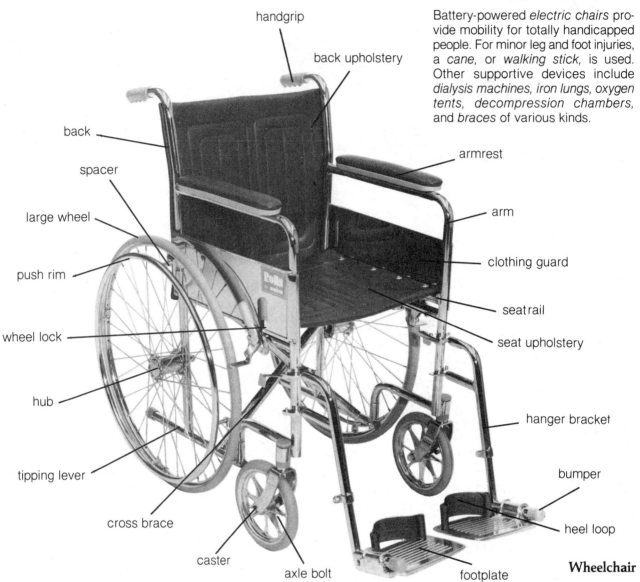

Supportive Devices

Battery-powered *electric chairs* provide mobility for totally handicapped people. For minor leg and foot injuries, a *cane*, or *walking stick*, is used. Other supportive devices include *dialysis machines*, *iron lungs*, *oxygen tents*, *decompression chambers*, and *braces* of various kinds.

handgrip

back upholstery

armrest

back

arm

spacer

large wheel

clothing guard

push rim

seat rail

wheel lock

seat upholstery

hub

hanger bracket

tipping lever

bumper

cross brace

heel loop

caster

axle bolt

footplate

Wheelchair

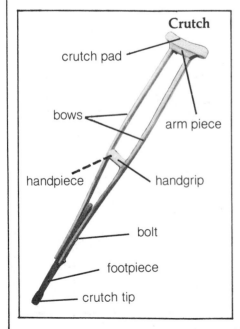

Crutch

crutch pad

bows

arm piece

handpiece

handgrip

bolt

footpiece

crutch tip

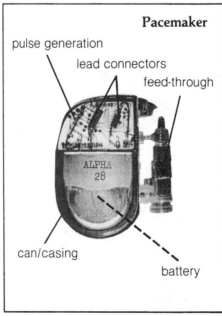

Pacemaker

pulse generation

lead connectors

feed-through

ALPHA 28

can/casing

battery

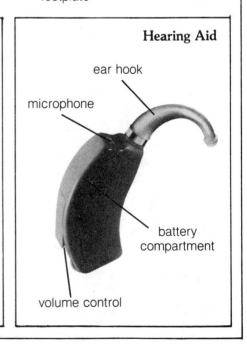

Hearing Aid

ear hook

microphone

battery compartment

volume control

Dental Corrective Devices

A *bridge* consists of one or more false teeth anchored between abutment teeth. The portion of the bridge that actually replaces the missing tooth or teeth is the *pontic*. A *crown* or *jacket crown* covers that part of the tooth normally protected by enamel. In *orthodontia,* the correction of the position of teeth, a *band* or *wire* is inserted in the slot and held in place by *rubber bands* looped over the tie wings.

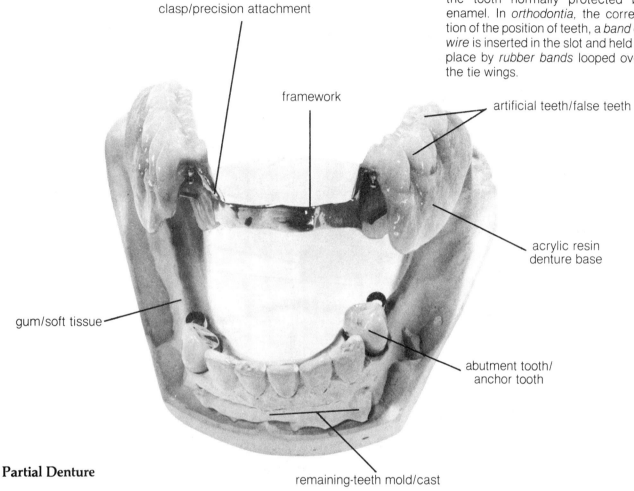

clasp/precision attachment

framework

artificial teeth/false teeth

acrylic resin denture base

gum/soft tissue

abutment tooth/ anchor tooth

remaining-teeth mold/cast

Partial Denture

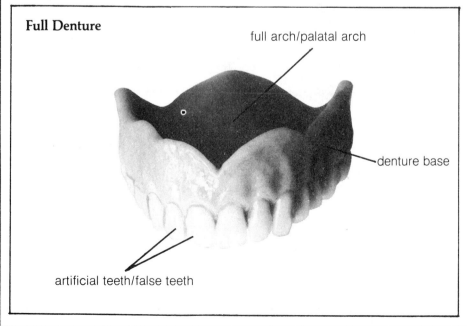

Full Denture

full arch/palatal arch

denture base

artificial teeth/false teeth

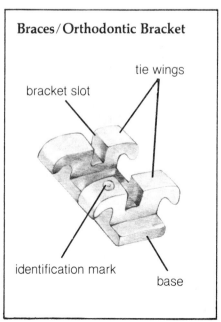

Braces/Orthodontic Bracket

tie wings

bracket slot

identification mark

base

Medical Tools

Dental Unit

A high-intensity *dental light* is usually attached to a dental unit, or *dental island.* Instrument trays may be attached to a *drift-free arm,* such as the one shown here, or to a *post-mounted arm.*

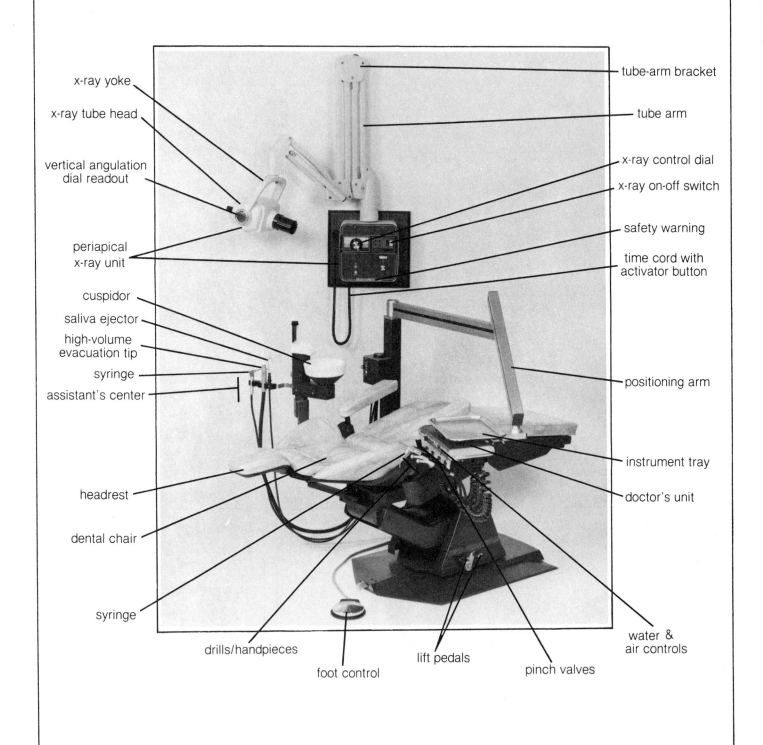

x-ray yoke

x-ray tube head

vertical angulation dial readout

periapical x-ray unit

cuspidor

saliva ejector

high-volume evacuation tip

syringe

assistant's center

headrest

dental chair

syringe

drills/handpieces

foot control

lift pedals

pinch valves

tube-arm bracket

tube arm

x-ray control dial

x-ray on-off switch

safety warning

time cord with activator button

positioning arm

instrument tray

doctor's unit

water & air controls

Dental Equipment

Fillings of *silver amalgam* or *inlays, cast restorations* of *gold, synthetic porcelain* or *acrylic resins,* are used to fill *cavities.* Teeth can also be fitted with *crowns* or *caps.*

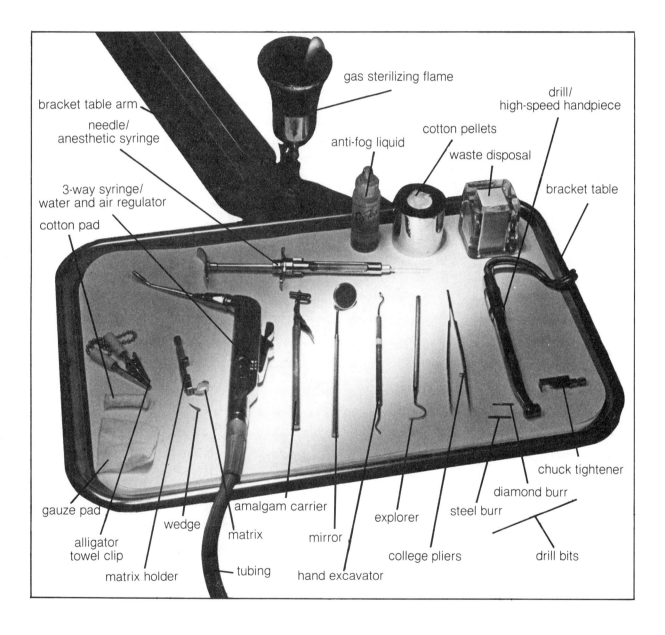

bracket table arm

needle/
anesthetic syringe

3-way syringe/
water and air regulator

cotton pad

gas sterilizing flame

anti-fog liquid

cotton pellets

waste disposal

drill/
high-speed handpiece

bracket table

gauze pad

alligator
towel clip

matrix holder

wedge

matrix

tubing

amalgam carrier

mirror

hand excavator

explorer

college pliers

steel burr

diamond burr

chuck tightener

drill bits

Medical Tools

Teeth

Each tooth has one or two *neighbors* and a biting *partner* in the opposite jaw. Teeth fit into *sockets*. The first set of teeth are *baby teeth,* or *milk teeth,* replaced in time by permanent teeth. A person with a fondness for sugary edibles is said to have a *sweet tooth.*

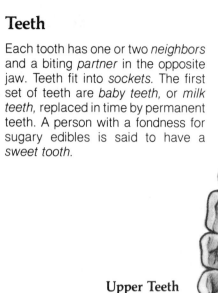

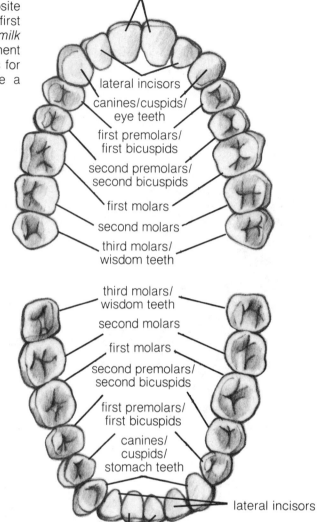

central incisors

lateral incisors

canines/cuspids/ eye teeth

first premolars/ first bicuspids

second premolars/ second bicuspids

first molars

second molars

third molars/ wisdom teeth

Upper Teeth

Lower Teeth

third molars/ wisdom teeth

second molars

first molars

second premolars/ second bicuspids

first premolars/ first bicuspids

canines/ cuspids/ stomach teeth

lateral incisors

central incisors

Permanent Teeth

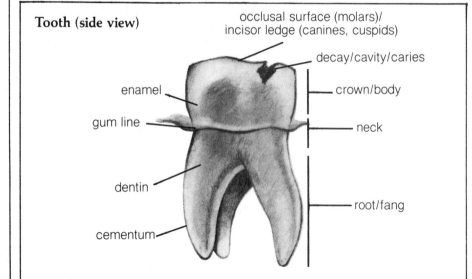

Tooth (side view)

occlusal surface (molars)/ incisor ledge (canines, cuspids)

decay/cavity/caries

crown/body

neck

root/fang

enamel

gum line

dentin

cementum

Tooth (top view)

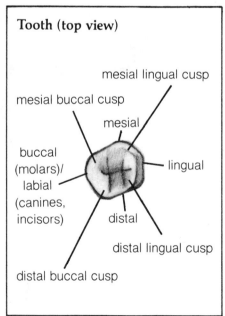

mesial lingual cusp

mesial buccal cusp

mesial

buccal (molars)/ labial (canines, incisors)

lingual

distal

distal lingual cusp

distal buccal cusp

Vault and Safe

Vaults are connected to *alarm systems*, which include *bells* and *silent alarms*. *Time locks* open safes or vaults at a predetermined time and prevent their being opened otherwise. A *strongbox* is a stoutly made box or chest for preserving valuable possessions. Most safes are insulated to protect against fire as well as theft. A home *money box*, *coin bank* or *piggy bank* is opened at the bottom or with a hammer.

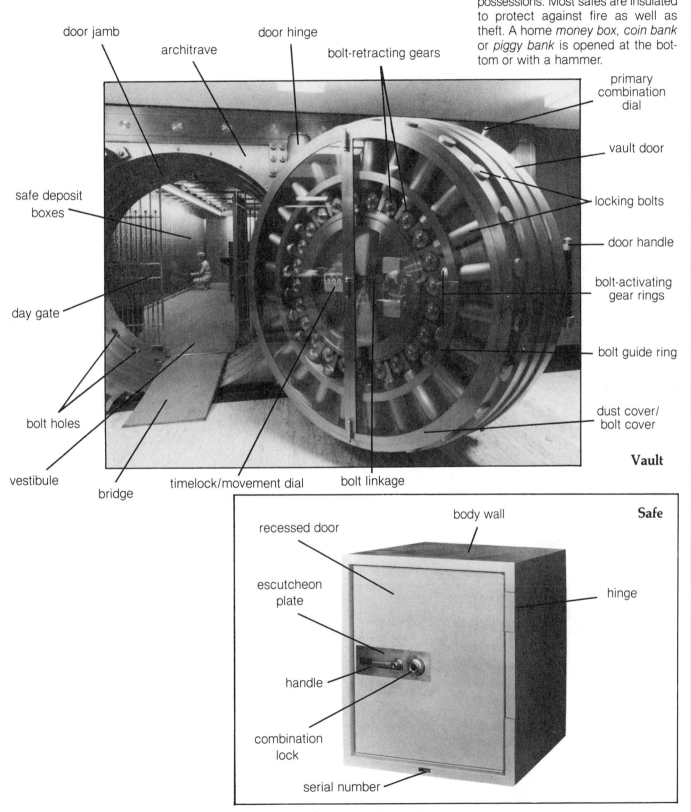

door jamb

architrave

door hinge

bolt-retracting gears

primary combination dial

vault door

locking bolts

door handle

bolt-activating gear rings

bolt guide ring

dust cover/ bolt cover

safe deposit boxes

day gate

bolt holes

vestibule

bridge

timelock/movement dial

bolt linkage

Vault

body wall

Safe

recessed door

escutcheon plate

hinge

handle

combination lock

serial number

Security Devices

Door Locks

Many mortise locks have two *buttons* below the latch bolt which allow the *outside knob* to be independently locked or unlocked. Bolts fit into a *striker plate,* attached to the door frame. A *latch* is a device which holds a door closed, but cannot be locked. A *catch* holds lightweight doors, such as cabinet doors, closed. A *lockset* has the features of a lock and a catch.

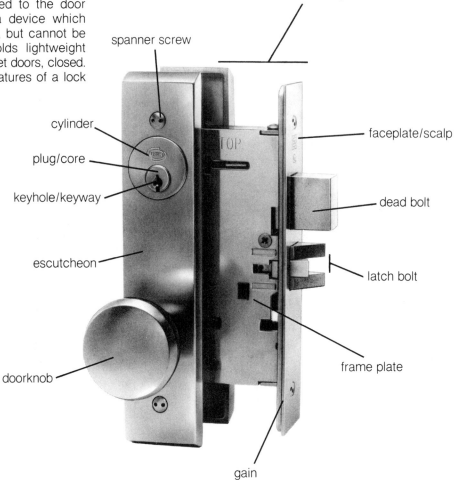

latch assembly

spanner screw

cylinder

plug/core

keyhole/keyway

escutcheon

doorknob

faceplate/scalp

dead bolt

latch bolt

frame plate

gain

Mortise Lock

Chain Lock/Door Bolt

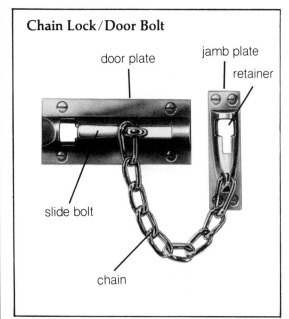

door plate

jamb plate

retainer

slide bolt

chain

Inter-grip Rim Lock

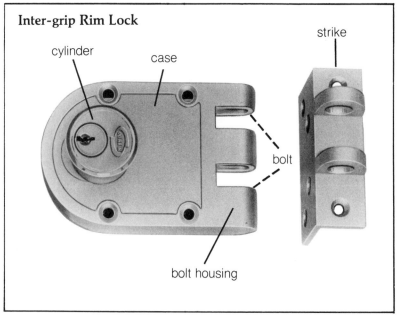

cylinder

case

strike

bolt

bolt housing

Key and Padlock

A key is inserted into a lock's cylinder via a *keyway*. The angled serrations, or *cuts*, on a key blade correspond to different sized *pin-tumblers*, or *pins*, within the lock cylinder. A key that has not yet been configured to any particular lock is a *blank*. A key used to open many common locks is a *skeleton key*.

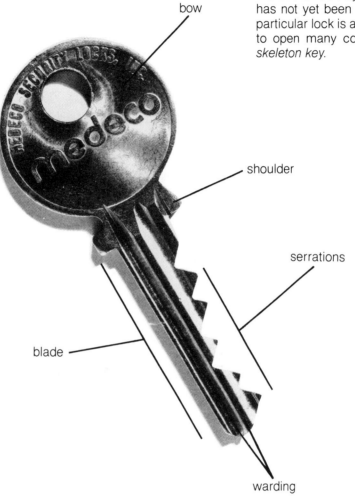

bow

shoulder

serrations

blade

warding

Key

Padlock

shackle

medeco

cylinder/plug

case/body

Keychain

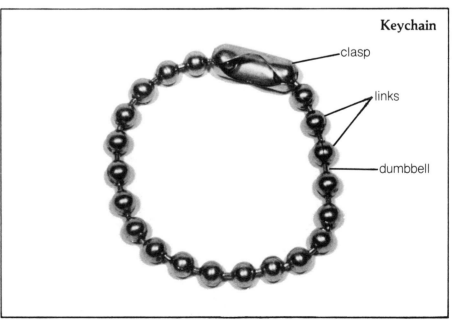

clasp

links

dumbbell

459

Hinge and Hasp

In addition to the *butt hinge,* seen here, there are *pivot hinges, full-surface hinges, half-surface hinges, spring hinges, strap hinges* and *continuous hinges.* Hinge pivot pins or *fixed pins,* used on smaller hinges, are available in a variety of ornamental *heads,* or *caps,* such as the ball tip seen here. A *safety hasp* is secured with a padlock or pin.

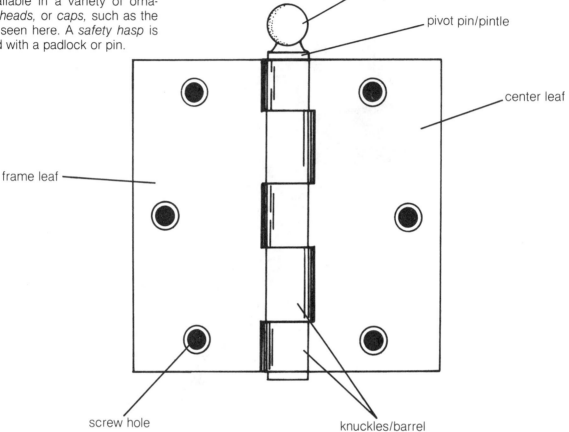

ball tip head

pivot pin/pintle

center leaf

frame leaf

screw hole

knuckles/barrel

Hinge

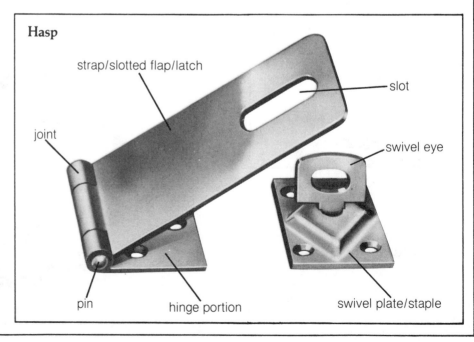

Hasp

strap/slotted flap/latch

slot

joint

swivel eye

pin

hinge portion

swivel plate/staple

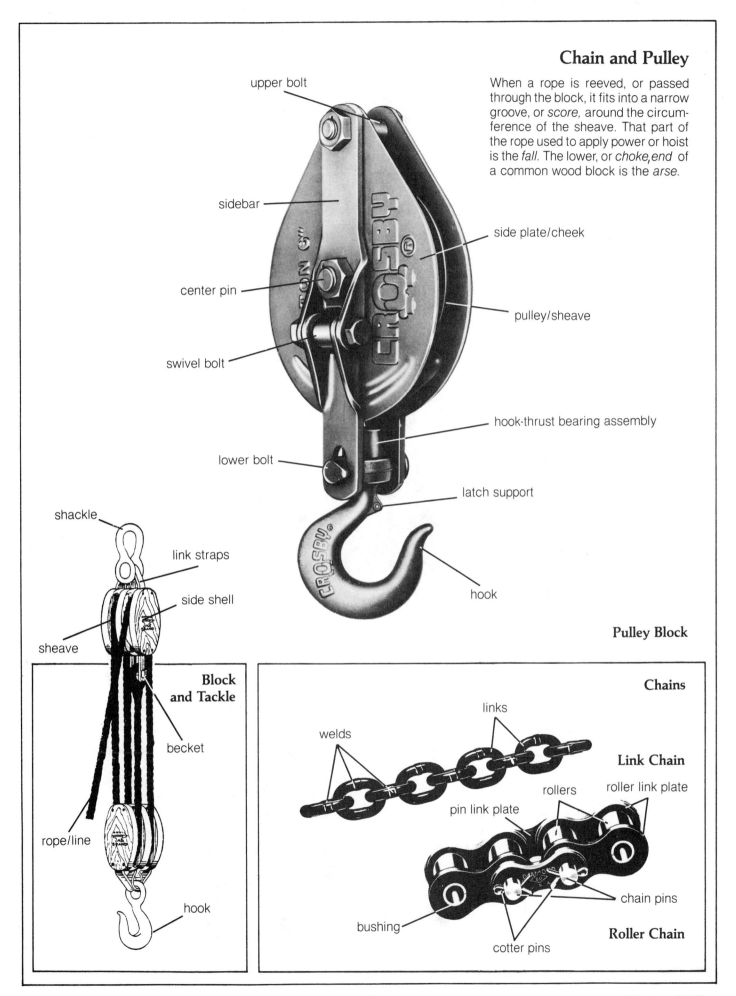

Chain and Pulley

When a rope is reeved, or passed through the block, it fits into a narrow groove, or *score,* around the circumference of the sheave. That part of the rope used to apply power or hoist is the *fall.* The lower, or *choke, end* of a common wood block is the *arse.*

upper bolt

sidebar

side plate/cheek

center pin

pulley/sheave

swivel bolt

hook-thrust bearing assembly

lower bolt

latch support

hook

Pulley Block

shackle

link straps

side shell

sheave

becket

rope/line

hook

Block and Tackle

Chains

links

welds

Link Chain

rollers

roller link plate

pin link plate

chain pins

bushing

cotter pins

Roller Chain

461

Chain and Pulley

Execution Devices

The blade on the guillotine is released by a *release cord* or *release button.* The Italian *mannaia* and the Scottish *maiden* were variations of the French guillotine. A *gibbet,* similar to a gallows, has a single, horizontal arm from which the noose was hung. On an electric chair, electrodes are attached to the prisoner's head and leg to complete the circuit. A *tumbrel* is any vehicle used to bring condemned people to the place of execution.

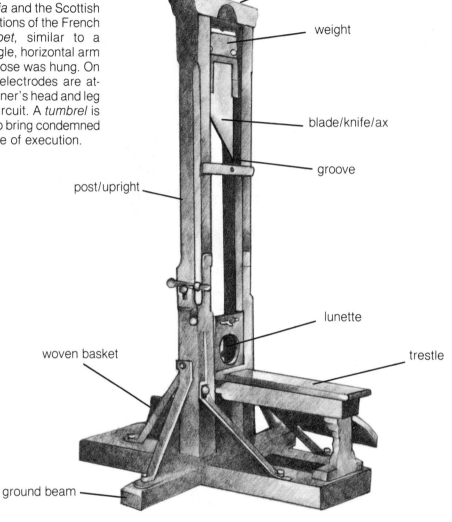

crossbeam

weight

blade/knife/ax

groove

post/upright

lunette

woven basket

trestle

ground beam

Guillotine

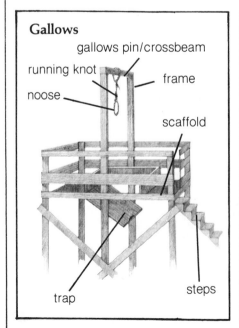

Gallows

gallows pin/crossbeam

running knot

frame

noose

scaffold

trap

steps

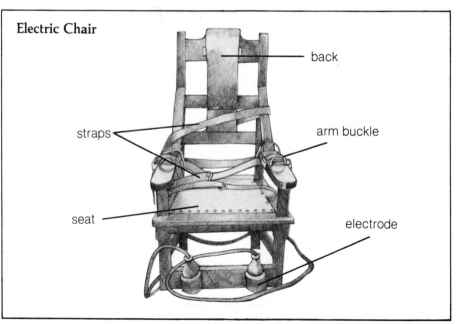

Electric Chair

back

straps

arm buckle

seat

electrode

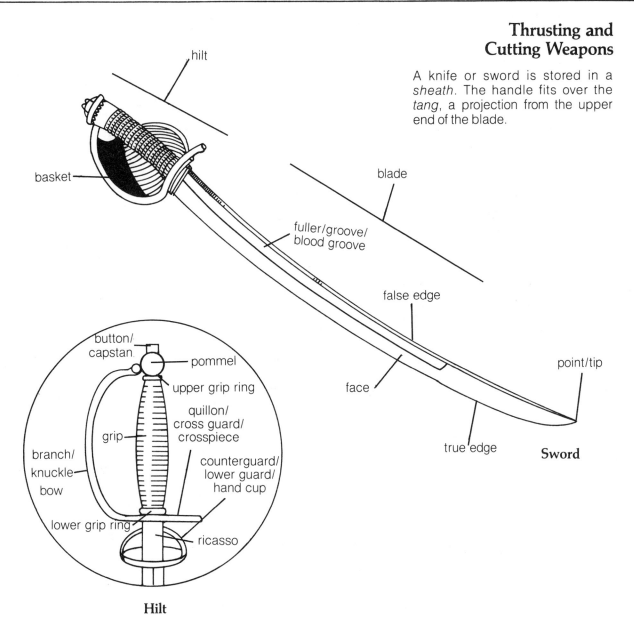

Thrusting and Cutting Weapons

A knife or sword is stored in a *sheath*. The handle fits over the *tang*, a projection from the upper end of the blade.

hilt

blade

fuller/groove/ blood groove

false edge

point/tip

face

true edge

Sword

basket

button/ capstan

pommel

upper grip ring

grip

quillon/ cross guard/ crosspiece

branch/ knuckle bow

counterguard/ lower guard/ hand cup

lower grip ring

ricasso

Hilt

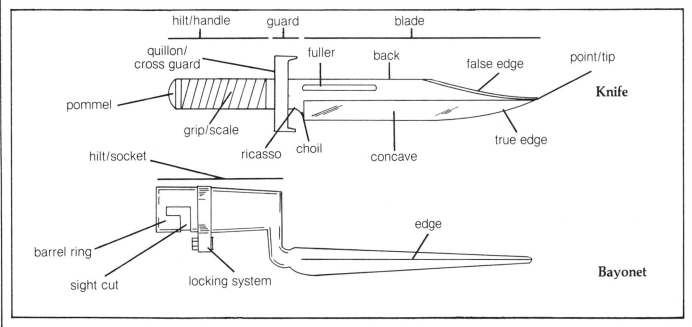

hilt/handle   guard   blade

quillon/ cross guard

fuller

back

false edge

point/tip

pommel

Knife

grip/scale

ricasso

choil

concave

true edge

hilt/socket

edge

barrel ring

sight cut

locking system

Bayonet

Medieval Arms

A round shield held at arm's length is called a *buckler,* while a shield held across the body by straps or handles called *enarmes* is a *target.* A shield offering protection during a siege is a *pavise.* Cutouts on the sides of a shield for holding spears to be thrown are called *bouches.* A shafted weapon having a *spear blade* and a pair of curved *lobes* at the base of the *spearhead* is a *partisan.*

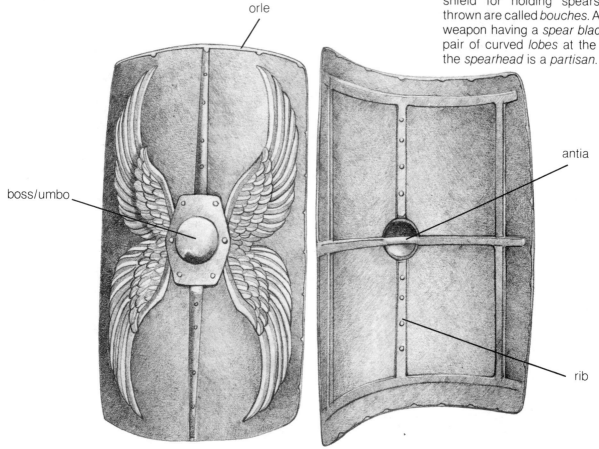

orle

boss/umbo

antia

rib

Shield

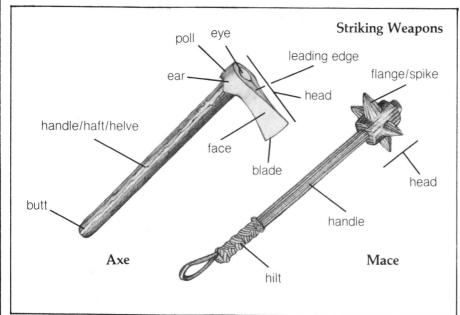

Striking Weapons

poll
eye
leading edge
ear
head
flange/spike
handle/haft/helve
face
blade
head
butt
handle
hilt

Axe

Mace

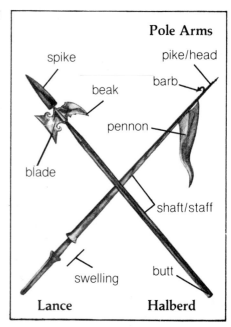

Pole Arms

spike
pike/head
beak
barb
pennon
blade
shaft/staff
swelling
butt

Lance

Halberd

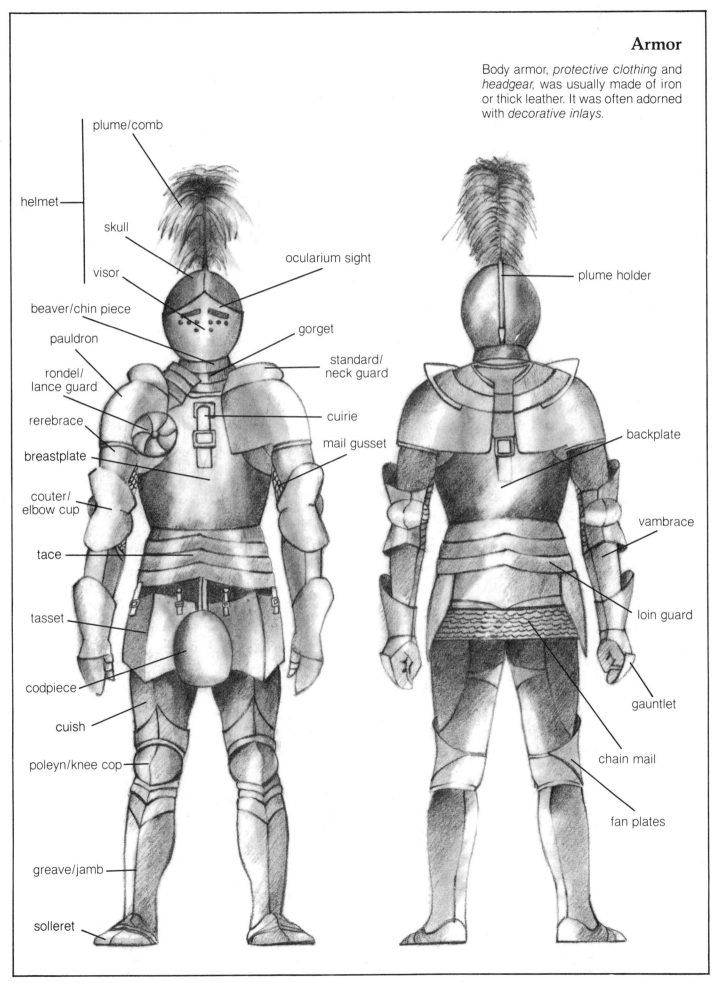

Armor

Body armor, *protective clothing* and *headgear*, was usually made of iron or thick leather. It was often adorned with *decorative inlays*.

plume/comb

helmet

skull

visor

oculariam sight

beaver/chin piece

pauldron

gorget

rondel/ lance guard

standard/ neck guard

rerebrace

cuirie

breastplate

mail gusset

couter/ elbow cup

tace

tasset

codpiece

cuish

poleyn/knee cop

greave/jamb

solleret

plume holder

backplate

vambrace

loin guard

gauntlet

chain mail

fan plates

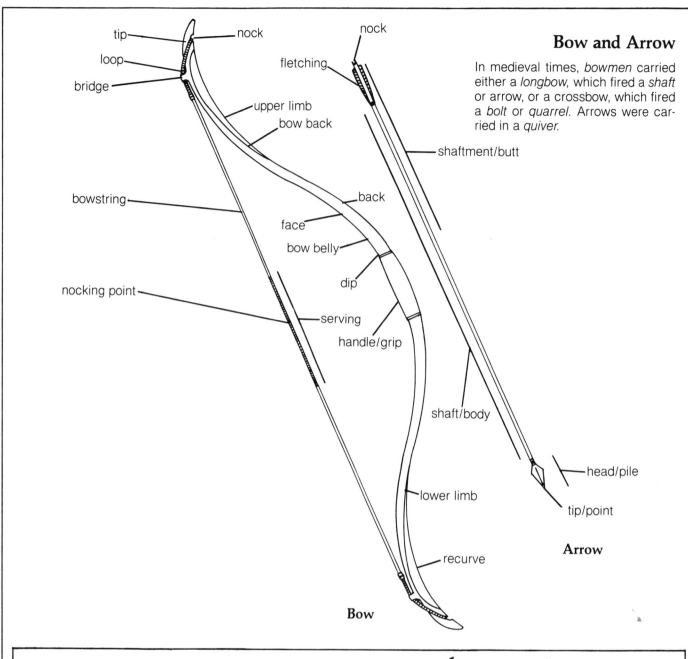

tip
nock
loop
bridge
nock
fletching
upper limb
bow back

Bow and Arrow

In medieval times, *bowmen* carried either a *longbow*, which fired a *shaft* or arrow, or a crossbow, which fired a *bolt* or *quarrel*. Arrows were carried in a *quiver*.

shaftment/butt

bowstring

back
face
bow belly
dip

nocking point

serving
handle/grip

shaft/body

head/pile

lower limb

tip/point

Arrow

recurve

Bow

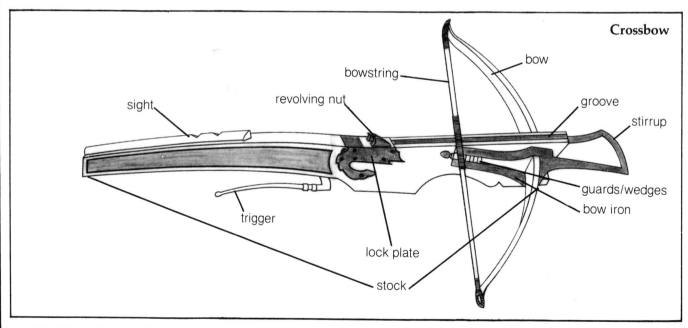

Crossbow

bow

bowstring

revolving nut

sight

groove

stirrup

trigger

guards/wedges
bow iron

lock plate

stock

Cannon and Catapult

Cannonballs fired by *muzzle-loaders* were transported in *caissons* and stacked in trays called *monkeys.* *Loaders* used a *swab* or *sponge* to get rid of residue, a *worm* to remove obstructions, and a *rammer* to drive the *projectile* into the *bore* at the muzzle, or *mouth,* of the cannon. Catapults were used to fire javelinlike shafts a quarter of a mile or more. Ballistas, using the same system of hurling, were employed to heave heavy stones short distances.

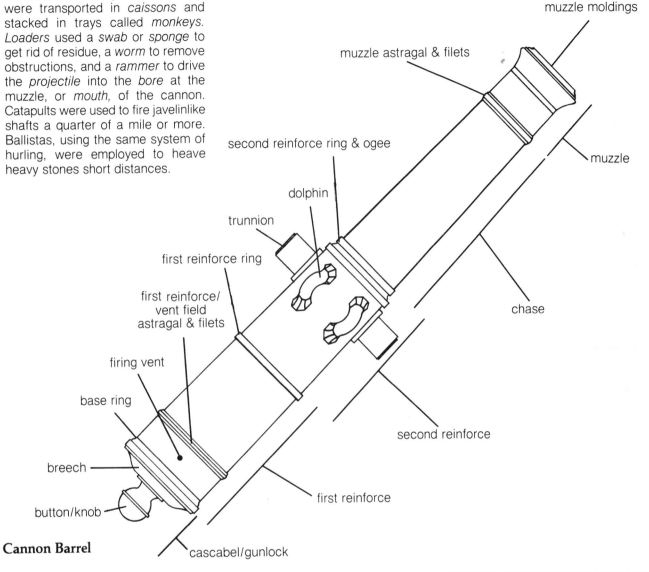

muzzle moldings

muzzle astragal & filets

muzzle

second reinforce ring & ogee

dolphin

chase

trunnion

first reinforce ring

first reinforce/ vent field astragal & filets

firing vent

base ring

second reinforce

breech

button/knob

first reinforce

cascabel/gunlock

Cannon Barrel

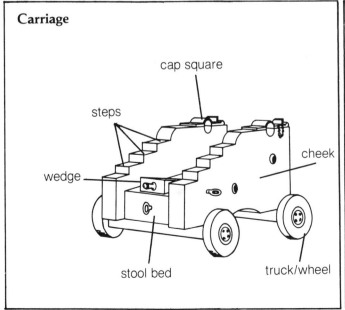

Carriage

cap square

steps

cheek

wedge

stool bed

truck/wheel

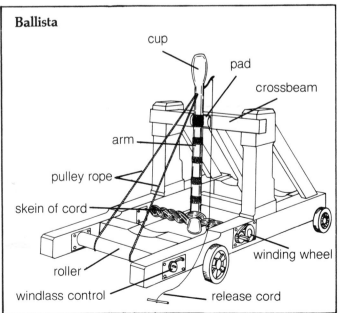

Ballista

cup

pad

crossbeam

arm

pulley rope

skein of cord

winding wheel

roller

windlass control

release cord

Weapons

Shotgun and Rifle

A shotgun fires small *pellets* through a *smooth bore,* while a rifle fires *bullets* through a *rifled barrel.* Shotgun barrels are usually tapered, or *choked,* to constrict the *shot pattern.* Rifles may be carried across the shoulder on a beltlike *sling* connected to the weapon by *sling swivels* and adjusted with bucklelike *claws.*

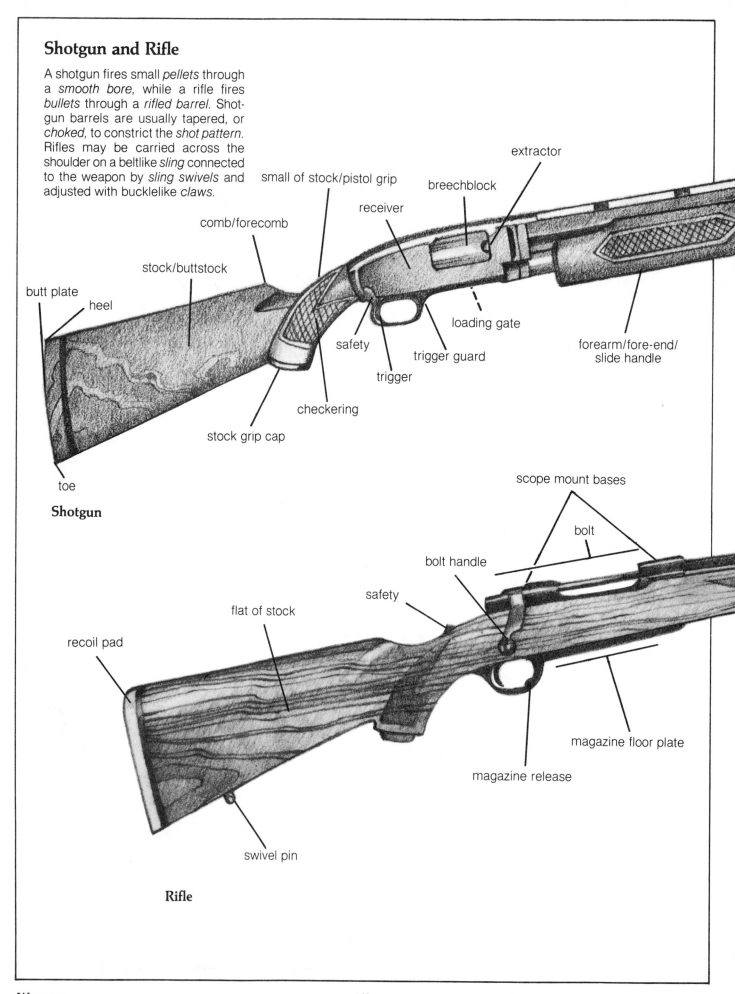

extractor

small of stock/pistol grip

breechblock

receiver

comb/forecomb

stock/buttstock

butt plate

heel

loading gate

forearm/fore-end/
slide handle

safety

trigger guard

trigger

checkering

stock grip cap

toe

Shotgun

scope mount bases

bolt

bolt handle

safety

flat of stock

recoil pad

magazine floor plate

magazine release

swivel pin

Rifle

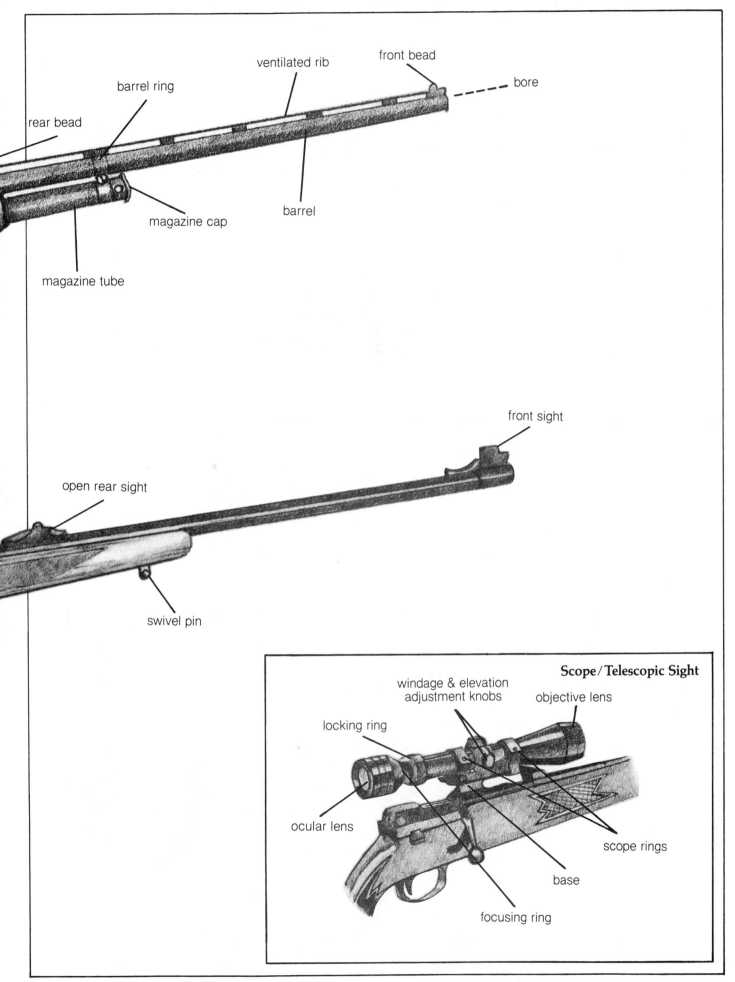

rear bead

barrel ring

ventilated rib

front bead

bore

magazine cap

barrel

magazine tube

front sight

open rear sight

swivel pin

Scope/Telescopic Sight

windage & elevation
adjustment knobs

objective lens

locking ring

ocular lens

scope rings

base

focusing ring

Weapons

Handguns

A *gun*, or *side arm*, is *fired* when a *firing pin* in the *breech* strikes the cartridge primer. A *silencer* dampens the sound of a gun's *discharge*. Grooves in the barrel, called *rifling*, cause a fired bullet to spiral for stability in flight. Cartridges are measured in *calibers*, their diameters in hundredths or thousandths of an inch written in a decimal fraction, or in *millimeters*. Handguns are carried in *holsters*.

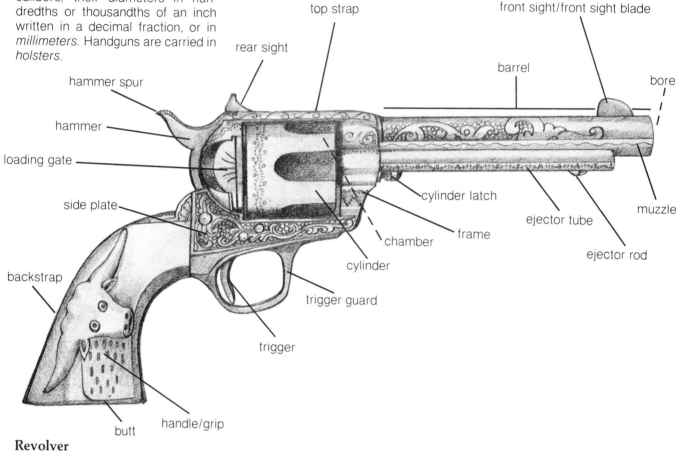

rear sight
top strap
front sight/front sight blade
barrel
bore
hammer spur
hammer
loading gate
cylinder latch
muzzle
side plate
frame
ejector tube
chamber
ejector rod
cylinder
backstrap
trigger guard
trigger
butt
handle/grip

Revolver

Cartridge

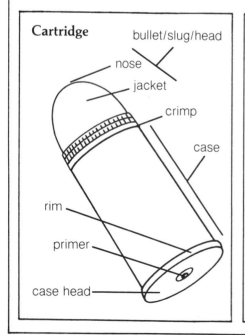

bullet/slug/head
nose
jacket
crimp
case
rim
primer
case head

Automatic Pistol

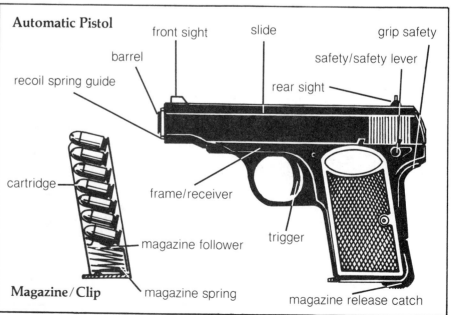

front sight
slide
grip safety
barrel
safety/safety lever
recoil spring guide
rear sight
cartridge
frame/receiver
magazine follower
trigger
magazine spring
Magazine/Clip
magazine release catch

Automatic Weapons

Multi-shot automatic weapons are grouped by weight: light, medium and heavy. The *air-cooled*, medium-weight machine gun shown here can be handled by one man on the ground or on a vehicle when mounted on *pintle mounts.* The light, hand-held automatic rifle is also able to deliver a rapid burst of continuous fire as long as the trigger is depressed. *Ammunition* is fed to it from *handle clips* or *banana clips.*

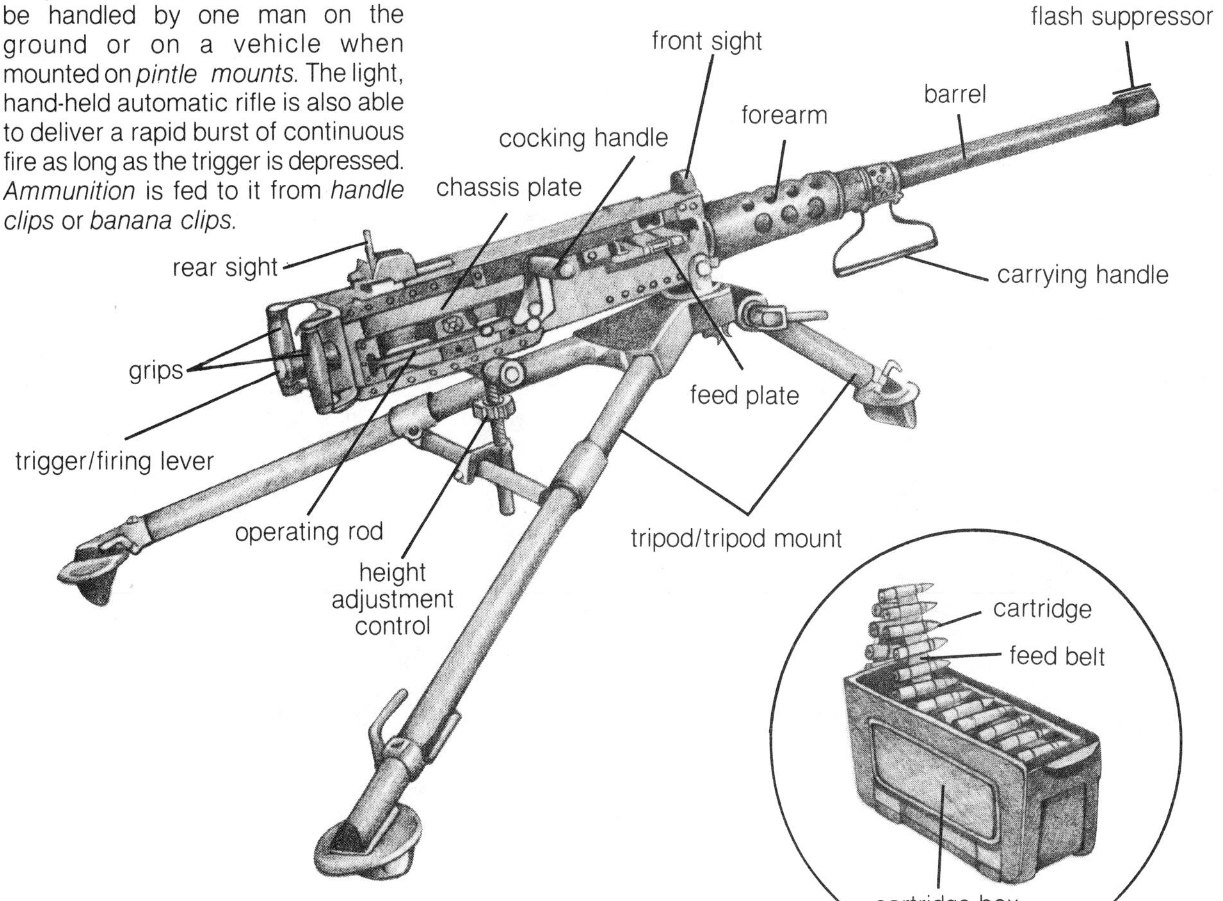

flash suppressor

front sight

forearm

barrel

cocking handle

chassis plate

carrying handle

rear sight

grips

feed plate

trigger/firing lever

operating rod

tripod/tripod mount

height
adjustment
control

cartridge

feed belt

cartridge box

Machine Gun

Ammunition Can

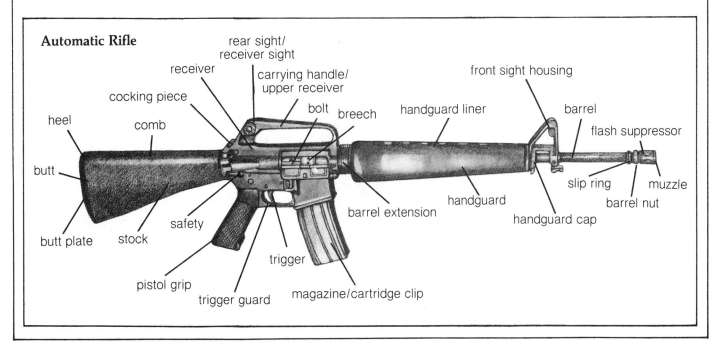

Automatic Rifle

rear sight/
receiver sight

receiver

carrying handle/
upper receiver

front sight housing

cocking piece

bolt   breech

handguard liner

barrel

heel   comb

flash suppressor

butt

safety

barrel extension

handguard

slip ring   muzzle

butt plate   stock

trigger

handguard cap   barrel nut

pistol grip

trigger guard

magazine/cartridge clip

Mortar and Bazooka

A mortar is a *muzzle-loading cannon*, or *midget howitzer*, used to throw *finned projectiles* at high angles. A bazooka is a portable shoulder weapon with an *open-breech smoothbore firing tube* that fires several types of *rockets*.

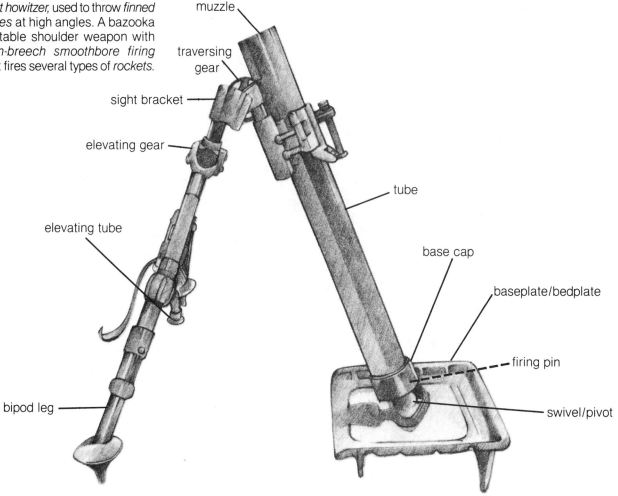

muzzle

traversing gear

sight bracket

elevating gear

elevating tube

tube

base cap

baseplate/bedplate

firing pin

swivel/pivot

bipod leg

Mortar

Bazooka / Rocket Launcher

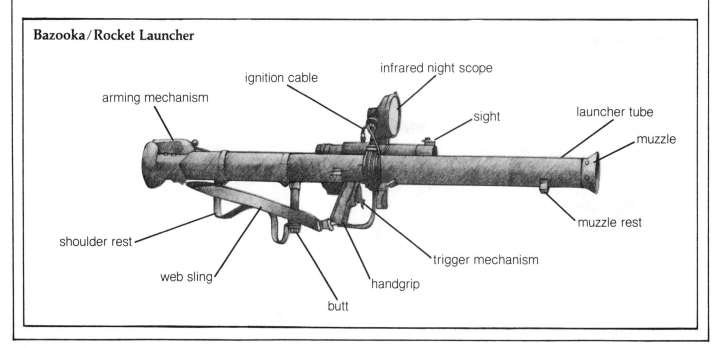

arming mechanism

ignition cable

infrared night scope

sight

launcher tube

muzzle

shoulder rest

web sling

butt

handgrip

trigger mechanism

muzzle rest

Grenade and Mine

When the type of grenade shown here is detonated, it bursts into numerous metal fragments called *shrapnel*. Other types of grenades include *smoke grenades* and *concussion grenades*. Streamlined *rifle grenades* have rear *fins* to provide stability in flight. A *"Molotov cocktail,"* a crude grenade often thrown at tanks to set them on fire, consists of a gasoline-filled bottle with a lighted *wick* at the top.

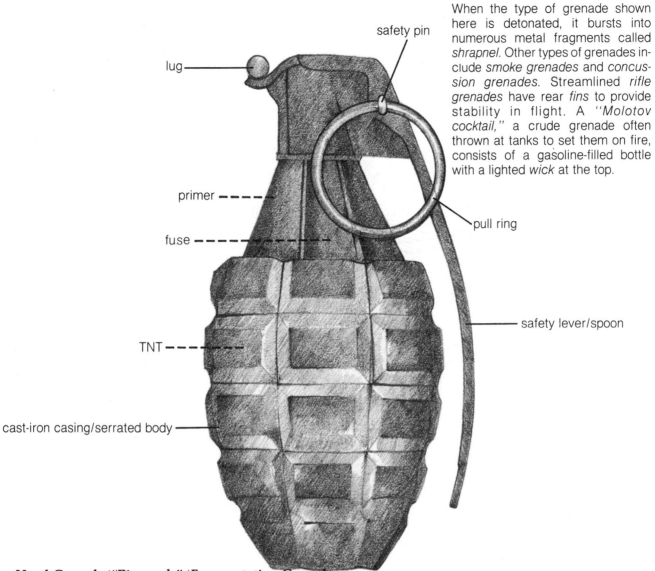

lug
safety pin
primer
fuse
TNT
cast-iron casing/serrated body
pull ring
safety lever/spoon

Hand Grenade/"Pineapple"/Fragmentation Grenade

Land Mine/Antitank Mine

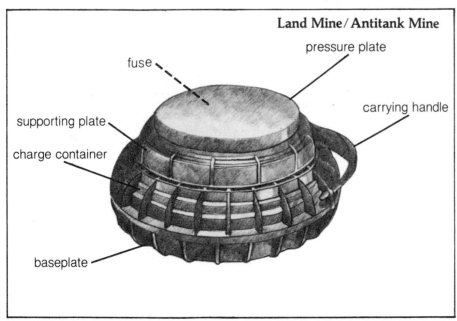

fuse
pressure plate
carrying handle
supporting plate
charge container
baseplate

Weapons

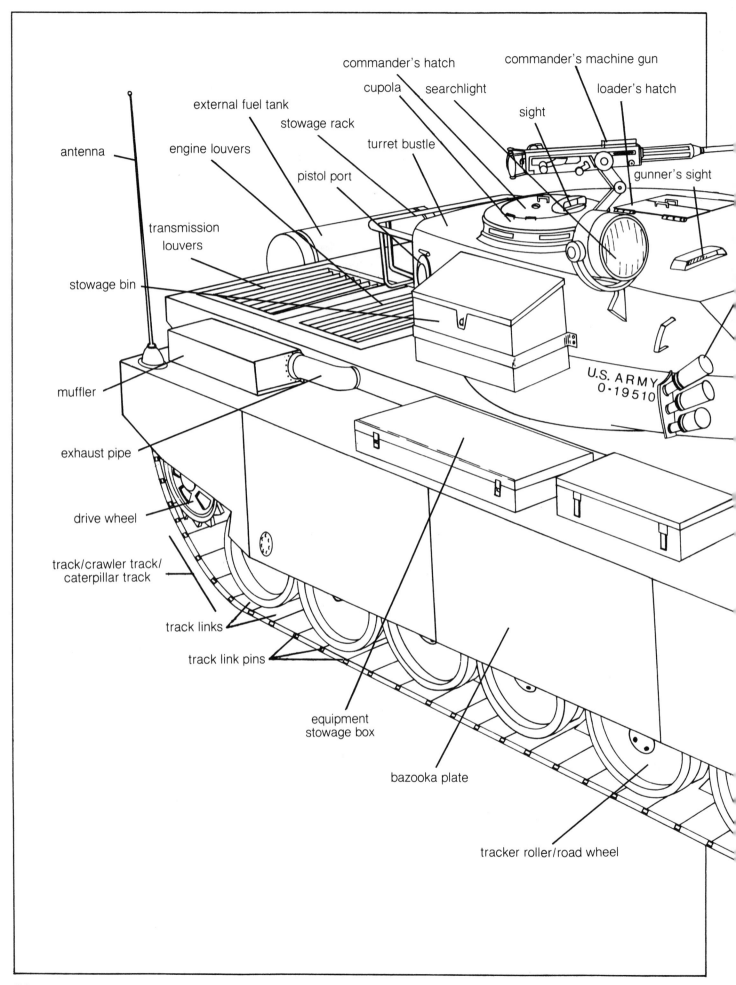

antenna

external fuel tank

engine louvers

stowage rack

commander's hatch

cupola

searchlight

commander's machine gun

loader's hatch

sight

turret bustle

pistol port

gunner's sight

transmission louvers

stowage bin

U.S. ARMY
0-19510

muffler

exhaust pipe

drive wheel

track/crawler track/
caterpillar track

track links

track link pins

equipment
stowage box

bazooka plate

tracker roller/road wheel

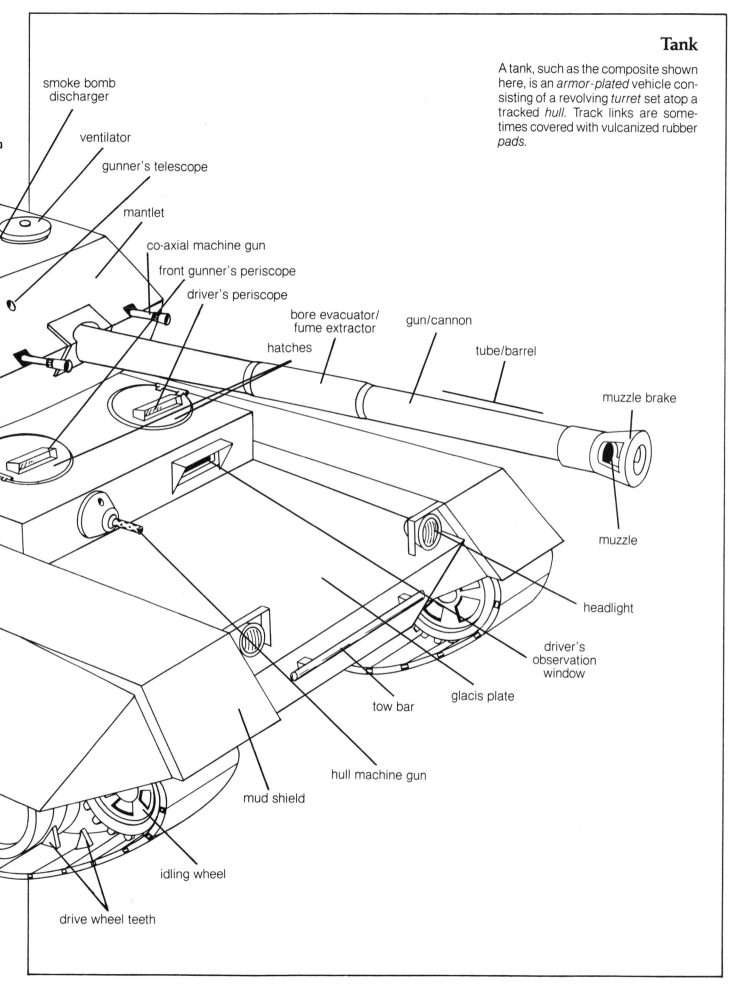

Tank

A tank, such as the composite shown here, is an *armor-plated* vehicle consisting of a revolving *turret* set atop a tracked *hull.* Track links are sometimes covered with vulcanized rubber *pads.*

smoke bomb discharger

ventilator

gunner's telescope

mantlet

co-axial machine gun

front gunner's periscope

driver's periscope

bore evacuator/ fume extractor

gun/cannon

tube/barrel

hatches

muzzle brake

muzzle

headlight

driver's observation window

glacis plate

tow bar

hull machine gun

mud shield

idling wheel

drive wheel teeth

Surface Fighting Ship

Beginning with *dreadnoughts*, or *battleships*, modern surface *warships*, such as this *destroyer*, or *tin can*, have the capability to protect *shipping lanes*, deter invasions or support military operations on land. Today military vessels carry *surface-to-air missiles* and *surface-to-surface missiles*, as well as a range of *defensive guided weapons*. Many are *nuclear-powered*.

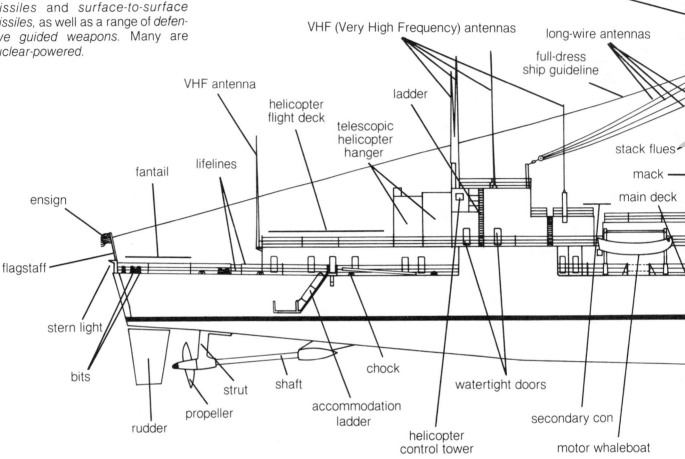

TACAN antenna

VHF (Very High Frequency) antennas

long-wire antennas

full-dress ship guideline

VHF antenna

helicopter flight deck

ladder

stack flues

telescopic helicopter hanger

mack

fantail

lifelines

main deck

ensign

flagstaff

stern light

chock

watertight doors

bits

strut

shaft

accommodation ladder

secondary con

rudder

propeller

helicopter control tower

motor whaleboat

Fighting Ship Types

scale 1:2,600

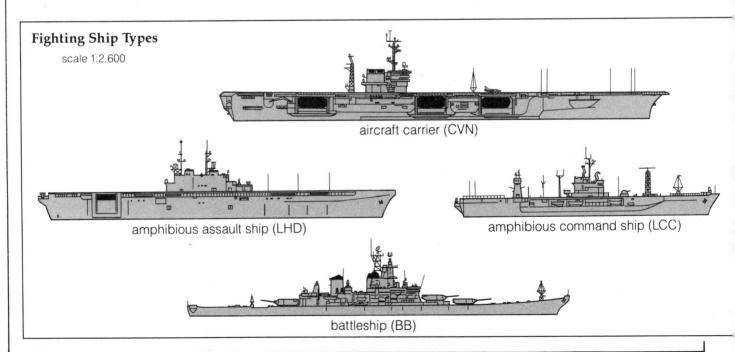

aircraft carrier (CVN)

amphibious assault ship (LHD)

amphibious command ship (LCC)

battleship (BB)

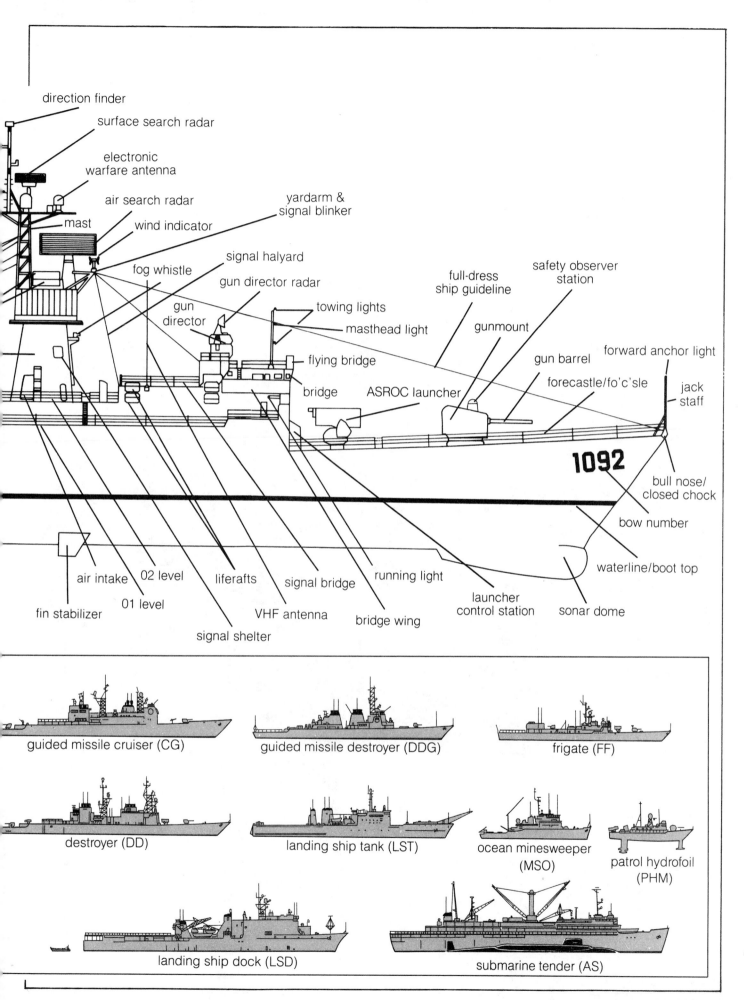

direction finder

surface search radar

electronic
warfare antenna

air search radar

wind indicator

mast

yardarm &
signal blinker

signal halyard

fog whistle

gun director radar

gun
director

towing lights

masthead light

full-dress
ship guideline

safety observer
station

gunmount

gun barrel

forward anchor light

flying bridge

forecastle/fo'c'sle

jack
staff

bridge

ASROC launcher

1092

bull nose/
closed chock

bow number

waterline/boot top

air intake

02 level

01 level

fin stabilizer

liferafts

signal bridge

VHF antenna

signal shelter

running light

bridge wing

launcher
control station

sonar dome

guided missile cruiser (CG)

guided missile destroyer (DDG)

frigate (FF)

destroyer (DD)

landing ship tank (LST)

ocean minesweeper
(MSO)

patrol hydrofoil
(PHM)

landing ship dock (LSD)

submarine tender (AS)

Fighting Ships

Aircraft Carrier

The superstructure on an aircraft carrier, or *flattop*, is called the *island*. On take-off, aircraft are assisted by steam-driven catapults located on the *flight deck* or *angled deck*.

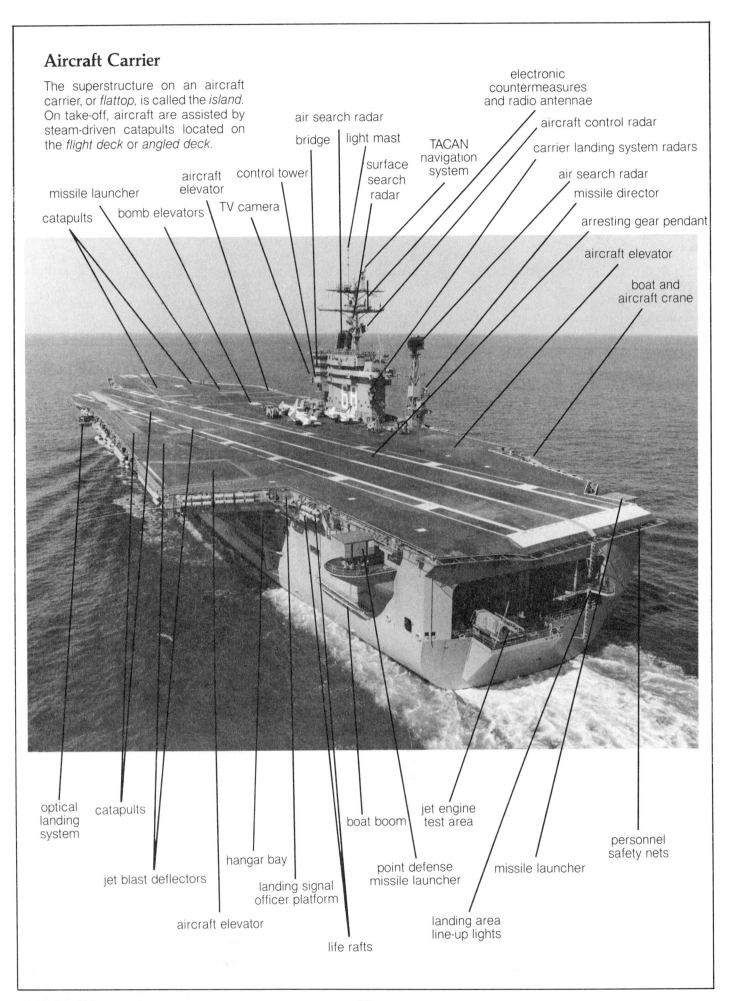

electronic countermeasures and radio antennae

aircraft control radar

carrier landing system radars

air search radar

missile director

arresting gear pendant

aircraft elevator

boat and aircraft crane

TACAN navigation system

air search radar

bridge   light mast

surface search radar

control tower

TV camera

aircraft elevator

bomb elevators

missile launcher

catapults

optical landing system

catapults

jet blast deflectors

hangar bay

aircraft elevator

landing signal officer platform

life rafts

boat boom

jet engine test area

point defense missile launcher

landing area line-up lights

missile launcher

personnel safety nets

Submarine

Submarines, formerly called *U-boats* or *pigboats*, have thick inner *pressure hulls* and lighter *outer hulls*. The space between hulls is divided into several *ballast tanks*, used to control the vessel's buoyancy and trim. The conning tower contains *radio* and *radar antennas* and various *periscopes*, used for observation and navigation. In older submarines the sail also contained a *snorkel tube*. Navigation underwater is accomplished by means of an *inertial guidance system*. In addition to missiles, submarines can carry *torpedoes*.

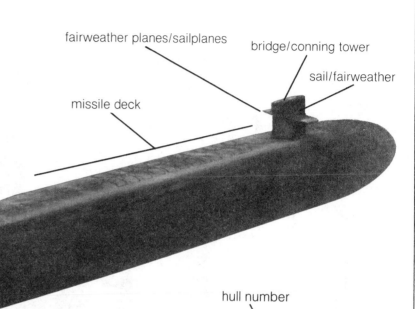

fairweather planes/sailplanes

bridge/conning tower

sail/fairweather

missile deck

rudder

propeller

diving plane

Fleet Ballistic Missile Submarine

hull number

Nuclear-Powered Attack Submarine

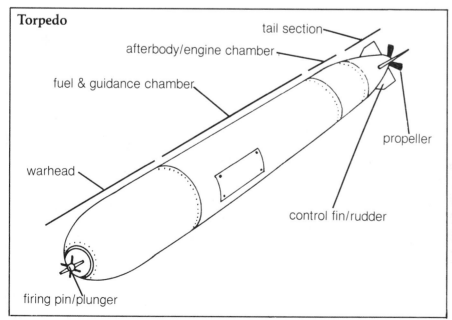

Torpedo

tail section

afterbody/engine chamber

fuel & guidance chamber

warhead

propeller

control fin/rudder

firing pin/plunger

Ballistic Missiles Launch Deck

hatch covers

launch tubes/silos

Submarines

Combat Aircraft

A fighter, such as the one shown here, has an advanced *airframe* with a *variable sweep wing* and a *long-range weapon system*. It is flown at speeds in excess of the speed of sound, or *mach speeds*.

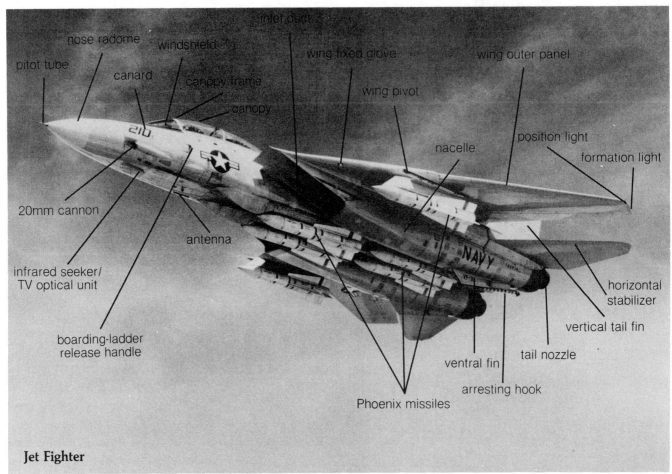

pitot tube
nose radome
canard
windshield
canopy frame
canopy
inlet duct
wing fixed glove
wing pivot
wing outer panel
position light
formation light
nacelle
20mm cannon
antenna
infrared seeker/ TV optical unit
boarding-ladder release handle
Phoenix missiles
ventral fin
arresting hook
tail nozzle
vertical tail fin
horizontal stabilizer

Jet Fighter

Combat Aircraft Wing Types

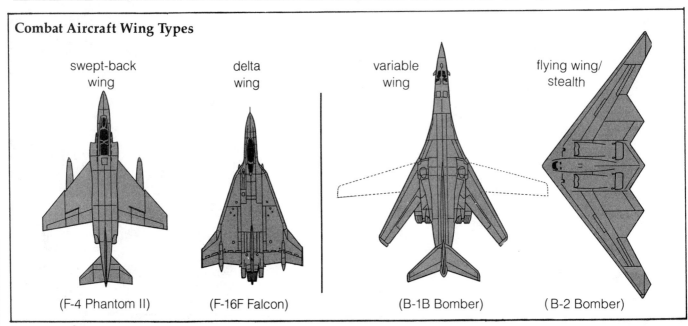

swept-back wing

delta wing

variable wing

flying wing/ stealth

(F-4 Phantom II)

(F-16F Falcon)

(B-1B Bomber)

(B-2 Bomber)

Pilot's Instrument Panel

Behind the *pilot* is a *flight officer*, or *missile control officer*, who monitors the *tactical information display*, *armament* and *electronic counter-armament panel* and *electronic countermeasures panel*.

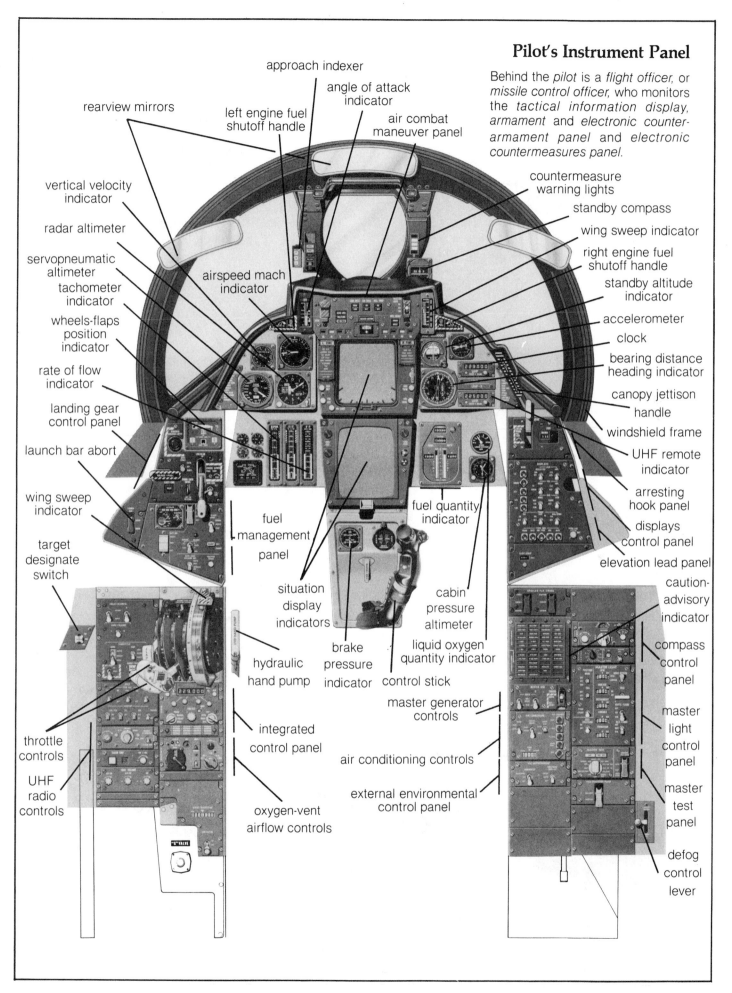

approach indexer

angle of attack indicator

air combat maneuver panel

rearview mirrors

left engine fuel shutoff handle

vertical velocity indicator

radar altimeter

servopneumatic altimeter

tachometer indicator

airspeed mach indicator

wheels-flaps position indicator

rate of flow indicator

landing gear control panel

launch bar abort

wing sweep indicator

target designate switch

throttle controls

UHF radio controls

fuel management panel

situation display indicators

hydraulic hand pump

integrated control panel

oxygen-vent airflow controls

brake pressure indicator

control stick

fuel quantity indicator

cabin pressure altimeter

liquid oxygen quantity indicator

master generator controls

air conditioning controls

external environmental control panel

countermeasure warning lights

standby compass

wing sweep indicator

right engine fuel shutoff handle

standby altitude indicator

accelerometer

clock

bearing distance heading indicator

canopy jettison handle

windshield frame

UHF remote indicator

arresting hook panel

displays control panel

elevation lead panel

caution-advisory indicator

compass control panel

master light control panel

master test panel

defog control lever

Missiles

Unlike the rocket-propelled *anti-ballistic missile*, or *ABM*, seen here, *intercontinental ballistic missiles*, or *ICBMs*, fly outside earth's atmosphere and have no stabilizing fins. *Multiple independently targeted reentry vehicles*, or *MIRVs*, have several warheads which disperse as the missile nears the target. Air- or ground-launched cruise missiles, sometimes powered by jet engines, fly in the lower atmosphere.

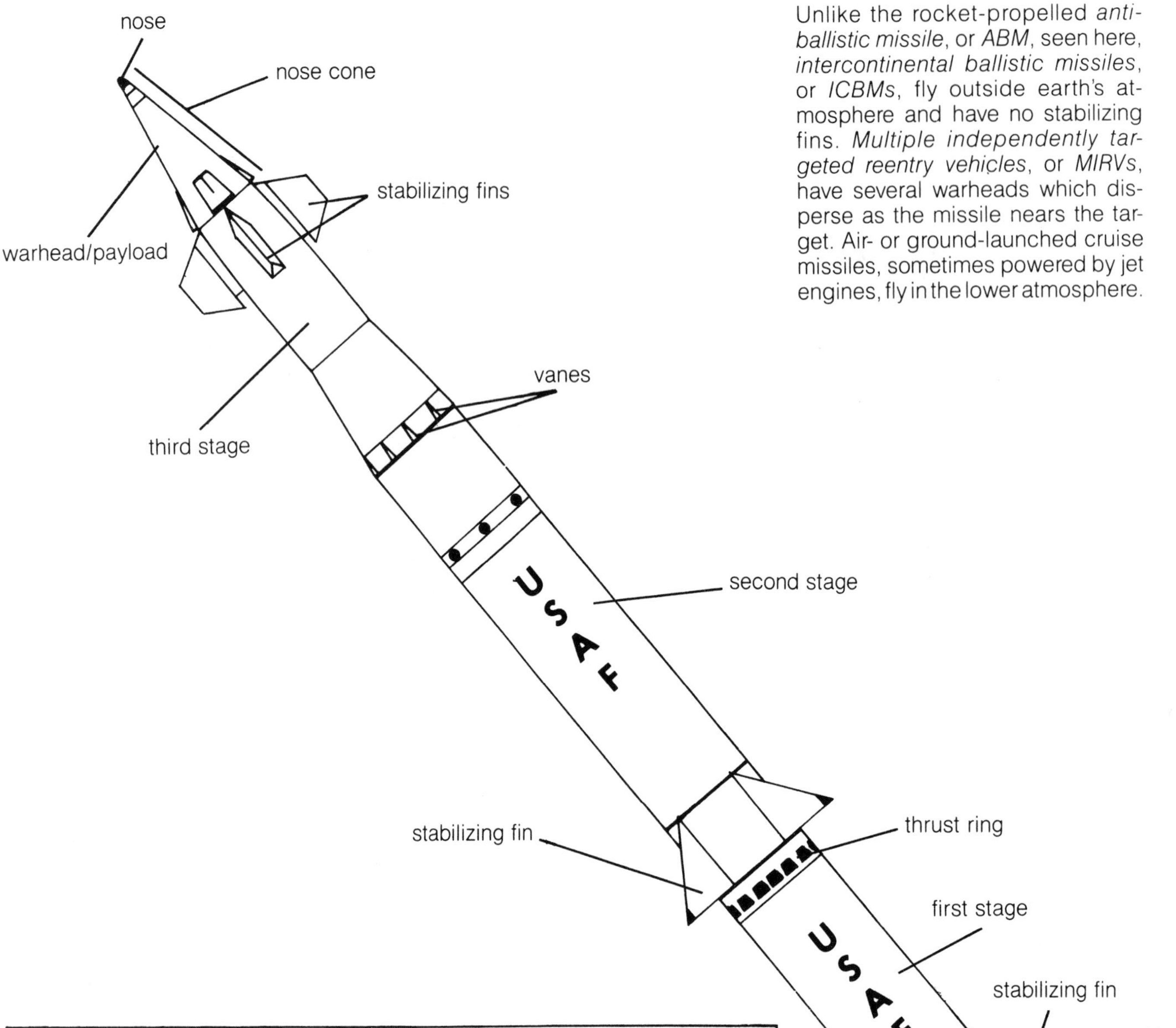

nose

nose cone

stabilizing fins

warhead/payload

vanes

third stage

second stage

U S A F

stabilizing fin

thrust ring

first stage

stabilizing fin

rear skirt

U S A F

thrust ring

expansion nozzles

Missile

Cruise Missile

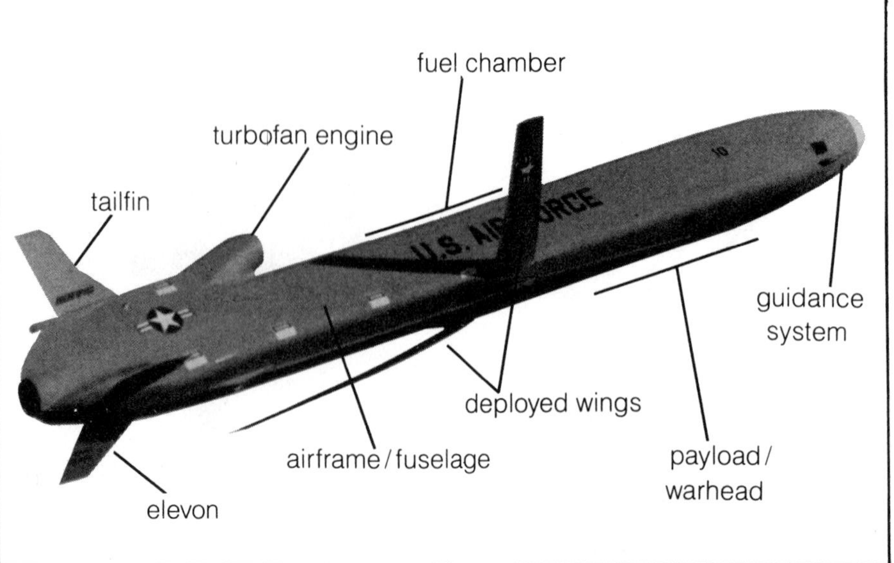

fuel chamber

turbofan engine

tailfin

U.S. AIR FORCE

guidance system

deployed wings

airframe/fuselage

payload/warhead

elevon

Uniforms, Costumes and Ceremonial Attire

The attire presented in this section ranges from vestments and formal dress used on special occasions to dress of distinctive design or fashion worn by members of particular groups. The parts of military or municipal attire, for example, serve to identify not only branch of service but rank and distinction as well.

Garb can be highly stylized or informal. Manchu Court dress, for example, was worn only on formal occasions, whereas the clothes commonly worn by cowboys, dictated by the demands of the profession, was casual.

In addition to the trappings that have come to typify characters in history— a general, pirate, miser, magician—this section also includes clothing used by performers such as clowns, ballet dancers and drum majorettes.

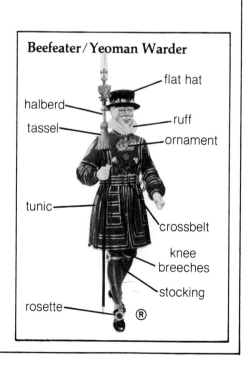

Beefeater / Yeoman Warder

flat hat
halberd
ruff
tassel
ornament
tunic
crossbelt
knee breeches
stocking
rosette

Royal Regalia

In coronations and investitures, a king wears a blunted sword called a *curtein* on his sash. Among a queen's foundation garments, or *underpinnings,* are a *corset, corselet, chemise* and *pantaloons.*

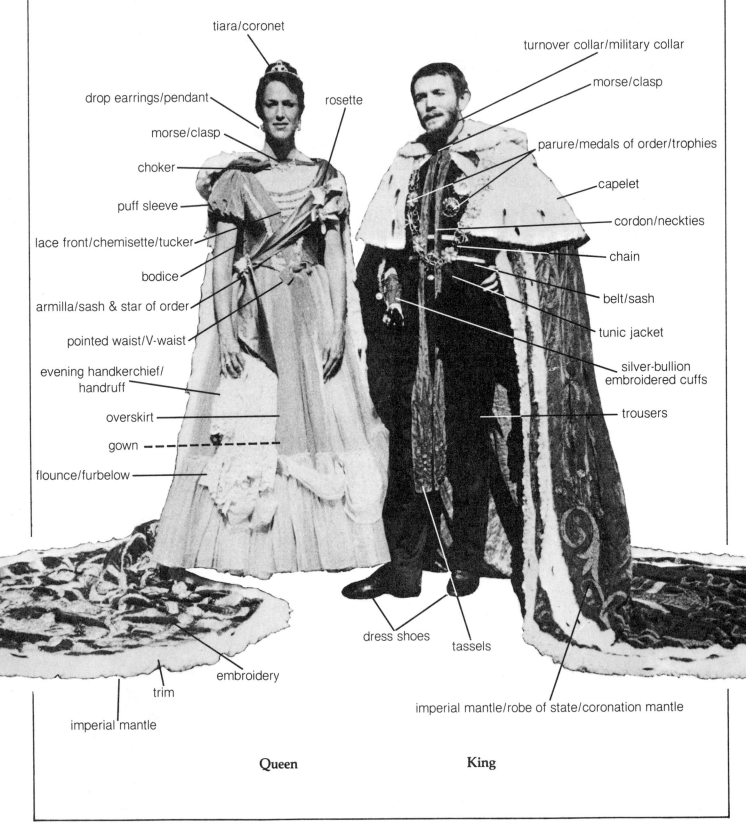

tiara/coronet

drop earrings/pendant

morse/clasp

choker

puff sleeve

lace front/chemisette/tucker

bodice

armilla/sash & star of order

pointed waist/V-waist

evening handkerchief/
handruff

overskirt

gown

flounce/furbelow

rosette

turnover collar/military collar

morse/clasp

parure/medals of order/trophies

capelet

cordon/neckties

chain

belt/sash

tunic jacket

silver-bullion
embroidered cuffs

trousers

dress shoes

tassels

imperial mantle/robe of state/coronation mantle

embroidery

trim

imperial mantle

Queen

King

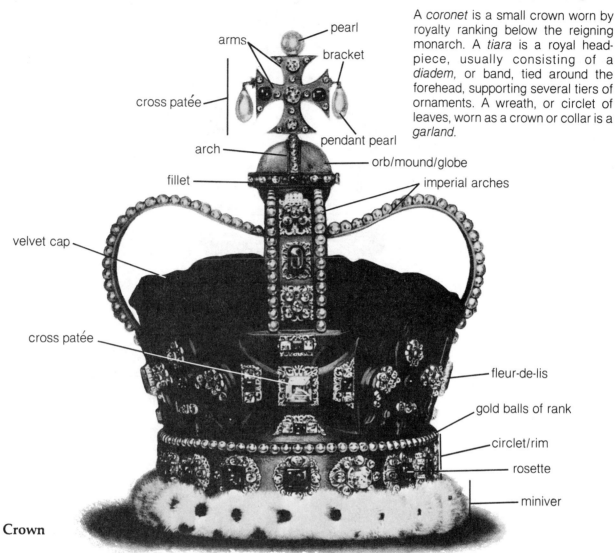

Royal Regalia

A *coronet* is a small crown worn by royalty ranking below the reigning monarch. A *tiara* is a royal head-piece, usually consisting of a *diadem,* or band, tied around the forehead, supporting several tiers of ornaments. A wreath, or circlet of leaves, worn as a crown or collar is a *garland.*

pearl

arms

bracket

cross patée

pendant pearl

arch

orb/mound/globe

fillet

imperial arches

velvet cap

cross patée

fleur-de-lis

gold balls of rank

circlet/rim

rosette

miniver

Crown

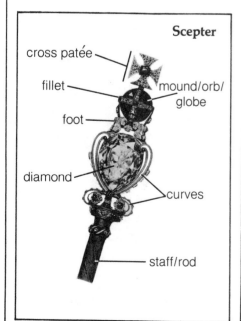

Scepter

cross patée

fillet

mound/orb/ globe

foot

diamond

curves

staff/rod

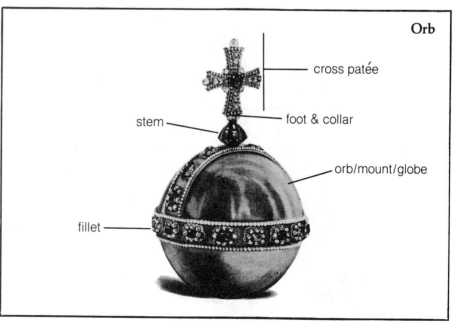

Orb

cross patée

stem

foot & collar

orb/mount/globe

fillet

Royal Vestments

Jewish Ritual Items

During regular service in a *Temple,* or *Synagogue,* excerpts are read by the *Rabbi,* who is assisted in leading the service by a *Cantor,* who sings the liturgy. Their vestments are the same as the rest of the congregation. During morning prayer, a *shel rosh,* similar to the tefillin, is worn on the forehead. Some Jews hang a *mezuzah,* a decorative box containing passages from the Torah, on the doorpost of their homes.

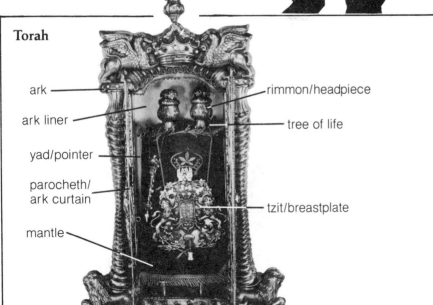

yarmulke/skullcap

tallith/prayer shawl

zecher lechurban/temple memorial bands

sidur/prayer book

zizith/fringes

Prayer Vestments

Torah

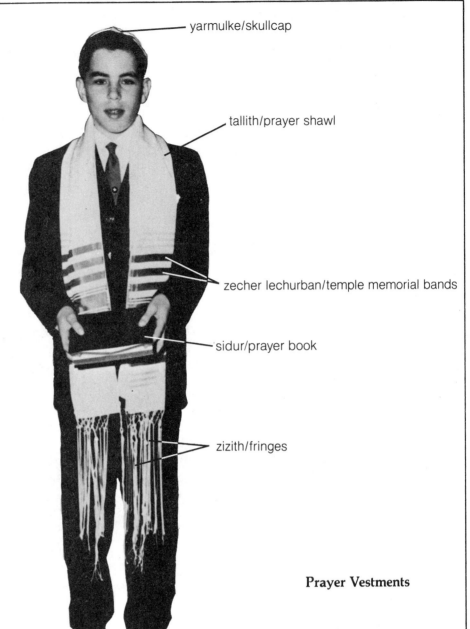

Ner Tamid/eternal light

ark

ark liner

yad/pointer

parocheth/ark curtain

mantle

rimmon/headpiece

tree of life

tzit/breastplate

Tefillin/Phylacteries

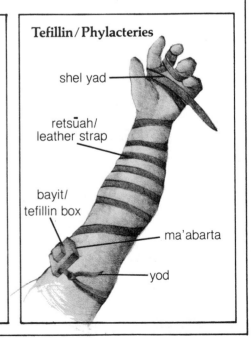

shel yad

retsūah/leather strap

bayit/tefillin box

ma'abarta

yod

Religious Vestments

The small square cap with three corners worn by Roman Catholic clergy is a *biretta*. Ropes, belts or sashes used to keep vestments closed are *cinctures*. Traditionally, the white band worn by nuns to encircle their faces is a *wimple*, while the wide cloth worn below it to cover their necks and shoulders is a *guimpe*. The ring worn by the Pope is the *Ring of the Fisherman*.

simple miter

precious miter

lappet

Roman collar

pectoral cross

stole

cope

cope piping

rochet

cassock

crosier/pastoral staff

dalmatic

Episcopal ring

chasuble

alb

cassock

Bishop　　　　**Cardinal**

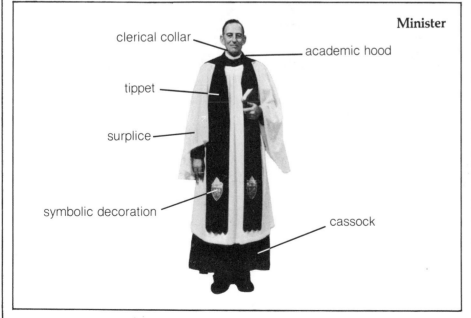

Minister

clerical collar

academic hood

tippet

surplice

symbolic decoration

cassock

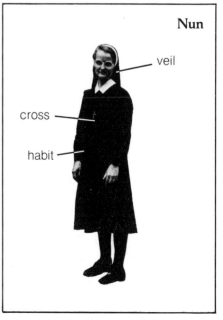

Nun

veil

cross

habit

Religious Attire

Bride and Groom

The bride, wearing white to symbolize purity, and a veil, symbol of modesty, is carrying a fan rather than the more traditional *wedding,* or *bridal, bouquet,* or *nosegay.* Some grooms wear semiformal evening dress at weddings: *tuxedos,* or *tuxes,* which are worn with *cummerbunds,* broad *waistbands, pleated* or *ruffled shirts* with *studs,* and *bow ties.*

picture hat/Gainsborough

veil

appliquéd lace/point d'appliqué

attached bertha/cascade collar/jabot

fan

princess waistline

modified leg-of-mutton sleeve/ modified bishop sleeve

fitted cuff

lace glove

train

scalloped hem

pumps

standing collar

white tie

boutonniere

formal shirt

cutaway coat/ morning coat

waistcoat/vest

French cuff

trousers

tail

Bridal Dress/Gown

Men's Formal Attire

Domestic Staff

Attire worn by male servants is called *livery*. Maids often wear a white linen bib attached at the neck and descending to just above the waist, as well as a knee-length or ankle-length apron.

standing collar / wing collar

four-in-hand tie

cook's cap

cutaway coat / morning coat

shirt-waist dress / shirt dress

knee-length apron

striped morning trousers

Butler

Cook

Maid

Chauffeur

serving cap

replaceable collar / detachable collar

bib

lace cuff

black tie

roll-collar shirt

black suit

Servants' Attire

Cowboy and Indian

On the range, cowboys, *cow punchers,* or *buckaroos,* carried *oilskin slickers,* a *tarp,* and heavy cotton or wool quilts to make up a *bedroll, crumb incubator, shakedown,* or *fleatrap.* Bullets, carried in *loops* on *cartridge belts,* were known as *blue whistlers* or *lead plums.* A cowboy's *ten-gallon hat* was held in place in a wind by buckskin thongs known as *bonnet strings.*

Members of most Indian tribes wore *leggings* and *moccasins.* Many decorated their faces with *war paint* prior to battle. Indians in the East shaved their heads except for a ridge of hair in the middle called a *roach.*

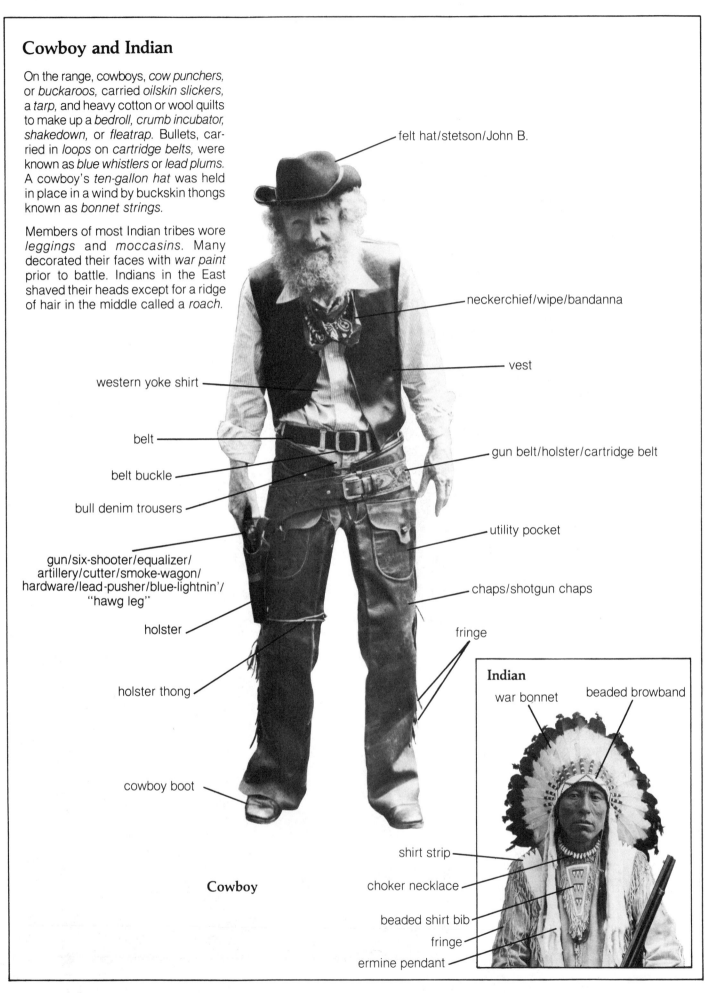

felt hat/stetson/John B.

neckerchief/wipe/bandanna

vest

western yoke shirt

belt

gun belt/holster/cartridge belt

belt buckle

bull denim trousers

utility pocket

gun/six-shooter/equalizer/
artillery/cutter/smoke-wagon/
hardware/lead-pusher/blue-lightnin'/
"hawg leg"

chaps/shotgun chaps

holster

fringe

holster thong

cowboy boot

Cowboy

Indian

war bonnet

beaded browband

shirt strip

choker necklace

beaded shirt bib

fringe

ermine pendant

Native Dress

Romans wore full-length, loose-fitting robes called *togas.* East Indian women wear *sarongs,* but Indian (Hindu) women wear *saris.* An ankle-length Middle East garment with long sleeves and a waist sash is called a *caftan.* The loose-fitting, sleeveless robes worn by Arabs are called *abas.*

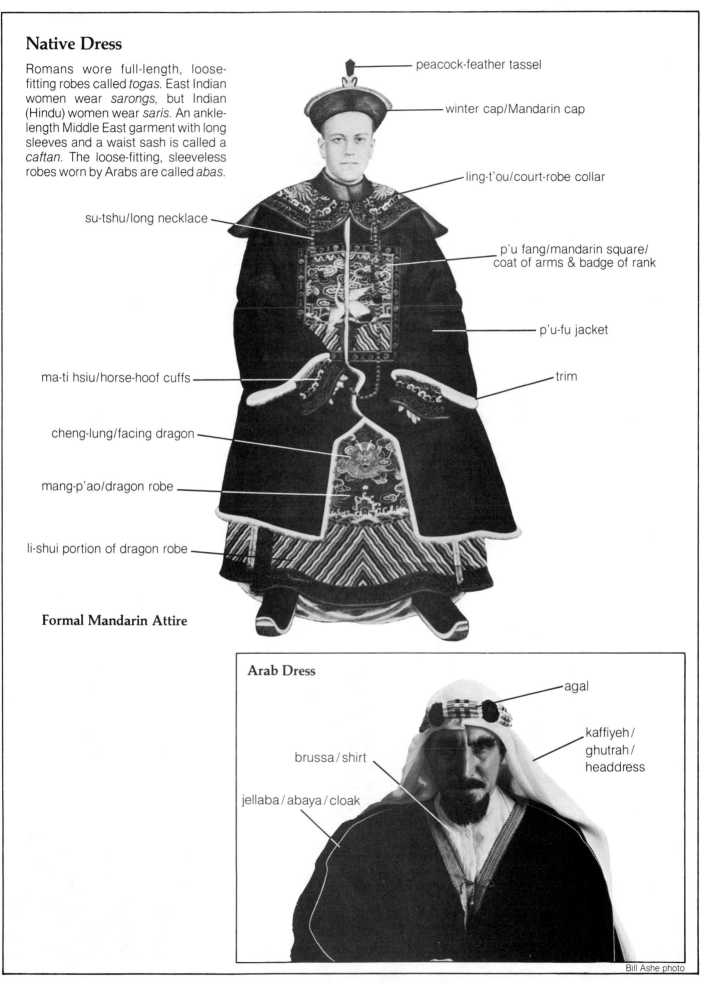

peacock-feather tassel

winter cap/Mandarin cap

ling-t'ou/court-robe collar

su-tshu/long necklace

p'u fang/mandarin square/ coat of arms & badge of rank

p'u-fu jacket

ma-ti hsiu/horse-hoof cuffs

trim

cheng-lung/facing dragon

mang-p'ao/dragon robe

li-shui portion of dragon robe

Formal Mandarin Attire

Arab Dress

agal

kaffiyeh/ ghutrah/ headdress

brussa/shirt

jellaba/abaya/cloak

Bill Ashe photo

Native Attire

Historical Costumes

Many characters in popular lore and history have become identified or associated with the clothing they wear. Other military attire worn by *Revolutionary* officers included a tunic, a plain jacket with a stiff collar, and a particularly heavy overcoat called a *greatcoat*.

cockade

cocked hat

epaulette

infantry button

wig

lapel

crossbelt

frock coat

embroidered buttonholes

button-down cuff

waistcoat

sword

gloves

scabbard

knee britches

coat skirt

boot

Revolutionary War General

Jim Leighton

eyepatch

tricorne

crossbelt

top hat

Franklin glasses

steeple-crowned hat

muffler

magic wand

scarf

robe

fingerless glove

pistol

purse

Pirate

photo by BODI

Miser

Jim Vaum

Wizard

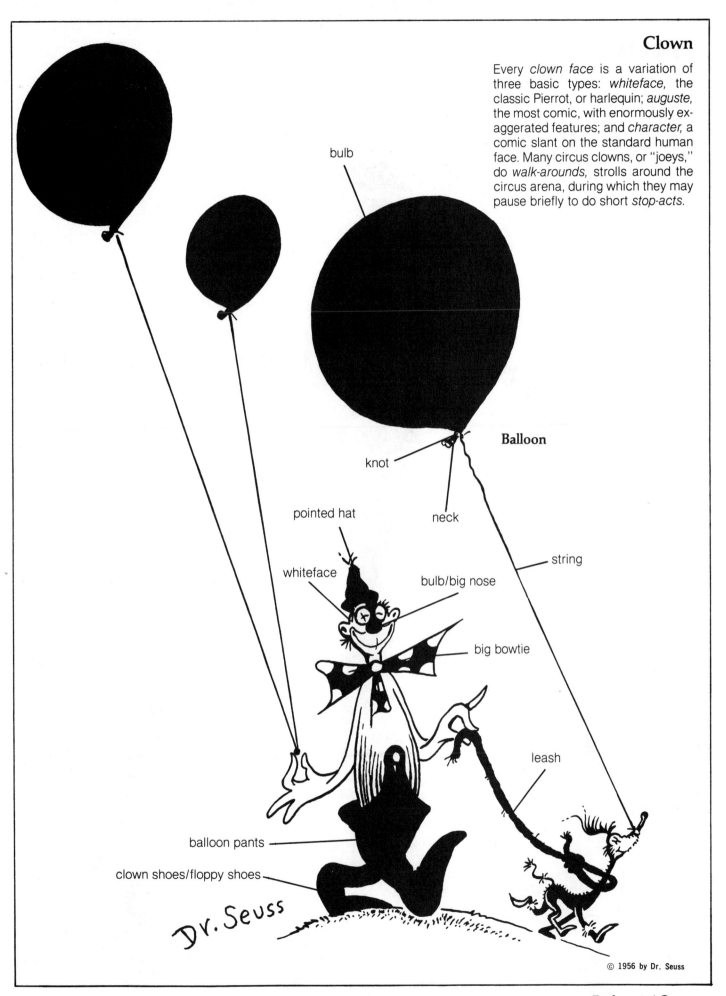

Clown

Every *clown face* is a variation of three basic types: *whiteface,* the classic Pierrot, or harlequin; *auguste,* the most comic, with enormously exaggerated features; and *character,* a comic slant on the standard human face. Many circus clowns, or "joeys," do *walk-arounds,* strolls around the circus arena, during which they may pause briefly to do short *stop-acts.*

bulb

Balloon

knot

neck

string

pointed hat

whiteface

bulb/big nose

big bowtie

leash

balloon pants

clown shoes/floppy shoes

Dr. Seuss

© 1956 by Dr. Seuss

Performers' Costumes

Ballet Dancer

The toeshoes worn by this *ballerina* are satin covered. Cloth mache has replaced wooden box toes. A short skirt of layered net often worn by female dancers is called a *tutu*.

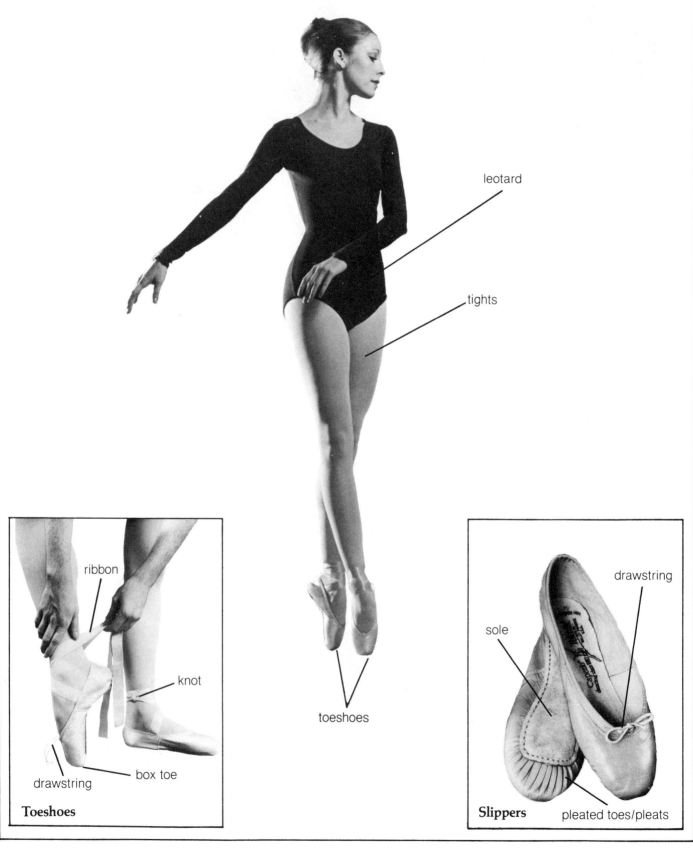

leotard

tights

toeshoes

Toeshoes

ribbon

knot

drawstring

box toe

Slippers

drawstring

sole

pleated toes/pleats

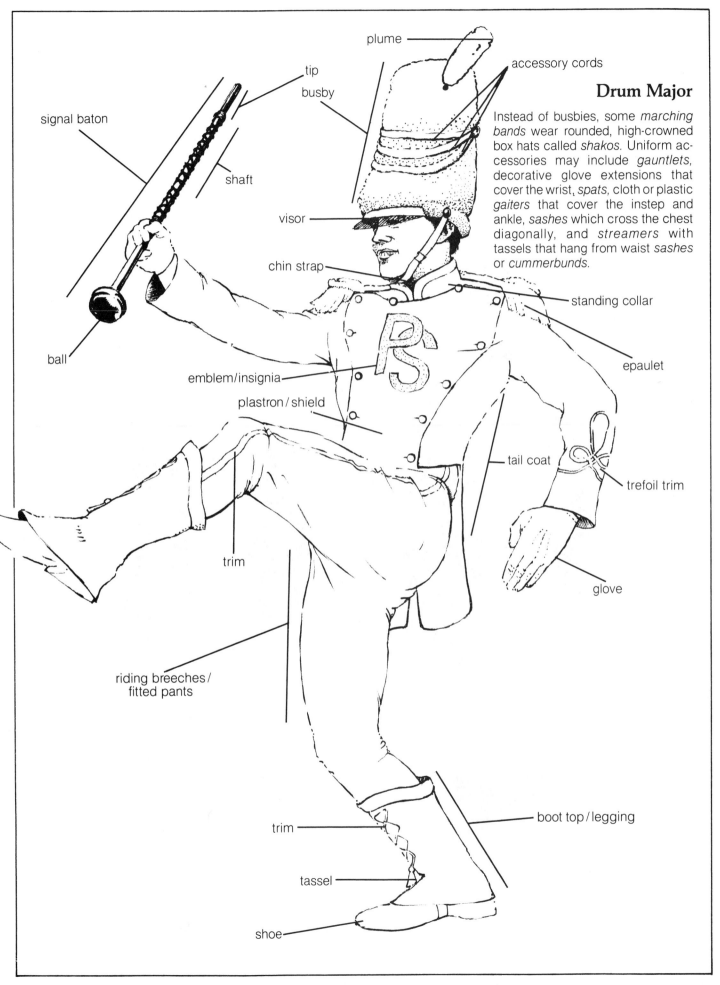

plume

accessory cords

tip

busby

Drum Major

Instead of busbies, some *marching bands* wear rounded, high-crowned box hats called *shakos*. Uniform accessories may include *gauntlets*, decorative glove extensions that cover the wrist, *spats*, cloth or plastic *gaiters* that cover the instep and ankle, *sashes* which cross the chest diagonally, and *streamers* with tassels that hang from waist *sashes* or *cummerbunds*.

signal baton

shaft

visor

chin strap

standing collar

ball

epaulet

emblem/insignia

plastron/shield

tail coat

trefoil trim

trim

glove

riding breeches/ fitted pants

boot top/legging

trim

tassel

shoe

495

Military Uniforms

The *uniform of the day* is worn for the season, day or occasion. A cloth band worn around the arm above the elbow, such as the one worn by *Military Police,* or *MPs,* is a *brassard.* A leather belt for a dress uniform is a *Sam Browne, or garrison, belt.* Service ribbons are worn on a *ribbon bar.* The only *neck decoration* awarded to members of the armed services is the *Medal of Honor.*

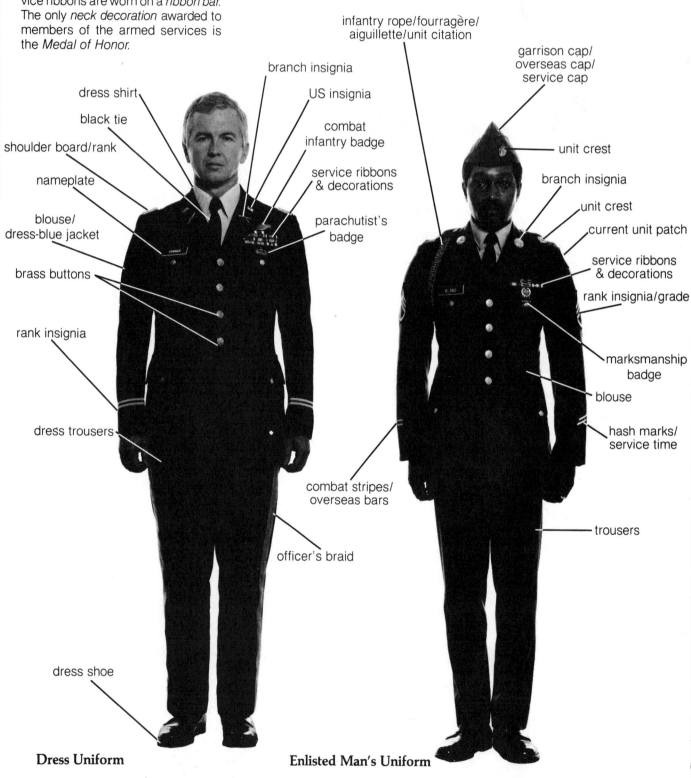

infantry rope/fourragère/ aiguillette/unit citation

branch insignia

US insignia

garrison cap/ overseas cap/ service cap

dress shirt

black tie

combat infantry badge

unit crest

shoulder board/rank

service ribbons & decorations

branch insignia

nameplate

parachutist's badge

unit crest

current unit patch

blouse/ dress-blue jacket

service ribbons & decorations

brass buttons

rank insignia/grade

rank insignia

marksmanship badge

blouse

dress trousers

hash marks/ service time

combat stripes/ overseas bars

trousers

officer's braid

dress shoe

Dress Uniform

Enlisted Man's Uniform

Military Uniforms

An *infantryman,* or "grunt," carries a *rain poncho* on his ammunition belt. A sailor, "swab," or " gob," may wear a *watch cap, leggings* and a *jersey* instead of a jumper. Sailors aboard ship keep their clothing in *seabags.*

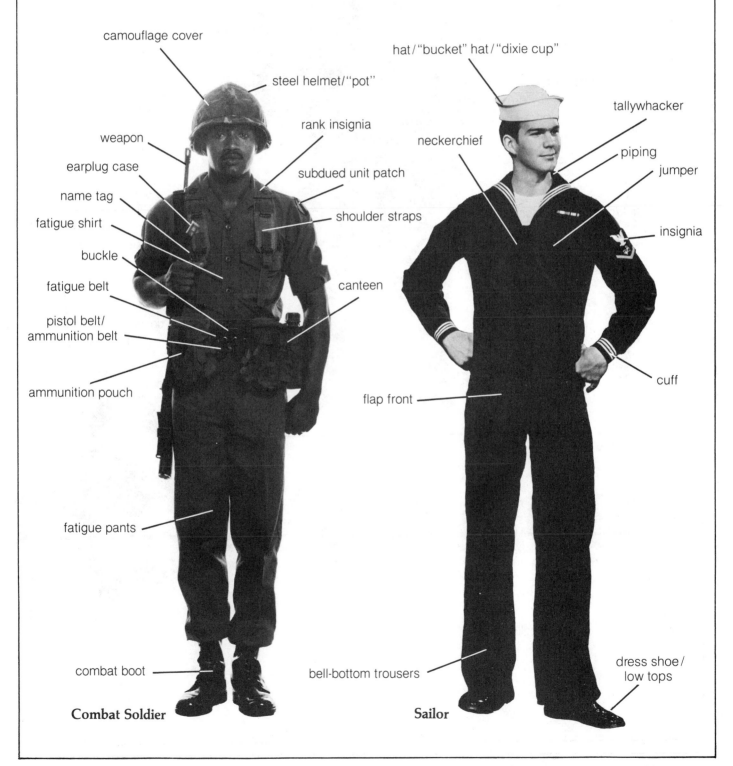

camouflage cover

hat/"bucket" hat/"dixie cup"

steel helmet/"pot"

tallywhacker

rank insignia

weapon

neckerchief

piping

earplug case

subdued unit patch

jumper

name tag

fatigue shirt

shoulder straps

insignia

buckle

fatigue belt

canteen

pistol belt/
ammunition belt

cuff

ammunition pouch

flap front

fatigue pants

combat boot

bell-bottom trousers

dress shoe/
low tops

Combat Soldier

Sailor

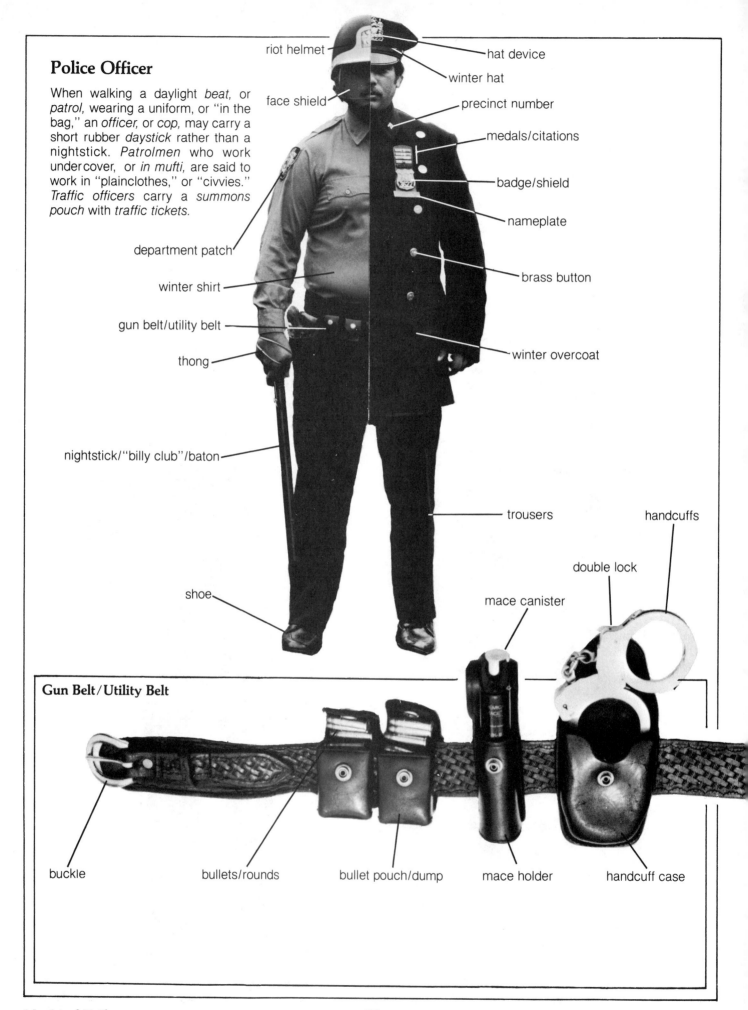

Police Officer

When walking a daylight *beat*, or *patrol*, wearing a uniform, or "in the bag," an *officer*, or *cop*, may carry a short rubber *daystick* rather than a nightstick. *Patrolmen* who work under cover, or *in mufti*, are said to work in "plainclothes," or "civvies." *Traffic officers* carry a *summons pouch* with *traffic tickets*.

riot helmet

hat device

winter hat

face shield

precinct number

medals/citations

badge/shield

nameplate

department patch

winter shirt

brass button

gun belt/utility belt

winter overcoat

thong

nightstick/"billy club"/baton

trousers

handcuffs

double lock

mace canister

shoe

Gun Belt/Utility Belt

buckle

bullets/rounds

bullet pouch/dump

mace holder

handcuff case

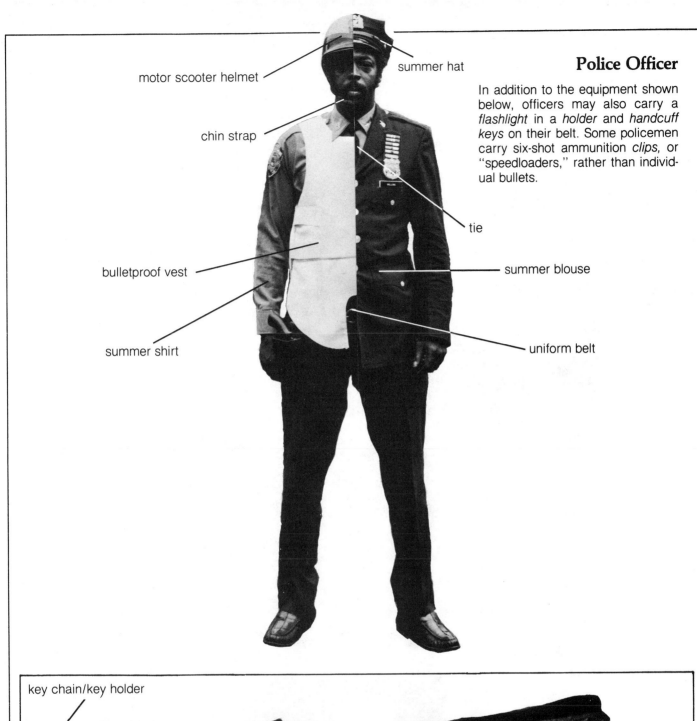

motor scooter helmet

summer hat

chin strap

Police Officer

In addition to the equipment shown below, officers may also carry a *flashlight* in a *holder* and *handcuff keys* on their belt. Some policemen carry six-shot ammunition *clips*, or "speedloaders," rather than individual bullets.

tie

bulletproof vest

summer blouse

summer shirt

uniform belt

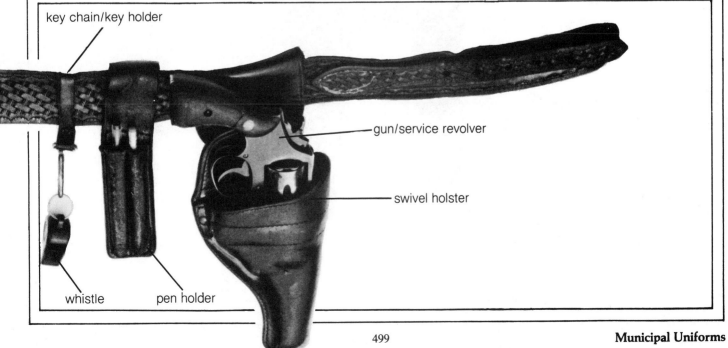

key chain/key holder

gun/service revolver

swivel holster

whistle

pen holder

Municipal Uniforms

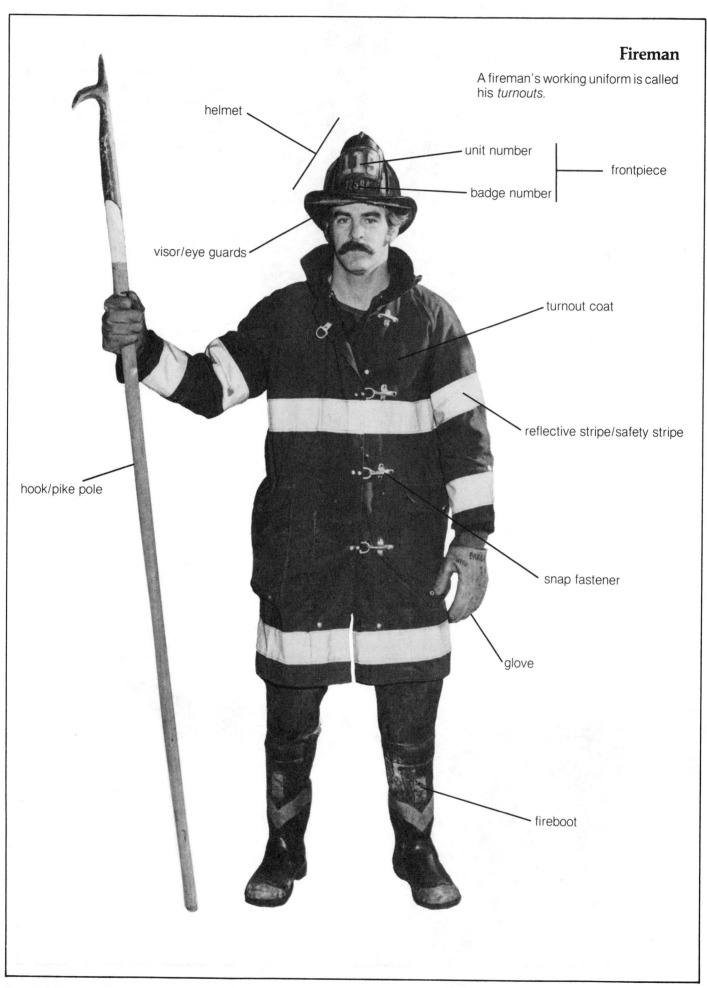

Fireman

A fireman's working uniform is called his *turnouts*.

helmet

unit number

frontpiece

badge number

visor/eye guards

turnout coat

reflective stripe/safety stripe

hook/pike pole

snap fastener

glove

fireboot

Signs and Symbols

While signs and symbols take the place of language or are used to represent meaning, either by suggestion, relationship or association, many have parts for which there are proper names. A flag is used as a sign of a nation, for example, or as a symbol of patriotism, yet it has distinctive components which are identifiable.

Other signs, such as editing and proofreading marks, also included in this section, are used to convey instructions, while sign language is a set of gestures used as a substitute for words or letters.

The fields of science, business and industry have all devised signs whose meanings have legal as well as instructional implications, and the world of transportation is largely controlled by traffic signs. Even hobos, whose pictographs appear here, use pictorial signs instead of written language to communicate messages.

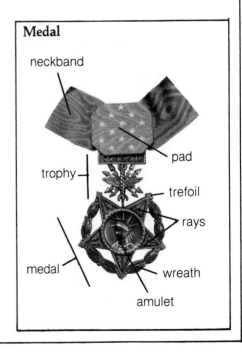

Medal

neckband

pad

trophy

trefoil

rays

medal

wreath

amulet

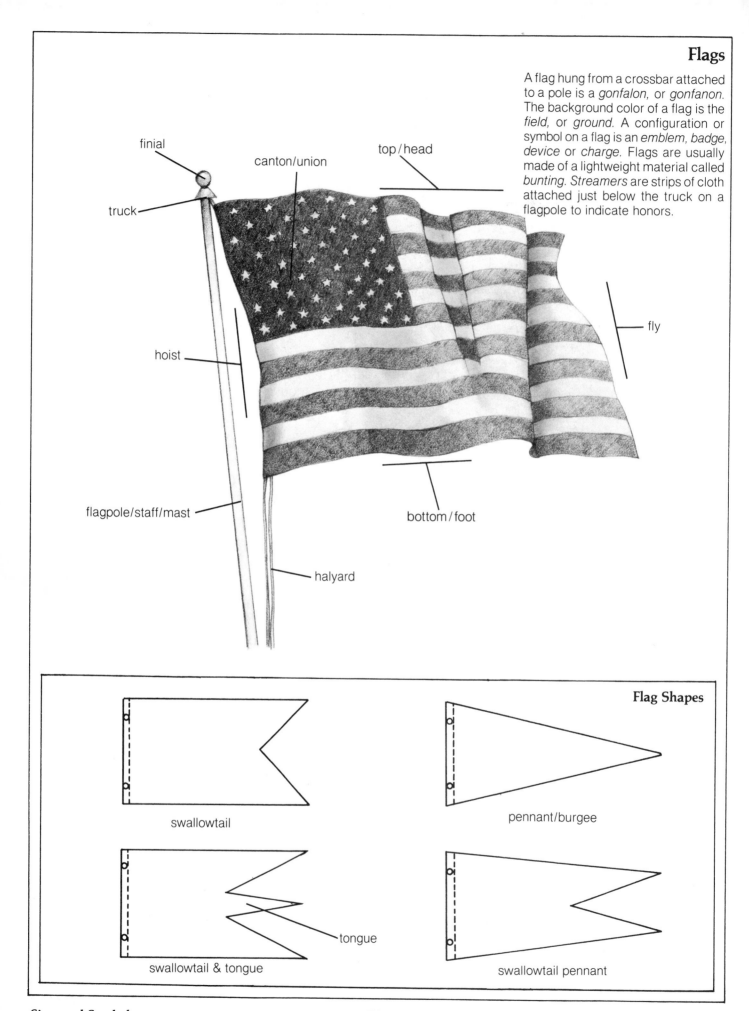

Flags

A flag hung from a crossbar attached to a pole is a *gonfalon*, or *gonfanon*. The background color of a flag is the *field*, or *ground*. A configuration or symbol on a flag is an *emblem*, *badge*, *device* or *charge*. Flags are usually made of a lightweight material called *bunting*. *Streamers* are strips of cloth attached just below the truck on a flagpole to indicate honors.

finial

canton/union

top/head

truck

hoist

fly

flagpole/staff/mast

bottom/foot

halyard

Flag Shapes

swallowtail

pennant/burgee

tongue

swallowtail & tongue

swallowtail pennant

Coat of Arms

Technically, a coat of arms, or *achievement of arms*, consists only of a shield, the surface of which is called the *field*. Everything surrounding a shield is *exterior decoration*. The entire grouping is known as *armorial achievement*. To the wearer's left but the viewer's right is the *sinister side*. The opposite side is the *dexter side*.

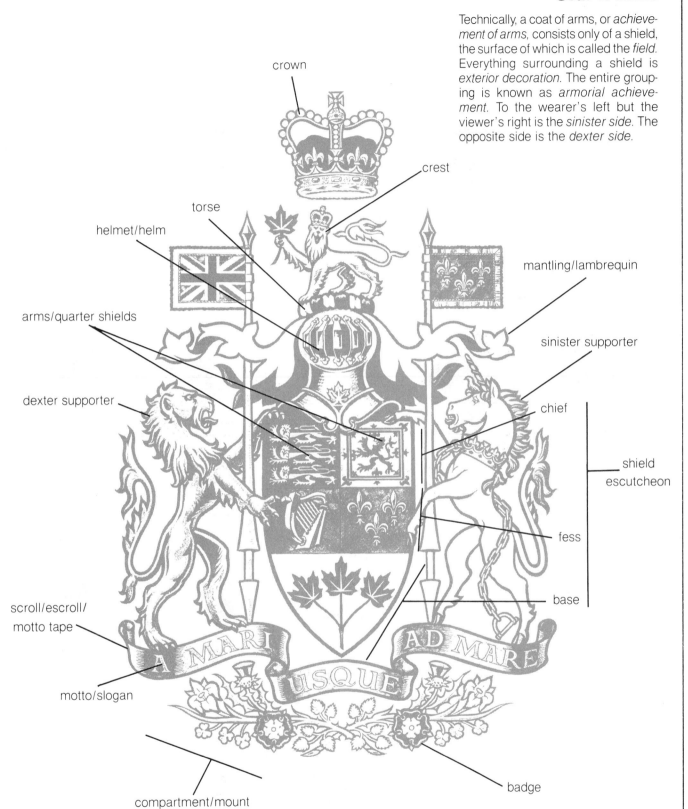

crown

crest

torse

helmet/helm

mantling/lambrequin

arms/quarter shields

sinister supporter

dexter supporter

chief

shield
escutcheon

fess

base

scroll/escroll/
motto tape

motto/slogan

badge

compartment/mount

A MARI

USQUE

AD MARE

Signs and Symbols

stop	yield	one way	one-way traffic/ do not enter	railroad crossing

no bicycles	no trucks	no U turn	no right turn	no left turn

interstate route	U.S. route	state route	trail	bike route

picnic area	camping	trailer park	hospital	telephone

Road Signs

With the exception of *route signs*, which are different shapes and colors, road signs are color-coded: red signs are *prohibit movement signs;* yellow are *warning signs;* white are *regulatory signs;* orange are *construction signs;* blue are *service signs;* green are *guide signs.* Octagonal red signs are used exclusively for *stop signs.* Rectangular signs with white letters on a green background are *destination signs.*

 signal ahead	two-way traffic	no-passing zone	divided highway ends	 merge
 merge left	winding road	slippery when wet	 hill	 school crossing
 pedestrian crossing	 bicycle crossing	farm machinery	 cattle crossing	 deer crossing

Signs and Symbols

Public Signs

Pasigraphy is a universal written language that uses signs and symbols rather than words, whereas *pictographs* can represent an object as well as a thought. A symbol or character that represents a word, syllable or phoneme is a *phonogram*. A symbolic representation of an idea rather than a word is an *ideogram* or *ideograph*.

 first aid

 information

 handicapped

 hotel/motel

 restaurant

 coffee shop

 bar

 no smoking

 toilets

 taxi stand

 bus transportation

 air transportation

 car rental

 rail transportation

 elevator

 baggage check-in

 baggage claim

 customs

 lost and found

 telephone

 mail

 gas station

 no parking

 parking

 mechanic

 picnic area

 campfires

 bicycle trail

 hiking trail

 playground

 launching ramp

 horse trail

 no entry

A gesture, the movement of the head, arm, hand or body to express reaction, emotion, opinion or a concept, can be one of friendship (as in a kiss, a hug, nose rubbing, back slapping) or one of anger (with a clenched fist or a raised middle finger).

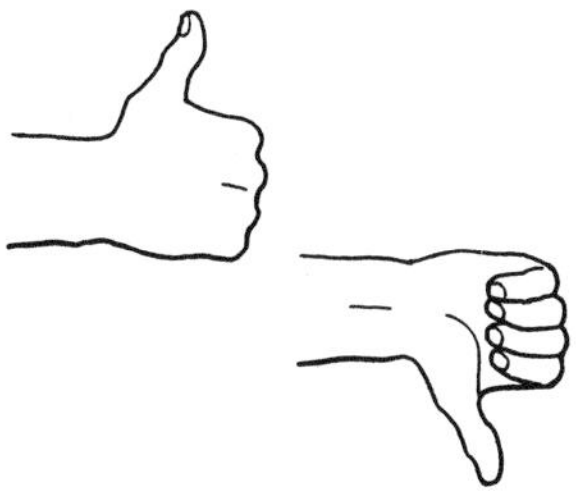

approval   disapproval

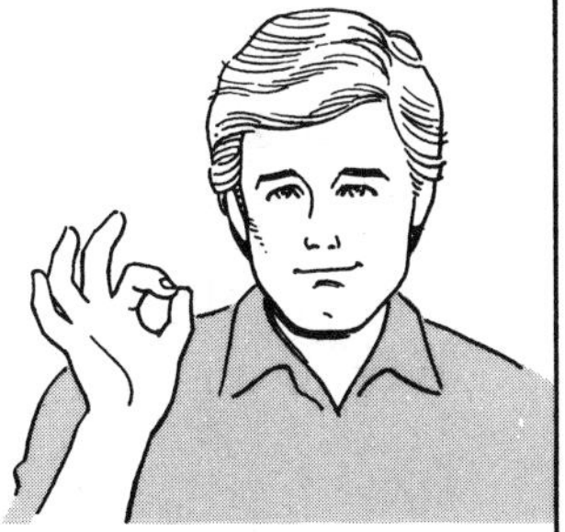

everything's OK / perfection

you're out / hitch-hiking

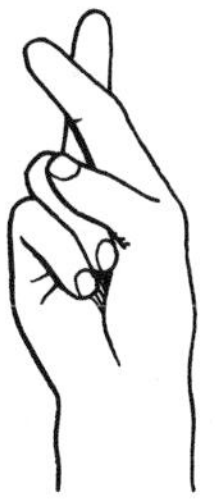

for good luck

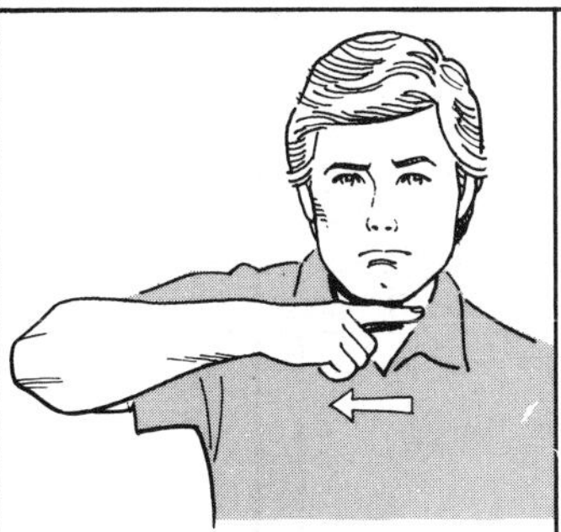

the end / cut it / "throat-cutting"

blunder / faux pas

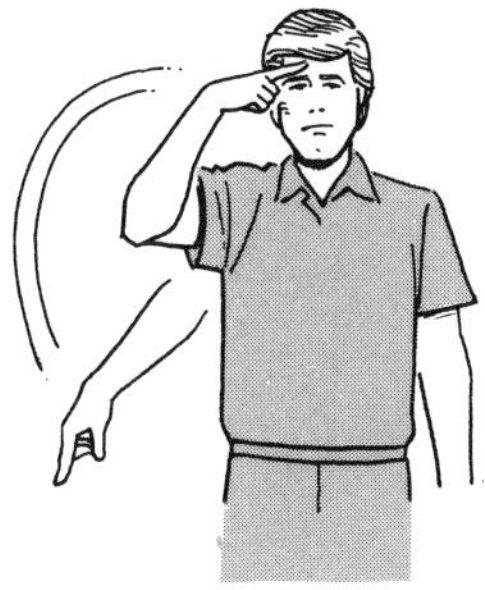

close escape / close call

no money

money / "pay up"

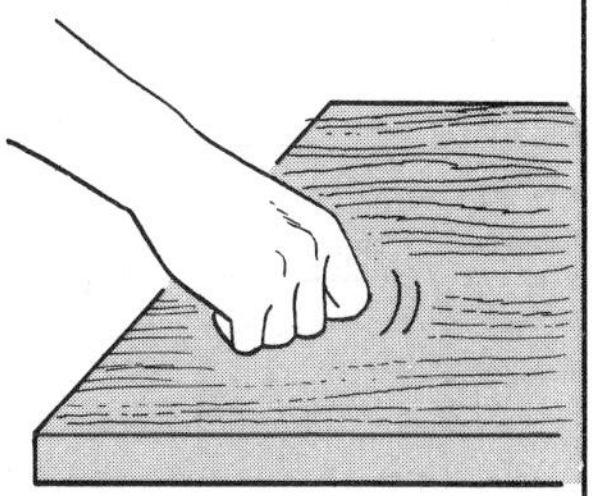

good luck / knock-on-wood

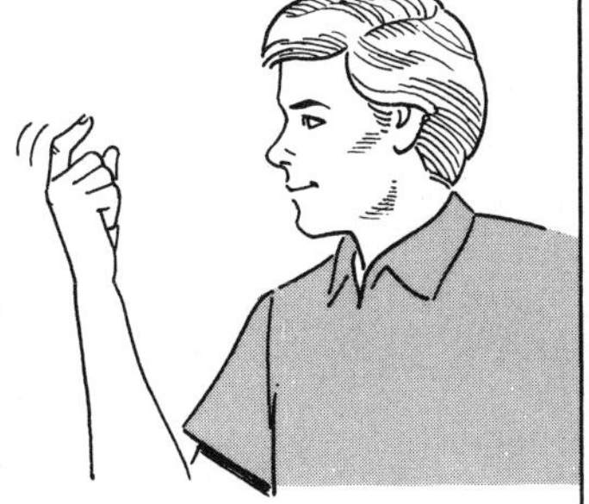

beckoning / come here

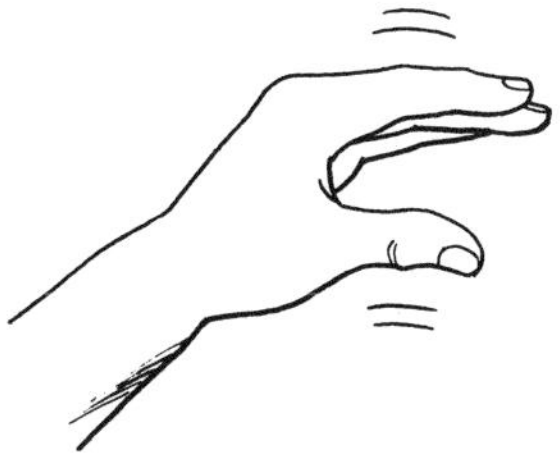

excessive talk / "yackety-yak"

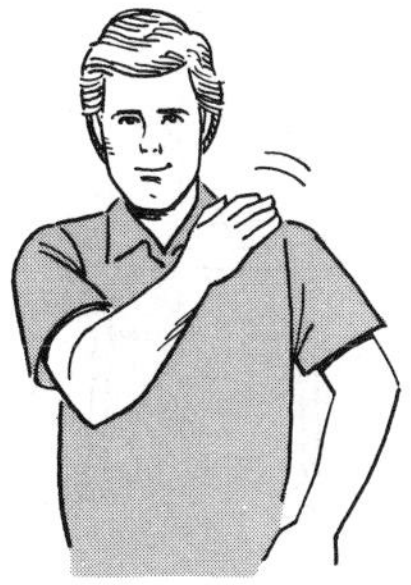

self-congratulation

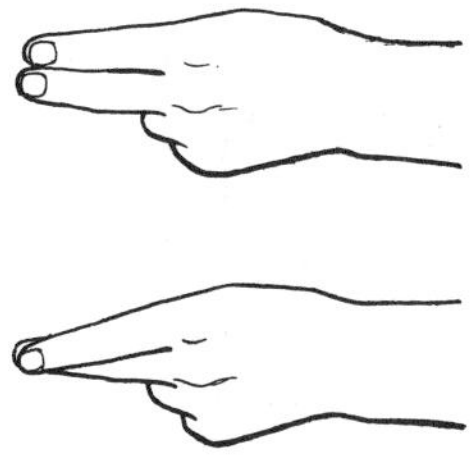

close relationship

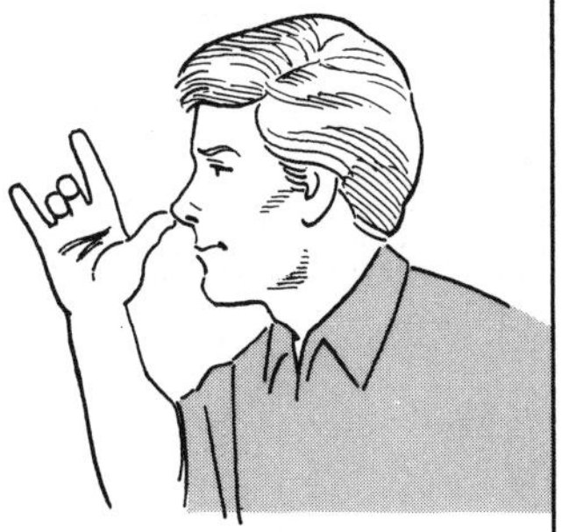

derision / mockery

victory / V-sign

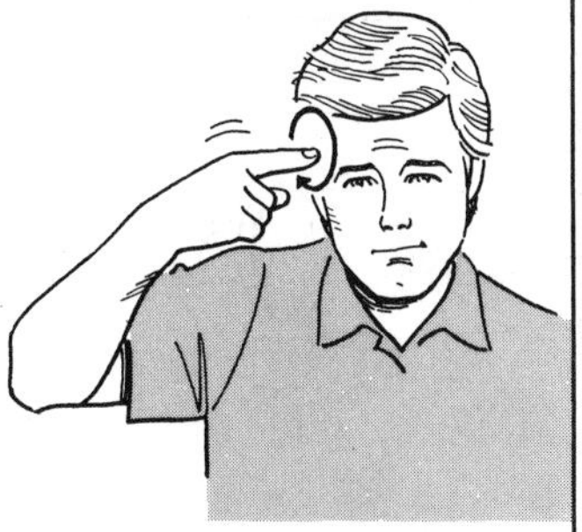

odd / foolish / "crazy"

annoyance / exasperation

Signs and Symbols

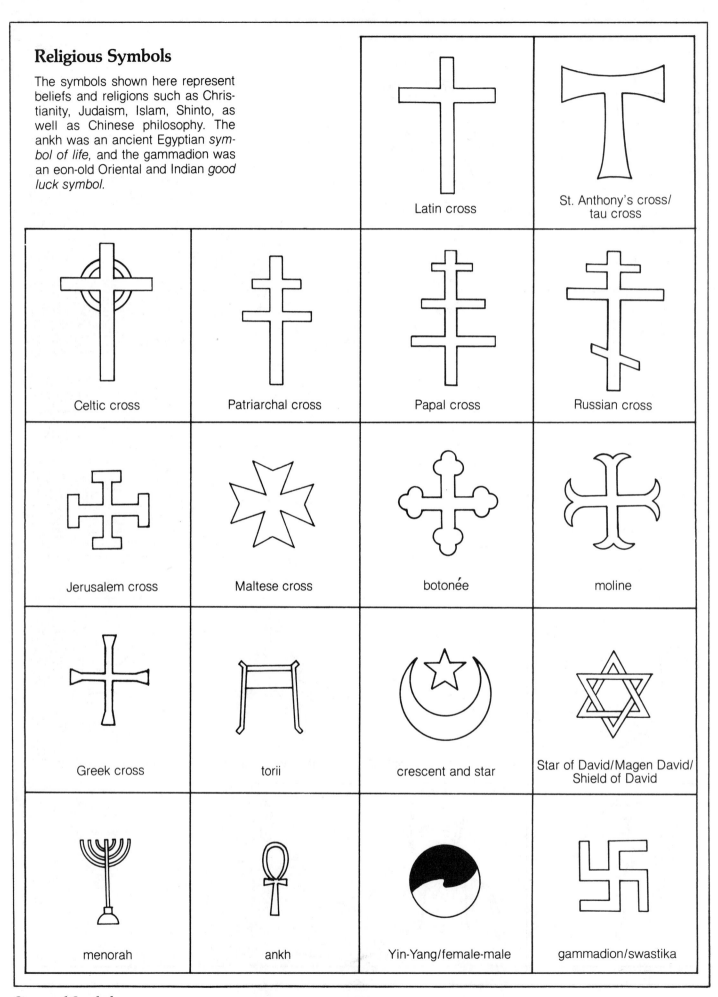

Religious Symbols

The symbols shown here represent beliefs and religions such as Christianity, Judaism, Islam, Shinto, as well as Chinese philosophy. The ankh was an ancient Egyptian *symbol of life,* and the gammadion was an eon-old Oriental and Indian *good luck symbol.*

Latin cross

St. Anthony's cross/ tau cross

Celtic cross

Patriarchal cross

Papal cross

Russian cross

Jerusalem cross

Maltese cross

botonée

moline

Greek cross

torii

crescent and star

Star of David/Magen David/ Shield of David

menorah

ankh

Yin-Yang/female-male

gammadion/swastika

Signs of the Zodiac

The *zodiac* is an imaginary belt in the heavens divided into twelve parts named for constellations, called *houses*. A *horoscope*, drawn by an *astrologer*, foretells the influence of these heavenly bodies on human affairs.

Spring Signs

Aries — The Ram
March 21—April 20

Taurus — The Bull
April 21—May 21

Gemini — The Twins
May 22—June 21

Summer Signs

Cancer — The Crab
June 22—July 22

Leo — The Lion
July 23—August 23

Virgo — The Virgin
August 24—September 23

Autumn Signs

Libra — The Balance
September 24—October 23

Scorpio — The Scorpion
October 24—November 22

Sagittarius — The Archer
November 23—December 21

Winter Signs

Capricorn — The Goat
December 22—January 20

Aquarius — The Water Bearer
January 21—February 19

Pisces — The Fish
February 20—March 20

Signs and Symbols

Symbols of Science, Business and Commerce

The symbols shown here are used in the medical and pharmaceutical fields, in chemistry, engineering and electronics, in mathematics and business, and by currency-exchange centers and banks. Also included are miscellaneous symbols used in other walks of life.

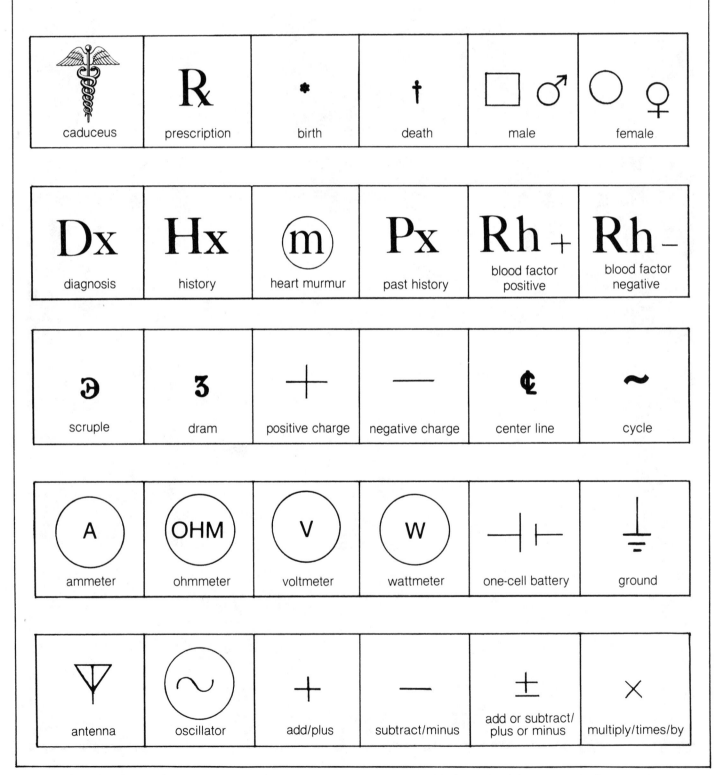

caduceus	prescription	birth	death	male	female
diagnosis	history	heart murmur	past history	blood factor positive	blood factor negative
scruple	dram	positive charge	negative charge	center line	cycle
ammeter	ohmmeter	voltmeter	wattmeter	one-cell battery	ground
antenna	oscillator	add/plus	subtract/minus	add or subtract/ plus or minus	multiply/times/by

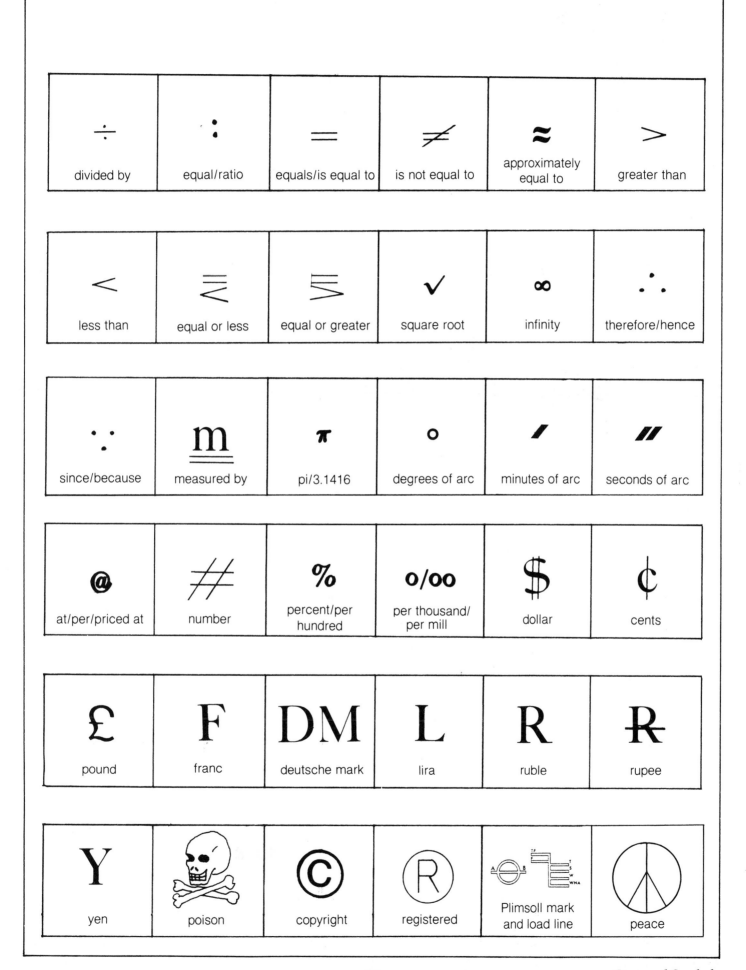

÷	∶	=	≠	≈	>
divided by	equal/ratio	equals/is equal to	is not equal to	approximately equal to	greater than

<	≦	≧	√	∞	∴
less than	equal or less	equal or greater	square root	infinity	therefore/hence

∵	m̲	π	°	′	″
since/because	measured by	pi/3.1416	degrees of arc	minutes of arc	seconds of arc

@	#	%	o/oo	$	¢
at/per/priced at	number	percent/per hundred	per thousand/ per mill	dollar	cents

£	F	DM	L	R	₨
pound	franc	deutsche mark	lira	ruble	rupee

Y		©	®		
yen	poison	copyright	registered	Plimsoll mark and load line	peace

Signs and Symbols

Symbolic Language

Sign language, used by deaf-mutes, substitutes *gestures* for spoken words. Embossed *dots* are used by blind people to read by touch. *Sema-phore* and *wigwag* are systems of signalling by hand-held flags.

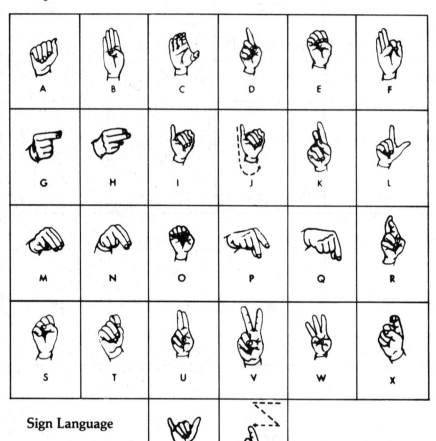

Sign Language

Braille

a	b	c	d	e	f	g	h	i	j	k	l	m

n	o	p	q	r	s	t	u	v	w	x	y	z

In addition to these *punctuation*, *diacritic* and *pronunciation symbols*, there are *phonetic symbols*, *abbreviations* and *contractions*.

'a' single quotation marks	**"a"** quotation marks	**′** foot/minute/prime	**″** inch/second/ double prime	**a'** apostrophe
(a) parentheses	**[a]** brackets/crotchets	**a-a** hyphen	**a—a** dash	**a/a** virgule/ slant/slash
, comma	**;** semicolon	**:** colon	**&** ampersand	***** asterisk
• period/full point	**• • •** ellipsis/marks of omission	**!** exclamation point/ bang/ecphoneme	**?** question mark/ eroteme	**‽** interrobang/ interabang
a̲ underline/ underscore	**ſh** ligature	**é** acute accent	**à** grave accent	**â** circumflex accent/ doghouse
ñ tilde	**ç** cedilla	**ā** macron	**ă** breve	**äi** dieresis/umlaut

Proofreader's Marks

The marks illustrated below are used for the purpose of standardizing the transmittal of corrections and queries between *editors* and/or *proofreaders* and *typesetters* and/or *printers*. When the corrected *copy* is set in *type* it is *proved,* or *proofed,* and additional marks are then made on the *galley proofs*. The first *impressions* of the corrected galleys are called *page proofs*.

Mark

```
                Enter HAMLET.

¶
⌐ Ham. To be, or not to be: that is the question:
∧
    Whether ('t is) nobler in the mind to suffer

    The slings⌢and arrows of outrageous fortune

⌐Or to take arms against a sea of troubles,

    And ⌐end \by opposing⌐ them? To die: to sleep:

    No ⌐More; and by a sleep to say we end

    The heart-ache and the (1000) natural shocks

    That flesh is heir to∧'t is a consummation

    Devoutly˅to˅be˅ wish'd.To˅die,˅ to sleep;

    ⌐To sleep: perchance to dream: ay, there's
    □□□ ⟵                         ⌐the rub;

    For in that sleep of death what dreams |may come|

    When we have (shuffled off) this mortal coil,

    Must give us pause. There's the res⌢pect

    That makes calamity of soǿ long life;

    For who would bear|the whips and scorns of time,

    The oppressor's wrong, the ⌐roud man|s contumely,

    The p⌐ngs of disprized love, the law's delay,
             i       o
    The ⌐ns⌐lence of office, and the spurns

    That patient (merit) of the unworthy takes,

    When he himself might⌐his quietus make

    With a bare bodkin∧who would fardels bear,

    to grunt and sweat under a weary life,
    ⎓
    But that the dread of something∧death,
```

Symbol	Meaning
ital	set in italics
¶	begin a paragraph
(G ?)	grammar?
⌐#⌐	close up partly/less space/take out space
⌐	move right/flush left
tr	transpose
lc	set in lower case
(*sp*)	spell out
⌒	insert comma
eq #	equalize space
[	move left/square up
[	move left – indent 3 ems
⎵	move down
au ?	query author
⌒	close up completely/take out space
⌿	delete
#	insert space/insert lead
⌐	insert apostrophe
a/	substitute letter
⹀	straighten type horizontally
rom	set in roman type
stet	let it stand
?	insert question mark
cap	set in capitals
after	insert/insert omitted matter

Hobo Signs

Symbols, inscriptions, phrases and signatures drawn in public places are collectively called graffiti. Those shown here are used among tramps and vagrants.

kindhearted lady	dishonest man	town asleep, cops inactive	town awake, cops active
housewife feeds for chores	tell pitiful story	town allows alcohol	town dislikes alcohol
dog	doctor	judge	chain gang
danger	man with gun	don't give up	be quiet
go	unsafe place	good for handout	officer

Tombstone and Coffin

A stone placed at the foot of a grave is a *footstone. Crypts,* or *vaults,* are wholly or partly underground *burial chambers. Mausoleums* are large aboveground *tombs.*

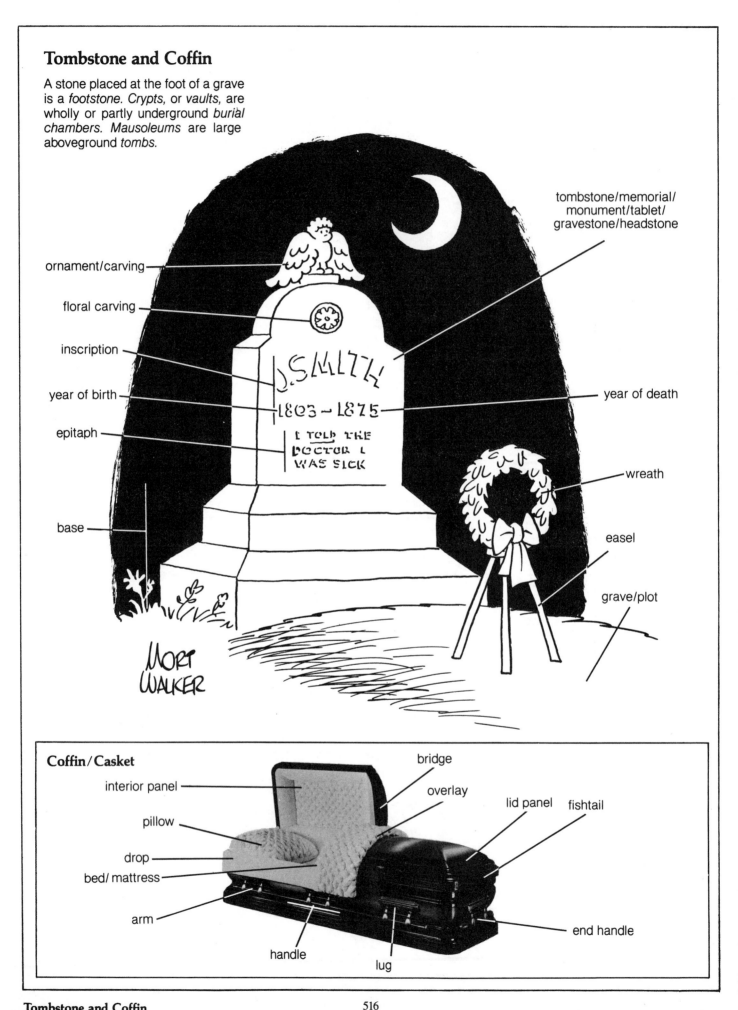

ornament/carving

floral carving

inscription

year of birth

epitaph

base

tombstone/memorial/ monument/tablet/ gravestone/headstone

year of death

wreath

easel

grave/plot

J.SMITH

1803 — 1875

I TOLD THE DOCTOR I WAS SICK

MORT WALKER

Coffin/Casket

interior panel

pillow

drop

bed/mattress

arm

handle

lug

bridge

overlay

lid panel

fishtail

end handle

Index

A

A: braille, 512; piano keyboard octave, 361; sheet music notation, 353; sign language, 512
aba, Arab robe, 491
abacus, 441; column, 73
ABA number, check, 226
abaya, Arab dress, 491
abbreviation: grammatical symbol, 513; magazine mailing label, 169
abdomen: grasshopper, 41; horse, 38; human, 24; lobster, 47; spider, 40
abdominal aorta, human, 28
abdominal board, universal gym, 344
ablation zone, glacier, 12
ABM, 482
abort, pilot's instrument panel, 481
abrasive material, sander, 421
abstraction, work of art, 368
abutment, arch, 72
abutment tooth, partial denture, 453
abyssal plain, continental margin, 15
academic career, résumé, 160
academic hood, minister, 487
acceleration contest, drag racing, 339
accelerator, 394
accelerator pedal, car, 110
accelerometer, pilot's instrument panel, 481
accent, grammatical symbol, 513
access arm, launch pad, 152
access door, turbine locomotive coupler, 117
accessory shoe, camera, 172
accessories: musical, 367; patio, 288; photographic, 176
accessories shelf, telescope, 443
accessory cords, drum major's busby, 495
accessory rail, surgical table, 450
accessory socket, movie camera, 174
access plate, water heater, 401
access road, highway cloverleaf, 114
accidental, music notation, 352
accommodation, sailboat, 135
accommodation ladder, destroyer, 476
accordion, 366
accordion gusset, shoulder bag, 222
accordion windows, wallet, 223
accounting summary, monthly statement, 227
account number: bank card, 226; check, 226; credit card, 227; monthly statement, 227
accumulation zone, glacier, 12
accumulator, dispenser, 267
ace, playing card, 348
A cell block, prison, 76
achene, strawberry, 55

achievement of arms, 503
Achilles' heel, 25
Achilles' tendon, 31; pad, running shoe, 302
acid-free backing, frame, 379
acorn, seed, 51
acorn nut, 411
acoustic guitar, 356
AC power cord, tape recorder, 177
acroterion, masonry gate post, 67
acrylic, painting medium, 370
acrylic resin, dental, 453, 455
act, circus, 90
act curtain, stage, 350
act drop, stage, 350
action bolt, roller skate, 324
action nut, roller skate, 324
activating lever, pencil sharpener, 277
activator button, dental x-ray, 454
active pointer, aneroid barometer, 18
active repeater satellite, 186
acute accent, grammatical symbol, 513
ACV, 145
Adam's apple, human, 25
adapter plate, tractor, 434
add, symbol, 510
adding machine, 441
addition, with abacus, 441
add-on segment weight, tractor planetary, 434
add or subtract, symbol, 510
address: check, 226; envelope, 159; letter, 159; magazine mailing label, 169; résumé, 160
adductor longus, human, 26
adductor muscle, scallop, 47
adductor policis, human, 26
adhesive: Band-aid, 451; roofing shingle, 68
adhesive tape, 451
adipose fin, fish, 45
adjustable arm, expansive bit, 419
adjustable barrel, hose nozzle, 428
adjustable bit gauge, drill, 419
adjustable buckle, brassiere, 195
adjustable channel, pliers, 414
adjustable C-clamp, 409
adjustable clip, jackhammer, 436
adjustable foot: potter's wheel, 373; surgical table, 450
adjustable frame, hacksaw, 416
adjustable fulcrum, diving board, 316
adjustable grill, patio accessory, 288
adjustable lamp, 239
adjustable mirror, cosmetic case, 285
adjustable neckband, ascot, 193
adjustable platform, computer workstation, 438
adjustable rear wing, racing car, 338
adjustable reference pointer, barometer, 18

adjustable screw, embroidery ring, 385
adjustable shoulder strap, bag, 222
adjustable stand, laboratory, 447
adjustable table extension, saw, 417
adjustable wheel tread, tractor planetary, 434
adjustable wrench, 415
adjuster, power mower wheel, 429
adjusting knob: knee kicker, 246; saw, 417
adjusting lever, plane, 420
adjusting nut, monkey wrench, 415
adjusting screw: expansive bit, 419; hitch and harrow, 434; pliers, 414; theodolite, 436; violin bow, 355
adjust knob, volt-ohm meter, 423
adjustment: microscope focus, 442; speculum, 448
adjustment control, machine gun, 471
adjustment knob: lamp, 239; medical examination table, 450; microscope, 442; nozzle, 428; rifle scope, 469
adjustment lever: child's car seat, 286; stroller, 286
adjustment lines, sewing pattern, 388
adjustment nut, plane, 420
adjustment screw: lithographic press, 376; monkey wrench, 415; plane, 420; ski binding, 326; volt-ohm meter, 423
administration building, prison, 76
ad service courts, tennis, 312
adult, insect, 41
advance control, cash register, 440
advanced life-support unit, ambulance, 123
adventitious root, 51
advertisement, magazine, 171
advertising panel: bus, 118; gas pump, 112; subway car, 119
adz, ice axe, 334
adze eye, hammer, 412
aerator, kitchen sink, 247
aerial: CB radio, 183; hovercraft, 145; jumbo jet, 148; tanker, 141
aerial displays, 382-383
aerial flash, fireworks, 382
aerialist, circus, 90
aerial platform, tower ladder, 124
aerial shell, 383
aerial tom-tom, 364
aeronautical light, nautical chart, 22
A flat, piano keyboard octave, 361
A-frame, Ferris wheel, 93
aft, boat, 132
aft cabin bunk, sailboat, 135
aft controls, tugboat, 144
aft equipment bay, lunar lander, 154

afterbody, torpedo, 479
after bulkhead, powerboat, 139
after-shave lotion, 217
after steering, fireboat, 144
aft monitor, fireboat, 144
aft superstructure, tanker, 141
against shooter, craps table, 347
agal, Arab dress, 491
agate line, newspaper, 168
agitator: spreader, 430; washing machine, 280
agitron, cartoon, 380
aglet: shoelace, 204; skate, 295; stringtie, 192
Agulhas Current, ocean, 6
aid: hearing, 452; public sign, 506; space shuttle navigation, 153
aiguillette, enlisted man's uniform, 496
aileron: glider, 147; jumbo jet, 148; single engine airplane, 147
aileron trim, 747 cockpit, 150
air bags, blimp, 156
air bladder, seaweed, 57
air blower, drag racing dragster, 339
air brake, shuttle, 152
airbrake hose, locomotive, 116
airbrake paddle, glider, 147
air bubble, monorail, 424
air cleaner: automobile engine, 107; bulldozer, 435; mechanical sweeper, 127; mower, 429; truck, 120
air combat maneuver panel, pilot's instrument panel, 481
air compressor, truck, 120
air conditioner, 402; camper, 130
air conditioner compressor, automobile engine, 111
air conditioning: control, pilot's instrument panel, 481; intake, bus, 118
air connect lines, truck, 120
air control: dental unit, 454; refrigerator, 249
air-cooled engine, 406
air-cooled machine gun, 471
aircraft: airport, 95; civil, 148-149; combat, 480; instrument panel, 481; 747 cockpit, 150; single engine, 147
aircraft carrier, 476, 478
aircraft tug, 95
air cushion vehicle (ACV), 145
air-data system, space shuttle, 152
air ducts, tunnel, 98
air filter: engine, 406; tractor, 434
airflow control, pilot's instrument panel, 481
airflow nozzle, hair dryer, 212
air foil, drag racing dragster, 339
airframe: cruise missile, 482; jet fighter, 480
air gauge, subway motorman's cab, 119
airglow ultraviolet spectrometer, satellite, 186
air hole: fountain pen, 158;

hair roller, 214; harmonica, 366; igloo, 85
air horn, truck, 120
air hose, skin diving, 331
air inlet: aircraft, 147, 149, 407; dishwasher, 250; surgical table, 450
air intake: destroyer, 477; heat exchanger, 403; hovercraft, 145; locomotive, 117; racing car, 338; truck, 120
air jet, Jacuzzi, 274
airline identification location marker, airport, 94
air-motor power pedal, surgical table, 450
air movement, cloud, 16
airplane, see aircraft
airplane-back, cufflink, 218
air plate, standpipe, 59
airport, 94-95
air pump, bicycle, 128
air regulator: dental, 455; laboratory burner, 437
air reservoir, locomotive, 116
air scoop: automobile, 106; blimp, 156
air search radar: aircraft carrier, 478; destroyer, 477
airship, 156
air speed indicator, 747 cockpit, 150, 151
airspeed mach indicator, pilot's instrument panel, 481
airtank: fire engine, 124; skin diving, 331
air temperature, 747 cockpit, 150
air traffic control: operator facility, 95; tower, 94; transporter, 747 cockpit, 151
air transportation, public sign, 506
air valve: blimp, 156; motorcycle, 129; subway motorman's cab, 119
air vent: automobile, 107, 110; Band-Aid, 451; furnace, 400; hair dryer, 212; intercity bus, 118; pressure cooker, 257; radiator, 400; VCR, 184
aisle: church, 87; courtroom, 89; House of Representatives, 74; theatre, 351
aisle display, 102
aisle number, supermarket, 102
ait, river, 13
alarm: clock radio, 233; elevator car button, 78; powerboat, 138; prison, 76; vault, 457
alarm panel, nuclear reactor control room, 393
alb, cardinal, 487
albedo, orange, 55
albumen, egg, 262
alcohol, ambulance, 123
alcohol percentage, wine label, 267
Alexander, playing card king, 348
algae, marine, 57
alignment control: gas laser, 395; radar, 444
alimentary canal, human, 27
Allen wrench, 415
alley: badminton court, 319; bowling, 317; tennis court, 312
alley light, police car, 122
all-fives, darts, 322
alligator, 42
alligator clip: dental towel, 455; and volt-ohm meter, 423
allosaurus, 43

all-purpose vehicle, 108
alluvial fan, river, 13
alp, mountain, 8
alpha-numeric keypad: answering machine, 181; cellular telephone, 181; computer workstation, 438; personal computer, 162
Alpine skiing, 326
altar, church, 87
altazimuth mounting, telescope, 453
alteration lines, sewing pattern, 388
alternate channel, picture-in-picture viewing, 185
alternator, automobile engine, 111
altimeter: pilot's instrument panel, 481; 747 cockpit, 150
altitude coarse-motion clamp, telescope, 443
altitude indicator, pilot's instrument panel, 481
altocumulus cloud, 16, 17
aluminum rim, drag racing dragster, 339
amalgam carrier, dental, 455
amateur radio operator, 183
amber starting light, drag racing, 339
ambu, ambulance, 123
ambulance, 123
ambulatory, church, 87
American Bankers Association routing number, check, 226
AM/FM controls, clock radio, 233
AM-FM radio scale, portable radio/cassette player, 182
AM/FM radio tuning dial, audio receiver, 179
amidships, boat, 132
ammeter, symbol, 510
ammunition: automatic weapon, 471; combat soldier, 497; fort, 82
amount: check, 226
amp, electric guitar, 363
amperage rating, circuit breaker box, 399
ampersand, grammatical symbol, 513
amphibian, 44
amphibious assault ship, 476
amphibious command ship, 476
amphibious hull, helicopter, 146
amphibious vehicle, 145
amplifier: guitar, 363; phonograph, 179
AM signal meter, phonograph, 179
amulet, medal, 501
amusement park, 92-93
anal fin, fish, 45
anal shield, snake, 43
anatomical snuffbox, human hand, 31
anatomy, literary, 25
anchor: boar, 132; diving board, 316; mattress cover, 271; passenger ship, 143; sailboat, 134; starting block, 304; tennis net, 312
anchorage, nautical chart, 22
anchor bolt, house, 60, 61
anchor chain: bear trap, 433; oil drilling platform, 101
anchor light, destroyer, 477
anchor spot, blackjack, 347
anchor spring, gas pump nozzle, 112
anchor tooth, denture, 453
anchor winch, oil drilling platform, 101

anchor windlass, tanker, 140
anchovies, pizza, 265
andiron, fireplace, 232
anemometer, weather station, 18
aneroid barometer, 18
angle: fort, 83; incline track, 92; lamp, 239; slide, 287; transit, 436
angled deck, aircraft carrier, 478
angle of attack indicator, pilot's instrument panel, 481
angle of light, relief map, 21
angler, fishing, 341
angle scale, circular saw, 417
angular adjustment, speculum, 448
angulation dial readout, dental x-ray unit, 454
anima, human, 25
animal: cell, 23; circus, 90, 91; composite, 48-49
animal trainer, 90
animal skin, igloo, 85
ankh, symbol, 508
ankle, human, 24, 31
ankle boot, harness racing pacer, 337
ankle extension, baseball catcher's shinguard, 290
ankle guard, hockey skate, 325
ankle sock, 207
ankle strap, woman's shoe, 205
anklet, 219
ankle weight, body building, 344; announcement microphone, 747 cockpit, 150
annoyance, gesture, 507
annual ring: lumber, 68; tree, 50
annulus, mushroom, 57
anode, laser, 395
anode plate, vacuum tube, 396
anorak, 201
answer button, answering machine, 181
answering machine, 181
answering machine capability, fax machine, 164
ant, 41
antenna: aircraft carrier, 478; airport control tower, 95; automobile, 106, 107; CB radio, 183; cellular telephone, 181; cordless phone, 180; destroyer, 476, 477; helicopter, 146; house, 63; insect, 41; jet fighter, 480; launch pad, 152; lobster, 47; lunar lander, 154; lunar rover, 155; police car, 122; portable radio/cassette player, 182; radar, 444; satellite, 186; single engine airplane, 147; spacesuit, 155; submarine, 479; symbol, 510; tank, 474; tanker, 141
antependium, church, 87
anterior chamber, eye, 30
anther, flower stamen, 53
antia, shield, 464
anti-ballistic missile (ABM), 482
anti-cavitation plate, outboard engine, 137
anti-fog liquid, dental, 455
anti-friction pad, ski binding, 326
antihelix, outer ear, 30
anti-kickback panel, saw, 417
antique, White House, 75

anti-reverse housing, fishing reel, 340
anti-rollback, incline track, 92
anti-shock trousers, paramedic equipment, 123
anti-skate dial, phonograph, 178
anti-submarine belt, drag racing driver, 339
antitank mine, 473
antitragus, outer ear, 30
antlers, ultimate beast, 48
anus, starfish, 46
anvil: stapler, 277; telegraph key, 157; vise, 409
anvil shears, gardening, 427
anvil toe, thundercloud, 17
aorta, heart, 28
aperture: microscope, 442; pencil sharpener, 277; physician's mirror, 448; univalve shell, 47
aperture key, camera, 172
aperture ring, zoom lens, 172
aperture scale: light meter, 176
apex: grass, 58; leaf, 52; pyramid, 71; univalve shell, 47
apostrophe: grammatical symbol, 513; proofreader's mark, 514
Appalachian dulcimer, 362
apparatus, animal cell, 23
apparel pocket, golf bag, 311
appendix, human, 27
appetizer, 263
apple, 55; baseball, 290; corer, 261
application package, computer, 438
applicator, beauty product, 217
applicator bottle, hair styling lotion, 214
appliqué: dress, 198; quilting, 385
appliquéd lace, bridal gown, 488
approach: airport runway, 94; bowling lane, 317; javelin throw, 301; pole vault, 305
approach indexer, pilot's instrument panel, 481
approval, gesture, 507
approximately equal to, symbol, 511
apron: airport, 95; ascot, 193; barn, 104; boxing ring, 309; bureau, 272; circus aerialist, 90; cook, 489; golf course, 311; house driveway, 63; necktie, 193; pool table, 320; table, 242; theatre, 351; window, 65
apsidal chapel, church, 87
apterium, bird, 39
APV, passenger car, 108
Aquarius, zodiac, 509
aquatint, printmaking, 377
Arab dress, 491
arbor lock, table saw, 417
arc: sextant, 137; Torah, 486
arcade, passengership, 142
arch, 72; church, 86; croquet, 318; denture, 453; dog, 36; football uniform, 292; house doorway, 62; human fingertip, 31; human foot, 31; kokoshniki, 70; organ, 360; royal crown, 485; saddle, 335; stage, 350, 351
arch cookie, sandal, 206
arched-top glass door, corner cabinet, 243
archer, zodiac, 509
architect, house blueprint, 62
architecture, international, 70-71
architrave: column entablature,

73; vault, **457**; White House, **75**
archival frame, **379**
arch-stones, arch, **72**
arco, stringed instrument, **355**
area code, telephone, **180**
area rug, **246**
A recreation yard, prison, **76**
arena, circus, **90**
areole, cactus, **56**
arête: glacier, **12**; mountain, **9**
Argine, playing card queen, **348**
Aries, zodiac, **509**
arithmetic function key calculator, **441**
ark, synagogue, **88**
arm: anchor, **132**; automobile, **161, 166**; ballista, **467**; bobby pin, **214**; cactus, **56**; candelabrum, **237**; chaise longue, **288**; clothes hanger, **281**; coffin, **516**; corkscrew, **251**; dental, **454, 455**; dishwasher, **250**; dog, **36**; drill bit, **419**; fishing reel, **340**; folding rule, **424**; frog, **44**; gas pump price-poster, **112**; guitar, **363**; hand shower, **274**; human, **24, 25**; jellyfish, **46**; lamp, **239**; launch pad, **152**; lounger, **235**; L-shaped square, **424**; lyre, **355**; microscope, **442**; movie projector, **175**; octopus, **46**; outboard engine, **137**; organ, **360**; overhead power line, **396**; phonograph turntable, **178**; piano, **361**; revolving sprinkler, **428**; rocking chair, **234**; sewing machine, **278**; sextant, **137**; shower, **274**; slot machine, **346**; sofa, **236**; starfish, **46**; toilet, **275**; toll booth gate, **114**; traffic light, **113**; type, **165**; wheelchair, **452**; *see also* arms
armament countermeasure panel, **481**
armament panel, pilot's, **481**
armature, sculpture, **372**
armboard extension, operating table, **450**
arm buckle, electric chair, **462**
armed guard, prison, **76**
arm grip, phonograph turntable, **178**
armhole: jacket, **188, 196**; undershirt, **194**
armhole seam, blouse, **197**
armilla, queen's regalia, **484**
arming mechanism, bazooka, **472**
armlet, jewelry, **219**
armoire, **272**
armor, **465**
armored cord, pay phone, **180**
armorial achievement, coat of arms, **503**
armor-plated vehicle, **474-475**
armory, castle, **81**
arm pad, lounger, **235**
arm piece, crutch, **452**
armpit: frog, **44**; human, **24**
arm post, rocking chair, **234**
arm protector, ice hockey goalie, **294**
armrail, commuter bus, **118**
armrest: Jacuzzi, **274**; lounger, **235**; rocking chair, **234**; sofa, **236**; wheelchair, **452**
arms: church, **87**; coat of, **503**; Manchu coat dress, **491**; medieval, **464**; royal crown, **485**; *see also* arm
aro, jai alai cesta, **314**
arrester, fireplace sparks, **232**

arresting gear pendant, aircraft carrier, **478**
arresting hook, jet fighter, **480**
arresting hook panel, pilot's instrument panel, **481**
arresting trap, **433**
arrow, **466**; bowling lane, **317**; road map, **20**
arrowhead, weather vane, **19**
arrow loop, castle, **80**
arse, wood block, **461**
art: book jacket, **167**; composition, **368-369**; in frame, **379**; magazine, **169, 170, 171**; newspaper, **168**
arteriole, human, **28**
artery, human; **27, 28**
article, magazine, **169, 170**
artificial abrasive material, sander, **421**
artificial teeth, denture, **453**
artificial turf, baseball field, **291**
artillery, cowboy, **490**
artist: cartoon, **380**; circus, **90**; painting, **370**; phonograph record, **178**
ASA-DIN exposure index, light meter, **176**
ascender, type, **165**
ascent air-data system, space shuttle, **152**
ascent stage, lunar lander, **154**
ascot, **193**
asdic, **444**
A sharp, piano keyboard octave, **361**
ash: cigar and cigarette, **228**; volcano, **10**
ash catcher, grill, **288**
ash dump, fireplace, **232**
ash lip, woodburning stove, **404**
ashpit, fireplace, **232**
ashtray, car, **11C**
asparagus, **54**
asphaltum, **376**
ASROC launcher, destroyer, **477**
assembly: backyard equipment, **287**; lamp, **239**; pulley block, **461**; scale, **446**
assigned weight, flat racing entry, **336**
assistance telephone, automatic teller machine, **226**
assistant quartermaster, frontier fort, **82**
assistant's center, dental unit, **454**
assist handle, truck tractor, **120**
association football, **297**
asterisk, grammatical symbol, **513**
asteroid, Milky Way, **2**
astragal: cannon barrel, **467**; column, **73**
A string, double bass, **355**
astrologer, **509**
asymmetrical closing, jacket, **196**
at, symbol, **511**
athletic sock, **207**
athletic supporter, **194**
athwartships, boat, **132**
Atlantic Drift, ocean, **6**
Atlantic North Equatorial Current, ocean, **6**
Atlantic South Equatorial Current, ocean, **6**
ATM, **226**
atmosphere, earth, **4**
atom smasher, **394**
attaché case, **285**
attached bertha, bridal gown, **488**

attaching point, inflatable, **133**
attaching socket, movie camera, **174**
attachment: denture, **453**; vacuum cleaner, **283**
attachment loop, basketball backstop, **296**
attachment plug, electrical, **398**
attachment screw thread, camera, **172**
attachment weight set, scale, **446**
attack indicator, pilot's instrument panel, **481**
attack line, volleyball court, **319**
attackman, lacrosse position, **298**
attic, house, **62, 63**
attitude indicator, space shuttle, **153**
audience, circus, **91**
audio control, police car, **122**
audio-input, movie projector, **175**
audio knob, Geiger counter, **445**
audio port, Geiger counter, **445**
audio power status, space shuttle, **153**
audio system, **179**
auditorium, prison, **76**
auditory canal, **30**
auger, **422**
auger bit, drill, **418, 419**
auguste face, clown, **493**
auricle, **30**
auricular, bird, **39**
author: book, **167**; magazine, **169**; music, **352**
authorized signature, traveler's check, **227**
autofeed bin, laser printer, **163**
autofocus 35 mm camera, **172**
auto gate, toll booth, **114**
auto inflation, hose, skin diving, **331**
autoloader latch, computer tape, **439**
automatic choke, automobile, **111**
automatic citrus juicer, **255**
automatic cue, phonograph turntable, **178**
automatic direction finder: helicopter, **146**; 747 cockpit, **150**
automatic inflator, skin diving, **331**
automatic line finder, typewriter, **161**
automatic music sensor, compact disc player, **178**
automatic noise limiter, CB radio, **183**
automatic nozzle, gas pump, **112**
automatic pilot disengage, 747 cockpit, **151**
automatic pistol, **470**
automatic rewind switch, tape measure, **424**
automatic rifle, **471**
automatic teller machine, **226**
automatic teller machine card, **226**
automatic temperature probe, microwave oven, **248**
automatic timer, coffee maker, **252**
automatic weapons, **471**
automobile: cutaway, **108-109**; drag racing, **339**; engine, **111**; exterior, **106-107**; Grand Prix racer, **338**; interior, **110**; police, **122**; *see also* car

autopilot display, space shuttle, **153**
autopilot engage switch, 747 cockpit, **150**
auto redial, cellular telephone, **181**
auto-reverse, portable radio/cassette player, **182**
auxiliary attaching socket, movie camera, **174**
auxiliary building, nuclear reactor, **392**
auxiliary car-station panel, elevator car, **78**
auxiliary contact, movie camera, **174**
auxiliary counterweight, lift bridge, **97**
auxiliary feedwater pump, nuclear reactor, **392**
auxiliary handle: hand drill, **418**; plane, **420**
auxiliary instruments arm, dental, **454**
auxiliary lens, microscope, **442**
auxiliary power feed, Walkman, **182**
auxiliary selector, movie camera, **174**
auxiliary tank, truck, **121**
avalanche area, mountain, **9**
aven, cave, **11**
aviation light, bridge, **97**
aviation lens, eyeglasses, **221**
awards, résumé, **160**
awl: combination square, **424**; knife, **426**
awn, grass, **58**
awning: barn, **104**; tent, **342**
ax: guillotine, **462**; ice climbing, **334**; medieval, **464**
axilla, frog, **44**
axillary bud, tree, **50**
axis: fern, **57**; peeler, **256**
axle: automobile, **109**; bicycle, **128**; child's wagon, **287**; Ferris wheel, **93**; Hansom cab, **131**; roller skate, **324**; stroller, **286**; tractor, **434**; wheelbarrow, **430**; wheelchair, **452**; windmill, **390**
axle gear, seeder, **430**
axle hole, tire, **105**
azimuth coarse-motion clamp, telescope, **443**

B

B: braille, **512**; music notation, **353**; piano keyboard octave, **361**; sign language, **512**
B-1 Bomber, **480**
B-2 Bomber, **480**
baby carriage, **286**
baby chair, **286**
baby teeth, **456**
baccarat, **346**
back: bird, **39**; bow, **466**; carpenter's saw, **416**; cat, **37**; chaise longue, **288**; chicken, **35**; chisel, **420**; coin, **225**; dog, **36**; easel, **370**; electric chair, **462**; horse, **38**; human, **24, 25**; knife, **256, 463**; playing card, **348**; polo position, **299**; rocking chair, **234**; saw tooth, **416**; shank button, **209**; sheep, **33**; sofa, **236**; stringed instrument, **355**; wave, **14** wheelchair, **452**
back arch, English saddle, **335**
back beam, hand loom, **387**
backboard, basketball backstop, **296**
backbone, hardback book, **167**
back boundary line, badminton court, **319**

519

backcombed hair, woman's, **213**
backcourt: basketball, **296**; handball, **313**; squash, **313**; tennis, **312**
back cover: hardback book, **167**; matchbook, **228**
back face, hardback book, **167**
backfill, underwater tunnel, **98**
back finger, handball glove, **313**
back flap, book jacket, **167**
backgammon, **345**
background, composition, **369**
back guard, stove, **248**
back half, piano, **361**
back housing, saddle, **335**
backing: carpet, **246**; frame, **379**; quilting, **385**; sandpaper, **421**; tent, **342**
back jaw, vise, **409**
back leg, bureau, **272**
back lid, grand piano, **361**
back light button, movie camera, **174**
back line, volleyball court, **319**
backlit composition, **368**
back margin, book page, **167**
back matter, book, **167**
back of book, magazine, **171**
back of hand, human, **31**
backpack, **343**; skin diving tank, **331**
backpack control box, spacesuit, **155**
backpacking, **343**
back pad, ice hockey goalie, **294**
back panel, man's jacket, **188**
backplate: armor, **465**; basketball backstop, **296**; shoulder bag, **222**; skin diving tank, **331**
backplate serial number, paper money, **224**
back quarter, boot, **206**
back rail, rocking chair, **234**
backrest: lounger, **235**; stroller, **286**
back roll protector, ice hockey player, **295**
backshore, shoreline, **14**
back sizer, football helmet, **292**
back sleeve seam, jacket, **188**
backspace key, typewriter, **161**
backstay: ice skates, **325**; sailboat, **134**
backstep, pumper, **125**
back-stick, easel, **370**
backstop: basketball, **296**; telegraph key, **157**; workbench, **408**
backstrap: brassiere, **195**; revolver, **470**; vest, **188**
backstretch, harness racetrack, **337**
backstrip, hardback book, **167**
backstroke swimming race, **316**
back upholstery, wheelchair, **452**
back-up light, tow truck bed, **126**
back wall: handball and squash courts, **313**; jai alai cancha, **314**
badge: coat of arms, **503**; fireman's helmet, **500**; flag, **502**; military, **496**; police, **498**
badge of rank, Manchu court dress, **491**
badminton, **319**
baffle, stove, **342**, **404**
bag: backpacking, **343**; bagpipe, **365**; blood pressure gauge, **449**; golf, **311**; hot air balloon, **332**; luggage, **285**;

lunar rover, **155**; packaging, **269**; paper, **266**; photographic, **176**; vacuum cleaner, **283**
bag compression strap, backpack, **343**
bag dispenser, spacesuit, **155**
baggage car, passenger train, **116**
baggage check-in, public sign, **506**
baggage claim, public sign, **506**
baggage compartment: bus, **118**; jumbo jet, **149**; single engine airplane, **147**
baggage rack, intercity bus, **118**
bag-holding button, garbage disposal, **247**
bagpipe, **365**
bag resuscitator, ambulance, **123**
bag stowage, lunar rover, **155**
bail: fishing reel, **340**; lantern, **342**; pail, **284**; screen, **175**; typewriter, **161**
bailey, castle, **80**, **81**
bail roller, typewriter, **161**
bait, mousetrap, **433**
baked dessert, **264**
bakery: frontier fort, **82**; prison, **76**
bakery department, supermarket, **103**
baking tray, toaster oven, **253**
balance: laboratory, **446-447**; monthly statement, **227**; zodiac, **509**
balance beam, gymnastics, **306**
balance dial, phonograph, **179**
balancer, trombone, **358**
balance weight, tire, **105**
balcony: minaret, **70**; pagoda, **71**; theatre, **351**; White House, **75**
bald spot, **211**
balistraria, castle, **80**
balk, lumber, **68**
ball: anchor, **132**; ballpoint pen, **158**; baseball, **290**; bowling, **317**; croquet, **318**; door, **64**; drum major's baton, **495**; field events hammer, **303**; foot, **31**; golf, **310**; handball, **313**; jai alai, **314**; lacrosse, **298**; Ping-Pong, **321**; pool table, **320**; roulette wheel, **346**; shower fitting, **274**; snap fastener, **208**; soccer, **297**; tea, **260**; tennis, **312**; thumb, **31**; toilet tank, **275**; type, **165**; typewriter, **161**
ballast: hot air balloon, **332**; lobster pot, **433**; railroad track, **115**
ballast tank, submarine, **479**
ball bearing: ballpoint pen, **158**; roller skate, **324**
ball-cock assembly, toilet, **275**
ballet dancer, **494**
ballista, **467**
ballistic missile, **482**; submarine, **479**
ballistic missile launch deck, submarine, **479**
ball joint, automobile, **108**
ball joint head, C-clamp, **409**
ball of rank royal crown, **485**
ballonets, blimp, **156**
balloon: cartoon, **380**, **381**; clown, **493**; hot air, **332**
balloon pants, clown, **493**
balloon pointer, comic strip, **381**
ballot, voting booth, **437**

ballot layout, electronic voting system, **437**
ballpark, **291**
ball-peen hammer, **412**
ball pocket, golf bag, **311**
ballpoint pen, **158**
ball rest, roulette wheel, **346**
ball return: bowling lane, **317**; pool table, **320**
ball side, snap fastener, **208**
ball storage box, pool table, **320**
ball tip head, hinge, **460**
baluster: column, **73**; staircase, **66**
balustrade: column, **73**; escalator, **79**; staircase, **66**
bamboo pole, pole vault, **305**
banana, **55**
banana clip, automatic rifle, **471**
band: baren, **374**; baseball uniform, **290**; cigar, **228**; cigarette, **228**; dance, **354**; dental, **453**; fire extinguisher, **284**; frontier fort, **82**; girdle, **195**; horse's hoof, **38**; hot air balloon, **332**; Jewish prayer shawl, **486**; marching; mattress cover, **271**; ring, **219**; skin diving tank, **331**; spinning wheel, **387**; spur, **335**; woman's hat, **203**; wristwatch, **220**
bandage, **451**; paramedic equipment, **123**; polo, **299**; racehorse, **336**
Band-Aid, **451**
bandanna: cowboy, **490**; skier's, **326**
band clamp, **409**
band organ, merry-go-round, **93**
band saw, **417**
band switch, portable radio/cassette player, **182**
bang: grammatical symbol, **513**; woman's hair, **213**
bangle, jewelry, **219**
banister, staircase, **66**
banjo, **362**
bank: check, **226**; elevator, **77**, **78**; name and address, **226**; newspaper, **168**; paper money, **224**; passenger ship, **142**; river, **13**; vault, **457**
bank card, **226**
bank card slot, automatic teller machine, **226**
bank indicator, 747 cockpit, **150**
bank logo, traveler's check, **227**
bank rod, fishing, **341**
banner: circus tent, **91**; football field, **293**; newspaper headline, **168**
banquette, permanent fort, **83**
baptistery, church, **87**
bar: backgammon board, **345**; backyard equipment, **287**; barbell, **344**; barbecue grill, **288**; bicycle, **128**; chain saw, **431**; commuter bus, **118**; courtroom, **89**; craps table, **347**; drag racing dragster, **339**; easel, **370**; electric razor, **210**; etching press, **377**; Ferris wheel, **93**; Grand Prix racer, **338**; hang glider, **333**; hurdle, **304**; hitch and harrow, **434**; horizontal bar, **306**; horse's foot, **38**; lithographic press, **376**; military uniform, **496**; mousetrap, **433**; movie

projector, **175**; music, **352**, **353**; necktie, **192**; parallel bars, **306**; passenger ship, **142**; public sign, **506**; railroad track, **115**; saddle, **335**; shoreline, **14**; slalom water ski, **329**; slot machine, **346**; suit hanger, **281**; table saw, **417**; tank, **475**; tow truck bed, **126**; type, **165**; typewriter, **161**
barb: barbed wire, **432**; bird, **39**; fishhook, **341**; lance, **464**; spring beard needle, **386**
barbed wire, **432**
barbell, body building, **344**
barbecue grill, **288**
barbershop, passenger ship, **142**
barbican, castle, **80**, **81**
Barcalounger, **235**
bar clamp, **409**
bare match end, aerial shell, **383**
baren, woodcut printing, **374**
bargeboard, house, **63**
barge carrier, **140**
barge cluster, pushboat, **144**
bargello stitchery, **385**
bark, wigwam, **84**
barley, **58**
bar line: music, **352**; newspaper, **168**
barn, **104**
barnacle, **47**
barometer, aneroid, **18**
barometric altimeter, 747 cockpit, **150**
barrack: castle, **81**; frontier fort, **82**
barred door, prison, **76**
barrel, **267**; automatic weapons, **468**, **469**, **470**, **471**; baseball bat, **291**; cannon, **467**; clarinet, **357**; cow, **32**; curling iron, **214**; dart, **322**; destroyer gun, **477**; fire hydrant, **125**; hair dryer, **212**; hinge, **460**; hypodermic syringe, **451**; man's shoe, **204**; pen, **158**; shirt cuff, **189**; spool, **384**; tank gun, **475**
barrel cap, lead pencil, **158**
barrel grille, hair dryer, **212**
barrel ring: bayonet, **463**; shotgun, **469**
barrel spiral galaxy, **2**
barrette, **214**
barrier, highway, **114**
barrier beach, **15**
barrier gate, toll booth, **114**
barrier island, **15**
bar scale, political map, **21**
bar tack, necktie, **193**
bar tip, chair saw, **431**
bartizan, castle, **80**
bascule bridge, **97**
base: acoustic guitar, **362**; badminton shuttlecock, **319**; baseball field, **291**; basket, **266**; basketball backstop, **296**; bear trap, **433**; blackjack, **347**; blender, **254**; canapé, **263**; candelabrum, **237**; cannon barrel ring, **467**; can opener, **251**; CB radio station, **183**; cellular telephone, **181**; citrus juicer, **255**; coat of arms, **503**; column, **73**; computer workstation, **438**; dental brace, **453**; denture, **453**; drag racing starting lights, **339**; dressing table, **272**; drill press, **419**; easel, **370**; elevator car, **78**; food processor, **254**; globe, **1**; grandfather clock, **233**;

hurdle, **304**; juice extractor, **255**; laboratory burner, **447**; laboratory scale, **447**; lantern, **342**; lawn sprinkler, **428**; leaf, **52**; light bulb, **238**; makeup, **216**; medical examination table, **450**; microscope, **442**; minaret, **70**; mortar cap, **472**; mousetrap, **433**; music stand, **367**; onion, **54**; parallel bars, **306**; pedestal table, **242**; pencil sharpener, **277**; percolator brewing basket, **252**; phonograph turntable, **178**; pole vault pole, **305**; pommel horse, **307**; pot, **373**; power saw, **417**; pyramid, **71**; refrigerator grille, **249**; rifle scope, **468, 469**; sandwich cookie, **264**; stapler, **277**; steam engine, **405**; telephone, **180**; television, **185**; thimble, **384**; tombstone, **516**; transistor chip, **396**; trimline phone, **180**; trophy, **289**; tuning fork, **367**; vacuum tube, **396**; vise, **409**; White House, **75**
baseball, **290-291**; darts, **322**
baseboard, and carpet, **246**
baseline: baseball field, **291**; Ping-Pong table, **321**; shuffleboard court, **319**; tennis court, **312**; type, **165**
basement, house, **60, 63**
basepath, baseball field, **291**
baseplate: land mine, **473**; mortar, **472**; railroad track, **115**; saber saw, **417**; sewing machine, **278**
base unit, cordless phone, **180**
basin: ambulance, **123**; dam, **100**; river, **13**; sink, **273**
basin compartment, sink, **247**
basket: basketball, **296**; bee, **41**; coffee maker, **252**; container, **266**; deep frying, **260**; garbage disposal, **247**; guillotine, **462**; hot air balloon, **332**; jai alai, **314**; juice extractor, **255**; refrigerator, **249**; sink, **247**; ski pole, **326**; sword, **463**; toll booth, **114**; typewriter type, **161**; washing machine, **280**
basketball, **296**
basket-release handle, garbage disposal, **247**
bass: accordion, **366**; bagpipe drone, **365**; bassoon joint, **357**; fiddle, **354, 355**; guitar, **363**; music clef, **353**; phonograph dial, **179**
bass and guitar, double-neck, **363**
bass clarinet, **354**
bass display, portable radio/cassette player, **182**
bass drum, **354, 364**
bass fiddle, **354, 355**
bassinet, **286**
bass neck, double-neck bass and guitar, **363**
bassoon, **354, 357**
bass speaker, portable radio/cassette player, **182**
basting brush, **259**
basting ladle, **259**
bastion: castle, **80, 81**; permanent fort, **83**
bat: badminton, **319**; baseball, **291**; brick wall, **69**; flat racing, **336**; Ping-Pong, **321**
bateau neck, sweater, **199**
bath, **274**

bath oil, **217**
batholith, volcano, **10**
bathtub, **274**
baton: drum major, **495**; police, **498**
bat pin, potter's wheel, **373**
batten: hand loom, **387**; stage, **350**
batten pocket, mainsail, **136**
batter, baseball, **290**
batter head, snare drum, **364**
batter's box, baseball, **291**
batter's circle, baseball, **291**
battery, **397**; automobile, **108**; buoy, **132**; electronic flash, **176**; Geiger counter, **445**; hearing aid, **452**; intercity bus, **118**; lunar rover, **155**; metal detector, **445**; movie camera, **174**; pacemaker, **452**; tape recorder, **177**; truck, **120, 121**
battery charger: medical examination equipment, **448**; tow truck, **126**
battery holder, camera, **172**
battery jumper cable, tow truck, **126**
battery pack: cellular telephone, **181**; video camera, **184**; video-still camera adaptor, **173**
battery-powered tape recorder, **177**
battery recharge contact, cordless phone, **180**
batting, quilting, **385**
batting glove, baseball, **290**
batting helmet, baseball, **290**
battlement, castle, **80**
battleship, **476**
bat weight, baseball, **290**
bay: aircraft carrier, **478**; barn, **104**; coastline, **7, 15**; space shuttle, **152**
bay bar, **15**
bay barrier, **15**
bayit, tefillin, **486**
baymouth, bar, **15**
bayonet, **463**
bayonet saw, **417**
bay window, house, **62, 63**
bazooka, **472**
bazooka plate, tank, **474**
B cell block, prison, **76**
beach, **14, 15**
beacon: helicopter, **146**; police car, **122**; single engine airplane, **147**
bead: abacus, **441**; beaker, **447**; cowboy hat, **202**; shotgun, **469**
beading: attaché case, **285**; Indian attire, **490**
bead line, bell, **iv**
beak: bird, **39**; chicken, **35**; clam, **47**; dolphin, **45**; halberd, **464**; turtle, **43**; type, **165**
beaker: coffee maker, **252**; laboratory, **447**
beam: abacus, **441**; automobile, **106**; boat, **132**; bus, **118**; drag racing, **339**; guillotine, **462**; gymnastic, **306**; hand loom, **387**; house, **61**; incline track, **92**; laboratory scale, **447**; laser, **395**; lumber, **68**; skyscraper, **77**; subway car, **119**; tow truck bed, **126**
beam abort, super collider, **394**
beam balance, laboratory, **446-447**
beam lens, laser, **395**
beam pipe, super collider, **394**

beam shroud, gas laser, **395**
beam splitter, holography, **395**
beanie cap, space shuttle, **152**
beard: man's, **211**; spring beard needle, **386**; turkey, **35**; type, **166**; ultimate beast, **49**; windmill, **390**
bearing: airport runway, **94**; fishing reel, **340**; laboratory scale, **446**; radar, **444**; roller skate, **324**; skateboard, **324**; socket wrench, **415**; transit, **436**
bearing distance heading indicator, pilot's instrument panel, **481**
bearing edge, horse's foot, **38**
bearing line, compass, **136**
bearing rail, bureau, **272**
bearing ring, radar, **444**
bearing surface, brick, **68**
bearpaw shoe, snowshoe, **327**
bear trap, **433**
bear trap binding, ski, **326**
beat, police, **498**
beater: bass drum, **364**; kitchen tool, **258**; vacuum cleaner, **283**
beauty products, **217**
beauty salon, passenger ship, **142**
beaver, armor, **465**
because, symbol, **511**
becket, block and tackle, **461**
beckoning, gesture, **507**
bed, **270-271**; brick, **68**; cannon carriage, **467**; child's wagon, **287**; coffin, **516**; etching press, **377**; hammock, **288**; highway, **114**; lithographic press, **376**; railroad track, **115**; river, **13**; slide, **287**; tower, ladder, **124**; trampoline, **308**; wheelbarrow, **430**
bed cloth, pool table, **320**
bedcover, **271**
bedding, **270-271**
bed handle, lithographic press, **376**
bed joint, brick wall, **69**
bed knife, sickle-bar mower, **429**
bed mold, column entablature, **73**
bedplate: mortar, **472**; steam engine, **405**
bedrail, **270**
bedroll: backpacking, **343**; cowboy, **490**
bedspread, **271**
bee, **41**
beef, **32**
Beefeater, **483**
beehive, woman's hair, **213**
begin paragraph, proofreader's mark, **514**
belfry, church, **86**
bell, **iv**; bassoon, **357**; boxing, **309**; buoy, **132**; candle snuffer, **237**; clarinet, **356**; cymbal, **364**; fire engine, **124, 125**; foil mounting, **315**; hammer, **412**; jellyfish, **46**; slot machine, **346**; steam locomotive, **116**; telephone, **180**; trombone, **358, 359**; vault, **457**
bell boot, harness racing pacer **337**
bell-bottom trousers, **191, 497**
bell brace, trombone, **358**
bell buoy, nautical chart, **22**
bell chest piece, stethoscope, **449**
bell cord, commuter bus, **118**
bellows: accordion, **366**;

bagpipe, **365**; fireplace, **232**; organ, **360**; paper bag, **266**
bellows pocket, parka, **201**
bellows strap, accordion, **366**
bell plug, fencing foil, **315**
bell rim, bugle, **359**
bell shade, lamp, **238**
bell wire, trumpet, **359**
belly: baluster, **73**; banjo, **362**; cat, **37**; horse, **38**; human, **25**; jumbo jet, **149**; mandolin, **362**; type, **166**; violin, **355**
bellybutton, **25**
belowdeck storage entrance, tanker, **140**
belt: automobile engine, **111**; backpack, **343**; belt sander, **421**; cardigan sweater, **199**; cowboy, **490**; drag racing driver, **339**; dress, **198**; football uniform, **292**; ice hockey player, **294**; jewelry, **219**; king's regalia, **484**; machine gun ammunition, **471**; man's, **190**; military, **496, 497**; Milky Way, **3**; mountain climbing, **334**; police, **498-499**; sander, **421**; shoulder bag, **222**; skirt, **197**; time, **5**; trench coat, **200**; trousers, **191**; waterskiing vest, **329**
belt carrier, trousers, **191**
belted waistband, woman's pants, **196**
belt safety guard, drill press, **419**
belt sander, **421**
belt-tension knob, drill press, **419**
bench: baseball field, **291**; basketball court, **296**; courtroom, **89**; football field, **293**; ice hockey rink, **295**; sled, **328**; toboggan, **328**
bench rule, **424**
bench saw, **417**
benchseat, powerboat, **139**
bench screw, woodcarving, **372**
bench top, workbench, **408**
bench vise, **409**
bend: fishhook, **341**; paper clip, **277**; tuba, **358**
bending magnet, super collider, **394**
Benguela Current, ocean, **6**
bent, roller coaster, **92**
bent gouge, woodcarving, **372**
bent side, grand piano, **361**
beret, **202**
berg, glacier, **12**
bergschrund, mountain, **9**
bergy bit, glacier, **12**
berm: permanent fort, **83**; shoreline, **14**
berry, tomato, **54**
berth, sailboat, **135**
berta, bridal gown, **488**
berthing hawser, passenger ship, **142**
besom, skirt, **197**
beta rod, radio antenna, **183**
betting: jai alai, **314**; odds, flat racing, **336**
bevel: chisel, **420**; scriber, **375**
bevel gear, hand drill, **418**
bevel scale, table saw, **417**
bezel: pendant, **219**; watch, **220, 304**
bezel facet, cut gemstone, **218**
B flat, piano keyboard octave, **361**
bias, fabric, **388**
bias switch, tape recorder, **177**
bias tape, garment seam, **196**
bib: fencing mask, **315**; Indian

shirt, **490**; lacrosse uniform, **298**; maid's uniform, **489**; man's shirt, **189**
bibcock, **273**
biceps, human, **26**
bicuspid, **456**
bicycle, **128**; body building, **344**
bicycle crossing, road sign, **505**
bicycle trail, public sign, **506**
bifocal eyeglasses, **221**
big bowtie, clown, **493**
big cage, circus, **90**
big 8, craps table, **347**
big guns, surfboard, **330**
big nose, clown, **493**
bight, coastline, **15**
big 6, craps table, **347**
big toe, human foot, **31**
big top, circus, **90**
bike: body building, **344**; harness racing, **337**
bike route, road sign, **504**
bilge, sailboat, **135**
bilge alarm, powerboat, **138**
bill: anchor, **132**; bird, **39**; duck, **35**; fishing plug, **341**; hook and eye, **208**; man's cap, **202**; paper money, **224**
bill compartment, wallet, **223**
billet, saddle, **335**
billfold, **223**
billiard table, **320**
billing, magazine cover, **169**
billing error information, monthly statement, **227**
billy club, police, **498**
bin: garbage disposal, **247**; jumbo jet, **148**; refrigerator, **249**; sideboard, **243**; silo, **104**; tank, **474**
binary code bars, Universal Product Code, **440**
binary star, **3**
binaural, stethoscope, **449**
binder: cigar, **228**; water ski, **329**
binding: baseball glove, **291**; hat, **202**; javelin, **303**; mattress, **271**; pole vault pole, **305**; shoe, **204**, **302**; ski, **326**, **327**, **329**; tennis racket, **312**
binding screw, electric plug, **398**
binnacle, compass, **136**
binoculars, **443**
binocular tube, microscope, **442**
bipod leg, mortar, **472**
bird, **39**; badminton, **319**; space shuttle, **152**
biretta, clergy, **487**
birth: racing entry, **336**; symbol, **510**
birth date, résumé, **160**
bishop: chess, **345**; vestments, **487**
bishop pawn, chess, **345**
bishop's arms, church, **87**
bishop sleeve, bridal gown, **488**
bishop's screen, church, **87**
bit: dental, **455**; destroyer, **476**; drain cleaner, **422**; fireboat, **144**; flat racing, **336**; gimlet, **418**; glacier, **12**; hand drill, **418**, **419**; harness racing, **337**; oil drilling, **101**; pipe, **229**; polo, **299**; screwdriver, **413**; stopwatch, **304**; tugboat, **144**
bite: bugle, **359**; scissors, **384**
bitee stick, ambulance, **123**
bit gauge, drill, **418**, **419**
bitty berg, glacier, **12**
bivalve shell, **47**

blackened copper surface, solar collector panel, **391**
black hole, **2**
black inner table, backgammon, **345**
blackjack, **347**
black match, aerial shell, **383**
black outer table, backgammon, **345**
black slot, roulette, **376**
black square, chessboard, **345**
black suit, chauffeur, **489**
black tie: chauffeur, **489**; military uniform, **496**
black wire, electrical receptacle, **398**
bladder: football, **292**; human, **27**; seeweed, **57**; spacesuit, **155**
blade: airplane propeller, **147**; ambulance, **123**; ax, **464**; bicycle, **128**; booties, ice skates, **325**; bulldozer, **435**; burnisher, **377**; can opener, **251**; cartridge fuse, **399**; chisel, **420**; cigar cutter, **228**; combination square, **424**; corkscrew, **251**; electric plug, **398**; fencing foil, **315**; fern, **57**; fishing rod, **341**; flower petal, **53**; food processor, **254**; gardening shears, **427**; gouge, **374**; grass, **58**; guillotine, **462**; halberd, **464**; hatchet, **412**; helicopter rotor, **146**; hoe, **427**; ice hockey stick, **295**; ice skates, **325**; juice extractor, **255**; key, **459**; knife, **244**, **256**, **426**, **463**; lawn mower, **429**; leaf, **52**; L-shaped square, **424**; outboard engine, **137**; partisan, **464**; peeler, **256**; Ping-Pong racket, **321**; plane, **420**; razor, **210**; rotogravure, **166**; rowboat oar, **133**; saw, **416**, **417**; scissors, **384**; screwdriver, **413**; scriber, **375**; seaweed, **57**; shoe horn, **207**; shovel, **427**; silk screen squeegee, **375**; skate, **295**; skin diving fin, **331**; speculum, **448**; sword, **463**; tape measure, **424**; windmill, **390**; woodcarving tool, **372**
blade-bevel handwheel, table saw, **417**
blade cartridge, razor, **210**
blade control lever, bulldozer, **435**
blade-elevating handwheel, saw, **417**
blade eye hook, bulldozer, **435**
blade guard, power saw, **417**
blade hole, cigar cutter, **228**
blade injector, shaver, **210**
blade screw, saw, **417**
blade shaft, can opener, **251**
blank: coin, **225**; key, **459**
blanket: bedding, **271**; police car, **122**; saddle, **335**
blanket bar, etching press, **377**
blanket cylinder, offset press, **166**
blank/search button, video-still camera, **173**
blazer jacket, woman's, **196**
bleach dispenser, washing machine, **280**
bleed: magazine, **171**; political map, **21**
bleed valve, steam engine, **405**
blender, **254**; pastry, **261**
blimp, **156**; camera, **174**
blind, window, **241**
blinder, flat racing, **336**
blinker: automobile, **106**;

destroyer, **477**; flat racing, **336**
blister: automobile fender, **107**; packaging, **268**
block: automobile engine, **111**; backgammon, **345**; bongo drum, **364**; football helmet, **292**; igloo, **85**; letter, **159**; postage stamps, **159**; pulley, **461**; racing, **304**; stapler, **277**; steam engine, swimming pool, **316**; and tackle, **461**; toothbrush, **215**; window shutters, **241**; woodcut printing, **374**; workbench, **408**
blocked man's hat, **202**
blocking, lacrosse, **298**
block number, city plan, **20**
block valve, nuclear reactor, **392**
blood factor symbols, **510**
blood groove, sword, **463**
bloodline, flat racing entry, **336**
blood-pressure cuff, **123**
blood-pressure gauge, **449**
blossom end, banana, **55**
blot, backgammon, **345**
blouse: baseball catcher, **290**; military, **496**; police, **499**; woman's, **197**
blower: drag racing dragster, **339**; heat exchanger, **403**
blow wheel, humidifier, **402**
blowhole: dolphin, **45**; flute, **357**
blow-in, magazine, **171**
blowpipe, bagpipe, **365**
blowout preventor, oil drilling, **101**
blucher, man's shoe, **204**
blue lightnin', cowboy, **490**
blue line, ice hockey rink, **295**
blueprint, house, **62**
Blue Room, White House, **75**
blue whistler, cowboy, **490**
bluff, nautical chart, **22**
blunder, gesture, **507**
blurb: book, **iv**, **167**; label, **268**; magazine, **169**, **170**
blurgit, cartoon, **381**
blush, makeup, **216**, **217**
boar, **34**
board: backgammon, **345**; barbecue grill, **288**; darts, **322**; diving, **316**; guitar, **362**; hand loom, **387**; horseracing, **336**, **337**; ice hockey rink, **295**; jai alai cancha, **314**; kitchen tool, **261**; merry-go-round, **93**; military uniform, **496**; organ, **360**; roller coaster, **92**; squash court, **313**; stage, **350**; track and field, **300**; universal gym, **344**; windsurfer, **330**
boarding, barn, **104**
boarding ladder: combat aircraft, **480**; tugboat, **144**
boat, **132**; craps table, **347**
boat boom, aircraft carrier, **478**
boat deck, passenger ship, **143**
boat neck, sweater, **199**
bob, clock pendulum, **233**
bobber, fishing, **341**
bobbin: sewing machine, **278**; spinning wheel, **387**; tatting shuttle, **386**
bobby pin, **214**
bobèche, candelabrum, **237**
bobsled, **328**
bodice: dress, **198**; queen's regalia, **484**
body: arrow, **466**; automobile, **106**; baren, **374**; binoculars, **443**; book, **167**; can, **267**;

carpenter's level, **424**; discus, **303**; drag racing dragster, **339**; drill bit, **419**; ear scope, **448**; faucet, **273**; fishing plug, **341**; garbage truck, **127**; guitar, **362**, **363**; hand grenade, **473**; human, **24-31**; internal combustion engine, **406**; letter, **159**; levigator, **376**; locking pliers, **414**; locomotive, **117**; nail clippers, **215**; newspaper story, **168**; padlock, **459**; pail, **284**; paper bag, **266**; percolator, **252**; pistol nozzle, **428**; phonograph headphone, **179**; piccolo, **356**; pot, **373**; printing press, **376**, **377**; saxophone, **357**; shirt, **189**; snake, **42**; sock, **207**; sweater, **199**; tooth, **456**; traffic light, **113**; type, **166**; video camera, **184**; window shade, **240**, **241**
body building, **344**
body case, rocket, **383**
body feather, chicken, **35**
body handle, pressure cooker, **257**
body lacing, snowshoe, **327**
body lock handle, garbage truck, **127**
body molding, automobile, **107**
body oil, **217**
body pad, ice hockey goalie, **294**
body panel, stagecoach, **131**
body-restraint strap, operating table, **450**
body rivet, pliers, **414**
body tube, microscope, **442**
body wall, safe, **457**
body whorl, univalve shell, **47**
bogie, bus, **118**
boiler: furnace, **400**; locomotive, **116**; pot, **257**; steam engine, **405**
bold face type, **165**; magazine, **170**, **171**
bole, tree, **50**
bollard, canal lock, **99**
bolo tie, **192**
bolster: chisel, **420**; knife, **256**; sofa, **236**; stagecoach, **131**
bolt, **411**; bicycle, **128**; saw, **417**, **431**; crossbow, **466**; crutch, **452**; door, **458**; fabric, **388**; house, **61**; hurdle, **304**; levigator, **376**; lock, **458**; plane knob, **420**; pliers, **414**; pulley block, **461**; railroad crossing signal, **115**; rifle, **468**, **471**; roller skate, **324**; ship's bell, **iv**; vault, **457**; vise, **409**; wheelchair, **452**
bolt-activating gear ring, vault, **457**
bolt cap, toilet, **275**
bolt cutter, **414**
bolt ring, **218**; identification bracelet, **187**
bolt-retracting gear, vault, **457**
bomb elevators, aircraft carrier, **478**
bombproof, permanent fort, **83**
bond, wall, **69**
bonded insulation filling, sleeping bag, **343**
bone: acoustic guitar, **362**; early calculator, **441**; girdle, **195**; human, **25**, **26**; meat, **262**; tile games, **345**
bone marrow, meat, **262**
bongos, **364**
bonnet, **203**; faucet, **273**; fire hydrant, **125**; Indian, **490**

522

bonnet string, cowboy, **490**
bony plate, stegosaurus, **43**
book, **167**; postage stamps,
  159; sample page; **iv**; type,
  165
boom: aircraft carrier, **478**;
  radio antenna, **183**; sailboat,
  134; tower ladder, **124**; tow
  truck, **126**; windsurfer, **330**
boom box, **182**
boom bumper, windsurfer, **330**
boom gallows, sailboat, **134**
boom light, truck bed, **126**
boom-to-mast clip, CB radio
  antenna, **183**
booster, space shuttle, **152**
booster fan, underwater
  tunnel, **98**
booster hose-reel, pumper, **124**
booster parachute canister,
  space shuttle, **152**
booster tank, pumper, **124**
boot, **206**; automobile, **106**;
  bassoon, **357**; cowboy, **490**;
  fireman, **500**; harness racing
  pacer, **337**; ice climbing, **334**;
  ice skate, **325**; panty hose,
  195; polo, **299**; race horse,
  336; rain, **207**; Revolutionary
  War general, **492**; roller
  skate, **324**; soccer, **297**; skin
  diving, **331**; skiing, **327**, **329**;
  soldier's, **497**; spark plug,
  111; stagecoach, **131**
booth, voting, **437**
boot hook, **207**
bootie, skin diving, **331**
bootjack, **207**
boot stripe, power boat, **138**
boot top: destroyer, **477**; drum
  major's shoe, **495**; sailboat,
  134
boozex, cartoon, **381**
borated-water storage tank,
  nuclear reactor, **392**
border: basket, **266**; book
  page, **iv**; canapé, **263**; check,
  226; comic strip, **380**;
  magazine cover, **169**; paper
  money, **225**; stage, **350**
bore: spool, **384**; thermometer,
  449; weapons, **467**, **468**, **469**,
  470
bore evacuator, tank gun, **475**
bosom, human, **25**
boson, **394**
boss, shield, **464**
bota, ski clothes, **327**
botonee, symbol, **508**
bottle, **267**, **268**; hair lotion
  applicator, **214**; opener, **251**,
  426
bottle rack, oil drilling
  platform, **101**
bottom: barrel, **267**; book
  page, **167**; flag, **502**; girdle,
  195; golf bag, **311**; man's
  shoe, **204**; parachute, **333**;
  piano, **361**; plane, **420**;
  screen, **175**; skillet, **257**;
  stove, **404**; sweater, **199**;
  vest, **188**; waterski, **329**;
  window shutter, **241**; zinc
  carbon cell, **397**; zipper, **209**
bottom bow, sousaphone, **358**
bottom girdle, hot air balloon,
  332
bottom pillow, stage coach,
  131
bottom plate, house, **61**
bottom rail: bureau, **272**; door,
  64; staircase, **66**; venetian
  blind, **241**; window, **65**
bottom sheet, bedding, **271**
bottom spring, **230**
bouffant hairdo, woman's, **213**
bounce-angle scale, electronic
  flash, **176**

bouche, shield, **464**
boundaries, map, **5**, **20**
boundary line, volleyball
  court, **319**
bouquet, bridal, **488**
bout: fencing, **315**; viola, **355**
boutonniere, jacket, **188**, **488**
bow, **466**; bear trap, **433**; bell,
  iv; beret, **202**; boat, **132**, **133**,
  144; bonnet, **203**; brace, **418**;
  crutch, **452**; cymbal, **364**;
  kettledrum, **364**; key, **459**;
  kite, **323**; man's hat, **202**;
  mousetrap, **433**; rake, **427**;
  saddle, **335**; scissors, **384**;
  sousaphone, **358**; sword hilt,
  463; trombone, **358**; violin,
  355; watch, **220**, **304**;
  windsurfer, **330**
bowel, human, **25**
bowl: basting ladle, **259**;
  brazier, **288**; dessert setting,
  245; electric wok, **257**; food
  processor, **254**; juice
  extractor, **255**; kitchen sink,
  247; mixing, **258**; pipe, **229**;
  roulette wheel, **346**; spoon,
  244; stemware, **244**; toilet,
  275; type, **165**
bowling, **317**
bowl release, minivacuum, **283**
bowl track, railroad yard, **96**
bowmen, **466**
bow numbers, destroyer, **477**
bow pulpit, sailboat, **134**
bowsprit, sailboat, **134**
bowstring, **466**
bow thruster, passenger ship,
  143
bow tie, **192**; clown, **493**;
  man's formal attire, **488**
bow window, house, **62**
box: automobile steering gear,
  108; ballet toeshoes, **494**;
  barn, **104**; baseball field,
  291; blackjack table, **346**;
  book page, **iv**; boot, **206**;
  bus, **118**; cigar cutter, **228**;
  circuit breaker, **399**;
  courtroom, **89**; craps table,
  347; dulcimer, **362**; easel,
  370; electrical receptacle,
  398; handball court, **313**; ice
  hockey rink, **295**; light
  fixture, **238**; lithographic
  press, **376**; machine gun
  cartridge, **471**; mail, **231**;
  map, **21**; metronome, **367**;
  money, **457**; packaging, **269**;
  paramedic equipment, **123**;
  parking meter, **113**; pole
  vault, **305**; pool table, **320**;
  prison, **76**; radar antenna,
  444; railroad crossing signal,
  115; razor blade injector,
  210; resonance, **367**; running
  shoe, **302**; seeder, **430**;
  sideboard, **243**; sketch, **371**;
  stagecoach, **131**; steam
  engine, **405**; subway
  motorman's cab, **119**; tank,
  474; tefillin, **486**; theatre,
  351; tow truck, **126**; tugboat,
  144; vault, **457**; wrench, **415**
boxcar, train, **117**
box drawer, desk, **276**
boxer, pugilist, **309**
boxer shorts, **194**
boxing, **309**
box kit, **323**
boxman, craps table, **347**
box ratchet, brace, **418**
box spring, bed, **271**
bra, **195**
brace, **418**; balance beam, **306**;
  basketball backstop, **296**;
  bridge, **97**; child's wagon,
  287; dental, **453**; fence gate,

69; guitar, **362**; house, **61**;
  kiln, **373**; kite, **323**; ladder,
  425; locomotive, **116**; man's,
  190; oil drilling platform,
  101; parallel bars, **306**;
  rocking chair, **234**; sponge
  mop, **283**; stage, **350**;
  stagecoach, **131**; supportive,
  452; table saw, **417**;
  toboggan, **328**; trombone,
  358; venetian blind, **241**;
  wheelbarrow, **430**;
  wheelchair, **452**; workbench,
  408
brace flange, trombone, **358**
brace pole, tent, **342**
brachial artery, human, **28**
brachial plexus, human, **29**
brachioradialis, human, **26**
bracket: butterfly table, **242**;
  child's wagon, **287**; citrus
  juicer, **255**; dental unit, **454**;
  grammatical symbol, **513**;
  house, **62**; inflatable, **133**;
  ladder, **425**; mortar, **472**;
  orthodontic, **453**; outboard
  engine, **137**; police car, **122**;
  radar antenna, **444**; railroad
  crossing signal, **115**; royal
  crown, **485**; sawhorse, **408**;
  ship's bell, **115**; tanker, **141**;
  tow truck bed, **126**; traverse
  rod, **240**; wheelbarrow, **430**;
  wheelchair, **452**
bracket slot, dental braces, **453**
bracket table, dental, **455**
bract: grass, **58**; lettuce, **262**;
  pineapple, **55**
brad, **410**
braid: military uniform, **496**;
  venetian blind, **241**;
  woman's hair, **213**; woman's
  hat, **203**
braided tail, polo pony, **299**
braille, **512**
brain: allosaurus, **43**; human,
  29; stegosaurus, **43**
brains, beef, **32**
brain stem, human, **29**
brake: bicycle, **128**; bobsled,
  328; bulldozer, **435**; car, **108**,
  110; chain saw, **431**;
  locomotive, **116**; motorcycle,
  129; 747 cockpit, **150**; ski
  binding, **326**; space shuttle,
  152; stagecoach, **131**;
  stroller, **286**; subway car,
  119; tank gun muzzle, **475**
brake caliper: automobile, **108**;
  bicycle, **128**; motorcycle, **129**
brake caster, easel, **370**
brake drum, automobile, **109**
brake duct, racing car, **338**
brake handle: 747 cockpit,
  150; subway motorman's
  cab, **119**
brake plate, ski binding, **326**
brake pressure indicator,
  pilot's instrument panel, **481**
branch: cactus, **56**;
  candelabrum, **237**; celery,
  262; hogan, **84**; horseshoe,
  38; military insignia, **496**;
  river, **13**; stirrup, **335**; sword
  hilt, **463**; tree, **50**; tuba, **358**
brand: branding iron, **432**; gas
  pump, **112**; label, **268**;
  pencil, **158**
branding iron, **432**
brand name, coupon, **103**
brand name ad space,
  supermarket, **102**
brand name logo, aisle
  display, **102**
brandy snifter, **245**

brass: musical instruments,
  354, **358**-**359**; sideboard, **243**
brassard, military police, **496**
brass button: military, **496**;
  police, **498**
brassie, golf club, **311**
brassiere, **195**
bratelles, dress, **198**
brayer, woodcut printing, **374**
brazier, patio, **288**
Brazil Current, ocean, **6**
bread: canapé base, **263**;
  Communion, **87**; loaf, **157**
breadbasket, human, **25**
bread rack, toaster, **253**
break, cat, **37**
break-arch, grandfather clock,
  233
breaker: circuit, **399**; magazine,
  170; shoreline, **14**; stained
  glass, **378**
breaker hammer, **436**
breakfront, **243**
breakout, political map, **21**
breakpoint, continental
  margin, **15**
breast: chicken, **35**; horse, **38**;
  human, **24**; lamb, **33**;
  poultry, **35**; woman's shoe
  heel, **205**
breastbeam, hand loom, **387**
breast collar, harness racing,
  337
breastplate: armor, **465**; polo,
  299; Torah, **486**
breast pocket: men's jacket,
  188; parka, **201**; shirt, **189**;
  woman's jacket, **196**
breast protector, fencing, **315**
breaststroke swimming race,
  316
breastworks, permanent fort,
  83
breath-hold diving, **331**
breathing aid, paramedic, **123**
breathing filter, drag racing
  fire suit, **339**
breath mark, music, **352**
B recreation yard, prison, **76**
breech: human, **25**; weapons,
  467, **470**, **471**
breechblock, shotgun, **468**
breeches, *see* trousers
breeches, polo, **299**
breeder reactor, nuclear
  power, **392**
breve, grammatical symbol,
  513
brewed coffee, **252**
brick: building material, **68**;
  lobster pot, **433**
brickmold, window, **65**
brick symbolia, cartoon, **380**
brick wall, **69**
bridal dress, **488**
bridge, **97**; aircraft carrier, **478**;
  airport, **94**; billiards, **320**;
  bow, **466**; bowling ball, **317**;
  castle, **80**, **81**; coffin, **516**;
  dental, **453**; destroyer, **477**;
  eyeglasses, **221**; guitar, **362**;
  highway cloverleaf, **114**;
  lacrosse stick, **298**; nose, **30**;
  passenger ship, **143**;
  railroad, **115**; spider web, **40**;
  submarine, **479**; tanker, **141**;
  vault, **457**; violin, **355**
bridge and socket assembly,
  sponge mop, **282**
bridge cover, guitar, **363**
bridge table, **242**
bridle: horseracing, **336**, **337**;
  kite leg, **323**; polo, **299**;
  waterskiing towline, **329**
briefcase, **285**
briffit, cartoon, **380**
brightness control, sonar, **444**
brilliance control, radar, **444**

brim, hat, 202, 203
briquette, charcoal, 288
brisket: beef, 32; dog, 36; horse, 38; sheep, 33
bristle: broom, 282; brow brush, 217; hairbrush, 212; painting brush, 370; paint brush, 425; toothbrush, 215
broadcast indicator, CB radio, 183
broad jump, 300
broguings, man's shoe, 204
broiler unit, stove, 248
broken leader, book page, iv
brooch, 218, 219
brook, 13
Brooklyn pocket, bowling, 317
broom, 282; mechanical sweeper, 127
brow, human, 25
browband, Indian, 490
brow brush, beauty product, 217
brow rest, eye scope, 448
brush: beauty product, 217; cooking utensil, 229; dog, 36; drum, 364; electric, 212; house painting, 425; painting, 370, 371; photographic supplies, 176; shaving, 210; ultimate beast's tail, 48; vacuum cleaner, 283
brush bag, lunar rover, 155
brush retainer screw, saber saw, 417
brushwood, wickiup, 84
brussa, Arab dress, 491
bubble: monovial, 424; theodolite, 436
buccal, tooth, 456
buccal cusp, tooth, 456
buckaroo, 490
buckboard, 131
bucket, 284; launch pad, 152; tower-ladder, 124
bucket hat, sailor, 497
bucket seat, car, 110
buckle: backpack, 343; brassiere, 195; combat soldier, 497; cowboy belt, 490; electric chair, 462; harness racing, 337; man's, 190; police gun belt, 498; sandal, 206; ski boot, 326; trench coat, 200; venetian blind, 241; waterskiing vest, 329; woman's hat, 203
buckler, medieval shield, 464
bud: flower, 53; potato, 54; taste, 30; tree, 50
buddy umbilical system bag, lunar rover, 155
buffalo horn, ultimate beast, 49
buffer: elevator shaft, 78; high-speed printer, 439; magnetic tape subsystem, 439; train track, 116
buffet, 243
buffet car, passenger train, 116
bug, ice cream cone, 265
buggy, horse-drawn, 131
bugle, 359
building, 77; city plan, 20; topographic map, 22; whole-timbered, 70
building material, 68
built-in flash: Polaroid, 173; video-still camera, 173
built-in microphone, tape recorder, 177
built-in phone, fax machine, 164
built-in speaker, personal cassette player, 182
bulb: balloon, 493; blood pressure gauge, 449; clown,

493; hourglass, 233; light, 238; onion, 54, 262; thermometer, 18, 449; vacuum tube, 396
bulb head, drain cleaner, 422
bulb of heel, horse, 38
bulkhead: passenger ship, 142; powerboat, 139; sailboat, 135; truck platform, 121
bulkhead mounting flange, aneroid barometer, 18
bulk storage: oil drilling platform, 101; refrigerator, 249
bull, 32; zodiac, 509
bull denim trousers, cowboy, 490
bulldozer, 435
bullet: cartridge, 470; police gun belt, 498; stick umbrella, 230
bulletproof vest, 499
bullhorn, police car, 122
bullion, 225
bull nose, destroyer, 477
bull's-eye, dart board, 322
bulwark: castle, 80, 81; passenger ship, 142; sailboat, 135
bump, razor blade injector, 210
bumper: automobile, 106, 107, 108; billiard cue, 320; bus, 118; citrus juicer, 255; football helmet, 292; knee kicker, 246; locomotive, 117; mechanical sweeper, 127; sled, 328; snowmobile, 130; toilet, 275; train track, 116; trombone, 359; vacuum cleaner, 283; wheelchair, 452; windsurfer, 330
bumper car, amusement park, 92
bumper steps, truck tractor,` 120
bun: sandwich, 263; woman's hair, 213
bundling, package, 269
bunghole, keg, 267
bunk, sailboat, 135
bunker, golf course, 405
bunting, flag, 502
buoy, 132; nautical chart, 22
buoyancy chamber, inflatable, 133
buoyancy compensator, skin diving, 331
bureau, dresser, 272
burette, laboratory, 447
burgee, flag, 502
burial chamber, 516
burner: barbecue grill, 288; camper stove, 342; candle, 237; chafing dish, 245; furnace, 400; hot air balloon, 332; laboratory, 447; stove, 248; tea kettle, 245; water heater, 401
burnisher, 377
burn sheet, ambulance, 123
burr: dental, 455; pipe, 422
burst, label, 268
bursting charge, aerial shell, 383
bus, 118
busby, drum major, 495
bus connection, circuit board, 439
bushing: automobile, 108; roller chain, 461
business, letter, 159
business card, 160
business career, résumé, 160
business-class section, jumbo jet, 148
bust, human, 25
bustle, tank, 474

bustline, dress, 198
bus transportation, public sign, 506
butane well, gas cigarette lighter, 228
butler, 489
butt: arrow, 466; ax, 464; bassoon, 357; bazooka, 472; billiard cue, 320; cigar, 228; cigarette, 228; fishing rod, 340; halberd, 464; latch needle, 386; pork, 34; revolver, 470; rifle, 471
butt cap; fishing rod, 340; tennis racket, 312
butte, mountain, 8
butt end, lacrosse stick, 298; paint brush bristle, 425
butter compartment, refrigerator, 249
butterfly net, 411
butterfly swimming race, 316
butterfly table, 242
butterfly tie, 192
butter knife, 244
butter plate, 244
butter stile, door, 64
butt hinge, 460
buttock: horse, 38; human, 24
button, 209; accordion, 366; answering machine, 181; ballpoint pen, 158; blender, 254; camera, 172; cannon barrel, 467; cardigan sweater, 199; chain saw, 431; compact disc player, 178; copier, 164; dental unit, 454; door lock, 458; elevator car, 78; escalator, 79; fencing foil, 315; garbage disposal, 247; guillotine, 462; human, 25; incandescent bulb, 238; jacket, 188, 196; lounger, 235; man's cap, 202; metronome, 367; military uniform, 496; movie camera, 174; organ, 360; plug fuse, 399; police car, 122; police uniform, 498; portable radio/cassette player, 182; potter's wheel, 373; remote control unit, 184; Revolutionary War general, 492; saxophone, 357; screen, 175; sewing machine, 280; skirt, 197; snake rattle, 43; sofa, 236; spur, 335; stopwatch, 304; suspenders, 190; sword hilt, 463; table saw, 417; tape recorder, 177; telegraph key, 157; trench coat, 200; trumpet, 359; vacuum cleaner, 283; vest, 188; Walkman, 182; woman's hat, 203
button-down collar, shirt, 189
button-down cuff, Revolutionary War general, 492
buttonhole: jacket, 188; Revolutionary War general, 492; shirt, 189; vest, 188
button mark, sewing pattern, 388
button nook, iron, 279
button-off collar, trench coat, 200
button-out robe lining, overcoat, 200
button rod, incandescent bulb, 238
button tab closings, pants, 191
button-through pocket, trench coat, 200
butt plate: rifle, 471; shotgun, 468
buttress, mountain, 8
butt section, fishing rod, 340

buttstock, shotgun, 468
buzzer button, video-still camera, 173
by, symbol, 510
byline: magazine, 169, 170; newspaper, 168
by-pass shears, gardening, 427

C

C: braille, 512; piano keyboard octave, 361; music notation, 353; sign language, 512
cab: airport control tower, 95; bulldozer, 435; elevator, 78; fire engine, 124, 125; horse-drawn, 131; locomotive, 116; subway, 119; tractor, 434; truck, 120
cabin: aircraft, 146, 147, 156; hovercraft, 145; sailboat, 134, 135; space shuttle, 152
cabinet: air conditioner, 402; ambulance, 123; china, 243; desk, 276; dishwasher, 250; elevator, 78; garbage disposal, 247; guitar amplifier, 363; humidifier, 402; phonograph, 179; television, 185; washing machine, 280
cabinet tip, screwdriver, 413
cabinetwork, house blueprint, 62
cabin pressure altimeter, pilot's instrument panel, 481
cabin trunk, powerboat, 138
cable: bazooka, 472; bicycle, 128; bridge, 97; circuit breaker box, 399; electrician's, 423; elevator shaft, 78; fencing strip, 315; gas pump, 112; motorcycle, 129; police car, 122; power line, 396; space suit, 155; stationary rings, 307; tow truck, 126; video-still camera adaptor, 173
cable stitch, sock, 207
caboose, train, 117
cabriolet, 131
cactus, 56
CAD, 438
caduceus, symbol, 510
Caesar, playing card king, 348
cafe curtain, 240
caftan, 491
cage: baseball catcher's, 290; buoy, 132; circus, 91; drag racing dragster, 339; football helmet, 292; hammer throw, 301; ice hockey goal, 294; jai alai cancha, 314; police car, 122
caisson, cannon, 467
cake, 264
cake plate, 245
calamus, bird feather, 39
calcaneus, human, 26
calculator, 441
calculator dial, electronic flash, 176
calendar, grandfather clock, 233
calendar day, globe, 5
calf, 32, 432; frog, 44; human, 24
caliber, cartridge, 470
calibration: blood pressure gauge, 449; Geiger counter, 445
California Current, ocean, 6
caliper: automobile disc brake, 108; bicycle, 128; motorcycle, 129
calk, horseshoe, 38
calliope, merry-go-round, 93
callout, book page, iv
calm, hurricane, 17

calving, glacier, 12
calyx, coral polyp, 46
cam: lawn sprinkler, 428; motorcycle, 129; plane, 420; pliers, 414
camber, skiing, 329
cambium, tree, 50
cambox, lithographic press, 376
camcorder, 184
came, lead, 378
cameo, 218
camera, 173; lunar rover, 155; satellite, 186; spacesuit, 155
camera connector, VCR, 184
camera platform, tripod, 176
camisole top, dress, 198
camouflage cover, soldier's helmet, 497
camper, 130
campfire, public sign, 506
camping, 342; road sign, 504
cam ring, brace, 418
can, 267; ammunition, 471; mercury battery, 397; nautical chart, 22; pacemaker, 452
canal lock, 99
canapé, 263
canard, jet fighter, 480
Canary Current, ocean, 6
cancel button, organ, 360
cancellation, envelope, 159
Cancer, zodiac, 509
cancha, jai alai, 314
candelabrum, 237
candidate's name column, voting booth, 437
candle, 237
candlepin, bowling, 317
candle slide, sideboard, 243
candlestick, 237; church, 87
cane, supportive device, 452
cane rod, fishing, 341
canine teeth, 456
canister: drain cleaner, 422; film roll, 172; police gun belt, 498; space shuttle, 152; windmill, 390
can ledge, can opener, 251
cannon, 467; horse, 38; jet fighter, 480; muzzle-loading, 472; tank, 475
cannonball, 467
cannula, hypodermic syringe, 451
canoe, roulette wheel, 346
can opener, 251; pocket knife, 426
canopy: bed, 270; bulldozer, 435; elevator, 78; glider cockpit, 147; jet fighter, 480; light fixture, 238; parachute, 333; stroller, 286; tent, 342; toll booth, 114
canopy jettison handle, pilot's instrument panel, 481
canteen, soldier's, 497
canthus, eye, 30
cantilevered suspension, racing car, 338
cantle, saddle, 335
canton, flag, 502
cantor, synagogue, 486
canvas: boxing ring, 309; painting, 370
canvas holder, easel, 370
canvas slot, sketch box, 371
canyon, 7, 13
cap: backpack, 343; baseball, 290; blender, 254; blood pressure gauge, 449; bottle, 268, 269; bulldozer, 435; can, 267; cartridge fuse, 399; chimney, 63, 232; chisel, 420; contact lens container, 221; cornet, 359; dental, 455; dishwasher, 250; dispenser,

267; engine, 111, 137, 406; fence gate, 67; fire hydrant, 125; fishing rod, 340; football, 292; hair styling, 214; hinge pin, 460; hockey skate, 325; lamp, 238; lantern, 342; magazine, 170; Manchu court dress, 491; man's, 202; military, 496, 497; mortar, 472; motorcycle, 129; mower, 429; mushroom, 57; pencil, 158; pin, 208; plane, 420; plug fuse, 399; polo, 299; racing, 336; razor, 210; railroad crossing signal, 115; rifle, 471; rocket, 383; royal crown, 485; saddle, 335; saw, 431; screen, 175; seeder, 430; shotgun, 468, 469; space shuttle, 152; standpipe, 59; stapler, 277; starting block, 304; stove, 342; tennis racket, 312; test tube, 447; thimble, 384; toilet, 275; track lighting, 239; traffic light, 113; umbrella, 230; venetian blind, 241; washing machine, 280; waterskiing towline, 329; windmill, 390
cape: land feature, 7; stonecutting, 342
capelet, king's, 484
capillary, human, 27
capillary bed, human, 28
capillary tube, thermometer, 449
capital: column, 73; political map symbol, 20; proofreader's mark, 514; type height, 165; White House, 75
Capitol building, 74
caplet, medicinal, 451
cap mounting, ballpoint pen, 158
cap nut, 411
capo, guitar, 362
capon, 35
cap opener, corkscrew, 251
cappuccino, 252
Capricorn, zodiac, 509
cap square, carriage, 467
capstan: sword hilt, 463; tape recorder, 177; tugboat, 144
capstem, strawberry, 55
capstone, gate post, 67
capsule: bottle, 267; medicinal, 451
captain's seat, 747 cockpit, 150
caption: book page, iv; cartoon, 380; magazine, 169, 171; newspaper, 168
car: amusement park ride, 92, 93; blimp, 156; drag racing, 339; elevator, 78; subway, 119; train, 96, 116, 117; see also automobile
carabiner, mountain climbing, 334
carapace, turtle, 43
carbide insert, masonry bit, 419
carbiner hole, ice ax, 242
carafe, coffee maker, 252
carapace, lobster, 47
carbon copy, letter, 159
carbon-layered forward wing edge, space shuttle, 152
carburetor: automobile, 111; chain saw, 431; motorcycle, 129
carcass, furniture, 272
card: automatic teller machine, 226; blister, 268; compass, 136; playing, 348
card case, wallet, 223

car deck, hovercraft, 145
card holder: bank card, 226; elevator car, 78; typewriter, 161
cardholder's address, monthly statement, 227
cardholder's name, monthly statement, 227
cardigan: jacket, 196; sweater, 199
cardinal, religious vestments, 487
cardinal points, weather vane, 19
card loop, typewriter, 161
card room, passenger ship, 142
card table, 242
card window, wallet, 223
career goal, résumé, 160
cargo, merchant ship, 140
cargo bay door, space shuttle, 152
cargo pocket, parka, 201
cargo ship, 140
cargo truck, airport, 95
caricature, cartooning, 380
caries, tooth, 456
carillon, iv
car lift, passenger ship, 142
carom, billiards, 320
carotid artery, human, 28
carousel: amusement park, 93; microwave oven, 248
carousel tray, slide projector, 175
carpal, human, 26
carpels, samara, 52
carpenter's level, 424
carpenter's saw, 416
carpet, 246; sweeper, 282; tack, 246
carpus: dog, 36; human hand, 31
car ramp, hovercraft, 145
car rental, public sign, 506
carriage: baby, 286; cannon, 467; horse-drawn, 131; hot air balloon; toaster, 253; typewriter, 161
carriage bolster, stagecoach, 131
carriage brace, child's wagon, 287
carrier: aircraft, 478; dental, 455; dress, 198; etching press roller, 377; fireplace wood, 232; harness racing, 337; microscope, 442; pencil sharpener, 277; traverse rod, 240
carrot, 54
carrying chair, ambulance, 123
carrying handle: golf bag, 311; landmine, 473; machine gun, 471; movie projector, 175; outboard engine, 137; photographic bag, 176; rifle, 471
car seat, child's, 286
car service area, railroad yard, 96
car-station panel, elevator, 78
art, lawn, 430
cart ad display, supermarket, 102
cartilage, human, 26
cartography, 5, 20
cartoon, stained glass, 378
cartooning, 380-381
cartridge: cowboy, belt, 490; film, 172, 174; laser printer, 163; pen, 158; phonograph turntable, 178; weapons, 470, 471
cartridge fuse, 399
cartridge slot, synthesizer, 363
caruncle, turkey, 35

carving: scrimshaw, 375; tombstone, 516
carving hammer, stonecutting, 342
cascable, cannon, 467
cascade collar, bridal gown, 488
case: attaché, 285; battery, 397; beauty product, 217; blood pressure gauge, 449; cellular telephone, 181; cosmetic, 285; handgun cartridge, 470; hardback book, 167; harmonica, 366; lock, 458; luggage, 288; metronome, 367; padlock, 459; pencil, 158; pitch pipe, 367; police gun belt, 499; screen, 175; sideboard, 243; stapler, 277; tape measure, 424; thermometer, 18; wallet, 223; watch, 220
casebound book, 167
casemate: castle, 80, 81; permanent fort, 89
casement window, 65
casework furniture, 243
cash drawer, automatic teller machine, 226
cash machine, 226
cash register, 440
cash value, coupon, 103
casing: calculator, 441; cartridge fuse, 399; door, 62, 64; electric meter, 399; hand grenade, 473; pacemaker, 452; pen, 158; pill, 451; pyramid, 71; slot machine, 346; telephone, 180; trumpet valve, 359; window, 65
casino, passenger ship, 142
cask, 267
casket, 516
casserole, 257
cassette: film, 172; operating table, 450; recorder, 177; tape, 177; Walkman, 182
cassette compartment, portable radio/cassette player, 182; Walkman, 182
cassette eject button, VCR, 184
cassette feed, laser printer, 163
cassette loading door, VCR, 184
cassette player, 182
cassette release lever, copier, 164
Cassini division, Saturn's rings, 3
cassock, 487
cast, denture, 453
caster: bed, 271; piano, 361; sofa, 236; wheelchair, 452
cast-iron casing, hand grenade, 473
castle, 80-81; chess, 345
castle pawn, chess, 345
castor, grand piano, 361
cast restoration, dental, 455
cat, 37; house, 61; circus, 90
catacomb, house, 62
catapult, 467; aircraft carrier, 478
cataract, river, 13
catch: door, 458; pistol, 470; swivel, 218
catcher: baseball, 290, 291; grill, 288; saw, 431
catch glove, ice hockey goalie, 294
catering truck, airport, 95
caterpillar track, tank, 474
cathedral, 86
cathedral hull, powerboat, 138
cathode, laser, 395
cathode ray tube: computer workstation, 438; personal

computer, 162; television, 185
cathode-ray tube screen, radar and sonar, 444
cathode wire, vacuum tube, 396
catta, 37
cattle, 32
cattle crossing, road sign, 505
cat trainer, circus, 90
catwalk: canal lock, 99; prison, 76; tanker, 140; tunnel, 98
caudal fin, fish, 45
caudal peduncle, fish, 45
caution signal: pilot's instrument panel, 481; toll booth, 114; traffic light, 113
cautionary statement, label, 269
cavalry yard, frontier fort, 82
cave, 11
cavern, 11
cavity, tooth, 455, 456
C-band antenna, lunar lander, 154
CB radio, 183; police car, 122
C cell block, prison, 76
C-clamp, 409
CD, compact disc player, 178
CD player, 178
cedilla, grammatical symbol, 513
ceiling: elevator car, 78; house, 61
celery, 262
cell: animal, 23; barometer, 18; battery, 397; electric meter, 399; flower, 53; kite, 323; octopus, 46; parachute, 333; prison, 76; solar power system, 391; telescope, 443
cellar, passenger ship, 143
cello, 354, 355
cello wrap, packaging, 269
cellular kite, 323
cellular telephone, 181
Celsius scale, thermometer; 18, 449
Celtic cross, symbol, 508
cementum, tooth, 456
cent, symbol, 511
center: basketball, 296; envelope, 159; ice hockey, 295; polo, 299; spider web, 40; theodolite, 436
centerable lens, microscope, 442
center aisle, theatre, 351
center beam, laboratory scale, 447
center bearing wall, house, 60
center circle: basketball court, 296; ice hockey rink, 295; soccer field, 297
center dent, cowboy hat, 202
center drawer: desk, 276; dressing table, 272
center field, baseball, 291
center field mark, soccer field, 297
center flag, soccer field, 297
center front panel, girdle, 195
center-front seam, skirt, 197
center hole, phonograph record, 178
centering: radar, 444; sonar, 444
centering screw, microscope, 442
center leaf, hinge, 460
center line: airport runway, 94; badminton court, 319; fencing strip, 315; ice hockey rink, 295; lacrosse field, 298; Ping-Pong table, 321; soccer field, 297; symbol, 510; volleyball court, 319

center mark, tennis court, 312
centerpiece, dessert setting, 245
center pin, pulley block, 461
center post: camera tripod, 176; tatting shuttle, 386
center ring, circus, 90-91
center slat, sled, 328
center span, bridge, 97
center spot, soccer field, 297
center stand, motorcycle, 129
center stile, door, 64
center strap, tennis net, 312
center weight, discus, 303
centigrade scale, thermometer, 18, 449
central cleft, horse's foot, 38
central computer, prison, 76
central disc, starfish, 46
central focusing drive, binoculars, 443
central incisor, tooth, 456
central instrument warning light, 747 cockpit, 151
central inventory control unit, cash register, 440
central nervous system, human, 29
central portal, church, 87
central processing unit, 438
Central Time, 5
central-vent volcano, 10
centriole, animal cell, 23
cents-off corner mark, label, 269
cents-off value, coupon, 103
cephalothorax, spider, 40
ceramic shell, plug fuse, 399
cerebellum, brain, 29
cerebral cortex, brain, 29
cerebrum, brain, 29
cereal grass, 38
cercus, grasshopper, 41
certificate holder, elevator car, 78
certification, gas pump, 112
certification plate, truck van, 121
cervical collar, ambulance, 123
cervical vertebrae, human, 26
cesta, jai alai, 314
chafing dish, 245
chain, 461; bear trap, 433; bicycle, 128; castle portcullis, 81; chain saw, 431; fire hydrant, 125; football sidelines, 293; gun belt, 499; grandfather clock, 233; hammock, 288; identification bracelet, 187; incline track, 92; jewelry, 219; king's regalia, 484; lock, 458; oil drilling platform, 101; spur, 335; swing, 287; tow truck bed, 126; zipper, 209
chain guard: bicycle, 128; lithographic press, 376; motorcycle, 129
chainlink fence, 67; prison, 76
chain lock, 458
chain mail, armor, 465
chain pin, roller chain, 461
chain reaction, nuclear reactor, 392
chain saw, 431
chain stopper, sink, 273
chair: ambulance, 123; dental, 454; electric, 462; powerboat, 139; reclining, 235; rocking, 234; wheeled, 452
chaise longue, 288
chalice, 87
chalk, billiards, 320
chamber: burial, 516; camera, 174; cave, 11; Capitol, 74; combustion jet engine, 407; decompression, 452;

fireplace, 232; revolver, 470; rocket, 407; stove, 404
chamber music ensemble, 354
champagne glass, 244
championship tee, golf course, 310
chancel, church, 87
chancellery, 86
chandelier: light fixture, 238; Senate, 74
changeout room, launch pad, 152
change pocket, jacket, 188
channel: backyard glider, 287; bowling lane, 317; canal lock, 99; CB radio, 183; laboratory scale, 447; lamp, 238; lead came, 378; nautical chart, 22; operating room table, 450; pliers, 414; police radio, 122; river, 13; stapler, 277; window, 65
channel index, picture-in-picture viewing, 185
channel number readout, picture-in-picture viewing, 185
channel selector, remote control unit, 184
channel set indicator, VCR, 184
chanter, bagpipe, 365
chapel: castle, 81; church, 86, 87; frontier fort, 82; passenger ship, 143; prison, 76
chaps, cowboy, 490
chapter: book, 167; grandfather clock, 233; pocket watch, 220
character: cartooning, 380; clown face, 493; mah-jongg tile, 345; typewriter, 161
charcoal: briquette, 288; sketch box, 371
charge, flag, 502
charge card, 227
charge container, land mine, 473
charged particle telescope, satellite, 186
charger, tow truck, 126
chariot, merry-go-round, 93
Charlemagne, playing card king, 348
Charlie, stagecoach, 131
charm, jewelry, 219
chart: electronic weather station, 18; nautical, 22
chart table, sailboat, 135
chase: cannon barrel, 467; wall, 69
chaser, engraving, 377
chassis: automobile, 106; racing car, 338-339; machine gun, 471
chasuble, cardinal, 487
château name, wine label, 267
chauffeur, 489
chauffeur's cab, fire engine, 124, 125
cheater, wrench, 415
check, 226; lacrosse, 298; lumber, 68; ticket, 349
check bars, Universal Product Code, 440
check bit, harness racing, 337
checkbook clutch, 223
check digit, bank card, 226
checker, 345
checkerboard, 345
checkering, shotgun, 468
check-in, public sign, 506
check issue date, 226
check letter, paper money, 224, 225

checkout area, supermarket, 103
checkout center, 440
checkout counter, 103
checkpoint, prison, 76
check rein, harness racing, 337
cheek: cannon carriage, 467; dog, 36; horse, 38; hammer, 412; human, 24; latch needle, 386; piano, 361; pulley block, 461
cheese, 263; pizza, 265; slicer, 256
chelicera, spider, 40
chemin de fer, 346
chemise: dress, 198; queen's underpinnings, 484
cheng-lung, Manchu court dress, 491
cherry: ice cream cone, 265; police car, 122
cherry picker, tower ladder, 124
chess, 345
chest: dog, 36; horse, 38; human, 24; organ, 360
chest and stomach pad, lacrosse uniform, 298
chest floor, cow, 32
chest of drawers, 272
chest piece, stethoscope, 449
chest press, universal gym, 344
chest protector: baseball catcher, 290; ice hockey goalie, 294
chest pull, body building, 344
chevelure, 211
chevron, airport runway, 94
chicken, 35
chief, coat of arms, 503
chief clerk, Senate, 74
chiffonier, 272
chignon, woman's hair, 213
children: backyard equipment, 286-287; gear, 286; playroom, passenger ship, 143
chime: barrel, 267; bell, iv
chimney: cave, 11; fireplace, 232; furnace, 400; house, 62, 63; mountain, 8; volcano, 10
chin: bird, 39; human, 24
china cabinet, 243
china guard, dishwasher, 244
China Room, White House, 75
chine, powerboat, 138
chinning bar, backyard, 287
chinning station, universal gym, 344
chin piece, armor, 465
chin rest, violin, 355
chin strap: cowboy hat, 202; drum major's busby, 495; football helmet, 292; ice hockey player, 295; police helmet, 499; polo, 299
chip: blackjack, 347; craps table, 347; transistor, 396
chisel, 372, 374, 420
chitin, crustacean, 47
chock: destroyer, 476, 477; mountain climbing, 334
choil, knife, 463
choir, church, 87
choir keyboard, organ, 360
choir riser, orchestra, 354
choke, car, 110, 111
choke end, wood block, 461
choke knob, chain saw, 431
choked barrel, shotgun, 468
choker necklace, 219; Indian, 490; queen's, 484
chopper, helicopter, 261
chopping board, 261
chopsticks, electric wok, 257
chord: lift bridge, 97; music, 352

chord buttons, accordion, 366
chordophone, 362
choropleth map, 21
Christmas tree, drag racing starting lights, 339
chromatophore, octopus, 46
chrome, automobile, 107
chronograph, spacesuit, 155
chronometer, 220
chromosome, cell, 23
chrysanthemum, fireworks, 382
chuck: beef, 32; brace, 418; drill, 418, 419; fishing rod, 340; screwdriver, 413; scriber, 375
chuck-a-luck, 346
chuck tightener, dental, 455
chukka, polo, 299
church, 86-87
church key, can opener, 251
chute: dam, 100; jumbo jet, 148; mountain, 8; mower, 429; parachuting, 333; racetrack, 337; running track, 300; saw, 417; toll basket, 114
cigar, 228
cigarette, 228
cigarette lighter, 228; car, 110
cilia, eye, 30
ciliary body, eye, 30
cinch: backpack strap, 343; cowboy hat, 202; fastener, 208; saddle, 335
cincture: column, 73; religious vestments, 487
cinder, volcano, 10
cine scale, light meter, 176
cinquefoil, church, 86
circle: baseball field, 291; basketball court, 296; geodesic dome, 85; ice hockey rink, 295; shot put, 301; theodolite, 436
circlet, royal crown, 485
circuit, electric, 399
circuit board, 439
circuit breaker, 399; space shuttle, 153
circuit closer lever, telegraph key, 157
circuit traces, circuit board, 439
circular saw, 417
circular slide rule, 441
circulating pump, solar heating system, 391
circulating water pump, nuclear reactor, 393
circulatory system, human, 27, 28
circumflex accent, grammatical symbol, 513
circus, 90-91
cirque, mountain, 8
cirque glacier, 9, 12
cirrocumulus cloud, 16
cirrostratus cloud, 16, 17
cirrus cloud, 16, 17
citation: enlisted man, 496; police, 498
Citizen's Band radio, 183
citrus juicer, 255
city plan, map, 20
city symbol, political map, 20
civil aircraft, 148-149
cladophyll, asparagus, 54
clam, 47
clamp, 409; cassette tape, 177; drill press, 419; finishing sander, 421; laboratory, 446; lamp, 239; outboard engine, 137; Ping-Pong net, 321; paw, 416; telescope, 443; theodolite, 436
clamp bar, suit hanger, 281
clamp collar, camera tripod, 176

clamp holder, pumper, 125
clamp screw: combination square, 424; outboard engine, 137; sewing machine, 278; theodolite, 436
clapboard siding, house, 63
clapper: bell, iv; buoy, 132
clarinet, 354, 356-357
clarstory, church, 86
clasp: denture, 453; hair roller, 214; identification bracelet, 187; keychain, 459; necktie, 192; pin, 208; royal regalia, 484
classification track, railroad yard, 96
class insignia, mainsail, 136
class interval, thematic map, 21
clavicle, human, 26
clavier, organ, 360
claw: allosaurus, 43; bee, 41; bird, 39; cat, 37; clothespin, 280; flower petal, 53; grasshopper, 41; hammer, 412; lizard, 43; lobster, 47; rifle sling, 468; ring, 219; spider, 40; turkey, 35; turtle, 43; ultimate beast, 48
clay choke, rocket, 383
cleaner: automobile engine, 111; mower, 429; nail clippers, 215; pipe, 229
cleaning supplies, photographic, 176
cleanout plug, sink drain, 273
cleansing cream, 216
clear: shuffleboard court, 318; weather map, 19
clearance light: bus, 118; truck, 121
clear key, calculator, 441
clear program button, compact disc player, 178
cleat: baseball, 290; football, 292; sailboat, 135; snowmobile, 130; tugboat, 144
cleavage, human, 25
clef, music, 352, 353
cleft: horse's foot, 38; human, 25
clerical collar, minister, 487
clerestory, church, 86
clerk, Congress, 74
clerk's table, courtroom, 89
clew: hammock, 288; mainsail, 136
cliff, 7, 9
climax basket, 266
climbing, mountain, 334
climbing net, backyard, 287
climbing wax, ski, 327
clinch, horse's hoof, 38
clinic, White House, 75
clip: ammunition, 499; bicycle, 128; bow tie, 192; CB radio antenna, 183; chest pull, 344; dental, 455; hair, 214; jackhammer, 436; juice extractor, 255; microscope, 442; pen, 158; pistol, 470; pistol nozzle, 428; rifle, 471; stethoscope, 449; suspenders, 190; telephone, 180; venetian blinds, 241; and volt-ohm meter, 423; wallet, 223; woodcarving, 372
clip-on bow tie, 192
clip-on sunglasses, 290
clipped mane, polo pony, 299
clippers, gardening, 427
cloche, 203
clock, 233; basketball backstop, 296; car, 110; darts, 322; nuclear reactor

control room, 393; organ, 360; pilot's instrument panel, 481; 747 cockpit, 150; stove, 248
clock timer, VCR, 184
cloister, mosque, 70
close, letter, 159
close call, gesture, 507
closed chock, destroyer, 477
closed-circuit track, road racing, 338
closed coat, sandpaper, 421
closed quad, magazine, 171
closed teeth, zipper, 209
close escape, gesture, 507
closer, brick wall, 69
close relationship, gesture, 507
closet, jumbo jet, 148
close up, proofreader's mark, 514
close way, permanent fort, 83
closure, 209; brassiere, 195; parka, 201; package, 268, 269; playpen, 286; swagger bag, 222; trousers, 191; woman's jacket and pants, 196
cloth: flat racing, 336; pool table, 320
cloth beam, hand loom, 387
clothes dryer, 281
clothesline, 280
clothespin, 280
clothing guard, wheelchair, 452
cloth lining, parka, 201
cloth said, windmill, 390
cloud, 2, 3, 16
cloudy, weather map, 19
cloven hoof, ultimate beast, 48
cloverleaf, highway, 114
clown, 493; circus act, 90
club: golf, 310, 311; playing cards, 348; police, 498
club-footed forestaysail, sailboat, 134
clubhouse, racetrack, 337
clubhouse turn, racetrack, 337
club insignia, soccer uniform, 297
clutch: automobile, 108, 110, 111; checkbook, 223; handbag, 222; lithographic press, 376; powerboat, 138
clutch lever: motorcycle, 129; outboard engine, 137
clutch nut, juice extractor, 255
clutter control, radar, 444
coach: bus, 118; horse-drawn, 131; passenger train, 116, 117; recreational vehicle, 130
coaches' box, baseball field, 291
coach roof, sailboat, 135
coach section, jumbo jet, 149
coal hod, fireplace, 232
coal tender, steam locomotive, 116
coaming, sailboat, 135
coaming padding, powerboat, 139
coarse-adjustment beam, laboratory scale, 447
coarse calibrate, Geiger counter, 445
coarse focus adjustment, microscope, 442
coarse-motion clamp, telescope, 443
coarse teeth, hair comb, 212
coast, nautical chart, 22
coastal shield, turtle, 43
Coast Guard station, nautical chart, 22
coastline, 7, 15
coat: animal cell, 23; butler, 489; drum major, 495; fireman, 500; man, 188, 488;

Revolutionary War general, 492; sandpaper, 421; ultimate beast, 48, 49
coating, sandpaper, 421
coat of arms, 503; Manchu court dress, 491
co-axial machine gun, tank, 475
cock: furnace, 400; internal combustion engine, 406; standpipe, 121
cockade, 492
cocked hat, 492
cocking handle, machine gun, 471
cocking piece, rifle, 471
cockpit: aircraft, 146, 147, 150-151; powerboat, 139; racing car, 338-339; sailboat, 134
coconut, 262; palm, 52
coda sign, music, 353
code: envelope, 159; magazine mailing label, 169; paper money, 224
codpiece: armor, 465; boxing, 309
coffeepot, tea set, 245
coffee shop, public sign, 506
coffee strainer, 260
coffin, 516
coffin corner, football field, 293
coherent light, laser, 395
coiffe, champagne cork, 267
coiffure, 213
coil: air conditioner, 402; automobile spring, 109; dipole magnet, 394; heat exchanger, 403; lasso, 432; metal detector, 445; postage stamps, 159; safety pin, 208; zipper, 209
coin, money, 225
coin bank, 457
coin box: parking meter, 113; pay phone, 180
coin chute, toll basket, 114
coin purse, wallet, 223
coin return: pay phone, 180; slot machine, 346
coin slot: parking meter, 113; pay phone, 180; slot machine, 346
col, mountain, 8
colander, 260
cold chisel, 420
cold cream, 216
cold front, 19
cold type, 166
cold-water faucet: bathtub, 274; Jacuzzi, 274; sink, 247, 273
cold-water pipe: solar heating system, 391; water heater, 401
collapsible legs, ironing board, 279
collar: ambulance, 123; ascot, 193; barbell, 344; bishop, 487; blouse, 197; bolt, 411; bridal gown, 488; camera tripod, 176; cardigan sweater, 199; dipole magnet, 394; drum major's coat, 495; fire extinguisher, 284; harness racing gear, 337; horizontal bar, 306; house beam, 61; jacket, 188, 488; kettledrum, 364; king's regalia, 484; Manchu court dress, 491; minaret, 70; minister, 487; power drill, 419; royal orb, 485; shirt, 189; shoe, 205; stove, 404; trench coat, 200; vacuum cleaner hose, 283
collarbone, human, 24

collection pan, air conditioner, **402**
collector: solar panel, **391**; transistor chip, **396**
college pliers, dental, **455**
collet, ring, **219**
collider, **394**
collimating screw, telescope, **443**
collision bulkhead, passenger ship, **142**
collop: human, **25**; meat, **262**
cologne, **217**
colon: grammatical symbol, **513**; human, **27**
colophon, book, **167**
color(s): horseracing, **336, 337**; typewriter ribbon, **161**
colored glass, **378**
color panel, soccer ball, **297**
color selector, toaster oven, **253**
colorstick, makeup, **216, 217**
colt, **38**
columbarium, church, **87**
columella, nose, **30**
column, **73**; abacus, **441**; basketball backstop, **296**; cave, **11**; citrus juicer, **255**; cupboard, **243**; drill press, **419**; magazine, **170, 171**; oil drilling platform, **101**; piano, **361**; skyscraper, **77**; surgical table, **450**; thermometer, **449**; voting booth, **437**
coma, comet, **3**
comb: armor, **465**; chicken, **35**; escalator, **79**; hair, **212**; razor, **210**; rifle, **471**; shotgun, **468**
combat aircraft, **480**
combat infantry badge, **496**
combat maneuver panel, pilot's instrument panel, **481**
combat soldier's uniform, **497**
comb holder, electric hairbrush, **212**
combination dial, vault, **457**
combination headlamp, automobile, **106**
combination lock, safe, **457**
combination pliers, **414**
combination screw, telegraph key, **157**
combination square, **424**
combination water ski, **329**
combination wrench, **415**
comb strip, electric hairbrush, **212**
combustion chamber: engine, **407**; rocket, **407**; stove, **404**
combustion jet engine, **407**
come box, craps table, **347**
come here, gesture, **507**
comet, **3**
comfort-cable temple, eyeglasses, **221**
comforter, bedding, **270**
comfort lining, spacesuit, **155**
comic book, **380**
comic strip, **380-381**
comma: grammatical symbol, **513**; proofreader's mark, **514**
commander's hatch, tank, **474**
commander's seat, space shuttle, **153**
command module, lunar lander, **154**
command post, White House, **75**
commemorative, coin, **215**
commemorative subject, stamp, **159**
commissary, prison, **76**
commissure, horse's foot, **38**
committee, room, Capitol, **74**
common iliac artery, human, **28**

common peroneal nerve, human, **29**
common rafter, house, **61**
common spiral galaxy, **2**
communication fuse, rocket, **383**
communication umbilical, spacesuit, **155**
Communion bread, **87**
Communion cup, **87**
commuter bus, **118**
compact, beauty product, **217**
compact disc, compact disc player, **178**
compact disc player, **178**
compactor, trash, **247**
companion benchseat, powerboat, **139**
companionway, sailboat, **134, 135**
company address, business card, **160**
company logo: business card, **160**; pumper, **125**
company name: business card, **160**; letter, **159**
company quarters, frontier fort, **82**
compartment: backpack, **343**; bus, **118**; camper, **130**; coat of arms, **503**; drag racing dragster, **339**; electronic flash, **176**; garbage disposal, **247**; hearing aid, **452**; jumbo jet, **148, 149**; refrigerator, **249**; sealed voting booth, **437**; sink, **247**; wallet, **223**
compass, **136**; airplane, **151, 481**; powerboat, **138**; skin diving, **331**; theodolite, **436**
compass bearing, airport runway, **94**
compass rose: nautical chart, **22**; political map, **20**
compensator sheave, elevator shaft, **78**
complimentary close, letter, **159**
composition: art, **368-369**; typeface, **165**
compound eye: bee, **41**; grasshopper, **41**
compound kite, **323**
compound leaves, **52**
compound microscope, **442**
compress, medicinal, **451**
compressed air: skin diving, **331**; truck tractor, **120**
compression member, geodesic dome, **85**
compression strap, backpack, **343**
compressor: automobile engine, **111**; heat exchanger, **403**
compressor fan, combustion engine, **407**
computer: **162, 438, 439**; prison, **76**; 747 cockpit, **150, 151**; space shuttle, **153**
computer aided design system, **438**
computer ring, light meter, **176**
computer system, **439**
computer tape, **439**
computer workstation, **438**
concave knife, **463**
concave lens, **221**
concave mirror, telescope, **443**
concave molding, grandfather clock, **233**
concealer, makeup, **216**
concentrating solar collector, **391**
concentric sculpture, clam shell, **47**
conceptacle, seaweed, **57**

concertmaster, orchestra, **354**
concha, outer ear, **30**
conchology, **47**
concourse, airport, **94**
concrete block foundation, house, **60**
concrete shield, nuclear reactor, **392**
concrete tunnel, super collider, **394**
concussion grenade, **473**
condensed type, **165**
condenser: heat pump, **403**; microscope, **442**; nuclear reactor, **392**
condenser coil, air conditioner, **402**
condiment, **263, 265**
conducting blade, cartridge fuse, **399**
conducting rivet, plug fuse, **399**
conductor: electrician's wire, **423**; track lighting, **239**
conductor's podium, orchestra, **354**
conduit, **98**; railroad crossing signal, **115**; volcano, **10**
cone: blimp, **156**; citrus juicer, **255**; combustion jet engine, **407**; ice cream, **265**; jumbo jet, **148, 149**; missile, **482**; phonograph receiver, **179**; pine, **52**; police car, **122**; potting, **373**; toll booth, **114**; volcano, **10**
Congress, **74**
conical buoy, nautical chart, **22**
connecting link, horizontal bar, **306**
connecting rod: steam engine, **405**; steam locomotive, **116**
connecting wire, field events hammer, **303**
connection: electric meter, **399**; pacemaker, **452**; parachute harness, **333**; pumper, **125**; sprinkler, **428**
conning tower, submarine, **479**
console: computer system, **439**; lunar rover, **155**; organ, **360**; powerboat, **138, 139**; skin diving tank, **331**
console door, electronic voting system, **437**
constellation, **2**
constriction, thermometer, **449**
construction, road map, **20**
construction sign, road, **505**
consumer requirements, coupon, **103**
contact: incandescent bulb, **238**; movie camera, **174**; plugfuse, **399**
contact lens, **221**
contact sport, **298**
container, **266-267**; blender, **254**; contact lens, **221**; land mine, **473**; paint spray gun, **425**
container ship, **140**
containment building, nuclear reactor, **392**
contemporary, house style, **63**
content: label, **268**; wine label, **267**
content heading, book page, **12**
contents page, magazine, **169**
contest, drag racing, **339**
continental margin, **15**
continued line, magazine, **171**
continuous battery monitor, Geiger counter, **445**
continuous hinge, **460**
contour: nautical chart, **22**; topographic map, **22**

contoured handgrip, camera, **172**
contour feathers, bird, **39**
contour line, map, **21, 22**
contra-bassoon, **354**
contraction, grammatical symbol, **513**
contractor's saw, **417**
contrast control, video-still camera, **173**
contrast indicator, fax machine, **164**
control: air conditioner, **402**; aircraft, **150, 151, 481**; automobile, **108, 110**; ballista, **467**; barbecue grill, **288**; blender, **254**; blood pressure gauge, **449**; bulldozer, **435**; camera, **174**; canal lock, **99**; cash register, **440**; CB radio, **183**; clock radio, **233**; clothes dryer, **281**; compass, **136**; dam, **100**; dental unit, **454**; dishwasher, **250**; drum, **364**; engine, **406, 407**; fire engine, **124, 125**; food processor, **254**; garbage disposal, **247**; garbage truck, **127**; girdle, **195**; guitar, **363**; hand glider, **333**; hearing aid, **452**; high-speed printer, **439**; hovercraft, **145**; humidifier, **402**; iron, **279**; lunar lander, **154**; lunar rover, **155**; machine gun height, **471**; metal detector, **445**; microscope, **442**; microwave oven, **248**; mower, **429**; nozzle, **428**; nuclear reactor, **392**; paint spray gun, **425**; parachute, **333**; passenger ship, **142**; phonograph, **178, 179**; police car, **122**; powerboat, **138, 139**; projector, **175**; radar, **444**; railroad crossing signal, **115**; saber saw, **417**; sealed voting booth, **437**; seeder, **430**; sonar, **444**; space shuttle, **153**; spacesuit, **155**; stove, **248, 342, 404**; subway, **119**; surgical table, **450**; synthesizer, **363**; telescope, **443**; toaster, **253**; toll booth, **114**; tow truck, **126**; tugboat, **144**; typewriter, **161**; vacuum tube, **396**; video camera, **184**; wristwatch, **220**
control button, answering machine, **181**
control console, computer, **439**
control functions, fax machine, **164**
controllable landing light, helicopter, **146**
control panel: dot matrix printer, **163**; nuclear reactor control room, **393**
control rod, window shutters, **241**
control-rod guide tube, nuclear reactor, **392**
control room, nuclear reactor, **393**
control room operator, nuclear reactor, **393**
control station, destroyer launcher, **477**
control structure, dam, **100**
control tower: aircraft carrier, **478**; airport, **94, 95**; destroyer, **476**
control unit: high-speed printer, **439**; magnetic tape subsystem, **439**
conversion marker, football field, **293**

conversion scale, nautical chart, 22
converter, vacuum cleaner, 283
convertible, 108; automobile, 106, 107
convertible sofa, 236
convenience door, dot matrix printer, 163
convex lens, 221
Conyne kite, 323
cook, 489
cookie, 264
cookie cutter, 261
cooking chopsticks, 257
cooking grid, barbecue grill, 288
cooking unit, camper, 130
cook's cap, 489
cook top, stove, 248
coolant port, dipole magnet, 394
coolant pump, nuclear reactor, 392
cooling fan clutch, automobile engine, 111
cooling/heating coils, heat exchanger, 403
cooling rack, kitchen, 260
cooling system: airport, 94; automobile, 108
cooling tower, nuclear reactor, 393
cool tip: curling iron, 214; percolator basket, 252
cop, police, 498
cope, bishop, 487
copier, 164
coping, masonry gate post, 67
coping saw, 416
copper foil, 378
copper surface, solar collector panel, 391
copra, 262
copy: letter, 159; magazine cover, 169
copyist, music, 353
copyright: book, 167; magazine, 169; music, 353; newspaper, 168; symbol, 511
coral, cave, 11
coral polyp, 46
coral reef, 46
cor anglais, 354, 357
corbel, castle, 80
corbeled arch, kokoshniki, 70
cord: air conditioner, 402; bagpipe, 365; ballista, 467; bedroll, 343; bus, 118; CB radio, 183; cellular telephone, 181; curling iron, 214; dental X-ray unit, 454; electrician's, 423; fastener, 208; fencing strip, 315; guillotine, 462; hand loom, 387; hot air balloon, 332; iron, 279; jackhammer, 436; juice extractor, 255; lamp, 238; movie camera microphone, 174; parachute, 333; Ping-Pong net, 321; saw, 417; snowshoe, 327; spinning wheel, 387; string tie, 192; tape recorder, 177; telephone, 180; thread, 384; track lighting, 239; traverse rod, 240; venetian blind, 241; windmill, 390
cord holder, ironing board, 279
cordial glass, 245
cording, mattress, 271
cordless phone, 180
cordlock, backpack, 343
cordon, king's regalia, 484
cord strain relief: CB radio microphone, 183; finishing sander, 421; hair dryer, 212;

hand drill, 419; saber saw, 417; toaster oven, 253
core: apple, 55; brayer, 374; earth, 4; human, 25; mortise lock, 458; nuclear reactor, 392; paint roller, 425; pineapple, 55; skyscraper, 77; typewriter, 161
core basket, nuclear reactor, 392
corer, apple, 261
core support assembly, nuclear reactor, 392
cork: bottle, 267; clarinet mouthpiece, 357
corkscrew, 251; pocket knife, 426
corn, 58
cornea, eye, 30
corner: boxing ring, 309; brick wall, 69; chessboard, 345; football field, 293; house, 62, 63; skyscraper, 77; violin, 355
corner cupboard, 243
corner cushion, boxing ring, 309
corner flag, soccer field, 297
corner index, playing cards, 348
cornering lamp, automobile, 106
corner kick area, soccer field, 297
corner mark, label, 269
corner post, house, 61
cornerstone, skyscraper, 77
cornet, 359
cornice: column entablature, 73; cupboard, 243; curtain, 240; house, 61, 62; merry-go-round, 93; minaret, 70; mosque, 70
cornsilk, 58
corolla, pea, 54
corona, column entablature, 73
coronary band, horse's hoof, 38
coronation mantle, king, 484
coronet: horse, 38; queen, 484; royal headpiece, 485
corpus callosum, human, 29
correctable ribbon, typewriter, 161
correction tape, typewriter, 161
corrective device, dental, 453
corrector magnet control, compass, 136
correspondence, 159
corridor, Capitol building, 74
corrugated brand name display, supermarket, 102
corrugated diaphragm chest piece, stethoscope, 449
corrugated fastener, 410
corrugated sole, ice climbing boot, 334
corrugated staple, silk screen, 375
corrugation: fastener, 410; speaker, 179
corselet, queen's, 484
corset, 195; queen's, 484
cosmetic case, 285
cosmic mass, 2
cosmic rays, 3
costal fold, salamander, 44
costal groove, salamander, 44
costilla, jai alai cesta, 314
costume, historical, 492
costume jewelry, 218
cotter pin, roller chain, 461
cotton, dental, 455
couch, upholstered, 236
couloir, mountain, 8

count, magazine mailing label, 169
counter: backgammon, 345; footware, 204, 205, 206, 302; pool table, 320; sink, 247; sailboat, 134; sealed voting booth, 437; tape recorder, 177; type, 165, 166
counterbalance, electronic weather station, 18
counter current, ocean, 6
counterfeit money, 224
counterguard, sword hilt, 463
counter hoop, drum, 364
countermeasures antenna, aircraft carrier, 478
countermeasure warning, pilot's instrument panel, 481
counterscarp, permanent fort, 83
countersink bit, drill, 418, 419
counterweight: elevator shaft, 78; lift bridge, 97; phonograph turntable, 178; railroad crossing signal, 115; stage pulley, 350; window, 65
counting rod, 441
coupe, automobile, 106
coupled truck, 120
coupler, locomotive, 116, 117
coupler-tilt tablet, organ, 360
coupling: gas pump, 112; hose, 428; train, 117
coupon, 103; magazine, 171
coupon machine, checkout counter, 103
course: brick wall, 69; drag racing, 339; harness racetrack, 337; meal, 263; river, 13
court: badminton, 319; barn, 104; basketball, 296; handball, 313; jai alai, 314; Ping-Pong table, 321; shuffleboard, 318; squash, 313; tennis, 312; volleyball, 319
court cards, 348
court clerk's table, courtroom, 89
court dress, Manchu, 491
courting seat, 236
courtroom, 89
couter, armor, 465
cove, 7
cove mold, staircase, 66
cover: automobile, 107, 111; bagpipe, 365; baseball, 290; basket, 266; battery, 397; blender, 254; book, 167; brayer, 374; cassette tape, 177; chain saw, 431; clarinet pad, 356; combat helmet, 497; copier, 164; desk, 276; fishing reel, 340; food processor, 254; football, 292; garbage disposal, 247; girdle, 195; hand loom, 387; ironing board, 279; jackhammer, 436; juice extractor, 255; kite, 323; laboratory scale, 446; magazine, 169; matchbook, 228; mattress, 271; motorcycle, 129; paint spray gun, 425; percolator basket, 252; playpen, 286; pocket watch, 220; portable word processor, 162; pots and pans, 257; sewing machine, 278; sketch box, 371; skyscraper, 77; smoke alarm, 284; swing, 287; tea kettle, 245; tepee, 84; theodolite, 436; toilet, 275; vault, 457; video-still camera adaptor, 173; Walkman, 182; wallet,

223; water ski, 329; window, 241
covered button cardigan sweater, 199
covered way, permanent fort, 83
cover key, video-still camera, 173
cover lock, video-still camera, 173
cover plate: electrical, 344; solar panel, 391
cover sheet, kite, 323
covert: bird, 39; permanent fort, 83; turkey, 35
coverup, makeup, 216
cow, 32
cowboy, 490; hat, 202
cowcatcher, locomotive, 116
cow hoof, ultimate beast, 48
cowl: bobsled, 328; helicopter, 146; outboard engine, 137
cowlick, 211
cowling: airplane, 147; outboard engine, 137; racing car, 338
cow puncher, 490
coxa: grasshopper, 41; spider, 40
CPU, 438; circuit board, 439; mainframe, 439
crab, 47; zodiac, 509
cracker, nut, 261
cradle, telephone, 180; telescope, 443; venetian blind, 241
craft, 132, 133
cramp, wall, 69
crampon, ice climbing, 334
cranial crest, toad, 44
cranium, human, 26
crank: brace, 418; drill, 418; easel, 370; engine, 405, 406, 407; fishing reel, 340; lawn sprinkler, 428; pencil sharpener, 277; printing press, 376, 377; truck platform, 121
crank arm, bicycle, 128
cranked axle, Hansom cab, 131
crankset, bicycle, 128
craps table, 347
crash helmet, 336, 338
crater, volcano, 10
cravat, 192
crawler track, tank, 474
crawler tractor, bulldozer, 435
crawl space, house, 60
crayfish, 47
crayon, lithographic, 376
crazy, gesture, 507
cream: makeup, 216, 217; sundae, 264
creamer, tea set, 245
crease: cowboy hat, 202; human hand, 31; ice hockey rink, 295; trousers, 191; woman's pants, 196
C recreation yard, prison, 76
credit, magazine, 169, 171
credit card, 227
credit card account, 227
credit card logo, traveler's check, 227
credit card slots, wallet, 223
credit line, newspaper, 168
creek: frontier fort, 82; river, 13
crenel, castle, 80
crepe sole, sandal, 206
crescendo, music, 352
crescendo, shoe, organ, 360
crescent, fingernail, 31
crescent and star, symbol, 508

crescent moon, **4**
crest: coat of arms, **503**; dam, **100**; dog, **36**; enlisted men's uniform, **496**; grandfather clock, **233**; horse, **38**; human, **25**; iceberg, **12**; mountain, **9**; rocking chair, **234**; screw thread, **410**; wave, **14**
crest fringe, lizard, **43**
crest rail, sofa, **236**
crevasse, mountain, **9**
crevice, mountain, **9**
crevice tool, vacuum cleaner, **283**
crew compartment, lunar lander, **154**
crewel, stitchery, **385**
crew neck sweater, **199**
crew's quarters, passenger ship, **142**
cricket, darts, **322**
crier, and minaret, **70**
crimp: cartridge, **470**; painting brush, **370**; spring board needle, **386**
crimper, electrician's wire stripper, **423**
cringle, mainsail, **136**
cripples, house, **61**
crisper, refrigerator, **249**
critical mass, nuclear power, **392**
crocheting, **386**
crocket, church, **86**
crockpot, **257**
crocodile, **42**
crocodilians, **42**
crook: of arm, **25**; bassoon, **357**; brasses, **358, 359**
crop: cow, **32**; flat racing, **336**; masonry gate post, **67**
croquet, **318**
crosier, cardinal, **487**
cross, **86, 487**; symbol, **508**
crossarm: power line, **396**; railroad crossing signal, **115**; weather station, **18**
crossbar: abacus, **441**; bicycle, **128**; football goalpost, **293**; hand glider, **333**; ice hockey goal, **294**; lyre, **355**; pole vault, **305**; sawhorse, **408**; snowshoe, **327**; suit hanger, **281**; weather vane, **19**
crossbeam: ballista, **467**; gallows, **462**; guillotine, **462**; hand loom, **387**
crossbelt, **483, 492**
crossbow, **466**
cross brace: ladder, **47**; wheelchair, **452**
crossbuck, railroad crossing signal, **115**
cross-country skiing, **327**
crosscut saw, **416, 417**
crosse, **298**
cross guard, knife, **463**
crosshatching: cartoon, **380**; and texture, composition, **369**
crosshead, steam engine, **405**
crossing: church, **87**; railroad, **115**
cross joint, brick wall, **69**
crossknot, bow tie, **192**
Cross of Christ, church, **87**
crossover, railroad yard, **96**
cross patée, royal regalia, **485**
crosspiece: bow tie, **192**; hand loom, **387**; kite, **323**; rocking chair, **234**; sword hilt, **463**; torii, **71**
cross section: cave, **11**; coral polyp, **46**; fireplace, **232**; frame, **379**; hurricane, **17**; insulated window, **65**; lumber, **68**; permanent fort,

83; river, **13**; stage, **350**; tree trunk, **50**; tunnel, **98**; volcano, **10**
cross stitching **385**
cross straps, overnight bag, **285**
cross strings, tennis racket **312**
cross strip: kite, **323**; wheelbarrow, **430**
cross support, pool table **320**
crosstie, railroad track, **115**
crosswise grain, fabric, **388**
crotch: underpants, **194**; trousers, **191**
crotchet: grammatical symbol, **513**; music, **352**
crotch strap: child's car seat, **286**; drag racing driver's belt, **339**
croup: dog, **36**; horse, **38**; pommel horse, **307**
croupier, roulette, **346**
crown: anchor, **132**; arch, **72**; bell, **iv**; bird, **39**; cactus, **56**; coat of arms, **503**; croquet wicket, **318**; cut gemstone, **218**; human, **25**; incline track, **92**; man's hair, **211**; man's hat, **202**; needle, **384**; palm, **52**; pineapple, **55**; royal, **485**; staple, **410**; tennis racket, **312**; tooth, **453, 455, 456**; tree, **50**; watch, **220, 304**; woman's hat, **203**
crown cap opener, **251**
crowning pavilion, minaret, **70**
crown stabilizer, football helmet, **292**
crow's nest: tanker, **140**; train caboose, **117**
CRT: computer workstation, **438**; personal computer, **162**; television, **185**
crucifix, church, **87**
cruise missile, **482**
crumb, bread, **263**
crumb incubator, cowboy's, **490**
crumble roller, hitch and harrow, **434**
crumb tray, toaster, **253**
crupper, harness racing, **337**
crusher claw, lobster, **47**
crust: earth, **4**; prepared food, **263, 265**
crustacean, **47**
crutch, **452**
crutch socket, operating table, **450**
crypt: burial chamber, **516**; Capitol, **74**
crystal, watch, **220**
Crystal Palace set piece, fireworks, **383**
crystal pool, cave, **11**
C sharp, piano keyboard octave, **361**
C-strap, motorcycle, **129**
cubbyhole, skull, **135**
cube: backgammon, **345**; slide projector, **175**
cucumber, **54**
cue: billiards, **320**; cassette tape recorder, button, **177**; phonograph turntable, **178**; shuffleboard, **318**
cuff: blood pressure gauge, **449**; blouse, **197**; bridal gown, **488**; fencing glove, **315**; golf bag, **311**; ice hockey goalie's glove, **294**; jacket, **196**; king's regalia, **484**; Manchu court dress, **491**; paramedic, **123**; parka, **201**; Revolutionary War general, **492**; sailor, **497**; shirt, **189, 488**; ski boot, **326**,

327; sweater, **199**; trousers, **191**
cuff checklist, spacesuit, **155**
cuff link, **218**
cuirie, armor, **465**
cuish, armor, **465**
cuissard, fencing, **315**
cull, lobster, **47**
culm, grass, **58**
culs, cut gemstone, **218**
cultivator, **434**
culture tube, laboratory, **447**
cummerbund, **488, 495**
cumulonimbus cloud, **16, 17**
cumulus congestus cloud, **16**
cup: armor, **465**; athletic supporter, **194**; ballista, **467**; baseball catcher, **290**; brassiere, **195**; bugle, **359**; citrus juicer, **255**; Communion, **87**; coral polyp, **46**; golf course, **311**; measuring, **258**; plumber's plunger, **422**; seed, **51**; sketch box, **371**; table setting, **245**; thimble, **384**; trombone, **358**; weather station, **18**
cupboard, **243**
cup level scale, coffee maker, **252**
cupola: barn, **104**; Capitol, **74**; kokoshniki, **70**; mosque, **70, 71**; tank, **474**; train caboose, **117**
curbside sidewall, truck van, **121**
curb window, bus, **118**
curd, cheese, **263**
curfew, fireplace, **232**
curl: pail, **284**; wave, **14**; woman's hair, **213**
curled position, windmill, **390**
curling iron, **214**
currency pocket, wallet, **223**
current: electrical, **398**; ocean, **6**
current temperature, thermometer, **18**
current unit patch, enlisted man's uniform, **496**
curriculum vitae, **160**
cursor: linear slide rule, **441**; radar, **444**
cursor control: computer workstation, **438**; personal computer, **162**
cursor keypad, portable word processor, **162**
curtain: cave, **11**; four-poster bed, **270**; living room, **240**; overnight bag, **285**; permanent fort, **83**; shower, **274**; stage, **350**; stagecoach, **131**; theatre, **351**; Torah, **486**; voting booth, **437**
curtain rod, **240**
curtain wall: castle, **81**; skyscraper, **77**
curtein, king's regalia, **484**
curve, royal scepter, **485**
curved jaw, combination pliers, **414**
curved slat, rocking chair, **234**
cushion: bowling lane, **317**; boxing ring, **309**; chaise longue, **288**; dog, **36**; jai alai cancha, **314**; lounger, **235**; phonograph headphone, **179**; pool table, **320**; roller skate, **324**; sofa, **236**
cusp, tooth, **456**
cuspid, **456**
cuspidor, dental unit, **454**
custodian's seal, voting booth, **437**
customized automobile, **106-107**

customs, public sign, **506**
cut: book, **167**; key blade, **459**; label, **268**; magazine, **170**
cutaway coat: butler's uniform, **489**; man's formal attire, **488**
cut gemstone, **218**
cuticle: human fingernail, **31**; leaf, **52**
cut it, gesture, **507**
cut line, newspaper, **168**
cutoff rule, magazine, **171**
cutout switch, 747 cockpit, **151**
cut section, stained glass, **378**
cutter: can opener, **251**; chain saw chain, **431**; cigar, **228**; cowboy, **490**; electric razor, **210**; glass, **378**; juice extractor, **255**; kitchen tool, **261**; pencil sharpener, **277**; pliers, **414**; wirestripper, **423**
cutter adjusting-screw, expansive bit, **419**
cutting board, **261**; barbecue grill, **288**
cutting edge: auger bit, **419**; bulldozer, **435**; chisel, **420**; nail clippers, **215**; plane, **420**
cutting line, sewing pattern, **388**
cutting surface, table saw, **417**
cutting teeth, lobster, **47**
cwm, mountain, **8**
cyc, stage, **350**
cyc flood, stage, **350**
cycle: internal combustion engine, **406**; symbol, **510**
cycle selector: clothes dryer, **281**; dishwasher, **250**; washing machine, **280**
cyclorama, stage, **350**
cyclorama floodlight, stage, **350**
cyclotron, **394**
cylinder: ambulance, **123**; automobile, **108, 111**; fire extinguisher, **284**; internal combustion engine, **406**; letterpress, **166**; lock, **458**; locomotive, **116**; offset-lithography, **166**; padlock, **459**; propane torch, **422**; revolver, **470**; rotogravure, **166**; skin diving, **331**; steam engine, **405**
cylinder desk, **276**
cylinder model, vacuum cleaner, **283**
cylindrical buoy, nautical chart, **22**
cylindrical slide rule, **441**
cymatium, column entablature, **73**
cymbal, **354, 364**
cytoplasm, animal cell, **23**

D

D: braille, **512**; music notation, **353**; piano keyboard octave, **341**; sign language, **512**
dabber, **377**
dado, column pedestal, **73**
daggerboard, windsurfer, **330**
dagger point position, windmill, **390**
dairy department, supermarket, **102**
daisy-wheel printer, **163**
daiwa, torii, **71**
dalmatic, cardinal, **487**
dal segno sign, music, **353**
dam, **100**; cave, **11**; horse, **38, 336**
dampening roller, offset-lithography, **166**
damper: fireplace, **232**; grill, **288**; woodburning stove, **404**

damper pedal, grand piano, 361
dance band, 354
dancing step, staircase, 66
dart: jacket, 188; sewing pattern, 388
dart board, 322
darts, 322
dash: book page, iv; car, 110; grammatical symbol, 513
dashboard: car, 110; Hansom cab, 131
dash-pot, toaster, 253
data display window, compact disc player, 178
data cache, circuit board, 439
data code, magazine mailing label, 169
data entry slider, synthesizer, 363
data file server, computer workstation, 438
data panel display, camera, 172
data processor, mainframe, 439
date: coin, 225; magazine, 169, 171; newspaper, 168; résumé, 160; traveler's check, 227; wine label, 267
date display control, wristwatch, 220
dateline: map, 5; newspaper, 168
date of issue, coupon, 103
davenport, 236
David, playing card king, 348
davit: fireboat, 144; powerboat, 138
day, globe, 5
daybed, sailboat, 135
day gate, vault, 457
daystick, police, 498
D cell block, prison, 76
DCmv scale, volt-ohm meter, 423
dead bolt, mortise lock, 458
dead-end cap, track lighting, 239
dead front plug, electrical, 398
dead lift, universal gym, 344
dead line, shuffle board court, 318
dead man's stick, subway motorman's cab, 119
dealer, blackjack, 347
dealer requirements, coupon, 103
deal patch, label, 269
death, darts, 322; symbol, 510
debit amount, check, 226
debossed label, 268
decal, child's wagon, 287
decanter, 245; coffee maker, 252
decathlon, 300
decay, tooth, 456
decelerator pedal, bulldozer, 435
decimal key, electronic calculator, 441
deck: aircraft carrier, 478; destroyer, 476; escalator, 79; fleet ballistic missile submarine, 479; house, 63; hovercraft, 145; jumbo jet, 148; kitchen sink, 247; magazine, 170; newspaper, 168; passenger ship, 142, 143; playing cards, 348; power mower, 429; powerboat, 138, 139; skateboard, 324; skyscraper, 77; sled, 328; stage, 350; surfboard, 330; toboggan, 328; truck platform, 121
deck brace, steam locomotive, 116

decked craft, 133
deckhouse, tanker, 141
deck manifold, tanker, 141
decompression chamber, 452
decorated initial, magazine, 170
decoration: cake, 264; canapé, 263; man's hat, 202; military uniform, 496; minister, 487
decorative engravings, scrimshaw, 375
decorative inlays, armor, 465
decorative perforations, man's shoe, 204
decorative stitching, 385
deep, continental margin, 15
deep-frying basket, 260
deep-frying thermometer, 258
deep gouge, woodcarving, 372
deep medium gouge, woodcarving, 372
deep throat, coping paw, 416
deer crossing, road sign, 505
deer ear, ultimate beast, 48
dee ring, Western saddle, 335
defendant's table, courtroom, 89
defenseman: ice hockey, 295; lacrosse, 298
defensive guided weapons, 476
defibrillator, paramedic equipment, 123
deflector: aircraft carrier, 478; power mower, 429
deflexor, hang glider, 333
defog control lever, pilot's instrument panel, 481
defroster, car windshield, 110
degree: longitude, 5; music notation, 353; political map, 20
degrees of arc, symbol, 511
dehumidifier, 236
delayed transmission capability, fax machine, 164
delete, proofreader's mark, 514
deli, supermarket, 103
delivery area, supermarket, 102
delta, 7, 13
delta-keel, kite, 323
delta wing, combat aircraft, 480
deltoid, human, 26
deluge gun, pumper, 125
deluxe suite, passenger ship, 143
demarcation groove, escalator, 79
demineralizer, nuclear reactor, 392
demisemiquaver, music, 353
demitasse cup, 245
Democrat, Congress, 74
demographic data code, magazine mailing label, 169
denier, support base, 207
denim trousers, cowboy, 490
denomination: money, 225; stamp, 159; traveler's check, 227
density adjustment, laser printer, 163
dental corrective devices, 453
dental equipment, 455
dental floss, 215
dental unit, 454
dentin, tooth, 456
denture, 453
department: business card, 160; magazine, 169
department patch, police, 498
deployed wing, cruise missile, 482
deposit box, vault, 457
deposit drawer, automatic teller machine, 226

deposit envelopes, automatic teller machine, 226
depository, ambulance, 123
depression contour, topographic map, 22
depth adjusting screw, hitch and harrow, 434
depth: nautical chart, 22; and perspective, 368
depth control, guitar amplifier, 363
depth discriminator switch, metal detector, 445
depth-effect hydrofoil, 145
depth gauge: 424; skin diving, 331
depth-of-field scale, camera, 172; zoom lens, 172
depth stop, drill press, 419
derailleur, bicycle, 128
derision, gesture, 507
derrick: oil drilling platform, 101; tanker, 141
derrière, human, 25
descender, type, 165
descending initial, magazine, 170
descent stage, lunar lander, 154
design: scrimshaw, 375; silk screen, 375; stamp, 159
designation: label, 268; topographic map, 22
designer's initials, coin, 225
desk, 276; grand piano, 361
desk phone, 180
deskside electronics cabinet, computer workstation, 438
desk top personal copier, 164
dessert, 264
dessert setting, 244, 245
destination sign: bus, 118; road, 505; subway car, 119
destroyer, 476, 477
detachable collar, maid's uniform, 489
detached house, 63
detail: house blueprint, 62; political map, 21; woman's jacket, 196
detection head, metal detector, 445
detector: elevator shaft, 78; metal, 445; super collider, 394
detent, levigator, 376
detergent dispenser, dishwasher, 250
deuce service courts, tennis, 312
deutsche mark, symbol, 511
development flight instrumentation control, space shuttle, 153
device: coin, 225; execution, 462; flag, 502; label, 268; police uniform, 498; supportive, 452
devilfish, 46
devotional candle, 237
dewbill, turkey, 35
dewcap, telescope, 443
dewclaw: cat, 37; cow, 32; dog, 36; ultimate beast, 48
dewlap: cow, 32; dog, 36; lizard, 43
dew point sensor, weather station, 18
dexter supporter, coat of arms, 503
D flat, piano keyboard octave, 361
diacritic grammatical symbol, 513
diadem, tiara, 485
diagnosis, symbol, 510
diagonal: telescope, 443; tweezers, 215

diagonally gaited pacer, 337
diagram: political map, 21; shuffleboard, 318; sundial, 389
dial: aneroid barometer, 18; clock radio, 233; dental unit, 454; electronic flash, 176; electric wok, 257; gas pump, 112; globe, 1; grandfather clock, 233; lawn sprinkler, 428; parking meter, 113; phonograph, 178, 179; sewing machine, 278; sundial, 389; tape recorder, 177; telephone, 180; toaster oven, 253; vault, 457; wristwatch, 220
dial memory index, fax machine, 164
dialogue, comic strip, 381
dial pad, fax machine, 164
dialysis machine, 452
diamond: baseball, 291; dental burr, 455; playing card, 348; roulette wheel, 346; royal scepter, 485
diamond stitch, suspenders, 190
diaphragm: aneroid barometer, 18; kazoo, 366; microscope, 442; speaker, 179; stethoscope, 449
diaphragm adjusting screw, theodolite, 436
dice, 347
dice boat, craps table, 347
dice table, 347
dickey, Hansom cab, 131
die: 347; coin, 225; pipe threader, 422
die cut, label, 268
dieresis, grammatical symbol, 513
diesel-fueled internal combustion engine, 406
diesel locomotive, 116
diestock, pipe threader, 422
differential, automobile, 109
differential thermostat, solar heating system, 391
differentiation code, magazine mailing label, 169
diffuser, light meter, 176
digestive system, human, 27
digit, human, 25, 31
digital artery, human, 28
digital display, clock radio, 233
digital speed readout, police car, 122
digital tape, computer workstation, 438
digital vein, human, 28
digiton, cartoon, 381
digitorium, piano, 361
dike, 100; volcano, 10
dimension: house blueprint, 62; and perspective, 368
diminuendo, music, 352
dimmer control, radar, 444
dimple: golf ball, 310; human, 25; necktie, 192
dinette table, sailboat, 135
dingbat, newspaper, 168
dinghy, 133
dining car, passenger train, 116
dining room, White House, 75
DIN socket, movie projector, 175
dink, 133
dinner knife, 244
dinner plate, 244
dinosaur, 43
diopter value, eye scope, 448
dip: bow, 466; ice cream cone, 265

531

dipping station, universal gym, **344**
diplomatic reception room, White House, **75**
dipole magnet, super collider, **394**
dipole superconducting magnet assembly, **394**
dipstick, **111, 406**
dip tube, dispenser, **267**
direct drive, chain saw, **431**
directional arrow, road map, **20**
directional letter, weather vane, **19**
directional light, automobile, **106**
directional-microphone contact, movie camera, **174**
directional signal, automobile, **106, 110**
direction finder: destroyer, **477**; helicopter, **146**; 747 cockpit, **150**
direction indicator: tape recorder, **177**; 747 cockpit, **150**
directions for use, package, **268**
director, fencing match, **315**
directory, elevator car, **78**
dirigible, **156**
dirigible mooring mast, skyscraper, **77**
dirndl skirt, **197**
dirt bike, **129**
dirt shoe, mechanical sweeper, **127**
disapproval, gesture, **507**
disc, *see* disk
discard holder, blackjack, **347**
disc brake: automobile, **108**; motorcycle, **129**
disc compartment, compact disc player, **178**
discharge chute, power mower, **429**
discharge tube: fire extinguisher, **284**; laser, **395**
discriminator adjustment, metal detector, **445**
discus, **301, 303**
dish: bathtub, **274**; chafing, **245**; table setting, **244-245**
dish rack, **260**
dishwasher, **250**
disk: bear trap, **433**; eye scope, **448**; harness racing sulky, **337**; incandescent bulb, **238**; light meter, **176**; phonograph, **178**; screwback earring, **218**; shuffleboard, **318**; starfish, **46**; stingray, **45**; video recorder, **184**; video-still camera, **173**
disk compartment, video-still camera, **173**
disk drive, synthesizer, **363**
diskette, personal computer, **162**
dispenser: dishwasher, **250**; kitchen sink, **247**; washing machine, **280**
displacement, chain saw, **431**
displacement hull, powerboat, **138**
display: calculator, **441**; cash register, **440**; CB radio, **183**; radar, **444**; space shuttle, **153**
display button, compact disc player, **178**
display control: pilot's instrument panel, **481**; sonar, **444**; wristwatch, **220**
display panel, video-still camera, **173**
display screen, cellular telephone, **181**

disposable bag, vacuum cleaner, **283**
disposable razor, **210**
distal, tooth, **456**
distal transverse, human hand, **31**
distance event, track and field, **300**
distance heading indicator, pilot's instrument panel, **481**
distance lens, eyeglasses, **221**
distance runner, shoe, **302**
distance scale, camera, **172, 174**; zoom lens, **172**
distilling equipment, laboratory, **447**
distortion pedal, guitar, **363**
distributary, river, **13**
distribution map, **21**
distribution of copies, letter, **159**
distribution point, man's hair, **211**
distributor, automobile engine, **111**
district, thematic map, **21**
ditch: castle, **81**; permanent fort, **83**
dite, cartoon, **380**
divan, **236**
dive break, glider, **147**
divers' oxygen bottle rack, oil drilling platform, **101**
diver's watch, skin diving, **331**
dive timer, skin diving, **331**
divided by, symbol, **511**
divided highway, **114**
divided highway ends, road sign, **505**
divider: highway, **114**; pocket knife, **426**; zipper, **209**
dividing line, domino, **345**
diving board, **316**
diving plane, submarine, **479**
diving platform, **316**
division: business card, **160**; thematic map, **21**; with slide rule, **441**
division line, basketball court, **296**
dixie cup, sailor, **497**
dock: horse, **38**; sheep, **33**
doctor blade, rotogravure, **166**
doctor's unit, dental, **144**
document feed guide, fax machine, **164**
document feed tray, fax machine, **164**
dodger cleat, inflatable, **133**
dog: **36**; bear trap, **433**; fishing reel, **340**; snack food, **265**; workbench, **408**
doghouse: grammatical symbol, **513**; oil drilling platform, **101**
dog's tooth, brick wall, **69**
Dolby, portable radio/cassette player, **182**
Dolby switch, Walkman, **182**
doldrums, wind, **6**
dollar, symbol, **511**
dolly, balance beam, **306**
dome: Capitol, **74**; compass, **136**; destroyer, **477**; dog, **36**; locomotive, **116**; mosque, **70, 71**; percolator, **252**; screwback earring, **218**; silo, **104**
dome cover, wok, **257**
domed shell, cupboard, **243**
domed structures, **85**
domestic hot-water tank, solar heating system, **391**
domestic staff, **489**
domino, **345**
donjon, castle, **80**
do not enter, road sign, **504**

don't-come box, craps table, **347**
don't-pass bar, craps table, **347**
donut, baseball bat, **290**
door: **64**; automobile, **106, 107**; barn, **104**; bath and shower, **274**; bolt, **458**; bus, **118**; church, **87**; clothes dryer, **281**; cupboard, **243**; destroyer, **476**; dishwasher, **250**; elevator car, **78**; fireplace ashpit, **292**; garage, **63**; garbage truck, **127**; grandfather clock, **233**; handball and squash courts, **313**; helicopter, **146**; house, **61, 62, 63**; jumbo jet, **149**; lobster pot, **433**; lock, **458**; locomotive, **117**; mailbox, **231**; mechanical sweeper, **127**; microwave oven, **248**; piano, **361**; powerboat, **139**; prison, **76**; refrigerator, **249**; safe, **457**; sealed voting booth, **437**; single engine airplane, **147**; space shuttle, **152**; stove, **248, 404**; subway car, **119**; synagogue ark, **88**; tent, **342**; tepee, **84**; toaster oven, **253**; vault, **457**; washing machine, **280**
doorknob, **64, 458**
doormat, **64**
door mirror, bus, **118**
doppler shift, **2**
dormer: barn, **104**; house, **62, 63**
dorsal fin, fish, **45**
dorsal scale, snake, **42**
dorso-lateral fold, frog, **44**
dosage, pill, **451**
dosage, prescription, **451**
dot: braille, **512**; curling iron, **214**; dice, **347**; domino, **345**; ice cream cone, **265**; music notation, **353**; sewing machine, **278**
dot matrix printer, **163**
dotted half note, music, **352**
dottle, pipe, **229**
double, dominos, **345**
double bar, music, **353**
double bar bridge, eyeglasses, **221**
double bass, **354, 355**
double bed, **270**
double-breasted jacket, **188**
double bull's eye, dart board, **322**
double-circuit tower, power network, **396**
double-clip palette cup, sketch box, **371**
double corner, chessboard, **345**
double cuff shirt, **189**
double-edged blade, shaver, **210**
double-end curve, staircase, **66**
double-front pocket, shoulder bag, **222**
double-hung window, **63, 67**
double interlining, necktie, **193**
double lancet window, church, **86**
double lock, police gun belt, **498**
double-pointed tack, **410**
double prime, grammatical symbol, **513**
double reed: bagpipe, **365**; English horn, **357**; oboe, **356**
double return, staircase, **66**
double ring, dart board, **322**
double-score ring, dart board, **322**
double seam, can, **267**
double slide zipper, parka, **201**

doubles line, Ping-Pong table, **321**
double spread, magazine, **170**
doubles service court, badminton, **319**
doubles sideline: badminton court, **319**; tennis court, **312**
double star, **3**
double top handles, swagger bag, **222**
double-truck, magazine, **170**
double vent, jacket, **188**
doubling, house, **61**
doubling cube, backgammon, **345**
dough blender, **261**
dowel, hammock, **288**
dowel bit, manual drill, **418**
down, bird, **39**
down haul, windsurfer, **330**
downhill skiing, **326**
down marker, football field, **293**
downpipe, house, **63**
downspout, house, **63**
downstream, river, **13**
downstream gate, canal lock, **99**
downstream stop log hoist, dam, **100**
downtube, bicycle, **128**
dozer, **435**
draft, boat, **132**
draftsman, house blueprint, **62**
draft tube, sleeping bag, **343**
drag, hot air balloon, **332**
dragee, sundae, **264**
drag knob, fishing reel, **340**
dragon, **48**; Manchu court dress, **491**
drag racing, **339**
drag shield, power mower, **429**
dragster, drag racing, **339**
drain: bathtub, **274** cleaner, **422**; sink, **247, 273**; washing machine basket, **280**; water heater, **401**
drain cock, furnace, **400**
drainer, kitchen tool, **259, 260**
draining rack, kitchen, **260**
draining spoon, kitchen utensil, **259**
drainpipe, house, **63**
drain tank, nuclear reactor, **392**
dram, symbol, **510**
drape: curtain, **240**; stage, **350, 351**
drapery, **240**; cave, **4**; four-poster bed, **270**
drawbridge, **97**; castle, **80**; permanent fort, **83**
drawer: bureau, **272**; cash register, **440**; compact disc player, **178**; desk, **276**; dressing table, **272**; garbage disposal, **247**; medical examination table, **450**; sideboard, **243**; workbench, **408**
drawer case, furniture, **272**
drawing, house, **62**
draw-knob, organ, **360**
drawstring: ballet slippers, **494**; parka, **201**
drawtube: microscope, **442**; telescope, **443**
draw-works, oil drilling platform, **101**
dreadnought, **476**
D recreation yard, prison, **76**
dredger, kitchen tool, **260**
dress, **198**; cook, **489**; native, **491**
dress-blue jacket, military, **496**
dressed pelt, **201**
dresser, **272**
dressing medicinal, **451**

dressing table, 272
dress shoe: king's, 484; military, 496; sailor, 497
dress suspenders, 190
dress uniform, military, 496
dried leaf, onion, 262
drift, ocean, 6
drift-free arm, dental unit, 454
drill: dental, 454, 455; hand, 418, 419; oil drilling platform, 101
drilling platform, oil, 101
drill press, 419
D-ring, trenchcoat, 200
drip coffee maker, 252
drip cup, citrus juicer, 255
drip edge, house, 62
drip hoop, overhead power line, 396
drip molding, automobile, 107
dripless candle, 237
drip pan, candelabrum, 237; stove, 248
dripstone, cave, 11; church, 86
drive: chain saw, 431; merry-go-round, 93
drive axle tire, bus, 118
drive chain: bicycle, 128; motorcycle, 129
drive joint, hitch and harrow, 434
drive mode key, camera, 172
driven element, CB radio antenna, 183
drive piece, socket wrench, 415
driver: golf club, 311; harness racing, 337; stagecoach, 131
driver's box, stagecoach, 131
driver's fire suit, drag racing, 339
driver sideview mirror, automobile, 106
driver's observation window, tank, 475
driver's seat: bus, 118; Hansom cab, 131
driveshaft: automobile, 109; outboard engine, 137
driveway apron, house, 63
drive wheel: can opener, 251; locomotive, 116; tank, 474, 475
drive yoke, hitch and harrow, 434
driving band, spinning wheel, 387
driving bit, harness racing, 337
driving glove, drag racing, 339
driving light, truck tractor, 120
driving suit, drag racing, 339
drone, bagpipe, 365
drone string, sitar, 362
drop: coffin, 516; roller coaster, 92; stage, 350; traverse rod, 240
drop armhole, woman's jacket, 196
drop box, blackjack, 346
drop cloth, painting, 425
drop earrings, queen's regalia, 484
drop feed button, sewing machine, 278
drop-in cartridge, movie film, 174
drop-leaf table, 242
drop-lid desk, 276
drop-out, bicycle, 128
dropped handlebar, bicycle, 128
dropped initial, magazine, 170
drop rail lock, playpen, 286
drop shoulder, woman's jacket, 196
drop-through fin cover, slalom water ski, 329
drug box, paramedic, 123

drug treatment, prescription, 451
drum, 354, 364; automobile brake, 109; clothes dryer, 281; humidifier, 402; sextant, 137; venetian blind, 241
drum brake, motorcycle, 129
drumlin, glacier, 12
drum major, 495
drum set, 364
drum shade, lamp, 238
drumstick: drum, 364; poultry, 35
drupe, peach, 55
dry-bulk carrier, 252
dry chemical fire extinguisher, 284
dryer: clothes, 281; hair, 214; lettuce, 260
dry fencing match, 315
drying, laundry, 280
dry measuring cup, 258
dry sink, 243
d.s., music notation, 353
D sharp, piano keyboard octave, 361
D string, double bass, 355
dual pneumatic liner system, football helmet, 292
dual rear wheel, tow truck, 126
dual scale thermometer, 18
dual wheel hub, tow truck, 126
dubbing control, movie projector, 175
ducat, 349
duck, 35
duckbill pliers, 414
duckpin, 317
duct: clothes dryer, 281; eye, 30; furnace, 400; heat exchanger, 403; jet fighter, 480; racing car, 338
dugout, baseball field, 291
dulcimer, Appalachian, 362
dumbbell: body building, 344; keychain, 459
dummy type, magazine, 170
dump: fireplace ashes, 232; police gun belt, 498
dump bin, aisle display, 102
dune: nautical chart, 22; shoreline, 14; topographic map, 22
dune buggy, 130
dust bag: sander, 421; vacuum cleaner, 283
dust cover: hardback book, 167; vault, 457
dust filter, minivacuum, 283
dust flap, folding box, 269
dustproof screw cover, theodolite, 436
dusting brush, vacuum cleaner, 283
dust jacket, hardback book, 167
dustpan, 282
dust panel, furniture, 272
dust ruffle, bedding, 270
Dutch door, 64
dwarf star, 3
dye, hair, 214
dynamic marking, music, 352
dynamic positioning equipment, oil drilling platform, 101

E

E: braille, 512; music notation, 353; piano keyboard octave, 361; sign language, 512
ear: ax, 464; cat, 37; corn, 58; dog, 36; grasshopper, 41; horse, 38; human, 24, 30; lizard, 43; pail, 284; pig, 34; pot, 373; rocking chair, 234;

scallop, 47; sheep, 33; tepee, 84; turkey, 35; turtle, 43; ultimate beast, 48
earclip, spring, 218
ear covert, bird, 39
ear cushion, audio headphone, 179
ear doctor, examination equipment, 448
eardrum, frog, 44
ear flap, baseball batting helmet, 290
earhole, football helmet, 292
ear hook, hearing aid, 452
earlobe, chicken, 35
earmark, cattle, 432
earphone jack, movie camera, 174
earphones, Walkman, 182
earpiece, desk, 180
earplug case, combat soldier's uniform, 497
earring, 219; findings, 218; queen's regalia, 484
ear scope, 448
earth, 3; core, 4; hogan, 84
earth dam section, dam, 100
earthen breastwork, permanent fort, 83
ear tip, stethoscope, 449
ear wire, findings, 218
easel: painting, 370, 371; tombstone, 516
East Australia Current, ocean, 6
Eastern Time, 5
east longitude, 5
East Room, White House, 75
east-west handbag, 222
easy chair, 235
eave: barn, 104; house, 61, 63
eave pole, tent, 342
E cell block, prison, 76
eachinus, column, 73
ecphoneme, grammatical symbol, 513
economy-class section, jumbo jet, 149
Eddy, kite, 323
edge: auger bit, 419; ax, 464; bayonet, 463; bugle, 359; cheese, 263; cheese plane, 256; coin, 225; cymbal, 364; drop-leaf table, 242; hang glider, 333; hatchet, 412; horse's foot, 38; ice skates, 325; knife, 256, 463; necktie, 192; paper bag, 266; razor blade, 210; ski, 326; space shuttle wing, 152; sword, 463
edge flap, jumbo jet, 148
edge marking, airport runway, 94
edger, lawn, 429
editing control, video camera, 184
edition, book, 167
edit key, synthesizer, 363
editorial cartoon, 380
education, résumé, 160
EENT specialist, 448
E flat, piano keyboard octave, 361
effector, nervous system, 29
efferent nerve, human, 29
egg, 262; insect, 41
eggbeater: helicopter, 146; kitchen tool, 258
egg cell, flower, 53
egg rack, refrigerator, 249
egg slicer, 261
eighth-inch mark, tape measure, 424
eighth-mile pole, harness racetrack, 337
eighth note, music, 352
eighth rest, music, 352

eight pin, bowling, 317
eject button, cassette tape recorder, 177; Walkman, 182
ejector, dental unit, 454
ejector chute, circular saw, 417
ejector rod, revolver, 470
elapsed time, drag racing, 339
elapsed time bezel, wristwatch, 220
elapsed time indicator, VCR, 184
elastic, mitten, 200
elastic band: baseball uniform, 290; mattress cover, 271
elastic facing: brassiere, 195; girdle, 195
elasticized waist: shirt, 197; woman's pants, 196
elastic webbing, suspenders, 190
elbow: cat, 37; dog, 36; fence gate, 67; horse, 38; human, 24
elbow cup, armor, 465
elbow pad: basketball, 296; football, 292; ice hockey, 295; rollerskating, 324
elbow protector, fencing, 315
electrical cable, spacesuit, 155
electrical conduit, railroad crossing signal, 115
electrical connection: meter, 399; truck, 120, 121
electrical current, switch, 398
electrical power control, space shuttle, 153
electrical system, automobile, 108
electric broom, 282
electric can opener, 251
electric chair, 462
electric cord, potter's wheel, 373
electric eye, Polaroid, 173
electric foil, fencing strip, 315
electric guitar, 363
electric hair brush, 212
electrician's pliers, 414
electrician's tools, 423
electricity: nuclear reactor, 392; solar power system, 391
electric kiln, 373
electric locomotive, 116; canal lock, 99
electric meter, 399; house, 63
electric organ, 360
electric pilot, stove, 248
electric potter's wheel, 373
electric range, 248
electric razor, 210
electric scoring machine, fencing strip, 315
electric sparks, fireworks, 383
electric starter, barbecue grill, 288
electric typewriter, 161
electric water heater, 401
electric wheelchair, 432
electric wire, railroad crossing signal, 115
electric wok, 257
electrocardiogram, 123
electrode: electric chair, 462; transistor, 396
electronic calculator, 441
electronic countermeasures antenna, aircraft carrier, 478
electronic countermeasure warning light, pilot's instrument panel, 481
electronic flash, photographic, 176
electronic game program, personal computer, 162
electronic lock, cellular telephone, 181
electronic organ, 360

electronics rack, space shuttle, 153
electronic touch button voting position, electronic voting system, 437
electronic warfare antenna, destroyer, 477
electronic weather station, 18
electron tube, 396
electropneumatic retarder, railroad yard, 96
element, CB radio antenna, 183; dishwasher, 250
element release lever, typewriter, 161
elephant, ultimate beast, 49
elevated track, subway, 119
elevating tube, mortar, 472
elevating wheel, slide projector, 175
elevation: house, 62; topographic map, 22
elevation adjustment knob, rifle scope, 469
elevation lead panel, pilot's instrument panel, 481
elevator, 78; aircraft carrier, 478; airplane, 147; blimp, 156; glider, 147; jumbo jet, 149; passenger ship, 142; public sign, 506; skyscraper, 77; stage, 350
elevator lock, camera tripod, 176
elevator platforms, desk, 276
elevator shaft, lift bridge, 97
elevon: cruise missile, 482; space shuttle, 152
eliminator, drag racing, 339
ellipsis, grammatical symbol, 513
elliptical galaxy, 2
embankment, railroad, 115
embattled parapet, castle, 80
emblem: drum major's coat, 495; flag, 502; paper money, 224
embossed label, 268
embouchure hole, flute, 357
embrasure, castle, 80
embroidered buttonhole, Revolutionary War general, 492
embroider cuff, king, 484
embroidered marquisette front, girdle, 195
embroidery, 385; queen's regalia, 484
emergency air vent, bus, 118
emergency brake: car, 110; subway car, 119
emergency channel: CB radio, 183; police radio, 122
emergency core-cooling system pump, nuclear reactor, 392
emergency escape chute, jumbo jet, 148
emergency exit, elevator shaft, 78
emergency light selector, police car, 122
emergency off switch, high-speed printer, 439
emergency stop: elevator car, 78; escalator, 79
emery board, 215
emesis basin, ambulance, 123
emission indicator, gas laser, 395
emitter, transistor chip, 396
empire shade, lamp, 238
EMT, fire engine, 124
enamel, tooth, 456
enarme, shield, 464
enclosing trap, 433
enclosure: air conditioner, 402; letter, 159

end: banana, 55; can, 267; clay modeling tool, 372; clothespin, 280; cupboard, 243; diving board, 316; domino, 345; fencing foil, 315; football, 292; lacrosse stick, 298; music, 353; spool, 384; suspenders, 190; theodolite, 436; tomato, 54; wrench, 415
end assembly, backyard equipment, 287
end-button, violin, 355
end cap: aisle display, 102; cartridge fuse, 399; seeder, 430; venetian blind, 241; waterskiing towline, 329
end cover, sewing machine, 278
end grain, lumber, 68
end handle, coffin, 516
end hook, tape measure, 424
endleaves, hardback book, 167
end line: basketball court, 296; football field, 293; Ping Pong table, 321; volleyball court, 319
end matter, book, 167
endocarp, peach, 55
end operating-screw handle, hand-screw clamp, 409
endoplasmic reticulum, animal cell, 23
endpapers, hardback book, 167
end piece: eyeglasses, 221; starting block, 304; zipper, 209
end pin, cello, 355
end plate, racing car, 338
end plug, vacuum tube, 396
endpost, fence gate, 67
end ring, fishing rod, 341
end slug, magazine, 171
end vise, workbench, 408
end wall, swimming pool, 316
end zone, football field, 293
energy: solar, 391; steam engine, 405
energy absorber: automobile bumper, 108; highway barrier, 114
energy storage capacitor, gas laser, 395
engage switch, 747 cockpit, 150
engine: automobile, 108, 110, 111; blimp, 156; bulldozer, 435; cruise missile, 482; fire fighter, 125; helicopter, 146; hovercraft, 145; internal combustion, 406; jet, 149, 407; lunar lander, 154; mechanical sweeper, 127; motorcycle, 129; outboard, 137; power mower, 429; racing car, 338, 339; single engine airplane, 147; space shuttle, 152; steam, 405; train, 116; truck tractor, 120
engine chamber, torpedo, 479
engine company number, pumper, 125
engineer, and transit, 436
engine fuel shutoff handle, pilot's instrument panel, 481
engine hour meter, powerboat, 138
engine instrumentation, 747 cockpit, 150, 151
engine louvers, tank, 474
engine mounting brackets inflatable, 133
engine oil-pressure gauge, powerboat, 138
engine room, passenger ship, 142

engine terminal, railroad yard, 96
engine test area, aircraft carrier, 478
English clock, darts, 322
English horn, 354, 357
English saddle, 335
engraved line, scrimshaw, 375
engraved plate, paper money, 224
engraving: identification bracelet, 187; knife, 375; and printing, 374, 377
enlarged scale detail inset, political map, 21
enlisted man's uniform, 496
ensemble, chamber music, 354
ensign, destroyer, 476
entablature, column, 73
entrails, fowl, 35
entrance: airport, 94; bus, 118; circuit breaker box, 399; highway cloverleaf, 114; igloo, 85; jai alai cancha, 314; lobster pot, 433; tanker belowdeck storage, 140; theatre, 351; White House, 75
entrée, meal, 263
entry, darts, 322
entry word, book page, iv
enumerating district, thematic map, 21
envelope, 159; animal cell, 23; hot air balloon, 332; vacuum tube, 396; Zeppelin, 156
environmental control, pilot's instrument panel, 481
environmental monitor, space shuttle, 153
epaulet: drum major's coat, 495; Revolutionary War general,; 492; trench coat, 200
épée, 315
epiglottis, tongue, 30
Episcopal ring, cardinal, 487
epitaph, tombstone, 516
equal, symbol, 511
equalizer: audio speaker, 179, 182; cowboy, 490
equalizer buckle, venetian blind, 241
equalize space, proofreader's mark, 514
equalizing switch, tape recorder, 177
equal or greater, symbol, 511
equal or less, symbol, 511
equals: calculator key, 441; symbol, 511
equator, 5, 6
equatorial counter current, ocean, 6
equatorial current, ocean, 6
equipment bay, lunar lander, 154
equipment status indicator, nuclear reactor control room, 393
equipment stowage box, tank, 474
erase button, video-still camera adaptor, 173
eraser, pencil, 158
erasure table, typewriter, 161
erecting telescope, field glasses, 443
ergostand, computer workstation, 438
ermine pendant, Indian, 490
eroteme, grammatical symbol, 513
escalator, 79
escape chute, jumbo jet, 148
escarp, permanent fort, 83
escarpment, continental margin, 15

escroll, coat of arms, 503
escutcheon: coat of arms, 503; mortise lock, 458
escutcheon plate: kitchen sink, 247; safe, 457
espresso coffee, 252
estate bottled, wine label, 267
estate name, wine label, 267
E string, double bass, 355
ET, drag racing, 339
etching, 377
eternal light: synagogue, 88; Torah, 486
evacuation tip, dental unit, 454
evaporator coil, air conditioner, 402
evening handkerchief, queen's regalia, 484
event: drag racing, 339; information, ticket, 349; track and field, 300
everything's OK, gesture, 507
ewe, 33
examination equipment, medical, 449
examination table, medical, 450
exasperation, gesture, 507
excavator, dental, 455
excessive talk, gesture, 507
exchanger, fireplace heat, 232
exclamation point, grammatical symbol, 506
execution device, 462
executive office, White House, 75
exercise, body building, 344
exercise yard, prison, 76
exhaust: automobile engine, 111; combustion jet engine, 407; drag racing dragster, 339; heat exchanger, 403; internal combustion engine, 406; locomotive, 117; motorcycle, 129; steam engine, 405; tank, 474; truck tractor, 120
exhaust duct: clothes dryer, 281; furnace, 400; tunnel, 98
exhaust line gas filter, gas laser, 395
exhaust port, outboard engine, 137; rocket, 407; skin diving tank, 331
exhaust tube, incandescent bulb, 238
exhibit hall, church, 87
exit: elevator, 78; jumbo jet, 149; theatre, 351
exit angle, slide, 287
exit bar, bus, 118
exit door, bus, 118
exit mirror, laser, 395
exit ramp, highway cloverleaf, 114
exocarp: orange, 55; pineapple, 55
exonomist, 225
exoskeleton, insect, 41
exosphere, earth, 4
expanding bit, drill, 418
expansion chamber, thermometer, 18
expansion nozzle, missile, 456
expansion tank, automobile, 108
expansive bit, drill, 419
expiration date: coupon, 103; credit card, 227; magazine mailing label, 169
exploration equipment, lunar lander, 154
explorer, dental, 455
exposure adjustment key, camera, 172
exposure index, light meter, 176
exposure label, gas laser, 395

exposure meter, **176**
exposure mode key, camera, **172**
expression pedal, organ, **360**
expressway, **114**
extended bay, barn, **104**
extender, paint roller, **425**
extending ball, pen, **158**
extension: automatic rifle barrel, **471**; baseball catcher's shinguard, **290**; dropleaf table, **242**; folding rule, **424**; operating table, **450**; political map, **21**; table saw, **417**; vacuum cleaner, **283**
extension handle, lunar rover, **155**
extension ladder, pumper, **124**
extension scoring light, fencing strip, **315**
extension tube: ambulance, **123**; screen, **175**
exterior, window, **65**
exterior decoration, coat of arms, **503**
exterior frame, tent, **342**
exterior panagraph gate, subway motorman's cab, **119**
exterior slope, permanent fort, **89**
external auditory canal, ear, **30**
external bud, potato, **54**
external door switch, dishwasher, **250**
external environmental control, pilot's instrument panel, **481**
external frame, **343**
external fuel tank: space shuttle, **152**; tank, **474**
external galaxy, **2**
external microphone, cassette tape recorder, **177**
external speaker, personal cassette player, **182**
external tank forward bay, space shuttle, **152**
extinct reptiles, **43**
extinguisher: candle, **237**; drag racing dragster, **339**
extra bass port, portable radio/cassette player, **182**
extra cheese, pizza, **265**
extractor: juice, **255**; shotgun, **468**
extrados, arch, **72**
extravehicular activity handrail, lunar lander, **154**
extravehicular visor, spacesuit, **155**
extremities, human, **31**
eye: ant, **41**; ax, **464**; bee, **41**; cat, **37**; cheese, **263**; fish, **45**; fishhook, **341**; fishing jig, **341**; frame, **379**; frog, **44**; grasshopper, **41**; hammer, **412**; hasp, **460**; hook and eye, **208**; human, **24**, **30**; hurricane, **17**; lobster, **47**; mallet, **412**; needle, **384**; octopus, **46**; pineapple, **55**; potato, **54**; sheep, **33**; snake, **42**; spider, **40**; spring beard needle, **386**; stirrup, **335**; tadpole, **44**; toad, **44**
eyeball, **30**
eyebolt, **411**
eyebrow, **30**; magazine, **171**; woman's, **213**
eye colorstick, **216**, **217**
eyecup: binoculars, **443**; video camera, **184**
eye doctor, examination equipment, **448**
eyedropper, **451**
eyeglasses, **221**

eye guards, fireman's helmet, **500**
eyelashes, **30**, **213**; liner, **216**, **217**
eyelet: baseball glove, **291**; ice skates, **325**; man's belt, **190**; cap, **202**; man's shoe, **204**; running shoe, **302**; shoulder bag, **222**
eyelid: frog, **44**; human, **30**
eyeliner, makeup, **216**
eyepatch, pirate, **492**
eye pencil, **217**
eyepiece: binoculars, **443**; camera, **174**; ear scope, **448**; eye scope, **448**; microscope, **442**; Polaroid, **173**; telescope, **443**; theodolite, **436**
eyeport shield, drag racing driver, **339**
eye scope, **448**
eye shadow, **217**
eye socket, **30**
eyespot, starfish, **46**
eyestay, running shoe, **302**
eye teeth, **456**
eyewires, eyeglasses, **221**

F

F: braille, **512**; music notation, **353**; piano keyboard octave, **361**; sign language, **512**
F-4 Phantom II, **480**
F-16F Falcon, **480**
fabric, **388**; embroidery, **385**; hand knitting, quilting, **385**; umbrella, **230**; weaving, **387**
fabric flowers, woman's hat, **203**
fabric ridge, embroidery ring, **385**
fabric temperature guide, iron, **279**
fabric-tension lock, screen, **175**
face: ax, **464**; bow, **466**; brick, **68**; check, **226**; clown, **493**; coin, **225**; croquet mallet, **318**; dart board, **322**; elliptical galaxy, **2**; file, **420**; gas pump, **112**; geodesic dome, **85**; golf club, **310**; grandfather clock, **233**; hammer, **412**; hand shower, **274**; lacrosse stick, **298**; lead came, **378**; lumber, **68**; mountain, **8**, **9**; obelisk, **71**; paper bag, **266**; Ping-Pong racket, **321**; playing cards, **348**; rasp, **420**; saw tooth, **416**; sheep, **33**; shower, **274**; slot machine, **346**; spider, **40**; starting block, **304**; sword, **463**; tennis racket, **312**; traffic light, **113**; type, **166**; voting booth, **437**; wall, **69**; wristwatch, **220**; zipper, **209**
face cards, **348**
face mask: baseball catcher, **290**; football helmet, **292**; ice hockey goalie, **294**; skin diving, **331**
face-off circle, ice hockey rink, **295**
faceplate: mortise lock, **458**; paper money, **225**; sewing machine, **278**; ski helmet, **326**
face shield, police, **498**
facet, cut gemstone, **218**
face value: money, **224**, **225**; stamp, **159**
facing: brassiere, **195**; girdle, **195**; necktie, **193**; skyscraper, **77**; woman's jacket, **196**
facing dragon, Manchu court dress, **491**

facsimile, fax machine, **164**
Fahrenheit scale, thermometer, **18**, **449**
fairing, helicopter, **146**; motorcycle, **129**
fair territory, baseball field, **291**
fairwater, outboard engine, **137**
fairway, golf course, **310**
fairweather, submarine, **479**
faja, jai alai player, **314**
fall: grand piano, **361**; pulley block rope, **461**; woman's hair, **213**
falling front desk, **276**
false edge, knife, **463**
false teeth, **453**
family name, typeface, **165**
fan: air circulating, **402**; automobile, **108**, **111**; bridal costume, **488**; combustion jet engine, **407**; heat exchanger, **403**; high jump, **300**; hovercraft, **145**; jumbo jet, **149**; lobster tail, **47**; subway car, **119**; underwater tunnel, **98**; vacuum cleaner, **283**
fan belt, **111**
fan clutch, **111**
fancy stitching, boot, **206**
fanfold paper, computer, **439**
fang: snake, **42**; spider, **40**; tooth, **456**
fanlight, door, **64**
fan plate, armor, **465**
fan switch, elevator, **78**
fantail: destroyer, **476**; passenger ship, **142**; windmill, **390**
fare box, commuter bus, **118**
farm machinery, road sign, **505**
far turn, harness racetrack, **337**
fascia, house, **60**, **61**
fastback, passenger car, **109**
fastener, **208**; corrugated, **410**; football helmet, **292**; hollow wall, **411**; overnight bag, **285**; spacesuit, **155**
fastening, bell, **iv**
fast forward: remote control unit, **184**; tape recorder, **177**
fast forward button, Walkman, **182**
fastigiated top, skyscraper, **77**
fast-rewind button, tape recorder, **177**
fat, meat, **262**
fat back, pork, **34**
father, flat racing entry, **336**
fathom, nautical chart, **22**
fatigue belt, **497**
fatigue pants, **497**
fatigue shirt, **497**
fauces, tongue, **30**
faucet, **273**; bathtub, **274**; hose coupling, **428**; Jacuzzi, **274**; kitchen sink, **247**
fault line, jai alai cancha, **314**
faux pas, gesture, **507**
fax machine, **164**
fax number, business card, **160**
F clef, music, **353**
feather: badminton shuttlecock, **319**; bird, **39**; chicken, **35**; turkey, **35**; weather vane, **19**; woman's hat, **203**
feather pen, **158**
feature spread, magazine, **170-171**
feature stripes, powerboat, **138**
feature well, magazine, **169**
Federal, house style, **63**
federal prescription number, prescription, **451**

Federal Reserve Bank seal, paper money, **224**
Federal Reserve note, **224**
federal route number, road map, **20**
feed: drill press, **419**; machine gun ammunition, **471**; track lighting, **239**
feed dog, sewing machine, **278**
feeder cap, blender, **254**
feeder waveguide, radar antenna, **444**
feeding pen, barnyard, **104**
feed knob, dot matrix printer, **163**
feed line, furnace, **400**
feed passage, barn, **104**
feed plate, machine gun, **471**
feed screw, auger bit, **419**
feed-through, pacemaker, **452**
feed tube: food processor, **254**; fountain pen, **158**
feedwater pump, nuclear reactor, **392**
fee indicator, toll booth, **114**
feeler: cat, **37**; lobster, **47**
feet: nautical chart, **22**; type, **166**
felloe, stagecoach, **131**
felt: film roll, **172**; pool table, **320**
felt cap, baseball gear, **290**
felt hat, cowboy, **490**
female, symbol, **510**
female coupling, hose connection, **428**
female ferrule, fishing rod, **340**
female flower, corn, **58**
female-male, symbol, **508**
female receptacle, electrical, **398**
femoral artery, human, **28**
femoral nerve, human, **29**
femoral vein, human, **28**
femur: frog, **44**; grasshopper, **41**; human, **26**; spider, **40**
fence: baseball field, **291**; house, **63**; prison, **76**; table saw, **417**
fence posts, **67**
fencing, **315**; barnyard, **104**
fencing shoe, **315**
fencing strip, wood fence, **67**
fender: automobile, **106**, **107**; bicycle, **128**; bulldozer, **435**; fireplace, **232**; lift bridge, **97**; motorcycle, **129**; saddle, **335**; tractor, **434**; tugboat, **144**
fender guard, gas pump automatic nozzle, **112**
fermata, music, **352**
fern, **57**
Ferris wheel, **93**
ferrule: billiard cue, **320**; burnisher, **377**; clay modeling tool, **372**; chisel, **420**; fishing rod, **340**; gouge, **374**; hoe, **427**; jump rope, **344**; paint brush, **425**; painting brush, **370**; pencil, **158**; rake, **427**; screwdriver, **413**; shoe tree, **207**; sousaphone, **358**; stick umbrella, **230**; tuba, **358**; woodcarving tool, **372**
fertilizer, **430**
fess, coat of arms, **503**
fetlock, horse, **38**
fettling tool, potter's wheel, **373**
F-hole, violin, **355**
fiber: nerve, **29**; paper money, **224**; rope, **132**
fiberglass pole, pole vaulting, **305**
fibula, human, **26**
fiddle: bass, **355**; tub, **366**
field: baseball, **291**; coat of

arms, **503**; coin, **225**; craps table, **347**; flag, **502**; football, **293**; lacrosse, **298**; mountain, **9**; polo, **299**; soccer, **297**; track and field, **300-301**
field events equipment, **303**
field fortification, **82**
fieldglasses, **443**
fife, marching band, **354**
15' marker, bowling lane, **317**
fifth wheel, truck trailer, **120**
51-in-5's, darts, **322**
50-point ring, dart board, **322**
50-yard line, football field, **293**
fighter, jet aircraft, **480**
fighting chair, powerboat, **139**
fighting kite, **323**
fighting ship, surface, **476-477**
figure skates, **325**
filament: coral polyp, **46**; flower stamen, **53**; incandescent bulb, **238**; vacuum tube, **396**
file, **420**; briefcase, **285**; chessboard, **345**; desk, **276**; nail, **215**; pocket knife, **426**
file handle, drill, **418**
filet, cannon barrel, **467**
file-type handle, coping saw, **416**
fill, sleeping bag, **343**
filler: cigar, **228**; inflatable, **133**; locomotive, **117**; man's belt, **190**; quilting, **385**
filler neck, automobile gas tank, **109**
filler tube: automobile engine power steering, **111**; toilet, **275**
fillet, royal regalia, **485**
filling, dental, **455**; dessert, **264**; quiche, **263**; sandwich, **263**; scrimshaw, **375**; sleeping bag, **343**
filling port, iron, **279**
fill opening, coffee maker, **252**
fill unit float, dishwasher, **250**
fill window, minivacuum, **283**
filly, horse, **38**
film, **172**; camera, **174**
film door, Polaroid, **173**
film door release, Polaroid, **173**
filming trigger, movie camera, **174**
film-loading port, movie projector, **175**
film pack, instant camera, **173**
film plate, **395**
film projector, **175**
film roll, **172**
film shade, Polaroid, **173**
film speed, lightmeter, **176**
film speed key, camera, **172**
filter: air conditioner, **402**; cigarette, **228**; dryer, **281**; coffee maker, **252**; drag racing driver's fire suit, **339**; engine, **111, 406**; heat exchanger, **403**; tractor, **434**; washing machine, **280**
filter carrier, microscope, **442**
fin: air conditioner, **402**; automobile, **107**; blimp, **156**; fish, **45**; glider, **147**; hovercraft, **145**; jet fighter, **480**; jumbo jet, **149**; missile, **482**; rifle grenade, **473**; single engine airplane, **147**; skin diving, **331**; stingray, **45**; surfboard, **330**; waterskiing, **329**; windsurfer, **330**
finance program, personal computer, **162**
fin cover, slalom water ski, **329**
findings, jewelry, **218**
fine-adjustment beam, laboratory scale, **447**

fine calibrate, Geiger counter, **445**
fine focus: microscope, **442**; telescope, **443**
fine tooth, hair comb, **212**
fine tuner: metal detector, **445**; violin, **355**
finger: baseball glove, **291**; frog, **44**; hair roller, **214**; handball glove, **313**; human, **24, 31**; laboratory clamp, **446**; lacrosse glove, **298**; ultimate beast, **49**
fingerboard: accordion, **366**; guitar, **362, 363**; violin, **355**
finger flange, hypodermic syringe, **451**
fingerless glove, miser, **492**
finger grip: hair clip, **214**; sewing machine, **278**
finger hole: bowling ball, **317**; desk phone, **180**
finger hook, trumpet, **359**
fingernail, **31**
finger pad, **31**
fingerplate, clarinet, **356**
fingerprint, human, **31**
finger pump, camp stove, **342**
finger stop, desk phone, **180**
fingertip: dog, **36**; human, **31**
finial: church, **86**; dressing table, **272**; flagpole, **502**; four-poster bed, **270**; gate post, **67**; grandfather clock, **233**; lamp, **238**; pagoda, **71**; woodburning stove, **404**
finish: drag racing, **339**; football, **292**; stained glass, **378**
finished copy tray, copier, **164**
finishing cap, umbrella, **230**
finishing nail, **410**
finishing sander, **421**
finishing wire, umbrella runner, **230**
finish line: harness racetrack, **337**; running track, **301**
finned projectile, mortar, **472**
fin-seal wrap, package, **269**
fin stabilizer, destroyer, **477**
fire, gemstone, **218**
fireback, fireplace, **232**
fireball, launch pad, **152**
fireboat, **144**
fireboot, **500**
fire bowl, brazier, **288**
firebox, fireplace, **232**
fire curtain, stage, **350**
fired handguns, **470**
fired pot, **373**
fire-eater, circus, **90**
fire engine, **124-125**
fire extinguisher, **284**; drag racing dragster, **339**; police car, **122**; tow truck, **126**
fire-fighting station, tanker, **141**
fire hydrant, **125**
fire irons, fireplace, **232**
fireman, **500**; suspenders, **190**
fire pit, tepee, **84**
fireplace, **232**
fire plug, **125**
fire screen, fireplace, **232**
fire stop, house, **60**
fire suit, drag racing driver's, **339**
fireworks, **382-383**
firing chamber, kiln, **373**
firing cone, potting, **373**
firing lever, machine gun, **471**
firing pin, torpedo, **479**
firing tube, bazooka, **472**
firing vent, cannon barrel, **467**
firn, mountain, **9**
first aid, public sign, **506**
first-aid box, fire engine, **124**
first-aid kit, police car, **122**

first base: baseball field, **291**; blackjack, **347**
first baseman's mitt, **291**
first bicuspid, **456**
first-class section, jumbo jet, **148**
first floor, White House, **75**
First Lady's office, White House, **75**
first meridian, globe, **5**
first molar, **456**
first officer's seat, 747 cockpit, **151**
first premolar, **456**
first quarter moon, **4**
first reef position, windmill, **390**
first reinforce, cannon barrel, **467**
first stage: missile, **482**; skin diving tank, **331**
first valve, trumpet, **359**
first valve slide: French horn, **358**; trumpet, **359**
first violin, **354**
fish, **45**; zodiac, **509**
fishing, **340-341**
fish ladder, dam, **100**
fishplate, railroad track, **115**
fish scaler, pocket knife, **426**
fish tail, coffin, **516**
fishtail chisel, woodcarving, **372**
fishtail gouge, woodcarving, **372**
fishway, dam, **100**
fission, nuclear reactor, **392**
fissure volcano, **10**
fist, human, **25**
fitted cuff, bridal gown, **488**
fitted pants, drum major, **495**
fitted pillow, sofa, **236**
fitted sheet, bedding, **271**
fitting: nozzle, **428**; pumper, **125**; saw, **416**; shoulder bag, **222**; shower, **274**; sink, **273**
five pin, bowling, **317**
5/8 pole, harness racetrack, **337**
5.25-inch disk format, diskette, **162**
five-unit beads, abacus, **441**
5 yard line, football field, **293**
fixed bridge, **97**
fixed glove, jet fighter, **480**
fixed hurdle, **304**
fixed jaw: C-clamp, **409**; monkey wrench, **415**
fixed pin, hinge, **460**
fixed service structure, launch pad, **152**
fixed-target collider, **394**
fixed window, **65**
fixings, ice cream, **265**
fixture, sink, **247**
flag, **502**; courtroom, **89**; football field, **293**; golf course, **311**; mailbox, **231**; music note, **353**; newspaper, **168**; parking meter, **113**; soccer field, **297**; swimming pool, **316**; track and field, **301**
flagged end, paint brush bristle, **425**
flagpole, **502**
flagstaff, destroyer, **476**
flake, tennis racket, **312**
flame: candle, **237**; dental, **455**; four-poster bed finial, **270**
flame bucket, launch pad, **152**
flame adjustment wheel, gas cigarette lighter, **228**
flan, coin, **225**
flange: barometer, **18**; hypodermic syringe, **451**; mace, **464**; sink, **273**; spool, **384**; trombone, **358**

flank: beef, **32**; cat, **37**; dog, **36**; horse, **38**; human, **25**; lamb, **33**; pelt, **201**; permanent fort, **83**; pork, **34**
flank billet, Western saddle, **335**
flap: backpack, **343**; baseball helmet, **290**; checkbook clutch, **223**; envelope, **159**; hasp, **460**; jumbo jet, **148**; magazine cover, **169**; man's shoe, **204**; matchbook, **228**; package, **269**; pocket, **188, 189, 196, 200**; saddle, **335**; sailor's uniform, **497**; shoulder bag, **222**; single engine airplane, **147**; slalom water ski, **329**; tepee, **84**; tow truck, **126**; wallet, **223**
flap lever, 747 cockpit, **151**
flare: police car, **122**; solar, **3**; trombone, **359**; trousers, **191**
flare fitting, plumbing, **422**
flaring tool, plumbing, **422**
flash: electronic, **176**; radar, **444**
flasher, locomotive, **117**
flash head: electronic flash, **176**; lunar lander, **154**
flashlight, police, **499**
flash suppressor, automatic weapon, **471**
flask, laboratory, **447**
flat: music, **352**; stage, **350**
flat bed, truck, **121**
flat-bottom hull, powerboat, **138**
flatcar, train, **117**
flat chisel, stonecutting, **372**
flat coast, nautical chart, **22**
flat diaphragm chest piece, stethoscope, **449**
flat four-cylinder automobile engine, **111**
flat grind, knife, **256**
flat hat, Beefeater, **483**
flat head, screw, **410**
flatiron, **279**
flat kite, **323**
flat of stock, rifle, **468**
flat pin, window shade roller, **241**
flat plate, solar heating system collector unit, **391**
flat racing, **336**
flat surface: perspective, **368**; printing, **166**
flattop, **478**
flatware, **244**
flavedo, orange, **55**
fleatrap, cowboy, **490**
fleet ballistic missile submarine, **479**
flesh, banana, **55**
fleshy root, carrot, **54**
fleshy tissue, succulent, **56**
fletching, arrow, **466**
fleur-de-lis, royal crown, **485**
flews, dog, **36**
flex, skateboard, **324**
flexible kite, **323**
flexible skirt, hovercraft, **145**
flexor, universal gym, **344**
flexor carpi radialis, human, **26**
flexor carpi ulnaris, human, **26**
flier, staircase, **66**
flies, stage, **350**
flight: dart, **322**; of steps, **66**
flight control position indicator, 747 cockpit, **150**
flight deck: aircraft carrier, **478**; destroyer, **476**; jumbo jet, **148**
flight feather, bird, **39**
flight instrumentation control, space shuttle, **153**
flight officer, airplane, **481**

flip, woman's hair, 213
flip chart, football down marker, 293
flipover, hurdle, 304
flip panel, football down marker, 293
flipper: dolphin, 45; skin diving, 331; turtle, 42
flitter candle, fireworks, 383
float: buoy, 132; dishwasher, 250; fishing, 341; toilet, 275
floating crank, brace, 418
floating pier, pontoon bridge, 97
floating position, oil drilling platform, 101
floe, glacier, 12
floeberg, glacier, 12
flood: river, 13; stage, 350
flood plain, 13, 15
floodlight, stage, 350
floor: barn, 104; basketball court, 296; canal lock, 99; and carpet, 246; cave, 11; church, 118; elevator car, 78; house, 60, 61, 62; kiln, 373; oil drilling platform, 101; skyscraper, 77; stage, 350; White House, 75
floorboards: inflatable, 133; playpen, 286
floor cable, fencing strip, 315
floor exercise, gymnastics, 306
floor glide, desk, 276
flooring, tent, 342
floor leader, House of Representatives, 74
floor-locking system pedal, surgical table, 450
floor pan, automobile, 109
floor plan: church, 87; house, 62
floor plate: escalator, 79; horizontal bar, 306; rifle, 468; stage, 350; stationary rings, 307
floor selector, elevator car, 78
floor support, playpen, 286
floor tom-tom, 364
floppy disk: computer, 438; personal computer, 162
floppy disk drive: computer workstation, 438; portable word processor, 162
floppy disk drive slot, personal computer, 162
floppy shoe, clown, 493
floral carving, tombstone, 516
floral organs, grass, 58
floral tube, apple, 55
floret, grass, 58
florist shop, passenger ship, 142
flotation device: skin diving, 331; jumbo jet, 148
flounce: dress, 198; queen's regalia, 484
flour shaker, 260
flow, volcano, 10
flow distributor head, nuclear reactor, 392
flower, 53; cactus, 56; corn, 58; grass, 58; woman's hat, 203
flow indicator, pilot's instrument panel, 481
flowstone, cave, 11
flue: destroyer, 476; fireplace, 232; house, 62; stove, 248, 404; water heater, 401
fluff, chicken, 35
fluid, solar collector panel, 391
fluke: anchor, 132; dolphin, 45
fluorescent banner, football field, 293
fluorescent bulb, lighting, 238
fluorescent light, oven, 248
flush, toilet, 275
flusher, sanitation vehicle, 127

flush left, proofreader's mark, 514
flush-left type, 170
flush-mount control actuator, Jacuzzi, 274
flute, 354, 356-357; auger bit, 419; screwdriver, 413
fluted spire, kokoshniki, 70
fluting, column, 73
flux, plumbing, 422
fly: flag, 502; man's underpants, 194
flybridge: powerboat, 138
flybridge monitor, fireboat, 144
fly deck, stage, 350
flyer: circus, 90; spinning wheel, 387; staircase, 66
fly front: blouse, 197; trousers, 191; woman's pants, 196
flying bridge: destroyer, 477; powerboat, 138
flying crate, kite, 323
flying horse, merry-go-round, 93
flying line, kite, 323
flying stovepipe, jet engine, 407
flying wing, combat aircraft, 480
fly line, stage, 350
fly rod, fishing, 341
fly tackle, windmill, 390
flywheel: automobile engine, 111; hitch and harrow, 434; steam engine, 405
FM: movie camera, 174; receiver, 179
foal, horse, 38
foam, fire extinguisher, 284
foam brush, house painting, 425
foam monitor, tanker, 141
fob: pocket watch, 220; trousers, 191; vest, 188
focal length: microscope, 442; movie camera, 174
focal point, composition, 369
fo'c'sle, destroyer, 477
focus: binoculars, 443; camera, 174; microscope, 442; projector, 175; rifle scope, 469; telescope, 443; theodolite, 436
focus collar, zoom lens, 172
focus control, video camera, 184
focusing lens, laser, 395
focusing magnet, super collider, 394
focusing ring, camera, 172
focus mode switch, camera, 172
fog, weather map, 19
fog whistle, destroyer, 477
foible, fencing foil, 315
foil: copper, 378; drag racing dragster, 339; electric, 315; fencing, 315; package, 269
fold: curtain, 240; frog, 44; salamander, 44
fold-down seat, automobile, 106
folder, briefcase, 285
folding box, package, 269
folding fan, 402
folding file, nail clippers, 215
folding leaf, drop-leaf table, 242
folding rule, 424
folding umbrella, 230
fold line, sewing pattern, 388
foley, 260
foliage, 52; carrot, 54
folio: book page, iv, 167; magazine, 169, 170; newspaper, 168
folk instruments, 366
follow block, stapler, 277

follower, magazine, 470
follow spring, stapler, 277
fondo, jai alai cesta, 314
food: desserts, 264; prepared, 263; raw, 262
food mill, 260
food processor, 254
foolish, gesture, 507
foot: attaché case, 285; basket, 266; bed, 270; bird, 39; book page, 167; boot, 206; bureau, 272; camera tripod, 176; cat, 37; cigar, 228; cigarette, 228; clam, 47; cymbal, 364; drop-leaf table, 242; electronic flash, 176; fishing reel, 340; flag, 502; food processor, 254; frog, 44; garbage disposal, 247; grammatical symbol, 506; horse, 38; human, 24, 31; hurdle, 304; juice extractor, 255; lounger, 235; mainsail, 136; pig, 34; pot, 373; potter's wheel, 373; rail, 115; royal regalia, 485; sewing machine, 278; shoulder bag, 222; shuffleboard court, 318; sideboard, 243; slide projector, 175; sofa, 236; stapler, 277; steamer basket, 257; stemware, 244; surgical table, 450; toaster, 253; ultimate beast, 49; windsurfer mast, 330; wok, 257
football, 292-293; association, 297
footballer, 297
foot binding, slalom water ski, 329
footboard: bed, 270; stagecoach, 131; operating table, 450
foot control, dental unit, 454
foothills, 7
footing: elevator shaft, 78; house, 60
foot joint, flute, 356
footline, book page, iv
footlight: circus, 90; stage, 350
footnote, magazine, 171
foot pad, kiln, 373
footpath, bridge, 97
foot peg: football field, 293; motorcycle, 129
footpiece, crutch, 452
footplate, wheelchair, 452
foot pocket, skin diving fin, 331
foot pump, paramedic equipment, 123
footrace, 300
footrest: baby's high chair, 286; car, 110; glider, 287; lounger, 235; medical examination table, 450; stroller, 286
foot spot, pool table, 320
footstool, 235
foot-switch input, guitar amplifier, 363
footstraps, windsurfer, 330
foot zipper, mainsail, 136
force cup, plumber's plunger, 422
fore and aft gangway, tanker, 140
forearm: dog, 36; frog, 44; horse, 38; human, 24; machine gun, 471; shotgun, 468
forearm pad, football uniform, 292
forebay, canal lock, 99
fore beam, hand loom, 387
forecast, weather, 18

forecastle, destroyer, 477
forecomb, shotgun, 468
forecourt: basketball, 296; handball, 313; squash, 313; tennis, 312
foredeck: powerboat, 138; sailboat, 134
fore-edge, book, 167
forefinger, hand, 31
forefoot: cat, 37; pig, 34; sailboat, 134
foregrip, fishing rod, 340
forehead: bird, 39; cat, 37; cow, 32; dog, 36; horse, 38; human, 24; sheep, 33
foreign price, magazine, 169
forel, book, 167
foreleg: bee, 41; cat, 37; sheep, 33
foreleg bandage, polo, 299
forelock, horse, 38
foremast, tanker, 140
forepart, shoe tree, 207
forepaw, pelt, 201
forepeak, sailboat, 135
foreshank: beef, 32; lamb, 33
foreslope, shoreline, 14
forestage, theatre, 351
forestay, sailboat, 135
forestaysail, sailboat, 134
forewing, grasshopper, 41
for good luck, gesture, 507
fork: bicycle, 128; branding iron, 432; fireplace logs, 232; kitchen utensil, 259; motorcycle, 129; river, 13; saddle, 335; spading, 427; stroller, 286; table setting, 244, 245; tuning, 367
form, etching press, 377
formal Mandarin attire, 491
formal shirt, man's, 488
formation light, jet fighter, 480
form tractor, high-speed printer, 439
Formula One racing car, 338
for shooter, craps table, 347
forte: fencing foil, 315; music notation, 352
fortification, 82, 83
fortress, castle, 80
45°-angle gauge, combination square, 424
45° vial, carpenter's level, 424
forward: basketball, 296; boat, 132; destroyer, 477; fireboat, 144; hovercraft, 145; lunar lander, 154; polo, 299; sailboat, 135; slide projector, 175; space shuttle, 152
forward-reverse button, potter's wheel, 373
foul light, drag racing, 339
foul line: baseball field, 291; basketball court, 296; bowling lane, 317; javelin throw, 301
foundation: beauty product, 216, 217; house, 60; skyscraper, 77; undergarment, 195
foundation lines, spider web, 40
foundation plan, house, 62
fount, lantern, 342
fountain, fireworks, 383
fountain pen, 158
4x4, passenger vehicle, 109
fourchette, glove, 200
four-cycle internal combustion engine, 406
four-cylinder automobile engine, 111
4-door sedan, 108
four-face traffic signals, 113
four-in-hand tie, 192-193
four-poster bed, 270

four pin, bowling, 317
fourragère, enlisted man's uniform, 496
four suit, domino, 345
14-stop, darts, 322
fourth toe, human foot, 31
fourth tooth, crocodile, 42
four-wheel drive jeep, 130
fovea centralis, eye, 30
fowl, 35
foxing: boot, 206; running shoe, 302
foyer, skyscraper, 77
fraction, political map, 21
fracture, volcano, 10
fragmentation grenade, 473
frame: 379; abacus, 441; attaché case, 285; automobile, 106, 109; automatic pistol, 470; backpack, 343; basket, 266; bed, 270, 271; bicycle, 128; binoculars, 443; brassiere, 195; card table, 242; carpenter's level, 424; C-clamp, 409; chaise longue, 288; circus, 90; coffee maker, 252; comic strip, 380; drill, 418; dressing table mirror, 272; eyeglasses, 221; film, 174; gallows, 462; garbage truck, 127; hammock, 288; hand loom, 387; hourglass, 233; house, 61; ironing board, 279; jai alai cesta, 314; jet fighter canopy, 480; Jew's harp, 366; lawn sprinkler, 428; man's belt buckle, 190; medical examination table, 450; paint roller, 425; piano, 361; pilot's instrument panel, 481; plane, 420; pocket watch, 220; revolver, 470; sailboat, 134; saw, 416; seeder, 430; sextant, 137; shutters, 241; silk screen, 375; skin diving tank, 331; skyscraper, 77; slot machine, 346; snowshoe, 327; solar collector panel, 391; stationary rings, 307; steam engine, 405; stroller, 286; swagger bag, 222; telegraph key, 157; tent, 342; tepee, 84; tractor, 434; trampoline, 308; umbrella, 230; wheelbarrow, 430; window, 65
frame cover, motorcycle, 129
frame leaf, hinge, 460
frame plate, mortise lock, 458
frame rail, truck tractor, 120
framework: denture, 453; yurt, 70; Zeppelin, 156
framing string, kite, 323
framing knob, movie projector, 175
franc, symbol, 511
frankfurter, 265
Franklin glasses, miser, 492
Franklin stove, 404
free arm, sewing machine, 278
freeboard, boat, 132
free-fall, parachuting, 333
free-reed instrument, 366
free-rotating mast, windsurfer, 330
free-sail system, windsurfer, 330
free-standing easel-back frame, 379
freestyle swimming race, 316
free-throw circle, basketball court, 296
freeway, 114
freewheel, bicycle, 128

freeze frame, picture-in-picture viewing, 185
freeze frame button, remote control unit, 184
freezer: powerboat, 139; refrigerator, 249; thermometer, 258
freezing rain, weather map, 19
freight, merchant ship, 140
freight car: railroad yard, 96; train, 116-117
French cuff, shirt, 189, 488
French door, 62, 64
French horn, 354, 358
French seam, tent, 342
frequency selector, police car, 122
frequently-used number listing, fax machine, 164
fresh air plate, standpipe, 59
fresh-air supply duct, tunnel, 98
fret: guitar, 362, 363; sitar, 362
friction post, jewelry findings, 218
frieze: column entablature, 73; drop-leaf table, 242; house, 62; White House, 75
frigate, 477
frill, bonnet, 203
fringe: cowboy, 490; dress, 198; golf course, 311; Indian, 490; Jewish prayer shawl, 486
frock coat, Revolutionary War general, 492
frog, 44; fastener, 208; horse's foot, 38; shovel, 427; violin bow, 355
from the sign, music notation, 353
frond: fern, 57; palm, 52; seaweed, 57
front: church, 87; desk, 276; eyeglasses, 221; glacier, 12; queen's regalia, 484; sailor's uniform, 497; steam locomotive boiler, 116; type, 166; weather map, 19; woman's pants, 196
frontal, church high altar, 87
frontal bone, human, 26
frontal lobe, brain, 29
front apron, 193
front-axle rod, child's wagon, 287
front bead, shotgun, 469
front beam, laboratory scale, 447
front boot, stagecoach, 131
front brace, wheelbarrow, 430
front brake, bicycle, 128
front bumper: automobile, 106; bus, 118
front cover: book, 167; dot matrix printer, 163
front crotch seam, trousers, 191
front derailleur, bicycle, 128
front disc brake, motorcycle, 129
front door: automobile, 106; bus, 118; sealed voting booth, 437; woodburning stove, 404
front end: diving board, 316; supermarket, 103
front end weight, tractor, 434
front face, book, 167
front fender, motorcycle, 129
front flap: book jacket, 167; matchbook, 228
front foot, stapler, 277
front gate, prison, 76
front grille, air conditioner, 402
front gunner's periscope, tank, 475

front half, grand piano, 361
front handle, sander, 421
front handlebar, chain saw, 431
front housing: can opener, 251; electric razor, 210
front hub: automobile, 108; bicycle, 128
front hydraulic fork, motorcycle, 129
frontier fort, 82
frontis, jai alai cancha, 314
frontispiece, magazine, 170
front jaw, vise, 409
front jockey, saddle, 335
front leg, bee, 41
front lid, grand piano, 361
front line: craps table, 347; handball, 313; squash, 313
front-loading washing machine, 280
front matter, book, 167
fronton, jai alai, 314
front panel: compact disc player, 178; jacket, 188; tape recorder, 177; toaster, 253
frontpiece, fireman's helmet, 500
front pilaster, cupboard, 243
front placket: blouse, 197; shirt, 189
front point, ice climbing boot, 334
front post: bureau, 272; hand loom, 387
front pulley, belt sander, 421
front-push plate, tow truck, 126
front quarter: automobile, 106; boot, 206
front rail: piano, 361; sled, 328
front rocker, slalom water ski, 329
front service door, gas pump, 112
front sight, weapon, 469, 470, 471
front sizer, football helmet, 292
front slit, man's underpants, 194
front spray nozzle, iron, 279
front stretcher, rocking chair, 234
front strut, hydrofoil, 145
front tab, razor blade injector, 210
front thread guide, sewing machine, 278
front tire, bus, 118
front tuck, blouse, 197
front walk, house, 63
front wall: jai alai cancha, 314; squash, 313; truck van, 121
front wheel: bicycle, 128; drag racing dragster, 339
front window: automobile, 106; camper, 130; tractor, 434
front wing: grasshopper, 41; racing car, 338
front yard, house, 62
frosting, cake, 264
frostfree refrigerator, 249
frozen food department, supermarket, 102
fruit, 55; grass, 58; palm, 52; slot machine, 346; woman's hat, 203
fruit & vegetable department, supermarket, 103
fruit bowl, 245
fruit compartment, refrigerator, 249
fruit juice extractor, 255
fruitlet, pineapple, 55
fruit wall, pea, 54
fry, fish, 45

frying basket, 260
frying pan, 257
F sharp, piano keyboard octave, 361
f-stop, zoom lens, 172
f-stop scale, light meter, 176
fuel, rocket, 407
fuel alarm, powerboat, 138
fuel assembly, nuclear reactor, 392
fuel cap, lantern, 342
fuel cell monitor, space shuttle, 153
fuel chamber: cruise missile, 482; torpedo, 479
fuel cock, internal combustion engine, 312
fuel filler, locomotive, 117
fuel gauge: barbecue grill, 288; powerboat, 138
fuel indicator, car, 110
fuel-line hose, automobile engine, 111
fuel management panel, pilot's instrument panel, 481
fuel nozzle, combustion jet engine, 407
fuel tank: camper, 130; camp stove, 342; drag racing dragster, 339; garbage truck, 127; motorcycle, 129; mower, 429; outboard engine, 137; space shuttle, 152; tank, 474; truck tractor, 120
fuel truck, airport, 95
fuel valve, lantern, 342
fulcrum, diving board, 316
full denture, 453
full-dress ship guideline, destroyer, 476, 477
fuller: horseshoe, 38; knife, 463; sword, 463
full face, elliptical galaxy, 2
full moon, 4
full nut, 411
full-organ button, organ, 360
full point, grammatical symbol, 513
full sail position, windmill, 390
full-service island, service station, 112
full-surface hinge, 460
fumarole, volcano, 10
fume extractor, tank gun, 475
function board, 439
function control, synthesizer, 363
function indicator: phonograph receiver, 179
function key: cash register, 440; computer workstation, 438; laser printer, 163; portable word processor, 162; synthesizer, 363
function selector: air conditioner, 402; phonograph receiver, 179
funerary structure, pyramid, 70
fungi, 57
funnel: citrus juicer, 255; kitchen, 258; lobster pot, 433; passenger ship, 142; tornado, 17
funny bone, 25
funny car, drag racing, 339
furbelow, queen's regalia, 484
furfurer, 201
furnace, 400
furniture guard, vacuum cleaner, 283
furniture nozzle, vacuum cleaner, 283
furrier, 201
furrow, horse's foot, 38
fuse: aerial shell, 383; cartridge, 399; hand

grenade, **473**; land mine, **473**; plug, **399**; radar, **444**

fuselage: cruise missile, **482**; helicopter, **146**; single engine airplane, **147**

fusible element, plug fuse, **399**

fuzz pedal, electric guitar, **363**

G

G: braille, **512**; music notation, **353**; piano keyboard octave, **361**; sign language, **512**

gable: barn, **104**; church, **86**; house, **63**

gadget bag, photographic, **176**

gaff, fishing, **341**

gage, drill, **418**

gain: mortise lock, **458**; sonar, **444**

Gainsborough, bride's hat, **488**

gaited horse, **337**

gaiter: drum major, **495**; ski clothes, **327**

gakuzuka, torii, **70, 71**

galaxy, Milky Way, **2, 3**

Galilean telescopes, opera glasses, **443**

gall bladder, human, **27**

gallery: cave, **11**; church, **86**; Congress, **74**; house, **63**; monocle, **221**; stage, **350**

galley, sailboat, **135**

galley module, jumbo jet, **148, 149**

gallon totalizer, gas pump, **112**

galloper, merry-go-round, **93**

gallows, **464**; sailboat, **134**

galluses, man's, **190**

galoshes, **207**

gam, human, **25**

gambling equipment, **346, 347**

gammadion, symbol, **508**

gangplank: passenger ship, **142**; tanker, **140**

gap, fishhook, **341**

garage: house, **63**; passenger ship, **142**; prison, **76**

garbage disposal, **247**

garbage truck, **127**

gardening implement, **427**

garland, royal regalia, **485**

garlic press, **261**

garment bag, **285**

garnish, poultry, **263**

garret, house, **62**

garrison belt, **496**

garrison cap, **496**

garter belt, ice hockey player, **294**

garter trolley, girdle, **195**

gas, volcano, **10**

gas bag, blimp, **156**

gas barbecue, **288**

gas cap, internal combustion engine, **406**

gas cigarette lighter, **228**

gas cloud, **3**

gas cock, water heater, **401**

gas control, laser, **395**

gas cylinder, plumber's torch, **422**

gas-fired water heater, **401**

gas-fueled internal combustion engine, **406**

gas gauge, car, **110**

gas inlet, laboratory burner, **447**

gash, razor blade injector, **210**

gasket: dishwasher, **250**; refrigerator, **249**

gaskin, horse, **38**

gas laser, holography, **395**

gasoline pump, **112**

gas regulator, laboratory burner, **447**

gas shutoff valve, standpipe, **59**

gas station, public sign, **506**

gas sterilizing flame, dental, **455**

gas supply line, water heater, **401**

gas tank: automobile, **107, 109**; barbecue grill, **288**; chain saw, **431**; internal combustion engine, **406**; mower, **429**

gaster, ant, **41**

gastight envelope, vacuum tube, **396**

gastrocnemius, human, **26**

gas-vent line, tanker, **141**

gate: airport, **94**; canal lock, **99**; dam, **100**; dropleaf table, **242**; flat racing, **336**; frontier fort, **82**; hurdle, **304**; mountain climbing carabiner, **334**; powerboat, **139**; prison, **76**; railroad crossing signal, **115**; sailboat, **134**; shotgun, **468**; subway motorman's cab, **119**; toll booth, **114**; vault, **457**

gatebar, hurdle, **304**

gated spillway, dam, **100**

gatefold, magazine, **171**

gatehouse: castle, **80, 81**; lift bridge, **97**

gate index, slide projector, **175**

gateleg table, **242**

gate pier, fence, **67**

gatepost, steel chain fence, **67**

gateway: castle, **81**; Shinto temple, **70, 71**

gather, bonnet, **203**

gathering: blouse, **197**; hardback book, **167**; woman's pants, **196**

gauge: barbecue grill, **288**; blood pressure, **449**; car, **110**; carpenter's level, **424**; combination square, **424**; drill, **419**; etching press, **377**; fire extinguisher, **284**; furnace, **388**; powerboat, **138**; pumper, **125**; railroad, **115**; 747 cockpit, **150**; skin diving, **331**; steam engine, **405**; subway motorman's cab, **119**; table saw, **417**; weather station, **18**

gauge needle, paramedic equipment, **123**

gauntlet: armor, **465**; drum major, **495**

gauze, **123, 451, 455**

gavel, **89, 412**

G clef, music, **352, 353**

gear: can opener, **251**; fishing, **341**; hand drill, **418**; mortar, **472**; seeder, **430**; single engine airplane, **147**; vault, **457**; venetian blinds, **241**

gearbox, automobile, **108**; etching press, **377**; hovercraft propeller, **145**; lithographic press, **376**; radar antenna, **444**; seeder, **430**

gear bracket, citrus juicer, **255**

gear cluster, bicycle, **128**

gear drive, chain saw, **431**

geared key chuck, power drill, **419**

gear housing, fishing reel, **340**

gear oil-pressure gauge, powerboat, **138**

gear ring, vault, **457**

gearshift: car, **110**; motorcycle, **129**

Geiger counter, **445**

gelatin casing, pill, **451**

gelatin shell, caplet, **451**

gelding, horse, **38**

gem clip, **277**

Gemini, zodiac, **509**

gemstone, **218**

gendarme, mountain, **9**

general, Revolutionary War, **492**

general merchandise, supermarket, **102**

general product category, Universal Product Code, **440**

generating plant, power network, **396**

generation, pacemaker, **452**

generator: nuclear reactor, **392**; steam engine, **405**

generator control, pilot's instrument panel, **481**

generic name, label, **268**

genitalia, human, **24**

geodesic dome, **85**

geographical boundaries, world, **5**

geologist, **4**

geometric stairs, staircase, **66**

gesso, **370**

gesture, **507**

gestures, sign language, **512**

getter, vacuum tube, **396**

geyser, volcano, **10**

G flat, piano keyboard octave, **361**

ghutrah, Arab dress, **491**

giant, circus, **90**

gibbet, **462**

gibbous moon, **4**

giblets, fowl, **35**

gig, horse-drawn carriage, **131**

gill: fish, **45**; mushroom, **57**; pelt, **201**

gimbal suspension, phonograph turntable, **178**

gimlet, **418**

gin pole, powerboat, **139**

giraffe, ultimate beast, **48**

girder: house, **60**; skyscraper, **77**; suspension bridge, **97**

girdle, **195**; cut gemstone, **218**; hot air balloon, **332**

girdle pad, football uniform, **292**

girth, racing, **336, 337**

girth & surcingle, polo, **299**

gizzard, fowl, **35**

glacial plain, mountain, **8**

glacier, **8, 9, 12**

glacis, permanent fort, **83**

glacis plate, tank, **475**

gladhand, truck van, **121**

gland, octopus, **46**

glass: basketball backboard, **296**; cupboard door, **243**; dressing table, **272**; eye dropper, **451**; electric meter casing, **399**; fluorescent bulb tube, **238**; frame, **379**; light bulb, **238**; sextant, **137**; solar panel cover plate, **391**; stained, **378**; table setting, **244, 245**

glass cutter, **378**

glasses: field, **443**; miser, **492**; ski touring, **327**

glass support, vacuum tube, **396**

glaze, pot, **373**

glazing, window, **67**

glide: desk, **276**; slalom water ski, **329**; surgical table, **450**

glider: backyard, **287**; hang, **333**

glide slope antenna, helicopter, **146**

glide slope indicator, airport runway, **94**

globe, **1, 5**; lantern, **342**; royal regalia, **485**

glochidia, cactus, **56**

gloss, makeup, **216**

glove, **200**; baseball, **290, 291**; boxing, **309**; bridal costume, **488**; drag racing driver's, **339**; drum major, **495**; fencing, **315**; fireman, **500**; hammer thrower, **303**; handball, **313**; ice hockey player, **294, 295**; jai alai cesta, **314**; jet fighter, **480**; lacrosse, **298**; miser, **492**; Revolutionary War general, **492**; skiing, **326**; skin diving, **331**

glove compartment, car, **110**

glume, grass, **58**

gluon, **394**

gluteus medius, human, **26**

gnomon, sundial, **389**

gnu beard, ultimate beast, **49**

goal: basketball, **296**; football, **293**; ice hockey, **294, 295**; lacrosse, **298**; soccer, **297**

goalie, lacrosse position, **298**

goal line, polo grounds, **299**; soccer, **297**

goal mouth, polo grounds, **299**

goal post, polo grounds, **299**

goaltender, lacrosse position, **298**

go around switch, 747 cockpit, **151**

goat, zodiac, **509**

goat beard, ultimate beast, **49**

goatee, men's beard, **211**

goggles: flat racing, **336**; ski helmet, **326**

gold: dental, **455**; ring, **219**

gold ball of rank, royal crown, **485**

golf ball, **310**

golf club, **310, 311**

golf course, **310, 311**; passenger ship, **142**

Golgi apparatus, animal cell, **23**

GO light, drag racing, **339**

gondola: blimp, **156**; Ferris wheel, **93**; merry-go-round, **93**

gonfalon, **502**

gonfanon, **502**

gong, drums, **364**

good luck, gesture, **507**

good luck symbol, **508**

goose, **35**

gooseneck: football goalpost, **293**; lamp, **239**

gore: hot air balloon, **332**; man's cap, **202**; sock, **207**; umbrella, **230**

gore area, highway cloverleaf, **114**

gorge: human, **25**; jacket, **188**; permanent fort, **83**; river, **13**

gorget, armor, **465**

gouge, **374, 420**; woodcarving, **372**

gouged sections, wood block, **374**

gourd, sitar, **362**

gour dam, cave, **11**

governor: internal combustion engine, **406**; power mower, **429**

governor-rope tension sheave, elevator shaft, **78**

gown, **198**; queen's regalia, **484**

grab iron, locomotive, **117**

grab rail, bathtub, **274**

grab strap, motorcycle, **129**

gracilis, human, **26**

grade: enlisted man's uniform, **496**; gasoline, **112**; pencil, **158**; railroad crossing, **115**

graduated guide, fishing rod, **341**

539

graduated scale, metronome, 367
graduation: beaker, 447; thermometer, 18, 449
grain: fabric, 388; lumber, 68; sandpaper, 421
grain pit, barnyard, 104
grammar, proofreader's mark, 514
grammatical symbol, 513
grand curtain, theater, 351
grand drape, stage, 350, 351
grand finale, fireworks, 382
grand valance, theater, 351
grandfather clock, 233
grandmother clock, 233
grand piano, 361
Grand Prix racing, 338
grandstand, harness racetrack, 337
granule, roofing shingle, 68
graphic, hot air balloon, 332
graphic device, label, 268
graphic scale, house blueprint, 62
graphics function selector, computer workstation, 438
graphics program, personal computer, 162
grasper, desk phone, 180
grasping foot, bird, 39
grass, 58; baseball field, 291
grass-catcher, lawn mower, 429
grasshopper, 41
grate: fireplace, 232; stove, 342
grater, kitchen tool, 261
graticule, political map, 21
grating, castle portcullis, 81
grave, 516
grave accent, grammatical symbol, 513
gravure, printing, 166, 374
grawlix, cartoon, 381
grease skimming brush, 259
great choir, church, 87
great circle, geodesic dome, 85
greatcoat, Revolutionary officer, 492
great door, barn, 104
greater than, symbol, 511
great keyboard, organ, 360
great saphenous vein, human, 28
greave, armor, 465
Greek cross, symbol, 508
Greek Revival, house style, 63
green, golf course, 311
greenback, paper money, 224
green light: drag racing, 339; traffic, 113
Green Room, White House, 75
Greenwich Mean Time, 5
Greenwich prime meridian, 5
green wire, electrical receptacle, 398
grenade, 473
grid: barbecue grill, 288; earth, 5; geodesic dome, 85; paint tray, 425; political map, 21; stage, 350; vacuum tube, 396
griddle, stove, 248, 404
gridiron, 293; stage, 350
grid marking, topographic map, 22
grid table extension, saw, 417
grill, barbecue, 288
grille: accordion, 366; air conditioner, 402; automobile, 106; CB radio antenna, 183; guitar amplifier, 363; hair dryer, 212; humidifier, 402; phonograph, 179; refrigerator, 249; tractor, 434; truck, 120
grind, knife, 256
grinder, kitchen tool, 261

grip: automatic weapon, 471; bobby pin, 214; bow, 466; carpenter's level, 424; chain saw, 431; chest pull, 344; field events hammer, 303; fishing rod, 340; foil mounting, 315; gardening shears, 427; golf club, 311; hair clip, 214; hammer, 412; javelin, 303; jump rope, 344; knife, 463; movie camera, 174; Ping-Pong racket, 321; revolver, 470; rowboat car, 133; seeder, 430; shoe horn, 207; shotgun, 468; ski pole, 326; squash racket, 313; stroller, 286; sword hilt, 463; tennis racket, 312; wheelbarrow, 430; wire stripper, 423
grip cap, shotgun, 468
gripper mark, nail, 410
gripping hole, clothespin, 280
grip safety, pistol, 470 grip tape, skateboard, 324
gristle, human, 26
grit, sandpaper, 421
groceries, supermarket, 103
groin, human, 25
grommet, tent, 342
groove: combination square, 424; corrugated fastener, 410; crossbow, 466; escalator, 79; guillotine, 462; horse, 38; phonograph record, 178; roulette wheel, 346; salamander, 44; ski, 326; sword, 463; type, 166
grospoint, stitchery, 385
grotto, 11
grotzen, pelt, 201
ground: flag, 502; symbol, 510
ground beam, guillotine, 462
ground coffee, 252
ground control, metal detector, 445
ground-effect machine, amphibious, 145
ground floor, White House, 75
grounding prong, electric plug, 344
grounding terminal, electrical receptacle, 398
ground steering tiller, 747 cockpit, 150
ground wire: circuit breaker box, 399; electrician's, 423; electrical receptacle junction box, 398
grout, tunnel, 98
growler, glacier, 12
growthline, clam shell, 47
growth ring, lumber, 68
grozing pliers, for stained glass, 378
grunting, 34
G sharp, piano keyboard octave, 361
G string, double bass, 355
guante, jai alai cesta, 314
guard: armor, 465; basketball, 296; crossbow, 466; dishwasher, 250; drill press, 419; elevator shaft, 78; foil mounting, 315; gas pump automatic nozzle, 112; guitar, 362, 363; ice hockey player, 295; knife, 256, 463; lacrosse stick, 298; lithographic press, 376; movie camera eyepiece, 174; mower, 429; prison, 76; revolver, 470; rifle, 471; safety pin, 208; saw, 417; sharpening steel, 256; shotgun trigger, 468; stagecoach, 131; sword hilt, 463; theodolite, 436; tow

truck, 126; washing machine, 280; wheelchair, 452
guard bars, Universal Product Code, 440
guard cone, potting, 373
guard house, frontier fort, 82
guardrail, highway, 114; slide, 287; tow truck, 126
guard socket, fencing foil, 315
guard tower, frontier fort, 82; prison, 76
gudgeon, window shade roller, 241
guest head, sailboat, 135
guidance chamber, torpedo, 479
guidance system: cruise missile, 482; submarine, 479
guide: fishing reel, 340; fishing rod, 340, 341; Hansom cab rein, 131; incline track, 92; jackhammer, 436; pencil sharpener, 277; power saw, 417; silk screen, 375; speculum, 448; toaster, 253
guide arm, toilet, 275
guide bar, saw, 417, 431
guide cone, potting, 373
guided missile cruiser, 477
guided missile destroyer, 477
guided weapons, defensive, 476
guideline, destroyer, 476, 477
guide lugs, nuclear reactor, 392
guide post, typewriter, 161
guide rail, elevator shaft, 78
guide ring, vault, 457
guide rod, workbench, 408
guide roller, cassette tape, 177
guide scope, telescope, 443
guide shoe, elevator shaft, 78
guide sign, road, 505
guide spring, pencil sharpener, 277
guide wall, dam, 100
guide wheel, roller coaster, 92
guillotine, 462
guimpe, nun, 487
guitar, 362, 363
gular region, salamander, 44
gulf, 7
Gulf Stream, ocean, 6
gullet, 25, 30; saddle, 335; saw teeth, 416
gull-wing hull, powerboat, 138
gully, mountain, 8
gum, and denture, 453
gum line, tooth, 456
gun, 470; cowboy, 490; jet fighter, 480; machine, 471; police, 499; police car, 122; pumper, 125; tank, 474, 475
gun barrel, destroyer, 477
gun belt: cowboy, 490; police, 498-499
gun director, destroyer, 477
gunlock, cannon barrel, 467
gunmount, destroyer, 477
gunner's periscope, tank, 475
gunship, helicopter, 146
gunwale: powerboat, 139; rowboat, 133
gusset: armor, 465; handbag, 222; house, 61
gut, human, 25
gutter: barn, 104; book, 167; bowling lane, 317; house, 63; magazine, 171; swimming pool, 316; gutter broom, mechanical sweeper, 127
gutter margin, book page, 167
guy brace, uneven parallel bars, 306
guy rope, circus tent, 91

guy wire: horizontal bar, 306; stationary rings, 307
gym, universal, 344
gymnasium, passenger ship, 143
gymnastics, 306-307
gynecologist, examination equipment, 448
gyro compass, 136

H

H: braille, 512; sign language, 512
habit, nun, 487
hackle, chicken, 35
hacksaw, 416, 422
haft, ax, 464
hailstone, 17
hair: human, 24, 211, 213; painting brush, 370; violin bow, 355
hair band, 214
hairbrush, electric, 212
hair clip, 214
hairdo, 214
hair dryer, 212
hairline: linear slide rule, 441; man's, 211; newspaper, 168
hairpiece, man's, 211
hairpin, 214
halberd: Beefeater, 483; medieval, 464
half, soccer, 297
half-court line, handball, 313
half-door, Hansom cab, 131
half-inch mark, tape measure, 424
half-jacket, fencing, 315
half-mile pole, harness racetrack, 337
half-moon, 4
half note, music, 352
half note rest, music, 352
half-surface hinge, 460
half-title logo, magazine, 170
halftone indicator, fax machine, 164
halfway line, soccer field, 297
haligan tool, police car, 122
hall: church, 87; mosque, 70-71; theatre, 351; White House, 75
hallmark, ring, 219
Hall of Columns, Capitol, 74
hallux, human foot, 20
halyard: destroyer, 477; flag, 502; sailboat, 134
ham, 34; human, 24; radio operator, 183
hammer: ball-peen, 412; carillon, iv; field events, 303; ice climbing, 334; jackhammer, 436; piano, 361; revolver, 470; stonecutting, 372; for testing reflexes, 449; telegraph key, 157
hammerhead crane, launch pad, 152
hammer throw, track and field, 301
hammock, 288
hance, arch, 72
hand: blackjack, 347; cattle ranch, 432; frog, 44; grandfather clock, 233; human, 24, 31; pocket watch, 220; stopwatch, 304; wristwatch, 220
handbag, 222
handball court, 313
hand brace, 418
hand controller, space shuttle, 153
hand crank, easel, 370
handcuff, police gun belt, 498
hand cup, sword hilt, 463

hand drill, **418, 419**
hand excavator, dental, **455**
hand flexor, body building, **344**
hand grenade, **473**
handgrip: bazooka, **472**; body building, **344**; carpenter's level, **424**; crutch, **452**; Jacuzzi, **274**; motorcycle, **129**; movie camera, **174**; pole vault pole, **305**; rocking chair, **234**; swimming pool, **316**; video camera, **184**; wheelbarrow, **430**; wheelchair, **452**
handguard, automatic rifle, **471**; chain saw, **431**
handgun, **470**
handhold: harness racing driver, **337**; lunar rover, **155**
handicap: drag racing, **339**; flat racing entry, **336**
handicapped, public sign, **506**
handkerchief, queen's regalia, **484**
handkerchief pocket, jacket, **188**
hand knitting, **386**
handle: attaché case, **285**; automobile door, **107**; ax, **464**; barbecue grill, **288**; baren, **374**; baseball bat, **291**; basket, **266**; blender, **254**; bow, **466**; brace, **418**; branding iron, **432**; brayer, **374**; broom, **282**; burnisher, **377**; candle snuffer, **237**; can opener, **251**; C-clamp, **409**; cellular telephone, **181**; chafing dish, **245**; cheese plane, **256**; chest pull, **344**; child's wagon, **287**; chisel, **420**; citrus juicer, **255**; clay modeling tool, **372**; clothespin, **280**; coffee maker, **252**; coffin, **516**; croquet mallet, **318**; dabber, **377**; drain cleaner, **422**; drill, **418, 419**; ear scope, **448**; etching press, **377**; faucet, **273**; field events hammer, **303**; finishing sander, **421**; fire engine, **125**; fire extinguisher, **284**; fishing reel, **340**; fishing rod, **340**; foil mounting, **315**; food mill, **260**; food processor, **254**; garbage disposal, **247**; garbage truck, **127**; gimlet, **418**; glass cutter, **378**; gouge, **374**; hair dryer, **212**; hammer, **412**; handbag, **222**; hand loom, **387**; hand shower, **274**; hoe, **427**, hot air balloon, **332**; ice hammer, **334**; internal combustion engine, **406**; iron, **279**; jackhammer, **436**; jet fighter, **480**; jump rope, **344**; knife, **244, 256, 463**; lacrosse stick, **298**; land mine, **473**; lithographic press, **376**; lorgnette, **221**; mace, **464**; mailbox, **231**; metal detector, **445**; microwave oven, **248**; mower, **429**; outboard engine, **137**; pail, **284**; painting brush, **370**; paint roller, **425**; paint spray gun, **425**; paper bag, **266**; parking meter, **113**; peeler, **256**; pencil sharpener, **277**; pilot's instrument panel, **481**; Ping-Pong racket, **321**; plane, **420**; playpen, **286**; pliers, **414**; plumber's plunger, **422**; pocket knife,

426; pommel horse, **307**; portable radio/cassette player, **182**; pots and pans, **257**; projector, **175**; radiator, **400**; rake, **427**; razor, **210**; refrigerator door, **249**; revolver, **470**; rifle, **471**; safe, **457**; scissors, **384**; saw, **416, 417, 431**; screen, **175**; screwdriver, **413**; scriber, **375**; seeder, **430**; **747** cockpit, **150, 151**; sewing machine, **278**; sextant, **137**; sharpening steel, **256**; shaver, **210**; shotgun, **468**; shovel, **427**; silk screen squeegee, **375**; single engine airplane, **147**; sink, **247, 273**; soldering iron, **378**; sponge mop, **282**; squash racket, **313**; stove, **342, 248, 404**; stroller, **286**; tea kettle, **245**; tennis racket, **312**; thrown pot, **373**; toilet, **275**; toothbrush, **215**; tuning fork, **367**; umbrella, **230**; vacuum cleaner, **283**; vault, **457**; video camera, **184**; vise, **408, 409**; voting booth, **437**; waterskiing towline, **329**; wheelbarrow, **430**; woodcarving tool, **372**; wrench, **415**
handlebar: bicycle, **128**; chain saw, **431**; snowmobile, **130**
handlebar mustache, **211**
handle grip: chain saw, **431**; seeder, **430**; stroller, **286**; vacuum cleaner, **283**
handler, boxing, **309**
handle release pedal, vacuum cleaner, **283**
handle screw, plane, **420**
hand lever: potter's wheel, **373**; spreader, **430**
hand loom, **387**
hand pad, football uniform, **292**
handpiece: crutch, **452**; dental, **454, 455**
hand protector, waterskiing towline, **329**
hand pump: blood pressure gauge, **449**; pilot's instrument panel, **481**
handrail: bus, **118**; elevator car, **78**; escalator, **79**; locomotive, **116, 117**; lunar lander, **154**; powerboat, **139**; roller coaster, **92**; sled, **328**; staircase, **66**; subway car, **119**
hand rope, racing sled, **328**
handruff, queen's regalia, **484**
handsaw, **416**
hand screw, **409**
handset, desk phone, **180**; cellular telephone, **181**
hand shower, **274**
hand slide, trombone, **359**
handstrap: bus, **118**; subway car, **119**; video-still camera, **173**
hand throttle, car, **110**
hand valve, solar heating system, **391**
hand warming slot, parka, **201**
handwheel: sewing machine, **278**; table saw, **417**
hangar, airport, **95**
hangar bay, aircraft carrier, **478**
hanger: dress, **198**; fishing plug, **341**; frame, **379**; harness racing, **337**; laboratory scale weight, **447**; lamp, **239**; screen, **175**; swing, **287**

hanger bracket, wheelchair, **452**
hang glider, **333**
hang hole: blister card, **268**; dustpan, **282**
hanging glacier, mountain, **8**
hanging locker, sailboat, **135**
hanging ring: can opener, **251**; skillet, **359**
hanging strip, window shutters, **241**
hanging weight, laboratory scale, **446**
hang ring, hair dryer, **212**
hang-up hole, toothbrush, **215**
hank, knitting yarn, **386**
Hansom cab, **131**
hardback book, **167**
hard copy, computer printer, **163**
hardcover book, **167**
hard disk, computer, **438**
hard-hat diving, **331**
hardness, pencil lead, **158**
hard suction connection hose, pumper, **125**
hardware: bureau, **272**; computer workstation, **438**; cowboy, **490**; shoulder bag, **222**
hardware sling, mountain climbing, **334**
hard-way bets, craps table, **347**
hare traction splint, paramedic equipment, **123**
harmonica, **366**
harness: drag racing driver, **339**; electrical wall switch, **398**; hang glider, **333**; harness racing, **337**; mountain climbing, **334**; parachute, **333**; skin diving tank, **331**
harness frame, hand loom, **387**
harness racing, **336, 337**
harp: orchestra, **354**; table lamp, **238**
harrow, tractor, **434**
hash mark: enlisted man's uniform, **496**; football field, **293**
hassock, lounger, **235**
hasp, **460**
hat: automobile engine, **111**; Beefeater, **483**; circus ringmaster, **90**; clown, **493**; cowboy, **490**; miser, **492**; pirate, **492**; police, **498, 499**; Revolutionary War general, **492**; sailor, **497**; skiing, **327**; wizard, **492**; woman's, **203**
hatband, **202, 203**
hat bow, beret, **202**
hatch: bus, **118**; fireboat, **144**; lunar lander, **154**; sideboard, **134**; tank, **474, 475**; tanker, **141**; tugboat, **144**
hatchback, passenger car, **109**
hatch cover, ballistic missile launch deck, **479**
hatchet, **412**
hatmaker, **202**
hat pin, woman's hat, **203**
hatter, men's hats, **202**
haunch: arch, **72**; human, **25**
hawg leg, cowboy, **490**
hawsehole: fireboat, **144**; passenger ship, **142, 143**
hawser: and canal lock, **99**; passenger ship, **142**; tugboat, **144**
hay door, barn, **104**
hay scale, frontier fort, **82**
hay yard, frontier fort, **82**
hazard, golf course, **310-311**
head: Allen wrench, **415**; anchor, **132**; arrow, **466**; automobile engine, **111**; ax,

464; badminton shuttlecock, **319**; barrel, **267**; bell, **iv**; billiard bridge, **320**; bolt, **411**; book page, **iv, 167**; bowling lane, **317**; brace, **418**; cartridge, **470**; C-clamp, **409**; chain saw, **431**; chisel, **420**; cigar, **228**; coin, **225**; combination square, **424**; comet, **3**; croquet mallet, **318**; dental x-ray tube, **454**; dispenser, **267**; drain cleaner, **422**; drill press, **419**; drum, **364**; electric razor, **210**; electronic flash, **176**; field events hammer, **303**; fish, **45**; fishing jig, **341**; flag, **502**; golf club, **310**; grasshopper, **41**; guitar, **362, 363**; hammer, **412**; hatchet, **412**; helicopter rotor, **146**; hinge fixed pin, **460**; human, **24**; javelin, **302**; knee kicker, **246**; knitting needle, **386**; lacrosse stick, **298**; lance, **464**; lettuce, **262**; levigator bolt, **376**; mace, **464**; magazine, **170, 171**; mainsail, **136**; match, **228**; mechanical sweeper gutter broom, **127**; movie camera microphone, **174**; music note, **353**; nail, **410**; newspaper, **168**; octopus, **46**; pelt, **201**; pin, **208**; polo mallet, **299**; saddle, **335**; sailboat, **135**; screw, **410**; screwdriver, **413**; shower, **274**; shuffleboard court, **318**; soldering iron, **378**; spring beard needle, **386**; squash racket, **313**; stemware, **244**; tambourine, **364**; table saw, **417**; tack, **410**; tape recorder, **177**; tennis racket, **312**; theodolite, **436**; toothbrush, **215**; venetian blinds, **241**
headband: hair ornament, **214**; hardback book, **167**; headphone, **179, 182**; physician's mirror, **448**; ski hat, **327**
headboard: four-poster bed, **270**; mainsail, **136**
head box, venetian blind, **241**
head channel, venetian blind, **241**
head collar, kettledrum, **364**
head cover, golf club, **311**
headdress, Arab dress, **491**
header: brick wall, **69**; drag racing dragster, **339**; house, **60, 61**; solar collector panel, **391**
headgear: armor, **465**; boxing, **309**
headguard, boxing, **309**
heading: book page, **iv**; draperies, **240**; letter, **159**; radar, **444**
heading alignment control, radar, **444**
head jamb, window, **65**
head joint: brick wall, **69**; flute, **357**
headlight: automobile, **106**; bulldozer, **435**; bus, **118**; locomotive, **116, 117**; medical examination equipment, **448**; motorcycle, **129**; snowmobile, **130**; tank, **475**; tractor, **434**; truck, **120**
headlight controls, car, **110**
headline: human hand, **31**; magazine, **170**; newspaper, **168**
head lock, camera tripod, **176**
head lug, bicycle, **128**

541

head margin, book page, 167
head mold, church, 86
head piece: book, 167; rocking chair, 234
headphone, audio, 179, 182
headphone jack: CB radio, 183; compact disc player, 178; metal detector, 445; receiver, 179; tape recorder, 177; VCR, 184; Walkman, 182
headphone level control, compact disc player, 178
headphones, Walkman, 182
headpiece, Torah, 486
headpin, bowling, 317
head post, four-poster bed, 270
headquarters, frontier fort, 82
headrail, venetian blind, 241
headrest: bumper car, 92; dental unit, 454; surgical table, 450
headsail, 136
head section: flute, 357; piccolo, 356
headset, bicycle, 128
headshell, phonograph turntable, 178
head spot, pool table, 320
headstay, sailboat, 136
head step, ladder, 425
headstone, grave, 516
heads-up, drag racing, 339
head tube, bicycle, 128
headwall, mountain, 9
health & beauty aids, supermarket, 102
hearing aid, 452
heart: fowl, 35; human, 25, 27, 28; lettuce, 262; playing cards, 348
hearth, fireplace, 232
heart line, human hand, 31
heart murmur, symbol, 510
heart of came, lead came, 378
heartwood, tree, 50
heat, drag racing, 339
heat-absorber plate, solar collector panel, 391
heat control: barbecue grill, 288; electric wok, 257
heater: camper, 130; water, 401
heater filament, vacuum tube, 396
heater wire, vacuum tube, 396
heat exchanger: 403; fireplace, 232; oil drilling platform, 101
heat indicator, electric hair brush, 212
heating controls, car, 110
heating/cooling coils, heat exchanger, 403
heating element: dishwasher, 250; soldering iron, 378; stove, 248
heating system, airport, 94
heating unit: camper, 130; solar heating system, 391
heat pump, 403
heat-resistant glass, light bulb, 238
heat-riser valve, automobile engine, 111
heat seal, foil pouch, 269
heat shield, lantern, 342
heat switch, hair dryer, 212
heat-transfer fluid, solar collector panel, 391
Hector, playing card jack, 348
heddle, hand loom, 387
heel: Achilles', 25; automatic rifle, 471; baseball glove, 291; boot, 206; bread, 263; carpenter's saw, 416; cat, 37; file, 420; frog, 44; golf club, 310; grand piano, 361; guitar, 362; horse, 38;

horseshoe, 38; human foot, 24, 31; human hand, 31; ice hockey goalkeeper's stick, 294; ice skate, 325; knife, 256; L-shaped square, 424; man's shoe, 204; paint brush, 425; panty hose, 195; plane, 420; rasp, 420; roller skate, 324; shoe tree, 207; shotgun, 468; ski binding, 326; tennis racket, 312; windmill, 390; woman's shoe, 205
heel band, spur, 335
heel binding, ski, 326
heel breast, woman's shoe, 205
heel cap: hockey skate, 325; skate, 295
heel chain, spur, 335
heel counter, running shoe, 302
heel cup, ski binding, 326
heel cup pivot, ski binding, 326
heel glide, slalom water ski, 329
heel gore, sock, 207
heelknob, dog, 36
heel lacing, snowshoe, 327
heel lift: boot, 206; woman's shoe, 205
heel loop, wheelchair, 452
heel patch, running shoe, 302
heel piece, slalom water ski, 329
heelplate, ski, 327, 329
heel rest, iron, 279
heel seam, sock, 207
heel seat, woman's shoe, 205
heel strap, skin diving fin, 331
heel tip, hockey skate, 325
heifer, 32
height: and perspective, 368; wave, 14
height adjustment: machine gun, 471; ski binding, 326; vacuum cleaner, 283
helical, settee, 288; staircase, 66
helicopter, 146
helicopter flight deck, destroyer, 476
helictite, cave, 11
helipad, White House, 75
heliport, oil drilling platform, 101
helium valve, blimp, 156
helix, outer ear, 30
helm: coat of arms, 503; sailboat, 134
helmath, windmill, 390
helmet: armor, 465; baseball batter, 290; coat of arms, 503; combat soldier, 497; downhill skiing, 326; drag racing driver's fire suit, 339; fireman, 500; flat racing, 336; football uniform, 292; Grand Prix racing, 338; harness racing, 337; ice hockey, 295; jai alai, 314; lacrosse, 298; police, 498, 499; polo, 299; roller skating, 324; spacesuit, 155
helmet diving, 331
helmet skirt, drag racing driver's fire suit, 339
helmseat, powerboat, 139
helve, axe, 464
hem: bridal gown, 488; dress, 198; jacket, 188; parka, 201; skirt, 197; window shade, 240, 241
hemmer foot, sewing machine, 278
hemming, necktie, 193
hen, 35
hence, symbol, 511

herb, prepared foods, 263
hex nut, 411; juice extractor, 255; table lamp, 238
hex wrench, 415
hibachi, 288
hide, ultimate beast, 49
hide rope, tepee, 84
hieroglyph, obelisk, 71
high altar, church, 87
high bar, gymnastics, 306
high beam, automobile, 106
high chair, 286
high fidelity phonograph, 179
high-frequency antenna, helicopter, 146
high-gain antenna, lunar rover, 155
high heat switch, hair dryer, 212
high-heel woman's shoe, 205
high hurdle, 304
high intensity lamp, 239
high jump, 300, 305
highlight, magazine, 170
highlighter, makeup, 216
highline, magazine, 171
high-low combination headlamp, automobile, 106
high-low scale, light meter, 176
high pressure, weather map, 19
high-pressure pump: fireboat, 144; paint spray gun, 425
high-pressure steam, steam engine, 405
high pressure water spray, tooth cleaner, 215
high pulley, universal gym, 344
high-resolution display, computer workstation, 438
high score, darts, 322
high-speed dubbing, portable radio/cassette player, 182
high-speed handpiece, dental, 455
high-speed printer, 439
high tide, 15
high-voltage power supply, gas laser, 395
high-volume evacuation tip, dental, 454
high water mark, topographic map, 22
highway, 114; map, 20, 22
high-wire act, circus, 90
hi-hat cymbal, 364
hiking trail, public sign, 506
hill, 7; road sign, 505; roller coaster, 92
hilt: bayonet, 463; billiard cue, 320; foil mounting, 315; knife, 463; mace, 464; sword, 463
hind bow, saddle, 335
hind foot: cat, 37; pig, 34; sheep, 33
hind paw, pelt, 201
hindquarters, 37
hind scalper, harness racing pacer, 337
hind shank, beef, 32
hind toe: cat, 37; chicken, 35
hind wing, grasshopper, 41
hinge, 460; binoculars, 443; book, 167; camera tripod, 176; cupboard, 243; eyeglasses, 221; folding rule, 424; hot dog roll, 265; kiln, 373; locomotive, 116; railroad signal, 115; safe, 457; scallop shell, 47; stapler, 277; stove oven door, 248; vault, 457; window shutters, 39; woodburning stove, 404

hinge cover: playpen, 286; refrigerator, 249
hinge portion, hasp, 460
hinge rod, power mower, 429
hip: barn, 104; bell, iv; horse, 38; human, 24
hip belt, backpack, 39
hip flexor, universal gym, 344
hipline, dress, 198
hip pad: football, 292; ice hockey, 295
hippodrome track, circus, 90
historical costumes, 492
history, symbol, 510
hitch, tractor, 434
hitch-hiking, gesture, 507
hite, cartoon, 380
hobble, harness racing gear, 337
hobble strap, saddle, 335
hock: chicken, 3; cow, 32; dog, 36; horse, 38; jet fighter, 480; pork, 34
hockey, ice, 294, 295
hockey skate, 325
hod, fireplace coal, 232
hoe, 427
hog, 34
hogan, 84
hogshead, 267
hoist: dam, 100; flag, 502; helicopter, 146
hoist cable, elevator shaft, 78
hoisting equipment, oil drilling platform, 101
hold, music notation, 352
holder: blackjack, 347; cassette tape recorder, 177; dental, 455; easel, 370; elevator car, 78; etching needle, 377; jackhammer, 436; laboratory, 446; lithographic press, 376; microscope slide, 442; police uniform, 498, 499; stroller, 286; telescope, 443; tom-tom, 364; track lighting, 239; two-suiter, 285
holder attaching screw, camera, 172
holdfast, seaweed, 57
holding prong, nail clippers, 215
holding tools, 409
hole: bagpipe, 365; blister card, 268; bowling ball, 317; button, 209; cheese, 263; cigar cutter blade, 228; clothespin, 280; film, 172, 174; fireboat, 144; fountain pen, 158; golf course, 311; guitar, 362; hair roller, 214; hinge, 460; hook and eye, 208; horseshoe, 38; ice axe, 334; igloo, 85; lantern, 342; man's belt, 190; man's underwear, 194; Milky Way, 2; needle, 384; oil drilling platform, 101; phonograph record, 178; snap fastener, 208; snowshoe, 327; spool, 384; stagecoach, 131; telephone, 180; tire, 105; tow truck bed, 126; vault, 457
hole punch, pocket knife, 426
hollow body, acoustic guitar, 363
hollow grind, knife, 256
hollow lower face, zipper, 209
hollow of throat, human, 25
hollow wall fastener, 411
hologram, 395; credit card, 227
holster, 470, 490, 499
home, White House, 75
home plate: baseball field, 291; blackjack, 347
home port, passenger ship, 142

home stake, croquet, 318
homestretch, harness racetrack, 337
honda, lasso, 432
honing surface, sharpening steel, 256
honors, résumé, 160
hood: automobile, 106; barn, 104; bassinet, 286; bus, 118; camera lens, 174; cobra, 42; compass, 136; fireplace, 232; fishing rod, 340; grandfather clock, 233; minister, 487; parka, 201; radar, 444; toboggan, 328; tractor, 434; truck, 120; vacuum cleaner, 283
hood door, grandfather clock, 233
hood release, car, 110
hoof: cow, 32; horse, 38; ultimate beast, 48
hook: block and tackle, 461; boot, 207; bulldozer, 435; fire engine, 124, 125; fireman, 500; fishing jig, 341; fishing plug, 341; frame, 379; garbage disposal, 247; hammock, 288; harness racing gear, 337; hearing aid, 452; ice skates, 325; latch needle, 386; parachute, 333; pendant, 219; pulley block, 461; shower curtain, 274; suit hanger, 281; tape measure, 424; tatting shuttle, 386; tow truck bed, 126; trumpet, 359; see also hook and eye
hookah, 229
hook and bar, fastener, 208
hook and bobbin case, sewing machine, 278
hook and eye: brassiere, 195; fastener, 208; pants, 191; skirt, 197; see also hook
hook and ring, mitten, 200
hook disgorger, pocket knife, 426
hooked-up truck, 120
hook grip, shoe horn, 207
hook panel, pilot's instrument panel, 481
hook tape, Velcro, 209
hook-thrust bearing assembly, pulley block, 461
hoop: banjo, 362; barrel, 267; basketball backstop, 296; croquet, 318; lasso, 432; lobster pot, 433
hopper: garbage truck, 127; mechanical sweeper, 127; seeder, 430
hopper car, train, 116
hop, skip, and jump, track and field, 300
horizontal bar, gymnastics, 306
horizontal centering, radar, 444
horizontal circle, theodolite, 436
horizontal direction indicator, 747 cockpit, 150
horizontal fin, blimp, 156
horizontal gauge, carpenter's level, 424
horizontally opposed automobile engine, 111
horizontal reduction, theodolite, 436
horizontal stabilizer: helicopter, 146; jet fighter, 480; jumbo jet, 149; single engine airplane, 147
horizon glass, sextant, 137

horizon indicator, 747 cockpit, 151
horizon line, perspective, 368
horizon mirror, sextant, 137
horizon sunshade, sextant, 137
horn: car, 110; cow, 32; fire engine, 124, 125; fire extinguisher, 284; French, 358; glacier, 12; motorcycle, 129; orchestra, 354; saddle, 335; shoe, 207; subway motorman's cab, 119; truck tractor, 120; ultimate beast, 48
horny scale: alligator, 42; crocodile, 42
horoscope, 509
hors d'oeuvre, 263
horse, 38; flat racing entry, 336; merry-go-round, 93; pommel, 307
horse-drawn carriage, 131
horsehide, baseball, 290
horse-hoof cuff, Manchu court dress, 491
horse latitudes, wind, 6
horsepower, internal combustion engine, 406
horseracing, 336-337
horse rod, merry-go-round, 93
horse shoe, 38
horse trail, public sign, 506
hose, 207; automobile engine, 111; baseball batter, 290; fireboat, 144; fire extinguisher, 284; gas pump, 112; hand saw, 274; kitchen sink, 247; lawn sprinkler, 428; locomotive, 116; panty, 195; pumper, 125; skin diving, 331; vacuum cleaner, 283
hose-handling derrick, tanker, 141
hose nozzle, fire hydrant, 125
hose reel: fireboat, 144; tower ladder, 124
hosel, golf club, 310
hospital: frontier fort, 82; passenger ship, 143; prison, 76; road sign, 504
hot air balloon, 332
hot corner, baseball field, 291
hot dog, 265
hotdogging board, surfboard, 330
hotel, airport, 94
hotel/motel, public sign, 506
hot foods department, supermarket, 103
hot gas pipe, heat exchanger, 403
hot metal, printing, 166
hot plate, coffee maker, 252
hot shoe, camera, 172
hot slot, electrical receptacle, 398
hot springs, volcano, 10
hot type, printing, 166
hot-water differential thermostat, solar heating system, 391
hot-water device, sink, 247
hot-water faucet: bathtub, 274; Jacuzzi, 274
hot water handle, sink, 247, 273
hot-water heater, 401; camper, 130
hot-water tank, solar heating system, 391
hot wire: electrical receptacle, 398; electrician's, 423
hourglass, 233
hour hand: clock, 233; watch, 220
hour line, sundial, 389

hour meter, powerboat engine, 138
house, craps, 346; foundation, 60; exterior, 62-63; frame, 61; roof truss, 61; zodiac, 509
house ad, magazine, 171
houseboat, 138
house car, train, 117
House corridor, Capitol, 74
housekeeper's room, White House, 75
House of Representatives chamber, Capitol, 74
house organ magazine, 169
house plan, White House, 75
house styles, 63
housing: automatic rifle, 471; automobile license plate, 106; belt sander, 421; CB radio microphone, 183; compass, 136; curling iron, 214; drill, 419; electric plug, 398; eye scope, 448; finishing sander, 421; fishing reel, 340; hair dryer, 212; harmonica, 366; jackhammer, 436; juice extractor, 255; laboratory clamp, 446; lawn sprinkler, 428; mechanical sweeper, 127; outboard engine, 137; paint spray gun, 425; phonograph headphone, 179; potter's wheel, 373; power mower, 429; razor, 210; saber saw, 417; saddle, 335; skate, 295; stationary rings, 307; tape measure, 424; toaster, 253; video camera, 184
hovercraft, 145
howitzer, midget, 472
hub: automobile, 108; bicycle, 128; cassette tape, 177; cupboard, 243; geodesic dome, 85; hypodermic syringe, 451; outboard engine, 137; racing car, 338; spider web, 40; stagecoach, 131; tow truck, 126; wheelchair, 452
hubble-bubble, 229
hubcap: automobile, 107
hubcap: child's wagon, 287; power mower, 429; seeder, 430
hull: boat, 132; drag racing, 339; helicopter, 146; submarine, 479; tank, 475; windsurfer, 330
hull column, oil drilling platform, 101
hull form, powerboat, 138
hull machine gun, tank, 475
hull mainsail: mainsail, 136; submarine, 479
human body, 24-31
Humboldt Current, ocean, 6
humerus, human, 26
humidifier, 402
humidity sensor, weather station, 18
humidor, cigar, 228
hump: frog, 44; crocodile, 42; railroad yard, 96; ultimate beast, 49
hump yard, railroad, 96
hung ceiling, elevator car, 78
hurdle, 304
hurdle race, track and field, 300
hurricane, 17; weather map, 19
hurst tool, police car, 122
husk: coconut, 262; corn, 58
hutch, side piece, 243
hydrant intake, pumper, 125

hydraulic filter breather, bulldozer, 435
hydraulic fluid tank, bulldozer, 435
hydraulic fork, motorcycle, 129
hydraulic hand pump, pilot's instrument panel, 481
hydraulic lifter, tower ladder, 124
hydraulic line, garbage truck, 127
hydraulic-pneumatic device, oil drilling platform, 101
hydraulic tank, garbage truck, 127
hydroelectric powerhouse, dam, 100
hydrofoil, 145
hydrogen venting arm, launch pad, 152
hydrometer, laboratory, 447
hypermarket, 102
hyphen, grammatical symbol, 513
hypodermic fang, snake, 42
hypodermic needle, 451
hypodermic syringe, 451
hydrosphere, earth, 4
hypospray, 451
hypothalamus, human, 29
hypothenar, human hand, 31

I

I: braille, 512; sign language, 512
ICBM, 482
ICC bumper, truck platform, 121
ice, thundercloud, 17
ice ax, mountain climbing, 334
iceberg, glacier, 12
icebox, 249; sailboat, 135
ice cliff, mountain, 9
ice climbing boot, 334
ice cream: cone, 265; scoop, 259; sundae, 264
ice crystal, clouds, 16
ice dispenser, refrigerator, 249
ice face, mountain, 8
icefall, mountain, 9
ice field, mountain, 9
ice hammer, mountain climbing, 334
ice hockey, 294-295
icemaker, refrigerator, 249
ice pack, 12
ice screw, mountain climbing, 334
ice sheet, 8
ice skates, 325
ice tray, refrigerator, 249
ice window, igloo, 85
icing, cake, 264
icing nozzle, 259
icing syringe, 259
idea balloon, cartoon, 381
identification: golf ball, 310; paper money, 224, 225; political map, 21
identification bracelet, 187
identification code, bank card, 226
identification mark, dental braces, 453
identification number, phonograph speaker, 121
identification tags, attaché case, 285
ideogram, public sign, 506
ideograph, public sign, 506
idler pinion, hand drill, 418
idle-speed, solenoid, automobile engine, 111
idling wheel, tank, 475
ID window, checkbook clutch, 223
igloo, 85
ignition, car, 110

ignition cable, bazooka, 472
ignition wire, automobile engine, 111
iguana, 43
iliac artery, human, 28
ilial crest, human, 25
ilium: allosaurus, 43; human, 26; stegosaurus, 43
illuminator, microscope, 442
illustration: book jacket, 167; book page, iv, 167; cartooning, 380; magazine, 170
image: church, 86; movie film, 174; offset-lithography, 166; rotogravure, 166; television, 185
image scanner, copier, 164
immature fruit, cucumber, 54
impact attenuation device, highway, 114
imperial arch, royal crown, 485
imperial mantle, royal regalia, 484
importer, wine label, 267
impost, arch, 72
impression, letterpress, 166
impression control, typewriter, 161
impression cylinder, printing press, 166
inboard aileron, jumbo jet, 148
inboard elevator, jumbo jet, 149
inboard engine, 137
inboard-outboard engine, 137
inboard spoiler, jumbo jet, 148
inbound line, football field, 293
incandescent bulb, lighting, 238
in-cannel, gouge, 420
inch, grammatical symbol, 513
inches of mercury, aneroid barometer, 18
inch mark, tape measure, 424
incident-light index, light meter, 176
incised line, scrimshaw, 375
incised printing, 377
incisor, tooth, 456
incline, roller coaster, 92
incline track, amusement park, 9
incore-instrument guide tube, nuclear reactor, 392
indent, proofreader's mark, 514
indented surface, thimble, 384
index: light meter, 176; newspaper, 168; playing card, 348; political map, 20; slide projector, 175; wristwatch, 220
index arm, sextant, 137
index column, voting booth, 437
index contour, topographic map, 22
indexer, pilot's instrument panel, 153
index finger, human hand, 31
index hole, diskette, 162
index mark, sextant, 137
index mirror, sextant, 137
index reference key, political map, 20
index sunshade, sextant, 137
Indian, 490
indicator: CB radio, 183; destroyer, 477; laboratory scale, 446; light meter, 176; organ, 360; phonograph turntable, 178; pilot's instrument panel, 481; roadmap, 20; 747 cockpit, 150, 151; ski binding, 326; space shuttle, 153; tape

recorder, 177; toll booth fee, 114; voting booth, 437
indicator light: airport runway, 94; coffee maker, 252; phonograph receiver, 179; 747 cockpit, 151; subway motorman's cab, 119; toaster oven, 253
indicia, magazine, 169
individual race, swimming pool, 316
individual lever, voting booth, 437
indoor floral department, supermarket, 103
inductor: dispenser, 267; elevator shaft, 78
inertial guidance system, submarine, 479
infantry badge, military uniform, 496
infantry banquette, permanent fort, 83
infantry button, Revolutionary War general, 492
infantryman, uniform, 496, 497
infantry rope, uniform, 496
inferior vena cava, human, 28
infield: baseball, 291; harness racetrack, 337
infinity, symbol, 511
inflatable anti-shock trousers, paramedic equipment, 123
inflation bulb, blood pressure gauge, 449
inflation needle, football, 292
infill, fence, 67
inflatable, 133
inflation hose, skin, diving, 331
inflation valve, tire, 105
inflator, skin diving, 331
inflorescence, grass, 58
information: ticket, 349; toll booth, 114
information display, pilot's instrument panel, 481
infrared lamp, hair styling, 214
infrared night scope, bazooka, 472
infrared radiometer, satellite, 186
infrared remote-control command, television, 185
infrared seeker, jet fighter, 480
infuser, tea, 260
infusion coffee maker, 252
ingredient, package, 268
ingress and egress platform, lunar lander, 154
initial: letter, 159; magazine, 170
injection, hypodermic syringe, 451
injector, razor blade, 210; super collider, 394
injector pipe, locomotive, 116
ink: octopus, 46; pen, 158; rotogravure, 166; rubbing, 376; well, 158
inked surface, wood block, 374
ink roller, offset-lithography, 166
inlay: armor, 465; dental, 455; sideboard, 243; sofa, 236
inlet: coastline, 15; combustion jet engine, 407; jet fighter, 480; laboratory burner, 447; surgical table, 450; toilet, 275
inlet nozzle, nuclear reactor, 392
in-line six automobile engine, 111
inmate, prison, 76
in mufti, police, 498
innards, human, 25
inner bailey, castle, 80, 81

inner basket, sink, 247
inner canthus, eye, 30
inner cornice, merry-go-round, 93
inner core, earth, 4
inner deck, escalator, 79
inner enclosure, air conditioner, 402
inner hearth, fireplace, 232
inner-liner pouch, package, 268
inner lip, univalve shell, 47
inner reflector, adjustable lamp, 239
inner ring, embroidery, 385
inner sash, window, 65
inner shell, nuclear reactor, 392
inner slide brace, trombone, 358-359
inner sole, shoe, 204, 205
inner spring, bed, 271
inner table, backgammon board, 345
inner ward, castle, 80, 81
inner wheel, Ferris wheel, 93
input, guitar amplifier, 363
input jack, cassette tape recorder, 177
input key, automatic teller machine, 226
input-output port, portable word processor, 162
input plug, movie projector, 175
inscription: money, 224; tombstone, 516
inseam: jacket, 188; trousers, 191
insect, 41
insert: clamp, 409; ice skates, 325; magazine, 171; proofreader's mark, 514
insert steel, jackhammer, 436
inset: magazine, 169, 170; political map, 21
inset picture, television, 185
inset sleeve, cardigan sweater, 199
inside address, letter, 159
inside cap, umbrella, 230
inside drive, merry-go-round, 93
inside leg seam, trousers, 191
inside margin, book page, 167
inside rail, harness racetrack, 337
inside sleeve seam, jacket, 188
insignia: drum major's coat, 495; mainsail, 136; military uniform, 496, 497
insole: boot, 206; man's shoe, 204; sandal, 206
inspection plate, buoy, 132
instant camera, 173
instant hot-water device, sink, 247
instant replay, picture-in-picture viewing, 185
instep: human foot, 31; shoe, 204, 205; sock, 207
instruction cache, circuit board, 439
instruction panel, automatic teller machine, 226
instructions: fire extinguisher, 284; furnace, 400; microwave oven, 248; parking meter, 113; pay telephone, 180; sheet music, 352; synthesizer, 363; water heater, 401
instrument, musical, 354-366
instrument approach, airport runway, 94
instrumentation, 747 engine, 151

instrumentation control, space shuttle, 153
instrument input, guitar amplifier, 363
instrument panel: airplane, 481; bulldozer, 435; lunar rover, 155; snowmobile, 130
instrument sensitivity, volt-ohm meter, 423
instrument tray, dental unit, 454
instrument warning light, 747 cockpit, 151
insulated grip, wire stripper, 423
insulated handle: chafing dish, 245; lineman's pliers, 414
insulated window, 65
insulating body, plug fuse, 399
insulating glass, window, 65
insulation: cartridge fuse, 399; electrician's wire, 423; solar collector panel, 391
insulator, overhead power line, 396
intaglio: and etching, 377; printing, 166
intake: bus, 118; destroyer, 477; racing car, 338, 339; silo, 104; turbine locomotive, 117; vacuum cleaner, 283
integrated circuit, circuit board, 439
integrated control panel, pilot's instrument panel, 481
integrated thermal meteoroid garment, 155
intensity control, radar, 444
interabang, grammatical symbol, 513
interaction hall, super collider, 394
interaction region, transistor chip, 396
intercarpal, human, 26
interchange, highway, 114
interchange symbol number, road map, 20
intercity bus, 118
intercolumniation, 73
intercom: prison, 76; 747 cockpit, 150
intercontinental ballistic missile (ICBM), 482
interdigital pad, human hand, 31
interest, monthly statement, 227
interface, ski binding, 326
interference rejector, radar, 444
inter-grip rim lock, 458
interlining, necktie, 193
interlocking timbered joint, Japanese architecture, 70
interior: Hansom cab, 131; window, 65
interior panel, coffin, 516
interior slope, permanent fort, 83
interlock control, gas laser, 395
intermediate hurdle, 304
intermediate lens, eyeglasses, 221
intermediate pipe, automobile, 108
internal combustion engine, 406
internal hard disk drive, personal computer, 162
internal jugular vein, human, 28
internal organs, human, 27
internal wave, 14
international architecture, 70-71
International Date Line, 5

International Standard Book
    Number, 167
interrobang, grammatical
    symbol, 513
interrupter, label, 268
intersection, highway, 114
interstate route: road map, 20;
    road sign, 504
interstellar cloud, 2
interval, thematic map, 21
intestine, human, 27
intrados, arch, 72
intravenous equipment,
    operating room table, 450
introduction, magazine, 170
intubation box, paramedic
    equipment, 123
inventory control number,
    paperback book, 167
inverted hub, two truck, 126
invisible zipper, 209
involuntary muscle, human, 26
ion particle cloud, 3
iris, eye, 30
iris diaphragm, microscope,
    442
iron, 279; branding, 432;
    crossbow, 466; fireplace,
    232; flat racing, 336; golf
    club, 311; hair styling, 214;
    plane, 420
iron curtain, stage, 350
ironing board, 279
iron lung, 452
iron man, cattle ranch, 432
irregular galaxy, 2
isarithmic map, 21
ISBN, book, 167
ischium: allosaurus, 43;
    human, 26; stegosaurus, 43
is equal to, symbol, 511
island, 7, 15; aircraft carrier,
    478; dental, 454; highway,
    114; river, 13; service
    station, 112; toll booth, 114
isle, 7
islet, 7
is not equal to, symbol, 511
isobar, weather map, 19
isopleth line, thematic map, 21
isotherm, weather map, 19
isotonic exercises, body
    building, 344
issue date: magazine, 169;
    newspaper, 168
issuer, paper money, 224;
    traveler's check, 227
issuing bank: credit card, 227;
    monthly statement, 227;
    traveler's check, 227
issuing country, stamp, 159
issuing Federal Reserve Bank's
    code number, paper money,
    225
isthmus, 7
Italianate, house style, 63
italic: proofreader's mark, 514;
    type, 165
italic refer, newspaper, 168
item-by-item tape, cash
    register, 440
IV equipment, operating room
    table, 450
ivory carving, scrimshaw, 375

J

J: braille, 512; sign language,
    512
jabot, bridal gown, 488
jack: CB radio, 183; garbage
    truck, 127; metal detector,
    445; movie camera, 174;
    phonograph receiver, 179;
    playing cards, 348; tape
    recorder, 177; volt-ohm
    meter, 423
jacket: cartridge, 470; diskette,
    162; fencing, 315; hardback

book, 167; kiln, 373; king's
    regalia, 484; locomotive,
    116; Manchu court dress,
    491; man's, 188; military
    uniform, 496; skin diving,
    331; sweater, 199; vacuum
    cleaner dust bag, 283;
    waterskiing, 329; woman's,
    196; zinc carbon cell, 397
jacket crown, dental, 453
jackhammer, 436
jack knife, 426
jack-plug socket, electric
    guitar, 363
jack staff, destroyer, 477
jack stud, house, 61
Jacuzzi, 274
jaguar coat, ultimate beast, 48
jail, 76
jai alai, 314
jalousie window, 65
jamb: arrow, 465; castle
    portcullis, 81; door, 64;
    vault, 457; window, 65
jamb plate, chain lock, 458
Japan Current, ocean, 6
jar: beauty product, 217;
    laboratory, 447
jarn, cartoon, 381
javelin, 301, 303
jaw: bear trap, 433; brace
    chuck, 418; cat, 37; clamp,
    409; drill, 419; fish, 45;
    human, 24; nail clippers,
    215; pliers, 414; snake, 42;
    vise, 408, 409; wire stripper,
    423; wrench, 415
jaw pad, football helmet, 292
jaws of life, police car, 122
jazz band, 354
jean pocket, trousers, 191
jeans, 191
jeep, 109, 130
Jehu, stagecoach, 131
jellaba, Arab dress, 491
jellyfish, 46
jersey: basketball, 296;
    football, 292; sailor, 497;
    soccer, 297
Jersey pocket, bowling, 317
Jerusalem cross, symbol, 508
jet: bath, 274; engine, 407;
    fighter, 480; hovercraft, 145;
    jumbo, 148
jet blast deflector, aircraft
    carrier, 478
jet bridge, airport, 94
jet engine test area, aircraft
    carrier, 478
jet nozzle, lawn sprinkler, 428
jetting fire crescendo,
    fireworks, 383
jettison handle, pilot's
    instrument panel, 481
jetty, nautical chart, 22
jewel drawer, dressing table,
    272
Jewish ritual items, 486
Jew's harp, 366
j-hook, tow truck bed, 126
jib: sail, 136; sailboat, 134
jibtop, 134
jib topsail, 134
jig, fishing, 341
jigsaw, 417
jingle, tambourine, 364
job descriptions, résumé, 160
jock, 194
jockey: flat racing, 336; saddle,
    335
jockey shorts, 194
jockstrap, 194
jockey wheel, bicycle, 128
jogger, running shoe, 302
jogging track, passenger ship,
    142
John B., cowboy hat, 490
'John Wayne,' can opener, 251

join, basket, 266
joint: automobile, 109; billiard
    cue, 320; brick wall, 69;
    folding rule, 424; hardback
    book, 167; hasp, 460; hitch
    and harrow, 434; human,
    26, 31; oil drilling platform,
    101; pliers, 414; silkscreen,
    375; timbered, 70; umbrella,
    230; windsurfer, 330
joint bar, railroad track, 115
joint-sealing compound,
    plumbing, 422
joist, house, 60, 61
joker, playing cards, 348
journal, 169
journal clerk, Congress, 12
journal printer, cash register,
    440
jowl, pork, 34
judge, 89; fencing match, 315
judge's box, ice hockey rink,
    295
judge's chambers, 89
judge's entrance, jai alai
    cancha, 314
judge's seat, courtroom, 89
judge's secretary's table,
    courtroom, 89
Judith, playing card queen, 348
jug, infusion coffee maker, 252
juggler, circus, 90
jugular groove, horse, 38
jugular vein, human, 28
juice extractor, 255
juicer, 255
juice rack, refrigerator, 249
jumbo jet, 148-149
jump, track and field, 300
jumper: merry-go-round, 93;
    parachuting, 333; sailor's
    uniform, 497; waterskiing,
    329
jumper cable, tow truck, 126
jumping: ski, 326; track and
    field, 300
jumping bed, trampoline, 308
jumping pit, high jump, 300
jump line: magazine, 171;
    newspaper, 168
jump plane, parachuting, 333
jump rope, body building, 344
junction, highway, 114
junction box: electrical
    receptacle, 398; light fixture,
    238
jungle gym, backyard, 287
Jupiter, planet, 3
jury box, courtroom, 89
juryroom, 89

K

K: braille, 512; sign language,
    512
kaffiyeh, Arab dress, 491
kame, mountain, 8
kangaroo crane, skyscraper, 77
kangaroo pouch, ultimate
    beast, 48
karat, ring, 219
kasagi, torii, 70-71
kazoo, 366
keel: box kite, 323; sailboard,
    134; turkey, 35; waterskiing,
    329
keep, castle, 80
keeper: dress, 198; man's belt,
    190; saddle, 335; tape
    recorder, 177; toaster, 253
keg, 267
kennel, passenger ship, 142
kerf, saw, 416
kernel, grass, 58
ketch hand, cattle ranch, 432
ketchup, and frankfurter, 265
kettle, tea service, 245
kettledrum, 354, 364
kettle grill, 288

key, 459; accordion, 366;
    anchor, 132; basketball
    court, 296; calculator, 441;
    camera, 172; can opener,
    251; cash register, 440;
    clarinet, 356; computer
    workstation, 438; drill press,
    419; flute, 356; fruit, 52;
    globe, 1; guitar, 362, 363;
    metronome, 367; organ, 360;
    piano, 361; political map,
    20; saw, 411; saxophone,
    357; synthesizer, 363;
    telegraph key, 157;
    television, 185; trombone,
    359; trumpet, 359;
    typewriter, 161
keyboard: accordion, 366;
    carillon, iv; cash register,
    440; computer, 439;
    computer workstation, 438;
    organ, 360; personal
    computer, 162; piano, 361;
    portable word processor,
    162; space shuttle computer,
    153; synthesizer, 363;
    typewriter, 161
keychain, 459; police gun belt,
    499
key chuck, power drill, 419
keydesk, pipe organ, 360
keyed point of interest, city
    plan, 20
keyhold, mortise lock, 458
key holder, police gun belt,
    498
keyhole, door, 64
keyless chuck, drill press, 419
key lever, telegraph, 157
keypad: computer workstation,
    438; fax machine, 164;
    personal computer, 162
key signature, music, 352
keyslip, grand piano, 361
keystone: arch, 72; arched
    window, 62; cupboard, 243;
    door, 64
keystone tip, screwdriver, 413
keyway, lock, 458, 459
kick, bottle, 267
kicker, magazine, 171
kicking pad, knee kicker, 246
kick plate, ice hockey rink, 295
kickstand, motorcycle, 129
kicktail, skateboard, 324
kick-wheel, potter's wheel,
    373
kidney, human, 27
kill, volleyball, 319
killer, darts, 322
killing trap, 433
kiln, 373
kiltie, man's shoe, 204
king: checkers, 345; chess, 345;
    playing cards, 348; royal
    regalia, 484
king block, igloo, 85
kingpin: bowling, 317; roller
    skate, 324; truck van, 121
king post: hang glider, 333;
    house, 61; tanker, 141
king row, checkers, 345
kingside men, chess, 345
kiss curl, woman's hair, 213
kitchen: lobster pot, 433;
    prison, 76
kitchen range, house
    blueprint, 62
kitchen sink, 247
kitchen spoon, 259
kitchen timer, 258
kite, 323
kitten, 37
klettershoe, mountain
    climbing, 334
knapsack, 343
knave, playing cards, 348
knee: cat, 37; cow, 32; dog, 36;

drop-leaf table, 242; frog, 44; horse, 38; human, 24
knee boot, harness racing, 337
knee breeches: Beefeater, 483; Revolutionary War general, 492
knee cup, armor, 465
kneehole: desk, 276; dressing table, 272
knee hose, fencing, 315
knee kicker, for carpet laying, 246
knee-length apron, cook's uniform, 489
knee machine, universal gym, 344
kneepad: basketball, 296; football, 292; ice hockey, 295; rollerskating, 324; ski pants, 326
knee roll, saddle, 335
knee sock, 207; ski clothes, 327
knickers: fencing, 315; ski clothes, 327
knife: corkscrew, 251; engraving, 375; guillotine, 462; kitchen, 256; mower, 429; painting, 370; pocket, 426; skin diving, 331; Swiss army, 426; table, 244; thrusting and cutting weapon, 463
knife box, sideboard, 243
knife case, sideboard, 243
knife man, cattle ranch, 432
knight, chess, 345
knight pawn, chess, 345
knitting needle, 386
knit vest, 199
knob: baseball bat, 291; bathtub, 274; bolt ring, 218; cannon barrel, 467; can opener, 251; chain saw, 431; citrus juicer, 255; coffee maker, 252; door, 64, 458; drain cleaner, 422; dressing table, 272; drill press, 419; drum, 364; fishing reel, 340; handbag, 222; knee kicker, 246; lacrosse stick, 298; lamp, 239; medical examination table, 450; microscope, 442; mower, 429; paint spray gun, 425; pencil sharpener, 277; phonograph receiver, 179; plane, 420; pots and pans, 257; projector, 175; propane torch, 422; rifle scope, 469; saw, 417; seeder, 430; telescope, 443; theodolite, 436; toaster, 253; typewriter, 161; venetian blind, 241; volt-ohm meter, 423; wind turbine, 390
knob nut and bolt, plane, 420
knocker, door, 64
knock-on-wood, gesture, 507
knot: ballet toeshoes, 494; balloon, 493; gallows, 462; lumber, 68; thread, 384; woman's hair, 213
knothole, lumber, 6
knuckle: dog, 36; hinge, 460; human hand, 31
knuckle bow, sword hilt, 463
kokoshniki, architecture, 70
kosher symbol, label, 268
kudu horn, ultimate beast, 48
Kuroshio Current, ocean, 6
kusabi, torii, 71

L

L: braille, 512; sign language, 512
label: baseball bat, 291; cartooning, 380; church, 86; diskette, 162; gas pump, 112; magazine, 169; necktie, 192; package, 268-269; phonograph record, 178; shirt, 189; wine bottle, 267
labeling, 268-269
labial, tooth, 456
laboratory equipment, 446-447
labrum, grasshopper, 41
laccolith, volcano, 10
lace: baseball, 290; baseball glove, 291; boxing glove, 309; bridal gown, 488; ice hockey, 295; ice skates, 325; man's shoe, 204; queen's regalia, 484; running shoe, 302; skate, 295
lace cuff, maid's uniform, 489
lace lock, ice climbing boot, 334
lacing: football, 292; lacrosse glove, 298; snowshoe, 327
lacrimal, eye, 30
lacrosse, 298
lacrosse field, 298
ladder, 425; circus aerialist, 90; destroyer, 476; Ferris wheel, 93; hydrofoil, 145; lunar lander, 154; powerboat, 139; silo, 104; slide, 287; tower ladder, 124; tugboat, 144; venetian blind, 241
ladle, 259
lagoon, 7, 15
La Hire, playing card jack, 348
lake, 7, 13; dam, 100; mountain, 8
lam, hand loom, 387
lamb, 33
lambrequin, coat of arms, 503
lamella, Jew's harp, 366
lamina, leaf, 52
lamp, 238; adjustable, 239; automobile, 106; blimp, 156; hair styling, 214; Hansom cab, 131; house, 63; locomotive, 116; speculum, 448; stagecoach, 131; track lighting, 239
lamp field diaphragm, microscope, 442
lampshade, 238
lance, medieval, 464
lance guard, armor, 465
Lancelot, playing card jack, 348
lancet window, church, 86
land feature, 7
landing, staircase, 66
landing area: aircraft carrier, 478; pole vault, 305
landing control, space shuttle, 153
landing gear, lunar lander, 154
landing gear controls: pilot's instrument panel, 481; 747 cockpit, 151
landing light, helicopter, 146
landing mat, gymnastics, 306
landing net, fishing, 341
landing pit, track and field, 300
landing ship dock, 477
landing ship tank, 477
landing system, aircraft carrier, 478
landing threshold, airport runway, 94
landing wheel: blimp, 156; glider, 147
landing-zone detector, elevator shaft, 78
landmark object, topographic map, 22
landmass, and continental shelf, 15
land mine, 473
lane: basketball court, 296; bowling, 317; highway, 114; running track, 300; swimming pool, 316; toll booth, 114
language, personal computer, 162
language, symbolic, 512
lantern, camping, 342
lanyard: cowboy hat, 202; stopwatch, 304
lap belt, drag racing driver, 339
lapel: jacket, 188, 196; Revolutionary War general, 492
lap-felled seam, tent, 342
lappet, bishop, 487
laptop, 162
large branch, tuba, 358
large intestine, human, 27
large shallow gouge, woodcarving, 372
large wheel, wheelchair, 452
lariat, ranching gear, 432
larva, insect, 41
laser, 395
laser and flares, fireworks, 383
laser beam, holography, 395
laser jet cartridge, laser printer, 163
laser pickup system, compact disc player, 178
laser printer, 163
lash brush, beauty product, 217
lashing, flat kite, 323
lasso, 432
latch: chain saw, 431; clothes dryer, 281; cupboard, 243; dishwasher, 250; door, 458; garbage disposal, 247; hasp, 460; laser printer, 163; mailbox, 231; mortise lock, 458; needle, 386; oven, 248; revolver, 470; trenchcoat, 200
latch needle, 386
latch support, pulley block, 461
lateral adjusting lever, plane, 420
lateral furrow, horse's foot, 38
lateral incisor, tooth, 456
lateral line, fish, 45
laterally gaited trotter, 337
lateral moraine, 8, 9, 12
lateral pulley, universal gym, 344
lath, lobster pot, 433
Latin cross, symbol, 508
latissimus dorsi, human, 26
latitude, parallel of, 5, 20
latticework tower, power network, 396
launch bar abort, pilot's instrument panel, 481
launch deck, submarine, 479
launcher: aircraft carrier, 478; destroyer, 477; rocket, 472
launcher tube, bazooka, 472
launching ramp, public sign, 506
launch pad, space shuttle, 152
launch tube, ballistic missile launch deck, 479
laundry: frontier fort, 82; passenger ship, 142; prison, 76
lava flow, volcano, 10
lavaliere, 219
lavatory, 273; bus, 118; jumbo jet, 148, 149
lawn cart, 430
lawn mower, 429
lawn sprinkler, 428
layout: dominos, 345; magazine, 170; roulette, 376
LCD: cellular telephone, 181; portable word processor, 162; wristwatch, 220
LCD display, synthesizer, 363
lead: internal combustion engine, 406; magazine, 170; newspaper, 168; pencil, 158; proofreader's mark, 514; and volt-ohm meter, 423
lead acid battery, 397
lead came, 378
lead connector, pacemaker, 452
leader: book page, iv; film, 172; fishhook, 341; house, 63; House of Representatives, 74
leader board, windmill, 390
leader-pusher, cowboy, 490
lead-in, magazine, 171
lead-in brace, toboggan, 328
leading edge: ax, 464; hang glider, 333; jumbo jet, 148
lead-in groove, phonograph record, 178
lead-in wire, bulb, 239
lead-out groove, phonograph record, 178
lead pencil, 158
lead pick-up, guitar, 363
lead pipe, trumpet, 359
lead plum, cowboy, 490
lead pusher, cowboy, 490
lead track, railroad yard, 96
lead weight: flat racing, 336; grandfather clock pendulum, 233; skin diving, 331
lead wire, vacuum tube, 396
leaf, 52; book, 167; canal lock, 99; carrot, 54; celery, 262; cigar, 228; corn, 58; fern, 57; grass, 58; hair clip, 214; hinge, 460; lettuce, 262; onion, 54, 262; pineapple, 55; table, 242; tree, 50
leaf springs, truck tractor, 120
lean tissue, meat, 262
leash: clown, 493; ski, 326
leather: bagpipe bag, 365; dabber pad, 377; dog, 36; flat racing, 336; football, 292; hot air balloon, 332; parka tab, 201; saddle bar, 335; stirrup, 335; suspenders, 190; tefillin strap, 486
lechurban, Jewish prayer shawl, 486
lecture hall, passenger ship, 143
lede: magazine, 170; newspaper, 168
LED electro-photographic developer, laser printer, 163
ledge: basket, 266; bathtub, 274; can opener, 251; mountain, 9
ledger, incline track, 92
ledger line, music, 353
leech, mainsail, 136
leeward side, boat, 132
left atrium, heart, 28
left bank, river, 13
left-channel volume unit meter, tape recorder, 177
left ear, newspaper, 168
left engine fuel shutoff handle, pilot's instrument panel, 481
left field, baseball, 291
left-handed strike pocket, bowling, 317
left-hand page, book, 167
left-hand steering lever, bulldozer, 435
left image, picture-in-picture viewing, 185
left pedestal, desk, 276
left service court: badminton, 319; handball, 313

left stereo speaker: portable radio/cassette player, 182; television, 185
left ventricle, heart, 28
left wing, easel, 370
leg: backyard equipment, 287; bee, 41; bridge, 97; bureau, 272; camera tripod, 176; cat, 37; chaise longue, 288; dog, 36; desk, 276; Ferris wheel, 93; fishing reel, 340; human, 24; ironing board, 279; kettledrum, 364; kiln, 373; kite, 323; lamb, 33; lobster, 47; lounger, 235; medical examination table, 450; mortar, 472; panty hose, 195; paper clip, 277; parallel bars, 306; piano, 361; playpen, 286; pool table, 320; poultry, 35; rocking chair, 234; sawhorse, 408; sheep, 33; sideboard, 243; stage, 350; staple, 410; steamer basket, 257; stove, 404; table, 242; table saw, 417; telescope, 443; tom-tom, 364; trampoline, 308; trousers, 191; tweezers, 215; wheelbarrow, 430; woman's pants, 196; workbench, 408; see also limb
legal tender, paper money, 224
leg brace: wheelbarrow, 430; workbench, 408
legend: magazine, 171; money, 224; political map, 21
legging: drum major's shoe, 495; Indian, 490; sailor, 497
leg hole, man's underpants, 194
legislative clerk, Senate, 74
leg leveler, parallel bars, 306
leg lock, screen, 175
leg-of-mutton sleeve, bridal gown, 488
leg press, universal gym, 344
leg strap, athletic supporter, 194
leg support, backyard equipment, 287
legume, pea, 54
lemon press, 261
lemon squeezer, 261
length adjuster, knee kicker, 246
lengthwise grain, fabric, 388
lengthwise grain line, sewing pattern, 388
lens: automobile, 106; binoculars, 443; camera, 172; ear scope, 448; eye, 30; eyeglasses, 221; holography, 395; microscope, 442; movie camera, 174; Polaroid, 173; projector, 175; radar, 444; rifle scope, 469; shapes, 221; skin diving mask, 331; solar power system, 391; telescope, 443; thermometer, 449; traffic light, 113; video camera, 184; video-still camera, 173
lens release button, camera, 172
lens-selection disc, eye scope, 448
lens suspensory ligament, eye, 30
lens tissue, photographic, 176
lenticel, tree, 50
Leo, zodiac, 509
leopard coat, ultimate beast, 48
leotard, ballet dancer, 494
lepton, 394

less space, proofreader's mark, 514
less than, symbol, 511
let it stand, proofreader's mark, 514
letter, 159; paper money, 224, 225; weather vane, 19
letter drawer, desk, 276
letterhead, 159
letterpress printing, 166
lettuce, 54, 262
lettuce dryer, 260
levee, 100; river, 13
level: carpenter's, 424; combination square, 424; transit, 436
level control, phonograph speaker, 179
leveler: parallel bars, 306; pool table, 320
leveling bubble, theodolite, 436
leveling foot: garbage disposal, 247; slide projector, 175
lever: bathtub, 274; bicycle, 128; bulldozer, 435; can opener, 251; child's car seat, 286; guitar, 363; electrical wall switch, 398; fire extinguisher, 284; fishing reel, 340; gas cigarette lighter, 228; gas pump, 112; hand grenade, 473; internal combustion engine, 406; iron, 279; jackhammer, 436; machine gun, 471; motorcycle, 129; movie projector, 175; nail clippers, 215; outboard engine, 137; pay phone, 180; pencil sharpener, 277; pilot's instrument panel, 481; pistol nozzle, 428; plane, 420; pliers, 414; potter's wheel, 373; 747 cockpit, 150, 151; sextant, 137; spreader, 430; stagecoach, 131; stroller, 286; surgical table, 450; telegraph key, 157; typewriter, 161; voting booth, 437; wheelchair, 452
lever arm, corkscrew, 251
lever cap, plane, 420
lever dolly, balance beam, 306
lever knob, pencil sharpener, 277
lever lock: pistol nozzle, 428; starting block, 304
lever-wrench pliers, 414
levigator, lithography, 376
Libra, zodiac, 509
library: passenger ship, 142; White House, 75
license plate: automobile, 106, 107; tow truck bed, 126
lickings, ice cream cone, 265
lid: automobile trunk, 107; barbecue grill, 288; basket, 266; camp stove, 342; can opener, 251; coffee maker, 252; coffin, 516; juice extractor, 255; kiln, 373; percolator, 252; piano, 361; pipe bowl, 229; pots and pans, 257; tea kettle, 245; toilet, 275; washing machine, 280
lie: golf, 310; ice hockey stick, 294
life, symbol of, 508
lifeboat: destroyer, 477; oil drilling platform, 101; passenger ship, 142; tanker, 141
life jacket, waterskiing, 329
lifeline: destroyer, 476; human hand, 31; inflatable, 133; sailboat, 134

lifepack, paramedic equipment, 123
life raft: aircraft carrier, 478; jumbo jet, 148; tugboat, 144
life ring, fireboat, 144
life-support system: ambulance, 123; racing car, 338; spacesuit, 155
lift: body building, 344; boot, 206; passenger ship, 142
lift bridge, 97
lift cord, venetian blind, 241
lift cylinder, bulldozer, 435
lifter: can opener, 251; kitchen utensil, 259; phonograph, 178; tower ladder, 124
lift fan, hovercraft, 145
lifting charge, aerial shell, 383
lifting column, surgical table, 450
lifting eye, buoy, 132
lifting ring, rowboat, 133
lift knob, toaster, 253
lift link, hitch and harrow, 434
lift lock: toaster, 253; venetian blind, 241
lift-net, tower ladder, 124
lift pedal, dental unit, 454
lift-out stem, steamer basket, 257
lift rod, sink, 273
lift section wrap, aerial shell, 383
lift span, bridge, 97
lift wires, toilet, 275
ligament, eye, 30
ligature: clarinet mouthpiece, 357; grammatical symbol, 513
light: aircraft carrier, 478; airport runway, 94; automobile, 106, 107; bulldozer, 435; buoy, 132; bus, 118; camera, 174; camper, 130; CB radio, 183; church, 87; coffee maker, 252; dental unit, 454; destroyer, 476, 477; door, 64; drag racing, 339; fencing strip, 315; fireboat, 144; fire engine, 124, 125; guitar amplifier, 363; helicopter, 146; house, 63; ice hockey, 294; jet fighter, 480; lift bridge, 97; locomotive, 117; lunar lander, 154; mechanical sweeper, 127; motorcycle, 129; nautical chart, 22; phonograph receiver, 179; pilot's instrument panel, 481; police car, 122; powerboat, 138; railroad crossing signal, 115; relief map, 21; sailboat, 134; 747 cockpit, 150, 151; sewing machine, 278; single engine airplane, 147; space shuttle, 153; speculum, 448; stage, 350; subway car, 119; synagogue, 88; taxi roof, 119; toaster oven, 253; toll booth, 114; Torah, 486; tow truck, 126; tractor, 434; traffic, 113; truck, 120, 121; tugboat, 144; voting booth, 437; washing machine, 280
light control, pilot's instrument panel, 481
light-diffuser panel, elevator car, 78
light-duty road, topographic map, 22
lighter, cigarette, 228
light-horn, nautical chart, 22
lighthouse, nautical chart, 22
lighting: and composition, 368; track, 239
lighting hole, lantern, 342

light mast, aircraft carrier, 478
light meter, photographic, 176
lightning, 17
lightning rod, launch pad, 152
light-reading index, light meter, 176
light selector, police car, 122
light source, composition, 369
light switch: elevator, 78; refrigerator, 249; stove oven, 248
light type, 169
ligule, grass, 58
limb: bow, 466; human, 24, 25; microscope, 442; sextant, 137; theodolite, 436; tree, 50; see also leg
limb top, microscope, 442
lime, crustacean chitin, 47
lime glass, light bulb, 238
limestone cup, coral polyp, 46
limited access highway, road map, 20
limiter, CB radio noise, 183
limit line, fencing strip, 315
limit switch, elevator shaft, 78
limousine, 109
Lincoln Suite, White House, 75
line: badminton court, 319; basketball court, 296; bell, iv; block and tackle, 461; boat, 132; book page, iv; bowling lane, 317; compass, 136; craps table, 347; drag racing, 339; fencing strip, 315; flat racing entry, 336; football field, 293; garbage truck, 127; globe, 5; handball court, 313; harness racetrack, 337; horse's foot, 38; hot air balloon, 332; ice hockey, 294, 295; jai alai cancha, 314; kite, 323; lasso, 432; magazine, 169, 171; map, 20, 21; movie film, 174; music notation, 352, 353; newspaper, 168; nuclear reactor, 392; parachute, 333; perspective, 368; power, 396; powerboat, 139; scrimshaw, 375; shuffleboard court, 318; squash court, 313; spider web, 40; stage, 350; sundial, 389; tanker, 141; telephone, 180; theatre, 351; track and field, 300, 301; tugboat, 144; volleyball court, 319; windmill, 390; windsurfer, 330
linear perspective, and composition, 368
linear slide rule, 441
line box, tugboat, 144
line finder, typewriter, 161
line guide, fishing reel, 340
line-in jack, tape recorder, 177
line lashing, kite, 323
lineman's pliers, 414
linen, ambulance, 123
linen locker, sailboat, 135
line of perspective, 368
liner: automatic rifle handguard, 471; fireplace flue, 232; football helmet, 292; glove, 200; gouge, 374; makeup, 216; ship, 140, 142; Torah, 486
line-recording level control, tape recorder, 177
line roller, fishing rod, 340
line space lever, typewriter, 161
line support, power network, 396
line symbol, political, map, 20
line-up light, aircraft carrier, 478

547

linework, map, 20
ling-t'ou, Manchu court dress, 491
lingual, tooth, 456
lingual cusp, tooth, 456
lining: beret, 202; garment, 196; hardback book, 167; man's belt, 190; man's shoe, 204; mitten, 200; parka, 201; saddle, 335; skate, 295; ski clothes, 327; sleeping bag, 343; trenchcoat, 200; tunnel, 98
link: bolt ring, 218; cartridge fuse, 399; chain, 461; chain saw chain, 431; hitch and harrow, 434; horizontal bar, 306; identification bracelet, 187; keychain, 459; parachute harness, 333; pendant, 219; sponge mop, 282; swivel, 218; tank track, 474; wristwatch band, 220
linkage: gardening shears, 427; vault, 457
link chain, 461
linking string, frankfurter, 265
link strap, block and tackle, 461
linseed oil, sketch, 371
lintel: church, 86; door, 64; fireplace, 232; house, 61; torii, 70-71
lint filter, washing machine, 280
lint trap, clothes dryer, 281
lion: ultimate beast, 48; zodiac, 509
lip: bell, iv; blender, 254; bottle, 267; cat, 37; coffee maker, 252; dustpan, 282; embroidery ring, 385; fishing plug, 341; human, 24; mousetrap, 433; mouth, 30; pot, 373; sink, 273; stemware, 244; stove, 404; theater, 351; univalve shell, 47
lip brush, 217
lip gloss, 216, 217
lip liner, 216, 217
lip rest, corkscrew, 251
lipstick, 216, 217
liqueur glass, 245
liquid: dental, 455; fruit, 255
liquid-bleach dispenser, washing machine, 280
liquid-bulk carrier, 142
liquid column, dual scale thermometer, 18
liquid-cooled internal combustion engine, 406
liquid crystal display: cellular telephone, 181; Geiger counter, 445; portable word processor, 162; wristwatch, 220
liquid fuel, rocket, 407
liquid measuring cup, 258
liquid oxygen: pilot's instrument panel indicator, 481; rocket, 407
lira, symbol, 511
li-shui portion of dragon robe, Manchu court attire, 491
listed number, telephone, 180
listing, magazine, 171
literal rendition, work of art, 368
literary anatomy, 25
lithographic crayon, 376
lithographic pencil, 376
lithographic press, 376
lithography, 166, 376
lithosphere, 4
litter, bin, 247
little finger, human hand, 31
little toe, human foot, 31

littoral zone, coastline, 15
live-bait well, powerboat, 139
liver: fowl, 35; human, 27
living quarters: oil drilling platform, 101; White House, 75
liwan, mosque, 70-71
lizard, 43
load bearing wall, house, 60
load cord, hot air balloon, 332
loader: cannon, 467; razor blade, 210
loader's hatch, tank, 474
loading bridge, airport, 94
loading door, stove, 404
loading gate: revolver, 470; shotgun, 468
loading platform, stage, 350
loading slot, razor blade, 210
load lever, typewriter, 161
load line, symbol, 511
load ring, hot air balloon, 332
load-size selector, washing machine, 280
loaf, bread, 263
loafer, man's shoe, 204
lobby, skyscraper, 77
lobe: leaf, 52; outer ear, 30; partisan, 464; ultimate beast, 49
lobster, 47
lobster cracker, 261
lobster pot, 433
local elevator, skyscraper, 77
local galaxy, 2
local organizer, backpack, 343
local political boundary, road map, 20
local route number, road map, 20
local street, city plan, 20
location marker, airport, 94
location of office, letter, 159
location of winery, wine label, 267
locator diagram, political map, 21
lock: attaché case, 285; bus, 118; canal lock, 99; cash register, 440; cymbal stand, 364; desk, 276; garbage disposal, 247; garbage truck, 127; handbag, 222; human, 25; hurdle, 304; ice climbing boot lace, 334; lift bridge, 97; mailbox, 231; movie projector, 175; organ, 360; parallel bars, 306; parking meter, 113; phonograph tone arm, 178; playpen, 286; police gun belt, 498; pommel horse, 307; pressure cooker, 257; safe, 457; screen, 175; sonar, 444; starting block, 304; tape recorder, 177; table saw, 417; toaster, 253; tripod, 176; trombone, 358; vault, 457; venetian blinds, 241; voting booth, 437; wheelchair, 452; window, 65
locked groove, phonograph record, 178
locker, sailboat, 135
locking bar, mousetrap, 433
locking bolt, vault, 457
locking pin, fire extinguisher, 284
locking plate, workbench vise, 408
locking pliers, 414
locking ring: rifle scope, 469; screwdriver, 413
locking screw, cassette tape, 176
locking system: balance beam, 306; bayonet, 463

locking tip, hypodermic syringe, 451
locking adjustable wrench, 415
lock key, typewriter shift, 161
locknut: lamp, 238; lithographic press, 376; roller skate, 324
lockout tool, tow truck, 126
lock plate, crossbow, 466
lock ring: fishing rod, 340; slide projector, 175
lock screw, lithographic press, 376
lock set, door, 458
lockside, canal lock, 99
lock stile, door, 64
lock switch: movie camera, 174; tape measure, 424; video-still camera, 173
lock wall, canal lock, 99
lock washer, lamp, 238
locomotive: canal lock, 99; railroad yard, 96; train, 116-117
lodge pole, tepee, 84
loft: barn, 104; golf clubs, 310; sleeping bag, 343; stage, 350
log chute, dam, 100
loge, theatre, 351
log fork, fire iron, 232
log hoist, dam, 100
logo: aisle display, 102; bank card, 226; baseball team, 290; bus, 118; credit card, 227; electric razor, 210; fire engine, 125; label, 268; letter, 159; locomotive, 117; magazine, 169, 170; mainsail, 136; newspaper, 168; pill, 451; prescription, 451; single engine airplane, 147
loin: beef, 32; lamb, 33; pork, 34
loin guard, armor, 465
loins: cat, 37; dog, 36; horse, 38; human, 25
longbow, 466
longeon, flat kite, 323
long-hair slot, electric razor, 210
long horse, gymnastics, 307
longitude, meridian of, 5, 20, 22
long joint, bassoon, 357
long jump, track and field, 300
long hose, football uniform, 292
long lid prop, grand piano, 361
long-life light bulb, 238
long necklace, Manchu court dress, 491
long-range weapon system, jet fighter, 480
long service line, badminton court, 319
longshore bar, 14
longshore trough, 14
long-term parking lot, airport, 94
long-wire antenna, destroyer, 476
lookout area, tanker, 140
lookout tower, passenger ship, 143
loom: rowboat oar, 133; weaving, 387
loop: basketball backstop, 296; bell, iv; book, 207; bow, 466; carpet, 246; checkbook clutch, 223; circus aerialist, 90; cowboy cartridge belt, 490; dress, 198; fastener, 208; hammock, 288; handbag, 222; human fingertip, 31; knitting, 386;

overhead power line, 396; roller coaster, 92; suspenders, 190; tent, 342; trench coat, 200; type, 165; wheelchair, 452
loop-former bar, movie projector, 175
loophole, castle, 80
loop label, necktie, 192
loop ramp, highway cloverleaf, 114
loop tape, Velcro, 209
loosefooted sail, windsurfer, 330
lore, bird, 39
lorgnette, 221
lost and found, public sign, 506
lotion, beauty product, 214, 217
lotion dispenser, kitchen sink, 247
loud, music notation, 352
loudness control, phonograph receiver, 179
loudspeaker: cellular telephone, 181; fire engine, 124, 125
lounge: jai alai cancha, 314; jumbo jet, 148; passenger train, 116
lounger, 235
louver: air conditioner, 402; church window, 86; tank, 474; window shutters, 241
loveseat, 236
low bar, uneven parallel bars, 306
low beam, automobile, 106
lower back-stick, easel, 370
lower bolt, pulley block, 461
lower bout, viola, 355
lower bow, bear trap, 433
lower case: proofreader's mark, 514; type, 165
lower chord, lift bridge, 97
lower compartment, backpack, 343
lower control arm, automobile, 108
lower eyelid, 30
lower face, zipper, 209
lower gate, canal lock, 99
lower-girdle facet, cut gemstone, 218
lower grid assembly, nuclear reactor, 392
lower grip ring, sword hilt, 463
lower guard, sword hilt, 463
lower handle, power mower, 429
lower housing, finishing sander, 421
lower jaw, snake, 42
lower joint, clarinet, 357
lower limb, bow, 466
lower link, hitch and harrow, 434
lower magnet, dipole magnet, 394
lower mandible, bird, 39
lower margin, book page, 167
lower pool, canal lock, 99
lower rack track, dishwasher, 250
lower rail, balustrade, 73
lower rudder, jumbo jet, 149
lower sash, window, 65
lower shell, turtle, 43
lower side-rail, truck van, 121
lower spray arm, dishwasher, 250
lower table, drill press, 419
lower tail crest, tadpole, 44
lower teeth, 456
lower thigh, dog, 36
lower vertical fin, blimp, 156

low-gain antenna: lunar rover, 155; satellite, 186
low heat switch, hair dryer, 212
low hurdle, 304
low-level outlet, dam, 100
low pressure, weather map, 19
low pulley, universal gym, 344
low tide, 15
low-tide terrace, 14
low tops, sailor, 497
low water controller, Jacuzzi, 274
lozenge, church, 86
L-shaped square, 424
L-steps, staircase, 66
lubber's line, compass, 136
lubricant port, saber saw, 417
lubricating valve, steam engine, 405
lucaflect, cartoon, 380
luff, mainsail, 136
lug: bicycle, 128; cassette tape, 177; coffin, 516; drum, 364; hand grenade, 473; nuclear reactor, 393; truck tractor, 120
luge, 328
luggage, 288
luggage rack: camper, 130; stagecoach, 131
lug hole, tire, 105
lug nuts, automobile, 106
lumber, building material, 68
lumber girder, 60
lumber post, 60
lumbrosacral plexus, human, 29
lumen, light, 238
luminous indices, wristwatch, 220
lunar lander, 154
lunar module, 154
lunar month, 4
lunar overshoe, spacesuit, 155
lunar rover, 155
lunette, guillotine, 462
lung: human, 27; iron, 452
lunge pads, ice skates, 325
lunt, pipe, 229
lunula, human fingernail, 31
lure, fishing, 341
lyre, 355; grand piano, 361
lyre holder, trumpet lyrics, music, 352
lysosome, animal cell, 23

M

M: braille, 512; sign language, 512
ma'abarta, tefellin, 486
mace: House of Representatives, 74; medieval, 464
mace canister, police gun belt, 498
machicolations, castle, 80
mach indicator: pilot's instrument panel, 481; 747 cockpit, 150
machine: acoustic guitar, 362; ambulance, 123; dialysis, 452; planting, 434; toll basket, 114; voting, 437
machine cabin, wind turbine, 390
machine gun, 471; tank, 474, 475
machine knitting needle, 386
machine-readable codeline, traveler's check, 227
machinery tower, lift bridge, 97
machine stop, etching press, 377
machinist's vise, workbench, 408
mach speed, jet fighter, 480

mack, destroyer, 476
macrame, 386
macron, grammatical symbol, 513
macula lutea, eye, 30
MADC scale, volt-ohm meter, 423
madreporite, starfish, 46
magazine: cover and contents page, 169; feature spread, 170, 171; film, 172; fort, 82; pistol, 470; rifle, 468, 471; shotgun, 469; stapler, 277
Magen David, 88, 508
magic wand, wizard, 492
magma reservoir, volcano, 10
magnesium star shell, fireworks, 383
magnet: pocket knife, 426; super collider, 394
magnetic compass, 136
magnetic disk, video-still camera, 173
magnetic lid lifter, can opener, 251
magnetic north, compass rose, 22
magnetic sound track, movie film, 174
magnetic strip, credit card, 227
magnetic tape, 177
magnetometer, satellite, 186
magnetometer stowage bags, lunar rover, 155
magnifier, pocket knife, 426
magnifying lens, radar, 444
magnifying power, microscope, 442
mag wheel: automobile, 106; motorcycle, 129
mah-jongg tile, 345
maid, 489
maiden: execution device, 462; spinning wheel, 387
mail: armor, 465; public sign, 506
mailbox, 231
mail drop, door, 64
mailing label, magazine, 169
main, furnace, 400
main body: flute, 356; furniture, 272
main breaker, circuit breaker box, 399
main bulkhead, passenger ship, 142
main cabin, sailboat, 135
main cable, suspension bridge, 97
main channel, river, 13
main circulating pump, solar heating system, 391
main compartment, backpack, 343
main control valve, camp stove, 342
main counterweight, lift bridge, 97
main-course table fork, 244
main cover title, magazine, 169
main curtain, theater, 351
main deck, destroyer, 476
main derrick, coin, 225
main engine, space shuttle, 152
main-engine heat exchanger, oil drilling platform, 101
main feedwater pump, nuclear reactor, 392
mainframe computer, 439
main gate, frontier fort, 82
main housing, curling iron, 214
main illustration, book page, iv
mainland, 7
mainland beach, 15

main landing gear, single engine airplane, 147
main line: lasso, 432; railroad yard, 96
main picture: picture-in-picture viewing, 185; television, 185
main ring, super collider, 394
main rod, steam locomotive, 116
mainsail, 136; sailboat, 134
main sanctuary, mosque, 70, 71
mainsheet, sailboat, 134
main slide, tuba, 358
main standard, football goalpost, 293
main strings, tennis racket, 312
main table, drill press, 419
maintenance safety rope, roller coaster, 92
main towing bit, tugboat, 144
maintube, telescope, 443
main undercarriage wheel, helicopter, 146
main vein, leaf, 52
majority secretary, Senate, 74
major road, 114
maker's imprint, playing cards, 348
maker's signature, check, 226
makeup, 216, 217
malacology, 47
maladicta balloon, cartoon, 381
malar, human, 24
male, symbol, 496
male coupling, hose connection, 428
male ferrule, fishing rod, 340
male flower, corn, 58
male plug, electrical, 398
maline, woman's hat, 203
malleolus, human foot, 31
mallet, 412; croquet, 318; drums, 364; kitchen tool, 261; polo, 299; woodcarving, 372
Maltese cross, symbol, 508
man: backgammon, 345; chess, 345; ranching, 432
manara, architecture, 70
manchette, lounger, 235
Manchu court dress, 491
mandible: ant, 41; bird, 39; fish, 45; grasshopper, 41; human, 26
mandolin, 362
mandoline, kitchen cutter, 261
mane: horse, 38; human, 25; polo pony, 299; ultimate beast, 48
maneuvering system, space shuttle, 152, 153
manger, barn, 104
mang-p'ao, Manchu court dress, 491
manifold: automobile engine, 111; tanker, 141
manometer, blood pressure gauge, 449
man's formal attire, 488
man's hair, 211
man's hat, 202
mansion, White House, 75
man's shirt, 189
man's shoe, 204
man's skate, 325
man's underwear, 92
manticore, legendary beast, 48
mantle: earth, 4; fireplace, 232; lantern, 342; octopus, 46; pyramid, 71; royal regalia, 484; Torah, 486
mantlepiece, fireplace, 232

mantlet, tank, 475
mantling, coat of arms, 503
manual, organ, 360
manual citrus juicer, 255
manual drill, 418
manual focusing, video camera, 184
manual operation button, vacuum cleaner, 283
manual-pump pedal, surgical table, 450
manual release, ski binding, 326
manual search button, compact disc player, 178
manual stabilizer trim lever, 747 cockpit, 150
manual typewriter, 161
manual zoom lever, movie camera, 174
manubrium, jellyfish, 46
manufacturer: gas pump, 112; lithographic press, 376; organ, 360; painting brush, 371; phonograph record, 178; phonograph speaker, 179; running shoe, 302; single engine airplane, 147; Universal Product Code, 440
manufacturer's imprint, prescription, 451
manure gutter, barn, 104
manure pit, barnyard, 104
map, 5, 20-22; subway car, 119
map pocket, parka, 201
marathon, 300; running shoe, 302
marbling, meat, 262
marching band, 354, 495
mare, 38
margin; book page, 167; jellyfish, 46; leaf, 52; magazine page, 171; map, 22; necktie, 193
marginal shield, turtle, 43
margin stop, typewriter, 161
marine algae, 57
marine life, 46
mark: basketball court, 296; coin, 225; dental braces, 453; grammatical symbol, 513; guitar, 362; label, 268, 269; military uniform, 496; monovial, 424; music notation, 352; nail, 410; proofreader's, 514; sextant, 137; tape measure, 424; topographic map, 22; type, 166
marked deck, playing card, 348
marker: airport, 84; bowling lane, 317; football field, 293; swimming pool lane, 316; tow truck, 126; wristwatch, 220
marker beacon, helicopter, 146
marker control, sonar, 444
marker lamp, locomotive, 116
marker light: bus, 118; fire engine, 124; locomotive, 117; truck van, 121
marking: airport runway, 94; blood pressure gauge, 449; hypodermic syringe, 451; music, 352; topographic map, 22
marking gauge, measuring tool, 424
mark of omission, grammatical symbol, 513
marksmanship badge, military uniform, 496
marrow, meat bone, 262
Mars, planet, 3
marsh: coastline, 15; river, 13; topographic map, 22
marshalling yard, railroad, 96

mars light, fire engine, 124, 125
mascara, 216, 217
masher kitchen utensil, 259
mask: baseball catcher, 290; fencing, 315; football helmet, 292; ice hockey goalie, 294; silk screen, 375; skin diving, 331; television, 185
masonry: building material, 68; permanent fort, 83; wall, 69
masonry bit, drill, 419
masonry gate post, fence, 67
mass: cosmic, 2; nuclear reactor, 392
massage-action hand shower, 274
massager shower, 274
mast: aircraft carrier, 478; CB radio antenna, 183; destroyer, 477; flag, 502; sailboat, 134; skyscraper, 77; space shuttle, 152; tanker, 140, 141; tugboat, 144; windsurfer, 330
mastabe, pyramid, 70
master control, pilot's instrument panel, 481
master cord, snowshoe, 327
master cylinder, automobile, 108
master number, phonograph record, 178
master slide, traverse rod, 240
master's quarters, tugboat, 144
masthead: magazine, 169; sailboat, 134
masthead light: destroyer, 477; fireboat, 144
mat: in frame, 379; gymnastics, 306; phonograph turntable, 178; wigwam, 84
match, 228; fencing, 315; polo, 299; soccer, 297
matchbook, 228
material identification, house blueprint, 62
match, soccer, 297
ma-ti hsiu, Manchu court dress, 491
matrix, dental, 455
mattress, 271; coffin, 516; playpen pad, 286
mature fruit, tomato, 54
mat window, frame, 379
mausoleum, 516
maw, human, 25
maxilla: fish, 45; human, 26
maximum security prison, 76
meadow, mountain, 8
mean high water mark, topographic map, 22
mean line, type, 165
mean time, 5
measure, music, 352; tape, 424
measured by, symbol, 511
measure of gold purity, ring, 219
measuring cup, 258
measuring diffuser, light meter, 176
measuring spoon, 258
measuring tool, 424; kitchen, 258; oil drilling platform, 101
meat: baseball bat, 291; beef, 32; coconut, 262; lamb, 33; pork, 34; poultry, 35; raw, 262
meat department, supermarket, 102
meat grinder, 261
meat keeper, refrigerator, 249
meat mallet, 261
meat thermometer, 258

mechanic, public sign, 506
mechanical floor, skyscraper, 77
mechanical power, steam engine, 405
mechanical stage control, microscope, 442
mechanical sweeper, 127
mechanical unit, piano, 361
mechanic's shops, frontier fort, 82
mechanism: bazooka, 472; fountain pen, 158; recliner, 235
mechanized voting machine, 437
medal, 501; collector, 225; military, 496; police, 498
medallion, boat, 206
medallion number, taxi, 119
Medal of Honor, 496
medal of order, king's regalia, 484
medial malleolus, human foot, 31
medial moraine, 9, 12
median, highway, 114
median furrow, horse, 38
median nerve, human, 29
medical examination equipment, 448
medical table, 450
medical treatment aids, 451
medication, 451; prescription, 451
medicine dropper, 451
medieval arms, 464
medium, painting, 370
medium gouge, woodcarving, 372
medley relay, track and field, 300
medley swimming race, 316
medulla, brain, 29
meeting rails, window, 65
melody part, accordion, 366
melody pipe, bagpipe, 365
melody string, sitar, 362
melon, silo, 104
member: basketball backstop, 296; geodesic dome, 85; house, 61
membrane, animal cell, 23
membranophone, 364
memo, check, 226
memorabilia, White House, 75
memorial, tombstone, 516
memorial band, Jewish prayer vestment, 486
memory control unit, circuit board, 439
memory data, cellular telephone, 181
memory function key, electronic calculator, 441
memory lock, organ, 360
meninges, brain, 29
menorah: symbol, 508; synagogue, 88
men's tee, golf course, 310
mentum, human, 24
menu: computer workstation, 438; personal computer, 162
menu key, cellular telephone, 181
Mercator grid, map, 22
merchant ship, 140
mercury: barometer, 18; battery, 397; blood pressure gauge, 449; planet, 3; thermometer, 449
mercury sphygmomanometer, 449
merge, road sign, 505
merge left, road sign, 505
meridian of longitude, 1, 5
merlon, castle, 80
merry-go-round, 93

mesentery, coral polyp, 46
mesh: Ping-Pong net, 321; playpen net, 286; silk screen, 375
mesial, tooth, 456
mesial buccal cusp, 456
mesial lingual cusp, 456
mesocarp: orange, 55; peach, 55
mesosphere, earth, 4
mess, frontier fort, 82
message display, magnetic tape subsystem, 439
message indicator light, answering machine, 181
mess hall, prison, 76
metacarpopalangeal crease, human hand, 31
metacarpus, cat, 37
metal: fuse cap, 399; vaulting pole, 305; printing type, 166; stapler cap, 277; umbrella rod, 230
metal detector, 445
metallic jacket, fencing, 315
metallic salts, aerial shell, 383
metal locator, 445
metal saw, pocket knife, 426
metal shop, prison, 76
metalworking vise, 409
metamorphosis, insect, 41
metatarsal arch, human foot, 31
metatarsals, human, 26
metatarsus: cat, 37; spider, 40
meteor, 2
meteorologist, weather monitoring equipment, 18
meter: CB radio, 183; and fuse box, 399; house, 63; nautical chart, 22; parking, 113; phonograph receiver, 179; powerboat, 138; tape recorder, 177; volt-ohm, 423
meter tape, envelope, 159
metronome, 367
mezuzah, Jewish ritual item, 486
mezzanine, theatre, 351
mezzo forte, music notation, 352
M-51 gun, jet fighter, 480
mica disc, incandescent bulb, 238
Michigan marker light, bus, 118
micro-dial indicator gauge, etching press, 377
micrometer drum, sextant, 137
microphone: CB radio, 183; hearing aid, 452; movie camera, 174; police car, 122; 747 cockpit, 150; tape recorder, 177; video camera, 184
microphone input plug, movie projector, 175
microphone jack: CB radio, 183; movie camera, 174; tape recorder, 177
microprocessor, circuit board, 439
microscope, 442, 447
microwave oven, 248
mid-angle, lamp, 239
midchannel nautical chart, 22
midcourt, basketball court, 296
midcourt line, basketball court, 296
middle finger, human hand, 31
middle joint, flute, 356
middle leg, bee, 41
middle operating-screw handle, clamp, 409
middle pick-up, guitar, 363
middle section, flute, 356
midfielder, lacrosse, 298

midfield line, lacrosse field, 298
midget, circus, 90
midget howitzer, 472
midget pliers, 414
midground, composition, 369
midnight, globe, 5
midrange audio speaker, 179
midrib: fern, 57; leaf, 52
midriff, human, 25
midsole: running shoe, 302; sandal, 206
midway line, soccer field, 297
mike stand, movie camera, 174
mike, video camera, 184
mileage indicator, road map, 20
milestone, highway, 114
mile track, harness racing, 337
military buckle, man's belt, 190
military collar, king's regalia, 484
military uniform, 496-497
milk, coconut, 262
milk teeth, 456
milk well, cow, 32
Milky Way galaxy, 2-3
mill, pepper grinder, 261
milled edge, coin, 225
millimeters, cartridge, 470
milliner, 203
minaret: architecture, 70; iceberg, 12
mind, human, 25
mine, 473
mineral detector, 445
miniature golf course, passenger ship, 142
minicar, 109
minim, music notation, 352
minimum payment, monthly statement, 227
minimum security prison, 76
minimus: foot, 31; hand, 31
minister, religious vestments, 487
minivacuum, 283
minivan, 108
miniver, royal crown, 485
minor coin, 225
minor road, highway, 114
minority secretary, Senate, 74
mint mark, coin, 225
minus, symbol, 510
minus square, shuffleboard court, 318
minute, grammatical symbol, 513
minute hand: grandfather clock, 233; stopwatch, 304; wristwatch, 220
minutes of arc, symbol, 511
mirliton, 366
mirror, 217; automobile, 106, 110; bus, 118; cosmetic case, 288; dental, 455; dressing table, 272; fire engine, 125; holography, 395; locomotive, 117; mechanical sweeper, 127; microscope, 442; physician's, 448; pilot's instrument panel, 481; racing car, 338; sextant, 137; telescope, 443; truck tractor, 120
MIRV, 482
miscellaneous information, monthly statement, 227
miser, costume, 492
missile, 482; jet fighter, 480; surface-to-air, 476; surface-to-surface, 476
missile control officer, and pilot's instrument panel, 481
missile deck, submarine, 479

missile launcher, aircraft carrier, **478**
mission specialist, space shuttle, **153**
mistigris, playing cards, **348**
miter: bishop, **487**; cardinal, **487**
miter clamp, **409**
mitered joint, silk screen, **375**
miter gauge, table saw, **417**
mitochondrion, animal cell, **23**
mitt, baseball, **290**, **291**
mitten, **200**; ski clothes, **327**
mixer, kitchen sink, **247**
mixing blades, food processor, **254**
mixing bowl, **258**
mixing tools, kitchen, **258**
moat: castle, **80**, **81**; mountain, **9**; permanent fort, **83**
mobile platform, space shuttle, **152**
moccasin: Indian, **490**; man's shoe, **204**
mockery, gesture, **507**
mode control, microwave oven, **248**
mode display window, laser printer, **163**
mode indicator, VCR, **184**
model: baseball glove, **291**; internal combustion engine, **406**
mode lever, surgical table, **450**
modeling end, clay modeling tool, **372**
model number: phonograph speaker, **179**; surgical table, **450**
mode mute, phonograph receiver, **179**
moderately loud, music, **352**
mode selection control, police car, **122**
mode selector: metal detector, **445**; 747 cockpit, **151**; sonar, **444**
modesty panel, desk, **276**
mode switch, Geiger counter, **445**
modified bishop sleeve, bridal gown, **488**
modified leg-of-mutton sleeve, bridal gown, **488**
modulation indicator, CB radio, **183**
modulation wheel, synthesizer, **363**
module, jumbo jet gallery, **148**; **149**
moisture collector pan, air conditioner, **402**
moisturizer, beauty product, **217**
molar, tooth, **456**
mold: church, **86**; denture, **453**
molding: automobile, **106**, **107**; church, **86**; cupboard, **243**; escalator, **79**; frame, **379**; grandfather clock, **233**; minaret, **70**
molding scoop, cooking utensil, **259**
moline, symbol, **508**
Molotov cocktail, **473**
money, **224-225**; gesture, **507**
money box, **457**
money slot, blackjack, **347**
money totalizer, gas pump, **112**
monitor, **184**; computer, **439**; computer workstation, **438**; fireboat, **144**; movie projector, **175**; personal computer, **162**; portable word processor, **162**; prison, **76**; space shuttle, **153**;

tanker, **141**; tape recorder, **177**; television, **185**
monkey, caisson, **467**
monkey bars, backyard equipment, **287**
monkey board, oil drilling platform, **101**
monkey ear, ultimate beast, **48**
monkey wrench, **415**
monocle, **221**
monocoque chassis, racing car, **338**
monorial, carpenter's level, **424**
Monroe Room, White House, **75**
monsoon, **6**
montgolfier hot air balloon, **332**
month, lunar, **4**
monthly statement, credit card, **227**
monticule, **7**
monument, tombstone, **516**
moon, **3**; phases, **4**
moon buggy, **155**
moon dial, grandfather clock, **233**
moon roof, automobile, **106**
mooring mast: airship, **156**; skyscraper, **77**
mooring winch, tanker, **140**
moose antler, ultimate beast, **48**
mop, **282**
moraine, **8**, **9**, **12**
morning coat: butler's uniform, **489**; man's formal attire, **488**
morning line, flat racing entry, **336**
morse, royal regalia, **484**
mortar, **472**; kitchen tool, **261**
mortar joint, brick wall, **69**
mortice hole, stagecoach, **131**
mortise, label, **269**
mortise lock, **458**
mosque, **70**
mosquito, **41**
mosquito netting screen, tent, **342**
mother, flat racing entry, **336**
mother-in-law, bowling pin, **317**
mother-of-all, spinning wheel, **387**
motion, steam engine, **405**
motion compensator, oil drilling platform, **101**
motor: automobile, **108**; automobile engine starter, **111**; power drill, **419**
motor cruiser, **133**
motor home, **130**
motor housing: blender, **254**; can opener, **251**; food processor, **254**; hair dryer, **212**; jackhammer, **436**; juice extractor, **255**; lawn sprinkler, **428**; potter's wheel, **373**; power drill, **419**; vacuum cleaner, **283**
motorman's cab, subway, **119**
motor mount, automobile engine, **111**
motor nerve, human, **29**
motor scooter helmet, police, **498**
motor whaleboat, destroyer, **476**
motto: coat of arms, **503**; money, **224**
mound: baseball field, **291**; royal regalia, **485**
mount: automobile engine, **111**; bagpipe, **365**; castle, **80**, **81**; coat of arms, **503**; film

slide, **172**; fire engine, **124**; fishing reel, **340**; machine gun tripod, **471**; pencil sharpener, **277**; polo, **299**
mountain, **8-9**; peak, **7**
mountain climbing, **334**
Mountain Time, **5**
mount base, rifle scope, **468**
mounting: ballpoint pen, **158**; bicycle caliper brake, **128**; drill press, **419**; electrical receptacle, **398**; electrical wall switch, **398**; electronic flash, **176**; fencing foil, **315**; frame, **379**; lamp, **239**; mailbox, **231**; ski binding, **326**; telescope, **443**
mouse, personal computer, **162**
mousetrap, **433**
mouth: beaker, **447**; bell, **iv**; bottle, **267**; cannon, **467**; coral polyp, **46**; fish, **45**; frog, **44**; hot air balloon, **332**; human, **24**, **30**; jellyfish, **46**; plane, **420**; river, **7**, **13**; starfish, **46**; suspenders, **190**; tadpole, **44**
mouth organ, **366**
mouthpiece: boxing, **309**; clarinet, **357**; French horn, **358**; harmonica, **366**; kazoo, **366**; pipe, **229**; skin diving, **331**; trombone, **358**; trumpet, **359**; tuba, **358**
mouthpiece key, saxophone, **357**
movable base, computer workstation, **438**
movable bridge, **97** *
movable control-arm, surgical table, **450**
movable fret, sitar, **362**
movable jaw: C-clamp, **409**; locking pliers, **414**; monkey wrench, **415**
move down, proofreader's mark, **514**
move left, proofreader's mark, **514**
movement, clock, **233**
movement dial, vault, **457**
move right, proofreader's mark, **514**
movie camera, **174**
movie projector, **174**
movie film, **174**
moving gate, racing, **336**
moving sidewalk, **79**
mower, lawn, **429**
MP, uniform, **496**
mucoprotein coat, animal cell, **23**
mud: hogan, **84**; nautical chart, **22**
mud flap, truck, **120**, **121**, **126**
mud shield, tank, **475**
muezzin, and minaret, **70**
muffler: automobile, **109**; bulldozer, **435**; internal combustion engine, **406**; miser, **492**; motorcycle, **129**; power mower, **429**; tank, **474**; tractor, **434**
muffler shield, chain saw, **431**
mufti, police, **498**
mug, shaving, **210**
mulching lawn mower, **429**
mule, canal lock, **99**
Mulligan, darts, **322**
mullion, church, **86**
multifoil window, church, **86**
multimeter, **423**
multi-picture key, television, **185**
multiple fruit, **55**
multiple independently

targeted reentry vehicle (MIRV), **482**
multiplication, with slide rule, **441**
multiply, symbol, **510**
multi-position surgical table, **450**
multipurpose electrician's tool, **423**
multipurpose vacuum cleaner brush, **283**
muntins, window, **65**
muscle: human, **26**; scallop, **47**
mushroom, **57**
music: accessories, **367**; notation, **352**
music arch, organ, **360**
music desk, grand piano, **361**
music ensemble, **354**
musician, orchestra, **354**
music selection button, compact disc player, **178**
music selection window, compact disc player, **178**
music selector, tape recorder, **177**
music stand, **367**
music wire pliers, **414**
Muslim temple, **70-71**
muslin wrapping, dabber, **377**
mussel, **47**
mustache, **211**
mustard, and frankfurter, **265**
mute, phonograph receiver, **179**
mutton, **33**
muttonchop whiskers, **211**
muzzle: automatic rifle, **471**; bazooka, **472**; cannon barrel, **467**; cat, **37**; cow, **32**; dog, **36**; horse, **38**; mortar, **472**; neck, **267**; revolver, **470**; sheep, **33**; tank gun, **475**
muzzle-loading cannon, **472**
mycelium, mushroom, **57**
mystery gas cloud, Milky Way, **3**

N

N: braille, **512**; sign language, **512**
nacelle, jet fighter, **480**
nail, **410**; bird, **39**; frame, **379**; human hand, **31**
nail cleaner: clippers, **215**; pocket knife, **426**
nail clippers, **215**
nail crease, horseshoe, **38**
nail file, **215**
nail hole, horseshoe, **38**
nail nick: corkscrew, **251**; pocket knife, **426**
nail polish, **217**
nail pulling slot, hatchet, **412**
name: business card, **160**; credit card, **227**; flat racing entry, **336**; label, **268**; letter, **159**; magazine mailing label, **169**; paper money, **225**; passenger ship, **142**; pencil brand, **158**; political map, **20**; résumé, **160**; tugboat, **144**
name column, voting booth, **437**
nameplate: automobile, **107**; can opener, **251**; fireboat, **144**; military uniform, **496**; newspaper, **168**; police uniform, **498**
name tag, soldier's uniform, **497**
nap, tennis ball, **312**
nape: bird, **39**; cat, **37**; human, **25**
napkin, **244**
nare, nose, **30**

narrow deep gouge, woodcarving, 372
narthex, church, 87
naso-labial groove, salamander, 44
native dress, 491
natural, music notation, 352
natural abrasive material, sander, 421
natural key, organ, 360
natural lever, river, 13
nautical chart, 22
nautical terminology, 132
nave, church, 87
navel, human, 24
navigation aerial, tanker, 141
navigational aid, space shuttle, 153
navigational instruments, 747 cockpit, 150, 151
navigation system, aircraft carrier, 478
navigator's station, sailboat, 135
neb: bird, 39; knife, 256
nebula, Milky Way, 2
neck: balloon, 493; bottle, 267, 268; broom, 282; cat, 37; column, 73; ear scope, 448; golf club, 310; guitar, 362; hammer, 412; horse, 38; human, 24, 25; knee kicker, 246; kokoshniki, 70; lamb, 33; lamp, 238; Ping-Pong racket, 321; pommel horse, 307; pot, 373; poultry, 35; saddle, 335; saxophone, 357; suit hangar, 281; sweater, 199; test tube, 447; tooth, 456; tub fiddle, 366; type, 166; undershirt, 194; violin, 355
neckband: ascot, 193; medal, 501; necktie, 192; shirt, 189
neckband label, 268
neck decoration, military uniform, 496
neck developer, body building, 344
neckerchief: cowboy, 490; sailor, 497
neck guard, armor, 465
necklace: Indian, 490; jewelry, 219; Manchu court dress, 491
neckline, woman's sweater, 196
neck roll: ambulance, 123; football uniform, 292
neck sock, drag racing driver, 339
necktie, 192-193; king's regalia, 484
needle: crochet, 386; dental, 455; etching, 377; football, 292; hypodermic, 451; knitting, 386; latch, 386; light meter, 176; mountain, 9; paramedic, 123; phonograph, 178; sewing, 384; sewing machine, 278; spring board, 386
needle-nose pliers, 414
needlepoint, 385
needlework, 386
negative charge, symbol, 510
negative terminal, battery, 397
negative test lead jack, volt-ohm meter, 423
neighbor, teeth, 456
Neptune, planet, 2
Ner Tamid, 88, 486
nerve, human, 29
nerve tissue, human, 29
nervous system, human, 29
nest: pliers, 414; spider, 40
net: aircraft carrier, 478; backyard equipment, 287;

badminton court, 319; basketball backstop, 296; circus aerialist, 90; fishing, 341; ice hockey goal, 294; ice hockey rink, 295; lacrosse, 298; Ping-Pong, 321; playpen, 286; soccer, 297; tennis, 312; volleyball court, 319
net contents, label, 268
netting: lobster pot, 433; woman's hat, 203
netting screen, tent, 342
network, power, 396
neuron, human, 29
neutral corner, boxing ring, 309
neutral terminal, electrical receptacle, 398
neutral wire: electrical receptacle, 398; electrician's, 423
neutral zone: ice hockey rink, 295; shuffleboard court, 318
neutrino, 394
neve, mountain, 9
new balance, monthly statement, 227
new crescent moon, 4
newel post, staircase, 66
newel skirt, escalator, 79
new gibbous moon, 4
new moon, 4
newspaper, 168
nib: auger bit, 419; bird, 39; fountain pen, 158
nichrome wire, toaster, 253
nick: corkscrew, 251; spool, 384; type, 166
nightclub, passenger ship, 142
night scope, bazooka, 472
night sign lamps, blimp, 156
nightstick, police, 498
nimbostratus cloud, 17
90 degree gauge, combination square, 424
90-degree turn, staircase, 66
nine pin, bowling, 317
nipple: eyedropper, 451; human, 24; lamp, 238
nittle, cartoon, 381
N number, hot air balloon, 332
no bicycles, road sign, 504
nock, bow and arrow, 466
node, grass, 58
no entry, public sign, 506
no-frost refrigerator, 249
noggin, human, 25
noise limiter, CB radio, 183
no left turn, road sign, 504
no money, gesture, 507
nonelectric fencing match, 315
non-glacial stream, mountain, 8
non-glaciated valley, 12
non-locking adjustable wrench, 415
non-overflow section dam, 100
non-porous backing, frame, 379
nonprecision approach marking, airport runway, 94
nonrigid lighter-than-air craft, 156
non-skid strip, bath and shower, 274
non-skid surface: diving platform, 316; Jacuzzi, 274
noon, 5
noose: gallows, 462; lasso, 432
no parking, public sign, 506
no-passing zone, road sign, 505
no right turn, road sign, 504
normal/metal tape switch, Walkman, 182
north, compass rose, 22

North Atlantic Drift, ocean, 6
North Equatorial Current, ocean, 6
north fork, river, 13
north latitude, globe, 5
North Pacific Drift, ocean, 6
North Pole pin, globe, 1
north porch, church, 87
north portal, church, 87
north portico, White House, 75
north-south handbag, 222
north tower, church, 87
north transept, church, 87
north wing, Capitol, 74
no-score ring, dart board, 322
nose: cartridge, 470; cat, 37; chain saw guide bar, 431; clown, 493; destroyer, 477; dog, 36; football, 292; human, 24, 30; missile, 482; pliers, 414; racing car, 338; skateboard, 324; surfboard, 330
nose bridge, airport, 94
nose bumper, football helmet, 292
nose cone: blimp, 156; glider, 147; missile, 482; snowmobile, 130
nose doctor, examination equipment, 448
nosegay, bride, 488
nose leather, cat, 37
nose pads, eyeglasses, 221
nosepiece, microscope, 442
nose radome, jet fighter, 480
nose shroud, drag racing driver's fire suit, 339
nose wheel, single engine airplane, 147
nosing, staircase, 66
no smoking, public sign, 506
nostril: alligator, 42; bird, 39; fish, 45; frog, 44; horse, 38; human, 30; snake, 43; tadpole, 44; toad, 44
notation: music, 352; pitch pipe, 367
notch: laboratory scale, 447; mountain, 8; sewing pattern, 388; spool, 384; telephone, 180; woman's jacket lapel, 196
note, music, 352, 353
not equal to, symbol, 511
note position letter and number, paper money, 224, 225
notice: envelope, 159; magazine, 169; sheet music, 353
no trucks, road sign, 504
no U turn, road sign, 504
nozzle: combustion jet engine, 407; faucet, 273; fireboat, 144; fire engine, 124, 125; gas pump, 112; icing syringe, 259; iron, 279; jet fighter, 480; lawn sprinkler, 428; lunar lander, 154; minivacuum, 283; missile, 482; paint spray gun, 425; propane plumber's torch, 422; satellite, 186; sprinkler, 428; vacuum cleaner, 283
nuchal shield, turtle, 43
nuclear envelope, animal cell, 23
nuclear membrane, animal cell, 23
nuclear-powered attack submarine, 479
nuclear-powered ship, 476-477
nuclear power reactor, 392-393
nucleolus, animal cell, 23
nucleus, animal cell, 23
nude heel, panty hose, 195

number: airport runway, 94; baseball uniform, 290; basketball player, 296; bus, 118; check, 226; destroyer, 477; envelope, 159; film slide, 172; football jersey, 292; hot air balloon, 332; laboratory scale, 446; lacrosse uniform, 298; magazine page, 169; mailbox, 231; mainsail, 136; map, 20; painting brush, 371; paper money, 224, 225; pencil, 158; phonograph record, 178; phonograph speaker, 179; police uniform, 498; racing program entry, 336; safe, 457; sealed voting booth, 437; soccer uniform, 297; submarine, 479; surgical table, 450; swimming pool lane, 316; symbol, 511; taxi, 119; telephone, 180; traveler's check, 227
number cloth, flat racing, 336
number entry keys, electronic calculator, 441
number plate: internal combustion engine, 406
number strip, telephone, 180
one bend, paper clip, 277
one leg, paper clip, 277
#1 wood, golf club, 311
two bend, paper clip, 277
two leg, paper clip, 277
#2 wood, golf club, 311
three bend, paper clip, 277
three leg, paper clip, 277
#3 wood, golf club, 311
four leg, paper clip, 277
numerals, pocket watch, 220
numeric keypad: computer workstation, 438; personal computer, 162; synthesizer, 363
numeric pad, cash register, 440
numismatist, 225
nun, religious vestments, 487
nun buoy, nautical chart, 22
nursery course, harness racetrack, 337
nut: automobile, 106; banjo, 362; crossbow, 466; faucet, 273; fire hydrant, 125; food, 55; guitar, 362, 363; hacksaw, 416; hurdle, 304; ice cream cone, 265; jewelry findings, 218; juice extractor, 255; lamp, 238; levigator, 376; monkey wrench, 415; mountain climbing, 334; nuts and bolts, 411; pendulum clock, 233; Ping-Pong net, 321; plane, 420; pliers, 414; radiator, 400; rifle, 471; roller skate, 324; sink drain, 273; tub fiddle, 366; violin and bow, 355
nutcracker, 261
nuts and bolts, 411; magazine article, 170
nyki, torii, 71

O

O: braille, 512; sign language, 512
oar, rowboat, 133
oarlock: inflatable, 133; rowboat, 133
oat, 58
obelisk, 71
object ball, pool table, 320
object beam, holography, 395
objective, microscope, 442; résumé, 160
objective end, theodolite, 436

objective lens: binoculars, **443**; rifle scope, **469**; telescope, **443**

objective outer cell, telescope, **443**

oboe, **354**, **356**

observation car, passenger train, **116**

observation deck, skyscraper, **77**

observation window, tank, **475**

observer station, destroyer, **477**

obstetrician, examination equipment, **448**

obverse side, coin, **225**

occipital lobe, brain, **29**

occiput, dog, **36**

occluded front, weather map, **19**

occlusal surface, tooth, **456**

occultation ultraviolet spectrometer, satellite, **186**

occupation, letter, **159**

ocean, **7**; basin, **15**; currents, **6**

oceanic crust, **15**

ocean liner, **142-143**

ocean minesweeper, **477**

ocellus, grasshopper, **41**

octane number, gasoline, **112**

octant, **137**

octave, piano, **361**

octopus, **46**; fireworks, **383**

oculama, cartoon, **381**

ocularium sight, armor, **465**

ocular lens: binoculars, **443**; rifle scope, **469**

oculus window, house, **62**

odd, gesture, **507**

odds, flat racing entry, **336**

odds board, jai alai cancha, **314**

odometer, car, **110**

oenophile negotiant, wine label, **267**

off-duty sign, taxi, **119**

offer, coupon, **103**

office: frontier fort, **82**; White House, **75**

office index column, voting booth, **437**

office location, letter, **159**

officer: airplane, **481**; police, **498**

officer's braid, military uniform, **496**

officer's lock and seal, voting booth, **437**

officers' quarters, frontier fort, **82**

office typewriter, **161**

office window, airport control tower, **95**

official reporter, Congress, **74**

off position, electrical wall switch, **398**

offset handle, wrench, **415**

offset-lithography, printing, **166**

offset screwdriver, **413**

offshore rig, oil drilling, **101**

off-the-road vehicle, **130**

ogee, cannon barrel, **467**

ogee section, dam, **100**

Ogier, playing card jack, **348**

ohmmeter, symbol, **510**

ohms scale, volt-ohm meter, **423**

oil: beauty product, **217**; painting medium, **370**; sketch box, **371**; woodcarving, **372**

oil buffer, elevator shaft, **78**

oil cap: automobile, engine, **111**; bulldozer, **435**

oil dipstick, engine, **111**, **406**

oil-drain plug, engine, **406**

oil drilling platform, **101**

oil filter, **111**

oil pan, **111**

oil pressure gauge: car, **110**; powerboat, **138**

oil-pump button, chain saw, **431**

oilskin slicker, cowboy, **490**

oil-tank cap, chain saw, **431**

oil water heater, **401**

old crescent moon, **4**

old gibbous moon, **4**

old lava flow, volcano, **10**

old Senate chamber, Capitol, **74**

omission, grammatical symbol, **513**

on and off lever, gas pump, **112**

on and off puck, craps table, **347**

on-deck batter's circle, baseball field, **291**

on-deck bat weight, baseball bat, **290**

1 1/4 mile chute, harness racetrack, **337**

one-arm bandit, **346**

one-button cuff, blouse, **197**

one-cell battery, symbol, **510**

1/8 pole, harness racetrack, **337**

one-eyed jack, playing card, **348**

1/2 pole, harness racetrack, **337**

180-degree turn, staircase, **66**

100-fathom curve, continental shelf, **15**

one pin, bowling, **317**

one-point perspective, **368**

1/4 pole, harness racetrack, **337**

1/16 pole, harness racetrack, **337**

one-unit beads, abacus, **441**

one way, road sign, **504**

one-way traffic, road sign, **504**

on guard line, fencing strip, **315**

onion, **262**, **265**

on-off button: iron, **279**; metal detector, **445**; metronome, **367**; police car, **122**; potter's wheel, **373**; remote control unit, **184**

on-off control, cash register, **440**

on-off switch: belt sander, **421**; camera, **172**; CB radio, **183**; coffee maker, **252**; compact disc player, **178**; curling iron, **214**; dental unit, **454**; electric hairbrush, **212**; electronic calculator, **441**; fax machine, **164**; guitar amplifier, **363**; hair dryer, **212**; lamp, **239**; laser printer, **163**; organ, **360**; phonograph receiver, **179**; portable radio/cassette player, **182**; power saw, **417**; razor, **210**; toaster oven, **253**; video-still camera, **173**

onomatopoeia, cartoon, **380**

on position, electrical wall switch, **398**

on-purchase signature, traveler's check, **227**

on-site bakery department, supermarket, **103**

01 level, destroyer, **477**

opaque background, thermometer, **449**

opaque balustrade, escalator, **79**

open and close: elevator car, **78**; voting booth, **437**

open-breech smoothbore firing tube, bazooka, **472**

open center spiral, staircase, **66**

open coat, sandpaper, **421**

open craft, **133**

open crown, man's hat, **202**

open end, wrench, **415**

opener, kitchen tool, **251**

open hole, bagpipe, **365**

open ID window, checkbook clutch, **223**

opening: eyedropper, **451**; harmonica, **366**; machinist's vise, **408**; pitch pipe, **367**

open outside pocket, shoulder bag, **222**

open rear sight, rifle, **469**

open-toed woman's shoe, **205**

open-top freight car, **116**

opera glasses, **443**

operating button, camera, **172**

operating control, movie projector, **175**

operating lever: fire extinguisher, **284**; jackhammer, **436**

operating nut, fire hydrant, **125**

operating panel, fax machine, **164**

operating rod, machine gun, **471**

operating room table, **450**

operating screw, clamp, **409**

operating table, **450**

operator: computer, **162**; radio, **183**

operator control panel, laser printer, **163**

operators facility, airport control tower, **95**

operculum, fish, **45**

ophthalmoscope, **448**

opisthenar, human hand, **31**

optical landing system, aircraft carrier, **478**

optical sound track, movie film, **174**

optical unit, jet fighter, **480**

optic nerve, eye, **30**

oral arm, jellyfish, **46**

oral surface, starfish, **46**

orange, **55**

orb: human, **25**; royal regalia, **485**; spider web, **40**

orbit, eye, **30**

orbital sander, **421**

orbiter, space shuttle, **152**, **153**

orchestra, **354**; theatre, **351**

orchestra pit, theatre, **351**

order number, paperback book, **167**

organ, **360**; church, **87**; merry-go-round, **93**

organizer, backpack, **343**

original document exit, fax machine, **164**

orle, shield, **464**

ornament: automobile hood, **106**; Beefeater, **483**; church, **86**; dressing table, **272**; earring, **218**; grandfather clock, **233**; running shoe, **302**; scallop shell, **47**; sofa, **236**; tombstone, **516**; trophy, **289**; woman's jacket, **196**

ornamented type, **165**

ornament pedestal, trophy, **289**

ornithischian, dinosaur, **43**

Ortez bar, tow truck bed, **126**

orthodontia, **453**

orthodontic bracket, **453**

oscillating lawn sprinkler, **428**

oscillator: metal detector, **445**; symbol, **510**

otoscope, **448**

Otto cycle internal combustion engine, **406**

ottoman, **235**

02 level, destroyer, **477**

ouch, jewelry, **219**

outboard aileron, jumbo jet, **148**

outboard bracket, inflatable, **133**

outboard elevator, jumbo jet, **149**

outboard engine, **137**

outboard flap, jumbo jet, **148**

outboard planetaries, tractor, **434**

outboard spoiler, jumbo jet, **148**

out-cannel, gouge, **420**

outdoor garden area, supermarket, **103**

outdoor pool, passenger ship, **142**

outer bailey, castle, **80**, **81**

outer canthus, eye, **30**

outer cell, telescope, **443**

outer core, earth, **4**

outer curtain wall, castle, **81**

outer ear, **30**

outer hearth, fireplace, **232**

outer hull, submarine, **479**

outer lip, univalve shell, **47**

outer panel, jet fighter, **480**

outer rim: coconut, **262**; Ferris wheel, **93**

outer ring, embroidery, **385**

outer sash, window, **65**

outer shell, parka, **201**

outer slide brace, trombone, **358**

outer table, backgammon, **345**

outer ward, castle, **80**, **81**

outerwear, **200**

outer wheel, Ferris wheel, **93**

outfield, baseball, **291**

outhaul line, windsurfer, **330**

outlet: dam, **100**; electrical, **398**; fire engine, **125**; kazoo, **366**

outlet nozzle, nuclear reactor, **392**

outline type, **165**

out of bounds: football field, **293**; golf course, **310-311**; jai alai cancha, **314**; squash, **313**

out-of-town prices, newspaper, **168**

output, computer, **163**

output meter, phonograph, **179**

output stacker, laser printer, **163**

outrigger: fire engine, **124**; house, **61**; powerboat, **139**

outseam, jacket, **188**

outside collar, barbell, **344**

outside flap pocket, shoulder bag, **222**

outside guard, theodolite, **436**

outside interests, résumé, **160**

outside knob, door, **458**

outside load bearing wall, house, **60**

outside margin, book page, **167**

outside pole, tepee, **84**

outside rail, harness racetrack, **337**

outside stile, window shutters, **241**

outside speaker selector, police car, **122**

outside wrap, aerial shell, **383**

outsole: boot, **206**; man's shoe, **204**; running shoe, **302**; woman's shoe, **205**

outwash, mountain, **8**

outwork, castle, **80**

oval head, screw, **410**

ovary: cucumber, **54**; flower pistil, **53**

ovary wall, tomato, **54**
oven: stove, **248**; toaster, **253**
oven thermometer, **258**
overcap, disposable razor, **210**
overcoat, **200**; police uniform, **498**
overflow drain, water heater, **401**
overflow pipe, furnace, **400**
overflow plate: bathtub, **274**; Jacuzzi, **274**
overflow section, dam, **100**
overflow tube, toilet, **275**
overflow vent, sink, **273**
overhang: house, **63**; mountain, **9**
overhead, sailboat, **135**
overhead baggage rack, bus, **118**
overhead bin, jumbo jet, **148**
overhead fan, **402**
overhead ladder, backyard equipment, **287**
overhead power line, **396**
overhead switch panel, 747 cockpit, **150**
overlay, coffin, **516**
overload, fuse box, **399**
overload reset button, table saw, **417**
overlook highway, **114**
overpass, highway cloverleaf, **114**
overpressure plug, pressure cooker, **257**
overrun area, airport runway, **94**
overseas bars, military uniform, **496**
overseas cap, military uniform, **496**
overserve line, jai alai cancha, **314**
overshoe, spacesuit, **155**
overskirt, queen's regalia, **484**
ovipositer, grasshopper, **41**
ovule, flower, **53**
owner, racing entry, **336**
owner's head, sailboat, **135**
owner's silks, racing entry, **336**
oxbow lake, river, **13**
oxen, **32**
oxford rule, magazine, **170**
oxter, human, **24**
oxygen, rocket, **407**
oxygen bottle rack, oil drilling platform, **101**
oxygen cylinder, ambulance, **123**
oxygen quantity indicator, pilot's instrument panel, **481**
oxygen tank, ambulance, **123**
oxygen tent, **452**
oxygen umbilical, spacesuit, **155**
oxygen unit, police car, **122**
oyster, **47**

P

P: braille, **512**; sign language, **512**
PA, mountain climbing, **334**
pacemaker, **452**
pacer, harness racing, **337**
Pacific Drift, ocean, **6**
Pacific Time, **5**
pack: backpacking, **343**; glacier, **12**; playing cards, **348**
packaging, **268-269**
packer controls, garbage truck, **127**
packing, faucet, **273**
packing nut: faucet, **273**; radiator, **400**
pad: ballista, **467**; Band-Aid, **451**; baren, **374**; basketball, **296**; bed, **271**; cassette tape,

177; cat, **37**; chaise longue, **288**; child's car seat, **286**; clarinet, **356**; crutch, **452**; dabber, **377**; dental, **455**; dog, **36**; fire engine, **124**; football uniform, **292**; handball glove, **313**; human hand, **31**; ice hockey player, **294**; **295**; kiln, **373**; knee kicker, **246**; launch, **152**; lounger, **235**; medal, **501**; medical examination table, **450**; paint roller, **425**; parallel bars, **306**; phonograph headphone, **179**; playpen, **286**; pommel horse, **307**; rifle, **468**; roller skate, **324**; rug, **246**; running shoe, **302**; saddle, **335**; sandal, **206**; sander, **421**; ski binding, **326**; stirrup, **335**; surgical table, **450**; tank, **475**; telephone, **180**; toboggan, **328**; trampoline, **308**
pad applicators, house painting, **425**
padded turnbuckles, boxing ring, **309**
padding: baseball catcher's mask, **290**; brassiere, **195**; carpet, **246**; fencing shoe, **315**; football goalpost, **293**; hockey skate, **325**; hot air balloon, **332**; playpen, **286**; powerboat, **139**; running shoe, **302**; ski clothes, **326**; woman's jacket, **196**
paddle: glider airbrake, **147**; for potting, **373**; Ping-Pong, **321**
paddock area, harness racetrack, **337**
padlock, **459**
pad pocket, football uniform, **292**
page: book, **iv**, **167**; magazine, **169**
pageboy, woman's hair, **213**
pagoda, **71**
pail, **284**
pail rest, ladder, **425**
pain-killer, paramedic equipment, **123**
paint: Indian, **490**; sketch box, **371**
paint brush, **425**
painter, **370**; rowboat, **133**
painting, **370-371**; merry-go-round, **93**; tools, **425**
paired string, mandolin, **362**
pair of pants, **191**
pajama pants, woman's, **196**
Palas, playing card queen, **348**
palatal arch, denture, **453**
palate, mouth, **30**
pale, wood fence, **67**
palette, sketch box, **371**
palette knife, **370**, **371**
palisade, frontier fort, **82**
pallet, tennis racket, **312**
pallet ship, **140**
palm: anchor, **132**; baseball glove, **397**; handball glove, **313**; human hand, **31**; lacrosse glove, **298**; tree, **52**
palm tree, fireworks, **383**
palpus, grasshopper, **41**
pan: air conditioner, **402**; automobile, **109**, **111**; bear trap, **433**; candelabrum, **237**; chafing dish, **245**; dustpan, **282**; kitchen, **257**; potter's wheel, **373**; roulette wheel, **346**
panagraph gate, subway motorman's cab, **119**

pancake makeup, **216**
pancake turner, **259**
pancreas, human, **27**
pane: postage stamps, **159**; window, **65**
panel: air conditioner, **402**; automobile, **106**, **107**, **109**; book page, **iv**; bureau, **272**; bus, **118**; cartoon, **39**; clothes dryer, **516**; coffin, **516**; cupboard door, **243**; curtain, **240**; desk, **276**; dishwasher, **250**; door, **64**; elevator car, **78**; football, **292**; football down marker, **293**; garbage disposal, **247**; girdle, **195**; hot air balloon, **332**; humidifier, **402**; jacket, **188**; jet fighter, **480**; lounger, **235**; mainsail, **136**; man's belt, **190**; mower, **429**; package, **268**; piano, **361**; pilot's instruments, **481**; satellite, **186**; saddle, **335**; 747 cockpit, **150**; sideboard, **243**; snowmobile, **130**; solar collector, **391**; stagecoach, **131**; steamer basket, **257**; subway car, **119**; tape recorder, **177**; toaster, **253**; tractor, **434**; trophy, **289**; umbrella, **230**; window shutter, **241**
panel assembly, football field, **293**
panel painting, merry-go-round, **93**
panier cases, motorcycle, **129**
pan lock, camera tripod, **176**
pantaloons, queen's underpinnings, **484**
pants, **191**; baseball batter, **290**; clown, **493**; combat soldier, **497**; football, **292**; ice hockey, **295**; skiing, **326**; skin diving, **331**; woman's, **196**; see also trousers
panty hose, **195**
Papal cross, symbol, **508**
paper: cigarette, **228**; copper foil backing, **378**; electrician's wire, **423**; hair styling, **214**; medical examination table, **450**; printing, **166**; silkscreen, **375**
paperback book, **167**
paper bag, **266**
paper bail, typewriter, **161**
paper clamp, finishing sander, **421**
paper clip, **277**
paper feed cassette, copier, **164**
paper guide, typewriter, **161**
paper handler, high-speed printer, **163**
paper money, **224-225**
paper release lever, dot matrix printer, **163**
paper roll compartment: fax machine, **164**; sealed voting booth, **437**
paper size indicator, laser printer, **163**
paper tape, cash register, **440**
papillary muscle, heart, **28**
papillote, poultry, **263**
parabolic mirror, physician's, **448**
parachute, **333**; silo, **104**; spider, **40**
parachute canister, space shuttle, **152**
parachute vent, hot air balloon, **332**
parachutist's badge, military uniform, **496**
parade: circus, **90**; fort, **83**
parade ground, fort, **82**, **83**

paraffin, candle, **237**
paragraph, proofreader's mark, **514**
parallel, staircase, **66**
parallel bars, **306**
parallel of latitude, **5**
parallel tracks, railroad yard, **96**
parallel-veined leaves, grass, **58**
paramedic equipment, **123**
parapet: castle, **80**, **81**; fort, **82**, **83**; house, **62**
parfait, dessert, **264**
parietal lobe, brain, **29**
parimutual betting, jai alai, **314**
park: amusement, **92-93**; road map, **20**
parka, **201**
parking, public sign, **506**
parking brake lever, 747 cockpit, **150**
parking light, truck tractor, **120**
parking lot, airport, **94**, **95**
parking meter, **113**
parking stand, hitch and harrow, **434**
parliamentarian, Congress, **74**
parlor, lobster pot, **433**
parocheth, Torah, **486**
parotoid gland, toad, **44**
parsley, and poultry, **263**
part: man's hair, **211**; poultry, **35**
partial denture, **453**
partial reflector, laser, **395**
particle accelerator, **394**
parting strip, window, **65**
parting tool, woodcarving, **372**
partisan, medieval weapon, **464**
partition: backpack, **343**; dishwasher, **250**; house, **60**
partly cloudy, weather map, **19**
partner, teeth, **456**
partner box, handball, **313**
parure: jewelry, **218**; king's regalia, **484**
pash, human, **25**
pasigraphy, **506**
pass, mountain, **8**
passage, barn, **104**
pass case, wallet, **223**
passenger cabin: hovercraft, **145**; hydrofoil, **145**
passenger car, train, **117**
passenger concourse, airport, **94**
passenger deck, ship, **143**
passenger grab strap, motorcycle, **129**
passenger loading bridge, airport, **94**
passenger ship **142-143**
passenger sideview mirror, automobile, **106**
passenger steps, Hansom cab, **131**
passenger terminal building, airport, **95**
passenger train, **116**
passe-partout, **379**
passive satellite, **186**
pass line: craps table, **347**; jai alai cancha, **314**
pastern: cow, **32**; dog, **36**; horse, **38**; sheep, **33**
past history, symbol, **510**
pastoral staff, cardinal, **487**
pastry, **264**
pastry blender, **261**
pastry brush, **259**
pastry pin, **259**

pastry wheel, 261
patch: label, 269; military uniform, 496, 497; paper bag, 266; police uniform, 498; running shoe, 302
patch pocket: cardigan, 199; woman's jacket, 196
patchwork quilting, 385
pate, human, 25
patella: human, 26; spider, 40
paten, for Communion bread, 87
path, golf course, 310
patient's address, prescription, 451
patient's name, prescription, 451
patio, 63; accessories, 288
Patriarchal cross, symbol, 508
patrol, police, 498
patrol hydrofoil, 477
patrolman, police, 498
pattern: sewing, 400; stained glass, 378; table setting, 245; wind, 6
patterned indented surface, thimble, 384
pattern scale, sewing machine, 276
pauldron, armor, 465
pause button: remote control unit, 184; tape recorder, 177
pavement light, church, 87
pavilion: cut gemstone, 218; minaret, 70
pavise, medieval shield, 464
paw: cat 37; dog, 36; human, 25; ultimate beast, 48
pawl: brace, 418; saw, 416, 417
pawn, chess, 345
payee: check, 226; traveler's check, 227
paying agent, traveler's check, 227
payload, missile, 482
payload changeout room, launch pad, 152
payload pallet, lunar rover, 155
payload specialist, space shuttle, 153
payment address, monthly statement, 227
payment information, monthly statement, 227
payoff chart, slot machine, 346
payoff return, slot machine, 346
pay phone, 180
pay up, gesture, 507
pea, 54; anchor, 132
peace, symbol, 511
peach, 55
peacock-feather tassel, Manchu court dress, 491
peak: bonnet, 203; glacier, 12; house, 61, 63; man's cap, 202; mountain, 7
pearl: cave, 11; royal crown, 485
pebble finish, football, 292
pectoral cross, bishop, 487
pectoral fin: fish, 45; stingray, 45
pectoralis major, human, 26
ped, 210
pedal: brass drum, 364; bicycle, 128; bulldozer, 435; car, 110; dental unit, 454; organ, 360; piano, 361; potter's wheel, 373; 747 cockpit, 150; starting block, 304; surgical table, 450; vacuum cleaner, 283
petal lip, mousetrap, 433
pedestal: animal tamer, 90; column, 73; computer workstation, 438; desk, 276;

diving board, 316; dressing table, 272; House of Representatives, 74; obelisk, 71; surgical table, 450; television, 185; trophy, 289
pedestal table, 242
pedestrian crossing, road sign, 505
pedestrian safety mirror, mechanical sweeper, 127
pedicel: flower, 53; grass, 58; spider, 40
pedipalpi, spider, 40
peduncle, flower, 53
peel, fruit, 55
peeler, 256, 261
peen, hammer, 412
peephole: door, 64; kiln, 373
peg: banjo, 362; croquet, 318; dulcimer, 362; guitar, 362, 363; sitar, 362; tent, 342; tepee, 84; violin, 355
pegbox, violin, 355
pellet: dental, 455; shotgun, 468
pelota, jai alai, 314
pelt, 201
pelvic fin, fish, 45
pelvic region, salamander, 44
pelvis: allosaurus, 43; stegosaurus, 43
pen: barnyard, 104; writing tool, 158
penalty area, soccer field, 297
penalty box: ice hockey rink, 295
penalty kick mark, soccer field, 297
penalty spot: polo grounds, 299; soccer field, 297
pen blade, pocket knife, 426
pencil: beauty product, 217; lithographic, 376; styptic, 210; writing tool, 158
pencil sharpener, 277
pendant: aircraft carrier, 478; Indian, 490; jewelry, 219; queen's regalia, 484
pendant pearl, royal crown, 485
pendentive, mosque, 71
pendulum: clock, 233; metronome, 367
pen holder: checkbook clutch, 223; police gun belt, 499
penhold grip, Ping-Pong, 321
pen loop, checkbook clutch, 223
pennant, 502; circus tent, 91
pennon, lance, 464
penny size, nail, 410
penstock control, dam, 100
Pentateuch, Torah, 88
pentathlon, track and field, 300
penthouse, barn, 104
pent roof, pagoda, 71
peonies, fireworks, 383
people-mover, 79
peplum, dress, 198
pepper, raw, 262
peppercorn, 262
pepper mill, 261
pepperoni, pizza, 265
per, symbol, 511
perambulator, 286
percent key, electronic calculator, 441
percolator, 252
percussion, orchestra, 354
perfection, gesture, 507
perforated panel, steamer basket, 257
perforated spreader, percolator brewing basket, 252
perforation: envelope, 159; foil pouch, 269; hair roller, 214;

man's shoe, 204; movie film, 174; stamp, 159
performance hall, theatre, 351
performance instruction, music, 352
performing rights organization, music, 353
perfume, 217
per hundred, symbol, 511
periapical dental x-ray unit, 454
pericarp, pea, 54
period: grammatical symbol, 513; wave, 14
periodical, 169
periople, horse's hoof, 38
periscope: submarine, 479; tank, 475
perishables, supermarket, 102
permanent current, ocean, 6
permanent end-of-aisle display, supermarket, 102
permanent fort, 83
permanent lotion, hair styling, 214
permanent rod, hair styling, 214
permanent teeth, 456
per mill, symbol, 511
peroneal artery, human, 28
peroxide, human, 123
personal cassette player/radio, 182
personal choice, voting booth, 437
personal computer, 162
personal foul, lacrosse, 298
personal identification number, ATM card, 226
personnel safety net, aircraft carrier, 478
perspective, and composition, 368
per thousand, symbol, 511
Peru Current, ocean, 6
pestle, kitchen tool, 261
petal, flower, 53
petiole: celery, 262; fern, 57; leaf, 52
petitpoint, stitchery, 385
petticoat, windmill, 390
pew, synagogue, 88
phalanges, human, 26, 31
pharmacy, supermarket, 102
pharynx, mouth, 30
phase of moon, 4
pheasant, 35
Phillips head, screw, 410
Phillips head screwdriver, pocket knife, 426
Phillips head tip, screwdriver, 413
philtrum, face, 30
phloem, tree, 50
Phoenix missile, jet fighter, 480
phone, 180
phone number, business card, 160
phonetic symbol, grammatical, 513
phonogram, public sign, 506
photo, magazine, 169, 170
photo and card case, wallet, 223
photocell, Polaroid, 173
photograph, book jacket, 167
photographic accessories, 176
photo holder, wallet, 223
phyllacteries, Jewish ritual items, 486
physician's address, prescription, 451
physician's mirror, 448
physician's name, prescription, 451
physician's phone number, prescription, 451

physician's room, White House, 75
physician's signature, prescription, 451
pi, symbol, 511
pianissimo, music notation, 353
piano, 361; music notation, 352
piano-accordion, 366
piano frame, 379
piccolo, 354, 356
pick: figure skates, 325; ice ax, 334; ice hammer, 334; pipe tool, 229; stringed instrument, 362
picket fence, 63, 67
pick guard, guitar, 362, 363
pick-up, guitar, 363
pick-up arm, fishing reel, 340
pick-up broom, mechanical sweeper, 127
pick-up selector, guitar, 363
picnic area: public sign, 506; road sign, 504
picnic shoulder, pork, 34
pictograph, public sign, 506
picture card, 348
picture exit slot, Polaroid, 173
picture frame, 379
picture hat, 203; bride's, 488
picture hook, 379
picture-in-picture viewing, 185
picture protection hood, Polaroid, 173
picture tube, television, 185
pie, 264
piece: backgammon, 345; cake, 264; chess, 345; coin, 225; crutch, 452; jewelry, 219; kite, 323; rifle, 471; slalom water ski, 329
piece goods, fabric, 388
pier: arch, 72; bridge, 97; dam, 100; house, 60; nautical chart, 22; skyscraper, 77
pierced ear findings, 218
piercer, can opener, 251
pierum assembly, nuclear reactor, 392
pig, 34
pig board, windsurfer, 330
pigboat, 479
piggin, container, 266
piggy bank, 457
pigment cell, octopus, 46
pigment filling, scrimshaw, 375
pigpen, 104
pigtail, woman's hair, 213
pike, lance, 464
pike pole, fireman, 500
pilaster: cupboard, 243; house, 62
pile: arrow, 484; carpet, 246; nuclear, 392; skyscraper, 77; Velcro, 209
pileus, mushroom, 57
pill, medicinal, 451
pillar: arch, 72; automobile windshield, 109; house, 62; mountain, 9; and obelisk, 70; torii, 71
pillbox, woman's hat, 203
pillow: bedding, 270; coffin, 516; lounger, 235; police car, 122; rocking chair, 234; sofa, 236; stagecoach, 131
pilot: airplane, 481; locomotive, 116
pilot boarding ladder, tugboat, 144
pilot chute, 333
pilot hole, screw, 410
pilothouse: fireboat, 144; tugboat, 144
pilot light: guitar amplifier, 363; stove, 248
pilot's seat, space shuttle, 153

pilot-wheel feed, drill press, **419**

pin: anchor, **132**; attachment plug, **398**; bowling, **317**; can opener, **251**; and carpet, **246**; compass, **136**; fastener, **208**; fire extinguisher, **284**; fluorescent bulb, **238**; gallows, **462**; gardening shears, **427**; globe, **1**; golf course, **311**; hacksaw, **416**; hair, **214**; hand grenade, **473**; hasp, **460**; jewelry, **219**; kitchen utensil, **259**; lock cylinder, **459**; mortar, **472**; nail clippers, **215**; pliers, **414**; potter's wheel, **373**; pulley block, **461**; revolver safety catch, **218**; rifle, **468**, **469**; roller chain, **461**; roller skate, **324**; sewing machine, **278**; stapler, **277**; starting block, **304**; stroller, **286**; tepee, **84**; track link, **474**; vacuum tube, **396**; window shade roller, **241**; woman's hat, **203**

pin binding, ski, **327**

pinbone, cow, **32**

pincer, lobster, **47**

pinch, man's hat, **202**

pinch roller, tape recorder, **177**

pinch valve, dental unit, **454**

pin connector, video-still camera adaptor, **173**

pincushion, **384**

pineapple, **55**; grenade, **473**

pine cone, **52**

Ping-Pong, **321**

pin hinge, stove, **404**

pinion, hand drill, **418**

pinkie, human hand, **31**

pinky ring, trumpet, **359**

pin link plate, roller chain, **461**

pin mark, type, **166**

pinna, **30**; fern, **57**

pinnacle: church, **86**; mountain, **9**

pinnule, fern, **57**

PIN number, ATM card, **226**

pin rail, stage, **350**

pinsetter, bowling, **317**

pinspotter, bowling, **317**

pintle, hinge, **460**

pintle mount, machine gun, **471**

pin-tumbler, lock cylinder, **459**

pinwood, clothespin, **280**

pip: apple, **55**; backgammon board, **345**; dice, **347**; domino, **345**; pineapple, **55**; playing card, **348**

pip card, **348**

pipe: automobile, **108**; bagpipe, **365**; furnace, **400**; heat exchanger, **403**; lamp, **238**; levigator, **376**; locomotive, **116**; motorcycle, **129**; oil drilling platform, **101**; organ, **360**; pitch, **367**; plumbing, **422**; pressure cooker, **257**; silo, **104**; smoking, **229**; solar heating system, **391**; space shuttle, **152**; standpipe, **59**; steam engine, **405**; steel chain fence gate, **67**; super collider, **394**; tank **474**; trumpet, **359**; water heater, **401**

pipe batten, stage, **350**

pipe cleaner, **229**

pipe cutter, plumbing, **422**

pipe-holding jaw, vise, **409**

pipeline, wave, **14**

pipe nozzle, fire engine, **124**

piper, bagpipe, **365**

pipe standard, parking meter, **113**

pipe threader, **422**

pipe tool, **229**

pipe umbrella, **229**

pipe wrench, plumbing, **422**

piping: baseball uniform, **290**; bishop's cope, **487**; boot, **206**; handball glove, **313**; jacket, **188**; man's belt, **190**; shoulder bag, **222**; woman's shoe, **205**

pipkin, **257**

pirate, costume, **492**

Pisces, zodiac, **509**

piste, fencing, **315**

pistil, flower, **53**

pistol, **470**; lobster, **47**; pirate, **492**

pistol belt, soldier, **497**

pistol grip: hacksaw, **416**; rifle, **471**; shotgun, **468**

pistol nozzle, **428**

pistol port, tank, **474**

piston: garbage truck, **127**; dispenser, **267**; organ, **360**; parallel bars, **306**; pommel horse, **316**; steam engine, **405**

piston displacement, chain saw, **431**

piston rod, steam engine, **405**

pit: barnyard, **104**; bowling lane, **317**; high jump, **305**; peach, **55**; pole vault, **305**; snake, **42**; theatre, **351**

pitch: plane blade, **420**; screw, **410**; soccer, **297**

pitch-control dial, tape recorder, **177**

pitcher's mound, baseball field, **291**

pitcher's rubber, baseball field, **291**

pitching wedge, golf club, **310**

pitch pipe, **367**

pitch trim, 747 cockpit, **151**

pitch wheel, synthesizer, **363**

pitmans, steam engine, **405**

piton, mountain climbing, **334**

pitot tube, jet fighter, **480**

pituitary gland, human, **29**

pivot: basketball, **296**; clamp, **409**; compass, **136**; dressing table mirror, **272**; jet fighter wing, **480**; laboratory, scale, **447**; metronome, **367**; mortar, **472**; pliers, **414**; roller skate, **428**; scissors, **384**; ski binding, **326**; wire stripper, **423**

pivot bolt, bicycle caliper brake, **128**

pivot gear housing, mechanical sweeper, **127**

pivot hinge, **460**

pivot pin: can opener, **251**; hinge, **460**

pivot point, bicycle caliper brake, **128**

pix, church, **87**

pizza, **265**

pizzicato, stringed instruments, **355**

place, flat racing, **336**

place bets, craps table, **347**

placenta, human, **54**

place setting, **244**

placket: blouse, **197**; parka, **201**; shirt, **189**

plain, **7**, **8**, **15**

plaintiff's table, courtroom, **89**

plait, woman's hair, **213**

plan: church, **87**; White House, **75**

planchet, coin, **225**

plane, **420**; monorail, **424**; perspective, **368**

plane iron, **420**

plane kite, **323**

plane surface, printing, **166**

planet, **2**, **3**

planetary, tractor, **434**

planetoid, **2**

planing hull, powerboat, **138**

plank, lumber, **68**

planographic printing, **376**

plant power network, **396**

plantar arch, human foot, **31**

Plantin typeface, **165**

planting box, pole vault, **305**

planting machine, **434**

planting pit, pole vault, **305**

plaque: identification bracelet, **187**; man's belt buckle, **190**; pyrometric cone, **373**

plasma membrane, animal cell, **23**

plasma science, satellite, **186**

plastic board, circuit board, **439**

plastic cap, stapler, **277**

plastic disc, harness racing sulky, **337**

plastic fruit, woman's hat, **203**

plastic lining, man's hat, **202**

plastic sheath, electrician's wire, **423**

plastic squeeze, bottle, **268**

plasti-shield, bottle, **269**

plastron: drum major's coat, **495**; fencing, **315**; turtle, **43**

plate: armor, **465**; automatic weapon, **471**; barbell, **344**; baseball field, **291**; baseball pitcher's spikes, **290**; bathtub, **274**; blackjack, **347**; beef, **32**; bicycle, **245**; chain lock, **458**; crossbow, **466**; escalator, **79**; flute, **356**; food mill, **260**; furnace, **400**; hasp, **460**; horizontal bar, **306**; house, **61**; identification bracelet, **187**; intaglio, **377**; internal combustion engine, **406**; iron, **279**; kitchen sink, **247**; laboratory scale, **446**; land mine, **473**; lithographic, **376**; locomotive, **116**; mandolin, **362**; mortise lock, **458**; onion, **54**; outboard engine, **137**; paper money, **224**; parking meter, **113**; pliers, **414**; pulley block, **461**; racing car, **338**; railroad track, **115**; rifle, **468**; roller chain, **461**; roller skate, **324**; safe, **457**; sewing machine, **278**; shotgun butt, **468**; ski binding, **326**; slalom water ski, **329**; solar collector panel, **391**; space shuttle, **152**; sponge mop, **282**; stage, **350**; standpipe, **59**; stationary rings, **307**; sundial, **389**; table setting, **244**, **245**; tank, **474**, **475**; theodolite, **436**; toaster, **253**; tow truck, **126**; tractor, **434**; trophy, **289**; typewriter, **161**; vacuum tube, **396**; vise, **408**

plate number: envelope, **159**; paper money, **225**

plate vial, theodolite, **436**

plateau, **7**

plate cylinder, printing, **166**

platen, typewriter, **161**

platform: aircraft carrier, **478**; camera tripod, **176**; circus aerialist, **90**; diving, **316**; elevator shaft, **78**; fire engine, **124**; helicopter, **146**; iceberg, **12**; lunar lander, **154**; merry-go-round, **93**; powerboat, **139**; slide, **287**; space shuttle, **152**; stage,

350; swimming pool, **316**; truck, **121**

platform car, train, **117**

platform shoe, woman's, **214**

platform tower, slide, **287**

platter, phonograph, **178**

playback control, video-still camera adaptor, **173**

playback unit, **184**; tape recorder, **177**; video-still camera, **173**

play button: answering machine, **181**; compact disc player, **178**; remote control unit, **184**; tape recorder, **177**; Walkman, **182**

player: basketball, **296**; ice hockey, **295**; jai alai cancha, **314**; lacrosse, **298**; orchestra, **354**; polo, **299**; soccer, **297**

player number, football uniform, **292**

playground: equipment, **287**; public signs, **506**

playing cards, **348**

playing surface, pool table, **320**

playpen, child's, **286**

playroom, passenger ship, **143**

plaza, skyscraper, **77**

pleat: ballet slippers, **494**; curtain, **240**; lounger, **235**; shirt, **189**; woman's pants, **196**

pleated pants, woman's, **196**

pleated ruffled shirt, man's, **488**

plectrum, stringed instrument, **362**

plenum assembly, nuclear reactor, **405**

plewd, cartoon, **381**

plexus, human, **25**

pliers, **414**; dental, **455**; stained glass, **378**

Plimsoll mark, symbol, **511**

plinth: column, **73**; grandfather clock, **233**

plot, grave, **516**

plow, **434**; can opener, **251**

plow anchor, sailboat, **134**

plug: ballpoint pen, **158**; electric, **398**; fishing, **341**; internal combustion engine, **406**; kiln, **373**; lawn sprinkler, **428**; locomotive boiler, **116**; mortise lock, **458**; movie projector, **175**; mower, **429**; padlock, **459**; paint spray gun, **425**; percolator, **252**; pots and pans, **257**; rocket, **383**; vacuum tube, **396**

plug body, phonograph headphone, **179**

plug fuse, **399**

plum, cowboy bullet, **490**

plumb, transit, **436**

plumber's friend, **422**

plumbing tool, **422**

plumb vial, carpenter's level, **424**

plume: armor, **465**; drum major's busby, **495**

plunge pool, dam, **100**

plunger: coffee maker, **252**; hypodermic syringe, **451**; juice extractor, **255**; plumbing tool, **422**; telephone, **180**; torpedo, **479**

plunger handle, camp stove, **342**

plunger snap lock, starting block, **304**

plunge step, shoreline, **14**

plus, symbol, **510**

plus or minus, symbol, **510**

Pluto, planet, **2**

pneumatic liner system, football helmet, 292
pneumoscopy port, ear scope, 448
pocket: backpack, 343; baseball glove, 291; bowling, 337; briefcase, 285; cardigan sweater, 199; cowboy, 490; football uniform, 292; golf bag, 311; handbag, 222; jacket, 188; lacrosse stick, 298; mainsail, 136; necktie, 193; parka, 201; pool table, 320; shirt, 189; skin diving gear, 331; skirt, 197; spacesuit, 155; trench coat, 200; trousers, 191; wallet, 223; woman's jacket and pants, 196; window shade, 241
pocket billiard table, 320
pocketbook, 222
pocket flap, backpack, 343
pocketknife, 426
pocket watch, 220
pod: jumbo jet engine, 149; pea, 54; racing car, 338
podium, symphony orchestra, 354
pogonotomy, 211
pogonotrophy, 211
point: arrow, 466; backgammon board, 345; ballpoint pen, 158; billiard cue, 320; chicken comb, 35; clown's hat, 493; dart, 322; drill bit, 419; etching needle, 377; fencing foil, 315; fish hook, 341; grammatical symbol, 513; hockey skate, 325; ice climbing boot, 334; jai alai cesta, 314; javelin, 302; knife, 256, 463; knitting needle, 386; laboratory scale, 446; land, 7; mainsail, 136; nail, 410; needle, 384; pencil, 158; pin, 208; rasp, 420; river, 13; saw tooth, 416; screw, 410; sharpening steel, 256; star fort, 83; sword, 463; tack, 410; violin bow, 355; weather vane, 19; wrench, 415; wrought iron fence, 67
point chisel, stonecutting, 372
point d'appliqué, bridal gown, 488
point defense missile launcher, aircraft carrier, 478
pointed waist, queen's regalia, 484
pointer: barometer, 18; comic strip, 381; laboratory scale, 447; Torah, 486; volt-ohm meter, 423; weather vane, 19
pointillism and texture, composition, 369
point of entry, darts, 322
point of hip, horse, 38
point of hock, horse, 38
point of interest, city plan, 20
point of shoulder, horse, 38
point ring, darts, 322
point size, type, 166
point symbol, political map, 21
poise, laboratory scale, 446
poison, symbol, 511
poisonous snake, 42
poker, fire iron, 232
polarity symbol, battery, 397
Polaroid, 173
pole: baseball field, 291; bumper car, 92; circus tent, 91; football field, 293; globe, 5; harness racetrack, 337; overhead power line, 396; pole vaulting, 305; powerboat, 139; skiing, 326;

327; stagecoach, 131; tent, 342; tepee, 84
pole arms, medieval, 464
pole grip, ski pole, 326
pole mount, fishing reel, 340
pole position, flat racing, 336
pole vault, 300, 305
poleyn, armor, 465
police car, 122
policeman's suspenders, 190
police officer, 498-499
polish, beauty product, 217
polisher, pipe cutter, 422
political boundary, map, 5, 20
political capital symbol, map, 20
political cartoon, 380
political map, 20-21
poll(s): ax, 464; cow, 32; hammer, 412; horse, 38; pig, 34; voting, 437
pollen, flower, 53
pollen basket, bee, 41
poll end, windmill, 390
pollen sac, flower stamen, 53
polling place, 437
polliwog, 44
pollution control valve, automobile engine, 111
polo, 299
polo & exercise bandage, polo, 299
polo grounds, 299
poly bag, packaging, 269
polygonal base, minaret, 70
polygonal tower, architecture, 71
polyp, coral, 46
pommel: foil mounting, 315; knife, 463; pommel horse, 307; saddle, 335; sword hilt, 463
pommel horse, 307
pompom, ski hat, 327
poncho, infantryman's uniform, 497
pond, topographic map, 22
pons, brain, 29
pontic, dental bridge, 453
pontoon, single engine airplane, 147
pontoon bridge, 97
ponytail, woman's hair, 213
pool, 320; canal lock, 99; cave, 11; dam, 100; passenger ship, 142, 143; swimming, 316
pool table, 320
popcorn, cave, 11
pop-up stopper, sink, 273
porcelain, dental, 455
porch: church, 87; house, 63
porcupine, ultimate beast, 48
pork, 34
port: drag racing driver's fire suit, 339; ear scope, 448; movie projector, 175; outboard; engine, 137; passenger ship, 142; rocket, 407; saber saw, 417; sailboat, 134; tank, 474
portable electrocardiogram, paramedic equipment, 123
portable life support system, spacesuit, 155
portable radio/cassette player, 182
portable telemetry radio, paramedic equipment, 123
portable typewriter, 161
portable word processor, 162
portal: church, 86-87; stage, 350, 351; underwater tunnel, 98
portcullis, castle, 81
port-engine clutch, powerboat, 138
portfolio, briefcase, 285

porthole, passenger ship, 142
portico: Capitol, 74; White House, 75
portlight: powerboat, 138; sailboat, 134
port quarter, boat, 132
portrait: money, 225; White House, 75
port side, boat, 132
port throttle, powerboat, 138
position: business card, 160; flat racing, 336; globe, 5
position indicator: elevator car, 78; 747 cockpit, 150; sonar, 444
positioning arm, dental unit, 454
positioning ratchet, chaise longue, 288
positioning scale, typewriter, 161
position letter, paper money, 224, 225
position light, jet fighter, 480
position lines, jai alai cancha, 314
position mark, guitar, 362
position number, paper money, 224
positive charge, symbol, 510
positive terminal, battery, 397
positive test lead jack, volt-ohm meter, 423
possession player, lacrosse, 298
post: battery, 397; bear trap, 433; bed, 270; bicycle, 128; boxing ring, 309; bureau, 272; camera tripod, 176; candelabrum, 237; fence, 67; guillotine, 462; hand loom, 387; hang glider, 333; house, 60, 61; jewelry findings, 218; kettledrum, 364; laboratory scale, 447; mailbox, 231; Ping-Pong net, 321; railroad crossing signal, 115; rocking chair, 234; snap fastener, 208; tanker, 141; tatting shuttle, 386; toilet, 275; typewriter guide, 161; wind turbine, 390
postage due notice, envelope, 159
post cap, railroad crossing signal, 115
poster arm, gas pump, 112
poster frame, garbage truck, 127
posterior chamber, eye, 30
posterior tibial nerve, human, 29
post footing, house, 60
posthole, fence, 67
post lamp, house, 63
postmark, envelope, 159
post-mounted arm, dental unit, 454
post office, Capitol, 74; supermarket, 102
post position: flat racing, 336; jai alai player, 314
postscript, letter, 159
pot, 373; combat soldier's helmet, 497; kitchen, 257; percolator, 252; tea set, 245
potato, 54; masher, 259; peeler, 261
pot fork, 259
pot holder, house painting, 425
potter's wheel, 373
pouch: athletic supporter, 194; combat soldier's uniform, 497; package, 268, 269; police gun belt, 498; tobacco, 259; ultimate beast, 48

pouf, footstool, 235
poult, turkey, 35
poultry, 35, 263
pound, symbol, 511
pound button, telephone, 180
pound lock, 99
pouring lip, blender, 254
pour spout, package, 268
powder: fortification, 82; makeup, 216, 217
powdered emery, nail file, 215
powder eye shadow, 217
power, steam engine, 405
powerboat, 138-139
power bore bit, drill, 418
power button: remote control unit, 184; tape recorder, 177; VCR, 184
power cable, police car, 122
power control: sonar, 444; space shuttle, 153
power cord: air conditioner, 402; camper, 130; curling iron, 214; lamp, 238; tape recorder, 177
power display, portable radio/cassette player, 182
power drill, 419
power feed, track lighting, 239
power handle, ear scope, 448
power head, chain saw, 431
powerhouse: dam, 100; prison, 76
power indicator, CB radio, 183
power key, television, 185
power knob, phonograph receiver, 179
power lawn mower, 429
power light, dot matrix printer, 163
power line, overhead, 396
power network, 396
power on indicator, phonograph turntable, 178
power output meter, phonograph receiver, 179
power pedal, surgical table, 450
power saw, 417
power station, dam, 100
power status, space shuttle, 153
power steering, automobile engine, 111
power supply module, cash register, 440
power switch: fax machine, 164; laser printer, 163; radar, 444
power takeoff, tractor, 434
power terminal, electrical wall switch, 344
power train, automobile, 108
power twister, body building, 344
power window control, car, 110
power-zoom control, camera, 174
prayer book, Jewish, 486
prayer hall, mosque, 70-71
prayer shawl, Jewish, 486
prayer vestment, Jewish, 486
pre-amp, phonograph, 179
preamplifier, guitar, 363
precautionary statement, label, 268
precinct number, police uniform, 498
precious miter, cardinal, 487
precipitation gauge, weather station, 18
precision approach marking, runway, 94
precision attachment, denture, 453
prediction, weather map, 19
prefix letter, paper money, 225

preheater hose, automobile engine, 111
prehensile lobe, ultimate beast, 49
preliminaries, book, 167
premolar, 456
preparation utensils, cooking, 259
prepared foods, 263
prepercle, fish, 45
pre-prepared food, supermarket, 102
pre-race betting odds, flat racing entry, 336
presbytery, church, 87
prescription, 451
prescription, symbol, 510
prescription number, prescription, 451
presentation mode selector, sonar, 444
preset, organ, 360
president: fencing match, 315; Senate, 74
President's executive office, White House, 75
President's living quarters, White House, 75
press: curling iron, 21; etching, 377; incandescent bulb, 238; kitchen tool, 261; lithographic, 376; printing, 166; universal gym, 344
presser, pipe tool, 229
presser foot, sewing machine, 278
presser plate, sponge mop, 282
pressure, weather map, 19
pressure altimeter, pilot's instrument panel, 481
pressure brush, house painting, 425
pressure cooker, 257
pressure cup, citrus juicer, 255
pressure cuff, blood pressure gauge, 449
pressure dial, sewing machine presser foot, 278
pressure gauge: fire extinguisher, 284; furnace, 400; gas laser, 395; skin diving, 331; steam engine, 405
pressure hull, submarine, 479
pressure indicator, pilot's instrument panel, 481
pressure pad, cassette tape, 177
pressure plate: key punch, 430; land mine, 473
pressure ratio gauge, 747 cockpit, 150
pressure regulator: pressure cooker, 257; steam engine, 405; water heater, 401
pressure relief valve: tanker, 140, 141; water heater, 401
pressure screw, etching press, 377
pressure sensor, weather station, 18
pressurized helmet, spacesuit, 155
pressurizer, nuclear reactor, 392
pre-starting light, drag racing, 339
preview, magazine, 169
price: book, 167; gas pump, 112; magazine, 169; newspaper, 168; ticket, 349
priced at, symbol, 511
price scanner, checkout counter, 103
price spot, label, 269
pricket, candlestick, 237
primary, bird, 39

primary cable, overhead power line, 396
primary cell: battery, 397; electric meter, 399
primary combination dial, vault, 457
primary combustion chamber, woodburning stove, 404
primary mirror, laser, 395
primary root, 51
primary selector control, sealed voting booth, 437
prime, grammatical symbol, 513
prime meridian, 5
primer: cartridge, 470; hand grenade, 473; painting, 370; rocket, 383
primer control, mower, 429
prime ribs, beef, 32
Prince of Wales handle, umbrella, 230
princess waistline, bridal gown, 488
principal doorway, church, 87
principal rafter, house, 61
principal street, city plan, 20
print, silk screen, 375
print band, high-speed printer, 439
printed image, 166
printed impression, 166
printer: cash register, 440; computer, 163
print head, high-speed printer, 439
printing: incised, 377; planographic, 376; processes, 166; silk screen, 273; woodcut, 374
printing surface: lithographic press, 376; type, 166
printmaking, 377; silk screen, 375
print-out bin, high-speed printer, 439
print sample: dot matrix printer, 163; laser printer, 163
print style control, dot matrix printer, 163
prison, 76
privacy curtain, electronic voting system, 437
probable morning line, flat racing, 336
probe jack, volt-ohm meter, 423
proboscis: mosquito, 41; ultimate beast, 49
proceed signal, traffic light, 113
produce department, supermarket, 103
product, coupon, 103
product label, 268
product number, pencil, 158
professional activities, résumé, 160
profile, shoreline, 14, 15
program, personal computer, 162
program information display, personal computer, 162
programmed flash, Polaroid, 173
program number, flat racing entry, 336
program reset button, camera, 172
prohibit movement sign, road, 505
projectile: cannon, 467; mortar, 472
projection, map, 20, 21
projection speed selector, movie projector, 175

project name, house blueprint, 62
projector, 175
prominence, solar, 2-3
promotional label, 268
prong: electric plug, 398; fork, 244, 259; man's belt, 190; nail clippers, 215; ring, 219; tuning fork, 367; vacuum tube, 396
pronunciation symbol, 513
proof-of-purchase seal, package, 268
proofreader's marks, 514
prop: grand piano, 361; stage, 350
propane gas, camper, 130
propane plumber's torch, 422
propellant, rocket, 383
propeller: destroyer, 476; hovercraft, 145; outboard engine, 137; single engine airplane, 147; submarine, 479; turboprop jet engine, 407
property, stage, 350
proposed road, road map, 20
proposition area, craps table, 347
prop root, corn, 58
prop stick, grand piano, 361
proscenium arch, stage, 350, 351
prosecutor's table, courtroom, 89
pro-style hair dryer, 212
protection pad, parallel bars, 306
protective cap, razor, 210
protective case, blood pressure gauge, 449
protective chain cover, swing, 287
protective clothing, armor, 465
protective counter, sealed voting booth, 437
protective cup: athletic supporter, 194; baseball catcher, 290; boxing, 309
protective glass, ice hockey rink, 295
protective padding, ski clothes, 326
protective shoulder, wristwatch, 220
protective sleeve, overhead power line, 396
protector: banjo, 362; baseball catcher, 290; ice hockey player, 294, 295; tow truck bed, 126; waterskiing towline, 329
proton, 394
proton-proton collision, 394
protruding upper face, zipper, 209
proximal transverse, human hand, 31
pubes, human, 25
pubis: allosaurus, 43; human, 26; stegosaurus, 43
public address switch, CB radio, 183
publications, résumé, 160
public counter, sealed voting booth, 437
public sign, 506
publisher, book, 167
puck: computer workstation, 438; craps table, 347; ice hockey, 294, 295
pudding fender, tugboat, 144
p'u fang, Manchu court dress, 491
puff, beauty product, 217
puff sleeve, queen's regalia, 484

p'u-fu, Manchu court dress, 491
pull: bureau, 272; dressing table, 272; sideboard, 243; traverse rod, 240; window shade, 240, 241
pull bail, screen, 175
pulley, 461; automobile engine, 111; belt sander, 421; block and tackle, 461; stage, 350; tow truck, 126; universal gym, 344; venetian blind, 241
pulley block, 461
pulley chain, castle portcullis, 81
pulley rope, ballista, 467
pulley safety guard, drill press, 419
pullover: hurdle, 304; sweater, 199, 327
pull-pin, fire extinguisher, 284
pullquote, magazine, 170
pull ring: hand grenade, 473; zipper slide, 209
pull strap, boot, 206
pull tab: package, 268; zipper, 209
pulmonary artery, human, 28
pulmonary vein, human, 28
pulp, fruit, 55, 255
pulpit: church, 87; sailboat, 134; synagogue, 88
pulsar, 3
pulse generation, pacemaker, 452
pulse point, and perfume, 217
pump: automobile engine, 111; bicycle, 128; blood pressure gauge, 449; dishwasher, 250; fireboat, 144; gas, 112; nuclear reactor, 392; paint spray gun, 425; paramedic equipment, 123; percolator brewing basket, 252; pilot's instrument panel, 481; rocket, 407; solar heating system, 391; woman's shoe, 205, 488
pumper, fire engine, 125
pumpkin, silo, 104
pump plunger handle, camp stove, 342
pump valve, lantern, 342
puncheon, 267
punch hole, man's belt, 190
punch line, comic strip, 381
punctuation, grammatical symbol, 513
punt: bottle, 267; fireboat, 144
punta, jai alai cesta, 314
pupa, insect, 41
pupil, eye, 30
pup tent, 342
purfling, violin, 355
purge valve, skin diving face mask, 331
purl, knitting, 386
purlicue, human hand, 31
purlin, house, 61
purl stitch, knitting, 386
purse, 222; miser, 492
push arm, bulldozer, 435
push axle tire, bus, 118
pushboat, 144
pushbutton: ballpoint pen, 158; drill press, 419; metal detector, 445; screen, 175; telephone, 180
pusher: food processor, 254; nail clippers, 215
pusher tug, 144
push knob, citrus juicer, 25
push-pin, wristwatch, 220
pushpit, sailboat, 134
push plate, tow truck bed, 126
push rim, wheelchair, 432
putter, golf club, 311

putting green, 311
puzzle solution, magazine, 171
pylon: helicopter, 146; hovercraft, 145; jumbo jet, 149
pyramid, 71
pyramidion, obelisk, 71
pyrometric cones, potting, 373

Q

Q: braille, 512; sign language, 512
quad, magazine column, 171
quadrant, 137
quadrant number, paper money, 224
quadredundant computer system, space shuttle, 153
quadrilateral structure, pyramid, 70
quality classification, wine label, 267
quality control line, wine label, 267
quantity, prescription, 451
quantity indicator, pilot's instrument panel, 481
quark, 3, 394
quarrel, crossbow, 466
quarter: boat, 206; horse's hoof, 38; man's shoe, 204
quarterdeck, passenger ship, 143
quarter glass, automobile, 107
quarter hoop, barrel, 267
quarter-inch mark, tape measure, 424
quartermaster, frontier fort, 82
quarter-mile pole, harness racetrack, 337
quarter moon, 4
quarter note, music, 352
quarter panel, automobile, 106, 107
quarter rest, music, 353
quarters: frontier fort, 82; oil drilling platform, 101; passenger ship, 142; tugboat, 144; White House, 75
quarter shield, coat of arms, 503
quasar, 3
quasihemidemisemiquaver, music, 352
quatrefoil, church, 86
quaver, music, 352
queen: chess, 345; playing cards, 348; royal regalia, 484
queen post, house, 61
queenside men, chess, 345
query author, proofreader's mark, 514
question index column, voting booth, 437
question mark: grammatical symbol, 513; proofreader's mark, 514
quiche, 263
quick claw, lobster, 47
quick match, rocket, 383
quick-release hook, parachute, 333
quiet button, dot matrix printer, 163
quill: bird feather, 39; brace, 418; pen, 158; ultimate beast, 48
quillon: knife, 463; sword hilt, 463
quilt, 270, 271
quilting, sleeping bag, 343
quimp, cartoon, 381
quiver, arrow, 466
quoin: brick wall, 69; masonry gate post, 67
quotation mark, 513

R

R: braille, 512; sign language, 512
rabbi, 486
rabbit ear, ultimate beast, 49
rabillo, jai alai cesta, 314
race: hand loom, 387; swimming, 316; track and field, 300
race track: Grand Prix, 338; harness, 337
Rachel, playing card queen, 348
rachis: bird feather, 39; fern, 57
racing: drag, 339; flat, 336; Grand Prix, 338; harness, 337; starting block, 304
racing colors, flat racing entry, 336
racing flat, 302
racing handlebar, bicycle, 128
racing slick, 338, 339
rack: automobile, 109; bathtub, 274; bicycle, 128; billiards, 320; blackjack, 320; bowling lane, 317; bus, 118; camper, 130; desk, 276; dishwasher, 250; kitchen tool, 260; lamb, 33; oil drilling platform, 101; outboard engine, 137; space shuttle, 153; stagecoach, 131; tank, 474; toaster, 253; wok, 257
racket: badminton, 319; Ping-Pong, 321; squash, 313; tennis, 312
radar: 444; aircraft carrier, 478; buoy, 132; destroyer, 477; fireboat, 144; hovercraft, 145; jumbo jet, 148; pilot's instrument panel, 481; police car, 122; 747 cockpit, 150; space shuttle, 153; submarine, 479; tanker, 141; tugboat, 144
radial: lumber, 68; scallop shell, 47; spider web, 40
radial artery, human, 28
radial nerve, human, 29
radiation belt, Milky Way, 3
radiator, 400; automobile, 108; bulldozer, 435; racing car, 338; solar power system, 391
radicle, root system, 51
radii, spider web, 40
radio: aircraft carrier, 478; ambulance, 123; Citizens Band, 183; clock, 233; hovercraft, 145; pilot's instrument panel, 481; police car, 122; 747 cockpit, 150; submarine, 479
radioactive-waste storage tank, nuclear reactor, 392
radio display, Walkman, 182
radio frequency acceleration system, super collider, 394
radio mast, skyscraper, 77
radiometer, satellite, 186
radio operator, 183
radio/tape mode switch, Walkman, 182
radio-translucent pad, surgical table, 450
radio tuning dial, phonograph receiver, 179
radio tuning wheel: portable radio/cassette player, 182; Walkman, 182
radio wave, 2-3
radius, human, 26
radome, jet fighter, 480
raft: aircraft carrier, 478; jumbo jet, 148; tugboat, 144
rafter: house, 61; lumber, 68

ragged-right type, magazine, 170
raglan sleeve: parka, 201; trench coat, 200
rail: backgammon board, 345; backyard equipment, 287; balustrade, 73; bathtub, 274; bed, 270; bridge, 97; bureau, 272; child's wagon, 287; church, 87; craps table, 347; door, 64; drag racing, 339; escalator, 79; fence, 67; flat racing, 336; harness racetrack, 337; ladder, 425; passenger ship, 142, 361; playpen, 286; pool table, 320; powerboat, 138, 139; railroad, 115; razor blade injector, 210; rocking chair, 134; sailboat, 134; skin diving fin, 331; sled, 328; slide, 287; snowmobile, 130; sofa, 236; sponge mop, 282; stage, 350; staircase, 66; stapler, 277; starting block, 304; subway, 119; surfboard, 330; surgical table, 450; tanker, 141; truck, 120, 121; venetian blind, 241; wheelchair, 452; window, 65
railing: highway, 114; tunnel, 98
railroad, 116-117
railroad crossing, 115; road sign, 504
railroad track, 115
railroad yard, 96
rail transportation, public sign, 506
rain, 17, 19
rain boot, 207
rain cap, bulldozer, 435
rain check, ticket, 349
raincoat, 200
rain gauge, weather station, 18
rain poncho, infantryman's uniform, 497
rain-snow clutter control, radar, 444
rake, 427
RAM, computer, 438
ram, 33; iceberg, 11; zodiac, 509
ram control, garbage truck, 127
ramjet, 407
rammer, cannon, 467
ramp: airport, 94; highway cloverleaf, 114; hovercraft, 145; theatre stage, 351
rampart: castle, 80, 81; fort, 83
ranching gear, 432
rand: boot, 206; mountain climbing, 334
random access memory, computer, 438
range: kitchen, 237; mountain, 7, 8; thematic map, 21
range control: police car, 122; radar, 444; sonar, 444
range indicator, movie camera, 174
rank: chessboard, 345; military uniform, 496, 497
rank badge, Manchu court dress, 491
rapid-response thermometer, 258
rapids, river, 13
rapid transit system, 119
rasp, 420
ratcatcher, passenger ship, 142
ratchet: brace, 418; chaise lounge, 288; screwdriver, 413
ratchet angle, incline track, 92
ratchet buckle, man's belt, 190

ratchet handle, socket wrench, 415
ratchet wheel, hand loom, 387
rate control, guitar amplifier, 363
rate of flow indicator, pilot's instrument panel, 481
rate plate, parking meter, 113
rating, clock, 233
ratio: political map, 21; symbol, 511
rattle, snake, 43
rattlesnake, 42-43
ravine, mountain, 8
raw ingredients, food, 262
ray: fish, 45; medal, 501; Milky Way, 3
razor, 210
razor blade, 210
RCS nozzle, lunar lander, 154
reaction, nuclear power, 392
reaction control system (RCS) thruster assembly, lunar lander, 154
reactor, nuclear, 392
reader service coupon, magazine, 171
reader surname, magazine mailing label, 169
reading clerk, House of Representatives, 74
reading lens, eyeglasses, 221
reading light, bus, 118
read only memory, computer, 438
readout, dental unit, 454
readout dash, newspaper, 168
read-write head, computer, 439
read-write window, diskette, 162
read-write window & shutter, diskette, 162
reamer: citrus juicer, 255; drill, 418; plumbing, 422
reaper, 434
rear anchor, diving board, 316
rear apron, necktie, 193
rear axle: automobile, 109; stroller, 286; tractor, 434; truck, 120; wagon, 287
rear bead, shotgun, 469
rear beam, laboratory scale, 447
rear bearing, fishing reel, 340
rear binding heel piece, slalom water ski, 329
rear boot, stagecoach, 131
rear brake, bicycle, 128
rear bumper, automobile, 107
rear cinch, saddle, 315
rear coil spring, automobile, 109
rear cover, dot matrix printer, 163
rear deflector, mower, 429
rear derailleur, bicycle, 128
rear door, automobile, 107
rear drive sprocket, motorcycle, 129
rear drop-out, bicycle, 128
rear drum brake, motorcycle, 129
rear end, automobile, 109
rear fender, motorcycle, 129
rear foot, stapler, 277
rear frame, wheelbarrow, 430
rear hood, fishing rod, 340
rear housing, razor, 210
rear jockey, saddle, 335
rear leg, bee, 41
rear lens cap, zoom lens, 172
rear light, bulldozer, 435
rear limit line, fencing strip, 315
rear post, hand loom, 387
rear quarter panel, automobile, 107

rear pulley, belt sander, 421
rear push plate, tow truck bed, 126
rear rigging ring, saddle, 335
rear section, bicycle, 128
rear shock absorber: automobile, 109; motorcycle, 129
rear sight, weapon, 469, 470, 471
rear skirt, missile, 482
rear spikers' line, volleyball court, 319
rear stretcher, rocking chair, 234
rear tire, bus, 118
rear wing, racing car, 338
rear toe binder, slalom water ski, 329
rearview mirror: bus, 118; car, 110; locomotive, 117; pilot's instrument panel, 481; truck, 120
rear wheel, tow truck, 126
rear window, automobile, 107
rear windshield, automobile, 107
rebote, jai alai cancha, 314
rebound tumbling, trampoline, 308
receipt: cash register, 440; toll booth, 114
received document exit, fax machine, 164
received document slot, fax machine, 164
receiver: automatic weapon, 470, 471; phonograph, 179; shotgun, 468; telephone, 180; television, 185
receiving track, railroad yard, 96
recent transactions, monthly statement, 227
receptacle: electrical, 398; flower, 53; pencil sharpener, 277; strawberry, 55
reception center, prison, 76
reception room, White House, 75
receptor, nervous system, 29
recessed back-up light, tow truck bed, 126
recessed door, safe, 457
recessed taillight, tow truck bed, 126
rechargeable battery pack, tape recorder, 177
rechargeable power handle, ear scope, 448
recirculating valve, automobile engine, 111
recliner, 235
recliner stand, child's car seat, 286
reclining seat, bus, 118
recoil pad, rifle, 468
recoil spring guide, automatic pistol, 470
recoil starter plate, internal combustion engine, 406
record: phonograph, 178
record button: remote control unit, 184; tape recorder, 177
recorder: tape, 177; weather station, 18
recording data control, video camera, 184
recording lever, movie projector, 175
recording phonograph, 178
red light, ice hockey, 294
red line: ice hockey, 295; squash, 313
record meter, tape recorder, 177
record size selector, phonograph turntable, 178

recreational vehicle, 109, 130
recreation area, road map, 20
recreation yard, prison, 76
rectangle, basketball backstop, 296
rectangular lens, eyeglasses, 221
rectangular spreader, 430
recto, book page, 167
rectory, 86
rectus, human, 26
recurve, bow, 466
red foul light, drag racing, 339
red light, traffic light, 113
red lighting, drag racing, 339
red line, squash court, 313
red marker light, truck van, 121
Red Room, White House, 75
red slot, roulette, 376
red supergiant star, 2
reduction, theodolite, 436
red wine glass, 244
reed: bagpipe, 365; clarinet, 357; English horn, 357; hand loom, 387; oboe, 356
reeding, coin, 225
reed selector switch, accordion, 366
reed tube opening, pitch pipe, 367
reef, coral, 46
reef cringle, mainsail, 136
reefer: refrigerator ship, 140; truck, 120
reef point, mainsail, 136
reel: fencing strip, 315; fireboat, 144; fishing, 340; movie camera, 174; movie projector, 175; mower, 429; tape measure, 424; tape recorder, 177; thread, 384
reel lawn mower, 429
reel seat, fishing rod, 340
referee, polo, 299
referee's crease, ice hockey rink, 295
reference beam, holography, 395
reference key, political map, 20
reference matter, book, 167
references, résumé, 160
reference slide, desk, 276
reference table, synthesizer, 363
refill data, prescription, 451
reflected-light window, light meter, 176
reflecting surface, solar power system, 391
reflecting telescope, 443
reflective identification, buoy, 132
reflective stripe, fireman's coat, 500
reflector: bicycle, 128; bus, 118; lamp, 239; mechanical sweeper, 127; railroad crossing signal, 115; truck van, 121
reflector satellite, 186
refracting telescope, 443
refrigeration van, truck, 120, 121
refrigerator, 249
refrigerator ship, 140
regalia, royal, 485
regional code, magazine mailing label, 169
regional name, political map, 20
regional temperature prediction, weather map, 19
region of interaction, transistor chip, 396
register, electric meter, 399

register buttons, accordion, 366
registered, symbol, 511
registered architect seal, house blueprint, 62
register mark, label, 268
registration guide, silk screen, 375
registration number, hot air balloon, 332
registration number, single engine airplane, 147
registry guide, silk screen, 375
regular section, magazine, 169
regulator: dental, 455; gas pump automatic nozzle, 112; laboratory burner, 447; pressure cooker, 257; skin diving, 331
regulatory sign, road, 505
rehabilitation, prison, 76
rehearsal marking, music, 352
rein, horseracing, 336, 337
reinforce, cannon barrel, 467
reinforced shoulder, waterskiing vest, 329
reinforced toe, panty hose, 195
reinforce ring, cannon barrel, 467
rein guide, Hansom cab, 131
relative bearing, radar, 444
relay race, track and field, 300
relay unit, lunar rover, 155
release: backpack, 343; ballista, 467; can opener, 251; chain saw, 431; guillotine, 462; hand loom, 387; jet fighter, 480; pistol, 470; pliers, 414; rifle, 468; sextant, 137; ski binding, 326; steam engine, 405; typewriter, 161
relief: printing, 166; stone sculpture, 372
relief map, 21
relief shading key, globe, 1
relief valve: nuclear reactor, 392; tanker, 140, 141; water heater, 401
reliever, saber saw, 417
religious symbol, 508
religious vestment, 487
relish, and frankfurter, 265
remaining-teeth mold, denture, 453
remnants of universal veil, mushroom, 57
remote control: slide projector, 175; television, 185
remote control unit, VCR, 184
remote filming jack, movie camera, 174
remote handset, cordless phone, 180
remote-operated block valve, nuclear reactor, 392
renal artery, human, 28
rendezvous radar antenna, lunar lander, 154
rendition, work of art, 368
repeat button: compact disc player, 178; tape recorder, 177
repeat control, phonograph turntable, 178
repeat sign, music, 352
replaceable collar, maid's uniform, 489
reporter, Congress, 74
representative fraction, political map, 21
reptiles, 42-43
Republican, Congress, 74
rerebrace, armor, 465
rescue, hoist, helicopter, 146
rescue platform, helicopter, 146
reservoir: blood pressure gauge, 449; dam, 100; iron,

279; locomotive, 116; pen, 158
reset: gas pump, 112; stopwatch, 304; table saw, 417; tape recorder, 177; water heater, 401
residence number, mailbox, 231
resin, dental, 453, 455
resist, silk screen, 375
resonance, stringed instruments, 355
resonance box, tuning fork, 367
resonator: banjo, 362; laser, 395; sitar, 362
respiratory system, human, 27
rest: bazooka, 472; child's glider, 287; corkscrew, 251; eye scope, 499; hypodermic syringe, 451; lantern, 342; music notation, 352, 353; music stand, 367
rest area, highway, 114
restaurant: Capitol, 74; passenger ship, 143; public sign, 506
restoration, dental, 455
restraining circle, basketball court, 296
restraint layer, spacesuit, 155
résumé, 160
resuscitator, ambulance, 123
retainer: air conditioner, 402; chain lock, 458; phonograph headphone, 179; saw, 417
retaining wall fence, 67
retarder, railroad yard, 96
retention device, ski, 326
reticulum, animal cell, 23
retina, eye, 30
retinal blood vessel, eye, 30
retractable blade guard, circular saw, 417
retractable footrest, medical examination table, 450
retractable paper support, typewriter, 161
retractable step, medical examination table, 450
retracting ball, pen, 158
retreat zone, fencing strip, 315
retrieving cable, gas pump, 112
retsūah, tefillin, 486
return: bowling lane, 317; traverse rod, 240
return address, envelope, 159
return duct, heat exchanger, 403
return end, cupboard, 243
return panel, elevator car, 78
return payment portion, monthly statement, 227
return pipe: furnace, 400; solar heating system, 391
return section, desk, 276
return top, desk, 276
reverse: locomotive, 116; money, 225; sewing machine, 278; slide projector, 175
reverse light, automobile, 107
reversible cord assembly, iron, 279
reversible motor, power drill, 419
revetment, canal lock, 99
review, magazine, 170
review button, tape recorder, 177
Revolutionary War general, costume, 492
revolver, 470, police gun belt, 499
revolver safety catch, jewelry findings, 218

revolving nosepiece, microscope, **442**
revolving nut, crossbow, **466**
revolving sprinkler, **428**
rewind button: remote control unit, **184**; tape recorder, **177**; video-still camera, **173**; Walkman, **182**
rewind starter, outboard engine, **137**
rewind switch, tape measure, **424**
rheostat control, microscope, **442**
rhinoceros horn, ultimate beast, **49**
rhizome, grass, **58**
rhumb line, globe, **5**
rhythm pick-up, guitar, **363**
riata, **432**
rib: basket, **266**; beef, **32**; cactus, **56**; celery, **262**; dog, **36**; hollow wall fastener, **411**; horse, **38**; human, **26**; jai alai cesta, **314**; laboratory burner, **447**; lamb, **33**; lampshade, **238**; mountain, **9**; parachute, **333**; scallop shell, **47**; shield, **464**; shotgun, **469**; skin diving fin, **331**; sock, **207**; sweater, **199**; umbrella, **230**; violin, **355**
ribbon: ballet toeshoe, **386**; bonnet, **203**; hair ornament, **214**; military uniform, **496**
ribbon cartridge typewriter, **161**
rib cage, human, **24**
ribosome, animal cell, **23**
rib pad, football uniform, **292**
ricasso: knife, **463**; sword hilt, **463**
rider, dress, **198**
ridge: barn, **104**; corrugated fastener, **410**; embroidery ring, **385**; file, **420**; mountain, **8, 9**
ridgeboard, house, **61**
ridgeline, house, **63**
ridgepole, house, **61**; tent, **342**
riding boot, polo, **299**
riding breeches, drum major, **495**
riding compartment, pumper, **125**
riding equipment, **335**
riding glove, polo, **299**
riding instructions, escalator, **79**
rifle, **468-469**; automatic, **471**
rifle grenade, **473**
rifle, gun, **470**
rig, **120**; oil drilling, **101**; wrecker, **126**
rigging: circus, **90**; hang glider, **333**; sailboat, **134**
rigging ring, saddle, **335**
right atrium, heart, **28**
right bank, river, **13**
right-channel volume unit meter, tape recorder, **177**
right engine fuel shutoff handle, pilot's instrument panel, **481**
right field, baseball, **291**
right-handed strike pocket, bowling, **317**
right-hand page, book, **167**
right-hand steering lever, bulldozer, **435**
right image, picture-in-picture viewing, **185**
right of way, railroad, **115**
right service court: badminton, **319**; handball, **313**
right stereo speaker: portable

radio/cassette player, **182**; television, **185**
right ventricle, heart, **28**
right wing, easel, **370**
rigid airships, **156**
rigid table, dull press, **419**
rim: basket, **266**; basketball backstop, **296**; bicycle wheel, **128**; bugle, **359**; button, **209**; cartridge, **470**; coconut, **262**; discus, **303**; Ferris wheel, **93**; merry-go-round, **93**; monocle, **221**; pail, **284**; pot, **373**; racing car, **338, 339**; royal crown, **485**; saucepan, **359**; sink, **247**; spool, **384**; stagecoach wheel, **131**; stemware, **244**; thimble, **384**; tire, **105**; toilet, **275**; trombone, **358**; wheelchair, **452**
rimmon, Torah, **486**
rimstone, cave, **11**
rind: cheese, **263**; orange, **55**
ring: anchor, **132**; basketball backstop, **296**; bayonet, **463**; bicycle, **128**; blender, **254**; boxing, **309**; brace, **418**; cannon barrel, **467**; can opener, **251**; cardinal, **487**; cinch fastener, **208**; circus, **90, 91**; clock, **233**; dart board, **322**; domed structure, **85**; embroidery, **385**; fire engine, **124, 125**; fishing rod, **340, 341**; grenade, **473**; hair dryer, **212**; hot air balloon, **332**; jewelry, **219**; kite, **323**; lampshade, **238**; light meter, **176**; lumber, **68**; missile, **482**; mitten, **200**; mushroom, **57**; projector, **175**; radar, **444**; rifle, **469, 471**; rowboat, **133**; saddle, **335**; Saturn, **2**; screwdriver, **413**; shotgun barrel, **469**; skillet, **359**; ski pole, **326**; stationary rings, **307**; stove, **342**; sword hilt, **463**; tent, **342**; tree, **50**; trumpet, **359**; vault, **457**; window shade pull, **241**
ring contact, incandescent bulb, **247**
ring finger, human hand, **31**
ring handle, scissors, **384**
ring key, clarinet, **356**
ringlet, woman's hair, **213**
ringmaster, circus, **90**
ring molding, minaret, **70**
Ring of the Fisherman, Pope, **487**
ringside, boxing, **309**
ring stand, laboratory, **447**
rink, ice hockey, **295**
riot gun, police car, **122**
riot helmet, police, **498**
rip cord, parachute, **333**
rip fence, saw, **417**
rip guide, saw, **417**
rip panel, hot air balloon, **332**
rip teeth, saw, **417**
ripper claw, lobster, **47**
ripping panel, hot air balloon, **332**
ripsaw, **416**
rise: arch, **72**; continental, **15**
riser: orchestra, **354**; parachute, **333**; staircase, **66**; trophy, **289**
riser pad, skateboard, **324**
ritard, music notation, **352**
ritual item, Jewish, **486**
river, **7, 13**; and underwater tunnel, **98**
rivet: attaché case, **285**; cheese plane, **256**; eyeglasses, **221**; jeans, **191**; knife, **256**; latch

needle, **386**; laboratory clamp, **446**; nail clippers, **215**; pliers, **414**; plug fuse, **399**; sandal, **206**; sharpening steel, **256**
riviêre, jewelry, **219**
rivulet, **13**
riwaq, mosque, **70**
roach, Indian, **490**
road: airport, **94**; highway, **114**; topographic map, **22**
roadbed: highway, **114**; railroad, **115**
road light, camper, **130**
road map, **20**
road racing, **338**
roadside sidewall, truck, **121**
road sign, **504-505**
road under construction, map, **20**
roadway: bridge, **97**; dam, **100**; highway, **114**; railroad, **115**; tunnel, **98**
road wheel: roller coaster, **92**; tank, **474**
roaring forties, wind, **6**
robe: judge, **89**; Manchu court dress, **491**; wizard, **492**
robe of state, king's regalia, **484**
rochet, bishop, **487**
rock: brazier, **288**; nautical chart, **22**
rocker: rocking chair, **234**; hitch and harrow, **434**; waterski, **329**
rocker panel, automobile, **106, 109**
rocket, **383, 407**; bazooka, **472**
rocket launcher, **472**
rocket motor nozzle, satellite, **186**
rockfill section, dam, **100**
rocking chair, **234**
rod: abacus, **441**; basket, **266**; belt buckle, **190**; CB radio antenna, **183**; child's wagon, **287**; coffee maker, **252**; drum, **364**; fishing, **340-341**; flute, **356**; garbage disposal, **247**; grandfather clock, **233**; hair styling, **214**; Hansom cab, **131**; incandescent bulb, **238**; launch pad, **152**; locomotive, **116**; machine gun, **471**; merry-go-round, **93**; metal detector, **445**; mower, **429**; music stand, **367**; nuclear reactor, **392**; powerboat, **139**; royal scepter, **485**; shower, **274**; stagecoach, **131**; steam engine, **405**; traverse, **240**; umbrella, **230**; window shutter, **277**; workbench, **408**
Rogallo kite, **323**
roll: ambulance, **123**; football uniform, **292**; frankfurter, **265**; hand loom, **387**; saddle, **335**; sandwich, **263**
roll bag, racing car, **338**
roll cage, drag racer, **339**
roll-collar shirt, chauffeur, **489**
rolled edge, necktie, **192**
rolled shoulder, shovel, **427**
roller: ballista, **467**; bulldozer, **435**; cassette tape, **177**; chain, **461**; etching press, **377**; fishing reel, **340**; hair, **214**; hitch and harrow, **434**; offset-lithography, **166**; painting, **425**; tank, **474**; tape recorder, **177**; typewriter, **161**; window shade, **241**; roller, woodcut printing, **374**
roller-coaster, **92**

roller guide shoe, elevator shaft, **78**
roller link plate, chain, **461**
roller foot, sewing machine, **278**
roller skate, **324**
roller support, saw, **417**
rolling pin, **259**
rolling stock, railroad, **96, 116-117**
roll on-roll off ship, **140**
roll pin, pliers, **414**
roll top, rocking chair, **234**
rolltop desk, **276**
roll-up blind, window, **241**
ROM, computer, **438**
Roman collar, bishop, **487**
roman type, **165**; proofreader's mark, **514**
rondel, armor, **465**
rood screen, church, **87**
roof: automobile, **106, 107, 109**; bus, **118**; church, **86**; house, **60, 61, 62, 63**; mountain, **8**; pagoda, **71**; skyscraper, **77**
roof air conditioner, camper, **130**
roofing shingle, **68**
roof light, subway, **119**
roof seam, tent, **342**
rook, chess, **345**
rook pawn, chess, **345**
room: cave, **11**; house blueprint, **62**; launch pad, **152**; White House, **75**
rooster, **35**
root: carrot, **54**; corn, **58**; grass, **58**; onion, **262**; outboard engine, **137**; screw, **410**; tertiary, **51**; tooth, **456**; tree, **50**
rope: **132**; ballista, **467**; block and tackle, **461**; boxing ring, **309**; bridge, **97**; circus tent, **91**; elevator shaft, **78**; military uniform, **496**; grandfather clock, **233**; hot air balloon, **332**; jump rope, **344**; mountain climbing, **334**; outboard engine, **137**; ranching gear, **432**; roller coaster, **92**; tent, **342**; tepee, **84**; toboggan, **328**; waterskiing towline, **329**
rope hole, sled, **328**
rope ladder, circus aerialist, **90**
rope strap, saddle, **335**
roping, hammock, **288**
Rose Room, White House, **75**
rosette: Beefeater, **483**; cupboard, **243**; guitar, **362**; queen's regalia, **484**; royal crown, **485**; sofa, **236**
rose window, church, **86**
rosette cap, traffic light, **113**
rose window, church, **86**
rotary beater, kitchen, **258**
rotary dial, telephone, **180**
rotary fairing, helicopter, **146**
rotary fan, **402**
rotary lawn mower, **429**
rotary press, printing, **166**
rotary spreader, **430**
rotating beacon: police car, **122**; single engine airplane, **147**
rotating frame, merry-go-round, **93**
rotating handle, food mill, **260**
rotating mast, windsurfer, **330**
rotating service structure, launch pad, **152**
rotational hand controller, space shuttle, **153**
rotational motion, steam engine, **405**
rotogravure, printing, **166**
rotor: automobile disc brake,

108; helicopter, 146; windmill, 390; wind turbine, 390
rotunda, Capitol, 74
rouge, 216, 217
rough, golf course, 310-311
roughneck, oil drilling, 101
rough sill, house, 61
rouleau, 440
roulette wheel, 346
round: beef, 32; boxing, 309; police ammunition, 498
round-bottom hull, powerboat, 138
round-end chisel, stonecutting, 372
round head, screw, 410
roundhouse, railroad yard, 96
rounding board, merry-go-round, 93
round pin, window shade roller, 241
round shank, screwdriver, 413
round-the-clock, darts, 322
roustabout, circus, 90
route: bus, 118; road map, 20; subway, 119
route sign, road, 505
routing number, check, 226
row, hand knitting, 386
rowboat, 133
rowel, spur, 335
row house, 63
royal regalia, 484-485
rubber: baseball pitcher, 291; shoe accessory, 207
rubber band, dental, 453
rubber blade, silkscreen squeegee, 375
rubber bumper, knee kicker, 246
rubber covering, brayer, 374
rubber face, Ping-Pong racket, 321
rubber foot, food processor, 254
rubber mat, phonograph turntable, 178
rubber plug, sink, 273
rubber-soled shoe, jai alai player, 314
rubber tip, bobby pin, 214
rubbing ink, 376
ruble, symbol, 511
rub rail: powerboat, 138; truck platform, 121
ruching, bonnet, 203
rucksack: backpacking, 343; ski touring, 327
rudder: blimp, 156; destroyer, 476; glider, 147; jumbo jet, 149; sailboat, 134; single engine airplane, 147; space shuttle, 152; submarine, 479
rudder pedal, 747 cockpit, 150
rudimentary root, 51
ruff, Beefeater, 483
ruffled shirt, man's, 488
rug, 246; hairpiece, 211
rule: magazine, 170, 171; measuring, 424
ruler, 424; pocket knife, 426
rumble seat, automobile, 106
rump: beef, 134; bird, 39; cat, 37; dog, 36; horse, 38; pelt, 201; sheep, 33
run: step tread, 66; track and field, 300
run and lock switch, movie camera, 174
rung: ladder, 425; rocking chair, 234
run light, movie camera, 174
runner: grass, 58; ice skates, 325; rug, 246; running shoe, 302; skate, 295; sled, 328; slide rule, 441; umbrella, 230

running board, automobile, 107
running foot: book page, iv; magazine, 171
running knot, gallows, 462
running light: camper, 130; destroyer, 477; fireboat, 144; single engine airplane, 147; tow truck, 126; tugboat, 144
running mold, church, 86
running noose, lasso, 432
running ornament, church, 86
running rigging, sailboat, 134
running shoe, 302
running title, magazine, 170
running track, 300
run number: bus, 118; paper money, 225
runway: airport, 94; bowling lane, 317; javelin throw, 301; pole vault, 305; stage, 351
rupee, symbol, 511
rural mailbox, 231
Russian Cross, symbol, 508
rustproof oil, woodcarving, 372
Rx, prescription symbol, 451

S
S: braille, 512; sign language, 512
saber saw, 417
sabot, blackjack, 347
sabre, 315
sabre and épée warning line, fencing strip, 315
sac: flower stamen, 53; octopus, 46
sacral hump, frog, 44
sacristy, church, 87
sacrum, human, 26
saddle: bicycle, 128; door, 64; guitar, 362; horse, 335, 336, 337; matchbook, 228; motorcycle, 129; mountain, 8; pipe, 229; polo, 299; pommel horse, 307; screen, 175
saddlebag, 335; motorcycle, 129
saddle blanket, polo, 299
saddle feather, chicken, 35
saddle head, dispenser, 267
saddle plate, iron, 279
safe, 457
safe deposit box, 457
safe side, file, 420
safety: elevator shaft, 78; weapon, 468, 470, 471
safety bar, Ferris wheel, 93
safety belt: car, 110; lunar rover, 155
safety binding, ski, 326
safety cable, elevator, 78
safety cable tension sheave, elevator, 78
safety cage, hammer throw, 301
safety catch, revolver, 218
safety-chain hole, tow truck bed, 126
safety control data, prescription, 451
safety cool tip, curling iron, 214
safety dome, train tank car, 116
safety edge, elevator door, 78
safety guard: drill press, 419; paint spray gun, 425
safety guardrail, slide, 287
safety hasp, 460
safety jacket, waterskiing, 329
safety ladder, Ferris wheel, 93
safety lever: hand grenade, 473; pistol, 470
safety line, inflatable, 133
safety loop, circus aerialist, 90

safety lug, cassette tape, 177
safety matches, 228
safety mirror, mechanical sweeper, 127
safety net: aircraft carrier, 478; circus aerialist, 90
safety observer station, destroyer, 477
safety pad, trampoline, 308
safety padding, football goalpost, 293
safety pin, 208; hand grenade, 473
safety rail: bathtub, 274; bridge, 97; powerboat, 139
safety razor, 210
safety rope, roller coaster, 92
safety shield, child's car seat, 286
safety shut-off, Jacuzzi, 274
safety stripe, fireman's coat, 500
safety trigger, chain saw, 431
safety valve, furnace, 400
safety warning, dental x-ray unit, 454
safety zone, polo grounds, 299
Sagittarius, zodiac, 509
sail, 134, 136; hang glider, 333; submarine, 479; windmill, 390; windsurfer, 330
sailboard, 330
sailboat, 134-135
sailing thwart, rowboat, 133
sailor, uniform, 497
sailplane, 147; submarine, 479
St. Anthony's cross, symbol, 508
salad bowl, 245
salad fork, 244
salad plate, 245
salad shaker, 260
salamander, 44
salient angle, 83
saline, paramedic equipment, 123
saliva ejector, dental unit, 454
sally port, frontier fort, 82
salon, sailboat, 135
salt shaker, 261
salutation, letter, 159
samara, 52
Sam Browne belt, 496
same name differentiation code, magazine mailing label, 169
same scale extension inset, political map, 21
sample bag dispenser, lunar rover, 155
sanctuary: church, 87; mosque, 70-71
sand, hourglass, 233
sand area, topographic map, 22
sandbag: ambulance, 123; hot air balloon, 332
sandbar: coastline, 14, 15; river, 13
sandbox: backyard, 287; locomotive, 116, 117
sander, 421
sandglass, 233
sandhill, nautical chart, 22
sandpaper, 421
sand shoe, truck van, 121
sand tower, railroad yard, 96
sand trap, golf course, 311
sand wedge, golf club, 310
sandwich, 263
sandwich cookie, 264
sanitary hose: baseball, 290; football uniform, 292
sanitary paper, medical examination table, 450
sanitation vehicle, 127
sanman, 127

sans serif type, 165
sapwood, tree, 50
sari, 491
sarong, 491
sartorius, human, 26
sash: drum major, 495; jai alai player, 314; royal regalia, 484; window, 65
satellite, 3, 186
Saturn, planet, 3
sauce, sundae, 264
saucepan, 257
saucer, 245
sauerkraut, and frankfurter, 265
sauna, passenger ship, 143
saurischian, dinosaur, 43
sausage, pizza, 265
saw, 416, 417; pocket knife, 426
sawbuck, 408
sawhorse, 408
saxophone, 357
S-band antenna, lunar lander, 154
S bend, tuba, 358
scabbard, Revolutionary War general, 492
scaffold, gallows, 462
scaffolding web, spider, 40
scale: bird foot, 39; blood pressure gauge, 449; camera, 174; coffee maker, 252; electronic flash, 176; fish, 45; frontier fort, 82; house blueprint, 62; hypodermic syringe, 451; kitchen, 258; knife, 426, 463; laboratory, 446-447; lettuce, 262; light meter, 176; metronome, 367; nautical chart, 22; pine cone, 52; political map, 21; saw, 417; sewing machine, 278; slide rule, 441; snake, 42; thermometer, 18, 449; typewriter, 161; volt-ohm meter, 423
scallop, 47; bridal gown hem, 488; curtain, 240
scalp, 211; mortise lock, 458
scalper, harness racing pacer, 337
scanner: cash register, 440; fax machine, 164; hovercraft, 145; radar, 444
scapha, outer ear, 30
scaphoid pad, sandal, 206
scapula, human, 26
scapular, bird, 39
scapular region, salamander, 44
scarf, pirate, 492
scarp, fort, 83
scend, wave, 14
scenery, stage, 350
scenic overlook, highway, 114
scent, 217
scepter, royal, 485
school: fish, 45; prison, 76
school crossing, road sign, 505
sciatic nerve, human, 29
scimitar antenna, lunar lander, 154
scintillometer, 445
scissor grip, body building, 344
scissors, 384; pocket knife, 426
sclera, eye, 30
scoop: ice cream cone, 265; kitchen tool, 258, 259; lacrosse stick, 298; pipe tool, 229
scoop stretcher, ambulance, 123
scooter car, amusement park, 92
scooter helmet, police, 499

scope: bazooka, 472; rifle, 469; telescope, 443
scopula, spider, 40
score: matchbook, 228; pulley block, 461
scoreboard, jai alai cancha, 314
score counter, pool table, 320
score ring, darts, 322
scorer's box, ice hockey rink, 295
scorer's table: basketball court, 296
scoring diagram, shuffleboard court, 318
scoring lines, golf club, 310
scoring machine, fencing strip, 315
scoring triangle, shuffleboard court, 318
Scorpio, zodiac, 509
scorpion, 48; zodiac, 509
scotch rule, magazine, 170
scotia, column, 73
scraper, lithographic press, 376
scratch line, track and field, 300, 301
screen: case, 175; church, 87; fireplace, 232; internal combustion engine, 406; jai alai cancha, 314; projector, 175; radar, 444; silk, 375; sonar, 444; television, 185; tent, 342
screendoor, 64
screen fence, 67
screen plug, mower, 429
scree slope, mountain, 8
screw, 410; banjo, 362; brayer, 374; cassette tape, 177; clamp, 409; combination square, 424; drill bit, 419; earring, 218; electric plug, 398; embroidery ring, 385; etching press, 377; eyeglasses, 221; faucet, 273; golf club, 310; hitch and harrow, 434; kettledrum, 364; lithographic press, 376; lock, 458; microscope, 442; outboard engine, 137; paramedic equipment, 123; plane, 420; pliers, 414; saw, 417; sewing machine, 278; ski binding, 326; telegraph key, 157; telescope, 443; theodolite, 436; violin, 355; violin bow, 355; vise, 409; volt-ohm meter, 423; woodcarving, 372; wrench, 415
screwback earring findings, 218
screw cap, test tube, 447
screwdriver, 413; pocket knife, 426
screwdriver bit, drill, 418
screw eye, frame, 379
screw hole, hinge, 460
screw nozzle, 428
screw thread, plug fuse, 399
scribed line, scrimshaw, 375
scriber, 375; combination square, 424
scrim, stage, 350
scrimshander, 375
scrimshaw, 375
scrip, collector, 225
Scripture, Torah, 88
scroll: coat of arms, 503; fence, 67; Torah, 88; violin, 355
scrolled arm, sofa, 236
scroll saw, 417
scrubboard, 280
scruff, human, 25
scruple, symbol, 510
scruto, stage, 350
scuba diving, 331

scuff leather, hot air balloon, 332
sculpting tools, 372
scupper: fireboat, 144; tugboat, 144
scythe, 429
sea, 7
seabag, 497
sea clutter control, radar, 444
seafood service section, supermarket, 103
seal: frame, 379; house architect, 62; package, 268-269; paper money, 224; voting booth, 437
sealant strip, roofing shingle, 68
sealed voting booth, 437
sealed vegetable compartment, refrigerator, 249
seam: blouse, 197; boot, 206; can, 267; football, 292; garment, 196; girdle, 195; hot air balloon, 332; inflatable, 133; jacket, 188; mainsail, 136; necktie, 192; sewing pattern, 388; skirt, 197; sock, 207; tennis ball, 312; tent, 342; trousers, 191; and zipper, 209
search coil, metal detector, 445
searchlight: fireboat, 144; tank, 474; tugboat, 144
search loop, metal detector, 445
seasonal current, ocean, 6
seasoning: frankfurter, 265; prepared food, 263
seasoning check, lumber, 68
sea star, 46
seat: ambulance, 123; automobile, 106, 107, 110, 286; backyard glider, 287; bicycle, 128; bumper car, 92; bus, 118; courtroom, 89; electric chair, 462; Ferris wheel, 93; fishing rod, 340; harness racing sulky, 337; inflatable, 133; lounger, 235; lunar rover, 155; motorcycle, 129; pants, 191; rocking chair, 234; rowboat, 133; saddle, 335; 747 cockpit, 150, 151; snowmobile, 130; sofa, 236; space shuttle, 153; stagecoach, 131; stroller, 286; subway car, 119; swing, 287; theatre, 351; toilet, 275; wheelchair, 452; woman's shoe heel, 205
seat belt, car, 110
seating area, supermarket, 103
seat location, ticket, 349
seaweed, 57
second, grammatical symbol, 513
secondary cable, overhead power line, 396
secondary cell, battery, 397
secondary combustion chamber, stove, 404
secondary con, destroyer, 476
secondary feather, 35, 39
secondary highway, 22
secondary root, 51
secondary tank, lunar lander, 154
secondary vein, leaf, 52
second base, baseball, 291
second bicuspid, 456
second bow, bell, iv
second channel, picture-in-picture viewing, 185
Second Empire, house style, 63
second floor, White House, 75
second hand, watch, 220, 304

second molar, 456
second premolar, 456
second reinforce, cannon barrel, 467
seconds bit, stopwatch, 304
seconds dial, grandfather clock, 233
seconds of arc, symbol, 511
second stage: missile, 482; skin diving tank, 331
second thigh: dog, 36; horse, 38
second toe, human foot, 31
second valve slide: French horn, 358; trumpet, 359
second violin, orchestra, 354
secretarial pedestal, desk, 276
secretary, Senate, 74
secretary's table, courtroom, 89
section: dam, 100; fishing rod, 340; jumbo jet, 148, 149; lumber, 68; magazine, 169; orange, 55; theatre, 351
sectional center, envelope, 159
sectional sofa, 236
section code, magazine mailing label, 169
sectioned floorboard, inflatable, 133
sector, track and field, 300
sector flag, hammer throw, 301
security system, prison, 76
sedan, automobile, 106
sediment bleed valve, water heater, 401
seed: 51; apple, 55; flower, 53; gardening, 430; grass, 58; pea, 54; peach, 55; pepper, 262; sandwich, 263; tomato, 54
seeder, gardening, 430
seeker, jet fighter, 480
seesaw, 287
see-through window, package, 269
segment: orange, 55; snake rattle, 43
segmented thumb, lacrosse glove, 298
seiche, 14
select button, dot matrix printer, 163
selection lever, voting booth, 437
selection plate, toaster, 253
selector: accordion, 366; air conditioner, 402; camera, 174; clothes dryer, 281; light meter, 176; movie projector, 175; phonograph, 178, 179; radar, 444; surgical table, 450; toaster oven, 253; volt-ohm meter, 423; washing machine, 280
selector control, sealed voting booth, 437
self-belt: dress, 198; trousers, 191
self-clasping hair roller, 214
self-cleaning oven, 248
self-congratulation, gesture, 507
self-filling mechanism, pen, 158
self-service gas station island, 112
self-starting timer, parking meter, 113
self-threading projector, 175
self-timer, camera, 172
self-timer indicator, camera, 172; Polaroid, 173
selling copy, magazine cover, 169
selvage: fabric, 388; weaving, 387

semaphore, 512
semibreve, music, 352
semicolon, grammatical symbol, 513
semiconductor, transistor, 396
semiflexible kite, 323
semi-hollow body, guitar, 363
semiquaver, music, 352
semirigid lighter-than-air craft, 156
semisubmersible design, oil drilling platform, 101
semitrailer, truck, 121
Senate side, Capitol, 74
sense organs, 30
sensitivity, volt-ohm meter, 423
sensitivity control, video camera, 184
sensor: electronic flash, 176; solar heating system, 391; weather station, 18
sensory nerve, human, 29
sepals, flower, 53
separation triangle, shuffleboard court, 318
separator wire, typewriter, 161
septum: nose, 30; heart, 28
septum linguae, tongue, 30
sequenced starting light, drag racing, 339
sequencer control, synthesizer, 363
sequins, woman's hat, 203
serac, mountain, 9
sergeant at arms, Senate, 74
serial number: internal combustion engine, 406; laboratory scale, 446; paper money, 224, 225; safe, 457; sealed voting booth, 437; surgical table, 450
series identification, paper money, 225
series number, painting brush, 371
serif, type, 165
serigraphy, 375
serrated body, hand grenade, 473
serrated edge: knife, 256; paper bag, 266
serration: coin, 225; key, 459
server, dessert, 245
service, tea, 245
service area: highway, 114; jai alai cancha, 314; railroad yard, 96; volleyball court, 319
service article, magazine, 170
service box, handball, 313; squash, 313
service cabinet, elevator, 78
service cap, military uniform, 496
service coupon, magazine, 171
service court: badminton, 319; barn, 104; handball, 313
service deli, supermarket, 103
service door, gas pump, 112
service line: handball, 313; jai alai, 314; squash, 313; tennis, 312
service mast, space shuttle, 152
service revolver, police gun belt, 499
service ribbon, military uniform, 496
service road, highway, 114
service sideline, tennis court, 312
service sign, road, 505
service station island, 112
service structure, launch pad, 152
service time, military, 496
service vehicle, airport, 95

service zone, handball, 313
serving, bow, 466
serving cap, maid's uniform, 489
serving player's line, jai alai, 314
serving silverware drawer, sideboard, 243
serving tray, 245; baby's high chair, 286
servopneumatic altimeter, pilot's instrument panel, 481
set: scale weights, 446; stage, 350; tea, 245; television, 185
setback, skyscraper, 77
set-in cap, magazine, 170
set-in sleeve: blouse, 197; jacket, 196
set of tail, dog, 36
setscrew: barbell, 344; faucet, 273
settee: patio, 288; sailboat, 135
setting: clock radio, 233; light meter, 176; ring, 219
setting dots, sewing machine, 278
setting indicator, ski binding, 326
setting lotion, hair, 214
setup: bowling lane, 317; chess, 345
7/8 mile chute, harness racetrack, 337
7/8 pole, harness racetrack, 337
747 cockpit, 150-151
seven furlong chute, harness racetrack, 337
seven pin, bowling, 317
70mm camera: lunar rover, 155; spacesuit, 155
sewer valve, camper, 130
sewing hole: hook and eye, 208; snap fastener, 208
sewing machine, 278
sewing pattern, 388
sew-through button, 209
sextant, 137
sforzando, organ, 360
shackle: block and tackle, 461; padlock, 459; pocket knife, 426
shade: and composition, 368; lamp, 238, 239; stagecoach, 131; track lighting 239; window covering, 240
shading: relief map, 21; and texture, composition, 369
shading key, globe, 1
shadow: and composition, 368; makeup, 216, 217; sundial, 389
shadow pin, compass, 136
shaft: arrow, 466; billiard cue, 320; bird feather, 39; boot, 206; bridge, 97; can opener, 251; cave, 11; column, 73; croquet mallet, 318; dart, 322; destroyer, 476; drum major's baton, 495; electric meter, 399; elevator, 78; golf club, 310; Hansom cab, 131; halberd, 464; harness racing, 337; ice ax, 334; ice hockey stick, 295; internal combustion engine, 406; javelin, 303; lacrosse stick, 298; lamp, 239; lance, 464; longbow, 466; metronome, 367; music stand, 367; oar, 133; obelisk, 71; pin, 208; printing press, 376, 377; ski pole, 326; squash racket, 313; stagecoach, 131; tennis racket, 312; umbrella, 230; underwater tunnel, 98; White House, 75
shaftment, arrow, 466

shake, wooden roofing shingle, 68
shakedown, cowboy, 490
shake-hands grip, Ping-Pong racket, 321
shaker: kitchen tool, 260; salt, 261
shako, drum major, 495
shallow gouge, woodcarving, 372
Shanghai, darts, 322
shank: anchor, 132; bolt, 411; boot, 206; brasses, 358; button, 209; cat, 37; chicken, 35; chisel, 420; shank, drill, 419; fishhook, 341; gimlet, 418; gouge, 374; hoe, 427; human, 25; lamb, 33; latch needle, 386; nail, 410; needle, 384; pipe, 229; ring, 219; screw, 410; screwdriver, 413; shoe, 204, 205; trombone, 358; type, 166
shape, pipe, 229
sharp: music, 352; organ, 360
sharpening oil, woodcarving, 372
sharpening steel, 256
sharpening stone: gouge, 374; woodcarving, 372
shaver, 210
shaving brush, 210
shawl, Jewish prayer vestment, 486
shawl collar, sweater, 199
shears, 384; gardening, 427; Indian, 427
sheath: cat, 37; grass, 58; knife, 463; nerve, 29; safety pin, 208; skin diving, 331; snake fang, 42; wire, 423
sheathing, house, 60
sheave: block and tackle, 461; elevator shaft, 78
shed, oil drilling platform, 101
sheep, 33
sheer line, powerboat, 139
sheet: ambulance, 123; bedding, 271; kite, 323; postage stamps, 159
sheet-fed press, printing, 166
sheet music notation, 352-353
sheet-transfer cylinder, offset-lithography, 166
shelf: cupboard, 243; fireplace, 232; igloo, 85; refrigerator, 249; stove oven, 248; telescope, 443
shelfback, book, 167
shelf break, continental margin, 15
shelf mount, telescope, 443
shelf sign, aisle display, 102
shell: attaché case, 285; baseball catcher's mask, 290; bivalve, 47; block and tackle, 461; brace chuck, 418; coconut, 262; cupboard, 243; drill, 419; drum, 356; egg, 262; fire extinguisher, 284; football helmet, 292; iron, 279; lamp, 238; lobster, 47; necktie, 192; nuclear reactor, 392; parka, 201; pea, 54; plug fuse, 399; quiche, 263; sleeping bag, 343; tambourine, 364; tart, 264; toaster, 253; turtle, 43; univalve, 47; vacuum tube, 396
shellfish, 47
shell fuse, aerial shell, 383
shell plate, mandolin, 362
shel rosh, Jewish ritual item, 486
shelter, destroyer, 477
shel yad, tefillin, 486
shield: car seat, 286; chain saw muffler, 431; coat of arms,

503; drag racing driver's fire suit, 339; drum major's coat, 495; hollow wall fastener, 411; lantern, 342; medieval, 464; merry-go-round, 93; mower, 429; nuclear, 392; police, 498; racing car, 338; tank, 475; toll basket, 114; tunnel, 98
Shield of David, 88, 508
shift, doppler, 2
shifter, bicycle, 128
shifting head, theodolite, 436
shift key, typewriter, 161
shift lever, bulldozer, 435
shimagi, torii, 70-71
shin, human, 24
shin boot, harness racing pacer, 337
shin pad, soccer, 297
shiner, brick wall, 69
shingle, roofing, 68
shinguard: baseball, 290; football, 292; ice hockey, 295
shin pad, ice hockey, 295
Shinto temple gateway, 70-71
ship: aircraft carrier, 478; cargo, 140-141; passenger, 142-143; submarine, 479; surface fighting, 476-477
shipboard lines, canal lock, 99
shipping lane, 476
shirring: blouse, 197; woman's pants, 196
shirt, 189; baseball, 290; cowboy, 490; Indian, 490; man's formal attire, 488; military, 496, 497; police, 499; polo, 299; soccer, 297
shirt dress, cook's uniform, 489
shirt-waist dress, cook's uniform, 489
shoaling wave, shoreline, 14
shoat, 34
shock absorber: automobile, 109; motorcycle, 129; single engine airplane, 147; snowmobile, 130
shoe: accessories, 207; blackjack, 347; boxing, 309; bridge, 97; bulldozer track, 435; clown, 339; drag racing driver, 339; drum major, 495; elevator shaft, 78; fencing, 315; football, 292; horse, 38; jai alai, 314; king's regalia, 484; ladder, 425; man's, 204; mechanical sweeper, 127; military, 496; mountain climbing, 334; organ, 360; police, 498; running, 302; sailor, 497; sander, 421; saw, 417; screen, 175; snowshoe, 327; soccer, 297; stagecoach, 131; woman's, 205
shoe brace, guitar, 362
shoe horn, 207
shoelace, 204
shoe shop, prison, 76
shoestring strap, dress, 198
shoe tree, 207
shoot: asparagus, 54; grass, 58
shooter: dice, 346; craps table, 347
shooting star, 2
shootout, soccer, 297
shop: frontier fort, 82; passenger ship, 142; prison, 76; railroad yard, 96
shopping cart, supermarket, 102
shore, 14
shoreline, 14; iceberg, 12; nautical chart, 22
short bar, easel, 370
short bar clamp, 409

short bent gouge, woodcarving, 372
short circuit, fuse box, 399
short lid prop, grand piano, 361
short line, handball, 313
short loin, beef, 32
short ribs, beef, 32
shorts: 191; basketball, 296; men's underwear, 194; soccer, 297
short service line, badminton court, 319
short stick, grand piano, 361
shortstop area, baseball, 291
short-term parking lot, airport, 95
shot, field events equipment, 303
shotgun, 468-469; stagecoach, 131
shotgun chaps, cowboy, 490
shot put, 301, 303
shot timer, basketball backstop, 296
shoulder: bell, iv; bottle, 267; broom, 282; cat, 37; chisel, 420; dog, 36; highway, 114; horse, 38; human, 24; key, 459; lamb, 33; mountain, 8; pencil, 158; pork, 34; razor blade, 210; shovel, 427; suit hanger, 281; tennis racket, 312; type, 166; waterskiing vest, 329; wave, 14; woman's jacket, 196; wristwatch, 220
shoulder bag, 222
shoulder blade: human, 24; stegosaurus, 43
shoulderboard, military uniform, 496
shoulder butt, pork, 34
shoulder harness, drag racing driver, 339
shoulder hook, frame, 379
shoulder pad: football, 292; ice hockey, 295
shoulder pad strap, backpack, 343
shoulder press, universal gym, 344
shoulder protector, ice hockey goalie, 294
shoulder rest, bazooka, 472
shoulder seam, jacket, 188
shoulder sling, mountain climbing, 334
shoulder strap: accordion, 366; brassiere, 195; child's car seat, 286; combat soldier, 497; golf bag, 311; handbag, 222; trench coat, 200
shoulder vise, workbench, 408
shoulder yoke blouse, 197
shovel, 427; fire iron, 232; ski, 326
show, flat racing, 336
shower: bath, 274; thunderstorm, 17; weather map, 19
shrapnel, grenade, 473
shredding disc, food processor, 254
shrimp, 47
shrine, pyramid, 70
shrinkwrap, packaging, 268
shroud: internal combustion engine, 406; parachute line, 333; sailboat, 134
shuffleboard, 318
shutoff handle, pilot's instrument panel, 481
shutoff valve: radiator, 400; standpipe, 59; toilet, 275; water heater, 401
shutter: house, 62, 63; laboratory burner, 447; windmill, 390; window, 241

shutter release: camera, 172; Polaroid, 173; video-still camera, 173
shutter scale, light meter, 176
shutter speed key, camera, 172
shuttle: badminton, 319; sewing machine, 278; space, 152; tatting, 386
shuttlecock, badminton, 319
shuttle race, hand loom, 387
siamese: hose, 428; standpipe, 59
sickle, chicken, 35
sickle-bar lawn mower, 429
side: accordion, 366; basket, 266; elliptical galaxy, 2; lumber, 68; organ, 360; piano, 361; skillet, 257; snap fastener, 208; violin, 355
sidearm, 470; juice extractor, 255
sidebar: courtroom, 89; magazine, 170; pulley block, 461
side belt, handbag, 222
side bit: fireboat, 144; tugboat, 144
sideboard, 243; ice hockey rink, 295; polo grounds, 299
side body molding, automobile, 107
sidebones, brassiere, 195
side broom balance assembly, mechanical sweeper, 127
sideburns, 211
side cleft, horse's foot, 38
side curtains, four-poster bed, 270
side cushion, sofa, 236
side cutter, pliers, 414
side deck, powerboat, 139
side drop, bedding, 270
side drum, 364
side fender, tugboat, 144
side flight, staircase, 66
side handle, drill, 418
side handrail, subway car, 119
side horse, gymnastics, 307
side jamb, window, 65
side leg, playpen, 286
sidelight: door, 64; Hansom cab, 131; house, 62; stagecoach, 131
sideline: basketball, 296; fencing strip, 315; football, 293; lacrosse field, 296; Ping-Pong, 321; polo grounds, 299; soccer field, 297; volleyball, 319
side link, chain saw chain, 431
sidelit composition, 368
side-loading collection truck, 127
side loading door, stove, 404
side loop, handbag, 222
side marker: automobile, 106; bus, 118; tow truck, 126
side panel: bureau, 272; bus, 118; curtain, 240; lounger, 235; package, 268; sideboard, 243; tractor, 434
side pieces, furniture, 243
side plate: pulley block, 461; racing car, 338; revolver, 470
side pocket, backpack, 343
side pod, racing car, 338
side rail: bed, 270; child's wagon, 287; ladder, 47
skin diving fin, 331; sled, 328; slide, 287; surgical table, 450; truck van, 121
side seam: boot, 206; trousers, 191
side shell, block and tackle, 461
sideshow, circus, 90
side sign: bus, 118; subway car, 119

side slats, sled, 328
side span, bridge, 97
sidestand, motorcycle, 129
side stretcher, rocking chair, 234
side vent, volcano, 10
sideview mirror: automobile, 106; mechanical sweeper, 127
sidewalk, moving, 79
sidewall: can, 267; circus tent, 91; horse's hoof, 38; man's hair, 211; slalom water ski, 329; squash, 313; swimming pool, 316; tire, 105; truck van, 121
side welt, boot, 206
side whiskers, 211
side window: bus, 118; camper, 130
siding: house, 62, 63; railroad yard, 96
sidur, Jewish prayer book, 486
sieve, 260
sifter, 260
sight: armor, 465; automatic weapons, 470, 471; bazooka, 472; crossbow, 466; pool table, 320; rifle, 469; tank, 474
sight bracket, mortar, 472
sight cut, bayonet, 463
sight glass, furnace, 400
sightseeing bus, 118
sign: bus, 118; music, 352, 353; public, 506-506; road, 504-505; subway car, 119
signal: automobile, 106; bus, 118; railroad crossing, 115; traffic light, 113
signal ahead, road sign, 505
signal baton, drum major, 495
signal bridge, destroyer, 477
signal deck, passenger ship, 143
signal halyard, destroyer, 477
signal intensity meter, metal detector, 445
signal light: automobile, 106; bus, 118; coffee maker, 252; mechanical sweeper, 127; motorcycle, 129; taxi, 119
signal meter, phonograph, 179
signal processor, synthesizer, 363
signal shelter, destroyer, 477
signal strength indicator, cellular telephone, 181
signal tower, passenger ship, 143
signature: baseball bat, 291; cartoon, 380; letter, 159; music, 352; prescription, 451
sign: taxi roof light, 119; toll booth, 114; zodiac, 509
sign language, 512
sign-off, magazine article, 170
silencer, 470
silent alarm, vault, 457
silent anti-reverse housing, fishing reel, 340
silicon photodiode, Polaroid, 173
silk: corn, 58; flat racing, 336
silk screen, 375
silk threads, spider, 40
sill: dam, 100; door, 64; house, 60, 61, 62; volcano, 10
sill cock, standpipe, 59
silo, 104; ballistic missile launch deck, 479
silver amalgam, dental, 455
silver-bullion embroidered cuff, king's regalia, 484
silver certificate, paper money, 224
silverware, 244

silverware drawer, sideboard, 243
simple eye, grasshopper, 41
simple microscope, 442
simple miter, bishop, 487
sin bin, ice hockey rink, 295
since, symbol, 511
single-breasted jacket, 188
single corner, checkerboard, 345
single cuff, shirt, 189
single engine airplane, 147
single lens reflex camera, 172
single-membered foot, ultimate beast, 49
single pleat, woman's pants, 196
single quotation mark, 513
single ring, dart board, 322
single-score ring, dart board, 322
single service court, badminton, 319
singles sideline: badminton, 319; tennis, 312
single system movie sound camera, 174
sinister side, coat of arms, 503
sinister supporter, coat of arms, 503
sink, 62, 247, 273; sailboat, 135; sidepiece, 243
sinker, fishing, 341
sinus, leaf, 52
siphon: clam, 47; octopus, 46
sire, horse, 38, 336
siren: fire engine, 124, 125; police car, 122
sirloin, beef, 32
sissy bar, motorcycle, 129
sitar, 362
situation display indicator, pilot's instrument panel, 481
six pin, bowling, 317
six-shooter, cowboy, 490
16mm camera, lunar rover, 155
sixteenth note, music, 352
sixteenth-of-a-mile pole, harness racetrack, 337
sixty-fourth note, music, 353
60-yard line, polo grounds, 299
size: electrician's wire, 423; nail, 410; painting brush, 371; tire, 105; type, 166
sizer, football helmet, 292
size selector, phonograph turntable, 178
skate: ice, 325; ice hockey, 295
skateboard, 324
skeg: outboard engine, 137; sailboat, 134; surfboard, 330; waterskiing, 329; windsurfer, 330
skein: ballista cord, 467; knitting yarn, 386
skeleton: coral polyp, 46; human, 26; skyscraper, 77; umbrella, 230
skeleton key, 459
skeleton tower, buoy, 132
sketch box, painting, 371
skewback: arch, 72; handsaw, 416
skew chisel, woodcarving, 372
skewer, 259
ski, 326, 327, 329; snowmobile, 130
skid, glider, 147
skiff, 133
skiing: cross-country, 327; downhill, 326; water, 329
skillet, 257
skimmer, 259
skimming brush, 259
skin: fruit, 55; geodesic dome, 85; igloo, 85; skyscraper, 77;

tepee, 84; vegetables, 54, 262; yurt, 70
skin diving, 331
skink, 42
skip rope, body building, 344
skirt: badminton shuttlecock, 319; bedding, 270; bureau, 272; drag racing driver's helmet, 339; dress, 198; escalator, 79; fishing jig, 341; fishing reel, 340; gas pump, 112; girdle, 195; hot air balloon, 332; hovercraft, 145; missile, 482; octopus, 46; palm, 52; racing car, 338; Revolutionary War general's coat, 492; saddle, 335; skin diving mask, 334; window, 65; window shade, 240; woman's, 197
skull: armor, 465; human, 26
skull cap: flat racing, 336; Jewish prayer vestment, 486
skull temple, eyeglasses, 221
sky, 2
skydiver, 333
sky drop, stage, 350
skyline, newspaper, 168
skyscraper, 77
slab: house, 60; lumber, 68
slacks, 191
slalom skiing, 326, 329
slant: gouge, 374; grammatical symbol, 513; type, 165
slant-front desk, 276
slash, grammatical symbol, 513
slash pocket, trousers, 191
slat: fence, 67; lobster pot, 433; rocking chair, 234; screen, 175; sled, 328; train stock car, 117; venetian blind, 241; window, 65; window shade, 241
sled, 328
sleeper, railroad track, 115
sleeping bag, backpacking, 343
sleeping box, truck cab, 120
sleeping car, passenger train, 116
sleeping shelf, igloo, 85
sleep key, television, 185
sleet, 17
sleeve: baluster, 73; barbell, 344; blouse, 197; bridal gown, 488; cardigan, 199; fencing, 315; jacket, 188, 196; jackhammer, 436; lamp, 238, 239; overhead power line, 396; parka, 201; queen's regalia, 484; scriber, 375; shirt, 189; sponge mop, 282; telescope, 443; trenchcoat, 200; windsurfer mast, 330
sleeve protector, banjo, 362
slice: bread, 263; cake, 264; pizza, 265; quiche, 263
slicer, vegetable, 261
slicing disc, food processor, 254
slick, racing, 338, 339
slicker, cowboy, 490
slide: backyard equipment, 287; cigar cutter, 228; cornet, 359; cowboy hat, 202; desk, 276; film, 172; French horn, 331; hand loom, 387; laboratory, 447; pistol, 470; projector, 175; rule, 424; string tie, 441; suspenders, 190; traverse rod, 240; trombone, 358, 359; trumpet, 359; tuba, 358; vise, 409; zipper, 209
slide bed, 287
slide bolt, chain lock, 458

565

slide bracket, hand shower, 274
slide fastener, 209
slide handle, shotgun, 468
slide holder, microscope, 442
slide hook, garbage disposal, 247
slide-out shelf, refrigerator, 249
slide plate, sewing machine, 278
slide projector, 175
slider, parachute, 333
slide rail, snowmobile, 130
slide rule, 441
slide support, 286
slide switch, minivacuum, 283
sliding block, steam engine, 405
sliding cover, desk, 276
sliding door: barn, 104; helicopter, 146; powerboat, 139
sliding eyepiece, ear scope, 448
sliding jaw, monkey wrench, 415
sliding pond, backyard, 287
sliding tandem wheels, truck, 121
slim fin, skin diving, 331
slim skirt, 197
sling: bazooka, 472; elevator shaft, 78; golf bag, 311; ice hammer, 334; mountain climbing, 334; rifle, 468
sling shoe, woman's, 205
slingshot dragster, 339
sling swivel, rifle, 468
slipcase, book, 167
slip-joint pliers, 414
slip nut, sink drain, 273
slipper, ballet, 494
slippery when wet, road sign, 505
slip printer, cash register, 440
slip ring, automatic rifle, 471
slip seat, rocking chair, 234
slip stitched seam, necktie, 192-193
slit: cheese plane, 256; man's underpants, 194; tepee, 84
slit pocket, skirt, 197
slogan, coat of arms, 503
slogan sign, aisle display, 102
sloop, sail, 136
slope: continental, 15; mountain, 8; permanent fort, 83; suit hanger, 281
slope indicator, runway, 94
sloping dormer, house, 62
slot: blackjack, 347; checkbook clutch, 223; clothespin, 280; dental brace, 453; electrical receptacle, 398; electrical switch, 398; hasp, 460; hovercraft, 145; parking meter, 113; pliers, 414; razor, 210; roulette wheel, 346; sandal, 206; screw head, 410; sketch box, 371; slot machine, 346; table saw, 417; telephone, 180; toaster, 253; toggle bolt, 411; toll basket, 114; wallet, 223
slot machine, 346
slotted lifter, kitchen tool, 259
slow down, music notation, 352
slow forward, remote control unit, 184
slow-motion control knobs, telescope, 443
slow-moving vehicle symbol, hitch and harrow, 434
SLR, 172
slug: book page, iv; cartridge,

470; magazine, 171; and parking meter, 113
sluice gate: canal lock, 99; dam, 100
slur, music notation, 352
small intestine, human, 27
small of back, human, 25
small of stock, shotgun, 468
small saphenous vein, human, 28
smock mill, 390
smoke alarm, 284
smoke bomb discharger, tank, 475
smoke chamber, fireplace, 232
smoke detector, 284
smoked sausage, 265
smoke ejector, fire engine, 124
smoke flap, tepee, 84
smoke grenade, 473
smokehouse, 104
smoke path, stove, 404
smoke shelf, fireplace, 232
smokestack, locomotive, 116
smoke-wagon, cowboy, 490
smooth bore, shotgun, 468
smoothbore firing tube, bazooka, 472
smooth-soled climbing shoe, 334
SMV symbol, hitch and harrow, 434
snack food, 265
snail, 47
snake, 42-43; plumbing tool, 422
snap, fishhook, 341
snap bar, suit hanger, 281
snap fastener, 208; fireman's coat, 500; parka, 201; spacesuit, 155; waterskiing vest, 329
snap lock, starting block, 304
snare drum, 364
snaste, candlewick, 237
sneaker, basketball, 296
snifter, 245
snood, 203; turkey, 35
snooker, billiards, 320
snooze alarm, clock radio, 233
snorkel, skin diving, 331
snorkel tube, submarine, 479
snot, candlewick, 237
snout: fish, 45; alligator, 42; crocodile, 42; glacier, 12; pig, 34; stingray, 45
snow, 19
snow block, igloo, 85
snow couloir, 8
snow cuff, ski boot, 327
snowfield, 9, 12
snow gully, 8
snowmobile, 130
snow plow, garbage truck, 127; hockey skate, 325
snow spoiler, snowmobile, 130
snow ring, ski pole, 326
snowshoe, 327
snuff, candlewick, 237
snuffbox, anatomical, 31
snuffer, candle, 237
soap dish: bathtub, 274; sink, 273
soap dispenser, 247
soaring, glider, 147
soccer, 297
sock, 207; baseball, 290; basketball, 296; drag racing driver, 339; fencing, 315; football, 292; ice hockey, 295; skiing, 327; soccer, 297; windsurfer, 330
socket: bayonet, 463; camera, 174; candlestick, 237; eye, 30; guitar, 363; lamp, 238; movie projector, 175; nozzle, 428; operating table, 450; rowboat, 133; shovel, 427;

snap fastener, 208; teeth, 456
socket wrench, 415
sod, hogan, 84
soda-acid fire extinguisher, 284
soda straw, cave, 11
sofa, 236
soffit, house, 61
soft, music notation, 352, 353
softback book, 167
softbound book, 167
softcover book, 167
soft dorsal fin, fish, 45
soft ground, printmaking, 377
soft lens, contact lens, 221
softnose, canal lock, 99
soft ray, fish, 45
soft suction connection hose, pumper, 125
soft tissue, and denture, 453
software, computer, 438
solar flare, 3
solar heating system, 391
solar panel: satellite, 186; weather station, 18
solar plexus, 25
solar power system, 391
solar prominence, 3
solar radiation sensor, weather station, 18
solar time, 5
solar system, 2-3
solder, plumbing, 422
soldering iron, 378
soldier: brick wall, 69; uniform, 496, 497
sole: ballet slippers, 494; boot, 206; golf club, 310; horse's foot, 38; human foot, 31; ice climbing boot, 334; ice skates, 325; man's shoe, 204; plane, 420; running shoe, 302; sailboat, 135; sandal, 206; sock, 207; woman's shoe, 205
solenoid, automobile engine, 111
soleplate: house, 61; iron, 279; rollerskate, 324
soleus, human, 26
solid body, guitar, 363
solid-rocket booster, space shuttle, 152
solid spoke wheel, motorcycle, 129
solitary confinement, prison, 76
solleret, armor, 465
solrad, cartoon, 381
solution: contact lens, 221; magazine puzzle, 171
sommelier, corkscrew, 251
sonar, 444
sonar autofocus transducer, Polaroid, 173
sonar dome, destroyer, 477
sonar rangefinder, Polaroid, 173
sostenuto pedal, piano, 361
soul, human, 25
sound, movie film, 174
sound box: dulcimer, 362; lyre, 355
sound hole: guitar, 260; violin, 355
sounding, nautical chart, 22
sounding board, guitar, 362
sounding datum reference, nautical chart, 22
soundome, sonar, 444
sound-test button, movie camera, 174
soundtrack, movie film, 174
soup spoon, 244
source: composition lighting, 369; coupon, 103
source code, magazine mailing label, 169

source lake, river, 13
sousaphone, 358
South Equatorial Current, ocean, 6
south fork, river, 13
south latitude, globe, 5
South Pole pin, globe, 1
south wing, Capitol, 74
sow, 34
space: music clef, 353; proofreader's mark, 514
space bar, typewriter, 161
space mark, basketball court, 296
spacer: typewriter, 161; wheelchair, 452
space shuttle, 152-153
spacesuit, 155
spade, 427; playing cards, 348
spade bit, drill, 418
spading fork, 427
spaghetti spoon, 259
spaghetti strap, dress, 198
spaghetti tongs, 259
spall, brick, 68
span: arch, 72; bowling ball, 317; bridge, 97
spandrel: arch, 72; mosque, 71
spandrel ornament, grandfather clock, 233
spangle, 219
spanner screw, mortise lock, 458
span wire, traffic light, 113
spar: kite, 323; sailboat, 134
spareribs, 34
spare tire, automobile, 106
spare wheel, truck, 120
spark-arrester: chain saw, 431; fireplace, 232
sparkgap trigger, gas laser, 395
spark plug: automobile engine, 111; internal combustion engine, 406
sparring, 309
spats, drum major, 495
spatula, 259
spawning, fish, 45
speaker: CB radio, 183; guitar amplifier, 363; House of Representatives, 74; metal detector, 445; phonograph, 179; projector, 175; sonar, 444; tape recorder, 177; telephone, 180; television, 185; theatre, 351
speaker grill, portable radio/cassette player, 182
speakerphone, answering machine, 181
speaker selector: phonograph, 179; police car, 122
spear: asparagus, 54; window shade roller, 241
spear blade: partisan, 464; pocket knife, 426
spearhead, partisan, 464
spear point, fence, 67
special-effect pedal, guitar, 363
special effects, synthesizer, 363
special-feature photo treatment, magazine, 170
special function button, telephone, 180
special instructions card holder, elevator car, 78
specialist, space shuttle, 153
specification: electric motor, 399; internal combustion engine, 406
specific edition, book, 167
specific product code, Universal Product Code, 440
specimen holder, microscope, 442
spectacles, 221
spectator seating, courtroom, 89

spectrometer, 445; satellite, 186
speculum, 448
speech balloon, comic strip, 380
speech selector, tape recorder, 177
speed, jet fighter, 480
speed bit, drill, 419
speed controls: blender, 254; car, 110; motorcycle, 129; phonograph turntable, 178; police car, 122; 747 cockpit, 150; tape recorder, 177
speedway racing, 338
spell out, proofreader's mark, 514
spelunking, 11
sphericasia, cartooning, 380
sphygmomanometer, 449
spice, 263
spider, 40; lampshade, 238
spigot, 247, 273
spike, 410; baseball batter, 290; castle portcullis, 81; fence, 67; football field, 293; halberd, 464; ice climbing, 334; mace, 464; pineapple, 55; railroad track, 115; stegosaurus, 43; track shoe, 302; volleyball, 319
spiked foot, camera tripod, 176
spiked heel, woman's shoe, 205
spikelet, grass, 58
spillway, dam, 100
spinal cord, human, 29
spinal nerve, human, 29
spindle: faucet, 273; movie projector, 175; phonograph turntable, 178; rocking chair, 234; roulette wheel, 346; screwdriver, 413; sewing machine, 278; spinning wheel, 387; stethoscope, 449; typewriter, 161; weather vane, 19
spindle hole, diskette, 162
spindle locking plate, workbench vise, 408
spindrift, wave, 14
spine: book, 167; cactus, 56; dust jacket, 167; hair comb, 314; kite, 323; starfish, 46; stegosaurus, 43; stingray, 45
spinnaker, sail, 136
spinner: dominos, 345; seeder, 430; single engine airplane, 147
spinneret, spider, 40
spinning reel, 340
spinning rod, 340-341
spinning wheel, 387
spiny dorsal fin, fish, 45
spiny ray, fish, 45
spiracle: grasshopper, 41; tadpole, 44
spiral: spider web, 40; staircase, 66
spiral bone, girdle, 195
spiral brush, vacuum cleaner, 283
spiral galaxy, 2
spiral ratchet screwdriver, 413
spiral tip, drain cleaner, 422
spire: church, 86; kokoshniki, 70; mountain, 9; univalve shell, 47
spirit level, 424
spit, of land, 7, 15, 22
spit curl, 211
spit key: trombone, 359; trumpet, 359
spitter, toll basket, 114
spitz, glacier, 12
splashboard: Hansom cab, 131; sink, 247
splash guard: truck, 120, 121, 126; washing machine, 280

splash pan, potter's wheel, 373
splash rim, sink, 273
splat, rocking chair, 234
splayed leg, butterfly table, 242
spleen, human, 25, 27
splint, 123, 451
split ballot, voting, 437
split end, paint brush bristle, 425
split line, pill, 451
split-rail fencing, barnyard, 104
split-rim wheel, tow truck, 126
split rudder, space shuttle, 152
split screen, picture-in-picture viewing, 185
splitter, table saw, 417
splitting tool, stonecutting, 372
spoiler: glider, 147; jumbo jet, 148; racing car, 338; snowmobile, 130
spoke: bicycle, 128; Ferris wheel, 93; geodesic dome, 85; harness racing sulky, 337; spider web, 40; stagecoach, 131
sponge: cannon, 467; mop, 282
sponge face, Ping-Pong racket, 321
sponge mop, 282
sponge-tip applicator, 217
sponson, helicopter, 146
spool, 384; film roll, 172; fishing reel, 340; typewriter, 161
spool pin, sewing machine, 278
spoon: golf club, 311; hand grenade, 473; kitchen, 258, 259; pipe tool, 259; table setting, 244
spore, fern, 57
sports car, 106
sports coupe, 108
sports deck, passenger ship, 143
sports wagon, 108
spot: billiard table, 320; blackjack, 347; bowling lane, 317; dice, 347; ice hockey rink, 295; label, 269; playing card, 348; sun, 3
spot label, 268
spotlight: circus, 91; pumper, 125; stage, 350; truck bed, 126
spot-meter reading index, light meter, 176
spotter, gymnastics, 306
spot weld, tweezers, 215
spout: bathtub, 274; beaker, 447; coffee maker, 252; faucet, 273; gas pump automatic nozzle, 112; Jacuzzi, 274; juice extractor, 255; package, 268; pot, 373; sink, 247, 273; tea kettle, 245
spray: bathtub, 274; dishwasher, 250; iron, 279; lawn sprinkler, 428; paint, 425; pistol nozzle, 428; shower, 274; sink, 247
spray adjuster, hand shower, 274
spread: book, 167; canapé, 263; magazine, 170-171; sandwich, 263; shirt collar, 189
spreader: gardening tool, 430; ladder, 425; powerboat, 139; sailboat, 134; saw, 417
spreading spinner, seeder, 430
spring: automobile, 109; ballpoint pen, 158; bear trap, 433; bed, 271; chest pull, 344; clothespin, 280; etching press, 377; gardening shears, 427; gas pump nozzle, 112; hair clip,

214; internal combustion engine, 406; lamp, 239; mousetrap, 433; pencil sharpener, 277; pistol magazine, 470; racing car, 338; sewing machine, 278; shoe tree, 207; sponge mop, 282; stapler, 277; trampoline, 308; truck, 120; umbrella, 230
spring-bar, wristwatch, 220
spring beard needle, 386
springboard: diving, 316; gymnastics, 307; trampoline, 308
spring catch, swivel, 218
spring clamp, 409
spring clip: juice extractor, 255; woodcarving, 372
spring earclip, 218
springer, arch, 72
spring guide, pistol, 470
spring hanger, lamp, 239
spring headband, headphones, 182
spring hinge, 460
springhouse, barnyard, 104
spring slot, clothespin, 280
spring wing, toggle bolt, 411
sprinkle: cake, 264; ice cream cone, 265
sprinkler, 428
sprocket, motorcycle, 129
sprocket drive housing, bulldozer, 435
sprocket hole: film, 172; movie film, 174
sprocket-tip cutting bar, chain saw, 431
spud, laboratory burner, 447
spur: auger bit, 419; chicken, 35; flat racing, 336; polo, 299; revolver hammer, 470; riding equipment, 335
spurl, cartoon, 381
spyglass, 443
squall cloud, 17
square: cannon carriage, 467; chessboard, 345; combination, 424; Manchu court dress, 491; shuffleboard court, 318
square nut, 411
square up, proofreader's mark, 514
square root: calculator key, 441; symbol, 511
square shank, screwdriver, 413
squash, vegetable, 54
squash court, 313
squean, cartoon, 381
squeegee, silk screen, 375
squeeze bottle, 268
squeezer, kitchen tool, 261
squelch control, CB radio, 183
squid, 46
S/RF meter, CB radio, 183
stabilizer: destroyer, 477; fire engine, 124; glider, 147; helicopter, 146; jet fighter, 480; jumbo jet, 149; missile, 482; parachute, 333; passenger ship, 143; single engine airplane, 147
stabilizer block, football helmet, 292
stabilizer trim, 747 cockpit, 150
stable, frontier fort, 82
stack: destroyer, 476; fireboat, 144; furnace, 400; passenger ship, 142; racing car, 338
stacker, high-speed printer, 439
stadia circle, theodolite, 436
stadium, baseball, 291
staff: cardinal, 487; destroyer, 476, 477; flag, 502; halberd,

464; lance, 464; music, 352-353; royal scepter, 485; weather vane, 19
stage, 350-351; microscope, 442; missile, 482
stagecoach, 131
staggeration, cartoon, 380
staggered starting line for distance events, track and field, 300
stained glass, 378
staircase design, house, 66
stairs: 66; house blueprint, 62; jumbo jet, 148; White House, 75
stake: basket frame, 266; croquet, 318; tent, 91, 342
stake pockets, truck platform, 121
stalactite, 11
stalagmite, 11
stalk: asparagus, 54; celery, 262; corn, 58; flower, 53; mushroom, 57; seaweed, 57
stalk end, tomato, 54
stall: railroad yard, 96; shower, 274
stallion, 38
stamen, flower, 53
stamp: coin, 225; envelope, 159; house blueprint, 62
stamp board, track and field, 300
stamp plate number, envelope, 159
stanchion: barn, 104; basketball backstop, 296; ice skates, 325; sailboat, 134; tow truck, 126
stand: cellular telephone, 181; chafing dish, 245; child's car seat, 286; courtroom, 89; curling iron, 214; cymbal, 364; etching press, 377; frame, 379; hammock, 288; kiln, 373; laboratory, 447; lithographic press, 376; movie camera microphone, 174; music, 367; pencil sharpener, 277; slot machine, 346
standard: armor, 465; football goalpost, 293; hose nozzle, 428; pole vault, 305; sled, 328; spinning wheel, 387; theodolite, 436
standard desk phone, 180
standard ratchet screwdriver, 413
stand brace, table saw, 417
standby altimeter, 747 cockpit, 150
standby altitude indicator, pilot's instrument panel, 481
standby compass: pilot's instrument panel, 481; 747 cockpit, 151
stand by/talk switch, cordless phone, 180
standee window, bus, 118
standing collar: butler's uniform, 489; drum major's coat, 495; man's formal attire, 488
standing rigging, sailboat, 134
standing sail, 136
stand leg, table saw, 417
standpipe, fire hydrant, 125
stang, fire engine, 124-125
staple, 410; hasp, 460; silk screen frame, 375
stapler, 277
star: Milky Way, 2-3; sea, 46
starboard: boat, 132; powerboat, 138
star button, telephone, 180
star case, rocket, 383

star diagonal, telescope, 443
star facet, cut gemstone, 218
starfish, 46
star fort, 83
star note, paper money, 224
Star of David, 88, 508
star of order, queen's regalia, 484
stars, aerial shell, 383
start button, copier, 164
starter: automobile, 108, 111; barbecue, 288; bulldozer, 435; chain saw, 431; clothes dryer, 281; elevator, 78; internal combustion engine, 406; mower, 429; outboard engine, 137; phonograph, 178; 747 cockpit, 151; stopwatch, 304
starting block: racing, 304; swimming pool, 316
starting gate, flat racing, 336
starting light, drag racing, 339
starting line: drag racing, 339; running track, 300
state abbreviation, magazine mailing label, 169
state dining room, White House, 75
state political division, thematic map, 21
state prescription number, prescription, 451
stateroom: passenger ship, 142; sailboat, 135
state route: road map, 20; road sign, 504
statesman's name, paper money, 225
static discharge wick, jumbo jet, 148
static line, parachuting, 333
station: dam, 100; nautical chart, 22; subway, 119; universal gym, 344
stationary front, weather map, 19
stationary jaw, wrench, 415
stationary leaf, table, 242
stationary rings, gymnastics, 307
stationery, 159
stationery rack, desk, 276
station guide, picture-in-picture viewing, 185
station model, weather map, 19
station wagon, 106, 108
Statue of Freedom, Capitol, 74
stave, barrel, 267
stay: bicycle, 128; checkbook clutch, 223; girdle, 195; running shoe, 302; shirt collar, 189; sousaphone, 358; wallet, 223
stay rope, bridge, 97
staysail, sailboat, 134
stealth bomber, 480
steam-and-dry iron, 279
steam engine, 405
steamer, pot, 257
steamer cap, fire hydrant, 125
steam generator, nuclear reactor, 392
steam heat, furnace, 400
steam line, nuclear reactor, 392
steam locomotive, 116
steam main, furnace, 400
steel: jackhammer, 436; sharpening, 256
steel blade, food processor, 254
steel burr, dental, 455
steel cage, circus, 90
steel guitar, 363
steel helmet, combat soldier, 497

steel inner shell, nuclear reactor, 392
steel pin, and carpet, 246
steel shield, tunnel, 98
steeplechase: harness racetrack, 337; hurdle, 304; track and field, 300
steeple-crowned hat, wizard, 492
steer, 32
steerable front strut, hydrofoil, 145
steerable high-gain antenna, satellite, 186
steering: automobile, 108, 110; bulldozer, 435; bumper car, 92; fireboat, 144; fire engine, 125; outboard engine, 137; 747 cockpit, 150; sled, 328; snowmobile, 130
stegosaurus, 43
stela, architecture, 71
stem: apple, 55; bicycle, 128; cactus, 56; candelabrum, 237; carrot, 54; celery, 262; faucet, 273; fern, 57; fishing reel, 340; flower, 53; grass, 58; hose nozzle, 428; laboratory burner, 447; latch needle, 386; leaf, 52; lettuce, 54; mushroom, 57; music, 353; onion, 54; pepper, 262; percolator brewing basket, 252; pipe, 229; potato, 54; powerboat, 138; razor blade injector, 210; rowboat, 133; royal orb, 485; steamer basket, 257; glassware, 244; spring beard needle, 386; thermometer, 449; tuning fork, 367; type, 165-166; watch, 220
stem press, incandescent bulb, 238
stemware, 244
stencil, silk screen, 375
stenographer's table, courtroom, 89
step: cannon carriage, 467; church, 87; escalator, 79; fire engine, 124; gallows, 462; Hansom cab, 131; house, 63; ladder, 425; locomotive, 116-117; medical examination table, 450; sailboat, 135; shoreline, 14; shovel, 427; staircase, 66; tractor, 434; truck, 120, 126; windsurfer mast, 330
stepladder, 425
step well, bus, 118
stereo camera, lunar rover, 155
stereo display, portable radio/cassette player, 182
stereo indicator light, phonograph receiver, 179
stereo key, television, 185
stereo/mono button, Walkman, 182
stereo sound LED display, VCR, 184
stereo speaker, television, 185
sterilizing flame, dental, 455
stern: boat, 132; destroyer, 476; dog, 36; sailboat, 134; tugboat, 144; windsurfer, 330
sterndrive engine, 137
sternocleidomastoid, human, 26
sternum, human, 26
stet, proofreader's mark, 514
stethoscope, 449
stetson, cowboy hat, 490
steward, corkscrew, 251
stew pot, 257
stick: ambulance, 123; beauty product, 217; billiard bridge,

320; car shift, 110; craps table, 347; folding rule, 424; golf course, 311; ice hockey, 295; internal combustion engine, 406; lacrosse, 298; piano, 361; pilot's instrument panel, 481; polo, 299; rocket, 383; space shuttle, 153; subway motorman's cab, 119; violin bow, 355; walking, 452
stick glove, ice hockey goalie, 294
stickman, craps table, 347
stick pin, 192
stick umbrella, 230
stiff backing, frame, 379
stiffening truss, bridge, 97
stifle: cow, 32; dog, 36; horse, 38
stigma, flower pistil, 53
stile: door, 64; rocking chair, 234; shutters, 241; sideboard, 243; window, 65
stiletto heel, 205
stilling basin, dam, 100
stimulator tip, toothbrush, 215
sting, bee, 41
stingray, 45
stipe: fern, 57; mushroom, 57
stipule, leaf, 52
stirrup: crossbow, 466; medical examination table, 450; saddle, 335-337
stirrup sock, baseball batter, 290
stitch and stitching, 384; baseball, 290; boot, 206; broom, 282; checkbook clutch, 223; decorative, 385; handbag, 222; knitting, 386; man's belt, 190; sandal, 206; sewing machine, 251; sleeping bag, 343; sock, 207; suspenders, 190
stitching line, sewing pattern, 388
stock: anchor, 132; bagpipe, 365; bell, iv; crossbow, 466; rifle, 468, 471; shotgun, 468; slide rule, 441; windmill, 390
stockade, frontier fort, 82
stockcar, train, 117
stock grip cap, shotgun, 468
stocking: Beefeater, 483; soccer, 297
stock pot, 257
stock saddle, 335
stogies, 228
stole, bishop, 487
stolon, grass, 58
stomach: human, 27, 31; jellyfish, 46
stomach teeth, 456
stone: backgammon, 345; dominos, 345; lithographic press, 376; peach, 55; pendant, 219; ring, 219; wall, 69; woodcarving, 372
stonecutting, 372
stool: boxing, 309; window, 65
stool bed, cannon carriage, 467
stoop, 66; door, 64; house, 63
stop: dam, 100; dog, 36; drill press, 419; elevator car, 78; etching press, 377; gardening shears, 427; mower, 429; organ, 360; remote control unit, 184; road sign, 504; subway, 119; tape recorder, 177; typewriter, 161; window, 65; zipper, 209
stop-act, clown, 493
stop action, picture-in-picture viewing, 185
stopboard, shot put, 301

stop button: compact disc player, 178; Walkman, 182
stoplight, truck, 121, 126
stopper: backpack, 343; bathtub, 274; hypodermic syringe, 451; sink, 273
stopping medium, silk screen, 375
stop plate, internal combustion engine, 406
stop sign, road, 505
stop signal, traffic light, 113
stopwatch, 220, 304
stop wire, umbrella runner, 230
storage: ambulance, 123; buoy, 132; camper, 130; car, 110; fire engine, 124, 125; garbage disposal, 247; gasoline pump, 112; laboratory scale, 447; nuclear reactor, 392; oil drilling platform, 101; pool table, 320; refrigerator, 249; stagecoach, 131; tanker, 140
storage area, supermarket, 102-103
storage drawer, oven, 248
storage solution, contact lens, 221
store ad space, supermarket, 102
storm, 19
storm door: house, 63; subway car, 119
storm flap, backpack, 343
storm igloo, 85
storm patch, trench coat, 200
storm surge, 14
story: minaret, 70; newspaper, 168; skyscraper, 77
stove: camping, 342; kitchen, 248; sailboat, 135; woodburning, 404
stovepipe leg, woman's pants, 196
stowage: jumbo jet, 148; lunar rover, 155; tank, 474
stowed derrick bracket, tanker, 141
straight arm, bobby pin, 214
straightaway, roller coaster, 92
straighten type horizontally, proofreader's mark, 514
straight gouge, 374
straight jaw, pliers, 414
straight leg: trousers, 191; woman's pants, 196
straight-line course, drag racing, 339
straight-line sander, 421
straight of goods, sewing pattern, 388
straight pin, 208
straight razor, 210
straight run, staircase, 66
straight side, grand piano, 361
straight ticket, voting, 437
straight tray, slide projector, 175
straight-up ribbed top, sock, 207
strainer: dishwasher, 250; juice extractor, 255; kitchen tool, 260
strain insulator, overhead power line, 396
strain reliever: curling iron cord, 214; hand drill cord, 419; toaster oven cord, 253
strait, 7
strand: barbed wire, 432; basket, 266; electrician's wire, 423; hair, 213, 214; land feature, 7; mop, 282; rope, 132; thread, 384
strap: accordion, 366; athletic supporter, 194; backpack,

343; baseball catcher, 290; bicycle, 128; block and tackle, 461; boot, 206; brassiere, 195; chain saw chain, 431; child's car seat, 286; cinch fastener, 208; cowboy hat, 202; drag racing driver, 339; dress, 198; electrical wall switch, 398; electric chair, 462; fencing half-jacket, 315; football helmet, 292; glove, 200, 313; golf bag, 311; hasp, 460; ice climbing boot, 334; ice hockey player, 295; man's undershirt, 194; motorcycle, 129; operating table, 450; overnight bag, 285; photographic, 176; police uniform, 499; sandal, 206; handbag, 222; saddle, 335; sandal, 206; skin diving gear, 331; ski pole, 326; stationary rings, 307; subway car, 119; tefillin, 486; trench coat, 200; umbrella, 230; waterskiing vest, 329; woman's shoe, 205; wristwatch, 220
strap hinge, 460
strapping, chaise longue, 288
strap lug, camera, 172
stratocumulus cloud, 16, 17
stratosphere, 4
stratus cloud, 16
straw, cave, 11
strawberry, 55
stream: mountain, 8; ocean, 6; river, 13; topographic map, 22
streamer: drum major's waist sash, 495; flagpole, 502
streamway, cave, 11
street, city plan, 20
street address, magazine mailing label, 169
street cleaner, 127
street zip, mailing label, 169
stretcher: ambulance, 123; brick wall, 69; drop-leaf table, 242; fire engine, 124; painting canvas, 370; rocking chair, 234; umbrella, 230; workbench, 408
stretch limo, 109
stretch pants, skiing, 326
strike: bell, iv; lock, 458
strike pocket, bowling, 317
striker, croquet, 318
striker plate, door lock, 458
striker wheel, cigarette lighter, 228
striking weapons, medieval, 464
string: balloon, 493; cowboy hat, 490; double bass, 355; frankfurter, 265; guitar, 362, 363; jai alai cesta, 314; kite, 323; mandolin, 362; orchestra section, 354; polo, 299; saddle, 335; sitar, 362; squash racket, 313; tennis racket, 312; tie, 192; tub fiddle, 366; violin, 355
string bass, 354
string brace, kite, 323
stringed instruments, 355, 362
string hole: tennis racket, 312; tub fiddle, 366
string tie, 192
strip: bath, 274; cartridge fuse, 399; fence, 67; fencing, 315; Indian shirt, 490; kite, 323; matchbook, 228; postage stamps, 159; roofing shingle, 68; staples, 277; tackless carpet, 246; wheelbarrow, 430; window shutters, 241

stripe: enlisted man's uniform, 496; powerboat, 138; runway, 94; toll booth, 114
striped morning trousers, butler's uniform, 489
stripper, wire, 423
strip title, comic strip, 380
strobe, photographic, 176
strobe flasher, locomotive, 117
stroller, child's, 286
strongbox, 457
strongbox storage, stagecoach, 131
strop, razor, 210
structural unit, piano, 361
structure: domed, 85; launch pad, 152; pyramids, 70
strut: bulldozer, 435; destroyer, 476; geodesic dome, 85; helicopter, 146; house, 61; hydrofoil, 145; racing car, 338; sled, 328
stub: candle, 237; pliers, 414; ticket, 285
stubble, beard, 211
stud: house, 61; man's formal attire, 488; organ, 360; running shoe tread, 302
stud hole, shirt, 189
stud side, snap fastener, 208
stuffing box, steam engine, 405
stuffsack, backpacking, 343
stump: rocking chair, 234; tree, 50
stupa, pagoda, 71
style: art, 368; flower pistil, 53; pea, 54
styled man's hat, 202
stylet, mosquito, 41
stylus, phonograph turntable, 178
styptic pencil, 210
subcategory, book page, iv
subclavian artery, human, 28
subclavian vein, human, 28
sub-control panel, VCR, 184
subdued unit patch, combat soldier, 497
subflooring, house, 60
subhead: book page, iv; magazine, 169-170; newspaper, 168
subject, work of art, 368
subleaflet, fern, 57
submarine, 479
submarine tender, 477
submerged foil hydrofoil, 145
submerged rock, nautical chart, 22
submersible watch, skin diving, 331
subnuclear particle, 3394
subordinate illustration, book page, iv
subscriber, magazine, 169
subsidiary coin, 225
subsidiary road, 114
substitute box area, basketball court, 296
substitute letter, proofreader's mark, 514
subtract, symbol, 510
subtraction, with abacus, 441
subtractive process, stone sculpture, 372
subway, 119; city plan, 20
succulent, 56
sucker, octopus, 46
suction cup, plumber's plunger, 422
suction machine, ambulance, 123
suction unit, paramedic equipment, 123
sudden death, darts, 322
sudden-death overtime, soccer, 297
suffix letter, paper money, 225

sugar bowl, 245
sugar cone, ice cream, 265
sugar shaker, 260
suicide king, playing cards, 348
suit: basketball, 296; chauffeur, 489; drag racing driver, 339; playing cards, 348; sails, 136
suitcase, 285
suit hanger, 281
suite, passenger ship, 143
sulky, harness racing, 337
summer berm, shoreline, 14
summer squash, 54
summer uniform, police, 499
summit, mountain, 8
summons pouch, police, 498
sump, nuclear reactor, 392
sun, 3
sundae, 264
sun deck, passenger ship, 142
sundial, 389
sunglasses, baseball gear, 290
sunglasses pocket, spacesuit, 155
sun roof, automobile, 106
sunshade: satellite, 186; sextant, 137; telescope, 443
sun spot, 3
sun visor, car, 110
super collider, 394
supercombo, 102
superconducting magnet, accelerator, 394
supercooled water, thundercloud, 17
supergiant star, 2
superior mesenteric artery, human, 28
superior slope, permanent fort, 83
superior vena cava, human, 28
supermarket, 102-103
supernova, 3
supersport, passenger car, 109
superstore, 102
superstructure, tanker, 141
super tanker, 140-141
supertweeter, phonograph speaker, 179
Super-Vee racing car, 338
supply duct, heat exchanger, 403
supply line, water heater, 401
supply pipe: solar collector panel, 391; space shuttle, 152; water heater, 401
supply reel: movie camera, 174; projector, 175; tape recorder, 177
support: backyard equipment, 287; camp stove, 342; citrus juicer, 255; desk, 276; Ferris wheel, 93; helicopter, 146; hot air balloon, 332; mailbox, 231; playpen, 286; pole vault, 305; pool table, 320; power line, 396; power saw, 417; pulley block, 461; rocking chair arm, 234; stroller, 286; traverse rod, 240; vacuum tube, 396; wheelbarrow, 430
support bar, drag racing dragster, 339
support beam: bus, 118; subway car, 119
supporter: athletic, 194; coat of arms, 503
support hose, 207
supporting members, fence, 67
supporting plate, land mine, 473
supportive devices, 452
support lacing, lacrosse glove, 298
support leg, truck, 121

support post, Ping-Pong net, 321
support system, racing car, 338
support tube, lamp, 239
support unit, basketball backstop, 296
support wire, incandescent bulb, 238
suppressor, automatic weapon flash, 471
sural nerve, human, 29
surbase, column pedestal, 73
surcingle, flat racing, 336
surf, 14
surface: brick, 68; desk, 276; diving platform, 316; lithographic press, 376; parachute, 333; and perspective, 368; pool table, 320; printing, 166; solar power system, 391; starfish, 46; table saw, 417; type, 166
surface fighting ship, 476-477
surface heating unit, oven, 248
surface-piercing hydrofoil, 145
surface search radar: aircraft carrier, 478; destroyer, 477
surface-to-air missiles, 476
surface-to-surface missiles, 476
surface wave, 14
surfboard, 331
surfing, 330
surgical table, 450
surname: basketball player, 296; magazine mailing label, 169
surplice, minister, 487
surveyor, and transit, 436
suspended ceiling, elevator car, 78
suspender, harness racing gear, 337
suspender cable, bridge, 97
suspenders, 190; ice hockey player, 294
suspension: phonograph turntable, 178; racing car, 338
suspension bridge, 97
suspension cable, stationary rings, 307
suspension line, parachute, 333
suspension pivot, laboratory scale, 447
suspension rope, hot air balloon, 332
suspension system: automobile, 108; football helmet, 292
suspension wheel, snowmobile, 130
sutler, frontier fort, 82
su-tshu, Manchu court dress, 491
suture, univalve shell, 47
swab, cannon, 467
swagger bag, 222
swalloop, cartoon, 380
swallowtail: flag, 502; surfboard, 330
swallowtail pennant, 502
swami belt, mountain climbing, 334
swamp: coastline, 15; river, 13
swan neck, house, 63
swash, wave, 14
swatch, fabric, 388
swastika, symbol, 508
sweatband, beret, 202
sweater, 199; skiing, 326, 327
sweat sock, 207
sweat soldering, plumbing, 422
sweep: brace, 418; windmill, 390
sweeper: carpet, 282; lawn, 429
sweep indicator, pilot's instrument panel, 481

sweet goods, 264
sweet spot, tennis racket, 312
sweet tooth, 456
swell, 14; saddle, 335
swelling, lance, 464
swell keyboard, organ, 360
swell shoe, organ, 360
swept-back wing, combat
   aircraft, 480
swim fin, skin diving, 331
swimming, 316
swimming foot, bird, 39
swine, 34
swing, backyard, 287
swing-away bar, suit hanger,
   281
swing chain, 287
swing gouge, woodcarving,
   372
swing hanger, 287
swinging gate, drop-leaf table,
   242
swing mirror, dressing table,
   272
swing seat, 287
Swiss army knife, 426
switch: accordion, 366;
   calculator, 441; camera, 172;
   car directional signal, 110;
   CB radio, 183; clothes dryer,
   281; cow, 32; curling iron,
   214; dental unit, 454;
   dishwasher, 250; drill press,
   419; electric, 398; electric
   hairbrush, 212; electric
   razor, 210; elevator, 78; fax
   machine, 164; finishing
   sander, 421; food processor,
   254; guitar amplifier, 363;
   hair dryer, 212; jackhammer,
   436; kiln, 373; lamp, 238,
   239; laser printer, 163;
   microphone, 183;
   minivacuum, 283; movie
   camera, 174; organ, 360;
   outboard engine, 137;
   phonograph receiver, 179;
   pilot's instrument panel,
   481; portable radio/cassette
   player, 182; radar, 444;
   railroad yard, 96; saw, 417,
   431; 747 cockpit, 150, 151;
   tape measure, 424; tape
   recorder, 177; telephone,
   180; toaster oven, 253;
   Walkman, 182
swivel: camera tripod, 176;
   C-clamp, 409; field events
   hammer, 303; fishhook, 341;
   hasp, 460; jewelry findings,
   218; jump rope, 344; mortar,
   472; peeler, 256; pulley
   block, 461; rifle, 468, 469;
   stationary rings, 307;
   stroller, 286; suit hanger,
   281; vise, 409
swivel holster, police gun belt,
   499
swivel mount, hand shower,
   274
sword, 463, 492
sword point position,
   windmill, 390
sword-swallower, circus, 90
symbol: grammatical, 513;
   label, 268, 269; of life, 508;
   mah-jongg tile, 345; map,
   20; religious, 508; science,
   business, and commerce,
   510-511
symbolia, cartoon, 381
symbolic date, coin, 225
symbolic decoration, minister,
   487
symbolic language, 512
sympathetic string, sitar, 362
symphony orchestra, 354
synagogue, 88, 486

synchronized dubbing,
   portable radio/cassette
   player, 182
synodic period, moon, 4
synoptic chart, weather, 19
synthesizer, 363
synthetic coil, zipper, 209
synthetic porcelain, dental, 455
syringe: dental, 454, 455;
   hypodermic, 451; kitchen,
   259; paramedic, 123
syrup, sundae, 264
system control panel, Polaroid,
   173
system diagram, portable
   radio/cassette player, 182

T

T: braille, 512; sign language,
   512; windsurfer, 330
tab: electrical receptacle, 398;
   eyeglasses, 221; handbag,
   222; package, 268; parka,
   201; powerboat, 138; racing
   car, 338; razor, 210; roofing
   shingle, 68; wallet, 223;
   zipper, 209
tabernacle, church, 87
table, 242; basketball court,
   296; courtroom, 89; cut
   gemstone, 218; dental, 455;
   drill press, 419; medical,
   450; Ping-Pong, 321; pocket
   billiards, 135; sailboat, 135;
   saw, 417; violin, 355
table arm, dental, 455
table lamp, 238
table lock, camera tripod, 176
table-locking clamp, drill
   press, 419
table position selector, surgical
   table, 450
table saw, 417
table setting, 244-245
tablet: computer workstation,
   438; medicinal, 451; organ,
   360; tombstone, 516
table tennis, 321
tabletop, dressing table, 272
tabling, mainsail, 136
tabloid newspaper, 168
tabulator control, typewriter,
   161
TACAN antenna, destroyer,
   476
Tacan navigation system,
   aircraft carrier, 478
tace, armor, 465
tach, car, 110
tachometer: car, 110;
   motorcycle, 129; pilot's
   instrument panel, 481;
   powerboat, 138
tack, 410; carpet, 246;
   mainsail, 136; necktie, 193;
   racehorse, 336; tambourine,
   364; umbrella, 230
tack cloth, painting, 425
tackle, fishing, 341
tackless strip, carpet, 246
taco, jai alai cesta, 314
tactical information display,
   pilot's instrument panel, 481
tadpole, 44
taenia, column entablature, 73
taffrail, sailboat, 134
tag: attaché case, 285; combat
   soldier's uniform, 461
tail: allosaurus, 43; cat, 37;
   coffin, 516; coin, 225; comet,
   3; cow, 32; dog, 36;
   fireworks, 383; fish, 45;
   horse, 38; house, 61; kite,
   323; lobster, 47; pelt, 201;
   pig, 34; single engine
   airplane, 147; skateboard,
   324; ski, 326, 329; snowshoe,
   327; stegosaurus, 43;

stingray, 45; surfboard, 330;
   ultimate beast, 48; weather
   station vane, 18; windsurfer,
   330
tail coat: circus ringmaster, 90;
   drum major, 495; man's
   formal attire, 488
tail crest, tadpole, 44
tail fan, lobster, 47
tail feather, 35, 39
tail fin: automobile, 107; cruise
   missile, 482; fish, 45; jet
   fighter, 480; jumbo jet, 149
tail nozzle, jet fighter, 480
tailored pillow, sofa, 236
tailor shop, prison, 76
tailor's loop, shirt, 189
tailpiece: banjo, 362; sink
   drain, 273; violin, 355
tailpipe, tow truck, 126
tail plane, jumbo jet, 149
tail pylon, helicopter, 146
tail rocker, slalom water ski,
   329
tail rotor, helicopter, 146
tail section: flute, 356;
   snowmobile, 130; torpedo,
   479
tail service mast, space shuttle,
   152
tail vise, workbench, 408
tail water, dam, 100
tail wheel, helicopter, 146
taintor gate, dam, 100
takeoff area, high jump, 305
takeoff board, track and field,
   300
takeoff engine, lunar lander,
   154
takeoff fan, high jump, 300
take out space, proofreader's
   mark, 514
take-up motion handle, hand
   loom, 387
take-up reel: movie camera,
   174; movie projector, 175;
   tape recorder, 177
take-up spool, typewriter, 161
talk switch, CB radio
   microphone, 183
tall-case clock, 233
tallith, Jewish prayer vestment,
   486
tallow, candle, 237
tally clerk, House of
   Representatives, 74
tally man, cattle ranch, 432
tallywhacker, sailor's uniform,
   497
talon: allosaurus, 43; bird, 39
talus slope, mountain, 8
tambourine, 354, 364
tamer, circus, 90
Tamid, 88, 486
tamper, pipe tool, 229
tandem wheels, truck, 121
tang: drill bit, 419; file, 420;
   knife, 244, 256, 463; rake,
   427; rasp, 420; skillet, 257
tangential section, lumber,
   68
tank, 474-475; ambulance, 123;
   automobile, 107, 108, 109;
   barbecue grill, 288; camper,
   130; camp stove, 342; chain
   saw, 431; drag racing
   dragster, 339; fire engine,
   124; garbage truck, 127;
   gasoline storage, 112;
   internal combustion engine,
   406; iron, 279; lantern, 342;
   lunar lander, 154; mower,

429; nuclear reactor, 392; oil
   drilling platform, 101;
   railroad yard, 96; skin
   diving, 331; solar heating
   system, 391; space shuttle,
   152; submarine ballast, 479;
   toilet, 275; truck, 120, 121;
   water heater, 401
tank car, train, 116
tanker, ocean-going, 140-141
tank forward bay, space
   shuttle, 152
tap, 273
tape: Band-Aid, 451; baseball
   bat, 291; boxing, 309; cash
   register, 440; cassette, 177;
   coat of arms, 503; envelope,
   159; garment seam, 196;
   measuring, 424; mountain
   climbing, 334; package, 269;
   Ping-Pong net, 321;
   skateboard, 324; tennis net,
   312; typewriter, 161; Velcro,
   209; venetian blind, 241;
   volleyball net, 319; zipper,
   209
tape control, portable
   radio/cassette player, 182
tape control button, Walkman,
   182
tape measure, 424
tape mode selector, portable
   radio/cassette player, 182
tape-monitor switch,
   phonograph receiver, 179
taper, 237
tape recorder, 177
tapered leg, woman's pants,
   196
tapered winder, staircase, 66
tape reel, magnetic tape
   subsystem, 439
taphole, keg, 267
tapper: buoy, 132; glass cutter,
   378
taproot, 51; carrot, 54
tare poise, laboratory scale,
   446
target: medieval shield, 464;
   radar, 444; railroad crossing
   signal, 115
target arrow, bowling lane,
   317
target designate switch, pilot's
   instrument panel, 481
target lock, sonar, 444
tassel: drum major's boot top,
   495; king's regalia, 484;
   Manchu court dress, 491;
   venetian blind, 241; window
   shade, 240; woman's hat,
   203
tasset, armor, 465
taste buds, tongue, 30
tasting spoon, 259
tatting shuttle, 386
tattooed lady, circus, 90
tau cross, symbol, 508
Taurus, zodiac, 509
taxi roof light, 119
taxi stand, public sign, 506
taxiway, airport, 95
t-bar, truck bed, 126
tea ball, 260
teacup, 245
tea infuser, 260
team insignia, soccer uniform,
   297
team logo, baseball, 290
team number, jai alai, 314
team race, swimming pool,
   316
team shirt, polo, 299
teamsters' mess, frontier fort,
   82
teamsters' quarters, frontier
   fort, 82
teapot, 245

tear-away jersey, football uniform, **292**
tear drop, surfboard, **330**
tear duct, eye, **30**
tear gland, eye, **30**
tear tape, package, **269**
teased hair, woman's, **213**
teaser: magazine, **171**; stage, **350**
tea set, **245**
tea spoon, **245**
tea strainer, **260**
teat: cow, **32**; pig, **34**
technical magazine, **169**
technician's set, ambulance, **123**
tee: golf, **310**; pagoda, **71**
teepee, **84**
teeterboard, circus, **90**
teeter-totter, backyard, **287**
teeth, *see* tooth
tefillin, Jewish ritual items, **486**
teflon pad, baren, **374**
telegraph aerial, tanker, **141**
telegraph key, **157**
telemetry radio, ambulance, **123**
telephone, **180**; public sign, **506**; road sign, **504**
telephone handset: answering machine, **181**; fax machine, **164**
telephone line, fax machine, **164**
telephone line hook-up, fax machine, **164**
telephone line jack, fax machine, **164**
telephone monitor, tape recorder, **177**
telephone pushbutton, answering machine, **181**
telescope, **443**; satellite, **186**; sextant, **137**; tank, **475**; theodolite, **436**
telescopic helicopter hangar, destroyer, **476**
telescopic sight, rifle, **469**
television, **184-185**; antenna, house, **63**; mast, skyscraper, **77**
television monitor, video-still camera, **173**
telex number, business card, **160**
telltale: mainsail, **136**; squash court, **313**
telson, lobster, **47**
tempera, painting medium, **370**
temperature: 747 cockpit, **150**; thermometer, **18**; weather map, **19**
temperature control: air conditioner, **403**; dryer, **281**; iron, **279**; microwave oven, **248**; toaster oven, **253**; washing machine, **280**
temperature gauge, car engine, **110**
temperature prediction, weather map, **19**
temperature scale, volt-ohm meter, **423**
temperature sensor: microwave oven, **248**; weather station, **18**
temple: eyeglasses, **221**; human, **24**; Jewish, **88, 486**; Muslim, **70-71**
temple gateway, Shinto, **70**
temple memorial band, Jewish prayer shawl, **486**
temporal lobe, brain, **29**
temporary traffic-control device, toll booth, **114**
tempura rack, wok, **257**
tenant floor, skyscraper, **77**

tender, **133**; locomotive, **116**
tenderloin, pork, **34**
tender truck, locomotive, **116**
tendon, human foot, **31**
tendon guard: hockey skate, **325**; skate, **295**
tendril, hair, **213**
ten-gallon hat, **202, 490**
tennis, **312**
10-off square, shuffleboard court, **318**
tenon, bagpipe, **365**
tenor drone, bagpipe, **365**
tenor drum, **364**
tenor joint, bassoon, **37**
tenpins, bowling, **317**
tension adjustment pin, gardening shears, **427**
tension arm, bobby pin, **214**
tension bar: razor, **210**; steel chain fence gate, **67**
tension clamp, lamp, **239**
tension control knob, snare drum, **364**
tension cord, Ping-Pong net, **321**
tension guide, sewing machine, **278**
tension hoop, banjo, **362**
tension ring, dome, **85**
tension rod: bass drum, **364**; man's buckle, **190**
tension screw: banjo, **362**; kettledrum, **364**; paramedic equipment, **123**
tension sheave, elevator shaft, **78**
tension wheel, bicycle, **128**
tent, **342**; circus, **90**; oxygen, **452**; yurt, **70**
tentacle: coral polyp, **46**; jellyfish, **46**; octopus, **46**; starfish, **46**
10-yard chain, football, **293**
10-yard line, football field, **293**
10.5-inch magnetic tape, computer tape, **439**
10.5-inch magnetic tape drive, computer system, **439**
tepal, flower, **53**
tepee, **84**
terminal: airport, **95**; electrical wall switch, **398**; fax machine, **164**; fence gate, **67**; railroad yard, **96**
terminal block, stove, **248**
terminal bud, tree, **50**
terminal moraine, **8, 12**
terminology, nautical, **132**
terminus, glacier, **12**
terrace: house, **63**; shoreline, **14**
terrace server, **245**
terreplein, permanent fort, **83**
territory, baseball field, **291**
tertiary root, **51**
test area, aircraft carrier, **478**
test button: police car, **122**; smoke alarm, **284**
test lead jack, volt-ohm meter, **423**
test panel, pilot's instrument, **481**
test tube, **447**
tether line, hot air balloon, **332**
text: book, **167**; magazine, **170**
textblock, book page, **iv**
texture, and composition, **369**
thalamus, brain, **29**
T-handle, pommel horse, **307**
theatre, **351**; passenger ship, **41**
the end, gesture, **507**
thematic map, **21**
thenar eminence, human hand, **31**
theodolite, **436**
therefore, symbol, **511**

thermal dot, curling iron, **214**
thermal energy, steam engine, **405**
thermal-storage tank, solar heating system, **391**
thermistor, weather station, **18**
thermometer, **449**; dual scale, **18**; kitchen, **258**; laboratory, **447**
thermosphere, earth, **4**
thermostat: refrigerator, **249**; solar heating system, **391**; stove, **404**; water heater, **401**
thick stroke, type, **165**
thick-walled inert laser pressure vessel, **395**
thigh: bird, **39**; cat, **37**; chicken, **35**; cow, **32**; dog, **36**; frog, **44**; horse, **38**; human, **24**; poultry, **35**
thigh pad, football uniform, **292**
thigh machine, universal gym, **344**
thimble, **384**; harness racing, **337**; stove, **404**
thin stroke, type, **165**
third base, baseball field, **291**
third eye, tuatara, **42**
third molar, **456**
third quarter moon, **4**
third rail, subway, **119**
third stage, missile, **482**
third toe, human foot, **31**
third valve, trumpet, **359**
third valve slide: French horn, **358**; trumpet, **359**
3480 magnetic tape cartridge, computer tape, **439**
3480 magnetic tape drive, computer system, **439**
thirty-second-inch mark, tape measure, **424**
thirty-second note, music, **353**
30-yard line, polo grounds, **299**
thong: cowboy holster, **490**; police nightstick, **498**; sandal, **206**
thoracic nerve, human, **29**
thorax, grasshopper, **41**
thorn, ultimate beast, **48**
thoroughbrace, stagecoach, **131**
thoroughbred, flat racing, **336**
thought balloon, cartoon, **380**
thread: bolt, **411**; plug fuse, **399**; screw, **410**; sewing, **384**; spider, **40**; weaving, **387**
threaded fitting, nozzle, **428**
threaded handle, paint roller, **425**
threaded neck, bottle, **268**
threaded pipe, **422**
thread guide, sewing machine, **278**
3-band display, portable radio/cassette player, **182**
3-band equalizer, Walkman, **182**
three dimensions, stone sculpture, **372**
3/8 pole, harness racetrack, **337**
301, darts, **322**
three pin, bowling, **317**
three-point line, basketball court, **296**
three-point perspective, **368**
3/4 pole, harness racetrack, **337**
3.25-inch disk format, diskette, **162**
three-ring circus, **90**
three-second lane, basketball court, **296**
3/16 pole, harness racetrack, **337**

three suit, domino, **345**
three-way light bulb, **238**
three-way syringe, dental, **455**
three-yard line, football, **293**
threshold: airport runway, **94**; door, **64**; house, **62**
throat: anchor, **132**; auger bit, **419**; bird, **39**; clamp, **409**; cornet, **359**; fireplace, **232**; human, **24, 25, 30**; lacrosse stick, **298**; latch needle, **386**; salamander, **44**; saw, **416**; shoe, **204, 205**; squash racket, **313**; tennis racket, **312**
throat-cutting, gesture, **507**
throat doctor, examination equipment, **448**
throat fan, lizard, **43**
throating, church, **86**
throat latch strap, trenchcoat, **200**
throat opening, vise, **408**
throatpiece, tennis racket, **312**
throat plate, sewing machine, **278**
throat protector, baseball catcher, **290**
throat pump, paramedic equipment, **123**
throttle: car, **110**; horse, **38**; internal combustion engine, **406**; motorcycle, **129**; outboard engine, **137**; pilot's instrument panel, **481**; powerboat, **138**
throttle latch, chain saw, **431**
throw: bedding, **270**; track and field, **301**
throwing circle, shot put, **301**
throwing sector, javelin, **300**
thrown pot, **373**
throw rug, **246**
thrust cone, jumbo jet, **149**
thruster: lunar lander, **154**; passenger ship, **143**; space shuttle, **152**
thrusting and cutting weapon, **463**
thrust lever, 747 cockpit, **151**
thrust ring, missile, **482**
thrust tube, ballpoint pen, **158**
thruway, **114**
thumb: baseball glove, **291**; dog, **36**; frog, **44**; human hand, **31**
thumbhole: bowling ball, **317**; painter's palette, **371**
thumbpiece, revolver safety catch, **218**
thumb press, curling iron, **214**
thumb rest: hypodermic syringe, **451**; iron, **279**
thumbscrew: blood pressure gauge, **449**; clarinet mouthpiece, **357**; drain cleaner, **422**; earring, **218**; laboratory clamp, **446**
thumb-string peg, banjo, **362**
thunder, **17**
thundercloud, **17**
thunderhead, **16, 17**
thunderstorm, **17, 19**
thurl, cow, **32**
thwart, rowboat, **133**
thyratron, gas laser, **395**
tiara, **219, 484, 485**
tibia: frog, **44**; grasshopper, **41**; human, **26**; spider, **40**
tibialis anterior, **26**
tibialis posterior, **26**
tibial nerve, human, **29**
ticket, **349**; police, **498**; voting, **437**
ticket pocket flap, jacket, **188**
ticket spitter, toll basket, **114**
tidal inlet, **15**
tidal marsh, **15**

tidal wave, 14
tide, 15
tie: man, 192-193, 488; military, 496; music notation, 353; package, 269; police, 499; railroad track, 115; saddle, 335; skirt, 197; wall, 69
tieback, curtain, 240
tie bar, 192
tie beam: house, 61; incline track, 92
tie brace, bridge, 97
tie clasp, 192
tie closure: blouse, 197; umbrella, 230
tie-down, inflatable, 133
tie holder, suitcase, 285
tie plate: railroad track, 115; stapler, 277
tie rod end, automobile, 108
tie strap, chain saw chain, 431
tie wing, dental brace, 453
tiger, circus, 90
tightener, dental, 455
tightrope act, circus, 90
tights, ballet dancer, 494
tight spiral, staircase, 66
tilde, grammatical symbol, 513
tile: domino, 345; mah-jongg, 345
till, cash register, 440
tiller: boat, 134; grass, 58; 747 cockpit, 150
tilt control, sonar, 444
tilt cord, venetian blind, 241
tilting arbor handwheel, saw, 417
tilting base, saw, 417
tilting knob, movie projector, 175
tilt lock, saw, 417
tilt rod, window shutters, 241
timber, 68; castle portcullis, 81
timbered joint, Japanese building, 70
timberline, 8
time: drag racing, 339; map, 5; parking meter, 113
time belt, 5
time cord, dental x-ray unit, 454
time dial, globe, 1
time dot, music, 353
timekeeper: House of Representatives, 74; ice hockey, 295
time lock, vault, 457
timer: basketball, 296; clothes dryer, 281; dishwasher, 250; kitchen, 258; parking meter, 113; skin diving, 331; stove, 248; traffic light, 113
timer digital display, microwave oven, 248
timer key, television, 185
timer set control, microwave oven, 248
times, symbol, 510
time signature, music, 352
Times Square, prison, 76
time zone, map, 5
time zone display control, wristwatch, 220
timing case cover, automobile engine, 111
timpani, 354, 364
tin, squash court, 313
tin can, surface fighting ship, 476
tine: fork, 244; hitch and harrow, 434; rake, 427
tip: arrow, 466; asparagus, 54; ballpoint pen, 158; bicycle, 128; billiard cue, 320; bobby pin, 214; bow, 466; cheese plane, 256; crutch, 452; curling iron, 214; dental

unit, 454; drain cleaner, 422; drum major's baton, 495; fencing foil, 315; fishing rod, 341; grass, 58; hypodermic syringe, 451; iceberg, 12; icing nozzle, 259; javelin, 302; knife, 256, 463; leaf, 52; man's belt, 190; nose, 30; outboard engine, 137; peeler, 256; pelt, 201; pliers, 414; saw, 431; screwdriver, 413; sharpening steel, 256; ski, 326, 329; soldering iron, 378; sword, 463; tent pole, 342; toothbrush, 215; tweezers, 215; umbrella, 230; univalve shell, 47; violin bow, 355; woman's shoe, 205
tip contact, incandescent bulb, 238
tip guard, hockey skate, 325
tipi, 84
tip-in, magazine, 171
tip-on label, 268
tippet, minister, 487
tipping, necktie, 193
tipping lever, wheelchair, 452
tip top, fishing rod, 341
tire, 105; automobile, 106, 107; bicycle, 128; bus, 118; drag racing dragster, 339; harness racing sulky, 337; motorcycle, 129; seeder, 430; stagecoach, 131; tractor, 434; truck, 120; wheelbarrow, 430
tissue: and denture, 453; fruit, 255; meat, 262; photographic supplies, 176; succulent, 56
Titan, 3
titanium salute, fireworks, 382
title: book, 167; business card, 160; comic strip, 380; magazine, 169, 170, 171; map, 21; music, 352; nautical chart, 22; phonograph record, 178
title block, house blueprint, 62
T-neck, ski clothes, 327
TNT, hand grenade, 473
toad, 44
toadstool, 57
toaster, 253
toaster oven, 253
tobacco, 228
tobacco pouch, 229
toboggan, 328
toe: bird, 39; boot, 206; cat, 37; chicken, 35; dog, 36; frog, 44; hockey skate, 325; golf club, 310; horseshoe, 38; horse's hoof, 38; human, 24, 31; ice skate, 325; man's shoe, 204; panty hose, 195; piano, 361; plane, 420; roller skate, 324; running shoe, 302; saw, 416; shotgun, 468; ski, 326, 327, 329; snowshoe, 327; sock, 207
toeboard, shot put, 301
toe cap, skate, 295
toe clip: bicycle, 128; horse's hoof, 38
toe disc, toad, 44
toe guard: elevator shaft, 78; mower, 429
toe-height adjustment screw, ski binding, 326
toenail: cat, 37; human, 31; turkey, 35; ultimate beast, 49
toe-piece release, ski binding, 326
toe plate: baseball pitcher, 290; refrigerator, 249
toe rail, sailboat, 134
toeshoe, ballet dancer, 494
toe strap, bicycle, 128

toe stud, organ, 360
toga, 491
toggle bolt, 411
toggle lever, pliers, 414
toggle link, sponge mop, 282
togglelock, backpack, 343
toilet, 275
toilet mirror, dressing table, 272
token, collector, 225
toll basket, 114
toll booth, highway, 114
tom, turkey, 35
tomato, 54
tomato sauce, pizza, 265
tomb, 516
tombolo, 7
tombstone, 516
tomcat, 37
tom-tom, 364
tone: tuning fork, 367; woodwind, 356, 358, 359
tone arm, phonograph turntable, 178
tone control: guitar, 363; tape recorder, 177
tone generator, synthesizer, 363
tone unit, piano, 361
tone-up wheel, body building, 344
tong(s): kitchen, 259; lunar rover, 155; oil drilling platform, 101; revolver safety catch, 218
tongue: bolt ring, 218; child's wagon, 287; cow, 32; curling iron, 214; film, 172; flag, 502; human, 30; Jew's harp, 366; L-shaped square, 424; man's belt, 190; man's shoe, 204; running shoe, 302; skate, 295, 324, 325; sled, 328; snake, 42
tongue-and-groove pliers, 414
tongue blade, 123, 449
tongue depressor, 449
tonsil, 30
tool: ice climbing, 334; pipe, 229; pocket knife, 426; police car, 122; sculpting, 372
tool stowage: bulldozer, 435; jackhammer, 436; lunar rover, 155; motorcycle, 129; tow truck, 126; workbench, 408
tooth, 456; allosaurus, 43; bear trap, 433; corrugated fastener, 410; denture, 453; fern, 57; file, 420; hair comb, 212; ice hammer, 334; knee kicker, 246; lobster, 47; pliers, 414; rake, 427; rasp, 420; saw, 416, 417; scissors, 384; scrimshaw, 375; snake, 42; suspenders, 190; tank drive wheel, 475; zipper, 209
toothbrush, 215
toothed chisel, 372
toothpick, pocket knife, 426
top: automobile, 107; balance beam, 306; battery, 397; button, 209; can, 267; circus, 90; desk, 276; fishing rod, 341; flag, 502; golf bag, 311; handbag, 222; hurdle, 304; juice extractor, 255; laboratory burner, 447; lettuce, 262; medical examination table, 450; microscope limb, 442; mountain, 8; parachute, 333; parallel bars, 306; piano, 361; rocking chair, 234; sideboard, 243; skyscraper, 77; sock, 207; stove, 404;

thimble, 384; violin, 355; workbench, 408; zipper, 209
top block, window shutters, 241
top cover, dot matrix printer, 163
tope, pagoda, 71
top exit, elevator, 78
top fabric, quilting, 385
top hat: circus ringmaster, 90; miser, 492
top housing, electric razor, 210
top link, hitch and harrow, 434
top lip, lacrosse stick, 298
toplit composition, 368
top-loading washing machine, 280
top margin, book page, 167
topographic map, 22
top pad, child's car seat, 286
top pillow, stagecoach, 131
topping: canapé, 263; dessert, 264
top plate: house, 61; typewriter, 161; violin, 355
top pocket flap, backpack, 343
top rail: backyard equipment, 287; bureau, 272; door, 64; fence gate, 67; playpen, 286; staircase, 66; window, 65
top ring, fishing rod, 341
top roller, etching press, 377
topsail, sailboat, 134
top sheet, bedding, 271
top spring, umbrella, 230
top stitching: checkbook clutch, 223; handbag, 222; man's belt, 190
top strap, revolver, 470
top thread guide, sewing machine, 278
top tube, bicycle, 128
toque, 203
Torah, 88, 486
torch, propane, 422
torii, 70-71, 508
tormentor: fire engine, 124; stage, 350
tornado, 17
torpedo, 479
torsade, wrought iron fence, 67
torse, coat of arms, 503
torso: cow, 32; human, 24; space suit, 155
tortoise, 43
torus, column, 73
tossut, igloo, 85
total air temperature, 747 cockpit, 150
totalizer, gas pump, 112
totalizer board, flat racing, 336
total reflector, laser, 395
tote board, horseracing, 336, 337
touchdown area, airport runway, 95
touch line: polo grounds, 299; soccer field, 297
touch-tone button: pay phone, 180; telephone, 180
toupee, 211
touring, ski, 327
tourist section, jumbo jet, 149
tournament darts, 322
towboat, 144
tow-cable pulley, tow truck, 126
towel bar: barbecue grill, 288; oven, 248
towel clip, dental, 455
towel rack, bathtub, 274
tower: aircraft carrier, 478; bridge, 97; castle, 80, 81; church, 86, 87; destroyer, 476; Ferris wheel, 93; fireboat, 144; frontier fort,

82; globe, 1; mountain, 9; nautical chart, 22; passenger ship, 143; polygonal, 71; powerboat, 139; power network, 396; prison, 76; railroad yard, 96; slide, 287; windmill, 390
tower bin, silo, 104
tower control, airport, 95
tower ladder, 124
towing gear: glider, 147; fire engine, 124, 125; tank, 475; tow truck, 126; tugboat, 144
towing light: destroyer, 477; tugboat, 144
towing ring, kite, 323
towline, waterskiing, 329
town: magazine mailing label, 169; map, 20; nautical chart, 22
towpath, canal lock, 99
tow ring, fire engine, 124, 125
tow truck, 126
tracery, church, 86
track: baseball field, 291; bulldozer, 435; canal lock, 99; circus, 90-91; dishwasher, 250; Grand Prix, 338; horseracing, 336, 337; incline, 92; lighting, 239; movie film, 174; passenger ship, 142; railroad, 96, 115; roller coaster, 92; snowmobile, 130; subway, 119; tank, 474; traverse rod, 240
track and field, 300-301
track cueing, compact disc player, 178
tracking adjuster, belt sander, 421
tracking-force dial, phonograph turntable, 178
track lighting, 239
track shoe, 302; bulldozer, 435
traction splint, 123
tractor, 434; bulldozer, 435; truck, 120
tractor dial, dot matrix printer, 163
tractor wheel, roller coaster, 92
trade magazine, 169
trademark: bank card, 226; baseball bat, 286; book, 167; credit card, 227; label, 268
trade winds, 6
trading post, 82
traffic control, 113; airport, 94, 95; toll booth, 114
traffic light, 113
traffic police officer, 498
traffic signals, 113
traffic ticket, 498
tragus, outer ear, 30
trail: public sign, 506; road sign, 504
trail bike, 129
trailer, 130
trailer connecter, truck, 120
trailing edge, jumbo jet, 148
trailing truck, locomotive, 116
trail rope, hot air balloon, 332
trail shoe, snowshoe, 327
train: bridal gown, 488; railroad, 96, 116-117; roller coaster, 92; subway, 119
trainer: circus, 90; flat racing entry, 336; running shoe, 302
training shoe, 302
tramp, merchant ship, 140
trampolets, 308
trampoline, 308
tranquilizer, 123
transaction button, automatic teller machine, 226
transaction receipt slot,

automatic teller machine, 226
transceiver: CB radio, 183; radar antenna, 444
transducer, sonar, 444
transept, church, 87
transfer call, answering machine, 181
transfer scale, light meter, 176
transfer to local elevator, skyscraper, 77
transformer, nuclear reactor, 393
transistor chip, 396
transit, 436
transit system, 119
transmission: automobile, 109; bulldozer, 435; tank, 474
transmit light, CB radio, 183
transmitter, telephone, 180
transom: door, 64; elevator car, 78; powerboat, 139; rowboat, 133
transom clamp, outboard engine, 137
transparency: film slide, 172; projector, 175
transparent balustrade, escalator, 79
transparent roof, bus, 118
transponder, 747 cockpit, 151
transportation, public sign, 506
transportation office, Capitol building, 74
transpose, proofreader's mark, 514
transverse arch, human foot, 31
transverse piece, kite, 323
trap, 433; clothes dryer, 281; gallows, 462; sink drain, 273
trapdoor: Hansom cab, 131; stage, 350
trapeze artist, circus, 90
trapezius, human, 26
trap plug, sink drain, 273
trapunto, quilting, 385
trash basket, 247
trash compactor, 247
trauma box, paramedic equipment, 123
traveler: sailboat, 134; stage, 350
traveler's check, 227
traverse arm, overhead power line, 396
traverse rod, 240
traversing gear, mortar, 472
tray: baby's high chair, 286; copier, 164; cosmetic case, 285; dental unit, 454; easel, 370; house painting, 425; slide projector, 175; tea set, 245; toaster, 253
tread: planetary wheel, 434; running shoe, 302; staircase, 66; stirrup, 335; tire, 105
treadboard, escalator, 79
treadle: hand loom, 387; spinning wheel, 387
treasure box, stagecoach, 131
Treasury seal, paper money, 225
treatment, magazine photo, 170
treatment aids, medical, 451
treble clef, music, 352
treble dial, phonograph receiver, 179
treble hook, fishing plug, 341
treble part, accordion, 366
treble pick-up, guitar, 363
tree, 50; saddle, 335; shoe, 207
tree of life, Torah, 486
trefoil: church, 86; drum major's coat, 495; medal, 501
tremolo arm, guitar, 363

trench: continental margin, 15; underwater funnel, 98
trench coat, 200
tress, 25, 213
trestle, guillotine, 462
triangle: orchestra, 354; shuffleboard court, 318
tributary, river, 13
triceps, human, 26
triceps exerciser, body building, 344
trick, spring beard needle, 386
trick, waterskiing, 329
tricorne, pirate, 492
tricycle, 128
trifecta, flat racing, 336
trifocal lenses, eyeglasses, 221
triforium, church, 86
trigger: bear trap, 433; chain saw, 431; crossbow, 466; drill, 419; gas pump automatic nozzle, 112; movie camera, 174; paint spray gun, 425; sander, 421; slalom water ski, 329; weapon, 468, 470, 471, 472
trigger control, gas laser, 395
trig-loop post, laboratory scale, 447
trim: automobile, 107; baseball uniform, 290; cake, 264; door, 64; drum major's uniform, 495; Manchu court dress, 491; pendant, 219; pool table, 320; queen's regalia, 484; running shoe, 302; 747 cockpit, 150; stove, 248; tennis racket, 312; window shade, 240; woman's hat, 203; woman's shoe, 205
trim-adjustment rack, outboard engine, 137
trimline phone, 180
trimmer: body building, 344; lawn, 429; razor, 210
trimming, woman's hat, 203
trimming end, clay modeling tool, 372
trim tab: powerboat, 138; racing car, 338
trip, fishing reel, 340
trip handle, toilet, 275
trip indicator, nuclear reactor control room, 393
triple jump, track and field, 300
triple ring, dart board, 322
triple-score ring, dart board, 322
triplet, music notation, 352
tripod: machine gun, 471; music stand, 367; photographic, 176; screen, 175; telescope, 443; transit, 436
trip odometer, car, 110
trochanter: grasshopper, 41; spider, 40
trolley, girdle, 195
trolley pole, bumper car, 92
trolling gear, fishing, 344
trombone, 354, 358-359
trophy, 289; king's regalia, 484; medal, 501
tropical storm, 19
troposphere, earth, 4
trotter, harness racing, 35
trough: barn, 104; humidifier, 402; longshore, 14; wave, 14
trousers, 191; bull denim, 490; butler, 489; cowboy, 490; jai alai player, 314; king's regalia, 484; man's formal attire, 488; military uniform, 496, 497; paramedic equipment, 123; police uniform, 498

trowel, 427
truck, 120-121; airport, 95; cannon carriage, 467; fire engine, 124; flagpole, 502; garbage, 127; locomotive, 116, 117; platform, 121; roller skate, 324; semitrailer, 121; skateboard, 324; tractor, 120
truck bed, tow truck, 126
true air speed indicator, 747 cockpit, 150
true bias, fabric, 388
true edge: knife, 463; sword, 463
true north, 22
true vertical, transit, 436
true-zero hook, tape measure, 424
trumpet, 354, 359
trunk: automobile, 107; cactus, 56; fish, 45; grandfather clock, 233; human, 24; octopus, 46; palm, 52; police car, 122; powerboat, 138; and root, 51; sailboat, 134; tree, 50; ultimate beast, 49
trunks, boxing, 309
trunnion: bulldozer, 435; cannon barrel, 467
truss: bridge, 97; roof, 61
trysail, 136
try square, 424
T-shirt, man's, 194
tsunami, 14
tuatara, 42
tub: bath, 274; dishwasher, 250; tub fiddle, 366; washing machine, 280
tuba, 354, 358
tube: ambulance, 123; automobile engine, 111; bazooka, 472; beauty product, 217; bicycle, 128; blood pressure gauge, 449; bolt ring, 218; dental unit, 454; dispenser, 267; eyedropper, 451; fire extinguisher, 284; food processor, 254; hurdle, 304; icing nozzle, 259; jet fighter, 480; laboratory burner, 447; laboratory clamp, 446; lamp, 238, 239; lawn sprinkler, 428; light bulb, 238; microscope, 442; mortar, 472; pen, 158; pitch pipe, 367; radiator, 400; screen, 175; shoe tree, 207; shotgun, 469; sketch box, 371; sleeping bag, 343; solar collector panel, 391; stethoscope, 449; submarine, 479; subway, 119; tank gun, 475; telescope, 443; television, 185; test, 447; thermometer, 449; toilet, 275; vacuum, 396; wave, 14
tuber, potato, 54
tubercles, stingray, 45
tube sock, 207
tub fiddle, 366
tubing: backyard glider, 287; dental, 455; plumbing, 422; stethoscope, 449
tub ring and filter, washing machine, 280
tuck: blouse, 197; cigar, 228
tucker, queen's regalia, 484
tuck flap, package, 269
tuft: lounger, 235; man's hair, 211; sofa, 236; toothbrush, 215
tug, 144; airport, 95
tugboat, 144
tumbling, trampoline, 308
tumbrel, execution vehicle, 462
tummy, human, 25

573

tuna tower, powerboat, **139**
tuner: audio, **179**; television, **185**
tunic: Beefeater, **483**; king's regalia, **484**
tuning fork, **367**
tuning gear: cornet, **359**; dulcimer, **362**; French horn, **358**; guitar, **362**; phonograph receiver, **179**; radar, **444**; sitar, **362**; trombone, **358-359**; trumpet, **359**
tunnel, **98**; igloo, **85**; prison, **76**; railroad, **115**; subway, **119**; super collider, **394**; wave, **14**
tunnel bottom, waterski, **329**
tunnel visor, traffic light, **113**
turban, woman's, **203**
turbine: combustion jet engine, **407**; nuclear reactor, **392**
turbine engine, helicopter, **146**
turbine locomotive, **116**
turbofan engine, cruise missile, **482**
turbofan jet engine, **149**, **407**
turboprop jet engine, **407**
turf: baseball field, **291**; polo grounds, **299**; racetrack, **336**, **337**
turkey, **35**
turn: lamp, **239**; racetrack, **337**
turnback, suit hanger, **281**
turnback cuff: blouse, **197**; jacket, **196**
turnbuckle, boxing ring, **309**
turned step, shovel, **427**
turner, kitchen utensil, **259**
turn indicator, 747 cockpit, **480**
turning, drop-leaf table, **242**
turning gear, can opener, **251**
turning signal, automobile, **106**
turning stake, croquet, **318**
turning wall, swimming pool, **316**
turn-lock, handbag, **222**
turnouts, fireman, **500**
turnover, **264**
turnover collar, king's regalia, **484**
turn signal light: bus, **118**; truck, **120**, **121**
turntable: fire engine, **124**; phonograph, **178**; railroad yard, **96**
turret: castle, **80**; stethoscope, **449**; tank, **475**
turtle, **43**
turtleneck: clothes, **327**; sweater, **199**
tusche stencil, silk screen, **375**
tush, ultimate beast, **49**
tusk, ultimate beast, **49**
tutu, ballerina, **494**
tuxedo, man's formal attire, **488**
TV camera: aircraft carrier, **478**; lunar rover, **155**; satellite, **186**
TV monitor, prison, **76**
TV optical unit, jet fighter, **480**
TV power status, space shuttle, **153**
TV/VCR mode, remote control unit, **184**
tweeter, audio speaker, **179**
tweezers, **215**; pocket knife, **426**
twelve foot marker, bowling lane, **317**
21, layout, **347**
25-point ring, dart board, **322**
20mm cannon, jet fighter, **48**
24-second clock, basketball, **296**
twig, tree, **50**

twilight zone, cave, **11**
twin bed, **270**
twine, frankfurter, **265**
twine tie, aerial shell, **383**
twinned stories, newspaper, **168**
twins, zodiac, **509**
twist: drill bit, **418**, **419**; paper clip, **277**
twisted handle, paper bag, **266**
twister, **17**; body building, **344**
twist-off cap, bottle, **269**
twist tie, package, **269**
two-button closing, woman's jacket, **196**
two-color eye pencil, **217**
two-cycle internal combustion engine, **406**
two-deck head, magazine, **171**
2-door coupe, **108**
2-piece casing, capsule, **451**
two-point perspective, **368**
two-pronged fork, **259**
two-suiter, **285**
two-stick kite, **323**
two-way traffic, road sign, **505**
two-way zipper, **209**
two-yard line, football, **293**
typanum: church, **86**; frog, **44**; grasshopper, **41**; toad, **44**
type, **165**; magazine, **170**, **171**; printing, **166**; typewriter, **161**; wine label, **267**
type display window, laser printer, **163**
type of subscription code, magazine mailing label, **169**
typewriter, **161**
typhoon, **17**
typist's initials, letter, **159**
typography, **165**
tzit, Torah, **486**

U

U: braille, **512**; sign language, **512**
U-boat, **479**
udder, cow, **32**
U-gouge, **374**
UHF radio, pilot's instrument panel, **481**; 747 cockpit, **150**
ullage, bottle, **267**
ulna, human, **26**
ulnar nerve, human, **29**
ultimate beast, **48-49**
ultraviolet spectrometer, satellite, **186**
umbilical: space shuttle, **152**; spacesuit, **155**
umbilical system bag, lunar rover, **155**
umbilicus, human, **24**
umbo, shield, **464**
umbo, clam, **47**
umbrella, **230**; golf, **311**; pipe, **229**; silo, **104**
umlaut, grammatical symbol, **513**
umpire, polo, **299**
umpire's area, baseball field, **291**
una corda pedal, piano, **361**
unattended reception capability, fax machine, **164**
undercarriage, stagecoach, **131**
undercarriage protector, tow truck bed, **126**
undercarriage wheels, helicopter, **146**
undercoat, bird, **39**
undercut, razor blade, **210**
underline, grammatical symbol, **513**
underpants, **194**
underpass, **114**
underpinnings, queen's regalia, **484**

underscore, grammatical symbol, **513**
under-seat bag stowage, lunar rover, **155**
underserve line, jai alai cancha, **314**
undershirt, **194**, **290**
underwater tunnel, **98**
underwear, man's, **194**
underwiring, brassiere, **195**
unexposed film, movie camera, **174**
unicycle, **128**
uniform: baseball, **290**; basketball, **296**; boxer, **309**; drag racing driver, **339**; fencing, **315**; football, **292**; ice hockey, **294**, **295**; jai alai, **314**; jockey, **336**, **337**; military, **496-497**; police, **498-499**; Revolutionary War general, **492**; skiing, **326**, **327**; skin diving, **331**
unimproved road, topographic map, **22**
union: flag, **502**; water heater, **401**
unistrut, Ferris wheel, **93**
unit: ambulance, **195**; masonry, **68**
unit citation, military uniform, **496**
unit column, abacus, **441**
unit crest, military cap, **496**
US insignia, military uniform, **496**
United States notes, paper money, **224**
U.S. interstate route number, road map, **20**
U.S. route, road sign, **504**
unit number, fireman's helmet, **500**
unit patch, military uniform, **496**, **497**
unit point, abacus, **441**
unit value, thematic map, **21**
univalve shell, **47**
universal cross connection, traffic light, **113**
universal drive joint, hitch and harrow, **434**
universal gym, **344**
universal joint: automobile, **109**; windsurfer, **330**
Universal Product Code, **440**; symbol, label, **269**
Universal Transverse Mercator grid marking, topographic map, **22**
universal veil, remnants, mushroom, **57**
universe, **2-3**
UPC code, coupon, **103**
UPC label, **440**
updraft, tornado, **17**
uphaul, windsurfer, **330**
upholstery: sofa, **236**; wheelchair, **452**
upper: ice skate, **325**; man's shoe, **204**; running shoe, **302**; sandal, **206**
upper arm: dog, **36**; frog, **44**; human, **24**; traffic light, **113**
upper back-stick, easel, **370**
upper ball joint, automobile, **108**
upper blade guard, saw, **417**
upper bolt, pulley block, **461**
upper bout, viola, **355**
upper bow, bear trap, **433**
upper case, type, **165**
upper chord, bridge, **97**
upper control arm, automobile, **108**
upper control line, parachute, **333**

upper deck, passenger ship, **143**
upper eyelid, frog, **44**
upper face, zipper, **209**
upper frame, piano, **361**
upper gate, canal lock, **99**
upper-girdle facet, cut gemstone, **218**
upper grid, nuclear reactor, **392**
upper grip ring, sword hilt, **463**
upper handle, mower, **429**
upper hatch, lunar lander, **154**
upper header, solar collector panel, **391**
upper housing, sander, **421**
upper jaw, fish, **45**
upper joint, clarinet, **357**
upper limb, bow, **466**
upper lounge, jumbo jet, **148**
upper magnet, dipole magnet, **394**
upper mandible, bird, **39**
upper panel, piano, **361**
upper plate, theodolite, **436**
upper shell, turtle, **43**
upper spray arm, dishwasher, **250**
upper tail crest, tadpole, **44**
upper teeth, **456**
upper thigh, dog, **36**
upper pool, canal lock, **99**
upper rack, dishwasher, **250**
upper rail, balustrade, **73**
upper receiver, rifle, **471**
upper rudder, jumbo jet, **149**
upper sash, window, **65**
upper side-rail, truck van, **121**
upper windshield, bus, **118**
upright: basketball backstop, **296**; croquet wicket, **318**; easel, **370**; etching press, **377**; football, **293**; guillotine, **462**; hand loom, **387**; horizontal bar, **306**; hurdle, **304**; lithographic press, **376**; parallel bars, **306**; pole vault, **305**; pommel horse, **307**; roller coaster, **92**; tow truck, **126**
upright handlebar, bicycle, **128**
upright piano, **361**
upright pole, tent, **342**
upright standard, theodolite, **436**
upright vacuum cleaner, **283**
uprush, wave, **14**
upstop wheel, roller coaster, **92**
upstream, river, **13**
upstream gate, canal lock, **99**
Uranus, planet, **3**
urine transfer connector, spacesuit, **155**
urn, bed finial, **270**
uropod, lobster, **47**
usage register, electric meter, **399**
use, label, **268**
used-blade box, razor blade injector, **210**
utility belt, police, **498-499**
utility pocket: cowboy, **490**; spacesuit, **155**
uvula, **30**

V

V: braille, **512**; sign language, **512**
VAC scale, volt-ohm meter, **423**
vacuum cleaner, **283**
vacuum gauge, gas laser, **395**
vacuum hose, automobile engine, **111**
vacuum jar, laboratory, **447**

vacuum mount, pencil sharpener, 277
vacuum relief valve, tanker, 140, 141
vacuum tube, 396
valance: curtain, 240; stage, 350; theater, 351
valley, 7; house roof, 63; non-glaciated, 12; river, 13
valley glacier, 12
value: coin, 225; thematic map, 21
value range, isarithmic map, 21
valve: automobile engine, 111; bicycle, 128; blood pressure gauge, 449; camper, 130; camp stove, 342; clam, 47; cornet, 359; drag racing dragster, 339; dental unit, 454; faucet, 273; football, 292; French horn, 358; furnace, 400; hot air balloon, 332; inflatable, 133; laboratory burner, 447; lantern, 342; motorcycle, 129; nuclear reactor, 392; playing cards, 348; plumber's torch, 422; radiator, 400; scallop, 47; skin diving, 331; solar heating system, 391; standpipe, 59; steam engine, 405; subway motorman's cab, 119; tanker, 140, 141; toilet, 275; trumpet, 359; water heater, 401
vambrace, armor, 465
vamp: boot, 206; man's shoe, 204; running shoe, 302; sandal, 206; woman's shoe, 205
van, truck, 121
Vandyke beard, 211
vane: barn, 104; bird feather, 39; missile, 482; weather, 18, 19; windmill, 390
vanishing point, perspective, 368
vanity, dresser, 272
vanogan, 108
varashield, truck cab, 120
variable range marker, radar and sonar, 444
variable spacer, typewriter, 161
variable-speed control, saw, 417
variable sweep wing, jet fighter, 480
variable wing, combat aircraft, 480
vase, church, 87
VASI, airport runway, 94
vastus medialis, human, 26
vault: bank, 457; burial chamber, 516; dome, 85; parking meter, 113; pay telephone, 180; pole, 300, 305
vaulter: gymnastics, 307; pole vault, 305
vaulting board, 307
vaulting horse, 307
V-berth, sailboat, 135
V-bottom hull, powerboat, 138
VCR, 184
VDC scale, volt-ohm meter, 423
vegetable, 54, 55, 262; juice extractor, 255; refrigerator compartment, 249
vegetable organ, grass, 58
vegetable slicer, 261
vehicle: airport, 95; armor-plated, 474–475
V-8 automobile engine, 111
veil: bride's, 488; nun's, 487; remnants of universal,

mushroom, 57; woman's hat, 203
vein: human, 27, 28; leaf, 52
Velcro closure, 209; football helmet, 292; parka cuff, 201
velocity indicator: pilot's instrument panel, 481; space shuttle, 153
velocity stack, racing car, 338
velvet cap, royal crown, 485
venetian blind, 241
vent: automobile, 107; Band-Aid, 451; battery, 397; bus, 118; cannon barrel, 467; furnace, 400; hair dryer, 212; hot air balloon, 332; house gable, 63; jacket, 188; paint spray gun, 425; radiator, 400; shoe tree, 207; skin diving fin, 331; stove, 248; truck van, 121; volcano, 10; water heater, 401
vent field astragal and filets, cannon barrel, 467
ventilated rib, shotgun, 469
ventilation building, underwater tunnel, 98
ventilation hatch, bus, 118
ventilation-heating controls, car, 110
ventilation pack, hovercraft, 145
ventilation umbilical, spacesuit, 155
ventilator: barn, 104; lantern, 342; locomotive, 117; subway car, 119; tank, 475
venting arm, launch pad, 152
vent pipe: house, 62; pressure cooker, 257
vent port, drag racing driver's fire suit, 339
ventral fin: fish, 45; jet fighter, 480
ventral scale, snake, 42
vent screw, outboard engine, 137
venturi windshield, powerboat, 139
venule, human, 28
Venus, planet, 3
veranda, house, 63
verge, barn, 104
vergeboard, house, 63
Vermeil Room, White House, 75
vernier, theodolite, 436
verso, book page, 167
vertebral column, human, 26
vertebral shield, turtle, 43
vertex, pyramid, 71
vertical, transit, 436
vertical adjustment, speculum, 448
vertical aerial, volleyball net, 319
vertical angulation dial readout, dental x-ray unit, 454
vertical brace: bridge, 97; oil drilling platform, 101
vertical centering, radar, 444
vertical circle, theodolite, 436
vertical exhaust, truck tractor, 120
vertical fin: blimp, 156; glider, 147; single engine airplane, 147
vertical gauge, carpenter's level, 424
vertical reduction, theodolite, 436
vertical speed indicator, 747 cockpit, 150
vertical stabilizer, jumbo jet, 149
vertical tail fin, jet fighter, 480
vertical updraft, tornado, 17

vertical velocity indicator, pilot's instrument panel, 481
very high frequency antenna, destroyer, 476
very soft, music notation, 353
vessel, 132
vest, 188; cowboy, 490; man's formal attire, 488; police, 499; ski clothes, 327, 329; sweater, 199
vestibule, vault, 457
vestment, Jewish ritual, 486
vestry, church, 87
V-gouge, 374
VHF aerial, jumbo jet, 148
VHF antenna: destroyer, 476, 477; helicopter, 146; lunar lander, 154
VHF radio, 747 cockpit, 151
vial: carpenter's level, 424; theodolite, 436
vibration damper pulley, automobile engine, 111
vibrissa: cat, 37; ultimate beast, 48
vice president, Senate, 74
victory, gesture, 507
video camera, 184
video cassette, 184
video key, television, 185
video recorder, 184
video screen, personal computer, 162
video-still camera, 173
video-still camera adaptor, 173
viewfinder: camera, 172; Polaroid, 173; telescope, 443
viewing hood, radar, 444
vignette: book, 167; label, 268
vintage, wine label, 267
viola, 354, 355
violation flag, parking meter, 113
violin, 354, 355
violoncello, 355
virgule, grammatical symbol, 513
virgin, zodiac, 509
Virgo, zodiac, 509
viscid spiral, spider web, 40
vise, workbench, 408
visor: armor, 465; drum major's busby, 495; fireman's helmet, 500; man's cap, 202; spacesuit, 155; traffic light, 113
visual-approach slope indicator light, airport runway, 94
visual code, coupon, 103
visual display, personal computer, 162
vite, cartoon, 380
vitellus, egg, 262
vitreous body, eye, 30
vitreous humor, eye, 30
V-neck, sweater, 199
vocational rehabilitation, prison, 76
voice, organ, 360
void, type, 165
volcanic rock, brazier, 288
volcano, 7, 10
volleyball court, 319
voltmeter: powerboat, 138; symbol, 510
volt-ohm meter, 423
volt-ohm milliammeter, 423
volume: stringed instruments, 355; wine label, 267
volume control: CB radio, 183; guitar, 363; hearing aid, 452; metal detector, 445; movie projector, 175; police radio, 122; portable radio/cassette player, 182; sonar, 444; tape recorder, 177; Walkman, 182

volume dial, audio receiver, 179
volume graduation, beaker, 447
volume key, television, 185
volume number, newspaper, 168
volume slider, synthesizer, 363
volume unit meter, tape recorder, 177
voluntary muscle, human, 26
volva, mushroom, 57
voting booth, 437
voting machines, mechanized, 437
votive candle, 237
voussoir, arch, 72
VRM range-intensity control, radar, 444
V-sign, gesture, 507
V-tail, surfboard, 330
V-waist, queen's regalia, 484

W

W: braille, 512; sign language, 512
wafer, Communion, 87
wafer ice cream cone, 265
waffle ice cream cone, 265
waftarom, cartoon, 381
wagon, child's toy, 287
wagon masters' quarters, frontier fort, 82
wagon pole, stagecoach, 131
wah-wah pedal, guitar, 363
waist: ant, 41; bell, iv; guitar, 362; hourglass, 233; human, 24; queen's regalia, 484; skirt, 197; viola, 355; woman's pants, 196
waistband: athletic supporter, 194; man's formal attire, 488; man's underpants, 194; panty hose, 195; skirt, 197; trousers, 291; woman's pants, 196
waistcoat: man's formal attire, 488; Revolutionary War general, 492
waistline: bridal gown, 488; dress, 198
waist trimmer, body building, 344
walk, house, 63
walk-around, clown, 493
walk board, roller coaster, 92
walkie-talkie radio, 183
walking leg, lobster, 47
walking race, 300
walking stick, 452
Walkman, 182
wall: barn, 104; baseball field, 291; brick, 69; canal lock, 99; and carpet, 246; cave, 11; circus tent, 91; dam, 100; dustpan, 282; elevator car, 78; fort, 83; handball court, 313; horse's hoof, 38; house, 60, 62; jai alai cancha, 314; mah-jongg, 345; lacrosse stick, 298; mountain, 9; oil drilling platform, 101; pea, 54; pepper, 262; prison, 76; safe, 457; squash court, 313; stage, 350; swimming pool, 316; tomato, 54; truck, 121; wave, 14
wallaby pouch, ultimate beast, 48
wallet, 223
wall fastener, 411
wall flange: aneroid barometer, 18; sink drain, 273
wall socket, electrical, 398
wall switch, electrical, 398
wall tent, 342
wall-to-wall carpet, 246

wand: venetian blind, 241; wizard, 492
waning moon, 4
war bonnet, Indian, 490
ward, castle, 80, 81
warding, key, 459
wardrobe, 272
warehouse store, 102
warhead: missile, 482; torpedo, 479
warm front, weather map, 19
warming element, percolator, 252
warming grid, barbecue grill, 288
warming unit, coffee maker, 252
warm liquid pipe, heat exchanger, 403
warm-up jersey, baseball batter, 290
warm-up suit, basketball, 296
warning, dental x-ray unit, 454
warning light: car, 110; fire engine, 124, 125; pilot's instrument panel, 481; railroad crossing signal, 115; 747 cockpit, 150, 151; space shuttle, 153; tractor, 434
warning lines, fencing strip, 315
warning sign, road, 505
warning track, baseball field, 291
warp, hand loom, 387
war paint, Indian, 490
warship, 476
warts, toad, 44
washbasin, sailboat, 135
washcloth rack, bathtub, 274
washer, 411; aerial shell, 383; faucet, 273; hose coupling, 428; lamp, 238; levigator, 376; parking meter, 113
washing machine, 280
washline, 280
washout plug, locomotive boiler, 116
washtub, 280
waste disposal, dental, 455
watch, 220; skin diving, 331
watchband, 220
watch cap, sailor's, 497
watch pocket: skirt, 197; trousers, 191; vest, 188
watchtower, train caboose, 117
water: dam, 100; thundercloud, 17
water bearer, zodiac, 509
water buffalo horn, ultimate beast, 49
water closet, sailboat, 135
watercolor, painting medium, 370
water control, dental unit, 454
watercourse, river, 13
water droplet, cave, 11
waterfalls, 13
water fill: camper, 130; iron, 279
watergate: castle, 81; frontier fort, 82
water glass, 244
water hazard: golf course, 310-311; steeplechase race, 304
water heater, 401; camper, 130
water hook, harness racing, 337
water jet, Jacuzzi, 274
water kettle, tea set, 245
water key: trombone, 359; trumpet, 359
water level sight glass, furnace, 400
waterline: boat, 132; destroyer, 477
water pipe, 229

water pressure gauge, pumper, 125
water regulator, dental, 455
water reservoir, coffee maker, 252
water return pipe, furnace, 400
waterskiing, 329
water spray: mechanical sweeper, 127; tooth cleaner, 215
water tank: iron, 279; railroad yard, 96; water heater, 401
water temperature gauge, powerboat, 138
watertight bulkhead, passenger ship, 142
watertight door, destroyer, 476
water tower, nautical chart, 22
wattage selector, CB radio, 183
wattle: chicken, 35; turkey, 35
wattmeter, symbol, 510
watts, phonograph, 179
wave, 14; radio, 3
wave-cut platform, iceberg, 12
waveguide, radar antenna, 444
wave height, 14
wavelength, 14; laser beam, 395
wax: candle, 237; ski, 327
waxing moon, 4
way, permanent fort, 83
W.C., sailboat, 135
weaponry, 463-482; combat soldier, 497; defensive guided, 476
weather boarding, barn, 104
weather deck, passenger ship, 143
weather ear, newspaper, 168
weather forecast, 18
weather map, 19
weather radarscope, 747 cockpit, 150
weather stripping, window, 65
weather vane, 19; barn, 104
weaving, 387
web: bird foot, 35, 39; circus aerialist, 90; horseshoe, 38; human hand, 31; knife, 256; spider, 40; toad, 44; weaving, 387
web area, wrench, 415
webbing: baseball glove, 291; suspenders, 190
web-fed press, printing, 166
web sling, bazooka, 472
wedding bouquet, bride, 488
wedge: cannon carriage, 467; crossbow, 466; dental, 455; hammer, 412; quiche, 263; running shoe, 302; sawhorse, 408; snowmobile, 130
weep hole: brick wall, 69; fence, 67
weft, weaving, 387
weight: barbell, 344; baseball bat, 290; bowling ball, 317; discus, 303; flat racing, 336; grandfather clock, 233; guillotine, 462; hurdle, 304; laboratory scale, 446, 447; lobster, 433; metronome, 367; skin diving, 331; tractor, 434; type, 165; universal gym, 344
weight floor, stage, 350
weights and measures certification, gas pump, 112
weight to be carried, flat racing entry, 336
weiner, 265
weld: link chain, 461; tweezers, 215
welded channel, backyard glider, 287
well: automobile, 106, 109; bus steps, 118; cigarette lighter,

228; ink, 158; magazine, 169; powerboat, 139; saucer, 245; Senate, 74; toaster, 253; workbench, 408
well-contents measuring tool, oil drilling platform, 101
welt: boot, 206; shoe, 204
welting: baseball glove, 291; lounger, 235; handbag, 222; mattress, 271
welt pocket flap, jacket, 188
West Australia Current, ocean, 6
West Coast mirror, truck, 120
westerlies, wind, 6
western pocket, trousers, 191
western saddle, 335
western yoke shirt, cowboy, 490
west front, church, 87
west longitude, 5
west portico, Capital, 74
west wind drift, ocean, 6
wet boot, slalom water ski, 329
wet compass, 747 cockpit, 151
wet suit, skin diving, 331
whaleboat, destroyer, 476
whalebone carving, scrimshaw, 375
whale's tooth, scrimshaw, 375
wharf, castle, 80, 81
wheat, 58
wheel: automobile, 106, 107; balance beam, 306; ballista, 467; bicycle, 128; blimp, 156; body building, 344; bumper car, 92; cannon carriage, 467; can opener, 251; child's wagon, 287; cigarette lighter, 228; drag racing dragster, 339; Ferris, 93; glass cutter, 378; hand loom, 387; helicopter, 146; humidifier, 402; locomotive, 116; motorcycle, 129; mower, 429; pastry cutter, 261; potter's, 373; powerboat, 138; roller coaster, 92; roller skate, 324; roulette, 346; sailboat, 134; seeder, 430; single engine airplane, 147; skateboard, 324; slide projector, 175; slot machine, 346; snowmobile, 130; spinning, 387; stagecoach, 131; stroller, 286; tank, 474, 475; tire, 105; tractor, 434; truck, 120, 121, 126; vacuum cleaner, 283; wheelbarrow, 430; wheelchair, 452
wheelbarrow, 430
wheelchair, 452
wheelhouse: hydrofoil, 145; tanker, 141
wheel of fortune, 346
wheels-flaps position indicator, pilot's instrument panel, 481
wheel speed fairing, single engine airplane, 147
wheel window, church, 86
whey, and cheese, 263
whip: flat racing, 336; harness racing, 337; stagecoach, 131; windmill, 390
whip roll, hand loom, 387
whirlpool bath, 274
whirlpool jet, bath, 274
whirlybird, 146
whisk, kitchen tool, 258
whiskers: cat, 37; man, 211; ultimate beast, 48
whistle: destroyer, 477; locomotive, 116; police gun belt, 499; subway motorman's cab, 119
white, egg, 262
whitecap, wave, 14

white dwarf star, 3
whiteface, clown, 493
White House, 75
white inner table, backgammon board, 345
white line, horse's foot, 38
white outer table, backgammon board, 345
white paint, sketch box, 371
white room, launch pad, 152
white square, chessboard, 345
white tie, man's, 488
whitewall tire, automobile, 107
white wine glass, 244
white wire, electrical receptacle, 398
whole note, music, 352
whole note rest, music, 352
whole-timbered building, 70
whorl: human fingertip, 31; univalve shell, 47
wick: candle, 237; jumbo jet, 148; Molotov cocktail, 473
wicket, croquet, 318
wickiup, 84
wide swing gouge, woodcarving, 372
wide tire, tractor, 434
width, and perspective, 368
widow, bowling pin, 317
widow's peak, hair, 211
widow's walk, house, 62
width, type, 165
wig, 211, 492
wiggle nail, 410
wigwag, symbolic language, 512
wigwam, 84
wild card, 348
wimple, nun, 487
win, flat racing, 336
winch: oil drilling platform, 101; sailboat, 134; tanker, 140; tow truck, 126
wind: fishing rod, 340; thunderstorm, 17
windage adjustment knob, rifle scope, 469
wind baffle, camp stove, 342
windbag, bagpipe, 365
windbreaker, automobile, 107
wind chest, organ, 360
wind direction sensor, weather station, 18
wind-door, garbage truck, 127
wind drift, ocean, 6
wind indicator, destroyer, 477
winding, fishing rod, 340
winding road, road sign, 505
wind instruments: brass, 358-359; wood, 356-357
windlass: ballista, 467; sailboat, 134; tanker, 140
windmill, 390
window, 65; airport control tower, 95; automobile, 106, 107; bridge, 97; bus, 118; camper, 130; checkbook clutch, 223; church, 86; house, 62, 63; igloo, 85; light meter, 176; lunar lander, 154; mainsail, 136; mat, 379; microwave oven, 248; package, 269; parking meter, 113; plug fuse, 399; powerboat, 139; slot machine, 346; stove oven door, 248; subway car, 119; tank, 475; tractor, 434; wallet, 223; washing machine door, 280; windsurfer, 330
window control, car, 110
window coverings, 240, 241
window flap, tent, 342
window shade, 240, 241
wind patterns, 6
windscreen: passenger ship,

142; 747 cockpit, **150**; single engine airplane, **147**
windshaft, windmill, **390**
windshield: automobile, **106, 107**; bus, **118**; jet fighter, **480**; powerboat, **139**; 747 cockpit, **150**; single engine airplane, **147**; snowmobile, **130**; space shuttle, **153**; truck, **120**
windshield defroster, **110**
windshield frame, pilot's instrument panel, **481**
windshield wiper: bus, **118**; car, **106, 110**; locomotive, **117**; subway motorman's cab, **119**
Windsor knot, necktie, **192**
wind speed sensor, weather station, **18**
windsurfer, **330**
wind system, **390**
wind turbine, **390**
wind vane, **18, 19**
wind wall, oil drilling platform, **101**
windward side, boat, **132**
wine, consecrated, **87**
wine bin, sideboard, **243**
wine cellar, passenger ship, **143**
wine department, supermarket, **102**
wine district, wine label, **267**
wine drawer, sideboard, **243**
wine glass, **244**
wine label, bottle, **267**
wine selector, wine label, **267**
wine steward's corkscrew, **251**
wing: baseball catcher's shinguard, **290**; bassoon, **357**; bird, **39**; bow tie, **192**; Capitol, **74**; cruise missile, **482**; dental braces, **453**; destroyer bridge, **477**; easel, **370**; grasshopper, **41**; house, **63**; hydrofoil, **145**; ice hockey, **295**; jet fighter, **480**; lamp, **238**; poultry, **35**; racing car, **338, 339**; safety razor, **210**; scallop, **45**; single engine airplane, **147**; space shuttle, **152**; stroller, **286**; tanker, **141**; theatre, **351**; toggle bolt, **411**; turkey, **35**; wallet, **223**
wing area, lacrosse field, **298**
wing-back cuff link, **218**
wing fixed glove, jet fighter, **480**
wing nut, **411**; hacksaw, **416**; hurdle, **304**; Ping-Pong net, **321**
wing strut, racing car, **338**
wing sweep indicator, pilot's instrument panel, **481**
wing tip: man's shoe, **204**; single engine airplane, **147**
wing type, combat aircraft, **480**
winter berm, shoreline, **14**
winter cap, Manchu court dress, **491**
winter squash, **54**
winter uniform, police, **498**
wipe, cowboy, **490**
wiper: bus windshield, **118**; car windshield, **106, 110**; locomotive windshield, **117**
wire: automobile engine, **111**;

barbed, **432**; circuit breaker box, **399**; dental, **453**; earring, **218**; electrical receptacle, **398**; electrician's, **423**; field events hammer, **303**; fire engine, **124**; frame, **379**; horizontal bar, **306**; incandescent bulb, **238**; plug fuse, **399**; railroad crossing signal, **115**; size, **423**; stationary rings, **307**; toaster, **253**; traffic light, **113**; trumpet, **359**; typewriter, **161**; vacuum tube, **396**
wire cutter: electrician's wire stripper, **423**; pliers, **414**
wire end, clay modeling tool, **372**
wire hood, champagne cork, **267**
wire knob, seeder, **430**
wireless aerial, tanker, **141**
wireline-logging unit, oil drilling platform, **101**
wire stripper: electrician's, **423**; pocket knife, **426**
wire support, camp stove, **342**
wiring tube, lamp, **239**
wisdom teeth, **456**
wishbone, poultry, **35**
wishbone boom, windsurfer, **330**
wisp, woman's hair, **213**
withdrawals, automatic teller machine, **226**
withers: cow, **32**; dog, **36**; sheep, **33**
witness cone, potting, **373**
witness stand, courtroom, **89**
wizard, costume, **492**
wok, **257**
woman's hair, **213**
woman's hat, **203**
woman's jacket, **196**
woman's pants, **196**
woman's shoe, **205**
woman's skate, **325**
women's tee, golf course, **310**
wood, jai alai cancha, **314**
wood block, **374, 461**
woodburning stove, **404**
wood carrier, fireplace, **232**
woodcarving tool, **372**
wood clamp, **409**
woodcut printing, **374**
wooded marsh, topographic map, **22**
wooden beam, tow truck bed, **126**
wooden mallet, woodcarving, **372**
wooden pipe, levigator, **376**
wooden roofing shingle, **68**
wooden siding, house, **62**
wooden spoon, **259**
wood fence, **67**
wood form, etching press, **377**
wood saw, pocket knife, **426**
wood shaft, umbrella, **230**
wood splice, house, **61**
woodwind, **354, 356-357**
woodworking vise, **409**
woodyard, frontier fort, **82**
woof, weaving, **387**
woofer, audio speaker, **179**
wool collar, trench coat, **200**
word, book page, **iv**
word processor, **162**

workbench, **408**
work bowl, food processor, **254**
work experience, résumé, **160**
working drawing, house, **62**
workingman, circus, **90**
workingman's suspenders, **190**
working surface, balance beam, **306**
workshelf, potter's wheel, **373**
work spotlight, tow truck bed, **126**
workstation, computer, **438**
work surface, desk, **276**
worktop, kitchen sink, **247**
worm: cannon, **467**; corkscrew, **251**
worm gear, venetian blind, **241**
woven backing, carpet, **246**
woven basket, guillotine, **462**
woven side, basket, **266**
woven wire fabric, steel chain fence, **67**
wrap: boxing, **309**; packaging, **269**
wrap belt, cardigan, **199**
wrapper: cigar, **228**; paperback book, **167**; Torah, **88**
wrapping, dabber, **377**
wreath: medal, **501**; tombstone, **516**
wreck, nautical chart, **22**
wrecker, **126**
wrench, **415**
wringer, **280**
wrist: cat, **37**; human, **24, 29**; steam engine crank, **405**
wristband, soccer, **297**
wristpad, lacrosse glove, **298**
wrist sling, ice hammer, **334**
wrist strap, ski pole, **326**
wristwatch, **220**
wrist weight, body building, **344**
write-in, voting, **437**
write-protect hole & slider, diskette, **162**
write-protect notch, diskette, **162**
writer's initials, letter, **159**
writing area, desk, **276**
writing arm, rocking chair, **234**
writing slide, desk, **276**
writing tip, pen, **158**
wrought iron fence, **67**

X

X: braille, **512**; sign language, **512**
x-height, type, **165**
x-indication, voting booth, **437**
x-ray cassette, operating room table, **450**
x-ray dental unit, **454**
xylem, tree, **50**
xylography, **374**

Y

Y: braille, **512**; sign language, **512**
yacht, **133**
yackety-yak, gesture, **507**
yad, Torah, **486**
y adjusting lever, plane, **420**
yankee, sailboat, **134**
yard: barn, **104**; frontier fort, **82**; house, **62**; prison, **76**
yardarm, destroyer, **477**

yard goods, fabric, **388**
yard line, football field, **293**
yardmaster, railroad yard, **96**
yarmulke, Jewish prayer vestment, **486**
yarn: knitting, **386**; rope, **132**; weaving, **387**
yarn loop, **246**
year of birth: flat racing entry, **336**; tombstone, **516**
year of death, tombstone, **516**
yellow traffic light, **113**
yen, symbol, **511**
Yeoman warder, **483**
yield, road sign, **504**
Yin-Yang, symbol, **508**
yod, tefillin, **486**
yoke: blouse, **197**; dental x-ray unit, **454**; dress, **198**; 747 cockpit, **150**; shirt, **189**; tennis racket, **312**; tuning fork, **367**; window, **65**
yoke cable, bicycle caliper brake, **128**
yoke shirt, cowboy, **490**
yolk, egg, **262**
you're out, gesture, **507**
yurt, **70**

Z

Z: braille, **512**; sign language, **512**
zebra coat, ultimate beast, **49**
zecher lechurban, Jewish prayer vestment, **486**
Zeppelin, **156**
zero adjust knob, volt-ohm meter, **423**
zero mark, wristwatch, **220**
zester, kitchen tool, **261**
ziggurat, pyramid, **70**
zigzag rule, **424**
zinc carbon cell, **397**
zip code: envelope, **159**; magazine mailing label, **169**
zip-out robe lining, overcoat, **200**
zipper, **209**; backpack, **343**; mainsail, **136**; package, **268**; parka, **201**; skirt, **197**; sleeping bag, **343**; trousers, **191**; woman's pants, **196**
zippered door, tent, **342**
zipper foot, sewing machine, **278**
zipper line, sewing pattern, **388**
zip plus four, mailing label, **169**
zizith, Jewish prayer shawl, **486**
zonal pattern, wind, **6**
zone: envelope, **159**; football field, **293**; glacier, **12**; handball court, **313**; ice hockey rink, **295**; shuffleboard court, **318**; time, **5**
zone marking, ice hockey rink, **295**
zoom collar, zoom lens, **172**
zoom control, video camera, **184**
zooming ring, movie projector, **175**
zoom lens, **172**; movie camera, **174**; video camera, **184**
zoom ring: movie camera, **174**; video camera, **184**

Credits

pages **2-3**, illustration by Neal Adams; **5**, time zone map courtesy of Hammond Incorporated, Maplewood, NJ; **8-9**, illustration by Dee Molenaar; **18**, photo courtesy of Science Associates Inc.; **20-21**, Japan map courtesy of Hammond Inc., thematic map of "Number of Irish Foreign Born 1930" courtesy of Carnegie Institution of Washington; **28, 29, 30**, anatomy cross sections courtesy of Hammond Inc.; **60-61**, illustrations courtesy of American Plywood Assoc.; **62**, illustration by Charles Addams, blueprint by Carl Hribar; **74-75**, photos by David Burnett, courtesy of Contact Press Images, Inc.; **76**, photo courtesy of State of N.Y. Dept. of Correctional Services; **77**, top photo courtesy of The Port Authority of New York & New Jersey, lower photo courtesy of Empire State Building; **78**, elevator shaft illustration courtesy of Westinghouse Elevator, elevator car illustration courtesy of Williamsburg Steel Products, Co.; **80**, photo courtesy of British Information Service; **86-87**, illustrations courtesy of Cathedral Church of St. John the Divine, N.Y.C.; **88**, courtesy of Temple Emanuel, N.Y.C.; **90-91**, courtesy of Ringling Brothers and Barnum & Bailey; **92-93**, roller coaster courtesy of Magic Mountain Amusement Park, Ferris wheel and merry-go-round courtesy of Rye Playland; **94-95**, airport photo courtesy of American Airlines; **96**, photo courtesy of Association of American Railroads; **97**, photos courtesy of Triborough Bridge and Tunnel Authority; **101**, photo by Carroll S. Grevemberg, Grevy Photography, New Orleans, LA; **102-103**, supermarket plan courtesy of *Progressive Grocer*, coupon courtesy of Folger's Coffee; **106-107**, AnyCar photos courtesy of Manufacturers Hanover Trust, N.Y.C.; **108-109**, photo courtesy of Buick Division, General Motors Corp.; **110**, photo courtesy of Alfa Romeo; **111**, photo courtesy of Bradford La Riviera Inc.; **114**, courtesy of Triborough Bridge & Tunnel Authority; **116-117**, steam locomotive photo courtesy of Association of American Railroads, turbine engine photo courtesy of National Railroad Passenger Corporation, panels courtesy of The Train Shop, Ltd.; **118**, coach courtesy of American Eagle, commuter bus interior courtesy of NY Metropolitan Transit Authority; **119**, courtesy of NY Metropolitan Transit Authority Museum; **120-121**, photos courtesy of Mack Trucks Corp.; **124-125**, photos courtesy of New York City Fire Department; **126**, tow truck courtesy of LST Towing, N.Y.C.; **127**, courtesy of NYC Department of Sanitation; **129**, photo courtesy of Kawasaki Motorcycles; **130**, camper photo courtesy of Winnebago Industries, Inc., snowmobile photo courtesy of Yamaha Motor Corp.; **131**, stagecoach courtesy of Wells Fargo Bank History Dept., hansom cab courtesy of The New-York Historical Society; **133**, photo courtesy of Dyer Jones, Warren, RI; **134-135**, illustrations courtesy of CSY Yacht Corp., Tampa, FL; **136**, compass photo courtesy of Aqua Meter Instrument Corp., Roseland, NJ; **137**, outboard photo courtesy of Mariner Outboards, Fond du Lac, WI, sextant photo courtesy of Weems & Plath, Annapolis, MD; **138-139**, illustration courtesy of Bertram Yachts, Miami, FL; **142-143**, illustration courtesy of Cunard Line Ltd., N.Y.C.; **144**, tugboat courtesy of Moran, fireboat courtesy of NYC Fire Department; **145**, hovercraft photo courtesy of British Hovercraft Corp. Ltd.; **146**, photo courtesy of Sikorsky; **147**, airplane photo courtesy of Piper Aircraft Corp.; **148-149**, illustration courtesy of Boeing; **150-151**, photo courtesy of Boeing; **152-153**, photo and illustration courtesy of NASA; **154-155**, illustrations courtesy of NASA; **156**, photo courtesy of Goodyear; **159**, calligraphy by Melissa, text by Sean Kelly; **161**, manual typewriter photo courtesy of Royal Business Machines, Inc.; **162**, top photo courtesy of Apple Computer Inc., bottom right photo courtesy of Sharp Electronics Corp.; **163**, top photo courtesy of Fujitsu America, San Jose, CA, bottom illustration after NEC Information Systems, Inc.; **164**, fax machine and copier photos courtesy of Sharp Electronics Corp.; **166**, illustrations courtesy of International Paper Company; **168**, courtesy of *The New York Times*, N.Y.C.; **169**, *Time* cover reprinted by permission from *Time* The Weekly Newsmagazine, copyright Time Inc., 1980, contents page reprinted courtesy of *Sports Illustrated* from the March 3, 1980 issue, copyright (c) 1980, Time, Inc.; **170-171**, prepared by *New York* Magazine, N.Y.C.; **172**, zoom lens photo courtesy of Tokina Optical Ltd.; **173**, video still camera photo courtesy of Sony; **174**, photo courtesy of Minolta Camera Co., Ltd.; **175**, movie projector photo courtesy of Minolta, slide projector photo courtesy of Kodak, screen courtesy of Da-Lite Screen Co.; **176**, light meter courtesy of Gossen-Luna Pro, electronic flash courtesy of Vivitar Corp., tripod courtesy of E. Leitz Inc.; **177**, reel-to-reel recorder photo courtesy of Pioneer Electronics, cassette tape photo courtesy of Sony; **178**, turntable photo courtesy of Pioneer Electronics Corp.; **179**, audio photos courtesy of Pioneer Electronics Corp.; **181**, cellular telephone photo courtesy of Panasonic, answering machine photo courtesy of Sony; **182**, bottom photo courtesy of Sharp Electronics Corp.; **183**, photo courtesy of Radio Shack; **184**, VCR photo courtesy of Panasonic, video camera courtesy of Sharp Electronics; **185**, television photo courtesy of Sony; **186**, illustration courtesy of NASA; **195**, panty hose photo courtesy of Hanes Corp.; **196-197**, illustrations by Calvin Klein; **201**, fur photo courtesy of Rosette, NY; **205**, courtesy of Andy Warhol; **207**, sock photo courtesy of Alexander Lee Wallan Inc.; **209**, photo courtesy of Velcro USA; **210**, electric razor photo courtesy of Sunbeam Corp.; **212**, hair dryer photo courtesy of Conair; **214**, curling iron photo courtesy of Conair; **216-217**, products courtesy of Avon Products, Inc., make-up by Tom Gearhard; **218-219**, ring and pendant illustrations courtesy of Jane Evans; **220**, wristwatch courtesy of Chronosport Inc., Rowayton, CT; **227**, traveler's check courtesy of Barclay's Bank, N.Y.C.; **237**, candle snuffer courtesy of Fortunoff Department Store, N.Y.C.; **244**, place setting courtesy of Rosenthal China Co.; **245**, dessert setting courtesy of Rosenthal China, panels courtesy of Gorham Division of Textron Inc.; **247**, sink courtesy of Elkay Manufacturing Co., disposal unit courtesy of Hobart Co.; **248**, stove and microwave oven photos courtesy of General Electric Co.; **251**, electric opener courtesy of Oster Corp., can piercer courtesy of Ekco Industries; **255**, vegetable juicer courtesy of Hamilton Beach, automatic juicer courtesy of Oster Corp., manual juicer courtesy of Acme Juicer Mfg. Corp.; **257**, pressure cooker courtesy of National Presto Industries, electric wok courtesy of Farberware; **258-261**, courtesy of H&P Mayer Corp.; **267**, pump dispenser courtesy of Calmar Division/Diamond Int'l.; **268-269**, illustration by The Schecter Group; **278**, courtesy of Viking Sewing Machine Co.; **279**, courtesy of Proctor-Silex; **281**, dryer courtesy of General Electric; **283**, vacuum cleaner courtesy of Hoover Co., minivacuum courtesy of Black & Decker; **284**, fire extinguisher courtesy of Amerex Corp., smoke alarm courtesy of General Electric; **286**, stroller courtesy of Perego/Pines, Milan, Italy, playpen and car seat courtesy of Century Products, Los Angeles, CA; **287**, wagon illustration courtesy of Flexible Flyer; **288**, barbecue courtesy of King Seeley Co.; **290**, models: Rod Carew, California Angels (batter), Ossie Virgil Jr., Philadelphia Phillies (catcher); **291**, glove courtesy of Rawlings Sporting Goods; **292**, model: James Ramey, New York Jets, helmet courtesy of Bike Athletic Co.; **294-295**, models: Ken Morrow (defenseman) and Billy Smith (goalie), New York Islanders; **296**, model: Mike Glenn, New York Knickerbockers; **298**, photos courtesy of STX Company; **299**, photo courtesy of *Polo* Magazine; **302**, running shoe courtesy of Adidas; **306-307**, photos courtesy of Nissen/Walter Kidde & Co.; **309**, model: Wendal Newton; **310-311**, equipment photos courtesy of Northwestern Golf Co.; **314**, courtesy of Bridgeport, Conn., Jai Alai, model: Donald Mazza; **315**, piste courtesy of George Santelli Fencing School, N.Y.C.; **320**, photo courtesy of Brunswick Corp.; **322**, courtesy of Darts Unlimited, N.Y.C.; **324**, photo courtesy of Chicago Roller Skates Inc.; **326**, equipment courtesy of Scandinavian Ski Shop; **327**, cross-country equipment courtesy of Scandinavian Ski Shop, snowshoe courtesy of The Snowcraft Corp.; **329**, ski courtesy of Connelly Skis, Inc.; **331**, equipment courtesy of Atlantic Divers World, NY; **332**, photo courtesy of The Balloon Works, Statesville, NC; **333**, parachute courtesy of Para-Flite Inc., US Parachuting Assoc., hang glider courtesy of United States Hang Gliding Assoc.; **334**, photos courtesy of George Willig, Topanga, CA; **335**, Western saddle courtesy of H. Kauffman and Sons, Inc., English saddle by Crosby, courtesy of Millers, N.Y.C.; **336**, program entry courtesy of Pimlico Race Track; **337**, Meadowlands Racetrack, East Rutherford, NJ, model: Courtney Foos; **338**, illustration by Jack Lane, courtesy of L'Art et L'Automobile Gallery, 354 E. 66th Street, N.Y.C., Jacques Vaucher; **339**, photos courtesy of National Hot Rod Association; **340-341**, fishing reel photo courtesy of Penn Reels, rod photo courtesy of Shakespeare Fishing Rods; **342**, photos courtesy of Coleman Co.; **343**, backpack photo courtesy of Johnson/Camp Trails; **344**, universal gym photo courtesy of Nissen; **346-347**, courtesy of Mr. Lucky Equipment, Rosedale, NY; **349**, ticket courtesy of Globe Ticket Co.; **351**, photo of the Bardavon Theatre courtesy of Robert Paul Molay; **352-353**, *Theme From What's What Book* written by John Hill, John Hill Music Inc.; **354**, illustration and photo courtesy of Chicago Symphony Orchestra; **360**, photo courtesy of Rodgers Organ, N.Y.C.; **365**, bagpipes courtesy of Larry Cole; **366**, accordion courtesy of Stuyvesant Music; **369**, painting courtesy of the Metropolitan Museum of Art, N.Y.C.; **370-371**, painting equipment courtesy of Grumbacher; **372**, Sculpture House, N.Y.C.; **374**, equipment courtesy of Rembrant Graphic Arts, NJ; **376-377**, courtesy of Rembrant Graphic Arts, NJ and Charles Brand Machinery Inc., NY; **378**, equipment courtesy of Glassmaster Guild; **380-381**, cartoon by Mike Witte, comic strip by Mort Walker, copyright 1978 King Features Syndicate, Inc.; **382**, photo courtesy of Fireworks By Grucci Inc., Brookhaven, NY; **383**, top and bottom right photos courtesy of Fireworks By Grucci Inc., Brookhaven, NY, center and bottom left photos courtesy of Zambelli Fireworks Mfg. Co., Inc., New Castle, PA; **385**, quilt courtesy of Fairfield Processing; **386**, shuttle courtesy of C.J. Bates & Son, Inc.; **387**, loom courtesy of LaClerc Weaving Looms; **390**, wind turbine photo courtesy of Grumman Corp.; **394**, super collider illustrations and photo courtesy of Universities Research Assoc., Washington, DC; **395**, gas laser diagram after *Lumonics*, hologram photo courtesy of AT&T Archives; **396**, transistor photo courtesy of Bell Laboratories; **402**, courtesy of Hampton Sales; **406**, courtesy of Teledyne Wisconsin Motor; **409**, photos courtesy of Adjustable Clamp Co.; **417**, table saw photo courtesy of ToolKraft, circular saw photo courtesy of Ski, saber saw photo courtesy of Rockwell International; **421**, sander photo courtesy of Rockwell International, belt sander courtesy of Black & Decker; **423**, voltmeter courtesy of Amprobe Instruments; **424**, folding rule courtesy of Stanley Tools, carpenter's level courtesy of ToolKraft; **425**, spray painter courtesy of Spray Tech Corp.; **426**, photo courtesy of Hoffritz; **427**, courtesy of Douglas Products; **428**, photos courtesy of L.R. Nelson Corp.; **429**, photo courtesy of Sears, Roebuck & Company; **430**, wheelbarrow courtesy of Jackson Mfg. Co., seeder courtesy of Cyclone Seeder Co., Inc.; **431**, chainsaw photo courtesy of Ski Corp.; **434**, tractor photo courtesy of J.I. Case; **436**, theodolite courtesy of Dietzgen Corp., jackhammer courtesy of Bosch Power Tools; **437**, photos courtesy of R.F. Shoup Corp., Radnor, PA; **438**, computer workstation photo courtesy of Intergraph Corp., Huntsville, AL; **439**, computer system and computer tapes photos courtesy of IBM Corp., White Plains, NY, circuit board photo courtesy of Intergraph Corp.; **440**, courtesy of NCR Corporation; **442**, photo courtesy of Carl Zeiss Inc.; **443**, telescope photo courtesy of Unitron Instruments Inc., binoculars photo courtesy of Minolta Camera Co., Ltd.; **444**, photos courtesy of Furuno U.S.A., Inc.; **445**, metal detector photo courtesy of White Electronics Inc., geiger counter photo courtesy of EDA Instruments; **446-447**, burner courtesy of Fisher Scientific Co., scale courtesy of Ohaus Scale Corp.; **448**, photos courtesy of Welch Allyn, Skaneateles Falls, NY; **449**, photos courtesy of Sybron Corp.; **450**, courtesy of Affiliated Hospital Products; **451**, prescription form courtesy of Scriptech; **452**, wheelchair photo courtesy of Invacare Corp., hearing aid photo courtesy of Dahlberg Electronics, pacemaker photo courtesy of Medtronic, Inc.; **453**, denture photo courtesy of Sterndent Corp., braces bracket photo courtesy of 'A' Company, Inc.; **454**, courtesy of Ritter Dental Corp.; **455**, courtesy of Dr. Herbert Spasser; **457**, photos courtesy of Mosler Safe Co.; **458**, Safe Hardware Corporation, Emhart Industries Inc.; **459**, lock photo courtesy of Medico Security Locks Inc.; **460**, hasp photo courtesy of Lawrence Brothers, Inc.; **461**, chains courtesy of Diamond Chain Co., block and pulley courtesy of The Crosby Group; **476-477**, illustration of DE 1092 courtesy of officers and men of *USS Thomas C. Hart*, drawings of ship types after *Jane's Fighting Ships*; **478-479**, photos courtesy of US Navy Department; **480-481**, fighter aircraft photos courtesy of Grumman; **482**, cruise missile photo courtesy of Boeing Aerospace; **483**, illustration courtesy of James Burrough Ltd., N.Y.C.; **484**, costumes courtesy of Eaves-Brooks Costume Co.; **486**, photo courtesy of Irving Fisher; **487**, minister photo courtesy of The Very Reverend Francis B. Sayre; **488**, photo courtesy of After Six Formal Wear; **489**, photos courtesy of Masterpiece Theatre, LWT, N.Y.C.; **490**, costume courtesy of Eaves-Brooks Costume Co., Indian courtesy of the Museum of the American Indian, N.Y.C.; **491**, Manchu Court Dress courtesy of Reginald Bragonier, Arab dress courtesy of Bill Ashe, model: Jan Leighton; **492**, model: Jan Leighton, pirate photograph by BODI, miser photograph by Michael Weiss; **493**, illustration by Ted Geisel; **494**, photo courtesy of Lois Greenfield/Capezio Ballet Makers; **496-497**, photos by Phil Koenig, soldiers courtesy of US Army, sailor courtesy of US Navy; **500**, photo courtesy of New York City Fire Department; **503**, courtesy of Government of Canada; **506**, symbols courtesy of *Handbook of Pictorial Symbols*, Rudolph Modley, Dover Publications, Inc., N.Y.C.; **514**, courtesy of Mary Grace and Maria Maggi; **516**, casket courtesy of Simmons Casket Co./Gulf and Western Casket Co.

Acknowledgements

The editors wish to express their special appreciation to the late Hugh Johnson for his friendship and support. Without him, WHAT'S WHAT would not exist.

Harold Adler, Adler Monument and Granite Works; Roslyn Alexander, librarian, Charles Evans Hughes High School; Jack Arnoff; Dave Lipsky, Juana Torres and Frank Coppinger, Army Corps of Engineers; Martin Bacheller, Hammond Inc.; Gwen Baker, Hammond Inc.; Roberta Baker, *Life* Magazine; Barney's Clothing Store; Sandy Bartram; Susan Bates Inc.; David Baxley, Triborough Bridge & Tunnel Authority; Mitch Becker, Globe Ticket Corp.; Paul Berkovitz, Algoma Net Company; Randy Black, Bike Athletic Corp.; Mitchell and George Tepper, Bond Street Suspender Inc.; Bonny Products; Carol Boswell and Gina Frantz, Boswell-Frantz Public Relations; Jerry Boxer, Abraham Boxer and Sons; Lee Bracy, Westinghouse Elevator Inc.; Benjamin Bragonier; Dana Bragonier; queen model Penelope Bragonier; Bill and Betty Brennan; Andreas Brown, Gotham Book Store; Donna Grucci Butler, Grucci Inc.; Cadillac Meat Company; Camrod Motorcycles; Carez Health Care Corp.; cross-country skiing model Catherine Carlen; Zack Carr, Calvin Klein Ltd.; Celeste Champagn, LWT Int'l.; Robert E. Lewis and William S. DeArment, Channellock Corp.; Betty Charak, Personality Hanger Inc.; Jerry Charles, Hollco Tools Coats and Clark, Inc.; accordion supplied by Larry Cole; Phil Colicchio, Oreo Cookies; Dita Comacho; Nancy Conforti, H & P Mayer Inc.; H. C. Cook, Inc., Division of Gem Products; Ron Coplon, Rubin Gloves Inc.; Richard Curtis, Richard Curtis Associates; Elmer Danch and Elaine Harr, Da-Lite Movie Screen Company; Frank Davis; John and Jessica Dorfman; Rose Dreger; Alfred Dunhill Inc.; Alex Dupuy, Columbia Computer Lab; Blaise Dupuy, The Box Studio; Ken Durst, Rawlings Inc.; John Edelmann; EKCO Housewares Corp.; Lt. Juan Torres and Ray Florida, NYC Emergency Medical Service; Lee Entwhistle, Eaves-Brooks Costumes Inc.; Herbert Eskelson, Para-Flite Inc.; Eye Center Inc.; Penny Farber, Foxmore Inc.; staff of Fashion Institute of Technology library; Arthur Ferguson, Metropolitan Transit Authority; Steve Fineberg, Feinberg Associates; Ira Finke, Ira Finke Photography; Nini Finkelstein, Ringling Brothers and Barnum & Bailey Circus; Irving and Sylvia Fisher; Anthony Forgione, Consolidated Wafer and Cone Corp.; Joann Forster, International School of Harness Racing at Roosevelt Raceway; William Free Advertising Agency; Bill Freeman, The Gill Track and Field Equipment Company; Steve Friedman; Lois Fry, Shakespeare Fishing Equipment; Fuller Brush Corp.; Louise Gaither, Executive Services Advertising; Gary Galante, Museum of the American Indian; cosmetic model make-up by Tom Gearhard; Irv Goldfinger, Forsyth Monument Works; Matthew Goldman; Bob Goldstein, M & F Hanger; Brian Goodman; Mary Grace; Kathy Graham, Bridgeport, Conn., Jai Alai; Thomas Grasso, Kay Jeep Eagle; J. F. Grgula, Structo Division, King-Seeley Thermos Co.; John Growth, School of Visual Arts; Mike Gue, Ethics Automobile Racing; Walter Guslawski, Williamsburg Steel Products; Stephen A. Halls, Jr., Digital Equipment Corp.; Dana Hammond, Hammond Inc.; Dean Hammond, President, Hammond Inc.; Kathy Hammond, Hammond Inc.; Stuart Hammond, Hammond Inc.; management and staff of Hampton Sales; Harvey Sound Corp.; Irving Heiberger, Marshall Clark Inc.; Joyce Heiberger, JBH Advertising; Kenneth Heinz, Welch-Allyn Corporation; Paul Heller, International Creative Management; Katharine Hill; Hoffritz Inc.; Ernst Hofmann, Hammond Inc.; Anne S. Hopkins, *Time* Magazine; Edward Irrizarry; Chris Jones, Hammond Inc.; Edward M. Kalail, Diebold Inc.; PO Ken Kaufman, NYPD, coauthor of *The Incredible Scooter Cops*; Scrooge's letter by Sean Kelly, former editor of *The National Lampoon*; Chris Kelly; Jessie O. Kempter, IBM; cowboy model by William Ketchum, Jr., author of *Western Memorabilia*; George Klauber, George Klauber Graphic Arts Studio; Morris and Ruth Kleinman; Drew Kuber, Hammond Inc.; Barbara Lach, Fermilab; Richard and Elyse Langsam; Larry Letizia, Joyson Motors; Leaf Tent and Sail Inc.; Charles Leib; Leland-Penn; Patricia Lewis; Robert Lewis, Chrysler Corporation; Teresa Longhitano; Mel and Cheryl London, authors of *Bread Winners*; Lionel V. Lorona, New York Public Library; Candace Love; Donald A. Macaulay; Joseph W. Maresca, Jr., SRI Institute; Daniel Mazzarella, Science Associates Inc.; Ken McAdams; Kay McDowell, US Postal Data Center; Frank 'Tug' McGraw, Philadelphia Phillies; Dave McNamara, Wilson Sporting Goods, Inc.; The Meadowlands Racetrack management; Jennifer Meyer, Hammond Inc.; John Meyers, Fisher Scientific Company; Ray Miller, VISA; Mr. Lucky School of Gambling; Macmillan Publishing Corp.; Captain Don Mitchell, Eastern Airlines; Jenny Moradfar; Ruth Grevey and Larry Osterman, Mosler Safe Corp.; Edward J. Murphy, Edward J. Murphy Corp.; Neckwear Association of America; Steve Nesbitt, Mark Hess, Tom Jacqua, NASA; New York Jets; New York Knickerbockers; New York Yankees; Don Morris and Suzanne Eagle, *New York* Magazine; PO George Legas and Steve Berenhaus, NYPD; John Nicholson; C. Michael Oldenberg, Centennial Management Corp.; Joan Rubin and Christine Martorana, Omega Fashions Ltd.; John Pace, National Cash Register; Shirley Palmer, *Progressive Grocer*; Rolando Pena; Arthur and Lois Perschetz, LTC Gerald Perschetz, U.S. Army (Ret.); Clarence Peskac, Dietzgen Corp.; Allen Petersen, Petersen Manufacturing Co., Inc.; Robert Pledge, Contact Press Images; Brigit Polk, The Factory; Marian Powers, *Time* Magazine; Andrew W. Prescott, Hammond Inc.; Donald Quest, Southwest Texas Drilling Co.; James Ramey, New York Jets; Jim Ramsey, Rodgers Organ Corp.; Mitch Rapaport, Scriptech; Mark Resnick, Hammond Inc.; Malcolm Ritter, Associated Press; Rock of Ages Corp.; Rosemary Rodgers, John Hill Music, Inc.; Linda Rosenblatt, R.D.H.; Joan Evanish, Judith Johnson and Canon West, Cathedral Church of St. John the Divine; Teddi Sann, Avon Products, Inc.; Gene Sayet, Executive Recording Ltd.; Frank and Harriet Sayre; Rosette Schecter, Furs by Rosette; Leslie Schwartz, Hammond Inc.; Deputy Police Commissioner 'Mickey' Schwartz, NYPD; Ann Scott, *Sports Illustrated*; Elizabeth Scott, Chicago Symphony Orchestra; Ray Scroggins, Wisconsin-Teledyne; Esther R. Selby, Zambelli Fireworks Mfg. Co.; Dr. John H. Seward, MD EENT; Joel Shaffer, Hammond Inc.; J. Ronald Shumate, Association of American Railroads; Craig Siebert; Harold Silver, Caldwell Button Corp.; Robert Simon, Wan, Simon and Black; Robert Smith; NY-NJ Port Authority; Dr. Herbert Spasser, D.D.S.; cosmetics model Tina Stahle; Stappers Equipment Corp.; Stuyvesant Music; Tom Szobe, Paragon Sporting Goods; Bob Taylor, Hedstrom Baby Furniture; Technigraph Studio; Marilyn Tempkins, Vivitar Inc.; calligraphy letterhead on Scrooge's letter by Melissa Topping; Tower Manufacturing; Paul Schulhaus, Russ Levin, Train Shop Ltd.; Bobbie Tupper, Park West Chapel; Helen Turi, General Motors Corp.; Helen Tutt, American Eagle; Tina T. Underwood, Intergraph; Universal Fastenings Inc.; Anna Urband, US Navy Public Relations; officers and men of the USS *Thomas C. Hart* (DE 1092); Jacques Vaucher, L'Art et L'Automobile Gallery; Ossie Virgil, Jr., Philadelphia Phillies; Dan Walden, Consolidated Edison Corp.; John Wanamaker; Sam Weinstein, Color Group; Western Union Corp.; Janet L. Wetmore, AT&T Archives; George Willig; king model Robert Wills; PO 'Scooter' Joe Wins, NYPD, coauthor of *The Incredible Scooter Cops*; John Wisdom; Laurie Wolford; Janet Wygall; Will Yolin, author of *The Complete Book of Kites and Kite Flying*; Richard Ziskin, American Umbrella Co.; Roger Zissu, Cowan, Liebowitz & Latman; Nell Znamierowski, Fashion Institute of Technology; and special thanks to the Hammond staff for their numerous contributions and assistance in producing this book.

Afterword

When we first created WHAT'S WHAT in 1981, it was
a major new undertaking, the first visual glossary
to appear in more than a century. While we were
confident that our research was meticulous, we also
recognized that errors were bound to creep into such
an ambitious project. So we asked readers to share
their special knowledge and observations with us.
Hundreds did. Most of the mail was embarrassing in
its flattery, much of it was touching. Letters from
parents of deaf children or children with learning
disabilities, for example, described the benefits and
pleasures derived by a very special reading audience.
Dozens of other letters proffered thoughtful criticism
that proved extremely valuable in preparing this
revision. We are indebted to all who wrote, and we
invite you to correspond with us in the future, for
whatever reason.

David Fisher
WHAT'S WHAT
357 West 19th St.
New York, N.Y,, 10011